WEST ACAD

LAW SCHOO

JES

Professor o

Universit

JOSI-

Distinguished University

Michael E. Moritz Coll

YA

Professor of Law I

Professor of Law I

MAI

Professor of Law,

University of Calif

LARI

President, Willia

JONA'

Professor

ARTI-

University Pro

Formerly Bruce Bromle

GRA

Professor of I

Professor of Law Emeritu

A. BEN

Earle K. S

University

JAM

Robert A. Sulliv

Univ

BUSINESS ORGANIZATIONS LAW AND POLICY

MATERIALS AND PROBLEMS

Ninth Edition

■ ■ ■

Jeffrey D. Bauman

Professor of Law and Co-Director,
Center for the Study of the Legal Profession
Georgetown University Law Center

Russell B. Stevenson, Jr.

Visiting Professor of Law
Georgetown University Law Center

Robert J. Rhee

John H. and Mary Lou Dasburg Professor of Law
University of Florida Levin College of Law

AMERICAN CASEBOOK SERIES®

American Casebook Series is a trademark registered in the U.S. Patent and Trademark Office.

COPYRIGHT © 1982, 1988, 1994 WEST PUBLISHING CO.
© West, a Thomson business, 1998, 2003, 2007
© 2010 Thomson Reuters
© 2013 LEG, Inc. d/b/a West Academic Publishing
© 2017 LEG, Inc. d/b/a West Academic
    444 Cedar Street, Suite 700
    St. Paul, MN 55101
    1-877-888-1330

West, West Academic Publishing, and West Academic are trademarks of West Publishing Corporation, used under license.

Printed in the United States of America

ISBN: 978-1-63460-594-6

For Linda and Margie, who lived through it all, with love.

For Don Schwartz, whose spirit continues to infuse this book.

For Nicki, Piers and Blake, our family.

PREFACE TO THE NINTH EDITION

The 9th edition of this casebook continues to be built around concept of prior editions that the best approach to teaching corporation law is to present students with a variety of problems that practitioners face, together with legal material relevant to their solution. This enables the teacher to structure class discussion around the way lawyers go about counseling clients on planning, structuring, and operating businesses rather than just extracting legal rules from appellate decisions, which, by the second year, most students have begun to find unsatisfying.

The change of name of the 9th edition from *Corporations: Law and Policy* to *Business Organizations: Law and Policy* reflects the addition to this edition of an entirely new section on Closely Held Entities in recognition of the division in modern practice between public corporations, and privately held business entities, including partnerships, closely held corporations, and limited liability companies. This section includes extensive materials on partnerships and limited liability companies designed to provide students the tools necessary to advise on the structure, formation, and operation of smaller businesses in the contemporary environment.

The addition of the new materials on closely held entities brought about a reorganization of the book, which is now organized into four parts. Part I "Introduction to Business Entities," covers the role of risk in business enterprises, and overview of terms and concepts explored in subsequent chapters, the nature of firms, limitations on limited liability, and the role of the large business corporation in society. Part II "Closely Held Entities," expands the coverage of prior editions from just close corporations to include partnerships and limited liability companies. Part III "Financing and Formation" provides introductions to accounting and valuation, financing the enterprise, and the selection of form and process of formation of the entity. Part IV "The Corporation," provides thorough coverage of major issues in corporation law, with an emphasis on the special problems of public corporations. Of course the book includes new developments since the last edition as well as consolidating and reorganizing the old materials.

Like the 8th edition, the 9th edition is premised on the belief that an understanding of basic business concepts, the role of statutes and regulations, and policy issues relevant to the history and direction of the law of business enterprises is essential to the business lawyer, and cannot be taught exclusively through the analysis of appellate opinions. Accordingly, unlike most books in this field, which consist largely of cases, the 9th edition continues to include much non-case material. It still begins with material designed to introduce basic business concepts essential to understanding business law including risk, valuation, and accounting. It also includes material, designed to be taught largely through problems, on the rapidly evolving law of corporate governance, the role of the corporation in society and the roles and ethical responsibilities of the business lawyer. As in the past, however, the book continues to deal with the more traditional questions of the law of business entities, including fiduciary duties, corporate litigation, transactions in control, and insider trading.

JEFFREY D. BAUMAN
RUSSELL B. STEVENSON, JR.
ROBERT J. RHEE

February 2017

SUMMARY OF CONTENTS

PART II. CLOSELY HELD ENTITIES

PART III. FINANCING AND FORMATION

PART IV. THE CORPORATION

TABLE OF CONTENTS

PART II. CLOSELY HELD ENTITIES

PART III. FINANCING AND FORMATION

TABLE OF CASES

The principal cases are in bold type.

———————

BUSINESS ORGANIZATIONS LAW AND POLICY

MATERIALS AND PROBLEMS

Ninth Edition

PART I

INTRODUCTION TO BUSINESS ENTITIES

■ ■ ■

Part I introduces basic concepts and terminologies that will be considered throughout the rest of the book. Chapter 1 shows how all businesses take risks, and that one of the functions of the legal structure of a business enterprise is the allocation of those risks and the expected returns among the participants in the enterprise. Chapter 2 describes the different entities that can be used to carry on a business and introduces some of the major concepts and terms that characterize them, including principles of agency. The remainder of the book returns to those concepts and terms repeatedly, exploring them in greater detail. Chapter 3 discusses in greater depth the rule of limited liability and the limits to that rule under the doctrine of veil piercing. Chapter 4 explores the idea that business entities are legal persons and the implications of that idea for some major questions of law and policy. It introduces the debate over whether corporations should be viewed as aggregates created by contract among their participants, or as entities separate from, and having broader social roles than, its constituent parts. Chapter 5 extends these concepts to consider the role of business enterprises, particularly large corporations, in our society, including issues such as the purpose of the corporation and corporate philanthropy.

CHAPTER 1

BUSINESS AND RISK

■ ■ ■

A. INTRODUCTION

Why, you may be thinking, have we chosen to begin this book with a chapter on risk? To begin, risk is an unavoidable characteristic of every business venture: it is an axiom of economics that without risk, there can be no reward. One of the principal features of the law of business enterprises is that it provides a framework for allocating and managing risk. This chapter considers different types of risk faced by businesses and introduces concepts about how business organizations can be structured and operated to manage those risks. A basic understanding of these concepts is essential to a lawyer's ability to advise business clients effectively. The purpose of this chapter is to establish a foundation on which to build much of the subsequent discussion of issues in the law of corporations and other business associations.

In any business venture, the parties have a shared interest in establishing a structure that produces the largest total return at the lowest cost. In the real world, this inevitably requires compromise. Each party to a venture will want to extract the maximum allocation of return while incurring the least risk. Only in a business owned and operated by a single individual will one party receive the entirety of the returns of the venture; the owner will obviously have to bear all of its risks. Most businesses are made up of multiple parties, including owners, employees, and lenders. These parties will have different preferences on how much risk they are willing to bear in exchange for an allocation of the rewards generated by the business. One of the goals of structuring a business enterprise is to minimize risks and to allocate risks and rewards among the parties in accordance with their preferences.

Among the uncertainties that organizers of a business face are the costs resulting from the employment of human beings in managing and operating the business. These costs, which are known as "agency costs," are of two general types. The first is a consequence of the fact that the efforts of that participants may vary, which may affect the value of the firm. Each person is likely to engage in a personal cost-benefit analysis and may choose to work less so long as the cost of diminishing her stake is less than the benefit she derives from slacking off (a phenomenon economists call "shirking"). The second type of agency costs arises from the desire of those charged with managing the firm to reduce shirking by monitoring the efforts of agents and contracting to yield the best effort, which may require establishing sanctions for failures to make suitable efforts. An important goal of structuring an enterprise is the minimization of these agency costs.

The legal structure of a business enterprise is determined by a combination of the law governing the type of organization (corporation, partnership, limited liability company, etc.) and the choices made in the structuring of the entity by the organizers. The ultimate goal is to maximize the value of the venture for all parties while allocating the risks and rewards of the venture in a manner that accommodates their desires.

Business is complex. Any given business enterprise has a unique combination of potential risks and returns, only some of which may be known at the start of the venture. Parties must decide how to distribute the risks of the future uncertainties of the business and how to create incentives that will encourage each of the parties to work for the best interest of the venture rather than exclusively for his or her own interest. Parties must create the structure of the venture at the outset, before its results are known. The lawyer's challenge is to advise a structure that creates the most efficient firm—one that minimizes agency cost, maximizes potential return, and minimizes unnecessary risks.

B. RISK AND RISK PREFERENCE

For our purpose, *risk* can be defined as the unpredictability of outcomes.[1] Any venture in which the outcome is unpredictable—including all business enterprises—carries risk. The most important risk in a business is that borne by those who invest in it. For example, an investment in the stock of a company is risky because at the time of the investment the future outcome is unpredictable: the stock price may increase, it may decrease, or it may remain constant. The company may pay dividends of varying amounts, or it may not. Investors in stock will have more of a chance of losing their money than if they put it away in a federally guaranteed, risk-free, interest-free checking account at the local bank. They only take the risk of investing in stock because they expect it to generate a return, whereas a checking account cannot result in losses but also it will not produce a return.

The *expected return* of an uncertain proposition is the sum of each possible outcome multiplied by the probability of that outcome. To demonstrate, consider the following scenarios:

---

[1] In economics, there is a formal distinction between "risk" and "uncertainty." Risk is calculable variance. For example, lotteries and table games in casinos involve risk. The probability of rolling a 6 on a fair, six-sided die is 16.7% (= 1 ÷ 6). Another form of risk probability can be derived from sufficient statistical data, such as the probability that a child will be born female. Uncertainty is variance of outcome that cannot be determined as a mathematical probability. Examples include the chance that next year will bring a global economic depression, that interest rates will increase by 0.10%, and that the stock price of a company will increase by 5%. For the purposes of this discussion, "risk" and "uncertainty" will be used synonymously.

Scenario 1.—Consider an investment in a U.S. Treasury bond, with an interest rate of 8%.[2] If we assume that, because it is backed by the full faith and credit of the United States, it is risk-free, the expected return is 100% times the $8 on a $100 face value bond:

Expected return = (100% × $8) = $8

Scenario 2.—Consider a different investment: if you have a 25% chance of making $4 from a business, a 25% chance of making $8, and a 50% chance of making $10, what is your expected return?

Expected return = (25% × $4) + (25% × $8) + (50% × $10) = $8

Scenario 3.—Now, consider this scenario: you have a 25% chance of *losing* $8 from a business, a 25% chance of making $8, and a 50% chance of making $16.

Expected return = (25% × –$8) + (25% × $8) + (50% × $16) = $8

All three scenarios produce the same expected value of $8. However, their risk profiles are different. Scenario 1 is risk-free because there is only one outcome of $8 (a spread of $0). Scenario 2 is moderately risky with a spread of $6 (between making $4 and making $10). Scenario 3 is even more risky with a spread of $24 (between the possibility of making $16 and the possibility of losing $8). Scenario 3 is more risky than Scenario 2 because the variance of outcomes is greater.

People have different preferences for risk. Some people like it; some don't; some are indifferent. To illustrate these preferences, consider a simple choice:

Choice 1: $1,000 sum certain

Choice 2: $2,000 or $0 depending on a 50/50 coin flip

The expected value of both choices if $1,000. The only difference is that Choice 1 is risk-free, and Choice 2 is risky because the outcome is variable.

If a person is risk averse, she does not like risk and therefore will select Choice 1. If a person is risk seeking, she likes risk and will select Choice 2. If a person is risk neutral, she is indifference to the two choices because their expected values are the same. A risk neutral person only considers the expected value and is indifferent to the risk profile.

Although people have different risk preferences, as a matter of empirical fact most people are risk averse. If you doubt this proposition, add a bunch of zeros to the above choices: for example, $1 million certain or a 50/50 coin flip for $2 million. Most everyone would choose the certain $1 million. Because most people are risk averse, there is a robust insurance market where insurance companies assume policyholders' fortuitous risk

---

[2]   Currently, as of 2017, the rates on Treasuries are much lower than 8%, but this inflated figure works better to illustrate the lesson.

for a premium that is more than the actuarial value of the risk. In other words, most people would rather pay a certain $1,300 in insurance premium rather than assume a 0.1% probability of suffering a $1 million loss. They would buy the insurance even though actuarial value of the loss is only $1,000 (0.1% × $1 million), which is less than the premium they have to pay to avoid the possibility of the loss. This vital social function justifies the existence of a robust insurance market. Insurance companies are also justified in charging more than the actuarial risk because they must pay employees and other expenses as well as earn a profit for shareholders.

Because people are risk averse, they will not risk their money in an investment unless they are compensated for doing something they otherwise not do (*i.e.*, take a risk with their money). The compensation for risk-taking is the expected return. An investor in a business venture expects to earn a return when she invests: she may invest $1,000 in a venture, putting this money at risk with the expectation that it will return $1,000 plus R, the expected return on her investment. If the risk of the investment is high, she will demand a higher R than if it is a relatively safe investment. Consequently, returns from investments in stocks are generally higher than returns on bonds, which return a fixed interest rate (subject to the continued solvency of the issuer) and are therefore less risky. Businesses that raise money from investors take this into account when deciding what type of securities to sell.

The success of a business depends heavily on how well it manages risk. Appetite for risk can affect decision making within the firm, particularly when the parties structure their business relationship in ways that create incentives to take on or avoid risk. Successful firms exploit favorable developments and minimize the effects of unfavorable ones. For example, even large corporations are significant consumers in the insurance market, and they purchase insurance to manage risk. How well a business manages risk depends on how the parties allocate different risks, which in turn determines the incentives of the firm's participants. However, it is impossible for a business to avoid dealing with risk.

Any business is exposed to many risks. Business risks can be categorized into controllable risks and non-controllable risks. Controllable risks are those that a party has some ability to control. For example, vineyard owners face risks associated with the type of grapes they grow, the amount and quality of work they do on the vineyard, and the adequacy of the equipment. The proper management of these risks depends on how well the parties conduct business operations. Success depends in part on how well incentives are structured maximize the incentives the participants to act in the best interest of the business and in part on the effectiveness of monitoring and sanctioning devices created to minimize agency costs.

Non-controllable risks, in contrast, consist of those over which the parties have no control and the elements of the controllable risks that remain after the parties have taken all reasonable steps to control them. For example, vineyard owners face risks associated with the weather, the demand for grapes, the quality and quantity of supply of grapes from other vineyards, and economic variables such as the level of interest rates, unemployment rate, and consumer sentiment.

C. ALLOCATING RISK AND RETURN

One of the key concerns in structuring any firm is how its risks are allocated among parties. The following hypothetical considers this issue in the context of a simple two-person firm: one party supplies capital to the business but wishes to do little or no work in it; the other party invests little or no financial capital but will do most or all of the work. Although a two-person firm is the simplest firm, this hypothetical illustrates the complexities of structuring a business enterprise.

Julia recently bought a vineyard in California's Napa Valley. The vineyard produces *vinifera* grapes that Julia hopes to sell to area winemakers. She does not plan to make wine on her own. She knows little about farming grapes and lives in Los Angeles. She knows that growing grapes is risky. Grape quality, crop yields and profits will depend on variables such as the weather, vineyard management and the market price of grapes at harvest. The size and quality of the crop also will depend on the effort and ability of the person who does the farming.

Julia meets Jonathan, a young man who has the equipment, expertise and desire to grow grapes. Julia and Jonathan consider a business relationship wherein Jonathan will manage Julia's vineyard. For now, they intend to cover only the coming year. They must decide Jonathan's compensation and duties. They consider two alternative structures:

- *Employment*: Julia will pay Jonathan a monthly salary. She will retain the net proceeds of the harvest, which is calculated as:

Net Proceeds = Sale of Grapes – Jonathan's Salary – Other Operating Expenses

- *Tenancy*: Jonathan will lease the land from Julia and pay her a yearly rent. He will bear all the operating expenses and will receive all the proceeds of the harvest.

Net Proceeds = Sale of Grapes – Lease Payment to Julia – Other Operating Expenses

These two arrangement are very different in terms of the risk borne by the parties. In the employment arrangement, Jonathan risks less since he receives a salary regardless of the outcome. His only risks are (1) that Julia does not pay him (in which case he can minimize his loss by stopping work), and (2) that the venture fails (in which case he has to find another job). On the other hand, Julia bears greater risk because she has claimed the residual return: the economic value remaining after payment to all others including Jonathan. Why would she do this (in essence choose to be paid last after all expenses)? The reason must be that, in her view, the expected return is sufficient *ex ante* compensation for bearing the risk.

In the tenancy arrangement, Jonathan risks more since *he* has claimed the residual return, after payment of all expenses including rent to Julia. Julia bears less risk because her return is a fixed rent irrespective of the outcome of the venture. If the venture fails, and Jonathan cannot pay rent, she reclaims the land as landlord.

How Julia and Jonathan structure their venture depends on their individual assessments of the risks and return from the venture. Their negotiations will also depend on a number of factors other than the risks of the venture. Consider how each of these factors might affect the allocation of risks: What if Julia is rich and Jonathan is poor (or vice versa)? What if Julia owns other vineyards or has experience growing grapes? What if the skill of operating a vineyard is in high demand in Napa Valley? What if Jonathan is an expert on viniculture and winemaking and understands the risks and rewards better than Julia?

1.   THE BUSINESS PROBLEM OF RISK MANAGEMENT

Even a simple business like a vineyard is exposed to a number of risks. Julia and Jonathan must manage these risks [*e.g.*, fire, pests, drought, crop disease, and market demand for wine.] Pests and crop disease can be mitigated somewhat through proper management, such as using pesticides and fungicides during the growing process. This aspect of risk management involves competent managers who know how to grow crops. Some of business risks, such as fire and crop disease, can be mitigated through traditional insurance. If these risks are considered significant enough, the manager of the vineyard would purchase insurance, the cost of which would be an expense to the business.

Other risks can be mitigated through more sophisticated financial transactions. If Julia and Jonathan are concerned that the price of grapes will drop by the time they harvest the grapes due to a nationwide fall in the demand for grapes, they can enter into a forward contract with another party. Before the harvest, they would agree to sell a fixed quantity of grapes for a prearranged price, thus locking in a sales price before the harvest. At the time of the sale, if the demand for grapes falls, Julia and Jonathan are better off because they would have sold the grapes at a higher price than the market spot price; if the demand for grapes increases, they are not better off *ex post*, but this was the financial bet required to protect against the downside risk. Sophisticated businesses, but probably not a simple vineyard, can also use specialized financial contracts to mitigate more exotic risks, such as weather and interest rates.

In addition to risk transfer, another way to manage risk is through diversification. A person or business can diversify by participating in numerous ventures, each of which involves different risks. For example, when an ordinary person buys stocks in several companies, such as General Electric, Coca-Cola, and Walt Disney, she has diversified her investments. She is not exposed solely to the risks of the market for industrial goods, beverages, or entertainment, but instead has investments in all of these business sectors. This reduces the possibility that she will sustain losses or low returns because one company or business sector does poorly. On the other hand (remember the greater the reward, the greater the risk) it also reduces the possibility of high returns because the company she picked does unusually well. One of the major social benefits of the stock market is that it enables investors easily to spread their risks through diversification. Even a single business enterprise can engage in diversification that would benefit its investors. For example, Walt Disney owns theme parks (Disney World), television studios (ABC and ESPN), and movie studios (Pixar and Lucasfilm).

The benefit of diversification can be illustrated with this simple example. In the above discussion, we said that due to risk aversion most people will choose a sum certain over a somewhat higher return that involves risk. In other words, most people will choose the sum certain even when the sum certain is less than the expected value of the lottery. Most people will choose Choice 1 in the following scenario even though the expected value is less than Choice 2:

Choice 1:   Sum certain of $9,000

Choice 2:   Either $20,000 or $0, depending on the flip of a coin.

However, consider the effect of a slight modification on the investor's choice. Choice 2 is modified in the following manner:

Choice 2*:   Either $200 or $0, depending on the flip of a coin, but you will repeat the wager 100 times.

Note that the expected value of Choice 2 in both cases is $10,000. If one thinks carefully about this proposition, however, even a risk averse person will most likely prefer the modified Choice 2*. Over the course of 100 coin flips, the risk associated with a single coin flip has been diversified away. It is still mathematically possible that all 100 coin flips would be a loser, but is extremely unlikely. If a person flips a coin 100 times, the chances are that approximately 50 flips will be a winner (give or take some variation around 50). If a person is unlucky and flips the winner only 45 times, she will earn $9,000, which would be the sum certain of Choice 1. If she flips 50 winners, she will earn $10,000. If she is lucky and flips the winner 55 times, she will earn $11,000. Accordingly, Choice 2* will be a more profitable choice except for a very risk averse individual who is unwilling to take the chance of losing more than 45 times out of 100. This example illustrates the benefit of investment in a corporation, which can invest in a number of different projects, as opposed to an investor making a single investment in a single venture.

Diversification can take many forms. If the main variable affecting a grape harvest is the amount of rainfall, an owner who is investing her financial capital might diversify her risk by investing in ten vineyards, provided each had a different expected rainfall. The vineyard owner could also diversify by investing in stocks and bonds, a strawberry patch, baseball trading cards, or Impressionist paintings, each of which involves risks that are different from, and somewhat independent of, the risks associated with a vineyard. In contrast, an employee who is investing human capital will find it nearly impossible to diversify that capital—even a person who works more than one job must forgo other employment opportunities.

How might this analysis affect the structure of the venture in the problem? Unlike Julia, Jonathan is investing human capital. Because he cannot work for more than one employer, he is not able to diversify his investment in the same way that Julia can spread financial capital around several investments. This inability may affect his attitude toward risk and his choice of how to arrange his relationship with Julia. He may demand concessions that lower his risk such as guaranteed salary, management control, and profit share.

Because controllable risks can be affected by the actions of principals and agents, how they are allocated requires a different analysis. Shirking is one type of controllable risk. For example, if the value of the harvest depends on whether Jonathan regularly sprays the vines with insecticides, a risk to the venture is that Jonathan will not make the effort to do so. The risk of shirking can be reduced by monitoring and disciplining devices that align the agent's incentives with the interests of the principal. However, the likelihood of shirking by Jonathan increases if he is guaranteed a lucrative employment contract irrespective of effort or outcome.

The difficulty in allocating risk among the parties is that the party who bears the consequences of the risk will have a greater incentive to control the risk, but the other party will not. In the spraying example, if Jonathan receives the same compensation no matter how many grapes are produced, he will have little incentive to rise early and spray the vines to prevent insect damage. In other words, there is a substantial risk that he will shirk, a risk he does not bear since it does not affect his compensation.[3] To avoid his self-interested shirking, Julia, who *does* bear the risk, must monitor Jonathan's work to ensure that he takes risk-reducing precautions. She thus incurs monitoring costs that would be avoided if a structure could be created to control the risk of shirking by putting it on Jonathan. From the perspective of economic efficiency, such a structure would be preferable because it would reduce the overall costs of the venture.

At the same time, however, the party who is in the best position to control risks might not be the best person to bear them. For example, suppose the agent has greater control over a particular risk, but that the principal is wealthier, less risk averse, or better able to diversify or insure. Who should bear the risk? Both parties would want the other to bear the risk, and both would be at least somewhat justified in their desire. There is a clear tension between the risk-controlling and the risk-bearing perspectives.

The spraying example illustrates this general problem. We might place all the risk on the principal, thus requiring her to monitor the agent to reduce shirking. In such case, the principal would bear the costs of monitoring and would have to come up with appropriate monitoring devices. However, because shirking *is* within the control of the agent, it might be better to have him bear the costs of his own shirking and thus avoid the necessity of monitoring. Neither of these allocations of risk is a perfect solution; each entails costs the parties would prefer to avoid and neither will eliminate completely the agent's shirking. What is required is an arrangement that will be the best compromise between the conflicting perspectives of risk controlling and risk bearing.

2.　ALLOCATING RISK TO THE OWNER

Some risks are most efficiently borne by the person who has the right to the firm's residual profits. For example, if Julia is richer or has other investment than Jonathan, she is probably less risk averse than him. As the person supplying the capital for the vineyard, she is presumptively its owner. She will be more willing to bear the risk of the success or failure of the business. On the other hand, Jonathan will prefer a fixed compensation because this is the least risky form of compensation. In this way, the owner accepts the uncertainty of business success or failure, and receives as compensation for this risk-taking the bulk of the returns if the business succeeds.

In this situation, the risk of the employee's shirking takes on greater significance for the owner, who must now directly or indirectly monitor the employee. Such monitoring consists of two parts. First, she must decide

---

[3]　More generally, the danger that a person who does not bear a risk will not take adequate steps to control that risk is referred to as *moral hazard*.

what constitutes optimal performance by the employee. Second, she must determine whether the desired level of performance is occurring or has occurred. The first part requires looking at shirking from an *ex ante* perspective, *i.e.*, before the employee has begun to work. The second part examines the employee's conduct from an *ex post* perspective, *i.e.*, after the employee has begun to work or has completed the work. In considering the costs and benefits of various monitoring devices, it is useful to keep these two perspectives in mind.

How might the principal monitor the agent? One solution would be direct supervision where the principal prescribes optimal standards, observes whether they are being met, and punishes the agent if they are not. This approach has obvious drawbacks. Deciding what the agent should do, obtaining information about whether she did it and disciplining wayward behavior is time-consuming and costly. It would undermine the main reason that the principal hired an agent, namely to delegate decision-making authority to another so the principal would have more time and leisure for other pursuits. Of course, the principal could hire a supervisor. Doing that, however, would create an additional problem: Who would supervise the supervisor? Maybe another supervisor, like a board of directors. In a small business, the principal might search for another less cumbersome solution.

An alternative monitoring device might be an employment contract between the owner and the employee. Such a contract would contain elements of both parts of monitoring: it would specify the employee's duties and it would prescribe the sanctions to be imposed if the employee failed to perform those duties.

In deciding whether such a contract is desirable, let us examine each part separately. Some aspects of the employee's work can be satisfactorily defined in a contract; other aspects are more problematic. Rather than looking at the terms of a contract as they might be drafted in the problem, consider a saleswoman for a clothing manufacturer whose job is to arrange for the clothing to be sold in stores in a given geographical area by meeting with buyers from those stores. A contract could be drafted with a provision specifying the number of hours the saleswoman was required to work and the number of stores she had to visit. Would such a provision be desirable? Where success is measured primarily by the quality of a person's effort, it is difficult to define the optimal level of that effort in a contract. The number of hours worked may not be as important as the way in which the hours were spent; the number of stores visited may not be as significant as what transpired in each store. Most important, a large number of hours spent working does not guarantee corresponding profits. Input does not always correlate with output.

Because of the *ex ante* drafting difficulty, shirking may continue even if there is a contract. This shirking does not vitiate the desirability of a contract; it may simply cause us to bring an *ex post* perspective to bear on the drafting. In the example of the saleswoman, consider the following provision: "Saleswoman will use her best efforts in selling employer's clothes. Any dispute over this issue will be resolved by an arbitrator mutually acceptable to the parties."

The term "best efforts" prescribes the saleswoman's efforts *ex ante*. In the terms we have used, although seemingly vague, it calls upon the employee to expend the same effort she would expend if she bore the entire risk. It also has the advantage of being given content after the fact by reference to the actual circumstances encountered by the employee and the steps she took to accomplish the task assigned to her.

From an *ex post* perspective, the enforcement mechanism of such a clause may be a useful monitoring device. In deciding whether to enforce the clause, the employer could use easily observable measures to alert her to the possibility that the employee was shirking. For example, the employer could compare the sales of the employee with those made in the previous year or by other salespeople. If, after such comparison, the owner also found that the venture's sales were high, she could infer that the saleswoman had used her best efforts. If, however, sales were low, the owner could then invoke the dispute resolution process to determine whether the saleswoman had, in fact, used her best efforts. Because the saleswoman could not know *ex ante* whether her employer would try to enforce the contract, her incentive to shirk would be reduced.

From an *ex ante* perspective, another problem encountered in devising an appropriate monitoring system is that the parties are unlikely to foresee all the contingencies that might arise over the life of the contract, particularly if the contract is for a long period of time. Moreover, some contingencies that are foreseeable may be so unlikely to occur that the costs of drafting provisions to deal with them would exceed the expected benefits. If, however, such a contingency did arise, how should the contract be construed? Some economists argue that a court should decide how the parties would have provided for the contingency if they had originally thought to do so.

At first blush, such a method of analysis may seem impossible and unrealistic. But economists who support this approach would argue that, although each party may have been concerned primarily with maximizing her own return from the venture rather than with the venture's total return, it is fair to assume each party would recognize that her share is likely to increase if the total return is greater. Therefore, a court should assume the parties would have adopted the provision maximizing the overall return.

Others, including some economists, question whether the provision that would maximize overall returns easily can be identified and suggest that, in any event, reasonable persons may well be more concerned with ensuring a fair division of returns than with maximizing total returns. These arguments will recur in a variety of contexts throughout this book.

Although less expensive than direct supervision by the owner, contracting is a costly method of specifying optimal performance for both parties. Information, negotiation and drafting costs all must be incurred (lawyers' time is not cheap). Moreover, the potential cost of enforcing contracts are high and cannot be disregarded, even if they never actually materialize Finally, keep in mind that the use of a contract shifts the ultimate resolution of a dispute to a third party—a court or an arbitrator— and thereby creates uncertainty for both parties to the contract.

3. ALLOCATING RISK TO THE EMPLOYEE

Thus far, we have assumed an organizational model that places the risk of the employee's shirking entirely on the owner. Under this model, the principal is likely to incur monitoring and disciplining costs, which will reduce, but not eliminate completely, the employee's shirking. A different organizational model would place the risk of shirking entirely on the employee.

Julia could rent the vineyard to Jonathan for a fixed rental and allow him to retain all the vineyard profits. This arrangement would create gains for Julia by reducing her monitoring costs. The bulk of the monitoring would be Jonathan's self-monitoring. If he works less hard, it will be because he values his non-work activities more than the fruits of his work; his reduced business profits will be counterbalanced by the value he places on those activities. The only immediate risk to Julia is that Jonathan will be unable to pay the rent if payment is delayed until the end.

A less drastic way of allocating risk to the agent is to base the employee's compensation on the success or failure of the business, thus rewarding or penalizing his efforts if they do not produce satisfactory results. For example, Julia and Jonathan might agree to the following: "Jonathan is to be paid an annual salary of $X. But if the vineyard's annual net income is less than $Y, his annual salary shall be reduced by $Z."

Is such a provision desirable? The relation between Jonathan's effort and Julia's ultimate profit probably depends on numerous factors. Some are beyond the control of either party; some that are within their control do not relate to the specific problem of shirking. If shirking is Julia's main concern, she can tie Jonathan's salary to the size or quality of the grape harvest. On the other hand, to the extent the profits of the vineyard *do* depend on Jonathan's efforts, such a clause creates incentives for Jonathan and reduces the need to monitor and discipline his performance.

Even when the risks of the venture are allocated to the employee, monitoring might still be necessary if the parties have differing time horizons. For example, if Jonathan will only work for one year and his compensation is based on grape sales for that year, he might want to prune the vines lightly so as to increase current yields. Julia, in contrast, may have a longer time horizon. She might be willing to forego higher yields this year if heavier pruning would produce better grapes, fetching higher prices, in later years. In such a case, Julia would have to monitor Jonathan to protect her longer-term interests.

Finally, consider the situation of Jonathan when he stops working for Julia. If he shirked for Julia, he might damage his reputation, reducing his value to other owners as a vineyard manager. Instead, Jonathan will want Julia and others to conclude that he worked diligently for her, a signal to future owners to increase his pay and reduce their monitoring of him. Thus, reputation serves as a self-effectuating monitoring device. It is particularly useful in both the employment and tenancy models because it does not involve any reallocation of the risks or returns of the venture. The drawback with reputation as a monitoring device is that its success may depend on the relevant labor market. If there is a shortage of vineyard managers, reputation will matter less. If there is a surplus, it will matter more.

Which allocation of risks is better? If risk is the main concern, the owner might be the better risk-bearer by virtue of her ability to diversify and insure, or simply because she prefers risk. This model, however, carries a price since she must incur monitoring/disciplining costs to reduce the costs of the employee's shirking. If shirking is the main concern, the employee might be the better risk-bearer since entitlement to higher compensation will give her incentives to maximize the venture's success. This model carries a different cost, namely that the employee might not be willing or able to bear all the risks.

4. MIDDLE GROUND SOLUTION

Is there is a satisfactory middle ground? Suppose the owner and the employee agree to divide the profits of the business in a mutually agreeable proportion. The employee would still receive a fixed salary, although the salary likely would be lower in exchange for a residual claim to the profits. The employee's incentive to shirk would be reduced since any shirking would decrease her share of the profits. The owner would still need to monitor, but not as much given the employee's greater interest in the success of the business.

Two problems remain with the middle ground solution that may ultimately make it unfeasible. As the employee's returns become increasingly dependent on the success of the business, the employee will become more concerned about control. For example, when Jonathan was paid a fixed salary he was willing to follow Julia's orders, at least up to a point. But in the middle ground, when he became a risk-bearer, his perspective shifted and he became more interested in operating the vineyard as he saw fit, without interference including deciding what expenditures to make in its operations. Although Julia is likely to give Jonathan more control, it is unlikely to be complete because she will worry about his making decisions that are contrary to her longer term interests and she will have a majority ownership interest.

The control problem is tied to the question of the appropriate allocation of profits. Julia will have sacrificed some of her returns from the vineyard in the hope of reducing her costs. On the other hand, the greater Jonathan's share of the profits (and hence the lower his salary), the more operating control he will want. And the greater his share of the profits, the more he will be asked to bear some of the risks of the venture beyond his capacity to bear them. *Ex ante*, with no previous working relationship between them, it is hard to know what the appropriate compensation structure should look like. At best, it will be a guess, and there is no principled way to know how good that guess will be.

The middle ground has other more nuanced dimensions. Over time, the employee will develop specialized knowledge while working for the owner. For example, as Jonathan becomes more familiar with grape growing and with Julia's vineyard, he will become more valuable to Julia. Consequently, he might opportunistically demand greater independence or a larger share of the profits since he knows it will be hard for Julia to replace him. But that greater specialization is a two-edged sword. His acquired skills and knowledge will be primarily valuable to Julia and her vineyard, on which he will be dependent. Julia might demand more effort from Jonathan or a reduced share of profits since it will be harder for him to go elsewhere where those skills and knowledge may be less valuable. Although we have limited our analysis to a one-year relationship, these questions become more important if that relationship continues after the first year.

D. BEYOND AGENCY COST

Although the discussion of risk allocation is central to the study of corporate law, it is not the whole story. In the context of the relatively simple problem in this chapter, it is easy to assume that the analytic focus should be on "agency costs." In other words, Julia is the principal who "owns" the business and she hires Jonathan as her agent. As the owner, she has the right to tell Jonathan how to run the business. As her agent, Jonathan has the duty to make the company as profitable as possible.

But suppose that the vineyard is very successful and continues to grow, and Julia wants to retire and cash out. She incorporates the business and sells shares to the public in an initial public offering. Now there are 2,000 people who own shares in Vineyard, Inc. Are they "owners" of the company in the same way Julia was? Are they principals, and are the executives of the company their agents? Do the shareholders collectively have the right to tell the managers how to run the business? What if the shareholders don't agree? Corporations have boards of directors, in part to address this problem. They are supposed to represent the shareholders in monitoring the performance of the managers and the other employees. What mechanisms are available to assure that the board carries out that responsibility effectively? Do they have a duty to make the company as profitable as possible in the way that Jonathan was expected to do for Julia?

Suppose the company employs thousands of people, has issued bonds to creditors, has a line of credit from a commercial bank, is the major employer in the town, and is party to an informal agreement with the regional water district not to use certain legal but possibly harmful pesticides. Must management maximize the company's profits for the shareholders regardless of the effects on all these other parties? Is it enough for these other "stakeholders" to protect themselves through contractual negotiations or by using the political process? Or should the company take into account these other interests?

In other words, does, and should, corporate law go beyond dealing with the problem of agency costs? That question and the wide range of possible answers will occupy us throughout the rest of this book and informs much of contemporary corporate law.

E. BUSINESS PLANNING

You should keep in mind that the problems and materials in this book intentionally cast you in the role of planner and counselor to your client, a role to which many law school courses do not always expose students. Because the laws of business organizations are largely enabling, private parties are, to varying degrees permitted by the form of organization they use, able to arrange their affairs as they would like. They thus often turn to a lawyer to assist as a planner and counselor.

This kind of planning calls on the lawyer to address a variety of questions, the resolution of which depends in part on the form of entity used and in part on tailoring the basic form to create a structure that best meets the needs of the client. These questions include the following:

- How are the economic interests in the entity to be divided?

- How will the entity be controlled?

- How are owners or managers incentivized to maximize production and reduce agency costs?

- How are the interests of owners protected against opportunistic behavior of other owners?

- What kinds of self-interested behavior is permissible and what are not?

- How can owners separate themselves from the enterprise?

The laws of business organizations can be used to create a business structure that addresses these issues. The answers to these questions can determine the success or failure of the individual's investment and the business venture as a whole.

Remember that business people want to succeed. They want to make money, and typically do not want to end up embroiled in litigation if they can avoid it. Although law school emphasizes litigation, many lawyers, particularly business lawyers, more frequently play the role of advisor than litigator. The materials in this book emphasize the use the law of business organizations to plan transactions.

At first, you may find the role of planner somewhat uncomfortable. A real client expects her lawyer to structure business transactions so as to maximize benefits and minimize legal and business costs. These transactions must be accomplished in a world fraught with uncertainty, often raising novel and difficult legal questions. Just as often there will be scant statutory and case law directly on point. The client, however, is interested in more than the arguments that can be made on either side. She is paying very high rates for the benefits of her lawyer's legal expertise, experience, and, most of all, judgment.

In this book, we frequently ask you to recommend a course of action to a client. Making such recommendations should help you develop the sound judgment highly prized in business lawyers. You will also have the chance to be creative by suggesting alternative approaches to surmount legal or business obstacles, and achieve your client's objectives. Doing that requires a lawyer to understand both the nature of the client's business and its objectives. It also should force a lawyer to consider the ethical ramifications of what she is being asked to do. Clients rarely want to hear, "That is illegal," or "You can't do it." They are paying their lawyers to figure out, within the constraints of ethics and law, how *to do* something. The experienced, creative lawyer provides value to the client (and society) by charting a lawful strategy that allows the client to accomplish her objectives.

CHAPTER 2

INTRODUCTION TO BUSINESS ENTITIES AND CONCEPTS

■ ■ ■

We study business organizations because they have a profound impact on society. They are the dominant engine of economic activity in the United States and most of the economically developed world. Little needs to be said about the economic, social, and political impact of companies like Microsoft, Google, McDonald's, General Electric, Bank of America, and Facebook. Today, even small businesses, such as the local pizzeria and the handyman, are conducted through business enterprises. Collectively, large and small, business organizations are important social institutions.

The chart below shows the change in the percentages of the different types of entity from 1990 to 2012.[1]

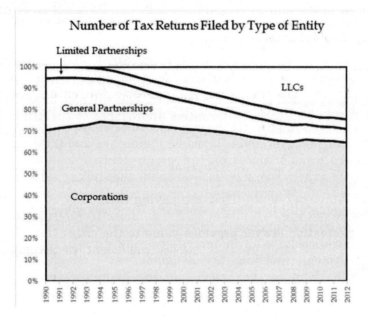

The above chart is interesting for several reasons. First, general partnerships are declining, and this decline is matched by a corresponding rise of LLCs. LLCs are the fastest growing entities in terms of entity

---

[1] Based on numbers of federal tax return filings reported by the IRS. https://www.irs.gov/uac/SOI-Tax-Stats-Integrated-Business-Data.

formation. Second, limited partnerships are a small and steady slice of the total business entities, and this is principally because they are most useful for specialized investment vehicles with passive limited partners as investors. Third, corporations are not growing, but they still constitute a large number of business entities.

A. TAXONOMY OF BUSINESS ORGANIZATION FORMS

In this book, we will study the major types of business organizations. As the above chart suggests, the universe of business organizations can be broadly split into two categories of business entities: corporations and non-corporate entities. After the introductory material in Part I of the book, Part II deals with closely held entities and Part IV with corporations.

1. CORPORATIONS

A corporation is the predominant structure through which publicly-owned businesses are conducted in United States and throughout the world, though interests in other entities such as limited partnerships may also be publicly traded as securities. Corporations range from giant, publicly-owned firms such as Microsoft to local family-owned businesses. Corporations can be classified based on either their tax status or the size of their shareholder base.

Tax status: The designations "C corporation" and "S corporation" refer to Subchapter C and Subchapter S of the Internal Revenue Code, which specify the tax treatment applicable to the entity. Most large corporations and all publicly-traded corporations are C corporations. They have two layers of taxation: (1) the corporation as an independent entity is an independent taxpayer and is taxed on its income, and (2) shareholders, who are separate and distinct from the corporation, are separate taxpayers and are taxed on their earnings, such as dividends and capital gains on sale of stock, made through ownership of shares. On the other hand, S corporations generally tend to be smaller corporations because there are significant restrictions on how the corporation can raise equity capital. Tax law treats S corporations as an aggregate of individuals. It permits pass-through treatment, meaning tax is applied at a single level of the shareholder as long as they meet the IRS requirements to be an S corporation.[2]

---

[2]   The IRS places significant restrictions on a corporation for it to receive this tax benefit. *See* https://www.irs.gov/businesses/small-businesses-self-employed/s-corporations. These restrictions include: (1) be a domestic corporation, (2) restricted to allowable shareholder (may be individuals, certain trusts and estates, but not partnerships, corporations, or non-resident alien shareholders), (3) have no more than 100 shareholders, (4) have only one class of stock, (5) not be an ineligible corporation (*i.e.* certain financial institutions, insurance companies, and domestic international sales corporations).

Non-profit corporation: Although the corporations that we discuss in this book are "for profit" corporations, corporations can be not-for-profit or "non-profit" corporations, which enjoy special tax benefits. These kinds of corporations are not studied in this book, which focuses on for profit business corporations.

Close corporation: A close corporation is a corporation whose shareholder base is closely held by a relatively small number of stockholders. For example, Delaware defines and requires a close corporation to have these features: (1) no more than 30 shareholders, (2) restrictions on transfer of shares, (3) no public offering of stock. Delaware General Corporation Law § 342. Corporation law may provide special rules concerning the governance of close corporations. For example, Delaware law provides that the business of the corporation can be managed by the stockholders of the corporation rather than by a board of directors. *Id.* § 351. A close corporation cannot be a public corporation, which has a large shareholder base and whose stock is publicly traded. Its shareholders are usually closely associated with managing the business, and in this respect, a close corporation often resembles the management structure of non-corporate entities.

Public corporation: A "public corporation" is a corporation whose stock is publicly traded, typically on stock exchanges.[3] Publicly traded means that the stock can be offered to the public at large, and anyone can become a shareholder simply by buying the stock. For a corporation to be able to issue shares to the public, it must go through a registration process under federal securities laws. On the other hand, a privately-held corporation, or a "private corporation," means that the corporation's stock cannot be traded publicly and is usually held by a small number of shareholders. Nonexclusive examples of private corporations are S corporations and close corporations, both of which have a limited number of shareholders. Public corporations tend to be larger, requiring investments from many public shareholders. Public corporations are C corporations and are not close corporations.

2.   NON-CORPORATE ENTITIES

Non-corporate entities are all other business entities that are not corporations. They are broadly categorized into partnerships and limited liability companies. Non-corporate entities can provide the firm structure for large, sophisticated business enterprises, such as significant business operations of Chrysler (limited liability company), Amazon (limited

---

[3]   A "public" company means that its shares (also called stock) is freely bought and sold in the public, typically through stock exchanges such as the New York Stock Exchange. A "public" company does not mean that is owned by or it is otherwise affiliated with the government. Nor does a "private" company mean it is owned by private citizens as opposed to the government. A private corporation refers to corporations that are privately-held and thus its shares are not publicly traded.

liability company) or Bloomberg (limited partnership), but the vast majority are smaller business enterprises.

General partnership: A general partnership is an association of two or more persons to carry on as co-owners a business for profit. Unlike entities that have limited liability, a general partnership can be created by partners without filing with the state. Because general partnerships do not have limited liability, partners are subject to unlimited personal liability for the debts and obligations of the partnership.

Limited partnership: A limited partnership is a partnership that is required to have at least one limited partner and one general partner. It is characterized by a formal separation of passive investors and managers. The limited partner is a passive investor in the partnership and enjoys the benefit of limited liability, which means that the limited partner is not vicariously liable for the debts and obligations of the limited partnership. On the other hand, general partners manage the business of the limited partnership. Like partners in a general partnership, they are vicariously liable for the debts and obligations of the limited partnership.

Limited liability company: A limited liability company (LLC) is typically characterized as a "hybrid" entity that has characteristics of both a corporation and a general partnership. Unlike a partnership and like a corporation, there is no requirement of two or more owners. An LLC can have a single owner (called a "member" in an LLC). Like a corporation's shareholders, all members of an LLC enjoy the benefit of limited liability. Most LLC statutes permit great contractual flexibility to design an LLC to resemble governance and management structures that resemble either partnership or corporations or some hybrid of the two. For example, LLCs can be designed to be member-managed, which resemble general partnerships, or manager-managed, which resemble corporations and limited partnerships.

A brief comment about the tax treatment of non-corporate entities is required. Unlike C corporations, partnerships and multi-member LLCs can opt to be treated as partnerships for tax purpose under Subchapter K of the Internal Revenue Code. The benefit is that Subchapter K treats partnerships as pass-through entities and thus tax them at the single level of partners. The entity and its partners avoid the two layers of taxation incurred by a C corporation and its shareholders. A single-member LLC is treated as an entity disregarded as separate from its owner for income tax purposes, meaning that the income is treated as the income of the sole member without regard to the entity. Anything beyond these differences in the taxation of corporations and partnership is for courses in partnership and corporate tax.

3.   WHY DIFFERENT ENTITIES?

As seen above, business entities can be categorized along several dimensions: (1) tax treatment is different between C corporations and partnerships, S corporations, and non-profit corporations; (2) enterprise purpose is different between non-profit corporations and for-profit businesses; (3) the number of "owners" is different between public corporations and firms with smaller numbers, such as S corporations, close corporations and many non-corporate entities.

In terms of the laws of business organizations, there are four commonly used, clearly defined business entities:

- General partnerships

- Limited partnerships

- Limited liability companies

- Corporations.

All 50 states have enacted statutes that enable the creation of general partnerships, limited partnerships, limited liability companies, and corporations. In the forthcoming chapters, this book will review these laws separately.

The existence of many legal entities raises the question: Why so many? The short, conclusory answer is that these entities provide different kinds of business structures and rules of internal governance that may be more suitable than the others given particular needs and circumstances of each business endeavor. We will learn that each entity has a different combination of features that make each more suitable than others given a particular business need. When advising in a business planning process, the lawyer's job is to advise on the selection of the most appropriate entity and then to custom tailor the entity for the particular need at hand. In the forthcoming chapters, we will consider the reasons for the different entities.

B.   WHY DO FIRMS EXIST?

A deeper question is: Why do firms exist at all? A "firm" is a legal entity used to assemble, organize and manage resources to carry on some economic activity. If business activities require cooperation among persons, why don't they engage in business by a series of individualized contracts with each other? To put this query more concretely, consider the system that produces the activities of ExxonMobil, a giant publicly traded oil company. In theory, it would be possible to replicate that system without a corporation by creating a complex series of contracts among all the individuals who participate in the business of ExxonMobil, including shareholders, creditors, managers, and employees. Why is it that, in a market economy in which individuals are free to contract with each other to create such a system, ExxonMobil is organized as a distinct legal entity? Economists have proposed a number of theories to answer that question.

The efficient functioning of any free market economy requires that producers be rewarded more or less in proportion to their productivity. In turn, there must be some means of monitoring productivity, determining the value of what is produced, and metering the rewards to the producer. In simple exchanges among individuals in an idealized free market, the price mechanism makes monitoring productivity and metering rewards unnecessary. The measure of productivity of individuals is their output; and the rewards for that productivity are determined by the free market price at which they can sell what they produce. Each producer can decide how hard to work, and the market determines the amount of the reward that she earns. Think of a contract for painting a house or catering service.

However, in a more complex economy individuals find it more productive to specialize and collaborate. An entrepreneurial individual may find it advantageous to spend her time designing and selling widgets and to hire a skilled mechanic to perform the work of making them. The establishment of this arrangement is not costless. The entrepreneur will have to bear the "information costs" of finding out how much the services of a qualified mechanic are worth, and locating one willing to take on the job. There will also be the costs of negotiating an agreement with the mechanic. Together, economists sometimes refer to these as "transaction costs." An entrepreneur must also be concerned that the mechanic may not perform his work as efficiently as possible, a problem theorists refer to as "shirking." To limit shirking, the entrepreneur will have to monitor the mechanic's work. Since monitoring may not be completely successful in eliminating shirking, she will bear the costs of any residual inefficiency.

In a famous 1937 article, Ronald Coase argued that firms come into existence because their hierarchical relationships can minimize the transaction and agency costs inherent in the principal-agent relationship.

> The main reason why it is profitable to establish a firm would seem to be that there is a cost of using the price mechanism. The most obvious cost of "organizing" production through the price mechanism is that of discovering what the relevant prices are. This cost may be reduced but it will not be eliminated by the emergence of specialists who will sell this information. The costs of negotiating and which takes place on a market must also be taken into account. Again, in certain markets, *e.g.*, produce exchanges, a technique is devised for minimising these contract costs; but they are not eliminated. It is true that contracts are not eliminated when there is a firm but they are greatly reduced. A factor of production (or the owner thereof) does not have to make a series of contracts with the factors with whom he is co-operating within the firm, as would be necessary, of course, if this co-

operation were as a direct result of the working of the price mechanism. For this series of contracts is substituted one.

R. H. Coase, *The Nature of the Firm*, 4 Economica 386 (1937).

Firms allow for the establishment of a centralized management with relatively simple contractual relationships with the firm's employees pursuant to which the management is able to provide incentives for good work and disincentives for shirking. This structure avoids the costs of creating numerous separate, detailed contracts with independent agents. It also allows for the creation of long-term business relationships in the form of employer-employee relationships, the precise details of which may not be spelled out in a contract. For example, the employee will be paid a specified sum to perform those tasks assigned by the firm from time to time, as the need arises. Moreover, because the management is closer to the employees, it is better able to monitor their work at a lower cost than if it had arms-length relationships with many agents.

Other economists have pointed out that this theory has conceptual weaknesses. Although recognizing that minimizing transaction and agency costs is one of the central economic problems faced by firms, they argue that Coase's theory fails to describe precisely how firms address that problem. In a frequently-cited article, Armen Alchian and Harold Demsetz point out that, like individuals in a market contracting in series, neither the employer nor the employee is bound by any contractual obligation to continue their relationship. *Production, Information Costs, and Economic Organization*, 62 Am. Econ. Rev. 777 (1972). Instead, Alchian and Demsetz posit that a firm acts as the "centralized contractual agent in a team productive process." In this capacity, the firm is in a position to monitor the productivity of each member of the team and allocate rewards to each in accordance with her contribution, thus providing appropriate incentives for efficient work. Firms are therefore able to minimize the transaction costs involved in monitoring and creating contractual relations among the various participants in the firm. It is often difficult to determine the relative contributions of the members of the team. For example, consider several scientists working to develop a new drug. Working together as a team, they are likely to be more productive than if they worked separately without cooperating. However, it may be difficult to figure out relative contribution for the purpose of distributing rewards for effort and outcome. A theoretical free market could provide a means of monitoring the members of a team to minimize shirking and allocate rewards efficiently. But the costs of this service would be higher in a free market than inside the hierarchical structure of a firm. Alchian and Demsetz assert that firms can perform this function at lower cost than market relationships among independent actors. Because the firm performs the monitoring function, it receives the rewards for that service in the form of the returns to the firm of the residual profits left after payment for the other resources used in production.

These theories agree that one of the principal reasons that firms exist is that they reduce the information, transaction and agency costs that would exist in a theoretical free market in which individuals cooperate only by contracting among themselves. None of them, however, provides a fully satisfactory explanation of how firms actually succeed in reducing those costs.

Some economists argue that this is not a defect in the theories at all. They propose viewing the firm as a "nexus of contracting relationships and which is also characterized by the existence of divisible residual claims on the assets and cash flows of the organization which can generally be sold without permission of the other contracting individuals." Michael C. Jensen & William H. Meckling, *Theory of the Firm: Managerial Behavior, Agency Costs and Ownership Structure*, 3 J. Fin. Econ. 305, 311 (1976). Under this view, the members of the firm agree to cooperate with each other by forming a set of incomplete contracts through which they subject themselves to some degree of control over their activities in exchange for receiving the benefits of being part of a more efficient organization. Proponents of this view emphasize that the firm is not an individual, but "a legal fiction which serves as a focus for a complex process in which the conflicting objectives of individuals . . . are brought into equilibrium within a framework of contractual relations." *Id.*

In order to reduce the transaction costs of negotiating a new set of relationships for each firm, we have evolved "standard form contracts," including the partnership, the public corporation, the privately-held corporation, and the limited liability company. The existence of those forms reduces the transaction costs of creating firms by enabling entrepreneurs to choose among a set of well-understood standard terms.

Whatever theoretical explanation one prefers for why firms exist, the empirical fact is that they do. Even if none of the theories discussed above provides a completely satisfactory explanation, they at least shed light on the nature of the problems that firms must address so that we can better understand the legal rules that have evolved to govern their structure and operation.

C. AGENCY

Business enterprises require coordinated action among businesspeople. Partners co-own a business. Members and managers of an LLC work together. The board of directors of a corporation delegates to officers. Even a sole proprietorship, the simplest kind of business enterprise, may employ many workers. Most of these relationships involve individuals performing tasks on behalf of the entity or another individual. These relationships invoke the law of agency.

1. AGENCY PRINCIPLES

"Agency is the fiduciary relationship that arises when one person (a 'principal') manifests assent to another person (an 'agent') that the agent shall act on the principal's behalf and subject to the principal's control, and the agent manifests assent or otherwise consents so to act." Restatement (Third) of Agency § 1.01. The principal and agent manifest assent through written or spoken words or other conduct. The consensual aspect of creating an agency does not require an enforceable contract. Many agents asset to act as an agent gratuitously. An agency creates a fiduciary relationship between the principal and the agent, the core of which is that agent must be loyal to the principal during the agency.

Agency is important because an agent has the legal power to bind the principal in legal relationships with third parties. Businesses require agents to work on their behalf. The corollary to this is that agents can bind the principals for whom they work or represent as to third parties, which can create unwanted liabilities for the principal. The practical implication is that agency has both benefits and costs for the principal.

The authority or power of an agent to bind the principal can be created in three ways. First, *actual authority* is created "when, at the time of the agent's act, the agent reasonably believes, in accordance with the principal's manifestations to the agent, that the principal wishes the agent so to act." *Id.* § 2.01. There must be a manifestation from the principal to the agent for the latter to act as an agent to take action designated or implied in the principal's manifestations to the agent and acts necessary or incidental to achieving the principal's objectives. The principal's manifestation to the agent can be spoken or written words or other conduct. Actual authority is not limited to specific, expressly stated instructions. Actual authority can be implied from words or conduct to the agent expressing the principal's manifestation.

Second, *apparent authority* is created "when a third party reasonably believes the agent has authority to act on behalf of the principal and that belief is traceable to the principal's manifestations." *Id.* § 2.03. Importantly, the agent who acts purportedly on behalf of the principal need not have had actual authority from the principal. The agent can legally bind the principal because the third party's belief of agency, and thus its dealings with the agent or actor, is traceable to the principal's conduct (manifestation of asset). Upon learning of the agent's action, the principal may be surprised and displeased with what the agent has done, but if there was apparent authority the principal is unhappily bound even if she never intended the result.

Third, *inherent agency power* is "the power of an agent which is derived not from authority, apparent authority or estoppel, but solely from the agency relation and exists for the protection of persons harmed by or dealing with a servant or other agent." This concept is found in Restatement (Second) of Agency § 8A, but the Restatement (Third) does not recognize it. It derives from a bucket of miscellaneous cases in which courts have found no authority or estoppel, but nevertheless held the agent's action binding as to the principal. The comment to § 8A states that there are two category of situations. The most familiar is the power of an employee to subject his employer to liability for torts in situations where the employer's liability cannot be based upon any ordinary tort theory because the employment is not a causative factor in any accepted sense. The other type of inherent power subjects the principal to contractual liability when an agent has acted improperly in entering into contracts. A common situation is when agent does something similar to what he is authorized to do, but violates or otherwise departs from orders.

A principal may be bound by an agent's or an actor's action in two other ways. *Estoppel* can bind a person where there was no agency authority or power when a third party "is justifiably induced to make a detrimental change in position because the transaction is believed to be on the person's account, if (1) the person intentionally or carelessly caused such belief, or (2) having notice of such belief and that it might induce others to change their positions, the person did not take reasonable steps to notify them of the facts." Restatement (Third) of Agency § 2.05.

Ratification binds a person to a prior act done by another, where the person would not otherwise be bound, if the person ratifies the act by manifesting assent that the act shall affect the person's legal relations, or engages in conduct that justifies a reasonable assumption that the person so consents. *Id.* § 4.01.

A hypothetical may help illustrate these concepts. Suppose that Priscilla Principal, a horse breeder, says to her agent, Andrew Agent, "Andy, please go down to the stables, put up a sign, '*Horses for Sale*,' and sell all of my horses for $500 apiece." Andrew has actual authority by express communication to sell the horses. He also probably has actual authority implied in the order to accept an apparently valid check in payment since, as long as Priscilla had not previously demanded cash in such transactions, it is reasonable to assume that she intended that Andrew accept checks. He may or may not have actual authority to accept a used car or a hogshead of tobacco worth $500, depending on what would be reasonably understood from the circumstances (such as the normal practices in the trade or in the locality) and from the prior dealings between him and Priscilla.

Suppose now that Priscilla gives him the same instructions but adds, "Whatever you do, don't sell Secretariat." She also sends out letters to prospective buyers saying, "I am selling off my horses. If you are interested, please see Andrew Agent at the stables. He is authorized to act for me." If Andrew sells Secretariat to a recipient of the letter, Priscilla is bound on the contract. By communicating what would appear to a reasonable person to be an intention to give Andrew the authority to sell any horse, including Secretariat, she has clothed him with apparent authority and is bound by his act, even though it was contrary to her actual instructions.

Finally, suppose that Andrew has never before sold any horses for Priscilla (and thus has no actual or inherent power), but he nevertheless purports to sell Secretariat to the stranger. When Priscilla learns of the sale, she declares, "Well, I guess that's okay. Five hundred dollars is a pretty good price for that old stud anyway." She has ratified the transaction and becomes bound as if Andrew had been authorized in the first place. Indeed, she may be deemed to ratify the transaction if she remains silent and takes no steps to rescind it.

The following case provides an example of how agency principles can work in unexpected ways to bind a person despite the subjective intents of the actors. In reading this case, think about these questions: (1) How was an agency relationship between Cargill and Warren created? (2) Why did Cargill act the way it did? (3) How could Cargill have accomplished its goals without getting trapped into liability?

GAY JENSON FARMS CO. v. CARGILL, INC.
309 N.W.2d 285 (Minn. 1981).

PETERSON, JUSTICE.

Plaintiffs, 86 individual, partnership or corporate farmers, brought this action against defendant Cargill, Inc. (Cargill) and defendant Warren Grain & Seed Co. (Warren) to recover losses sustained when Warren defaulted on the contracts made with plaintiffs for the sale of grain. After a trial by jury, judgment was entered in favor of plaintiffs, and Cargill brought this appeal. We affirm.

This case arose out of the financial collapse of defendant Warren Seed & Grain Co., and its failure to satisfy its indebtedness to plaintiffs. Warren, which was located in Warren, Minnesota, was operated by Lloyd Hill and his son, Gary Hill. Warren operated a grain elevator and as a result was involved in the purchase of cash or market grain from local farmers. The cash grain would be resold through the Minneapolis Grain Exchange or to the terminal grain companies directly. Warren also stored grain for farmers and sold chemicals, fertilizer and steel storage bins. In addition, it operated a seed business which involved buying seed grain from farmers, processing it and reselling it for seed to farmers and local elevators.

Lloyd Hill decided in 1964 to apply for financing from Cargill. Cargill's officials from the Moorhead regional office investigated Warren's operations and recommended that Cargill finance Warren.

Warren and Cargill thereafter entered into a security agreement which provided that Cargill would loan money for working capital to Warren on "open account" financing up to a stated limit, which was originally set as $175,000. Under this contract, Warren would receive funds and pay its expenses by issuing drafts drawn on Cargill through Minneapolis banks. The drafts were imprinted with both Warren's and Cargill's names. Proceeds from Warren's sales would be deposited with Cargill and credited to its account. In return for this financing, Warren appointed Cargill as its grain agent for transaction with the Commodity Credit Corporation. Cargill was also given a right of first refusal to purchase market grain sold by Warren to the terminal market.

A new contract was negotiated in 1967, extending Warren's credit line to $300,000 and incorporating the provisions of the original contract. It was also stated in the contract that Warren would provide Cargill with annual financial statements and that either Cargill would keep the books for Warren or an audit would be conducted by an independent firm. Cargill was given the right of access to Warren's books for inspection.

In addition, the agreement provided that Warren was not to make capital improvements or repairs in excess of $5,000 without Cargill's prior consent. Further, it was not to become liable as guarantor on another's indebtedness, or encumber its assets except with Cargill's permission. Consent by Cargill was required before Warren would be allowed to declare a dividend or sell and purchase stock.

Officials from Cargill's regional office made a brief visit to Warren shortly after the agreement was executed. They examined the annual statement and the accounts receivable, expenses, inventory, seed, machinery and other financial matters. Warren was informed that it would be reminded periodically to make the improvements recommended by Cargill.[3] At approximately this time, a memo was given to the Cargill official in charge of the Warren account, Erhart Becker, which stated in part: "This organization (Warren) needs very strong paternal guidance."

In 1970, Cargill contracted with Warren and other elevators to act as its agent to seek growers for a new type of wheat called Bounty 208. Warren, as Cargill's agent for this project, entered into contracts for the growing of the wheat seed, with Cargill named as the contracting party. Farmers were paid directly by Cargill for the seed and all contracts were

---

[3]   Cargill headquarters suggested that the regional office check Warren monthly. Also, it was requested that Warren be given an explanation for the relatively large withdrawals from undistributed earnings made by the Hills, since Cargill hoped that Warren's profits would be used to decrease its debt balance. Cargill asked for written requests for withdrawals from undistributed earnings in the future.

performed in full. In 1971, pursuant to an agency contract, Warren contracted on Cargill's behalf with various farmers for the growing of sunflower seeds for Cargill. The arrangements were similar to those made in the Bounty 208 contracts, and all those contracts were also completed. Both these agreements were unrelated to the open account financing contract. In addition, Warren, as Cargill's agent in the sunflower seed business, cleaned and packaged the seed in Cargill bags.

During this period, Cargill continued to review Warren's operations and expenses and recommend that certain actions should be taken.[4] Warren purchased from Cargill various business forms printed by Cargill and received sample forms from Cargill which Warren used to develop its own business forms.

Cargill wrote to its regional office in 1970 expressing its concern that the pattern of increased use of funds allowed to develop at Warren was similar to that involved in two other cases in which Cargill experienced severe losses. Cargill did not refuse to honor drafts or call the loan, however. A new security agreement which increased the credit line to $750,000 was executed in 1972, and a subsequent agreement which raised the limit to $1,250,000 was entered into in 1976.

Warren was at that time shipping Cargill 90% of its cash grain. When Cargill's facilities were full, Warren shipped its grain to other companies. Approximately 25% of Warren's total sales was seed grain which was sold directly by Warren to its customers.

As Warren's indebtedness continued to be in excess of its credit line, Cargill began to contact Warren daily regarding its financial affairs. Cargill headquarters informed its regional office in 1973 that, since Cargill money was being used, Warren should realize that Cargill had the right to make some critical decisions regarding the use of the funds. Cargill headquarters also told Warren that a regional manager would be working with Warren on a day-to-day basis as well as in monthly planning meetings. In 1975, Cargill's regional office began to keep a daily debit position on Warren. A bank account was opened in Warren's name on which Warren could draw checks in 1976. The account was to be funded by drafts drawn on Cargill by the local bank.

In early 1977, it became evident that Warren had serious financial problems. Several farmers, who had heard that Warren's checks were not being paid, inquired or had their agents inquire at Cargill regarding Warren's status and were initially told that there would be no problem with

---

4   Between 1967 and 1973, Cargill suggested that Warren take a number of steps, including: (1) a reduction of seed grain and cash grain inventories; (2) improved collection of accounts receivable; (3) reduction or elimination of its wholesale seed business and its specialty grain operation; (4) marketing fertilizer and steel bins on consignment; (5) a reduction in withdrawals made by officers; (6) a suggestion that Warren's bookkeeper not issue her own salary checks; and (7) cooperation with Cargill in implementing the recommendations. These ideas were apparently never implemented, however.

payment. In April 1977, an audit of Warren revealed that Warren was $4 million in debt. After Cargill was informed that Warren's financial statements had been deliberately falsified, Warren's request for additional financing was refused. In the final days of Warren's operation, Cargill sent an official to supervise the elevator, including disbursement of funds and income generated by the elevator.

After Warren ceased operations, it was found to be indebted to Cargill in the amount of $3.6 million. Warren was also determined to be indebted to plaintiffs in the amount of $2 million, and plaintiffs brought this action in 1977 to seek recovery of that sum. Plaintiffs alleged that Cargill was jointly liable for Warren's indebtedness as it had acted as principal for the grain elevator.

The matter was bifurcated for trial in Marshall County District Court. In the first phase, the amount of damages sustained by each farmer was determined by the court. The second phase of the action, dealing with the issue of Cargill's liability for the indebtedness of Warren, was tried before a jury.

The jury found that Cargill's conduct between 1973 and 1977 had made it Warren's principal. Warren was found to be the agent of Cargill with regard to contracts for: (1) the purchase and sale of grain for market; (2) the purchase and sale of seed grain; (3) the storage of grain. The court determined that Cargill was the disclosed principal of Warren. It was concluded that Cargill was jointly liable with Warren for plaintiffs' losses, and judgment was entered for plaintiffs.

Cargill seeks a reversal of the jury's findings or, if the jury findings are upheld, a reversal of the trial court's determination that Cargill was a disclosed principal.

The major issue in this case is whether Cargill, by its course of dealing with Warren, became liable as a principal on contracts made by Warren with plaintiffs. Cargill contends that no agency relationship was established with Warren, notwithstanding its financing of Warren's operation and its purchase of the majority of Warren's grain. However, we conclude that Cargill, by its control and influence over Warren, became a principal with liability for the transactions entered into by its agent Warren.

Agency is the fiduciary relationship that results from the manifestation of consent by one person to another that the other shall act on his behalf and subject to his control, and consent by the other so to act. In order to create an agency there must be an agreement, but not necessarily a contract between the parties. An agreement may result in the creation of an agency relationship although the parties did not call it an agency and did not intend the legal consequences of the relation to follow. The existence of the agency may be proved by circumstantial evidence which shows a course of dealing between the two parties. When an agency relationship is to be proven by circumstantial evidence, the principal must be shown to have consented to the agency since one cannot be the agent of another except by consent of the latter.

Cargill contends that the prerequisites of an agency relationship did not exist because Cargill never consented to the agency, Warren did not act on behalf of Cargill, and Cargill did not exercise control over Warren. We hold that all three elements of agency could be found in the particular circumstances of this case. By directing Warren to implement its recommendations, Cargill manifested its consent that Warren would be its agent. Warren acted on Cargill's behalf in procuring grain for Cargill as the part of its normal operations which were totally financed by Cargill. Further, an agency relationship was established by Cargill's interference with the internal affairs of Warren, which constituted de facto control of the elevator.

A creditor who assumes control of his debtor's business may become liable as principal for the acts of the debtor in connection with the business. Restatement (Second) of Agency § 14 O (1958). It is noted in comment a to section 14 O that:

> A security holder who merely exercises a veto power over the business acts of his debtor by preventing purchases or sales above specified amounts does not thereby become a principal. However, if he takes over the management of the debtor's business either in person or through an agent, and directs what contracts may or may not be made, he becomes a principal, liable as a principal for the obligations incurred thereafter in the normal course of business by the debtor who has now become his general agent. The point at which the creditor becomes a principal is that at which he assumes de facto control over the conduct of his debtor, whatever the terms of the formal contract with his debtor may be.

A number of factors indicate Cargill's control over Warren, including the following:

(1) Cargill's constant recommendations to Warren by telephone;

(2) Cargill's right of first refusal on grain;

(3) Warren's inability to enter into mortgages, to purchase stock or to pay dividends without Cargill's approval;

(4) Cargill's right of entry onto Warren's premises to carry on periodic checks and audits;

(5) Cargill's correspondence and criticism regarding Warren's finances, officers salaries and inventory;

(6) Cargill's determination that Warren needed "strong paternal guidance";

(7) Provision of drafts and forms to Warren upon which Cargill's name was imprinted;

(8) Financing of all Warren's purchases of grain and operating expenses; and

(9) Cargill's power to discontinue the financing of Warren's operations.

We recognize that some of these elements, as Cargill contends, are found in an ordinary debtor-creditor relationship. However, these factors cannot be considered in isolation, but, rather, they must be viewed in light of all the circumstances surrounding Cargill's aggressive financing of Warren.

On the whole, there was a unique fabric in the relationship between Cargill and Warren which varies from that found in normal debtor-creditor situations. We conclude that, on the facts of this case, there was sufficient evidence from which the jury could find that Cargill was the principal of Warren within the definitions of agency set forth in Restatement (Second) of Agency §§ 1 and 140.

Affirmed.

2. AGENCY AUTHORITY IN NON-CORPORATE ENTITIES

Partnership and LLC statutes provide default provisions related to the authority of partners, members, and managers. In general partnerships, each partner has equal rights in the management and conduct of the partnership business." Revised Uniform Partnership Act § 401(f) ("RUPA"). The agency authority of partners is part and parcel of this rule.

RUPA § 301. Partner Agent of Partnership

(1) Each partner is an agent of the partnership for the purpose of its business. An act of a partner, including the execution of an instrument in the partnership name, for apparently carrying on in the ordinary course the partnership business or business of the kind carried on by the partnership binds the partnership, unless the partner had no authority to act for the partnership in the particular matter and the person with whom the partner was dealing knew or had received a notification that the partner lacked authority.

(2) An act of a partner which is not apparently for carrying on in the ordinary course the partnership business or business of the kind carried on by the partnership binds the partnership only if the act was authorized by the other partners.

Partners are agents of the partnership and have actual authority for carrying on the ordinary course of business for the partnership unless they have been deprived of that authority as a result of the terms of the partnership agreement or some other agreement. They do not, however, have apparent authority to take bind the partnership outside the ordinary course of partnership business. Of course, as subsection (2) provides, a partner may be given actual authority to act outside the ordinary course of partnership business.

A limited partnership requires a general partner, who manages the business of the partnership, and one or more limited partners, who are considered passive investors with no authority to conduct business for the entity. The statutory rules of agency reflect this dichotomy. Uniform Limited Partnership Act (2001) § 302 ("ULPA (2001)") provides: "A limited partner does not have the right or the power as a limited partner to act for or bind the limited partnership." As to the general partner of a limited partnership, ULPA (2001) § 402 restates the agency authority principles set forth in the above RUPA § 301.

The rules of agency in LLCs can be different from the rules in partnership. An LLC can be member-managed, which resembles a general partnership, or manager-managed, which resembles a limited partnership or a corporation. The original Uniform Limited Liability Company Act ("ULLCA") recognizes this distinction. ULLCA § 301 follows the rules of general partnership in that each member is an agent of the LLC in a member-managed LLC. However, when an LLC is manager-managed, members are not agents, and the managers have agency authority that reflect the authority of a general partner in a general partnership or a limited partnership. Under the ULLCA, agency authority is vested in the persons who manage the LLC, which is either members or managers (or both).

In the more recent uniform statute, the Revised Uniform Limited Liability Company Act ("RULLCA") changes the default rules of agency. RULLCA § 301(a) provides: "A member is not an agent of a limited liability company solely by reason of being a member." Unlike the ULLCA, which is modeled on the framework of the rules in general partnership and limited partnership, the RULLCA does not provide default agency rules based on one's status as a member or manager. When working with an LLC, it is important to check each jurisdiction's statute as the rules of agency may vary considerably. The following passage explains the change from the ULLCA and the RULLCA.

LARRY E. RIBSTEIN, *AN ANALYSIS OF THE REVISED UNIFORM LIMITED LIABILITY COMPANY ACT*

3 Va. L. & Bus. Rev. 35, 57–59 (2008).

One of the most distinctive features of LLC law is "chameleon" management—a firm's ability to choose from two sets of default rules, providing for management by managers or by members. RULLCA includes new rules that threaten the viability of this advantageous feature.

The LLC approach to management is best understood against the background of partnership law. The time-honored partnership rule is that each partner has "positional" authority as a partner to bind the firm. This is based on the idea that a partner's ownership interest gives her special concern for the welfare of the firm and therefore the right incentives and interests in the firm to participate in management. A significant problem with the partnership rule is that a centrally managed partnership cannot easily deny partners the apparent authority to bind the firm, because this requires notifying third parties of limitations on members' authority. By contrast, the limited partnership form offers the advantage of permitting the firm to limit the authority of non-managing members by providing that only general partners can bind the firm. Limited partnerships, however, have the potential drawback of inflexibility in the distinction between general and limited partners. The limited partnership control rule traditionally penalized limited partners who participate in control by making them liable as general partners. Although the most recent uniform law abandons this rule, the rule is still found in many states' statutes. Also, limited partnership law maintains a clear default rule of centralized management that may be inappropriate for many closely held firms.

The LLC form offers a compromise between the general and limited partnership rules by providing a way to allocate management authority while preserving partnership-type flexibility. LLC statutes generally require the firm to disclose in the certificate if it is managed by members or by managers. An LLC managed by members is like a partnership: each member has the power, as such, to bind the firm, at least as to ordinary matters, while all the members must agree as to extraordinary matters. If it is managed by managers, it is like a limited partnership, as the actual and apparent authority attributed to members devolves to the managers, and the members have no default power to bind the firm to third parties. Unlike a limited partnership under many statutes, the members can freely contract among themselves to allocate management power, for example, by permitting some members to exercise certain powers even in a manager-managed firm. Most statutes, however, provide that these allocations are not effective as to third parties unless they have knowledge or notice of limitations on statutory authority.

This combination of flexibility and clarity has potential costs for third parties dealing with LLCs. Limiting a member's power in centrally managed LLCs forces third parties to check the certificate to determine whether the firm has opted for management by managers. Even then it may not be obvious who the managers are, since there are generally no rules requiring public disclosure of this information. This structure puts some burden on third parties, thereby increasing their costs of dealing with LLCs. Yet it also limits the costs incurred by LLC members of determining who may bind the firm. State statutes have experimented with a variety of approaches in an effort to achieve the right balance, and the courts have been bringing some clarity to these issues by interpreting the statutory provisions.

RULLCA essentially abandons the careful compromise and distinctive features embodied in the dominant state statutory approach, as well as seeking to halt its evolution, by imposing brand new agency rules on LLCs. While RULLCA preserves the distinction between member-managed and manager-managed LLCs, it undercuts the effect of the distinction. The firm need not disclose its status in the articles and, more importantly, members and managers have no statutory default agency power to bind the LLC. By eliminating positional agency power, RULLCA unmoors itself not only from every other LLC statute, but also from the LLC's partnership antecedents clarified in generations of partnership precedents. At the same time, RULLCA does not align the LLC with any other model. The RULLCA LLC becomes a sui generis business form regarding the important category of agency rules.

The reporters' main rationale for the change was that the standard LLC rule is a trap for the unwary because third parties may not be aware of whether an LLC is member-managed or manager-managed. In other words, the expectations of a third party dealing with an LLC member may be frustrated if, for example, the third party assumes the member has the power to bind and is unaware that the LLC is manager-managed and that the member is not a manager.

3. AGENCY AUTHORITY IN CORPORATIONS

The power and authority to manage the business and affairs of the corporation resides in the board of directors. *See* Delaware General Corporation Law § 141(a) ("DGCL") ("The business and affairs of every corporation organized under this chapter shall be managed by or under the direction of a board of directors. . . ."); Model Business Corporation Act § 8.01(b) ("MBCA") ("All corporate powers shall be exercised by or under the authority of the board of directors of the corporation, and the business and affairs of the corporation shall be managed by or under the direction, and subject to the oversight, of its board of directors. . . .").

In many corporations—and all public corporations—the board delegates day-to-day management authority to officers and employees. Officers of corporations often have two titles, a "legal" title and a "business" title. Although the DGCL and the MBCA do not specify any particular titles for officers, many older corporate statutes require that there be at least a President, a Secretary, and a Treasurer. That requirement has survived in practice, so that even where there is no statutory requirement, many corporations designate individuals to hold those offices. Today most public company senior officers also have "business" titles, such as Chief Executive Officer (CEO), Chief Financial Officer (CFO), Chief Operation Officer (COO), etc. These titles, while not specified in the statute, are often associated with a "legal" title so that, for example, an individual may be designated as President and Chief Executive Officer. Normally the bylaws specify what titles are to be used and give some indication of the responsibilities of the officer who fills each office.

The principal officers of a corporation are as follows.

Chief Executive Officer (President). The senior officer with the greatest authority usually is designated the Chief Executive Officer (CEO). At one time, the corporation's President usually was the chief executive. More recently, though, titles have become less uniform. In some companies the President still is the CEO. In others, especially large corporations, the CEO is likely to hold only that title, and perhaps as well the "Chair of the Board," the director who presides over board meetings.

Chief Financial Officer. Corporations generally have a Chief Financial Officer (CFO). The Treasurer is the officer who manages the corporation's cash management function. The CFO generally is responsible for the corporation's financial records. The CFO can be the Treasurer as well, but sometimes a separate officer acts as the treasurer who reports to the CFO. In public companies, the CEO and CFO are separate officers, but in small companies the positions can reside in a single officer.

Secretary. Some corporate statutes still require that the corporation have one officer charged with responsibility for preparing minutes of directors' and shareholders' meetings and authenticating the corporation's books and records. That person often has the title of Secretary. If a corporation has a General Counsel, she is often the Secretary.

General Counsel. Many corporations have a General Counsel or Chief Legal Officer (CLO), who is the principal in-house lawyer and is responsible for managing the corporation's legal affairs. The General Counsel is not only the chief legal adviser to the corporation, but she is a business manager in that she supervises the work of lawyers who work in the corporation as employees (called "in-house" lawyers), and the work done for the corporation by outside counsel.

Vice Presidents. Large corporations will also have a layer of Vice Presidents (and sometimes Executive Vice Presidents or Senior Vice Presidents) who, like other officers, report to the CEO. Vice Presidents often head a business unit or a division of the corporation, or a major function such as operations, marketing, or engineering.

Most modern statutes allow officers and their roles to be designated in the corporation's bylaws or by action of its board of directors. The MBCA, for example, provides simply: "A corporation has the officers described in its bylaws or appointed by the board of directors in accordance with the bylaws." MBCA § 8.41. The comment to § 8.41 states:

> These methods of investing officers with formal authority do not exhaust the sources of an officer's actual or apparent authority. Many cases state that specific corporate officers, particularly the chief executive officer, may have implied authority merely by virtue of their positions. This authority, which may overlap the express authority granted by the bylaws, generally has been viewed as extending only to ordinary business transactions, through some cases have recognized unusually broad implied authority of the chief executive officer or have created a presumption that corporate officers have broad authority, thereby placing on the corporation the burden of showing lack of authority. Corporate officers may also be vested with apparent (or ostensible) authority by reason of corporate conduct on which third persons reasonably rely.

One pragmatic concern is the extent to which the third party must investigate the authority of the officer. Given that actual authority is within the knowledge of the corporation, rather than the third party, courts have developed rules of thumb to facilitate dealings between the corporation and third parties. For example, courts assume that the CEO, whether known as the president or by some other title, has authority to bind the corporation in transactions entered into in the "ordinary course of business."

> The rule most widely cited is that the president only has authority to bind his company by acts arising in the usual and regular course of business but not for contracts of an "extraordinary" nature. The substance of such a rule lies in the content of the term "extraordinary" which is subject to a broad range of interpretation.

> The growth and development of this rule occurred during the late nineteenth and early twentieth centuries when the potentialities of the corporate form of enterprise were just being realized. As the corporation became a more common vehicle for the conduct of business it became increasingly evident that many

corporations, particularly small closely held ones, did not normally function in the formal ritualistic manner hitherto envisaged. While the boards of directors still nominally controlled corporate affairs, in reality officers and managers frequently ran the business with little, if any, board supervision. The natural consequence of such a development was that third parties commonly relied on the authority of such officials in almost all the multifarious transactions in which corporations engaged. The pace of modern business life was too swift to insist on the approval by the board of directors of every transaction that was in any way "unusual."

The judicial recognition given to these developments has varied considerably. Whether termed "apparent authority" or an "estoppel" to deny authority, many courts have noted the injustice caused by the practice of permitting corporations to act commonly through their executives and then allowing them to disclaim an agreement as beyond the authority of the contracting officer, when the contract no longer suited its convenience.

Lee v. Jenkins Brothers, 268 F.2d 357, 365–366 (2d Cir. 1959) (holding that a life pension offered by the company's president to attract a new executive was within the president's apparent authority).

Generalization is more difficult with respect to subordinate officers. Their authority depends on the how a board has delegated responsibility within the particular corporation's management structure. Thus, any given case will turn on a court's assessment of the facts and circumstances of the transaction at issue. A third party who deals with a corporation's subordinate officers generally bears the burden of demonstrating that an act was within the officer's authority.

In some circumstances when authority is doubtful, the third party has a heightened burden to investigate the officer's authority. Courts require a third party who knows that a given transaction will benefit some officer personally to inquire in greater depth as to whether the officer has valid authority to enter into the transaction. For example, in *Branding Iron Motel, Inc. v. Sandlian Equity, Inc.*, 798 F.2d 396 (10th Cir. 1986), a lender could not rely on the usual evidence that a motel president had apparent authority to enter into a mortgage, when the lender knew the president was the ultimate beneficiary of the mortgage. In *Schmidt v. Farm Credit Services*, 977 F.2d 511 (10th Cir. 1992), a lender could not rely on a board resolution authorizing the president to sign a loan agreement, but had to make further inquiries, since the lender knew the president would benefit personally from the loan.

Even when authority appears not to exist, the corporation's inaction following a transaction with a third party can have binding effect. For example, in *Scientific Holding Co., Ltd. v. Plessey Inc.*, 510 F.2d 15 (2d Cir.

1974), during the negotiations for the sale of a business, the president and chief operating officer of the selling corporation expressed doubts about his authority to sign an amendment to the purchase agreement. Although the purchaser was on notice of the officer's lack of authority, he nonetheless signed. Several months later when the purchaser sought to enforce the amended agreement, the corporation repudiated it. The court agreed that the officer's authority to sign to the amendment was unclear. But even if he lacked authority, the corporation's "failure to repudiate the amendment for lack of authorization [from March] until mid-July estopped it from doing so later." The amended agreement stood.

The following two cases present typically complex factual situations. Keep in mind that the parties to the transactions are corporations that can only act through human agents. In reading this case, think about this question: Under what circumstances can these human beings bind their principal corporations?

SUMMIT PROPERTIES, INC. v. NEW TECHNOLOGY ELECTRICAL CONTRACTORS, INC.

2004 WL 1490327 (D. Ore. 2004).

STEWART, JANICE M., MAGISTRATE JUDGE:

On June 4, 2003, plaintiff, Summit Properties, Inc. ("Summit"), filed a Complaint alleging claims against defendants, New Technology Electrical Contractors, Inc. ("New Tech") and its parent company, Integrated Electrical Services ("IES"). The parties dispute the validity of a lease that Summit, as landlord, allegedly entered into with New Tech and IES, as tenants, for the property located at 6950 N.E. Campus Way, Hillsboro, Oregon ("the Campus Way Property").

[Coleman sold New Tech to IES, but remained as president of New Tech. His employment agreement with New Tech provided that:]

> Mr. Coleman shall perform such specific duties and shall exercise such specific authority as may be assigned to him from time to time by the board of directors. In performing his duties, Mr. Coleman shall be subject to the direction and control of the board of directors. Mr. Coleman further agrees that he will, in all aspects of his employment, comply with the instructions, policies, and rules of New Tech established from time to time by New Tech.

After the sale to IES, New Tech continued to do business as it had previously. [New Tech was the lessee in two buildings owned by Milestone. Coleman owned Milestone, New Tech's lessor. After the sale, New Tech's business grew and the managers of IES, New Tech's parent, decided to move to a new building at Campus Way. In April 2001, Crouser, New Tech's

Vice President of Finance, signed the lease on behalf of "New Tech Electric, Inc." Coleman signed the lease on behalf of Milestone.]

After the lease was signed and the improvements were underway, Summit learned that the Campus Way Property was for sale and being marketed by Grub & Ellis, as subject to a seven-year lease with New Tech. Before deciding to buy the property, Summit sought to fulfill its duties of due diligence by thoroughly investigating the circumstances surrounding the lease. In a report forwarded by Summit's president, Yoshio Kurosaki ("Kurosaki"), to Summit's Board members on July 18, 2001, Grub & Ellis alerted potential purchasers that "IES is not a financial guarantor of the lease, but does represent a strong financial backer, committed to the success of the company [New Tech]." However, in an e-mail dated July 19, 2001, to the real estate broker handling the transaction with Summit, Coleman wrote that "New Tech is a D.B.A. of IES and when I, as an officer of New Tech, am signing on behalf of IES [*sic*]. So IES is the guarantee [*sic*]. That's what I've just been told." Additionally, on August 6, 2001, Milestone's attorney wrote to Summit as follows:

> Apparently your client has misunderstood certain comments regarding which specific entity is obligated under the [Campus Way Property lease]. This letter serves to clarify the identity of the party obligated to perform the duties of the tenant under the lease.

> The lease agreement ... identified [Milestone] as the landlord and [New Tech] as the sole tenant. This lease is in full force and effect. The signature block clearly indicates that New Tech Electric, Inc. is the tenant under the agreement with no evidence of any subsidiary or parent company of New Tech Electric, Inc. as having signed the lease or having any authority to execute this lease on behalf of New Tech. The lease contains no references to any guarantor or guaranty of this lease. *Therefore, by way of clarification, I wish to reiterate that New Tech Electric, Inc. is the only tenant and sole obligee of the tenant's duties as provided in this lease.* Mr. Coleman confirmed to me that New Tech generates revenue more than adequate to meet its obligation under the lease.

After reviewing the lease and receiving these reports, Summit requested certain modifications to the lease. A broker for Grub & Ellis met with Kurosaki and informed Coleman by letter dated August 14, 2001, that Summit would lift its remaining contingencies and submit a deposit if certain modifications were made in the lease, including a clarification that the lessee was "New Tech Electric, Inc. a wholly owned subsidiary of Integrated Electrical Services.".

To provide the clarification as to the name of the tenant, on August 16, 2001, Holan sent the following letter addressed to Summit:

New Technology Electrical Contractors, Inc. (formerly known as New Technology Acquisition Corporation), a Delaware corporation, is a wholly owned subsidiary of Integrated Electrical Services, Inc.

A few hours later, Coleman faxed Summit four replacement pages to the lease that made several changes, including identifying the tenant as "New Technology Electrical Contractors, Inc., a wholly owned subsidiary of Integrated Electrical Services, Inc." An unsigned copy of these documents was placed in the New Tech lease file maintained by IES in Houston.

The next day, August 17, 2001, Summit informed Milestone that it had "become comfortable with the financial situation of the tenant" and would remove the contingencies it previously placed on the purchase.

[New Tech and Coleman moved their offices to the Campus Way Property a few weeks later. Shortly after the move, Robert Stalvey, the Chief Operating Officer of IES's Electrical Division attended the open house celebrating the move to the Campus Way Property. After the party, Stalvey wrote this letter addressed to Coleman at the Campus Way Property:]

> The new facility is just awesome. It was immediately apparent that much thought and planning went into the project. I have no doubt that it will serve New Tech very efficiently and will improve everyone's spirit and attitude. I could see, hear, and even feel a sense of family, dedication, integrity and moral conviction that makes me extremely proud that New Tech is part of the IES team.

IES publicized New Tech's move in its newsletter. Signs identifying IES and New Tech as the tenant of the Campus Way Property were displayed prominently on the side of the building. Pursuant to the lease, New Tech paid the rent, property taxes, maintenance costs, and insurance on the property during this period.

New Tech's economic fortunes deteriorated after its move to the Campus Way Property, coinciding with the collapse of the Oregon high-tech market it served. As a result of New Tech's loss of business, IES directed New Tech to sublet some or all of the Campus Way building. New Tech began that process in about July 2002 and continued through late June 2003. Given the bleak economic conditions in the Sunset Corridor where the Campus Way Property is located, New Tech's brokers, Cushman & Wakefield, could identify only one prospective tenant for the property. The effort to sublet the property eventually failed, and New Tech asked that the signs advertising the space available for sublet be removed in late June 2003. By 2002, Stalvey asked Coleman, Crouser, and Milestone several times for a copy of the lease on the Campus Way Property. However, Stalvey did not receive a copy of the lease until August 2002, when he traveled to Oregon in order to fire Coleman. Stalvey claims he did not look at it at that time, but instead placed it in his briefcase.

Coleman signed a severance agreement with IES on September 3, 2002, but IES' Lease Committee did not review the lease for the Campus Way Property until sometime in 2003. IES' investigators concluded that the lease was executed without the requisite corporate authority.

On April 4, 2003, New Tech and IES served Summit with a complaint in a Texas lawsuit alleging that the misconduct of Coleman and Crouser rendered the lease "void *ab initio* or voidable." On July 10, 2003, New Tech delivered the keys to the Campus Way Property to Summit, together with prorated July rent (covering three days). Since then, New Tech has performed none of its lease obligations.

Although Summit signed a listing agreement on July 23, 2003 to re-lease the Campus Way Property, it has not found a new tenant. New Tech argues that the lease lacked proper corporate authority. [Summit responds that Coleman reviewed the lease with his superiors at IES and mailed copies of the lease to them.]

Some testimony indicates that New Tech and IES' executives thought the proper procedure for a local official and affiliate to enter into a lease with IES or one of its subsidiaries was for the affiliate to pass it onto his regional superiors, who would then handle the remainder of the approval process and inform the affiliate of the result.

On the other hand, IES and New Tech have submitted an affidavit from Robert Stalvey, who was a high level IES official during many of the events in question, which demonstrates that the lease and its modifications violated IES' leasing policies in several respects. According to IES, the length of the term of affiliate leases was limited to five years. IES' policy prohibited affiliated leases from being signed by employees of the affiliated party and required pre-approval from the General Counsel. In most instances, these affiliated leases were also signed by the General Counsel, who was also an officer of the subsidiary company, although a few are signed by the parties as part of an acquisition or with pre-approval. Also, IES required that affiliated leases be approved by both the Accounting Department and the Legal Department. Finally, affiliated leases were subject to final review and approval by IES' Board of Directors, and all affiliate leases had to be reviewed at this level before any lease could be considered validly executed with full authority. According to Warnock, at the time in question, such leases were also typically executed by the General Counsel, John Wombuell, rather than by the parties involved on both sides of the transaction. The Campus Way property lease and its subsequent modifications violated all of these provisions.

Accordingly, a genuine issue of fact remains as to whether the lease was properly entered into by Crouser and thereby binding on New Tech.

Even if the lease did not receive proper corporate approval, Summit contends that Crouser had apparent authority to sign the lease.

Apparent authority can be created in a number of ways, including the principal appointing the agent to a managing position. "A managing agent is presumed to have the authority to do those acts which managing agents normally do, unless the principal has by some action given notice to third parties of the limitations on the agent's authority." Oregon follows the rule that "persons dealing with a known agent have a right to assume, in the absence of information to the contrary, that the agency is general," not subject to specific restrictions. However, a third-party has no right to rely on the apparent authority of an agent if he knows that the agent has no actual authority or is aware of facts that should put the third party on inquiry.

New Tech argues that Crouser's position as Vice President of Finance did not cloak him with apparent authority to bind it to a lease. However, Summit does not claim that it relied solely on Crouser's title. Instead, Summit contends that New Tech and IES made specific representations concerning the lease which reasonably led it to believe that they consented to Crouser acting on their behalf.

New Tech next argues that Crouser did not have apparent authority because Summit never spoke about the lease to anyone at IES or New Tech, other than Coleman. Whether Summit communicated directly with anyone at IES or New Tech is irrelevant. What matters is whether third parties, such as Summit, reasonably relied on representations made to the general public.

Through their conduct, New Tech and IES represented both to the public and to Summit that the lease was valid and, hence, that Crouser had authority to enter into the lease on behalf of New Tech. Although Coleman owned Milestone, he also was the president of New Tech, and represented during correspondence and negotiations with Summit that the lease was valid. At the very least, he failed to disabuse the notion that the lease was valid. Moreover, prior to purchasing the Campus Way Property, Summit questioned the identity of the tenant and its relationships to IES and requested changes in the lease that clarified New Tech's corporate status. IES' senior counsel responded to Summit by verifying that New Tech was IES' wholly owned subsidiary. By virtue of the Grub and Ellis' report and the prior letter from Milestone's attorney, Summit knew that IES was not a guarantor of the lease. However, IES had the opportunity when responding to Summit's inquiry to disabuse Summit of any notion that the lease was valid. It did not do so. Instead, it impliedly confirmed the validity of the lease.

Accordingly, a genuine issue of material fact remains as to whether Crouser had apparent authority to enter into the lease agreements and whether Summit reasonably relied on that authority.

Summit contends that because New Tech occupied the Campus Way Property from October 2001 until July 2003, it ratified the lease by reaping its benefits. Common law ratification is frequently used to force corporations to meet the terms of an unauthorized contract, often without any discussion of the fairness of the contract. This is the type of ratification for which the legal standards set out above apply. It is also the type of ratification Summit is contending occurred.

Furthermore, IES cannot raise an issue that the lease lacked proper corporate authority because it was unaware of the lease until the Lease Committee discovered it or Stalvey obtained a copy of it. Prior to receiving a copy of the lease in August 2002, Stalvey had ample knowledge such an agreement was in place and that IES and New Tech were benefitting under the lease. Indeed, Stalvey visited the premises himself for New Tech's open house in the fall of 2001. Furthermore, copies of the lease and reports concerning the lease were found in the files of unbiased IES employees in the accounting and legal departments. At the very least, IES ratified the lease by doing nothing between August 2002, when Stalvey obtained a copy of the lease, and 2003 when the Lease Committee reviewed the lease. IES and New Tech's counsel admitted at oral argument that it was sheer negligence for IES' Lease Committee not to have reviewed the lease prior to 2003, even though Stalvey obtained a copy in August 2002.

Finally, the evidence also demonstrates that at the very least, New Tech and IES acquiesced to the lease. Both New Tech and IES' employees occupied the Campus Way Property for a period of almost two years, with both companies engaging in numerous activities to maintain the premises, advertise them, and take advantage of them. Under these circumstances, by accepting even a portion of the benefits under the lease, both companies ratified all of the lease transaction.

Ratification is usually an issue best left to the factfinder, but no material issues of fact exist regarding whether New Tech and IES ratified the lease. Therefore, to the extent the lease is otherwise enforceable, the lease is valid as to New Tech without regard to any failures to adhere to internal corporate procedure in approving the lease.

MENARD, INC. v. DAGE-MTI, INC.

726 N.E.2d 1206 (Ind. 2000).

SULLIVAN, JUSTICE.

Menard, Inc., offered to purchase 30 acres of land from Dage-MTI, Inc., for $1,450,000. Arthur Sterling, Dage's president, accepted the offer in a written agreement in which he represented that he had the requisite authority to bind Dage to the sale. The Dage board of directors did not approve and refused to complete the transaction. We hold that as president, Sterling possessed the inherent authority to bind Dage in these circumstances.

BACKGROUND

[Dage, is a closely held Indiana corporation that manufactures specialized electronics equipment. It has a six-member board of directors. Sterling, besides being a director, had served as president of Dage for at least 20 years.

For many years, Sterling operated Dage without significant input from or oversight by the board. In the summer of 1993, however, Kerrigan (a new investor in Dage and member of the board) sought to subject Dage management to board control. Kerrigan hired a New York financial consultant to assess the company's performance, and retained a New York attorney to represent his interests in Dage.

In October 1993, Sterling first informed other directors that Menard (a home improvement chain) had expressed interest in purchasing a 30-acre parcel of land owned by Dage. When Menard gave a formal offer to Sterling to purchase 10.5 acres of the 30-acre parcel, Sterling forwarded the offer to all the Dage directors with a cover note acknowledging that board approval was necessary on the offer. Ultimately, the board rejected this offer, and Sterling informed Menard's agent that the Dage board had objected to various provisions of the offer.

Sterling then called Kerrigan and informed him that Menard would make a second offer for the entire 30-acre parcel. Sterling presented a proposed consent resolution to the board that authorized Sterling to "offer and sell" the 30-acre parcel. Sterling and Kerrigan (along with his financial consultant and lawyer) discussed the offer and Sterling was told that in soliciting offers for the 30-acre parcel, he was not to negotiate the terms of a sale. Kerrigan's lawyer Gorinsky reminded Sterling that any offer from Menard would require Board review and acceptance.

In early December, Menard forwarded a second proposed purchase agreement to Sterling. This agreement contained the same provisions that the Board found objectionable in the first proposed agreement, but unlike the first offer was for the entire 30-acre parcel for $1,450,000.

After a week-long series of discussions, and unknown to any other Dage board members, Sterling negotiated several minor changes in the Menard offer and then signed the revised offer on behalf of Dage. Menard accepted. In the agreement, Sterling as president of Dage represented as follows: "The persons signing this Agreement on behalf of the Seller are duly authorized to do so and their signatures bind the Seller in accordance with the terms of this Agreement."

Upon learning of the signed agreement with Menard, the Dage board instructed Sterling to extricate Dage from the agreement. Later, the board hired counsel to inform Menard of its intent to question the agreement's enforceability, though it was until March 1994 that Dage first gave notice to Menard of this intent.

Menard ultimately filed suit to require Dage to specifically perform the agreement and to secure the payment of damages. Following a bench trial, the trial court ruled in favor of Dage. The court of appeals affirmed, finding that Sterling did not have express or apparent authority to bind the corporation in the land transaction.]

DISCUSSION

Two main classifications of authority are generally recognized: "actual authority" and "apparent authority." Actual authority is created "by written or spoken words or other conduct of the principal which, reasonably interpreted, causes the agent to believe that the principal desires him so to act on the principal's account." Apparent authority refers to a third party's reasonable belief that the principal has authorized the acts of its agent; it arises from the principal's indirect or direct manifestations to a third party and not from the representations or acts of the agent. On occasion, Indiana has taken an expansive view of apparent authority, including within the discussion the concept of "inherent agency power."

"Inherent agency power is a term used . . . to indicate the power of an agent which is derived not from authority, apparent authority or estoppel, but solely from the agency relation and exists for the protection of persons harmed by or dealing with a servant or other agent." This "status based" form of vicarious liability rests upon certain important social and commercial policies, primarily that the business enterprise should bear the burden of the losses created by the mistakes or overzealousness of its agents because such liability stimulates the watchfulness of the employer in selecting and supervising the agents. And while representations of the principal to the third party are central for defining apparent authority, the concept of inherent authority differs and originates from the customary authority of a person in the particular type of agency relationship so that no representations beyond the fact of the existence of the agency need be shown.

We find the concept of inherent authority—rather than actual or apparent authority—controls our analysis in this case. Menard did not negotiate and ultimately contract with a lower-tiered employee or a prototypical "general" or "special" agent, with respect to whom actual or apparent authority might be at issue. Menard dealt with the president of the corporation, whom the law recognizes as one of the officers who are the means, the hands and the head, by which corporations normally act.

II

Our determination that the inherent agency concept controls our analysis does not end the inquiry, however. The Restatement (Second) of

Agency § 161 provides that an agent's inherent authority subjects his principal to liability for acts done on his account which [(1)] usually accompany or are incidental to transactions which the agent is authorized to conduct if, although they are forbidden by the principal, [(2)] the other party reasonably believes that the agent is authorized to do them and [(3)] has no notice that he is not so authorized.[3]

A

As to whether Sterling acted within the usual and ordinary scope of his authority as president, the trial court found that Sterling, a director and substantial shareholder of Dage, had served as Dage's president from its inception; had managed the affairs of Dage for an extended period of time with little or no Board oversight; and had purchased real estate for Dage without Board approval. However, the trial court reached the conclusion that "the record persuasively demonstrates that the land transaction in question was an extraordinary transaction" for Dage, which manufactures electronic video products. Thus, the court concluded that "Sterling was not performing an act that was appropriate in the ordinary course of Dage's business."

Given that the trial court found that Sterling, as president of the company since its inception, had managed its affairs for an extended period of time with little or no Board oversight and, in particular, had purchased real estate for Dage in the past without Board approval, we conclude that Sterling's actions at issue here were acts that "usually accompany or are incidental to transactions which [he was] authorized to conduct." Restatement (Second) of Agency § 161.

B

Next, we must determine whether Menard reasonably believed that Sterling was authorized to contract for the sale and purchase of Dage real estate. While Sterling's apparent authority to bind Dage was "vitiated" by Menard's knowledge that the sale of Dage real estate required Board approval, this information did not defeat Sterling's inherent authority as Dage president to bind the corporation in a "setting" where he was the sole negotiator.

Because the inherent agency theory "originates from the customary authority of a person in the particular type of agency relationship, we look to the agent's indirect or direct manifestations to determine" whether Menard could have "reasonably believed" that Sterling was authorized to

---

[3] Relevant to the case before us is the observation that if one appoints an agent to conduct a series of transactions over a period of time, it is fair that he should bear losses which are incurred when such an agent, although without authority to do so, does something which is usually done in connection with the transactions he is employed to conduct. Restatement (Second) of Agency § 161 cmt. a (1958). In this case, the Board positioned its corporate president, Sterling, to "conduct a series of transactions [ ] with Menard concerning the sale of Dage real estate." We find this section of the Restatement applicable to this case.

contract for the sale and purchase of Dage real estate. And considering that the "agent" in this case is a general officer of the corporation (as opposed to an "appointed general agent" or "company general manager"), we find that Menard "should not be required to scrutinize too carefully the mandates of [this] permanent agent[ ] who [did] no more than what is usually done by [a corporate president]." Restatement (Second) of Agency § 161 cmt. a.

Here, the facts establish that Menard reasonably believed that Sterling was authorized to contract for the sale and purchase of Dage real estate. "Sterling held himself out as president of Dage . . . he had served as president of Dage since its inception". He was a substantial shareholder and member of the six-person Board of Directors; he had managed the affairs of Dage for an extended period of time with little or no Board oversight and he had purchased real estate for Dage without Board approval. And although "early in the transaction, Sterling advised [Menard] that he was required to go back to his partners to obtain authority to sell the entire thirty acres, Sterling later confirmed that he had the authority from his Board of Directors to proceed."

We find it reasonable that Menard did not question the corporate president's statement that he had "authority from his Board of Directors to proceed" with the land transaction. We also find it reasonable for Menard not to scrutinize Sterling's personal "acknowledgment that he signed the agreement for the purchase and sale of the real estate by authority of Dage's board of directors." We believe this especially to be the case where (1) Sterling himself was a member of the Board, (2) the agreement contained an express representation that "the persons signing this Agreement on behalf of the Seller are duly authorized to do so and their signatures bind the Seller in accordance with the terms of this Agreement," and (3) Menard was aware that Dage's corporate counsel, Patrick Donoghue, was involved in the review of the terms of the agreement.

D

In *Koval*, this Court said: "if one of two innocent parties must suffer due to a betrayal of trust—either the principal or the third party—the loss should fall on the party who is most at fault. Because the principal puts the agent in a position of trust, the principal should bear the loss." *Koval*, 693 N.E.2d at 1304.

That maxim has particular resonance here. The record fails to reveal a single affirmative act that Dage took to inform Menard of Sterling's limited authority with respect to the 30-acre parcel, and the Board did not notify Menard that Sterling had acted without its authority until 104 days after it learned of Sterling's action. By this time, Sterling had taken additional steps to close the transaction. Dage's failure to act should not now form the basis of relief, penalizing Menard and depriving it of its bargain.

SHEPHARD, CHIEF JUSTICE, dissenting.

A board of directors authorizes the president to sell some real estate but requires that the sale be submitted to the board for approval or disapproval. The president understands that he must submit any sale to the board. He tells the potential buyer that he must submit it. The buyer knows that its offer must be submitted to the board after the president signs the sales agreement. The agreement is in fact submitted to the board and disapproved. Our Court holds that the agreement is binding anyway.

In the end, it is difficult to know how lawyers will advise their clients after today's decision. Where all parties to a corporate transaction understand that board approval is required and that it may or may not be forthcoming, the black letter law cited in today's opinion points toward a conclusion that the buyer's offer was not accepted by the seller.

While I agree with the general legal principles laid out by the majority, those principles seem undercut by the resolution of this case.

As the above cases illustrate, lawyers are often called on to protect the corporation from unauthorized actions by corporate executives and to advise third parties on the existence of corporate authority. For example, we can assume that Menard was represented by counsel who should also have been attentive to questions of corporate authority. What should Menard's lawyer have insisted on to resolve the question of Sterling's authority and to avoid the costly litigation that ultimately went to the state's supreme court? The court noted that "Menard was aware that Dage's corporate counsel, Patrick Donoghue, was involved in the review of the terms of the agreement." Could Menard rely on the presence of Dage's corporate counsel in the negotiations, since corporate counsel is presumably supposed to protect the corporation from any unauthorized actions?

Counsel representing a party involved in a major transaction with a corporation usually will insist on receiving adequate evidence that the individuals who purport to act on behalf of the corporation have authority. What is required is evidence that the officer has been delegated authority to act on behalf of the corporation. This can come from a number of sources: (1) a provision of statutory law, (2) the articles of incorporation, (3) a bylaw of the company, (4) a resolution of the board of directors, or (5) evidence that the corporation had allowed the officer to act in similar matters and has recognized, approved or ratified those actions.

Usually, the best evidence of delegated authority will be a copy of the minutes of the board of directors' meeting at which a resolution formalizing the board's grant of authority was adopted. The resolution, in addition to approving the transaction in question, should designate the CEO or some other officer to execute the documents and do the other acts necessary to consummate the transaction. In the case of a particularly significant transaction, the minutes might include, as an attachment, a copy of the contract that the board has authorized the officer to sign.

Somewhat less important transactions may be covered by more general delegations of authority. For example, the bylaws might state the officer's general authority or a board might generally authorize the CEO or other officer to enter into contracts of a certain type or up to a certain value. If a party to a transaction with the corporation has doubts as to the authority of the official with whom she is dealing, she can request a copy of the resolution delegating such authority and the minutes of the board meeting at which the resolution was adopted.

But a question remains. How can a third party be sure the minutes and resolution are genuine? Customary practice is to have the secretary of the corporation (or other officer charged with maintaining the corporation's books and records) certify the minutes and resolution. The secretary generally is held to have apparent authority to certify such documents, so that a corporation is bound by the secretary's certification. Thus, a third party seeking to confirm an officer's authority can proceed with confidence after the secretary has certified the minutes and resolution, and need not ask the directors personally to swear that the board voted to authorize the officer to act.

D. OVERVIEW OF BASIC LEGAL ATTRIBUTES OF FIRMS

Business entities have important characteristics that define the essential nature of each entity. Some of these characteristics are the same or similar across business entities. Others are different. These similarities and differences solve problems for business actors and create their own tensions within each firm as well. They constitute basic considerations in business planning and legal advice.

As different entity forms are presented in detail, the following section may serve as a reference for distinguishing the basic legal attributes of different entities.

1. LEGAL PERSONHOOD

Business entities are legal persons.[4] They are separate and distinct from their equityholders (*i.e.*, partners of partnerships, members of LLCs, and shareholders of corporations). Entity personhood is necessary because

---

[4]   *See, e.g.,* Revised Uniform Partnership Law § 201(a) ("A partnership is an entity distinct from its partners."); Revised Uniform Limited Liability Company Act § 104(a) ("A limited liability company is an entity distinct from its members."); Model Business Corporation Act § 3.02 ("every corporation . . . has the same powers as an individual to do all things necessary to carry out its business and affairs").

entities needs the legal powers of an individual. For example, entities need the power to sign contracts, own and sell property, sue and be sued, and do all other things necessary to conduct business.

At least for corporations, legal personhood goes a step further. Constitutional jurisprudence has established that corporations have certain constitutional rights, including due process and first amendment speech rights (we will discuss this topic further in Chapter 4).

2. LIMITED LIABILITY

The rule of limited liability is one of the most fundamental rules of business entities, and certainly of corporation law. Limited liability entities (*i.e.*, corporations, limited partnerships, and LLCs) provides limited liability protection to its equityholders (*i.e.*, shareholders, limited partners, and members).[5] Importantly, partners in a general partnership do not have limited liability.[6] Limited liability means that an equityholder cannot be held vicariously for the debts and obligations of the entity. The rule flows from the concept of legal personhood. It is said that the entity, as a separate and distinct person, is responsible for its own debts and obligations.

Limited liability does not mean that an equityholder is not liable for his or her own actions that create liability. Obviously, if a person is directly liable (*e.g.*, is negligent and causes a loss), liability flows directly irrespective of whether she was an equityholder in a limited liability entity. Limited liability simply means that one cannot be held liable by virtue of one's status as an equityholder. It creates a floor on one's investment loss. One cannot lose money beyond one's initial investment in the firm. Therefore, the purchase of Enron stock for $100 does not mean that the shareholder can be held liable for the outstanding debts and obligations of Enron at the time of its demise, a potentially massive amount of unpaid liability. The shareholder has simply lost the entire $100 investment.

Additionally, the rule of limited liability does not mean that creditors cannot contract for their protection. Creditors to smaller corporations and other limited liability entities often demand that equityholders personally guarantee provision of credit to the firm, which means an increase in the

---

[5]   *See, e.g.,* Model Business Corporation Act § 6.22(b) ("a shareholder of a corporation is not personally liable for the acts or debts of the corporation except that he may become personally liable by reason of his own acts or conduct"); Revised Uniform Limited Liability Company Act § 304(a) ("The debts, obligations, and liabilities of a limited liability company, whether arising in contract, tort, or otherwise: (1) are solely the debts, obligations, and liabilities of the limited liability company; and (2) do not become the debts, obligations, and liabilities of a member or manager solely by reason of the member or manager acting as member or manager."); Uniform Limited Partnership Act (2001) § 303 ("A limited partner is not personally liable, directly or indirectly, by way of contribution or otherwise, for an obligation of the limited partnership solely by reason of being a limited partner, even if the limited partner participates in the management and control of the limited partnership.").

[6]   *See* Revised Uniform Partnership Act § 306(a) ("all partners are liable jointly and severally for all obligations of the partnership").

equityholders' financial exposure. It is not uncommon to find such guarantees when creditors lend to smaller limited liability entities.

3.   PERPETUAL EXISTENCE

Legal persons do not have biological clocks and thus do not have temporal limitations. They can potentially have perpetual existence. Because they are separate and distinct from their equityholders, the deaths of the latter do not affect a firm's legal existence as long as there are other equityholders of the firm.[7] Business entities created under modern statutes can exist in perpetuity. For example, perpetual existence permits the Ford Motor Company to continue existence today though it was incorporated in 1903 and Henry Ford died in 1947.

Perpetual existence does not mean that a business entity *will* exist in perpetuity. All firms are subject to dissolution and wind up. Business entities expire for a number of reasons, including: (1) they are designed *ex ante* to have a fixed dissolution date; (2) they are voluntarily dissolved and wind up by their equityholders at some point; (3) they go bankrupt and are liquidated; (4) they merge into or combine another company and disappear.

4.   EQUITYHOLDERS

An *equityholder* is an economic concept that describes the interests of partners in a partnership, members in an LLC, and shareholders in a corporation. An equityholder is an investor in a firm, and she is entitled to the firm's equity. The firm's equity has two components: (1) profits, and (2) net assets. In the accounting definition, profit is defined as sales proceed (revenue) remaining after all expenses, including the compensation of creditors and employees, are paid. If one has a lemonade stand, profits are the revenue from sales after all expenses are paid including lemonade ingredients, employee wages, and interest payment on debt. Net assets are the firm's assets net of liabilities that must be paid to creditors. An entitlement to profits and net assets indicates that an equityholder is the person who stands last in the financial queue.

Why would anyone choose to be last in line? The last in line is the riskiest position because others have priority in payment. But it is the position that may have the greatest expected value because the equityholder is entitled to everything remaining after all others have been paid. For example, at the inception of Google, it may have been good to be an employee earning just a decent salary, but it would have been much better to have been a shareholder. Of course, the risk of having been a Google shareholder is that perhaps the company would become like

---

[7]   Under the Uniform Partnership Act (UPA), an older partnership statute adopted by a minority of states, this comment could not be said so unequivocally. The death of a partner causes the dissolution of the partnership, which simply means a change in the relation of the partners. UPA § 29, § 31(4). In parts of the statutes, the UPA conceptualizes the partnership as an aggregate of its partners as opposed to a distinct entity.

countless other failed entrepreneurial ventures instead of being a technology giant. No one has a crystal ball, and the shareholders of Google took a greater risk than its employees. Equityholders in business entities have different names: "partners" in a partnership; "members" in an LLC; "shareholders" or "stockholders" in a corporation.

Importantly, there is no reason why there must or should be a single class of equityholder. How investors allocate financial and governance rights among themselves is a matter of contracting among the firm, its managers, and equityholders. Business organization laws permit each firm to organize and structure the firm to fit its needs. Corporations can, and often do, issue two or more different classes of stock with different financial and governance rights attached to them. For example, a corporation can issue common stock and preferred stock, where the holders of preferred stock have certain priority rights to dividends and liquidation over common stockholders. Partnerships and LLCs can structure their equity to provide different sets of rights as well. With this said, in many cases a firm may find that having one class of equity makes the most sense.

Equityholders are frequently said to "own" the firm or is the "owner" of the company.[8] From a formal legal analysis, this is not correct. Ownership of property connotes control and the right to exclude. Business entities are not "owned" in a legal sense of property ownership. The concept of separate and distinct entity rightfully precludes this conclusion. A shareholder of a corporation as its "owner" cannot demand to be let into the corporate headquarter; he cannot direct his corporate "employees" to sign a contract; he cannot direct the board of directors to make a dividend payment. Partnership law makes clear that a partner is not a co-owner of partnership property and has no interest in partnership property, which is owned by the partnership as a legal person. *See* Revised Uniform Partnership Act § 501 ("A partner is not a co-owner of partnership property and has no interest in partnership property which can be transferred, either voluntarily or involuntarily.").

More accurately, equityholders own the bundle of financial and governance rights inherent in their stakes in the entity. For example, a shareholder is entitled to dividends when declared by the board of directors and she is entitled to vote for board members and certain fundamental transaction; a partner is entitled to his allocation of profit from the partnership and his right to manage the partnership. Thus, when one says shareholders and partners are "owners," the statement is really shorthand for the idea that equityholders have residual financial claims and certain

---

[8] For example, in a famous manifesto on the corporation's obligation to maximize profit, Milton Friedman stated: "In a free-enterprise, private-property system, a corporate executive is an employee of the owners of the business." *The Social Responsibility of Business is to Increase its Profits*, N.Y. Times (Sept. 13, 1970).

governance rights provided either in the enabling statute or the private ordering among the equityholders.

5. MANAGERS

The business and affairs of business entities are managed, either by natural or legal persons. The laws of business organizations authorizes managers certain powers to manage the enterprise. Different entity forms have fundamentally different rules of management structure and authority.

General partnerships: The default rule[9] is that partners will manage the business and that they will manage in a communitarian, collective way. "Each partner has equal rights in the management and conduct of the partnership business." Revised Uniform Partnership Act § 401(f). A prototypical, if not simple, arrangement is a law partnership between two attorneys where both have equal financial and management rights.

Importantly, the default management rights of general partners can be privately ordered such that certain partners can have greater management rights by virtue of having a greater partnership interest or simply the delegation of greater rights. A general partnership can also delegate management authority to non-partners. However, the statute imbues all general partners with significant management rights through various provisions in the statute, such as provisions dealing with agency authority.

Limited partnerships: The definition of a limited partnership requires as a *mandatory* statutory rule is that there must at least one general partner and one limited partner. There can be multiple general and limited partners, but there must be one of each. The general partner of a limited partnership "has equal rights in the management and conduct of the limited partnership's activities." Uniform Limited Partnership Act

---

[9]   As explained in Section D.4 of this chapter and subsequent chapters, the enabling statutes for partnerships and LLCs provide default terms that apply to the business entity in the event that the partners or members do not otherwise contract for different terms governing their rights and duties in the firm.

(2001) § 406(a). On the other hand, a limited partner is conceived as a passive investor. Thus, a limited partner "does not have the right or the power as a limited partner to act for or bind the limited partnership." *Id.* § 302.

A limited partnership is an entity that has a rigid, statutorily-required manager and passive investor relationship. Thus, enterprises using this form is typically some sort of an investment vehicle such as real estate investments and investment funds, which require professional managers and capital-providing passive investors.

Limited liability companies: An LLC is perhaps the most flexible business entity form. It can be "member-managed" LLC in which members collectively manage the LLC in a way that partners manage a general partnership, the default rule of equal management rights. Revised Uniform Limited Liability Company Act § 407(b). An LLC can be "manager-managed" LLC, which can resemble the management structures of limited partnerships or corporations. *Id.* § 407(c).

A manager of an LLC can be a member in the way that a general partner of a limited partnership is a partner. However, a manager can be, but need not be, a member of the LLC. *Id.* § 407(c)(6). A manager-managed LLC can mimic the form of corporate governance by installing a formal "board of directors." However, unlike a corporation, nothing in the statute requires that an LLC be managed in a particular way. Statutes in most states enable the constituents of an LLC to form a governance structure through private ordering.

Corporations: A corporation is required to have a board of directors. *See, e.g.,* MBCA § 8.01(a) ("each corporation must have a board of directors"). A fundamental tenet of corporation law is that the board has the power to manage the business and affairs of the corporation. *Id.* § 8.01(b). Like shareholders in a close corporation, shareholders in a public corporation can have a substantial or controlling stake in the corporation; in such case, they can exert significant influence on the corporation's management. However, shareholders generally do not manage the corporation. They are generally passive investors, and for public companies especially they are typically a diffuse group. Their principal governance role comprise of two functions: (1) to vote for the board of directors, and (2) to vote on amendments to charter documents and certain fundamental transactions, such as mergers and acquisitions.

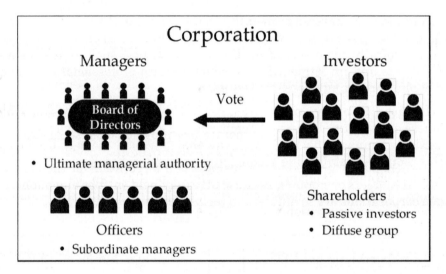

The board of directors selects the officers of the corporation, typically, a chief executive officer (CEO) who is the top officer, a chief financial officer (CFO) who is directly responsible for managing the company's finances, one or more vice presidents who directly manage business units or functions, and a secretary who is responsible for preparing board minutes and authenticating corporate records. The board of directors does not run the day-to-day business operations. Officers do this. Most corporate statutes do not specify which officers a corporation must have. Corporate bylaws generally describe the duties of the officers.

6. SEPARATION OF OWNERSHIP AND CONTROL

More than any other entity, the corporation exemplifies the concept of the separation of ownership and control. Shareholders do not own the assets of the corporation, but through the ownership of shares they have an ownership interest in the corporation. In early twentieth century when public corporations were becoming prominent, Adolf Berle and Gardiner Means observed the following.

> Though the American law makes no distinction between the private corporation and the quasi-public, the economics of the two are essentially different. The separation of ownership from control produces a condition where the interests of owner and of ultimate manager may, and often do, diverge, and where many of the checks which formerly operated to limit the use of power disappear. Size alone tends to give these giant corporations a social significance not attached to the smaller units of private enterprise. By the use of the open market for securities, each of these corporations assumes obligations towards the investing public which transform it from a legal method clothing the rule of a few individuals into an institution at least nominally serving investors who have embarked their funds in its enterprise.

Adolf A. Berle & Gardiner C. Means, The Modern Corporation and Private Property (1932).

In the early twenty-first century, the concept of separation of ownership and control still exists and is a major facet of the corporate form. *See* N. Am. Catholic Educ. Prog. Foundation, Inc. v. Gheewalla, 930 A.2d 92, 101 (Del. 2007) ("Delaware corporate law provides for a separation of control and ownership. The directors of Delaware corporations have 'the legal responsibility to manage the business of a corporation for the benefit of its shareholders owners.' "). Because privately-held entities and publicly-traded corporations are so different in terms of the number of equityholders and more generally the size of the business enterprise, the monitoring and accountability mechanisms present different problems and potential solutions. However, in the modern era, there is also a group of shareholders who are not passive investors. They take significant stakes in companies, for example stakes as large as 5 to 20 percent or even larger, with an eye toward having a direct say in management, governance, corporate strategy, and other matters of corporate internal affairs. These investors are called "activist shareholders," many of whom operate through investment funds called hedge funds.

Activist Investor

Problem: Chesapeake Marine Services

This problem is intended to help introduce terms and concepts applicable to a corporation. We will examine all of them in greater detail in later chapters.

Chesapeake Marine Services, Inc., ("Chesapeake") is a Delaware corporation whose business consists principally of the provision of barge and towing services. It also maintains a small shipyard in which it services its own vessels and does some work for others. Its certificate of incorporation contains the following provisions:

> FOURTH. A. The Corporation shall have the authority to issue 1,000,000 shares of Common Stock, par value $.01 per share.

> TENTH. Wherever approval by a vote of the shareholders is required by statute for any action, such approval shall be by the holders of two-thirds of the outstanding shares entitled to vote thereon.

Chesapeake has 1,000,000 common shares outstanding, all of which are held by descendants of Louis Lambert and Richard Tyler, Chesapeake's founders. Theresa Tyler, Richard's granddaughter, holds 300,000 shares and is the president Chief Executive Officer of the corporation. Larry Lambert, Louis' only grandson, is a director and the largest shareholder, with 350,000 shares. Larry also owns a half interest in United Harbor Services, Inc. ("United") a somewhat smaller firm that is a competitor of Chesapeake's in the towing business. He was once the Chief Operating Officer of Chesapeake but resigned when he acquired his interest in United. The remaining shares of Chesapeake are distributed among other members of the Lambert and Tyler families. The five-member board consists of Theresa, her brother and sister, Larry, and Larry's mother.

In the last two years, Chesapeake's business has been growing, and Theresa wants to expand the facilities of the shipyard and purchase two more vessels. Moreover because of the growth of the business, it needs more working capital, and recently it has had to delay payments to suppliers, resulting in the loss of discounts for prompt payment. As a consequence, Theresa believes Chesapeake needs more capital. Her brother and sister agree with her, but the two Lamberts do not.

Theresa has asked the board to approve a plan to raise additional equity capital by selling more common stock. Larry has declared that he is opposed to the plan and says he will do everything he can to block it.

You have known Theresa for some time, and you have advised her occasionally on business-related legal issues, though you have not done any work for Chesapeake. She has now come to you for advice. She asks you the following questions:

    1.   As a general matter, what options might be available to Chesapeake to raise additional capital?

    2.   Can Larry block the plan to raise new equity capital? How?

    3.   Is Larry's interest in a competing business a relevant consideration?

    4.   Why does the certificate of incorporation contain a limit on the number of shares of common stock that can be issued?

5.   Is Article TENTH of the certificate of incorporation consistent with Delaware law? Why did the founders of the company include it?

In a follow-up conversation Theresa confirms that she has been unable to obtain any form of credit financing. Based on your earlier advice, she is concerned that Larry will be able to block any sale of common stock by Chesapeake. She asks you about the following alternative plan which was suggested to her by an investment banker she knows:

- Chesapeake forms a subsidiary and transfers the business and assets of the shipyard to it in exchange for shares of the subsidiary's stock.

- The subsidiary then sells additional shares to a wealthy investor whom Theresa believes may be willing to invest in the business.

- The subsidiary uses some of the capital thus raised to expand the shipyard's operations and loans some to its parent to use for working capital and to purchase a new vessel.

1.   What possible legal obstacles would you want to explore before advising Theresa on the viability of this alternative? Is Larry in a position to block it? What about his interest in the competing business?

2.   Assuming you determine to proceed with this proposal, what formal legal steps would be required?

E.   BASIC TERMS AND CONCEPTS OF BUSINESS ENTITIES

1.   SOURCES OF LAWS OF BUSINESS ORGANIZATIONS

The laws of business organizations, including corporate law, are primarily a matter of state law. Every state has a set of statutes enabling the creation of general partnerships, limited partnerships, limited liability companies, and corporations. These statutes constitute the first source of laws. Like all statute-based laws, there are gaps in the statutes or interpretive uncertainties. When required, the common law process of judicial decisions and precedent constitute the second source of laws. Thus, the laws of business organizations are a combination of statute and common law.

Federal laws apply in specific areas affecting business organizations. Business organizations are subject to federal tax laws. Aside from tax law, federal law plays little direct role in the rules of governance and internal affairs of private business entities (*i.e.*, entities that not publicly traded or reporting companies under federal securities laws). The laws of non-corporate business entities are almost exclusively governed by state law in respect of their internal affairs. With respect to publicly traded corporations, state corporation laws are supplemented by an array of federal laws regulating, among other things, securities and proxies, disclosures to the public, accounting matters, and mergers and acquisitions. Federal statutes such as the Sarbanes-Oxley Act, the Dodd-Frank Act, the Williams Act, and federal securities laws contain provisions that regulate particular aspects of the conduct of corporations, boards of directors, and officers. Thus, for public companies especially, one can fairly say that state law principally governs corporation law, but federal law substantially supplements laws related to such matters as structure of boards, obligations of boards and management, shareholder rights and powers.

State statutes control the organization and governance of non-corporate entities. With respect to general partnerships and limited partnerships, the uniform laws as promulgated by the National Conference of Commissioners on Uniform State Laws are heavily influential. The commission has promulgated several versions of statutes governing general partnerships and limited partnerships. The major uniform statutes are:

General partnership

- Revised Uniform Partnership Act (1997) ("RUPA")[10]

Limited partnership

- Revised Uniform Limited Partnership Act (1976) ("RULPA")
- Uniform Partnership Act (2001) ("ULPA (2001)")

Limited liability company

- Revised Uniform Limited Liability Company Act (2006) ("RULLCA")

Most states have enacted some version of uniforms laws for general partnerships and limited partnership. With respect to limited partnerships, a significant minority of states have adopted the ULPA (2001), and a majority of states have adopted the RULPA (as discussed in Chapter 7, these two statutes are very different).

There is greater variance in LLC statutes, however. At last count, only 17 states and the District of Columbia have adopted the RULLCA. Other states have adopted their own statutes. The greater diversity in laws may be due to the fact that LLCs are the newest entities of the three major non-corporate entities, and states may be still experimenting with their laws.

The laws governing corporations are principally state law. There is no general federal corporation statute. Every state has enacted a statute

---

[10] A small minority of states have adopted the earlier version of the statute, Uniform Partnership Act (1914).

enabling the creation of corporations. Like the laws of non-corporate entities, several statutes are influential. The two most influential statutes are:

Corporation

- Model Business Corporation Act ("MBCA")
- Delaware General Corporation Act ("DGCL")

The MBCA is the product of the Committee on Corporate Laws of the American Bar Association. It is a model act, and thus it must be adopted by a state. A significant majority of states have adopted some version of the MBCA with individual tweaks by each state legislatures. The adoption of the MBCA has the effect of promoting uniformity in state corporation law.[11]

unique

The DGCL is *sui generis*—unlike any other state statute both in form and substance—but its influence on corporate law is outsized. Although Delaware is a small state by land size and population with few industries physically present within state borders, it figures large in corporation law. A majority of the public companies listed on the New York Stock Exchange are Delaware incorporated companies. Unlike most states, the Delaware legislature amends the DGCL annually to take account of new developments, practices and judicial decisions in corporate law. Additionally, Delaware courts have an expertise and a highly developed corporate law jurisprudence that other state courts often follow even though the statutes in those states differ from the DGCL. More than any other jurisdiction, Delaware law depends heavily on the common law process to make corporation law, even though the DGCL is a comprehensive, artfully drafted statute. Because of the unique position Delaware has occupied in corporate law for decades, its courts have developed the most extensive body of corporate jurisprudence in the country and have had a great influence on the evolution of corporate law in the United States.[12]

NOTE

The above statutes are typically referred to by their acronyms. These acronyms are confusing, a veritable alphabet soup of entities and statutes, but one must overcome this confusion. Throughout the remainder of this book, the statutes will be cited by their acronyms.

---

[11] Unlike other areas of law where the American Law Institute has adopted Restatements that collect and synthesize judge-made rules, there is no Restatement for corporate law. Instead, in 1994, the Institute adopted a series of principles of corporate law and corporate governance. ALI Principles of Corporate Governance: Analysis and Recommendations (1994) The ALI Principles have achieved some influence in corporate law cases although not nearly as much as have ALI Restatements in other areas of the law.

[12] *See generally* Randy J. Holland, *Delaware's Business Courts: Litigation Leadership*, 34 J. Corp. L. 771 (2009) (describing advantages and expertise of Delaware's business courts).

2. INTERNAL AFFAIRS AND CHOICE OF LAW

There is no requirement that business entities form in the state of its principal place of business or where its participants reside. All business entities that have limited liability must be created through a filing with a state, and businesspersons can choose any jurisdiction to file.[13] Thus, an important characteristic of American business organization law is its animating choice of law rule: the law of the state of filing governs the "internal affairs" of the business entity.

The internal affairs are any matters relating to the internal affairs and governance of the entity among its managers and equityholders. Under the internal affairs doctrine, disputes between managers and owners as to the internal affairs of the entity are governed by the law of the state of organization rather than the law of the state in which the litigation is brought or even where the entity has its principal office or business activity. However, each state applies its own law to the external activities of business entities within the state. For example, suppose that Utah prohibits gambling and Delaware permits it. A Delaware corporation cannot establish a casino in Utah even though its internal affairs are governed by Delaware law. On the other hand, if there is dispute between the managers and the shareholders of the corporation on matters governed by corporation law, a Utah court must apply Delaware corporation law even if the action is brought in Utah state court and the Delaware corporation's headquarter and principal business activities are located in Utah.

3. CHARTER DOCUMENTS

It is quite easy to *legally* create a business entity (to do it *properly* is a different matter). Although general partnerships can be created without filing anything with a state, all entities to which state law grants limited liability must register with the state. The information *required* in the document they must file is minimal, although it can include provisions that are not required. The purpose of the filing is principally to create the entity with a specific name indicating its limited liability status, an address, a statutory agent so that it is subject to service of process, and for a corporation the number of shares of stock it is authorized to issue.[14] For

---

[13] An exception is general partnerships, where "the law of the jurisdiction in which a partnership has its chief executive office governs relations among the partners and between the partners and the partnership." RUPA § 106(a). General partnerships are not subject to a choice of forum because, unless they have filed to become a limited liability partnership, they are not a limited liability entity.

[14] It is also important to note that states do not permit the creation of limited liability entities and filing and other administrative services for free. States charge filing fees and franchise taxes. The annual revenue from these services are substantial. Thus, states have an economic incentive to provide laws that are attractive to businesspersons in light of the fact that there is a choice of forum. This fact has spawned a significant debate in academic scholarship on whether state competition is a "race to the bottom" or a "race to the top" in terms of the quality of the law. *Compare* William L. Cary, *Federalism and Corporate Law: Reflections Upon Delaware*, 83 Yale

non-corporate entities, the filing is typically called the certificate or articles of organization. For a corporation, it is typically called the certificate or articles of incorporation. For convenience, we will generally refer to the required filing as the "certificate."

For non-corporate entities, the certificate is threadbare;[15] and for corporations, the mandatory requirements of the certificate are not much more involved.[16] The actual task of creating a business entity is not difficult. A non-lawyer or a web-based service can do this task. This ministerial task of creating an entity by filing with a state is not where business lawyers provide value added services to most business clients. Instead, *how* the entity is created requires the work of sophisticated business lawyers

Although the certificates of simple corporations can be threadbare, the certificates of large, sophisticated, or public corporations contain many more provisions. Among other things, the certificate may contain important terms relating to different classes of stock such as preferred stock, provisions exculpating directors from liability for money damages for breach of fiduciary duty, and indemnification of directors and officers. The complexity of a large, sophisticated, or public corporation necessitates these additional terms even though they are not required by corporation law.

Every corporation also has *bylaws*, which set forth the details of the corporation's internal governance arrangements, such as procedures for calling and holding meetings, titles and functions of inferior officers, voting procedures, etc. A corporation's certificate cannot conflict with the statute under which the corporation is organized, and a corporation's bylaws cannot conflict with the statute or the certificate. For public corporations subject to the disclosure requirements of the federal securities laws, the certificate and bylaws can often be found as attachments to disclosure documents filed with the Securities and Exchange Commission. Public

---

L.J. 663, 664–666 (1974) (suggesting that the development of corporate law has been a "race for the bottom" due to jurisdictional competition to attract incorporation business: "In Brandeis' words, the race was not one of diligence but of laxity."), with Ralph K. Winter, Jr., *State Law, Shareholder Protection, and the Theory of the Corporation*, 6 J. Legal Stud. 251, 254–62, 290 (1977) (challenging Cary's argument that corporate law is a race to the bottom and instead "the competition between states for charters will tend toward optimal legal systems regulating the market for capital").

[15] For example, the RULLCA § 201(b) provides: "A certificate of organization must state: (1) the name of the limited liability company, which must comply with Section 108; (2) the street and mailing address of the initial designated office and the name and street and mailing address of the initial agent for service of process of the company; and (3) if the company will have no members when the [Secretary of State] files the certificate, a statement to that effect."

[16] For example, the MBCA § 2.02 provides: "The articles of incorporation must set forth: (1) a corporate name for the corporation that satisfied the requirements of section 4.01; (2) the number of shares the corporation is authorized to issue; (3) the state address of the corporation's initial registered office and the name of its initial registered agent at that office; and the name and address of each incorporator."

corporations also provide links to these documents on their websites, usually under the tab "Investor Relations."

4. PRIVATE ORDERING

Business entity statutes are often called "enabling laws" because they enable the creation of the entity and the structure of the business in a way the business sees fit. *See Williams v. Geier*, 671 A.2d 1368, 1381 (Del. 1996) ("At its core, the Delaware General Corporation Law is a broad enabling act which leaves latitude for substantial private ordering, provided the statutory parameters and judicially imposed principles of fiduciary duty are honored."). It is important to understand that the laws of business organizations permit a certain degree of private ordering of the internal rules of governance. State business entity statutes have some mandatory provisions setting forth the relationships among managers and owners. However, they also provide in large part a set of "default rules." Managers and owners can change these default rules to suit their needs.

For non-corporate business entities, partnership and LLC statutes permit a great deal of private ordering. Private ordering means that the statute enables partners and members to create (contract for) their own internal rules of the business organization or opt out of many (but not all) rules in the statute. Statutory rules that may be changed or eliminated by parties are often referred to as "default rules" or "default statutory rules" (*i.e.*, applicable statutory rules absent a specific agreed upon rule of the parties). In this respect, the law of business organizations is closely aligned with contract law. For example, general partnership and LLC statutes generally leave it to partners and members to determine the management structure. General partnerships and LLCs can be managed in a communitarian way with each partner or member having equal management rights, or they can establish a central decisionmaking authority such as a board or executive committee. There is no legal requirement of a particular management structure. The matter is subject to contracting. Another example is that partnership and LLC laws permit a certain degree of private ordering fiduciary duties of partners, members, and managers. These issues will be discussed further in the forthcoming chapters. At this point, it is important to note that most sophisticated non-corporate entities will opt out of many statutory default provisions, and instead partners and members will elect to privately order the rules of internal governance themselves.

Corporation statutes also permit a great deal of private ordering, but they impose many more mandatory terms. For example, corporate law mandates that, unless the corporation is a close corporation, it must be managed through a board of directors; a corporation must maintain certain formalities such as having annual meeting of shareholders; the fiduciary duties of directors of a corporation are mandatory and set by law. Such requirements are generally not found in the laws of general partnerships and LLCs.

In addition to creating the entity, the organic documents of a business entity also contain a variety of provisions that implement the scheme of private ordering that the organizers wish to establish. For corporations, the basic organic documents are the *certificate (or articles) of incorporation* and the *bylaws*. In closely-held corporations there are often, in addition, contracts among the shareholders or between the shareholders and the corporation. The certificate of incorporation must be filed with the state, but the bylaws and contracts need not be. For non-corporate entities, the charter documents are the *partnership agreement* for partnerships and the *operating agreement* for LLCs. Limited partnerships and LLCs must file a certificate with the state. There is not requirement to file partnership agreements and operating documents, however, as they are essentially contracts entered into by partners or members.

5. STAKEHOLDERS

Business organization laws create a framework for determining the powers of managers, the rights of equityholders, and the relationship among the firm, managers, and equityholders. Of course, business enterprises can affect more interests than those of their managers and equityholders. Other "stakeholders" include creditors, employees, customers, and the community—all of whom have real and legitimate interests in the actions of the business enterprise. The firm's activities necessarily affects creditors, employees, customers, and the community. Yet business organization laws do not systematically deal with these relationships in the way that they do with the relationship between managers and equityholders.

Creditors of a business include suppliers who sell goods on credit and lenders who provide capital in exchange for a promise to make periodic interest payments and to return the principal of the loan after a specified time. With one exception, the laws of business organizations are generally not designed to protect the rights of creditors. Although managers generally owe fiduciary duties to equityholders, they generally do not owe such duties to creditors, who must protect themselves by *ex ante* contracting, including covenants in bond or loan documents that restrict certain actions. Bankruptcy law also protects creditors because they are entitled to payment first, before shareholders.

The one way the laws of business entities do concern themselves with the rights of creditors is to prohibit distributions to equityholders that would make the entity insolvent.[17] This rule protects creditors against

---

[17] *See, e.g.,* MBCA § 6.40(c) ("No distribution may be made if, after giving it effect . . . the corporation would not be able to pay its debts as they become due in the usual course of business . . . ."); RULLCA § 405(a) ("A limited liability company may not make a distribution if after the

opportunistic equityholders who could otherwise use their control of the entity to strip it of the assets required to make good on its obligations.

Employees and customers of business entities also have significant interests in them. The law of business enterprises, however, is not generally designed to protect those interests. Employees must look to contract law, employment law, and laws governing workplace safety, anti-discrimination, etc., to protect their interests. Customers, are relegated to contract law, and laws governing product safety.

Finally, the communities in which business entities operate can often be stakeholders because of the significant effects businesses can have on them. They depend on business enterprises to employ their citizens, pay taxes, contribute to various cultural and community affairs, protect the local environment, and generally act as responsible citizens. When a major business such as a large corporation leaves a community, the exit can be a serious blow to its health or even survival. However, the laws of business organizations do not systematically address the relationship between a business entity and the community. There are two exceptions. One is that all corporation law authorize the corporation to make charitable contributions.[18] The other is that the corporation laws of some states explicitly (statutorily) permit consideration of the public and other constituents when a board of directors makes a decision.[19] (These issues will be discussed later in this book.)

6. FIDUCIARY DUTIES

Perhaps the most important concept in business organization laws is that of *fiduciary duties*. The word "fiduciary" comes from the Latin *fides,* meaning faith or confidence, and was originally used in the common law to describe the nature of the duties imposed on a trustee. Today, the basic notion survives that managers and equityholders (in some circumstances) owe enforceable duties to the entity and to other equityholders. Historically, courts have articulated these fiduciary duties as comprising a *duty of care* and a *duty of loyalty.*

---

distribution . . . the company would not be able to pay its debts as they become due in the ordinary course of the limited liability company's activities . . . ."); ULPA (2001) § 508(b) ("A limited partnership may not make a distribution if after the distribution . . . the limited partnership would not be able to pay its debts as they become due in the ordinary course of the limited partnership's activities . . . ."). The RUPA does not have a similar provision because it is unnecessary to protect creditors; partners do not have limited liability and thus are liable for the debts and obligations of the partnership. Revised Uniform Partnership Act § 306(a).

[18] *See, e.g.,* MBCA § 3.02(13) (empowering the corporation "to make donations for the public welfare or for charitable, scientific, or educational purposes").

[19] *See, e.g.,* Florida Statute § 607.0830(3) ("In discharging his or her duties, a director may consider such factors as the director deems relevant, including the long-term prospects and interests of the corporation and its shareholders, and the social, economic, legal, or other effects of any action on the employees, suppliers, customers of the corporation or its subsidiaries, the communities and society in which the corporation or its subsidiaries operate, and the economy of the state and the nation.").

We will study fiduciary duties as they exist for each type of entity. For now, we generalize. Fiduciaries duties serve to align the manager's efforts toward the interest of the firm's equityholders. Because equityholders have residual claims that are risky and are not subject to highly particularized contractual protections in the way that creditors are protected, fiduciary duties provide "gap-filling" or "catch-all" provisions that essentially oblige managers to make reasonable or fair efforts toward advancing the interests of equityholders in a myriad of potentially complex business situations.

Fiduciary duties impose two different kinds of obligations. The duty of care obliges a manager to exercise a degree of care in making business decisions. It is qualified, however, by a fundamental rule called the *business judgment* rule (BJR). While the duty of care may appear to expose a manager to potential liability for breach similar to that for breach of the duty of care in a tort action, the BJR limits that exposure significantly. It creates a presumption that, in making a business decision, the directors of an enterprise acted on an informed basis, in good faith and in the honest belief that the action taken was in the best interests of the enterprise. It requires courts to give great deference to the decisions of managers; thus it allows managers to take risks on behalf of the firm without fear of personal liability for any resulting losses. A complaining plaintiff may overcome the presumption of the BJR only by showing that a decision was not informed, not in good faith, or not made in the honest belief that it was in the best interest of the firm.

The duty of loyalty requires managers to place the best interests of the entity above their own personal interests. The duty has a broad reach. For example, it may arise when the firm enters into a transaction with a manager, when the manager engages in outside transactions in which the firm also may have an interest, when the manager is involved in setting executive compensation and defeating a shareholder litigation. Underlying the duty of loyalty is the requirement that a manager has acted in good faith. A manager who has not done so cannot be considered to have acted loyally toward the firm.

The *derivative suit* was developed to give equityholders a means of addressing breaches of fiduciary duty by managers. It is an action in equity brought by a shareholder on behalf of the entity. It was originally developed as part of the law of corporations, but it has been adapted to the laws of non-corporate entities as well. A derivative suit is brought against the entity for failure to bring an action in law against some third party, most often an allegedly careless or unfaithful manager, who is also a defendant in the suit. The entity (the real party at interest) is a nominal defendant and the plaintiff-equityholder controls prosecution of the suit. Any recovery, either through a judgment or settlement, belongs to the entity for whose benefit the suit has been brought. The attorney for the plaintiff receives a court-approved fee from the entity for having conferred a benefit on it bringing the suit.

––––––––––

The following case is an early illustration of a court struggling with the question of director fiduciary duties. The court discusses both the duty of loyalty and the duty of care and the effect on the latter of the BJR. Consider these questions: (1) Who normally decides how to manage a radio campaign? Why? (2) What was the potential problem in this particular radio advertisement campaign? What problem does it pose for the best interest of the corporation and its shareholders? (3) How did the court ultimately resolve the issue?

BAYER V. BERAN
49 N.Y.S.2d 2 (Sup.Ct. 1944).

SHIENTAG, JUSTICE:

These derivative stockholders' suits present for review two transactions upon which plaintiffs seek to charge the individual defendants, who are directors, with liability in favor of the corporate defendant, the Celanese Corporation of America. Before taking up the specific transactions complained of, I shall consider generally certain pertinent rules to be applied in determining the liability of directors of a business corporation such as is here involved.

Directors of a business corporation[are not trustees and are not held to strict accountability as such.]Nevertheless, [their obligations are analogous to those of trustees.]Directors are agents; they are fiduciaries. The fiduciary has two paramount obligations: responsibility and loyalty. Those obligations apply with equal force to the humblest agent or broker and to the director of a great and powerful corporation. They lie at the very foundation of our whole system of free private enterprise and are as fresh and significant today as when they were formulated decades ago. The responsibility—that is, the care and the diligence—required of an agent or of a fiduciary, is proportioned to the occasion. It is a concept that has, and necessarily so, a wide penumbra of meaning—a concept, however, which becomes sharpened in its practical application to the given facts of a situation.

The concept of loyalty, of constant, unqualified fidelity, has a definite and precise meaning. The fiduciary must subordinate his individual and private interests to his duty to the corporation whenever the two conflict. In an address delivered in 1934, Mr. Justice, now Chief Justice, Stone declared that the fiduciary principle of undivided loyalty was, in effect, "the precept as old as Holy Writ, that 'a man cannot serve two masters'. More than a century ago equity gave a hospitable reception to that principle and the common law was not slow to follow in giving it recognition. No thinking man can believe that an economy built upon a business foundation can long endure without loyalty to that principle". He went on to say that "The separation of ownership from management, the development of the corporate structure so as to vest in small groups control of resources of great numbers of small and uninformed investors, make imperative a fresh and active devotion to that principle if the modern world of business is to perform its proper function."

A director is not an insurer. On the one hand, he is not called upon to use an extraordinary degree of care and prudence; and on the other hand it is established by the cases that it is not enough for a director to be honest, that fraud is not the orbit of his liability. The director may not act as a dummy or a figurehead. He is called upon to use care, to exercise judgment, the degree of care, the kind of judgment that one would give in similar situations to the conduct of his own affairs.

The director of a business corporation is given a wide latitude of action. The law does not seek to deprive him of initiative and daring and vision. Business has its adventures, its bold adventures; and those who in good faith, and in the interests of the corporation they serve, embark upon them, are not to be penalized if failure, rather than success, results from their efforts. The law will not permit a course of conduct by directors, which would be applauded if it succeeded, to be condemned with a riot of adjectives simply because it failed. Directors of a commercial corporation may take chances, the same kind of chances that a man would take in his own business. Because they are given this wide latitude, the law will not hold directors liable for honest errors, for mistakes of judgment. The law will not interfere with the internal affairs of a corporation so long as it is managed by its directors pursuant to a free, honest exercise of judgment uninfluenced by personal, or by any considerations other than the welfare of the corporation.

To encourage freedom of action on the part of directors, or to put it another way, to discourage interference with the exercise of their free and independent judgment, there has grown up what is known as the "business judgment rule". Questions of policy of management, expediency of contracts or action, adequacy of consideration, lawful appropriation of corporate funds to advance corporate interests, are left solely to their honest and unselfish decision, for their powers therein are without limitation and free from restraint, and the exercise of them for the common and general interests of the corporation may not be questioned, although the results show that what they did was unwise or inexpedient. Indeed, although the concept of "responsibility" is firmly fixed in the law, it is only in a most unusual and extraordinary case that directors are held liable for negligence in the absence of fraud, or improper motive, or personal interest.

The "business judgment rule", however, yields to the rule of undivided loyalty. This great rule of law is designed "to avoid the possibility of fraud and to avoid the temptation of self-interest." It is designed to obliterate all divided loyalties which may creep into a fiduciary relation. Included within its scope is every situation in which a trustee chooses to deal with another in such close relation with the trustee that possible advantage to such other person might influence, consciously or unconsciously, the judgment of the trustee. The dealings of a director with the corporation for which he is the fiduciary are therefore viewed with jealousy by the courts. Such personal transactions of directors with their corporations, such transactions as may tend to produce a conflict between self-interest and fiduciary obligation, are, when challenged, examined with the most scrupulous care, and if there is any evidence of improvidence or oppression, any indication of unfairness or undue advantage, the transactions will be voided. Their dealings with the corporation are subjected to rigorous scrutiny and where any of their contracts or engagements with the corporation are challenged the burden is on the director not only to prove the good faith of the transaction but also to show its inherent fairness from the viewpoint of the corporation and those interested therein.

While there is a high moral purpose implicit in this transcendent fiduciary principle of undivided loyalty, it has back of it a profound understanding of human nature and of its frailties. It actually accomplishes a practical, beneficent purpose. It tends to prevent a clouded conception of fidelity that blurs the vision. It preserves the free exercise of judgment uncontaminated by the dross of divided allegiance or self-interest. It prevents the operation of an influence that may be indirect but that is all the more potent for that reason. The law has set its face firmly against undermining the rule of undivided loyalty by the disintegrating erosion of particular exceptions.

The first, or "advertising", cause of action charges the directors with negligence, waste and improvidence in embarking the corporation upon a radio advertising program beginning in 1942 and costing about $1,000,000 a year. It is further charged that they were negligent in selecting the type of program and in renewing the radio contract for 1943. More serious than these allegations is the charge that the directors were motivated by a noncorporate purpose in causing the radio program to be undertaken and in expending large sums of money therefor. It is claimed that this radio advertising was for the benefit of Miss Jean Tennyson, one of the singers on the program, who in private life is Mrs. Camille Dreyfus, the wife of the president of the company and one of its directors; that it was undertaken to "further, foster and subsidize her career"; to "furnish a vehicle" for her talents.

Eliminating for the moment the part played by Miss Tennyson in the radio advertising campaign, it is clear that the character of the advertising, the amount to be expended therefor, and the manner in which it should be used, are all matters of business judgment and rest peculiarly within the discretion of the board of directors. Under the authorities previously cited, it is not, generally speaking, the function of a court of equity to review these matters or even to consider them. Had the wife of the president of the company not been involved, the advertising cause of action could have been disposed of summarily. Her connection with the program, however, makes it necessary to go into the facts in some detail.

[The court reviewed the history of the decision to launch a program of radio advertising.]

So far, there is nothing on which to base any claim of breach of fiduciary duty. Some care, diligence and prudence were exercised by these directors before they committed the company to the radio program. It was for the directors to determine whether they would resort to radio advertising; it was for them to conclude how much to spend; it was for them to decide the kind of program they would use. [It would be an unwarranted act of interference for any court to attempt to substitute its judgment on these points for that of the directors, honestly arrived at.] The expenditure was not reckless or unconscionable. Indeed, it bore a fair relationship to the total amount of net sales and to the earnings of the company. The fact that the company had offers of more business than it could handle did not, in law, preclude advertising. Many corporations not now doing any business in their products because of emergency conditions advertise those products extensively in order to preserve the good will, the public interest, during the war period. The fact that the company's product may not now be identifiable did not bar advertising calculated to induce consumer demand for such identification. That a program of classical and semiclassical music was selected, rather than a variety program, or a news commentator program, furnishes no ground for legal complaint. True, variety programs have a wider popular appeal than do musicals, but it would be a very sad thing if the former were the only kind of radio programs to be used. Some of the largest industrial concerns in the country have recognized this and have maintained fine musical programs on the radio for many years.

Now we have to take up an unfortunate incident, one which cannot be viewed with the complacency displayed by some of the directors of the company. This is not a closely held family corporation. The Doctors Dreyfus and their families own about 135,000 shares of common stock, the other directors about 10,000 shares out of a total outstanding issue of 1,376,500 shares. Some of these other directors were originally employed by Dr. Camille Dreyfus, the president of the company. His wife, to whom he has been married for about twelve years, is known professionally as Miss Jean Tennyson and is a singer of wide experience.

Dr. Dreyfus, as was natural, consulted his wife about the proposed radio program; he also asked the advertising agency, that had been retained, to confer with her about it. She suggested the names of the artists, all stars of the Metropolitan Opera Company, and the name of the conductor, prominent in his field. She also offered her own services as a paid artist. All of her suggestions as to personnel were adopted by the advertising agency. While the record shows Miss Tennyson to be a competent singer, there is nothing to indicate that she was indispensable or essential to the success of the program. She received $500 an evening. It would be far-fetched to suggest that the directors caused the company to incur large expenditures for radio advertising to enable the president's wife to make $24,000 in 1942 and $20,500 in 1943.

Of course it is not improper to appoint relatives of officers or directors to responsible positions in a company. But where a close relative of the chief executive officer of a corporation, and one of its dominant directors, takes a position closely associated with a new and expensive field of activity, the motives of the directors are likely to be questioned. The board would be placed in a position where selfish, personal interests might be in conflict with the duty it owed to the corporation. That being so, the entire transaction, if challenged in the courts, must be subjected to the most rigorous scrutiny to determine whether the action of the directors was intended or calculated to "subserve some outside purpose, regardless of the consequences to the company, and in a manner inconsistent with its interests." *Gamble v. Queens County Water Co.*, 123 N.Y. 91, 99, 25 N.E. 201, 202 (1890).

After such careful scrutiny I have concluded that, up to the present, there has been no breach of fiduciary duty on the part of the directors. The president undoubtedly knew that his wife might be one of the paid artists on the program. The other directors did not know this until they had approved the campaign of radio advertising and the general type of radio program. The evidence fails to show that the program was designed to foster or subsidize "the career of Miss Tennyson as an artist" or to "furnish a vehicle for her talents". That her participation in the program may have enhanced her prestige as a singer is no ground for subjecting the directors to liability, as long as the advertising served a legitimate and a useful corporate purpose and the company received the full benefit thereof.

The musical quality of "Celanese Hour" has not been challenged, nor does the record contain anything reflecting on Miss Tennyson's competence as an artist. There is nothing in the testimony to show that some other soprano would have enhanced the artistic quality of the program or its advertising appeal. There is no suggestion that the present program is inefficient or that its cost is disproportionate to what a program of that character reasonably entails. Miss Tennyson's contract with the advertising agency retained by the directors was on a standard form, negotiated through her professional agent. Her compensation, as well as that of the other artists, was in conformity with that paid for comparable work. She received less than any of the other artists on the program. Although she appeared with greater regularity than any other singer, she received no undue prominence, no special build-up. Indeed, all of the artists were subordinated to the advertisement of the company and of its products. The company was featured. It appears also that the popularity of the program has increased since it was inaugurated.

It is clear, therefore, that the directors have not been guilty of any breach of fiduciary duty, in embarking upon the program of radio advertising and in renewing it. It is unfortunate that they have allowed themselves to be placed in a position where their motives concerning future decisions on radio advertising may be impugned. The free mind should be ever jealous of its freedom. Power of control carries with it a trust or duty to exercise that power faithfully to promote the corporate interests, and the courts of this State will insist upon scrupulous performance of that duty. Thus far, that duty has been performed and with noteworthy success. The corporation has not, up to the present time, been wronged by the radio advertising attacked in the complaints.

7.   EQUITABLE LIMITATIONS

In actions involving business entities, courts apply principles of equity in reviewing the actions of managers and provide equitable remedies. Importantly, the Delaware Court of Chancery, which is the trial court having jurisdiction over actions involving the internal affairs of Delaware corporations and non-corporate entities, is a court of equity. Among other powers, the court can apply principles of equity and provide equitable remedies including injunctions, which are important remedies in blocking unlawful actions or stopping transactions such as mergers and acquisitions.

———————

The following case illustrates a court's application of equity. Consider the questions: (1) If the board's action was legal, why did the Delaware Supreme Court strike down the defendant board's conduct? (2) What conduct was unfair and what made it so?

SCHNELL V. CHRIS-CRAFT INDUSTRIES, INC.
285 A.2d 437 (Del. 1971).

[Plaintiffs, a group of Chris-Craft shareholders, were dissatisfied with the company's economic performance. They resolved to seek control by electing a new board of directors at Chris-Craft's next annual shareholders' meeting. On October 16, 1971, as required by federal law, they filed documents announcing their intentions with the Securities and Exchange Commission.

On October 18, Chris-Craft's board met and amended the corporation's by-laws, which had previously fixed January 11 as the date of the annual meeting, to authorize the board to set an annual meeting date at any time in December or January. The board then proceeded to schedule the upcoming meeting for December 8, thereby reducing by more than a month the time available to the insurgents to solicit the support of other shareholders. The board also set the place of the meeting in Cortland, New York, a small town far from any transportation hubs. The board said it changed the meeting date because weather conditions made it difficult to get to Cortland in January and because holding the meeting well before Christmas would reduce problems with the mail. Meanwhile, however, the board took a number of other actions to impede the insurgents, including resisting providing them with the list of stockholders to which they were entitled under Delaware law.

The trial court found that the defendants' actions, including the change in the date of the annual meeting, were designed to obstruct the plaintiffs' efforts to gain control. But the court declined to reschedule the meeting on its original date, holding that the plaintiffs had delayed too long in seeking judicial relief. On appeal, the Supreme Court reversed.]

HERRMANN, JUSTICE:

It will be seen that the Chancery Court considered all of the reasons stated by management as business reasons for changing the date of the meeting; but that those reasons were rejected by the Court below in making the following findings:

"I am satisfied, however, in a situation in which present management has disingenuously resisted the production of a list of its stockholders to plaintiffs or their confederates and has otherwise turned a deaf ear to plaintiffs' demands about a change in management designed to lift defendant from its present business doldrums, management has seized on a relatively new section of the Delaware Corporation Law for the purpose of cutting down on the amount of time which would otherwise have been available to plaintiffs and others for the waging of a proxy battle. Management thus enlarged the scope of its scheduled October 18 directors' meeting to include the by-law amendment in controversy after the stockholders committee had filed with the S.E.C. its intention to wage a proxy fight on October 16.

"Thus plaintiffs reasonably contend that because of the tactics employed by management (which involve the hiring of two established proxy solicitors as well as a refusal to produce a list of its stockholders, coupled with its use of an amendment to the

Delaware Corporation Law to limit the time for contest), they are given little chance, because of the exigencies of time, including that required to clear material at the S.E.C., to wage a successful proxy fight[20] between now and December 8. * * * ."

In our view, those conclusions amount to a finding that management has attempted to utilize the corporate machinery and the Delaware Law for the purpose of perpetuating itself in office; and, to that end, for the purpose of obstructing the legitimate efforts of dissident stockholders in the exercise of their rights to undertake a proxy contest against management. These are inequitable purposes, contrary to established principles of corporate democracy. The advancement by directors of the by-law date of a stockholders' meeting, for such purposes, may not be permitted to stand.

When the by-laws of a corporation designate the date of the annual meeting of stockholders, it is to be expected that those who intend to contest the reelection of incumbent management will gear their campaign to the by-law date. It is not to be expected that management will attempt to advance that date in order to obtain an inequitable advantage in the contest.

Management contends that it has complied strictly with the provisions of the new Delaware Corporation Law in changing the by-law date. The answer to that contention, of course, is that [inequitable action does not become permissible simply because it is legally possible.]

Accordingly, the judgment below must be reversed and the cause remanded, with instructions to nullify the December 8 date as a meeting date for stockholders; to reinstate January 11, 1972 as the sole date of the next annual meeting of the stockholders of the corporation; and to take such other proceedings and action as may be consistent herewith regarding the stock record closing date and any other related matters.

————

A number of other cases, most of them involving mergers or recapitalizations, have taken what seems, on the surface at least, to be a rather different view of actions that comply with all relevant statutory provisions. In these cases, plaintiffs have argued that defendants were making use of a mechanism provided in one section of the statute to accomplish a result that they could not have accomplished had they pursued it in an arguably more straightforward fashion. Consider this question: In what way is *Bove* distinguishable from *Schnell* with respect to the court's exercise of equitable power?

---

[20] Shareholders in public companies rarely attend annual meetings. They vote by granting a proxy—a written authority to vote their shares—to some other person. In the event of a contest for control, both management and dissident shareholders solicit proxies from shareholders. [Ed.]

BOVE v. COMMUNITY HOTEL CORP. OF NEWPORT, R.I.

249 A.2d 89 (R.I. 1969).

JOSLIN, JUSTICE.

[The holders of preferred stock had the right to receive 24 years of unpaid dividends before the corporation could pay any dividends on its common stock. [Management wanted to eliminate the preferred stockholders' claim so that the corporation could sell new common stock and raise needed capital.] Under Rhode Island law, the dividend claims could be eliminated by amending the charter, but such an amendment required unanimous approval of the preferred stockholders, which would not be forthcoming. Consequently, management decided to pursue another alternative. It created a new corporation with nominal assets and proposed to merge the old corporation into it in a transaction that would eliminate the old preferred stock and the associated claims for dividends. The merger required the approval of two-thirds, rather than all, of the preferred stock. If the merger was approved, preferred stockholders who voted against it had the option of demanding to be paid a judicially determined "fair value" for their stock, rather than accepting stock in the surviving corporation. Some preferred stockholders, however, sought to enjoin the merger.]

The plaintiffs argue that the primary, and indeed, the only purpose of the proposed merger is to eliminate the priorities of the preferred stock with less than the unanimous consent of its holders. Assuming that premise, a preliminary matter for our consideration concerns the merger of a parent corporation into a wholly-owned subsidiary created for the sole purpose of achieving a recapitalization which will eliminate the parent's preferred stock and the dividends accumulated thereon, and whether such a merger qualifies within the contemplation of the statute permitting any two or more corporations to merge into a single corporation.

It is true, of course, that to accomplish the proposed recapitalization by amending Community Hotel's articles of association under relevant provisions of the general corporation law would require the unanimous vote of the preferred shareholders, whereas under the merger statute, only a two-third vote of those stockholders will be needed. Concededly, unanimity of the preferred stockholders is unobtainable in this case, and plaintiffs argue, therefore, that to permit the less restrictive provisions of the merger statute to be used to accomplish indirectly what otherwise would be incapable of being accomplished directly by the more stringent amendment procedures of the general corporation law is tantamount to sanctioning a circumvention or perversion of that law.

The question, however, is not whether recapitalization by the merger route is a subterfuge, but whether a merger which is designated for the sole purpose of cancelling the rights of preferred stockholders with the consent of less than all has been authorized by the legislature. The controlling statute is § 7–5–2. Its language is clear, all-embracing and unqualified. It authorizes any two or more business corporations *which were or might have been organized* under the general corporation law to merge into a single corporation; and it provides that the merger agreement shall prescribe " * * * the terms and conditions of consolidation or merger, the mode of carrying the same into effect * * * *as well as the manner of converting the shares of each of the constituent corporations into shares or other securities of the corporation resulting from or surviving such consolidation or merger,* with such other details and provisions as are deemed necessary." (italics ours) Nothing in that language even suggests that the legislature intended to make *underlying purpose* a standard for determining permissibility. Indeed, the contrary is apparent since the very breadth of the language selected presupposes a complete lack of concern with whether the merger is designed to further the mutual interests of two existing and nonaffiliated corporations or whether alternatively it is purposed solely upon effecting a substantial change in an existing corporation's capital structure.

Moreover, that a possible effect of corporate action under the merger statute is not possible, or is even forbidden, under another section of the general corporation law is of no import, it being settled that the several sections of that law may have independent legal significance, and that the validity of corporate action taken pursuant to one section is not necessarily dependent upon its being valid under another.

We hold, therefore, that nothing within the purview of our statute forbids a merger between a parent and a subsidiary corporation even under circumstances where the merger device has been resorted to solely for the purpose of obviating the necessity for the unanimous vote which would otherwise be required in order to cancel the priorities of preferred shareholders.

CHAPTER 3

LIMITS TO LIMITED LIABILITY

■ ■ ■

A. INTRODUCTION TO VEIL PIERCING

Limited liability is a fundamental characteristic of the corporation and other entities that provide limited liability to equityholders. A principal advantage of limited liability entities such as corporations and LLCs is that equityholders' potential losses are limited to the amount they have invested in the enterprise. They are not vicariously liable for the debts and obligations of the entity solely based on their status as equityholders.[1] Unless the entity is disregarded in a case such as those considered in this chapter, the maximum equityholders' can lose is the amount of their investment. This follows from the rule that the entity is separate and distinct from its owners. As a legal person, it is responsible for its own debts and liabilities, and its creditors can look only to the entity's assets for payment of their claims.

In certain circumstances, however, courts allow claimants to disregard the entity form and recover directly from its equityholders. Corporate statutes generally do not specify when limited liability is to be disregarded. Instead, courts have created a doctrine called "piercing the corporate veil," which is an equitable remedy.[2] More recently courts have begun applying the same concept to LLCs, though for them "piercing the corporate veil" is a misnomer. It is perhaps more accurate to speak of "disregarding the entity."

Whether a corporation's veil should be pierced is the most litigated issue in corporate law, and is the corporation law issue most often confronted by attorneys who specialize in other areas of law. *See* Robert B. Thompson, *Piercing the Corporate Veil: An Empirical Study*, 76 Cornell L. Rev. 1036 (1991). Piercing issues arise both when a defendant corporation may not have assets sufficient to satisfy a plaintiff's claims and when a plaintiff sues a shareholder for tactical reasons, such as to litigate a claim

---

[1] *See* MBCA § 6.22(a) ("a shareholder of a corporation is not personally liable for the acts or debts of the corporation except that he may become personally liable by reason of his own acts or conduct"); RULLCA § 304(a) ("The debts, obligations, and liabilities of a limited liability company, whether arising in contract, tort, or otherwise: (1) are solely the debts, obligations, and liabilities of the limited liability company; and(2) do not become the debts, obligations, and liabilities of a member or manager solely by reason of the member or manager acting as member or manager.").

[2] Since corporations were the first entity providing broad limited liability protection (limited partnership did not historically protect general partners and limited partners were subject to the "control rule"), the doctrine of veil piercing developed in corporate law.

in a jurisdiction the plaintiff prefers or to introduce evidence of a shareholder's wealth that might lead a jury to increase an award of punitive damages.

1. DOCTRINAL CONFUSION

Both law students and practicing attorneys often find judicial decisions in piercing cases to be confusing, partly because of the courts' propensity to rely on metaphors. Courts often use other colorful phrases in "piercing" cases, describing corporations as the "agent," "alias," "alter ego," "corporate double," "dummy," or "instrumentality" of their shareholders. None of these terms is particularly instructive. As Judge Cardozo observed in *Berkey v. Third Avenue Railway Co.*, 155 N.E. 58, 61 (N.Y. 1926): "Metaphors in law are to be narrowly watched, for starting as devices to liberate thought, they end often by enslaving it." Instead, an attorney must look beyond the metaphors and closely examine cases on their unique facts.

FRANKLIN A. GEVURTZ, PIERCING: AN ATTEMPT TO LIFT THE VEIL OF CONFUSION SURROUNDING THE DOCTRINE OF PIERCING THE CORPORATE VEIL
76 Ore. L. Rev. 853, 854–858 (1997).

Courts in piercing cases almost invariably begin at the same point of departure: Piercing is an equitable remedy the court can impose in order to avoid injustice. Fair enough. The problem, of course, is to go beyond this broad generality and determine what specific facts establish such an injustice, and why. Unfortunately, three judicial foibles have made a mess of this area of the law.

To begin with, many writers have criticized the courts' tendency in this area to reason by pejorative. For example, courts often explain their decision to pierce by announcing that the corporation was a mere "sham" or "shell," or the defendant's "alter ego" or "instrumentality." At best, such terms are unhelpful. All too often, they confuse the issue.

Terms like "sham" and "shell" seem to convey a lack of substance to the corporation. To the extent this refers to inadequate capitalization, it would be clearer to state this and discuss whether inadequate capitalization should provide grounds to pierce in the situation at hand. Otherwise, it is easy for the court and litigants to start wandering off looking for additional ways in which a corporation can lack substance. For instance, this can lead to a focus on the non-observance of rituals or "corporate formalities," which rarely has much to do with the equities of piercing in a given situation.

Worse, terms such as these sometimes lead to a search of the defendant's purpose for establishing the corporation. This, in turn, can convey the impression that creating a corporation for the purpose of enjoying the benefits of owning a business while, at the same time, avoiding personal liability, should be grounds to pierce. This cannot be correct. Most corporations exist for the purpose of achieving limited liability for their owners. It would be perverse to grant limited liability to anyone who did not care about it and deny it to everyone who sought it.

A second foible is to follow what one might call a "template" approach. Under this approach, a court either quotes or constructs a list of facts, which, in prior cases, accompanied decisions to pierce the corporate veil. The court then compares the list with the facts in the situation at hand and pierces if enough of the facts present fit the list.

The template approach is a godsend to students, litigants, and courts who recognize the weakness of reasoning by pejorative, but still wish to remain aloof from analysis based on policy. Unfortunately, it leads to difficulties. To begin with, listing facts from prior opinions without an evaluation of why these facts should or should not lead to piercing inevitably introduces facts into these sort of lists, which, upon reflection, seem of questionable significance. For example, many such lists [include] the non-payment of dividends. It is hard to understand why a creditor should complain about the non-payment of dividends, which, after all, are payments from the corporation to its shareholders and leave less money in the company for its creditors. In fact, loan agreements and corporation statutes commonly limit dividends for the protection of creditors.

A second difficulty with the template approach is that the relevance of some facts in the list, even when present in a given case, may depend upon the circumstances. [Consider undercapitalization, which most such lists include. Often ignored] is the question of whether undercapitalization, which should be of significance in dealing with tort claimants, should be relevant to the claim of a contract creditor who might have checked the financial status of the corporation before dealing with it.

Finally, this sort of multi-factor approach carries tremendous indeterminacy. Must all factors on the list be present? Is the presence of any one factor enough? If the answer to these two questions is, as seems to be the rule from the opinions, no, then how many factors does one need and which factors are more important than the others? The opinions provide little guidance.

The third foible is to employ a character test. Consciously or subconsciously, many courts in piercing cases appear to engage in a sort of general review of the defendant's business ethics. Is this an honest business person who simply suffered misfortune, or is this some sort of "sharp operator"? A stark illustration in a recent case is the court's pointing to the defendant's tax fraud as among the facts leading to piercing. The problem, of course, is that the defendant's tax fraud in this case had absolutely nothing to do with the plaintiff's (who was a private creditor) claim. We might all agree that tax or other fraud is wrong, but to allow recovery by parties who were not the victims creates a windfall.

———————

Similarly, Professor Bainbridge observes: "Those who like tidy opinions that admit to easy application will not care for veil piercing law. Judicial opinions in this area tend to open with vague generalities and close with conclusory statements with little or no concrete analysis in between. There simply are no bright-line rules for deciding when courts will pierce the corporate veil." Stephen M. Bainbridge, *Abolishing Veil Piercing*, 26 J. Corp. L. 479, 513 (2001). Indeed, in reading the materials in this chapter, it is useful to ask what the consequences would be in a world in which there was always limited liability (no veil piercing) and in which there was no limited liability (always veil piercing).

2.   PUBLIC VS. CLOSELY-HELD CORPORATIONS

Some commentators argue that limited liability is justified primarily because it promotes efficiency by facilitating the organization of large, publicly-held corporations.

FRANK H. EASTERBROOK & DANIEL R. FISCHEL, THE ECONOMIC STRUCTURE OF CORPORATE LAW
41–44 (1991).

Publicly held corporations dominate other organizational forms when the technology of production requires firms to combine both the specialized skills of multiple agents and large amounts of capital. Limited liability reduces the costs of this separation and specialization of functions in a number of respects.

First, limited liability decreases the need to monitor agents. To protect themselves, investors could monitor their agents more closely. The more risk they bear, the more they will monitor. But beyond a point extra monitoring is not worth the cost. Limited liability makes passivity a more rational strategy and so potentially reduces the cost of operating the corporation.

Second, limited liability reduces the costs of monitoring other shareholders. Under a rule exposing equity investors to unlimited liability, the greater the wealth of other shareholders, the lower the probability that any one shareholder's assets will be needed to pay a judgment. Thus existing shareholders would have incentives to engage in costly monitoring of other shareholders to ensure that they do not transfer assets to others or sell to others with less wealth. Limited liability makes the identity of other shareholders irrelevant and thus avoids these costs.

Third, by promoting free transfer of shares, limited liability gives managers incentives to act efficiently. Although individual shareholders lack the expertise and incentive to monitor the actions of specialized agents, the ability of investors to sell creates opportunities for investors as a group and constrains agents' actions. [The] potential for displacement gives existing managers incentives to operate efficiently in order to keep share prices high.

With limited liability, the value of shares is set by the present value of the income stream generated by a firm's assets. The identity and wealth of other investors is irrelevant. Shares are fungible; they trade at one price in liquid markets. Under a rule of unlimited liability shares would not be fungible. Their value would be a function of the present value of future cash flows and the wealth of shareholders. Their lack of fungibility would impede their acquisition. Limited liability allows a person to buy a large bloc without any risk of being surcharged, and thus it facilitates beneficial control transactions. A rule that facilitates transfers of control also induces managers to work more effectively to stave off such transfers, and so it reduces the costs of specialization whether or not a firm is acquired.

Fourth, limited liability makes it possible for market prices to reflect additional information about the value of firms. With unlimited liability, shares would not be homogeneous commodities and would no longer have one market price. Investors would be required to expend greater resources analyzing the prospects of the firm to know whether "the price is right." When all can trade on the same terms, though, investors trade until the price of shares reflect the available information about a firm's prospects. Most investors need not expend resources searching for additional information.

Fifth, limited liability allows more efficient diversification. Investors can cut risk by owning a diversified portfolio of assets. Firms can raise capital at lower costs because investors need not bear the special risk associated with nondiversified holdings. This applies only under a rule of limited liability or some good substitute.

Sixth, limited liability facilitates optimal investment decisions. When investors hold diversified portfolios, managers maximize investors' welfare by investing in any project with a positive net present value. In a world of unlimited liability managers would reject as "too risky" some projects with positive net present values. Investors would want them to do this because it would be the best way to reduce risks. By definition this would be a social loss, because projects with net present value are beneficial uses of capital. The increased availability of funds for projects with positive net values is the real benefit of limited liability.

———————

Easterbrook and Fischel note that the economic efficiency arguments supporting limited liability have limited applicability to close corporations. In companies owned by a small number of investors who also are managers, there is much less separation of management and risk bearing than in a public corporation and the absence of a market for close corporations' stock makes irrelevant the fact that limited liability increases the efficiency of the market for a corporation's stock. In addition, limited liability is more likely to generate external costs because the shareholder-managers of a close corporation have more to gain personally by taking risks that may shift losses to creditors than do the managers of a public company. Easterbrook and Fischel conclude that courts should reduce the extent to which third parties bear these costs by disregarding limited liability more frequently in close corporations.

Presser disagrees. Pointing to the principal historical justification for limited liability, he contends that it is precisely in the context of the smaller firm that limited liability should be most protected. It is important to keep in mind, in this regard, that limited liability only protects a shareholder *qua* shareholder. Stephen B. Presser, Piercing the Corporate Veil. A shareholder who also acts as a corporate manager or employee can be held liable personally for her own tortious actions, as can any other corporate manager or employee. *See* MBCA § 6.22(b); *see generally* Robert B. Thompson, *Unpacking Limited Liability: Direct and Vicarious Liability of Corporation Participants for Torts of the Enterprise*, 47 Vand. L. Rev. 1 (1994). Professor Leebron takes a middle position. He suggests that limited liability should exist for close corporation shareholders subject to two conditions: (1) shareholders should not be allowed to reduce capital available for involuntary creditors by using debt they have personally guaranteed, rather than equity, to finance the corporation and (2) shareholder-managers should be required to carry adequate insurance for foreseeable tort liabilities. Leebron asserts that these conditions would protect against the major abuses that typically concern the advocates of unlimited liability for shareholders of close corporations. *See* David W. Leebron, *Limited Liability, Tort Victims, and Creditors*, 91 Colum. L. Rev. 1565, 1636 (1991).

3. INDIVIDUAL SHAREHOLDERS VS. CORPORATE GROUPS

Another question is whether disregarding separate incorporation should be easier in a holding company structure. As originally conceived, the corporation was an "enterprise" formed to carry on all the operations of a given business. *See* Adolf A. Berle, Jr., *The Theory of Enterprise Entity*, 47 Colum. L. Rev. 343 (1947). Early statutes prohibited one corporation from holding the stock of another. But these prohibitions disappeared and many corporations began to operate through subsidiaries that were more or less indistinguishable parts of a larger enterprise. Courts initially responded by employing enterprise theories to hold parent corporations responsible for the liabilities of these subsidiaries.

More recently, courts have tended to apply the same rule of limited liability to individual and corporate shareholders. Professor Blumberg has argued that the principal justification for limited liability—encouraging investors to fund new business ventures—disappears in the case of the parent or affiliate of a subsidiary corporation. Although it may seem unjust to hold individual shareholders liable for the actions of a corporation's directors or managers, this argument seems less persuasive when applied to a parent corporation that controls and directs a subsidiary. And the purpose of limited liability to promote investment by dispersed individual investors is inapplicable when one corporation capitalizes another corporation. Thus, eliminating limited liability for corporate groups will not adversely affect the capital markets. Phillip I. Blumberg, *Limited Liability and Corporate Groups*, 11 J. Corp. L. 573 (1986).

Professor Bainbridge agrees that "from a policy perspective, the considerations justifying limited liability insofar as individual shareholders seem far less powerful when applied to corporate shareholders." Bainbridge, *supra*, at 529. He notes, in particular, the danger that large corporations will seek to externalize risks associated with their businesses by using thinly-capitalized subsidiaries to conduct high risk activities. Stephen M. Bainbridge, *Abolishing Veil Piercing*, 26 J. Corp. L. 479 (2001).

Bainbridge argues that the best approach to this problem is to retain (or, perhaps more accurately, to reinvigorate) the doctrine of enterprise liability. This would promote analytic clarity because, were courts to rely on the theory of enterprise liability, rather than on veil piercing, they "would acknowledge the important conceptual distinctions between holding an individual liable and holding a larger corporate enterprise liable." Moreover, this approach would force courts to recognize that the key issue in the parent-subsidiary context "is whether the firm has split up a single business enterprise into multiple corporations with the goal of externalizing specific risks."

RICHARD A. POSNER, AN ECONOMIC ANALYSIS OF LAW
439–440 (7th ed. 2007).

PIERCING THE CORPORATE VEIL

Even if a large, publicly held corporation operates through wholly owned subsidiaries, so long as those subsidiaries are in unrelated businesses, maximization of the enterprise's profits will require that the profits of each subsidiary be maximized separately, and the assets, costs, and debts of each subsidiary should be the same as they would be if they were separate firms, so creditors are not prejudiced by being limited to their rights against the particular subsidiary with which they dealt. The danger of abuse of the corporate form is the greatest in the case of the small business, where operation of the constituent corporations as separate profit centers is less necessary to assure efficient management.

Even when the activities of affiliated corporations are closely related—when for examples the produce complementary goods-each corporation normally will be operated as a separate profit center. It is true that if there are substantial cost savings from common ownership, as in some cases where the affiliated corporations operate at successive stages in the production of a good, the two corporations will be managed differently from separately owned corporations in the same line of business, their operations will be more closely integrated than would be those of independent corporations. But it would be perverse to penalize such a corporation for its superior efficiency by withdrawing from it the privilege of limited liability that its nonintegrated competitors enjoy.

The important difference between a group of affiliates engaged in related businesses and one engaged in a number of unrelated businesses is that in the former case the creditor is more likely to be misled into thinking he's dealing with a single corporation. But notice that where there is no misrepresentation, abrogating the limited liability of affiliated corporations would not reduce the risks of any class of creditors; it would merely increase their costs of information.

B. TORT CREDITORS

Limited liability makes sense with respect to voluntary contract creditors, such as lenders and trade creditors, compared to involuntary tort creditors. A voluntary creditor knows she is dealing with a no-recourse corporation and can bargain for a risk premium, shareholder guarantees, or restrictions on distributions. A tort creditor, by comparison, cannot easily self-protect. Thus, one might expect that courts would pierce the corporate veil more readily for tort claimants compared to contract creditors.

Surprisingly, according to Professor Thompson's study, courts pierce the corporate veil more often in contract cases (42%) than in tort actions (31%). Robert B. Thompson, *Piercing the Corporate Veil: An Empirical Study*, 76 Cornell L. Rev. 1036 (1991). What explains this counter-intuitive result? One explanation may be that many contract cases involve misrepresentations that undermine the expectation of a non-recourse relationship. Thompson's study, however, found that courts pierce in 34% of contract cases that did not involve misrepresentation claims and in only 27% of the tort cases that did not involve misrepresentation claims.

WALKOVSZKY V. CARLTON
223 N.E.2d 6 (N.Y. 1966).

FULD, JUDGE.

This case involves what appears to be a rather common practice in the taxicab industry of vesting the ownership of a taxi fleet in many corporations, each owning only one or two cabs.

The complaint alleges that the plaintiff was severely injured four years ago in New York City when he was run down by a taxicab owned by the defendant Seon Cab Corporation and negligently operated at the time by the defendant Marchese. The individual defendant, Carlton, is claimed to be a stockholder of 10 corporations, including Seon, each of which has but two cabs registered in its name, and it is implied that only the minimum automobile liability insurance required by law (in the amount of $10,000) is carried on any one cab. Although seemingly independent of one another, these corporations are alleged to be 'operated as a single entity, unit and enterprise' with regard to financing, supplies, repairs, employees and garaging, and all are named as defendants. The plaintiff asserts that he is also entitled to hold their stockholders personally liable for the damages sought because the multiple corporate structure constitutes an unlawful attempt 'to defraud members of the general public' who might be injured by the cabs.

The defendant Carlton has moved to dismiss the complaint on the ground that as to him it 'fails to state a cause of action'. The court at Special Term granted the motion but the Appellate Division, by a divided vote, reversed, holding that a valid cause of action was sufficiently stated.

The law permits the incorporation of a business for the very purpose of enabling its proprietors to escape personal liability but, manifestly, the privilege is not without its limits. Broadly speaking, the courts will disregard the corporate form, or, to use accepted terminology, 'pierce the corporate veil', whenever necessary 'to prevent fraud or to achieve equity'. In determining whether liability should be extended to reach assets beyond those belonging to the corporation, we are guided, as Judge Cardozo noted, by 'general rules of agency.' In other words, whenever anyone uses control of the corporation to further his own rather than the corporation's business, he will be liable for the corporation's acts 'upon the principle of *respondeat superior* applicable even where the agent is a natural person.' Such liability, moreover, extends not only to the corporation's commercial dealings but to its negligent acts as well.

In the *Mangan* case, the plaintiff was injured as a result of the negligent operation of a cab owned and operated by one of four corporations affiliated with the defendant Terminal. Although the defendant was not a stockholder of any of the operating companies, both the defendant and the operating companies were owned, for the most part, by the same parties.

The defendant's name (Terminal) was conspicuously displayed on the sides of all of the taxis used in the enterprise and, in point of fact, the defendant actually serviced, inspected, repaired and dispatched them. These facts were deemed to provide sufficient cause for piercing the corporate veil of the operating company—the nominal owner of the cab which injured the plaintiff—and holding the defendant liable. The operating companies were simply instrumentalities for carrying on the business of the defendant without imposing upon it financial and other liabilities incident to the actual ownership and operation of the cabs.

In the case before us, the plaintiff has explicitly alleged that none of the corporations "had a separate existence of their own" and, as indicated above, all are named as defendants. However, it is one thing to assert that a corporation is a fragment of a larger corporate combine which actually conducts the business. (*See* Berle, *The Theory of Enterprise Entity*, 47 Col. L.Rev. 343, 348–350.) It is quite another to claim that the corporation is a "dummy" for its individual stockholders who are in reality carrying on the business in their personal capacities for purely personal rather than corporate ends. Either circumstance would justify treating the corporation as an agent and piercing the corporate veil to reach the principal but a different result would follow in each case. In the first, only a larger corporate entity would be held financially responsible while, in the other, the stockholder would be personally liable. Either the stockholder is conducting the business in his individual capacity or he is not. If he is, he will be liable; if he is not, then it does not matter—insofar as his personal liability is concerned—that the enterprise is actually being carried on by a larger "enterprise entity."

The individual defendant is charged with having "organized, managed, dominated and controlled" a fragmented corporate entity but there are no allegations that he was conducting business in his individual capacity. Had the taxicab fleet been owned by a single corporation, it would be readily apparent that the plaintiff would face formidable barriers in attempting to establish personal liability on the part of the corporation's stockholders. The fact that the fleet ownership has been deliberately split up among many corporations does not ease the plaintiff's burden in that respect. The corporate form may not be disregarded merely because the assets of the corporation, together with the mandatory insurance coverage of the vehicle which struck the plaintiff, are insufficient to assure him the recovery sought. If Carlton were to be held individually liable on those facts alone, the decision would apply equally to the thousands of cabs which are owned by their individual drivers who conduct their businesses through corporations organized pursuant to section 401 of the Business Corporation Law, and carry the minimum insurance required by [the Vehicle and Traffic Law]. These taxi owner-operators are entitled to form such corporations, and we agree with the court at Special Term that, if the insurance coverage required by statute "is inadequate for the protection of the public, the remedy lies not with the courts but with the Legislature." It may very well be sound policy to require that certain corporations must take out liability insurance which will afford adequate compensation to their potential tort victims. However, the responsibility for imposing conditions on the privilege of incorporation has been committed by the Constitution to the Legislature and it may not be fairly implied, from any statute, that the Legislature intended, without the slightest discussion or debate, to require of taxi corporations that they carry automobile liability insurance over and above that mandated by the Vehicle and Traffic Law.

This is not to say that it is impossible for the plaintiff to state a valid cause of action against the defendant Carlton. However, the simple fact is that the plaintiff has just not done so here. While the complaint alleges that the separate corporations were undercapitalized and that their assets have been intermingled, it is barren of any "sufficiently particular(ized) statements" that the defendant Carlton and his associates are actually doing business in their individual capacities, shuttling their personal funds in and out of the corporations "without regard to formality and to suit their immediate convenience." Such a "perversion of the privilege to do business in a corporate form" would justify imposing personal liability on the individual stockholders. Nothing of the sort has in fact been charged, and it cannot reasonably or logically be inferred from the happenstance that the business of Seon Cab Corporation may actually be carried on by a larger corporate entity composed of many corporations which, under general principles of agency, would be liable to each other's creditors in contract and in tort.[3]

In point of fact, the principle relied upon in the complaint to sustain the imposition of personal liability is not agency but fraud. Such a cause of action cannot withstand analysis. If it is not fraudulent for the owner-operator of a single cab corporation to take out only the minimum required liability insurance, the enterprise does not become either illicit or fraudulent merely because it consists of many such corporations. The plaintiff's injuries are the same regardless of whether the cab which strikes him is owned by a single corporation or part of a fleet with ownership fragmented among many corporations. Whatever rights he may be able to assert against parties other than the registered owner of the vehicle come into being not because he has been defrauded but because, under the principle of *respondeat superior*, he is entitled to hold the whole enterprise responsible for the acts of its agents.

---

[3]   In his affidavit in opposition to the motion to dismiss, the plaintiff's counsel claimed that corporate assets had been 'milked out' of, and 'siphoned off' from the enterprise. Quite apart from the fact that these allegations are far too vague and conclusory, the charge is premature. If the plaintiff succeeds in his action and becomes a judgment creditor of the corporation, he may then sue and attempt to hold the individual defendants accountable for any dividends and property that were wrongfully distributed * * * .

In sum, then, the complaint falls short of adequately stating a cause of action against the defendant Carlton in his individual capacity.

The order of the Appellate Division should be reversed.

KEATING, JUDGE (dissenting).

The defendant Carlton, the shareholder here sought to be held for the negligence of the driver of a taxicab, was a principal shareholder and organizer of the defendant corporation which owned the taxicab. The corporation was one of 10 organized by the defendant. The sole assets of these operating corporations are the vehicles themselves and they are apparently subject to mortgages.[*]

From their inception these corporations were intentionally undercapitalized for the purpose of avoiding responsibility for acts which were bound to arise as a result of the operation of a large taxi fleet having cars out on the street 24 hours a day and engaged in public transportation. And during the course of the corporations' existence all income was continually drained out of the corporations for the same purpose.

The issue presented by this action is whether the policy of this State, which affords those desiring to engage in a business enterprise the privilege of limited liability through the use of the corporate device, is so strong that it will permit that privilege to continue no matter how much it is abused, no matter how irresponsibly the corporation is operated, no matter what the cost to the public. I do not believe that it is.

Under the circumstances of this case the shareholders should all be held individually liable to this plaintiff for the injuries he suffered. At least, the matter should not be disposed of on the pleadings by a dismissal of the complaint. "If a corporation is organized and carries on business without substantial capital in such a way that the corporation is likely to have no sufficient assets available to meet its debts, it is inequitable that shareholders should set up such a flimsy organization to escape personal liability. The attempt to do corporate business without providing any sufficient basis of financial responsibility to creditors is an abuse of the separate entity and will be ineffectual to exempt the shareholders from corporate debts. It is coming to be recognized as the policy of law that shareholders should in good faith put at the risk of the business unencumbered capital reasonably adequate for its prospective liabilities. If capital is illusory or trifling compared with the business to be done and the risks of loss, this is a ground for denying the separate entity privilege." (Ballantine, Corporations (rev.ed., 1946), § 129, pp. 302–303.)

In *Minton v. Cavaney*, 56 Cal.2d 576, 15 Cal.Rptr. 641, 364 P.2d 473, the Supreme Court of California had occasion to discuss this problem in a

---

[*] It appears that the medallions, which are of considerable value, are judgment proof. (Administrative Code of City of New York § 436–2.0.)

negligence case. The corporation of which the defendant was an organizer, director and officer operated a public swimming pool. One afternoon the plaintiffs' daughter drowned in the pool as a result of the alleged negligence of the corporation.

Justice Roger Traynor, speaking for the court, outlined the applicable law in this area. "The figurative terminology 'alter ego' and 'disregard of the corporate entity'," he wrote, "is generally used to refer to the various situations that are an abuse of the corporate privilege. The equitable owners of a corporation, for example, are personally liable when they treat the assets of the corporation as their own and add or withdraw capital from the corporation at will; when they hold themselves out as being personally liable for the debts of the corporation; Or *when they provide inadequate capitalization and actively participate in the conduct of corporate affairs.*" (56 Cal.2d, p. 579, 15 Cal.Rptr., p. 643, 364 P.2d p. 475; italics supplied.)

Examining the facts of the case in light of the legal principles just enumerated, he found that "(it was) undisputed that there was no attempt to provide adequate capitalization. (The corporation) never had any substantial assets. It leased the pool that it operated, and the lease was forfeited for failure to pay the rent. Its capital was 'trifling compared with the business to be done and the risks of loss.' "

It seems obvious that one of 'the risks of loss' referred to was the possibility of drownings due to the negligence of the corporation. And the defendant's failure to provide such assets or any fund for recovery resulted in his being held personally liable.

The defendant Carlton claims that, because the minimum amount of insurance required by the statute was obtained, the corporate veil cannot and should not be pierced despite the fact that the assets of the corporation which owned the cab were "trifling compared with the business to be done and the risks of loss" which were certain to be encountered. I do not agree.

The Legislature in requiring minimum liability insurance of $10,000, no doubt, intended to provide at least some small fund for recovery against those individuals and corporations who just did not have and were not able to raise or accumulate assets sufficient to satisfy the claims of those who were injured as a result of their negligence. It certainly could not have intended to shield those individuals who organized corporations, with the specific intent of avoiding responsibility to the public, where the operation of the corporate enterprise yielded profits sufficient to purchase additional insurance. Moreover, it is reasonable to assume that the Legislature believed that those individuals and corporations having substantial assets would take out insurance far in excess of the minimum in order to protect those assets from depletion. Given the costs of hospital care and treatment and the nature of injuries sustained in auto collisions, it would be unreasonable to assume that the Legislature believed that the minimum provided in the statute would in and of itself be sufficient to recompense "innocent victims of motor vehicle accidents for the injury and financial loss inflicted upon them."

The defendant, however, argues that the failure of the Legislature to increase the minimum insurance requirements indicates legislative acquiescence in this scheme to avoid liability and responsibility to the public. In the absence of a clear legislative statement, approval of a scheme having such serious consequences is not to be so lightly inferred.

The defendant contends that the court will be encroaching upon the legislative domain by ignoring the corporate veil and holding the individual shareholder. This argument was answered by Mr. Justice Douglas in *Anderson v. Abbott, supra,* [321 U.S.] 366–367, 64 S.Ct. p. 540, where he wrote that: "In the field in which we are presently concerned, judicial power hardly oversteps the bounds when it refuses to lend its aid to a promotional project which would circumvent or undermine a legislative policy. To deny it that function would be to make it impotent in situations where historically it has made some of its most notable contributions. If the judicial power is helpless to protect a legislative program from schemes for easy avoidance, then indeed it has become a handy implement of high finance. *Judicial interference to cripple or defeat a legislative policy is one thing; judicial interference with the plans of those whose corporate or other devices would circumvent that policy is quite another.* Once the purpose or effect of the scheme is clear, once the legislative policy is plain, we would indeed forsake a great tradition to say we were helpless to fashion the instruments for appropriate relief." (Emphasis added.)

The defendant contends that a decision holding him personally liable would discourage people from engaging in corporate enterprise.

What I would merely hold is that a participating shareholder of a corporation vested with a public interest, organized with capital insufficient to meet liabilities which are certain to arise in the ordinary course of the corporation's business, may be held personally responsible for such liabilities. Where corporate income is not sufficient to cover the cost of insurance premiums above the statutory minimum or where initially adequate finances dwindle under the pressure of competition, bad times or extraordinary and unexpected liability, obviously the shareholder will not be held liable.

The only types of corporate enterprises that will be discouraged as a result of a decision allowing the individual shareholder to be sued will be those such as the one in question, designed solely to abuse the corporate privilege at the expense of the public interest.

For these reasons I would vote to affirm the order of the Appellate Division.

———————

Following the remand, Walkovsky amended his complaint to allege
that Carlton had conducted business in his individual capacity. Carlton
again moved to dismiss but this time the trial court denied his motion. The
intermediate appellate court affirmed, with one judge dissenting on the
ground that rather than set forth facts, Carlton had only "vaguely and
prematurely pleaded conclusions." 287 N.Y.S.2d 546, 547 (2d Dept. 1968)
(Rabin, J. dissenting). The Court of Appeals also affirmed in a
memorandum decision, 244 N.E.2d 55 (N.Y. 1968), and the parties settled
the case.

Notice that in *Walkovszky* the plaintiff sought liability from two
sources: (1) the ten taxicab corporations and corporate garage under
common ownership, and (2) Carlton individually. The case was appealed
only on the issue of Carlton's liability. The possibility of "enterprise
liability" against corporations that are operated as a single economic unit
expands the assets available to corporate creditors, without imposing
liability on corporate shareholders. In some instances, this may be enough.
But in *Walkovszky* the assets of the other corporations were heavily
mortgaged or otherwise judgment-proof.

RADASZEWSKI V. TELECOM CORP.

981 F.2d 305 (8th Cir.1992).

RICHARD S. ARNOLD, CHIEF JUDGE.

This is an action for personal injuries filed on behalf of Konrad
Radaszewski, who was seriously injured in an automobile accident on
August 21, 1984. Radaszewski, who was on a motorcycle, was struck by a
truck driven by an employee of Contrux, Inc. The question presented on
this appeal is whether the District Court had jurisdiction over the person
of Telecom Corporation, which is the corporate parent of Contrux. This
question depends, in turn, on whether, under Missouri law, Radaszewski
can "pierce the corporate veil," and hold Telecom liable for the conduct of
its subsidiary, Contrux, and Contrux's driver.

I.

In general, someone injured by the conduct of a corporation or one of
its employees can look only to the assets of the employee or of the employer
corporation for recovery. The shareholders of the corporation, including, if
there is one, its parent corporation, are not responsible. This is a conscious
decision made by the law of every state to encourage business in the
corporate form. Obviously the decision has its costs. Some injuries are
going to go unredressed because of the insolvency of the corporate
defendant immediately involved, even when its shareholders have plenty
of money. To the general rule, though, there are exceptions. There are
instances in which an injured person may "pierce the corporate veil," that
is, reach the assets of one or more of the shareholders of the corporation

whose conduct has created liability. In the present case, the plaintiff seeks to hold Telecom Corporation liable for the conduct of an employee of its wholly owned subsidiary, Contrux, Inc.

Under Missouri law, a plaintiff in this position needs to show three things.

> (1)   Control, not mere majority or complete stock control, but complete domination, not only of finances, but of policy and business practice in respect to the transaction attacked so that the corporate entity as to this transaction had at the time no separate mind, will or existence of its own; and

> (2)   Such control must have been used by the defendant to commit fraud or wrong, to perpetrate the violation of a statutory or other positive legal duty, or dishonest and unjust act in contravention of plaintiff's legal rights; and

> (3)   The aforesaid control and breach of duty must proximately cause the injury or unjust loss complained of.

Collet v. American National Stores, Inc., 708 S.W.2d 273, 284 (Mo.App.1986).

[Because Telecom, as such, has had no contact with Missouri, whether Missouri courts have jurisdiction over Telecom depends on whether the corporate veil of Contrux can be pierced. The parties have argued the case as one of jurisdiction, and so will we, but in fact the underlying issue is whether Telecom can be held liable for what Contrux did.]

II.

[To satisfy] the second element of the *Collet* formulation, plaintiff cites no direct evidence of improper motivation or violation of law on Telecom's part. He argues, instead, that Contrux was undercapitalized.

Undercapitalizing a subsidiary, which we take to mean creating it and putting it in business without a reasonably sufficient supply of money, has become a sort of proxy under Missouri law for the second *Collet* element. The reason, we think, is not because undercapitalization, in and of itself, is unlawful (though it may be for some purposes), but rather because the creation of an undercapitalized subsidiary justifies an inference that the parent is either deliberately or recklessly creating a business that will not be able to pay its bills or satisfy judgments against it. This point has been made clear by the Supreme Court of Missouri. In *May Department Stores Co. v. Union Electric Light & Power Co.*, 341 Mo. 299, 327, 107 S.W.2d 41, 55 (1937), the Court found an improper purpose in a case where a corporation was "operating it without sufficient funds to meet obligations to those who must deal with it." Similarly, in *Consolidated Sun Ray, Inc. v. Oppenstein*, 335 F.2d 801 (8th Cir.1964), we said:

Making a corporation a supplemental part of an economic unit and operating it without sufficient funds to meet obligations to those who must deal with it would be circumstantial evidence tending to show either an improper purpose or reckless disregard of the rights of others.

Id. at 806–07.

Here, the District Court held, and we assume, that Contrux was undercapitalized in the accounting sense. Most of the money contributed to its operation by Telecom was in the form of loans, not equity, and, when Contrux first went into business, Telecom did not pay for all of the stock that was issued to it. Telecom in effect concedes that Contrux's balance sheet was anemic, and that, from the point of view of generally accepted accounting principles, Contrux was inadequately capitalized. Telecom says, however, that this doesn't matter, because Contrux had $11,000,000 worth of liability insurance available to pay judgments like the one that Radaszewski hopes to obtain. No one can say, therefore, the argument runs, that Telecom was improperly motivated in setting up Contrux, in the sense of either knowingly or recklessly establishing it without the ability to pay tort judgments.

In fact, Contrux did have $1,000,000 in basic liability coverage, plus $10,000,000 in excess coverage. This coverage was bound on March 1, 1984, about five and one-half months before the accident involving Radaszewski. Unhappily, Contrux's insurance carrier became insolvent two years after the accident and is now in receivership. But this insurance, Telecom points out, was sufficient to satisfy federal financial-responsibility requirements [applicable to interstate carriers such as Contrux].

The District Court rejected this argument. Undercapitalization is undercapitalization, it reasoned, regardless of insurance. The Court said:

The federal regulation does not speak to what constitutes a properly capitalized motor carrier company. Rather, the regulation speaks to what constitutes an appropriate level of *financial responsibility*.

This distinction escapes us. The whole purpose of asking whether a subsidiary is "properly capitalized," is precisely to determine its "financial responsibility." If the subsidiary is financially responsible, whether by means of insurance or otherwise, the policy behind the second part of the *Collet* test is met. Insurance meets this policy just as well, perhaps even better, than a healthy balance sheet.

At the oral argument, counsel for Radaszewski described the insurance company in question as "fly-by-night." He pointed out, and this is in the record, that the insurance agency that placed the coverage, Dixie Insurance Agency, Inc., was, like Contrux, a wholly owned subsidiary of Telecom. (Apparently the $1,000,000 primary policy is still in force. It is only the $10,000,000 excess policy that is inoperative on account of the insolvency of the excess carrier, Integrity Insurance Co.) Plaintiff argues that if the case went to trial he could show that the excess carrier "was an insurance company with wobbly knees for years before its receivership." He also says that the excess carrier was not strong enough even to receive a minimum rating in the Best Insurance Guide. Finally, plaintiff suggests that Contrux bought "its insurance from a financially unsound company which most certainly charged a significantly lower premium."

Insurance is unquestionably relevant on the issue of "undercapitalization." The existence of insurance goes directly to the question of the subsidiary's financial responsibility. Here, it is beyond dispute that Contrux had insurance, and that it was considered financially responsible under the applicable federal regulations. We see nothing sinister in the fact that the insurance was purchased through an agency wholly owned by Telecom. This is a common business practice. The assertion that a reduced premium was paid is wholly without support in the record. It is based on speculation only. There is no evidence that Telecom or Contrux knew that the insurance company was going to become insolvent, and no reason, indeed, that we can think of why anyone would want to buy insurance from a company that he thought would become insolvent.

[I]nformation [that Integrity had operated for several years at a loss], in our view, supports at most an inference that Contrux may have made an error in business judgment in placing its excess coverage with Integrity. It furnishes no genuine support for an inference of improper purpose.

The doctrine of limited liability is intended precisely to protect a parent corporation whose subsidiary goes broke. That is the whole purpose of the doctrine, and those who have the right to decide such questions, that is, legislatures, believe that the doctrine, on the whole, is socially reasonable and useful. We think that the doctrine would largely be destroyed if a parent corporation could be held liable simply on the basis of errors in business judgment. Something more than that should be shown, and *Collet* requires something more than that. In our view, this record is devoid of facts to show that "something more."

HEANEY, SENIOR CIRCUIT JUDGE, dissenting.

I respectfully dissent. The record is more than sufficient to support a prima facie showing that personal jurisdiction over Telecom exists.

In every respect on the basis of the record now before us, Contrux was nothing but a shell corporation established by Telecom to permit it to operate as a nonunion carrier without regard to the consequences that might occur to those who did business with Contrux or those who might be affected by its actions.

The majority asks why anyone would want to buy insurance from an insolvent company. An answer readily comes to mind. The purchase was a cheap way of complying with federal regulations and furthered the illusion to all concerned that Contrux was a viable company able to meet its responsibilities.

As the matter now stands, the innocent victim may have to bear most of the costs of his disabling injuries without having the opportunity to prove that Contrux was intentionally undercapitalized. I believe this is wrong and inconsistent with Missouri law. I would thus remand for trial.

Piercing to Benefit Tort Creditors

In *Browning-Ferris Industries of Illinois, Inc. v. Ter Maat*, 195 F.3d 953 (7th Cir.1999), Chief Judge Posner asserted that he could "think of only two arguments for piercing the corporate veil" in a case brought by an involuntary creditor. The first is disregard of corporate formalities, a factor that Professors Gevurtz and Bainbridge both contend should be irrelevant to such piercing claims. Judge Posner, however, suggested that if the owners of a corporation "have so far neglected the legal requirements (requirements not intended solely for the protection of creditors) for operating in the corporate form[,] they should be taken to have forfeited its protections, forfeiture thus operating to enforce the legal requirements that the state has seen fit to impose on investors who want the benefits of limited liability." In his view, "if the formalities have been flouted, it becomes hard to see how the investors could reasonably have relied on the protections of limited liability; they would have known they were skating on thin ice. In such a case the investment-encouraging function of limited liability is attenuated."

Posner's second argument relates to undercapitalization: "that enterprises engaged in potentially hazardous activities should be prevented from externalizing the costs of those activities, by being required to maintain or at least endeavor to maintain a sufficient capital cushion to be answerable in a tort suit should its activities give rise to liability, on pain of its shareholders' and affiliates' losing their limited liability should the corporation fail to do this." However, Posner stated:

> This argument has not carried the day in any jurisdiction that we are aware of, presumably because of the risks that it would impose on shareholders and because the potential victims of the corporation's hazardous activities can be protected without making inroads into limited liability by requiring enterprises engaged in such activities to post a bond large enough to assure that any judgment against the corporation will be collectible. Courts do, it is true, frequently mention "undercapitalization" as a separate ground from neglect of corporate formalities for

piercing the corporate veil. They do not do so on the basis of unusual risks to potential tort victims or other involuntary creditors, however, though conceivably such concerns are in the background of their thinking.

Whether or not one agrees with Judge Posner's characterization of the case law, it seems beyond dispute that courts tend to pierce the veil where they find undercapitalization. Of the cases studied by Professor Thompson in which the corporate veil was pierced, undercapitalization was identified by the court in only 19% of the contract cases and 13% of the tort cases. But in those cases where the court found a corporation to be undercapitalized, it pierced the veil in almost three cases out of four.

Determining whether a corporation is undercapitalized can present difficult questions. One is whether the adequacy of a corporation's capital should be measured as of the time it was organized or as of some later date. Clearly, if a corporation begins operating with sufficient capital to finance its anticipated business needs and then loses money over time, the purpose of limited liability would be defeated if the shareholders were required to invest additional capital on pain of losing the shield of limited liability. But what if a corporation, organized with capital sufficient to finance its anticipated business activities, subsequently enters a much riskier line of business? If the corporation's capital is trivial in relation to the risks involved in that new line of business, should its shareholders be required to contribute additional capital? Logic suggests that courts should require a corporation to increase its capital as the risks associated with its business grow. However, this logic has not been widely accepted. One reason may be that courts feel ill equipped to take on the task of deciding how much additional capital should be required.

Because most businesses buy insurance that limits their exposure to the risks of accidents, undercapitalization issues may arise less frequently in tort cases. Both *Walkovsky* and *Radaszewski* held that a corporation's purchase of the minimum liability insurance required by law effectively moots a claim that it is undercapitalized. In neither case was the court required to consider when a corporation should be considered underinsured, and therefore undercapitalized, in the absence of any minimum mandatory insurance requirement. The *Radaszewski* court's statement that "[i]nsurance is unquestionably relevant on the issue of 'undercapitalization'" implies that courts should consider the amount of a corporation's insurance coverage when passing on a piercing claim by a tort claimant. However, there does not appear to be any case in which a court, in the absence of a mandatory insurance requirement, has discussed whether a corporation should be deemed to be undercapitalized because it was underinsured. This result may reflect plaintiffs' failure to make this argument, underinsured defendants' propensity to settle when this argument is raised, or courts' reluctance to address this argument when it has been raised.

C. CONTRACT CREDITORS

FREEMAN V. COMPLEX COMPUTING CO., INC.
119 F.3d 1044 (2d Cir.1997).

MINER, CIRCUIT JUDGE:

While pursuing graduate studies under a fellowship at Columbia University in the early 1990s, [defendant Jason] Glazier co-developed computer software with potential commercial value and negotiated with Columbia to obtain a license for the software. Columbia apparently was unwilling to license software to a corporation of which Glazier was an officer, director, or shareholder. Nonetheless, Columbia was willing to license the software to a corporation that retained Glazier as an independent contractor. The licensed corporation then could sublicense the product to others for profit.

Accordingly, in September of 1992, [Complex Computing Co., Inc. ("C3")] was incorporated, with an acquaintance of Glazier's as the sole shareholder and initial director, and Seth Akabas (a partner of Glazier's counsel in this action) as the president, treasurer and assistant secretary. In November of 1992, another corporation, Glazier, Inc., of which Glazier was the sole shareholder, entered into an agreement with C3 (the "consulting agreement").[1] Under the consulting agreement, Glazier, Inc. was retained as an independent contractor (titled as C3's "Scientific Advisor") to develop and market Glazier's software, which was licensed from Columbia, and to provide support services to C3's clients. Glazier was designated the sole signatory on C3's bank account, and was given a written option to purchase all of C3's stock for $2,000.

In September of 1993, C3 entered into an agreement with [plaintiff Daniel Freeman] (the "C3-Freeman Agreement"), under which Freeman agreed to sell and license C3's computer software products for a five-year term. In exchange, C3 agreed to pay Freeman commissions on the revenue received by C3 over a ten-year period from the client-base developed by Freeman, including the revenue received from sales and licensing, maintenance and support services. The C3-Freeman Agreement included provisions relating to Freeman's compensation if C3 terminated the agreement prior to its expiration, or if C3 made a sale that did not result

---

[1] Although the consulting agreement was between C3 and Glazier, Inc., numerous provisions in the agreement made express reference to Glazier personally. For example, the consulting agreement provided that it was terminable if Glazier himself was unable to perform or supervise performance of Glazier, Inc.'s obligations.

in revenues because of a future merger, consolidation, or stock acquisition. The agreement included an arbitration clause.

Schedule 1 of the C3-Freeman Agreement listed the customers from whom Freeman would receive commissions. Although C3's president signed the C3-Freeman Agreement, Glazier personally signed the periodic amendments to Schedule 1. On March 24, 1994, Glazier signed an amended Schedule 1 that listed as customers, among numerous others, Thomson Financial, Banker's Trust and Chemical Bank. The amendment provided that "[t]o date, Dan Freeman has performed—and will continue to perform—material marketing services" as regards these customers.

On August 22, 1994, C3 and Thomson Investment Software, a unit or affiliate of Thomson [Trading Services, Inc. ("Thomson")], entered into a licensing agreement that granted Thomson exclusive worldwide sales and marketing rights of C3's products. Freeman contends that the licensing agreement resulted from efforts made by him over approximately nine months to bring the transaction to fruition.

In October of 1994, C3 gave Freeman the requisite 60-days notice of the termination of its agreement with him. The letter of termination, signed by Glazier, explained that C3's exercise of its option to terminate Freeman's employment was "an action to combat the overly generous termination clause we committed to, and to force a renegotiation of your sales contract."

Glazier was hired in January of 1995 as Thomson Investment Software's Vice President and Director of Research and Development at a starting salary of $150,000 plus additional payments of "incentive compensation" based in part upon the revenues received by Thomson in connection with the sale or license of products developed by Glazier. On the same day, Thomson and C3 entered into an assets purchase agreement (the "Thomson Agreement" or "assets purchase agreement"). As part of the transaction, Thomson assumed C3's intellectual products, trademarks and tradenames. It also assumed most of the liabilities and obligations of existing agreements involving C3, including agreements with C3 customers such as Banker's Trust and Chemical Bank. The Thomson Agreement set forth a list of C3 agreements assumed by Thomson, but expressly excluded the C3-Freeman Agreement. Thomson paid a total of $750,000, from which Glazier was paid $450,000 as a "signing bonus" in connection with his new employment contract; and C3 was paid $300,000, $100,000 of which was held by Thomson in an escrow account to indemnify Thomson for legal expenses in defending itself against claims arising from the assets purchase agreement, as well as for other expenses.

In May of 1995, Freeman commenced the action giving rise to this appeal. He estimated that he was due more than $100,000, and that the moneys due him in the future under the agreement would be in excess of $5 million.

In a memorandum opinion dated June 28, 1996, the district court found that both C3 and Glazier should be compelled to arbitrate their disputes with Freeman in accordance with the C3-Freeman Agreement. The district court found that Glazier was subject to the arbitration clause of the C3-Freeman Agreement because he "did not merely dominate and control C3—to all intents and purposes, he was C3" and because he held the "sole economic interest of any significance" in the corporation. The district court intended the judgment to "dispose[ ] of all claims asserted herein between and among [Freeman, C3 and Glazier]."

II. Piercing the Corporate Veil

Glazier argues on appeal that the district court erred in piercing the corporate veil to compel him to arbitrate Freeman's claims pursuant to the arbitration provision of the C3-Freeman Agreement. First, he contends that he cannot be held liable on a veil-piercing theory because he is neither a shareholder, officer, director or employee of C3. Second, Glazier argues that the district court's determination that he controlled C3 does not justify piercing the corporate veil in the absence of a factual finding that he used his control over C3 to wrong Freeman. We reject the former contention, but agree that the district court erred in piercing the corporate veil before finding that Glazier used his domination of C3 to wrong Freeman.

A. Glazier's Equitable Ownership of C3

Glazier contends that he should not be held personally liable under a veil-piercing theory because he is not a shareholder, officer, director, or employee of C3. We reject this argument.

New York courts have recognized for veil-piercing purposes the doctrine of equitable ownership, under which an individual who exercises sufficient control over the corporation may be deemed an "equitable owner", notwithstanding the fact that the individual is not a shareholder of the corporation. As the Appellate Division explained in *Lally v. Catskill Airways, Inc.*, a nonshareholder defendant may be, "in reality," the equitable owner of a corporation where the nonshareholder defendant "exercise[s] considerable authority over [the corporation] . . . to the point of completely disregarding the corporate form and acting as though [its] assets [are] his alone to manage and distribute."

Because Glazier "exercised considerable authority over [the corporation] . . . to the point of completely disregarding the corporate form and acting as though [its] assets were his alone to manage and distribute," he is appropriately viewed as C3's equitable owner for veil-piercing purposes. If there were board meetings, no minutes were kept from August 1994 through May 1995. Glazier agreed to personally indemnify C3's sole shareholder and director against any liability arising from the performance of his duties as C3's director. The president of C3 never attended a meeting of the Board of Directors. No shareholder received dividends or other distributions, despite the corporate income of $563, 257 in 1994 and $200,000 from the assets sale to Thomson.

Glazier used C3 to sell his intellectual product and powers, including the software that he had co-developed at Columbia and which Columbia licensed to C3. Through payments from C3 to Glazier, Inc., he received the vast majority of the resulting revenues.[5] Both Glazier, Inc. and C3 were located at Glazier's apartment, and Glazier was the sole signatory on C3's bank account. Glazier, Inc.'s consulting agreement with C3 expressly provided that it was terminable if Glazier himself was unable to perform or supervise the performance of Glazier, Inc.'s obligations to C3, which were described as "marketing [C3's] software products, developing new software products, enhancing [C3's] existing software products, and providing support services to [C3's] clients." These obligations essentially described C3's entire business.

Glazier himself gave Thomson a resume stating that from 1992 to the present, Glazier was the principal, owner and manager of C3, and that Glazier, Inc. was the predecessor to C3. C3 paid over $8000 to the law firm that represented Glazier personally in his negotiations with Thomson. These negotiations resulted in Thomson employing Glazier and paying him a $450,000 signing bonus. C3 then paid Glazier, through Glazier, Inc., an additional $210,000 out of the proceeds of the assets and other funds that were in the C3 bank account following the assets purchase. After payment of taxes and other expenses, this left only $10,000 in C3's account. Freeman contends that this balance renders C3 unable to fulfill its alleged obligations to him. Additionally, Glazier had an option to purchase all the shares of C3 from its sole shareholder for $2000. Thus, at his discretion, he could have become the sole shareholder for a small payment.

The district court found that "[t]o regard [Glazier] as anything but the sole stockholder and controlling person of C3 would be to exalt form over substance." Under the unique facts of the instant case, viewed in their totality, we agree that it is appropriate to treat Glazier as an "equitable owner" for veil-piercing purposes.

B. Piercing the C3 Veil

The presumption of corporate independence and limited shareholder liability serves to encourage business development. *See Wm. Passalacqua Builders, Inc. v. Resnick Developers S., Inc.*, 933 F.2d 131, 139 (2d Cir.1991). Nevertheless, that presumption will be set aside, and courts will pierce the corporate veil under certain limited circumstances. Specifically,

---

[5] The consulting agreement provided that C3 would not pay anyone compensation unless Glazier, Inc. had first received its share in full. The consulting agreement obligated C3 to pay Glazier, Inc. annual compensation of $150,000, with "cost-of-living" adjustments. In addition, it was to pay Glazier, Inc. a bonus for each calendar year equal to 60% of the first $200,000 in revenues received by C3, 70% of the next $200,000, 80% of the third $200,000, and 85% of all revenues received thereafter.

such "[l]iability . . . may be predicated either upon a showing of fraud or upon complete control by the dominating [entity] that leads to a wrong against third parties." As we explained in *Wm. Passalacqua Builders*, to pierce the corporate veil under New York law, a plaintiff must prove that "(1) [the owner] ha[s] exercised such control that the [corporation] has become a mere instrumentality of the [owner], which is the real actor; [(2) such control has been used to commit a fraud or other wrong;] and (3) the fraud or wrong results in an unjust loss or injury to plaintiff." *Id.* (internal quotation omitted).

[handwritten: equity]

To the extent that we have restated this test in cases such as *Carte Blanche (Singapore) Pte., Ltd. v. Diners Club International, Inc.*, 2 F.3d 24 (2d Cir.1993), in which we stated that veil-piercing will be allowed "in two broad situations: to prevent fraud or other wrong, or where a parent dominates and controls a subsidiary," the element of domination and control never was considered to be sufficient of itself to justify the piercing of a corporate veil. Unless the control is utilized to perpetrate a fraud or other wrong, limited liability will prevail. As we explained in *Electronic Switching Industries, Inc. v. Faradyne Electronics Corp.*, even if a plaintiff showed that the dominator of a corporation had complete control over the corporation so that the corporation "had no separate mind, will, or existence of its own," New York law will not allow the corporate veil to be pierced in the absence of a showing that this control "was used to commit wrong, fraud, or the breach of a legal duty, or a dishonest and unjust act in contravention of plaintiff's legal rights, and that the control and breach of duty proximately caused the injury complained of."

In determining whether "complete control" exists, we have considered such factors as: (1) disregard of corporate formalities; (2) inadequate capitalization; (3) intermingling of funds; (4) overlap in ownership, officers, directors, and personnel; (5) common office space, address and telephone numbers of corporate entities; (6) the degree of discretion shown by the allegedly dominated corporation; (7) whether the dealings between the entities are at arms length; (8) whether the corporations are treated as independent profit centers; (9) payment or guarantee of the corporation's debts by the dominating entity, and (10) intermingling of property between the entities. No one factor is decisive. In this case, there is little question that Glazier exercised "complete control" over C3.

*[handwritten: * Total control or Separation]*

As discussed in the context of equitable ownership, the record is replete with examples of Glazier's control over C3. Therefore, the district court's finding of control was not erroneous. However, the district court erred in the decision to pierce C3's corporate veil solely on the basis of a finding of domination and control. "While complete domination of the corporation is the key to piercing the corporate veil, . . . such domination, standing alone, is not enough; some showing of a wrongful or unjust act toward plaintiff is required." Thus, while we accept the district court's factual finding that Glazier controlled C3, we remand to the district court the issue of whether Glazier used his control over C3 to commit a fraud or other wrong that resulted in unjust loss or injury to Freeman. Though there is substantial evidence of such wrongdoing, a finding on this issue must be made in the first instance by the district court before veil-piercing occurs.

GODBOLD, SENIOR CIRCUIT JUDGE, concurring in part, dissenting in part.

I concur in affirming the district court's holding that Glazier was in total control of C3. I see no need, however, to remand the case to the district court for it to determine whether "Glazier used his control over C3 to commit a fraud or other wrong that resulted in an unjust loss or injury to Freeman." The record before us discloses fraud or other wrong by Glazier, through C3, resulting in an unjust loss or injury to Freeman. Consequently C3's corporate veil is to be pierced, and, without more, arbitration should proceed against Glazier as well as C3.

In some "corporate veil" cases one must search the record for evidence shedding light on whether an individual's control of the corporation has been used to commit a fraud or wrong resulting in unjust loss or injury. Not in this case. Here it all hangs out.

C3 is Glazier's creature, subject to his "complete control" ("he [Glazier] was C3"). C3 agreed with Freeman for him to sell and license C3's software products for five years and to receive commissions for ten years on revenue received from Freeman's clients. Plus, if C3 merged or consolidated, Freeman was to receive an additional payment of 10 percent of the total consideration conveyed. The agreement contained a termination clause. C3 could terminate on sixty days notice, but Freeman was entitled to receive all compensation for services previously rendered as well as the commissions that accrued over a ten year period (presumably to include 10 percent of the consideration for a buy out or merger).

An arbitration clause was included: "Any controversy or claim arising out of or related to this Agreement or any breach thereof . . . shall be settled by arbitration."

Approximately a year after the C3-Freeman agreement was made C3 entered into an agreement with Thomson Trading Services, Inc., an account developed by Freeman, to make Thomson its exclusive worldwide marketer. Thomson took over existing C3 agreements, but not C3's agreement with Freeman. That agreement remained C3's responsibility. But C3 has paid Freeman nothing.

It remained for C3 to get rid of Freeman. It did so by a purported termination of the C3-Freeman agreement. C3 recited that it was exercising its option to terminate as "an action to combat the overly generous termination clause we committed to, and to force a renegotiation of your sales contract." In short, Freeman was not to receive the benefits guaranteed him by the termination clause; the termination was to force him to give up the "overly generous" termination benefits he was entitled to receive. The asserted termination was not to implement the provision for termination but in derogation of it.

By this Tinker-to Evans-to-Chance play:

—C3's business has gone to Thomson.

—Thomson has handsomely rewarded Glazier.

—Thomson, in acquiring C3, has not assumed responsibility for the Freeman agreement.

—Glazier is enjoying the generous fruits of the C3-Thomson deal while C3 has been reduced to a shell.

—Freeman has been stripped of his benefits, paid nothing, and hung out to dry, on the asserted ground that benefits (past and future) agreed to be paid to him by C3 were too generous.

This is fraud by Glazier—a fully revealed rip off. But if one shrinks from the word "fraud" it is at least a "wrongful injury." We should not hesitate to say so at the appellate level, for the record is clear.

———

On remand, the district court found that Glazier's actions constituted fraudulent or other wrongful behavior because they left Freeman as "a general creditor of an essentially defunct corporation with virtually no assets." *Freeman v. Complex Computing Co., Inc.*, 979 F.Supp. 257, 260 (S.D.N.Y.1997). The court entered an order compelling Glazier to arbitrate plaintiff's claim.

KINNEY SHOE CORP. V. POLAN
939 F.2d 209 (4th Cir.1991).

CHAPMAN, SENIOR CIRCUIT JUDGE:

Plaintiff-appellant Kinney Shoe Corporation ("Kinney") brought this action against Lincoln M. Polan ("Polan") seeking to recover money owed on a sublease between Kinney and Industrial Realty Company ("Industrial"). Polan is the sole shareholder of Industrial. The district court found that Polan was not personally liable on the lease between Kinney and Industrial. Kinney appeals asserting that the corporate veil should be pierced, and we agree.

The district court based its order on facts which were stipulated by the parties. In 1984 Polan formed two corporations, Industrial and Polan Industries, Inc., for the purpose of re-establishing an industrial manufacturing business. The certificate of incorporation for Polan Industries, Inc. was issued by the West Virginia Secretary of State in November 1984. The following month the certificate of incorporation for

Industrial was issued. Polan was the owner of both corporations. Although certificates of incorporation were issued, no organizational meetings were held, and no officers were elected.

In November 1984 Polan and Kinney began negotiating the sublease of a building in which Kinney held a leasehold interest. The building was owned by the Cabell County Commission and financed by industrial revenue bonds issued in 1968 to induce Kinney to locate a manufacturing plant in Huntington, West Virginia. Under the terms of the lease, Kinney was legally obligated to make payments on the bonds on a semi-annual basis through January 1, 1993, at which time it had the right to purchase the property. Kinney had ceased using the building as a manufacturing plant in June 1983.

The term of the sublease from Kinney to Industrial commenced in December 1984, even though the written lease was not signed by the parties until April 5, 1985. On April 15, 1985, Industrial subleased part of the building to Polan Industries for fifty percent of the rental amount due Kinney. Polan signed both subleases on behalf of the respective companies.

Other than the sublease with Kinney, Industrial had no assets, no income and no bank account. Industrial issued no stock certificates because nothing was ever paid in to this corporation. Industrial's only income was from its sublease to Polan Industries, Inc. The first rental payment to Kinney was made out of Polan's personal funds, and no further payments were made by Polan or by Polan Industries, Inc. to either Industrial or to Kinney.

Kinney filed suit against Industrial for unpaid rent and obtained a judgment in the amount of $166,400.00 on June 19, 1987. A writ of possession was issued, but because Polan Industries, Inc. had filed for bankruptcy, Kinney did not gain possession for six months. Kinney leased the building until it was sold on September 1, 1988. Kinney then filed this action against Polan individually to collect the amount owed by Industrial to Kinney. Since the amount to which Kinney is entitled is undisputed, the only issue is whether Kinney can pierce the corporate veil and hold Polan personally liable.

The district court held that Kinney had assumed the risk of Industrial's undercapitalization and was not entitled to pierce the corporate veil. Kinney appeals, and we reverse.

We have long recognized that a corporation is an entity, separate and distinct from its officers and stockholders, and the individual stockholders are not responsible for the debts of the corporation. This concept, however, is a fiction of the law " 'and it is now well settled, as a general principle, that the fiction should be disregarded when it is urged with an intent not within its reason and purpose, and in such a way that its retention would produce injustices or inequitable consequences.' " *Laya v. Erin Homes, Inc.*,

352 S.E.2d 93, 97–98 (W.Va.1986) (quoting *Sanders v. Roselawn Memorial Gardens, Inc.*, 152 W.Va. 91, 159 S.E.2d 784, 786 (1968)).

Piercing the corporate veil is an equitable remedy, and the burden rests with the party asserting such claim. A totality of the circumstances test is used in determining whether to pierce the corporate veil, and each case must be decided on its own facts. The district court's findings of facts may be overturned only if clearly erroneous. *Id.*

Kinney seeks to pierce the corporate veil of Industrial so as to hold Polan personally liable on the sublease debt. The Supreme Court of Appeals of West Virginia has set forth a two prong test to be used in determining whether to pierce a corporate veil in a breach of contract case. This test raises two issues: first, is the unity of interest and ownership such that the separate personalities of the corporation and the individual shareholder no longer exist; and second, would an equitable result occur if the acts are treated as those of the corporation alone. Numerous factors have been identified as relevant in making this determination.

The district court found that the two prong test of *Laya* had been satisfied. The court concluded that Polan's failure to carry out the corporate formalities with respect to Industrial, coupled with Industrial's gross undercapitalization, resulted in damage to Kinney. We agree.

It is undisputed that Industrial was not adequately capitalized. Actually, it had no paid in capital. Polan had put nothing into this corporation, and it did not observe any corporate formalities. As the West Virginia court stated in *Laya*, " '[i]ndividuals who wish to enjoy limited personal liability for business activities under a corporate umbrella should be expected to adhere to the relatively simple formalities of creating and maintaining a corporate entity.' " *Laya*, 352 S.E.2d at 100 n. 6 (quoting *Labadie Coal Co. v. Black*, 672 F.2d 92, 96–97 (D.C.Cir.1982)). This, the court stated, is " 'a relatively small price to pay for limited liability.' " Another important factor is adequate capitalization. "[G]rossly inadequate capitalization combined with disregard of corporate formalities, causing basic unfairness, are sufficient to pierce the corporate veil in order to hold the shareholder(s) actively participating in the operation of the business personally liable for a breach of contract to the party who entered into the contract with the corporation." *Laya*, 352 S.E.2d at 101–02.

In this case, Polan bought no stock, made no capital contribution, kept no minutes, and elected no officers for Industrial. In addition, Polan attempted to protect his assets by placing them in Polan Industries, Inc. and interposing Industrial between Polan Industries, Inc. and Kinney so as to prevent Kinney from going against the corporation with assets. Polan gave no explanation or justification for the existence of Industrial as the intermediary between Polan Industries, Inc. and Kinney. Polan was obviously trying to limit his liability and the liability of Polan Industries, Inc. by setting up a paper curtain constructed of nothing more than

Industrial's certificate of incorporation. These facts present the classic scenario for an action to pierce the corporate veil so as to reach the responsible party and produce an equitable result. Accordingly, we hold that the district court correctly found that the two prong test in *Laya* had been satisfied.

In *Laya*, the court also noted that when determining whether to pierce a corporate veil a third prong may apply in certain cases. The court stated: "When, under the circumstances, it would be reasonable for that particular type of a party [those contract creditors capable of protecting themselves] entering into a contract with the corporation, for example, a bank or other lending institution, to conduct an investigation of the credit of the corporation prior to entering into the contract, such party will be charged with the knowledge that a reasonable credit investigation would disclose. If such an investigation would disclose that the corporation is grossly undercapitalized, based upon the nature and the magnitude of the corporate undertaking, such party will be deemed to have assumed the risk of the gross undercapitalization and will not be permitted to pierce the corporate veil." The district court applied this third prong and concluded that Kinney "assumed the risk of Industrial's defaulting" and that "the application of the doctrine of 'piercing the corporate veil' ought not and does not [apply]." While we agree that the two prong test of *Laya* was satisfied, we hold that the district court's conclusion that Kinney had assumed the risk is clearly erroneous.

Without deciding whether the third prong should be extended beyond the context of the financial institution lender mentioned in *Laya*, we hold that, even if it applies to creditors such as Kinney, it does not prevent Kinney from piercing the corporate veil in this case. The third prong is permissive and not mandatory. This is not a factual situation that calls for the third prong, if we are to seek an equitable result. Polan set up Industrial to limit his liability and the liability of Polan Industries, Inc. in their dealings with Kinney. A stockholder's liability is limited to the amount he has invested in the corporation, but Polan invested nothing in Industrial. This corporation was no more than a shell—a transparent shell. When nothing is invested in the corporation, the corporation provides no protection to its owner; nothing in, nothing out, no protection. If Polan wishes the protection of a corporation to limit his liability, he must follow the simple formalities of maintaining the corporation. This he failed to do, and he may not relieve his circumstances by saying Kinney should have known better.

For the foregoing reasons, we hold that Polan is personally liable for the debt of Industrial, and the decision of the district court is reversed and this case is remanded with instructions to enter judgment for the plaintiff.

———————

Piercing to Benefit Contract Creditors

Piercing most often occurs in a contract case where a "corporation had led potential creditors to believe that it was more solvent than it really was." *Browning-Ferris Industries*, 195 F.3d at 959. *Freeman* involved such conduct. In most cases in which no misrepresentation has been made, courts have refused to pierce. For example, *Paul Steelman, Ltd. v. Omni Realty*, 885 P.2d 549 (Nev. 1994), held that absent evidence that the original capital of a corporate general partner of a limited partnership was a sham, the fact that the corporation was undercapitalized would not support a decision to pierce the corporate veil. The court noted: "It is unfortunate that Steelman's recovery is limited to the assets of two insolvent entities; but Steelman alone is responsible for not protecting against the eventuality that occurred [*i.e.*, the insolvency of the general partner] by insisting on individual guarantees from shareholders who were financially capable of satisfying its claims."

Similarly, in *Theberge v. Darbro, Inc.*, 684 A.2d 1298 (Me.1996), the court refused to hold the sole shareholder of a corporation to which plaintiffs had loaned money liable for the corporation's debt, even though the shareholder had assured plaintiffs orally that he would "stand behind" the corporation's obligations. Reversing a trial court judgment in favor of plaintiffs, the court reasoned:

> The [trial] court found, and the record supports, that the defendants did not act illegally or fraudulently, but, rather, conducted themselves 'shrewdly' and employed 'sharp business practices.' The court determined that defendants did not formally, personally, guarantee the transaction and that the plaintiffs were sophisticated real estate professionals who understood the significance of a personal guarantee.

> [Others who had advanced funds to this real estate venture took action to secure the amounts they were owed.] The plaintiffs, by contrast, failed to obtain any such guarantee from any of the defendants and instead opted to proceed with the transaction. We decline to reconstruct the agreement negotiated between the parties to effect a result beyond the plain meaning of that bargain.

D. PARENT-SUBSIDIARY CORPORATIONS

The division of a business enterprise into multiple corporations is done for the convenience and profit maximization of the owners. Sometimes the relationship is that of parent and subsidiary: one corporation owns the stock of another. Sometimes one corporation owns the stock of many corporations, all of whom are subsidiaries of the parent and affiliates of each other. In the first case, a plaintiff who asserts an injury caused by a corporate subsidiary will seek to reach the assets of the parent to satisfy the judgment. In the second instance, the plaintiff will attempt to recover from the affiliates if neither the corporation that caused the injury nor the parent corporation has sufficient assets. While it may be appropriate to respect the limited liability of individual shareholders of a *parent* corporation, when does it make sense to treat related corporations as separate entities?

GARDEMAL V. WESTIN HOTEL CO.
186 F.3d 588 (5th Cir.1999).

DEMOSS, CIRCUIT JUDGE:

Plaintiff-appellant, Lisa Cerza Gardemal ("Gardemal"), sued defendants-appellees, Westin Hotel Company ("Westin") and Westin Mexico, S.A. de C.V. ("Westin Mexico"), under Texas law, alleging that the defendants were liable for the drowning death of her husband in Cabo San Lucas, Mexico. The district court dismissed the suit in accordance with the magistrate judge's recommendation that the court grant Westin's motion for summary judgment, and Westin Mexico's motion to dismiss for lack of personal jurisdiction. We affirm the district court's rulings.

In June 1995, Gardemal and her husband John W. Gardemal, a physician, traveled to Cabo San Lucas, Baja California Sur, Mexico, to attend a medical seminar held at the Westin Regina Resort Los Cabos ("Westin Regina"). The Westin Regina is owned by Desarollos Turisticos Integrales Cabo San Lucas, S.A. de C.V. ("DTI"), and managed by Westin Mexico. Westin Mexico is a subsidiary of Westin, and is incorporated in Mexico. During their stay at the hotel, the Gardemals decided to go snorkeling with a group of guests. According to Gardemal, the concierge at the Westin Regina directed the group to "Lovers Beach" which, unbeknownst to the group, was notorious for its rough surf and strong undercurrents. While climbing the beach's rocky shore, five men in the group were swept into the Pacific Ocean by a rogue wave and thrown against the rocks. Two of the men, including John Gardemal, drowned.

Gardemal, as administrator of her husband's estate, brought wrongful death and survival actions under Texas law against Westin and Westin Mexico, alleging that her husband drowned because Westin Regina's concierge negligently directed the group to Lovers Beach and failed to warn her husband of its dangerous condition. Westin then moved for summary judgment, alleging that although it is the parent company of Westin Mexico, it is a separate corporate entity and thus could not be held liable for acts committed by its subsidiary. The magistrate judge agreed with Westin, and recommended that Westin be dismissed from the action. In reaching its decision the magistrate judge rejected Gardemal's assertion that the state-law doctrines of alter-ego and single business enterprise allowed the court to disregard Westin's separate corporate identity. [The magistrate also granted Westin Mexico's motion to dismiss on the ground that it had insufficient minimum contacts to bring it within the personal jurisdiction of the court. The district court accepted the magistrate judge's recommendations and dismissed Gardemal's suit.] We affirm.

In this action Gardemal seeks to hold Westin liable for the acts of Westin Mexico by invoking two separate, but related, state-law doctrines. Gardemal first argues that liability may be imputed to Westin because Westin Mexico functioned as the alter ego of Westin. Gardemal next contends that Westin may be held liable on the theory that Westin Mexico operated a single business enterprise. We consider first the issue of whether Westin may be held liable on an alter-ego theory.

Under Texas law the alter ego doctrine allows the imposition of liability on a corporation for the acts of another corporation when the subject corporation is organized or operated as a mere tool or business conduit. Alter ego is demonstrated "by evidence showing a blending of identities, or a blurring of lines of distinction, both formal and substantive, between two corporations." An important consideration is whether a corporation is underfunded or undercapitalized, which is an indication that the company is a mere conduit or business tool.

On appeal Gardemal points to several factors which, in her opinion, show that Westin is operating as the alter ego of Westin Mexico. She claims, for example, that Westin owns most of Westin Mexico's stock; that the two companies share common corporate officers; that Westin maintains quality control at Westin Mexico by requiring Westin Mexico to use certain operations manuals; that Westin oversees advertising and marketing operations at Westin Mexico through two separate contracts; and that Westin Mexico is grossly undercapitalized. Gardemal places particular emphasis on the last purported factor, that Westin Mexico is undercapitalized. She insists that this factor alone is sufficient evidence that Westin Mexico is the alter ego of Westin. We are not convinced.

The record, even when viewed in a light most favorable to Gardemal, reveals nothing more than a typical corporate relationship between a parent and subsidiary. It is true, as Gardemal points out, that Westin and Westin Mexico are closely tied through stock ownership, shared officers, financing arrangements, and the like. But this alone does not establish an alter-ego relationship. As we explained in *Jon-T Chemicals, Inc.,* there must be evidence of complete domination by the parent.

> The control necessary . . . is not mere majority or complete stock control but such domination of finances, policies and practices that the controlled corporation has, so to speak, no separate mind, will or existence of its own and is but a business conduit for its principal.

Thus, "one-hundred percent ownership and identity of directors and officers are, even together, an insufficient basis for applying the alter ego theory to pierce the corporate veil."

In this case, there is insufficient record evidence that Westin dominates Westin Mexico to the extent that Westin Mexico has, for practical purposes, surrendered its corporate identity. In fact, the evidence suggests just the opposite, that Westin Mexico functions as an autonomous business entity. There is evidence, for example, that Westin Mexico banks in Mexico and deposits all of the revenue from its six hotels into that account. The facts also show that while Westin is incorporated in Delaware, Westin Mexico is incorporated in Mexico and faithfully adheres to the required corporate formalities. Finally, Westin Mexico has its own staff, its own assets, and even maintains its own insurance policies.

Gardemal is correct in pointing out that undercapitalization is a critical factor in our alter-ego analysis, especially in a tort case like the present one. But as noted by the district court, there is scant evidence that Westin Mexico is in fact undercapitalized and unable to pay a judgment, if necessary. This fact weighs heavily against Gardemal because the alter ego doctrine is an equitable remedy which prevents a company from avoiding liability by abusing the corporate form. "We disregard the corporate fiction . . . when the corporate form has been used as part of a basically unfair device to achieve an inequitable result." In this case, there is insufficient evidence that Westin Mexico is undercapitalized or uninsured. Moreover, there is no indication that Gardemal could not recover by suing Westin Mexico directly. As a result, equity does not demand that we merge and disregard the corporate identities of Westin and Westin Mexico. We reject Gardemal's attempt to impute liability on Westin based on the alter-ego doctrine.

Likewise, we reject Gardemal's attempt to impute liability to Westin based on the single business enterprise doctrine. Under that doctrine, when corporations are not operated as separate entities, but integrate their resources to achieve a common business purpose, each constituent corporation may be held liable for the debts incurred in pursuit of that business purpose. Like the alter-ego doctrine, the single business enterprise doctrine is an equitable remedy which applies when the corporate form is "used as part of an unfair device to achieve an inequitable result."

On appeal, Gardemal attempts to prove a single business enterprise by calling our attention to the fact that Westin Mexico uses the trademark "Westin Hotels and Resorts." She also emphasizes that Westin Regina uses Westin's operations manuals. Gardemal also observes that Westin allows Westin Mexico to use its reservation system. Again, these facts merely demonstrate what we would describe as a typical, working relationship between a parent and subsidiary. Gardemal has pointed to no evidence in the record demonstrating that the operations of the two corporations were so integrated as to result in a blending of the two corporate identities. Moreover, Gardemal has come forward with no evidence that she has suffered some harm, or injustice, because Westin and Westin Mexico maintain separate corporate identities.

Reviewing the record in the light most favorable to Gardemal, we conclude that there is insufficient evidence that Westin Mexico was Westin's alter ego. Similarly, there is insufficient evidence that the resources of Westin and Westin Mexico are so integrated as to constitute a single business enterprise. Accordingly, we affirm the district court's grant of Westin's motion for summary judgment on that issue.

OTR ASSOCIATES V. IBC SERVICES, INC.

801 A.2d 407 (N.J.App. 2002).

PRESSLER, P.J.A.D.

The single dispositive issue raised by this appeal is whether the trial court, based on its findings of fact following a bench trial, was justified, as a matter of law, in piercing the corporate veil and thus holding a parent corporation liable for the debt incurred by its wholly owned subsidiary. We are satisfied that the facts, both undisputed and as found, present a textbook illustration of circumstances mandating corporate-veil piercing.

Plaintiff OTR Associates, a limited partnership, owns a shopping mall in Edison, New Jersey, in which it leased space in 1985 for use by a Blimpie franchisee, Samyrna, Inc., a corporation owned by Sam Iskander and his wife. The franchise agreement, styled as a licensing agreement, had been entered into in 1984 between Samyrna and the parent company, International Blimpie Corporation [(Blimpie)]. Blimpie was the sole owner of a subsidiary named IBC Services, Inc. (IBC), created for the single purpose of holding the lease on premises occupied by a Blimpie franchisee. Accordingly, it was IBC that entered into the lease with OTR in July 1985 and, on the same day and apparently with OTR's consent, subleased the space to the franchisee. The history of the tenancy was marked by regular and increasingly substantial rent arrearages, and it was terminated by a dispossess judgment and warrant for removal in 1996. In 1998 OTR commenced this action for unpaid rent, then in the amount of close to $150,000, against Blimpie. The action was tried in December 2000, and judgment was entered in favor of OTR against Blimpie in the full amount of the rent arrearages plus interest thereon, then some $208,000. Blimpie appeals, and we affirm.

We consider the facts in the context of the well-settled principles respecting corporate-veil piercing. Nearly three-quarters of a century ago, the Court of Errors and Appeals, in *Ross v. Pennsylvania R.R. Co.,* 106 N.J.L. 536, 538, 539, 148 A. 741 (E. & A.1930), made clear that while "ownership alone of capital stock in one corporation by another, does not create any relationship that by reason of which the stockholding company would be liable for torts of the other," nevertheless "[w]here a corporation holds stock of another, not for the purpose of participating in the affairs of the other corporation, in the normal and usual manner, but for the purpose of control, so that the subsidiary company may be used as a mere agency or instrumentality for the stockholding company, such company will be liable for injuries due to the negligence of the subsidiary." The conceptual basis of the rule enunciated by *Ross,* which is equally applicable to contractual obligations, is simply that "[i]t is where the corporate form is used as a shield behind which injustice is sought to be done by those who have control of it that equity penetrates the [corporate] veil." And, as the Supreme Court phrased it in *State, Dep't. of Envtl. Prot. v. Ventron Corp.,* 94 N.J. 473, 500, 468 A.2d 150 (1983), "[t]he purpose of the doctrine of piercing the corporate veil is to prevent an independent corporation from being used to defeat the ends of justice, . . . to perpetrate fraud, to accomplish a crime, or otherwise to evade the law."

Thus, the basic finding that must be made to enable the court to pierce the corporate veil is "that the parent so dominated the subsidiary that it had no separate existence but was merely a conduit for the parent." But beyond domination, the court must also find that the "parent has abused the privilege of incorporation by using the subsidiary to perpetrate a fraud or injustice, or otherwise to circumvent the law." And the hallmarks of that abuse are typically the engagement of the subsidiary in no independent business of its own but exclusively the performance of a service for the parent and, even more importantly, the undercapitalization of the subsidiary rendering it judgment-proof.

Finally, we point out that these principles are hardly novel to New Jersey, constituting rather a fundamental doctrine of corporate jurisprudence.

Blimpie concedes that it formed IBC for the sole purpose of holding the lease on the premises of a Blimpie franchisee. It is also clear that IBC had virtually no assets other than the lease itself, which, in the circumstances, was not an asset at all but only a liability since IBC had no independent right to alienate its interest therein but was subject to Blimpie's exclusive control. It had no business premises of its own, sharing the New York address of Blimpie. It had no income other than the rent payments by the franchisee, which appear to have been made directly to OTR. It does not appear that it had its own employees or office staff. We further note that Blimpie not only retained the right to approve the premises to be occupied by the franchisee and leased by IBC, but itself, in its Georgia headquarters, managed all the leases held by its subsidiaries on franchisee premises. As explained by Charles G. Leaness, presently Executive Vice President of Blimpie and formerly corporate counsel as well as vice-president and secretary of IBC, in 1996, the year of IBC's eviction for non-payment of rent, he was Blimpie's Corporate Counsel Compliance Officer. Blimpie, he testified, is exclusively a franchising corporation with "hundreds and hundreds" of leases held by its wholly-owned leasehold companies, which are, however, overseen by Blimpie's administrative assistants, that is "people in our organization that . . . do this [communicate with landlords] as their everyday job. Because we have—you know—there are various leases, various assignments." Leaness also made clear that the leasing companies, whose function he explained as assisting franchisees in negotiating leases, "don't make a profit. There's no profit made in a leasehold."

Domination and control by Blimpie of IBC is patent and was not, nor could have been, reasonably disputed. The question then is whether Blimpie abused the privilege of incorporation by using IBC to commit a fraud or injustice or other improper purpose. We agree with the trial judge that the evidence overwhelmingly requires an affirmative answer. The *leit motif* of the testimony of plaintiff's partners who were involved in the dealings with IBC was that they believed that they were dealing with Blimpie, the national and financially responsible franchising company, and never discovered the fact of separate corporate entities until after the eviction. While it is true that IBC never apparently expressly claimed to be Blimpie, it not only failed to explain its relationship to Blimpie as a purported independent company but it affirmatively, intentionally, and calculatedly led OTR to believe it was Blimpie. Illustratively, when OTR was pre-leasing space in the mall, the first approach to it was the appearance at its on-site office of two men in Blimpie uniforms who announced that they wanted to open a Blimpie sandwich shop. One of the men was the franchisee, Iskander. The other was never identified but presumably was someone with a connection to Blimpie. It is also true that the named tenant in the lease was IBC Services, Inc., but the tenant was actually identified in the first paragraph of the lease as "IBC Services, Inc. having an address at c/o International Blimpie Corporation, 1414 Avenue of the Americas, New York, New York." It hardly required a cryptographer to draw the entirely reasonable inference that IBC stood for International Blimpie Corporation The suggestion, unmistakably, was that IBC was either the corporate name or a trading-as name and that International Blimpie Corporation was the other of these two possibilities.

Beyond the circumstances surrounding the commencement of the tenancy relationship, the correspondence through the years between plaintiff and the entity it believed to be its tenant confirmed plaintiff's belief that Blimpie was its tenant. Blimpie's letters to OTR were on stationary headed only by the Blimpie logo. There is nothing in any of that correspondence that would have suggested the existence of an independent company standing between the franchisor and the franchisee, and, indeed, the correspondence received by OTR from its lessee typically referred to the sub-tenant, Samyrna, as "our franchisee."

We agree with the trial judge that the inference is ineluctable and virtually conceded by Blimpie that IBC was created as a judgment-proof corporation for the sole purpose of insulating Blimpie from any liability on the lease in the event of the franchisee's default, a purpose found by the trial judge to have been deliberately concealed by Blimpie by its conduct in creating the impression from the outset of the tenancy relationship and throughout its duration that it and IBC were one and the same. We reject Blimpie's contention of the irrelevancy of its conduct after execution of the lease that tended to confirm to plaintiff that it was the actual tenant. As we have noted, the franchisee was habitually late and in arrears in its rent payments. We think it clear that if OTR had any suspicion that its tenant was a judgment-proof corporation, it would not have forborne over the years as the arrearages continued to accumulate but would have taken steps to regain possession long before the tenant's obligations reached $150,000.

As we understand Blimpie's defense and its argument on this appeal, it asserts that it is entitled to the benefit of the separate corporate identities merely because IBC observed all the corporate proprieties—it had its own officers and directors albeit interlocking with Blimpie's, it filed annual reports, kept minutes, held meetings, and had a bank account. But that argument begs the question. The separate corporate shell created by Blimpie to avoid liability may have been mechanistically impeccable, but in every functional and operational sense, the subsidiary had no separate identity. It was moreover not intended to shield the parent from responsibility for its subsidiary's obligations but rather to shield the parent from its own obligations. And that is an evasion and an improper purpose, fraudulently conceived and executed. The corporate veil was properly pierced.

The judgment appealed from is affirmed.

E. VEIL-PIERCING IN LIMITED LIABILITY COMPANIES

Although the LLC is a relatively new entity form, the established case law shows that courts across many jurisdictions have applied the doctrine of piercing the corporate veil to LLCs. Most cases apply the principles and formulations applicable to corporations. However, the LLC has fewer requirements of formalities of maintaining the form than the corporation (for example, corporations are required to have annual shareholder meetings). The uniform law recognizes this difference: "The failure of a limited liability company to observe any particular formalities relating to the exercise of its powers or management of its activities is not a ground for imposing liability on the members or managers for the debts, obligations, or liabilities of the limited liability company." RULLCA § 304(b).

NETJETS AVIATIONS, INC. V. LHC COMMUNICATIONS, LLC
537 F.3d 168 (2d Cir. 2008).

KEARSE, CIRCUIT JUDGE:

[Plaintiffs NetJets Aviation, Inc., and NetJets Sales, Inc. (collectively "NetJets"), appeal from a summary judgment of the district court dismissing their claims against defendant Laurence S. Zimmerman, as the alter ego of LHC Communications, LLC ("LHC"), for breach of contract and account stated.]

NetJets is engaged in the business of leasing fractional interests in airplanes and providing related air-travel services. LHC is a Delaware limited liability company whose sole member-owner is Zimmerman. Most of the facts with respect to the relationship between NetJets and LHC are not in dispute.

On August 1, 1999, LHC entered into two contracts with NetJets. In the first (the "Lease Agreement"), NetJets leased to LHC a 12.5 percent interest in an airplane, for which LHC was to pay NetJets a fixed monthly rental fee. The lease term was five years, with LHC having a qualified right of early termination. The second contract (the "Management Agreement") required NetJets to manage LHC's interest in the leased airplane and to provide services such as maintenance and piloting with respect to that airplane, or substitute aircraft, at specified hourly rates. It required LHC to pay a monthly management fee, as well as fuel charges, taxes, and other fees associated with LHC's air travel. The Management Agreement allotted to LHC use of the airplane for an average of 100 hours per year for the five-year term of the lease ("LHC air hours"), and it provided that if the leased airplane were unavailable at a time when LHC wished to use it, NetJets would provide substitute aircraft. NetJets regularly sent LHC invoices for the services provided under the Lease and Management Agreements.

In July 2000, LHC terminated its agreements with NetJets. LHC's chief financial officer ("CFO") James P. Whittier sent a letter, addressed to a NetJets vice president, stating, in pertinent part, that "[t]he present outstanding is $440,840.39 and we are requesting that you apply the deposit of $100,000 against the outstanding and contact this office to resolve the balance."

As requested, NetJets contacted LHC and applied the $100,000 deposit against LHC's debt; however, it did not receive payment of the remaining balance of $340,840.39. In 2001, LHC ceased operations.

For the reasons that follow, we conclude that NetJets is entitled to trial on its contract and account-stated claims against Zimmerman as LHC's alter ego.

NetJets's Claims Against Zimmerman

A limited liability company (or "LLC"), formed by one or more entities and/or individuals as its "members," is an entity that, as a general matter, provides "tax benefits akin to a partnership and limited liability akin to the corporate form." The shareholders of a corporation and the members of an LLC generally are not liable for the debts of the entity, and a plaintiff seeking to persuade a Delaware court to disregard the corporate structure faces "a difficult task,"

Nonetheless, in appropriate circumstances, the distinction between the entity and its owner "may be disregarded" to require an owner to answer for the entity's debts. In general, with respect to the limited liability of owners of a corporation, Delaware law permits a court to pierce the corporate veil "where there is fraud or where [the corporation] is in fact a mere instrumentality or alter ego of its owner." Given the similar liability shields that are provided by corporations and LLCs to their respective owners, "[e]merging caselaw illustrates" that "situations that result in a piercing of the limited liability veil are similar to those [that warrant] piercing the corporate veil." J. Leet, J. Clarke, P. Nollkamper & P. Whynott, *The Limited Liability Company* § 11:130, at 11–7 (rev. ed.2007); *see also id.* at 11–9 ("Every state that has enacted LLC piercing legislation has chosen to follow corporate law standards and not develop a separate LLC standard.").

To prevail under the alter-ego theory of piercing the veil, a plaintiff need not prove that there was actual fraud but must show a mingling of the operations of the entity and its owner plus an "overall element of injustice or unfairness."

> "[A]n alter ego analysis must start with an examination of factors which reveal how the corporation operates and the particular defendant's relationship to that operation. These factors include whether the corporation was adequately capitalized for the corporate undertaking; whether the corporation was solvent; whether dividends were paid, corporate records kept, officers and directors functioned properly, and other corporate formalities were observed; whether the dominant shareholder siphoned corporate funds; and whether, in general, the corporation simply functioned as a facade for the dominant shareholder."

> "[N]o single factor c[an] justify a decision to disregard the corporate entity, but . . . some combination of them [i]s required, and . . . *an overall element of injustice or unfairness must always be present, as well.*"

As the above discussion indicates, "[n]umerous factors come into play when discussing whether separate legal entities should be regarded as alter egos," and "[t]he legal test for determining when a corporate form should be ignored in equity cannot be reduced to a single formula that is neither over-nor under-inclusive," Stated generally, the inquiry initially focuses on whether "those in control of a corporation" did not "treat[ ] the corporation as a distinct entity"; and, if they did not, the court then seeks "to evaluate the specific facts with a standard of 'fraud' or 'misuse' or some other general term of reproach in mind," such as whether the corporation was used to engage in conduct that was "inequitable," or an "unfair trade practice," or "illegal."

Simply phrased, the standard may be restated as: "whether [the two entities] operated as a single economic entity such that it would be inequitable for th[e] Court to uphold a legal distinction between them." Our Court has stated this as a two-pronged test focusing on (1) whether the entities in question operated as a single economic entity, and (2) whether there was an overall element of injustice or unfairness.

Finally, we note that the plaintiff need not prove that the corporation was created with fraud or unfairness in mind. It is sufficient to prove that it was so used.

These principles are generally applicable as well where one of the entities in question is an LLC rather than a corporation. In the alter-ego analysis of an LLC, somewhat less emphasis is placed on whether the LLC observed internal formalities because fewer such formalities are legally required. *See, e.g.,* Delaware Limited Liability Company Act, Del.Code Ann. tit. 6, § 18–101 *et seq.* ("DLLCA") (requiring little more than that an LLC execute and file a proper certificate of formation, *see id.* § 18–201(a), maintain a registered office in Delaware, *see id.* § 18–104(a)(1), have a registered agent for service of process in Delaware, *see id.* § 18–104(a)(2), and maintain certain records such as membership lists and tax returns, *see id.* § 18–305(a)). On the other hand, if two entities with common ownership "failed to follow legal formalities *when contracting with each other* it would be tantamount to declaring that they are indeed one in the same."

With respect to the question of whether LHC and Zimmerman operated as a single entity, the record contains, *inter alia,* financial records of LHC and deposition testimony from Zimmerman and LHC's CFO, Whittier. The evidence discussed below, taken in the light most favorable to NetJets, shows, *inter alia,* that LHC, of which Zimmerman is the sole member-owner, was started with a capitalization of no more than $20,100; that LHC proceeded to invest millions of dollars supplied by Zimmerman, including some $22 million in an internet technology company eventually called Bazillion, Inc. ("Bazillion"); and that Zimmerman put money into LHC as LHC needed it, and took money out of LHC as Zimmerman needed it.

Whittier, who had known Zimmerman since 1980 and worked with him full time from 1996 until April 2002 was LHC's only officer other than Zimmerman (*see* Affidavit of Laurence Zimmerman dated October 14, 2004. In addition to LHC, Zimmerman directly or indirectly owned or controlled a number of companies, including Landover Telecom Corporation, LandTel N.V., IP II Partners, LP, Fox Lair Holdings Corporation, and Kimlar Consulting Corporation. During most of the period 1996 to April 2002, Whittier "got paid from either Mr. Zimmerman or one of his corporations."

Zimmerman formed LHC in 1998; for most of its operating life, it shared office space with some of Zimmerman's other companies; LHC employed no more than five-to-seven people at any given time; and some of its employees worked for both LHC and Zimmerman's other companies or for LHC and Zimmerman personally. Whittier ran much of LHC's day-to-day operations based on instructions, general or specific, received from Zimmerman.

Zimmerman formed LHC "to be used as an investment vehicle for Mr. Zimmerman for him to make investments." "With regards to investments, Mr. Zimmerman reviewed investments. If he decided to go forward after his review, he would make an investment through [LHC] to an investment corporation he wanted to invest in." Although Zimmerman sought Whittier's advice as to the best way of accomplishing something he had decided he wanted to do, the ultimate decisions were always made by Zimmerman. "There were no decisions, financial decisions, made with regard to LHC without Mr. Zimmerman's approval."

Whittier testified that LHC also "was an operating company which maintained a consulting agreement with another entity called Landtel NV." But LandTel, which was wholly owned by Zimmerman's Landover Telecom—and was apparently LHC's only paying client—did not come into existence until January 2000, and LHC records do not show receipt of any consulting fees from LandTel until July 2000. Until LandTel was formed, therefore, the day-to-day LHC operations run by Whittier apparently consisted only of making Zimmerman's investments and carrying on Zimmerman's personal business:

Q.   What was your role with regard to LHC?

A.   I was acting chief financial officer.

Q.   What were your responsibilities as chief financial officer?

A.   They were defined by Mr. Zimmerman. I *basically tried to carry out what Mr. Zimmerman's wishes were.*

. . . .

Q.   What did your day-to-day responsibilities with regard to Mr. Zimmerman include?

A.   They varied. It was working on a potential investment that LHC might make; it was overseeing the consulting agreement that it had, might have had, that it did have with Landtel, and *it was personal business*.

Q.   By "personal business," do you mean the *personal business of Mr. Zimmerman?*

A.   *Sure.*

Q.   *Do you mean anything else by "personal business?"*

A.   *No.*

Whittier's compensation was paid sometimes by LHC and sometimes by Zimmerman personally.

In connection with Zimmerman's personal business, LHC's records show numerous transfers of money by Zimmerman to LHC, as well as numerous transfers of money from LHC to Zimmerman. Some of the transfers by Zimmerman to LHC were for the purpose of having LHC make investments, principally in Bazillion. Other transfers by Zimmerman to LHC were made for the purpose of meeting LHC's operating expenses:

> To the extent that the corporation had to pay operating expenses like rent, telephone, copy, employees, if there was not sufficient capital in the corporation, he would then advance the money personally to the corporation to meet these obligations.

Whittier testified that Zimmerman would transfer funds to LHC "as needed." Often those funds would come from Zimmerman's personal bank accounts. However, because Zimmerman generally waited until the eleventh hour to provide money to meet LHC's operating needs, sometimes "shortcuts" were taken by having the money come to LHC directly from one of Zimmerman's other companies such as Landover Telecom, Kimlar, Fox Lair, or IP II, none of which had any business relationship with LHC.

Whittier testified also that "[m]onies would go . . . *out of LHC* based on the need." For example, Zimmerman would take money out of LHC to "mak[e] an investment in another entity." In addition, at several brokerage firms, Zimmerman had personal accounts that were unrelated to LHC's operations; he had many margin calls in those accounts because he "utilized margin debt very aggressively," especially with respect to two stocks whose market prices dropped sharply in 2000. Zimmerman had LHC make payments to meet some of these margin calls in his personal accounts. On May 15 and 16, 2000, for example, LHC wired a total of $2 million to Salomon Smith Barney to meet margin calls or reduce the margin debt on Zimmerman's personal brokerage accounts. On August 22 and October 6, 2000, LHC sent Paine Webber, another firm at which Zimmerman personally had "big brokerage accounts," checks totaling $2 million. Some of the money that LHC used to pay Zimmerman's margin calls was "loan money" that Zimmerman had put into LHC. Other money used to meet Zimmerman's margin calls was money that LHC received from a third party ("Riverside") purchasing a share of an LHC asset. Thus, the $2 million that LHC paid to Salomon Smith Barney in May 2000 was money that Riverside paid LHC to buy participation in a Bazillion convertible subordinated note owned by LHC. Riverside "bought [participation in the note] directly from LHC"; but Riverside's payment to LHC was used to meet margin calls in Zimmerman's personal brokerage accounts.

LHC also transferred money to Zimmerman, or to third persons on his behalf, in connection with his living expenses. For example, LHC made payments to Fox Lair (consistently called "Fox Liar" in LHC's general ledger), a Zimmerman corporation that owned a $15 million New York apartment on Park Avenue, which was characterized by Zimmerman as "a corporate residence" but was used by no one other than Zimmerman and his family. Fox Lair needed money "to pay phone bills and cleaning people and things of that nature"; according to LHC's ledgers, from December 5, 2000, through July 2, 2001, Fox Lair received some $70,000 from LHC. In addition, LHC made periodic payments to the Screen Actors Guild (of which Zimmerman's wife was a member) for health insurance for Zimmerman and his family; LHC purchased a Bentley automobile at a cost of approximately $350,000 for Zimmerman's personal use, placing title in his name; and LHC made a payment of $110,000, characterized in its general ledger as "Loan receivable" and in its check register as "Interest Expense," to a person who had no connection with LHC but who held a mortgage on a property owned by Zimmerman personally.

In addition, many of the air hours to which LHC was entitled under its agreements with NetJets were used by Zimmerman personally. Of the 40-odd LHC flights invoiced by NetJets, Zimmerman acknowledges that "approximately 6" were for vacations for himself and/or his wife. But in addition to those six, there were at least an equal number of flights that apparently had no relation to LHC's business. These flights included several that transported Zimmerman's family to and from Europe or to and from one of Zimmerman's five homes. Zimmerman contends that use of LHC air hours for these purposes was "part of [his compensation] package" and "[o]ne of the perks of being the chairman." That may be; but for purposes of determining whether Zimmerman and LHC were alter egos, it is pertinent that Zimmerman made all of LHC's financial decisions; Zimmerman alone decided what his perks and package would be.

In LHC's general ledger, each of the transfers of money between LHC and Zimmerman—in either direction—is labeled "Loan receivable." They were also so labeled regardless of whether Zimmerman's payment to LHC was to be used to make an investment or was to be used for operating expenses. Whittier, who had responsibility for LHC's financial records, testified that the ledger treated Zimmerman's payments to and withdrawals from LHC as loans and loan repayments in order to allow Zimmerman to make withdrawals as he needed money, without having to pay taxes on the moneys withdrawn. Thus, aside from Zimmerman's initial capital contribution to LHC (which Whittier thought was $100), "any monies that Mr. Zimmerman . . . deposited into LHC should have been designated as loans." The decision that those transactions would be labeled loans or loan repayments was made by Zimmerman.

"There were no written agreements" with regard to any of Zimmerman's loans; nor were there any "set repayment program" or agreements as to repayment terms: "Money was put in as needed and when money was not needed and Mr. Zimmerman needed money elsewhere, he might transfer it out. *That was his decision to make.*" "*There was no procedure.* Money was put in and taken out as needed."

In all, LHC's financial records for the period January 1, 2000, through June 18, 2002, show—in addition to some two dozen transactions between LHC and Zimmerman's other companies—approximately 60 transfers of money directly from Zimmerman to LHC and approximately 60 transfers of money out of LHC directly to Zimmerman. In sum, there is evidence that, *inter alia,* Zimmerman created LHC to be one of his personal investment vehicles; that he was the sole decisionmaker with respect to LHC's financial actions; that Zimmerman frequently put money into LHC as LHC needed it to meet operating expenses; that LHC used some of that money, as well as some moneys it received from selling shares of one of its assets, to pay more than $4.5 million to third persons for Zimmerman's personal expenses including margin calls, mortgage payments, apartment expenses, and automobiles; and that with no written agreements or documentation or procedures in place, Zimmerman directly, on the average of twice a month for 2½ years, took money out of LHC at will in order to make other investments or to meet his other personal expenses. This evidence is ample to permit a reasonable factfinder to find that Zimmerman completely dominated LHC and that he essentially treated LHC's bank account as one of his pockets, into which he reached when he needed or desired funds for his personal use. Accordingly, we reject Zimmerman's contention that the district court should have granted summary judgment in his favor on the ground that he and LHC did not operate as a single economic entity.

The district court ruled that NetJets had not adduced sufficient evidence to show that there was any fraud or unfairness in Zimmerman's operation of LHC because the court believed it could not consider, with regard to that issue, any of the factors that showed that Zimmerman and LHC operated as a single entity. But nothing prevents a court, in determining whether there is sufficient evidence of fraud or unfairness, from taking into account relevant evidence that is also pertinent to the question of whether the two entities in question functioned as one.

Much of the evidence described in above, along with other evidence discussed below, reveals that NetJets adduced sufficient evidence of fraud, illegality, or unfairness to warrant a trial on its contract and account-stated claims against Zimmerman as LHC's alter ego. For example, in an effort to parry NetJets's contention that LHC was undercapitalized, Zimmerman submitted an affidavit from LHC's accountant stating that "it was not intended by Zimmerman to treat the monies paid into LHC as loans" and that all of Zimmerman's payments into LHC were in fact capital contributions. Yet, as discussed above, Whittier testified that Zimmerman instructed him that those payments were to be characterized as loans, in order to allow Zimmerman to take money out of LHC at will and to do so without tax consequences.

Further, although the Balaban affidavit stops short of giving an opinion as to how to characterize Zimmerman's withdrawals of money from LHC, it would appear that, if his payments to LHC were capital contributions as the Balaban affidavit opines, LHC's payments to Zimmerman would be properly characterized as distributions. Yet the DLLCA provides generally, with some qualifications, that an LLC "shall not make a distribution to a member to the extent that at the time of the distribution, after giving effect to the distribution, all liabilities of the limited liability company . . . exceed the fair value of the assets of the limited liability company." Del.Code tit. 6, § 18–607(a). Given that LHC ceased operating and was unable to pay its debt to NetJets, if Zimmerman's withdrawals left LHC in that condition those withdrawals may well have been prohibited by § 18–607(a). A factfinder could infer that Zimmerman's payments to LHC were deliberately mischaracterized as loans in order to mask the fact that Zimmerman was making withdrawals from LHC that were forbidden by law, and could thereby properly find fraud or an unfair siphoning of LHC's assets.

The record also includes other evidence from which a reasonable factfinder could find that Zimmerman operated LHC in his own self-interest in a manner that unfairly disregarded the rights of LHC's creditors. For example, it could find

> —that although LHC was apparently unable in 2000 to pay its $340,840.39 (net of LHC's deposit) debt to NetJets, in that year LHC bought, and gave Zimmerman title to, a Bentley automobile for $350,210.95;

> —that LHC's only paying client for its consulting services began paying LHC for those services in July 2000 (the month in which LHC terminated its agreements with NetJets), sending LHC a first payment of approximately $675,000 on July 9, and that on that day Zimmerman withdrew that amount and more from LHC;

> —that from the point at which LHC terminated its relationship with NetJets in July 2000 until the end of 2001—the year in which

NetJets ceased operations—LHC's records of its transactions directly with Zimmerman indicate that Zimmerman withdrew from LHC approximately $750,000 more than he put in;

—and that, excluding moneys put into LHC solely for its investments in Bazillion, the total amount of money taken out of LHC by Zimmerman and his other companies appears to exceed the amount that he and those companies put into LHC by some $3 million.

From this record, a reasonable factfinder could properly find that there was an overall element of injustice in Zimmerman's operation of LHC. Summary judgment should not have been entered dismissing NetJets's breach-of-contract and account-stated claims against Zimmerman.

F. FRAUDULENT CONVEYANCE AND EQUITABLE SUBORDINATION

Veil piercing is not the only method that courts use to protect creditor interests. Another method is to set aside transactions that defraud creditors under the Uniform Fraudulent Conveyance Act (UFCA), codified in the U.S. Bankruptcy Code and many state statutes. The UFCA protects creditors from two general types of transfers: (1) transfers with the intent to defraud creditors, and (2) transfers that constructively defraud creditors. Showing intentional fraud requires that the court find an actual intent by the debtor to "hinder, delay or defraud." But constructive fraud can be shown if the debtor makes a transfer while insolvent or near insolvency— if the transfer lacks fair consideration.

In the bankruptcy context, the UFCA is used rather than veil piercing to set aside transfers by the corporation to its shareholders when the transfer undermines creditor claims. The courts set aside the transfer and apply it against the corporation's debts to its creditors. For example, the UFCA has been used to set aside "excess" salary payments from a corporation to its sole shareholder that far exceeds the value of the shareholder's services to the corporation.

The UFCA helps explain why courts consider corporate formalities and the intermingling of corporate and personal assets in veil piercing cases. The disregard of corporate formalities often provides indirect evidence of fraudulent conveyances; the intermingling of corporate and personal assets may provide direct evidence of fraudulent conveyances.

But the UFCA has limitations—compared to veil piercing. First, the UFCA requires a specific finding of a fraudulent transaction, which may be difficult to establish. Second, unlike veil piercing, which imposes unlimited liability on shareholders, the UFCA only allows a court to set aside specific fraudulent conveyances, which may not satisfy a creditor's entire claim.

The doctrine of equitable subordination is another method to protect creditors interests. This doctrine, applicable only in federal bankruptcy proceedings, subordinates—or pushes to the back of the line—some creditors' claims (particularly those of corporate insiders) to reach an equitable result. Subordination thus allows outside creditors to receive payment before insiders. The result is significant since priority in bankruptcy often determines which creditors will get paid.

Before courts invoke the equitable subordination doctrine, there must be a showing of fraudulent conduct, mismanagement, or inadequate capitalization. Some cases explicitly reject inadequate capitalization as the sole basis for subordination. As a baseline, courts generally look to whether a claimant engaged in some form of "inequitable conduct" and whether the misconduct resulted in injury to the bankrupt's creditor or conferred an unfair advantage on the claimant.

Equitable subordination also has limitations compared to veil piercing and fraudulent conveyance principles. Equitable subordination does not increase the overall size of the pie available to creditors. Nor does it hold shareholders personally liable for corporate obligations. It only alters the normal priority of insider claims against the available corporate resources.

CHAPTER 4

THE BUSINESS ENTITY AND
LEGAL PERSONALITY

■ ■ ■

A. INTRODUCTION

With the exception of the sole proprietorship, all business entities are treated by the law as endowed with "legal personality." At a basic level, corporate personality is necessary to do business through a business entity. This convenient fiction gives corporations, partnerships, and limited liability companies the same rights as natural persons with respect to owning property, entering into contracts, and suing and being sued. Also, legal personality provides a basic legal rationale for the rule of limited liability, which states that the debts and liabilities of a limited liability entity, such as a corporation and an LLC, generally cannot be imputed to equityholders and managers, who are deemed to be separate and distinct from the entity. In other words, the debts and liabilities of legal person are its own and cannot be imputed to others via vicarious liability.

That business entities are considered "persons" for some purposes, however, does not necessarily mean that they are "persons" for all purposes. The extent to which the law should treat business entities differently from natural persons involves a conceptual question that the law has never fully resolved: whether corporations, partnerships, and LLCs should be treated as distinct "legal persons" or whether they consist simply of convenient forms in which their owners can associate to carry on a business. If the answer is the former, the law should look primarily, if not exclusively, to the characteristics of the entity to determine what rights it has. If, on the other hand, the entity is seen as an association of natural persons, it follows that it is necessary to take into account the rights of the owners in determining what rights to extend to the entity. The law in this area has developed primarily in cases involving corporate "legal personality," which is the main focus of this chapter.

In constitutional law, the issue is often framed as whether a corporation is entitled to the same constitutional rights as a natural person. The Supreme Court first discussed this issue in *Trustees of Dartmouth College v. Woodward*, 17 U.S. (4 Wheat.) 518 (1819). In 1769, the British Crown had granted articles of incorporation to the trustees of Dartmouth College. After the American Revolution, New Hampshire, as successor to the Crown, enacted three laws amending Dartmouth's charter so as to give state officials a major role in the governance of the college. Dartmouth sued to invalidate the amendments, claiming they violated the contract clause of the U.S. Constitution (Art. I, § 10). The New Hampshire Supreme Court rejected Dartmouth's claim, and the college appealed to the Supreme Court.

The Court, in an opinion by Chief Justice Marshall, held New Hampshire's action was invalid because the charter constituted a contract between the state and the college that was "within the letter of the Constitution and within its spirit also." In a well-known passage, the Chief Justice described a corporation's basic attributes in terms suggesting that a corporation is both a fictional entity created by the state and the product of a contract among private parties:

> A corporation is an artificial being, invisible, intangible, and existing only in contemplation of law. Being the mere creature of law, it possesses only those properties which the charter of its creation confers upon it, either expressly, or as incidental to its very existence. These are such as are supposed best calculated to effect the object for which it was created. Among the most important are immortality, and, if the expression may be allowed, individuality; properties, by which a perpetual succession of many persons are considered as the same, and may act as a single individual. They enable a corporation to manage its own affairs, and to hold property, without the perplexing intricacies, the hazardous and endless necessity, of perpetual conveyances for the purpose of transmitting it from hand to hand. It is chiefly for the purpose of clothing bodies of men, in succession, with these qualities and capacities, that corporations were invented, and are in use. By these means, a perpetual succession of individuals are capable of acting for the promotion of the particular object, like one immortal being. But this being does not share in the civil government of the country, unless that be the purpose for which it was created. Its immortality no more confers on it political power, or a political character, than immortality would confer such power or character on a natural person. It is no more a state instrument, than a natural person exercising the same powers would be.

Id. at 636–37.

The Court also held that a state could not unilaterally amend the provisions of a corporate charter it had granted. Justice Story, concurring, suggested that states could avoid this problem by granting charters subject to a reserved right to amend them. States seized upon this suggestion and began to include in all corporate charters a clause reserving the state's power to amend or repeal any authority granted to the corporation. When general corporation laws came into vogue, states added similar reserved powers clauses to their constitutions, their general corporation laws, or both. Currently, all states reserve the power to amend the corporate charters they issue.

Subsequent to *Dartmouth College*, the Court has had several more occasions to examine the extent to which a corporation is entitled to the rights and privileges that the Constitution provides to natural persons. *Santa Clara County v. Southern Pacific Railroad Co.*, 118 U.S. 394 (1886), perhaps the most important of these cases, held that a corporation is entitled to equal protection of the law under the Fourteenth Amendment. *Minneapolis & St. Louis Railway Co. v. Beckwith*, 129 U.S. 26 (1888), decided two years later, extended the holding of *Santa Clara* and ruled that a corporation also is entitled to due process of law. *Hale v. Henkel,* 201 U.S. 43 (1906), subsequently established that a corporation is protected against unreasonable searches and seizures by the Fourth Amendment, but also held that the Fifth Amendment's protection against self-incrimination is not available to a corporation. More recently, the Court has been required to consider whether speech by corporation is protected under the First Amendment, a subject considered in the next section.

B. THE RIGHTS OF CORPORATIONS UNDER THE FIRST AMENDMENT

Problem: Regulating Corporate Lobbying

You are the legislative assistant to Kathleen Bruin, who recently was elected a Columbia State Senator. In recent years, there have been frequent reports that corporations had exerted tremendous influence on the Columbia Legislature, and Sen. Bruin campaigned heavily on the promise that, if elected, she would work to reduce corporations' political influence. Now in office, Sen. Bruin would like to introduce a bill that would amend the Columbia Business Corporation Law (which is based on the Model Business Corporations Act) to allow any shareholder to recover from the directors of a Columbia corporation in a derivative suit "any corporate funds or other resources used, directly or indirectly, (1) to communicate, other than in a public hearing, directly with any member or employee of the Legislature of Columbia to secure or defeat the passage of any pending or proposed legislation by said legislature, or (2) to support or opposed the election of any candidate for public office, unless such use of corporate funds has been expressly authorized, after full disclosure of the position the corporation intends to advance, by a vote of the holders of 80 percent of said corporation's voting stock."

Sen. Bruin has asked for your opinion as to whether this legislation raises any serious issues under the First Amendment, and whether, if so, it would be helpful to make a distinction between public corporations those that are closely-held. She would also like to know how likely you think it is that the bill would achieve her goal of limiting the influence of large corporations on the Columbia Legislature or on elections for public office.

The legal fiction that a corporation is a "person" is a convenient means of endowing the corporation with the ability to enter in to contracts and to sue and be sued. However, this does not necessarily mean that corporations must have all of the legal rights of a natural person. One question that has been particularly contentious is the extent to which corporations have rights under the First Amendment. In 1907, Congress enacted the Tillman Act, which prohibits corporations from contributing money to federal political campaigns. There are two possible reasons for this prohibition. It can be seen as reflecting a fear that corporate managers were exercising control over large accumulations of capital in ways that unduly influenced political decisions. Alternatively, such contributions may be considered as giving away other people's money—shareholders' money—without any restraints. Whether viewed as a fear of big business or an agency cost problem, corporate political expenditures have remained controversial for over a century.

In *First National Bank of Boston v. Bellotti*, 435 U.S. 765 (1978), the Court held unconstitutional a Massachusetts statute that prohibited certain expenditures by banks and business corporations for the purpose of influencing the vote on referendum proposals other than those that materially affected the property, business or assets of the corporation. The banks wanted to spend money to publicize their views on a proposed constitutional amendment that would have permitted the legislature to impose a graduated tax on the income of individuals. The parties disagreed as to the effect that the adoption of a personal income tax would have on appellants' business but did not dispute that the banks' managements believed that the tax would have a significant effect on their businesses. Largely because of this perceived effect, the Court held that the First Amendment protected the right of banks to speak out on the issue.

Subsequently, in *Austin v. Michigan Chamber of Commerce*, 494 U.S. 652 (1990), a decision that appears inconsistent with *Bellotti*, the Court upheld the constitutionality of a Michigan statute that prohibited corporations from using corporate funds for contributions or independent expenditures in support of or in opposition to candidates for election to state office. More recently, the Supreme Court expressly overruled *Austin* in *Citizens United v. Federal Election Commission*, 558 U.S. 310 (2010), which struck down a federal prohibition of the use of corporate funds for "electioneering communication."

As you read the excerpts from these three cases, focus on the arguments made by the majority in *Austin,* and the dissents in *Bellotti* and *Citizens United.* In evaluating these arguments and the counter-arguments that ultimately prevailed, consider that it is usually impossible for shareholders of publicly held corporations to defeat incumbent directors in an election contest and that there are substantial procedural and substantive hurdles in prosecuting a derivative suit.

FIRST NATIONAL BANK OF BOSTON V. BELLOTTI
435 U.S. 765 (1978).

JUSTICE POWELL, writing for the Court.

Finally, appellee argues that § 8 protects corporate shareholders, an interest that is both legitimate and traditionally within the province of state law. The statute is said to serve this interest by preventing the use of corporate resources in furtherance of views with which some shareholders may disagree. This purpose is belied, however, by the provisions of the statute, which are both underinclusive and overinclusive.

The underinclusiveness of the statute is self-evident. Corporate expenditures with respect to a referendum are prohibited, while corporate activity with respect to the passage or defeat of legislation is permitted, even though corporations may engage in lobbying more often than they take positions on ballot questions submitted to the voters. Nor does § 8 prohibit a corporation from expressing its views, by the expenditure of corporate funds, on any public issue until it becomes the subject of a referendum, though the displeasure of disapproving shareholders is unlikely to be any less.

The fact that a particular kind of ballot question has been singled out for special treatment undermines the likelihood of a genuine state interest in protecting shareholders. It suggests instead that the legislature may have been concerned with silencing corporations on a particular subject.

The overinclusiveness of the statute is demonstrated by the fact that § 8 would prohibit a corporation from supporting or opposing a referendum proposal even if its shareholders unanimously authorized the contribution or expenditure. Ultimately shareholders may decide, through the procedures of corporate democracy, whether their corporation should engage in debate on public issues.[34] Acting through their power to elect the board of directors or to insist upon protective provisions in the corporation's charter, shareholders normally are presumed competent to protect their own interests. In addition to intracorporate remedies, minority

---

[34] Appellee does not explain why the dissenting shareholder's wishes are entitled to such greater solicitude in this context than in many others where equally important and controversial corporate decisions are made by management or by a predetermined percentage of the shareholders.

[Moreover,] no shareholder has been "compelled" to contribute anything. Apart from the fact, noted by the dissent, that compulsion by the State is wholly absent, the shareholder invests in a corporation of his own volition and is free to withdraw his investment at any time and for any reason.

shareholders generally have access to the judicial remedy of a derivative suit to challenge corporate disbursements alleged to have been made for improper corporate purposes or merely to further the personal interests of management.

Assuming, arguendo, that protection of shareholders is a "compelling" interest under the circumstances of this case, we find "no substantially relevant correlation between the governmental interest asserted and the State's effort" to prohibit appellants from speaking.

JUSTICE WHITE (joined by JUSTICES BRENNAN and MARSHALL), dissenting:

Indeed, what some have considered to be the principal function of the First Amendment, the use of communication as a means of self-expression, self-realization, and self-fulfillment, is not at all furthered by corporate speech. It is clear that the communications of profitmaking corporations are not "an integral part of the development of ideas, of mental exploration and of the affirmation of self." They do not represent a manifestation of individual freedom or choice. Shareholders in such entities do not share a common set of political or social views, and they certainly have not invested their money for the purpose of advancing political or social causes or in an enterprise engaged in the business of disseminating news and opinion. In fact, as discussed infra, the government has a strong interest in assuring that investment decisions are not predicated upon agreement or disagreement with the activities of corporations in the political arena.

Of course, it may be assumed that corporate investors are united by a desire to make money, for the value of their investment to increase. Since even communications which have no purpose other than that of enriching the communicator have some First Amendment protection, activities such as advertising and other communications integrally related to the operation of the corporation's business may be viewed as a means of furthering the desires of individual shareholders. This unanimity of purpose breaks down, however, when corporations make expenditures or undertake activities designed to influence the opinion or votes of the general public on political and social issues that have no material connection with or effect upon their business, property, or assets. Although it is arguable that corporations make such expenditures because their managers believe that it is in the corporations' economic interest to do so, there is no basis whatsoever for concluding that these views are expressive of the heterogeneous beliefs of their shareholders whose convictions on many political issues are undoubtedly shaped by considerations other than a desire to endorse any electoral or ideological cause which would tend to increase the value of a particular corporate investment.

There is an additional overriding interest related to the prevention of corporate domination which is substantially advanced by Massachusetts' restrictions upon corporate contributions: assuring that shareholders are not compelled to support and financially further beliefs with which they disagree where, as is the case here, the issue involved does not materially affect the business, property, or other affairs of the corporation. The State has not interfered with the prerogatives of corporate management to communicate about matters that have material impact on the business affairs entrusted to them, however much individual stockholders may disagree on economic or ideological grounds. Nor has the State forbidden management from formulating and circulating its views at its own expense or at the expense of others, even where the subject at issue is irrelevant to corporate business affairs. But Massachusetts has chosen to forbid corporate management from spending corporate funds in referenda elections absent some demonstrable effect of the issue on the economic life of the company. In short, corporate management may not use corporate monies to promote what does not further corporate affairs but what in the last analysis are the purely personal views of the management, individually or as a group.

The Court assumes that the interest in preventing the use of corporate resources in furtherance of views which are irrelevant to the corporate business and with which some shareholders may disagree is a compelling one, but concludes that the Massachusetts statute is nevertheless invalid because the State has failed to adopt the means best suited, in its opinion, for achieving this end. It proposes that the aggrieved shareholder assert his interest in preventing the expenditure of funds for nonbusiness causes he finds unconscionable through the channels provided by "corporate democracy" and purports to be mystified as to "why the dissenting shareholder's wishes are entitled to such greater solicitude in this context than in many others where equally important and controversial corporate decisions are made by management or by a predetermined percentage of the shareholders.". It should be obvious that the alternative means upon the adequacy of which the majority is willing to predicate a constitutional adjudication is [not] able to satisfy the State's interest.

There is no apparent way of segregating one shareholder's ownership interest in a corporation from another's. It is no answer to respond, as the Court does, that the dissenting "shareholder is free to withdraw his investment at any time and for any reason." Clearly the State has a strong interest in assuring that its citizens are not forced to choose between supporting the propagation of views with which they disagree and passing up investment opportunities.

Finally, even if corporations developed an effective mechanism for rebating to shareholders that portion of their investment used to finance political activities with which they disagreed, a State may still choose to restrict corporate political activity irrelevant to business functions on the grounds that many investors would be deterred from investing in corporations because of a wish not to associate with corporations propagating certain views. The State has an interest not only in enabling individuals to exercise freedom of conscience without penalty but also in eliminating the danger that investment decisions will be significantly influenced by the ideological views of corporations. While the latter concern may not be of the same constitutional magnitude as the former, it is far from trivial. Corporations, as previously noted, are created by the State as a means of furthering the public welfare. One of their functions is to determine, by their success in obtaining funds, the uses to which society's resources are to be put. A State may legitimately conclude that corporations would not serve as economically efficient vehicles for such decisions if the investment preferences of the public were significantly affected by their ideological or political activities. It has long been recognized that such pursuits are not the proper business of corporations. The common law was generally interpreted as prohibiting corporate political participation.

Austin v. Michigan Chamber of Commerce, 494 U.S. 652 (1990), involved a First Amendment challenge to a Michigan statute that prohibited corporations from using their funds to make direct contributions to the campaigns of candidates for state office or to support those campaigns indirectly. In the majority opinion upholding the statute, Justice Marshall wrote:

> The State contends that the unique legal and economic characteristics of corporations necessitate some regulation of their political expenditures to avoid corruption or the appearance of corruption. *See* FEC v. National Conservative Political Action Committee, 470 U.S. 480, 496–497, 105 S.Ct. 1459, 1468, 84 L.Ed.2d 455 (1985) ("[P]reventing corruption or the appearance of corruption are the only legitimate and compelling government interests thus far identified for restricting campaign finances"). State law grants corporations special advantages—such as limited liability, perpetual life, and favorable treatment of the accumulation and distribution of assets—that enhance their ability to attract capital and to deploy their resources in ways that maximize the return on their shareholders' investments. These state-created advantages not only allow corporations to play a dominant role in the Nation's economy, but also permit them to use "resources amassed in the economic marketplace" to obtain "an unfair advantage in the political marketplace."

In response to the argument that these concerns were not great enough to justify a limitation on independent expenses, Justice Marshall wrote:

> [T]his Court has . . . recognized that a legislature might demonstrate a danger of real or apparent corruption posed by such

expenditures when made by corporations to influence candidate elections. Michigan's regulation aims at a different type of corruption in the political arena: the corrosive and distorting effects of immense aggregations of wealth that are accumulated with the help of the corporate form and that have little or no correlation to the public's support for the corporation's political ideas. We emphasize that the mere fact that corporations may accumulate large amounts of wealth is not the justification for § 54; rather, the unique state-conferred corporate structure that facilitates the amassing of large treasuries warrants the limit on independent expenditures. Corporate wealth can unfairly influence elections when it is deployed in the form of independent expenditures, just as it can when it assumes the guise of political contributions. We therefore hold that the State has articulated a sufficiently compelling rationale to support its restriction on independent expenditures by corporations.

Justice Scalia filed a dissent that, among other things, addressed the argument—made by Justice Brennan in a concurring opinion—that allowing corporations to use their assets for political purposes is unfair to shareholders who disagree with the corporation's position:

> But even if the object of the prohibition could plausibly be portrayed as the protection of shareholders . . . that would not suffice as a "compelling need" to support this blatant restriction upon core political speech. A person becomes a member of that form of association known as a for-profit corporation in order to pursue economic objectives, *i.e.*, to make money. Some corporate charters may specify the line of commerce to which the company is limited, but even that can be amended by shareholder vote. Thus, in joining such an association, the shareholder knows that management may take any action that is ultimately in accord with what the majority (or a specified supermajority) of the shareholders wishes, so long as that action is designed to make a profit. That is the deal. The corporate actions to which the shareholder exposes himself, therefore, include many things that he may find politically or ideologically uncongenial: investment in South Africa, operation of an abortion clinic, publication of a pornographic magazine, or even publication of a newspaper that adopts absurd political views and makes catastrophic political endorsements. His only protections against such assaults upon his ideological commitments are (1) his ability to persuade a majority (or the requisite minority) of his fellow shareholders that the action should not be taken, and ultimately (2) his ability to sell his stock. It seems to me entirely fanciful, in other words, to suggest that the Michigan statute makes any significant contribution

towards insulating the exclusively profit-motivated shareholder from the rude world of politics and ideology.

CITIZENS UNITED V. FEDERAL ELECTION COMMISSION
558 U.S. 310 (2010).

JUSTICE KENNEDY delivered the opinion of the Court.

Federal law prohibits corporations and unions from using their general treasury funds to make independent expenditures for speech defined as an "electioneering communication" or for speech expressly advocating the election or defeat of a candidate. Limits on electioneering communications were upheld in *McConnell v. Federal Election Comm'n* (2003). The holding of *McConnell* rested to a large extent on an earlier case, *Austin v. Michigan Chamber of Commerce* (1990). *Austin* had held that political speech may be banned based on the speaker's corporate identity.

In this case we are asked to reconsider *Austin* and, in effect, *McConnell*. We hold that *stare decisis* does not compel the continued acceptance of *Austin*. The Government may regulate corporate political speech through disclaimer and disclosure requirements, but it may not suppress that speech altogether. We turn to the case now before us.

I

Citizens United is a nonprofit corporation. It brought this action in the United States District Court for the District of Columbia. A three-judge court later convened to hear the cause. The resulting judgment gives rise to this appeal.

Citizens United has an annual budget of about $12 million. Most of its funds are from donations by individuals; but, in addition, it accepts a small portion of its funds from for-profit corporations.

In January 2008, Citizens United released a film entitled *Hillary: The Movie*. We refer to the film as *Hillary*. It is a 90-minute documentary about then-Senator Hillary Clinton, who was a candidate in the Democratic Party's 2008 Presidential primary elections. *Hillary* mentions Senator Clinton by name and depicts interviews with political commentators and other persons, most of them quite critical of Senator Clinton. *Hillary* was released in theaters and on DVD.

Before the Bipartisan Campaign Reform Act of 2002 (BCRA), federal law prohibited—and still does prohibit—corporations and unions from using general treasury funds to make direct contributions to candidates or independent expenditures that expressly advocate the election or defeat of a candidate, through any form of media, in connection with certain qualified federal elections. BCRA § 203 amended § 441b to prohibit any "electioneering communication" as well. An electioneering communication is defined as "any broadcast, cable, or satellite communication" that "refers to a clearly identified candidate for Federal office" and is made within 30 days of a primary or 60 days of a general election. Corporations and unions are barred from using their general treasury funds for express advocacy or electioneering communications. They may establish, however, a "separate segregated fund" (known as a political action committee, or PAC) for these purposes. The moneys received by the segregated fund are limited to donations from stockholders and employees of the corporation or, in the case of unions, members of the union.

Citizens United wanted to make *Hillary* available through video-on-demand within 30 days of the 2008 primary elections. It feared, however, that both the film and the ads would be covered by § 441b's ban on corporate-funded independent expenditures, thus subjecting the corporation to civil and criminal penalties. In December 2007, Citizens United sought declaratory and injunctive relief against the FEC. It argued that (1) § 441b is unconstitutional as applied to *Hillary*; and (2) BCRA's disclaimer and disclosure requirements are unconstitutional as applied to *Hillary* and to the three ads for the movie.

III

The First Amendment provides that "Congress shall make no law . . . abridging the freedom of speech." Laws enacted to control or suppress speech may operate at different points in the speech process. The law before us is an outright ban, backed by criminal sanctions. Section 441b makes it a felony for all corporations—including nonprofit advocacy corporations—either to expressly advocate the election or defeat of candidates or to broadcast electioneering communications within 30 days of a primary election and 60 days of a general election.

Section 441b's prohibition on corporate independent expenditures is thus a ban on speech. As a "restriction on the amount of money a person or group can spend on political communication during a campaign," that statute "necessarily reduces the quantity of expression by restricting the number of issues discussed, the depth of their exploration, and the size of the audience reached." *Buckley v. Valeo* (1976) (per curiam). Were the Court to uphold these restrictions, the Government could repress speech by silencing certain voices at any of the various points in the speech process. If § 441b applied to individuals, no one would believe that it is merely a time, place, or manner restriction on speech. Its purpose and effect are to silence entities whose voices the Government deems to be suspect.

Quite apart from the purpose or effect of regulating content, moreover, the Government may commit a constitutional wrong when by law it identifies certain preferred speakers. By taking the right to speak from some and giving it to others, the Government deprives the disadvantaged person or class of the right to use speech to strive to establish worth, standing, and respect for the speaker's voice. The Government may not by these means deprive the public of the right and privilege to determine for itself what speech and speakers are worthy of consideration. The First Amendment protects speech and speaker, and the ideas that flow from each.

[I]t is inherent in the nature of the political process that voters must be free to obtain information from diverse sources in order to determine how to cast their votes. At least before *Austin*, the Court had not allowed the exclusion of a class of speakers from the general public dialogue.

We find no basis for the proposition that, in the context of political speech, the Government may impose restrictions on certain disfavored speakers. Both history and logic lead us to this conclusion.

A

The Court has recognized that First Amendment protection extends to corporations. This protection has been extended by explicit holdings to the context of political speech. Under the rationale of these precedents, political speech does not lose First Amendment protection "simply because its source is a corporation." *Bellotti*. The Court has thus rejected the argument that political speech of corporations or other associations should be treated differently under the First Amendment simply because such associations are not "natural persons."

At least since the latter part of the 19th century, the laws of some States and of the United States imposed a ban on corporate direct contributions to candidates. Yet not until 1947 did Congress first prohibit independent expenditures by corporations and labor unions in § 304 of the Labor Management Relations Act 1947. In passing this Act Congress overrode the veto of President Truman, who warned that the expenditure ban was a "dangerous intrusion on free speech." For almost three decades thereafter, the Court did not reach the question whether restrictions on corporate and union expenditures are constitutional.

In *Buckley*, the Court addressed various challenges to the Federal Election Campaign Act of 1971 (FECA) as amended in 1974. These amendments created an independent expenditure ban separate from that applied to individuals as well as corporations and labor unions. *Buckley* invalidated [the] restrictions on independent expenditures, with only one Justice dissenting. Notwithstanding this precedent, Congress recodified [the] corporate and union expenditure ban at § 441b four months after *Buckley* was decided. Section 441b is the independent expenditure restriction challenged here.

Less than two years after *Buckley*, *Bellotti* reaffirmed the First Amendment principle that the Government cannot restrict political speech based on the speaker's corporate identity. *Bellotti* struck down a state-law prohibition on corporate independent expenditures related to referenda issues.

It is important to note that the reasoning and holding of *Bellotti* did not rest on the existence of a viewpoint-discriminatory statute. It rested on the principle that the Government lacks the power to ban corporations from speaking.

Bellotti did not address the constitutionality of the State's ban on corporate independent expenditures to support candidates. In our view, however, that restriction would have been unconstitutional under *Bellotti*'s central principle: that the First Amendment does not allow political speech restrictions based on a speaker's corporate identity.

Thus the law stood until *Austin*. *Austin* "uph[eld] a direct restriction on the independent expenditure of funds for political speech for the first time in [this Court's] history." (KENNEDY, J., dissenting). There, the Michigan Chamber of Commerce sought to use general treasury funds to run a newspaper ad supporting a specific candidate. Michigan law, however, prohibited corporate independent expenditures that supported or opposed any candidate for state office. A violation of the law was punishable as a felony. The Court sustained the speech prohibition.

[T]he *Austin* Court identified a new governmental interest in limiting political speech: an antidistortion interest. *Austin* found a compelling governmental interest in preventing "the corrosive and distorting effects of immense aggregations of wealth that are accumulated with the help of the corporate form and that have little or no correlation to the public's support for the corporation's political ideas."

B

In its defense of the corporate-speech restrictions in § 441b, the Government notes the antidistortion rationale on which *Austin* and its progeny rest in part, yet it all but abandons reliance upon it. It argues instead that two other compelling interests support *Austin*'s holding that corporate expenditure restrictions are constitutional: an anticorruption interest, and a shareholder-protection interest. We consider the three points in turn.

1

As for *Austin*'s antidistortion rationale, the Government does little to defend it. And with good reason, for the rationale cannot support § 441b.

If the First Amendment has any force, it prohibits Congress from fining or jailing citizens, or associations of citizens, for simply engaging in political speech. If the antidistortion rationale were to be accepted, however, it would permit Government to ban political speech simply because the speaker is an association that has taken on the corporate form.

Political speech is "indispensable to decisionmaking in a democracy, and this is no less true because the speech comes from a corporation rather than an individual." *Bellotti* (the worth of speech "does not depend upon the identity of its source, whether corporation, association, union, or individual"); *Buckley* ("[T]he concept that government may restrict the speech of some elements of our society in order to enhance the relative voice of others is wholly foreign to the First Amendment"). This protection for speech is inconsistent with *Austin*'s antidistortion rationale. *Austin* sought to defend the antidistortion rationale as a means to prevent corporations from obtaining " 'an unfair advantage in the political marketplace' " by using " 'resources amassed in the economic marketplace.' " But *Buckley* rejected the premise that the Government has an interest "in equalizing the relative ability of individuals and groups to influence the outcome of elections." *Buckley* was specific in stating that "the skyrocketing cost of political campaigns" could not sustain the governmental prohibition. The First Amendment's protections do not depend on the speaker's "financial ability to engage in public discussion."

Either as support for its antidistortion rationale or as a further argument, the *Austin* majority undertook to distinguish wealthy individuals from corporations on the ground that "[s]tate law grants corporations special advantages—such as limited liability, perpetual life, and favorable treatment of the accumulation and distribution of assets." This does not suffice, however, to allow laws prohibiting speech. "It is rudimentary that the State cannot exact as the price of those special advantages the forfeiture of First Amendment rights." *Id.* (SCALIA, J., dissenting).

It is irrelevant for purposes of the First Amendment that corporate funds may "have little or no correlation to the public's support for the corporation's political ideas." *Id.* (majority opinion). All speakers, including individuals and the media, use money amassed from the economic marketplace to fund their speech. The First Amendment protects the resulting speech, even if it was enabled by economic transactions with persons or entities who disagree with the speaker's ideas.

Austin interferes with the "open marketplace" of ideas protected by the First Amendment. It permits the Government to ban the political speech of millions of associations of citizens. Most of these are small corporations without large amounts of wealth.[1] This fact belies the Government's argument that the statute is justified on the ground that it prevents the "distorting effects of immense aggregations of wealth." *Austin*. It is not even aimed at amassed wealth.

---

[1]   [The Court cites statistics showing that 96% of the 3 million businesses that belong to the U. S. Chamber of Commerce have fewer than 100 employees; and more than 75% of corporations whose income is taxed under federal law have less than $1 million in receipts per year. —Ed.]

The censorship we now confront is vast in its reach. By suppressing the speech of manifold corporations, both for-profit and nonprofit, the Government prevents their voices and viewpoints from reaching the public and advising voters on which persons or entities are hostile to their interests. Factions will necessarily form in our Republic, but the remedy of "destroying the liberty" of some factions is "worse than the disease." The Federalist No. 10 (J. Madison). Factions should be checked by permitting them all to speak and by entrusting the people to judge what is true and what is false.

Even if § 441b's expenditure ban were constitutional, wealthy corporations could still lobby elected officials, although smaller corporations may not have the resources to do so. And wealthy individuals and unincorporated associations can spend unlimited amounts on independent expenditures. Yet certain disfavored associations of citizens—those that have taken on the corporate form—are penalized for engaging in the same political speech.

When Government seeks to use its full power, including the criminal law, to command where a person may get his or her information or what distrusted source he or she may not hear, it uses censorship to control thought. This is unlawful. The First Amendment confirms the freedom to think for ourselves.

C

Due consideration leads to this conclusion: *Austin* should be and now is overruled. We return to the principle established in *Buckley* and *Bellotti* that the Government may not suppress political speech on the basis of the speaker's corporate identity. No sufficient governmental interest justifies limits on the political speech of nonprofit or for-profit corporations.

V

The judgment of the District Court is reversed with respect to the constitutionality of § 441b's restrictions on corporate independent expenditures. The judgment is affirmed with respect to BCRA's disclaimer and disclosure requirements. The case is remanded for further proceedings consistent with this opinion.

It is so ordered.

JUSTICE STEVENS, with whom JUSTICE GINSBURG, JUSTICE BREYER, and JUSTICE SOTOMAYOR join, concurring in part and dissenting in part.

The real issue in this case concerns how, not if, the appellant may finance its electioneering. Citizens United is a wealthy nonprofit corporation that runs a political action committee (PAC) with millions of dollars in assets. Under the Bipartisan Campaign Reform Act of 2002 (BCRA), it could have used those assets to televise and promote *Hillary: The Movie* wherever and whenever it wanted to. It also could have spent unrestricted sums to broadcast *Hillary* at any time other than the 30 days before the last primary election. Neither Citizens United's nor any other corporation's speech has been "banned." All that the parties dispute is whether Citizens United had a right to use the funds in its general treasury to pay for broadcasts during the 30-day period. The notion that the First Amendment dictates an affirmative answer to that question is, in my judgment, profoundly misguided. Even more misguided is the notion that the Court must rewrite the law relating to campaign expenditures by for-profit corporations and unions to decide this case.

The basic premise underlying the Court's ruling is its iteration, and constant reiteration, of the proposition that the First Amendment bars regulatory distinctions based on a speaker's identity, including its "identity" as a corporation. While that glittering generality has rhetorical appeal, it is not a correct statement of the law. Nor does it tell us when a corporation may engage in electioneering that some of its shareholders oppose. It does not even resolve the specific question whether Citizens United may be required to finance some of its messages with the money in its PAC. The conceit that corporations must be treated identically to natural persons in the political sphere is not only inaccurate but also inadequate to justify the Court's disposition of this case.

In the context of election to public office, the distinction between corporate and human speakers is significant. Although they make enormous contributions to our society, corporations are not actually members of it. They cannot vote or run for office. Because they may be managed and controlled by nonresidents, their interests may conflict in fundamental respects with the interests of eligible voters. The financial resources, legal structure, and instrumental orientation of corporations raise legitimate concerns about their role in the electoral process. Our lawmakers have a compelling constitutional basis, if not also a democratic duty, to take measures designed to guard against the potentially deleterious effects of corporate spending in local and national races.

III

The So-Called "Ban"

The laws upheld in *Austin* and *McConnell* leave open many additional avenues for corporations' political speech. Consider the statutory provision we are ostensibly evaluating in this case. It has no application to genuine issue advertising—a category of corporate speech Congress found to be far more substantial than election-related advertising—or to Internet, telephone, and print advocacy. Like numerous statutes, it exempts media companies' news stories, commentaries, and editorials from its electioneering restrictions, in recognition of the unique role played by the institutional press in sustaining public debate. It also allows corporations to spend unlimited sums on political communications with their executives and shareholders, to fund additional PAC activity through trade associations, to distribute voting guides and voting records, to underwrite voter registration and voter turnout activities, to host fundraising events for candidates within certain limits, and to publicly endorse candidates through a press release and press conference.

So let us be clear: Neither *Austin* nor *McConnell* held or implied that corporations may be silenced; the FEC is not a "censor"; and in the years since these cases were decided, corporations have continued to play a major role in the national dialogue. Laws such as § 203 target a class of communications that is especially likely to corrupt the political process, that is at least one degree removed from the views of individual citizens, and that may not even reflect the views of those who pay for it. Such laws burden political speech, and that is always a serious matter, demanding careful scrutiny. But the majority's incessant talk of a "ban" aims at a straw man.

Identity-Based Distinctions

. . . [I]t is the identity of corporations, rather than individuals, that the Legislature has taken into account. Not only has the distinctive potential of corporations to corrupt the electoral process long been recognized, but within the area of campaign finance, corporate spending is also "furthest from the core of political expression, since corporations' First Amendment speech and association interests are derived largely from those of their members and of the public in receiving information." Campaign finance distinctions based on corporate identity tend to be less worrisome, in other words, because the "speakers" are not natural persons, much less members of our political community, and the governmental interests are of the highest order. Furthermore, when corporations, as a class, are distinguished from noncorporations, as a class, there is a lesser risk that regulatory distinctions will reflect invidious discrimination or political favoritism.

IV

Austin and Corporate Expenditures

1.   Antidistortion

The fact that corporations are different from human beings might seem to need no elaboration, except that the majority opinion almost completely elides it. *Austin* set forth some of the basic differences. Unlike natural persons, corporations have "limited liability" for their owners and managers, "perpetual life," separation of ownership and control, "and favorable treatment of the accumulation and distribution of assets that enhance their ability to attract capital and to deploy their resources in ways that maximize the return on their shareholders' investments." Unlike voters in U. S. elections, corporations may be foreign controlled. Unlike other interest groups, business corporations have been "effectively delegated responsibility for ensuring society's economic welfare"; they inescapably structure the life of every citizen. " '[T]he resources in the treasury of a business corporation,' " furthermore, "are not an indication of popular support for the corporation's political ideas." "They reflect instead the economically motivated decisions of investors and customers. The availability of these resources may make a corporation a formidable political presence, even though the power of the corporation may be no reflection of the power of its ideas."

It might also be added that corporations have no consciences, no beliefs, no feelings, no thoughts, no desires. Corporations help structure and facilitate the activities of human beings, to be sure, and their "personhood" often serves as a useful legal fiction. But they are not themselves members of "We the People" by whom and for whom our Constitution was established.

These basic points help explain why corporate electioneering is not only more likely to impair compelling governmental interests, but also why restrictions on that electioneering are less likely to encroach upon First Amendment freedoms. Corporate speech is derivative speech, speech by proxy. A regulation such as BCRA § 203 may affect the way in which individuals disseminate certain messages through the corporate form, but it does not prevent anyone from speaking in his or her own voice.

It is an interesting question "who" is even speaking when a business corporation places an advertisement that endorses or attacks a particular candidate. Presumably it is not the customers or employees, who typically have no say in such matters. It cannot realistically be said to be the shareholders, who tend to be far removed from the day-to-day decisions of the firm and whose political preferences may be opaque to management. Perhaps the officers or directors of the corporation have the best claim to be the ones speaking, except their fiduciary duties generally prohibit them from using corporate funds for personal ends. Some individuals associated with the corporation must make the decision to place the ad, but the idea that these individuals are thereby fostering their self-expression or cultivating their critical faculties is fanciful. It is entirely possible that the corporation's electoral message will conflict with their personal convictions. Take away the ability to use general treasury funds for some of those ads, and no one's autonomy, dignity, or political equality has been impinged upon in the least.

Austin recognized that there are substantial reasons why a legislature might conclude that unregulated general treasury expenditures will give corporations "unfai[r] influence" in the electoral process and distort public debate in ways that undermine rather than advance the interests of listeners. The legal structure of corporations allows them to amass and deploy financial resources on a scale few natural persons can match.

NOTE

Not surprisingly, *Citizens United* has been extremely controversial. Drawing on Justice Kennedy's emphasis on disclosure in his opinion, efforts have shifted toward seeking greater disclosure of corporate political expenditures. According to a 2012 report by Institutional Shareholder Services, over sixty percent of corporations in the S & P 100 have agreed to adopt policies requiring disclosure of companies' political expenditures and more corporations are likely to do so in the future. Nevertheless, many corporations do not provide such disclosure, and the information provided by those who do is not uniform and may not be adequate to satisfy those who are troubled by the Court's decision. Citing these concerns, in 2011 a group of law professors petitioned the SEC to adopt rules mandating disclosure of corporate political expenditures. In late 2015, Congress passed a budget bill that prohibited the Commission from adopting any such rule during fiscal 2016, although the bill does not prevent it from doing so thereafter. Meanwhile, under pressure from investors, over half of the S&P 500 corporations have undertaken at least some disclosure of their political activities, and for the 2016 proxy season investors have submitted more than 100 shareholder proposals calling for greater disclosure.

C. A SEPARATE ENTITY OR AN ASSOCIATION OF INDIVIDUALS?

The following case raises the controversial question whether corporation should enjoy the First Amendment's protections of religious freedom. Although it involved the interpretation of a statute rather than the application of the protections of the Constitution to a corporate "person," it illustrates the conceptual question whether a corporation is a truly separate entity with distinct rights or merely a convenient legal construct enabling individuals to associate and act together, which thus is imbued with the rights of its individual owners. In reading this case, think about how the conception of the corporation can be framed: (1) What are the implications of conceiving a corporation as separate entity and distinct from its shareholders or as an aggregation of its shareholders? (2) What if these corporations are publicly traded corporations rather than closely held corporations? (3) Is it relevant that the activities in question in *Burwell* and *Citizens United* do not directly relate to economic activity and profit making?

BURWELL v. HOBBY LOBBY STORES, INC.
134 S.Ct. 2751 (2014).

[The opinion decides two separate cases brought by three closely held corporations, Conestoga Wood Specialties Corporation, Mardel, Inc., and Hobby Lobby Stores, Inc. The plaintiff corporations claimed that the mandate in the regulations under the Patient Protection and Affordable

Care Act (ACA) that employers include contraceptive coverage in their health insurance plans violated the Restoration of Religious Freedom Act (RFRA) and the Free Exercise clause of the First Amendment.

Conestoga, a Pennsylvania corporation, is owned by Norman and Elizabeth Hahn and their three sons, all devout members of the Mennonite Church. Hobby Lobby, an Oklahoma corporation, is owned by David and Barbara Green and their three children, all devout Christians. One of the Green sons owns Mardel, Inc., which operates a chain of Christian bookstores. The Hahns and the Greens all believe that abortion, including any method of birth control that can be considered to lead to the abortion of a fertilized ovum, is morally wrong.]

JUSTICE ALITO delivered the opinion of the Court.

We must decide in these cases whether the Religious Freedom Restoration Act of 1993 (RFRA), 107 Stat. 1488, 42 U.S.C. § 2000bb *et seq.*, permits the United States Department of Health and Human Services (HHS) to demand that three closely held corporations provide health-insurance coverage for methods of contraception that violate the sincerely held religious beliefs of the companies' owners. We hold that the regulations that impose this obligation violate RFRA, which prohibits the Federal Government from taking any action that substantially burdens the exercise of religion unless that action constitutes the least restrictive means of serving a compelling government interest.

In holding that the HHS mandate is unlawful, we reject HHS's argument that the owners of the companies forfeited all RFRA protection when they decided to organize their businesses as corporations rather than sole proprietorships or general partnerships. The plain terms of RFRA make it perfectly clear that Congress did not discriminate in this way against men and women who wish to run their businesses as for-profit corporations in the manner required by their religious beliefs.

Under RFRA, a Government action that imposes a substantial burden on religious exercise must serve a compelling government interest, and we assume that the HHS regulations satisfy this requirement. But in order for the HHS mandate to be sustained, it must also constitute the least restrictive means of serving that interest, and the mandate plainly fails that test. There are other ways in which Congress or HHS could equally ensure that every woman has cost-free access to the particular contraceptives at issue here and, indeed, to all FDA-approved contraceptives.

In fact, HHS has already devised and implemented a system that seeks to respect the religious liberty of religious nonprofit corporations while ensuring that the employees of these entities have precisely the same access to all FDA-approved contraceptives as employees of companies whose owners have no religious objections to providing such coverage. The employees of these religious nonprofit corporations still have access to insurance coverage without cost sharing for all FDA-approved contraceptives; and according to HHS, this system imposes no net economic burden on the insurance companies that are required to provide or secure the coverage.

[The "system" to which the Court refers is an exemption for religious organizations from the requirement to provide contraceptive services. Under this exemption, a group-health-insurance issuer whose client is exempted must exclude contraceptive coverage from the client's plan and provide separate payments for contraceptive services for plan participants without imposing any cost-sharing requirements on the organization or its employees.]

Although HHS has made this system available to religious nonprofits that have religious objections to the contraceptive mandate, HHS has provided no reason why the same system cannot be made available when the owners of for-profit corporations have similar religious objections. We therefore conclude that this system constitutes an alternative that achieves all of the Government's aims while providing greater respect for religious liberty. And under RFRA, that conclusion means that enforcement of the HHS contraceptive mandate against the objecting parties in these cases is unlawful.

III

A

RFRA prohibits the "Government [from] substantially burden[ing] *a person's* exercise of religion even if the burden results from a rule of general applicability" unless the Government "demonstrates that application of the burden to *the person*—(1) is in furtherance of a compelling governmental interest; and (2) is the least restrictive means of furthering that compelling governmental interest." The first question that we must address is whether this provision applies to regulations that govern the activities of for-profit corporations.

HHS contends that neither these companies nor their owners can even be heard under RFRA. According to HHS, the companies cannot sue because they seek to make a profit for their owners, and the owners cannot be heard because the regulations, at least as a formal matter, apply only to the companies and not to the owners as individuals. HHS's argument would have dramatic consequences.

Consider this Court's decision in *Braunfeld v. Brown*, 366 U.S. 599 (1961) (plurality opinion). In that case, five Orthodox Jewish merchants who ran small retail businesses in Philadelphia challenged a Pennsylvania Sunday closing law as a violation of the Free Exercise Clause. Because of their faith, these merchants closed their shops on Saturday, and they argued that requiring them to remain shut on Sunday threatened them with financial ruin. The Court entertained their claim (although it ruled against them on the merits), and if a similar claim were raised today under RFRA against a jurisdiction still subject to the Act, the merchants would be entitled to be heard. According to HHS, however, if these merchants chose to incorporate their businesses—without in any way changing the size or nature of their businesses—they would forfeit all RFRA (and free-exercise) rights. HHS would put these merchants to a difficult choice: either give up the right to seek judicial protection of their religious liberty or forgo the benefits, available to their competitors, of operating as corporations.

As we have seen, RFRA was designed to provide very broad protection for religious liberty. By enacting RFRA, Congress went far beyond what this Court has held is constitutionally required. Is there any reason to think that the Congress that enacted such sweeping protection put small-business owners to the choice that HHS suggests? An examination of RFRA's text, to which we turn in the next part of this opinion, reveals that Congress did no such thing.

As we will show, Congress provided protection for people like the Hahns and Greens by employing a familiar legal fiction: It included corporations within RFRA's definition of "persons." But it is important to keep in mind that the purpose of this fiction is to provide protection for human beings. A corporation is simply a form of organization used by human beings to achieve desired ends. An established body of law specifies the rights and obligations of the *people* (including shareholders, officers, and employees) who are associated with a corporation in one way or another. When rights, whether constitutional or statutory, are extended to corporations, the purpose is to protect the rights of these people. For example, extending Fourth Amendment protection to corporations protects the privacy interests of employees and others associated with the company. Protecting corporations from government seizure of their property without just compensation protects all those who have a stake in the corporations' financial well-being. And protecting the free-exercise rights of corporations like Hobby Lobby, Conestoga, and Mardel protects the religious liberty of the humans who own and control those companies.

In holding that Conestoga, as a "secular, for-profit corporation," lacks RFRA protection, the Third Circuit wrote as follows:

> "General business corporations do not, *separate and apart from the actions or belief systems of their individual owners or employees,* exercise religion. They do not pray, worship, observe sacraments or take other religiously-motivated actions separate and apart from the intention and direction of their individual actors."

All of this is true—but quite beside the point. Corporations, "separate and apart from" the human beings who own, run, and are employed by them, cannot do anything at all.

B

As we noted above, RFRA applies to "a person's" exercise of religion, and RFRA itself does not define the term "person." We therefore look to the Dictionary Act, which we must consult "[i]n determining the meaning of any Act of Congress, unless the context indicates otherwise." 1 U.S.C. § 1.

Under the Dictionary Act, "the wor[d] 'person' . . . include[s] corporations, companies, associations, firms, partnerships, societies, and joint stock companies, as well as individuals."

We see nothing in RFRA that suggests a congressional intent to depart from the Dictionary Act definition, and HHS makes little effort to argue otherwise. We have entertained RFRA and free-exercise claims brought by nonprofit corporations, and HHS concedes that a nonprofit corporation can be a "person" within the meaning of RFRA.

This concession effectively dispatches any argument that the term "person" as used in RFRA does not reach the closely held corporations involved in these cases. No known understanding of the term "person" includes *some* but not all corporations. The term "person" sometimes encompasses artificial persons (as the Dictionary Act instructs), and it sometimes is limited to natural persons. But no conceivable definition of the term includes natural persons and nonprofit corporations, but not for-profit corporations.

The principal argument advanced by HHS and the principal dissent regarding RFRA protection for Hobby Lobby, Conestoga, and Mardel focuses not on the statutory term "person," but on the phrase "exercise of religion." According to HHS and the dissent, these corporations are not protected by RFRA because they cannot exercise religion. Neither HHS nor the dissent, however, provides any persuasive explanation for this conclusion.

Is it because of the corporate form? The corporate form alone cannot provide the explanation because, as we have pointed out, HHS concedes that nonprofit corporations can be protected by RFRA. The dissent suggests that nonprofit corporations are special because furthering their religious "autonomy . . . often furthers individual religious freedom as well." But this principle applies equally to for-profit corporations: Furthering their religious freedom also "furthers individual religious freedom." In these cases, for example, allowing Hobby Lobby, Conestoga, and Mardel to assert RFRA claims protects the religious liberty of the Greens and the Hahns.

If the corporate form is not enough, what about the profit-making objective? In *Braunfeld,* 366 U.S. 599, 81 S.Ct. 1144, 6 L.Ed.2d 563, we entertained the free-exercise claims of individuals who were attempting to make a profit as retail merchants, and the Court never even hinted that this objective precluded their claims. As the Court explained in a later case, the "exercise of religion" involves "not only belief and profession but the performance of (or abstention from) physical acts" that are "engaged in for religious reasons." *Smith,* 494 U.S., at 877, 110 S.Ct. 1595. Business practices that are compelled or limited by the tenets of a religious doctrine fall comfortably within that definition. Thus, a law that "operates so as to make the practice of . . . religious beliefs more expensive" in the context of business activities imposes a burden on the exercise of religion. *Braunfeld, supra,* at 605, 81 S.Ct. 1144;

If, as *Braunfeld* recognized, a sole proprietorship that seeks to make a profit may assert a free-exercise claim, why can't Hobby Lobby, Conestoga, and Mardel do the same?

Some lower court judges have suggested that RFRA does not protect for-profit corporations because the purpose of such corporations is simply to make money. This argument flies in the face of modern corporate law. "Each American jurisdiction today either expressly or by implication authorizes corporations to be formed under its general corporation act for *any lawful purpose* or business." 1 J. Cox & T. Hazen, Treatise of the Law of Corporations § 4:1, p. 224 (3d ed. 2010) (emphasis added). While it is certainly true that a central objective of for-profit corporations is to make money, modern corporate law does not require for-profit corporations to pursue profit at the expense of everything else, and many do not do so. For-profit corporations, with ownership approval, support a wide variety of charitable causes, and it is not at all uncommon for such corporations to further humanitarian and other altruistic objectives. Many examples come readily to mind. So long as its owners agree, a for-profit corporation may take costly pollution-control and energy-conservation measures that go beyond what the law requires. A for-profit corporation that operates facilities in other countries may exceed the requirements of local law regarding working conditions and benefits. If for-profit corporations may pursue such worthy objectives, there is no apparent reason why they may not further religious objectives as well.

In any event, the objectives that may properly be pursued by the companies in these cases are governed by the laws of the States in which they were incorporated—Pennsylvania and Oklahoma—and the laws of those States permit for-profit corporations to pursue "any lawful purpose" or "act," including the pursuit of profit in conformity with the owners' religious principles.

HHS and the principal dissent express concern about the possibility of disputes among the owners of corporations, but that is not a problem that arises because of RFRA or that is unique to this context. The owners of closely held corporations may—and sometimes do—disagree about the conduct of business. And even if RFRA did not exist, the owners of a company might well have a dispute relating to religion. For example, some might want a company's stores to remain open on the Sabbath in order to make more money, and others might want the stores to close for religious reasons. State corporate law provides a ready means for resolving any conflicts by, for example, dictating how a corporation can establish its governing structure. Courts will turn to that structure and the underlying state law in resolving disputes.

For all these reasons, we hold that a federal regulation's restriction on the activities of a for-profit closely held corporation must comply with RFRA.

[The Court goes on to hold that the contraceptive mandate "substantially burdens" the exercise of religion; that there were less-burdensome alternatives available that would have accomplished the goal of providing contraceptive services; and that the regulations therefore violate RFRA.]

JUSTICE GINSBURG, with whom JUSTICE SOTOMAYOR joins, and with whom
    JUSTICE BREYER and JUSTICE KAGAN join as to all but Part III-C-1,
    dissenting.

In a decision of startling breadth, the Court holds that commercial enterprises, including corporations, along with partnerships and sole proprietorships, can opt out of any law (saving only tax laws) they judge incompatible with their sincerely held religious beliefs. Compelling governmental interests in uniform compliance with the law, and disadvantages that religion-based opt-outs impose on others, hold no sway, the Court decides, at least when there is a "less restrictive alternative." And such an alternative, the Court suggests, there always will be whenever, in lieu of tolling an enterprise claiming a religion-based exemption, the government, *i.e.,* the general public, can pick up the tab.

The Court does not pretend that the First Amendment's Free Exercise Clause demands religion-based accommodations so extreme, for our decisions leave no doubt on that score. Instead, the Court holds that Congress, in the Religious Freedom Restoration Act of 1993 (RFRA), dictated the extraordinary religion-based exemptions today's decision endorses. In the Court's view, RFRA demands accommodation of a for-profit corporation's religious beliefs no matter the impact that accommodation may have on third parties who do not share the corporation owners' religious faith—in these cases, thousands of women employed by Hobby Lobby and Conestoga or dependents of persons those corporations employ. Persuaded that Congress enacted RFRA to serve a far less radical purpose, and mindful of the havoc the Court's judgment can introduce, I dissent.

Any First Amendment Free Exercise Clause claim Hobby Lobby or Conestoga might assert is foreclosed by this Court's decision in *Employment Div., Dept. of Human Resources of Ore. v. Smith,* 494 U.S. 872. . . . The First Amendment is not offended, *Smith* held, when "prohibiting the exercise of religion . . . is not the object of [governmental regulation] but merely the incidental effect of a generally applicable and otherwise valid provision."

RFRA's compelling interest test, as noted, applies to government actions that "substantially burden *a person's exercise of religion.*" This reference, the Court submits, incorporates the definition of "person" found in the Dictionary Act, which extends to "corporations, companies, associations, firms, partnerships, societies, and joint stock companies, as well as individuals." The Dictionary Act's definition, however, controls only where "context" does not "indicat[e] otherwise." Here, context does so indicate. RFRA speaks of "a person's *exercise of religion.*" Whether a corporation qualifies as a "person" capable of exercising religion is an inquiry one cannot answer without reference to the "full body" of pre-*Smith* "free-exercise caselaw." There is in that case law no support for the notion that free exercise rights pertain to for-profit corporations.

Until this litigation, no decision of this Court recognized a for-profit corporation's qualification for a religious exemption from a generally applicable law, whether under the Free Exercise Clause or RFRA. The absence of such precedent is just what one would expect, for the exercise of religion is characteristic of natural persons, not artificial legal entities. As Chief Justice Marshall observed nearly two centuries ago, a corporation is "an artificial being, invisible, intangible, and existing only in contemplation of law." *Trustees of Dartmouth College v. Woodward,* 4 Wheat. 518, 636, 4 L.Ed. 629 (1819). Corporations, Justice Stevens more recently reminded, "have no consciences, no beliefs, no feelings, no thoughts, no desires." *Citizens United v. Federal Election Comm'n,* 558 U.S. 310, 466, 130 S.Ct. 876, 175 L.Ed.2d 753 (2010) (opinion concurring in part and dissenting in part).

Religious organizations exist to foster the interests of persons subscribing to the same religious faith. Not so of for-profit corporations. Workers who sustain the operations of those corporations commonly are not drawn from one religious community. Indeed, by law, no religion-based criterion can restrict the work force of for-profit corporations. The distinction between a community made up of believers in the same religion and one embracing persons of diverse beliefs, clear as it is, constantly escapes the Court's attention. One can only wonder why the Court shuts this key difference from sight.

The Court notes that for-profit corporations may support charitable causes and use their funds for religious ends, and therefore questions the distinction between such corporations and religious nonprofit organizations. Again, the Court forgets that religious organizations exist to serve a community of believers. For-profit corporations do not fit that bill. Moreover, history is not on the Court's side. Recognition of the discrete characters of "ecclesiastical and lay" corporations dates back to Blackstone, and was reiterated by this Court centuries before the enactment of the Internal Revenue Code. See *Terrett v. Taylor,* 9 Cranch 43, 49, 3 L.Ed. 650 (1815) (describing religious corporations); *Trustees of Dartmouth College,* 4 Wheat., at 645 (discussing "eleemosynary" corporations, including those "created for the promotion of religion").

Citing *Braunfeld v. Brown,* 366 U.S. 599, 81 S.Ct. 1144, 6 L.Ed.2d 563 (1961), the Court questions why, if "a sole proprietorship that seeks to make a profit may assert a free-exercise claim, [Hobby Lobby and Conestoga] can't . . . do the same?" But even accepting, *arguendo,* the premise that unincorporated business enterprises may gain religious accommodations under the Free Exercise Clause, the Court's conclusion is unsound. In a sole proprietorship, the business and its owner are one and the same. By incorporating a business, however, an individual separates herself from the entity and escapes personal responsibility for the entity's obligations. One might ask why the separation should hold only when it serves the interest of those who control the corporation. In any event, *Braunfeld* is hardly impressive authority for the entitlement Hobby Lobby and Conestoga seek. The free exercise claim asserted there was promptly rejected on the merits.

The Court's determination that RFRA extends to for-profit corporations is bound to have untoward effects. Although the Court attempts to cabin its language to closely held corporations, its logic extends to corporations of any size, public or private.[19] Little doubt that RFRA claims will proliferate, for the Court's expansive notion of corporate personhood—combined with its other errors in construing RFRA—invites

---

[19] The Court does not even begin to explain how one might go about ascertaining the religious scruples of a corporation where shares are sold to the public. No need to speculate on that, the Court says, for "it seems unlikely" that large corporations "will often assert RFRA claims." *Ante,* at 2774. Perhaps so, but as Hobby Lobby's case demonstrates, such claims are indeed pursued by large corporations, employing thousands of persons of different faiths, whose ownership is not diffuse. "Closely held" is not synonymous with "small." Hobby Lobby is hardly the only enterprise of sizable scale that is family owned or closely held. For example, the family-owned candy giant Mars, Inc., takes in $33 billion in revenues and has some 72,000 employees, and closely held Cargill, Inc., takes in more than $136 billion in revenues and employs some 140,000 persons.

Nor does the Court offer any instruction on how to resolve the disputes that may crop up among corporate owners over religious values and accommodations. The Court is satisfied that "[s]tate corporate law provides a ready means for resolving any conflicts," but the authorities cited in support of that proposition are hardly helpful. See Del.Code Ann., Tit. 8, § 351 (2011) (certificates of incorporation may specify how the business is managed); 1 J. Cox & T. Hazen, Treatise on the Law of Corporations § 3:2 (3d ed. 2010) (section entitled "Selecting the state of incorporation"); id., § 14:11 (observing that "[d]espite the frequency of dissension and deadlock in close corporations, in some states neither legislatures nor courts have provided satisfactory solutions"). And even if a dispute settlement mechanism is in place, how is the arbiter of a religion-based intracorporate controversy to resolve the disagreement, given this Court's instruction that "courts have no business addressing [whether an asserted religious belief] is substantial"?

for-profit entities to seek religion-based exemptions from regulations they deem offensive to their faith.

For the reasons stated, I would reverse the judgment of the Court of Appeals for the Tenth Circuit and affirm the judgment of the Court of Appeals for the Third Circuit.

NOTE

The extension of corporate personality in *Citizens United* and *Hobby Lobby* to the realms of free speech and religious liberty has significant social implications. A number of legal commentators have criticized *Citizens United*. Some have argued on constitutional grounds. *See, e.g.,* Deborah Hellman, *Money Talks but It Isn't Speech*, 95 Minn. L. Rev. 953 (2011). From the perspective of corporate law, some scholars have criticized *Citizens United* on the ground that a corporation's principal activity should be the business of profit-making and that corporate shareholders cannot easily monitor the political activities of managers and corporate managers cannot easily discern the political leanings of shareholders. *See* Leo E. Strine Jr. & Nicholas Walter, *Conservative Collision Course?: The Tension Between Conservative Corporate Law Theory and* Citizens United, 100 Cornell L. Rev. 335 (2015). Furthermore, a number of corporate law scholars have argued in *Hobby Lobby* that a corporation is a separate and distinct from shareholders and therefore the latter's religious beliefs cannot be imputed to the corporation. *See Amicus Curiae* Brief of Corporate and Criminal Law Professors in Support of Petitioners (Jan. 2014). *But see* Alan J. Meese & Nathan B. Oman, Hobby Lobby, *Corporate Law, and the Theory of the Firm*, 127 Harv. L. Rev. F. 273 (2014).

CHAPTER 5

THE CORPORATION AND SOCIETY

∎ ∎ ∎

A. INTRODUCTION

Corporations come in many sizes. Although new smaller businesses tend today to be organized as LLCs, there remain many very small corporations. This chapter focuses on large corporations and the important and distinct role they play in American society. They possess independent concentrations of substantial economic power, and many would argue that they possess social and political power as well. Thus we return to some of the fundamental questions underlying corporate law: Is the corporation essentially private in nature or does it serve some public ends? Is it essentially contractual in nature or is it a creature of the state and to which it is responsible? Should it be run solely for the benefit of shareholders, or does it have responsibility to other stakeholders as well; and if the answer is both, then how should the balance be struck?

We begin by considering the economic and legal framework and assessing the arguments for and against the proposition that large corporations do have a social responsibility. They often are exhorted to be socially responsible, but what exactly does this mean? That is a polarizing question. Corporate social responsibility is not a self-defining concept. At one end of the spectrum are commentators such as the late Nobel Prize-winning economist Milton Friedman who argued that that a corporation's only responsibility to society is to maximize returns for shareholders within the boundaries of the law. At the other end are those who believe that large corporations have an obligation to take into account broader societal interests as well as just those of shareholders. Under this view, corporations should incorporate in their policies and decision making the interests of other constituencies including consumers, employees, suppliers, creditors, and the communities in which they operate.

The global economic environment has made corporate social responsibility even more challenging. Multinational corporations confront complicated legal and moral questions when they conduct business overseas. Simply complying with domestic laws and regulations may no longer be enough. Multinational companies must take into account the potentially serious legal, regulatory, and business risks that the company may face abroad. The transnational perspective also illustrates the varied nature of the current battleground of ideas over the proper role of the corporation in society. Non-shareholder constituencies wield much greater power in European countries than they do in the United States. The influence of such stakeholders in European corporate governance requires European companies to balance the interests of non-shareholder groups in their corporate decision making. As a result, the corporate social responsibility movement has gained greater acceptance in Europe than it has in the United States.

We next turn to the lawyer's role in advising corporate clients on matters that may involve corporate social responsibility. What legal, professional and ethical responsibilities does a lawyer bear for the actions of her corporate client? Should she confine her advice simply to legal questions or to stopping the corporation from taking unlawful actions? To what degree should she inject extra-legal factors in her recommendations? Is the relationship between lawyer and client such that the lawyer may have some moral responsibility for the ultimate outcome?

The question that underlies all the material in the chapter is how to assure some degree of legitimacy or accountability to the corporation's actions. What devices are available to make it "accountable?" To whom is it accountable? What is the nature of its accountability?

Critics claim that the managers of large corporations function as a sort of economic oligarchy making decisions that significantly affect employees, consumers, and suppliers as well as the broader community (even a global community), without being accountable to any of these constituency groups. To the extent this is correct, it is necessary to determine whose interests corporations should seek to serve, and in what priority: those of their shareholders, those of other corporate constituencies ("stakeholders"), or those of society at large. That determination, in turn, leads to a consideration of the mechanisms by which managers' discretion should be harnessed and the extent to which market forces, social or business norms, government regulation, and the corporate governance system are sufficient.

B. FRAMING THE ISSUES

Problem: Exogen, Inc.—Part 1

You are an outside director of Exogen, a company that manufactures components for the engines of automobiles and other vehicles. You have been on the board for eight years and are very familiar with its business. One of the solvents used in the company's manufacturing process, Durasol, has been implicated as a potential carcinogen in recent scientific studies. The data from this research is consistent with internal information and reports about the dangers of Durasol that Exogen has in its possession. The Occupational Health and Safety Administration (OSHA) has begun to consider the possibility of banning the use of Durasol because of its effect on workers who come in contact with it or breathe in its fumes. OSHA officials have approached the company about the possibility of voluntarily discontinuing the use of the solvent.

Exogen officials privately have concluded that they eventually will have to discontinue the use of Durasol. They are concerned, however, that doing so will significantly increase the costs of manufacturing, since the substance that would have to be used in its place is considerably more expensive. The company is in the process of moving its major manufacturing operations to Indonesia, and expects those operations to be up and running within three years. Indonesia regulates substances used in the manufacturing process more leniently than does the United States, and Exogen would be able to use Durasol in its operations there. If the company could delay OSHA efforts to ban the solvent for three years, Exogen would be able to sustain its profits by continuing to use Durasol in its United States plants during that period. At the end of that time, its major manufacturing activities would take place in Indonesia, where it would not have to worry about the OSHA ban.

Company officials have considered a legal campaign that could accomplish this goal. This campaign could consist of a number of strategies. First, rather than voluntarily cease using Durasol, Exogen could insist that OSHA institute formal procedures to prohibit use of the solvent. This would require hearings, the opportunity for Exogen to present data that question whether the harms of Durasol have been adequately established, the chance to respond to adverse testimony, and other elaborate procedural measures. In addition, Exogen has learned that the daughter of the OSHA official who would play a major role in the OSHA proceedings works for an insurance subsidiary of Panoply Corporation. Panoply is a multinational holding company that has just purchased a small corporation that manufactures a solvent that some companies might use if Durasol were banned. Exogen plans to hold on to this information until OSHA formally prohibits use of Durasol, then challenge the OSHA action on the ground that the lead agency official has a conflict of interest because of his daughter's employment with Panoply. If it loses, Exogen plans to appeal to the U.S. Court of Appeals and, if necessary, seek review by the Supreme Court. All these steps should comprise a legal strategy that would delay OSHA prohibition of Durasol for at least three years.

How should the board proceed? What interests, if any, besides those of shareholders may the board consider? How should the board determine what those interests are? What is the risk of personal liability for the directors if their decision results in harm to the corporation?

1. JUDICIAL APPROACHES

DODGE v. FORD MOTOR CO.
170 N.W. 668 (Mich. 1919).

[Although the principal issue in this famous case was whether the corporation could be compelled to pay a dividend, the case is also significant for its discussion of the role of a corporation in society, a discussion that was elicited by Henry Ford's insistence in describing his motives for business decisions in terms of social rather than economic values.

Ford Motor Company was organized in 1903 with an initial capital of $150,000. Henry Ford took 225 of the 1,500 shares authorized, the Dodge brothers took 50 shares each, and several others subscribed to a few shares each. At the time the suit was brought, the company's capital was $2,000,000, the plaintiffs owned 10% of the outstanding stock, and Ford owned 58% and completely dominated the company.

The company paid regular quarterly dividends amounting to $1,200,000 per year and, in addition, had paid during the years 1911 through 1915 a total of $41 million in "special dividends." In 1916, Ford had "declared it to be the settled policy of the company not to pay in the future any special dividends, but to put back into the business for the future all of the earnings of the company other than the regular dividend."

This suit was brought by the Dodge brothers, two minority shareholders, against the Ford Motor Company, Henry Ford, and other members of the board of directors, to compel the payment of a dividend, to enjoin construction of the company's River Rouge plant, and for other relief. Ford's business then principally involved assembling cars using parts supplied by others. The Dodge brothers owned 22% of Ford's stock and were among Ford's largest suppliers. In addition, they had begun manufacturing cars in competition with Ford. Ford's decision to withhold dividends deprived the Dodge brothers of cash they needed to finance the expansion of their manufacturing operations, and Ford's plan to reduce the selling price of its cars placed additional competitive pressure on those operations. The lower court granted all the relief requested by plaintiffs.

The defendants appealed from a lower court order directing the corporation to pay a dividend of $19 million, enjoining it from building a smelter at the River Rouge plant and restraining it from "increasing of the fixed capital assets," or "holding of liquid assets in excess of such as may be reasonably required in the proper conduct and carrying on of the business and operations" of the corporation.]

OSTRANDER, C.J.:

To develop the points now discussed, and to a considerable extent they may be developed together as a single point, it is necessary to refer with some particularity to the facts.

When plaintiffs made their complaint and demand for further dividends, the Ford Motor Company had concluded its most prosperous year of business. The demand for its cars at the price of the preceding year continued. It could make and could market in the year beginning August 1, 1916, more than 500,000 cars. Sales of parts and repairs would necessarily increase. The cost of materials was likely to advance, and perhaps the price of labor; but it reasonably might have expected a profit for the year of upwards of $60,000,000. In justification [of their dividend policy and business plan], the defendants have offered testimony tending to prove, and which does prove, the following facts: It had been the policy of the corporation for a considerable time to annually reduce the selling price of cars, while keeping up, or improving, their quality. As early as in June, 1915, a general plan for the expansion of the productive capacity of the concern by a practical duplication of its plant had been talked over by the executive officers and directors and agreed upon; not all of the details having been settled, and no formal action of directors having been taken. The erection of a smelter was considered, and engineering and other data in connection therewith secured. In consequence, it was determined not to reduce the selling price of cars for the year beginning August 1, 1915, but to maintain the price and to accumulate a large surplus to pay for the proposed expansion of plant and equipment, and perhaps to build a plant for smelting ore. It is hoped, by Mr. Ford, that eventually 1,000,000 cars will be annually produced. The contemplated changes will permit the increased output.

The plan, as affecting the profits of the business for the year beginning August 1, 1916, and thereafter, calls for a reduction in the selling price of the cars. It is true that this price might be at any time increased, but the plan called for the reduction in price of $80 a car. The capacity of the plant, without the additions thereto voted to be made (without a part of them at least), would produce more than 600,000 cars annually. This number, and more, could have been sold for $440 instead of $360, a difference in the return for capital, labor, and materials employed of at least $48,000,000. In short, the plan does not call for and is not intended to produce immediately a more profitable business, but a less profitable one; not only less profitable than formerly, but less profitable than it is admitted it might be made. The apparent immediate effect will be to diminish the value of shares and the returns to shareholders.

It is the contention of plaintiffs that the apparent effect of the plan is intended to be the continued and continuing effect of it, and that it is deliberately proposed, not of record and not by official corporate declaration, but nevertheless proposed, to continue the corporation henceforth as a semi-eleemosynary institution and not as a business institution. In support of this contention, they point to the attitude and to the expressions of Mr. Henry Ford.

Mr. Henry Ford is the dominant force in the business of the Ford Motor Company. No plan of operations could be adopted unless he consented, and no board of directors can be elected whom he does not favor. One of the directors of the company has no stock. One share was assigned to him to qualify him for the position, but it is not claimed that he owns it. A business, one of the largest in the world, and one of the most profitable, has been built up. It employs many men, at good pay.

"My ambition," said Mr. Ford, "is to employ still more men, to spread the benefits of this industrial system to the greatest possible number, to help them build up their lives and their homes. To do this we are putting the greatest share of our profits back in the business."

"With regard to dividends, the company paid sixty per cent on its capitalization of two million dollars, or $1,200,000, leaving $58,000,000 to reinvest for the growth of the company. This is Mr. Ford's policy at present, and it is understood that the other stockholders cheerfully accede to this plan."

He had made up his mind in the summer of 1916 that no dividends other than the regular dividends should be paid, "for the present."

"Q. For how long? Had you fixed in your mind any time in the future, when you were going to pay? A. No.

"Q. That was indefinite in the future? A. That was indefinite; yes, sir."

The record, and especially the testimony of Mr. Ford, convinces that he has to some extent the attitude towards shareholders of one who has dispensed and distributed to them large gains and that they should be content to take what he chooses to give. His testimony creates the impression, also, that he thinks the Ford Motor Company has made too much money, has had too large profits, and that, although large profits might be still earned, a sharing of them with the public, by reducing the price of the output of the company, ought to be undertaken. We have no doubt that certain sentiments, philanthropic and altruistic, creditable to Mr. Ford, had large influence in determining the policy to be pursued by the Ford Motor Company—the policy which has been herein referred to.

It is said by his counsel that—

Although a manufacturing corporation cannot engage in humanitarian works as its principal business, the fact that it is organized for profit does not prevent the existence of implied powers to carry on with humanitarian motives such charitable works as are incidental to the main business of the corporation.

And again:

> As the expenditures complained of are being made in an
> expansion of the business which the company is organized to carry
> on, and for purposes within the powers of the corporation as
> hereinbefore shown, the question is as to whether such
> expenditures are rendered illegal because influenced to some
> extent by humanitarian motives and purposes on the part of the
> members of the board of directors.

[The cases referred to by counsel], after all, like all others in which the
subject is treated, turn finally upon the point, the question, whether it
appears that the directors were not acting for the best interests of the
corporation. We do not draw in question, nor do counsel for the plaintiffs
do so, the validity of the general proposition stated by counsel nor the
soundness of the opinions delivered in the cases cited. The case presented
here is not like any of them. The difference between an incidental
humanitarian expenditure of corporate funds for the benefit of the
employees, like the building of a hospital for their use and the employment
of agencies for the betterment of their condition, and a general purpose and
plan to benefit mankind at the expense of others, is obvious. There should
be no confusion (of which there is evidence) of the duties which Mr. Ford
conceives that he and the stockholders owe to the general public and the
duties which in law he and his codirectors owe to protesting, minority
stockholders. A business corporation is organized and carried on primarily
for the profit of the stockholders. The powers of the directors are to be
employed for that end. The discretion of directors is to be exercised in the
choice of means to attain that end, and does not extend to a change in the
end itself, to the reduction of profits, or to the nondistribution of profits
among stockholders in order to devote them to other purposes.

There is committed to the discretion of directors, a discretion to be
exercised in good faith, the infinite details of business, including the wages
which shall be paid to employees, the number of hours they shall work, the
conditions under which labor shall be carried on, and the price for which
products shall be offered to the public.

It is said by appellants that the motives of the board members are not
material and will not be inquired into by the court so long as their acts are
within their lawful powers. As we have pointed out, and the proposition
does not require argument to sustain it, it is not within the lawful powers
of a board of directors to shape and conduct the affairs of a corporation for
the merely incidental benefit of shareholders and for the primary purpose
of benefiting others, and no one will contend that, if the avowed purpose of
the defendant directors was to sacrifice the interests of shareholders, it
would not be the duty of the courts to interfere.

We are not, however, persuaded that we should interfere with the
proposed expansion of the business of the Ford Motor Company. In view of

the fact that the selling price of products may be increased at any time, the ultimate results of the larger business cannot be certainly estimated. The judges are not business experts. It is recognized that plans must often be made for a long future, for expected competition, for a continuing as well as an immediately profitable venture. The experience of the Ford Motor Company is evidence of capable management of its affairs. It may be noticed, incidentally, that it took from the public the money required for the execution of its plan, and that the very considerable salaries paid to Mr. Ford and to certain executive officers and employees were not diminished. We are not satisfied that the alleged motives of the directors, in so far as they are reflected in the conduct of the business, menace the interests of shareholders. It is enough to say, perhaps, that the court of equity is at all times open to complaining shareholders having a just grievance.

The decree of the court below fixing and determining the specific amount to be distributed to stockholders is affirmed. In other respect, the said decree is reversed.

———————

Scholars often cite *Dodge v. Ford* for the proposition that the directors' sole legal duty is to maximize shareholder profits. Alternatively, they argue that the case supports the normative conclusion that the ultimate goal of a public corporation should be shareholder wealth maximization. But does the opinion support either proposition? In other words, can the opinion be read to hold that there is an independent fiduciary duty to maximize shareholder profit, the breach of which can result in a cognizable shareholder derivative suit for a breach of fiduciary duty? And, what is the implication of such a duty on the managerial authority of the board and the concept of the separation of ownership and control?

Note that the court seems to suggest that "an incidental humanitarian expenditure for the benefit of the employees" would be permissible. Further, the court states that "a business corporation is organized and carried on *primarily* for the profit of the stockholders." (Emphasis added) Thus it would appear that for the court, the discretion to engage in activity that is not profit maximizing is not prohibited but rather is limited by the requirement that such activity be "incidental" to the primary purpose of the corporation. A close reading of the opinion (and other contemporary cases) suggests that the court is more concerned with majority shareholder oppression of minority shareholders than it is with the broader question of shareholder wealth maximization. As the court states, "There should be no confusion (of which there is evidence) of the duties which Mr. Ford conceives that he and the stockholders owe to the general public *and the duties which in law he and his codirectors owe to protesting, minority stockholders*." (Emphasis added). And, of course, the court refused to enjoin the proposed expansion of the company even though that expansion would reduce short term profits. *See*, D. Gordon Smith, *The Shareholder Primacy Norm*, 23 J. Corp. L. 277, 315 (1997–1998).

Henry Ford asserted on numerous occasions that he wanted only a small profit from his venture:

> I hold this [view] because it enables a large number of people to buy and enjoy the use of a car and because it gives a larger number of men employment at good wages. Those are the two aims I have in life. But I would not be counted a success if I could not accomplish that and at the same time make a fair amount of profit for myself and the men associated with me in the business.

> And let me say right here, that I do not believe that we should make such an awful profit on our cars. A reasonable profit is right, but not too much. So it has been my policy to force the price of the car down as fast as production would permit, and give the benefits to users and laborers, with resulting surprisingly enormous benefits to ourselves.

Allan Nevins & Frank E. Hill, Ford: Expansion and Challenge 1915–1933, 97 (1957). *See* Henry Ford, My Life and Work: An Autobiography of Henry Ford at 92 (1922) ("Take the industrial idea; what is it? The true industrial idea is not to make money. The industrial idea is to express a serviceable idea, to duplicate a useful idea, by as many thousands as there are people who need it.").

Can Ford's refusal to "make such an awful profit" be justified as sound business practice in that it lays the foundation for substantial future profits? The court seemed to think that the parts of his testimony it quotes belied that justification. The following more recent case, in an opinion by a respected judge of the Delaware Chancery Court, presents even more squarely the question of whether directors can manage a corporation for purposes other than to maximize profits for shareholders.

---

eBay Domestic Holdings, Inc. v. Newmark
16 A.3d 1, 6 (Del.Ch. 2010).

[craigslist, Inc., was founded by Craig Newmark (Craig) in 1995. Since its beginning, it has operated largely as a community service that allows its users to advertise goods and services for sale and connect with potential buyers. It is now the most-used classified ad site in the country. Despite its success, it operates as a small business. Its headquarters are in an old Victorian house in a residential San Francisco neighborhood; and it employs approximately thirty-four employees. It has never had more than three stockholders. Prior to 2004 they were Craig; James Buckmaster (Jim), the President and CEO; and Phillip Knowlton.

Craig and Jim believed strongly that craigslist should be run as a community service, but Knowlton wanted to monetize its success. Eventually the tension between Knowlton and the other two shareholders was resolved when Knowlton agreed to sell his stock to eBay. eBay offered to purchase the stock of Craig and Jim as well, but they refused to sell. Because it would be a minority stockholder, eBay sought an agreement pursuant to which it would receive certain contractual rights to protect its investment. Ultimately eBay paid Knowlton $16 million for his stock and paid $8 million to each of Craig and Jim in exchange for rights it received under a stock purchase agreement (the "SPA") and a stockholders' agreement (the "Shareholder Agreement"). As part of the transaction, craigslist also adopted a new Delaware charter providing for a three-person board elected by cumulative voting.

After the transaction closed in August of 2004 Craig owned 42.6% of craigslist, Jim owned 29%, and eBay owned 28.4%. This ensured that eBay would be able to elect one member of the board. Craig and Jim entered into a separate voting agreement pursuant to which they agreed to vote their shares so as to elect one board member selected by each of them.

From the beginning, it was eBay's wish that it would eventually be able to acquire all of craigslist or otherwise use the craigslist platform to enter the classified advertising business in the United States. Meanwhile, however, it insisted on retaining the right to enter into competition with craigslist in the United States, although the Shareholders' Agreement provided that eBay would lose certain of its protective rights if it did.

eBay eventually realized that it would not succeed in turning craigslist into a profit-maximizing business, as Craig and Jim, who controlled the corporation, insisted on continuing to operate the company as a community service. In March 2005, eBay launched an international classified service. Because it did not operate in the United States, this did not trigger a loss of its protective rights. There was, however, evidence at the trial that suggested that in developing its new service, eBay had made use of confidential information obtained from craigslist, in violation of one of the provisions of the Shareholders' Agreement.

Finally, eBay gave up on its efforts to make use of the craigslist platform and, in June 2007 it began offering classified ad service in the United States, thus triggering the loss of some of its rights under the Shareholders' Agreement. Recognizing the conflict between their desires and those of eBay, Jim and Craig suggested to eBay that they buy back its shares. When that suggestion was rebuffed, they determined to take steps to keep eBay out of the craigslist boardroom and to limit its ability to purchase any more stock of craigslist. Working with their counsel, they implemented three measures (the "2008 Board Actions") designed to achieve these ends: (1) an amendment to the charter and bylaws to provide for a staggered board; (2) a stockholder rights plan (the "Rights Plan"); and

(3) an offer to issue one new share of craigslist stock in exchange for every five shares on which a craigslist stockholder granted a right of first refusal in favor of craigslist.

Chancellor Chandler's lengthy opinion considers each of these measures, holding that the staggered board amendments were lawful, but that in adopting the Rights Plan issuing more stock Jim and Craig had breached their fiduciary duty as directors. The following excerpt addresses only the adoption of the Rights Plan. Such plans, colloquially known as "poison pills—or just "pills"—are widely used by public companies as effective anti-takeover devices. They have the effect of significantly diluting any stock purchased by a hostile tender offeror unless the acquisition is approved by the board of the target. They are described in greater detail in Chapter 22.

CHANDLER, CHANCELLOR

II. ANALYSIS

Jim and Craig owe fiduciary duties to eBay because they are directors and controlling stockholders of craigslist, and eBay is a minority stockholder of craigslist. All directors of Delaware corporations are fiduciaries of the corporations' stockholders. Similarly, controlling stockholders are fiduciaries of their corporations' minority stockholders. Even though neither Jim nor Craig individually owns a majority of craigslist's shares, the law treats them as craigslist's controlling stockholders because they form a control group, bound together by the Jim-Craig Voting Agreement, with the power to elect the majority of the craigslist board.

eBay's complaint asserts that Jim and Craig breached the fiduciary duties they owed to eBay by implementing the 2008 Board Actions. eBay argues that the implementation of the 2008 Board Actions was a breach of fiduciary duty because the SPA and the Shareholders' Agreement limits the actions craigslist can take in response to eBay's Competitive Activity, and, by implementing the 2008 Board Actions, Jim and Craig used their fiduciary positions to cause craigslist to take actions beyond those permitted by the SPA and the Shareholders' Agreement. eBay also asserts that by enacting the 2008 Board Actions, Jim and Craig used their fiduciary positions to secure rights and benefits for themselves that they were not able to secure when they negotiated the SPA and the Shareholders' Agreement with eBay in 2004.

Any time a stockholder challenges an action taken by the board of directors, the Court must first determine the appropriate standard of review to use in analyzing the challenged action. Identifying the appropriate standard of review ensures that the Court applies the proper level of judicial scrutiny to the board's decision-making process.

A.   The Rights Plan

I will review Jim and Craig's adoption of the Rights Plan using the intermediate standard of enhanced scrutiny, typically referred to as the *Unocal* test.[1] Framed generally, enhanced scrutiny "requires directors to bear the burden to show their actions were reasonable." The directors must "(1) identify the proper corporate objectives served by their actions; and (2) justify their actions as reasonable in relationship to those objectives."

Enhanced scrutiny has been applied universally when stockholders challenge a board's use of a rights plan as a defensive device. In the typical scenario, the decision to deploy a rights plan will fall within the range of reasonableness if the directors use the plan in a good faith effort to promote stockholder value. Using a rights plan to promote stockholder value is a legitimate exercise of board authority that accords with the directors' fiduciary duties.

Like any strong medicine, however, a pill can be misused. The Delaware Supreme Court understood from the outset that a rights plan can be deployed inappropriately to benefit incumbent managers and directors at the stockholders' expense. Therefore when deploying a rights plan, "directors must at minimum convince the court that they have not acted for an inequitable purpose." And more than mere subjective good faith is required. Human judgment can be clouded by subtle influences like the prestige and perquisites of board membership, personal relationships with management, or animosity towards a bidder. Because of the omnipresent specter that directors could use a rights plan improperly, even when acting *subjectively* in good faith, *Unocal* and its progeny require that this Court also review the use of a rights plan *objectively*. Like other defensive measures, a rights plan cannot be used preclusively or coercively; nor can its use fall outside the "range of reasonableness."

The ample case law addressing rights plans almost invariably involves publicly traded corporations with a widely dispersed, potentially disempowered, and arguably vulnerable stockholder base. In cases involving rights plans to date, Delaware courts have typically and understandably approved the use of rights plans to remedy the collective action problems that stockholders [of publicly-held corporations] face, including but not limited to the classically coercive prisoner's dilemma imposed by a two-tiered offer. At the same time, Delaware courts have guarded against the overt risk of entrenchment and the less visible, yet

---

[1]   The court refers to the test established in *Unocal Corp. v. Mesa Petroleum Co.*, 493 A.2d 946 (Del. 1985), in which the Delaware Supreme Court held that, in reviewing measures designed to prevent a takeover, a court should not defer to the business judgment of the board but should review its decision using an "enhanced standard" somewhere between the deference shown under the business judgment rule and the "entire fairness" standard used in reviewing decisions as to which the board has a conflict of interest. The *Unocal* case is considered in Chapter 21.

more pernicious risk that incumbents acting in subjective good faith might nevertheless deprive stockholders of value-maximizing opportunities.

In this unique case, I do not face those same concerns. Jim and Craig are not dispersed, disempowered, or vulnerable stockholders. They are the majority. Jim and Craig are not using the Rights Plan improperly to preclude craigslist stockholders from considering and opting for a value-maximizing transaction. As the majority, Jim and Craig can consider and opt-for a value-maximizing transaction whenever they want.

Nor are Jim and Craig using the Rights Plan to protect their board seats. Together Jim and Craig own an overwhelming majority of craigslist's voting power, and they have entered into the Jim-Craig Voting Agreement which ensures that each votes the other onto the board.

Thus, the two main issues I confront are: First, did Jim and Craig properly and reasonably perceive a threat to craigslist's corporate policy and effectiveness? Second, if they did, is the Rights Plan a proportional response to that threat?

I have carefully considered Jim and Craig's contentions in this case and the evidence they presented in support of those contentions. I conclude, based on all of the evidence, that Jim and Craig in fact did *not* adopt the Rights Plan in response to a reasonably perceived threat or for a proper corporate purpose.

Jim and Craig contend that they identified a threat to craigslist and its corporate policies that will materialize after they both die and their craigslist shares are distributed to their heirs. At that point, they say, "eBay's acquisition of control [via the anticipated acquisition of Jim or Craig's shares from some combination of their heirs] would fundamentally alter craigslist's values, culture and business model, including departing from [craigslist's] public-service mission in favor of increased monetization of craigslist." To prevent this unwanted potential future reality, Jim and Craig have adopted the Rights Plan *now* so that their vision of craigslist's culture can bind *future* fiduciaries and stockholders from beyond the grave.

Promoting, protecting, or pursuing nonstockholder considerations must lead at some point to value for stockholders. When director decisions are reviewed under the business judgment rule, this Court will not question rational judgments about how promoting non-stockholder interests—be it through making a charitable contribution, paying employees higher salaries and benefits, or more general norms like promoting a particular corporate culture—ultimately promote stockholder value. Under the *Unocal* standard, however, the directors must act within the range of reasonableness.

Ultimately, defendants failed to prove that craigslist possesses a palpable, distinctive, and advantageous culture that sufficiently promotes stockholder value to support the indefinite implementation of a poison pill.

Jim and Craig did not make any serious attempt to prove that the craigslist culture, which rejects any attempt to further monetize its services, translates into increased profitability for stockholders. I am sure that part of the reason craigslist is so popular is because it offers a free service that is also extremely useful. It may be that offering free classifieds is an essential component of a successful online classifieds venture. After all, by offering free classifieds, craigslist is able to attract such a large community of users that real estate brokers in New York City gladly pay fees to list apartment rentals in order to access the vast community of craigslist users. Likewise, employers in select cities happily pay fees to advertise job openings to craigslist users. Neither of these fee-generating activities would have been possible if craigslist did not provide brokers and employers access to a sufficiently large market of consumers, and brokers and employers may not have reached that market without craigslist's free classifieds.

Giving away services to attract business is a sales tactic, however, not a corporate culture. To the extent business measures like loss-leading products, money-back coupons, or putting products on sale are cultural artifacts, they reflect the American capitalist culture, not something unique to craigslist. The existence of a distinctive craigslist "culture" was not proven at trial.

The defendants also failed to prove at trial that when adopting the Rights Plan, they concluded in good faith that there was a sufficient connection between the craigslist "culture" (however amorphous and intangible it might be) and the promotion of stockholder value. No evidence at trial suggested that Jim or Craig conducted any informed evaluation of alternative business strategies or tactics when adopting the Rights Plan. Jim and Craig simply disliked the possibility that the Grim Reaper someday will catch up with them and that a company like eBay might, in the future, purchase a controlling interest in craigslist. They considered this possible future state unpalatable, not because of how it affects the value of the entity for its stockholders, but rather because of their own personal preferences. Jim and Craig therefore failed to prove at trial that they acted in the good faith pursuit of a proper *corporate* purpose when they deployed the Rights Plan. Based on all of the evidence, I find instead that Jim and Craig resented eBay's decision to compete with craigslist and adopted the Rights Plan as a punitive response. They then cloaked this decision in the language of culture and *post mortem* corporate benefit. Although Jim and Craig (and the psychological culture they embrace) were the only known beneficiaries of the Rights Plan, such a motive is no substitute for their fiduciary duty to craigslist stockholders.

Jim and Craig did prove that they personally believe craigslist should not be about the business of stockholder wealth maximization, now or in the future. As an abstract matter, there is nothing inappropriate about an organization seeking to aid local, national, and global communities by providing a website for online classifieds that is largely devoid of monetized elements. Indeed, I personally appreciate and admire Jim's and Craig's desire to be of service to communities. The corporate form in which craigslist operates, however, is not an appropriate vehicle for purely philanthropic ends, at least not when there are other stockholders interested in realizing a return on their investment. Jim and Craig opted to form craigslist, Inc. as a *for-profit Delaware corporation* and voluntarily accepted millions of dollars from eBay as part of a transaction whereby eBay became a stockholder. Having chosen a for-profit corporate form, the craigslist directors are bound by the fiduciary duties and standards that accompany that form. Those standards include acting to promote the value of the corporation for the benefit of its stockholders. The "Inc." after the company name has to mean at least that. Thus, I cannot accept as valid for the purposes of implementing the Rights Plan a corporate policy that specifically, clearly, and admittedly seeks *not* to maximize the economic value of a for-profit Delaware corporation for the benefit of its stockholders—no matter whether those stockholders are individuals of modest means[106] or a corporate titan of online commerce. If Jim and Craig were the only stockholders affected by their decisions, then there would be no one to object. eBay, however, holds a significant stake in craigslist, and Jim and Craig's actions affect others besides themselves.

Directors of a for-profit Delaware corporation cannot deploy a rights plan to defend a business strategy that openly eschews stockholder wealth maximization—at least not consistently with the directors' fiduciary duties under Delaware law.

The avowed purpose of the Rights Plan is to protect the craigslist "culture" at some point in the future unrelated to when eBay sells some or all of its shares. As long as Jim and Craig have control, however, they can maintain the craigslist "culture" regardless of whether eBay sells some or all of its shares. The Rights Plan neither affects when eBay can sell its shares nor affects when the craigslist culture can change. It therefore does not have a reasonable connection to Jim and Craig's professed goal. Assuming Jim and Craig sought to establish a corporate *Academie Francaise* to protect the cultural integrity of craigslist's business model, the Rights Plan simply does not serve that goal. It therefore falls outside the range of reasonableness. On the factual record presented at trial, therefore, the defendants also failed to meet their burden of proof under the second prong of *Unocal*.

Because defendants failed to prove that they acted to protect or defend a legitimate corporate interest and because they failed to prove that the rights plan was a reasonable response to a perceived threat to corporate policy or effectiveness, I rescind the Rights Plan in its entirety.

2.   A HISTORICAL VIEW

Dodge v. Ford, provoked considerable scholarly debate about the social responsibility issues in the case. In the early 1930s, two leading corporate law scholars, Adolf A. Berle, Jr. and E. Merrick Dodd first framed the argument. Berle believed that corporate powers were held in trust "at all times exercisable only for the ratable benefit of all the shareholders." Adolf A. Berle, Jr., *Corporate Powers as Powers in Trust*, 44 Harv. L. Rev. 1049 (1931). Dodd contended that the business corporation was properly seen "as an economic institution which has a social service as well as a profit making function." E. Merrick Dodd, *For Whom Are Corporate Managers Trustees?*, 45 Harv. L. Rev. 1145, 1148 (1932).

Twenty years later, the New Jersey Supreme Court seemed to vindicate both points of view. In *A.P. Smith Manufacturing Co. v. Barlow*, 98 A.2d 581 (N.J. 1953), it upheld the validity of a corporate gift to Princeton University. But in reaching this conclusion, the court accepted the company's argument that its gift at least arguably advanced its long-run business interests. As Professor Berle observed, the effect of the decision was to recognize that "[m]odern directors are not limited to running business enterprise for maximum profit, but are in fact and recognized in law as administrators of a community system." The Corporation in Modern Society, *Foreword* at xii (Edward S. Mason, ed.1960).

In 1954, Professor Berle conceded that Dodd had won the argument, at least for the moment. However, he did not acknowledge that Dodd had been correct. Notwithstanding Professor Berle's concession, there is a strong argument to be made on his behalf. Perhaps the most well-known opponent of corporate social responsibility was Professor Milton Friedman. Friedman argued that the only social responsibility of a corporation is to maximize profits for its shareholders. That's all. Shareholders may choose to be socially responsible by contributing their own money to social causes, but this is not the job of business. In Friedman's view, "there is one and only one social responsibility of business—to use its resources and engage in activities designed to increase its profits so long as it stays within the rules of the game, which is to say, engages in open and free competition, without deception or fraud." Milton Friedman, Capitalism & Freedom, 133–34 (1962). *See* Milton Friedman, *The Social Responsibility of Business Is to Increase Its Profits*, N.Y. Times, Sept. 13, 1970, § 6 (Magazine), at 32–33 (arguing that a corporation should "make as much money as possible while confirming to the basic rules of the society").

Over the last few years, the pendulum has swung toward Berle's and Friedman's position. "[S]hareholder wealth maximization is a widely accepted social norm among business leaders. That social norm, in turn, has a profound effect on the behaviors and attitudes of those who manage firms. Even in the absence of a clear and unequivocal legal obligation, managers are encouraged to think of their role as properly directed to producing value for shareholders. That is, managers are primed to think that a focused pursuit of shareholder returns is part of their role morality." James D. Nelson, *The Freedom of Business Association*, 115 Colum. L. Rev. 461, 500–02 (2015). *See also* Henry Hansmann & Reinier Kraakman, *The End of History for Corporate Law*, 89 Geo. L.J. 439, 439 (2001) ("There is no longer any serious competitor to the view that corporate law should principally strive to increase long-term shareholder value.").

This "widely accepted social norm" represents a significant departure from the norm that prevailed during much of the early and mid-twentieth century. Consider, for example, the following excerpt from a 1971 report prepared by a subcommittee of the Committee for Economic Development, an organization whose members read like a Who's Who of large American businesses: "The modern professional manager also regards himself, not as an owner disposing of personal property as he sees fit, but as a trustee balancing the interest of many diverse participants and constituents in the enterprise, whose interests sometimes conflict with those of others. The chief executive of a large corporation has the problem of reconciling the demands of employees for more wages and improved benefit plans, customers for lower prices and greater values, vendors for higher prices, government for more taxes, stockholders for higher dividends and greater capital appreciation-all within a framework that will be constructive and acceptable to society." Research and Policy Comm., Committee. for Economic Development, Social Responsibilities of Business Corporations, 22 (1971).

WILLIAM T. ALLEN, OUR SCHIZOPHRENIC CONCEPTION OF THE BUSINESS CORPORATION
14 Cardozo L.Rev. 261, 263–65, 272–73 (1992).

Modern corporation law statutes were, and still are, "enabling" statutes in the broadest sense of that term. They are almost literally empty, and those few mandatory features that remain—such as the requirement of an annual meeting of shareholders, or a right to inspect the company's books and records for a proper corporate purpose—are themselves under attack from some quarters as paternalistic clogs on efficiency.

Two inconsistent conceptions have dominated our thinking about corporations since the evolution of the large integrated business corporation in the late nineteenth century. Each conception could claim dominance for a particular period, or among one group or another, but neither has so commanded agreement as to exclude the other from the discourses of law or the thinking of business people.

In the first conception, the corporation is seen as the private property of its stockholder-owners. The corporation's purpose is to advance the purposes of these owners (predominantly to increase their wealth), and the function of directors, as agents of the owners, is faithfully to advance the financial interests of the owners. I call this the property conception of the corporation, because it sees the corporation as the property of its stockholders. This model might almost as easily be called a contract model, because in its most radical form, the corporation tends to disappear, transformed from a substantial institution into just a relatively stable corner of the market in which autonomous property owners freely contract.

The second conception sees the corporation not as the private property of stockholders, but as a social institution. According to this view, the corporation is not strictly private; it is tinged with a public purpose. The corporation comes into being and continues as a legal entity only with governmental concurrence. The legal institutions of government grant a corporation its juridical personality, its characteristic limited liability, and its perpetual life. This conception sees this public facilitation as justified by the state's interest in promoting the general welfare. Thus, corporate purpose can be seen as including the advancement of the general welfare. The board of directors' duties extend beyond assuring investors a fair return, to include a duty of loyalty, in some sense, to all those interested in or affected by the corporation. This view could be labeled in a variety of ways: the managerialist conception, the institutionalist conception, or the social entity conception. All would be descriptive, since the corporation is seen as distinct from each of the individuals that happens to fill the social roles that its internal rules and culture define. The corporation itself is, in this view, capable of bearing legal and moral obligations. To law and economics scholars, who have been so influential in academic corporate law, this model is barely coherent and dangerously wrong.

These two, apparently inconsistent, conceptions have coexisted in our thinking over the last century. For most of the century the lack of agreement on the ultimate nature and purpose of the business corporation has not generated intense conflict. A host of macro-economic factors— secularly rising prosperity, a lack of global competition, and the absence of powerful shareholders—probably account for this placid status quo. By the 1980s however, emerging global competition, capital market innovation, and the growth and evolution of institutional investors, among other factors, made possible the takeover movement, which glaringly exposed our inconsistent thinking about the nature of the business corporation.

The law "papered over" the conflict in our conception of the corporation by invoking a murky distinction between long-term profit maximization and short-term profit maximization. Corporate expenditures which at first blush did not seem to be profit maximizing, could be squared with the property conception of the corporation by recognizing that they might redound to the long-term benefit of the corporation and its shareholders. Thus, without purporting to abandon the idea that directors ultimately owe loyalty only to stockholders and their financial interests, the law was able to approve reasonable corporate expenditures for charitable or social welfare purposes or other actions that did not maximize current profit.

There is a utility in this long-term/short-term device. Though employment of this distinction is subject to obvious manipulation, it can nevertheless resolve the tension between these differing conceptions of the corporation in a way that offers the possibility of some judicial protection to shareholders, while affording substantial room to the multi-constituency, social entity conception to operate. With this distinction, judicial review of particular decisions is available under the fiduciary duty standard. But corporate directors are also afforded very considerable latitude to deal with all groups or institutions having an interest in, or who are affected by, the corporation. The long-term/short-term distinction preserves the form of the stockholders oriented property theory, while permitting, in fact, a considerable degree of behavior consistent with a view that sees public corporations as owing social responsibilities to all affected by their operation.

Thus, while early on much ink was spilled on the question to whom should directors be responsible, in practice the question of the nature of the corporation seemed essentially unproblematic until the emergence of the cash tender offer of the 1980s. The long-term/short-term distinction proved a serviceable, if an intellectually problematic way, for the corporation law to avoid choosing between the alpha of property and the omega of relationships.

———————

Leo Strine is the Chief Justice of the Delaware Supreme Court and a highly-regarded judge and scholar of corporate law whose opinions and other writings are sprinkled throughout this book. Here are excerpts from two of his law review articles that touch on this debate

LEO STRINE, THE DANGERS OF DENIAL: THE NEED FOR A CLEAR-EYED UNDERSTANDING OF THE POWER AND ACCOUNTABILITY STRUCTURE ESTABLISHED BY THE DELAWARE GENERAL CORPORATION LAW

50 Wake Forest L. Rev. 761, 766–67 (2015).

Dodge v. Ford and *eBay* are hornbook law because they make clear that if a fiduciary admits that he is treating an interest other than stockholder wealth as an end in itself, rather than an instrument to stockholder wealth, he is committing a breach of fiduciary duty.

If we wish to make the corporation more socially responsible, we must do it the proper way. If we believe that other constituencies should be given more protection within corporation law itself, then statutes should be adopted giving those constituencies enforceable rights that they can wield.

But a more effective and direct way to protect interests such as the environment, workers, and consumers would be to revive externality regulation. We must also address the incentives and duties of institutional investors—who act as the direct stockholders of most public companies—so that these investors behave in a manner more consistent with the longer-term investment horizon of the human beings whose capital they control.

But lecturing others to do the right thing without acknowledging the actual rules that apply to their behavior, and the actual power dynamics to which they are subject, is not a responsible path to social progress. Rather, it provides an excuse for avoiding the tougher policy challenges that must be overcome if we are to make sure that for-profit corporations become vehicles for responsible, sustainable, long-term wealth creation.

3. ALI PRINCIPLES OF CORPORATE GOVERNANCE

Corporation statutes do not mandate that a corporation must primarily pursue profit, let alone maximize shareholder wealth. They simply provide that a corporation can engage in any lawful activity. *See, e.g.,* DGCL § 101(b); MBCA § 3.01(a). The charters of most public corporations track the statute. *See, e.g.,* Restated Certificate of Incorporation of Facebook, Inc., Art. III (May 22, 2012) ("The purpose of the corporation is to engage in any lawful act or activity for which corporations may be organized under the General Corporation Law of the State of Delaware."). However, the American Law Institute's Principles of Corporate Governance squarely address the issue in the model act.

---

§ 2.01 The Objective and Conduct of the Corporation

(a) Subject to the provisions of Subsection (b), a corporation should have as its objective the conduct of business activities with a view to enhancing corporate profit and shareholder gain.

(b) Even if corporate profit and shareholder gain are not thereby enhanced, the corporation, in the conduct of its business:

(1) Is obliged, to the same extent as a natural person, to act within the boundaries set by law;

(2) May take into account ethical considerations that are reasonably regarded as appropriate to the responsible conduct of business; and

(3) May devote a reasonable amount of resources to public welfare, humanitarian, educational, and philanthropic purposes.

COMMENT

e. Corporate objective and corporate conduct. The subject matter of these Principles is the governance of business corporations. The business corporation is an instrument through which capital is assembled for the activities of producing and distributing goods and services and making investments. These Principles take as a basic proposition that a business corporation should have as its objective the conduct of such activities with a view to enhancing corporate profit and shareholder gain. The provisions of Subsection (b) reflect a recognition that the corporation is a social as well as an economic institution, and accordingly that its pursuit of the economic objective must be constrained by social imperatives and may be qualified by social needs.

f. The economic objective. In very general terms, Subsection (a) may be thought of as a broad injunction to enhance economic returns, while Subsection (b) makes clear that certain kinds of conduct must or may be pursued whether or not they enhance such returns (that is, even if the conduct either yields no economic return or entails a net economic loss). In most cases, however, the kinds of conduct described in Subsection (b) could be pursued even under the principle embodied in Subsection (a). Such conduct will usually be consistent with economic self-interest, because the principle embodied in Subsection (a)—that the objective of the corporation is to conduct business activities with a view to enhancing corporate profit and shareholder gain—does not mean that the objective of the corporation must be to realize corporate profit and shareholder gain in the short run. Indeed, the contrary is true: long-run profitability and shareholder gain are at the core of the economic objective. Activity that entails a short-run cost to achieve an appropriately greater long-run profit is therefore not a departure from the economic objective. An orientation toward lawful, ethical, and public-spirited activity will normally fall within this description. The modern corporation by its nature creates interdependencies with a variety of groups with whom the corporation has a legitimate concern, such as employees, customers, suppliers, and members of the communities in which the corporation operates. The long-term profitability of the corporation generally depends on meeting the fair expectations of such groups. Short-term profits may properly be subordinated to recognition that responsible maintenance of these interdependencies is likely to contribute to long-term profitability and shareholder gain. The corporation's business may be conducted accordingly.

4.　PENNSYLVANIA BUS. CORP. LAW

A significant number of corporation statutes have "constituency" provisions, which provide that a board may consider the interests of constituents other than shareholders when managing the business and affairs of the corporation. *See* Einer Elhauge, *Sacrificing Corporate Profits in the Public Interest*, 80 N.Y.U. L. Rev. 733, 737 (2005) (noting that over half the states have passed constituency provisions); D. Gordon Smith, *The Shareholder Primacy Norm*, 23 J. Corp. L. 277, 279–80, 289 (1998) (same). The following is Pennsylvania's statute.

---

§ 1715　Exercise of Powers Generally

(a)　In discharging the duties of their respective positions, the board of directors, committees of the board and individual directors of a business corporation may, in considering the best interests of the corporation, consider to the extent they deem appropriate:

(1)　The effects of any action upon any or all groups affected by such action, including shareholders, employees, suppliers, customers and creditors of the corporation, and upon communities in which offices or other establishments of the corporation are located.

(2)　The short-term and long-term interests of the corporation, including benefits that may accrue to the corporation from its long-term plans and the possibility that these interests may be best served by the continued independence of the corporation.

(3)　The resources, intent and conduct (past, stated and potential) of any person seeking to acquire control of the corporation.

(4)　All other pertinent factors.

(b)　The board of directors, committees of the board and individual directors shall not be required, in considering the best interests of the corporation or the effects of any action, to regard any corporate interest or the interests of any particular group affected by such action as a dominant or controlling interest or factor. The consideration of interests and factors in the manner described in this subsection and in subsection (a) shall not constitute a violation of section 1712 (relating to standard of care and justifiable reliance).

Importantly, neither the Delaware General Corporation Law nor the Model Business Corporation Act have a constituency provision. However, the silence of these statutes does not mean that they command profit maximization as the statutes are also silent on this point as well. Rather, the broad managerial authority given to the board to manage the business and affairs of the corporation, and under the authority the board can most likely consider all the implications of its decisions on the long-run best interest of the corporation. Indeed, Delaware courts have specifically noted that, in the takeover realm, a board may consider all relevant factors in making decisions. *See Paramount Communications, Inc. v. Time, Inc.*, 571 A.2d 1140, 1150 (Del. 1989) ("[A] board of directors, while always required to act in an informed manner, is not under any *per se* duty to maximize shareholder value in the short term, even in the context of a takeover"); Unocal Corp. v. Mesa Petroleum Co., 493 A.2d 946, 955 (Del. 1985) (noting that in making decisions in the realm of takeovers "the impact on 'constituencies' other than shareholder (*i.e.*, creditors, customers, employees, and perhaps even the community generally)").

C.   THE SPECIAL PROBLEM OF MULTINATIONAL CORPORATIONS

As the Exogen problem makes clear, multinational corporations encounter special legal and moral questions when they operate in a global environment. First, United States corporations face increased risks when they conduct business overseas. While those that operate through foreign subsidiaries or foreign partners are largely shielded from legal liability, international business operations are not without social and economic risk. Environmental concerns, labor issues, and political corruption are but some of the potential problems multinational corporations face when they do business abroad. These problems are particularly acute for businesses that carry on operations in developing countries where local laws and regulations may impose fewer restrictions on corporate conduct.

Technological advances such as the ability to produce and communicate information over the Internet have made corporate conduct and misconduct visible on a global scale. Multinational corporations whose foreign practices fall below accepted standards expose themselves to negative media coverage, consumer boycotts, and public protests that can severely damage a company's image and reputation. United States Customs regulations ban the importation of goods into the United States that are produced using unlawful child or forced labor. Finally, multinational corporations may face potential legal exposure under such laws as the Foreign Corrupt Practices Act, which prohibits corporations and their agents from bribing foreign governments to further their business interests abroad, as well as the Alien Tort Claims Act, which plaintiffs have used with some success to hold United States corporations accountable for alleged complicity in human rights abuses perpetrated by the governments of countries where these corporations do business.

Multinational corporations must also take into account different cultural perspectives in connection with their foreign business practices. Cynthia Williams and John Conley explain:

> Scholars of corporate governance commonly divide the world into two spheres: the Anglo-American "outsider" system and the continental European "insider" system. In addition to having distinct corporate governance structures, inhabitants of these two spheres make different assumptions about corporate goals. In general, the Anglo-American approach is understood to valorize "shareholder value," while the European approach includes a broader social class of "stakeholders"—employees, creditors, suppliers, communities, and even the environment—within the ambit of managerial concern.

Cynthia Williams & John Conley, *An Emerging Third Way, The Erosion of the Anglo-American Shareholder Value Construct*, 38 Cornell Int'l L.J. 493 (2005).

One consequence of the European stakeholder-based model of corporate governance is that it has allowed European corporations to take into account broader interests and longer time horizons in corporate decision making. Many European countries have adopted measures that require corporations to respond explicitly to the concerns of employees and other nonshareholder constituencies. As a result, the corporate social responsibility movement has achieved greater prominence in Europe than it has in the United States.

For example, France, Belgium, Germany, and the United Kingdom require pension funds to disclose the extent to which they take ethical, social, and environmental information into account in their investment portfolios. Denmark, the Netherlands, Norway, and Sweden require companies to provide extensive environmental information in their annual reports even though these matters have little, if any, direct affect on short-term share prices. The European Union has also endorsed sustainable growth as a proper corporate goal and has paid attention to the social and environmental consequences of corporate actions.

France is perhaps the best example of the continental European approach to corporate social responsibility. In 2001, France enacted the "New Economic Regulations" ("NRE"), which amended French company law to require French companies to disclose social and environmental information. Article 116 of the NRE requires all French companies traded on the French stock exchange (the Bourse de Paris) to provide detailed information about the environmental, labor, community involvement, health, and safety in the company's annual reports to shareholders. For example, French listed companies must disclose specific environmental information about the use of natural resources, information about emissions and pollutants, efforts by the company to reduce environmental impacts, accounting reserves for environmental risks, and any environmental fines or monetary penalties. The required social disclosures include detailed information about the company's labor arrangements, working hours and overtime, gender equity, collective bargaining agreements, health and safety provisions, use of subcontractors, as well as information about the company's territorial impact and regional development practices. Listed French companies must disclose this social and economic information for the company's domestic activities as well as for its operations abroad.

Globalization is also affecting the social responsibility movement in the United Kingdom. While the UK has long followed the American shareholder-centered model of corporate governance, Williams and Conley observe that the UK may be adopting a "third way" that merges elements of the American shareholder and European stakeholder approaches. As they explain, the UK is subject to institutional pressures that do not currently exist in the United States or are present in much weaker form. These forces include actions by public institutions (the EU and the UK government) and private actors (pension funds and insurance companies, labor unions, consumers, and nongovernmental organizations). Williams and Conley believe that these relatively stronger pro-stakeholder influences, have moved the UK towards a model of corporate governance that increasingly considers other constituency groups in corporate decision making.

For a less optimistic view of the European CSR movement, consider Olivier Delbard's argument in *CSR Legislation in France and the European Regulatory Paradox: An Analysis of EU CSR Policy and Sustainability Reporting Practice*, 8 Corporate Governance 397 (2008). Dr. Delbard contends that while the EU has both strong and mandatory environmental legislation, corporate social responsibility rules—a logical extension of environmental legislation—tend towards voluntary compliance. As such, it is left to the individual EU member states to implement their own CSR policy. Though some countries have undertaken to regulate certain categories of companies, depending on their size or sector, France alone requires that all publicly listed French companies comply with its CSR law.

Further, Dr. Delbard notes that there appears to be at least some backsliding in the realm of CSR at the EU member state level. For example, citing the potential to stifle innovation and competitiveness, the UK abandoned its plans for compulsory reporting of environmental and social risk information by British-based companies listed on the London Stock Exchange. Instead, the UK opted for a less stringent regime that would allow businesses more flexibility in how they handle CSR.

When the European Commission launched its "Alliance for CSR" in 2006, it noted the program's "completely voluntary" nature and stressed that there would be neither independent monitoring nor mandatory conditions. Chris Smyth, *Can Europe Show the Way on CSR?*, Fin. Times, Apr. 5, 2006. In response to the announcement by UNICE (now BusinessEurope), a business federation, sent a letter to its members stating that the announcement constituted good news for industry, and that "a few passages in the communication must be interpreted as verbal concessions to other stakeholders, which will however have no real impact." Trade unions and NGOs responded angrily to the Alliance's announcement, contending that the Alliance would be ineffectual and no more than a public relations exercise.

D. CORPORATE CHARITABLE CONTRIBUTIONS

Some corporate expenditures may be viewed as not necessarily directly increasing profits or otherwise adding to shareholder value. Business decisions such as building a new plant long have been viewed as within the ambit of the board of directors. Social expenditures such as charitable contributions, however, may not fit comfortably within the traditional decision making structure.

In thinking about such expenditures, consider who actually decides which organization should receive a charitable contribution. What criteria are relevant to the decision? What does it mean to say that the "the corporation" supports a particular organization?

There are two principal concerns in these expenditures: how to protect the interests of shareholders who may not agree with the choices that corporate management has made and how to create a system of managerial accountability with respect to such expenditures. As you read the following materials consider the following questions.

1. Must the corporation be seen solely as a profit-maximizing entity with limits on everything else it does? If not, what kind of standard would adequately make the directors accountable to the shareholders?

2. Modern corporate statutes authorize corporations to make charitable contributions. What limits are there on these contributions? Must the contribution be in furtherance of the corporation's business purpose, *i.e.*, must there be a direct corporate benefit arising from the contribution? If there is a corporate benefit, how is a charitable contribution different from advertising or other forms of marketing?

3. What is the proper role of shareholders? Should they be forced to sell their shares if they disagree about the beneficiary of a corporate contribution? Or should they be given a greater voice in corporate charitable contributions? If so, what form should that voice take?

Problem: Union Airlines

You are general counsel for Union Airlines, Inc., a major U.S. domestic air carrier headquartered in Georgetown, Columbia. The company has $2 billion in assets and generates $1.5 billion in annual revenues. Due to increased competition and higher fuel prices, Union's profits have declined steadily and it has posted large losses for the last three years.

Wright, the company's chief executive officer has told you that Union intends to make a corporate donation of $1 million to the Georgetown Opera Company to help it survive a financial crisis that threatens to prevent the Opera from opening the current season. He has also suggested that Union would be prepared to disclose its charitable giving policies in its next proxy statement, including mentioning its gift to the Opera, and to seek shareholder approval of those policies.

1. Wright would like your opinion on the legality of the gift. What should you tell him?

2. Would your opinion change if Wright were a member of the board of directors of the Opera and that this contribution would fulfill his annual obligation either to personally contribute or arrange for the contribution of $50,000?

3. Would your opinion change if you learned that Wright had been trying for years to join the board of directors of the Opera, perhaps the most socially prestigious board in Georgetown, and that the proposed gift appeared to be an unspoken quid pro quo for an invitation to Wright to join that board?

1. JUDICIAL ATTITUDES

THEODORA HOLDING CORP. V. HENDERSON
257 A.2d 398 (Del.Ch. 1969).

[For many years, Girard Henderson dominated the affairs of Alexander Dawson, Inc., through his controlling interest in that corporation. In 1955, he transferred as part of a separation agreement 11,000 shares of common stock to his wife, Theodora Henderson. Ms. Henderson owned in her own name 3,000 of first preferred, 12,000 of second preferred, and 22,000 of third preferred stock of Alexander Dawson, Inc. In 1967, Mrs. Henderson formed the Theodora Holding Corporation (plaintiff) and transferred in those 11,000 shares of Alexander Dawson, Inc. common stock (At the time of the transfer the market value of this stock was $15,675,000 and had a net asset value of $28,996,000). During that year of the disputed charitable donation, the combined dividends paid by Alexander Dawson, Inc. on the preferred and common stock held Mrs. Henderson and her corporation totaled $286,240.

From 1960 to 1966, Girard Henderson had caused Alexander Dawson, Inc. to make annual corporate contributions ranging from $60,000 to more than $70,000 to the Alexander Dawson Foundation ("the Foundation"), which Henderson had formed in 1957. All contributions were unanimously approved by the shareholders. In 1966, Alexander Dawson, Inc. donated to the Foundation a large tract of land valued at $467,750 for the purpose of establishing a camp for under-privileged boys. In April 1967, Mr. Henderson proposed that the board approve a $528,000 gift of company stock to the Foundation to finance the camp. One director, Theodora Ives, objected and suggested that the gift be made instead to a charitable corporation supported by her mother (Girard Henderson's ex-wife) and herself. Girard Henderson responded by causing a reduction in the Alexander Dawson, Inc. board of directors from eight members to three. The board thereafter approved the gift of stock to the Foundation.

Theodora Holding Corp. then brought suit against certain individuals, including Girard Henderson, challenging the gift and seeking an accounting and the appointment of a liquidating receiver for Alexander Dawson, Inc.]

MARVEL, VICE CHANCELLOR.

Title 8 Del.C. § 122 provides as follows:

Every corporation created under this chapter shall have power to—

(9) Make donations for the public welfare or for charitable, scientific or educational purposes, and in time of war or other national emergency in aid thereof.

There is no doubt but that the Alexander Dawson Foundation is recognized as a legitimate charitable trust by the Department of Internal Revenue. It is also clear that it is authorized to operate exclusively in the fields of "religious, charitable, scientific, literary, or educational purposes, or for the prevention of cruelty to children or animals". Furthermore, contemporary courts recognize that unless corporations carry an increasing share of the burden of supporting charitable and educational causes that the business advantages now reposed in corporations by law may well prove to be unacceptable to the representatives of an aroused public. The recognized obligation of corporations towards philanthropic, educational and artistic causes is reflected in the statutory law of all of the states, other than the states of Arizona and Idaho.

In *A.P. Smith Mfg. Co. v. Barlow*, 13 N.J. 145, 98 A.2d [581], appeal dismissed, 346 U.S. 861, 74 S.Ct. 107, 98 L.Ed. 373, a case in which the corporate donor had been organized long before the adoption of a statute authorizing corporate gifts to charitable or educational institutions, the Supreme Court of New Jersey upheld a gift of $1500 by the plaintiff corporation to Princeton University, being of the opinion that the trend towards the transfer of wealth from private industrial entrepreneurs to corporate institutions, the increase of taxes on individual income, coupled with steadily increasing philanthropic needs, necessitate corporate giving for educational needs even were there no statute permitting such gifts, and this was held to be the case apart from the question of the reserved power of the state to amend corporate charters. The court also noted that the gift tended to bolster the free enterprise system and the general social climate in which plaintiff was nurtured. And while the court pointed out that there was no showing that the gift in question was made indiscriminately or to a pet charity in furtherance of personal rather than corporate ends, the actual holding of the opinion appears to be that a corporate charitable or educational gift to be valid must merely be within reasonable limits both as to amount and purpose.

I conclude that the test to be applied in passing on the validity of a gift such as the one here in issue is that of reasonableness, a test in which the provisions of the Internal Revenue Code pertaining to charitable gifts by corporations furnish a helpful guide. The gift here under attack was made from gross income and had a value as of the time of giving of $528,000 in a year in which Alexander Dawson, Inc.'s total income was $19,144,229.06, or well within the federal tax deduction limitation of 5% of such income. The contribution under attack can be said to have "cost" all of the stockholders of Alexander Dawson, Inc. including plaintiff, less than $80,000, or some fifteen cents per dollar of contribution, taking into consideration the federal tax provisions applicable to holding companies as well as the provisions for compulsory distribution of dividends received by such a corporation. In addition, the gift, by reducing Alexander Dawson, Inc.'s reserve for unrealized capital gains taxes by some $130,000, increased the balance sheet net worth of stockholders of the corporate defendant by such amount. It is accordingly obvious, in my opinion, that the relatively small loss of immediate income otherwise payable to plaintiff and the corporate defendant's other stockholders had it not been for the gift in question, is far out-weighed by the overall benefits flowing from the placing of such gift in channels where it serves to benefit those in need of philanthropic or educational support, thus providing justification for large private holdings, thereby benefiting plaintiff in the long run. Finally, the fact that the interests of the Alexander Dawson Foundation appear to be increasingly directed towards the rehabilitation and education of deprived but deserving young people is peculiarly appropriate in an age when a large segment of youth is alienated even from parents who are not entirely satisfied with our present social and economic system.

On notice, an order in conformity with the holdings of this opinion may be presented.

KAHN V. SULLIVAN
594 A.2d 48 (Del. 1991).

HOLLAND, JUSTICE:

[The case involves a challenge to a decision by the board of directors of Occidental Petroleum Corporation to make a charitable donation to construct and fund an art museum to house some of the collection of

Armand Hammer, Occidental's chief executive officer and chairman of the board. The collection was extremely valuable and had been exhibited throughout the world for many years prior to the decision to make the donation. Occidental shareholders brought a derivative suit that challenged the validity of the gift. Prior to trial, the parties agreed to a settlement whose terms required approval by the Court of Chancery. Despite the objections of some shareholders, the court approved the settlement.]

On December 15, 1988, the Board was presented with a detailed plan for the Museum proposal. The Board approved the concept and authorized a complete study of the proposal. Following the December 15th Board meeting, the law firm of Dilworth, Paxson, Kalish & Kauffman ("Dilworth") was retained by the Board to examine the Museum proposal and to prepare a memorandum addressing the issues relevant to the Board's consideration of the proposal.[6] The law firm of Skadden, Arps, Slate, Meagher & Flom ("Skadden Arps") was retained to represent the new legal entity which would be necessitated by the Museum proposal. Occidental's public accountants, Arthur Andersen & Co. ("Arthur Andersen"), were also asked to examine the Museum proposal.

On or about February 6, 1989, ten days prior to the Board's prescheduled February 16 meeting, Dilworth provided each member of the Board with a ninety-six page memorandum. It contained a definition of the Museum proposal and the anticipated magnitude of the proposed charitable donation by Occidental. It reviewed the authority of the Board to approve such a donation and the reasonableness of the proposed donation. The Dilworth memorandum included an analysis of the donation's effect on Occidental's financial condition, the potential for good will and other benefits to Occidental, and a comparison of the proposed charitable contribution by Occidental to the charitable contributions of other corporations.

During the February 16 Board meeting, a Dilworth representative personally presented the basis for that law firm's analysis of the Museum proposal, as set forth in its February 6 written memorandum. Following the Dilworth presentation, the Board resolved to appoint the Special Committee, comprised of its eight independent and disinterested outside directors, to further review and to act upon the Museum proposal. The Board then adjourned to allow the Special Committee to meet.

The Special Committee consisted of individuals who collectively had approximately eighty years of service on Occidental's board of directors. Those Board members were not officers of Occidental, and were not associated with the Museum or the Foundation.

---

[6]   At the time of its selection, Dilworth also represented Dr. Hammer personally.

The minutes of the February 16, 1989 meeting of the Special Committee outline its consideration of the Museum proposal. Those minutes reflect that many questions were asked by members of the Special Committee and were answered by the representatives of Dilworth, Skadden Arps, or Arthur Andersen. As a result of its own extensive discussions, and in reliance upon the experts' opinions, the Special Committee concluded that the establishment of the Museum, adjacent to Occidental's corporate offices in Los Angeles, would provide benefits to Occidental for at least the thirty-year term of the lease. The Special Committee also concluded that the proposed museum would establish a new cultural landmark for the City of Los Angeles.

On February 16, 1989, the Special Committee unanimously approved the Museum proposal, [which committed Occidental to spend more than $85 million for a museum, to be identified as "The Armand Hammer Museum of Art and Cultural Center," to which the Art collection would be transferred. Occidental would receive public recognition for its role in establishing the Museum by the naming of the courtyard, library, or auditorium of the museum for Occidental.]

On April 25, 1989, Occidental reported the Special Committee's approval of the Museum proposal to its shareholders in the proxy statement for its annual meeting to be held May 26, 1989. On May 2, 1989, the first shareholder action ("the Kahn action") was filed, challenging Occidental's decision to establish and fund the Museum proposal. The Sullivan action was filed on May 9, 1989.

On June 9, 1989, the plaintiffs in the Kahn action moved for a preliminary injunction to enjoin the proposed settlement in the Sullivan action and also for expedited discovery.

In denying the motion for injunctive relief, the Court of Chancery identified six issues to be addressed at any future settlement hearing:

> (1) the failure of the Special Committee appointed by the directors of Occidental to hire its own counsel and advisors or even to formally approve the challenged acts; (2) the now worthlessness of a prior donation by Occidental to the Los Angeles County Museum; (3) the huge attorney fees which the parties have apparently decided to seek or not oppose; (4) the egocentric nature of some of Armand Hammer's objections to the Los Angeles County Museum being the recipient of his donation; (5) the issue of who really owns the art; and (6) the lack of any direct substantial benefit to the stockholders.

At its July 20 meeting, the Special Committee also reviewed the July 19, 1989 decision and order of the Court of Chancery denying Kahn's request for injunctive relief in the Sullivan action. In response to one of the concerns expressed by the Court of Chancery, the Special Committee resolved to retain independent Delaware counsel with no prior connection to Occidental or its officers.

The parties to the Sullivan action presented the Court of Chancery with a fully executed Stipulation of Compromise, Settlement and Release agreement ("the Settlement") on January 24, 1990. [The Settlement provided substantial recognition of Occidental for its donation, the loan and ultimate transfer of all of Hammer's collections to the Museum, a limit of $50–$60 million on Occidental's contributions and payment of plaintiffs' attorneys fees not to exceed $1.4 million.]

On August 7, 1990, the Court of Chancery found the Settlement to be reasonable under all of the circumstances. The Court of Chancery concluded that the claims asserted by the shareholder plaintiffs would likely be dismissed before or after trial. While noting its own displeasure with the Settlement, the Court of Chancery explained that its role in reviewing the proposed Settlement was restricted to determining in its own business judgment whether, on balance, the Settlement was reasonable.[23] The Court opined that although the benefit to be received from the Settlement was meager, it was adequate considering all the facts and circumstances.

In an appeal from the Court of Chancery, following the approval of a settlement of a class action, the function of this Court is more limited in its nature. This Court does not review the record to determine the intrinsic fairness of the settlement in light of its own business judgment. This Court reviews the record "solely for the purpose of determining whether or not the Court of Chancery abused its discretion by the exercise of its business judgment."

The proponents of the Settlement argued that the business judgment rule could undoubtedly have been invoked successfully by the defendants as a complete defense to the shareholder plaintiffs' claims. The Objectors presented several alternative arguments in support of their contention that the shareholder plaintiffs would have been able to rebut the defense based on the protection which the presumption of the business judgment rule provides.

---

[23] The Court of Chancery noted:

Despite this Court's expressed displeasure with the settlement efforts, as set forth in its July 19, 1989 opinion in Kahn, the settlement now before the Court is only slightly changed from the June 3, 1989 Memorandum of Understanding.

[Therefore] the settlement in the Court's opinion leaves much to be desired. The Court's role in reviewing the proposed Settlement, however, is quite restricted. If the Court was a stockholder of Occidental it might vote for new directors, if it was on the Board it might vote for new management and if it was a member of the Special Committee it might vote against the Museum project. But its options are limited in reviewing a proposed settlement to applying Delaware law to the facts adduced in the record and then determining in its business judgment whether, on balance, the settlement is reasonable.

The Court of Chancery carefully considered each of the Objectors' arguments in response to the merits of the suggested business judgment rule defense. It concluded that if the Sullivan action proceeded, it was highly probable in deciding a motion to dismiss, a motion for summary judgment, or a post-trial motion, the actions of "the Special Committee would be protected by the presumption of propriety afforded by the business judgment rule." Specifically, the Court of Chancery concluded that it would have been decided that the Special Committee, comprised of Occidental's outside directors, was independent and made an informed decision to approve the charitable donation to the Museum proposal. These conclusions by the Court of Chancery are supported by the record and are the product of an orderly and logical deductive process.

Following its analysis and conclusion that the business judgment rule would have been applicable to any judicial examination of the Special Committee's actions, the Court of Chancery considered the shareholder plaintiffs' claim that the Board and the Special Committee's approval of the charitable donation to the Museum proposal constituted a waste of Occidental's corporate assets. In doing so, it recognized that charitable donations by Delaware corporations are expressly authorized by 8 Del.C. § 122(9). It also recognized that although § 122(9) places no limitations on the size of a charitable corporate gift, that section has been construed "to authorize any reasonable corporate gift of a charitable or educational nature." *Theodora Holding Corp. v. Henderson*, Del.Ch., 257 A.2d 398, 405 (1969). Thus, the Court of Chancery concluded that the test to be applied in examining the merits of a claim alleging corporate waste "is that of reasonableness, a test in which the provisions of the Internal Revenue Code pertaining to charitable gifts by corporations furnish a helpful guide." We agree with that conclusion.

The Objectors argued that Occidental's charitable contribution to the Museum proposal was unreasonable and a waste of corporate assets because it was excessive. The Court of Chancery recognized that not every charitable gift constitutes a valid corporate action. Nevertheless, the Court of Chancery concluded, given the net worth of Occidental, its annual net income before taxes, and the tax benefits to Occidental, that the gift to the Museum was within the range of reasonableness established in *Theodora Holding Corp. v. Henderson*. Therefore, the Court of Chancery found that it was "reasonably probable" that plaintiffs would fail on their claim of waste. That finding is supported by the record and is the product of an orderly and logical deductive process.

In examining the Settlement, the Court of Chancery evaluated not only the nature of the shareholder plaintiffs' claims but also the possible defenses to those claims. After carefully evaluating the parties' respective legal positions, the Court of Chancery opined that "the [shareholder plaintiffs'] potential for ultimate success on the merits [in the Sullivan action] is, realistically, very poor."

After considering the legal and factual circumstances of the case *sub judice*, the Court of Chancery examined the value of the Settlement.

The Court of Chancery characterized the proponents' efforts to quantify the monetary value of most of the Settlement benefits as "speculative." The Court of Chancery also viewed the estimate that naming the building for Occidental would have a ten million dollar value to Occidental with "a good deal of skepticism." Nevertheless, the Court of Chancery found that Occidental would, in fact, receive an economic benefit in the form of good will from the charitable donation to the Museum proposal. It also found that Occidental would derive an economic benefit from being able to utilize the Museum, adjacent to its corporate headquarters, in the promotion of its business.

Finally, the Court of Chancery applied its own independent business judgment in deciding whether the Settlement was fair and reasonable. The Court of Chancery found that "the benefit [of the Settlement] to the stockholders of Occidental is sufficient to support the Settlement and is adequate, if only barely so, when compared to the weakness of the plaintiffs' claims." The Court of Chancery concluded that "although the Settlement is meager, it is adequate considering all the facts and circumstances."

The reasonableness of a particular class action settlement is addressed to the discretion of the Court of Chancery, on a case by case basis, in light of all of the relevant circumstances. In this case, we find that all of the Court of Chancery's factual findings of fact are supported by the record. We also find that all of the legal conclusions reached by the Court of Chancery were based upon a proper application of well established principles of law. Consequently, we find that the Court of Chancery did not abuse its discretion in deciding to approve the Settlement in the Sullivan action. Therefore, the decision of the Court of Chancery is Affirmed.

Dr. Hammer's decision to renege on his oral promise to donate the Art Collection to LACMA was precipitated by LACMA's rejection of his insistence that an entire floor of LACMA's Frances and Armand Hammer Building be remodeled to house the Art Collection and that the names of other donors, currently inscribed over galleries on that floor, be removed. Consequently, LACMA and Dr. Hammer never discussed other demands that LACMA found objectionable, such as that the main entrance to the floor be outfitted with a full length portrait of Hammer, that each work in the Collection be separately identified as donated by Hammer, that LACMA never sell any of the works in the Collection, that the collection be exhibited together on the special floor, and that no other works be exhibited with the Collection.

Dr. Hammer dominated Occidental from the time he took control of the company until his death at age 92. Until 1980, when the SEC discovered the practice and objected to it, Dr. Hammer required that every person elected to Occidental's board sign and deliver to him an undated letter of resignation. At least five of the eight members of the Special Committee joined the board prior to the time he discontinued this practice. Dr. Hammer also apparently viewed himself as indispensible to Occidental's success. He dismissed four experienced executives hired by Occidental as his potential successor, concluding that none of them were up to the job.

While Occidental agreed to pay counsel fees to the Sullivan plaintiffs of up to $1.4 million, the Vice-Chancellor awarded a fee of only $800,000, reflecting, to some degree, his skepticism about the merits of the settlement. *See Sullivan v. Hammer*, [CCH] Fed. Sec. L. Rep. & 95,415, 1990 WL 114223 (Del.Ch.1990). Counsel for the other plaintiffs, however, were awarded no fees for their efforts.

On Hammer's death, Time Magazine's obituary made the following observations:

> In life, which he departed in December at the age of 92, Hammer was a textbook case of furor Americanus: a bullying blowhard with an ego like a Mack truck, whose main aim was to parlay a genius for negotiation (which he had) into a Nobel Peace Prize (which, luckily for the prestige of that award, he never got).

> Nowhere was Hammer's rage for fame more obtrusive than in his role as a collector of old masters and Impressionists, which he flew around the world as promotion for Oxy and himself. Hammer's proudest feat was his 1980 purchase, for $5.12 million (a big price then), of a manuscript by Leonardo da Vinci called the Codex Leicester, which he renamed the Codex Hammer.

> [After the LACM finally turned him down,] Hammer announced, he would make his gift to the world in the form of his own museum.

> The building cost $60 million; the endowment fund is $38 million. It is a tribute to his gall that Hammer managed to get Oxy to pay out such sums, when he owned less than 1% of Oxy stock, on the questionable ground that the museum would pump up the company's prestige.

> Before his death, Hammer claimed the collection was worth $450 million, but most of it is junk: a mishmash of second- or third-rate work by famous names.

Robert Hughes, *America's Vainest Museum*, Time Magazine (January 28, 1991).

2. PERSPECTIVES ON CORPORATE CHARITY

In the early 1900s, many courts held that corporate charitable contributions were ultra vires, *i.e.*, beyond the powers granted by the articles of incorporation with respect to the operation of the corporation's business. In response to these decisions, every state amended its corporate law to explicitly authorize such contributions without limiting that authority to donations that could be viewed as increasing corporate profits.

If the business judgment rule protects directors from liability for decisions that do not enhance corporate profits, why were these statutes necessary? Professor Einer Elhauge argues:

> The answer seems to be simply that it was only in the donative area that an explicit legal statement was necessary. For operational decisions, the managerial authority to run the corporation subject only to deferential business judgment rule review had historically give managers enough discretion to have their operational decisions molded by social and moral forces. An explicit legislative statement was thus not necessary to preserve this discretion. In contrast, because many courts were striking down corporate donations under the ultra vires doctrine, legislatures had to enact statutes making the corporate power to donate explicit if they wanted to preserve this profit-sacrificing managerial discretion.

Einer Elhauge, *Sacrificing Corporate Profits in the Public Interest*, 80 N.Y.U. L.Rev. 733, 839 (2005).

> For Elhauge, the conclusion is clear.

> [G]iven that such donation authority clearly does exist, operational decisions in the public interest should also be authorized. If managers had donation authority but not operational authority, managers who wanted to advance public interest causes would simply substitute donations for profit-sacrificing operational decision, and the limitation on the latter would tend to cause them to the former even when the latter is more efficient.

Recent commentators have increasingly argued that charitable contributions are little more than disguised advertising that is designed to make the corporation seem more socially responsible:

> When a corporation voluntarily engages in socially responsible activity, it does so to advertise its behavior, differentiate its produce, increase its market share, and boost profits. For

example, enter any Starbucks and you are surrounded by advertisements explaining how socially conscious Starbucks is. BP is now "Beyond Petroleum" in an attempt to persuade consumers that the firm is not "Big Oil." The list goes on and on, begging, the question, is there a difference between traditional advertising and advertising a company's socially responsible behavior? Both are attempts to increase sales and profits. A firm would no sooner make an anonymous donation to charity than it would buy 30 seconds of silence on the radio.

Andrew C. Coors & Wayne Winegarden, *"Corporate Social Responsibility —Or Good Advertising?"* Regulation (Spring, 2005).

If that argument is correct, should shareholders have a greater voice in corporate charitable contributions? Professors Victor Brudney and Allan Ferrell have proposed changing the existing corporate decision making process so that shareholders will have such a voice. Victor Brudney & Allan G. Ferrell, *Corporate Charitable Giving*, 69 U. Chicago L. Rev. 1191 (2002). Under their plan, the board of directors would decide the amount of money that the corporation would distribute as goodwill giving in a particular year. The board would then allow the company's shareholders to select the beneficiaries of the donation. The company could donate only to the causes that the shareholders chose and to no others.

Brudney and Ferrell defend this "shareholder choice" proposal on several grounds. First, they observe that corporate charitable giving is a discrete expenditure. Unlike most corporate expenditures which involve integrated operational decisions, donations that seek to create goodwill (gifts given to universities, museums, or social service enterprises), have little, if any, direct effect on the company's business activities. Moreover, unlike corporate decisions that seek to enhance corporate profit, no special managerial competence is required to select the beneficiaries of charitable donations. As Brudney and Ferrell explain, corporate charitable giving essentially is a moral choice about what kind of "good" society needs or should have. The board does not have any special moral competence to make such choices, at least with assets that are not "its." Additionally, Brudney and Ferrell argue that if the justification of corporate philanthropy is that it satisfies the corporation's debt to society, shareholders should decide how to satisfy that debt since they have a greater claim over the company's assets.

Brudney and Ferrell recognize that there are tradeoffs in allowing shareholders a greater voice. First, they note that there may be a diluting effect on the value of the goodwill claimed for such gifts. They predict that individual stockholders would not make as large an aggregate contribution to charitable enterprises as would corporate management. There is also a concern that by mandating deference to shareholders, the board might decline to approve as much charitable giving because it could not choose the recipients and because it would lose the satisfaction (and the benefits) it currently receives from gifting to particular beneficiaries. These factors, they note, could produce a net reduction in the amounts charities receive from goodwill giving.

Shareholder choice may also redistribute corporate charitable contributions. Brudney and Ferrell predict that shareholder choice will result in a substantial portion of the corporate charitable funds being diverted to religious causes. Shareholders are also more likely than corporate managers to fund conservative causes, social services, and organizations that espouse more radical, social and political views. Brudney and Ferrell explain that corporate management is more constrained in its choice of recipients. Managers are also more likely to select charities that promote a "stable" climate for business. Managers are also more likely to select beneficiaries that the government is under popular pressure to fund to avoid unpopular regulatory and burdensome tax consequences. Finally, the management culture imposes its own limitations on management's conception of "worthy" recipients.

In 2008, individuals' charitable contributions totaled 75% of all contributions while corporate charitable giving, including corporate foundations, accounted for 5%. Corporate contributions averaged less than 2% of pretax profits. The reasons for corporate generosity are not entirely altruistic; the Internal Revenue Code permits corporations to deduct charitable contributions up to 10 percent of their taxable income when they compute their taxes.

The recent financial crisis and stock market decline has exacerbated the continuing decline in certain types of corporate charitable giving and the long-range consequences of reduced corporate giving remain unclear, particularly for certain types of non-profit organizations. The following stories describe the change in one company's contributions from 1999 to 2007 and the changed emphasis in the justification for those contributions. For better or for worse (and you should decide which), the latter story accurately reflects much contemporary corporate behavior.

In 1999 Phillip Morris (now Altria) donated $60 million to charitable programs including hunger relief, domestic violence, and fine arts. In an effort to rebuild its image, it launched a $100 million program to highlight the company's goodwill efforts:

> In fighting on so many fronts, the [tobacco] industry has spread its cash far beyond its traditional campaign contributions and large infusions of soft money to the Republican Party. In Washington, in state capitals, and even down to the city and county levels, the tobacco companies have expended vast resources on lobbying. They've supported whole armies of attorneys, consultants, and expert witnesses. They've lavishly funded political allies, ranging from conservative think tanks like

the Cato Institute, the Heritage Foundation, the Washington Legal Foundation, and the Progress & Freedom Foundation to liberal groups like the American Civil Liberties Union. They've sponsored sports events, from airy Virginia Slims tennis tournaments to gritty NASCAR races. And recently, worried about increasing restrictions on tobacco advertising, they've funded the start-up of entirely new, corporate-sponsored magazines, in which, of course, they impose no advertising restrictions on themselves.

The money Philip Morris spends on charitable, educational, and cultural institutions may not look like it's part of that same war chest. But antismoking activists say that the company's corporate giving program is an integral part of its defense strategy. Not only do such contributions provide Philip Morris with a veneer of respectability, but critics worry that by carefully choosing the recipients of million-dollar grants the company is quietly buying the neutrality and, in some cases, the grudging support of important parts of the American body politic.

"They're buying silence," says [Cliff] Douglas [an attorney who has fought big tobacco companies for years]. "For years, the health community, in its effort to combat tobacco, has sought the buying of many affected communities and has had great difficulty enlisting their support." Citing Philip Morris contributions over the years to groups like the NAACP, the Urban League, the National Organization for Women, the National Council of La Raza, and many others, Douglas says, "Many of them were either silent or provided testimony to Congress opposing tobacco-control legislation."

An ace in the hole for Philip Morris is its long-standing relationship with the highbrow fine arts community. For decades the company has provided substantial support to leading institutions like New York's Whitney Museum of American Art and the Solomon R. Guggenheim Museum, Philip Morris's partnership with the Whitney began in 1967, perhaps not coincidentally just after the first report of the U.S. surgeon general on the cancer-causing nature of tobacco smoke. In 1983 the two established the Whitney Museum of American Art at Philip Morris, housed in the tobacco company's New York world headquarters. Over the years, the company has funneled millions of dollars to icons of the New York cultural establishment, including the Lincoln Center—which in the 1980s handed out cigarettes in bags of favors to patrons—the Joffrey Ballet, the Brooklyn Academy of Music, the American Ballet Theater, and the Brooklyn Museum of Art, among others.

On occasion, there's been an explicit quid pro quo. In 1994, when the New York City Council was considering restrictions on smoking in public places, Philip Morris threatened to leave the city-taking its arts funding with it—and the company leaned on grantees to join it in opposing the bill; some did. And when Philip Morris tried to wrap itself in the Bill of Rights by sponsoring a nationwide celebration of that constitutional document, among those appearing prominently in the company's campaign was Judith Jamison, artistic director of the Alvin Ailey American Dance Theater.

Robert Dreyfuss, *'Philip Morris Money'* 3/27/00 American Prospect 2022.

Times have changed. Consider how Altria now views funding the arts.

When the Altria Group announced in the fall that it was planning to spin off its Kraft Foods division, Wall Street cheered. But among cultural institutions, the response was considerably less upbeat: as part of the restructuring, Altria, formerly Philip Morris, is phasing out its significant support for the arts, which has funneled $210 million to cultural groups over the last four decades.

"It's the end of an era," said Sharon Gersten Luckman, the executive director of Alvin Ailey American Dance Theater. "Altria and Philip Morris supported dance and Ailey for over 25 years. They were at the forefront. There wouldn't be an Ailey if it weren't for them."

Altria's decision is just part of the changing landscape of corporate financing of the arts. Over the last decade, the portion of corporate philanthropy dedicated to the arts has dropped by more than half, according to the Giving USA Foundation, an educational and research program of the American Association of Fundraising Counsel. In 2004, the most recent year for which figures are available, support for the arts was 4 percent of total corporate philanthropy, compared with 9.5 percent in 1994—part of a general shift in giving toward health and social services.

When companies do support culture, they are increasingly paying for it out of their marketing budgets, which means strings are attached to the funds: from how a corporation's name will appear in promotional materials, to what parties it can give during an exhibition, to the number of free or discounted tickets available to its employees.

"Corporations are not Medicis; they never have been, they're not supposed to be," said Nancy Perkins, a senior vice president at

Payne, Forrester & Associates, fund-raising consultants. "They're not in business to be philanthropic."

As a lead sponsor of City Center's Fall for Dance program over the three years of its existence, Time Warner had its logo splashed on everything from 160,000 festival brochures to 150,000 regular-season brochures to 400 subway posters and 5,500 bus ads. Its gift was in the six figures, City Center said, declining to be more specific.

Arlene Shuler, president and chief executive of City Center, said providing this kind of exposure for a major sponsor was not a problem. In fact, she said, it was City Center's idea to put the Time Warner logo on every ticket envelope. "We are very aware of the kind of recognition they deserve," she said.

Time Warner was also happy with the deal, said Lisa Quiroz, the company's senior vice president for corporate responsibility. Time Warner gives to arts groups whose activities have "a direct connection to our business," she said, and Fall for Dance brought in audiences of different ages and ethnicities, one of the company's goals.

"It's becoming increasingly metrics-driven: you've got to show how your money has been leveraged and how that's been to the benefit of your company," Ms. Quiroz said. "Ten years ago, you didn't hear people talking about measuring the impact of your dollars."

Robin Pogrebin, "As Corporate Support Shifts Its Focus, Arts Organizations Are Adjusting," New York Times (February 21, 2007) p.B1.

Perhaps the problem of accountability for charitable contributions is exacerbated by the fact that neither the federal securities laws nor state corporate law require that such contributions be disclosed to the shareholders. This lack of disclosure, coupled with the broad standards of a decision such as *Theodora Holding*, gives corporate managers wide latitude with relatively little effective monitoring when they exercise that discretion.

Proponents of greater accountability argue that greater disclosure would enable stakeholders to monitor managers' performance more effectively. Those who oppose this point of view contend that corporations should be concerned exclusively with maximizing the profits they can earn within the law and that market forces, government regulation and the mechanisms of the corporate governance system, sufficiently constrain managers' discretion. There is also doubt that the SEC would be willing (or politically able) to require such disclosure. Former SEC Chairman, Richard Breeden has said, "[I]f I were still in government, I would not want to touch the issue of "regulating" corporate philanthropy with a 500 foot pole."

E. BENEFIT CORPORATIONS

A significant development in corporate social responsibility is the creation of a new type of business entity, the benefit corporation or "B Corp." Under model benefit corporation legislation, directors, in addition to having a fiduciary duty to shareholders, also have a legal duty to other stakeholder interests including employees, suppliers, customers, society and the environment. For more on benefit corporations and the model legislation *see* http://www.benefitcorp.org.

Benefit corporations operate in the same way as regular business corporations. They engage in ordinary commercial activities and can issue stock to finance their operations. At the same time, the legislation to which they are subject imposes different governance requirements.

Although state benefit corporation statutes vary, there is a commonality to them. Such statutes require that benefit corporations have a stated purpose of creating a "general public benefit" that the corporations are permitted to identify in their articles of incorporation. Examples would include (but not be limited to) preserving the environment; improving human health; promoting the arts, sciences or the advancement of knowledge; or providing low-income or underserved individuals or communities with beneficial products or services.

Directors of benefit corporations are required to consider a broader range of stakeholder interests than would be the case in an ordinary business corporation. Among other interests, they must consider the interests of shareholders, employees and the workplace, customers, community and societal factors and the local and global environment. The corporation itself must deliver an annual benefit report to the shareholders, post it on its website and file it with the state. That report must include, among other disclosures, an assessment of the overall social and environmental performance of the benefit corporation against an independent third-party standard.

The first benefit corporation statute was enacted in 2010. As of the date of this casebook, approximately 18 states have adopted such legislation and it is being considered by at least 15 more states. *See* Andrew Kassoy, Bart Houlahan & Joel Coen Gilbert, Impact governance and management: Fulfilling the promise of capitalism to achieve a shared and durable prosperity (2016), available at http://www.brookings.edu/research/papers/2016/07/01-b-corporations-kassoy-houlahan-gilbert. The nonprofit B Lab has certified over 1,700 corporations around the world as meeting its defined standards for true B Corps, They include such well-known names as Ben & Jerry's, Method Products, Honest Company, Warby Parker; Kickstarter, HootSuite, Seventh Generation, Patagonia and Triodos Bank.

The Delaware public benefit corporation statute, enacted in 2013, differs from the model statute in several significant aspects. While the model statute specifies the interests that the directors must consider, Delaware requires only that directors "consider the interests of those materially affected by the operation of the corporation, in addition to the pecuniary interests of the stockholders of a Delaware corporation." Further, while the model statute requires that the benefit report be given to the general public, Delaware limits the reporting requirements simply to the shareholders. There is also no requirement in Delaware that the report assess the corporation's performance against a third-party standard instead of being self-reported.

While the B Corp movement represents a significant milestone in the history of corporate social responsibility, the extent of its practical impact on the business community is so far unclear. Neither *Dodge v. Ford* nor *eBay* should be read to prevent directors and managers of for profit corporations from taking social considerations into account in managing their businesses. While *eBay* might well have come out differently had craigslist been organized as a B Corp, Chancellor Chandler seems to suggest that as long as Craig and Jim continue to control the board of directors, ordinary Delaware corporate law gives their operational decisions the protection of the business judgment rule, leaving them free to continue to operate the company as they wish. The corporate statutes of Delaware and most other states already authorize many of the things that are permitted in benefit corporation statutes. *See, e.g.,* MBCA 3.02 (13) (corporations have the power "to make donations for the public welfare or for charitable, scientific, or educational purposes").

F. THE ROLE OF THE LAWYER

The corporate scandals in the early 2000s often involved complex financial transactions that were difficult to understand even after they became publicly known. In many cases, such transactions could not have been undertaken without the assistance of skilled professionals, particularly lawyers and accountants. As Judge Stanley Sporkin said in talking of an earlier financial fraud:

> Where were these professionals when these clearly improper actions were being consummated? Why didn't any of them speak up or disassociate themselves from the transaction? Where also were the outside accountants and attorneys when these transactions were effectuated? What is difficult to understand is that with all the professional talent involved (both accounting and legal) why at least one professional would not have blown the whistle to stop the overreaching that took place in this case.

Lincoln Savings & Loan Association v. Wall, 743 F.Supp. 901, 920 (D.D.C.1990).

Enron and other scandals renewed the focus on the lawyer's role in financial frauds. Professor Milton C. Regan. Jr. has observed that transactional lawyers face a distinctive ethical challenge because their stock in trade is the creative manipulation of legal form. The law's tolerance of some divergence between legal form and economic substance has helped to create a background assumption that such divergence is normal and not problematic. As Professor Regan notes, however, a point is reached where the divergence becomes wide enough that the law will treat it as fraud. To understand the lawyer's role in Enron, he argues that lawyers must appreciate the complexity of the ethical judgments that Enron's counsel faced and to imagine the world as these lawyers may have seen it at the time the events unfolded. As he explains, "proposed transactions don't come labeled as problematic and intricate legal structures rarely are obviously fraudulent." How might Enron's lawyers have interpreted information that in retrospect seems incriminating? To what situational cues were they sensitive or blind, and why? What precisely does it mean to say that Enron's lawyers "blessed," "signed off" on, or "approved" the company's transactions? Milton C. Regan, Jr. *Teaching Enron*, 74 Fordham L. Rev. 1139 (2005).

The following materials consider the lawyer's responsibilities—legal, professional, ethical and moral—for the transactions in which their corporate clients engage. The materials raise the broader question of what it means to be a corporate lawyer in differing contexts. That is a recurring question in this casebook and, ultimately, in your professional life.

Problem: Exogen, Inc.—Part 2

Assume you are in-house general counsel at Exogen; and the CEO comes to you and asks for your advice on how to deal with the Durasol problem. He tells you that someone has suggested to him that the company proceed with the legal strategy outlined described in Part 1, above. How would you respond? Are you being asked for legal advice or something else?

Assume now that you are a partner in an outside law firm that is the principal outside counsel for Exogen, and the in-house counsel asks about the legal strategy outlined above. How would you respond? To what extent, if any, would your advice change if you were a partner in a law firm that Exogen is considering retaining for the first time in this matter?

AMERICAN BAR ASSOCIATION, MODEL RULES OF PROFESSIONAL CONDUCT

(2002).

Rule 2.1   Advisor

In representing a client, a lawyer shall exercise independent professional judgment and render candid advice. In rendering advice, a lawyer may refer not only to law but to other considerations such as moral, economic, social and political factors, that may be relevant to the client's situation.

COMMENT

[1] A client is entitled to straightforward advice expressing the lawyer's honest assessment. Legal advice often involves unpleasant facts and alternatives that a client may be disinclined to confront. In presenting advice, a lawyer endeavors to sustain the client's morale and may put advice in as acceptable a form as honesty permits. However, a lawyer should not be deterred from giving candid advice by the prospect that the advice will be unpalatable to the client.

[2] Advice couched in narrowly legal terms may be of little value to a client, especially where practical considerations, such as cost or effects on other people, are predominant. Purely technical legal advice, therefore, can sometimes be inadequate. It is proper for a lawyer to refer to relevant moral and ethical considerations in giving advice. Although a lawyer is not a moral advisor as such, moral and ethical considerations impinge upon most legal questions and may decisively influence how the law will be applied.

[3] A client may expressly or impliedly ask the lawyer for purely technical advice. When such a request is made by a client experienced in legal matters, the lawyer may accept it at face value. When such a request is made by a client inexperienced in legal matters, however, the lawyer's responsibility as advisor may include indicating that more may be involved than strictly legal considerations.

. . .

[5] In general, a lawyer is not expected to give advice until asked by the client. However, when a lawyer knows that a client proposes a course of action that is likely to result in substantial adverse legal consequences to the client, the lawyer's duty to the client under Rule 1.4 may require that the lawyer offer advice if the client's course of action is related to the representation.

HON. POTTER STEWART, PROFESSIONAL ETHICS FOR THE BUSINESS LAWYER: THE MORALS OF THE MARKETPLACE
31 Bus.Law. 463 (1975).

It goes without saying, of course, that every lawyer has a duty to keep the confidences of his client, that every lawyer in whom is confided a trust must conduct himself as a trustee, that every lawyer should keep his word and deal honorably in all his associations. And it certainly is the duty of every lawyer and every association of lawyers, to denounce and to eliminate from our midst those who have betrayed our profession for their own ugly or dishonest purposes.

But beyond these and a few other self-evident precepts of decency and common sense, a good case can be made, I think, for the proposition that the ethics of the business lawyer are indeed, and perhaps should be, no more than the morals of the market place. The first rule for a business lawyer is to provide his total ability and effort to his client. But is this an ethical standard, or no more than a response to the economic forces of the market place? After all, the first rule in any occupation is to be competent. The business lawyer is in the business of providing legal advice for a businessman. If he performs that job with diligence, conscientiousness, and knowledgeable ability, his client will reap the benefits and reward him accordingly. If not, unless he is particularly lucky or married to the boss' daughter, the lawyer will find his client less than eager to retain indefinitely a professional adviser who habitually directs him down the wrong path.

In short, it can fairly be argued that many aspects of what we call "ethics" are not really ethics at all, but are merely corollaries of the axiom of the better mousetrap, an axiom that is itself derived from enlightened self-interest.

WILLIAM T. ALLEN, CORPORATE GOVERNANCE AND A BUSINESS LAWYER'S DUTY OF INDEPENDENCE
38 Suffolk U. L. Rev. 1 (2004).

This short essay addresses a topic important to both corporate governance and, perhaps more importantly, vital to the satisfaction that we lawyers can draw from our professional lives: our conception of the duties of a lawyer when she engages in advising and assisting corporate clients.

To whom do business lawyers owe duties and what is the nature of those duties? Rather than discussing external controls of the legal profession, such as licensing and lawyer disciplinary rules or processes, the topic of this essay is the internal or personal controls that a business lawyer may or should feel.

The loyalty that a lawyer owes extends beyond the duties to keep client's confidences, to give honest, competent advice unaffected by conflicting interests, and to exercise energy and imagination in pursuit of clients' lawful ends. Certainly these are a lawyer's core obligations in representing a client. But there is another aspect of a lawyer's duty that we do not much notice and have not for a long time—the duty of independence. The duty of independence is the lawyer's duty to the legal system itself and to the substantive values that it incorporates. This duty has its greatest role not in the defense of clients in court, but when business lawyers advise their clients with respect to prospective compliance with regulatory or private law and in structuring and disclosing material transactions.

The value of professional independence of judgment has always been reflected in our professional identity, but it has never been central to it. As lawyers, our main and favorite identification is as the loyal, energetic, and imaginative defender of clients: as zealous advocate.

The zealous advocacy ideal envisions the lawyer in a litigation setting. That setting, however, builds in powerful checks on the costs of the advocacy ideal. An adversary is represented by a lawyer. There are mandated discovery rights provided to both sides. Truth is tested by cross examination and a disinterested and expert judge will decide disputed questions. These factors make the costs of the zealous advocacy model in the litigation setting reasonable. But when the zealous advocacy mentality is adopted by business lawyers advising on law compliance, transaction planning, disclosure, and other advisory matters, none of these counter-balancing forces are present. In the business context, adoption of the zealous advocacy ideal is likely to give rise to unacceptable social costs.

In the short run, at least, a skilled lawyer who is willing to facilitate advantageous transactions that do not clearly and unarguably violate the law is useful to some clients. But the relative indeterminacy of many legal commands creates a very broad range over which a lawyer's imagination can roam. Unless legal advice and advocacy are rooted in principles finer than zealous advocacy, that conception can easily degenerate into socially wasteful conduct.

Dominated as we are today by the advocacy conception of what loyalty to clients means, it probably seems strange to consider the nature or scope of a business lawyer's duty of independence. But it was not always so. The old Canons of Professional Ethics of the City Bar Association of the City of New York, for example, reflected the value of a lawyer's moral autonomy quite explicitly. They stated, for example, that "the office of attorney does not permit, much less does it demand of him for any client, violation of law or any manner of fraud or chicanery." And, in the next sentence: "[A lawyer] must obey his own conscience and not that of his client." Under this principle, a lawyer's moral scruples should affect the decision to deploy a legal strategy. It is the lawyer's moral judgment, not that of the client, that acts as the final safeguard against lawyer involvement in socially destructive activity. In the end, clients may do as they choose. They may risk breaking the law. They may engage in action that violates the discernable spirit of the law, while arguably keeping to the letter. But business clients do not deserve the assistance of a lawyer in accomplishing such actions. Of course, lawyers owe loyalty to clients. They must be kept fully informed. Client confidences must be kept inviolate. They may at any time discharge a lawyer. But, in the vision that underlies the old City Bar Association code, lawyers are seen not as amoral tools of their clients, but as professionals who are morally responsible for the results that their actions help to bring about.

This is a morally attractive view of professional responsibility. It is reflected quite powerfully in the text of Canon 32 of the original 1908 Canons of Ethics of the American Bar Association:

"No client, corporate or individual, however powerful, nor any cause, civil or political, however important is entitled to receive, nor should any lawyer render, any service or advice involving disloyalty to the law . . . or deception or betrayal to the public . . . . The lawyer . . . advances the honor of his profession and the best interest of his client when he renders service or gives advice tending to impress upon the client, his undertaking exact compliance with the strictest principles of moral law. He must also observe the statute law, though until a statute shall have been construed and interpreted by competent adjudication, he is free and entitled to advise as to its validity and as to what he conscientiously believes to be its just meaning and extent."

This statement envisions lawyers who are not simple zealous advocates of their clients' legal interests, limited presently only by a command not to take frivolous positions. It calls upon lawyers to exercise independent judgment concerning the detectible spirit animating the law (that is, "what he conscientiously believes to be its just meaning and extent"). It also encourages a lawyer to "advance . . . the best interest of his client" through impressing upon the client "exact compliance with the strictest principles of moral law." Clearly, lawyers who satisfy these ideals were seen as independent actors: counselors who conceptualized their mission as guiding clients to comply with what these experts understood to be the best interpretation of the law.

Today, however, the formal organs of the profession fail to recognize this history or to acknowledge a professional duty of independence. The modern rules reflect our modern perspective. Lawyers are seen as zealous advocates with few duties to the public other than refraining from deceiving the court, lying on behalf of clients, or violating or facilitating the violation of law.

How do we explain this movement from the bar's acknowledgement in the early and mid-twentieth century of the moral autonomy of lawyers as a condition that co-existed with a lawyer's status as a loyal agent of her client? The answer lies not in the profession itself and its organization, but in the social conditions in which lawyers practice their craft. These circumstances differ vastly from those of forty or fifty years ago. Today, lawyers in private practice are more dependent upon their corporate clients and do not typically possess the leverage that lawyers previously had with such clients.

The conception of a lawyer [sic] independence is not canonical. It is the result of individual consideration. It is for everyone to formulate the

the more narrowly defined roles of "reputational intermediary" and "transaction cost engineer," are roles that lawyers willingly assume and the performance of which justifies a significant portion of their fees. Monitoring conduct often means monitoring the flow of information provided by clients to investors and regulators who trust the accuracy of clients' information because they trust the clients' lawyers. Responsibility not to betray trust that comes with these roles is part of the bargain. Corporate lawyers are not soldiers, and they are certainly not conscripts required to launch sneak attacks on unsuspecting victims at the whim of their clients.

Finally, lawyers should accept moral responsibility when they perform functions in corporate governance that they have chosen collectively as well as individually. The Berle-Means corporation that gives lawyers so much responsibility and so many opportunities to earn fees is the product of law as well as economics. Regulations, many of which have been drafted by lawyers, severely limit participation in corporate governance by nonshareholder constituencies and by many institutional shareholders, leaving these constituencies with primarily legal levers to control corporate conduct. Management, not to be outdone, has been provided with legal levers of its own. For lawyers to deny any responsibility when they pull these levers for clients is self serving to say the least.

Briefly, how is interdependent lawyering, or practicing law knowing that lawyers can be morally responsible for client conduct, different from the presumably independent lawyering illustrated by so many of the unfortunate examples discussed in this Article? First, if lawyers believe that ethical dilemmas of their clients can become their own, some lawyers may change the way they choose their clients. Legal representation might be allocated in part by moral commitments of lawyers in addition to by the market. Lawyers might also consider the merits of a particular client's transactional objectives relative to the objectives of others whom the lawyer could represent instead. Finally, the impact on lawyers' own moral character, and that of their partners and associates, from representing a particular client might be considered. Despite Lord Erskine's dire prediction, our liberties are unlikely to be threatened by the notion that everybody is not entitled to a lawyer for every purpose.

Interdependent lawyering might also involve giving more than legal advice. If clients contemplate leveraged buyouts, for example, lawyers could inform them of moral, political, and economic advantages of deals that increase long-term goodwill with the community, employees, and regulatory authorities, instead of deals that exclusively emphasize short-term profits. If clients contemplate discharging pollutants that Congress intended to prohibit but agency regulations arguably allow, lawyers could explain to clients that taking advantage of regulatory loopholes involves moral dilemmas, legal risk, and loss of reputation. They could also urge clients to consider the purpose as well as the letter of the law. When lawyers participate in client conduct and acknowledge that they are morally, if not legally, responsible for that conduct, such advice cannot rightfully be regarded as unwarranted intermeddling.

PART II

CLOSELY HELD ENTITIES

■ ■ ■

Part II is devoted to the law related to closely held business entities. Chapter 6 focuses on the close corporation and the issues practitioners must address in creating and structuring them. Chapter 7 discusses general partnerships and limited partnerships. Chapter 8 discusses the fastest growing type of closely-held entity, the limited liability company. These chapters discuss the key role of private ordering in this form.

CHAPTER 6

CLOSE CORPORATIONS

▪ ▪ ▪

A. INTRODUCTION

At the outset it is important to note that there is no generally accepted definition of a "close corporation." The following case discusses the nature of close corporations and the particular kinds of problems seen in them.

DONAHUE V. RODD ELECTROTYPE CO. OF NEW ENGLAND, INC.
328 N.E.2d 505 (Mass. 1975).

TAURO, CHIEF JUSTICE:

The plaintiff, Euphemia Donahue, a minority stockholder in the Rodd Electrotype Company of New England, Inc. (Rodd Electrotype), a Massachusetts corporation, brings this suit against the directors of Rodd Electrotype, Charles H. Rodd, Frederick I. Rodd and Mr. Harold E. Magnuson, against Harry C. Rodd, a former director, officer, and controlling stockholder of Rodd Electrotype and against Rodd Electrotype (hereinafter called defendants). The plaintiff seeks to rescind Rodd Electrotype's purchase of Harry Rodd's shares in Rodd Electrotype and to compel Harry Rodd "to repay to the corporation the purchase price of said shares, $36,000, together with interest from the date of purchase." The plaintiff alleges that the defendants caused the corporation to purchase the shares in violation of their fiduciary duty to her, a minority stockholder of Rodd Electrotype.

The trial judge, after hearing oral testimony, dismissed the plaintiff's bill on the merits. He found that the purchase was without prejudice to the plaintiff and implicitly found that the transaction had been carried out in good faith and with inherent fairness. The Appeals Court affirmed with costs.

[After several corporate and stock purchase transactions, Harry Rodd owned 200 shares of Rodd Electrotype and Joseph Donahue owned 50 shares. Subsequently, Harry engaged in a series of gifts to his three children, resulting in Charles Rodd, Frederick Rodd, and Phyllis Mason each owning 51 shares. The directors of the company (Charles, Frederick and the company's lawyer) authorized the president, Charles, to repurchase on behalf of the company 45 shares of Harry's stock for $800 per share ($36,000). This transaction divested Harry totally. When the

Donahues found about the stock repurchase, they sought to have the company repurchase their shares on equal terms as Harry received. The company refused to do so.]

In her argument before this court, the plaintiff has characterized the corporate purchase of Harry Rodd's shares as an unlawful distribution of corporate assets to controlling stockholders. She urges that the distribution constitutes a breach of the fiduciary duty owed by the Rodds, as controlling stockholders, to her, a minority stockholder in the enterprise, because the Rodds failed to accord her an equal opportunity to sell her shares to the corporation. The defendants reply that the stock purchase was within the powers of the corporation and met the requirements of good faith and inherent fairness imposed on a fiduciary in his dealings with the corporation. They assert that there is no right to equal opportunity in corporate stock purchases for the corporate treasury. For the reasons hereinafter noted, we agree with the plaintiff and reverse the decree of the Superior Court. However, we limit the applicability of our holding to 'close corporations,' as hereinafter defined. Whether the holding should apply to other corporations is left for decision in another case, on a proper record.

Close Corporations. In previous opinions, we have alluded to the distinctive nature of the close corporation, but have never defined precisely what is meant by a close corporation. There is no single, generally accepted definition. Some commentators emphasize an "integration of ownership and management." Others focus on the number of stockholders and the nature of the market for the stock. In this view, close corporations have few stockholders; there is little market for corporate stock. The Supreme Court of Illinois adopted this latter view: "For our purposes, a close corporation is one in which the stock is held in a few hands, or in a few families, and wherein it is not at all, or only rarely, dealt in by buying or selling." We accept aspects of both definitions. We deem a close corporation to the typified by: (1) a small number of stockholders; (2) no ready market for the corporate stock; and (3) substantial majority stockholder participation in the management, direction and operations of the corporation.

As thus defined, the close corporation bears striking resemblance to a partnership. Commentators and courts have noted that the close corporation is often little more than an "incorporated" or "chartered" partnership. The stockholders "clothe" their partnership "with the benefits peculiar to a corporation, limited liability, perpetuity and the like." In essence, though, the enterprise remains one in which ownership is limited to the original parties or transferees of their stock to whom the other stockholders have agreed, in which ownership and management are in the same hands, and in which the owners are quite dependent on one another for the success of the enterprise. Many close corporations are "really partnerships, between two or three people who contribute their capital, skills, experience and labor." Just as in a partnership, the relationship among the stockholders must be one of trust, confidence and absolute loyalty if the enterprise is to succeed. Close corporations with substantial assets and with more numerous stockholders are no different from smaller close corporations in this regard. All participants rely on the fidelity and abilities of those stockholders who hold office. Disloyalty and self-seeking conduct on the part of any stockholder will engender bickering, corporate stalemates, and, perhaps, efforts to achieve dissolution.

Although the corporate form provides the above-mentioned advantages for the stockholders (limited liability, perpetuity, and so forth), it also supplies an opportunity for the majority stockholders to oppress or disadvantage minority stockholders. The minority is vulnerable to a variety of oppressive devices, termed "freezeouts," which the majority may employ. An authoritative study of such "freeze-outs" enumerates some of the possibilities: "The squeezers (those who employ the freeze-out techniques) may refuse to declare dividends; they may drain off the corporation's earnings in the form of exorbitant salaries and bonuses to the majority shareholder-officers and perhaps to their relatives, or in the form of high rent by the corporation for property leased from majority shareholders . . . ; they may deprive minority shareholders of corporate offices and of employment by the company; they may cause the corporation to sell its assets at an inadequate price to the majority shareholders. . . ." In particular, the power of the board of directors, controlled by the majority, to declare or withhold dividends and to deny the minority employment is easily converted to a device to disadvantage minority stockholders.

The minority can, of course, initiate suit against the majority and their directors. Self-serving conduct by directors is proscribed by the director's fiduciary obligation to the corporation. However, in practice, the plaintiff will find difficulty in challenging dividend or employment policies. Such policies are considered to be within the judgment of the directors. This court has said: "The courts prefer not to interfere . . . with the sound financial management of the corporation by its directors, but declare as general rule that the declaration of dividends rests within the sound discretion of the directors, refusing to interfere with their determination unless a plain abuse of discretion is made to appear." Judicial reluctance to interfere combines with the difficulty of proof when the standard is "plain abuse of discretion" or bad faith to limit the possibilities for relief. Although contractual provisions in an "agreement of association and articles of organization" or in by-laws have justified decrees in this jurisdiction ordering dividend declarations, generally, plaintiffs who seek judicial assistance against corporate dividend or employment policies do not prevail.

Thus, when these types of "freeze-outs" are attempted by the majority stockholders, the minority stockholders, cut off from all corporation-related revenues, must either suffer their losses or seek a buyer for their shares.

Many minority stockholders will be unwilling or unable to wait for an alteration in majority policy. Typically, the minority stockholder in a close corporation has a substantial percentage of his personal assets invested in the corporation. The stockholder may have anticipated that his salary from his position with the corporation would be his livelihood. Thus, he cannot afford to wait passively. He must liquidate his investment in the close corporation in order to reinvest the funds in income-producing enterprises.

At this point, the true plight of the minority stockholder in a close corporation becomes manifest. He cannot easily reclaim his capital. In a large public corporation, the oppressed or dissident minority stockholder could sell his stock in order to extricate some of his invested capital. By definition, this market is not available for shares in the close corporation. In a partnership, a partner who feels abused by his fellow partners may cause dissolution by his "express will . . . at any time" and recover his share of partnership assets and accumulated profits. If dissolution results in a breach of the partnership articles, the culpable partner will be liable in damages. By contrast, the stockholder in the close corporation or "incorporated partnership" may achieve dissolution and recovery of his share of the enterprise assets only by compliance with the rigorous terms of the applicable chapter of the General Laws. "The dissolution of a corporation which is a creature of the Legislature is primarily a legislative function, and the only authority courts have to deal with this subject is the power conferred upon them by the Legislature." To secure dissolution of the ordinary close corporation, the stockholder, in the absence of corporate deadlock, must own at least fifty per cent of the shares or have the advantage of a favorable provision in the articles of organization. The minority stockholder, by definition lacking fifty per cent of the corporate shares, can never "authorize" the corporation to file a petition for dissolution by his own vote. He will seldom have at his disposal the requisite favorable provision in the articles of organization.

Thus, in a close corporation, the minority stockholders may be trapped in a disadvantageous situation. No outsider would knowingly assume the position of the disadvantaged minority. The outsider would have the same difficulties. To cut losses, the minority stockholder may be compelled to deal with the majority. This is the capstone of the majority plan. Majority "freeze-out" schemes which withhold dividends are designed to compel the minority to relinquish stock at inadequate prices. When the minority stockholder agrees to sell out at less than fair value, the majority has won.

Because of the fundamental resemblance of the close corporation to the partnership, the trust and confidence which are essential to this scale and manner of enterprise, and the inherent danger to minority interests in the close corporation, we hold that stockholders in the close corporation owe one another substantially the same fiduciary duty in the operation of the enterprise that partners owe to one another. In our previous decisions, we have defined the standard of duty owed by partners to one another as the "utmost good faith and loyalty." Stockholders in close corporations must discharge their management and stockholder responsibilities in conformity with this strict good faith standard. They may not act out of avarice, expediency or self-interest in derogation of their duty of loyalty to the other stockholders and to the corporation.

We contrast this strict good faith standard with the somewhat less stringent standard of fiduciary duty to which directors and stockholders[20] of all corporations must adhere in the discharge of their corporate responsibilities. Corporate directors are held to a good faith and inherent fairness standard of conduct and are not "permitted to serve two masters whose interests are antagonistic." "Their paramount duty is to the corporation, and their personal pecuniary interests are subordinate to that duty."

The more rigorous duty of partners and participants in a joint adventure, here extended to stockholders in a close corporation, was described by then Chief Judge Cardozo of the New York Court of Appeals in Meinhard v. Salmon, 164 N.E. 545 (N.Y. 1928): "Joint adventurers, like copartners, owe to one another, while the enterprise continues, the duty of the finest loyalty. Many forms of conduct permissible in a workaday world for those acting at arm's length, are forbidden to those bound by fiduciary ties. . . . Not honesty alone, but the punctilio of an honor the most sensitive, is then the standard of behavior."

Application of this strict standard of duty to stockholders in close corporations is a natural outgrowth of the prior case law. In a number of cases involving close corporations, we have held stockholders participating in management to a standard of fiduciary duty more exacting than the traditional good faith and inherent fairness standard because of the trust and confidence reposed in them by the other stockholders.

[W]e have imposed a duty of loyalty more exacting than that duty owed by a director to his corporation or by a majority stockholder to the minority in a public corporation because of facts particular to the close corporation in the cases. In the instant case, we extend this strict duty of loyalty to all stockholders in close corporations. The circumstances which justified findings of relationships of trust and confidence in these particular cases exist universally in modified form in all close corporations.

[The court stated the rule of equal opportunity in stock purchases by close corporations, which provides equal access to these benefits for all stockholders. It held that, in any case in which the controlling stockholders have exercised their power over the corporation to deny the minority such equal opportunity, the minority shall be entitled to appropriate relief. The

---

[20] The rule set out in many jurisdictions is: "The majority has the right to control; but when it does so, it occupies a fiduciary relationship toward the minority, as much so as the corporation itself or its officers and directors."

purchase of Harry Rodd's shares by the corporation was a breach of the duty which the controlling stockholders owed to the minority stockholders. The plaintiff and her son were not offered an equal opportunity to sell their shares to the corporation. The court suggested two remedies: (1) undo the stock repurchase, or (2) provide the same repurchase opportunity to the minority shareholder.]

———————

In *Donahue*, the court stated that a close corporation "bears striking resemblance to a partnership." This characterization has a level of truth and must be understood in historical context. A close corporation is fundamentally characterized by a small number of stockholders; thus, stockholders participate in management and there is typically no ready market the equity. These attributes are prototypical characteristics of a general partnership. When the case was decided in 1975, if equityholders sought to participate in management, the available choice of entities was principally a general partnership or a corporation, and only the corporation provided limited liability.[1]

Corporations and partnerships differ fundamentally, but the distinction becomes blurred in close corporations. The tax treatment of corporations and partnerships differ, but some corporations, including close corporations, can quality as an S corporation under federal tax law, which would permit a single level of taxation. The default governance rules of corporations and partnerships materially differ in many respects. But some corporation statutes permit written shareholder agreements that mimic the management of a close corporation to that of a partnership. *See* DGCL § 354 (permitting written shareholder agreement "by the parties to the agreement or by the stockholders of the corporation to treat the corporation as if it were a partnership or to arrange relations among the stockholders or between the stockholders and the corporation in a manner that would be appropriate only among partners").

Delaware corporation law draws a distinction between a closely-held corporation and a close corporation. A closely-held corporation is simply a corporation whose shares are held by a limited number of shareholders. A close corporation has a formal legal definition and is subject to somewhat more flexible governance requirements than an ordinary corporation. Subchapter XIV of the Delaware corporation statute requires that a corporation must elect treatment as a close corporation by filing a

———————

[1]   Although the first LLC statute was enacted in Wyoming in 1977, the form did not achieve wide acceptance among practitioners until the 1990s. Likewise, the limited liability partnership was introduced in the 1990s. The Revised Uniform Partnership Act was also adopted in the 1990s, which provided that the partnership was an entity is distinct from its partners and thus the partnership may continue in perpetuity despite the dissociation of partners (*see* RUPA § 201(a) and § 603(a)). A limited partnership would not permit limited partners to participate in management without risking the loss of limited liability under the "control" rule.

certificate of incorporation consistent with Subchapter IV and maintaining its requirements.

DGCL § 342: Close Corporation Defined; Contents of Certificate of Incorporation

(a) A close corporation is a corporation organized under this chapter whose certificate of incorporation contains the provisions required by § 102 of this title and, in addition, provides that:

(1) All of the corporation's issued stock of all classes, exclusive of treasury shares, shall be represented by certificates and shall be held of record by not more than a specified number of persons, not exceeding 30; and

(2) All of the issued stock of all classes shall be subject to 1 or more of the restrictions on transfer permitted by § 202 of this title; and

(3) The corporation shall make no offering of any of its stock of any class which would constitute a "public offering" within the meaning of the United States Securities Act of 1933 [15 U.S.C. § 77a et seq.] as it may be amended from time to time.

Problem: Precision Tools—Part 1

Precision Tools, Inc. is a corporation formed under the law of Columbia, a hypothetical jurisdiction. It makes specialized, precision components for manufacturers of communication equipment. Precision Tools has a staff of highly skilled machinists who produce components that meet demanding specifications. The company's largest customer, from which it derives more than one-third of its sales, is Majestic Radio Corporation, a major producer of two-way radio equipment. The company's founders, Harry Stern and John Starr, own and manage the business, but are contemplating retirement. They seek to sell Precision Tools.

Jessica Bacon, 30, a writer for business publications, specializes in smaller businesses and the people who own and operate them. Precision Tools is one of the companies about which she has written. Jessica has discussed Precision Tools with Michael Lane, 32, an engineer at a large computer company. Michael believes that the telecommunications industry will continuing growing and large companies will need dependable suppliers of precision components. Michael thinks the company could capitalize on this trend; its machinists are highly skilled; and its machinery is state of the art. Michael and Jessica have concluded that Precision Tools could grow rapidly under new management.

If Jessica and Michael acquire Precision Tools, they plan to expand the company's product line and will need working capital to purchase additional equipment. Michael comes from a financially modest background, is married, has two young children and owns his home. He can invest $100,000 and would have to borrow money in order to invest a greater amount. Jessica, who has no dependents, could invest $200,000 in Precision Tools. In addition, she has a $175,000 stock portfolio and is likely to inherit more than a million dollars on the death of her father who is retired and in ill health.

Bernie Gould, Michael and Jessica's mutual friend, says he could invest about $600,000 in their new business. Bernie, 62, owns an insurance brokerage business and plans to retire in a few years. Bernie is married and has a son, Bill, who is a college junior. Bill is a technology buff and is enthusiastic about his father's potential involvement in Precision Tools. Bernie is too busy to help with day-to-day management but could, however, offer his substantial business experience to the venture. If he invests, he will want some voice in major business decisions.

Jessica, Michael and Bernie agree that Michael will manage the business and that Jessica, who obtained an M.B.A. degree before becoming a reporter, will oversee its finances. Michael and Jessica will be full-time employees.

The three anticipate that their new venture, already a going concern, will be profitable from the beginning. But they recognize the possibility of losses in the first few years due to expansion and added borrowing costs.

You have represented Michael in past business dealings. When he approached you about representing the potential purchasers in this matter, he asks: "The three of us want to invest in this venture. We're really excited about the potential of this business; and we hope to grow it quickly and probably eventually take it public. What do we do?"

What are some of the large issues that you can identify for the purpose of planning this business?

NOTE

In this and forthcoming chapters, we will continue to consider the facts in Precision Tools as we consider entity choice and other issues in business planning. We will assume that the applicable law is the law of Columbia.

B. RESTRICTIONS ON BOARD AUTHORITY AND SHAREHOLDER VOTING ARRANGEMENTS

In a close corporation, there may be no reason to maintain a formal separation of ownership and control. Like partners in a general partnership, shareholders often wish to involve themselves directly in the

Court refused to find any enforcement mechanism, thus rendering empty the parties' promises to pool their votes. A provision for specific performance would probably have solved the enforceability and remedy problem.

Problem: Precision Tools—Part 2

Suppose that Michael Lane, Jessica Bacon, and Bernie Gould were to form a close corporation to acquire Precision Tools. They present you with the following issues.

Bernie explains that his interest in "having some voice" in the business means he wants to elect half of the board. The three have tentatively agreed on a four-member board of directors, consisting of the three of them and an additional director chosen by Bernie.

What advice would you give to the parties on having a four-person board?

Why might the parties want to be on the board of directors?

Without any special arrangements, how will the board be chosen under the rules set forth in corporate statutes?

If one of the three investors has a small investment but is still wants to get a board seat a condition to his or her investment, how can this be accomplished?

Michael, Jessica and Bernie also agree to use their best efforts to elect each other to the board, along with a fourth director designated by Bernie. Over time, Bernie becomes dissatisfied with Michael as CEO, even though Jessica continues to support him. Bernie and his designee then begin to vote against proposals by Michael and Jessica at board meetings, including a proposal to expand Precision Tools' business by buying one of Precision Tools' principal suppliers at a very attractive price. Bernie explained that he intends to continue to block all major new investments because he has no confidence in Michael's ability to manage the company.

What is the likelihood that Michael and Jessica would succeed in a suit to hold Bernie liable for the losses Precision Tools has incurred because of his negative votes, assuming that they can prove Precision Tools has in fact been damaged?

Under the MBCA, how likely is it that a Columbia court would follow Smith v. Atlantic Properties?

C. MINORITY PROTECTION DEVICES

A minority shareholder in a close corporation is in a vulnerable position. Without some check on control, a minority shareholder can be exposed to the tyranny of the majority. In a public corporation, the plight of the minority is not really a problem because the vast majority of public shareholders have minute stakes in the corporation. The difference is that these shareholders can readily exit their investment by selling their stock in the capital markets. Shareholders in a close corporation seldom have that option.

A close corporation can be structured to provide minority shareholders some degree of protection. Such protective measures can be related to shareholder action, board action, or management action.

The most basic control devices are those designed to protect shareholders from decisions by the board of directors that are adverse to their interests. Three choices are available: (1) arrangements that ensure board representation; (2) arrangements that give some or all shareholders the ability to veto board decisions with which they disagree; or (3) arrangements that provide for dispute resolution or exit options. Shareholders in a close corporation can negotiate to establish the proper balance between the power of the majority and protection of the minority.

Importantly, control devices designed to protect the minority shareholder may be worth very little if the majority shareholder retains the power to eliminate those protections, whether through expansion of the board or amendment of the corporation's articles or bylaws. Consequently, if control devices are to remain effective, they must be supplemented by provisions designed to give the minority shareholder a veto over board or shareholder decisions that would alter or eliminate the protective measures.[2] In other words, the protective device must itself be protected as well to ensure the integrity of the original design.

Other than election of directors, the ordinary and default rule of voting in most corporations is majority vote of a quorum of votes. The MBCA provides the default rule of shareholder voting.

---

[2]   MBCA § 7.27(b) anticipates the potential problem of an end-around through amendment of the articles of incorporation and provides: "An amendment to the articles of incorporation that adds, changes, or deletes a greater quorum or voting requirement must meet the same quorum requirement and be adopted by the same vote and voting groups required to take action under the quorum and voting requirements then in effect or proposed to be adopted, whichever is greater."

> **MBCA § 7.25. Quorum and Voting Requirements for Voting Groups**
>
> (a) Shares entitled to vote as a separate voting group may take action on a matter at a meeting only if a quorum of those shares exists with respect to that matter. Unless the articles of incorporation provides otherwise, a majority of the votes entitled to be cast on the matter by the voting group constitutes a quorum of that voting group for action on that matter.
>
> . . .
>
> (c) If a quorum exists, action on a matter (other than the election of directors) by a voting group is approved if the votes cast within the voting group favoring the action exceed the votes cast opposing the action, unless the articles of incorporation require a greater number of affirmative votes.

The articles of incorporation may provide for a greater quorum or voting requirement of shareholders in both routine actions and fundamental changes such as mergers and acquisitions.[3] *Id.* § 7.27. Similarly, the default rule of director voting is a majority of a quorum of directors, again subject to any contrary provision in the articles of incorporation or bylaws. *Id.* § 8.24.

1. SUPERMAJORITY VOTING

The most straightforward way to create veto rights for minority shareholders is to require that a supermajority of directors or shareholders approve all or certain specified actions. One approach is to require unanimous approval. Many lawyers follow the practice of setting the supermajority requirement sufficiently high to make opposition of one shareholder or one director sufficient to block board or shareholder action. A requirement that a board action be approved by 80% of the directors, for example, effectively requires unanimity if the board has four or fewer members.

The reason for the caution in this area is that a few courts have struck down extraordinary majority voting requirements for one reason or another. *See Benintendi v. Kenton Hotel*, 60 N.E.2d 829 (N.Y. 1945)

---

[3] Google, of course, is a public company and not a close corporation. However, its certificate of incorporation provides an example of a different quorum requirement: "*Change in Control Transaction.* The Corporation shall not consummate a Change in Control Transaction without first obtaining the affirmative vote, at a duly called annual or special meeting of the stockholders of the Corporation, of the holders of the greater of: (A) a majority of the voting power of the issued and outstanding shares of capital stock of the Corporation then entitled to vote thereon, voting together as a single class, and (B) sixty percent (60%) of the voting power of the shares of capital stock present in person or represented by proxy at the stockholder meeting called to consider the Change in Control Transaction and entitled to vote thereon, voting together as a single class." Amended and Restated Certificate of Incorporation, Article IV, Section 3 (October 2, 2015).

(holding that bylaw provisions requiring unanimity for any action by either the board or the shareholders were invalid as against public policy because they made it difficult for the corporation to conduct its business and created a substantial risk of deadlock). However, courts have come to accept the fact that departures by close corporations from the traditional corporate model do not inevitably entail untoward results. For example, *Sutton v. Sutton*, 637 N.E.2d 260 (N.Y. 1994), upheld as valid under N.Y.B.C.L. § 616(b) a provision in a corporation's articles of incorporation requiring unanimous shareholder approval to transact any business, "including amendment to the articles of incorporation." Moreover, many legislatures have enacted statutory provisions that authorize, specifically or by implication, high vote requirements in the articles or bylaws. *See, e.g.*, MBCA § 2.02, § 7.25(c), § 8.24(c); N.Y.B.C.L. § 616, § 709.

2. CLASS VOTING

A simple technique for ensuring shareholder representation on the board or shareholder decisions is class voting. Class voting entails dividing the voting stock into two or more classes, each of which is entitled to elect a certain number of directors or approve transactions as a class. Consider the simple case of a corporation with three shareholders, each of whom wishes to have a seat on the board. The shareholders can readily accomplish this end by having the corporation authorize three classes of shares, each of which is entitled to elect one director, and issuing a different class to each shareholder. The changes that can be built on this basic device are limited only by the imagination of the drafter. For example, classes of stock can be created that have differing numbers of votes, or even no vote at all (as long as at least one class can vote).

Class voting has potential pitfalls. One is simply inherent in any provision that strays from majority rule (required if minority protection is deemed necessary), which is the potential for deadlock or obstruction. If the minority is given too much authority (from the perspective of the majority shareholder), it may be able to obstruct or to create an impasse, leading to rent-seeking behavior. But this is an issue that can be dealt with through planning and drafting for contingencies in the articles of incorporation.

3. CUMULATIVE VOTING

A more complex technique for ensuring shareholder representation on the board is cumulative voting. There are two principal methods for conducting an election of directors. With straight voting, each share is entitled to one vote for each open directorship, and at the annual meeting directors are elected one at a time to fill each slot. Most corporation statutes provide that directors are elected by a plurality of the votes cast, so the nominee who receives the greatest number of votes for a particular board seat is elected, even if she receives less than a majority of the votes cast. *See* MBCA § 7.28(a) ("Unless otherwise provided in the articles of incorporation, directors are elected by a plurality of the votes cast by the shares entitled to vote in the election at a meeting at which a quorum is present."). In a straight voting regime, therefore, a shareholder or group of shareholders controlling more than 50% of the shares can, as a matter of legal certainty, elect all of the members of the board.[4]

Cumulative voting allows shareholders to elect directors in rough proportion to the shares they own even if that number is less than 50%. In most states, cumulative voting is available if the parties "opt in" in the articles.[5] *See* MBCA § 7.28; DGCL § 214; N.Y.B.C.L. § 618. If they own the requisite number of shares, they can be guaranteed minority representation on the board. With cumulative voting, each share again carries a number of votes equal to the number of directors to be elected, but a shareholder may "cumulate" her votes. Cumulating simply means multiplying the number of votes a shareholder is entitled to cast by the number of directors for whom she is entitled to vote. If there is cumulative voting, the shareholder may cast all her votes for one candidate or allocate them in any manner among a number of candidates.

The number of shares required to elect a given number of directors under a cumulative voting regime may be calculated by the following formula:

$$X = \frac{S \times d}{D + 1} + 1$$

where X = Number of shares required to elect directors

          S = Number of shares represented at the meeting

          d = Number of directors it is desired to elect

          D = Total number of directors to be elected

To understand this formula, it is helpful to work through a simple example. Suppose that three directors are to be elected at a meeting at which 1000 shares are represented and will vote. To elect one director a minority group would have to control 251 shares. With that number, the minority group would have 753 votes (= 251 × 3), which would all be cast

---

[4] In a public company, due to diffuse shareholdings, a substantial minority stake can have de facto control. For example, a shareholder that owns 40% of the voting shares needs only another 10% of the shares (plus one share) to win a vote by a majority. In practice the 40% may be enough all by itself, because the normal requirement is a majority of the votes cast, and in public companies many shareholders don't bother to vote.

[5] In a few states, cumulative voting is mandatory for closely-held corporations. *See, e.g.*, Cal. Corp. Code § 708.

for one candidate. The majority would have 2247 votes (= 749 × 3). If the majority distributed these equally among three candidates, each would receive 749 votes, and the one candidate receiving the minority's 753 votes would be guaranteed a seat. In other words, holding just over 25% of the shares guarantees the election of one of three directors. (Note that the reason for the "+ 1" at the end of the formula is to avoid the tie that would occur if, in this example, the minority controlled only 250 votes. Then it would be possible for four candidates each to receive 750 votes.)

Cumulative voting does not provide the minority shareholder with majority representation. It simply ensures that a holder with a large enough minority position is assured of board representation, which would not be the case in straight voting. Does minority representation through class voting or cumulative voting matter where the remaining shareholders still control the vote? It may matter in three ways. First, the remaining shareholders may not be a cohesive block. If factions are split, the minority representation may matter quite a bit. Second, cumulative voting may give larger minority shareholders a voice and promotes divergent points of view, which may result in better decision-making. Third, and perhaps most important, minority representation may discourage self-dealing and other improper conduct by the majority faction because of more information available to, and monitoring by, the minority's board representative.

The majority can undermine the effectiveness of cumulative voting. One method is to classify the board of directors (usually into three classes), and stagger the election of directors so only a fraction of the total number of directors are elected each year. This means fewer vacancies to be filled each year, which requires a larger minority position be guaranteed of electing a director. Another way of undermining cumulative voting is to decrease the board size, again increasing the percentage of shares necessary for a minority shareholder to elect one director. The courts have generally upheld this technique, even though it undermines cumulative voting. A planner may guard against the implementation of these techniques by inserting anti-circumvention provisions in the articles, such as requiring a supermajority vote to stagger the board or reduce the number of directors.

Problem: Precision Tools—Part 3

Assume Bernie, Jessica and Michael have agreed to allocate 40% of the voting common stock to Jessica, 40% to Michael, and 20% to Bernie. They have also agreed that Jessica and Michael will each get to elect one director, and Bernie will get to elect two. Consider the effect on board representation if the parties use cumulative voting to elect directors. Assuming a four-member board of directors and 1,000 shares of voting stock issued and outstanding.

If all the shares are voted, how many shares must Bernie have to (1) assure his election to the board, (2) elect two directors, and (3) win control of a majority of the board (three positions)?

Assume that the parties decide not to use cumulative voting or the capital structure to achieve their goals of board representation.

Would a voting agreement accomplish their purposes? What basic provisions should it include? Are there legal restrictions that affect its validity?

If a party to the agreement does not comply with her obligations, what enforcement mechanisms, if any, should the agreement contain? Assume that the applicable law is: (1) MBCA §§ 2.02, 7.22, 7.30, 7.31, 7.32; (2) DGCL § 218.

To protect the agreed voting arrangement, you consider a high vote requirement (such as 80%) to amend the articles of incorporation or the bylaws.

What are the advantages and disadvantages of such a requirement? To which issues should the requirement apply? If such requirement is desirable, should it relate to actions by the shareholders, the directors, or both? Assume that the applicable law is: MBCA §§ 2.02, 7.25, 7.27, 7.32, 8.24, 10.21.

The parties have agreed that Michael will be the president and chief executive officer of the new company; Jessica will be vice-president and chief financial officer; and Bernie will be secretary. Michael will have control over the operational part of the business, and Jessica will run its financial end. Because both Michael and Jessica will derive most of their income from the business, each will be paid a reasonable salary. For now, Bernie will not be paid a salary for his more limited participation.

Jessica and Michael would like to guarantee their officerships. Without such a guarantee, they are concerned the other directors might remove them. They would also like an assured compensation for the first few years. Bernie understands their concerns and is willing to enter into an arrangement to fulfill these objectives, but wants a cap on their salaries. Since he will not have a salary, he also wants the corporation to pay dividends should it show a profit.

The three ask you about the validity of an agreement that would bind them "to use their best efforts" to elect each other to their respective officerships, to have Michael and Jessica each paid a salary of $100,000 per year, and to have the corporation pay a dividend annually equal to one-third of its net profits. They also want to fix the amount spent on research and development in the next few years.

Advise Michael and Jessica how to implement their understanding. In this connection, consider: (1) whether the agreement can be between only

Michael and Jessica, or whether it must be unanimous; (2) whether the provisions of the agreement can or must be put in the corporation's articles of incorporation or bylaws, and whether they need be in writing. Assume that the applicable law is: (1) DGCL §§ 350, 351, 354; (2) MBCA §§ 2.02, 7.32.

D. CONTRACTUAL TRANSFER PROVISIONS

Because starting a corporate venture is relatively easy, close corporation participants may also assume that exiting from their venture will be just as simple. They may assume that they will be able to withdraw and be paid their ratable share, much as partnership law permits partners to withdraw from a partnership. The traditional rules of corporate law, however, create a permanent structure in which shareholders cannot liquidate their investment except by selling to others, selling the corporation itself or, rarely, by dissolving the corporation. In a close corporation, there is no readily available trading market for the corporation's shares. Thus, without control or a contractual right to sell their shares, the shareholders in a close corporation own an illiquid investment.

The organizers of a closely-held corporation should also be concerned about what will happen if one of the shareholders dies or does manage to find a buyer for her shares. In a partnership or an LLC, a transferee of a partnership or membership interest can only acquire an economic interest in the entity. The transferee requires approval by the remaining partners or members to be admitted as a partner or member with rights of control. This is not true in a corporation, as the transfer of stock carries with it all of the voting rights associated with that stock, often enabling the transferee to elect one or more board members. The remaining stockholders, who initially thought of the departing stockholder as a "partner" (in the business rather than the legal sense) may object to taking on a new "partner." To deal with this set of issues, lawyers advising on the creation of a close corporation generally advise the shareholders to enter into an agreement that places restrictions on the transfer of shares and, perhaps, attempts to provide some form of liquidity for the estate of a decedent shareholder or a shareholder who wishes to withdraw from the business.

1. PURPOSES AND LEGALITY OF TRANSFER PROVISIONS

When a closely-held enterprise is organized as a partnership, each partner has the power to veto the admission into the partnership of a new member. RUPA § 401(i). In a corporation, however, free transferability of shares is the default rule. In a close corporation, where the participants may want to control who are the shareholders, special arrangements are necessary to restrict the ability of shareholders to transfer their shares.

Stock transfer agreements can accomplish three purposes. (1) They can allow the shareholders to exercise some control over whom they might be doing business with in the future. (2) They can ensure the continuance of a desired balance of control that might be undone if shares are transferred to an unwanted third party. (3) Finally, they can provide a means for disposing of otherwise illiquid shares.

Liquidity is particularly important in estate planning. Creating a mechanism for the estate of a close corporation shareholder to sell the decedent's shares, for which no ready market exists, makes possible paying the decedent's personal debts, the expenses of administering the estate, and federal and state estate taxes. The mechanism, such as a buy-sell agreement, must address how the purchase will be funded and how a price for the stock will be established. In setting that price, the planner must consider the risk that the taxing authorities may claim that the shares are worth substantially more than the price established by agreement. A buy-out provision also allows the estate to diversify the assets to be passed on to the heirs.

Historically, the validity and enforceability of transfer restrictions was somewhat controversial, given the general American legal principle that unreasonable restraints on alienation of personal property are void. As a result, a number of older decisions questioned the validity of corporate transfer restrictions. Over time, courts came to recognize the importance of such restrictions and became more tolerant in their approach. Today most corporate statutes expressly authorize transfer restrictions. *See* MBCA § 6.27; DGCL § 202. Some statutes even require them for close corporations.

2. TYPES OF TRANSFER PROVISIONS

Transfer restrictions that seek to preserve the ownership and control structure of a close corporation can take several different forms.

Right of first refusal. Before a shareholder can sell her shares to a third person, she must first offer them to the corporation or to the remaining shareholders (or both) at the same price and on the same terms and conditions offered by the outsider. Typically, the right, if extended to the other shareholders, is given in proportion to their respective holdings. If any shareholder is unable to purchase or declines to do so, her allocation may be taken up proportionately by the remaining shareholders.

First option provision. Unlike a right of first refusal, the offer to the corporation or the remaining shareholders is made at a price and on terms fixed by agreement rather than by the outside offer. Even if the agreement calls for a right of first refusal, including a first option provision is useful to deal with non-sale transfers such as gifts or devises.

Consent. Transfers can be conditioned on the consent of the board of directors or the other shareholders. Modern statutes allow the parties to provide for a consent restriction if such "prohibition is not manifestly unreasonable."

In creating these restrictions, the planner must bear in mind that there are a variety of ways for a shareholder to dispose of her shares. The most common are by sale or bequest. But the planner should also consider the possibility of inter vivos transfers by way of gifts, creation of trusts, pledges, or other means by which the right to vote the shares and receive dividends might pass to someone other than the original owner. For example, in *Seven Springs Farm, Inc. v. Croker*, 801 A.2d 1212 (Pa. 2002), the Pennsylvania Supreme Court held that a merger in which the majority of a close corporation agreed to sell to another company did not trigger an agreement that restricted the sale or "other disposition" of company shares, unless first offered to the corporation and the other shareholders. Without deciding whether a "conversion" constituted a "disposition" under the agreement, the court held that a merger is a corporate act, not a shareholder act governed by the agreement. Although through the merger the majority shareholders were able to obtain cash for their shares without triggering the right of first refusal, the court stated:

> This is an area of law where formalities are important, as they are the method by which sophisticated businessmen make their contractual rights definite and limit the authority of the courts to redo their deal. It is important to note that the parties to the case had legal assistance in drafting the Buy-Sell Agreement. Their lawyers must be charged with the knowledge not only that "one consequence of Pennsylvania's strict construction approach is that controlling shareholders can use mergers, acquisitions and dissolution to avoid share transfer restrictions, but also that this result can be prevented by express coverage of merger and acquisitions in the transfer restriction."

Id. at 1220.

In addition, transfer provisions often specify the liquidity rights of shareholders who withdraw from the business.

Sale option. The withdrawing shareholder can receive an option to sell her shares (typically all) to the corporation or the remaining shareholders upon the occurrence of specified events, such as the death of the shareholder or the termination of his or her employment with the corporation.

Buy-sell agreement. More commonly, the obligation to buy is combined with a reciprocal obligation to sell. A "buy-sell agreement" compels the corporation or the remaining shareholders to purchase the shares of another shareholder upon the occurrence of specified events, such as the death of a shareholder. If the designated purchaser is the corporation, the agreement is known as an "entity purchase" agreement or "redemption agreement." If the purchase obligation falls on the other shareholders, the agreement is known as a "cross-purchase" arrangement. Frequently the two approaches are combined.

Transfer provisions are most commonly negotiated and adopted when the close corporation is formed. What is the status of a shareholder who purchases shares (from the corporation or a shareholder) after the transfer provisions became effective? Whether the newcomer is bound may depend on how the transfer provisions are documented—in the articles of incorporation, a bylaw provision, or a separate contract among the shareholders. The newcomer may not be bound if the restriction is in a shareholders' agreement to which she is not a party. It is customary, therefore, to make transfer restrictions a part of the bylaws or the articles.

To be valid against a purchaser of shares without notice, a transfer restriction must be "noted conspicuously" on the stock certificate itself. MBCA § 6.27(b). The term "conspicuous" is defined in MBCA § 1.40(3). Even if not conspicuous, a transfer restriction is enforceable against a transferee with knowledge.

Can transfer restrictions be adopted without the consent of all the shareholders? In *Tu-Vu Drive-In Corp. v. Ashkins*, 391 P.2d 828 (Cal. 1964), the court upheld transfer restrictions in a bylaw added by the board of directors three years after the corporation was organized. The bylaw gave a right of first refusal to the other shareholders and then to the corporation, before any shareholder could sell to an outsider. Later, when one of the minority shareholders granted to an outsider an option to purchase her shares, the majority shareholder sought a declaratory judgment that the bylaw was enforceable. The question, according to the court, was whether the restriction was an unreasonable restraint on alienation. Holding that it was not, the court said, "In the light of the legitimate interests to be furthered by the by-law the defendant's asserted right becomes 'innocuous and insubstantial.' The by-law merely proscribes the defendant's choice of transferees while insuring to her the price and terms equal to those offered by the outsider."

3. VALUATION OF RESTRICTED SHARES

Recall the discussion of valuation methodologies in Chapter 9. The technique for valuing shares subject to a transfer agreement is of critical importance. Consider the following options.

Book value. This is a popular method but one that may lead to inequitable results. As we will see in Chapter 9, the book value of a company may bear little relationship to its value as an ongoing concern. Moreover, despite its apparent simplicity, book value turns out to be remarkably ambiguous. Does it, for example, include intangible assets, especially "goodwill"? What about income taxes that are accrued but unpaid, and may not appear on the books? If the corporation carries insurance on life of the shareholder whose death triggers a buy-sell provision, are the insurance proceeds included? Should assets that have appreciated substantially be written up? If book value is used, these and other questions should be anticipated and resolved in the agreement.

Capitalized earnings. An agreement may establish a formula for capitalizing the earnings of the business.[6] Like book value, however, this technique presents certain difficulties of drafting. It is especially critical that the earnings of the business be carefully defined. Moreover, a capitalization rate that captures the nature of the business when formed may not be appropriate as the business matures and diversifies.

Right of first refusal. When a principal concern is that one of the shareholders may sell his interest to an outsider, a provision that requires the shareholder, before selling, to offer his shares to the corporation (or the other shareholders) with the same price and terms offered by the outsider has great appeal. This approach may, however, substantially increase illiquidity, since a prospective buyer may well be put off by the risk of negotiating a sale only to have the shares bought by the corporation or other shareholders. Moreover, this approach is useful only for prospective sales to third parties and not for the transfer of shares by gift, devise, or inheritance.

Appraisal. Some of these pitfalls can be avoided by leaving the valuation to a later appraisal by a neutral third party according to a predetermined procedure. For example, a convenient technique is to provide for arbitration according to the rules of the American Arbitration Association or some other recognized arbitral organization. The disadvantage is that a professional appraisal of an ongoing business is expensive.

Mutual agreement. Another technique is for the parties to the agreement to set a value for the shares and to revise it at stated intervals, usually annually. While this may lead to a fairer price,

---

[6]   Capitalizing earnings means that earnings are assume to generate in perpetuity and thus a perpetuity formula is applied to calculate the value of the perpetual earnings stream, which is: Value = Earnings ÷ Discount Rate. For example, if the expected earnings is 100 and the discount rate is 10%, the value of the firm based on the capitalized earnings method is: $100 \div 10\% = 1{,}000$.

it is subject to a number of drawbacks. The parties may forget to revalue the shares. They may not have enough comparative information or skill to value the company's business. And for psychological reasons, they may avoid contemplating the possibility of a falling out or of one of them departing.

A valuation method is of little use if the person obligated to purchase lacks the financial ability to do so. Unless some means of funding is provided, both the shareholders and the corporation may find themselves without the ready ability to purchase the shares. A corporate repurchase might require selling parts of the business, and the corporation might even be prevented by statutory restrictions from making the purchase under applicable legal capital rules.

If the putative purchaser is the corporation, one means of funding the purchase is the establishment of a sinking fund in which the corporation regularly sets aside money to be saved for that purpose. A second, and more common, technique is for the corporation to purchase and maintain life insurance on the lives of the shareholders in an amount adequate to fund all or a substantial part of any repurchase for which the corporation may become obligated on their death. Planners will often link the agreement's valuation of the shares to the level of insurance coverage. A third method of funding is to defer payment by the use of promissory notes or installment obligations.

Problem: Precision Tools—Part 4

Jessica, Michael and Bernie mentioned to you their concern about what would happen to their interests in the corporation should one of them die, withdraw, or have their employment involuntarily terminated. You advised them that shareholders in close corporations, particularly when advised by counsel, often enter into an agreement that addresses the transfer of stock in specified circumstances. They have asked you to draft such an agreement.

What events should trigger the applicability of the transfer provisions? The death of one of the parties? The termination of employment—should it make a difference if the termination is voluntary or involuntary? Should the parties be allowed to make a gift of their stock? To family? Third parties? To pledge the stock as collateral for a loan?

Who should have the option (or be required) to purchase the shares subject to the transfer provisions? In what circumstances should the transfer be mandatory—that is, should the agreement require that upon the triggering event, the shareholder is obligated to sell and the prospective purchaser to buy? Alternatively, when should the transfer be subject to the option of one or more of the parties?

Assuming that more than one person has an interest in purchasing the shares, in what order should there be a right of refusal? If no one exercises the right to purchase the shares under the agreement, should the seller be free to sell to a third party without restriction?

How should the price at which any transfers take place be determined? Should it vary depending upon the occasion for the transfer? Should the agreement specify a price or should it set forth a formula to fix the price? How often should such a determination be made? Whether or not there is a formula, what should happen if the parties fail to agree upon the price?

How should any purchase options be funded?

In what instrument(s) should the transfer provisions be included? Consider MBCA § 2.02 and DGCL § 202.

E. DISSENSION AND OPPRESSION

All too frequently in a closely-held business (such as close corporations, partnerships, and LLCs), a day comes when the owners cease to get along with each other. The case law is replete with examples of highly personalized disputes among family members, friends, and business partners. One principal source of difficulty is that differences over matters of business policy or practice frequently arise from personal or family conflicts. When money and personal relationships mix, it sometimes ends unpleasantly. Individuals who join a corporate venture seldom think about the possibility that one day they may have a parting of ways. Often, this uncomfortable subject will be raised by counsel.

Developing appropriate control mechanisms can be expensive. The cost may include the direct cost involved in anticipating possible areas of disagreement and designing control mechanisms to deal with them. The indirect cost of potential deadlock and obstruction made possible by granting control rights to a minority shareholder may also be significant. As a result, many close corporations are formed without any special dispute resolution mechanisms.

In a close corporation, a minority shareholder is subject to two kinds of potential vulnerabilities. First, the majority can cut off minority shareholders from realizing any return, thus leaving them holding illiquid stock that generates no current income. Second, the majority can exercise control to frustrate the preferences of the minority.

How courts respond to dissension in close corporations has turned on two factors. The first factor is how the courts view close corporations. Courts in some states, building on the approach set forth in *Donahue v. Rodd Electrotype Co. of New England, Inc.*, 328 N.E.2d 505 (Mass. 1975), have analogized the relationship among close corporation participants to that of partners, holding shareholders to high standards of fairness to one another. Courts in other states, Delaware in particular, have rejected that approach, holding that, in general, in accordance with traditional norms of corporate law, shareholders of closely-held corporations have no fiduciary duties to one another. *Nixon v. Blackwell*, 626 A.2d 1366 (Del. 1993) (excerpted below). Delaware corporations can, however, elect to be treated as "close corporations" under a separate section of the DGCL, in which case different rules apply.

The second factor is whether the legislature in the relevant jurisdiction has included in its corporate statute provisions aimed at protecting shareholders in close corporations. Many state laws now authorize courts to order dissolution or to take other remedial actions to protect shareholders who show that the majority has oppressed the minority.

1. FIDUCIARY DUTY

WILKES V. SPRINGSIDE NURSING HOME, INC.
353 N.E.2d 657 (Mass. 1976).

HENNESSEY, CHIEF JUSTICE:

On August 5, 1971, the plaintiff (Wilkes) filed a bill in equity for declaratory judgment in the Probate Court for Berkshire County, naming as defendants T. Edward Quinn (Quinn), Leon L. Riche (Riche), the First Agricultural National Bank of Berkshire County and Frank Sutherland MacShane as executors under the will of Lawrence R. Connor (Connor), and the Springside Nursing Home, Inc. (Springside or the corporation). Wilkes alleged that he, Quinn, Riche and Dr. Hubert A. Pipkin (Pipkin) entered into a partnership agreement in 1951, prior to the incorporation of Springside, which agreement was breached in 1967 when Wilkes's salary was terminated and he was voted out as an officer and director of the corporation. Wilkes sought, among other forms of relief, damages in the amount of the salary he would have received had he continued as a director and officer of Springside subsequent to March, 1967.

A judgment was entered dismissing Wilkes's action on the merits. We granted direct appellate review. On appeal, Wilkes argued in the alternative that (1) he should recover damages for breach of the alleged partnership agreement; and (2) he should recover damages because the defendants, as majority stockholders in Springside, breached their fiduciary duty to him as a minority stockholder by their action in February and March, 1967.

We reverse so much of the judgment as dismisses Wilkes's complaint and order the entry of a judgment substantially granting the relief sought by Wilkes under the second alternative set forth above.

In 1951, Wilkes, Riche, Quinn, and Pipkin purchased a building to use as a nursing home. Ownership of the property was vested in Springside, a corporation organized under Massachusetts law.

Each of the four men invested $1,000 and subscribed to ten shares of $100 par value stock in Springside.[6] At the time of incorporation, it was understood by all of the parties that each would be a director of Springside and each would participate actively in the management and decision making involved in operating the corporation.[7] It was, further, the understanding and intention of all the parties that, corporate resources permitting, each would receive money from the corporation in equal amounts as long as each assumed an active and ongoing responsibility for carrying a portion of the burdens necessary to operate the business.

The work involved in establishing and operating a nursing home was roughly apportioned, and each of the four men undertook his respective tasks.

At some time in 1952, it became apparent that the operational income and cash flow from the business were sufficient to permit the four stockholders to draw money from the corporation on a regular basis. Each of the four original parties initially received $35 a week from the corporation. As time went on the weekly return to each was increased until, in 1955, it totalled $100.

In 1959, after a long illness, Pipkin sold his shares in the corporation to Connor, who was known to Wilkes, Riche and Quinn through past transactions with Springside in his capacity as president of the First Agricultural National Bank of Berkshire County. Connor received a weekly stipend from the corporation equal to that received by Wilkes, Riche and Quinn. He was elected a director of the corporation but never held any other office. He was assigned no specific area of responsibility in the operation of the nursing home but did participate in business discussions and decisions as a director and served additionally as financial adviser to the corporation.

Beginning in 1965, personal relationships between Wilkes and the other shareholders began to deteriorate. As a consequence of the strained relations among the parties, Wilkes, in January of 1967, gave notice of his intention to sell his shares for an amount based on an appraisal of their value. In February of 1967 a directors' meeting was held and the board exercised its right to establish the salaries of its officers and employees.[10]

---

[6]   On May 2, 1955, and again on December 23, 1958, each of the four original investors paid for and was issued additional shares of $100 par value stock, eventually bringing the total number of shares owned by each to 115.

[7]   Wilkes testified before the master that, when the corporate officers were elected, all four men "were guaranteed directorships." Riche's understanding of the parties' intentions was that they all wanted to play a part in the management of the corporation and wanted to have some "say" in the risks involved; that, to this end, they all would be directors; and that "unless you [were] a director and officer you could not participate in the decisions of [the] enterprise."

[10]   The by-laws of the corporation provided that the directors, subject to the approval of the stockholders, had the power to fix the salaries of all officers and employees. This power, however, up until February, 1967, had not been exercised formally; all payments made to the four

A schedule of payments was established whereby Quinn was to receive a substantial weekly increase and Riche and Connor were to continue receiving $100 a week. Wilkes, however, was left off the list of those to whom a salary was to be paid. The directors also set the annual meeting of the stockholders for March, 1967.

At the annual meeting in March, Wilkes was not reelected as a director, nor was he reelected as an officer of the corporation. He was further informed that neither his services nor his presence at the nursing home was wanted by his associates.

The meetings of the directors and stockholders in early 1967, the master found, were used as a vehicle to force Wilkes out of active participation in the management and operation of the corporation and to cut off all corporate payments to him. Though the board of directors had the power to dismiss any officers or employees for misconduct or neglect of duties, there was no indication in the minutes of the board of directors' meeting of February, 1967, that the failure to establish a salary for Wilkes was based on either ground. The severance of Wilkes from the payroll resulted not from misconduct or neglect of duties, but because of the personal desire of Quinn, Riche and Connor to prevent him from continuing to receive money from the corporation. Despite a continuing deterioration in his personal relationship with his associates, Wilkes had consistently endeavored to carry on his responsibilities to the corporation in the same satisfactory manner and with the same degree of competence he had previously shown. Wilkes was at all times willing to carry on his responsibilities and participation if permitted so to do and provided that he receive his weekly stipend.

We turn to Wilkes's claim for damages based on a breach of the fiduciary duty owed to him by the other participants in this venture. In light of the theory underlying this claim, we do not consider it vital to our approach to this case whether the claim is governed by partnership law or the law applicable to business corporations. This is so because, as all the parties agree, Springside was at all times relevant to this action, a close corporation as we have recently defined such an entity in Donahue v. Rodd Electrotype Co. of New England, Inc., 328 N.E.2d 505 (Mass 1975).

In Donahue, we held that "stockholders in the close corporation owe one another substantially the same fiduciary duty in the operation of the enterprise that partners owe to one another." As determined in previous decisions of this court, the standard of duty owed by partners to one another is one of "utmost good faith and loyalty." Thus, we concluded in Donahue, with regard to "their actions relative to the operations of the enterprise and the effects of that operation on the rights and investments of other stockholders," "stockholders in close corporations must discharge

participants in the venture had resulted from the informal but unanimous approval of all the parties concerned.

their management and stockholder responsibilities in conformity with this strict good faith standard. They may not act out of avarice, expediency or self-interest in derogation of their duty of loyalty to the other stockholders and to the corporation."

In the Donahue case we recognized that one peculiar aspect of close corporations was the opportunity afforded to majority stockholders to oppress, disadvantage or "freeze out" minority stockholders. In Donahue itself, for example, the majority refused the minority an equal opportunity to sell a ratable number of shares to the corporation at the same price available to the majority. The net result of this refusal, we said, was that the minority could be forced to "sell out at less than fair value," since there is by definition no ready market for minority stock in a close corporation.

"Freeze outs," however, may be accomplished by the use of other devices. One such device which has proved to be particularly effective in accomplishing the purpose of the majority is to deprive minority stockholders of corporate offices and of employment with the corporation. F.H. O'Neal, "Squeeze-Outs" of Minority Shareholders 59, 78–79 (1975). This "freeze-out" technique has been successful because courts fairly consistently have been disinclined to interfere in those facets of internal corporate operations, such as the selection and retention or dismissal of officers, directors and employees, which essentially involve management decisions subject to the principle of majority control. As one authoritative source has said, "Many courts apparently feel that there is a legitimate sphere in which the controlling directors or shareholders can act in their own interest even if the minority suffers." F.H. O'Neal, supra at 59 (footnote omitted).

The denial of employment to the minority at the hands of the majority is especially pernicious in some instances. A guaranty of employment with the corporation may have been one of the "basic reasons why a minority owner has invested capital in the firm." The minority stockholder typically depends on his salary as the principal return on his investment, since the "earnings of a close corporation are distributed in major part in salaries, bonuses and retirement benefits." 1 F.H. O'Neal, Close Corporations § 1.07 (1971).[13] Other noneconomic interests of the minority stockholder are likewise injuriously affected by barring him from corporate office. Such action severely restricts his participation in the management of the enterprise, and he is relegated to enjoying those benefits incident to his status as a stockholder. In sum, by terminating a minority stockholder's employment or by severing him from a position as an officer or director, the majority effectively frustrate the minority stockholder's purposes in entering on the corporate venture and also deny him an equal return on his investment.

---

[13] We note here that the master found that Springside never declared or paid a dividend to its stockholders.

The distinction between the majority action in Donahue and the majority action in this case is more one of form than of substance. Nevertheless, we are concerned that untempered application of the strict good faith standard enunciated in Donahue to cases such as the one before us will result in the imposition of limitations on legitimate action by the controlling group in a close corporation which will unduly hamper its effectiveness in managing the corporation in the best interests of all concerned. The majority, concededly, have certain rights to what has been termed "selfish ownership" in the corporation which should be balanced against the concept of their fiduciary obligation to the minority.

Therefore, when minority stockholders in a close corporation bring suit against the majority alleging a breach of the strict good faith duty owed to them by the majority, we must carefully analyze the action taken by the controlling stockholders in the individual case. It must be asked whether the controlling group can demonstrate a legitimate business purpose for its action. In asking this question, we acknowledge the fact that the controlling group in a close corporation must have some room to maneuver in establishing the business policy of the corporation. It must have a large measure of discretion, for example, in declaring or withholding dividends, deciding whether to merge or consolidate, establishing the salaries of corporate officers, dismissing directors with or without cause, and hiring and firing corporate employees.

When an asserted business purpose for their action is advanced by the majority, however, we think it is open to minority stockholders to demonstrate that the same legitimate objective could have been achieved through an alternative course of action less harmful to the minority's interest. If called on to settle a dispute, our courts must weigh the legitimate business purpose, if any, against the practicability of a less harmful alternative.

Applying this approach to the instant case it is apparent that the majority stockholders in Springside have not shown a legitimate business purpose for severing Wilkes from the payroll of the corporation or for refusing to reelect him as a salaried officer and director. The master's subsidiary findings relating to the purpose of the meetings of the directors and stockholders in February and March, 1967, are supported by the evidence. There was no showing of misconduct on Wilkes's part as a director, officer or employee of the corporation which would lead us to approve the majority action as a legitimate response to the disruptive nature of an undesirable individual bent on injuring or destroying the corporation. On the contrary, it appears that Wilkes had always accomplished his assigned share of the duties competently, and that he had never indicated an unwillingness to continue to do so.

It is an inescapable conclusion from all the evidence that the action of the majority stockholders here was a designed "freeze out" for which no legitimate business purpose has been suggested. Furthermore, we may infer that a design to pressure Wilkes into selling his shares to the corporation at a price below their value well may have been at the heart of the majority's plan.[14]

In the context of this case, several factors bear directly on the duty owed to Wilkes by his associates. At a minimum, the duty of utmost good faith and loyalty would demand that the majority consider that their action was in disregard of a long-standing policy of the stockholders that each would be a director of the corporation and that employment with the corporation would go hand in hand with stock ownership; that Wilkes was one of the four originators of the nursing home venture; and that Wilkes, like the others, had invested his capital and time for more than fifteen years with the expectation that he would continue to participate in corporate decisions. Most important is the plain fact that the cutting off of Wilkes's salary, together with the fact that the corporation never declared a dividend, assured that Wilkes would receive no return at all from the corporation.

The question of Wilkes's damages at the hands of the majority has not been thoroughly explored on the record before us. Wilkes, in his original complaint, sought damages in the amount of the $100 a week he believed he was entitled to from the time his salary was terminated up until the time this action was commenced. However, the record shows that, after Wilkes was severed from the corporate payroll, the schedule of salaries and payments made to the other stockholders varied from time to time. In addition, the duties assumed by the other stockholders after Wilkes was deprived of his share of the corporate earnings appear to have changed in significant respects. Any resolution of this question must take into account whether the corporation was dissolved during the pendency of this litigation.

Therefore our order is as follows: So much of the judgment as dismisses Wilkes's complaint and awards costs to the defendants is reversed.

NIXON V. BLACKWELL
626 A.2d 1366 (Del. 1993).

[Plaintiffs, descendants of the founder of E.C. Barton & Co., held Class B non-voting stock. Plaintiffs claimed that the directors of the corporation had treated them unfairly by establishing an employee stock ownership plan ("ESOP") and purchasing key man life insurance to enable defendants and other employees to sell their stock while providing no comparable

---

[14] This inference arises from the fact that Connor, acting on behalf of the three controlling stockholders, offered to purchase Wilkes's shares for a price Connor admittedly would not have accepted for his own shares.

liquidity for Class B shareholders. The Delaware Supreme Court agreed with the Vice Chancellor that the Corporation had not provided substantially equal treatment to employee and non-employee shareholders, but held that this lack of parity was not unfair because the ESOP and key man insurance advanced legitimate corporate objectives.]

VEASEY, CHIEF JUSTICE:

NO SPECIAL RULES FOR A "CLOSELY-HELD CORPORATION" NOT QUALIFIED AS A "CLOSE CORPORATION" UNDER SUBCHAPTER XIV OF THE DELAWARE GENERAL CORPORATION LAW

We wish to address one further matter which was raised at oral argument before this Court: Whether there should be any special, judicially-created rules to "protect" minority stockholders of closely-held Delaware corporations.

The case at bar points up the basic dilemma of minority stockholders in receiving fair value for their stock as to which there is no market and no market valuation. It is not difficult to be sympathetic, in the abstract, to a stockholder who finds himself or herself in that position. A stockholder who bargains for stock in a closely-held corporation and who pays for those shares can make a business judgment whether to buy into such a minority position, and if so on what terms. One could bargain for definitive provisions of self-ordering permitted to a Delaware corporation through the certificate of incorporation or bylaws by reason of the provisions in 8 Del.C. §§ 102, 109, and 141(a). Moreover, in addition to such mechanisms, a stockholder intending to buy into a minority position in a Delaware corporation may enter into definitive stockholder agreements, and such agreements may provide for elaborate earnings tests, buy-out provisions, voting trusts, or other voting agreements. *See, e.g.,* 8 Del.C. § 218.

The tools of good corporate practice are designed to give a purchasing minority stockholder the opportunity to bargain for protection before parting with consideration. It would do violence to normal corporate practice and our corporation law to fashion an ad hoc ruling which would result in a court-imposed stockholder buy-out for which the parties had not contracted.

In 1967, when the Delaware General Corporation Law was significantly revised, a new Subchapter XIV entitled "Close Corporations; Special Provisions," became a part of that law for the first time. While these provisions were patterned in theory after close corporation statutes in Florida and Maryland, "the Delaware provisions were unique and influenced the development of similar legislation in a number of other states." *See* Ernest L. Folk, III, Rodman Ward, Jr., and Edward P. Welch, 2 Folk on the Delaware General Corporation Law 404 (1988). Subchapter XIV is a narrowly constructed statute which applies only to a corporation which is designated as a "close corporation" in its certificate of incorporation, and which fulfills other requirements, including a limitation to 30 on the number of stockholders, that all classes of stock have to have at least one restriction on transfer, and that there be no "public offering." 8 Del.C. § 342. Accordingly, subchapter XIV applies only to "close corporations," as defined in section 342. "Unless a corporation elects to become a close corporation under this subchapter in the manner prescribed in this subchapter, it shall be subject in all respects to this chapter, except this subchapter." 8 Del.C. § 341. The corporation before the Court in this matter, is not a "close corporation." Therefore it is not governed by the provisions of Subchapter XIV.[19]

One cannot read into the situation presented in the case at bar any special relief for the minority stockholders in this closely-held, but not statutory "close corporation" because the provisions of Subchapter XIV relating to close corporations and other statutory schemes preempt the field in their respective areas. It would run counter to the spirit of the doctrine of independent legal significance, and would be inappropriate judicial legislation for this Court to fashion a special judicially-created rule for minority investors when the entity does not fall within those statutes, or when there are no negotiated special provisions in the certificate of incorporation, bylaws, or stockholder agreements.

Nixon did not leave minority shareholders without any remedy for overreaching by the majority. Although the court rejected the Massachusetts view, in a passage not included in the excerpt above, the court held that, because the ESOP benefited shareholders who were directors in a way different from the non-employee shareholders, the board's action in creating the ESOP was to be judged under the "entire fairness" standard rather than the business judgment rule. In this case, however, the court found that the defendants had met the burden of proving that the transaction was entirely fair.

---

[19] We do not intend to imply that, if the Corporation had been a close corporation under Subchapter XIV, the result in this case would have been different.

"[S]tatutory close corporations have not found particular favor with practitioners. Practitioners have for the most part viewed the complex statutory provisions underlying the purportedly simplified operational procedures for close corporations as legal quicksand of uncertain depth and have adopted the view that the objectives sought by the subchapter are achievable for their clients with considerably less uncertainty by cloaking a conventionally created corporation with the panoply of charter provisions, transfer restrictions, by-laws, stockholders' agreements, buy-sell arrangements, irrevocable proxies, voting trusts or other contractual mechanisms which were and remain the traditional method for accomplishing the goals sought by the close corporation provisions."

David A. Drexler, Lewis S. Black, Jr., and A. Gilchrist Sparks, III, Delaware Corporation Law and Practice § 43.01 (1993).

2. WHAT IS "OPPRESSION"?

As the cases illustrate, oppression is often in the eye of the beholder. Should the "oppression" analysis take into consideration the prerogatives of the majority to manage the business as it sees fit? Should "oppression" depend on the wrongful conduct of the majority or the frustrated expectations of the minority, whether or not the majority was wrongful? Should reasonable expectations be fixed at the beginning of the corporate relationship? Or do expectations evolve over time?

"The increasing use of the reasonable expectations standard reflects a move away from an exclusive search for egregious conduct by those in control of the enterprise and toward greater consideration of the effect of conduct on the complaining shareholder, even if no egregious conduct by controllers can be shown." Robert B. Thompson, *Corporate Dissolution and Shareholders' Reasonable Expectations*, 66 Wash. U.L.Q. 193, 219–220 (1988). More recently, Professor Douglas Moll has observed:

> A minority shareholder's chance of success in an "oppression" action depends on the perspective from which shareholder oppression is viewed. On the one hand, some courts view shareholder oppression from a majority perspective—a perspective that focuses primarily on the conduct of the majority. On the other hand, some courts view shareholder oppression from a minority perspective—a perspective that focuses primarily on the effect of that conduct on the minority shareholder. Whereas a majority-perspective court finds oppression liability when the majority's actions are not justified by a legitimate business purpose, a minority-perspective court generally finds oppression liability when majority actions, whether justified or not, harm the interests of a minority shareholder. The choice of perspective can make an outcome-determinative difference in a number of cases.

Douglas K. Moll, *Shareholder Oppression in Close Corporations: The Unanswered Question of Perspective*, 53 Vand. L. Rev. 749 (2000).

From which perspective should shareholder oppression be viewed? To answer this question, Moll constructs hypothetical bargains between rational close corporation participants. He argues that a modified minority perspective best captures the likely understandings that reasonable investors would have reached if, at the venture's inception, they had bargained over minority protection and majority prerogatives. Indeed, because the close corporation investment is typically comprised of more than a mere financial stake in the corporation's success, Moll asserts that reasonable close corporation shareholders would not reach an understanding that any majority conduct benefitting the corporation is permissible. The majority perspective is flawed due to its assumption that close corporation shareholders are solely concerned with maximizing the investment returns.

Judge Easterbrook and Professor Fischel, on the other hand, oppose judicial decisions and state statutes that provide for dissolution if the majority shareholders frustrate a minority shareholder's "reasonable expectations." They argue that this vague and open-ended standard provides disgruntled minority shareholders with an opportunity to coerce majority shareholders by threatening in bad faith to initiate lawsuits seeking dissolution. Frank H. Easterbrook & Daniel R. Fischel, *Close Corporations and Agency Costs*, 38 Stan. L. Rev. 271, 288 (1986).

Another question of perspective that permeates the oppression cases is when reasonable expectations should be gauged—at the time of investment or over the course of the corporation's life? Courts take different approaches. In his review of the various interpretations of reasonable expectations in oppression cases, Professor Moll found that the leading judicial formulation has focused on the minority shareholder's expectations at the time he invested in the business. Douglas K. Moll, *Shareholder Oppression and Reasonable Expectations: Of Change, Gifts, and Inheritances in Close Corporation Disputes*, 86 Minn. L. Rev. 717 (2002). But Moll asserts a "time of investment" focus may be problematic if changed post-investment expectations are the basis for the oppression claim. Such a focus may also fail to account for non-investing shareholders who received their shares by inheritance or gift, and may not have had any specific reasonable expectations at the time their shares were acquired.

Using an "investment model" for understanding oppression, Moll argues that "reasonable expectations" should be understood as a bargain struck between majority and minority shareholders over a specific entitlement the minority is to receive in return for her investment in the company. Because majority and minority shareholders may strike these "investment bargains" throughout their participation in a close corporation, Moll asserts that the oppression doctrine should look for evidence of such bargains during the entirety of the shareholders' relationship, rather than merely at the time of investment. Moreover, although non-investing stockholders may not commit money capital to the company, their mutual understandings with the majority, if proven, should be protected as investment bargains.

3. REMEDIES

Many modern statutes grant courts the power to dissolve the corporation if a shareholder establishes that: (a) the directors are deadlocked, and the deadlock cannot be broken by shareholders and it is injuring the corporation or impairing the conduct of its business; (b) the shareholders are deadlocked and have not been able to elect directors for two years; (c) corporate assets are being wasted; or (d) those in control of the corporation are acting "in a manner that is illegal, oppressive or fraudulent." *See* MBCA § 14.30(2). Over the last three decades, courts have used these statutes to craft broad protections for minority shareholders who complain of "oppression" by majority shareholders.

The Official Comment to MBCA § 14.30 advises courts to be "cautious" when considering claims of oppression "so as to limit such cases to genuine abuse rather than instances of acceptable tactics in a power struggle for control of a corporation." In addition, MBCA § 14.34 authorizes any close corporation or any shareholder of a close corporation "to purchase all shares owned by the petitioning shareholder at the fair value of the shares" within 90 days after a petition is filed under § 14.30(2) or, if authorized by the court, at some later date, which can be a date after the court has found that the petitioning shareholder was being oppressed.

These statutes raise three important interpretive questions. First, when is majority conduct "oppressive"? Second, when a court finds oppression, what remedy is appropriate—dissolution or buy-out? Third, where a corporation or shareholder elects to exercise buy-out rights under MBCA § 14.34, how is the "fair value" of the complaining shareholder's stock to be determined?

Corporate statutes usually provide that a corporation can be dissolved with the approval of the board of directors and the shareholders. In the case of both voluntary and court-ordered dissolutions, corporate existence is terminated in an orderly fashion: the corporation sells off its assets, pays off its creditors, and distributes whatever remains to its shareholders. But a dissident shareholder who brings suit seeking dissolution often will be less interested in terminating the corporation's legal existence than in using the threat of dissolution as leverage to bargain for a better price for her stock.

Whether a threat of dissolution is effective may depend on the nature of the corporation's business. If a business derives its value almost entirely from the corporation's tangible assets, shareholders who wish to continue to operate the business probably will have to pay fair market value for those assets, since other prospective purchasers could use them to equally good effect. But if a business derives most of its value from its economic good will supplied by the presence of the majority, dissolution may disserve the minority's interests. In such a situation, the majority may be able to purchase the corporation's tangible assets for their fair market value and to capture the associated good will at no additional cost and a mandatory buyout of her shares at their "fair market value" will better serve the minority's interests. That is so because, in valuing the minority's shares, most courts take account of the value of the corporation's economic good will.

At first glance, dissolution or a mandatory buyout may appear a sensible solution to oppression. But on closer examination, the problem is more complex. First, how will the remedy affect other corporate constituents, such as employees or creditors? Would a remedy that forces the sale of some business assets affect the corporation's viability? Second, will dissolution (or even a buyout) enable one shareholder group to acquire the business at a price unfair to others? Third, is the petitioning shareholder merely seeking to liquidate an investment, or is there another, darker agenda?

IN THE MATTER OF KEMP & BEATLEY, INC.

473 N.E.2d 1173 (N.Y. 1984).

COOKE, CHIEF JUDGE:

When the majority shareholders of a close corporation award de facto dividends to all shareholders except a class of minority shareholders, such a policy may constitute "oppressive actions" and serve as a basis for an order made pursuant to section 1104—a of the Business Corporation Law dissolving the corporation. In the instant matter, there is sufficient evidence to support the lower courts' conclusion that the majority shareholders had altered a long-standing policy to distribute corporate earnings on the basis of stock ownership, as against petitioners only. Moreover, the courts did not abuse their discretion by concluding that dissolution was the only means by which petitioners could gain a fair return on their investment.

I

The business concern of Kemp & Beatley, incorporated under the laws of New York, designs and manufactures table linens and sundry tabletop items. The company's stock consists of 1,500 outstanding shares held by eight shareholders. Petitioner Dissin had been employed by the company for 42 years when, in June 1979, he resigned. Prior to resignation, Dissin served as vice-president and a director of Kemp & Beatley. Over the course of his employment, Dissin had acquired stock in the company and currently owns 200 shares.

Petitioner Gardstein, like Dissin, had been a long-time employee of the company. Hired in 1944, Gardstein was for the next 35 years involved in various aspects of the business including material procurement, product design, and plant management. His employment was terminated by the company in December 1980. He currently owns 105 shares of Kemp & Beatley stock.

Apparent unhappiness surrounded petitioners' leaving the employ of the company. Of particular concern was that they no longer received any distribution of the company's earnings. Petitioners considered themselves to be "frozen out" of the company; whereas it had been their experience when with the company to receive a distribution of the company's earnings according to their stockholdings, in the form of either dividends or extra compensation, that distribution was no longer forthcoming.

Gardstein and Dissin, together holding 20.33% of the company's outstanding stock, commenced the instant proceeding in June 1981, seeking dissolution of Kemp & Beatley pursuant to section 1104–a of the Business Corporation Law. Their petition alleged "fraudulent and oppressive" conduct by the company's board of directors such as to render petitioners' stock "a virtually worthless asset." Supreme Court referred the matter for a hearing, which was held in March 1982.

Upon considering the testimony of petitioners and the principals of Kemp & Beatley, the referee concluded that "the corporate management has by its policies effectively rendered petitioners' shares worthless, and the only way petitioners can expect any return is by dissolution". Petitioners were found to have invested capital in the company expecting, among other things, to receive dividends or "bonuses" based upon their stock holdings. Also found was the company's "established buyout policy" by which it would purchase the stock of employee shareholders upon their leaving its employ.

The involuntary-dissolution statute (Business Corporation Law, § 1104–a) permits dissolution when a corporation's controlling faction is found guilty of "oppressive action" toward the complaining shareholders. The referee considered oppression to arise when "those in control" of the corporation "have acted in such a manner as to defeat those expectations of the minority stockholders which formed the basis of their participation in the venture." The expectations of petitioners that they would not be arbitrarily excluded from gaining a return on their investment and that their stock would be purchased by the corporation upon termination of employment, were deemed defeated by prevailing corporate policies. Dissolution was recommended in the referee's report, subject to giving respondent corporation an opportunity to purchase petitioners' stock.

Supreme Court confirmed the referee's report. It, too, concluded that due to the corporation's new dividend policy petitioners had been prevented from receiving any return on their investments. Liquidation of the corporate assets was found the only means by which petitioners would receive a fair return. The court considered judicial dissolution of a corporation to be "a serious and severe remedy." Consequently, the order of dissolution was conditioned upon the corporation's being permitted to purchase petitioners' stock. The Appellate Division affirmed, without opinion.

At issue in this appeal is the scope of section 1104–a of the Business Corporation Law. Specifically, this court must determine whether the provision for involuntary dissolution when the "directors or those in control of the corporation have been guilty of oppressive actions toward the complaining shareholders" was properly applied in the circumstances of this case. We hold that it was, and therefore affirm.

II

Judicially ordered dissolution of a corporation at the behest of minority interests is a remedy of relatively recent vintage in New York.

Section 1104–a (subd. [a], par. [1]) describes three types of proscribed activity: "illegal", "fraudulent", and "oppressive" conduct. The first two terms are familiar words that are commonly understood at law. The last, however, does not enjoy the same certainty gained through long usage. As no definition is provided by the statute, it falls upon the courts to provide guidance.

The statutory concept of "oppressive actions" can, perhaps, best be understood by examining the characteristics of close corporations and the Legislature's general purpose in creating this involuntary-dissolution statute. It is widely understood that, in addition to supplying capital to a contemplated or ongoing enterprise and expecting a fair and equal return, parties comprising the ownership of a close corporation may expect to be actively involved in its management and operation. The small ownership cluster seeks to "contribute their capital, skills, experience and labor" toward the corporate.

As a leading commentator in the field has observed: "Unlike the typical shareholder in the publicly held corporation, who may be simply an investor or a speculator and cares nothing for the responsibilities of management, the shareholder in a close corporation is a co-owner of the business and wants the privileges and powers that go with ownership. His participation in that particular corporation is often his principal or sole source of income. As a matter of fact, providing employment for himself may have been the principal reason why he participated in organizing the corporation. He may or may not anticipate an ultimate profit from the sale of his interest, but he normally draws very little from the corporation as dividends. In his capacity as an officer or employee of the corporation, he looks to his salary for the principal return on his capital investment, because earnings of a close corporation, as is well known, are distributed in major part in salaries, bonuses and retirement benefits." (O'Neal, Close Corporations [2d ed.], § 1.07, at pp. 21–22)

Shareholders enjoy flexibility in memorializing these expectations through agreements setting forth each party's rights and obligations in corporate governance. In the absence of such an agreement, however, ultimate decision-making power respecting corporate policy will be reposed in the holders of a majority interest in the corporation (see, *e.g.*, Business Corporation Law, §§ 614, 708). A wielding of this power by any group controlling a corporation may serve to destroy a stockholder's vital interests and expectations.

As the stock of closely held corporations generally is not readily salable, a minority shareholder at odds with management policies may be without either a voice in protecting his or her interests or any reasonable means of withdrawing his or her investment. This predicament may fairly be considered the legislative concern underlying the provision at issue in this case; inclusion of the criteria that the corporation's stock not be traded on securities markets and that the complaining shareholder be subject to oppressive actions supports this conclusion.

Defining oppressive conduct as distinct from illegality in the present context has been considered in other forums. The question has been resolved by considering oppressive actions to refer to conduct that substantially defeats the "reasonable expectations" held by minority shareholders in committing their capital to the particular enterprise (see, *e.g.*, Exadaktilos v. Cinnaminson Realty Co., 167 N.J.Super. 141, 153–156, 400 A.2d 554, affd. 173 N.J.Super. 559, 414 A.2d 994). This concept is consistent with the apparent purpose underlying the provision under review. A shareholder who reasonably expected that ownership in the corporation would entitle him or her to a job, a share of corporate earnings, a place in corporate management, or some other form of security, would be oppressed in a very real sense when others in the corporation seek to defeat those expectations and there exists no effective means of salvaging the investment.

Given the nature of close corporations and the remedial purpose of the statute, this court holds that utilizing a complaining shareholder's "reasonable expectations" as a means of identifying and measuring conduct alleged to be oppressive is appropriate. A court considering a petition alleging oppressive conduct must investigate what the majority shareholders knew, or should have known, to be the petitioner's expectations in entering the particular enterprise. Majority conduct should not be deemed oppressive simply because the petitioner's subjective hopes and desires in joining the venture are not fulfilled. Disappointment alone should not necessarily be equated with oppression.

Rather, oppression should be deemed to arise only when the majority conduct substantially defeats expectations that, objectively viewed, were both reasonable under the circumstances and were central to the petitioner's decision to join the venture. It would be inappropriate, however, for us in this case to delineate the contours of the courts' consideration in determining whether directors have been guilty of oppressive conduct. As in other areas of the law, much will depend on the circumstances in the individual case.

The appropriateness of an order of dissolution is in every case vested in the sound discretion of the court considering the application (see Business Corporation Law, § 1111, subd. [a]). Under the terms of this statute, courts are instructed to consider both whether "liquidation of the corporation is the only feasible means" to protect the complaining shareholder's expectation of a fair return on his or her investment and whether dissolution "is reasonably necessary" to protect "the rights or interests of any substantial number of shareholders" not limited to those complaining (Business Corporation Law, § 1104–a, subd. [b], pars. [1], [2]). Implicit in this direction is that once oppressive conduct is found, consideration must be given to the totality of circumstances surrounding the current state of corporate affairs and relations to determine whether some remedy short of or other than dissolution constitutes a feasible means of satisfying both the petitioner's expectations and the rights and interests of any other substantial group of shareholders (see, also, Business Corporation Law, § 1111, subd. [b], par. [1]).

By invoking the statute, a petitioner has manifested his or her belief that dissolution may be the only appropriate remedy. Assuming the petitioner has set forth a prima facie case of oppressive conduct, it should be incumbent upon the parties seeking to forestall dissolution to demonstrate to the court the existence of an adequate, alternative remedy. A court has broad latitude in fashioning alternative relief, but when fulfillment of the oppressed petitioner's expectations by these means is doubtful, such as when there has been a complete deterioration of relations between the parties, a court should not hesitate to order dissolution. Every order of dissolution, however, must be conditioned upon permitting any shareholder of the corporation to elect to purchase the complaining shareholder's stock at fair value (see Business Corporation Law, § 1118).

One further observation is in order. The purpose of this involuntary dissolution statute is to provide protection to the minority shareholder whose reasonable expectations in undertaking the venture have been frustrated and who has no adequate means of recovering his or her investment. It would be contrary to this remedial purpose to permit its use by minority shareholders as merely a coercive tool. Therefore, the minority shareholder whose own acts, made in bad faith and undertaken with a view toward forcing an involuntary dissolution, give rise to the complained-of oppression should be given no quarter in the statutory protection.

III

There was sufficient evidence presented at the hearing to support the conclusion that Kemp & Beatley had a long-standing policy of awarding de facto dividends based on stock ownership in the form of "extra compensation bonuses." Petitioners, both of whom had extensive experience in the management of the company, testified to this effect. Moreover, both related that receipt of this compensation, whether as true dividends or disguised as "extra compensation", was a known incident to ownership of the company's stock understood by all of the company's principals. Finally, there was uncontroverted proof that this policy was changed either shortly before or shortly after petitioners' employment ended. Extra compensation was still awarded by the company. The only difference was that stock ownership was no longer a basis for the payments; it was asserted that the basis became services rendered to the corporation. It was not unreasonable for the fact finder to have determined that this change in policy amounted to nothing less than an attempt to exclude petitioners from gaining any return on their investment through the mere recharacterization of distributions of corporate income. Under the circumstances of this case, there was no error in determining that this conduct constituted oppressive action within the meaning of section 1104–a of the Business Corporation Law.

Nor may it be said that Supreme Court abused its discretion in ordering Kemp & Beatley's dissolution, subject to an opportunity for a buy-out of petitioners' shares. After the referee had found that the controlling faction of the company was, in effect, attempting to "squeeze-out" petitioners by offering them no return on their investment and increasing other executive compensation, respondents, in opposing the report's confirmation, attempted only to controvert the factual basis of the report. They suggested no feasible, alternative remedy to the forced dissolution. In light of an apparent deterioration in relations between petitioners and the governing shareholders of Kemp & Beatley, it was not unreasonable for the court to have determined that a forced buy-out of petitioners' shares or liquidation of the corporation's assets was the only means by which petitioners could be guaranteed a fair return on their investments.

Accordingly, the order of the Appellate Division should be modified, with costs to petitioners-respondents, by affirming the substantive determination of that court but extending the time for exercising the option to purchase petitioners-respondents' shares to 30 days following this court's determination.

As courts have come to understand that a dissolution order essentially forces one faction to buy out the other, courts have increasingly ordered a buyout on specified terms. The MBCA permits majority shareholders in a close corporation to avoid dissolution by electing to buy out at "fair value" the shares of a shareholder who petitions for involuntary dissolution. MBCA § 14.34. As the Official Comment explains, this provision gives the majority a "call" right of minority's shares to prevent strategic abuse of the dissolution procedure. Under this optional procedure, the shareholders who elect to purchase must give notice to the court within 90 days of the petition and then negotiate with the petitioning shareholder. If after 60 days the negotiations fail, the court must stay the proceedings for involuntary dissolution and order a buyout and determine the "fair value" of the petitioner's shares. If the petitioner had "probable grounds" for relief under the misconduct provisions of the involuntary dissolution statute, the award may include the petitioner's litigation costs (attorney and expert fees).

One question that arises under a buyout statute or when a court finds oppression and orders a buyout is what weight should be given to a shareholder agreement on transfers of stock. In *In the Matter of Pace Photographers, Ltd.*, 525 N.E.2d 713 (N.Y. 1988), a shareholder agreement fixed the price at which stock could be purchased if any shareholder decided to "sell, hypothecate, transfer, encumber or otherwise dispose of" his stock. The court held that the agreement did not control the price at which the stock should be transferred when the corporation elected to buy a petitioning shareholder's stock pursuant to New York's buyout statutes (N.Y.B.C.L. § 1118), because the agreement did not include a dissolution proceeding under N.Y.B.C.L. § 1104–a in its list of voluntary transactions that would trigger the pricing provision.

Courts in other states have relied on their inherent equity authority to devise remedies other than dissolution where they have found minority shareholders have been oppressed or a deadlock exists. In *Baker v. Commercial Body Builders, Inc.*, 507 P.2d 387 (Ore. 1973), the court listed ten possible forms of relief that it could order short of outright dissolution:

(a) The entry of an order requiring dissolution of the corporation at a specified future date, to become effective only in the event that the stockholders fail to resolve their differences prior to that date.

(b) The appointment of a receiver, not for the purposes of dissolution, but to continue the operation of the corporation for the benefit of all of the stockholders, both majority and minority, until differences are resolved or "oppressive" conduct ceases.

(c) The appointment of a "special fiscal agent" to report to the court relating to the continued operation of the corporation, as a protection to its minority stockholders, and the retention of jurisdiction of the case by the court for that purpose.

(d) The retention of jurisdiction of the case by the court for the protection of the minority stockholders without appointment of a receiver or "special fiscal agent."

(e) The ordering of an accounting by the majority in control of the corporation for funds alleged to have been misappropriated.

(f) The issuance of an injunction to prohibit continuing acts of "oppressive" conduct and which may include the reduction of salaries or bonus payments found to be unjustified or excessive.

(g) The ordering of affirmative relief by the required declaration of a dividend or a reduction and distribution of capital.

(h) The ordering of affirmative relief by the entry of an order requiring the corporation or a majority of its stockholders to purchase the stock of the minority stockholders at a price to be determined according to a specified formula or at a price determined by the court to be a fair and reasonable price.

(i) The ordering of affirmative relief by the entry of an order permitting minority stockholders to purchase additional stock under conditions specified by the court.

(j) An award of damages to minority stockholders as compensation for any injury suffered by them as the result of "oppressive" conduct by the majority in control of the corporation.

Id. at 395–96.

Problem: Precision Tools—Part 5

When Michael, Jessica and Bernie formed Precision Tools, they entered into a written shareholder voting agreement that provided each would vote for a board of directors made up of the three of them and a fourth person to be designated by Bernie. Pursuant to their mutual understanding, which they did not reduce to writing, Michael was elected president and CEO and Jessica was elected vice-president and chief financial officer.

After operating under this agreement for three years, Jessica and Bernie became increasingly dissatisfied with Michael's performance as president. They decided that he was not an effective executive, that he was indecisive, and that he had allowed Precision Tools' overhead expenses to grow excessively. They were particularly distressed that, for the first time, the company had operated at a loss. They also were upset by what they perceived to be serious personality clashes between Michael and several key employees. All this led Jessica and Bernie to conclude that unless steps were taken to remove Michael, the company's decline would continue.

At the company's next board of directors meeting, Michael defended his performance and argued that the company's losses were due to a difficult business environment. Nonetheless, Jessica, Bernie and Bernie's designee voted to remove Michael as an officer and employee and to appoint Jessica president and CEO at a salary substantially higher than Michael had been paid. They also voted not to pay dividends for the foreseeable future and to use all available funds for business development.

After the board meeting Michael wrote a strongly-worded email blaming Jessica for not informing him of the company's financial problems. Bernie and Jessica responded with emails accusing Michael of causing the company's deteriorating employee morale and failing as the company head. When Michael came to the headquarters to clear out his office, Jessica had a private security guard escort him from the building. She also had the company computer passwords changed so that Michael would not be able to access any company information.

Jessica and Bernie then wrote Michael a certified letter and suggested that, although as a director he would be permitted to attend future board meetings, his presence at the company would no longer be welcomed. They requested that he sell his shares back to the corporation at a price fixed by an outside valuation firm—payable over three years and based on what his shares would be worth to an outside purchaser. They reminded him that the board had voted not to pay dividends for the foreseeable future and to use all available funds for business development.

You have known Michael since college, but you have done no legal work for him or for Precision Tools. He is very upset about what has happened and has consulted you about what legal remedies he might have.

Assume that a Columbia court would adopt the same approach the Massachusetts Supreme Judicial Court has followed in cases involving close corporations. Is it likely that Michael would succeed in a suit to restore him to his position as president and/or compel the payment of dividends?

If Columbia has not addressed a case like Michael's, should it follow the Massachusetts approach? Is the approach of the Delaware Supreme Court preferable? Is there some other methodology that might be more appropriate?

Assume you have concluded that bringing a suit along these lines would not be advisable, can Michael establish that he has been oppressed by Jessica and Bernie? If he could prove oppression, what relief could he obtain? Consider whether your answer varies if Precision Tools is incorporated in: (1) New York (Matter of Kemp & Beatley, Inc.); (2) MBCA §§ 14.30, 14.32, 14.34; (3) DGCL §§ 226, 352, 353, 355.

Should Michael, Jessica and Bernie have included a contractual buyout in a shareholders' agreement, before making their initial investments in Precision Tools? How do existing statutory oppression remedies affect your analysis? How might each of the parties have reacted to suggestions made by the others?

CHAPTER 7

PARTNERSHIPS

■ ■ ■

A. INTRODUCTION

Partnerships are the oldest form of business after sole proprietorships, and they have long existed alongside corporations. All 50 states recognize and enable the formation of general partnerships and limited partnerships. In this book, a "general partnership" is defined as a partnership that does not have limited liability. Most states have enacted in some version of the Revised Uniform Partnership Act (1997) ("RUPA"). The laws of limited partnerships in most states are variations of two uniform statutes: Revised Uniform Limited Partnership Act (1976) ("RULPA"), and Uniform Limited Partnership Act (2001) ("ULPA (2001)").

B. GENERAL PARTNERSHIPS

As limited liability entities have become prominent, general partnerships are becoming less preferred by businesspersons. More pointedly, sophisticated businesses prefer to create a limited liability entity such as a corporation or LLC because the risk of liability is greater than the relatively minimal administrative burden of filing with the state to become a limited liability entity. The calculus applies to even smaller, simpler businesses, which explains the rapid rise of LLCs since the 1990s. However, general partnerships are important to study because general partnerships are sometimes formed by businesspersons (with specific intent to do so or not) and because their legal structure is the root source of the laws of non-corporate entities including LLCs.

1. DEFINITION OF PARTNERSHIP

A partnership is "an association of two or more persons to carry on as co-owners a business for profit." RUPA § 101(6). Partnerships differ in a fundamental way from corporations and LLCs because partnerships require two or more equityholders (partners) whereas corporations and LLCs need only a single equityholder (shareholder or member). "Persons" need not be natural persons (*e.g.*, a partnership between Bill Gates and Steve Jobs). Persons can also mean legal persons, such as another partnership or corporation (*e.g.*, a partnership between Microsoft and Apple).

Two or more persons must be co-owners of a business for profit. A key attribute of "co-owners" is sharing in profit of the partnership business. This does not mean that employees cannot per se share in profit. Many businesses have profit-share plans in which employees share some of the profit with the owners of the business. But co-owners predominantly own the profits of the firm, and a claim to profit is the principal benefit of owning a business as opposed to working as an employee for a fixed salary. Another key attribute of co-owners is that they have control of the management of the business. This does not mean that each partner is a totalitarian dictator in the firm or has a veto on all matters. Rather, partners collectively controls the business in a way that employees collectively do not.

Profit is a specific economic and accounting term. It means the residual claim on revenue after all expenses are paid. Revenue, sometimes called "sales" or "gross receipts" or "gross returns," is the proceeds received from the sale of goods or services. For example, suppose a partnership sells real estate transaction services; it earns a fee of 100 for each transaction; in a year, it consummates 100 transactions. Its revenue is 10,000 (= 100 × 100). Revenue is not profit because a firm incurs expenses associated with doing business. Profit is net of all expenses. For example, the partnership may have to pay for rent, utilities, and employees (who are not partners). Suppose these expenses constitute on average 70% of revenue. Profit is what remains after deducting expenses (thus, profit is called "residual" income or profit in economic-speak). Profit is calculated as: Revenue – Expenses = Profit. For example, a firm sells 10,000 in products and services and incurs expenses of 7,000: (10,000 – 7,000) = 3,000 profit. Of course, there is no guarantee of profit in a market system. A firm's expenses may exceed revenue, in which case there is a "loss" or "net loss."

2. FORMATION

To form a limited liability entity such as an LLC or a corporation, an organizer or promoter must file a certificate with a state agency, typically the secretary of state. This is a ministerial act for non-corporate limited liability entities because the information content in a filing is typically bare bone. Albeit ministerial, the act of filing is important because the state grants the authority to form a business entity with limited liability. However, since a general partnership is not a limited liability entity, it can be formed without filing with the state.

A general partnership can be formed by two or more persons without filing with the state. Instead, it is formed by the mutual asset of partners.

RUPA § 202: Formation of Partnership

(a) . . . the association of two or more persons to carry on as co-owners a business for profit forms a partnership, whether or not the persons intend to form a partnership. . . .

(c) In determining whether a partnership is formed, the following rules apply: . . .

   (2) The sharing of gross returns does not by itself establish a partnership, even if the persons sharing them have a joint or common right or interest in property from which the returns are derived.

   (3) A person who receives a share of the profits of a business is presumed to be a partner in the business, unless the profits were received in payment:

      (i) of a debt by installments or otherwise;

      (ii) for services as an independent contractor or of wages or other compensation to an employee; . . .

      (v) of interest or other charge on a loan, even if the amount of payment varies with the profits of the business, including a direct or indirect present or future ownership of the collateral, or rights to income, proceeds, or increase in value derived from the collateral

---

Section 202(a) states that partners can form a partnership "whether or not the persons intend to form a partnership." Subjective intent to form a partnership is not a prerequisite to form a partnership. Parties, mostly unsophisticated persons without proper legal advice, can intend to form a partnership, but in fact do not because they failed to satisfy the definition of a partnership. *See, e.g., Fenwick v. Unemployment Compensation Commission*, 44 A.2d 172 (N.J.App. 1945) (holding that parties had employer-employee relationship even though they called themselves "partners"). Conversely, parties may not have intended to form a partnership or have had no intent at all, but in fact they formed a partnership because the satisfied the definition of a partnership. *See, e.g., In re Marriage of Hassiepen*, 646 N.E.2d 1348 (Ill.App. 1995) (holding that husband and wife were partners in a partnership despite their lack of specific intent, thus permitting only half of the husband's income to be subject to his ex-wife's claim of child support). Even sophisticated businesspersons can inadvertently form a partnership. *See, e.g., Minute Maid Corp. v. United Foods, Inc.*, 291 F.2d 577 (5th Cir. 1961) (holding that an inventory financing and storage agreement between two businesses created a partnership despite their lack of specific intent, thus permitting a creditor of one partner in the course of transactions on behalf of the partnership to seek satisfaction of a debt against the other partner). There is a common fact pattern in these kinds of cases. When a creditor is not paid by a debtor, it may seek payment from a third party on the argument that the debtor and the third party were actually partners in a partnership. Partners are liable for the debts and obligations of the partnership to the creditor. Accordingly, if a creditor can prove the existence of a partnership, it can satisfy its debt from the other partners.

Since the creation of a limited liability entity requires a filing with the state, it always requires a conscious intent to create an entity. However, a general partnership can be formed or not formed, irrespective of specific intent to do so. The inquiry is whether two or more persons carry on as co-owners of a business for profit, irrespective of specific intent. When parties unknowingly form a partnership, the laws of general partnerships provide a set of default rules that govern the entity even though the partners have not considered the creation of a partnership agreement.

The case below concerns whether a creditor of a firm was really a partner in a partnership with the firm. In reading this case, think about these questions: (1) What practical difference does it make if one is a creditor or a partner? (2) What rights did the creditor negotiate for itself and why did they negotiate for them? (3) How do these rights bear on the question of whether the defendant was really (legally) a creditor or a partner?

MARTIN V. PEYTON
158 N.E. 77 (N.Y. 1927).

ANDREWS, J.

Much ancient learning as to partnership is obsolete. Today, only those who are partners between themselves may be charged for partnership debts by others. There is one exception. Now and then, a recovery is allowed where in truth such relationship is absent. This is because the debtor may not deny the claim.

Partnership results from contract, express or implied. If denied it may be proved by the production of some written instrument; by testimony as to some conversation; by circumstantial evidence. If nothing else appears, the receipt by the defendant of a share of the profits of the business is enough.

Assuming some written contract between the parties the question may arise whether it creates a partnership. If it be complete; if it expresses in good faith the full understanding and obligation of the parties, then it is for the court to say whether a partnership exists. It may, however, be a mere sham intended to hide the real relationship. Then other results follow. In passing upon it effect is to be given to each provision. Mere words will not blind us to realities. Statements that no partnership is intended are not conclusive. If as a whole a contract contemplates an association of two or more persons to carry on as co-owners a business for profit a partnership there is. On the other hand, if it be less than this no partnership exists. Passing on the contract as a whole, an arrangement for sharing profits is to be considered. It is to be given its due weight. But it is to be weighed in connection with all the rest. It is not decisive. It may be merely the method adopted to pay a debt or wages, as interest on a loan or for other reasons.

In the case before us the claim that the defendants became partners in the firm of Knauth, Nachod & Kuhne, doing business as bankers and brokers, depends upon the interpretation of certain instruments. "The plaintiff's position is not," we are told, "that the agreements of June 4, 1921, were a false expression or incomplete expression of the intention of the parties. We say that they express defendants' intention and that that intention was to create a relationship which as a matter of law constitutes a partnership."

Remitted then, as we are, to the documents themselves, we refer to circumstances surrounding their execution only so far as is necessary to make them intelligible. And we are to remember that although the intention of the parties to avoid liability as partners is clear, although in language precise and definite they deny any design to then join the firm of K. N. & K.; although they say their interests in profits should be construed merely as a measure of compensation for loans, not an interest in profits as such; although they provide that they shall not be liable for any losses or treated as partners, the question still remains whether in fact they agree to so associate themselves with the firm as to "carry on as co-owners a business for profit."

In the spring of 1921 the firm of K. N. & K. found itself in financial difficulties. John R. Hall was one of the partners. He was a friend of Mr. Peyton. From him he obtained the loan of almost $500,000 of Liberty bonds, which K. N. & K. might use as collateral to secure bank advances. This, however, was not sufficient. The firm and its members had engaged in unwise speculations, and it was deeply involved. Mr. Hall was also intimately acquainted with George W. Perkins, Jr., and with Edward W. Freeman. He also knew Mrs. Peyton and Mrs. Perkins and Mrs. Freeman. All were anxious to help him. He, therefore, representing K. N. & K., entered into negotiations with them. While they were pending a proposition was made that Mr. Peyton, Mr. Perkins and Mr. Freeman or some of them should become partners. It met a decided refusal. Finally an agreement was reached. It is expressed in three documents, executed on the same day, all a part of the one transaction. They were drawn with care and are unambiguous. We shall refer to them as "the agreement," "the indenture" and "the option."

We have no doubt as to their general purpose. The respondents were to loan K. N. & K. $2,500,000 worth of liquid securities, which were to be returned to them on or before April 15, 1923. The firm might hypothecate them to secure loans totalling $2,000,000, using the proceeds as its business necessities required. To insure respondents against loss K. N. & K. were to turn over to them a large number of their own securities which may have been valuable, but which were of so speculative a nature that they could not be used as collateral for bank loans. In compensation for the loan the respondents were to receive 40 per cent of the profits of the firm until the return was made, not exceeding, however, $500,000 and not less than $100,000. Merely because the transaction involved the transfer of securities and not of cash does not prevent its being a loan within the meaning of section 11. The respondents also were given an option to join the firm if they or any of them expressed a desire to do so before June 4, 1923.

Many other detailed agreements are contained in the papers. Are they such as may be properly inserted to protect the lenders? Or do they go further? Whatever their purpose, did they in truth associate the respondents with the firm so that they and it together thereafter carried on as co-owners a business for profit? The answer depends upon an analysis of these various provisions.

As representing the lenders, Mr. Peyton and Mr. Freeman are called "trustees." The loaned securities when used as collateral are not to be mingled with other securities of K. N. & K., and the trustees at all times are to be kept informed of all transactions affecting them. To them shall be paid all dividends and income accruing therefrom. They may also substitute for any of the securities loaned securities of equal value. With their consent the firm may sell any of its securities held by the respondents, the proceeds to go, however, to the trustees. In other similar ways the trustees may deal with these same securities, but the securities loaned shall always be sufficient in value to permit of their hypothecation for $2,000,000. If they rise in price the excess may be withdrawn by the defendants. If they fall they shall make good the deficiency.

So far there is no hint that the transaction is not a loan of securities with a provision for compensation. Later a somewhat closer connection with the firm appears. Until the securities are returned the directing management of the firm is to be in the hands of John R. Hall, and his life is to be insured for $1,000,000, and the policies are to be assigned as further collateral security to the trustees. These requirements are not unnatural. Hall was the one known and trusted by the defendants. Their acquaintance with the other members of the firm was of the slightest. These others had brought an old and established business to the verge of bankruptcy. As the respondents knew, they also had engaged in unsafe speculation. The respondents were about to loan $2,500,000 of good securities. As collateral they were to receive others of problematical value. What they required seems but ordinary caution. Nor does it imply an association in the business.

The trustees are to be kept advised as to the conduct of the business and consulted as to important matters. They may inspect the firm books and are entitled to any information they think important. Finally they may veto any business they think highly speculative or injurious. Again we hold this but a proper precaution to safeguard the loan. The trustees may not initiate any transaction as a partner may do. They may not bind the firm by any action of their own. Under the circumstances the safety of the loan depended upon the business success of K. N. & K. This success was likely to be compromised by the inclination of its members to engage in speculation. No longer, if the respondents were to be protected, should it be allowed. The trustees, therefore, might prohibit it, and that their prohibition might be effective, information was to be furnished them. Not dissimilar agreements have been held proper to guard the interests of the lender.

As further security each member of K. N. & K. is to assign to the trustees their interest in the firm. No loan by the firm to any member is permitted and the amount each may draw is fixed. No other distribution of profits is to be made. So that realized profits may be calculated the existing capital is stated to be $700,000, and profits are to be realized as promptly as good business practice will permit. In case the trustees think this is not done, the question is left to them and to Mr. Hall, and if they differ then to an arbitrator. There is no obligation that the firm shall continue the business. It may dissolve at any time. Again we conclude there is nothing here not properly adapted to secure the interest of the respondents as lenders. If their compensation is dependent on a percentage of the profits still provision must be made to define what these profits shall be.

The "indenture" is substantially a mortgage of the collateral delivered by K. N. & K. to the trustees to secure the performance of the "agreement." It certainly does not strengthen the claim that the respondents were partners.

Finally we have the "option." It permits the respondents or any of them or their assignees or nominees to enter the firm at a later date if they desire to do so by buying 50 per cent or less of the interests therein of all or any of the members at a stated price. Or a corporation may, if the respondents and the members agree, be formed in place of the firm. Meanwhile, apparently with the design of protecting the firm business against improper or ill-judged action which might render the option valueless, each member of the firm is to place his resignation in the hands of Mr. Hall. If at any time he and the trustees agree that such resignation should be accepted, that member shall then retire, receiving the value of his interest calculated as of the date of such retirement.

This last provision is somewhat unusual, yet it is not enough in itself to show that on June 4, 1921, a present partnership was created nor taking these various papers as a whole do we reach such a result. It is quite true that even if one or two or three like provisions contained in such a contract do not require this conclusion, yet it is also true that when taken together a point may come where stipulations immaterial separately cover so wide a field that we should hold a partnership exists. As in other branches of the law a question of degree is often the determining factor. Here that point has not been reached.

3. PRIVATE ORDERING AND MANDATORY PROVISIONS

In partnerships, the private ordering of the partners is set forth in the partnership agreement. The partnership statute provides a template for ordering the partnership, but one of the principal purposes of drafting a partnership agreement is to modify some of the default statutory provisions and provide additional provisions as needed to establish the economic and management relationships desired by the partners.

The partnership statute provides the default terms that apply in the event that partners have not contracted for the matter in the partnership agreement. For example, RUPA § 103(a) provides:

> [R]elations among the partners and between the partners and the partnership are governed by the partnership agreement. To the extent the partnership agreement does not otherwise provide, this [Act] governs relations among the partners and between the partners and the partnership.

All sophisticated partnerships will have a written partnership agreement. Significant businesses or sophisticated parties generally engage business attorneys to draft these agreements. In many states, a partnership agreement or provisions thereof need not be written, but obviously a written agreement is best practice.

All partnership statutes contain a few provisions regarding matters that partnership agreements may not change. RUPA § 103(b) provides these mandatory terms and states that a partnership agreement may not:

- Unreasonably restrict the right of access to books and records

- Eliminate the duty of loyalty, but the partnership agreement may identify specific types or categories of activities that do not violate the duty of loyalty, if not manifestly unreasonable

- Eliminate the obligation of good faith and fair dealing, but the partnership agreement may prescribe the standards by which the performance of the obligation is to be measured, if the standards are not manifestly unreasonable

- Unreasonably reduce the duty of care

- Vary the right of a court to expel a partner for reasons stated in the statute

As we have learned in Chapter 6 on close corporations, the economic and governance interests of shareholders in a corporation can be structured through various means: the certificate of incorporation, bylaws, shareholder agreements, and employment contracts. In non-corporate entities such as partnerships, the economic and governance interests are found in the partnership agreement. If drafted properly, the partnership agreement should address:

- The allocation of economic interests (profits, losses and rights to distributions)

- Management structure

- Governance rights (voting powers),

- Agency authority

- Events of dissociation,

- Rights and duties upon dissociation

- Dissolution and rights on dissolution

4.   KEY STATUTORY DEFAULT RULES

The following are key statutory default rules found in most partnership statutes. These are default terms, and they apply when the partners have not separately agreed to a different rule in the partnership agreement. In practice, partners will typically change some of the statutory terms, at least, in the partnership agreement.

Equal financial rights.—RUPA § 401(b) provides the following default rule regarding the allocation of profits and losses: "Each partner is entitled to an equal share of the partnership profits and is chargeable with a share of the partnership losses in proportion to the partner's share of the profits." In terms of financial and governance rights, partnership law presumes a communitarian association where equality is the rule. Under the default rule, even if partners contribute different amounts of capital to the partnership they are treated equally with respect to the allocation of profits and losses. In practice, this rule of equality may not be suitable or equitable, and partners may provide that the allocation of profits and losses will depend on each partner's contribution to the partnership in the form of capital or labor, or on any other formula established by the partnership agreement.

When partners contribute the same form of capital (such as money), the allocation of profits and losses may be as simple as the percentage contribution of capital. However, partners can contribute capital in different forms—money, property, or labor. When forms of contributions are different, partners must determine how the contributions are valued if they seek to have contributions determine financial rights.

A good example of this problem is seen in *Kovacik v. Reed*, 315 P.2d 314 (Cal. 1957). There, one partner contributed $10,000 and the other labor capital. They agreed to share profits equally, but did not discuss the possibility of a loss. The partnership ultimately suffered losses, and the partner who provided money capital lost $8,680 of his $10,000 capital contribution. He sued the other partner, who contributed labor only, to share the loss of money capital. The California Supreme Court held:

> Where, however, as in the present case, one partner or joint adventurer contributes the money capital as against the other's skill and labor, all the cases cited, and which our research has discovered, hold that neither party is liable to the other for contribution for any loss sustained. Thus, upon loss of the money the party who contributed it is not entitled to recover any part of it from the party who contributed only services. The rationale of this rule is that where one party contributes money and the other contributes services, then in the event of a loss each would lose his own capital the one his money and the other his labor. Another view would be that in such a situation the parties have, by their agreement to share equally in profits, agreed that the value of their contributions the money on the one hand and the labor on the other were likewise equal; it would follow that upon the loss, as here, of both money and labor, the parties have shared equally in the losses.

Cases like *Kovacik* can, of course, be prevented by proper consideration of financial rights in the partnership agreement. It seems that the partners there were overly optimistic since they did not consider the potential that the venture may actually lose money.

Finally, partnership financial rights are inextricably related to tax laws. Contributions of property and distributions by the partnership to partners have significant tax consequences.

Equal management rights.—Consistent with a communitarian view of the enterprise, partnership statutes provides: "Each partner has equal rights in the management and conduct of the partnership business." RUPA § 401(f). In conducting the business and affairs of the partnership, each partner is an agent of the partnership. *Id.* § 301. If partners disagree on a matter in the ordinary course of business, the matter is decided by a majority vote of partners. *Id.* § 401(j).

Again, equal management is a statutory default rule, and the partnership agreement can alter it. For example, significant management authority may be placed in a group of managing partners or a formal body such as an executive board. The management structure will depend on the circumstance of each business. When there are two partners, each having an active role, equal rights may work, though there is always the risk of an impasse through a one-partner veto. When there are hundreds of partners, such as a large law firm, equal rights may be inefficient. A centralized management structure such as a managing partner or an executive board may work better.

Transfer of equity interest.—The laws of corporations and partnerships fundamentally differ on the rules of transfer of ownership interest. Partnership law provides: "The only transferable interest of a partner in the partnership is the partner's share of the profits and losses of the partnership and the partner's right to receive distributions. The interest is personal property." RUPA § 502. Because financial rights are personal property, they are freely transferable, but governance rights are not. A mother cannot donate her entire partnership interest to her son, thus making her son a partner in the partnership. The core policy is that partnerships and LLCs are envisioned as a close and intimate business association where an important consideration of forming the entity is the specific identity of partners or members. "A person may become a partner only with the consent of all of the partners." *Id.* § 401(i) As a result, governance rights are not alienable and they can be granted only by permission of other partners and members, whereas financial rights are personal property and freely transferable.

Corporation law does not have a default restriction on alienability of shares. Generally, the financial and governance rights inherent in stock are inseparable and are alienable as a bundle. Whereas the laws of non-corporate entities value the right of specific equityholders to associate with each other voluntarily, corporation law recognizes that decoupling financial interest and governance rights among a potentially broad group of shareholders could be inefficient and potentially lead to mischief. Corporation law presumes free alienability of shares, subject to contractual restrictions[1] and restrictions on offer and sale of securities under federal securities law (*e.g.*, shares cannot be offered to the public at large without registration under federal securities laws). Free alienability of stock is a necessary condition for public companies because their shares must be freely traded by the public at large.

Dissociation.—Partners come and go, and partnerships form and dissolve. Under the RUPA framework, the departure of a partner results

---

[1] "A restriction on the transfer or registration of transfer of shares is authorized: (1) to maintain the corporation's status when it is dependent on the number or identity of its shareholders; (2) to preserve exemption under federal or state securities law; (3) for any other reasonable purpose." MBCA § 6.27(c).

in the dissociation of the partner from the partnership. The following events cause dissociation of the partner: (1) express will of partner to withdraw, (2) expulsion under the partnership agreement or unanimous vote of partners, (3) expulsion by court order,[2] (4) partner's disqualification due to death, incapacity, bankruptcy, or dissolution (for partners that are entities). RUPA § 601. A partner always has the power to dissociate (a person cannot be forced to work in involuntary servitude), but may not have the right to depart. A wrongful dissociation occurs when by doing so the partner breaches the partnership agreement or leaves earlier than an agreed time. *Id.* § 602(b). A partner that wrongfully dissociates is liable to the partnership and to the other partners for any damages caused by the dissociation. *Id.* § 602(c).

When a partner dissociates, "the partnership *shall* cause the dissociated partner's interest in the partnership to be purchased for a buyout price." *Id.* § 701(a) (emphasis added). Before considering the buyout price, note an important lesson on private ordering here: the "shall" in this provision is not a mandatory term in the same way that "shall" in a statute usually means a mandatory obligation. This provision is not a nonwaivable mandatory provision as identified in RUPA § 103(b). Thus, it is subject to private ordering. Whether a partner is entitled to a buyout and if so the buyout calculation are subject to the partnership agreement. If the partnership agreement is silent on the issue, the buyout term in RUPA § 701 becomes the default term that then becomes mandatory.

The buyout price is the amount that would have been distributable to the dissociating partner in a wind up of the partnership if, on the date of dissociation, the assets of the partnership were sold at a price equal to the greater of the liquidation value or the value based on a sale of the entire business as a going concern without the dissociated partner. *Id.* § 701(b).

5. FIDUCIARY DUTY

RUPA § 404 provides a basic statement regarding the fiduciary duties of partners in a general partnership. The statute has been further refined by an extensive body of case law. The following case provides a classic formulation the fiduciary duty of loyalty in the context of a partnership. In reading this case, think about these questions: (1) In what way did Salmon breach his fiduciary duty to Meinhard? (2) What would have been minimally required to avoid liability? (3) What was the power relationship between Salmon and Meinhard? (4) In what way might Meinhard have

---

[2] The RUPA provides a mechanism for partners to be expelled through judicial action. The bases for such action are: (1) the partner engaged in wrongful conduct that adversely and materially affected the partnership business; (2) the partner willfully or persistently committed a material breach of the partnership agreement or of a duty owed to the partnership or the other partners; or (3) the partner engaged in conduct relating to the partnership business which makes it not reasonably practicable to carry on the business in partnership with the partner. RUPA § 601(5).

been vulnerable in this relationship? (5) What purpose does fiduciary duty serve in promoting business enterprises such as the venture between Salmon and Meinhard?

MEINHARD V. SALMON
164 N.E. 545 (N.Y. 1928).

CARDOZO, C. J.

On April 10, 1902, Louisa M. Gerry leased to the defendant Walter J. Salmon the premises known as the Hotel Bristol at the northwest corner of Forty-Second street and Fifth Avenue in the city of New York. The lease was for a term of 20 years, commencing May 1, 1902, and ending April 30, 1922. The lessee undertook to change the hotel building for use as shops and offices at a cost of $200,000. Alterations and additions were to be accretions to the land.

Salmon, while in course of treaty with the lessor as to the execution of the lease, was in course of treaty with Meinhard, the plaintiff, for the necessary funds. The result was a joint venture with terms embodied in a writing. Meinhard was to pay to Salmon half of the moneys requisite to reconstruct, alter, manage, and operate the property. Salmon was to pay to Meinhard 40 percent of the net profits for the first five years of the lease and 50 percent for the years thereafter. If there were losses, each party was to bear them equally. Salmon, however, was to have sole power to 'manage, lease, underlet and operate' the building. There were to be certain pre-emptive rights for each in the contingency of death.

They were coadventurers, subject to fiduciary duties akin to those of partners. As to this we are all agreed. The heavier weight of duty rested, however, upon Salmon. He was a coadventurer with Meinhard, but he was manager as well. During the early years of the enterprise, the building, reconstructed, was operated at a loss. If the relation had then ended, Meinhard as well as Salmon would have carried a heavy burden. Later the profits became large with the result that for each of the investors there came a rich return. For each the venture had its phases of fair weather and of foul. The two were in it jointly, for better or for worse.

When the lease was near its end, Elbridge T. Gerry had become the owner of the reversion. He owned much other property in the neighborhood, one lot adjoining the Bristol building on Fifth Avenue and four lots on Forty-Second Street. He had a plan to lease the entire tract for a long term to someone who would destroy the buildings then existing and put up another in their place. In the latter part of 1921, he submitted such a project to several capitalists and dealers. He was unable to carry it through with any of them. Then, in January, 1922, with less than four months of the lease to run, he approached the defendant Salmon. The result was a new lease to the Midpoint Realty Company, which is owned and controlled by Salmon, a lease covering the whole tract, and involving a huge outlay. The term is to be 20 years, but successive covenants for renewal will extend it to a maximum of 80 years at the will of either party.

The lease between Gerry and the Midpoint Realty Company was signed and delivered on January 25, 1922. Salmon had not told Meinhard anything about it. Whatever his motive may have been, he had kept the negotiations to himself. Meinhard was not informed even of the bare existence of a project. The first that he knew of it was in February, when the lease was an accomplished fact. He then made demand on the defendants that the lease be held in trust as an asset of the venture, making offer upon the trial to share the personal obligations incidental to the guaranty. The demand was followed by refusal, and later by this suit.

Joint adventurers, like copartners, owe to one another, while the enterprise continues, the duty of the finest loyalty. Many forms of conduct permissible in a workaday world for those acting at arm's length, are forbidden to those bound by fiduciary ties. A trustee is held to something stricter than the morals of the market place. Not honesty alone, but the punctilio of an honor the most sensitive, is then the standard of behavior. As to this there has developed a tradition that is unbending and inveterate. Uncompromising rigidity has been the attitude of courts of equity when petitioned to undermine the rule of undivided loyalty by the 'disintegrating erosion' of particular exceptions. Only thus has the level of conduct for fiduciaries been kept at a level higher than that trodden by the crowd. It will not consciously be lowered by any judgment of this court.

The owner of the reversion, Mr. Gerry, had vainly striven to find a tenant who would favor his ambitious scheme of demolition and construction. Baffled in the search, he turned to the defendant Salmon in possession of the Bristol, the keystone of the project. He figured to himself beyond a doubt that the man in possession would prove a likely customer. To the eye of an observer, Salmon held the lease as owner in his own right, for himself and no one else. In fact he held it as a fiduciary, for himself and another, sharers in a common venture. If this fact had been proclaimed, if the lease by its terms had run in favor of a partnership, Mr. Gerry, we may fairly assume, would have laid before the partners, and not merely before one of them, his plan of reconstruction. The pre-emptive privilege, or, better, the pre-emptive opportunity, that was thus an incident of the enterprise, Salmon appropriate to himself in secrecy and silence. He might have warned Meinhard that the plan had been submitted, and that either would be free to compete for the award. If he had done this, we do not need to say whether he would have been under a duty, if successful in the competition, to hold the lease so acquired for the benefit of a venture than about to end, and thus prolong by indirection its responsibilities and duties. The trouble about his conduct is that he excluded his coadventurer from any chance to compete, from any chance to enjoy the opportunity for benefit that had come to him alone by virtue of his agency. This chance, if nothing more, he was under a duty to concede. The price of its denial is an extension of the trust at the option and for the benefit of the one whom he excluded.

We have no thought to hold that Salmon was guilty of a conscious purpose to defraud. Very likely he assumed in all good faith that with the approaching end of the venture he might ignore his coadventurer and take the extension for himself. He had given to the enterprise time and labor as well as money. He had made it a success. Meinhard, who had given money, but neither time nor labor, had already been richly paid. There might seem to be something grasping in his insistence upon more. Such recriminations are not unusual when coadventurers fall out. They are not without their force if conduct is to be judged by the common standards of competitors. That is not to say that they have pertinency here. Salmon had put himself in a position in which thought of self was to be renounced, however hard the abnegation. He was much more than a coadventurer. He was a managing coadventurer. For him and for those like him the rule of undivided loyalty is relentless and supreme. A different question would be here if there were lacking any nexus of relation between the business conducted by the manager and the opportunity brought to him as an incident of management. For this problem, as for most, there are distinctions of degree. If Salmon had received from Gerry a proposition to lease a building at a location far removed, he might have held for himself the privilege thus acquired, or so we shall assume. Here the subject-matter of the new lease was an extension and enlargement of the subject-matter of the old one. A managing coadventurer appropriating the benefit of such a lease without warning to his partner might fairly expect to be reproached with conduct that was underhand, or lacking, to say the least, in reasonable candor, if the partner were to surprise him in the act of signing the new instrument. Conduct subject to that reproach does not receive from equity a healing benediction.

[The court granted equitable remedy in favor of Meinhard in the form of trust on a minority stake in Salmon's corporation, which was the lessee.]

The following is RUPA's formulation of fiduciary duty. Importantly, note the limiting nature of the language of the statute: *i.e.*, fiduciary duty "is limited to" the formulation stated in the statute. This approach attempts to "cabin in" judicial formulation of fiduciary duty as seen in cases like *Meinhard v. Salmon*, which apply stringent requirements of proper conduct (*e.g.*, "Not honesty alone, but the punctilio of an honor the most sensitive, is then the standard of behavior.").

RUPA § 404: General Standards of Partner's Conduct

(a) The only fiduciary duties a partner owes to the partnership and the other partners are the duty of loyalty and the duty of care set forth in subsections (b) and (c).

(b) A partner's duty of loyalty to the partnership and the other partners is limited to the following:

> (1) to account to the partnership and hold as trustee for it any property, profit, or benefit derived by the partner in the conduct and winding up of the partnership business or derived from a use by the partner of partnership property, including the appropriation of a partnership opportunity;
>
> (2) to refrain from dealing with the partnership in the conduct or winding up of the partnership business as or on behalf of a party having an interest adverse to the partnership; and
>
> (3) to refrain from competing with the partnership in the conduct of the partnership business before the dissolution of the partnership.

(c) A partner's duty of care to the partnership and the other partners in the conduct and winding up of the partnership business is limited to refraining from engaging in grossly negligent or reckless conduct, intentional misconduct, or a knowing violation of law.

(d) A partner shall discharge the duties to the partnership and the other partners under this [Act] or under the partnership agreement and exercise any rights consistently with the obligation of good faith and fair dealing.

(e) A partner does not violate a duty or obligation under this [Act] or under the partnership agreement merely because the partner's conduct furthers the partner's own interest.

Consistent with modern trend in the laws of business organizations, the RUPA permits some degree of contracting for and around fiduciary duty. The duty of loyalty and the obligation of good faith may not be eliminated, but the partnership agreement may identify specific conduct that do not violate the duty if it is not manifestly unreasonable. The duty of care may be reasonably reduced.

RUPA § 103(b): Effects of Partnership Agreement; Nonwaivable Provisions

The partnership agreement may not:

(3) eliminate the duty of loyalty under Section 404(b) . . . but:

  (i)   the partnership agreement may identify specific types or categories of activities that do not violate the duty of loyalty, if not manifestly unreasonable; or

  (ii) all of the partners or a number or percentage specified in the partnership agreement may authorize or ratify, after full disclosure of all material facts, a specific act or transaction that otherwise would violate the duty of loyalty;

(4) unreasonably reduce the duty of care under Section 404(c) . . . ;

(5) eliminate the obligation of good faith and fair dealing under Section 404(d), but the partnership agreement may prescribe the standards by which the performance of the obligation is to be measured, if the standards are not manifestly unreasonable;

Partners may have legitimate reasons to contract about fiduciary duty. For example, the duty of loyalty prohibits "the appropriation of a partnership opportunity." In *Meinhard*, the court held that "Salmon appropriate to himself in secrecy and silence" a partnership opportunity and that Salmon was held to "not honesty alone, but the punctilio of an honor the most sensitive." This is a high bar. This standard may conflict with the realities of the relationships and circumstances in a partnership. A simple example illustrates the point: A partner in a general partnership that manages professional sports teams may also be a partner in a sports team, thus creating a potential conflict of interest in both roles as a partner in different partnerships doing business, albeit slightly different activities, in the same industry. One answer to this situation is that, realizing the potential for conflict of interest, the partners of both partnerships decide that the person should not be a partner unless she relinquishes her position in the other partnership. But business can be complex. Suppose the other partners believe that, despite the potential conflict, the partner brings value to the business. This is the kind of situation in which contracting can provide solutions.

For partners and lawyers, the contours of fiduciary duty are determined by a combination of common law, the statute, and the partnership agreement. The RUPA provides that the partnership agreement may carve out conduct that is not a breach of the duty of loyalty if not manifestly unreasonable and may reasonably reduce the duty of care.

The partners may contract with these standards in mind. However, courts must then determine what is reasonable or not. Thus, we can see that fiduciary duties and contracting for them is a complex area that can present challenges to parties and their lawyers.

6. UNLIMITED LIABILITY

Many businesses fail and close. When they terminate, they undergo a process of dissolution and winding up. All business organization statutes provide terms for how that is accomplished. The general concept is the same across all business entities. First, assets are marshalled and sold in a liquidation. Second, creditors are always paid first before equityholders because they hold the priority financial position. Third, if the assets net of liabilities paid are positive, the equityholders distribute these net assets among themselves according to some formula in the statute or in the charter document. This is the happier ending of a business. In the unhappy ending, liabilities are greater than assets of the firm. Creditors are not fully satisfied. The rule of limited liability applies in this situation, generally precluding the imposition of the remaining liabilities of the firm on its equityholders. Creditors are left unsatisfied, and they cannot seek recourse against equityholders. Of course, in this case, the equityholders recover nothing since all assets are distributed to creditors.

A critically important feature of general partnerships is that they do not offer limited liability to partners since in general partnerships, partners do not have limited liability. They are liable for the remaining debts and obligations of the partnership if the partnership's assets are insufficient to satisfy all creditors: "all partners are liable jointly and severally for all obligations of the partnership." RUPA § 306(a). The lack of limited liability protection is the major disadvantage of the general partnership form.

If a general partnership is so inadequate in this respect, why form a partnership at all? In fact, many businesses, and particularly sophisticated businesses, opt to form a limited liability entity instead. But partnerships can be formed "accidentally" if the partners intend to engage together in a business for profit, even if they do not have a subjective awareness they have formed a partnership. For these enterprises, the law of partnership provides the default internal rules of the business organization.

Also, a general partnership may be suitable if limited liability is not a significant concern for partners. The partners may believe that the business has sufficient capitalization or insurance (though it is not unheard of that over-optimism has led many business owners to ruin). The partners may themselves be limited liability entities: for example, a partnership between two corporations or two LLCs. Lastly, the partners may believe that liability can be strictly controlled through vigorous monitoring of partners, employees, and agents of the partnership.

Notwithstanding these considerations, it is worth emphasizing that many businesses, and particularly sophisticated ones, find that the benefit of limited liability exceeds the cost of filing and maintaining a limited liability entity such as an LLC, a limited partnership, or a corporation.

7. LIMITED LIABILITY PARTNERSHIP (LLP)

A limited liability partnership (LLP) is a general partnership in which the partners enjoy the benefit of limited liability.

RUPA § 306: Partner's Liability

(c) An obligation of a partnership incurred while the partnership is a limited liability partnership, whether arising in contract, tort, or otherwise, is solely the obligation of the partnership. A partner is not personally liable, directly or indirectly, by way of contribution or otherwise, for such an obligation solely by reason of being or so acting as a partner.

Except the liability of partners and related issues, all the rules of general partnerships in the RUPA apply to LLPs.

Texas enacted the first LLP statute in the 1991. Since then, all 50 states permit the creation of an LLP. Because an LLP is a limited liability entity, its formation requires filing with the state. Although LLPs provide limited liability to partners, its use in practice has been principally in professional services firms such as law firms, accounting firms, and architecture firms.[3]

Even with limited liability, a business that is not suitable for the general partnership form will be unsuitable for an LLP. Although limited liability is important, it is not the only feature that businesspersons and their lawyers should consider when choosing an entity. If limited liability were the only consideration, the business world would not have a needed alternative limited liability entities, principally the LLC. The rise and prominence of LLCs indicate that there are other important distinctions between general partnerships, limited partnerships, and LLCs. Each entity is a bundle of features that can be custom tailored to fit the needs of a particular business. How much these features benefit the business

---

[3] Some states restrict the use of LLPs to professional firms. For example, California limits LLPs to the following activities: "(i) each of the partners of which is a licensed person or a person licensed or authorized to provide professional limited liability partnership services in a jurisdiction or jurisdictions other than this state, (ii) is licensed under the laws of the state to engage in the practice of architecture, practice of public accountancy, or the practice of law, or (iii)(I) is related to a registered limited liability partnership that practices public accountancy or, to the extent permitted by the State Bar, practices law or is related to a foreign limited liability partnership and (II) provides services related or complementary to the professional limited liability partnership services provided by, or provides services or facilities to, that registered limited liability partnership or foreign limited liability partnership." Cal. Code § 16101(8).

(including other laws such as tax treatment) and how easily they can be privately ordered should determine the choice of entity.

C. LIMITED PARTNERSHIPS

A limited partnership differs from a general partnership in two fundamental ways. First, limited partnerships requires two classes of partners—at least one general partner and one limited partner. Second, limited partners, but not general partners, of a limited partnership have limited liability. This two-class partner system separates the roles of partners into managers and passive investors.

There are two prevalent statutes: RULPA and ULPA (2001). These statutes work very differently. The RULPA is not a standalone statute. It provides additional terms applicable only to limited partnerships, but otherwise it "links" to the general partnership statute to provide a complete of set of rules. *See* RULPA § 1105 ("In any case not provided for in this [Act] the provisions of the Uniform Partnership Act govern."). On the other hand, the ULPA (2001) is an independent standalone statute. As with general partnerships statutes, the limited partnership statutes provide default rules, and they permit a significant degree of contracting in the partnership agreement.

1. MANAGEMENT STRUCTURE

The business of a limited partnership is managed by the general partner: "a general partner of a limited partnership has the rights and powers and is subject to the restrictions of a partner in a partnership without limited partners." RULPA § 403(a). Limited partners are passive investors and do not have the right or the power to act for or bind the limited partnership. ULPA (2001) § 302.

2. FIDUCIARY DUTY

A general partner owes the same fiduciary duties as a partner in a general partnership. *Compare* ULPA (2001) § 408, *with* RUPA § 404. However, because a limited partner is conceived of as a passive investor who does not participate in the control of the business, she "does not have any fiduciary duty to the limited partnership or to any other partner solely by reason of being a limited partner." ULPA (2001) § 305(a). A limited partner is bound by the partnership agreement. As such, she must "exercise any rights consistently with the obligation of good faith and fair dealing." *Id.* § 305(b).

As discussed above, the RUPA permits a certain degree of contracting for fiduciary duties, but does not permit their complete elimination. RUPA § 103(b). The ULPA (2001) takes a similar approach:

ULPA (2001) § 110(b): Effect of Partnership Agreement; Nonwaivable Provisions

A partnership agreement may not: . . .

(5) eliminate the duty of loyalty under Section 408, but the partnership agreement may:

(A) identify specific types or categories of activities that do not violate the duty of loyalty, if not manifestly unreasonable; and

(B) specify the number or percentage of partners which may authorize or ratify, after full disclosure to all partners of all material facts, a specific act or transaction that otherwise would violate the duty of loyalty;

(6) unreasonably reduce the duty of care under Section 408(c);

(7) eliminate the obligation of good faith and fair dealing under Sections 305(b) and 408(d), but the partnership agreement may prescribe the standards by which the performance of the obligation is to be measured, if the standards are not manifestly unreasonable. . . .

Since a majority of the jurisdictions have adopted the uniform laws, the above provision represents the majority approach toward contracting for fiduciary duties. Delaware takes a significantly different approach.

Delaware Revised Uniform Limited Partnership Act § 17–1101: Construction and application of chapter and partnership agreement

(c) It is the policy of this chapter to give maximum effect to the principle of freedom of contract and to the enforceability of partnership agreements.

(d) To the extent that, at law or in equity, a partner or other person has duties (including fiduciary duties) to a limited partnership or to another partner or to another person that is a party to or is otherwise bound by a partnership agreement, the partner's or other person's duties may be expanded or restricted or eliminated by provisions in the partnership agreement; provided that the partnership agreement may not eliminate the implied contractual covenant of good faith and fair dealing.

3. OBLIGATION OF GOOD FAITH AND FAIR DEALING

Statutes and courts provide that partners have an obligation of good faith and fair dealing. Note the lexicon of "duty" and "obligation." Statutes and courts classify good faith and fair dealing as an "obligation" but not "duty." For example, RUPA § 404(a) states that the "only fiduciary duties a partner owes to the partnership and the other partners are the duty of loyalty and the duty of care." Confusing matters further is the fact that bad faith actions may be relevant in a duty of loyalty analysis, which, as we shall see later, is the law in Delaware for corporations. Whereas fiduciary duties are derived from the principles of the law of trusts, courts typically characterize the obligation of good faith and fair dealing as a contract principle. Note also that partnership statutes specifically prohibit the elimination of the obligation of good faith and fair dealing,[4] even in jurisdictions that permit maximum degree of contractual flexibility in the design of business firms.[5]

The following cases provide a discussion of the difference between fiduciary duty and the obligation of good faith and fair dealing. Both cases concern limited partnerships, but the principle of fiduciary duty and obligation of good faith and fair dealing are the same for general partnerships. In reading the cases, think about these questions: (1) What is the relationship between the implied covenant of good faith and fair dealing and the partnership agreement? (2) What is the core purpose of the doctrine of the obligation of good faith and fair dealing? (3) What is relevance of the temporal focus?

GERBER V. ENTERPRISE PRODUCTS HOLDINGS, LLC

67 A.3d 400 (Del. 2013).

JACOBS, JUSTICE:

[Limited partners in a limited partnership brought class action against the managers of the partnership. They challenged the sale of a portion of partnership and subsequent triangular merger of partnership into a wholly-owned subsidiary of purchaser. They argued that the action

---

[4] *See, e.g.,* RUPA § 103(b)(5) ("The partnership agreement may not . . . eliminate the obligation of good faith and fair dealing . . . but the partnership agreement may prescribe the standards by which the performance of the obligation is to be measured, if the standards are not manifestly unreasonable."); ULPA (2001) § 110(b)(7) (same formulation); RULLCA § 110(c)(same formulation).

[5] *See* Delaware Limited Partnership Act § 17–1101(d) ("To the extent that, at law or in equity, a partner or other person has duties (including fiduciary duties) to a limited partnership or to another partner or to another person that is a party to or is otherwise bound by a partnership agreement, the partner's or other person's duties may be expanded or restricted or eliminated by provisions in the partnership agreement; provided that the partnership agreement may not eliminate the implied contractual covenant of good faith and fair dealing."); Delaware Limited Liability Company Act § 18–1101(c) (same formulation).

breached the partnership agreement and the implied covenant of good faith and fair dealing. The court adopted the following quote from *ASB Allegiance Real Estate Fund v. Scion Breckenridge Managing Member, LLC*, 50 A.3d 434, 440–42 (Del.Ch. 2012), as the correct statement of law in Delaware on the distinction between fiduciary duty and the obligation of good faith and fair dealing.]

The implied covenant seeks to enforce the parties' contractual bargain by implying only those terms that the parties would have agreed to during their original negotiations if they had thought to address them. Under Delaware law, a court confronting an implied covenant claim asks whether it is clear from what was expressly agreed upon that the parties who negotiated the express terms of the contract would have agreed to proscribe the act later complained of as a breach of the implied covenant of good faith—had they thought to negotiate with respect to that matter. While this test requires resort to a counterfactual world—what if—it is nevertheless appropriately restrictive and commonsensical.

The temporal focus is critical. Under a fiduciary duty or tort analysis, a court examines the parties as situated at the time of the wrong. The court determines whether the defendant owed the plaintiff a duty, considers the defendant's obligations (if any) in light of that duty, and then evaluates whether the duty was breached. Temporally, each inquiry turns on the parties' relationship as it existed at the time of the wrong. The nature of the parties' relationship may turn on historical events, and past dealings necessarily will inform the court's analysis, but liability depends on the parties' relationship when the alleged breach occurred, not on the relationship as it existed in the past.

An implied covenant claim, by contrast, looks to the past. It is not a free-floating duty unattached to the underlying legal documents. It does not ask what duty the law should impose on the parties given their relationship at the time of the wrong, but rather what the parties would have agreed to themselves had they considered the issue in their original bargaining positions at the time of contracting. "Fair dealing" is not akin to the fair process component of entire fairness, *i.e.*, whether the fiduciary acted fairly when engaging in the challenged transaction as measured by duties of loyalty and care whose contours are mapped out by Delaware precedents. It is rather a commitment to deal "fairly" in the sense of consistently with the terms of the parties' agreement and its purpose. *Likewise "good faith" does not envision loyalty to the contractual counterparty, but rather faithfulness to the scope, purpose, and terms of the parties' contract. Both necessarily turn on the contract itself and what the parties would have agreed upon had the issue arisen when they were bargaining originally.*

The retrospective focus applies equally to a party's discretionary rights. The implied covenant requires that a party refrain from arbitrary or unreasonable conduct which has the effect of preventing the other party to the contract from receiving the fruits of its bargain. *When exercising a discretionary right, a party to the contract must exercise its discretion reasonably.* The contract may identify factors that the decision-maker can consider, and it may provide a contractual standard for evaluating the decision. Express contractual provisions always supersede the implied covenant, but even the most carefully drafted agreement will harbor residual nooks and crannies for the implied covenant to fill. In those situations, what is "arbitrary" or "unreasonable"—or conversely "reasonable"—depends on the parties' original contractual expectations, not a "free-floating" duty applied at the time of the wrong.

DIECKMAN V. REGENCY GENERAL PARTNER LP
155 A.3d 358 (Del. 2017).

SEITZ, JUSTICE.

In this appeal, we again wade into the details of a master limited partnership agreement[6] to decide whether the complaint's allegations can overcome the general partner's use of conflict resolution safe harbors to dismiss the case. The parties are identified by a host of confusing abbreviations, but the gist of the appeal is as follows.

The plaintiff is a limited partner/unitholder in the publicly-traded master limited partnership ("MLP"). The general partner proposed that the partnership be acquired through merger with another limited partnership in the MLP family. The seller and buyer were indirectly owned by the same entity, creating a conflict of interest. Because conflicts of interest often arise in MLP transactions, those who create and market MLPs have devised special ways to try to address them. The general partner in this case sought refuge in two of the safe harbor conflict resolution provisions of the partnership agreement—"Special Approval" of the transaction by an independent Conflicts Committee, and "Unaffiliated Unitholder Approval."

---

[6]   Author's note: The SEC provides the following description of a master limited partnership.

Generally, Master Limited Partnerships (MLPs) are exchange-traded investments that are focused on exploration, development, mining, processing, or transportation of minerals or natural resources. MLPs hold cash-generating assets such as oil and gas properties or pipelines. MLPs have certain characteristics that can make them attractive to some investors, including partnership tax consequences, limited liability to investors for the MLP's debts, and anticipated consistent distributions of cash. However, like all investments, MLPs have risks investors should consider before making an investment decision. *Those risks include governance features that can favor management over other investors, potential conflicts of interest,* and concentrated exposure to a single industry or commodity. Since most MLPs are clustered in the energy sector, they can therefore be sensitive to shifts in oil and gas prices. The 2015–16 decreases in oil prices are an example.

Investor Bulletin: Master Limited Partnerships—An Introduction, U.S. Securities and Exchange Commission (May 18, 2016) (emphasis added), available at https://www.sec.gov/oiea/investor-alerts-bulletins/ib_mlpintro.html.

In the MLP context, Special Approval typically means that a Conflicts Committee composed of members independent of the sponsor and its affiliates reviewed the transaction and made a recommendation to the partnership board whether to approve the transaction. Unaffiliated Unitholder Approval is typically just that—a majority of unitholders unaffiliated with the general partner and its affiliates approve the transaction. Under the partnership agreement, if either safe harbor is satisfied, the transaction is deemed not to be a breach of the agreement.

The partnership agreement required that the Conflicts Committee be independent, meaning that its members could not be serving on affiliate boards and were independent under the audit committee independence rules of the New York Stock Exchange. The plaintiff alleged in the complaint that the general partner failed to satisfy the Special Approval safe harbor because the Conflicts Committee was itself conflicted. According to the plaintiff, one of the Committee's two members began evaluating the transaction while still a member of an affiliate's board, and then resigned from the affiliate's board four days after he began his review to then become a member of the Conflicts Committee. On the same day the transaction closed, the committee member was reappointed to the seat left vacant for him on the affiliate's board.

The plaintiff also alleged that the general partner failed to satisfy the Unaffiliated Unitholder Approval safe harbor because the general partner made false and misleading statements in the proxy statement to secure that approval. In the 165-page proxy statement sent to the unitholders, the general partner failed to disclose the conflicts within the Conflicts Committee. Instead, the proxy statement stated that Special Approval had been obtained by an independent Conflicts Committee.

The general partner moved to dismiss the complaint and claimed that, in the absence of express contractual obligations not to mislead investors or to unfairly manipulate the Conflicts Committee process, the general partner need only satisfy what the partnership agreement expressly required—to obtain the safe harbor approvals and follow the minimal disclosure requirements. In other words, whatever the general partner said in the proxy statement, and whomever the general partner appointed to the Conflicts Committee, was irrelevant because only the express requirements of the partnership agreement controlled and displaced any implied obligations not to undermine the protections afforded unitholders by the safe harbors.

The Court of Chancery side-stepped the Conflicts Committee safe harbor, but accepted the general partner's argument that the Unaffiliated Unitholder Approval safe harbor required dismissal of the case. The court held that, even though the proxy statement might have contained materially misleading disclosures, fiduciary duty principles could not be used to impose disclosure obligations on the general partner beyond those in the partnership agreement, because the partnership agreement disclaimed fiduciary duties. Further, the court agreed with the defendants that the only express disclosure requirement of the agreement in the event of a merger—that the general partner simply provide either a summary of, or a copy of, the merger agreement—displaced any implied contractual duty to disclose in the proxy statement material facts about the conflicts within the Conflicts Committee.

We view the central issue in the dispute through a different lens than the Court of Chancery. The Court of Chancery was correct that the implied covenant of good faith and fair dealing cannot be used to supplant the express disclosure requirements of the partnership agreement. But the court focused too narrowly on the partnership agreement's disclosure requirements. Instead, the center of attention should have been on the conflict resolution provision of the partnership agreement.

The partnership agreement's conflict resolution provision is a powerful tool in the general partner's hands because it can be used to shield a conflicted transaction from judicial review. But the conflicts resolution provision also operates for the unitholders' benefit. It ensures that, before a safe harbor is reached by the general partner, unaffiliated unitholders have a vote, or the conflicted transaction is reviewed and recommended by an independent Conflicts Committee.

The partnership agreement does not address how the general partner must conduct itself when seeking the safe harbors. But where, as here, the express terms of the partnership agreement naturally imply certain corresponding conditions, unitholders are entitled to have those terms enforced according to the reasonable expectations of the parties to the agreement. The implied covenant is well-suited to imply contractual terms that are so obvious—like a requirement that the general partner not engage in misleading or deceptive conduct to obtain safe harbor approvals—that the drafter would not have needed to include the conditions as express terms in the agreement.

We find that the plaintiff has pled sufficient facts, which we must accept as true at this stage of the proceedings, that neither safe harbor was available to the general partner because it allegedly made false and misleading statements to secure Unaffiliated Unitholder Approval, and allegedly used a conflicted Conflicts Committee to obtain Special Approval. Thus, we reverse the Court of Chancery's order dismissing Counts I and II of the complaint.

I.

[The case involves a web of cross-ownerships and cross-interests among entities. The plaintiff, Adrian Dieckman, is a unitholder of Regency Energy Partners LP ("Regency"), a publicly-traded Delaware limited partnership engaged in the gathering and processing, contract compression, treating and transportation of natural gas and the transportation, fractionation and storage of natural gas liquids. Regency General Partner LP ("General Partner LP") is the general partner of Regency. Regency is governed by a partnership agreement ("LP Agreement"). Energy Transfer Partners L.P. ("ETP") is the general partner of Sunoco LP and a 43% owner of limited partnership interests in Sunoco. Energy Transfer Equity, L.P. ("ETE") indirectly own Regency's general partner and ETP's general partner, which means that ETE indirectly controls both limited partnerships. A simplified version of the cross-relationships is the following.

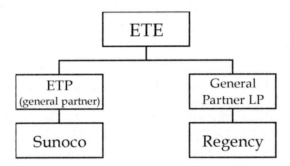

The remaining defendants are the six members of General Partner LP's board of directors: two of whom were James Bryant and Richard Brannon. Bryant and Brannon served on the Conflicts Committee of the General Partner's board.]

According to the complaint and the proxy statement distributed to unitholders, the ETP and ETE boards met to discuss a merger between ETP and Regency. ETP eventually made a merger proposal to Regency, where Regency would be merged into ETP for a combination of cash and stock using an exchange ratio of 0.4044 ETP common units for one Regency common unit, and a $137 million cash payment. Because of the undisputed conflicts of interest in the proposed merger transaction, the General Partner looked to the conflict resolution provisions of the LP Agreement.

Under § 7.9(a) of the LP Agreement, entitled "Resolution of Conflicts of Interest; Standards of Conduct and Modification of Duties," unless otherwise provided in another agreement, the General Partner can resort to several safe harbors to immunize conflicted transactions from judicial review:

> [A]ny resolution or course of action by the General Partner or its Affiliates in respect of such conflict of interest shall be permitted and deemed approved by all Partners, and shall not constitute a breach of this Agreement . . . or of any duty stated or implied by law or equity, if the resolution or course of action in respect of such

conflict of interest is (i) approved by Special Approval, (ii) approved by the vote of a majority of the Common Units (excluding Common Units owned by the General Partner and its Affiliates), (iii) on terms no less favorable to the Partnership than those generally being provided to or available from unrelated third parties, or (iv) fair and reasonable to the Partnership, taking into account the totality of the relationships between the parties involved (including other transactions that may be particularly favorable or advantageous to the Partnership).

The General Partner sought the protections of the safe harbors by Special Approval under § 7.9(a)(i) and Unaffiliated Unitholder Vote under § 7.9(a)(ii). Special Approval is defined in the LPA as "approval by a majority of the members of the Conflicts Committee." The Conflicts Committee must be:

[A] committee of the Board of Directors of the general partner of the General Partner composed entirely of two or more directors who are not (a) security holders, officers or employees of the General Partner, (b) officers, directors or employees of any Affiliate of the General Partner[,] or (c) holders of any ownership interest in the Partnership Group other than Common Units and who also meet the independence standards required of directors who serve on an audit committee of a board of directors established by the Securities Exchange Act of 1934, as amended, and the rules and regulations of the Commission thereunder and by the National Securities Exchange on which the Common Units are listed or admitted to trading.

For purposes of subsection (b), "Affiliate" is defined as any person "that directly or indirectly through one or more intermediaries controls, is controlled by or is under control with, the Person in question." Sunoco and the General Partner are both controlled by ETE, and are "Affiliates," under the LP Agreement. Thus, Sunoco board members were not eligible to serve as members of the General Partner's Conflicts Committee. Nor was it clear that they would meet the audit committee independence rules of the New York Stock Exchange.

The General Partner appointed Brannon and Bryant to the Conflicts Committee. The complaint alleges that before the proposed transaction, Brannon was a Sunoco director. On January 16, 2015, ETE appointed Brannon to the General Partner's board, while still a director of Sunoco. The plaintiff claims that, from January 16–20, while a member of both boards, Brannon consulted informally on the proposed transaction. According to the complaint, Brannon then temporarily resigned from the Sunoco board on January 20, and on January 22, became an official member of the Conflicts Committee when formal resolutions were passed creating the Committee. Brannon and Bryant then negotiated on behalf of

Regency with ETP and recommended the merger transaction to the General Partner. On April 30, 2015, the day that the merger closed, Brannon was reappointed to the Sunoco board, and Bryant was also appointed to Sunoco board.

The plaintiff claims that the negotiations between the Conflicts Committee and ETP were ceremonial and only lasted a few days. According to the complaint, between January 23 and January 25, the Conflicts Committee made a perfunctory and slightly increased counteroffer to ETP's offer, which would have achieved a 15% premium to the closing price of common units. ETP rejected the counteroffer, and the parties settled on ETP's opening bid of a 13.2% premium to the January 23 closing price. The Conflicts Committee recommended that the General Partner pursue the transaction on the original terms proposed by ETP, which the General Partner approved on January 25. The plaintiff alleges that the entire process from start to finish lasted nine days.

The LP Agreement only required minimal disclosure when a merger transaction was considered by the unitholders—a summary of, or a copy of, the merger agreement. But the General Partner went beyond the minimal requirements in the LP Agreement. To gain Unaffiliated Unitholder Approval and the benefit of the safe harbor, the General Partner filed a 165-page proxy statement and disseminated it and a copy of the merger agreement to the unitholders.

The proxy statement stated that the "Conflicts Committee consists of two independent directors: Richard D. Brannon (Chairman) and James W. Bryant." It also stated that the Conflicts Committee approved the transaction, and such approval "constituted 'Special Approval' as defined in the Regency partnership agreement." The proxy statement did not inform unitholders about the circumstances of Bryant's alleged overlapping and shifting allegiances, including reviewing the proposed transaction while still a member of the Sunoco board, his nearly contemporaneous resignation from the Sunoco board and appointment to the General Partner's board and then the Conflicts Committee, or Brannon's appointment and Bryant's reappointment to the Sunoco board the day the transaction closed. At a special meeting of Regency's unitholders on April 28, 2015, a majority of Regency's unitholders, including a majority of its unaffiliated unitholders, approved the merger.

II.

We start with the settled principles of law governing Delaware limited partnerships. The Delaware Revised Uniform Limited Partnership Act ("DRUPLA") gives "maximum effect to the principle of freedom of contract." [DRUPLA § 17–1101(c)] One freedom often exercised in the MLP context is eliminating any fiduciary duties a partner owes to others in the partnership structure. [DRUPLA § 17–1101(d)] The act allows drafters of

Delaware limited partnerships to modify or eliminate fiduciary-based principles of governance, and displace them with contractual terms.

With the contractual freedom accorded partnership agreement drafters, and the typical lack of competitive negotiations over agreement terms, come corresponding responsibilities on the part of investors to read carefully and understand their investment. Investors must appreciate that "with the benefits of investing in alternative entities often comes the limitation of looking to the contract as the exclusive source of protective rights." In other words, investors can no longer hold the general partner to fiduciary standards of conduct, but instead must rely on the express language of the partnership agreement to sort out the rights and obligations among the general partner, the partnership, and the limited partner investors.

Even though the express terms of the agreement govern the relationship when fiduciary duties are waived, investors are not without some protections. For instance, in the case of an ambiguous partnership agreement of a publicly traded limited partnership, ambiguities are resolved as with publicly traded corporations, to give effect to the reading that best fulfills the reasonable expectations an investor would have had from the face of the agreement. The reason for this is simple. When investors buy equity in a public entity, they necessarily rely on the text of the public documents and public disclosures about that entity, and not on parol evidence. And, of course, another protection exists. The DRUPLA provides for the implied covenant of good faith and fair dealing, which cannot be eliminated by contract.

The implied covenant is inherent in all contracts and is used to infer contract terms "to handle developments or contractual gaps that the asserting party pleads neither party anticipated." It applies "when the party asserting the implied covenant proves that the other party has acted arbitrarily or unreasonably, thereby frustrating the fruits of the bargain that the asserting party reasonably expected." The reasonable expectations of the contracting parties are assessed at the time of contracting. In a situation like this, involving a publicly traded MLP, the pleading-stage inquiry focuses on whether, based on a reading of the terms of the partnership agreement and consideration of the relationship it creates between the MLP's investors and managers, the express terms of the agreement can be reasonably read to imply certain other conditions, or leave a gap, that would prescribe certain conduct, because it is necessary to vindicate the apparent intentions and reasonable expectations of the parties.

The Court of Chancery decided that the implied covenant could not be used to remedy what the plaintiff alleged were faulty safe harbor approvals because the LP Agreement waived fiduciary-based standards of conduct and contained an express contractual term addressing what disclosures were required in merger transactions. According to the court, the implied covenant had "no work to do" because the express disclosure requirement displaced the implied covenant.

The Court of Chancery erred by focusing too narrowly on whether the express disclosure provision displaced the implied covenant. Instead, it should have focused on the language of the safe harbor approval process, and what its terms reasonably mean. Although the terms of the LP Agreement did not compel the General Partner to issue a proxy statement, it chose to undertake the transaction, which the LP Agreement drafters would have known required a pre-unitholder vote proxy statement. Thus, the General Partner voluntarily issued a proxy statement to induce unaffiliated unitholders to vote in favor of the merger transaction. The favorable vote led not only to approval of the transaction, but allowed the General Partner to claim the protections of the safe harbor and immunize the merger transaction from judicial review. Not surprisingly, the express terms of the LP Agreement did not address, one way or another, whether the General Partner could use false or misleading statements to enable it to reach the safe harbors.

We find that implied in the language of the LP Agreement's conflict resolution provision is a requirement that the General Partner not act to undermine the protections afforded unitholders in the safe harbor process. Partnership agreement drafters, whether drafting on their own, or sitting across the table in a competitive negotiation, do not include obvious and provocative conditions in an agreement like "the General Partner will not mislead unitholders when seeking Unaffiliated Unitholder Approval" or "the General Partner will not subvert the Special Approval process by appointing conflicted members to the Conflicts Committee." But the terms are easily implied because "the parties must have intended them and have only failed to express them because they are too obvious to need expression." Stated another way, "some aspects of the deal are so obvious to the participants that they never think, or see no need, to address them."

Our use of the implied covenant is based on the words of the contract and not the disclaimed fiduciary duties. Under the LP Agreement, the General Partner did not have the full range of disclosure obligations that a corporate fiduciary would have had. Yet once it went beyond the minimal disclosure requirements of the LP Agreement, and issued a 165-page proxy statement to induce the unaffiliated unitholders not only to approve the merger transaction, but also to secure the Unaffiliated Unitholder Approval safe harbor, implied in the language of the LP Agreement's conflict resolution provision was an obligation not to mislead unitholders.

Further, the General Partner was required to form a Conflicts Committee comprised of members who:

> [A]re not (a) security holders, officers or employees of the General Partner, (b) officers, directors or employees of any Affiliate of the

General Partner or (c) holders of any ownership interest in the Partnership Group other than Common Units and who also meet the independence standards required of directors who serve on an audit committee of a board of directors established by the Securities Exchange Act of 1934, as amended, and the rules and regulations of the Commission thereunder and by the National Securities Exchange on which the Common units are listed or admitted to trading.

As with the contract language regarding Unaffiliated Unitholder Approval, this language is reasonably read by unitholders to imply a condition that a Committee has been established whose members genuinely qualified as unaffiliated with the General Partner and independent at all relevant times. Implicit in the express terms is that the Special Committee membership be genuinely comprised of qualified members and that deceptive conduct not be used to create the false appearance of an unaffiliated, independent Special Committee.

The plaintiff has agreed that the LP Agreement's safe harbor provisions, if satisfied, would preclude judicial review of the transaction. But we find that the plaintiff has pled sufficient facts to support his claims that those safe harbors were unavailable to the General Partner. Instead of staffing the Conflicts Committee with independent members, the plaintiff alleges that the chair of the two-person Committee started reviewing the transaction while *still* a member of an Affiliate board. Just a few days before the General Partner created the Conflicts Committee, the same director resigned from the Affiliate board and became a member of the General Partner's board, and then a Conflicts Committee member.

Further, after conducting the negotiations with ETE over the merger terms and recommending the merger transaction to the General Partner, the two members of the Conflicts Committee joined an Affiliate's board the day the transaction closed. The plaintiff also alleges that the Conflicts Committee members failed to satisfy the audit committee independence rules of the New York Stock Exchange, as required by the LP Agreement. In the proxy statement used to solicit Unaffiliated Unitholder Approval of the merger transaction, the plaintiff alleges that the General Partner materially misled the unitholders about the independence of the Conflicts Committee members. In deciding to approve the merger, a reasonable unitholder would have assumed based on the disclosures that the transaction was negotiated and approved by a Conflicts Committee composed of persons who were not "affiliates" of the general partner and who had the independent status dictated by the LP Agreement. This assurance was one a reasonable investor may have considered a material fact weighing in favor of the transaction's fairness.

The plaintiff has therefore pled facts raising sufficient doubt about the General Partner's ability to use the safe harbors to shield the merger transaction from judicial review. Thus, we reverse the judgment of the Court of Chancery dismissing Counts I and II of the complaint.

4.　FINANCIAL RIGHTS

Financial rights in limited partnerships are fundamentally different from those in a general partnership. Recall that equal allocation of profit and loss is the default rule in general partnerships. The default rule in limited partnerships is different: "If the partnership agreement does not so provide in writing, profits and losses shall be allocated on the basis of the value, as stated in the partnership records . . . , of the contributions made by each partner to the extent they have been received by the partnership and have not been returned." RULPA § 503. This rule resembles the scheme in corporations; the more shares you have, the more you are entitled to the financial benefits. A limited partnership is conceived as an investment vehicle, which explains the departure from a general partnership's rule of equal shares.

Like shareholders in a corporation, a general or limited partner may exit the investment at some point. Here, the RULPA and the ULPA (2001) have different rules on a partner's rights upon dissociation.

RULPA § 604: Distribution upon Withdrawal

Except as provided in this Article, upon withdrawal any withdrawing partner is entitled to receive any distribution to which he [or she] is entitled under the partnership agreement and, if not otherwise provided in the agreement, he [or she] is entitled to receive, within a reasonable time after withdrawal, the fair value of his [or her] interest in the limited partnership as of the date of withdrawal based upon his [or her] right to share in distributions from the limited partnership.

As a default rule, the RULPA grants each partner the power to withdraw including the withdrawal of his investment in the partnership. It values the freedom of partners over the benefit of locking in capital.

The ULPA (2001) values the benefit of locking in capital. It provides: "A person does not have a right to receive a distribution on account of dissociation." ULPA (2001) § 505. The rule benefits the limited partnership because it prevents capital from leaving the firm, which may destabilize the partnership or require the partnership to seek additional capital from remaining partners.

Limited partnerships are planned entities. They cannot be formed "accidentally" the way that general partnerships can be formed. Promoters file with the state to create a limited partnership. The statutes require that the partnership maintain records of financial matters including the financial interests of all partners. There will be a written partnership agreement. Accordingly, matters of financial rights will be subject to private ordering by the partners keeping in mind that limited partnership are primarily investment vehicles where general partners manage an investment on behalf of limited partners who primarily contribute capital to the enterprise. In thoughtfully designed limited partnerships, the partnership agreement will address the financial and exit rights of partners.

5. LIMITED LIABILITY

Like a partner in a general partnership, a general partner in a limited partnership is exposed to personal liability for the debts and obligations of the limited partnership. However, limited partners have the benefit of limited liability.

RULPA § 303: Liability to Third Parties

(a) Except as provided in subsection (d), a limited partner is not liable for the obligations of a limited partnership unless he [or she] is also a general partner or, in addition to the exercise of his [or her] rights and powers as a limited partner, he [or she] participates in the control of the business. However, if the limited partner participates in the control of the business, he [or she] is liable only to persons who transact business with the limited partnership reasonably believing, based upon the limited partner's conduct, that the limited partner is a general partner.

(b) A limited partner does not participate in the control of the business within the meaning of subsection (a) solely by doing one or more of the following:

(1) being a contractor for or an agent or employee of the limited partnership or of a general partner or being an officer, director, or shareholder of a general partner that is a corporation;

(2) consulting with and advising a general partner with respect to the business of the limited partnership;

(3) acting as surety for the limited partnership or guaranteeing or assuming one or more specific obligations of the limited partnership;

(4) taking any action required or permitted by law to bring or pursue a derivative action in the right of the limited partnership;

(5) requesting or attending a meeting of partners;

(6) proposing, approving, or disapproving, by voting or otherwise, one or more of the following matters:

    (i)   the dissolution and winding up of the limited partnership;

    (ii)   the sale, exchange, lease, mortgage, pledge, or other transfer of all or substantially all of the assets of the limited partnership;

    (iii)   the incurrence of indebtedness by the limited partnership other than in the ordinary course of its business;

    (iv)   a change in the nature of the business;

    (v)   the admission or removal of a general partner;

    (vi)   the admission or removal of a limited partner;

    (vii)   a transaction involving an actual or potential conflict of interest between a general partner and the limited partnership or the limited partners;

    (viii)   an amendment to the partnership agreement or certificate of limited partnership; or

    (ix)   matters related to the business of the limited partnership not otherwise enumerated in this subsection (b), which the partnership agreement states in writing may be subject to the approval or disapproval of limited partners;

(7) winding up the limited partnership pursuant to Section 803; or

(8) exercising any right or power permitted to limited partners under this [Act] and not specifically enumerated in this subsection (b).

The RULPA § 303(a) denies limited liability protection to a limited partner if "he [or she] participates in the control of the business." If a limited partner participates in the control of the business, then the "control rule" in effect treats the limited partner as a general partner. The statute provides a safe harbor for activities that are not deemed to be participating in the control of the business, among which are: (1) being a contractor for, or an agent or employee of, the limited partnership or of a general partner, or being an officer, director, or shareholder of a general partner that is a corporation; (2) consulting with and advising a general partner with respect to the business of the limited partnership; (3) requesting or attending a meeting of partners; and (4) proposing, approving, or disapproving, by voting or otherwise, certain business matters. *Id.* § 303(b). As the statute frames it, the key inquiry is whether the limited partner participates in the *control* of the business.

Clearly, when a creditor is left unsatisfied on its claim against the limited partnership and its general partner, it will inquire, at least, whether the limited partners could be said to have participated in the control the business. These are, of course, factual inquiries. With respect to the scope of the control rule, RULPA § 303(a) has undergone revision. The original 1976 version provided:

> [A] limited partner is not liable for the obligations of a limited partnership unless he is also a general partner or, and in addition to the exercise of his rights and powers as a limited partner, he takes part in the control of the business. *However, if the limited partner's participation in the control of the business is not substantially the same as the exercise of the powers of a general partner, he is liable only to persons who transact business with the limited partnership with actual knowledge of his participation in control.*

Thus, the 1976 version imposed liability on limited partners if they participate in the control of the business irrespective of the creditor's knowledge of that participation. In many cases, a creditor would not know of a limited partner's participation in the control if the creditor deals only with a general partner and the limited partner exercises control within the partnership. In these cases, the limited partner would be held liable. However, if the participation in the control "is not substantially the same" as the general partner's control, the limited partner is liable only to a creditor who has actual knowledge of his participation in control.

In 1985, RULPA § 303(a) was amended and the second sentence now reads (see boxed statutory text for the full provision): "However, if the limited partner participates in the control of the business, he is liable only to persons who transact business with the limited partnership reasonably believing, based upon the limited partner's conduct, that the limited partner is a general partner."

A case that illustrates import of the 1985 amendment is *Gateway Potato Sales v. G.B. Investment Co.*, 822 P.2d 490 (Ariz.App. 1991). There, a creditor provided trade credit (supplies) to a limited partnership. He believed that the partnership was a general partnership, and not a limited partnership. The general partner of the limited partnership represented that its partner was a large financial institution and that it was actively involved in the operation of the business. On this understanding, the creditor provided trade credit. He did not contact or otherwise deal with the limited partner. Because the state had adopted the 1976 version of RULPA § 303, the court held that the lack of dealings between the creditor and the limited partner did not preclude potential liability: "The Arizona statute continues to impose liability on a limited partner whenever the 'substantially the same as' test is met, even though the creditor has no knowledge of the limited partner's control. It follows then that no contact between the creditor and the limited partner is required to impose liability." Subsequently, the Arizona legislature amended the statute to reflect the 1985 amendment to RULAP § 303(a). *See* Shimko v. Guenther, 505 F.3d 987 (9th Cir. 2007) ("By adopting the language 'reasonably believing . . . that the limited partner is a general partner,' the drafters restricted the liability of limited partners to third party creditors to situations where the third party was misled about the limited partner's actual status and potential liability.").

Having decided that a creditor need not have dealt with or known of the limited partner's participation of control, the court in the following excerpt analyzed the issue of the limited partner's exercise of control. In reading this case, think about these questions: (1) What is "control"? (2) How do you advise a limited partner who seeks to participate in the governance of the limited partnership in light of the statute (RULPA) and the case law?

GATEWAY POTATO SALES V. G.B. INVESTMENT CO.
822 P.2d 490 (Ariz.App. 1991).

TAYLOR, JUDGE.

[The limited partner, G.B. Investment, testified that G.B. Investment had exerted no control over the daily management and operation of the limited partnership. This testimony was contradicted, however, by the affidavit testimony of the general partner, Ellsworth, who stated that G.B. Investment's employees, Darl Anderson and Thomas McHolm, controlled the day-to-day affairs of the limited partnership. Ellsworth provided the following affidavit.]

[ELLSWORTH AFFIDAVIT]

a.   During the early months of the Partnership, Thomas McHolm and/or Darl Anderson were at the Partnership's offices on a daily basis directing the operation of the Partnership, and thereafter, they were at the Partnership's offices at least 2–3 times per week reviewing the operations of the business, directing changes in operations, and instructing me to make certain changes in operating the Partnership's affairs;

b.   G.B. Investment Company was solely responsible for obtaining a $150,000.00 line-of-credit loan for the Partnership with Valley National Bank of Arizona, and it also signed documents guaranteeing the repayment of the loan;

c.   As the President of the general partner, I was not permitted to make any significant independent business decisions concerning the operations of the Partnership, but was directed to have all business decisions approved with Darl Anderson and/or Thomas McHolm, or was directed to carry out decisions made by Darl Anderson and/or Thomas McHolm. For example, instead of using Partnership funds to pay certain creditors and suppliers, I was directed by Darl Anderson and/or Thomas McHolm to use the Partnership funds to purchase additional machinery and equipment;

    d.   Prior to constructing improvements to the packaging facilities of the Partnership, Thomas McHolm and/or Darl Anderson had to approve all construction bids, individually selected some of the suppliers and subcontractors, and individually selected the equipment to be installed;

    e.   Thomas McHolm and/or Darl Anderson dictated the accounting procedures to be followed by the Partnership, reviewed the Partnership's books and accounts almost continually, dictated that the Partnership use the same accounting firm as that of G.B. Investment Company to do the Partnership accounting tasks, undertook the responsibility of having prepared all Partnership tax forms and returns, and I only signed tax returns after they had been prepared by G.B. Investment Company's accountants and reviewed by Darl Anderson or some other employee/agent of G.B. Investment Company;

    f.   During a great portion of the duration of the Partnership, Thomas McHolm and/or Darl Anderson oversaw the daily operations of the Partnership because I had to have all expenditures approved by Thomas McHolm and/or Darl Anderson and Darl Anderson had to approve and sign checks issued by the Partnership, including without limitation payroll checks and invoices for telephone charges, utilities, publications, interest payments, bank card charges, supplies, etc. Copies of a sampling of the invoices and the corresponding checks are attached hereto as Exhibit 2;

    g.   After it was decided to add a hydrocooler to the processing and packaging facilities of the Partnership, Thomas McHolm individually selected the refrigeration equipment and chose the contractor to install the refrigeration equipment on the hydrocooler, and even saw to it that G.B. Investment Company (not the Partnership) directly paid the contractor for all of his services;

    h.   Thomas McHolm insisted that the Partnership use a particular supplier, to-wit: Allied Packaging, to supply packaging materials to the Partnership, he further took an active role in reviewing and modifying the art work for use on the packaging items, and personally approved the bid submitted for the art work;

    i.   At least on two separate occasions, approximately in August, 1986 and again in November, 1986, Darl Anderson caused sums of monies (approximately $8,000 and $7,000 respectively) to be withdrawn from the Partnership account (No. 2270–8018) with Valley National Bank without the prior knowledge or consent of myself, as the President of the general partner of the Partnership. These monies were paid directly to G.B. Investment, and the withdrawals caused other checks of the Partnership to be dishonored due to insufficient funds and left the Partnership without sufficient funds to meet its payroll obligations;

j.   Darl Anderson and/or Thomas McHolm caused certain expenses of the Partnership to be paid directly by G.B. Investment Company, to-wit: refrigeration equipment; and

k.   After the Partnership defaulted on its loan payments to Valley National Bank, a loan which had been guaranteed by G.B. Investment Company, Darl Anderson, without my knowledge or consent, instructed the Valley National Bank to proceed with declaring the loan to be in default and to pursue its remedies under its Security Agreement with the Partnership, to-wit: to sell the equipment and machinery that it held as collateral at a foreclosure auction. At the foreclosure auction held on March 3, 1987, by Valley National Bank, Darl Anderson, on behalf of G.B. Investment Company, bought the equipment and machinery previously owned by Sunworth Corporation.

[ANALYSIS]

Whether a limited partner has exercised the degree of control that will make him liable to a creditor has always been a factual question. Our current Arizona statute lists activities that a limited partner may undertake without participating in controlling the business. It also states that other activities may be excluded from the definition of such control. Where activities do not fall within the "safe harbor" [of RULPA § 303(b)], it is necessary for a trier-of-fact to determine whether such activities amount to "control."

We conclude that the evidence [the creditor] presented in this case should have allowed it to withstand summary judgment. The affidavit testimony of Ellsworth raises the issue whether he was merely a puppet for the limited partner, G.B. Investment. While a few of the activities Ellsworth listed may have fallen within the protected areas listed in [RULPA § 303(b)], others did not. Ellsworth's detailed statement raises substantial issues of material facts.

As evident from the above case and the evolution of the RULPA § 303(a), the issue of control can be complicated on the facts. The ULPA (2001) fundamentally changes the concept of a limited partner's liability. It eliminates the control rule altogether and thus broadens the protection to limited partners. ULPA (2001) § 303 provides:

An obligation of a limited partnership, whether arising in contract, tort, or otherwise, is not the obligation of a limited partner. A limited partner is not personally liable, directly or indirectly, by way of contribution or otherwise, for an obligation of the limited partnership solely by reason of being a limited partner, *even if the limited partner participates in the management and control of the limited partnership.*

Thus, in a jurisdiction that has adopted the ULPA (2001), a limited partner has limited liability even though the limited partner participates in the control of the limited partnership.

6. LIMITED LIABILITY LIMITED PARTNERSHIP (LLLP)

The ULPA (2001) enables the creation of a limited liability limited partnership ("LLLP"). An LLLP is a limited partnership where the general partner, in addition to the limited partner, is protected by limited liability. ULPA (2001) § 404(c) provides the model provision:

An obligation of a limited partnership incurred while the limited partnership is a limited liability limited partnership, whether arising in contract, tort, or otherwise, is solely the obligation of the limited partnership. A general partner is not personally liable, directly or indirectly, by way of contribution or otherwise, for such an obligation solely by reason of being or acting as a general partner.

Unlike the limited liability partnership (LLP), which has been adopted by all states, the limited liability limited partnership (LLLP) has not been universally adopted. There may be several reasons for this.

First, a combination of the current availability of entity forms can provide similar limited liability protection for a general partner in a limited partnership even though the general partner is subject to personal liability. The general partner can itself be a limited liability entity. Recall that a partner can be a natural or legal person. For example, Real Estate, L.P. is a limited partnership that invests in real estate, and its general partner is Management, LLC, which manages Real Estate, L.P.'s properties. The general partner, Management, LLC, is subject to unlimited liability, but it is a limited liability entity and its members are shielded from liability arising from the activities of Management, LLC in its role as general partner of Real Estate, L.P.

Second, if personal liability of a general partner in a limited partnership is a significant concern, other entity forms provide liability protection for all equityholders (such as a corporation, an LLC, or an LLP), and these entities can be structured through private ordering to mimic a two-tiered partnership and management structure where one equityholder is an active manager and the other is either a passive investor or a partner that has less management power than the managing partner. Indeed, most

LLC statutes permit a basic dichotomy of LLCs into a "manager-managed" and a "member-managed" LLC in which the former resembles a limited partnership and the latter resembles a general partnership. Thus, the current menu of entities can provide the essential features of an LLLP.

CHAPTER 8

LIMITED LIABILITY COMPANIES

■ ■ ■

A. INTRODUCTION

Corporations and partnerships are old forms of business entities. They were well in use by businesses throughout the twentieth century. The limited liability company ("LLC") is the newest entity form. Wyoming enacted the first LLC statute in 1977. However, the LLC form did not achieve prominence until 1997 when the IRS permitted LLCs to be taxed as partnerships, thus avoiding the entity-level taxation of corporations. Since then, the LLC has grown quickly to become a favored form for businesses with a small number of owners. All 50 states and the District of Columbia now have LLC statutes. Unlike the laws of partnerships where some version of the uniform laws have been adopted almost universally, LLC statutes among states are more variable. There are two uniform laws: Uniform Limited Liability Company Act (1996) ("ULLCA"), and Revised Uniform Limited Liability Company Act (2006) ("RULLCA"). LLC statutes have undergone significant revisions over the past several decades as the LLC form has grown in popularity. The RULLCA is the more prominent uniform law, but many states have adopted their own statutes from scratch, Delaware being a prominent example.

Because an LLC has limited liability, a filing is required to create the entity. In most states, the filing requirement is ministerial and the information content of the certificate is bare bones, similar to the process for limited partnerships. Some states may also require publication of the filing in designated publications or media forums.

1. MEMBERS

The equityholders of an LLC are called "members." They are the equity counterpart to a partner in a partnership or a shareholder in a corporation. One obvious advantage of an LLC over a partnership is that an LLC requires only one member, whereas a partnership requires at least two partners. The two-person requirement of a partnership is a significant limitation. In this regard, an LLC is like a corporation, which requires only one shareholder. The benefit of a single equityholder can be significant for both small businesses and larger or more sophisticated ones.

Consider a simple business owned by a single owner with 20 employees and $2 million in revenue. The owner wants to operate the business through an entity because she does not want to put her personal wealth at risk through exposure to the potential liability from the business. A general partnership clearly would not work because there is no liability protection. To form a limited liability partnership or a limited partnership she would have to find a partner, and would have to assume all the commitments that partnership law imposes: *e.g.*, respecting partners' rights and abiding by a partner's fiduciary obligations to the partnership and other partners. This may be undesirable from a business or legal perspectives. She could create a corporation where she would be the sole shareholder. But a corporation could also present complications. She would need to be concerned about tax planning and must abide by the more stringent and formal requirements imposed by corporation law (which we discussed in Chapter 6).

Now consider a large corporation that wishes to conduct a specific business through a wholly-owned entity. It can create a corporation in which the parent company is the sole shareholder of the subsidiary, a solution that is relatively common. Alternatively, it could create an LLC in which it is the sole member. This option may be preferable because of its more flexible requirements for management and governance.

The LLC form may also be useful in the context of a limited partnership. Recall that the general partner of a limited partner has the same liability exposure as a partner in a general partnership (unless the ULPA (2001) provision permitting a limited liability limited partnership is in effect). The organizer of a venture for which the limited partnership form might be appropriate has two options for avoiding this liability exposure. She can form an LLC in which she is the sole member and have it act as the general partner of the limited partnership. Alternatively, she can simply create an LLC in which she is the managing member and the other members are passive just as they would be as limited partners. As with the other situations described above, using the LLC form would be less attractive, if not altogether impossible, if the LLC required more than one member.

2. CONTRACTING

Except for a few mandatory rules, the laws of general partnerships and limited partnerships provide the default rules of internal affairs and governance, and they permit a significant degree of private ordering. In practice, when parties have deliberately created a partnership to engage in business, the partnership agreement provides the actual rules of internal affairs and governance. The same is true for LLCs, if not more so. In practice, the operating agreement establishes the LLC's rules of operations and governance. Consider the following observation by the Delaware chancery court.

It is frequently observed that LLCs "are creatures of contract," which they primarily are. The Delaware Limited

Liability Company Act provides that "[i]t is the policy of this chapter to give maximum effect to the principle of freedom of contract and to the enforceability of limited liability company agreements." 6 Del. C. § 18–110(b). Because of this freedom, the parties have broad discretion to use an LLC agreement to define the character of the company and the rights and obligations of its members. One attraction of the LLC form of entity is the statutory freedom granted to members to shape, by contract, their own approach to common business 'relationship' problems. Virtually any management structure may be implemented through the company's governing instrument.

Using the contractual freedom that the LLC Act bestows, the drafters of an LLC agreement can create an LLC with bespoke governance features or design an LLC that mimics the governance features of another familiar type of entity. The choices that the drafters make have consequences. If the drafters have embraced the statutory default rule of a member-managed governance arrangement, which has strong functional and historical ties to the general partnership (albeit with limited liability for the members), then the parties should expect a court to draw on analogies to partnership law. If the drafters have opted for a single managing member with other generally passive, non-managing members, a structure closely resembling and often used as an alternative to a limited partnership, then the parties should expect a court to draw on analogies to limited partnership law. If the drafters have opted for a manager-managed entity, created a board of directors, and adopted other corporate features, then the parties to the agreement should expect a court to draw on analogies to corporate law. Depending on the terms of the agreement, analogies to other legal relationships may also be informative.

It is important not to embrace analogies to other entities or legal structures too broadly or without close analysis, because the flexibility inherent in the limited liability company form complicates the task of fixing such labels or making such comparisons.

Obeid v. Hogan, 2016 WL 3356851 (Del.Ch. 2016) (some quotation marks and internal citations omitted).

The chief advantage of the LLC is its flexibility. It is often characterized as a "hybrid" entity that has features of both partnerships and corporations. It requires only one equityholder, like a corporation and unlike a partnership. It provides limited liability to all members and managers, like a corporation and unlike a partnership. It can allow flow-through taxation, like a partnership, but unlike a public corporation. It permits a flexible management structure, more like a partnership than a corporation.

LLCs are not subject to the automatic application of many decades of the legal frameworks of partnership or corporation law. Courts still often look for guidance on issues such as fiduciary duty and governance in the LLC to judicial rulings from partnership or corporation law. Those rulings do not, however, constitute binding precedent; and the LLC permits great freedom in self-ordering. Indeed, many LLC statutes explicitly tout a policy of maximum freedom of contract. *See, e.g.,* 6 Del.C. § 18–1101(b) (stating a policy "to give the maximum effect to the principle of freedom of contract and to the enforceability of limited liability company agreements"); Fla. Stat. § 605.0111(1) (same); Md.C. § 4A–102(A) (same); Nev.Rev.Stat. § 86.286(4)(B) (same).

The following passage discusses the advantage of the freedom from the mandatory requirements of the uniform partnership laws. Note the references to flexibility in setting fiduciary duty and the fiduciary standard set in *Meinhard v. Salmon* that applies to general partnerships, at least in New York. The court notes that some aspects of partnership laws, including aspects of fiduciary duty, can be "disclaimed."

> The LLC, a relatively modern form of corporate governance, not only has the benefit of limited liability, but also the virtually limitless possibilities of customization. One of the beauties of the LLC is that members can specifically and explicitly determine how their company is to be run. Unlike traditional fiduciaries that necessarily are bound by "the punctilio of an honor the most sensitive" (*see People v. Grasso,* 50 A.D.3d 535, 546 (1st Dept. 2008), quoting *Meinhard v. Salmon,* 164 N.E. 545 (N.Y. 1928)), LLC members are permitted to disclaim some of the most fundamental fiduciary obligations. *See, e.g., Kagan v. HMC-New York, Inc.,* 94 A.D.3d 67, 72–73 (1st Dept. 2012) (LLC members may disclaim fiduciary duties by explicitly doing so in the operating agreement), citing *Kelly v. Blum,* 2010 WL 629850, at *10 (Del.Ch. 2010). Moreover, while New York has its own set of LLC laws, those are merely default rules that can easily be overridden by the LLC's operating agreement. Hence, when a member complains that his rights were violated based on traditional notions of equity and corporate fair play, courts must be wary not to lose sight of the nature of the LLC and provide members with rights they did not bargain for and, in many cases, expressly disclaimed. This court, sitting in New York's commercial part, recognizes that the flexibility an LLC provides sophisticated business people is an essential tool for modern capital activity. At its heart is predictability. Courts should be wary of undermining that predictability.

Barry v. Clermont York Associates LLC, 28 N.Y.S.3d 647 (Table) (N.Y. Sup.Ct. 2015).

3. MANAGEMENT

Because it is entirely a matter of contract, the management structure of an LLC is highly malleable. Most LLC statutes permit an LLC that is managed by its members (similar to the default statutory rules of a general partnership) or by managers (similar to mandatory statutory provisions of a corporation or a limited partnership). The RULLCA explicitly recognizes the two forms of management structure: a member-managed LLC, which resembles a general partnership, and a manager-managed LLC, which resembles a limited partnership or a corporation with respect to management structure.

RULLCA § 407: Management of Limited Liability Company

(a) A limited liability company is a member-managed limited liability company unless the company qualifies as a manager-managed limited liability company under Section 110(10).

(b) In a member-managed limited liability company, the following rules apply:

(1) The management and conduct of the limited liability company is vested in the members collectively.

(2) Each member has equal rights in the management and conduct of the limited liability company's activities.

(3) A difference arising among members as to a matter in the ordinary course of the activities of the limited liability company may be decided by a majority of the members.

(4) An act outside the ordinary course of activities of the limited liability company may be undertaken only with the consent of all the members.

(5) The operating agreement may be amended only with the consent of all members.

(c) In a manager-managed limited liability company, the following rules apply:

(1) Except as otherwise expressly provided in this [act], any matter relating to the activities of the company may be exclusively decided by the managers.

---

(2) Each manager has equal rights in the management and conduct of the activities of the limited liability company.

(3) A difference arising among managers as to a matter in the ordinary course of the activities of the company may be decided by a majority of the managers.

(4) The consent of all the members is required to: (A) sell, lease, exchange, or otherwise dispose of all, or substantially all, of the company's property, with or without the good will, other than in the usual and regular course of the company's activities; (B) approve a merger, conversion or domestication under [Article] 10; (C) undertake any other act outside the ordinary course of activities of the company; and (D) amend the operating agreement.

(5) A manager may be chosen at any time by the consent of a majority of the members and remains a manager until a successor has been chosen, unless the manager sooner resigns, is removed, dies, or, in the case of a manager that is not an individual, terminates. A manager may be removed at any time by the consent of a majority of the members without notice or cause.

(6) A person need not be a member in order to be a manager, but the dissociation of a member that is also a manager removes the person as a manager. If a person that is both a manager and a member ceases to be a manager, that cessation does not by itself cause the person to dissociate as a member.

(7) A person's ceasing to be a manager does not discharge any debt, obligation or liability to the limited liability company or members which the person incurred while a manager.

Although customization can be as flexible as the limits of contracting permits, most management structures take the broad form of "member-managed" or "manager-managed." A member-managed LLC resembles the communitarian management structure of general partnerships; and a manager-managed LLC resembles the centralized management authority of limited partnerships and corporations.

The case below is an antitrust case involving Major League Soccer (MLS). The case was decided on antitrust grounds, and not on the law of limited liability companies, but it provides a good illustration of the flexibility possible in structuring an LLC. The case is excerpted here for its facts. The facts describe the business model of the enterprise and the use of the LLC form. As of 2013, the 19 teams in MLS had a combined value of $1.96 billion, generated $494 million in revenue and $34 million in operating profit. Chris Smith, *Major League Soccer's Most Valuable Teams*, Forbes (Nov. 20, 2013). Professional soccer in America is big business, and it is operated through an LLC. In reading this case, think about these questions: (1) How was Major League Soccer organized? (2) How did the LLC form facilitate this organization?

FRASER V. MAJOR LEAGUE SOCCER, L.L.C.

284 F.3d 47 (1st Cir. 2002).

BOUDIN, CHIEF JUDGE.

Professional soccer players sued Major League Soccer, LLC ("MLS"), nine independent operator/investors in MLS, and the United States Soccer Federation, Inc. ("USSF"), alleging violations of Sherman Act sections 1 and 2, 15 U.S.C. §§ 1–2, and Clayton Act section 7, *id.* § 18, and seeking injunctive relief and monetary damages.[1] The district court granted summary judgment for defendants on the section 1 and Clayton Act counts. After a twelve-week long trial on the section 2 count, the jury returned a special verdict leading to judgment in favor of defendants. Players now appeal the disposition of all three counts. We begin with a statement of the background facts.

Despite professional soccer's popularity abroad, the sport has achieved only limited success in this country. Several minor leagues have operated here (four such leagues exist today), but before the formation of MLS, only one other U.S. professional league—the North American Soccer League ("NASL")—had ever obtained Division I, or top-tier, status. Launched in 1968, the NASL achieved some success before folding in 1985; MLS attributes the NASL's demise in part to wide disparities in the financial resources of the league's independently owned teams and a lack of centralized control.

In 1988, the USSF, the national governing body of soccer in the United States, 36 U.S.C. § 220501 *et seq.*, was awarded the right to host the 1994 World Cup soccer tournament in the U.S. by the Federation Internationale de Football Association ("FIFA"), soccer's international governing body. In consideration for the coveted sponsorship rights, the USSF promised to establish a viable Division I professional soccer league in the U.S. as soon as possible.

The USSF decided as early as 1988 to sanction only one Division I professional league. The concern was that sanctioning rival leagues would dilute revenues, drive up costs, and thereby dim the long-term prospects for Division I soccer in the U.S. Indeed, MLS contends no other country has sanctioned more than one Division I league within its borders, although arrangements in other countries could be variously described.

Just before World Cup USA play began, in early December 1993, three organizations presented competing plans to develop a Division I professional soccer league to the USSF National Board of Directors. The three competing organizers were: League One America; the American Professional Soccer League ("APSL"), an existing Division II league; and Major League Professional Soccer ("MLPS"), the precursor to MLS, headed by the USSF's own president, Alan Rothenberg.

At its December 5, 1993, meeting the USSF board tentatively selected MLPS as the exclusive Division I professional soccer league in the U.S., based upon its relatively strong capitalization, higher proposed spending, business plan and management. The board also reaffirmed its intention to sanction only one Division I league. But in January 1995, the USSF announced that it would consider sanctioning additional leagues which could meet rigorous new financial and operating standards beginning with the 1998 season.

In the wake of a successful World Cup USA, MLS was officially formed in February 1995 as a limited liability company ("LLC") under Delaware law. The league is owned by a number of independent investors (a mix of corporations, partnerships, and one individual) and is governed by a management committee known as the board of governors. Some of the investors are passive; others are also team operators as explained below.

MLS has, to say the least, a unique structure, even for a sports league. MLS retains significant centralized control over both league and individual team operations. MLS owns all of the teams that play in the league (a total of 12 prior to the start of 2002), as well as all intellectual property rights, tickets, supplied equipment, and broadcast rights. MLS sets the teams' schedules; negotiates all stadium leases and assumes all related liabilities; pays the salaries of referees and other league personnel; and supplies certain equipment.

At issue in this case is MLS's control over player employment. MLS has the "sole responsibility for negotiating and entering into agreements with, and for compensating, Players." In a nutshell, MLS recruits the players, negotiates their salaries, pays them from league funds, and, to a large extent, determines where each of them will play. For example, to balance talent among teams, it decides, with the non-binding input of team operators, where certain of the league's "marquee" players will play.

However, MLS has also relinquished some control over team operations to certain investors. MLS contracts with these investors to operate nine of the league's teams (the league runs the other three). These investors are referred to as operator/investors and are the co-defendants in this action. Each operator/investor has the "exclusive right and obligation to provide Management Services for a Team within its Home Territory" and is given some leeway in running the team and reaping the potential benefits therefrom.

Specifically, the operator/investors hire, at their own expense and discretion, local staff (including the general managers and coaches of their respective teams), and are responsible for local office expenses, local promotional costs for home games, and one-half the stadium rent (the same portion as MLS). In addition, they license local broadcast rights, sell home tickets, and conduct all local marketing on behalf of MLS; agreements regarding these matters do not require the prior approval of MLS. And they control a majority of the seats on MLS's board, the very same body which runs the league's operations. Among other things, the board is responsible for hiring the commissioner and approving national television contracts and marketing decisions, league rules and policies (including team player budgets), and sales of interests.

The operator/investors also play a limited role in selecting players for their respective teams. While the operating agreements provide that the operator/investors will not bid independently for players against MLS, they may trade players with other MLS teams and select players in the league's draft. Such transactions, however, must follow strict rules established by the league. Most importantly, no team may exceed the maximum player budget established by the management committee.

In return for the services of the operator/investors, MLS pays each of them a "management fee" that corresponds (in large part) to the performance of their respective team. The management fee equals the sum of one-half of local ticket receipts and concessions; the first $1,125,000 of local broadcast revenues, increasing annually by a percentage rate, plus a 30% share (declining to 10% by 2006) of any amount above the base amount; all revenues from overseas tours; a share of one-half the net revenues from the MLS Championship Game and a share of revenues from other exhibition games.

The remaining revenues of the league are distributed in equal portions to all investors. Thus, while the investors qua investors share equally in the league's profits and losses, the individual team operators qua operators fare differently depending at least in part on the financial performance of their respective teams. It bears mentioning, however, that neither the league nor, apparently, any of its teams has yet made a profit.

Although the league retains legal title to the teams, the operator/investors may transfer their operating rights, within certain limits, and retain much of the value created by their individual efforts and investments. Investors may transfer their ownership stakes and operating rights to other current investors without obtaining prior consent; transfers to outside investors, however, require a two-thirds majority vote of the board. For its part, MLS may terminate any operating agreement on its own initiative if, by a two-thirds vote of the board, an operator/investor is determined to have failed to act in the best interests of the league. If so, it must still pay such operator/investor fair market value for its operating rights and ownership interest.

The league began official play in 1996. The following February of 1997, eight named players sued MLS, the USSF, and the operator/investors under various antitrust theories.

B. FIDUCIARY DUTY

There are two noteworthy aspects of fiduciary duties in LLCs. First, the locus and nature of fiduciary duties must reflect the management structure of the LLC. Second, LLC statutes generally permit some degree of flexibility in defining and limiting fiduciary duties in the operating agreement.

1. FIDUCIARY DUTY OF MEMBERS AND MANAGERS

The RULLCA provides a default rule that reflects the two basic types of management structure.

RULLCA § 409: Standards of Conduct for Members and Managers

(a)   A member of a member-managed limited liability company owes to the limited liability company and, subject to Section 901(b), the other members the fiduciary duties of loyalty and care stated in subsections (b) and (c).

(b)   The duty of loyalty of a member in a member-managed limited liability company includes the duties:

> (1)   to account to the company and to hold as trustee for it any property, profit, or benefit derived by the member: (A) in the conduct or winding up of the company's activities; (B) from a use by the member of the company's property; or (C) from the appropriation of a limited liability company opportunity;

> (2)   to refrain from dealing with the company in the conduct or winding up of the company's activities as or on behalf of a party having an interest adverse to the company; and

> (3)   to refrain from competing with the company in the conduct of the company's activities before the dissolution of the limited liability company.

(c) Subject to the business judgment rule, the duty of care of a member of a member-managed limited liability company in the conduct and winding up of the company's activities is to act with the care that a person in a like position would reasonably exercise under similar circumstances and in a manner the member reasonably believes to be in the best interests of the company. In discharging duties under this subsection, a member may rely in good faith upon opinions, reports, statements, or other information provided by another person that the member reasonably believes is a competent and reliable source for the information.

(d) A member shall discharge the duties under this [act] or under the operating agreement and exercise any rights consistently with the contractual obligation of good faith and fair dealing.

(e) It is a defense to a claim under subsection (b)(2) and any comparable claim in equity or at common law that the transaction was fair to the limited liability company.

(f) All of the members may authorize or ratify after full disclosure of all material facts a specific act or transaction that otherwise would violate the duty of loyalty.

(g) In a manager-managed limited liability company:

> (1) subsections (a), (b), (c) and (e) apply to the manager or managers and not the members;
>
> (2) the duty stated under subsection (b)(3) continues until winding up is completed;
>
> (3) subsection (d) applies both to members and managers;
>
> (4) subsection (f) applies only to members; and
>
> (5) A member of a manager-managed limited liability company does not have any fiduciary duty to the limited liability company or to any other member solely by reason of being a member.

There are several aspects of RULLCA § 409 that are worth noting. Compare RULLCA § 409(b) with RUPA § 404(b). RUPA provides: "A partner's duty of loyalty to the partnership and the other partners is *limited to* the following. . . ." RULLCA provides: "The duty of loyalty of a member in a member-managed limited liability company *includes* the duties. . . ." The language difference "limited to" and "includes" is significant. RUPA attempts to cabin in fiduciary duty of loyalty to the specific enumerated duties in the statute. RULLCA implies that the specific enumerated duties are not exclusive to the statute. *See generally*

Larry E. Ribstein, *An Analysis of the Revised Uniform Limited Liability Company Act*, 3 Va. L. & Bus. Rev. 35, 62–63 (2008).

With respect to the duty of care, subsection § 409(c) explicitly incorporates the corporate law principle of deference to management decisions, by reference to the "business judgment rule." We have already considered that rule briefly in Chapter 2 and will discuss it in greater detail in the chapters on corporation law. It is significant in that it provides substantial protection to managers from liability for alleged breach of their duty of care. It is noteworthy that the business judgment rule is not found in RUPA, and courts are divided on its applicability to partnership cases. *See* Elizabeth S. Miller & Thomas E. Rutledge, *The Duty of Finest Loyalty and Reasonable Decisions: The Business Judgment Rule in Unincorporated Business Organizations?*, 30 Del. J. Corp. L. 343 (2005).

Lastly, note that irrespective of the management structure, all members and managers are subject to the obligation of good faith and fair dealing. In all business enterprises (partnerships, LLCs, and corporations), this obligation is mandatory and nonwaivable.

2. CONTRACTING FOR FIDUCIARY DUTY

As mentioned above, fiduciary duty in LLCs is subject to contracting in the operating agreement. The purpose of contracting is to change the default rules to the specific circumstance of the parties of interest. For example, suppose that A and B decide that forming a business enterprise between the two would be mutually beneficial. However, B has a preexisting participation in another business enterprise that could foreseeably conflict with an interest in the contemplated business between A and B. In this situation, A and B can head off any potential problems with fiduciary duty in the future by contracting for fiduciary duty in a way that resolves the anticipated conflict of interest to the extent permitted by statute.

RULLCA provides for contracting of fiduciary duty, but it places limits on such contracting.

RULLCA § 110: Operating Agreement; Scope, Function and Limitations

(c)   An operating agreement may not:

(4)   subject to subsections (d) through (g), eliminate the duty of loyalty, the duty of care, or any other fiduciary duty;

(5)   subject to subsection (d) through (g), eliminate the contractual obligation of good faith and fair dealing under Section 409(d);

(6)   to refrain from competing with the company in the conduct of the company's activities before the dissolution of the limited liability company.

(d)   If not manifestly unreasonable, the operating agreement may:

(1)   eliminate the duty: (A) to account, as required in Section 409(b)(1) and (g), to the limited liability company and to hold as trustee for it any property, profit, or benefit derived by the member in the conduct or winding up of the company's business, from a use by the member of the company's property, or from the appropriation of a limited liability company opportunity; (B) to refrain, as required in Section 409(b)(2) and (g), from dealing with the company in the conduct or winding up of the company's business as or on behalf of a party having an interest adverse to the company; and(C) to refrain, as required by Section 409(b)(3) and (g), from competing with the company in the conduct of the company's business before the dissolution of the company.

(2)   identify specific types or categories of activities that do not violate the duty of loyalty;

(3)   subject to subsection (d) through (g), eliminate the contractual obligation of good faith and fair dealing under Section 409(d);

(4)   alter the duty of care, except to authorize intentional misconduct or knowing violation of law;

(5)   prescribe the standards by which to measure the performance of the contractual obligation of good faith and fair dealing under Section 409(d);

The case below concerns contracting for fiduciary duty. In reading this case, think about these questions: (1) Consider the circumstance of the prospective members before the formation of the LLC. Why was the operating agreement on fiduciary duty drafted in this way? (2) In hindsight, from the perspective of the Hunt Sports Group, how could the operating agreement have been better drafted and yet meet the *ex ante* concerns of all members?

McConnell v. Hunt Sports Enterprises

725 N.E.2d 1193 (Ohio App. 1999).

TYACK, JUDGE.

On June 17, 1997, John H. McConnell and Wolfe Enterprises, Inc. filed a complaint for declaratory judgment against Hunt Sports Enterprises, Hunt Sports Enterprises, L.L.C., Hunt Sports Group, L.L.C. ("Hunt Sports Group"), and Columbus Hockey Limited ("CHL"). CHL was a limited liability company formed under R.C. Chapter 1705.

In 1996, the National Hockey League ("NHL") determined it would be accepting applications for new hockey franchises. In April 1996, Gregory S. Lashutka, the mayor of Columbus, received a phone call from an NHL representative inquiring as to Columbus's interest in a hockey team. As a result, Mayor Lashutka asked certain community leaders who had been involved in exploring professional sports in Columbus to pursue the possibility of applying for an NHL hockey franchise. Two of these persons were Ronald A. Pizzuti and McConnell.

Pizzuti began efforts to recruit investors in a possible franchise. Pizzuti approached Lamar Hunt, principal of Hunt Sports Group, as to Hunt's interest in investing in such a franchise for Columbus. Hunt was already the operating member of the Columbus Crew, a professional soccer team whose investors included Hunt Sports Group, Pizzuti, McConnell, and Wolfe Enterprises, Inc. Hunt expressed an interest in participating in a possible franchise. The deadline for applying for an NHL expansion franchise was November 1, 1996.

On October 31, 1996, CHL was formed when its articles of organization were filed with the secretary of state. The members of CHL were McConnell, Wolfe Enterprises, Inc., Hunt Sports Group, Pizzuti Sports Limited, and Buckeye Hockey, L.L.C. Each member made an initial capital contribution of $25,000. CHL was subject to an operating agreement that set forth the terms between the members. Pursuant to section 2.1 of CHL's operating agreement, the general character of the business of CHL was to invest in and operate a franchise in the NHL.

On or about November 1, 1996, an application was filed with the NHL on behalf of the city of Columbus. In the application, the ownership group was identified as CHL, and the individuals in such group were listed as Pizzuti Sports Limited, McConnell, Wolfe Enterprises, Inc., and Hunt Sports Group. A $100,000 check from CHL was included as the application fee. Also included within the application package was Columbus's plan for an arena to house the hockey games. There was no facility at the time, and the proposal was to build a facility that would be financed, in large part, by a three-year countywide one-half percent sales tax. The sales tax issue would be on the May 1997 ballot.

On May 6, 1997, the sales tax issue failed. The day after, Mayor Lashutka met with Hunt, and other opportunities were discussed. The mayor also spoke with Gary Bettman, commissioner of the NHL, and they discussed whether an alternate plan for an arena was possible. Dimon McPherson, chairman and chief executive officer of Nationwide Insurance Enterprise ("Nationwide"), met with Hunt, and they discussed the possibility of building the arena despite the failure of the sales tax issue. Hunt was interested, and Nationwide began working on an arena plan. The mayor spoke with Bettman and let him know that alternate plans would be pursued, and Mr. Bettman gave Columbus until June 4, 1997 to come up with a plan.

By May 28, Nationwide had come up with a plan to finance an arena privately and on such date, Nationwide representatives met with representatives of Hunt Sports Group. Hunt Sports Group did not accept Nationwide's lease proposal. On May 29, Nationwide representatives again met with representatives of Hunt Sports Group. Again, Hunt Sports Group indicated that the lease proposal was unacceptable and that the NHL team would lose millions with this proposal. The June 4 NHL deadline was discussed. Hunt Sports Group stated that it would continue to evaluate the proposal, and it wanted the weekend to do so. Nationwide informed [Hunt Sports Group] that it needed an answer by close of business Friday, May 30.

On May 30, McPherson called McConnell and requested that they meet and discuss "where [they] were on the arena." McPherson "could see that the situation now was slipping away, and [he] just didn't want that to happen," so he went to see McConnell for advice and counsel. McConnell testified that the conversation was "totally out of the blue. [McPherson] said that Nationwide was going to finance and build an arena, and that he had offered the Hunt group the opportunity to pick up the lease and bring a franchise in. That was news to me. It was out of the blue." McPherson told McConnell about [Hunt Sports Group's] rejection of the lease proposal and discussed the NHL's June 4 deadline. McConnell stated that if Hunt would not step up and lease the arena and, therefore, get the franchise, McConnell would. Hunt Sports Group did not contact Nationwide on May 30.

On Saturday, May 31, McPherson told Nationwide's board of directors that there was not yet a lease commitment but that if Hunt Sports Group did not lease the arena, McConnell would. On Monday, June 2, City Council passed the resolution that set forth the terms for Nationwide to build an arena downtown. McPherson met with Bettman and told him that Nationwide would be building an arena in downtown Columbus.

McPherson also told Bettman that if need be, McConnell would purchase the franchise on his own. On or about Tuesday, June 3, McConnell was informed that [Hunt Sports Group] had not yet accepted the lease proposal. On June 3, Hunt Sports Group told Nationwide that it still found the terms of the lease to be unacceptable. On June 3 or June 4, McConnell, in a conversation with the NHL, orally agreed to apply for a hockey franchise for Columbus. On June 4, McPherson returned a call from Hunt, and Hunt informed McPherson that he was still interested in pursuing an agreement with Nationwide.

On June 4, the NHL franchise expansion committee met. Bettman informed the committee that Nationwide would build an arena, and McConnell was prepared to go forward with the franchise even if he had to do it himself. The committee was told that Hunt Sports Group's involvement was an open issue, but McConnell as an owner was more than adequate. The expansion committee recommended Columbus to the NHL board of governors as one of four cities to be granted a franchise.

On June 5, the NHL sent Hunt a letter requesting that he let the NHL know whether he was going forward with his franchise application. In a June 6 letter to the NHL, Hunt responded that CHL intended to pursue the franchise application. Hunt informed the NHL that he had arranged a meeting with the members of CHL to be held on June 9. Hunt indicated that the application was contingent upon entering into an appropriate lease for a hockey facility.

On June 9, a meeting took place at Pizzuti's office. Those present at the meeting included McConnell, Hunt, Pizzuti, John F. Wolfe, chairman of Wolfe Enterprises, Inc., and representatives of Buckeye Hockey, L.L.C. and Ameritech. The NHL required that the ownership group be identified and that such ownership group sign a lease term sheet by June 9. Brian Ellis, president and chief operating officer of Nationwide, presented the lease term sheet to those present at the meeting, left the meeting, and went to a different room.

Hunt indicated the lease was unacceptable. Ameritech and Buckeye Hockey, L.L.C. indicated that if Hunt found it unacceptable, then they too found it unacceptable. Pizzuti and Wolfe agreed to participate along with McConnell. John Christie, president of JMAC, Inc., the personal investment company of the McConnell family, left the meeting and joined Ellis. Christie informed Ellis that McConnell had accepted the term sheet and was signing it in his individual capacity. The term sheet contained a signature line for "Columbus Hockey Limited" as the franchise owner. Ellis phoned his secretary and had her omit the name "Columbus Hockey Limited" on her computer from under the signature line and fax the change. McConnell then signed the term sheet as the owner of the franchise. Christie faxed the signed lease term sheet to Bettman that day along with a cover letter and a description of the ownership group. Such ownership group was identified as John H. McConnell, majority owner, Pizzuti Sports, L.L.C., John F. Wolfe, and "[u]p to seven (7) other members."

On or about June 25, the NHL board of governors awarded Columbus a franchise with McConnell's group as owner. Hunt Sports Group, Buckeye Hockey, L.L.C. and Ameritech have no ownership interest in the hockey franchise.

[In their complaint, McConnell and Wolfe Enterprises, Inc. requested a declaration that section 3.3 of the CHL operating agreement allowed members of CHL to compete with CHL. Specifically, McConnell and Wolfe Enterprises, Inc. sought a declaration that under the operating agreement, they were permitted to participate in McConnell ownership group and obtain the franchise. The trial court granted summary judgment in favor of McConnell and Wolfe Enterprises, Inc. It found that section 3.3 of the operating agreement was clear and unambiguous and allowed McConnell and Wolfe Enterprises, Inc. to compete against CHL and obtain the NHL franchise. McConnell also sought a declaration that McConnell, Wolfe Enterprises, Inc., and other members of the McConnell ownership group had not violated any fiduciary duties in connection with the hockey franchise and arena lease. After a jury trial, the trial court granted McConnell and Wolfe Enterprises, Inc.'s motion for directed verdicts on the fiduciary duty issue].

[OPERATING AGREEMENT]

As indicated above, count one of the first amended complaint sought a declaration that section 3.3 of CHL's operating agreement allowed members to compete against CHL to obtain an NHL franchise. [McConnell] contends section 3.3 is plain and unambiguous and allows what occurred here—[McConnell ownership group] competing for and obtaining the NHL franchise. [Hunt Sports Group] asserts, in part, that the trial court's interpretation of section 3.3 was incorrect and that section 3.3 is ambiguous and subject to different interpretations. Therefore, [Hunt Sports Group] contends extrinsic evidence should have been considered, and such evidence would have shown the parties did not intend section 3.3 to mean members could compete against CHL and take away CHL's only purpose.

The construction of written contracts is a matter of law. The purpose of contract construction is to discover and effectuate the intent of the parties, and the intent of the parties is presumed to reside in the language they chose to use in the agreement. If a contract is clear and unambiguous, there is no issue of fact to be determined, and the court cannot create a new contract by finding an intent not expressed in the clear language employed by the parties. Only where the language of a contract is unclear or ambiguous or when the circumstances surrounding the agreement invest the language of the contract with a special meaning, will extrinsic evidence be considered in an effort to give effect to the parties' intentions.

The test for determining whether a term is ambiguous is that common words in a written contract will be given their ordinary meaning unless manifest absurdity results or unless some other meaning is clearly evidenced from the face or overall content of the contract. A writing will be read as a whole, and the intent of each part will be gathered from a consideration of the whole. For the reasons that follow, we conclude that section 3.3 is plain and unambiguous and allowed members of CHL to compete against CHL for an NHL franchise.

Section 3.3 of the operating agreement states:

> "*Members May Compete.* Members shall not in any way be prohibited from or restricted in engaging or owning an interest in any other business venture of any nature, including any venture which might be competitive with the business of the Company."

[Hunt Sports Group] emphasizes the word "other" in the above language and states, in essence, that it means any business venture that is different from the business of the company. [Hunt Sports Group] points out that under section 2.1 of the operating agreement, the general character of the business is "to invest in and operate a franchise in the National Hockey League." Hence, [Hunt Sports Group] contends that members may only engage in or own an interest in a venture that is not in the business of investing in and operating a franchise with the NHL.

[Hunt Sports Group's] interpretation of section 3.3 goes beyond the plain language of the agreement and adds words or meanings not stated in the provision. Section 3.3, for example, does not state "[m]embers shall not be prohibited from or restricted in engaging or owning an interest in any other business venture that is different from the business of the company." Rather, section 3.3 states: "any other business venture *of any nature.*" (Emphasis added.) It then adds to this statement: "including any venture which might be competitive with the business of the Company." The words "any nature" could not be broader, and the inclusion of the words "any venture which might be competitive with the business of the Company" makes it clear that members were not prohibited from engaging in a venture that was competitive with CHL's investing in and operating an NHL franchise. Contrary to [Hunt Sports Group]'s contention, the word "other" simply means a business venture other than CHL. The word "other" does not limit the type of business venture in which members may engage.

Hence, section 3.3 did not prohibit [McConnell] from engaging in activities that may have been competitive with CHL, including [McConnell's] participation in [McConnell ownership group]. Accordingly, summary judgment in favor of [McConnell] was appropriate, and [McConnell] was entitled to a declaration that section 3.3 of the operating agreement permitted [McConnell] to request and obtain an NHL hockey franchise to the exclusion of CHL.

We have already determined that section 3.3 permitted [McConnell] to request and obtain an NHL franchise. [Hunt Sports Group] points to section 4.1(c)(v) of the operating agreement in further support of its argument that McConnell breached the operating agreement in forming [McConnell ownership group]. Section 4.1 states:

Approval by Members. * * * [N]o Member shall take any action *on behalf of the Company* unless such actions are approved by a vote of the specified number of Members:

* * *

"(c) The following actions require the approval of Members owning all of the Units allocated to the Members:

* * *

"(v) do any other act that would make it impossible to carry on the ordinary business of the Company[.] (Emphasis added.)

As to any argument that McConnell breached section 4.1(c)(v) in forming [McConnell ownership group] and competing against CHL, there is no genuine issue of material fact, and [McConnell] is entitled to judgment as a matter of law. The voting requirements in section 4.1 apply only to actions taken "on behalf of the Company." In forming [McConnell ownership group] and in obtaining the NHL franchise, McConnell was obviously not taking action on behalf of CHL. Therefore, McConnell did not breach section 4.1(c)(v) in failing to obtain the vote of all CHL members prior to taking such action.

In summary, there are no genuine issues of material fact, [McConnell is] entitled to judgment as a matter of law and reasonable minds could only conclude that section 3.3 of the operating agreement allowed [McConnell] to request and obtain an NHL franchise to the exclusion of CHL, McConnell did not breach the operating agreement by forming [McConnell ownership group] and competing against CHL.

[FIDUCIARY DUTY]

As to the fiduciary duty issue, the trial court found, in part, that [McConnell] had not engaged in any kind of willful misconduct, misrepresentation, or concealment. Therefore, the trial court concluded that [McConnell] had not breached any fiduciary duty in seeking and obtaining the NHL franchise and in negotiating with Nationwide concerning the arena lease. For the reasons that follow, we conclude that a directed verdict was appropriate.

The term "fiduciary relationship" has been defined as a relationship in which special confidence and trust is reposed in the integrity and fidelity of another, and there is a resulting position of superiority or influence acquired by virtue of this special trust. In the case at bar, a limited liability company is involved which, like a partnership, involves a fiduciary relationship. Normally, the presence of such a relationship would preclude direct competition between members of the company. However, here we have an operating agreement that by its very terms allows members to compete with the business of the company. Hence, the question we are presented with is whether an operating agreement of a limited liability company may, in essence, limit or define the scope of the fiduciary duties imposed upon its members. We answer this question in the affirmative.

A fiduciary has been defined as a person having a duty, *created by his or her undertaking,* to act primarily for the benefit of another in matters *connected with such undertaking. Strock v. Pressnell,* 527 N.E.2d 1235, 1243 (Ohio 1988). A claim of breach of fiduciary duty is basically a claim for negligence that involves a higher standard of care. In order to recover, one must show the existence of a duty on the part of the alleged wrongdoer not to subject such person to the injury complained of, a failure to observe such duty, and an injury proximately resulting therefrom. These principles support our conclusion that a contract may define the scope of fiduciary duties between parties to the contract.

Here, the injury complained of by [Hunt Sports Group] was, essentially, [McConnell] competing with CHL and obtaining the NHL franchise. The operating agreement constitutes the undertaking of the parties herein. In becoming members of CHL, [Hunt Sports Group] and [McConnell] agreed to abide by the terms of the operating agreement, and such agreement specifically allowed competition with the company by its members. As such, the duties created pursuant to such undertaking did not include a duty not to compete. Therefore, there was no duty on the part of [McConnell] to refrain from subjecting [Hunt Sports Group] to the injury complained of herein.

We find further support for our conclusion in case law concerning close corporations and partnerships. In *Cruz v. S. Dayton Urological Assoc., Inc.,* 700 N.E.2d 675 (Ohio App. 1997), the plaintiff filed suit against his former shareholders in a close corporation, alleging, in part, breach of fiduciary duty. The plaintiff had been a shareholder in a professional corporation organized for the practice of medicine. The plaintiff was employed by the corporation pursuant to a written agreement. Such agreement provided that the corporation or employee could terminate the employment contract unilaterally and without specification of cause upon ninety days' written notice. The plaintiff was terminated after the other shareholders voted to terminate him.

The court of appeals recognized that shareholders have a fiduciary duty to each other and that such duty is heightened in a close corporation setting. The court cited *Gigax v. Repka,* 615 N.E.2d 644, 649–650 (Ohio App. 1992), wherein such court concluded that a minority shareholder/ employee in a close corporation was not an at-will employee who was terminable at any time by the majority shareholders. Rather, the *Gigax* court concluded that the fiduciary duty that partners owe each other requires that removal of a partner be based upon legitimate business reasons.

The *Cruz* plaintiff claimed the other shareholders breached their fiduciary duty by terminating him without a legitimate business reason. However, the *Cruz* court distinguished *Gigax,* noting that in *Gigax* the shareholder/employee had not entered into an employment agreement with the corporation that permitted termination without cause. The court of appeals stated that when the plaintiff agreed that the corporation could terminate him without specification of cause, he relieved the corporation and shareholders of any duty they owed him to terminate him only for good cause.

The *Cruz* case stands for the proposition that close corporation employment agreements may limit the scope of fiduciary duties that otherwise would apply absent certain provisions in such agreements. The same principle has been applied in situations involving partnerships that are subject to partnership agreements.

"Operating agreement" is defined in R.C. 1705.01(J) as all of the valid written or oral agreements of the members as to the affairs of a limited liability company and the conduct of its business. R.C. 1705.03(C) sets forth various activities limited liability companies may engage in and indicates such are subject to the company's articles of organization or operating agreement. Indeed, many of the statutory provisions in R.C. Chapter 1705 governing limited liability companies indicate they are, in various ways, subject to and/or dependent upon related provisions in an operating agreement. Here, the operating agreement states in its opening paragraph that it evidences the mutual agreement of the members in consideration of their contributions and promises to each other. Such agreement specifically allowed its members to compete with the company.

Given the above, we conclude as a matter of law that it was not a breach of fiduciary duty for [McConnell] to form [McConnell ownership group] and obtain an NHL franchise to the exclusion of CHL. In so concluding, we are not stating that *no* act related to such obtainment could be considered a breach of fiduciary duty. In general terms, members of limited liability companies owe one another the duty of utmost trust and loyalty. However, such general duty in this case must be considered in the context of members' ability, pursuant to operating agreement, to compete with the company.

3. DELAWARE APPROACH

Delaware takes a radically different approach toward contracting for fiduciary duty. It permits the complete *elimination* of fiduciary duty of members and managers through contracting.[1]

Delaware Limited Liability Company Act § 18–1101. Construction and application of chapter and limited liability company agreement

(b) It is the policy of this chapter to give the maximum effect to the principle of freedom of contract and to the enforceability of limited liability company agreements.

(c) To the extent that, at law or in equity, a member or manager or other person has duties (including fiduciary duties) to a limited liability company or to another member or manager or to another person that is a party to or is otherwise bound by a limited liability company agreement, the member's or manager's or other person's duties may be expanded or restricted or *eliminated* by provisions in the limited liability company agreement; provided, that the limited liability company agreement may not eliminate the implied contractual covenant of good faith and fair dealing.

The potential for complete elimination of fiduciary duties, particularly the duty of loyalty, is an extreme proposition. Consider a simple hypothetical in which there is a legally valid provision in the operating agreement that eliminates all fiduciary duty. The LLC is manager-managed; the manager decides to engage in a transaction in the LLC sells assets at a price that is highly favorable to another business that he owns. The conflict of interest is apparent. However, there would be no accountability under a fiduciary duty framework because the operating agreement eliminated the manger's fiduciary duty.

The question of whether default fiduciary duties existed for Delaware LLCs has a colorful history. In a prior version of the Delaware statute, there was no mention of fiduciary duties. In *Auriga Capital, Corp. v. Gatz Properties, LLC*, 40, A.3d 839 (Del.Ch. 2012), a case involving allegations by minority members of self-dealing by an LLC's manager and majority member, Chancellor Leo Strine suggested that the Delaware statute, albeit silent on the existence of fiduciary duty, implicitly provided default fiduciary duties in the event that parties did not contract for them in the operating agreement:

---

[1] Nevada also takes this approach. Nev.Rev.Stat. § 86.286(5) ("such duties may be expanded, restricted or *eliminated* by provisions in the operating agreement").

Thus, because the LLC Act provides for principles of equity to apply, because LLC managers are clearly fiduciaries, and because fiduciaries owe the fiduciary duties of loyalty and care, the LLC Act starts with the default that managers of LLCs owe enforceable fiduciary duties.

Id. at 851.

On appeal, the Delaware Supreme Court upheld the chancery court's decision on the ground that the operating agreement required "a fair price" in these kinds of transactions. *Gatz Properties, LLC v. Auriga Capital, Corp.,* 59 A.3d 1206, 1214–16 (Del. 2012). However, the court held that a contract analysis sufficed to resolve the case, and it chastised the chancery court for delving into the issue of whether the Delaware LLC statute provided default fiduciary duties:

We remind Delaware judges that the obligation to write judicial opinions on the issues presented is not a license to use those opinions as a platform from which to propagate their individual world views on issues not presented. A judge's duty is to resolve the issues that the parties present in a clear and concise manner. To the extent Delaware judges wish to stray beyond those issues and, without making any definitive pronouncements, ruminate on what the proper direction of Delaware law should be, there are appropriate platforms, such as law review articles, the classroom, continuing legal education presentations, and keynote speeches.

Id. at 1220. The public rebuke was even covered by the media. Peter Lattman, *In Unusual Move, Delaware Supreme Court Rebukes a Judge,* N.Y. Times (Nov. 9, 2012).

Ultimately the Delaware legislature resolved the conflict by affirming the chancery court's approach. It amended section 18–1104 of the LLC statute to provide (amendment in italics): "In any case not provided for in this chapter, the rules of law and equity, including *the rules of law and equity relating to fiduciary duties and* the law merchant, shall govern." In Delaware, there are now default fiduciary duties in the event that parties do not contract for them; but if parties do contract for fiduciary duties, the statute permits their modification or complete elimination. There is also a rich irony: subsequent to writing the opinion in *Gatz,* former chancellor Strine was appointed to be the chief justice of the Delaware Supreme Court.

The case below involves the interpretation of a limited partnership's partnership agreement and specifically the provisions dealing with contracting for fiduciary duty. This chapter concerns LLCs, and not limited partnerships. However, in Delaware, the statutory provisions governing the ability to contract for fiduciary duty are the same for LLCs and limited partnerships.[2] Therefore, the lesson in the following case applies both to Delaware limited partnerships and LLCs.

In reading this case, think about these questions: (1) What are the ownership and management structures of the limited partnership? (2) In what way did the partnership agreement relate to the general partner's fiduciary duty?

NORTON V. K-SEA TRANSP. PARTNERS L.P.

67 A.3d 354 (Del. 2013).

STEELE, CHIEF JUSTICE.

In this appeal, we consider a general partner's obligations under a limited partnership agreement. The plaintiffs allege that the general partner obtained excessive consideration for its incentive distribution rights when an unaffiliated third party purchased the partnership. Importantly, the plaintiffs do not allege that the general partner breached the implied covenant of good faith and fair dealing. We conclude that the limited partnership agreement's conflict of interest provision created a contractual safe harbor, not an affirmative obligation. Therefore, the general partner needed only to exercise its discretion in good faith, as the parties intended that term to be construed, to satisfy its duties under the agreement. The general partner obtained an appropriate fairness opinion, which, under the agreement, created a conclusive presumption that the general partner made its decision in good faith. Therefore we AFFIRM the Court of Chancery's dismissal of the complaint.

I.   FACTUAL AND PROCEDURAL BACKGROUND

The Parties

This case arises out of the Merger of K-Sea Transportation Partners L.P. (K-Sea or the Partnership) and Kirby Corporation. K-Sea operates a barge and tugboat fleet that transports refined petroleum products

---

[2]   *Compare* Delaware Revised Limited Partnership Act § 17–1101(c) ("It is the policy of this chapter to give maximum effect to the principle of freedom of contract and to the enforceability of partnership agreements."); *id.* § 17–1101(d) ("To the extent that, at law or in equity, a partner or other person has duties (including fiduciary duties) to a limited partnership or to another partner or to another person that is a party to or is otherwise bound by a partnership agreement, the partner's or other person's duties may be expanded or restricted or eliminated by provisions in the partnership agreement; provided that the partnership agreement may not eliminate the implied contractual covenant of good faith and fair dealing."); *with* Delaware Limited Liability Company Act § 18–1101(b) ("It is the policy of this chapter to give the maximum effect to the principle of freedom of contract and to the enforceability of limited liability company agreements."); *id.* § 18–1101(c) ("To the extent that, at law or in equity, a member or manager or other person has duties (including fiduciary duties) to a limited liability company or to another member or manager or to another person that is a party to or is otherwise bound by a limited liability company agreement, the member's or manager's or other person's duties may be expanded or restricted or eliminated by provisions in the limited liability company agreement; provided, that the limited liability company agreement may not eliminate the implied contractual covenant of good faith and fair dealing.").

between American ports. Before the Merger, K-Sea was a publicly traded Delaware limited partnership. The Fourth Amended and Restated Agreement of Limited Partnership (the LPA) created K-Sea's governance structure. Plaintiffs Edward F. Norton III and Ken Poesl (Norton) represent a class consisting of K-Sea's unaffiliated former common unitholders.

K-Sea's general partner is K-Sea General Partner L.P. (K-Sea GP), which is also a Delaware limited partnership. K-Sea GP's general partner is K-Sea General Partner GP LLC (KSGP), a Delaware limited liability company that ultimately controls K-Sea. Anthony S. Abbate, Barry J. Alperin, James C. Baker, Timothy J. Casey, James J. Dowling, Brian P. Friedman, Kevin S. McCarthy, Gary D. Reaves II, and Frank Salerno served on KSGP's board of directors (the K-Sea Board) during the Merger negotiations. Directors Abbate, Alperin, and Salerno comprised the K-Sea Board's Conflicts Committee. K-Sea, K-Sea GP, KSGP, and the K-Sea Board members are the Defendants in this action.

K-Sea's Capital Structure and Ownership

At the time of the Merger, K-Sea's equity was divided among K-Sea GP, the common unitholders, and a class of preferred units held by KA First Reserve, LLC (KAFR). The common unitholders held 49.8% of the total equity, KAFR held 49.9%, and K-Sea GP's general partner interest comprised the remaining 0.3%.

In addition to its general partner interest, K-Sea GP held incentive distribution rights (IDRs) through a wholly owned affiliate. These IDRs entitled K-Sea GP to increasing percentages of K-Sea's distributions once payments to the limited partners exceeded certain levels. K-Sea GP would not receive payments on the IDRs until *quarterly* distributions reached $0.55 per unit. K-Sea's conservative estimates indicated that *annual* distributions would not reach $0.55 per unit until 2015. Norton extrapolates these projections to show that K-Sea would not reach the $0.55-per-unit quarterly threshold until the mid-2030s. Based on these projections, the IDRs were worth as little as $100,000.

Kirby Approaches K-Sea and Negotiates the Merger

Shortly after the phantom unit grant, Kirby's CEO communicated with McCarthy, who also served as a director designee of KAFR, to discuss a strategic transaction between Kirby and K-Sea. On February 2, 2011, McCarthy informed Dowling, the K-Sea Board's Chairman, of those discussions. K-Sea and Kirby then extended a confidentiality agreement they had previously signed, and K-Sea provided Kirby with due diligence.

On February 9, 2011, Kirby offered to pay $306 million for K-Sea's common and preferred units. After discussing the offer with the K-Sea Board, McCarthy rejected it and informed Kirby that future offers should include consideration for K-Sea GP's general partner interest and its IDRs.

Kirby responded the next day with a $316 million offer for all of K-Sea's equity interests, but McCarthy again rejected the offer as inadequate. On February 15, 2011, Kirby offered $329 million for K-Sea, which included an $18 million payment for the IDRs (the IDR Payment).

K-Sea Activates its Conflicts Committee to Consider the Merger

When the K-Sea Board met to consider Kirby's new offer, it acknowledged that the IDR Payment created a "possible conflict of interest" and referred the proposed Merger to the Conflicts Committee for a recommendation. Under the LPA, the Conflict Committee's approval of a transaction would constitute "Special Approval," which purportedly would limit the unitholders' ability to challenge the transaction.

The Conflicts Committee hired Stifel, Nicolaus & Co. (Stifel) and DLA Piper LLP as its independent financial and legal advisors, respectively. Stifel valued K-Sea's common units using a distribution discount model based on K-Sea's internal projections. After valuing the common units, Stifel opined that the consideration K-Sea's unaffiliated common unitholders received was fair from a financial viewpoint. The fairness opinion expressly did not consider "the fairness of the amount or nature of any compensation to any of the officers, directors or employees of K-Sea or its affiliates . . . relative to the compensation of the public holders of K-Sea's equity securities."

The K-Sea Board Approves the Merger and the Transaction Closes

After reviewing Stifel's fairness opinion, the Conflicts Committee unanimously recommended the Merger to the K-Sea Board, which also approved it. Like Stifel's fairness opinion, the Conflicts Committee's recommendation did not refer to the IDR Payment. K-Sea and Kirby then entered into a definitive merger agreement and disseminated a Form S–4 recommending that the common unitholders vote in favor of the Merger. A majority of K-Sea's unitholders voted in favor of the transaction, and the Merger closed on July 1, 2011. As finally negotiated, K-Sea's common unitholders received $8.15 per unit and K-Sea GP received $18 million for the IDRs. The consideration represented a 26% premium over K-Sea's March 11, 2011 closing price.

III. ANALYSIS

What Contractual Standards Apply to the Merger?

Limited partnership agreements are a type of contract. We, therefore, construe them in accordance with their terms to give effect to the parties' intent. We give words their plain meaning unless it appears that the parties intended a special meaning. When interpreting contracts, we construe them as a whole and give effect to every provision if it is reasonably possible. A meaning inferred from a particular provision cannot control the agreement if that inference conflicts with the agreement's overall scheme. We consider extrinsic evidence only if the contract is ambiguous. A contract is not ambiguous "simply because the parties do not agree upon its proper construction," but only if it is susceptible to two or more reasonable interpretations. If the contractual language at issue is ambiguous and if the limited partners did not negotiate for the agreement's terms, we apply the *contra proferentem* principle and construe the ambiguous terms against the drafter.

The Delaware Revised Uniform Limited Partnership Act (DRULPA) gives "maximum effect to the principle of freedom of contract and to the enforceability of partnership agreements." 6 Del. C. § 17–1101(c). Parties may expand, restrict, or eliminate any fiduciary duties that a partner or other person might otherwise owe, but they "may not eliminate the implied contractual covenant of good faith and fair dealing." 6 Del. C. § 17–1101(d).

The LPA's Provisions Governing Mergers and Creating Contractual Fiduciary Duties

Unfortunately, limited partnership agreements that attempt to modify, rather than eliminate, fiduciary duties often create a Gordian knot of interrelated standards in different sections of the agreement. This LPA requires us to parse several provisions to determine which standards apply to the Merger. The LPA creates procedures for mergers in Article XIV. Section 14.2 of Article XIV establishes that K-Sea GP must approve any proposed merger. K-Sea GP may consent to a merger "in the exercise of its discretion." Section 7.9(b), which attempts to clarify the nebulous "discretion" standard, provides:

> Whenever this Agreement . . . provides that [K-Sea GP] . . . is permitted or required to make a decision (i) in its "sole discretion" or "discretion," . . . except as otherwise provided herein, [K-Sea GP] . . . shall be entitled to consider only such interests and factors as it desires and shall have no duty or obligation to give any consideration to any interest of, or factors affecting, the Partnership . . . [or] any Limited Partner . . . [and] (ii) it may make such decision in its sole discretion (regardless of whether there is a reference to "sole discretion" or "discretion") unless another express standard is provided for. . . .

Therefore, when K-Sea GP decides whether to consent to a merger, it may "consider only such interests and factors as it desires and shall have no duty or obligation to give any consideration to any interest of, or factors affecting" K-Sea or its limited partners. The limited partners' ultimate right to reject a merger under Section 14.3 practically limits that discretion however.

The LPA limits Section 14.2's broad grant of discretion in Section 7.10(d), which provides:

> Any standard of care and duty imposed by [the LPA] or [DRULPA] ... shall be modified, waived or limited, to the extent permitted by law, as required to permit [K-Sea GP] to act under [the LPA] ... and to make any decision pursuant to the authority prescribed in [the LPA], *so long as such action is reasonably believed by [K-Sea GP] to be in, or not inconsistent with, the best interests of the Partnership.*

If K-Sea GP were subject to common law fiduciary duties, it could not consent to a merger in its sole discretion. Therefore, Section 7.10(d) eliminates any duties that otherwise exist and replaces them with a contractual fiduciary duty—namely, that K-Sea GP must reasonably believe that its action is in the best interest of, or not inconsistent with, the best interests of the Partnership.

Finally, the LPA broadly exculpates all Indemnitees (which no party disputes includes all the Defendants) so long as the Indemnitee acted in "good faith." Although the LPA regrettably does not define "good faith" in this context, we cannot discern a rational distinction between the parties' adoption of this "good faith" standard and Section 7.10(d)'s contractual fiduciary duty, *i.e.*, an Indemnitee acts in good faith if the Indemnitee reasonably believes that its action is in the best interest of, or at least, not inconsistent with, the best interests of K-Sea. If we take seriously our obligation to construe the agreement's "overall scheme," we must conclude that the parties' insertion of a free-standing, enigmatic standard of "good faith" is consistent with Section 7.10(d)'s conceptualization of a reasonable belief that the action taken is in, or not inconsistent with, the best interests of the Partnership. In this LPA's overall scheme, "good faith" cannot be construed otherwise.

Thus, while the LPA does not require K-Sea GP to consider any particular interest or factor affecting the Partnership when exercising its discretion, K-Sea GP still must reasonably believe that its ultimate course of action is not inconsistent with K-Sea's best interests. Therefore, unless another provision supplants this standard, in order to state a claim that withstands Rule 12(b)(6), Norton must allege facts supporting an inference that K-Sea GP had reason to believe that it acted inconsistently with the Partnership's best interests when approving the Merger.

In order to state a claim that survives a motion to dismiss under Rule 12(b)(6), Norton must plead facts supporting a reasonable inference that K-Sea GP, the only defendant with a duty relating to the Merger's approval, acted inconsistently with the Partnership's best interests. If Norton's complaint cannot establish a breach of the contract's "good faith" standard, we need not reach whether the phantom unit grant disqualified the Conflicts Committee members and invalidated the Special Approval process.

Here, Norton has alleged that the IDR Payment created a conflict of interest between K-Sea GP and the Partnership because K-Sea GP obtained consideration that did not flow to the common unitholders. At the motion to dismiss stage we must draw all inferences in Norton's favor. We therefore could conclude that K-Sea GP used its position to extract an excessive amount of consideration for its IDRs at the expense of the limited partners. That permits us to infer that K-Sea GP may not have acted in good faith when it approved the Merger and submitted it to the unitholders for approval. That raises the next issue, which is whether Norton has pled a cognizable claim that K-Sea GP did not act in good faith.

Did the Investment Banker's Fairness Opinion Create a Conclusive Presumption of Good Faith?

In addressing that issue, we must consider yet another LPA provision addressing K-Sea GP's obligation to act in "good faith." That provision creates a conclusive presumption that K-Sea GP has acted in good faith if K-Sea GP relies on a competent expert's opinion. Section 7.10(b) provides that

> [K-Sea GP] may consult with . . . investment bankers . . . and any act taken or omitted to be taken in reliance upon the opinion . . . of such Persons as to matters that [K-Sea GP] reasonably believes to be within such Person's professional or expert competence *shall be conclusively presumed to have been done or omitted in good faith* and in accordance with such opinion.

The Conflicts Committee obtained Stifel's opinion that the consideration that Kirby paid to K-Sea's unaffiliated common unitholders was financially fair. No party alleges that Stifel lacked the requisite expertise to render that opinion. Norton nowhere claims that the opinion did not state that the Merger was fair, nor does he allege that the analyses underlying the fairness opinion were flawed. Rather, he alleges that K-Sea extracted a larger portion of the consideration than the IDRs' value justified. We note also that Norton does not claim on appeal that Defendants' actions breached the implied covenant of good faith and fair dealing.

Norton argues that K-Sea GP is not entitled to a conclusive presumption of good faith because Stifel did not specifically address the IDR Payment's fairness—the reason why K-Sea GP activated the Conflicts Committee. He concedes that the unaffiliated unitholders received a fair price, and he correctly notes that a limited partnership's value is not a single number, but a range of fair values. While we understand Norton's frustration, the LPA's provisions control.

The LPA does not require K-Sea GP to evaluate the IDR Payment's reasonableness separately from the remaining consideration. Section 7.9(a) explicitly states that nothing in the LPA shall be construed to require K-Sea GP to consider the interests of any person other than the Partnership.

That Section authorizes (but does not require) K-Sea GP to consider the "relative interests of any party to such conflict." These provisions indicate that K-Sea GP was not required to consider whether the IDR Payment was fair, but only whether the Merger as a whole was in the best interests of the Partnership (which included the general partner and the limited partners). Because of those clear provisions, Norton had no reasonable contractual expectation that K-Sea GP or the Conflict Committee's retained investment banker would specifically consider the IDR Payment's fairness.

Because Stifel's opinion satisfied the LPA's requirements, we next address whether that opinion entitles *K-Sea GP* to a conclusive presumption of good faith. Although the Conflicts Committee of the K-Sea Board actually obtained the fairness opinion, it is unreasonable to infer that the entire K-Sea Board did not rely on the opinion that a K-Sea Board subcommittee obtained. Similarly, because K-Sea GP is a "pass-through" entity controlled by KSGP, the only reasonable inference is that K-Sea GP relied on the fairness opinion. K-Sea GP is therefore conclusively presumed to have acted in good faith when it approved the Merger and submitted it to the unitholders for a vote. That process satisfied K-Sea GP's contractual duty to exercise its discretion in "good faith" (as this LPA defines the term).

Norton willingly invested in a limited partnership that provided fewer protections to limited partners than those provided under corporate fiduciary duty principles. He is bound by his investment decision. Here, the LPA did not require K-Sea GP to consider separately the IDR Payment's fairness, but granted K-Sea GP broad discretion to approve a merger, so long as it exercised that discretion in "good faith". Reliance on Stifel's opinion satisfied this standard. By opining that the consideration Kirby paid to the unaffiliated unitholders was fair, Stifel's opinion addressed the IDR Payment's fairness, albeit indirectly. Kirby presumably was willing to pay a fixed amount for the entire Partnership. If K-Sea GP diverted too much value to itself, at some point the consideration paid to the unaffiliated unitholders would no longer be "fair."

Furthermore, the LPA does not leave K-Sea's unitholders unprotected. K-Sea GP's approval merely triggered submission of the Merger to the unitholders for a majority vote. If the unitholders were dissatisfied with the Merger's terms, "their remedy [was] the ballot box, not the courthouse." Here K-Sea GP is conclusively presumed to have approved the Merger in good faith, and a majority of the unitholders voted to consummate it. The LPA required nothing more.

C. LIMITED LIABILITY

Unlike a general partnership and a limited partnership, in which the general partner is personally liable for the debts and obligations of the partnership, all members and managers of LLCs are entitled to the benefit of limited liability: "The debts, obligations, and liabilities of a limited liability company, whether arising in contract, tort, or otherwise: (1) are solely the debts, obligations, and liabilities of the limited liability company; and (2) do not become the debts, obligations, and liabilities of a member or manager solely by reason of the member or manager acting as member or manager." RULLCA § 304(a).

———————

The case below concerns the scope of the liability protection in LLCs. In reading this case, think about these questions: (1) What are differences, if any, between the limited liability protection of limited partners in limited partnerships and members and managers in LLCs? (2) In what way do the substantive liability rules in torts affect the liability of members and managers in LLCs and the rule of limited liability in LLCs? (2) If Sun Studs was a corporation, would the Court have imposed liability under the Employers Liability Law on the President and CEO?

CORTEZ V. NACCO MATERIAL HANDLING GROUP, INC.
337 P.3d 111 (Ore. 2014) (en banc).

KISTLER, J.

Plaintiff worked for a lumber mill, Sun Studs, LLC. One evening while he was walking from one area of the mill to another, a forklift hit and severely injured him. After receiving workers' compensation benefits, plaintiff brought this action against Swanson Group, Inc., which owns Sun Studs, as well as other defendants. Plaintiff alleged that Swanson was liable for negligently failing (or for negligently failing to require Sun Studs) to provide a safe workplace and for failing to provide competent safety personnel. Plaintiff also alleged that Swanson was liable under the Employers Liability Law (ELL), which requires employers to take certain safety measures. Swanson moved for summary judgment, and the trial court granted its motion on the ground that the workers' compensation statutes provided the exclusive remedy for plaintiff's injuries. The court entered a limited judgment in Swanson's favor.

The Court of Appeals affirmed the trial court's judgment regarding plaintiff's ELL claim, reversed its judgment regarding plaintiff's negligence claim, and remanded the negligence claim for further proceedings. We reverse the Court of Appeals decision. We affirm the trial court's judgment regarding plaintiff's negligence claim, reverse its judgment regarding plaintiff's ELL claim, and remand the ELL claim to the trial court for further proceedings.

Because Sun Studs is currently organized as a limited liability company (LLC), we discuss that form of organization briefly before setting out the facts. An LLC is a relatively new form of business organization. The persons who own an LLC are its "members." ORS 63.001(21). The members can manage the LLC themselves, or they can appoint a manager or group of managers to manage the company. ORS 63.001(19), (20). The statutes accordingly distinguish between member-managed and manager-managed LLCs.[1]

LLCs share many attributes of limited partnerships, but they differ from that form of business organization in at least one respect: in Oregon, a "member or manager [of an LLC] is not personally liable for a * * * liability of the [LLC] solely by reason of being or acting as a member or manager." ORS 63.165(1). By contrast, in Oregon, a limited partner will become personally liable for the limited partnership's obligations if the limited partner "participates in the control of the business." ORS 70.135; see Ribstein and Keatinge, *Limited Liability Companies* § 1.6 ("Unlike limited partners, LLC members do not lose their limited liability for participating in control of the business.").

With that background in mind, we turn to the facts of this case. In 2001, Swanson Group, Inc., purchased a lumber mill, Sun Studs, Inc., and reorganized that business as a limited liability company. Swanson is the sole member of Sun Studs, LLC, and it elected to manage Sun Studs, making Sun Studs a member-managed LLC. Sun Studs is one of several timber-related LLCs that Swanson owns and manages. Swanson sets general policies and priorities for those LLCs. Sun Studs, like the other LLCs that Swanson owns, has its own employees, who are responsible for the day-to-day operation of the mill and also for implementing Swanson's general directives.

Regarding safety, Swanson provided the LLCs that it owned with a safety manual, which stated general policies and served as a "template" that each LLC could customize to its particular operations. Swanson delegated day-to-day responsibility for safety at Sun Studs to Sun Studs' mill manager and HR director. Specifically, Swanson delegated responsibility "to [Sun Studs' mill manager and HR director] to carry out the safety program and to follow as close as they can the template provided by [Swanson]." It was "up to [Sun Studs' mill manager and HR director] to identify and rectify any safety violations or unsafe workplace issues or safety hazard type issues" at the worksite.

Ash was Swanson's HR director and supervised his counterpart at Sun Studs. Swanson's executive vice president explained the relationship between Ash and Sun Studs' HR director:

> "So the practical way it works is that Mr. Ash would provide what I would say is oversight in the overall direct setting: [Ash would tell Sun Studs HR director,] [y]ou need to have these types of

---

[1] The persons appointed as the managers of a manager-managed LLC may but need not be members of the LLC. ORS 63.001(19).

programs. Here's the steps you need to take to implement. Here's the things you need to do. Here's the programs you need to ensure you've implemented. I'm here at this point if you [Sun Studs' HR director] need any help. Or if you want any support on your safety committee meetings or in your training sessions, then I'll [Ash] help you with that."

Harris was Swanson's vice president of operations. In that capacity, Harris supervised Sun Studs' mill manager. Swanson's executive vice-president explained the relationship between Harris and Sun Studs' mill manager:

"Mr. Harris was more of: You need to make sure you're doing what you have got to do safety-wise. You need to make sure that you're compliant. I'm going to be checking on you and making sure that I'm satisfied with your efforts in the safety program and the safety process."

Swanson's executive vice-president explained that the "[p]rimary responsibility for safety" rested with Sun Studs' HR director and mill manager.

Ash and Harris conducted periodic performance reviews of Sun Studs' managers. Ash and Harris also served as a resource to whom Sun Studs' HR director and mill manager could turn if they had a problem that required "corporate level upper-end" decision-making. On one occasion, Ash attended a safety committee meeting at Sun Studs to ensure that Sun Studs' supervisors did not need any help or further assistance. Otherwise, Swanson executives did not visit Sun Studs to monitor safety conditions or set safety policy. If Ash or Harris observed a safety violation when either of them was on Sun Studs' worksite, each person had authority to direct Sun Studs to correct the violation.

In this case, plaintiff suffered severe injuries one evening when another Sun Studs employee drove a forklift down a dark corridor and accidently hit him. Plaintiff filed a claim for and received workers' compensation benefits from Sun Studs. He then filed this action against Swanson, as well as other defendants. Plaintiff alleged in his amended complaint that Swanson was negligent. Plaintiff also claimed that Swanson had violated the ELL, based on similar allegations.

I. ORS 63.165(1)

Swanson does not dispute that a reasonable juror could infer from the evidence on summary judgment that Sun Studs was negligent in failing to have appropriately marked crosswalks, in failing to provide adequate lighting, in failing to require workers to wear fluorescent vests, and in failing to have forklifts equipped with audible and visual movement and backup alarms. Swanson also does not dispute that a reasonable juror could infer from the evidence on summary judgment that it had the authority, as the member-manager of Sun Studs, to require Sun Studs to provide safer conditions. Swanson notes, however, that ORS 63.165(1) shields LLC members and managers from personal liability for "acting" as a member-manager.[12] Swanson reasons that, under ORS 63.165(1), "merely having the authority to require the LLC to prevent a workplace accident * * * is not sufficient for personal liability to attach to a managing-member for every act of negligence that arises out of the operations of the LLC's business."

Swanson argues that it will be liable as Sun Studs' member-manager only when an officer or director of a corporation would be liable for a corporate employee's negligence—that is, only if Swanson "actively participated" in Sun Studs' negligence. Swanson contends that the evidence on summary judgment does not permit an inference that it either actually knew of the conditions at Sun Studs that allegedly led to plaintiff's injuries or that it actively participated in the creation of those conditions.

Plaintiff takes a different view of both ORS 63.165(1) and the evidence. He argues that the sole function of ORS 63.165(1) is to make clear that LLC members and managers are immune from vicarious liability for the LLC's debts, obligations, and liabilities. Plaintiff reasons that, to the extent a member or a manager is independently liable to an employee or a third party, ORS 63.165(1) provides no protection from that liability. Plaintiff argues that a reasonable juror could infer that Swanson "retain[ed] control over job site safety" and, having retained control, failed to provide (or to require Sun Studs to provide) a safe workplace.

A.   *Statutory Immunity under ORS 63.165(1)*

ORS 63.165(1) provides: "The debts, obligations and liabilities of a limited liability company, whether arising in contract, tort or otherwise, are solely the debts, obligations and liabilities of the limited liability company. A member or manager is not personally liable for a debt, obligation or liability of the limited liability company solely by reason of being or acting as a member or manager."

In many respects, the two sentences in subsection (1) mirror each other. The first sentence provides that the "debts, obligations and liabilities" of an LLC are "solely" the debts, obligations, and liabilities of the LLC. The second sentence provides that a member or a manager of an LLC is not personally liable for the LLC's debts, obligations, and liabilities "solely by reason of being or acting as a member or manager" of the LLC. Each sentence makes clear that a member or a manager of an LLC is not

---

[12] An LLC member can be a passive owner of the LLC, much like a corporate shareholder. Alternatively, an LLC member can manage the LLC either in a member-managed LLC or in a manager-managed LLC, if the member is designated as the manager of the manager-managed LLC. Ribstein and Keatinge, *Limited Liability Companies* § 2.3. We assume that the issues that arise from extending immunity to LLC members and managers for "acting" in those capacities primarily will involve persons (whether members or managers) who manage the LLC.

vicariously liable for the LLC's debts, obligations, and liabilities, as a general partner will be vicariously liable for the partnership's obligations.

The use of the word "being" in the second sentence in ORS 63.165(1) is consistent with that interpretation. Merely "being" a member or manager does not make that person liable for the LLC's obligations. However, the use of the word "acting" in the second sentence interjects ambiguity into the text. On the one hand, "acting" could mean that a member or manager is not personally liable for any debts, obligations or liabilities of the LLC that arise solely by reason of the "actions" that a member or manager takes in that person's official capacity. Read broadly, the phrase "acting as a member or manager" would provide members and managers immunity not only from vicarious liability but also from personal liability for their actions in managing an LLC.

On the other hand, the word "acting" may play a more modest role. It may simply confirm that a member or manager of an LLC is not vicariously liable for the LLC's debts, obligations, and liabilities. Specifically, the word "acting" could serve to make clear that, unlike a limited partner who will become vicariously liable if he or she participates in the control of the business, a member or manager of an LLC will not be vicariously liable for actively managing the LLC's business. *Cf.* ORS 70.135(1) (providing that, although a limited partner is ordinarily not vicariously liable for the limited partnership's liabilities, a limited partner will become vicariously liable for those liabilities if he or she participates in the control of the business). The text, specifically the word "acting," is capable of more than one interpretation, and we turn to the context.

The context does little to clarify the text's meaning. Essentially, it reveals that, as initially enacted in 1993, ORS 63.165(1) shielded an LLC member or manager from liability for the LLC's obligations only for "being" a member or manager. As noted, granting immunity for "being" a member or manager implies only that the grant of immunity extends to vicarious liability.

In 1999, the legislature amended the part of ORS 63.165 (1993) at issue by adding the word "acting." The addition of the word "acting" could have been intended to expand the scope of ORS 63.165(1) to include not only immunity from vicarious liability but also immunity from liability for all "actions" that a member or manager of an LLC takes in his or her official capacity. Alternatively, the legislature could have added "acting" to make clear that a member or manager of an LLC will not be vicariously liable either for "being" a member or manager of an LLC or for "acting" as such, *i.e.,* for exercising control over the LLC. That is, the legislature may have wanted only to clarify that a member or manager of an LLC enjoys greater immunity than a limited partner does. *Cf.* ORS 70.135(1) (1997).[14]

The legislative history of ORS 63.165 shows that the 1993 legislature enacted the initial version of that statute to protect members and managers from vicarious liability for the LLC's obligations even when the member or manager actively managed the LLC. A member of a taskforce charged with advising the legislature on LLCs told the 1993 House Judiciary Subcommittee on Civil Law: "The limited liability company gives flexibility for members to participate as little or as much as they wish * * * as opposed to a limited partner[ship] where the limited partner[s] cannot [participate] without running the risk of becoming general partners."

In clarifying ORS 63.165(1), the 1999 legislature relied on the recently published Uniform Limited Liability Company Act (ULLCA) (1996) and adopted verbatim subsections 303(a) and (b) from that uniform statute.[3] The comment to those 1996 ULLCA provisions sheds some light on the 1999 legislature's intent. The relevant part of the comment to Section 303 explains:

> "A member or manager is responsible for acts or omissions to the extent those acts or omissions would be actionable in contract or tort against the member or manager if that person were acting in an individual capacity. Where a member or manager delegates or assigns the authority or duty to exercise appropriate company functions, the member or manager is ordinarily not personally liable for the acts or omissions of the officer, employee, or agent [of the LLC] if the member or manager has complied with the duty of care set forth in Section 409(c)."

The first sentence in the comment makes clear that the use of the word "acting" in section 303 of the ULLCA, and by extension in ORS 63.165(1), was not intended to immunize members and managers from personal liability for their actions in managing an LLC. Rather, members and managers remain personally liable for the actions that they take on behalf of an LLC to the same extent that they would be liable "if [they] were acting in an individual capacity."

---

[14] We note that the most recent version of the Uniform Limited Partnership Act (2001) abolishes the so-called "control rule" for determining when a limited partner will become personally liable for the partnership's liabilities. Oregon still retains that rule. *See* ORS 70.135(1).

[3] Author's note: Uniform Limited Liability Company Act § 303 provides:

(a) Except as otherwise provided in subsection (c), the debts, obligations, and liabilities of a limited liability company, whether arising in contract, tort, or otherwise, are solely the debts, obligations, and liabilities of the company. A member or manager is not personally liable for a debt, obligation, or liability of the company solely by reason of being or acting as a member or manager.

(b) The failure of a limited liability company to observe the usual company formalities or requirements relating to the exercise of its company powers or management of its business is not a ground for imposing personal liability on the members or managers for liabilities of the company.

Having identified that, as a general rule, members or managers will remain personally liable for their own acts, the comment goes on to identify one instance in which members or managers ordinarily will not be personally liable. The second sentence quoted above recognizes that, when a member or manager of an LLC delegates authority to carry out company functions, as an officer or director of a corporation might, the member or manager ordinarily will not be personally liable for a subordinate's negligence. We do not read the second sentence as establishing statutory immunity in that situation. Rather, the second sentence recognizes that, as a matter of common law, a member or manager ordinarily will not be personally liable for a subordinate's negligence.

Unlike limited partners, members or managers who participate in or control the business of an LLC will not, as a result of those actions, be vicariously liable for the LLC's debts, obligations, or liabilities. However, a member or manager remains responsible for his or her acts or omissions to the extent those acts or omissions would be actionable against the member or manager if that person were acting in an individual capacity. *See* ULLCA § 303 comment (1996). Because ORS 63.165(1) does not shield Swanson from responsibility for its own negligent acts in managing Sun Studs, we turn to the question whether, as a matter of Oregon negligence law, there was evidence from which a reasonable juror could find that Swanson was liable for the injuries that plaintiff suffered.

B.   *Oregon Negligence Law*

Swanson argues that its relationship to plaintiff is governed by a "particular standard of conduct"—namely, those standards that apply to corporate officers and directors. Swanson argues, and plaintiff does not dispute, that this court has recognized that "[a] director of a corporation is not liable for any tort of other subordinate agents in which he did not participate." *Pelton v. Gold Hill Canal Co.,* 72 Or. 353, 357–58 (1914) (holding that a corporation's directors were not liable for conversion when the manager of the corporation sold, without the directors' knowledge or participation, wheat entrusted to the corporation).

Swanson argues that, in acting as the member-manager of Sun Studs, its role was comparable to that of a corporate officer and should be judged by the same standard. We agree with both the premise and conclusion of that argument. As Swanson's argument implicitly recognizes, an LLC gives its members flexibility in choosing a management structure. *See* Ribstein and Keatinge, *Limited Liability Companies* § 2.3.[15] In this case, the evidence on summary judgment showed that Swanson had adopted a corporate model; that is, in managing safety at Sun Studs, Swanson acted

---

[15] Ribstein and Keatinge explain that, "[w]hile the management structure of an LLC is limited only by the owners' imagination," there are three "fundamental" or typical structures: a corporate or "representative management" structure; a limited partnership or "entrenched management" structure; and a general partnership or "direct management" structure. *Limited Liability Companies* § 2.3.

in the same way that an officer in a corporation would. Swanson delegated primary responsibility for safety to Sun Studs' HR director and mill manager but retained oversight authority of their implementation of Swanson's safety policies. Having agreed with Swanson's premise, we also agree with its conclusion that the negligence standards that apply to corporate officers and managers apply to Swanson.

Turning to the applicable common-law negligence standard, we note that this court has held that a director or an officer of a corporation will be liable for a subordinate's tortious acts if the officer knew of those acts or participated in them. In this case, a reasonable juror could infer that Swanson "participated" in worksite safety at Sun Studs in three respects: Swanson formulated a general safety policy that it directed Sun Studs to implement; it delegated primary authority for safety at Sun Studs to Sun Studs' HR director and mill manager; and Swanson undertook to oversee those persons' implementation of Swanson's general safety policies. However, there was no evidence from which a reasonable juror could infer that Swanson negligently had formulated the general safety plan that it directed Sun Studs to implement. Similarly, a reasonable juror could not infer that Swanson negligently delegated primary responsibility for safety to Sun Studs' HR director and mill manager. Finally, there was no evidence from which a reasonable juror could infer that Swanson negligently exercised the oversight authority that it retained over Sun Studs' implementation of Swanson's safety policies.

II. THE ELL

The ELL "imposes a heightened statutory standard of care on a person or entity who either is in charge of, or responsible for, any work involving risk or danger." *Woodbury v. CH2M Hill, Inc.*, 335 Or. 154, 159 (2003).[20] In this case, the "work involving risk or danger" was driving forklifts through the areas of the mill in which Sun Studs' employees customarily walked. The question on which plaintiff's ELL claim turns is whether Swanson was a person "having charge of, or responsibility for" that work. On that issue, this court has held that, in addition to a worker's direct employer, liability under the ELL "can be imposed on a person or entity who (1) is engaged with the plaintiff's direct employer in a 'common enterprise'; (2) retains the right to control the manner or method in which the risk-producing activity was performed; or (3) actually controls the manner or method in which the risk producing activity is performed."

Swanson was not plaintiff's "direct employer," and the Court of Appeals held that a reasonable juror could not infer that Swanson was

---

[20] The ELL provides: "Generally, all owners, contractors or subcontractors and other persons having charge of, or responsibility for, any work involving a risk or danger to the employees or the public shall use every device, care and precaution that is practicable to use for the protection and safety of life and limb, limited only by the necessity for preserving the efficiency of the structure, machine or other apparatus or device, and without regard to the additional cost of suitable material or safety appliance [*sic*] and devices." ORS 654.305.

plaintiff's "indirect employer" for the purposes of the ELL; that is, the Court of Appeals held that a reasonable juror could not infer that Swanson was engaged in a common enterprise with Sun Studs, that Swanson actually controlled the risk-producing activity, or that Swanson retained the right to control that activity. On review, we agree with the Court of Appeals that Swanson was not liable under the ELL on a common-enterprise or actual-control theory of responsibility. We disagree, however, that a reasonable juror could not infer that Swanson retained the right to control the method or manner in which the risk-producing activity was performed.

To establish that Swanson "retained the right to control" a risk-producing activity, plaintiff must either "identify some source of legal authority for that perceived right" or evidence from which a retained right could be inferred. In this case, Swanson was the sole member-manager of Sun Studs. As such, the governing statutes gave Swanson the right to manage Sun Studs' business. *See* ORS 63.130(1)(a) (explaining that, in member-managed LLCs, each member has equal rights in the management and conduct of the LLC's business). Although Swanson chose to delegate responsibility for day-to-day decisions to Suns Studs' mill manager and HR director, Swanson retained the right, under ORS 63.130, to manage all aspects of Sun Studs' operation, including the way that forklifts operated in the mill and the safety conditions in their area of operation.

Beyond that, there was evidence from which a reasonable juror could infer that, even though Swanson had chosen to delegate primary authority to Sun Studs to operate the mill and regulate the way that forklifts were used, Swanson retained the right to do so itself. In this case, Swanson's executive vice president acknowledged that Swanson "could have made all of th[e safety] changes" when it first acquired Sun Studs that Sun Studs later made in response to plaintiff's accident. Similarly, the executive vice-president agreed "that if the Swanson group people wanted to change either the design or the equipment used in the yard at Sun Studs, they could do that." A reasonable juror could infer from that evidence that, as the LLC statutes state, Swanson retained the right to manage the day-to-day operations of Sun Studs, including the operation of the forklifts and attendant safety procedures. Put differently, a reasonable juror could infer that Swanson "retain[ed] the right to control the manner or method in which the risk-producing activity was performed."

We recognize that some tension may exist between our resolution of plaintiff's negligence and ELL claims. Any tension results, however, from the differences between the common-law tort standards and the broader statutory standards that the legislature adopted in the ELL. Our negligence cases have held that, in the absence of knowledge or participation, corporate officers and directors are not liable for their employees' negligence. That is so even though corporate officers, having delegated responsibility to others to carry out tasks, retain the right to control how those tasks are carried out. Our ELL cases, however, have held that persons who retain the right to control how others carry out risk-producing activities are liable under the ELL. Our resolution of plaintiff's claims reflects those differing standards.

The decision of the Court of Appeals is reversed. The judgment of the circuit court is affirmed in part and reversed in part, and the case is remanded to the circuit court for further proceedings.

D. DISSOCIATION AND DISSOLUTION

In business organizations, equityholders leave the firm and sometimes the firm dissolves and winds up its business. In non-corporate entities, the rules for dissociation of partners and members and dissolution of the firm are similar. They derive from the rules applicable to general partnerships.

1. DISSOCIATION

In partnership, a partner can be dissociated from the partnership for a number of reasons. RUPA § 601 defines some of the events causing dissociation.

- *Express will:* Partner's express will to withdraw

- *Per partnership agreement:* Event agreed to in the partnership agreement, or expulsion pursuant to the partnership agreement

- *Expulsion by partners:* Partner's expulsion by the unanimous vote of the other partners if: (i) it is unlawful to carry on the partnership business with that partner; (ii) there has been a transfer of all or substantially all of that partner's transferable interest in the partnership; or (iii) partner that is a legal person has or will dissolved

- *Expulsion by court:* On application by the partnership or another partner, the partner's expulsion by judicial determination because: (i) the partner engaged in wrongful conduct that adversely and materially affected the partnership business; (ii) the partner willfully or persistently committed a material breach of the partnership agreement or of a duty owed to the partnership or the other partners; or (iii) the partner engaged in conduct relating to the partnership business which makes it not reasonably practicable to carry on the business in partnership with the partner

- *Death, dissolution, or bankruptcy:* Partner's bankruptcy, receivership, liquidation, death, incapacity, or termination

Importantly, the above are default terms, and the partnership agreement can specify the events of dissociation. There is a rationale for each of the default terms. Partners have the power to leave the partnership at will because the law cannot force a partner to associate with other partners if he or she no longer wishes to do so. The partnership agreement may provide specific terms relating to dissociation, including mechanisms in which partners can expel other partners. Because a partnership is a voluntary association of partners, partners can expel each other, but they cannot do so arbitrarily or to take advantage of one another; instead, the reasons must be related to some aspect of the business of the partnership such as a situation where it would be unlawful for the partnership to continue with the partner. If a partner, whether a natural or legal person, is incapacitated in some way, such as death, disability, or insolvency, the incapacitation can be detrimental to the partnership. Finally, the partnership or a partner can petition the court to expel a partner, but again for good reason. These reasons may be that the partner is engaging in wrongful activity including willful breach of the partnership agreement, or that "it not reasonably practicable to carry on the business in partnership with the partner."

A partner has the power to dissociate, but does not have the right to do so if the dissociation is wrongful. RUPA § 602(a)-(b). A partner has a right to dissociate if it is not a breach of the partnership agreement and there is no other indicia of wrongful conduct. When a dissociation is wrongful, including expulsion by other partners or the court, the dissociated partner may be liable for any harm to the partnership. *Id.* § 602(b).

The rules applicable to LLCs and limited partnerships of the uniform statutes are generally derived from the above general partnership rules. *See* RULLCA §§ 601–602; ULPA (2001) §§ 601–602 (limited partners), §§ 603–604 (general partners). Default terms for dissociation include the following events: (1) at will, (2) operation of the operating agreement, (3) expulsion by other members, and (4) judicial expulsion.[4]

Clearly, when drafting an operating agreement, the attorney should consider the issue of member dissociation and the default rules in the statute. The issues to consider are the following: (1) When does a member have a right to dissociate? (2) When can a member be expelled? (3) In either case, what is the member entitled to in terms of his or her interest in the

---

[4]   Because the ULC and the RULLC have not been as widely adopted as the uniform laws for partnerships, the variation in LLC statutes across jurisdictions is greater than for the laws of general partnership and limited partnership. Importantly, Delaware has enacted its own LLC statute that is, like its corporation law, *sui generis*. The Delaware statute provides: "A member may resign from a limited liability company only at the time or upon the happening of events specified in a limited liability company agreement and in accordance with the limited liability company agreement. Notwithstanding anything to the contrary under applicable law, unless a limited liability company agreement provides otherwise, a member may not resign from a limited liability company prior to the dissolution and winding up of the limited liability company." Delaware Limited Liability Company Act, 6 Del.C. § 18–603.

LLC? (4) What are the events of dissociation by operating of the operating agreement? (5) Upon a dissociation by operation of the operating agreement, what is the member entitled to in terms of his or her interest in the LLC?

2.   DISSOLUTION AND WINDING UP

An LLC may eventually dissolve and terminate its business. There are a number of reasons why it may do so. The members may agree that the business has run its course. The members may no longer wish to work together in a common venture. It may no longer be practicable to conduct business. The statute typically provides the terms for dissolution, including dissolution by judicial decree on petition by one of the members.

RULLCA § 701: Events Causing Dissolution

(a)   A limited liability company is dissolved, and its business must be wound up, upon the occurrence of any of the following:

    (1)   an event or circumstance that the operating agreement states causes dissolution;

    (2)   the consent of all the members;

    (3)   the passage of 90 consecutive days during which the limited liability company has no members;

    (4)   on application by a member, the entry by [appropriate court] of an order dissolving the company on the grounds that:

        (A)   the conduct of all or substantially all of the company's activities is unlawful; or

        (B)   it is not reasonably practicable to carry on the limited liability company's activities in conformity with the certificate of organization and the operating agreement; or

    (5)   on application by a member, the entry by [appropriate court] of an order dissolving the company on the grounds that the managers or those members in control of the company:

        (A)   have acted, are acting, or will act in a manner that is illegal or fraudulent; or

        (B)   have acted or are acting in a manner that is oppressive and was, is, or will be directly harmful to the applicant.

(b)   In a proceeding brought under subsection (a)(5), the court may order a remedy other than dissolution.

Although the RULLCA provides for considerable flexibility in self-ordering, the operating agreement may not curtail the court's power to adjudicate a claim for judicial dissolution. *See* RULLCA § 110(c)(7) ("An operating agreement may not . . . vary the power of a court to decree dissolution in the circumstances specified in Section 701(a)(4) and (5).").

––––––––––

The case below concerns a member's petition for judicial dissolution of a Delaware LLC. It concerns a common fact pattern found in cases involve impasse and deadlock—a 50/50 venture where the owners are at loggerheads. In reading this case, think about these questions: (1) On what legal ground did the member petition for judicial dissolution? (2) What is the relationship between Delaware corporation law and LLC law? (3) Why did the court determine that the operating agreement did not govern the remedy in this case?

HALEY V. TALCOTT
864 A.2d 86 (Del.Ch. 2004).

STRINE, VICE CHANCELLOR.

Plaintiff Matthew James Haley has moved for summary judgment of his claim seeking dissolution of Matt and Greg Real Estate, LLC ("the LLC"). Haley and defendant Gregory Talcott are the only members of the LLC, each owning a 50% interest in the LLC. Haley brings this action in reliance upon § 18–802 of the Delaware Limited Liability Company Act which permits this court to "decree dissolution of a limited liability company whenever it is not reasonably practicable to carry on the business in conformity with a limited liability company agreement." The question before the court is whether dissolution of the LLC should be granted, as Haley requests, or whether, as Talcott contends, Haley is limited to the contractually-provided exit mechanism in the LLC Agreement.

Haley and Talcott have suffered, to put it mildly, a falling out. There is no rational doubt that they cannot continue to do business as 50% members of an LLC. But the path to separating their interests is complicated by a second company, Delaware Seafood, also known as the Redfin Seafood Grill ("Redfin Grill"), a restaurant that, at the risk of slightly oversimplifying, was owned by Talcott and, before the falling out, operated by Haley under an employment contract that gave him a 50% share in the profits. The LLC owns the land that the Redfin Grill occupies under an expired lease. The resolution of the current case and the ultimate fate of the LLC therefore critically affect the continued existence of a second business that one party owns and that the other bitterly contends, in other litigation pending before this court, wrongly terminated him.

The question before the court is essentially how the interests of the members of the LLC are to be separated. Haley asserts that summary judgment is appropriate because it is factually undisputed that it is not reasonably practicable for the LLC to carry on business in conformity with a limited liability company agreement (the "LLC Agreement") that calls for the LLC to be governed by its two members, when those members are in deadlock. Therefore, urges Haley, the LLC should be judicially dissolved immediately. Such an end will force the sale of the LLC's real property, which is likely worth, at current market value, far more than the mortgage that the LLC must pay off if it sells.

In response, Talcott stresses that the LLC Agreement provides an alternative exit mechanism that allows the LLC to continue to exist, and argues that Haley should therefore be relegated to this provision if he is unhappy with the stalemate. In other words, Talcott argues that it is reasonably practicable for the LLC to continue to carry on business in conformity with its LLC Agreement because the exit mechanism creates a fair alternative that permits Haley to get out, receiving the fair market value of his share of the property as determined in accordance with procedures in the LLC Agreement, while allowing the LLC to continue. Critically, the exit provision would allow Talcott to buy Haley out with no need for the LLC's asset (*i.e.*, the land) to be sold on the open market. The LLC could continue to exist and own the land (with its favorable mortgage arrangement) and Talcott, as owner of both entities, could continue to offer the Redfin Grill its favorable rent.

But the problem with Talcott's argument is that the exit mechanism is not a reasonable alternative. A principle attraction of the LLC form of entity is the statutory freedom granted to members to shape, by contract, their own approach to common business "relationship" problems. If an equitable alternative to continued deadlock had been specified in the LLC Agreement, arguably judicial dissolution under § 18–802 might not be warranted. In this case, however, Talcott admits that the exit mechanism provides no method to relieve Haley of his obligation as a personal guarantor for the LLC's mortgage. Haley signed an agreement with the lender personally guaranteeing the entire mortgage of the LLC (as did Talcott) in order to secure the loan. Without relief from the guaranty, Haley would remain personally liable for the mortgage debt of the LLC, even after his exit. Because Haley would be left liable for the debt of an entity over which he had no further control, I find that the exit provision specified in the LLC Agreement and urged by Talcott is not sufficient to provide an adequate remedy to Haley under these circumstances.

With no reasonable exit mechanism, I find that Haley is entitled to exercise the only practical deadlock-breaking remedy available to him, and one that is also alluded to in the LLC Agreement, the right to seek judicial dissolution. Haley argues, convincingly, that the analysis under § 18–802 for an evenly-split, two-owner LLC ordinarily should parallel the analysis under 8 Del. C. § 273, which enables this court to order the judicial dissolution of a joint venture corporation owned by deadlocked 50% owners. Because Haley has demonstrated an indisputable deadlock between the two 50% members of the LLC, and that deadlock precludes the LLC from functioning as provided for in the LLC Agreement, I also grant Haley's motion for summary judgment and order dissolution of Matt and Greg Real Estate, LLC.

I. *Factual Background*

Haley and Talcott each have a 50% interest in Matt & Greg Real Estate, LLC, a Delaware limited liability company they formed in 2003. The creation of the company, however, is only a recent event in the history between the parties.

Haley and Talcott have known each other since the 1980s. In 2001 Haley was the manager of the Rehoboth location of The Third Edition, a restaurant owned by Talcott that also had a location in Washington, D.C. In 2001, Haley found the location for what would become the Redfin Grill. Talcott contributed substantial start-up money and Haley managed the Redfin Grill without drawing a salary for the first year.

The structure of the agreements between the parties forming the Redfin Grill is complex and the subject of additional litigation before this court. For reasons that are not relevant, Haley and Talcott chose to create and operate the Redfin Grill as an entity solely owned by Talcott, with Haley's rights and obligations being defined by a series of contracts. Those agreements, all dated November 30, 2001, included an Employment Agreement, a Retention Bonus Agreement, and a Side Letter Agreement (together, the "Employment Contract"), as well as an Agreement regarding an option to purchase real estate (the "Real Estate Agreement").

The Employment Contract, although structured as an agreement between an employer and an employee, makes clear that the parties were operating the business as a joint venture. The Employment Contract specified that Haley reported to Talcott and that Talcott had the right to reevaluate and revise Haley's decisions, but indicated that "such action is not anticipated." It also provided that Haley's "bonus" would be one half of the net profits of the Redfin Grill, after the initial loan from Talcott was repaid. Moreover, Talcott would materially breach the Employment Contract, and Haley could end his employment for cause, if Talcott amended Haley's duties such that his position as "Operations Director" became one of "less dignity, responsibility, importance or scope." The Employment Contract further clarified Haley's importance to the enterprise by awarding him one half of any proceeds from any sale of the Redfin Grill. Finally, the Employment Contract limited Talcott's ability to remove Haley from his active role:

[N]otwithstanding the language in the Employment Agreement relating to termination, individually, I [Talcott] will assure you that the Employment Agreement will not be terminable under any circumstances unless an event occurs that would entitle you payment of a Retention Bonus as set forth in the Retention Bonus Agreement that is part of this transaction. Such an event would be a "Business Sale". . . .

The Employment Contract therefore establishes a relationship more similar to a partnership than a typical employer/employee relationship.

The equivalent nature of the parties' contributions is further confirmed by the Real Estate Agreement. In that agreement, Talcott granted Haley the right to participate in an option to purchase the property where the Redfin Grill was situated which is located at 1111 Highway One in Bethany Beach, Delaware (the "Property"). Talcott had obtained the option personally when the Redfin Grill first leased the Property from the then-owner in February of 2001. Talcott provided this valuable right to participate for the nominal price of $10.00. The agreement provided that if the option were exercised, Haley would shoulder 50% of the burden of the purchase, and would be either a 50% owner of the land or a 50% owner of the entity formed to hold the land.

From late 2001 into 2003, under Haley's supervision, the Redfin Grill grew into a successful business. By the second year of its existence, the start-up money had been repaid to Talcott with interest, both parties were drawing salaries (Talcott's substantially smaller since he was not participating in day-to-day management), and the parties each received approximately $150,000 in profit sharing.

In 2003, the parties formed Matt & Greg Real Estate, LLC to take advantage of the option to purchase the Property that was the subject of the Real Estate Agreement. The option price was $720,000 and the new LLC took out a mortgage from County Bank in Rehoboth Beach, Delaware, for that amount, exercised the option, and obtained the deed to the Property on or about May 23, 2003. Importantly, both Haley and Talcott, individually, signed personal guaranties for the entire amount of the mortgage in order to secure the loan. The Redfin Grill continued to operate at the site, paying the LLC $6,000 per month in rent, a payment sufficient to cover the LLC's monthly obligation under the mortgage. Thus by mid-2003, the parties appeared poised to reap the fruits of their labors; unfortunately, at that point their personal relationship began to deteriorate.

Haley, having managed the restaurant from the time it opened in May 2001, and having formalized his management position in the Employment Contract, apparently believed that the relationship would be reformulated to provide him a direct stock ownership interest in the Redfin Grill at some point. The reasons underlying that belief are not important here, but in late October they caused a rift to develop between the parties. On or about October 27, 2003, the conflict that had been brewing between the parties led to some kind of confrontation. As a result, Talcott sent a letter of understanding to Haley dated October 27, 2003, purporting to accept his resignation and forbidding him to enter the premises of the Redfin Grill.

Haley responded with two separate letters from his counsel to Talcott. In the first, Haley asserts that he did not resign, and that he regarded Talcott's October 27, 2003 letter of understanding as terminating him without cause in breach of the Employment Contract. Haley goes on to express his intent to pursue legal remedies, an intent that he acted upon in the related case in this court.

In his second letter, Haley purported to take several positions expressly as a 50% member in the LLC including: (1) rejecting the new lease proposed by Talcott for the Redfin Grill; (2) voting to revoke any consent to possession by the Redfin Grill and terminating any lease by which the Redfin Grill asserts the right to possession; and (3) voting that the Property be put up for sale on the open market.

Of course, as a 50% member, Haley could not force the LLC to take action on these proposals because Talcott opposed them. As a result, the pre-existing status quo continued by virtue of the stalemate—a result that Talcott favored. The Redfin Grill's lease has expired and, as a consequence, the Redfin Grill continues to pay $6,000 per month to the LLC in a month-to-month arrangement. The $6,000 rent exceeds the LLC's required mortgage payment by $800 per month, so the situation remains stable. With only a 50% ownership interest, Haley cannot force the termination of the Redfin Grill's lease and evict the Redfin Grill as a tenant; neither can he force the sale of the Property, land that was appraised as of June 14, 2004 at $1.8 million. In short, absent intervention by this court, Haley is stuck, unless he chooses to avail himself of the exit mechanism provided in the LLC Agreement.

That exit mechanism, like judicial dissolution, would provide Haley with his share of the fair market value of the LLC, including the Property. Section 18 of the LLC Agreement provides that upon written notice of election to "quit" the company, the remaining member may elect, in writing, to purchase the departing member's interest for fair market value. If the remaining member elects to purchase the departing member's interest, the parties may agree on fair value, or have the fair value determined by three arbitrators, one chosen by each member and a third chosen by the first two arbitrators. The departing member pays the reasonable expenses of the three arbitrators. Once a fair price is determined, it may be paid in cash, or over a term if secured by: (1) a note signed by the company and personally by the remaining member; (2) a security agreement; and (3) a recorded UCC lien. Only if the remaining member fails to elect to purchase the departing member's interest is the company to be liquidated.

The LLC agreement describes additional details regarding the term and interest rate of any installment payments and defines penalty, default, and acceleration terms to be contained in the securing note. Although these details are not critical to a comparison between a contractual separation under the LLC Agreement and a judicial dissolution, they demonstrate the level of detail that the parties considered in crafting the exit mechanism. But despite this level of detail, the exit provision does not expressly provide a release from the personal guaranties that both Haley and Talcott signed to secure the mortgage on the Property. Nor does the exit provision state that any member dissatisfied with the status quo must break an impasse by exit rather than a suit for dissolution.

Rather than use the exit mechanism, Haley has simultaneously sought: (1) dissolution of the LLC; and (2) relief in an employment litigation filed against Talcott and Redfin Grill, a case also pending in this court. Haley does not view himself as being obligated by the LLC Agreement to be the one who exits; moreover, he would bear the cost of the exit mechanism and that mechanism, as will be discussed, would not release him from the guaranty.

Haley continues to be interested in the Redfin Grill, and has expressed his desire to buy Talcott out of both the LLC and the Redfin Grill itself if given the opportunity. Talcott, by urging the exit remedy provided in the LLC Agreement, has expressed his desire to buy Haley out of the LLC and has no interest in selling the Redfin Grill. Haley continues to refuse to use the exit mechanism.

Pragmatically, the current impasse arises because we have two willing buyers and no willing sellers. Haley alleges that, given this practical dilemma, and his evident inability to effect his desired direction for the LLC, judicial dissolution is his only practicable remedy.

III. Legal Analysis

Haley alleges that pursuant to 6 Del. C. § 18–802 the court should exercise its discretion and dissolve the LLC because it is not reasonably practicable for it to continue the business of the company in conformity with the LLC Agreement. Section 18–802 provides in its entirety:

> On application by or for a member or manager the Court of Chancery may decree dissolution of a limited liability company whenever it is not reasonably practicable to carry on the business in conformity with a limited liability company agreement.

Here, the key facts about the parties' ability to work together are not rationally disputable. Therefore, my decision on the motion largely turns on two legal issues: (1) if the doctrine of corporate deadlock is an appropriate analogy for the analysis of a § 18–802 claim on these facts; and (2) if so, and if action to break the stalemate is necessary to permit the LLC to function, whether, because of the contract-law foundations of the Delaware LLC Act, Haley should be relegated to the contractual exit mechanism provided in the LLC Agreement.

Case Law Under § 273 Of The Delaware General Corporate Law ("DGCL") Provides An Appropriate Framework For Analysis

Section 18–802 of the Delaware LLC Act is a relatively recent addition to our law, and, as a result, there have been few decisions interpreting it. Nevertheless, § 18–802 has the obvious purpose of providing an avenue of relief when an LLC cannot continue to function in accordance with its chartering agreement. Thus § 18–802 plays a role for LLCs similar to the role that § 273 of the DGCL plays for joint venture corporations with only two stockholders. When a limited liability agreement provides for the company to be governed by its members, when there are only two members, and when those members are at permanent odds, § 273 provides relevant insight into what should happen. To wit, Section 273(a) provides, in relevant part, that:

> If the stockholders of a corporation of this state, having only 2 stockholders each of whom own 50% of the stock therein, shall be engaged in a joint venture and if such stockholders shall be unable to agree upon the desirability of discontinuing such joint venture and disposing of the assets used in such venture, either stock holder may, unless otherwise provided in the certificate of incorporation of the corporation or in a written agreement between stockholders, file with the Court of Chancery a petition stating that it desires to discontinue such joint venture and to dispose of the assets used in such venture in accordance with a plan to be agreed on by both stockholders or that, if no such plan shall be agreed upon by both stockholders, the corporation be dissolved.

Section 273 essentially sets forth three pre-requisites for a judicial order of dissolution: (1) the corporation must have two 50% stockholders, (2) those stockholders must be engaged in a joint venture, and (3) they must be unable to agree upon whether to discontinue the business or how to dispose of its assets. Here, by analogy, each of the three provisions is indisputably met.

First, there is no dispute that the parties are 50% members of the LLC.

Second, there is no rational doubt that the parties intended to be and are engaged in a joint venture. The relationship between Haley and Talcott indicates active involvement by both parties in creating a restaurant for their mutual benefit and profit, and the Employment Contract shows that Haley was to be the "Operations Director" of the Redfin Grill, a position that, according to the Side Letter Agreement, would only be terminated if the restaurant was sold. Haley was also entitled to a 50% share of the Redfin Grill's profits. In short, Haley and Talcott were in it together for as long as they owned the restaurant, equally sharing the profits as provided in the Employment Contract.

Most importantly, Haley never agreed to be a passive investor in the LLC who would be subject to Talcott's unilateral dominion. Instead, the LLC agreement provided that: "no member/managers may, *without the agreement of a majority vote of the managers' interest,* act on behalf of the company." Thus, Haley is entitled to a continuing say in the operation of the LLC.

Finally, the evidence clearly supports a finding of deadlock between the parties about the business strategy and future of the LLC.

Moreover, there is no evidentiary support for Talcott's suggestion that the parties are not at an impasse. The parties have not interacted since their falling out in October, 2003. Clearly, Talcott understands that the end of Haley's managerial role from the Redfin Grill profoundly altered their relationship as co-members of the LLC. After all, it has left Haley on the outside, looking in, with no power. Of course, Talcott insists that the LLC can and does continue to function for its intended purpose and in conformity with the agreement, receiving payments from the Redfin Grill and writing checks to meet its obligations under the mortgage on Talcott's authority. But that reality does not mean that the LLC is operating in accordance with the LLC Agreement. Although the LLC is technically functioning at this point, this operation is purely a residual, inertial status quo that just happens to exclusively benefit one of the 50% members, Talcott, as illustrated by the hands-tied continuation of the expired lease with the Redfin Grill. With strident disagreement between the parties regarding the appropriate deployment of the asset of the LLC, and open hostility as evidenced by the related suit in this matter, it is not credible that the LLC could, if necessary, take any important action that required a vote of the members. Abundant, uncontradicted documents in the record demonstrate the inability of the parties to function together.

For all these reasons, if the LLC were a corporation, there would be no question that Haley's request to dissolve the entity would be granted. But this case regards an LLC, not a corporation, and more importantly, an LLC with a detailed exit provision. That distinguishing factor must and is considered next.

Even Given The Contractual Emphasis Of The Delaware LLC Act,
The Exit Remedy Provided In The LLC Agreement Is
An Insufficient Alternative To Dissolution

The Delaware LLC Act is grounded on principles of freedom of contract. For that reason, the presence of a reasonable exit mechanism bears on the propriety of ordering dissolution under 6 Del. C. § 18–802. When the agreement itself provides a fair opportunity for the dissenting member who disfavors the inertial status quo to exit and receive the fair market value of her interest, it is at least arguable that the limited liability company may still proceed to operate practicably under its contractual charter because the charter itself provides an equitable way to break the impasse.

Here, that reasoning might be thought apt because Haley has already "voted" as an LLC member to sell the LLC's only asset, the Property, presumably because he knew he could not secure sole control of both the LLC and the Redfin Grill. Given that reality, so long as Haley can actually extract himself fairly, it arguably makes sense for this court to stay its hand in an LLC case and allow the contract itself to solve the problem.

Notably, reasoning of this nature has been applied in the § 273 context. Even under § 273, this court's authority to order dissolution remains discretionary and may be influenced by the particular circumstances. Talcott rightly argues that the situation here is somewhat analogous to that in *In re Delaware Bay Surgical Services* where this court declined to dissolve a corporation under § 273 in part because a mechanism existed for the repurchase of the complaining member's 50% interest.

But, this matter differs from *Surgical Services* in two important respects. First, in *Surgical Services,* the respondent doctor had owned the company before admitting the petitioner to his practice as a 50% stakeholder. The court found that both parties clearly intended, upon entering the contract, that if the parties ended their contractual relationship, the respondent would be the one permitted to keep the company. By contrast, no such obvious priority of interest exists here. Haley and Talcott created the LLC together and while the detailed exit provision provided in the formative LLC Agreement allows either party to leave voluntarily, it provides no insight on who should retain the LLC if both parties would prefer to buy the other out, and neither party desires to leave. In and of itself, however, this lack of priority might not be found sufficient to require dissolution, because of a case-specific fact; namely, that Haley has proposed—as a member of the LLC—that the LLC's sole asset be sold. But I need not—and do not—determine how truly distinguishing that fact is, because forcing Haley to exercise the contractual exit mechanism would not permit the LLC to proceed in a practicable way that accords with the LLC Agreement, but would instead permit Talcott to penalize Haley without express contractual authorization.

Why? Because the parties agree that exit mechanism in the LLC Agreement would not relieve Haley of his obligation under the personal guaranty that he signed to secure the mortgage from County Bank. If Haley is forced to use the exit mechanism, Talcott and he both believe that Haley would still be left holding the bag on the guaranty. It is therefore not equitable to force Haley to use the exit mechanism in this circumstance. While the exit mechanism may be workable in a friendly departure when both parties cooperate to reach an adequate alternative agreement with the bank, the bank cannot be compelled to accept the removal of Haley as a personal guarantor. Thus, the exit mechanism fails as an adequate remedy for Haley because it does not equitably effect the separation of the parties. Rather, it would leave Haley with no upside potential, and no protection over the considerable downside risk that he would have to make good on any future default by the LLC (over whose operations he would have no control) to its mortgage lender. Thus here, unlike in *Surgical Services,* the parties do not, in fact, "have at their disposal a far less drastic means to resolve their personal disagreement."

IV. Conclusion

For the reasons discussed above, I find that it is not reasonably practicable for the LLC to continue to carry on business in conformity with the LLC Agreement. The parties shall confer and, within four weeks, submit a plan for the dissolution of the LLC. The plan shall include a procedure to sell the Property owned by the LLC within a commercially reasonable time frame. Either party may, of course, bid on the Property.

IT IS SO ORDERED.

––––––––––––

Problem: Precision Tools—Part 6

We return to the Precision Tools, Inc. problem. Jessica Bacon, Michael Lane, and Bernie Gould have approached you about representing them in planning the business. Speaking for the three, Michael asks: "The three of us are partners in this venture. We're really excited about the potential of this business. We want to form a company to conduct our business. We don't think a corporation makes for us. We've heard that we can form a partnership. That seems appealing since we *are* partners. We've also heard about limited liability companies. What should we do? Does it really matter we form a partnership or a limited liability company?"

What is your advice?

PART III

FINANCING AND FORMATION

■ ■ ■

Part III discusses financing and formation of the entity. Chapter 9 introduces basic concepts of accounting and valuation, an understanding of which is essential to the business lawyer. Chapter 10 discusses how business entities are financed and the different kinds of securities and economic interests that a business can issue. Lastly, Chapter 11 addresses the formation of business entities, including the choice of form, with the proviso that, aside from close corporations, we have yet to undertake a substantial study of the corporation.

CHAPTER 9

FINANCIAL ACCOUNTING AND VALUATION

■ ■ ■

A. FINANCIAL ACCOUNTING

A basic understanding of financial accounting is critically important for a business lawyer. The reality of practice is that you cannot escape accounting and numbers in law practice. If you doubt this proposition, go to any public company's website and take a quick look at their Form 10–K, which is a document drafted and filed by securities lawyers and read by a company's business lawyers on a routine basis.[1] This brief 10-minute exercise will dispel any notion that a business lawyer can practice without any familiarity with key quantitative concepts like accounting, finance, and valuation. Whether you practice corporate law or litigation, and whether you work in the private sector, a non-profit organization or government, you inevitably will confront financial accounting.

The importance of a lawyer's having at least some understanding of accounting is seen in a 2013 Harvard Law School survey of 124 practicing lawyers at major law firms.[2] The survey asked lawyers to rank important knowledge and skills. The following is their response.

> **Question #3, Rating Knowledge/Skills Bases:** "Please indicate how important the following knowledge bases/skills are for your associates." (1 = Not at all Useful; 3 = Somewhat Useful; 5 = Extremely Useful)

---

[1] All SEC filings and corporate documents such as certificate of incorporation and bylaws are found in the "Investor Relations" page of the corporation's website. Form 10–K is a required SEC filing for public companies and it discloses, among other things, the company's audited financial statements. Form 10–Q is a quarterly filing that contains unaudited financial statements.

[2] John C. Coates IV, Jesse M. Fried & Kathryn E. Spiers, *What Courses Should Law Students Take? Lessons from Harvard's BigLaw Survey*, 64 Journal of Legal Education 443 (2015).

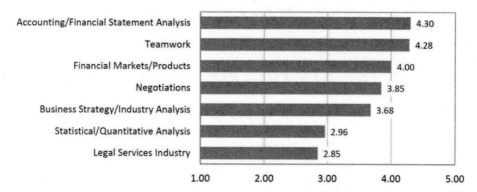

We see that understanding of accounting and financial products were ranked #1 and #3. This is not surprising. Parenthetically, the skill ranked #2 was teamwork. This is also not surprising as business transactions are done in teams and the ability to work in, manage, and coordinate teams is an important business skill.

The chapter is designed to introduce basic accounting concepts to law students who have *no* training in accounting or finance. It is written to provide law students an overview of the broad concepts. Lawyers must be effective users of accounting and financial information. Securities lawyers work with the client's management and accountants to prepare required SEC filings, much of which are financial statements and filing containing detailed financial and accounting information. Mergers and acquisitions lawyers work with investment bankers and accountants. Securities and corporate litigators are constantly involved in disputes about valuation, financial prospects, and accounting issues. A major piece of corporate legislation, the Sarbanes-Oxley Act, involved major legal reforms of accounting and reporting processes.

When preparing and presenting accounting information, most firms, and all public corporations, use Generally Accepted Accounting Principles (GAAP). GAAP is a complex series of rules than a set of principles. These rules do not embody immutable scientific or mathematical truths. Instead, they represent the often judgments and policy preferences of a group of highly-qualified accounting professionals from the Financial Accounting Standards Board (FASB). As the perceptions, judgments and preferences of the members of the FASB change over time, so do the rules of GAAP that govern how financial information is presented.

GAAP consist of a series of conventions, many of which are not immediately intuitive. The goal of these conventions is to resolve potential policy choices as to the most appropriate method of presenting financial information, given the frequent impossibility of providing truly accurate and reliable information at reasonable cost.

GAAP assume that a business is a "going concern" that will continue in operation for the foreseeable future. A firm is required to apply the same accounting concepts, standards, and procedures from one period to the next. Firms also are supposed to disclose all material information and follow a "conservatism" principle that profits not be anticipated and that probable losses be recognized as soon as possible. The principle of conservatism also requires that, with some exceptions, values in the balance sheet be recorded at historical cost (*i.e.*, original cost of purchase). Since values change over time (think of the original purchase price of a building bought in Manhattan in 1900 and compare it to its value in 2000), the "book values" may differ significantly from the "market values."

An excellent example of how GAAP financial statements can differ from financial reality is seen in *Kahan v. United States Sugar Corp.*, 1985 WL 4449 (Del.Ch. 1985). There, United States Sugar made a cash self-tender offer for its shares (an offer to buy back shares from shareholders). The issue was whether the disclosure to shareholders relating to the tender offer price of $68 per share was materially inaccurate. The incentive to tender shares to the company depends on the value of the company; this value in turn depends, in part at least, on the value of the company's assets. The company's primary assets were Florida muckland, which the court described as: "Muckland is a unique type of soil formed form the overflow of Lake Okeechobee in south central Florida. It is so fertile that little fertilizer is needed to produce high yield sugar crops and it is the perfect soil for the raising of sugar cane but has limited other uses." In the proxy statement to shareholders, the company disclosed the value of the muckland (as recorded on its books in accordance with GAAP) at book value (the historical cost of purchase), but did not disclose the land's current market value. The court found the disclosure to be faulty:

> There was a failure to clearly indicate in the proxy materials that the book value of the land, which was the principal asset of U.S. Sugar, was based primarily on the 1931 acquisition costs of the land and that in 1982 the internal real estate department of the corporation had rendered an informal opinion to management that the fee simple holdings of land was in excess of $408 million ($83 per share).

Although financial statements appear precise, those numbers often reflect subjective judgments. Transactions can often be conceptualized in different ways, all of them consistent with GAAP. People naturally have a tendency to want to use the flexibility inherent in GAAP to present financial information in a way that best serves their interests. A manager will want the business to appear as profitable as possible. A divorcing spouse will try to minimize her income and the value of her assets. A person selling a business will attempt to make the business appear free of risks. An accountant will want to keep her clients happy, by painting the picture of their business that they want to see. These are human beings, after all. You should keep in mind two fundamental aspects of accounting that matter crucially to law and policy:

- Because accounting data are a product of selected policies and principles, there is no such thing as objective truth in accounting. Accounting data should be understand as data produced by these policies and principles, including the limitations inherent therein.

- Because accounting policies and principles permit certain degree of discretion in selection of rules and judgment as to values, people naturally are inclined to present financial information in a manner that suits their interests.

Financial statements are produced through a three-stage process. First is the "recording and controls" stage in which a company records in its books information concerning every transaction in which it is involved. Second is the "accounting" stage in which the company classifies and analyzes the information and presents it in a set of financial statements. Third is the "audit" stage in which the company, usually with the assistance of independent public accountants, verifies the accuracy of the information it has recorded and the manner in which it has presented the financial statements. At each stage, there are opportunities for managers and accountants to make judgments and estimates, and to be truthful and forthcoming—or not.

Although public companies always go through these three stages, private companies often do not. The audit and accounting process is expensive, and many small companies are not in a position to pay to have their financial statements audited. As you might suspect, the managers of private companies might not produce entirely accurate financial statements, either because they don't have the time and resources to do so or they don't care enough. Someone who was considering buying a private business would want to know who prepared the financial statements, what they did, and whether any third party reviewed them. An acquirer would certainly want answers to these questions, particularly if the company's financial statements are not audited.

Inevitably, reading financial statements is an art, not a science. Notwithstanding the fact that numbers are involved, this is not mathematics. It is more like a forensic investigation, an attempt to construct a plausible story about the value and risks of a business. The goal of financial statements is to convey information, but financial statements alone rarely tell the entire story. The first part of becoming a sophisticated user of financial statements is to understand their basic components. That is the goal here, and no more.

The materials that follow will help you to understand the basics of financial accounting. These are, however, just the basics. The financial statements of public companies today stretch to dozens of pages, with detailed footnotes describing, among other things, contingent liabilities, stock option grants, and complex financial instruments. However, there are three fundamental financial statements, which are typically presented in three pages.

- **Balance sheet**
- **Income statement**
- **Cash flow statement**

The balance sheet records the amount of the firm's assets, liabilities, and equity as of fiscal year end. The income statement records the firm's yearly revenue, expenses, and profit or loss. The cash flow statement records the firm's yearly cash inflows and outflows. At the outset, it is important to understand the temporal aspect of these financial statements. The income statement and the cash flow statement provides the sum all activities for the entire year related to the generation of revenue, the outlay of expenses, and the flows of cash. The balance sheet is a snapshot of the firm's assets, liabilities, and equity on the last day of the fiscal year. For example, suppose the fiscal year of a company runs from July 1, 2xx0, to June 30, 2xx1.[3]

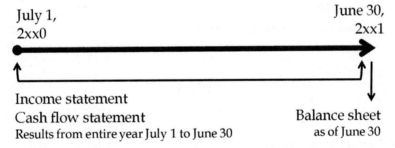

July 1,
2xx0

June 30,
2xx1

Income statement
Cash flow statement
Results from entire year July 1 to June 30

Balance sheet
as of June 30

1. PRECISION TOOLS FINANCIAL STATEMENTS

The pages that follow include the most recent financial statements of Precision Tools, Inc., the company now owned by Stern and Starr. Michael, Jessica, and Bernie are interested in purchasing Precision Tools. A discussion of financial statements will be made more concrete if it is had in conjunction with reviewing an actual set of financial statements.

These financial statements are presented upfront because they will be referenced throughout the discussion of the balance sheet, income statement, and cash flow statement that follow.

---

[3] The fiscal year of a company need not match the calendar year running from January 1 to December 31, though many companies have matching fiscal and calendar years. For example, the fiscal year of Walt Disney Company ends in late September and early October of each year.

PRECISION TOOLS, INC.
BALANCE SHEET

	December 31	
	2xx2	2xx1
Assets		
Current Assets		
Cash	225,000	412,000
Accounts Receivable (Net of reserve for doubtful accounts)	2,070,000	1,717,000
Inventories	1,965,000	1,670,000
Prepaid expenses	60,000	55,000
Total Current Assets	4,320,000	3,854,000
Property, Plant, and Equipment		
Land*	1,160,000	1,160,000
Buildings**	3,000,000	3,000,000
Machinery**	1,500,000	1,358,000
Office Equipment**	340,000	305,000
Total PP & E	6,000,000	5,823,000
Accumulated Depreciation***	(2,430,000)	(2,055,000)
Intangible Assets****	150,000	0
Total Long-term Assets	3,720,000	3,768,000
Total Assets	8,040,000	7,622,000
Liabilities and Equity		
Current Liabilities		
Accounts payable	1,350,000	1,237,000
Demand Note payable, 11%	0	500,000
Accrued expenses payable	375,000	350,000
Other liabilities	1,050,000	855,000
Total Current Liabilities	2,775,000	2,942,000
Long-term Notes payable, 12.5% due 12/15/2x17	3,000,000	3,000,000
Total Liabilities	5,775,000	5,942,000
Stockholders' Equity		
Common stock (1,000 shares authorized and outstanding)		
Paid-in capital	300,000	300,000
Retained earnings	1,965,000	1,380,000
Total Equity	2,265,000	1,680,000
Total Liabilities and Equity	8,040,000	7,622,000

* The land was purchased 15 years ago for $1,160,000, the price shown on the balance sheet. A comparable property nearby recently sold for $1,500,000

** The machinery and equipment are in good repair. The fair market value of the building and equipment are about $300,000 more than historical cost.

*** Depreciation is on a level (straight line) basis over the estimated useful life.

**** Intangible assets include the $150,000 cost of a patent acquired during 2012.

STATEMENT OF INCOME

Years ended December 31

	2xx2	2xx1	2xx0
Net sales	11,250,000	10,500,000	10,200,000
Operating Expenses			
Cost of goods sold	7,470,000	6,975,000	6,910,000
Gross Profit	3,780,000	3,525,000	3,290,000
Depreciation expense	375,000	360,000	300,000
Selling, general, and administrative*	1,950,000	1,830,000	1,725,000
Research and development	75,000	188,000	180,000
Total Operating Expense	2,400,000	2,378,000	2,205,000
Operating Income	1,380,000	1,147,000	1,085,000
Interest expense	480,000	562,000	562,000
Income before taxes	900,000	585,000	523,000
Income taxes	315,000	204,000	183,000
Net Income	585,000	381,000	340,000

* Includes salaries paid to Stern and Starr totaling $130,000 in 2012; $100,000 in 2011; and $100,000 in 2010, and bonuses totaling $120,000 in 2012; $100,000 in 2011; and $80,000 in 2010.

STATEMENT OF CASH FLOWS

Years ended December 31

	2xx2	2xx1	2xx0
From Operating Activities			
Net Income	585,000	381,000	340,000
Decrease (Increase) in accts receivable	(353,000)	(51,000)	(48,000)
Decrease (Increase) in inventories	(295,000)	(42,000)	49,000
Decrease (Increase) in prepaid expenses	(5,000)	(5,000)	4,000
Increase (Decrease) in accounts payable	113,000	37,000	30,000
Increase (Decrease) in accrued exp. payable	25,000	10,000	7,000
Depreciation	375,000	360,000	300,000
Total from Operating Activities	445,000	690,000	682,000
From Investing Activities			
Sales (Purchases) of machinery	(142,000)	(567,000)	(394,000)
Sales (Purchases) of office equipment	(35,000)	(40,000)	(37,000)
Sales (Purchases) of intellectual prop.	(150,000)	0	0
Total from Investing Activities	(327,000)	(607,000)	(431,000)
From Financing Activities			
Increase (Decrease) in short -term debt	(305,000)	(60,000)	(53,000)
Total from Financing Activities	(305,000)	(60,000)	(53,000)
Increase (Decrease) in Cash Position	**(187,000)**	**23,000**	**198,000**

2.　THE BALANCE SHEET

The balance sheet presents the firm's assets, liabilities and equity. A firm's *asset* is defined as a probable future economic benefit obtained or controlled by the firm as a result of an identified past transaction or event. Assets can be tangible, such as real property, plant, equipment, and inventory. They can also be intangible, such as intellectual property, goodwill, and financial assets, including accounts receivables and securities. For example, if Computer Inc. sells a $1 million computer mainframe on credit to Software Inc., it creates an asset in the form of the account receivable for the future payment of $1 million, which is an obligation resulting from a past contractual transaction with Software.

Obviously, this account receivable represents a probable economic benefit to the firm, and therefore meets the definition of an asset.

A firm's *liability* is defined as a probable future sacrifice of an economic benefit by the firm arising from a present obligation to transfer an asset or to provide a service to another person in the future as a result of an identified past transaction or event. For example, if Computer Inc. sells a $1 million computer mainframe on credit to Software Inc., Software has an obligation resulting from a past contractual transaction with Computer to transfer $1 million to Computer Inc.; and this obligation meets the definition of a liability. Liabilities include financial obligations such as account payables, bank loans, bonds, and taxes owed. They also include obligations to perform future services, such as warranty services for products sold.

The calculation of *equity* is simply a mathematical plug. It is the difference between assets and liabilities: Equity = Assets − Liabilities. Therefore, equity is frequently called "net assets" (*i.e.*, assets net of liabilities) or "net worth" (*i.e.*, worth net of liabilities). When referring to the value of equity in the balance sheet, it is sometimes called *book value of equity* (or "book value" for short).

Beyond the mathematical formula, equity is an economic concept. Recall that partners, members, and shareholders are equityholders. Creditors own the firm's liabilities: for example, a bank loan is a liability on the borrowing firm's balance sheet, and an asset (a note receivable from the borrower) on the balance sheet of the creditor bank. On the other hand, equityholders have the economic claim on a firm's equity. Thus, the shareholders of a corporation are entitled to all the assets of the firm after all obligations to creditors have been satisfied. Equityholders own the net assets.

The mathematical formula for equity (net assets) reveal the fundamental attribute of a balance. The balance sheet must balance according to this formula:[4]

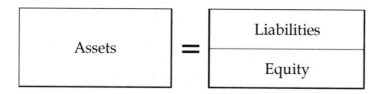

There is no exception to this formula. If assets are 100 and liabilities are 80, then equity is 20. If assets are 100 and liabilities are 120, then equity is −20. This is a case of negative equity (which is synonymously referred to as equity being "underwater"). Notice in Precision Tools' balance sheet, the

---

⁴   The formula is sometimes stated as: (Assets = Liabilities + Net Worth) or (Assets − Liabilities = Owners' Equity).

balance sheet balances: in 2xx2, total assets are $8,040,000, total liabilities $5,775,000, and equity $2,265,000.

The balance sheet conveys important information about economic ownership of a firm. A firm needs assets to do business. It needs factories and machines to make things, building to house things and people, inventory to sell customers, and cash to do business. When a business sells goods or services, it also generates assets (cash and account receivables). The balance sheets says that the assets of a firm (the left side of the balance sheet) are owned by creditors and equityholders (the right of the balance sheet). In other words, the assets of the firm must be claimed by creditors and equityholders.

These claimants do not own the assets in the sense of legal ownership; the corporation, the partnership, or the LLC, as a separate and distinct legal person, is the legal owner of the assets. However, creditors and equityholders have economic claims on the assets. For creditors, if their debts are not paid, they have legal claims against the firm including the right to throw the firm into bankruptcy. If a firm dissolves and winds up, the equityholders have legal claims on the assets after payment of all obligations to creditors. Otherwise, when a firm operates as a going concern, the value of their equity interest is dependent upon the value of the firm's equity. Shareholders have an economic interest that is directly linked to the value of the equity in the corporation. Thus, the balance sheet tells us that assets needed by a firm to do business are claimed by creditors and equityholders, who together finance the business enterprise.

Assets and liabilities on the balance sheet can also be categorized into temporal characteristics: current assets and noncurrent (long-term) assets, and current liabilities and noncurrent (long-term) liabilities. In this scheme, equity is categorized as long-term financing.

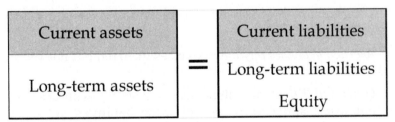

A current asset is a short durational asset that a firm expects to monetize, sell or exchange within the firm's normal operating cycle or one year. Current assets are typically cash, receivables, and inventory. A firm normally expects to sell inventory and collect on receivables within a year. Assets that are more permanent, such as real property, plant and equipment are long-term assets. In the Precision Tools balance sheet, we see the following asset items.

Current Assets

- *Cash*

- *Accounts receivable*

- *Inventories:* stockpile of products to be sold or materials to be used in the production process

- *Prepaid expenses:* expenses that have been prepaid in anticipation of those expenses (*e.g.*, insurance premiums)

Long-term Assets

- *Property, plant and equipment* (called PP&E)

- *Accumulated depreciation:* accumulated depreciation of the asset that deduct from the value of the assets recorded in the balance sheet as a contra asset (note that a negative number in accounting is represented in parentheses)

- *Intangible assets:* typically intellectual property (in the case of Precision Tools a patent) and goodwill

A current liability is a short durational debt or obligation that a firm expects to pay within the firm's normal operating cycle or one year. Examples include account payables such as amounts owed to traded creditors who provide inventory goods on short credit. A noncurrent liability is a longer term debt or obligation, which is a form of financing the firm through debt. An example is a bond issued by the corporation that matures in 30 years. In the Precision Tools balance sheet, we see the following liabilities items.

Current Liabilities

- *Accounts payable*

- *Demand note payable:* short-term debt to a creditor payable upon demand

- *Accrued expenses payable:* expenses incurred but not yet paid by the firm

- *Other liabilities:* miscellaneous category that captures other liabilities, and descriptions of these liabilities are usually provided in the notes to the financial statements

Long-term Liabilities

- *Long-term note payable:* long-term debt obligations (in the case of Precision Tools, the long-term debt is due in 15 years in year 2x17 as of the current year of the balance sheet 2xx2)

Equity is considered long-term financing provided by the firm's equityholders. In a corporation, they are shareholders. In the Precision Tools balance sheet, we see the following equity items.

- *Common stock:* the aggregate par value of stock issued by the corporation.[5]

- *Additional paid-in capital* (or *paid-in capital*): The difference between the total amount paid for common stock and the aggregate par value of the stock.

- *Retained earnings:* the profit that has not been distributed to shareholders and thus retained by the corporation (in the event there is a loss, the retained earnings account is reduced by the amount of the loss)

Together, these represent the balance sheet value of the common stock, which for Precision Tools is also the stockholders' equity or net worth.[6]

It is important to understand conceptually the temporal categorization of a firm's balance sheet into (1) current assets and liabilities and (2) long-term assets, liabilities, and equity. Current assets and current liabilities are considered a part of *working capital*: capital needed to conduct day-to-day operations. For example, day-to-day operations involves compiling and selling inventory, receiving cash or obligations from customers and paying bills, and paying employees. The ability to do these things are seen in the current assets and current liabilities. A key measure of a firm's liquidity (which is the ability of a firm to meet its current obligations) is the calculation of net working capital (NWC).

$$\text{NWC} \quad = \quad \text{Current Assets} \quad - \quad \text{Current Liabilities}$$

The net working capital equation can be restated into a ratio known as the "liquidity ratio":

$$Liquidity \ Ratio \quad = \quad \frac{Current \ Assets}{Current \ Liabilities}$$

To understand the meaning of these calculation, consider the implication of positive, contrasted with negative net working capital; or alternatively, a liquidity ratio of greater than or less than 1.0. If you were

---

[5] A corporation can issue stock with a "par value." Par value is an arbitrary number, typically a low amount. With par value stock, the categories recording stock issuances are two. An item typically labeled "stock" or "common stock" records the aggregate of par value. An item typically labeled "additional paid in capital" records the aggregate issuance consideration less the aggregate par value. For example, a corporation sells 100 shares of stock at the issue price of $100 per share for stock that has a par value of $0.01 per share. The corporation receives total consideration: $100 × 100 shares = $10,000. Of this amount, the aggregate par value is: Common stock = $0.01 × 100 shares = $1. The additional paid in capital is: $99.99 × 100 shares = $9,999. Accordingly, the balance is recorded as: "Common stock $1" and "Additional paid in capital $9,999." We will consider par value and its implications in greater detail in Chapter 11.

[6] If Precision Tools had an outstanding issue of preferred stock, it would be allocated a portion of the total stockholders' equity.

a creditor, what critical information would these calculations provide? Remember that by definition, a firm expects to reduce its current assets to cash within a year and to pay its current liabilities within a year. How likely is it that it will be able to do the latter, if current assets are less than current liabilities?

Long-term assets are capital assets that are expected to be used in a production function over a long period of time: for example, factories, machinery, real property, intellectual property, and substantial investments. These assets must be funded by long-term financing. To understand this, one should think about financing a massive hydroelectric dam project in the Amazon jungle with a series of short-term bank loans that mature within one year. What would be the problem with this financing arrangement? The options for financing capital assets are long-term debt and equity. The financiers of a business are thus shareholders, who provide equity financing, and lenders, who provide long-term debt financing. Corporation law involves in part the rights of shareholders. (The rights of creditors are principally found in the debt contract, and thus contract and bankruptcy laws are the most relevant sources of law.)

Although a complete understanding of how balance sheet items are recorded is beyond the scope of this introduction to accounting, one can get a sense of this process through the following examples.

A corporation that has just been created by filing with the state is simply an entity that exists on paper. In the beginning, it has no assets or liabilities, and thus equity is zero.

The corporation issues 100,000 shares of common stock with par value of $0.01 at $100 per share. The total cash proceeds from the issuance is $10,000,000 (= $100 × 100,000). The transaction would be recorded on the balance sheet as a credit of $10,000,000 to cash on the left side and debits of $1,000 (= $0.01 × 100,000, representing the par value of the stock) and $9,999,000 (= $9.99 × 100,000, representing the remainder of the amount paid by the stockholders) on the right side.[7] The corporation needs financing in addition to this equity financing. It issues a 30-year bond with principal amount of $5 million to creditors (bondholders). This transaction would be recorded as a credit of $5,000,000 to cash on the left side and a debit of $5,000,000 to liabilities on the right side. As must be the case, these entries balance such that (Assets = Liabilities + Equity), as they always must.

---

[7]   We will consider the reason for the division between "Common stock" and "Additional paid-in capital" in Chapter 11. The terms "credit" and "debit" are formal accounting terms relating to the double-entry bookkeeping system. An explanation of this recording system is beyond the scope of this book. For the purpose here, a debit to assets means an increase in assets (thus, a credit is a decrease in assets). Also, a credit to liabilities or equity means an increase in these items (thus, a debit is a decrease in liabilities or equity). These are accounting terms and concepts. They have no deeper meaning, and you should take them for what they are.

Assets		Liabilities	
Cash	15,000,000	Bond	5,000,000
		Equity	
		Stock (100,000 shares)	1,000
		Paid in capital	9,999,000
TOTAL ASSETS	15,000,000	TOTAL LIABILITY & EQUITY	15,000,000

With $15 million on hand, the corporation purchases a building for $8 million and equipment for $5 million. These transactions involve only the left side of the balance sheet. Conceptually, the transactions are exchange of one form of an asset (cash) into another form of an asset (PP&E). The balance sheet must balance.

Assets		Liabilities	
Cash	2,000,000	Bond	5,000,000
Property, Plant, Equipment		**Equity**	
Building	8,000,000	Stock (100,000 shares)	1,000
Equipment	5,000,000	Paid in capital	9,999,000
TOTAL ASSETS	15,000,000	TOTAL LIABILITY & EQUITY	15,000,000

The corporation now engages in business: employees are hired; products are made; transactions are done with counterparties; goods are sold to customers. Most of these activities are recorded in the income statement, which ultimately connects to the balance sheet as detailed in the statement of cash flows. Thus the three sections of the financial statements are interconnected. A detailed analysis of how this is done is beyond the scope of this book. Here, we focus on two matters that connect the balance sheet and the income statement.

First, PP&E remain static as book values in the left side of the ledger, but we know that they decline in value due to use or obsolescence. Depreciation is a diminution of the value of the asset through use. Depreciation is not difficult to understand. Suppose you buy a $30,000 car and use it for one year. The car is obviously no longer worth $30,000. Suppose it is worth $25,000. The $5,000 difference is depreciation. The same concept applies for capital assets such as buildings and equipment. (In accounting convention, land is assumed not to depreciate.)

Second, at the end of the year, the corporation will have either a net loss or a net profit. Let's assume the optimistic scenario. The corporation made a profit of $1 million. The corporation can choose to distribute this profit to shareholders in the form of a cash dividend, or it can retain this profit. If the corporation retains profit, the amount is recorded in the balance sheet as an equity item called "retained earnings."

Let's assume that depreciation for both the building and equipment was $700,000, and the happy scenario that the corporation earned profit of $1 million, all of which was received in cash. The corporation distributed dividend to shareholders of $500,000 and retained the remaining profit.

Assets		Liabilities	
Cash	3,200,000	Bond	5,000,000
Property, Plant, Equipment		Equity	
Building	8,000,000	Stock (100,000 shares)	1,000
Equipment	5,000,000	Paid in capital	9,999,000
Accumulated depreciation	(700,000)	Retained earnings	500,000
TOTAL ASSETS	15,500,000	TOTAL LIABILITY & EQUITY	15,500,000

A new entry is added on the left side of the balance sheet for accumulated depreciation (a negative number since it is a contra asset). A new entry for recording retained earnings is created for equity. Notice that cash increased from $2 million to $3.2 million. We can explain an increase of $500,000 by the fact that profit was retained by this amount and thus cash would increase by the amount of retained profit. How do we explain the other $700,000? It is an increase cash that is matched by the amount of the depreciation. Depreciation is a noncash expense (when your car depreciates, do you lose the cash in your bank account by the amount of the depreciation?). It simply is an economic cost, but no cash changes hand in the way that the corporation pays its employees in cash. Accordingly, the company's cash flow would reflect a greater amount of cash inflow than the retained profit amount. The balance sheet still balances, because the addition to the Equity accounts on the right hand side of the balance is $700,000 less than it would be had we not recognized a depreciation expense of that amount.

Lastly, the corporation purchases $1.5 million in inventory, but has not paid the invoice yet, and it pays $1 million to bondholders to reduce the principal amount.

Assets		Liabilities	
Cash	2,200,000	Bond	4,000,000
Inventory	1,500,000	Account payable	1,500,000
Property, Plant, Equipment		Equity	
Building	8,000,000	Stock (100,000 shares)	1,000
Equipment	5,000,000	Paid in capital	9,999,000
Accumulated depreciation	(700,000)	Retained earnings	500,000
TOTAL ASSETS	16,000,000	TOTAL LIABILITY & EQUITY	16,000,000

3. THE INCOME STATEMENT

The income statement records a firm's profit-making activities, the fundamental operating activity of a business firm. A business firm sells goods and services for the purpose of making a profit, and the aggregate or the receipts from sales is called revenue. To produce goods or services, a firm must expend resources, the values of which are recorded as expenses. If revenue is greater than total expenses, a firm has earned net profit. If total expenses are greater than revenue, a firm has incurred a net loss.

$$\text{Revenue} \quad - \quad \text{Expenses} \quad = \quad \text{Net Profit or Loss}$$

Clearly, net profit is very important to any firm. If a firm cannot generate sustained net profits, it will ultimately fail for it cannot continue indefinitely without profit sustaining the business. However, net profit is a residual profit remaining after all expenses have been paid. The payment of these expenses represents claims by claimants other than shareholders on the firm's revenue.

The income statement can be categorized into four major components, and the lines items proceed in this order: (1) operations, (2) debt service, (3) tax service, (4) residual profit. The income statement is fundamentally organized as follows.

FUNCTION	LINE ITEMS	DESCRIPTION OF LINE ITEM
	Revenue	Receipts from sale of goods and services
	— Cost of goods sold	"COGS" is direct cost of production of goods and services, including wages, supplies, parts, and all other direct costs of producing the firm's goods or services
Operations	Gross profit	= Revenue − COGS
	— Sales, general & administrative	"SG&A" is the overhead and administrative expenses that are not directly related to the production of goods and services but are a part of the firm's operations
	Operating profit (or income)	= Revenue − COGS − SG&A
Debt service	— Interest expense	Expense associated with the payment of interest on debt to creditors, but this does not include repayment of principal
	Pretax profit	= Operating profit − Interest
Tax service	— Tax expense	Taxes paid to government
Equity	Net profit/(loss)	Residual income (or loss) after deducting all expenses from revenue

The concept of the income statement is that a business firm sells products and service. Revenue is the gross sale proceeds. If a widget sells for $10 per unit and the firm sells 100,000 widgets, its revenue is $1 million (= $10 × 100,000). Various constituents of the firm have claims on this money, and the income statement deducts these claims in the order of priority. The income statement has an intuitive logic that is easily understood. One can imagine a line of people who have economic claims on the economic benefit generated by the firm through the sale of goods and services. This line has a specific priority, which looks like this.

LINE ITEMS		CLAIMANTS
Revenue	⟶	All claimants
• COGS and SG&A	⟶	• Suppliers, vendors, employees
• Interest expense	⟶	• Creditors
• Taxes	⟶	• Government
• Net profit (loss)	⟶	• Equityholders

Revenue is the gross return that is divided up among all claimants. From revenue, the claims of specific claimants are paid in the order of: (1) suppliers, vendors, employees; (2) creditors; (3) government; (4) equityholders.

In the Precision Tools income statement, we see the same organization of expense items.

- *Cost of goods sold* (COGS)
- *Depreciation expense*
- *Sales and administrative expense* (SG&A)
- *Research and development* (R&D)
- *Interest expense*
- *Income taxes*

Notice that depreciation expense is shown as a single item. In many income statements, depreciation expense is allocated to COGS and SG&A, and shown as a separate item for each. Also, the income statement provides a separate item for R&D expense.

It is important to understand that there are different ways to measure "profit" or "earnings": (1) gross profit, (2) operating profit, (3) earnings before interest and tax (EBIT), (4) earnings before interest, tax, depreciation and amortization (EBITDA), (5) pretax profit, and (6) net profit. These various profit measures can be confusing, but each is a different measure that conveys different information.

Gross profit is a measure of how much the firm earns when the COGS is deducted from revenue. Operating profit is gross profit less depreciation, SG&A expense, and R&D expense. It represents the profits of the corporation before the costs of capital and taxes. If there are no special or nonrecurring items, then EBIT is simply the operating profit. From operating profit, creditors, and the government take their share, leaving net profit after taxes, which is essentially part of cost of capital, for the shareholders.

Earnings before interest, tax, depreciation and amortization (EBITDA) is not a line item that is seen in the income statement. It must be calculated by adding depreciation and amortization expense (D&A) to EBIT. Depreciation is the diminution of value of tangible assets. Amortization is the diminution of value of intangible assets, such as intellectual property or goodwill. Creditors are keenly interested in EBIT and EBITDA. The reason is simple: interest expense is paid from operating profit plus any other sources of cash. Since depreciation and amortization expense are noncash expenses, the income statement recognizes these expenses (thus, having the effect of reducing profit), but the EBIT figure understates the inflow of cash into the firm because EBIT includes the deduction of D&A.

Pretax profit is the profit from which taxes are calculated. Note that interest expense is deducted from the calculation of pretax profit. This is called the "interest tax shield." Interest expense reduces pretax profit, thus reducing tax liability. For example, compare the difference when interest expense gets a tax deduction versus no deduction.

Tax deduction

Operating profit	3,000
Interest expense	(1,000)
Pretax profit	2,000
Tax @ 30%	(600)
Net profit	1,400

No tax deduction

Operating profit	3,000
Tax @ 30%	(900)
After-tax profit	2,100
Interest expense	(1,000)
Net profit	1,100

With the interest tax deduction, tax liability is lower. As a result, net profit increases by the amount of the lower tax liability (when compared with a tax scheme in which there is no interest expense deduction). The total wealth of all capital providers (creditors and shareholders) increase: compare 2,400 for creditors and shareholders with the tax deduction, with 2,100 with no tax deduction. The 300 difference in payments to shareholders and creditors is the difference in the tax payments between the two scenarios.

Net profit is the residual profit remaining after payment to all other claimants. It is the economic claim belonging to shareholders. Notice that shareholders take the greatest risk because they are the last claimants. All other claimants have priority interests and are protected by contract law. Upon nonpayment, trade counterparties, employees, creditors, and the government have legal claims for unpaid amounts. Shareholders are the residual claimants standing last in the financial queue. Corporation law provides their principal protection.

If law students need confirmation that accounting is really useful in business law practice, consider the following example. As mentioned above, EBITDA is a common used accounting measure in credit contracts. Section 4.04, "Limitation on Indebtedness," in *Model Negotiated Covenants and Related Definitions,* 61 Bus. Law. 1439 (2006) (Drafted by Committee on Trust Indentures and Indenture Trustees, ABA Section of Business Law), provides a model covenant term that creditors use to limit the amount of debt that a debtor firm can undertake as a condition of the credit contract:

> The Company shall not, and shall not permit any Restricted Subsidiary to, Incur, directly or indirectly, any Indebtedness; provided, however, that the Company [and its Restricted Subsidiaries] [and its Guarantors] shall be entitled to Incur Indebtedness if, on the date of such Incurrence and after giving effect thereto on a pro forma basis, no Default has occurred and is continuing and the Consolidated Coverage Ratio exceeds to 1.0
>
> . . . .

The model covenant defines "Consolidated Coverage Ratio" as:

> the ratio of (x) the aggregate amount of Consolidated EBITDA for the period of the most recent four consecutive fiscal quarters ending at least 45 days prior to the date of such determination to (y) Consolidated Interest Expense for such four fiscal quarters [which is the following equation]

$$Consolidated\ Coverage\ Ratio\ = \frac{x}{y} = \frac{Consolidated\ EBITDA}{Consolidated\ Interest\ Expense}$$

The model covenant defines Consolidated EBITDA as:

> the sum of Consolidated Net Income, plus the following to the extent deducted in calculating such Consolidated Net Income: (1) all income tax expense of the Company and its consolidated Restricted Subsidiaries; (2) Consolidated Interest Expense; (3) depreciation and amortization expense of the Company and its consolidated Restricted Subsidiaries (excluding amortization expense attributable to a prepaid operating expense that was paid in cash in a prior period); . . .

It should be obvious that anyone who represents either corporations that issue bonds using such an indenture or investors who purchase them needs to have a basic understanding of the meaning of these accounting terms and how they are used in corporate finance.

4. STATEMENT OF CASH FLOWS

The statement of cash flows for an accounting period provides information on how much cash is generated and how much is used, and by what activities, during the period. (It is thus sometimes called the "Statement of Sources and Uses of Cash.") It is necessary because cash flow is not correlated with the way the economic transactions in which firms engage are recorded on the balance sheet and income statement. Some transactions are simply noncash transactions. For example when a firm sells product on credit, it records an account receivable on its income statement, even though it has not received cash payment. When it buys products on credit it must record an account payable indicating that it has incurred a payment obligation, but has not paid the vendor yet. Even though no cash has changed hands, these economic activities are recognized in the income statement. Likewise, depreciation and amortization also reduce a firm's profit although they do not involve any expenditure of cash.

As a consequence of noncash expenses and timing issues related to payments, the income statement usually does not reflect the actual inflows and outflows of cash. A firm must use cash, not income, to pay its bills, repay its debts, and make distributions to its owners. Cash, not income, must be on hand when the firm needs it. Over a period of many years, a firm's total income and cash flow usually will approximate each other. But over a shorter period of time, income and cash flow may differ substantially. As one accounting adage goes, "income is a fiction, but cash is a fact." Since cash is important—some even say it is king—the statement of cash flow fills in the gap in information by reconciling the income statement with actual changes in the firm's cash position.

The cash flow statement has three components: (1) cash flow from operations, (2) cash flow from financing, (3) cash flow from investing. The statement of cash flow is fairly simply, relative to other accounting statements, because it is designed to count cash. The most difficult conceptual component is the cash flow from operations.

The cash flow from operations shows represents cash generated and used in all aspects of the business associated with the production and selling of a firm's product. It must capture all receipts of payment for the sale of goods and services and all payments to employees and vendors. The calculation starts from the false assumption that net income reflects cash. Since this is untrue, one must correct for the differences between reported net income and the net cash generated by operations.

The first correction is to add back depreciation and amortization since both are expenses deducted from revenues in calculating profits but are noncash expenses. The second correction is to adjust for receivables and payables. Accounts receivable represent revenues are created when revenue is recognized, but there is no change in cash when they are created. If receivables increase from the prior year, it means that the firm has recognized more revenue than it has received cash for, with the result that cash flow is lower than if receivables had remained the same. If payables increase from the prior year, it means that the firm has paid for fewer products and services than it has recognized expenses for, which means that cash flow is higher than it would have been if payables had remained the same. The opposite is true for a decrease in receivables or a decrease in payables. The cash flow from operations is calculated by adding to net income depreciation and amortization expenses, and adding or subtracting, as appropriate, changes in accounts receivable and accounts payable.

Cash flow from operations

Net income

+ Depreciation and amortization expense

+/− Change in receivables

+/− Change in payables

Cash flow from operations

The cash flow from investing is a fairly simple calculation. Any sale of investments results in cash inflow. Any purchase of investments results in cash outflow. Investments can be varied: for example, intellectual property, PP&E, investments in securities, and whole companies or business units.

Cash flow from investing

+ Sale of investments by company (assets)

− Purchase of investments by company (assets)

Cash flow from investing

The cash flow from financing is also fairly simple. Financing activities result in cash inflows and outflows. If a company raises cash by issuing debt or equity, there is a cash inflow. If a company pays off the principal of debt or buys back stock from shareholders, there is a cash outflow. The payment of cash dividends to shareholders is a cash outflow. However, the payment of interest on debt is not calculated here. Instead, since interest expense is a part of the income statement, the cash effect is factored into the cash flow from operations.

Cash flow from operations

+ Issurance of securities (stocks and bonds)

– Repayment of bonds to bondholders

– Stock buyback by company

– Payment of dividends to stockholders

Cash flow from financing

Once the three components of the cash flow statement are calculated, the three are added to calculate the entire year's cash flow. Suppose the cash flow from operations, investing, and financing are +300, —200, and +100, respectively. The entire year's cash flow is 200. This is equal to the change in cash from that reported on the previous year's balance sheet to that reported in the new one. For example, the cash flow statement from Precision Tools states that the company had cash outflow of $187,000 in year 2xx2, in the previous year 2xx1 the cash balance on the balance sheet was $412,000. Therefore, the cash balance on year 2xx2 in the balance sheet should be (and is) $225,000.

5. OTHER PARTS OF THE FINANCIAL STATEMENTS

Public companies are required by federal securities law to file financial statements with the SEC in a filing called a Form 10–K. This document is dense and chock full of information, including audited financial statements. Additionally, reporting companies are also required to file unaudited quarterly financial reports as part of Form 10–Q. These documents along with documents related to corporate governance, such as the certificate of incorporation and bylaws, are found in a company's website under the tab "Investor Relations."

Even if they are not subject to reporting under the securities laws, firms with substantial businesses normally hire independent accounting firms to audit their financial statements and accounting processes. Not only is this a means of assuring that financial statements are accurate, but third-parties, including suppliers, lenders, and investors often expect to see audited financial statements.

An independent accounting firm conducts an audit. It produces an *auditor's report*. If the accounting firm is satisfied that the company's books and records are consistent with the applicable accounting standard, it issues an *unqualified opinion*, which certifies that the financial statements "present fairly, in all material respects" the financial position of the company. If the company's financial statements do not meet this standard, the auditor issues a *qualified opinion*, which indicates a material deficiency in the financial statements. The following excerpt from Nike, Inc.'s 2015 Form 10–K is the unqualified opinion of PricewaterhouseCoopers, Nike's independent auditor.

> In our opinion, the consolidated financial statements listed in the index appearing under Item 15(a)(1) present fairly, in all material respects, the financial position of NIKE, Inc. and its subsidiaries at May 31, 2015 and 2014, and the results of their operations and their cash flows for each of the three years in the period ended May 31, 2015 in conformity with accounting principles generally accepted in the United States of America. In addition, in our opinion, the financial statement schedule listed in the index appearing under Item 15(a)(2) presents fairly, in all material respects, the information set forth therein when read in conjunction with the related consolidated financial statements. Also in our opinion, the Company maintained, in all material respects, effective internal control over financial reporting as of May 31, 2015, based on criteria established in *Internal Control— Integrated Framework (2013)* issued by the Committee of Sponsoring Organizations of the Treadway Commission (COSO).

Public companies are also required by federal securities laws to maintain adequate *internal controls* over their financial reporting. Internal controls consist of a firm's internal processes and procedures used to provide reasonable assurance that the firm is complying with applicable laws and has an adequate financial reporting process. The financial statements of public companies contain reports on the internal controls of the company by both the independent accounting firm and the management of the company. The following is an excerpt of Nike management's 2015 certification of internal controls in its Form 10–K.

> Management is responsible for establishing and maintaining adequate internal control over financial reporting, as such term is defined in Rule 13(a)–15(f) and Rule 15(d)–15(f) of the Securities Exchange Act of 1934, as amended. Internal control over financial reporting is a process designed to provide reasonable assurance regarding the reliability of financial reporting and the preparation of the financial statements for external purposes in accordance with generally accepted accounting principles in the United States of America. Internal control over financial reporting includes those policies and procedures that: (i) pertain to the maintenance of records that, in reasonable detail, accurately and fairly reflect the transactions and dispositions of assets of the Company; (ii) provide reasonable assurance that transactions are recorded as necessary to permit preparation of financial

statements in accordance with generally accepted accounting principles, and that receipts and expenditures of the Company are being made only in accordance with authorizations of our management and directors; and (iii) provide reasonable assurance regarding prevention or timely detection of unauthorized acquisition, use or disposition of assets of the Company that could have a material effect on the financial statements.

. . .

Under the supervision and with the participation of our Chief Executive Officer and Chief Financial Officer, our management conducted an evaluation of the effectiveness of our internal control over financial reporting based upon the framework in *Internal Control—Integrated Framework (2013)* issued by the Committee of Sponsoring Organizations of the Treadway Commission (COSO). Based on the results of our evaluation, our management concluded that our internal control over financial reporting was effective as of May 31, 2015.

The financial statements for public companies also contain a section called "management's discussion and analysis" (MD&A), where management discusses and analyzes the year-end results and financial statement. MD&A highlights operating results that management deems important to note, which may include comparisons to prior year's results, segmentation results on various business lines or geographic results, explanations of financial results, and other information.

Additionally, most financial statements are accompanied by extensive notes, which are essential to an understanding of the numbers because they explain (1) important accounting policies adopted by the company and its auditors including the assumptions and estimates that are necessary to producing financial statements, and (2) how various line items in the financial statements have been calculated. Accounting policies may include policies on revenue recognition, depreciation, valuation of derivatives and hedging strategies, and inventory policies. Many items are self-explanatory, such as "cash." However, many items stated in the financial statements are not immediately apparent, for example items that may be called "affiliated investments" (what exactly are these?). Also, even with items that are recognizable, such as "deferred taxes," a reader may want more details about these items. The notes may explain these matters.

Problem: Precision Tools—Part 7

The following are questions about the financial statements of Precision Tools that Michael, Jessica and Bernie might want to ask:

Balance sheet

- Assess the company's liquidity situation. Is it in a good position to fund current operations?

- What are the key capital assets of Precision Tools? How has the company financed its capital assets?

- How much equity does Precision Tools have in relation to long-term debt?

Income statement

- What are the operating profit and net income as a percentage of revenue?

- Assess the progression of financial results from year 2xx0 to 2xx2.

- Explain how Precision Tools increased net income by almost $200,000 in 2xx2.

Statement of cash flow

- Was there a net cash inflow or outflow in 2xx2?

- Assess the progression of cash flow from operations from 2xx0 to 2xx2. What accounts for the differences in these years?

- If Precision Tools has the same net cash flow in 2xx3, what will be its cash position in 2xx3? What are the implications?

6.   PARTNERSHIP ACCOUNTING

Most business enterprises apply GAAP to produce and maintain financial reports. However, accounting for partnerships and LLCs also requires maintaining "capital accounts" for each partner. Shares of stock in a corporation are fungible in that a share of stock in the same class of stock is the same; thus, one investor's ownership is the same as the other's except that she may own more shares than the other. Partnership or an LLC can be issued in "units" that mimic the fungibility of stock. However, through contracting, non-corporate entities often have individualized arrangements as to capital contribution, profit/loss allocation, governance rights, rights of each partner to draw from the account, and distribution rights. For example, if a partnership anticipates that it will sustain losses during the early years, the partners might agree to allocate those losses all to partners who have other sources of income against which they can offset those losses. As a matter of practical necessity, partnerships and LLCs maintain capital accounts to keep track of each partner's interest. Indeed, because limited partnerships are typically investment vehicles where limited partners are passive investors, they are legally required to maintain capital accounts.[8]

A capital account maintains a record of contributions, profit/loss allocation, draws and distributions. Consider a simple example of four partners who contribution different amounts and profit/loss allocation mirror the percentage contribution. At the beginning of the partnership, the capital account looks like this.

Partner	Beginning Capital	Profit Made		Capital Contribution	Draw and Distribution	Ending Capital
		%	Allocation			
Amy	100	10%	-	-	-	-
Ben	200	20%	-	-	-	-
Clare	300	30%	-	-	-	-
Don	400	40%	-	-	-	-
Total	1,000	100%	-	-	-	-

In the first year of business, the partnership made a profit of 2,000, and various partners made different additional contributions and took different draws. A contribution adds capital to a partner's capital account. A draw is a permissible amount taken by a partner from his or her capital account, and thus subtracts capital from the capital account. The following table provides a record of the capital accounts.

Partner	Beginning Capital	Profit Made		Capital Contribution	Draw and Distribution	Ending Capital
		%	Allocation			
Amy	100	10%	200	500	(150)	650
Ben	200	20%	400	200	-	800
Clare	300	30%	600	-	(200)	700
Don	400	40%	800	300	(100)	1,400
Total	1,000	100%	2,000	1,000	(450)	3,550

Note that the additional contribution of capital, and in different amounts, by Amy, Ben, and Don, may result in a new formula for the allocation of profit and loss, though the above table assumes that the formula remains unchanged.

---

[8] "A limited partnership shall maintain . . . a record stating: (A) the amount of cash, and a description and statement of the agreed value of the other benefits, contributed and agreed to be contributed by each partner; (B) the times at which, or events on the happening of which, any additional contributions agreed to be made by each partner are to be made; (C) for any person that is both a general partner and a limited partner, a specification of what transferable interest the person owns in each capacity; and (D) any events upon the happening of which the limited partnership is to be dissolved and its activities wound up." ULPA (2001) § 111(9).

If interests in the business are fungible and categorized into discrete units (such as shares of stock in a corporation), a firm simply needs to keep track of the number of units issued and the identity of the holder. The equity value held by a holder is simply the total equity value of the firm multiplied by the percentage of equity held. However, if economic interests are individualized, a capital account is needed to maintain each equityholder's capital in the firm.

B. VALUATION

1. INTRODUCTION

For many constituents, the value of the firm is important. Let's consider a corporation. A creditor will want to know the corporation's value before it lends money. A shareholder will want to know before she buys stock. An acquirer will want to know before it submits an offer to buy the corporation. The corporation will want to know before it acquires another firm by giving its shares to the target corporation's shareholders as consideration. A credit rating agency will want to know before it rates the corporation's debt. A regulator may want to know the financial health of a regulated company.

The equity value of a firm is most important. For a corporation, the equity value is the aggregate value of the outstanding shares. If a corporation is publicly traded the market price of its shares provides useful information about the value of the corporation, but does not necessarily determine what it would be worth to someone interested in buying the entire company. The aggregate value of all publicly traded shares is called the market capitalization (or "market cap"): Market Cap = (Shares Outstanding) × (Share Price). If a corporation is private, there is no market price, and the value of the corporation is more difficult to determine.

A share of stock represents a discrete unit of economic claim on the corporation's total equity value. If a shareholder owns all 100 of the outstanding shares of a corporation (meaning shares held by shareholders), she owns 100% of the equity. However, if there are 10,000 shares outstanding, she owns 1% of the equity.

Importantly, the stock price is not, *in and of itself*, a measure of value. Suppose corporations A and B have stock prices of $200 and $100, respectively. Is corporation A twice as valuable as B? Uncertain, without more information. Suppose A has only 1 share outstanding and B has 2 shares. The total equity values are the same. In other words, corporation A can decrease its stock price to match the stock price of B by splitting its 1 share into 2 shares in a transaction known as a "stock split." This would have the effect of decreasing A's stock price to $100 per share. Likewise, corporation B can increase its stock price to match the stock price of A by combining 2 shares of stock into 1 share in what is called a "reverse stock split," which would have the effect of increasing B's stock price to $200 per share. We see that the stock price, *in and of itself*, is an arbitrary number. Only when the stock price is compared to some financial measure is stock price relevant to the concept of value. In other words, a stock price of $1,000 per share may not necessarily be so impressive; nor is a stock of $10 per share necessarily humble.

When considering the complexities of valuation, consider the underlying lesson in the following parable of attempting to value an apple tree.

2.   THE OLD MAN AND THE TREE: A PARABLE OF VALUATION

Once there was a wise old man who owned an apple tree. The tree was a fine tree, and with little care it produced a crop of apples each year which he sold for $100. The man was getting old, wanted to retire to a different climate and he decided to sell the tree. He enjoyed teaching a good lesson, and he placed an advertisement in the Business Opportunities section of Wall Street Journal Online in which he said he wanted to sell the tree for "the best offer."

The first person to respond to the ad offered to pay the $50 which, the offeror said, was what he would be able to get for selling the apple tree for firewood after he had cut it down. "You are a very foolish person," said the old man. "You are offering to pay only the salvage value of this tree. That might be a good price for a pine tree or perhaps even this tree if it had stopped bearing fruit or if the price of apple wood had gotten so high that the tree was more valuable as a source of wood than as a source of fruit. But my tree is worth much more than $50."

The next person to come to see the old man offered to pay $100 for the tree. "For that," said she, "is what I would be able to get for selling this year's crop of fruit which is about to mature."

"You are not quite so foolish as the first one," responded the old man. "At least you see that this tree has more value as a producer of apples than it would as a source of firewood. But $100 is not the right price. You are not considering the value of next year's crop of apples, nor that of the years after. Please take your $100 and go elsewhere."

The next person to come along was a young man who had just started business school. "I am going to major in marketing," he said. "I figure that the tree should live for at least another fifteen years. If I sell the apples for $100 a year, that will total $1,500. I offer you $1,500 for your tree."

"You, too, are foolish," said the man. "Surely the $100 you would earn by selling the apples from the tree fifteen years from now cannot be worth $100 to you today. In fact, before the recent financial crisis, if you had placed $41.73 in a bank account paying 6% interest, compounded annually, that small sum would grow to $100 at the end of fifteen years with no risk to you because your deposit is federally insured. Therefore the present value of $100 worth of apples fifteen years from now, assuming an interest rate of 6%, would have been only $41.73, not $100. The same principle applies even when interest rates are substantially lower. Pray," said the old man, "take your $1,500 and invest it more safely until you have graduated from business school and know more about finance."

Before long, there came a wealthy physician, who said, "I don't know much about apple trees, but I know what I like. I'll pay the market price for it. The last fellow was willing to pay you $1,500 for the tree, and so it must be worth that."

"Doctor," advised the old man, "you should get yourself a knowledgeable investment adviser. If there were truly a market in which apple trees were traded with some regularity, the prices at which they were sold might be a good indication of their value. But there is no such market. And the isolated offer I just received tells very little about how much my tree is really worth—as you would surely realize if you had heard the other foolish offers I have heard today. Please take your money and buy a vacation home."

The next prospective purchaser to come along was an accounting student. When the old man asked "What price are you willing to give me?" the student first demanded to see the old man's books. The old man had kept careful records and gladly brought them out. After examining them the accounting student said, "Your books show that you paid $75 for this tree ten years ago. Furthermore, you have made no deductions for depreciation. I do not know if that conforms with generally accepted accounting principles, but assuming that it does, the book value of your tree is $75. I will pay that."

"Ah, you students know so much and yet so little," chided the old man. "It is true that the book value of my tree is $75, but any fool can see that it is worth far more than that. You had best go back to school and see if you can find some books that will show you how to use your numbers to better effect."

The next prospective purchaser was a young stockbroker who had recently graduated from business school. Eager to test her new skills she, too, asked to examine the books. After several hours she came back to the old man and said she was now prepared to make an offer that valued the tree on the basis of the capitalized earnings of the tree.

For the first time the old man's interest was piqued, and he asked her to go on.

The young woman explained that while the apples were sold for $100 last year, that figure did not represent profits realized from the tree. There were expenses attendant to the tree, such as the cost of fertilizer, the expense of pruning the tree, the cost of the tools, expenses in connection with picking the apples, carting them into town and selling them. Somebody had to do these things, and a portion of the salaries paid to those persons ought to be charged against the revenues from the tree. Moreover, the purchase price, or cost, of the tree was an expense. A portion of the cost is taken into account each year of the tree's useful life. Finally, there were taxes. She concluded that the profit from the tree was $50 last year.

"Wow!" kidded the old man, to see how she'd respond. "And here I thought I'd made $100 off that tree."

"That's because you failed to match expenses with revenues, in accordance with generally accepted accounting principles," she explained. "You don't actually have to write a check to be charged with what accountants consider to be your expenses. For example, you bought a pickup some time ago and you used it part of the time to cart apples to market. The truck will last a while, and each year some of the original cost has to be matched against revenues. A portion of the amount has to be spread out over the next several years even though you expended it all at one time. Accountants call that depreciation. I'll bet you never figured that in your calculation of profits."

"Now we're getting to the nitty gritty," he replied. "Tell me more."

"I also went back into the books for a few years and I saw that in some years the tree produced fewer apples than in other years, the prices varied and the costs were not exactly the same each year. Taking an average of only the last three years, I came up with a figure of $45 as a fair sample of the tree's earnings. But that is only half of what we have to do so as to figure the value."

"So, what's the other half?" he asked.

"The tricky part," she told him. "We now have to figure the value to me of owning a tree that will produce average annual earnings of $45 a year. If I believed that the tree was a one year wonder, I would say 100% of its value—as a going business—was represented by one year's earnings. But if I believe, as both you and I do, that the tree is more like a corporation, in that it will continue to produce earnings year after year, then the key is to figure out an appropriate rate of return. In other words, I will be investing my capital in the tree, and I need to compute the value to me of an investment that will produce $45 a year in income. We can call that amount the capitalized value of the tree's earnings."

"Do you have something in mind?" he asked.

"I'm getting there. If this tree produced entirely steady and predictable earnings each year, it would be risk-free, like a U.S. Treasury bond, and I'd settle to a return equal to what I'd get on that. But its earnings are not guaranteed; so I'll need a higher return to be willing to take the additional risk. After all, apples could become a glut on the market one day, and I'd have to cut the price and increase the costs of selling them. Or some doctor could discover a link between eating an apple a day and heart disease. A drought could cut the yield of the tree. Or, heaven forbid, the tree could become diseased and die. These are all risks. And of course we do not know what will happen to costs that we know we have to bear."

"You are a gloomy one," reflected the old man. "There are some emerging technologies, you know, that may be able to increase the yield of the tree. This tree could help spawn a whole orchard."

"I recognize that the profits may be more than $45 as well as less," she assured him. "That is part of what we mean by risk. The one thing we know is that we don't know with certainty what's going to happen in the future. But you want your money now; and if am going to pay you, I'm going to have to live with the risk. That's fine with me, but my investment resources are limited. I have to choose between your tree and the strawberry patch down the road. I cannot make both investments, and the purchase of your tree will deprive me of any alternative investments. That means I have to compare the opportunities and risks of buying your tree with those of investing my money elsewhere.

"To determine a proper rate of return," she continued, "I have looked at investment opportunities that are comparable to the apple tree, particularly in the agribusiness industry, where these factors have been taken into account. I have concluded that 20% would be an appropriate rate of return. In other words, assuming that the average earnings from the tree over the last three years (which seems to be a representative period) are indicative of the return I will receive, I am prepared to pay a price for the tree that will give me a 20% return on my investment. I am not willing to accept any lower rate of return because I don't have to; I can always buy the strawberry patch instead. That means the value of the apple tree should equal an amount of money that will generate $45 per year at a rate of 20%. Therefore, we can determine its value by dividing $45 by 20%: $45 divided by 0.2—or multiplied by 5, which is the same thing—equals $225. That's my offer."

"Well, okay," he prodded, "but what about something I've heard of called price-earnings ratio. Can't we use that?"

"That's what Wall Street types call it, but it's basically the same thing," she replied. They determine the price-earnings ratio, or P/E—which they sometimes call a "multiplier"—of a public company, by dividing its price by its earnings for the last twelve months. In theory, at least, the price of the stock is a function of the market's prediction of the company's stream of future earnings, including their growth, and the risk associated with actually achieving those earnings. The higher the expected earnings growth, the higher the multiplier; but the greater the risk of achieving that growth, the lower. To the extent that the market really is a good predictor of value, it should be possible to use the same P/E to value a comparable company that is not publicly traded. You'd just multiply that company's earnings for the last twelve months by the P/E of the comparable public company. But, since no two companies are exactly alike, deciding what multiplier to use is a tricky business requiring a lot of judgment."

"With a small business it's even harder to use this technique because the earnings to which the multiplier will be applied are often harder to determine and it's harder to find comparables. If you want to use it, you have to look at past earnings, make a judgment on the representative baseline, and then apply the multiplier. As with a public company, the choice of the multiplier is only a guess as to what the future will bring— both risks and rewards. Since there aren't any publicly traded apple trees, I've used what I estimate would be the right multiplier for businesses that appear to have a similar risk profile as your tree. That's why I chose the strawberry patch."

The old man sat back and said he greatly appreciated the lesson. He would have to think about her offer, and he asked if she could come by the next day.

When the young woman returned she found the old man emerging from a sea of work sheets, small print columns of numbers and a calculator. "Glad to see you," he said. "I think we can do some business."

"It's easy to see how you Wall Street smarties make so much money, buying people's property for less than its true value. I think I can get you to agree that my tree is worth more than you figured."

"I'm open-minded," she assured him.

"The number you worked so hard over my books to come up with was something you called profits, or earnings that I earned in the past. I'm not so sure it tells you anything that important."

"Of course it does," she protested. "Profits measure efficiency and economic utility."

"Maybe," he mused, "but it sure doesn't tell you how much money you've got. I looked in my safe yesterday after you left and I saw I had some stocks that hadn't ever paid much of a dividend to me. And I kept getting reports each year telling me how great the earnings were, but I sure couldn't spend them. The only way that I could have gotten money from those stocks would be to sell them. It's just the opposite with the tree. You figured the earnings were lower because of some amounts I'll never have to spend. It seems to me these earnings are an idea worked up by the accountants. Now I'll grant you that ideas, or concepts as you call them, are important and give you lots of useful information, but you can't fold them up, and put them in your pocket."

Surprised, she asked, "What is important, then?"

"Cash flow," he answered. "I'm talking about dollars you can spend, or save or give to your children. This tree will go on for years yielding revenues after costs. And it is the future, not the past, that we're trying to predict."

"Don't forget the risks," she reminded him. "And the uncertainties."

"Quite right," he observed. "I think we can deal with that. Chances are that you and I could agree, after a lot of thought, on the possible range of future revenues and costs. I suspect we would estimate that for the next five years, there is a 25% chance that the cash flow will be $40, a 50% chance it will be $50 and a 25% chance it will be $60. That makes the expected value of the cash flow $50. (You can do the math.) Then let us figure that for ten years after that the average will be $40. And that's it. The tree doctor tells me it can't produce any longer than that. Now all we have to do is figure out what you pay today to get $50 a year from now, two years from now, and so on for the first five years until we figure what you would pay to get $40 a year for each of the ten years after that. Then, throw in the 50 bucks we can get for firewood at that time, and that's that."

"Simple," she said. "You want to discount to the present value of future cash flow, including salvage value. Of course you need to determine the rate at which you discount."

"Precisely," he noted. "That's what all these charts and the calculator are doing." She nodded knowingly as he showed her discount tables that revealed what a dollar received at a later time is worth today, under different assumptions of the discount rate. It showed, for example, that at an 8% discount rate, a dollar delivered a year from now is worth 92 cents today, simply because 92 cents today, invested at 8%, will produce $1 a year from now.

"You could put your money in a bank today and receive 1 or 2% interest, insured. Before the recent financial crisis when the return went to almost zero, you could also put your money into obligations of the United States Government which would have earned 5% interest. (These numbers will vary with prevailing interest rates. The principle remains the same.) Anywhere else you put your money deprives you of the opportunity to earn that rate.

Discounting by the risk free rate will only compensate you for the time value of the money you invest in the tree rather than in government securities. But the cash flow from the apple tree is not riskless, sad to say, so we need to use a higher discount rate to compensate you for the risk in your investment. But the 20% P/E ratio you used is a bit high for a discount rate, considering that the riskless rate is already unusually low and this time we're talking about a stream of real cash, not just those fictional GAAP profits. Let us agree to use a discount rate of 15%, which is about the rate that is applied to investments with this level of risk. You can check that out with my cousin who just sold his strawberry patch yesterday.

According to my figures, the present value of the anticipated annual net revenues is $267.42, and today's value of the firewood is $6.14, making a grand total of $273. I'll take $270 even. You can see how much I'm allowing for the risk you are taking because if I discounted the stream at even 5% (which, as we said, is higher than today's risk free rate), it would come to $482.53, and if I used a lower risk free rate, the present value would be even higher."

After a few minutes reflection, the young woman said to the old man, "It was a bit foxy of you yesterday to let me appear to be teaching you something. Where did you learn so much about finance as an apple grower?"

"Don't be foolish, my young friend," he counseled her. "Wisdom comes from experience in many fields. Socrates taught us how to learn. I'll tell you a little secret; I took a Corporations course in law school."

The young woman smiled at this last confession. "I have enjoyed this little exercise but let me tell you something that some of the financial whiz kids have told me. Whether we figure value on the basis of the discounted cash flow method or the capitalization of earnings, so long as we apply both methods perfectly we should come out at exactly the same point."

"Of course!" the old man exclaimed. "Some of the wunderkinds are catching on. But the clever ones are looking not at old earnings, but doing what managers are doing and projecting earnings into the future. The question is, however, which method is more likely to be misused. I prefer to calculate by my method because I don't have to monkey around with depreciation. You have to make these arbitrary assumptions about useful life and how fast you're going to depreciate. Obviously that's where you went wrong in your figuring."

"You are a crafty old devil," she rejoined. "There are plenty of places for your calculations to go off. It's easy to discount cash flows when they are nice and steady, but that doesn't help you when you've got some lumpy expenses that do not recur. For example, several years from now that tree will require some extensive pruning and spraying operations that simply do not show up in your cash flow projections. The labor and chemicals for that once-only occasion throw off the evenness of your calculations. But I'll tell you what, I'll offer you $250. My cold analysis tells me I'm overpaying, but I really like that tree. I think the psychic rewards of sitting in its shade must be worth something."

"It's a deal," said the old man. "I never said I was looking for the highest offer, but only the *best* offer."

3. COMPARABLE COMPANY ANALYSIS

One way to value a company is to compare it other similar companies. Because information about them is more readily available, it is easier to use public companies as the "comparables." The first step in the analysis is to calculate the market cap of the comparable company. Of course as we've seen, the market cap alone does not indicate a company's value. What is important is the ratio between the market cap and some other financial measure, or put another way, the multiple the market cap is of the other measure.

An easy way to think about multiples is to analogize to the housing market. Each housing market has a range of values of homes. An average home in Manhattan may sell for a price of $1,000 per square foot. If a home has 2,000 square feet, we would expect that its value would be approximately $2 million by using the price per square foot multiple: $2 million = 2,000 s.f. × $1,000. An average home in Gainesville may sell for $150 per square foot, and a home in Washington, D.C., $600 per square foot. Thus, the same 2,000 square foot home in Gainesville and Washington would be valued at $300,000 and $1.2 million. The price per square foot is a multiple that gives some indication of the value of homes in different housing markets. These different values are driven by different valuation multiples applicable in each market.

For business corporations, the valuation multiples are based on financial measures. The most prevalent market value measure is the price-to-earnings ratio. The "P/E" multiple calculates the multiple of the market cap to the company's earnings.

$$\text{Price to earning (PE) multiple} = \frac{\text{Market cap}}{\text{Earnings}}$$

This formula can be rewritten on a per share basis, which produces the same value (think about why).

$$\text{Price to earning (PE) multiple} = \frac{\text{Share price}}{\text{Earnings per share}}$$

Another common multiple is the price-to-book ratio. The "P/B" multiple calculates the market cap to the company's book value of equity.

$$\text{Price to book (PB) multiple} = \frac{\text{Market cap}}{\text{Book value}}$$

This multiple compares the market price of shares to the book value. This is a measure of the difference between the market value of equity to the accountant's value of equity.

For rapidly growing companies that are plowing a large percentage of revenues back into the business, current earnings may be less important than revenues. A multiple sometimes used in this situation is the multiple market cap is of revenues.

$$\textit{Market cap to revenue multiple} \;\; = \;\; \frac{\textit{Market cap}}{\textit{Revenue}}$$

The calculation of these multiples is fairly mechanistic, and sophisticated business people to not take them as a definitive measure of value but only as useful information to be used in reaching a judgment about value. Suppose, for example, Alpha Tech is undergoing an initial public offering (IPO) in which its shares will be sold to the public for the first time. Thus far, it has been a private company and so there are no public trading prices on its shares. The company is offering 10 million shares to the public for sale. How does it put a price on those shares? The pricing must obviously be based on the value of the company. If it is too high, it will be difficult to sell the stock, and if it is too low, the company will be leaving money on the table. Thus, if those charged with pricing the offering value the company at $100 million, the shares must be priced at $10 per share; if they value it at $50 million, the shares must be $5 per share.

Like the value of homes in particular real estate markets, the company and its investment bankers typically rely heavily on comparables when pricing the offering. If one seeks to value Nike, for example, one might compare it to Under Armour, Adidas, and Puma.

Suppose the company going public is a technology company that provides laser technology for self-driving cars. Assume there are four public companies that similarly compete to provide technology to the global auto industry and that their valuation multiples are as follows:

Company	Market cap ($m)	Earnings ($m)	Book value ($m)	P/E multiple	P/B multiple
Beta Tech	100	2	15	50.0	6.7
Chi Tech	200	5	50	40.0	4.0
Delta Tech	750	25	250	30.0	3.0
Epsilon Tech	1,200	50	600	24.0	2.0
Average of all companies				36.0	3.9
Average of small companies				45.0	5.3
Average of big companies				27.0	2.5

We see that each comparable company has a different set of multiples, but they are within a range. The P/E multiples range from 24 to 50, and the P/B multiple from 2.0 to 6.7. Furthermore, we see that small companies enjoy a valuation premium to larger companies.

Suppose the above comparables were prepared so that we can value Alpha Tech. Alpha Tech has earnings of $10 million and a book value of

$100 million. What is its value? There are a number of potential approaches.

- Use the average multiple for P/E

- Use the average multiple for P/B

- Use the average multiple for P/E and P/B

- Use the multiples for the small cap companies (Beta Tech and Chi Tech) on the argument that small companies like Alpha Tech have higher valuation multiples than larger companies like Delta Tech and Epsilon Tech

These valuation multiples produce different implied valuations for Alpha Tech. The following is a summary.

	Multiple	Earnings ($m)	Book value ($m)	Implied value ($m)
Average P/E	36.0	10		360
Average P/B	3.9		100	390
Average P/E and P/B				375
Average P/E of small cap	45.0	10		450
Average P/B of small cap	5.3		100	530
Average of small cap				490
Average of all implied values				433

The resulting valuations range from $360 million (the average P/E multiples) to $533 million (the average P/B multiples of small cap companies). Suppose the company and its investment bankers select the average of all methods as the best valuation ("best" defined as the highest valuation that the public market would accept, and thus the IPO will be successful). The valuation is $434 million. With 10 million shares offered, the IPO price would be $43.40 per share.

The same kind of analysis would apply to value for a company for purchase by an acquirer, or to value the sales price of a target company that initiates a sales process. In another context, a company may initiate a valuation study to determine how it is valued in the market relative to its peers. For example, Delta Tech in the above example may seek to determine whether the market is "undervaluing" or "overvaluing" its stock relative to Beta, Chi, and Epsilon.

4. DISCOUNTED CASH FLOW ANALYSIS

Comparable company analyses are based on market values of the company and its peers. Market values give essential insights into the fundamental value of a company. However, markets are not perfect. At any given time, markets may fluctuate for various reasons, only some of which may be directly relevant to the company's value. Markets can also misprice assets over a longer period, such as when financial markets experience "bubbles" and "crashes" (systemic rises and decline of market valuations that are usually unsupported by factors relevant to valuations). In addition to market price-based valuation techniques, there are other techniques to derive a theoretical value of the company that depend on analyzing the company's financial performance in the abstract rather than by comparison.

The principal such technique is called the *discounted cash flow* analysis (DCF). Under the DCF, the theoretical value of a firm is the present value of its future stream of free cash flow, discounted by the riskiness of that cash flow. This is a highly technical analysis that must be done by competent financial analyst. However, the concept in broad principle is fairly simple.

A firm generates economic benefit for all of its constituents. It is expected to do so as a going concern indefinitely into the future. The economic value of a firm to investors is simply the value of the future free cash flows that the firm generates through its business. Let's define free cash flow non-technically as cash freely available to its investors after the firm pays all other expenses. This free cash flow is then discounted to take into account the riskiness of the cash flow and the time value of money.

Let's start with a simple hypothetical. Suppose a firm is expected to generate no cash for four years and then free cash flow of $100 in the fifth, and it needs to raise capital to accomplish that. The economic transaction is clear: the firm asks an investor to provide capital and in return the firm expects to provide free cash flow in the future to the investor (claimant). The future free cash flow must be enticing enough for the investor to forego other investment opportunities. In this case, assume that the investor requires a 10% compounded return for this opportunity to be worthwhile (the investor is risking her money in this investment and thus she requires a 10% rate of return to compensate her for the risk she is taking). At what price should the investor purchase this return of $100 expected in five years by making an investment in the firm now (thus providing the firm cash now)? The process of discounting provides the answer.

An important concept here is that a dollar today is always worth more than a dollar tomorrow. That is because, if you invest a dollar today, at an interest rate of say 10%, you will have $110 in a year. Or, conversely, to get $100 a year from now, you only have to invest $90.91 today.

The formula for discounting (equating) a future value to present value is:

$$Present\ value\ =\ \frac{Future\ value}{(1 + R)^T}$$

where R is the discount rate and T is time. Thus, the present value of $100 in the future is equal to $100 ÷ (1 + 10\%) = $90.91.

A simple way to understand the present value equation is to think about an investor who invests $62.09 now (today) in the firm and leaves the money there for five years. The firm uses the capital and it earns an annual return on that capital for the investor that generates a rate of 10%. After investing $62.09, the investor will have $100 in five years.

$$Present\ value\ of\ investment\ =\ 62.09\ =\ \frac{100}{(1 + 10\%)^5}$$

In other words, a future value of $100 discounted by 10% for five years results in a present value equivalent of $62.09. (In the real world, of course, the investment negotiations will almost certainly result in a round number, like $62 for the investment, given the uncertainties involved in determining the present value.)

Another way to look at this is to turn it around and ask the question what a dollar invested today will be worth in the future at a given rate of return. Suppose, for example, that the investor invests $62.09 today at a 10% rate of return. The future value is calculated by this formula:

$$Future\ value = Present\ value \times (1 + R)^T$$

$$Future\ value = 62.09 \times (1 + 10\%)^5 = 100$$

Consider now what happens to the investment amount if the investor's return rates change. If the investor's required return is 15%, she would only pay to the firm for which she expects to get $100 five years in the future. She pays a lower price for the investment, which results in a higher rate of return (15%):

$$Present\ Value\ =\ \frac{100}{(1 + 15\%)^5}\ =\ 49.72$$

As the investor requires more return, the present value (the amount that she is willing to pay cash today for the expectation of a future payout) must decrease, and vice versa.

What does this have to do with the DCF analysis? Everything. A corporation is expected to produce a stream of free cash flows (FCF) indefinitely into the future as a going concern. This stream of free cash flows represents the return to investors. Since these returns are in the future, they must be discounted to present value. They must be discounted to present value by a discount rate that provides a suitable rate of return R for the investor. The formula is:

$$Value = \frac{FCF_1}{(1+R)^1} + \frac{FCF_2}{(1+R)^2} + \ldots + \frac{FCF_n}{(1+R)^n}$$

where FCF_n = FCF in the nth year.

The DCF analysis is simply a sum of a series of present value calculations. The theoretical value of the firm is the present values of a stream of expected free cash flows provided to investors discounted by a suitable discount rate.[9]

It should be evident that a DCF analysis involves estimating two key factors. First is the projection of future free cash flows. Obviously, the greater the amounts, the greater would be the valuation. Second is the discount rate, which is equal to the desired rate of return. The greater the discount rate, the lower would be valuation. Like the choice of multiples in a comparable company analysis, the projections of free cash flows and discount rate are subject to a degree of uncertainty, flexibility, and ultimately judgment.

The scope of this book does not encompass a detailed analyses of the calculation of free cash flow and the discount rate. With respect to the latter, the economic theory is required to quantity what should be an investor's expected return. The theory, called the capital asset pricing model, is beyond the scope of this introduction to valuation. At this point in the study of business law, an understanding of the basic principle of the DCF suffices.

Problem: Precision Tools—Part 8

Assume that the relevant P/E and P/B multiples for Precision Tools are 11.0 and 2.5, respectively. What are the implied equity valuations?

Precision Tools is a private company. Assume that you are interested in putting together a comparable company analysis. What kind of public companies would be suitable comparable companies?

If you were investing $100,000 in Precision Tools, what rate of return would you expect? Explain why you selected the rate.

---

[9]   In the real world, the uncertainty associated with projections of FCF in future years means that the DCF analysis encompasses only five to seven years of FCF. After that, the typical analysis assumes a "terminal value" equal to what the company might sell for or, alternatively, the present value of an infinite stream of FCF at some fixed dollar amount.

CHAPTER 10

FINANCING THE ENTERPRISE

■ ■ ■

A. CORPORATE SECURITIES

Any business enterprise requires capital, the amount of which depends on the type of business. A utility company requires massive amounts of capital to finance power plants and distribution facilities. A full service investment bank requires large amounts of capital to engage in broker/dealer activities. A professional services enterprise, such as a law firm or architecture firm, needs only sufficient capital to rent office space, purchase furniture and office equipment, and handle short-term cash needs. A business enterprise will have equityholders who provide equity financing and creditors who provide debt financing. In this chapter, we will focus on corporate financing.

Corporations can raise money by issuing securities that offer investors the possibility of a return on their investment. The rights associated with securities can vary, and corporations have considerable flexibility in tailoring the terms of their securities. There are several standard types of securities, each of which has a different profile with respect to rights of control, claims on profits and residual assets, and risk assumed. Corporate securities can be divided into two broad categories: *equity* and *debt*.

1. EQUITY SECURITIES

The equity security in a corporation is stock.[1] Stocks are generally of two kinds: *common stock* and *preferred stock*. Within these two broad categories constituting equity securities, there can be any number of variations. Corporation law permits the creation of different classes of stock, enabling corporations to design their capital structure to suit their needs, as the following section of the DGCL makes clear.

---

[1] Corporate statutes permit the creation of nonstock corporations. *See* DGCL § 102. Many nonstock corporations are used for nonprofit purposes. Public corporations are stock corporations. Stock is the discrete unit of equity ownership that makes large scale public trading feasible.

> **DGCL § 151. Classes and Series of Stock; Redemption; Rights.**
>
> (a) Every corporation may issue 1 or more classes of stock or 1 or more series of stock within any class thereof, any or all of which classes may be of stock with par value or stock without par value and which classes or series may have such voting powers, full or limited, or no voting powers, and such designations, preferences and relative, participating, optional or other special rights, and qualifications, limitations or restrictions thereof, as shall be stated and expressed in the certificate of incorporation or of any amendment thereto, or in the resolution or resolutions providing for the issue of such stock adopted by the board of directors pursuant to authority expressly vested in it by the provisions of its certificate of incorporation.

When a stock corporation is created, it will issue at least one class of common stock. Indeed, many corporations have only one class of common stock. Common stock has two key attributes. "The articles of incorporation must authorize: (1) one or more classes or series of shares that together have unlimited voting rights, and (2) one or more classes or series of shares (which may be the same class or classes as those with voting rights) that together are entitled to receive the net assets of the corporation upon dissolution." MBCA § 6.01(b). Common stockholders enjoy indirect, albeit sometimes abstract, control of governance through the right to vote for the board of directors and certain fundamental transactions such as some kinds of mergers and acquisitions transactions (these rights are discussed in greater detail in Chapter 15). In a liquidation, they have the right to remaining residual assets after payment of all liabilities and preferred rights of preferred stockholders.

This combination of voting rights and a residual claim on profits and assets creates a governance structure that provides shareholders with a strong incentive to ensure that the corporation is operated efficiently. If shareholders elect competent directors and monitor their performance effectively, they will realize the benefits of those directors' sound business decisions. Their stake in the net profits and residual assets of the corporation will increase. If shareholders elect incompetent directors or fail to monitor their performance effectively, they will bear the loss.

Because common shareholders have the most incentive to maximize the value of the firm, they are the primary beneficiaries of the fiduciary duties that corporate law imposes on the board of directors. As we will see, courts defer to a considerable degree to directors' business judgments, but they do so on the assumption that directors have acted in good faith and in the corporation's best interests. This deference extends to director decisions concerning whether a corporation should retain profits to reinvest profits (as opposed to distributing them to shareholders). In addition, directors have a duty to refrain from engaging in transactions that will provide them unfair personal benefits at the corporation's expense. In short, directors have broad discretion to manage, but must bear in mind that they are managing other people's money and that they have obligations to do so carefully and loyally.

When a corporation is formed, the articles of incorporation will create *authorized* shares. A change in the authorized shares requires an amendment of the articles. Until shares are first sold to stockholders, they are *authorized but unissued*. When sold, they are *authorized and issued* or *authorized and outstanding* (or simply "outstanding shares"). If they are repurchased by the corporation, they become *authorized and issued, but not outstanding*. Under the terminology of Delaware corporation law, shares repurchased by the company are called *treasury stock*.

Because authorized shares limit the number of shares that a corporation can issue, public companies at least have large number of authorized shares (in absolute terms). For example, as of December 31, 2015, Bank of America had 12,800,000,000 authorized shares, of which 10,380,265,063 were issued and outstanding. The number of authorized shares must permit a broad shareholder base that is the hallmark of public ownership. It must also permit a board of directors to raise future equity financing by selling additional shares to the public. For public companies, the convenience and flexibility of a large number of authorized shares is apparent.

Private corporations may have a different set of considerations. For example, shareholders may want to tightly regulate future equity issuances along with the potential for the addition of new shareholders. To further this end, a private corporation may authorize a limited number of shares, which would limit a board of director's ability to issue shares to a prospective shareholders that the current shareholders may not desire. To issue more shares in the future, the corporation would need a shareholder vote to amend the articles to increase the number of authorized shares. This vote requirement can protect minority shareholders and preserve existing control relationships. However, such a limitation can also create problems. In particular, it might enable one or more shareholders to prevent the company from raising needed additional capital by blocking the vote to authorize additional shares.

Clearly, the number of shares held by a shareholder is less important than the *percentage* of shares held. For example, assume that a shareholders hold 1 million shares. If a corporation has issued 1 million shares, the shareholder owns 100% of the equity. She has total control of the voting for the board of directors, and thus direct control of the corporation. However, if the corporation has issued 1 billion shares, the shareholder's 1 million shares constitute 0.1% of outstanding shares (equivalent to 1 in 1,000), a minute fraction and no de facto control or influence at all.

As we have seen, corporation law permits multiple classes of common stock. Some corporations have two or more classes of stock with different voting rights, effectively giving one of the classes disproportionate control over the board. For example, assume that a corporation has 100 shares of Class A stock with 1 vote per share and 25 shares of Class B stock with 4 votes per share. Assume that the other rights of the two classes are the same. The holders of A and B stock would each have 50% of the vote, even though B stockholders have only a 20% economic stake in the corporation (= 25 B shares ÷ 125 total shares). Another practice is to give each class the right to elect a specified number of directors. Several prominent companies like Berkshire Hathaway, Ford Motor, Google, and Facebook have multiple classes of stock with different voting rights.

A second type of equity security is *preferred stock*. Larger public companies often use preferred stock as part of their capital structures; preferred stock is universally used in venture capital financing; and it is sometimes used in structuring small businesses. However, although all corporations must issue common stock, the majority do not issue preferred.

As the name suggests, a preferred stock has certain contractually stated preferences over common stock. The two most common preferences are dividend and liquidation preferences. Preferred stock also often has special voting rights, particularly when used in venture financing. The contractual rights of preferred stockholders are found in the articles of incorporation or amendments thereto.

Dividend priority means that dividends to preferred stockholders must be paid first before common stockholders can be paid dividends. Most commonly, preferred stock will state a fixed dividend, for example 8% of the original issuance price of the stock. However, some preferred stock have a more complex formula. The dividend can be tied to some floating (variable) financial index. As the index changes, the dividend rate changes as well. Preferred stock may also bear a "participating dividend," meaning that after the holders receive their dividend priority payment, they "participate" in any dividends paid on the common stock. Because payments to preferred stockholders are dividends, and not interest payments on debt, they are paid out of net income or the equity account on the balance sheet, and unlike interest payments, they are not deductible by the corporation for tax purposes.

Dividends on preferred stock can be *cumulative* or *noncumulative*. If cumulative dividends are not paid when due, the right to receive that dividend accumulates, and all accrued dividend arrearages must be paid before any dividends can be paid on common stock. If preferred stock is noncumulative, any dividend not paid is foregone and does not accumulate as an owed arrearage.

Liquidation priority means that in a liquidation, the preferred stockholder is paid a contractually stated liquidation price ahead of any payment to common stockholders. However, as is the case with common stock, the preferred stock's equity of redemption is subordinate to the claims of creditors. Consequently, when a corporation does not have assets sufficient to pay its debts, the preferred stockholders receive nothing in the event of liquidation.

Preferred stock sometimes represents a permanent commitment of capital to a corporation and sometimes does not. The latter occurs when there is a right to require the redemption of preferred stock if and when specified events should occur. The right to require redemption may be held by the stockholder, by the corporation, or by both. The amount for which stock is to be redeemed generally is equal to the preference to which it is entitled in the event of liquidation, although it is not uncommon to provide that, when stock can be redeemed by the corporation, some premium above that amount must be paid.

Preferred stock can have voting rights, and will be deemed to have voting rights equal to those of common stock unless the articles of incorporation provide otherwise. But the voting rights of preferred stock often are limited to specified issues and circumstances. Preferred stock often is given the right to elect some or all of a corporation's directors if dividends owed on such stock are not paid for some designated period. Such provisions reflect the nature of the contract between holders of preferred stock and the corporation: the holders relinquish their right to participate in control in exchange for a priority claim to periodic dividends, but if the corporation fails to pay those dividends, holders of preferred stock then become entitled to exert control.

The standard features of preferred stock described above may be supplemented by a variety of others, including the right to convert preferred stock into common stock at some specified ratio. Such "convertible preferred stock" are commonly used in venture capital investments in which venture capitalists take the priority position by holding preferred stock, but have the upside participation rights of common stock through the conversion right. The right to convert is essentially contractual in nature and must be spelled out in the articles of incorporation. Moreover, because preferred stock is stock and thus equity, their holders benefit from the fiduciary duties of the board and management. However, most courts, influenced by the adage that "no man can serve two masters," have taken the position that the only protections to which holders of preferred are entitled are those found in the preferred stock contract (the articles of incorporation). Thus, conflicts between preferred and common stockholders are resolved in favor of common stockholders when the contract is silent on the issue.

Preferred stock is sometimes characterized as a "hybrid" instrument, having characteristics of debt and equity. The fixed dividend on preferred stock resembles the fixed interest rate on debt instruments. The holders of preferred stock, like creditors, have priority over common stockholders, though their rights are subordinate to holders of debt. On the other hand, preferred stock is like equity in that dividends on preferred are declared and paid at the option of the board of directors, unlike interest on debt, which must be paid or the corporation is in default. Also like common stock, preferred stock often carries voting rights, though the voting right may be more limited than that of common stockholders.

Corporations often sell preferred stock in lieu of debt. The two have obvious similarities. The price at which a company can sell preferred stock is influenced by factors similar to those that determine the price at which it can borrow—the dividend rate, the redemption features, whether the preferred can be converted into common stock and, if so, at what price. Consequently, the requirement that the terms of preferred stock be spelled out in the articles of incorporation can pose real timing problems, especially in the case of a public company. It usually takes a minimum of 30 days to obtain shareholder approval of an amendment to the articles of incorporation authorizing new preferred stock. By the end of that period, market conditions are likely to have changed enough so that whatever terms were specified at the beginning of the period no longer must be modified.

Most corporation statutes address this timing problem by permitting shareholders to authorize *blank check preferred stock*, the essential characteristics of which—rights to dividends, liquidation preferences, redemption rights, voting rights, and conversion rights—can be set by the board of directors at the time the stock is sold. Such an authorization may facilitate the sale of preferred stock, but it also enhances substantially the power of a corporation's board of directors by allowing it to issue preferred stock with rights that may impinge materially on those of common stock without first obtaining explicit shareholder approval. For example, many corporate boards use blank check preferred stock as part of "poison pill" rights plans, because the issuance does not require shareholder approval.

2. DEBT SECURITIES

Debt securities represent liabilities of a corporation. There is a wide array of debt instruments, the terms of which are defined by contract. Debt can be categorized into different levels of seniority, which determine priority rights in terms of payment of principal during a liquidation. Debt can be junior, mezzanine, and senior. Debt can also be categorized into durations (short, medium, and long term). Short-term instruments are payable in a year or less and include bank loans provided by a single bank or a syndicate of banks. They also include commercial paper: short-term notes with a maturity of no more nine months, which are exempt from registration under federal securities laws. Medium-term instruments include notes sold to investors or longer duration bank loans. Long-term instruments can be called notes, debentures, or bonds. Some are secured by a mortgage on corporate assets. Others are unsecured and backed only by the general credit of the corporation. Whether they are formally denominated notes, debentures or bonds, all long-term debt instruments are often loosely referred to as "bonds," even though their terms can vary significantly.

The terms of a bond usually are fixed by a complex contract known as an *indenture* that specifies the rights and obligations of the bondholders and the corporation and is administered by an indenture trustee. Even if an indenture is not used, there are certain fundamental terms that are set forth in every debt contract. For example, the debt contract obliges the corporate borrower to repay a fixed amount of principal on a particular date. The contract typically requires that *interest* be paid at periodic intervals. The interest might be fixed throughout the term of the contract or based on a floating rate that varies over time. The interest obligation does not depend on whether the corporation earned a profit. If the corporation fails to pay interest on a bond when interest is due, it will be deemed in default. Typically, an event of default will cause the entire principal amount of the bond to become due immediately, and this "acceleration" entitles the bondholders to pursue all legal remedies for which they have bargained, including the right to initiate bankruptcy proceedings.

Like convertible preferred stock, debt can also have the right to convert to common stock. The conversion right must be found in the debt contract. The formula for the conversation is set forth in the contract. Bonds may also be redeemable or "callable" at a fixed price at the option of the borrower. This right can be valuable to a corporation; if interest rates decline, it can borrow the money needed to repay outstanding high-interest bonds at a lower interest rate and then use it to finance a redemption of those high-interest bonds. The debt contract will specify a redemption price, which is usually more than the principal amount of the debt.

Because the terms and conditions of debt securities are fixed entirely by contract and often are the result of extensive negotiations, many other provisions may be included in a debt contract. For example, the contract may include provisions, known as *covenants*, requiring the borrower to perform certain obligations, such as making available annual audited financial statements. *Negative covenants* require the borrower to refrain from taking certain actions that might jeopardize the position of the bondholders, such issuing new debt, selling assets outside the ordinary course, or making distributions to shareholders unless certain financial conditions are met.

Bonds generally do not carry the right to vote.[2] Because the relationship between the corporation and the bondholders is fundamentally contractual, directors are not considered to be fiduciaries for the bondholders. The interest of creditors are generally protected only to the extent that they have negotiated appropriate protections in the debt contracts.

Unless the articles of incorporation provide otherwise, a corporation's board of directors has the authority to issue debt securities without shareholder approval. The board decides whether the corporation should incur new debt, in what amount, and on what terms and conditions. The board must involve shareholders only if it decides to issue bonds that will be convertible into stock and the corporation does not have enough stock authorized to satisfy the bonds' conversion rights. In such a case, the board must seek shareholder approval of an amendment to the articles of incorporation increasing the number of authorized shares. However, shareholders are not asked or required to approve issuance of the convertible debt securities.

The use of long-term debt as part of a corporation's capital structure creates a tension between debt and equity investors. Both have stakes in the long term health of the corporation and both benefit if the corporation accumulates funds in excess of the amount it needs for current operations. But holders of debt and equity have agreed to different trade-offs between risk and reward, and each thus has a different perspective on the degree of risk that a corporation should assume. A creditor prefers a risk-reward corporate strategy that maximizes the probability that the issuer can pay the creditor's principal and interest, which may mean lower return for lower risk taken. A shareholder prefers a risk-reward corporate strategy that maximizes the firm's wealth, which may mean higher return for higher risk taken.

Unless she has bargained for a right to convert her debt into stock, a bondholder has accepted rights to fixed payments of interest and repayment of her capital in lieu of the possibly higher, but uncertain, returns available to holders of equity securities, especially common stock. The holder of common stock has assumed more risk, but also can exercise more control over the conduct of the corporation's business. A debtholder is viewed as an outsider entitled only to the protection specified in her contract. In contrast, the holder of common stock is protected by directors' fiduciary obligations, including their obligation to deal with other holders

---

[2] *See* MBCA § 7.21(a) ("Only shares are entitled to vote."). *But see* DGCL § 221 ("Every corporation may in its certificate of incorporation confer upon the holders of any bonds, debentures or other obligations issued or to be issued by the corporation the power to vote . . . .").

of corporate securities in whatever fashion advances the interests of the common stockholders.

3. OPTIONS

In addition to debt and equity, companies often issue options, which are the right to buy stock, typically common stock, at a specified time and price. In addition, investors in publicly-traded stocks often create options by contracting with other investors, although these options do not constitute part of a corporation's capital structure and do not appear on its financial statements. Options are one form of broad class of financial instruments called derivatives. Derivatives are instruments that derive their value from some other thing. In the case of options, the some other thing is the asset price that is the subject of options. Options can be complicated, but lawyers have no choice but to understand them. Corporate lawyers in particular frequently deal with options, in part because most publicly traded companies and many private companies award stock options as compensation to managers and employees. Business litigators also encounter options in various contexts.

A *call option* is the right, but not the obligation, to buy a specified asset (such as the company's stock) at a fixed price. A *put option* is the right, but not the obligation, to sell a specified asset at a fixed price. The option price is called its *exercise price* or *strike price*. Options issued by corporations may usually be exercised at any time before some fixed date. Exchange-traded options created by investors may usually be exercised only on a particular date. The specified asset can be anything, such as the stock of a company, bonds, commodities such as orange juice or gold, or any other asset that is capable of identification, specification, and delivery.

Consider a simple, but common, use of call options. A corporation's current stock price is $10 per share. In addition to her salary and other compensation, the corporation issues to its CEO an option to purchase 100,000 shares of stock,[3] with a strike (or exercise) price of $15 per share exercisable at any time up to ten years. The idea of the option is that it gives the CEO an incentive to work hard to increase the share price. If, after some time, the company's stock price has increased to $25 per share. The CEO can purchase from the company 100,000 shares of common stock, paying only the $15 per share exercise price, thus making a profit of $10 per share or $1 million. Of course, if the stock price never goes above $15 per share, the options will expire worthless (and the CEO may be out of a job depending on how poorly the stock has performed over the past five years of her tenure).

---

[3] Colloquially such an option is sometimes referred to as "100,000 options" to purchase a single share, even though the option document itself is usually written as single option to purchase 100,000 shares, exercisable in whole or in part.

Another important aspect of a call option is that there is no theoretical limit on potential profit of the option holder. For example, if the stock price increased from $10 to $115, the option would be "in-the-money" by $100. This would make her payday on the option profit $10 million (= $100 profit × 100,000 options).

Corporations sometimes issue *warrants*, simply another form of call option, in connection with capital-raising transactions. For example, in order to induce investors to purchase bonds, corporations sometimes issue warrants to purchase stock at a future time at an exercise price that is usually above the current market price. If the stock price increases above the exercise price, the investment return of a purchaser of the bond will be improved by the amount of profit it makes on exercise of the warrant.

A put option is the right to sell an asset. (For obvious reasons, corporations do not issue put options on their stock; such options are created only by contracts among investors.) The holder of a put option profits if the asset price declines in value. For example, assume that the current stock price is $10 per share, and the strike price on the put option is $8 per share. The holder is betting that the stock price will decline below the strike price. If the stock goes down to $5 per share, she can sell the stock to the issuer of the put option for a fixed price of $8 per share even though the trading price is $5 per share. In theory, the option holder could "settle" the option by buying stock in the market for $5 and selling it at $8 to the issuer of the put option. In practice, exchange traded options are usually settled by a cash payment between the writer of the option and its holder.

Options, can be used to hedge other positions or to speculate on the markets, but any further discussion of them is beyond the scope of this book.

Problem: Precision Tools—Part 9

Michael Lane, Jessica Bacon, and Bernie Gould have agreed to organize and incorporate Precision Tools Corporation as a Columbia corporation and to have Precision Tools pay $3 million to acquire all of the assets, tangible and intangible, of Precision Tools, Inc. and assume all of the liabilities listed on the company's balance sheet. In addition to financing the purchase of the business by Precision Tools, Michael, Jessica and Bernie want to provide Precision Tools with an additional $300,000 to finance an expansion of the business. Thus, they need to raise a total of $3,300,000.

Michael and Jessica each are prepared to commit $300,000 to Precision Tools. Jessica can provide that amount in cash, but Michael cannot raise more than $150,000. However, he is willing to sign a note obligating him to pay Precision Tools the additional $150,000. In exchange for their investments, Michael and Jessica each expect to receive 40% of Precision Tools' common stock.

Bernie will invest $900,000 in cash in Precision Tools. In exchange for $150,000 of his investment, he will receive 20% of Precision Tools' common stock. Bernie is prepared to use the remaining $750,000 either to purchase preferred stock or to make a long-term loan to Precision Tools. Whatever the form of that investment, Bernie wants to be assured that he will receive at least $75,000 in income from Precision Tools every year before any payments (other than salary) are made to Michael and Jessica and that, if Precision Tools is liquidated, the $750,000 will be repaid before any payments are made with respect to Precision Tools' common stock.

In addition to the $1,350,000 of cash that Michael, Jessica, and Bernie will invest, Precision Tools has arranged to borrow $800,000 from Columbia National Bank. Precision Tools has agreed to repay that principal amount in four annual installments of $200,000 each, the first of which will be due in five years, and to pay interest at 10% percent per annum on the unpaid principal. The bank will not have any right to participate in the management of Precision Tools or any right to receive payments other than those just described. However, the bank has required Precision Tools and Bernie to agree that, whatever form Bernie's $750,000 investment takes, Bernie's funds will remain committed to Precision Tools until the bank's loan has been repaid in full and, in the event Precision Tools is liquidated, Bernie's claims will be subordinated to those of the bank.

Even with the $800,000 loan from the bank, Michael, Jessica, and Bernie would be $1,150,000 short of the total they need. However, Stern and Starr, who are eager to retire, have agreed to cover this shortfall by accepting a note for $1,150,000 of the $3 million purchase price. The note will require Precision Tools to make annual interest payments of $115,000 (equal to 10% of the face value of the note) and to repay the principal of $1,150,000 to Stern and Starr in 10 years. If Precision Tools fails to make any interest payment when due, the entire $1,150,000 in principal will become due immediately. Stern and Starr will not have any right to participate in the management of Precision Tools or any right to receive payments other than those just described.

What are the interests of each of these the parties with regard to (1) participating in the management of Precision Tools, (2) receiving current income with respect to their investments, and (3) recovering the capital they are committing to Precision Tools?

How does the form of the parties' proposed investments advance and protect their interests?

How does it allocate risk-bearing among the parties?

Would it be better for Bernie to receive preferred stock or a debt security in exchange for the $750,000 of his proposed investment that will not be allocated to common stock?

What business and legal risks does the choice entail for Precision Tools and the three investors?

If Bernie elects to purchase preferred stock, how should the terms of that stock be structured to protect Bernie's interest in receiving income of $75,000 a year with respect to this portion of his investment?

B. CORPORATE CAPITAL STRUCTURE

The term "capital structure" describes how a company has raised funds using corporate securities. Some corporations have an all equity capital structure consisting only of common stock. Other corporations have large amounts of debt. Some corporations have complicated capital structures, with numerous slices of debt and equity, each of which has different claims on the corporation.

Investing is a voluntary act. People with funds to invest will buy a security only if they perceive it to be more attractive than other available investments. Consequently, a corporation cannot simply select a capital structure and impose it on potential investors. They must design a capital structure for the firm in general, and specify the terms of the securities it will issue so that investors find the rights embodied in those securities sufficiently attractive to justify investing in them. The choice of capital structure—the mix of debt and equity—is an economic and financial decision. Economic theory states that there is an optimal capital structure. There are a number of considerations that a financial manager takes into account when determining how to finance the corporation. The following discussion considers only the most basic aspects of what is a very complicated subject.

There are two basic considerations: tax benefit and leverage or its converse, insolvency risk. As discussed in the previous chapter, a corporation enjoys a tax benefit from issuing debt. The government subsidizes the use of debt by permitting corporations to deduct interest expense paid on debt before taxes are assessed. Thus, debt increases the value of the firm because the firm benefits from the interest tax shield.

For example, assume that an investor takes a 10% ownership stake in the total capital of each of Firms A and B.

- Firm A: 100% equity-financed with $20,000 in equity

- Firm B: 50/50 financed by $10,000 of debt and $10,000 of equity

Assume that the cost of debt is 10%, which is the interest payment. The two firms are otherwise identical: making and selling the same widgets, and generating the same revenues, operating costs, and thus operating income. In a world *without taxes*, the investor's returns on the 10% ownership stakes in Firm A and Firm B are identical.

	Firm A	Firm B
Capital		
Equity	20,000	10,000
Debt at 10%	0	10,000
Operating income	3,000	3,000
Interest payment	0	(1,000)
Net income	3,000	2,000
Investor's 10% of equity	300	200
Investor's 10% of debt	0	100
Total return to investor	300	300

However, as Benjamin Franklin noted many years ago, "in this world nothing can be said to be certain, except death and taxes." Let's assume a tax rate to be 30%. The debt service of 1,000 is deducted from operating income because of the interest tax shield.

	Firm A	Firm B
Capital		
Equity	20,000	10,000
Debt at 10%	0	10,000
Operating income	3,000	3,000
Interest payment	0	(1,000)
Pretax profit	3,000	2,000
Tax payment at 30%	(900)	(600)
Net income	2,100	1,400
Investor's 10% of equity	210	140
Investor's 10% of debt	0	10
Total return to investor	210	240

Tax matters. A 10% investor in Firm A has 10% of the after-tax net income of $2,100, which is $210. A 10% owner of Firm B has 10% of the interest payment of $1,000 and 10% of the after-tax net income of $1,400, which combined is $240. The difference of $3 is explained by the fact that Firm B benefited from paying $300 less in taxes than Firm A, and the $30 represents the investor's 10% claim on this benefit.

Debt also creates "leverage" in that it increases the profits of the equityholders when a company is profitable and increases the losses when it is not. Consider the example of the two companies above. If the operating income of both is $3,000, the equity holders in A, who have invested $20,000 in equity, receive a return on equity of 10.5% ($2,100 ÷ $20,000). The equityholders in B, who have invested only $10,000 in equity, receive a higher rate of return on equity of 14% (=$1,400 ÷ $10,000). But suppose that times are bad, and the operating income of the two companies is only $1,000. Now the picture looks like this:

when times are bad

	Firm A	Firm B
Capital		
Equity	20,000	10,000
Debt at 10%	0	10,000
Operating income	1,000	1,000
Interest payment	0	(1,000)
Pretax profit	1,000	0
Tax payment at 30%	300	0
Net income	700	0

The holders of equity in Firm A see a 3.5% ($700 ÷ $20,000) return on their investment, but the holders of equity in the leveraged firm B have 0% return on their investment. Thus, borrowing to create leverage is a two-edged sword for stockholders, increasing their returns in profitable times, and decreasing them in lean times.

A capital structure of 50% equity and 50% debt like the one in the example is not unusual for a mature, profitable company. But the greater the proportion of debt, the greater the leverage and the greater are the risks to equityholders if the company is not doing well. Imagine a highly-leveraged firm that is capitalized with $9,000 of debt and $1,000 of equity; the cost of debt is 10%; and the firm has operating profit of $950. The firm must pay $900 in interest every year, leaving only a $50 margin of error. If the firm generates less than $900 in operating profit it will eventually be unable to pay the interest on the debt and will find itself in default. When that happens, the holder of the debt will have the right to demand immediate payment of the $9,000 principal amount, probably forcing the company into bankruptcy.

For most mature companies, some amount of debt is desirable both for tax reasons and because leverage increases the return to equityholders. The optimal capital structure considers the optimal point between the benefit of debt and the cost of bankruptcy. As debt increases, the value of the firm increase to the optimal point, and then the cost of bankruptcy begins to overtake the benefit. The firm value declines, and at some point it dips below the value of a firm that has been wholly financed by equity.

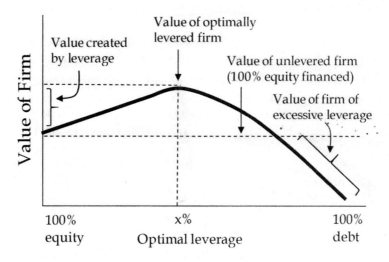

C. LEGAL CAPITAL

As we have seen, a creditor's claims against a corporation's income and assets have priority over the claims of shareholders. This priority is valuable. It is the reason why, generally, creditors expect and accept lower returns than shareholders. The creditor's best protection is the credit contract it negotiates with the corporation and thus falls in the realm of contract law. *See* American Bar Foundation, Commentaries on Indentures, at 2 (1971) ("Short of bankruptcy, the debt security holder can do nothing to protect himself against actions of the borrower which jeopardize its ability to pay the debt unless he ... establishes his rights through contractual provisions set forth in the debt agreement or indenture."). Not all creditors are in a position to negotiate the kind of protective covenants typical of a bond or a bank loan, however. Vendors that sell goods and services to corporations on credit (the usual practice in business) typically just rely on their customer's creditworthiness. Corporation law has long attempted to afford some protection to these creditors against opportunistic behavior by the corporation and its shareholders: in particular the possibility that shareholders would take large amounts of money out of the corporation by dividends or otherwise and leave the company unable to pay its debts. The least effective and most anachronistic of these protections is the regulation of legal capital. Although modern developments have rendered the concept of legal capital meaningless as a practical matter, it survives as a relic of the past, and it still can create mischief for those who do not understand it.

Legal capital rules dates back to the rise of the early corporations. During the 19th century and much of the 20th century, protecting creditors was a major preoccupation of corporation law. By the 1970s, if not earlier, it became clear that the legal capital rules no longer protected creditors and probably never had. Stimulated by the revision of the legal capital provisions of the MBCA, many state abandoned the concept of legal capital. But in some states, including Delaware, traditional legal capital rules remain in force, though ineffective in protecting creditors.

As the name connotes, legal capital is a legal concept of the corporation's equity capital structure and the value of capital. The basic idea is this: corporation law requires the corporation to hold a minimum level of equity capital that the board of directors assigns as a fixed stock value. This statutory minimum value is called the "par value" or "stated value." The aggregate of the par value of shares issued forms the legal capital that affixes a minimum stock value and establishes a minimum level of the corporation's equity capital. For example, the corporation's stock has a par value of $10 per share and it issues 10,000 shares: the legal capital is $100,000 (= par value × shares issued).

In an earlier era, a statutorily fixed share value was thought to protect against "watered stock," which occurs when the issuing corporation sells stock for a consideration that is less than what earlier stockholders paid. This was thought to be an improper transfer of value from existing shareholders, who paid "legitimate" consideration, to new shareholders whose interest is diluted. Because legal capital purported to affix a statutory value to stock, the concept of legal capital eventually was seen to protect creditors as well. The corporation must hold a minimum level of equity capital, and it cannot distribute this capital to shareholders. Thus, the legal capital rule purportedly protected creditors from shareholder opportunism by keeping a minimum level of equity in the corporation. This assumption here is, of course, that stock value must be maintained or rise, but can never fall.

The idea that the law can affix value to stock is too simplistic. The basic problem is that underlying economics and market prices determine the value of stock—not the board's fiat. Stock value can indeed decline in the market. In other words, the board of directors cannot control the value of a stock by simply saying so in the form of a par value in the charter. Although a corporation may originally sell stock for its par value, the value of the stock thereafter will be determined by the market; and obviously, the trading market is not bound by any fiat price.

To see the problem created by these realities, consider a situation where the corporation sets the par value of $100 per share and sells it at that price. The par value, it is wrongly believed, "protects" the initial shareholders and also sets a minimum amount of equity to protect creditors. However, assume that the corporation does not prosper, and the market price of the stock drops to $50 per share. The market has set the price. The corporation now seeks to raise new equity, perhaps because it is not doing so well and needs new equity capital. The legal capital rules dictate that it must sell them at the par value of $100, even though the stock trades at $50. Why would any new potential investor buy overpriced shares? The corporation will be unable to raise needed equity.

Legal capital rules still exists in some jurisdictions, including Delaware, but they are a functionless legal relic. The pragmatic circumvention around the ineffective concept of legal capital came in the form of the board's authority to determine the amount of "par value" or "stated capital." A board cannot issue shares for *less* than par value, but no rule precludes a board from issuing shares for *more* than par value. Corporations can, therefore, issue stock with a very low par value, known as "low-par stock." This protects against the possibility that the price of future issuances of stock—which will be determined by economic factors—would ever be below the par value. Another means of avoiding the pitfalls of par value is to issue without a par value, or "no-par stock," which Delaware and other states that have preserved the par value concept, also permit.

The original prophylactic intent of legal capital (never really meaningful in the first place) has been nullified. In jurisdictions that have maintained the vestige of the rules in their statutes, like Delaware, well-advised corporations avoid its pitfalls by issuing no par stock or setting an arbitrarily low par value. A common par value is $0.01, and some corporations set par at a fraction of a penny.

The ineffectiveness of legal capital is seen in the accounting treatment of an equity issuance. The aggregate par value of issued shares is noted as "stock," or "capital," or "common stock" in a separate line item on the equity side of the balance sheet. The amount in excess of the par value is noted as "additional paid in capital" or "paid in capital" (*i.e.*, capital contributed in excess of par value). For example, assume that the par value is $0.001 (one-tenth of a penny) and the corporation issues 100 million shares for $10 per share. The total proceeds from the stock issue is $1 billion ($10 per share × 100 million shares). A tiny fraction of the total proceed is designated as capital ($100,000 legal capital = $0.001 par value × 100 million shares). This amount is added to a line item labeled in the equity portion of the balance sheet typically labeled as "common stock" or "stock" or "capital." The remaining $999,900,000 is credited to a separate line in the equity portion as "additional paid in capital" or "paid in capital."

Consider this example from the 2015 Form 10–K of Facebook, Inc., a Delaware corporation. The social media company reported the following items of the balance sheet as of December 31, 2015 (all amounts in $ millions): assets $49,407, liabilities $5,189, and equity $44,218. The components of the equity account were the following items.

Common stock[4]	—
Additional paid-in-capital	34,886
Retained earnings	9,787
Other equity items	(455)
Total shareholders' equity	44,218

Facebook has dual class stock, Class A and Class B. The two classes differ on voting rights, but otherwise have the same par value. It issued 2,293,000,000 Class A shares and 552,000,000 Class B share, both with $0.000001 par value. The total shares outstanding of Class A and B are 2,845,000,000. "Common stock," reported as "—", indicates no value that can be recorded as a round up to the $ million scale. The actual legal capital is $2,845, which is calculated as:

$$\$2,845 = 2,845,000,000 \text{ shares} \times \$0.000001 \text{ par value}$$

Compare $2,845 to the additional paid-in-capital of $34,886,000,000, which is the excess of par value paid by Facebook shareholders. One wonders whether the $2,845 in legal capital serve any serious protection to creditors in light of the size of the balance sheet.

Because the legal capital rule is so obviously ineffective in protecting creditors (and current shareholders as well), creditors have shown no interest in the concept of legal capital. *See* Bayless Manning & James J. Hanks, Jr., Legal Capital 95 (4th ed. 2013). They have not argued for stricter rules or for the inclusion of the concept into the laws of newer business entities such as the limited liability company. They understand that their ability to contract for their rights, such as covenants and liens, constitutes the most important protection mechanism. For example, in the case of Facebook, creditors can see that the company has assets of $49,407 million and most of this was financed by equity ($44,218 million). However,

---

[4] The precise information for "common stock" as stated in the balance sheet, including authorized and outstanding shares, is this: "Common stock, $0.000006 par value; 5,000 million Class A shares authorized, 2,293 million [in 2015] and 2,234 million [in 2014] shares issued and outstanding, including 8 million and 13 million outstanding shares subject to repurchase, as of December 31, 2015 and December 31, 2014, respectively; 4,141 million Class B shares authorized, 552 million [in 2015] and 563 million [in 2014] shares issued and outstanding, including 3 million and 6 million outstanding shares subject to repurchase, as of December 31, 2015 and December 31, 2014, respectively."

if Facebook was highly levered, this fact would also be factored into their negotiations with Facebook for the provision of credit.

In the face of economic and legal reality, MBCA § 6.21 eliminated the "traditional (but arbitrary)" concept of setting par value and stated capital. Instead, the statute requires the board to determine the adequacy of the consideration for stock, and that determination is conclusive insofar as the adequacy of consideration relates to whether the shares are fully paid and thus nonassessable. The commentary states: "Practitioners and legal scholars have long recognized that the statutory structure embodying 'par value and 'legal capital' concepts is not only complex and confusing but also fails to serve the original purpose of protecting creditors and senior security holders from payments to junior security holders." MBCA § 6.21, official comment (Dec. 2010).

The MBCA also abandons traditional restrictions on the quality of consideration. Section 6.21 permits sale of stock for future services or promissory notes. Again, the statutory scheme relies on the board's judgment that the values exist. Section 6.21(c) makes clear that shares are fully paid and non-assessable after the corporation has received the bargained-for consideration. The Official Comment notes that whether shares are validly issued depends solely on whether proper corporate procedures have been followed.

D. LIMITATION ON DISTRIBUTIONS

Corporations can make distributions to shareholders in the form of cash dividends or distribution of other assets such as interests in other firms owned by the corporation. They can use their assets to repurchase some of their outstanding stock, which will have exactly the same economic impact to creditors as a decision to distribute those assets as a dividend. In both instances of dividend or repurchase of shares, the assets used will no longer be available to satisfy creditors' claims. Consequently, statutes generally classify both dividends and payments made to repurchase stock as "distributions" and impose essentially the same restrictions on both.

Excessive distributions can harm creditors by reducing the assets available to pay them what they are due when it is due. Consequently, shareholders and creditors have conflicting interests with regard to the size and frequency of distributions to shareholders. Because directors generally are elected by holders of common stock, the danger exists that they will favor these shareholders' interests, to the prejudice of creditors, if their power to authorize distributions is unrestricted. To deal with this danger, corporate law traditionally has sought to protect creditors' interests with regard to distributions. Recognizing that the interests of preferred stockholders also can be jeopardized by overly-generous distributions to holders of common stock, corporate law also has sought to protect their interests.

1. STATUTORY LIMITATIONS ON DISTRIBUTIONS

One approach to statutory limitations on distributions to shareholders is seen in Delaware, which still depends on the concept of legal capital. In the following case, *Klang v. Smith's Food & Drug Centers, Inc.*, the corporation repurchased its shares even though the balance sheet showed a negative equity value, which means that net assets were negative. The issue in the case is whether, in light of the negative book value, the corporation can make a distribution. In reading this case, these Delaware statute provisions are relevant.

DGCL § 170.   Dividends;   payment;   wasting   asset corporations.

(a) The directors of every corporation, subject to any restrictions contained in its certificate of incorporation, may declare and pay dividends upon the shares of its capital stock either:

    (1) Out of its surplus, as defined in and computed in accordance with §§ 154 and 244 of this title; or

    (2) In case there shall be no such surplus, out of its net profits for the fiscal year in which the dividend is declared and/or the preceding fiscal year.

DGCL § 160.   Corporation's   powers   respecting ownership, voting, etc., of its own stock; rights of stock called for redemption.

(a) Every corporation may purchase, redeem, receive, take or otherwise acquire, own and hold, sell, lend, exchange, transfer or otherwise dispose of, pledge, use and otherwise deal in and with its own shares; provided, however, that no corporation shall:

    (1) Purchase or redeem its own shares of capital stock for cash or other property when the capital of the corporation is impaired or when such purchase or redemption would cause any impairment of the capital of the corporation. . . .

DGCL § 154. Determination of amount of capital; capital, surplus and net assets defined.

Any corporation may, by resolution of its board of directors, determine that only a part of the consideration which shall be received by the corporation for any of the shares of its capital stock which it shall issue from time to time shall be capital; but, in case any of the shares issued shall be shares having a par value, the amount of the part of such consideration so determined to be capital shall be in excess of the aggregate par value of the shares issued for such consideration having a par value, unless all the shares issued shall be shares having a par value, in which case the amount of the part of such consideration so determined to be capital need be only equal to the aggregate par value of such shares. . . . The excess, if any, at any given time, of the net assets of the corporation over the amount so determined to be capital shall be surplus. Net assets means the amount by which total assets exceed total liabilities.

In reading this case, think about these questions: (1) How can there be surplus under the Delaware statute when the book value of the company was negative? (2) What concept of value did the court adopt?

KLANG v. SMITH'S FOOD & DRUG CENTERS, INC.
702 A.2d 150 (Del.1997).

VEASEY, CHIEF JUSTICE:

Smith's Food & Drug Centers, Inc. ("SFD") is a Delaware corporation that owns and operates a chain of supermarkets in the Southwestern United States. Slightly more than three years ago, Jeffrey P. Smith, SFD's Chief Executive Officer, began to entertain suitors with an interest in acquiring SFD.

On January 29, 1996, SFD entered into an agreement with The Yucaipa Companies ("Yucaipa"), a California partnership also active in the supermarket industry. Under the agreement, the following would take place:

(1)   Smitty's Supermarkets, Inc. ("Smitty's"), a wholly-owned subsidiary of Yucaipa that operated a supermarket chain in Arizona, was to merge into Cactus Acquisition, Inc. ("Cactus"), a subsidiary of SFD, in exchange for which SFD would deliver to Yucaipa slightly over 3 million newly-issued shares of SFD common stock; [and]

(2)   SFD was to undertake a recapitalization, in the course of which SFD would assume a sizable amount of new debt, retire old

debt, and offer to repurchase up to fifty percent of its outstanding shares (other than those issued to Yucaipa) for $36 per share.

SFD hired the investment firm of Houlihan Lokey Howard & Zukin ("Houlihan") to examine the transactions and render a solvency opinion. Houlihan eventually issued a report to the SFD Board replete with assurances that the transactions would not endanger SFD's solvency, and would not impair SFD's capital in violation of 8 *Del.C.* § 160. On May 17, 1996, in reliance on the Houlihan opinion, SFD's Board determined that there existed sufficient surplus to consummate the transactions, and enacted a resolution proclaiming as much. On May 23, 1996, SFD's stockholders voted to approve the transactions, which closed on that day. The self-tender offer was over-subscribed, so SFD repurchased fully fifty percent of its shares at the offering price of $36 per share.

[A corporation may not repurchase its shares if, in so doing, it would cause an impairment of capital, unless expressly authorized] by Section 160.[4] A repurchase impairs capital if the funds used in the repurchase exceed the amount of the corporation's "surplus," defined by 8 *Del.C.* § 154 to mean the excess of net assets over the par value of the corporation's issued stock.

Plaintiff asked the Court of Chancery to rescind the transactions in question as violative of Section 160.

In an April 25, 1996 proxy statement, the SFD Board released a pro forma balance sheet showing that the merger and self-tender offer would result in a deficit to surplus on SFD's books of more than $100 million. A balance sheet the SFD Board issued shortly after the transactions confirmed this result. Plaintiff asks us to adopt an interpretation of 8 *Del.C.* § 160 whereby balance-sheet net worth is controlling for purposes of determining compliance with the statute. Defendants do not dispute that SFD's books showed a negative net worth in the wake of its transactions with Yucaipa, but argue that corporations should have the presumptive right to revalue assets and liabilities to comply with Section 160.

Plaintiff advances an erroneous interpretation of Section 160. We understand that the books of a corporation do not necessarily reflect the current values of its assets and liabilities. Among other factors, unrealized appreciation or depreciation can render book numbers inaccurate. It is unrealistic to hold that a corporation is bound by its balance sheets for purposes of determining compliance with Section 160. Accordingly, we adhere to the principles of *Morris v. Standard Gas & Electric Co.*, 63 A.2d 577 (Del.Ch.1949), allowing corporations to revalue properly its assets and liabilities to show a surplus and thus conform to the statute.

---

[4] The provisions of Section 160 permitting a corporation to purchase its shares out of capital are not implicated in this case.

It is helpful to recall the purpose behind Section 160. The General Assembly enacted the statute to prevent boards from draining corporations of assets to the detriment of creditors and the long-term health of the corporation. That a corporation has not yet realized or reflected on its balance sheet the appreciation of assets is irrelevant to this concern. Regardless of what a balance sheet that has not been updated may show, an actual, though unrealized, appreciation reflects real economic value that the corporation may borrow against or that creditors may claim or levy upon. Allowing corporations to revalue assets and liabilities to reflect current realities complies with the statute and serves well the policies behind this statute.

Plaintiff contends that SFD's repurchase of shares violated Section 160 even without regard to the corporation's balance sheets. Plaintiff claims that the SFD Board was not entitled to rely on the solvency opinion of Houlihan, which showed that the transactions would not impair SFD's capital given a revaluation of corporate assets.

On May 17, 1996, Houlihan released its solvency opinion to the SFD Board, expressing its judgment that the merger and self-tender offer would not impair SFD's capital. Houlihan reached this conclusion by comparing SFD's "Total Invested Capital" of $1.8 billion—a figure Houlihan arrived at by valuing SFD's assets under the "market multiple" approach—with SFD's long-term debt of $1.46 billion. This comparison yielded an approximation of SFD's "concluded equity value" equal to $346 million, a figure clearly in excess of the outstanding par value of SFD's stock. Thus, Houlihan concluded, the transactions would not violate 8 *Del.C.* § 160.

Plaintiff contends that Houlihan's analysis relied on inappropriate methods to mask a violation of Section 160. Noting that 8 *Del.C.* § 154 defines "net assets" as "the amount by which total assets exceeds total liabilities," plaintiff argues that Houlihan's analysis is erroneous as a matter of law because of its failure to calculate "total assets" and "total liabilities" as separate variables.

We believe that plaintiff reads too much into Section 154. The statute simply defines "net assets" in the course of defining "surplus." It does not mandate a "facts and figures balancing of assets and liabilities" to determine by what amount, if any, total assets exceeds total liabilities. The statute is merely definitional. It does not require any particular method of calculating surplus, but simply prescribes factors that any such calculation must include. Although courts may not determine compliance with Section 160 except by methods that fully take into account the assets and liabilities of the corporation, [Houlihan's methods were not erroneous as a matter of law simply because they used Total Invested Capital and long-term debt as analytical categories rather than "total assets" and "total liabilities."]

We are satisfied that the Houlihan opinion adequately took into account all of SFD's assets and liabilities. The record contains, in the form of the Houlihan opinion, substantial evidence that the transactions complied with Section 160. Plaintiff has provided no reason to distrust Houlihan's analysis. In cases alleging impairment of capital under Section 160, the trial court may defer to the board's measurement of surplus unless a plaintiff can show that the directors failed to fulfill their duty to evaluate the assets on the basis of acceptable data and by standards which they are entitled to believe reasonably reflect present values. In the absence of bad faith or fraud on the part of the board, courts will not substitute our concepts of wisdom for that of the directors. Here, plaintiff does not argue that the SFD Board acted in bad faith. Nor has he met his burden of showing that the methods and data that underlay the board's analysis are unreliable or that its determination of surplus is so far off the mark as to constitute actual or constructive fraud. Therefore, we defer to the board's determination of surplus, and hold that SFD's self-tender offer did not violate 8 *Del.C.* § 160.

The MBCA abandons restrictions based on legal capital and employs a more functional approach to regulating distributions, using two tests to determine whether a distribution is possible:

MBCA § 6.40(c)

No distribution may be made if, after giving it effect:

(1) the corporation would not be able to pay its debts as they become due in the usual course of business; or

(2) the corporation's total assets would be less than the sum of its total liabilities plus (unless the articles of incorporation permit otherwise) the amount that would be needed, if the corporation were to be dissolved at the time of the distribution, to satisfy the preferential rights upon dissolution of shareholders whose preferential rights are superior to those receiving the distribution.

The Official Comment to § 6.40 characterizes the first of these tests as the "equity insolvency test" and the second as the "balance sheet test." Both tests require the exercise of judgment by a corporation's board of directors. If directors judge incorrectly, they face personal liability, but this danger is mitigated by the statement in the Official Comment that decisions concerning distributions should to be evaluated on the same basis as any other exercise of business judgment.

In applying the equity insolvency test, directors usually can assume that the company will continue as a going concern. The Official Comment suggests several benchmarks directors may wish to consider, but no bright line tests. Where solvency appears to be a matter of concern, directors may find it helpful to analyze a company's liquidity and cash flows, using both reports on the results of operations and any forecasts or budgets management has prepared.

The balance sheet test can be based on (1) specified financial statements or (2) fair valuation or other reasonable methods. The MBCA does not mandate the use of financial statements prepared in accordance with GAAP but the Official Comment notes that "directors should in all circumstances be entitled to rely" on such financial statements.

Since statutes that relied on concepts of legal capital provided little protection to creditors, the approach of MBCA § 6.40 seems more sensible; however it furnishes little meaningful protection to creditors. Directors cannot render the corporation insolvent by approving a distribution, but the MBCA does not preclude them from going to the edge. No cushion is required. By contrast, Calif. Corp. Code § 500 requires that a corporation's liquid and hard assets (total assets less certain intangibles) after a distribution equal at least 125% of liabilities and that directors employ GAAP in making this computation. One explanation for the different approaches is that the drafters of the MBCA appear to have decided that corporate law is not the vehicle through which creditors should be protected. They can rely on contract, or on fraudulent conveyance law, such as the Uniform Fraudulent Conveyance Act. A similar attitude is reflected in other aspects of corporate law, which provides that managers' fiduciary duties run only to shareholders, allow only shareholders to bring derivative actions and rarely allow creditors to "pierce the corporate veil" and reach the assets of shareholders of insolvent corporations.

If a corporation does make a distribution that violates statutory restrictions, it jeopardizes the interests of creditors. Corporation law creates a remedy for any actual losses creditors sustain, by making the directors who authorized the unlawful distribution personally liable to them. A director held liable for an unlawful distribution in turn has an action for contribution against shareholders who received a distribution knowing that it was improper. While shareholders of a Delaware corporation can exculpate directors from liability for many breaches of the duty of due care, they cannot provide such exculpation for unlawful distributions.

In addition to the restriction of DGLC § 160, Delaware common law also has a prohibition against insolvency-inducing distributions to shareholders that is similar to MBCA § 6.40(c). In *SV Inv. Partners, LLC v. ThoughtWorks, Inc.*, 7 A.3d 973 (Del.Ch. 2010), the Delaware chancery court noted:

> Delaware follows these principles. Since at least 1914, this Court has recognized that, *in addition* to the strictures of Section 160, "[t]he undoubted weight of authority" teaches that a

"corporation cannot purchase its own shares of stock when the purchase diminishes the ability of the company to pay its debts, or lessens the security of its creditors." In *Farland v. Wills,* 1975 WL 1960 (Del.Ch. 1975), this Court enjoined payments by a corporation to its sole stockholder, including a repurchase of stock. The Court held that it was not necessary "to conclude preliminarily that there was an actual impairment of capital" under Section 160 of the DGCL. Rather, the Court enjoined the repurchase on the legal principle that "[a] corporation should not be able to become a purchaser of its own stock when it results in a fraud upon the rights of or injury to the creditors."

A corporation may be insolvent under Delaware law either when its liabilities exceed its assets, or when it is unable to pay its debts as they come due. Although a corporation cannot be balance-sheet insolvent and meet the requirements of Section 160, a corporation can nominally have surplus from which redemptions theoretically could be made and yet be unable to pay its debts as they come due.

2. LIMITATION ON THE BOARD'S DISCRETION

The statutory limitations on distributions to shareholders involve circumstances where creditors are affected. The corporation is in some sort of financially precarious situation when, arguably, the distribution is said to impair capital under the Delaware framework or makes the corporation functionally insolvent under the MBCA framework. When a corporation is not in this financial vicinity, the decision to make a distribution is within the discretion of the board of directors. It is a business decision that is driven by financial and business considerations. Accordingly, courts give substantial deference to decisions on distributions.

––––––––––

The case below states the basic rule that the decision on dividends is subject to the business judgement rule. The case presents a classic statement of the business judgment rule. In reading this case, think about these questions: (1) Was the board decision substantively wrong as a matter of proper financial management? (2) Does it matter that the board was right or wrong on the substance of the business decision?

KAMIN V. AMERICAN EXPRESS CO.

383 N.Y.S.2d 807 (Sup.Ct. 1976).

GREENFIELD, JUSTICE:

The individual defendants, who are the directors of the American Express Company, move for an order dismissing the complaint for failure to state a cause of action, and alternatively, for summary judgment.

The complaint is brought derivatively by two minority stockholders of the American Express Company, asking for a declaration that a certain dividend in kind is a waste of corporate assets, directing the defendants not to proceed with the distribution, or, in the alternative, for monetary damages. The motion to dismiss the complaint requires the Court to presuppose the truth of the allegations.

The complaint alleges that in 1972 American Express acquired for investment 1,954,418 shares of common stock of Donaldson, Lufkin and Jenrette, Inc. (DLJ), a publicly traded corporation, at a cost of $29.9 million. It is further alleged that the current market value of those shares is approximately $4.0 million. On July 28, 1975, the Board of Directors of American Express declared a special dividend to all stockholders of record pursuant to which the shares of DLJ would be distributed in kind. Plaintiffs contend further that if American Express were to sell the DLJ shares on the market, it would sustain a capital loss of $25 million, which could be offset against taxable capital gains on other investments. Such a sale, they allege, would result in tax savings to the company of approximately $8 million, which would not be available in the case of the distribution of DLJ shares to stockholders.

The crucial allegation alleges: "All of the defendant Directors engaged in or acquiesced in or negligently permitted the declaration and payment of the Dividend in violation of the fiduciary duty owed by them to Amex to care for and preserve Amex's assets in the same manner as a man of average prudence would care for his own property."

There is no claim of fraud or self-dealing, and no contention that there was any bad faith or oppressive conduct. The law is quite clear as to what is necessary to ground a claim for actionable wrongdoing. "In actions by stockholders, which assail the acts of their directors or trustees, courts will not interfere unless the powers have been illegally or unconscientiously executed; or unless it be made to appear that the acts were fraudulent or collusive, and destructive of the rights of the stockholders. Mere errors of judgment are not sufficient as grounds for equity interference, for the powers of those entrusted with corporate management are largely discretionary."

The question of whether or not a dividend is to be declared or a distribution of some kind should be made is exclusively a matter of business judgment for the Board of Directors. "Courts will not interfere with such discretion unless it be first made to appear that the directors have acted or are about to act in bad faith and for a dishonest purpose. It is for the directors to say, acting in good faith of course, when and to what extent dividends shall be declared * * * The statute confers upon the directors this power, and the minority stockholders are not in a position to question this right, so long as the directors are acting in good faith * * * "

A complaint must be dismissed if all that is presented is a decision to pay dividends rather than pursuing some other course of conduct. A complaint which alleges merely that some course of action other than that pursued by the Board of Directors would have been more advantageous gives rise to no cognizable cause of action. Courts have more than enough to do in adjudicating legal rights and devising remedies for wrongs. The directors' room rather than the courtroom is the appropriate forum for thrashing out purely business questions which will have an impact on profits, market prices, competitive situations, or tax advantages.

It is not enough to allege, as plaintiffs do here, that the directors made an imprudent decision, which did not capitalize on the possibility of using a potential capital loss to offset capital gains. More than imprudence or mistaken judgment must be shown. "Questions of policy of management, expediency of contracts or action, adequacy of consideration, lawful appropriation of corporate funds to advance corporate interests, are left solely to their honest and unselfish decision, for their powers therein are without limitation and free from restraint, and the exercise of them for the common and general interests of the corporation may not be questioned, although the results show that what they did was unwise or inexpedient."

The objections raised by the plaintiffs to the proposed dividend action were carefully considered and unanimously rejected by the Board at a special meeting called precisely for that purpose at the plaintiffs' request. The minutes of the special meeting indicate that the defendants were fully aware that a sale rather than a distribution of the DLJ shares might result in the realization of a substantial income tax saving. Nevertheless, they concluded that there were countervailing considerations primarily with respect to the adverse effect such a sale, realizing a loss of $25 million, would have on the net income figures in the American Express financial statement. Such a reduction of net income would have a serious effect on the market value of the publicly traded American Express stock. This was not a situation in which the defendant directors totally overlooked facts called to their attention. They gave them consideration, and attempted to view the total picture in arriving at their decision. While plaintiffs contend that according to their accounting consultants the loss on the DLJ stock would still have to be charged against current earnings even if the stock were distributed, the defendants' accounting experts assert that the loss would be a charge against earnings only in the event of a sale, whereas in the event of distribution of the stock as a dividend, the proper accounting treatment would be to charge the loss only against surplus.

What we have here as revealed both by the complaint and by the affidavits and exhibits, is that a disagreement exists between two minority stockholders and a unanimous Board of Directors as to the best way to handle a loss already incurred on an investment. The directors are entitled to exercise their honest business judgment on the information before them, and to act within their corporate powers. That they may be mistaken, that other courses of action might have differing consequences, or that their action might benefit some shareholders more than others presents no basis for the superimposition of judicial judgment, so long as it appears that the directors have been acting in good faith. The question of to what extent a dividend shall be declared and the manner in which it shall be paid is ordinarily subject only to the qualification that the dividend be paid out of surplus. The Court will not interfere unless a clear case is made out of fraud, oppression, arbitrary action, or breach of trust. The plaintiffs have failed as a matter of law to make out an actionable claim.

The discretion given to the board under the business judgment rule is substantial. In the context of a public corporation, if a shareholder seeks dividend but the corporation does not pay them (many public corporations do not pay dividends), she can exit the investment and invest the money in companies that pay dividends. However, a shareholder in a private corporation, and particularly a close corporation, may be locked into the investment because the shares are not liquid (freely tradable in an existing market). The board's decision on dividends are consequential.

A shareholder in a close corporation often is well advised to enter into an agreement requiring that the corporation pay dividends under appropriately defined circumstances. She generally cannot easily sell her stock, and if she is not employed by the company and receives no dividends (whether labeled as such or disguised as salary or bonus payments), she receives no meaningful economic return from her investment. Courts have become sensitive to such situations, and tend to uphold agreements relating to the payment of dividends and otherwise extend protections to minority shareholders who have been denied such a return.

Shareholders face an uphill battle when they bring an action to compel the board of directors to declare a dividend. Most attempts by shareholders to compel boards of directors to declare dividends have involved closely-held companies. *Gottfried v. Gottfried*, 73 N.Y.S.2d 692 (Sup.Ct. 1947), is typical. The plaintiff-shareholders alleged that (1) there was bitter animosity between the directors (who were the majority shareholders) and the plaintiffs (the minority shareholders); (2) the majority shareholders sought to coerce the minority shareholders to sell their stock to them at a grossly inadequate price; (3) the majority shareholders wanted to avoid heavy personal income taxes on any dividends that might be declared; (4) the majority shareholders, who were on the corporation's payroll, paid themselves excessive salaries and bonuses and borrowed money from the corporation; and (5) the nonpayment of dividends was designed to compel the minority shareholders, who were not on the corporation's payroll, to sell their stock to the majority shareholders.

Although the court expressed sympathy for the minority shareholders, who had been discharged from the corporate payroll, it did not find that the hostility and dissension among shareholders provided a sufficient basis on which to conclude that the refusal to pay dividends was due to the directors' "bad faith." According to the court "The essential test of bad faith is to determine whether the policy of the directors is dictated by their personal interests rather than corporate welfare. Directors are fiduciaries. Their [beneficiaries] are the corporation and the stockholders as a body. Circumstances appraised in the light of the financial condition and requirements of the corporation, will determine the conclusion as to whether the directors have or have not been animated by personal, as distinct from corporate considerations."

The court found that bonuses and corporate loans to the majority shareholders were a long-standing company practice. In addition, the remuneration to one defendant could not be considered excessive because he had played an important role in the "tremendous expansion" of the company's subsidiary, Hanscom Baking Corporation, between 1933 and 1946. In dismissing the complaint and directing judgment for the defendants, the court concluded:

> The testimony discloses that many general considerations affected the policy of the Board of Directors in connection with dividend payments. Some of the major factors were as follows: The recognition that earnings during the war years might be abnormal and not representative of normal earning capacity; the pressing need for heavy expenditures for new equipment and machinery, replacement of which had been impossible during the war years; heavy expenditures required to finance the acquisition and equipment of new Hanscom stores in harmony with the steady growth of the business; the increased initial cost of opening new stores because, under present conditions, it has become difficult to lease appropriate sites necessitating actual acquisition by ownership of locations; the erection of a new bakery for Hanscom at a cost of approximately $1,000,000 inasmuch as the existing plant is incapable of producing the requirements of Hanscom sales which are running at the rate of approximately $6,000,000 per annum; unstable labor conditions with actual and threatened strikes; several pending actions involving large sums of money

under the Federal Fair Labor Standards Act; a general policy of financing expansion through earnings requiring long-term debt.

The plaintiffs oppose many of these policies of expansion. There is no evidence of any weight to the effect that these policies of the Board of Directors are actuated by any motives other than their best business judgment. If they are mistaken, their own stock holdings will suffer proportionately to those of the plaintiffs. With the wisdom of that policy the court has no concern. It is this court's conclusion that these policies and the expenditures which they entail are undertaken in good faith and without relation to any conspiracy, scheme and plan to withhold dividends for the purpose of compelling the plaintiffs to sell their stock or pursuant to any other sinister design.

73 N.Y.S.2d at 700–01.

The case below one of those rare cases in which a court found that the board of directors acted in bad faith by withholding dividends from minority shareholders. The factual background of this famous action is set forth in Chapter 4, as is the portion of the court's decision refusing to enjoin Ford's plans to expand production and lower the price of its cars, even though demand at current prices exceeded Ford's production capacity. The following portion of the opinion deals with the Dodge brothers' request, which the trial court granted, for an order compelling Ford to pay a special dividend of $19 million—an amount equal to one-half of Ford's cash surplus—in addition to the $1.2 million regular dividend Ford had declared.

DODGE v. FORD MOTOR CO.
170 N.W. 668 (Mich. 1919).

[T]he case for plaintiffs must rest upon the claim that in any event the withholding of the special dividend asked for by plaintiffs is arbitrary action of the directors requiring judicial interference.

The rule which will govern courts in deciding these questions is not in dispute.

In Cook on Corporations (7th Ed.) 545, it is expressed as follows:

The board of directors declare the dividends, and it is for the directors, and not the stockholders, to determine whether or not a dividend shall be declared.

When, therefore, the directors have exercised this discretion and refused to declare a dividend, there will be no interference by the courts with their decision, unless they are guilty of a willful abuse of their discretionary powers, or of bad faith or of a neglect of duty. It requires a very strong case to induce a court of equity to order the directors to declare a dividend, inasmuch as equity has no jurisdiction, unless fraud or a breach of trust is involved. There have been many attempts to sustain such a suit, yet, although the courts do not disclaim jurisdiction, they have quite uniformly refused to interfere. The discretion of the directors will not be interfered with by the courts, unless there has been bad faith, willful neglect, or abuse of discretion.

Accordingly, the directors may, in the fair exercise of their discretion, invest profits to extend and develop the business, and a reasonable use of the profits to provide additional facilities for the business cannot be objected to or enjoined by the stockholders.

When plaintiffs made their complaint and demand for further dividends, The Ford Motor company had completed its most prosperous year of business [and had earned a profit of almost $60 million]. It had assets of more than $132,000,000, a surplus of almost $112,000,000, and its cash on hand and municipal bonds were nearly $54,000,000. Its total liabilities, including capital stock, was a little over $20,000,000. Considering only these facts, a refusal to declare and pay further dividends appears to be not an exercise in discretion on the part of the directors but an arbitrary refusal to do what the circumstances required to be done.

[The court reviewed Ford's plans to finance a major expansion of its business.]

Assuming the general plan and policy of expansion and the details of it were for the best ultimate interest of the company and therefore of its shareholders, what does it amount to in justification of a refusal to declare and pay a special dividend or dividends? The Ford Motor Company was able to estimate with nicety its income and profit. It could sell more cars than it could make. Having ascertained what it would cost to produce a car and to sell it, the profit upon each car depended upon the selling price. That being fixed, the yearly income and profit was determinable, and, within slight variations, was certain.

There was appropriated—voted—for the smelter $11,325,000. Assuming that the plans required an expenditure sooner or later of $9,895,000 for duplication of the plant, and for land and other expenditures $3,000,000, the total is $24,220,000. The company was continuing business, at a profit—a cash business. If the total cost of proposed expenditures had been immediately withdrawn in cash from the cash surplus (money and bonds) on hand August 1, 1916, there would have remained nearly $30,000,000.

Defendants say, and it is true, that a considerable cash balance must be at all times carried by such a concern. But, as has been stated, there was a large daily, weekly, monthly, receipt of cash. The output was practically continuous and was continuously, and within a few days, turned into cash. Moreover, the contemplated expenditures were not to be immediately made. The large sum appropriated for the smelter plant was payable over a considerable period of time. So that, without going further, it would appear that, accepting and approving the plan of the directors, it was their duty to distribute on or near the 1st of August, 1916, a very large sum of money to stockholders.

The decree of the court below fixing and determining the specific amount to be distributed to stockholders is affirmed. In other respects, the said decree is reversed.

CHAPTER 11

FORMING THE ENTITY

■ ■ ■

A. ADVISING THE ENTITY

If organizing a business entity simply involved complying with the statutory requirements, there might be no reason for a lawyer's involvement. Unfortunately, life is not that simple. Although a partnership or an LLC can be created without a written agreement among the partners or members, such an entity is highly unlikely to address adequately the preferences of the founders. Nor, if a corporation is the appropriate form, would a simple corporation created with the minimal required charter and a set of bylaws taken out of a form book. As we have seen, all business entity statutes leave the organizers of a business entity relatively free to engage in a complex system of private ordering designed to deal with fundamental issues of structure, governance, finance, control, and the allocation of profit and risk.

In the representation of a new business enterprise involving more than one individual, the first question that the lawyer must answer before accepting the representation is "who is the client." The question is important because the lawyer has specific duties to clients that she does not have to non-clients. At first glance, determining the client would not seem to be a difficult task. An attorney-client relationship is either formed explicitly by a formal contractual agreement or implicitly by the client requesting, and the attorney performing, legal services for the client. Restatement (Third) The Law Governing Lawyers § 14. In practice, however, where there are multiple parties to a transaction, as with Precision Tools, it is not always easy to determine whether each of the parties is a client; whether the entity is (or will be) a client; and whether the lawyer's prior representation of one of the parties will raise a conflict of interest in the current representation.

Keep in mind the practical consequences of determining the identity of the client. Once a lawyer-client relationship is established, the lawyer must "comply with obligations concerning the client's confidences and property, avoid impermissible conflicting interests, deal honestly with the client, and not employ advantages arising from the client-lawyer relationship in a manner adverse to the client." Restatement (Third) The Law Governing Lawyers § 16. Under Model Rule 1.4, a lawyer has the duty promptly to inform the client of any situation requiring the client's informed consent, to consult with the client about her objectives and how they will be accomplished, to keep the client reasonably informed and to promptly comply with the client's information requests. With limited exceptions not relevant to the incorporation process, Model Rule 1.6 forbids the lawyer to disclose information about a client without the client's informed consent. And Model Rule 1.7 requires a lawyer to get informed consent before representing one or more clients who may have a conflict of interest or to decline the representation altogether. Finally, only clients can assert the attorney-client privilege, seek disqualification of the attorney in litigation because of the attorney's conflict of interest, or sue for malpractice.

The potential for conflict is present whenever there is multiple representation. The potential is stronger when the enterprise is closely held and the same individuals will be owners, managers and employees, whose goals and interests may differ. This is particularly true when the individuals are making different contributions to the capital of the enterprise and possibly expecting to own different shares.

Multiple representation means that no party will have her own advocate in that process. At the outset, the actual or potential conflicts may be clearer to the lawyer than to the parties themselves, and once the conflicts have been identified, the parties may expect the lawyer to suggest the most desirable way of resolving them. The lawyer as planner may find it difficult to maintain a neutral role since every solution involves tradeoffs among the parties. How does the lawyer respond? To whom, if anyone, at this stage (before an entity even exists), does the lawyer owe her loyalty?

There are, of course, arguments in favor of multiple representation. Although they may have divergent interests, the parties start with a common goal, going into business together, and divergent interests do not always rise to the level of conflicts of interest. The parties are likely to want to minimize their organizational expenses before the business has begun, and the cost of each party retaining her own lawyer at this stage may seem excessive. Thus, Model Rule 1.7 of the American Bar Association Model Rules of Professional Conduct permits multiple representation, albeit with the informed consent of the parties after full disclosure of the consequences. There is also distinguished precedent. Justice Brandeis, when a private practitioner, sometimes became what he called "lawyer for the situation," representing what most of us would consider to be conflicting interests in a variety of transactions. Most of us, however, are not Justice Brandeis, and assuming the role of the lawyer for the situation may be difficult, attractive as that role might appear to be.

Problem: Precision Tools—Part 10

We return to the Precision Tools problem. Assume that Jessica, Michael and Bernie have come to you with a plan to acquire the business and assets of Precision Tools and need to create an entity to do so. You are a junior partner in a midsize law firm. You have represented Michael in past business dealings unrelated to Precision Tools, and he has suggested that the three of them come to see you to for legal assistance.

What ethical and legal concerns affect your decision to accept the representation?

If you do accept the representation, who will your client(s) be? Michael? Michael, Bernie and Jessica individually, or collectively? The entity that will be created?

If you do accept the representation, how much do you expect to charge for your work? Of what do you expect that work will consist? Assume that your hourly billing rate is $300.

As a result of your recent representation of Michael, you have learned that he and his wife are considering a divorce. Because he has significantly more earning power and fewer assets than she does, he is afraid that the financial settlement will require him to be responsible for child support and, conceivably, for spousal maintenance payments.

May you disclose this information to Jessica and Bernie? Must you? Would it make a difference if you had never represented Michael and discovered this information in a private conversation with him? How would you respond if he asked you specifically not to tell Jessica and Bernie about his marital situation?

1. AMERICAN BAR ASSOCIATION MODEL RULES OF PROFESSIONAL CONDUCT[1]

> **Rule 1.4   Communication**
>
> (a) A lawyer shall:
>
> (1) promptly inform the client of any decision or circumstance with respect to which the client's informed consent, as defined in Rule 1.0(e), is required by these Rules;
>
> (2) reasonably consult with the client about the means by which the client's objectives are to be accomplished;
>
> (3) keep the client reasonably informed about the status of the matter;
>
> (4) promptly comply with reasonable requests for information; and

> (5) consult with the client about any relevant limitation on the lawyer's conduct when the lawyer knows that the

---

[1]   State ethics rules often vary from the Model Rules and it is important that a lawyer consult the specific rules of her jurisdiction.

client expects assistance not permitted by the Rules of Professional Conduct or other law.

(b) A lawyer shall explain a matter to the extent reasonably necessary to permit the client to make informed decisions regarding the representation.

Rule 1.6   Confidentiality of Information

(a) A lawyer shall not reveal information relating to the representation of a client unless the client gives informed consent, the disclosure is impliedly authorized in order to carry out the representation or the disclosure is permitted by paragraph (b).

(b) A lawyer may reveal information relating to the representation of a client to the extent the lawyer reasonably believes necessary:

(1) to prevent reasonably certain death or substantial bodily harm;

(2) to prevent the client from committing a crime or fraud that is reasonably certain to result in substantial injury to the financial interests or property of another and in furtherance of which the client has used or is using the lawyer's services;

(3) to prevent, mitigate or rectify substantial injury to the financial interests or property of another that is reasonably certain to result or has resulted from the client's commission of a crime or fraud in furtherance of which the client has used the lawyer's services;

(4) to secure legal advice about the lawyer's compliance with these Rules;

(5) to establish a claim or defense on behalf of the lawyer in a controversy between the lawyer and the client, to establish a defense to a criminal charge or civil claim against the lawyer based upon conduct in which the client was involved, or to respond to allegations in any proceeding concerning the lawyer's representation of the client; or

(6) to comply with other law or a court order.

(7) [Omitted]

Rule 1.7   Conflict of Interest: Current Clients

(a)   Except as provided in paragraph (b), a lawyer shall not represent a client if the representation involves a concurrent conflict of interest. A concurrent conflict of interest exists if:

(1)   the representation of one client will be directly adverse to another client; or

(2)   there is a significant risk that the representation of one or more clients will be materially limited by the lawyer's responsibilities to another client, a former client or a third person or by a personal interest of the lawyer.

(b)   Notwithstanding the existence of a concurrent conflict of interest under paragraph (a), a lawyer may represent a client if:

(1)   the lawyer reasonably believes that the lawyer will be able to provide competent and diligent representation to each affected client;

(2)   the representation is not prohibited by law;

(3)   the representation does not involve the assertion of a claim by one client against another client represented by the lawyer in the same litigation or other proceeding before a tribunal; and

(4)   each affected client gives informed consent, confirmed in writing.

Rule 1.13   Organization as Client

(a)   A lawyer employed or retained by an organization represents the organization acting through its duly authorized constituents.

(b)   If a lawyer for an organization knows that an officer, employee or other person associated with the organization is engaged in action, intends to act or refuses to act in a matter related to the representation that is a violation of a legal obligation to the organization, or a violation of law that reasonably might be imputed to the organization, and that is likely to result in substantial injury to the organization, then the lawyer shall proceed as is reasonably necessary in the best interest of the organization. Unless the lawyer reasonably believes that it is not necessary in the best interest of the organization to do so, the lawyer shall refer the matter to higher authority in the organization, including, if warranted by the circumstances, to the highest authority that can act on behalf of the organization as determined by applicable law.

(c)   Except as provided in paragraph (d), if

(1) despite the lawyer's efforts in accordance with paragraph (b) the highest authority that can act on behalf of the organization insists upon or fails to address in a timely and appropriate manner an action or a refusal to act, that is clearly a violation of law, and

(2) the lawyer reasonably believes that the violation is reasonably certain to result in substantial injury to the organization, then the lawyer may reveal information relating to the representation whether or not Rule 1.6 permits such disclosure, but only if and to the extent the lawyer reasonably believes necessary to prevent substantial injury to the organization.

(d) Paragraph (c) shall not apply with respect to information relating to a lawyer's representation of an organization to investigate an alleged violation of law, or to defend the organization or an officer, employee or other constituent associated with the organization against a claim arising out of an alleged violation of law.

(e)   A lawyer who reasonably believes that he or she has been discharged because of the lawyer's actions taken pursuant to paragraphs (b) or (c), or who withdraws under circumstances that require or permit the lawyer to take action under either of those paragraphs, shall proceed as the lawyer reasonably believes necessary to assure that the organization's highest authority is informed of the lawyer's discharge or withdrawal.

(f)   In dealing with an organization's directors, officers, employees, members, shareholders or other constituents, a lawyer shall explain the identity of the client when the lawyer knows or reasonably should know that the organization's interests are adverse to those of the constituents with whom the lawyer is dealing.

(g) A lawyer representing an organization may also represent any of its directors, officers, employees, members, shareholders or other constituents, subject to the provisions of Rule 1.7. If the organization's consent to the dual representation is required by Rule 1.7, the consent shall be given by an appropriate official of the organization other than the individual who is to be represented, or by the shareholders.

2.   THE ENTITY THEORY OF REPRESENTATION

Many jurisdictions have adopted the "entity theory" as embodied in Model Rule 1.13. The heart of the theory is that the lawyer represents the entity, rather than its officers, directors, employees and owners (though, with informed consent, the lawyer may also represent them). The entity theory appears to adopt the paradigm of the publicly-held corporation: the corporation is an individual, standing apart from its constituents, and hence, any attorney hired to represent the corporation represents the corporation as a distinct legal entity and not its constituents.

JESSE BY REINECKE V. DANFORTH
485 N.W.2d 63 (Wisc. 1992).

[In 1985, Drs. Danforth and Ullrich were part of a group of twenty-three physicians who retained Douglas Flygt (Flygt), an attorney with the law firm of DeWitt, Porter, Huggett, Schumacher & Morgan, S.C. (DeWitt). The physicians asked DeWitt to assist them in creating a corporation for the purpose of purchasing and operating a magnetic resonance imaging machine (MRI). Flygt incorporated MRIGM in 1986 and continued to serve as its corporate counsel. The twenty-three physicians became the shareholders of MRIGM, and Dr. Danforth became president of the corporation.

In May 1988, the Jesse family sued Drs. Danforth and Ullrich for medical malpractice unrelated to the activities of MRIGM. The plaintiffs retained Eric Farnsworth, also an attorney with DeWitt. Farnsworth had conducted an internal conflict of interest check at DeWitt, but had not found the defendants listed as clients of the firm. Drs. Danforth and Ullrich moved to disqualify DeWitt, alleging that the firm had a conflict of interest. They argued that they were clients of DeWitt because of Flygt's pre-incorporation of the twenty-three physicians and because of other advice that Flygt had provided to the defendants.]

DAY, JUSTICE:

We begin with SCR 20:1.7, the conflict of interest rule [which parallels the 1983 Model Rule 1.7]. The question is, who did or does DeWitt represent, *i.e.,* who were and are DeWitt's clients?

It is undisputed that DeWitt, through Farnsworth, represents Jean Jesse in this case. What remains disputed is whether Drs. Danforth or Ullrich were ever or are currently clients of DeWitt.

The entity rule contemplates that where a lawyer represents a corporation, the client is the corporation, not the corporation's constituents.

The clear purpose of the entity rule was to enhance the corporate lawyer's ability to represent the best interests of the corporation without automatically having the additional and potentially conflicting burden of representing the corporation's constituents.

If a person who retains a lawyer for the purpose of organizing an entity is considered the client, however, then any subsequent representation of the corporate entity by the very lawyer who incorporated the entity would automatically result in dual representation. This automatic dual representation, however, is the very situation the entity rule was designed to protect corporate lawyers against.

We thus provide the following guideline: where (1) a person retains a lawyer for the purpose of organizing an entity and (2) the lawyer's involvement with that person is directly related to that incorporation and (3) such entity is eventually incorporated, the entity rule applies retroactively such that the lawyer's pre-incorporation involvement with the person is deemed to be representation of the entity, not the person.

In essence, the retroactive application of the entity rule simply gives the person who retained the lawyer the status of being a corporate constituent during the period before actual incorporation, as long as actual incorporation eventually occurred.

This standard also applies to privileged communications under SCR 20:1.6. Thus, where the above standard is met, communications between the retroactive constituent and the corporation are protected under SCR 20:1.6. And, it is the corporate entity, not the retroactive constituent, that holds the privilege. This tracks the Comment to SCR 20:1.13 which states in part: "When one of the constituents of an organizational client communicates with the organization's lawyer in that person's organizational capacity, the communication is protected by Rule 1.6."

However, where the person who retained the lawyer provides information to the lawyer not directly related to the purpose of organizing an entity, then it is the person, not the corporation which holds the privilege for that communication.

Applying the above standard to the case at hand, we observe that the evidence cited and quoted by the defendants demonstrates that the above standard is met and that DeWitt represented MRIGM, not Drs. Danforth or Ullrich.

For example, defendants Drs. Danforth and Ullrich point to Flygt's affidavit wherein Flygt states that he was contacted "*to assist a group of physicians in Milwaukee in organizing an entity to own and operate one or more facilities.*" (Emphasis added.)

Dr. Danforth points to a January 29, 1986 letter from Flygt to Dr. Danforth wherein Flygt stated:

I would suggest that the *corporation* come to a quick resolution of the subchapter S corporation question. (Emphasis added).

Drs. Danforth and Ullrich point to a May 5, 1986 letter from Flygt to Dr. Danforth which states that "to the extent that there are common expenses of the partnership, such as drafting documents, etc., *it would be appropriate to have the entity pay those fees while the attorneys fees of each individual group are its own cost.*" (Emphasis added).

[Drs.] Danforth and Ullrich point to a May 13, 1987 memorandum Flygt wrote to the "Shareholders" of MRIGM. This memorandum begins, "The purpose of this letter is to advise you as to a decision *which must be made by the corporation* at this time." (Emphasis added).

This evidence overwhelmingly supports the proposition that the purpose of Flygt's pre-incorporation involvement was to provide advice with respect to organizing an entity and that Flygt's involvement was directly related to the incorporation. Moreover, that MRIGM was eventually incorporated is undisputed.

In addition, with respect to Flygt's advice concerning the structure of the entity, the fact that a particular corporate structure may benefit the shareholders or the fact that there was communication between Flygt and the shareholders concerning such structuring does not mean that Drs. Danforth and Ullrich were the clients of the law firm. Again, the very purpose of the entity rule is to preclude such automatic dual representation.

Drs. Danforth and Ullrich also contend that they provided certain confidential information to attorney Flygt that should disqualify DeWitt under SCR 20:1.6, the confidential information rule. Defendants point to questionnaires Flygt provided to the physicians involved in the MRI project which inquire, in part, as to the physicians' personal finances and their involvement in pending litigation.

Because MRIGM, not the physician shareholders, was and is the client of DeWitt, and because the communications between Drs. Danforth and Ullrich were directly related to the purpose of organizing MRIGM, we conclude that Drs. Danforth or Ullrich cannot claim the privilege of confidentiality.

STATE BAR OF ARIZONA, OPINION NO. 02–06

(September 2002).

1.   Can a lawyer represent an entity that does not yet exist?

Yes, as long as the incorporators understand that they are retaining counsel on behalf of the yet-to-be-formed entity and will need to ratify this corporate action, *nunc pro tunc,* once the entity is formed. According to ER 1.13(a), a lawyer may represent an "organization." The Comments to the Rule explain that an "organizational client is a legal entity, but it cannot act except through its officers, directors, employees, shareholders and other constituents. . . . The duties defined in this comment apply equally to unincorporated associations."

Under this statute, a corporation does not exist as a separate legal entity until its articles of incorporation are filed with the Corporation Commission. Section 10–204 of the Arizona Revised Statutes further cautions that individuals who attempt to transact business as a corporation, knowing that no corporation exists, will be jointly liable for their actions. Presumably, however, a newly formed corporation may ratify pre-incorporation acts of the corporation, *nunc pro tunc.*

A decision from Wisconsin specifically holds that a lawyer hired to form an entity can represent the to-be-formed entity, not the incorporators, and the "entity" rule applies retroactively. *Jesse v. Danforth,* 485 N.W.2d 63 (Wis.1992). This view would be consistent with the "entity" theory of representation, under ER 1.13(a). The "entity" theory holds that a lawyer may represent the corporation and does not, necessarily, represent any of the constituents that act on behalf of the entity—even if it is a closely held corporation.

An alternative view is the "aggregate" theory in which the lawyer is found to represent the incorporators/constituents collectively as joint clients. *See Griva v. Davison,* 637 A.2d 830 (D.C.1994). Under the aggregate theory, a lawyer represents multiple co-clients during formation of the corporation and then once the entity is formed, the clients must determine whether the lawyer will continue to represent all of the constituents *and* the entity, or just the entity. Who a lawyer *may* represent depends upon whether the lawyer's independent professional judgment would be materially limited because of the lawyer's duties to another client or third person.

Thus, a lawyer may represent an entity during the formation process, as long as the constituents who are acting on behalf of the yet-to-be-formed entity understand and agree to the entity being the client.

2.   Can a lawyer represent *only* the yet-to-be-formed entity and not the constituents?

Who a lawyer represents depends upon the reasonable perceptions of those who have consulted with the lawyer. When two or more individuals consult with a lawyer about forming an entity, it is the responsibility of the lawyer at that initial meeting to clarify who the lawyer will represent. ER 1.13 provides that a lawyer may represent an entity and the Rule suggests that the lawyer will not automatically be considered counsel for the constituents.

[U]nless a lawyer *wants* to be counsel to all of the incorporators and the entity, the lawyer should specify that the lawyer does *not* represent the constituents collectively, the lawyer only represents the entity. If an engagement letter or oral representation by the lawyer suggests that the constituents are represented as an aggregate, then the lawyer will have ethical obligations to *each* constituent. Aggregate representation also is ethically proper if the disclosure to each client includes an explanation that the lawyer may have to withdraw from representing *each* client if a conflict arises *among* the clients.

3.   What disclosures should a lawyer make to the incorporating constituents to obtain their informed consent to the limited representation of the entity?

The underlying premise of the conflict Rules is loyalty to clients. Where a lawyer's independent professional judgment for a client is materially limited due to *anything or anyone,* a conflict may exist. Thus, in order to avoid inadvertent conflicts caused by misunderstandings of constituents in corporate representations, it is crucial for lawyers to specify exactly who they represent, who they do *not* represent, and how information conveyed to the lawyer by constituents of an entity client will be treated, for confidentiality purposes.

Therefore, it is crucial that a lawyer specify in the engagement agreement if the lawyer is not representing the constituents of an entity client.

Even if the engagement letter specifies that the constituents are not clients, lawyers still should regularly caution constituents that they are not clients—particularly when they consult with counsel. Lawyers who represent entities also must be aware of the *entity's* potential fiduciary duties to the constituents, so that the lawyer does not run afoul of those statutory or common law obligations. For instance, there are cases that have held that lawyers may have fiduciary duties to non-clients, depending upon whether the *entity* represented had fiduciary duties to the third parties.

With respect to confidentiality obligations, lawyers should specify how information conveyed to the lawyer will be treated for confidentiality purposes. If the firm is representing only the entity, constituents must be advised that their communications to the lawyer will be conveyed to the other decision-makers for the entity and are not confidential as to the entity. The information is confidential, however, according to Rule 1.6(a), to the "outside world." Similarly, information shared by one co-client that is necessary for the representation of the other joint clients will be shared with the other co-clients because there is no individual confidentiality when a joint representation exists.

Finally, if the lawyer has chosen to represent multiple clients, including the constituents and the entity, the lawyer should explain, at the beginning of the joint representation, that in the event that a conflict arises among the clients, the lawyer most likely will need to withdraw from representing *all* of the co-clients. However, some commentators, including the *Restatement Third,* note that the engagement agreement may provide that in the event of a conflict, the lawyer may withdraw from representing one of the co-clients and continue to represent the remaining clients.

3. THE AGGREGATE THEORY OF REPRESENTATION

The entity theory may not apply easily when the entity is in the process of being formed or the same people are likely to constitute all or a majority of the owners and managers (as in a close corporation). For example, *Jesse* leaves open the question of whether the entity theory applies retroactively when the pre-organization activities fail, and the entity never comes into existence. In this situation, who is (or has been) the client?

An alternative to the entity theory is the aggregate theory, which posits that instead of representing the shareholders individually, the lawyer represents all of the owners individually in addition to the entity. Unlike the entity theory, under the aggregate theory, a lawyer has no duty to keep information confidential among the owners if the information relates to the representation, nor does the attorney-client privilege obtain if there is litigation between the owners.

One case illustrating the use of the aggregate theory is *Opdyke v. Kent Liquor Mart,* 181 A.2d 579 (Del.Ch. 1962). In that case, one of three original shareholders asserted that the lawyer who incorporated the company breached his duty to the plaintiff by purchasing stock in the corporation from the other stockholders, a transaction adverse to the plaintiff, who had wanted to buy the stock himself. In holding that the lawyer had breached his duty to the plaintiff, the court acknowledged the entity theory, but stated:

> [I]n determining the existence or non-existence of the important relationship of attorney and client a broader approach is required. The question is, what in fact was the relationship between Brown [the attorney] and the three men?

It is clear to us that Brown was, at the beginning of the venture, and also at its end, the attorney for the three men. The corporation was simply a form for the carrying on of a joint venture. For our present purpose Brown must be regarded as the attorney for three joint adventurers. When they fell out he undertook to resolve their differences. He very properly told them that he could not represent any one of them against another. This was so, not because of the corporate form of the enterprise, but because of the well-settled rule that if a lawyer is retained by two clients and they get into a dispute he cannot ordinarily represent either. Indeed, Brown's justifiable insistence on this neutrality was a recognition, conscious or not, of his fiduciary duty to all three men. That he was acting in his capacity as a lawyer admits of no doubt. Why were they discussing the matter in his office if not to obtain his help and counsel in their difficulty? * * *

But by these very acts he had emphasized his role of counselor to the three men. In suggesting the settlement he was discharging a characteristic function of the legal adviser. He could not escape the fiduciary obligations of this relationship by insisting that he was acting only for a corporation.

181 A.2d at 583–84.

Some commentators have supported the aggregate theory on the grounds that reasons of economy and efficiency justify multiple representation in a close corporation. *See, e.g.,* Lawrence E. Mitchell, *Professional Responsibility and the Close Corporation: Toward a Realistic Ethic*, 74 Cornell L.Rev. 466 (1982). ("[B]ecause counsel's conduct will . . . directly affect each of these shareholders, it should be recognized that counsel owes a duty to each of them.")

4. THE REASONABLE EXPECTATIONS TEST

In determining who is the client when there is multiple representation, some courts have adopted the "reasonable expectations" test rather than trying to apply either the entity or the aggregate theory. Under this test, as set forth in *Westinghouse Elec. Corp. v. Kerr-McGee Corp.*, 580 F.2d 1311 (7th Cir.1978), if an attorney leads an individual or entity to believe that they are a client and the belief is reasonable under the circumstances, an attorney-client relationship will be created, whether or not the client enters into a formal retainer agreement.

The reasonable expectations test is most difficult to apply in disputes involving closely-held enterprises where the founders, owners, and managers (often the same people) may all expect that the lawyer also represents them in a personal capacity. There is surprisingly little case law determining whether that belief is reasonable and the relevant decisions lack analytic coherence. In *Rosman v. Shapiro*, 653 F.Supp. 1441

(S.D.N.Y.1987), the court applied the reasonable expectations test to disqualify counsel for a corporation in litigation between the corporation's two shareholders. The court noted that although corporate counsel does not usually also become counsel for the shareholders, "where, as here, the corporation is a close corporation consisting of only two shareholders with equal interests in the corporation, it is indeed reasonable for each shareholder to believe that the corporate counsel is in effect his own individual attorney." In so finding, the court relied upon evidence which established that Rosman and Shapiro jointly consulted the attorney for legal advice concerning the creation of a corporation through which they would conduct their business. Thus the court held that "it would exalt form over substance to conclude that [the attorneys] only represented [the company], solely because Rosman and Shapiro chose to deal through a corporate entity."

In its decision, *Rosman* appears to equate a corporation with a partnership. In dealing with the latter, some courts have found that a lawyer representing a partnership also "represents all the partners as to matters of partnership business" as joint clients. The same, presumably, would be true for the members of a member-managed LLC. If, as the court seems to do in *Rosman*, it determines that the entity functions as if it were a partnership, it may also decide that the attorney represents the entity's constituents rather than the entity itself. In *Hecht v. Superior Court (Ferguson)*, 237 Cal.Rptr. 528 (2d Dist. 1987), for example, the court noted that prior to incorporation, the parties had run the business for many years as if it were a partnership and had viewed each other as partners. In addition, they had formed the corporation not to change the nature of their working relationship, but for tax reasons. Indeed, as the court noted, the new corporation had been "formed as a statutory close corporation, which is akin to a partnership in its informality." Under those circumstances, it was reasonable for the plaintiff to believe that she was being represented by the "corporation's" attorney. The difficulty with this method of analysis, as we saw in the previous chapter, is that there are fundamental conceptual differences between the two forms of organization so that it is difficult to determine when a corporation should be treated as a corporation and when as a partnership.

The capacity in which the constituent acts when dealing with the entity's lawyer is another factor courts have considered in determining the existence of the attorney-client relationship. If the court determines that the constituent sought legal advice on personal affairs or that the attorney represented her in a personal matter, the court may be more likely to find that an attorney-client relationship exists. Likewise, the absence of such personal representation may indicate to the court that no attorney-client relationship exists. Often, in examining the nature of the relationship, the courts will look to any previous association between the possible client and the attorney in order to determine whether there was any past personal representation before the lawyer became counsel for the entity.

Courts seem divided on assigning significance to who paid the lawyer's fees. Some courts have held that the payment of the attorney's fees by the entity and not the potential client does not disprove the existence of the attorney-client relationship. Other courts have implied that the entity's payment is inconsistent with the conclusion that an attorney-client relationship exists between the lawyer and the individual. Still other courts have stated that the method of payment, while not dispositive of the existence of the attorney-client relationship, may be indicative of who the client is.

Even if no attorney-client relationship has been established between the constituents and the closely held entity's attorney, some courts have held that the attorney may have a fiduciary duty to each of the individual owners. Whether such a duty exists can be either a question of law or of fact. If such a fiduciary relationship is found to exist, the attorney could be responsible to a third party for a variety of duties, including negligence or fraud.

GEOFFREY C. HAZARD, JR.,
ETHICS IN THE PRACTICE OF LAW
(1978).

The problem of deciding who is the client arises when a lawyer supposes that a conflict of interest prevents him from acting for all the people involved in a situation. That is, if the interests of the potential clients were in harmony, or could be harmonized, no choice would have to be made between them and the lawyer could act for all. When the lawyer feels that he can act for all, it can be said simply that he has several clients at the same time. When the clients are all involved in a single transaction, however, the lawyer's responsibility is rather different from what it is when he represents several clients in transactions that have nothing to do with each other. This difference is suggested by the proposition that a lawyer serving more than one client in a single transaction represents "the situation."

The term is the invention of Louis D. Brandeis, Justice of the United States Supreme Court and before that practitioner of law in Boston. It emerged in a hearing in which Brandeis's professional ethics as a lawyer had been questioned.

If Brandeis was wrong, then "lawyering for the situation" is marginally illicit professional conduct because it violates the principle of unqualified loyalty to client. But if Brandeis was right, and the record of good practitioners testifies to that conclusion, then what is required is not interdiction of "lawyering for the situation" but reexamination of what is meant by loyalty to client. That is, loyalty to client, like loyalty to country, may take different forms.

It is not easy to say exactly what a "lawyer for the situation" does. Clearly, his functions vary with specific circumstances. But there are common threads. The beginning point is that no other lawyer is immediately involved. Hence, the lawyer is no one's partisan and, at least up to a point, everyone's confidant. He can be the only person who knows the whole situation. He is an analyst of the relationship between the clients, in that he undertakes to discern the needs, fears, and expectations of each and to discover the concordances among them. He is an interpreter, translating inarticulate or exaggerated claims and forewarnings into temperate and mutually intelligible terms of communication. He can contribute historical perspective, objectivity, and foresight into the parties' assessment of the situation. He can discourage escalation of conflict and recruitment of outside allies. He can articulate general principles and common custom as standards by which the parties can examine their respective claims. He is advocate, mediator, entrepreneur, and judge, all in one. He could be said to be playing God.

Playing God is a tricky business. It requires skill, nerve, detachment, compassion, ingenuity, and the capacity to sustain confidence. When mishandled, it generates the bitterness and recrimination that results when a deep trust has been betrayed. Perhaps above all, it requires good judgment as to when such intercession can be carried off without unfairly subordinating the interests of one of the parties or having later to abort the mission.

When a relationship between the clients is amenable to "situation" treatment, giving it that treatment is perhaps the best service a lawyer can render to anyone. It approximates the ideal forms of intercession suggested by the models of wise parent or village elder. It provides adjustment of difference upon a holistic view of the situation rather than bilaterally opposing ones. It rests on implicit principles of decision that express commonly shared ideals in behavior rather than strict legal right. The basis of decision is mutual assent and not external compulsion. The orientation in time tends to be a hopeful view of the future rather than an angry view of the past. It avoids the loss of personal autonomy that results when each side commits his cause to his own advocate. It is the opposite of "going to law."

One would think that the role of "lawyer for the situation" would have been idealized by the bar in parity with the roles of partisan advocate and confidential adviser. The fact that it has not been may itself be worth exploring.

It is clear that a "lawyer for the situation" has to identify clearly his role as such. But beyond saying that he will undertake to represent the best interests of all, a lawyer cannot say specifically what he will do or what each of the clients should do in the situation. (If the outcome of the situation were clearly foreseeable, presumably the lawyer's intercession would be unnecessary.) Moreover, he cannot define his role in the terms of the direction of his effort, for his effort will not be vectored outward toward third persons but will aim at an interaction among the clients. Hence, unlike advocacy or legal counseling involving a single client, lawyering for a situation is not provided with a structure of goals and constraints imposed from outside. The lawyer and the clients must create that structure for themselves, with the lawyer being an active participant. And like the other participants he cannot reveal all that is on his mind or all that he suspects the others may have on their minds, except as doing so aids movement of the situation along lines that seem productive.

A lawyer can proceed in this role only if the clients trust him and, equally important, he trusts himself. Trust is by definition ineffable. It is an acceptance of another's act without demanding that its bona fides be objectively provable; to demand its proof is to confess it does not exist. It is a relationship that is uncomfortable for the client but perhaps even more so for the lawyer. Experienced as he is with the meanness that people can display to each other, why should the lawyer not doubt his own susceptibility to the same failing? But trust is involved also in the role of confidential adviser and advocate. Why should lawyers regard their own trustworthiness as more vulnerable in those roles than in the role of "lawyer for the situation"?

Perhaps it is because the legal profession has succeeded in defining the roles of confidential adviser and advocate in ways that substantially reduce the burden of being trustworthy in these roles. The confidential adviser is told that he may not act to disclose anything about the client, except an announced intention to commit a crime. Short of this extremity, the rules of role have it that the counsellor has no choices to make between the interests of his client and the interest of others. His commitment is to the client alone. Correlatively, the advocate is told that he may assert any claim on behalf of a client except one based on fabricated evidence or one empty of any substance at all. Short of this extremity, the advocate also has no choices to make.

The "lawyer for the situation," on the other hand, has choices to make that obviously can go against the interests of one client or another, as the latter perceives it. A lawyer who assumes to act a intercessor has to evoke complete confidence that he will act justly in the circumstances. This is to perform the role of the administered justice itself, but without the constraints inherent in that process (such as the fact that the rules are written down, that they are administered by independent judges, and that outcomes have to be justified by references to reason and precedent). The role of lawyer for the situation therefore may be too prone to abuse to be explicitly sanctioned. A person may be entrusted with it only if he knows that in the event of miscarriage he will have no protection from the law. In this respect, acting as lawyer for the situation can be thought of as similar to a doctor's "authority" to terminate the life of a hopeless patient: It can properly be undertaken only if it will not be questioned afterwards. To this extent Brandeis's critics may have been right.

Yet it seems possible to define the role of intercessor, just as it has been possible to define the role of the trustee or guardian. The role could be defined by contrast with those of confidential counselor and advocate, perhaps to the advantage of clarity in defining all three. At minimum, a recognition of the role of lawyer for the situation could result in a clearer perception by both clients and lawyers of one very important and socially estimable function that lawyers can perform and do perform.

B. CHOICE OF ENTITY AND FORMATION

As a practical matter, there are four principal forms of business entity available for the organizers of a new venture: general partnership, limited partnership, LLC, and corporation. The choice among them depends on matching the economics of the venture, its plans for the future, the preferences of the individual owners, and tax considerations with the characteristics of each of these different forms of entity. One must also consider the important ways in which these entities in their default forms can be modified and the key non-tax issues involved in deciding which form to choose. The following discussion summarizes some of the principal characteristics of the various entities that are relevant to the choice of form.

1. LIMITED LIABILITY

Limited liability is the most important consideration in the formation of a business entity. The rule of limited liability states that an equityholder of a firm is not liable for the debts, obligations, and liabilities of the firm solely by reason of being an equityholder. *All things considered, the equityholders of any firm would prefer to have limited liability than not.* Absent a reason to believe that personal liability of equityholders is not a significant issue, a bona fide business enterprise of some scale would most likely prefer to operate as a limited liability entity. Nowadays, with a panoply of limited liability entities that can suit diverse needs, the formation of a limited liability entity is the presumptive default choice.

The benefit of limited liability is granted by the state, and thus a firm must file with the state to become a limited liability entity. Corporations, LLCs, limited partnerships, and limited liability partnerships provide limited liability protection to equityholders. But in a general partnership the partners can be held jointly and severally liable for partnership obligations, whether contractual or in tort. Importantly, although all of the limited liability entities provide protection from liability, certain aspects of limited liability differ among various business forms.

In a limited partnership, only limited partners have limited liability protection, and they are still subject to the "control rule" under the RULPA scheme.[2] Like partners in a general partnership, a general partner in a limited partnership is still subject to personal liability for the debts and obligations of the limited partnership. If a person who wishes to serve as a general partner seeks a liability shield, then he or she must form a limited liability entity (such as a corporation or an LLC) that then serves as the general partner.[3]

The LLC statutes provide limited liability protection for members and managers without the constraints seen in limited partnerships. In this sense, the liability protection is more similar to corporations than general partnerships and limited partnerships.

It is important to recognize that none of these forms of entity provide absolute protection against liability. In addition to the exceptions discussed above, as discussed in Chapter 3, all of them are subject to the doctrine of "veil piercing," pursuant to which the liability "veil" will be disregarded under certain circumstances.

2. CONTINUITY OF EXISTENCE

Unless the certificate of incorporation provide otherwise, a corporation exists in perpetuity. Its existence is independent of any particular shareholder. This is implied in the legal fact that a corporation is a legal person distinct from its shareholders. A corporation continues to exist in perpetuity until its constituents voluntarily dissolve the business, creditors force its liquidation under the laws of bankruptcy, or the state or the court dissolves the corporation under specified authority set forth in the statute.

For limited and general partnerships, the issue of continued existence is more nuanced. Like corporations, modern LLC and limited partnership

---

[2] Under the ULPA (2001), the "control rule" has been eliminated and limited partners benefit from limited liability with that restriction. ULPA (2001) § 303 ("An obligation of a limited partnership, whether arising in contract, tort, or otherwise, is not the obligation of a limited partner. A limited partner is not personally liable, directly or indirectly, by way of contribution or otherwise, for an obligation of the limited partnership solely by reason of being a limited partner, even if the limited partner participates in the management and control of the limited partnership."). Additionally, if the limited partnership is a limited liability limited partnership, the general partners also receive limited liability protection. ULPA (2001) § 404(c) ("An obligation of a limited partnership incurred while the limited partnership is a limited liability limited partnership, whether arising in contract, tort, or otherwise, is solely the obligation of the limited partnership. A general partner is not personally liable, directly or indirectly, by way of contribution or otherwise, for such an obligation solely by reason of being or acting as a general partner.").

[3] A partner in a partnership need not be a natural person. "Partnership" means an association of two or more persons to carry on as co-owners a business for profit formed under Section 202, predecessor law, or comparable law of another jurisdiction. RUPA § 101(6). "Person" means an individual, corporation, business trust, estate, trust, partnership, association, joint venture, government, governmental subdivision, agency, or instrumentality, or any other legal or commercial entity. RUPA § 101(10).

statutes provide that, absent a contrary provision in the organic documents, these entities exist in perpetuity. *See, e.g.,* RULLCA § 104(c) ("A limited liability company has perpetual duration."); ULPA (2001) § 104(c) ("A limited partnership has a perpetual duration.").[4] For a general partnership, a dissociation of a partner need not result in dissolution of the partnership. The statute provides two distinct pathways for a partnership to move forward: it can either continue as a business (RUPA Article 7, §§ 701–705), or it can wind up the business (RUPA Article 8, §§ 801–807).[5] Obviously, since a partnership is fundamentally defined as having at least two co-owners of a business, if there is only one co-owner due to the dissociation of the other from the business and another partner does not join the venture, there can be no partnership. An LLC does not face this problem because there can be single-member LLCs.

3.   MANAGEMENT AND CONTROL

Management and control is another factor that should be considered in the selection of an entity. The management of a corporation is centralized in its board of directors, which is charged with managing or overseeing the corporation's business and affairs. The board delegates authority over day-to-day operations to officers whom they appoint.

In a general partnership, management authority is vested in all the partners, each of whom has full authority to bind the partnership. The default statutory rule is that each partner has an equal voice, regardless of the amount of her capital contribution. Decisions generally are made by majority vote of the partners, but extraordinary changes, such as modification of a partner's decision-making authority, require the unanimous consent of all partners. In practice, partners often agree to modify the default rules by provision in the partnership agreement. For example, many partnership agreements provide that a partner's voice in management will be in proportion to her capital contribution. Thus, a partner who contributes 60% of the capital would be entitled to 60% of the voting power. Some partnership agreements, including those of many large law firms, assign exclusive responsibility for managing various aspects of the partnership's business to one partner or a committee of partners.

---

[4]   Under the original 1976 version of the RULPA (which is an older statute than the ULPA (2001)), the certificate of limited partnership that must be filed with the state mandates that it shall set forth "the latest date upon which the limited partnership is to dissolve." RULPA § 201(a)(4). Obviously, a mandatory dissolution date makes the venture temporally finite. The ULPA (2001) eliminates this required termination date and permits a perpetual entity similar to corporations.

[5]   Under the older UPA, a partnership dissolves when there has been a "change in the relation of the partners caused by any partner ceasing to be associated in the carrying on as distinguished from the winding up of the business." UPA § 29. This rule conceptualizes the partnership not as an entity that is separate and distinct from its partners, but as an aggregate of its partners such that a change in the composition of the aggregate results in a dissolution of the partnership.

In a limited partnership, the law mandates a formal dichotomy between partners who manage the partnership (general partners) and partners who are passive investors in the partnership (limited partners). If this separation is encroached upon by the limited partner participating in the control of the limited partnership, the limited partner may lose the benefit of limited liability under the RULPA (but not under the ULPA (2001)). Under the default statutory rules, the management rights of general partners are largely coterminous with the management rights of partners in a general partnership.

In terms of management and control, the LLC is the most flexible form of entity. Most statutes permit either a member-managed LLC or a manager-managed LLC. A member-managed LLC resembles a general partnership; all members have the authority to make management decisions and to act as agents for the LLC. A manager-managed LLC resembles a corporation or a limited partnership; it has a centralized management structure. Members are not agents of the entity and make only major decisions. The managers—who can be members as well but need not be—make most ordinary business decisions and have the authority to act as agents of the LLC. The organizers are not bound by these general principles, but can customize the management structure in whatever way they choose by appropriate provisions in the operating agreement.

4.   TRANSFERABILITY OF INTERESTS

One of the distinctive features of the corporation is that, absent a contrary agreement, its shareholders are free to transfer their stock without obtaining the consent of other shareholders. In a close corporation, however, free transferability can pose problems because the success of such firms often depends upon the ability of the owners to work with each other and the shareholders may have agreed to arrangements that enable each shareholder to be represented on the board or participate in the management of the business. A problem may arise if one shareholder dies, sells or otherwise transfers her stock to some person with whom the other shareholders would prefer not to be associated. To avoid such a problem, the certificate of incorporation or a shareholders agreement often contain restrictions on the transferability of stock. Even without such restrictions, free transferability may be of little practical value because of the lack of a ready market for stock in a close corporation.

Similarly, in partnerships (both general and limited) current partners normally do not want to have new partners thrust upon them without their consent. The default rule provides that all current partners must consent to the transfer of a partnership interest and the admission of a new partner. *See, e.g.,* RUPA § 401(i) ("A person may become a partner only with the consent of all of the partners."); ULPA (2001) § 301(3) ("A person becomes a limited partner . . . with the consent of all the partners.").

However, partners can transfer their economic interests in the partnership while retaining their governance rights. In such a case, the transferee can share in the partnership's profits without a voice in management. Such an arrangement permits partners to pledge their financial interest in the partnership to obtain personal loans without having to obtain the consent of the other partners.

The default rule for LLCs is also that new members can be admitted only with the consent of all the existing members. *See, e.g.,* RULLCA § 401(d)(3). Again, however, the rights of members to receive distributions in accordance with the operating agreement these rights are considered "transferable interests" (*Id.* § 102(21)) and can be transferred without disassociating the member from the LLC or causing its dissolution. (*Id.* § 502).

5. MANDATORY RULES AND CONTRACT DESIGN

The laws of business organizations differ as to the degree in which promoters and constituents can design their entity by contract. Two characteristics that are most often the subject of contract design are management structure and fiduciary duties.

The most inflexible structures are the corporation and the limited partnership. A corporation requires a board of directors in which ultimate managerial authority is vested. A limited partnership requires a dichotomy of partners in which the general partner manages the partnership and the limited partners are passive investors.

Another important area involving the scope of contracting is fiduciary duty. In partnerships and LLCs, the statutes provide the basic framework of fiduciary duties. *See, e.g.,* RUPA § 404; ULPA (2001) §§ 305, 408; RULLCA § 409. The uniform laws generally provide that the partnership or operating agreement may not eliminate fiduciary duties. However, they allow considerable flexibility in modifying the scope of fiduciary duty through the partnership or operating agreement. *See, e.g.,* RUPA § 103; ULPA (2001) § 110; RULLCA § 110. If not manifestly unreasonable, the partnership or operating agreement may (1) identify specific types or categories of activities that do not violate the duty of loyalty, (2) reasonably reduce the duty of care, and (3) prescribe the standards by which to measure the performance of the contractual obligation of good faith and fair dealing. A few jurisdictions permit the complete elimination of fiduciary duty, though the contractual obligation of good faith and fair dealing cannot be waived. *See* Delaware Limited Liability Company Act § 18–1101(c) ("[Fiduciary duties] may be expanded or restricted or eliminated by provisions in the limited liability company agreement; provided, that the limited liability company agreement may not eliminate the implied contractual covenant of good faith and fair dealing."); Nevada Rev. Stat. § 86.286(5) ("such duties may be expanded, restricted or *eliminated* by provisions in the operating agreement"). Partnership or operating agreements that fail to address fiduciary duties are subject to traditional concepts of contract interpretation. Thus, a failure to contract for fiduciary duties in the partnership or operating agreement invokes the common law of fiduciary duties, as articulated in cases like *Meinhard v. Salmon*, which we considered in Chapter 7.

In a corporation, directors, officers and controlling shareholders owe fiduciary duties of care and loyalty to the corporation and to the shareholders. Unlike statutes governing partnerships and LLCs, most corporate statutes do not permit eliminating or narrowing the scope of fiduciary duties by contract.[6] Instead, they generally provide that the corporate charter may contain a provision exculpating directors from liability for a breach of the duty of care, though not for a breach of the duty of loyalty. *See* DGCL § 102(b)(7); MBCA § 2.02(b)(4).

6.   TAXATION

The major tax consideration in choice of form is whether the entity pays taxes on its income or whether the income "passes through" and is taxable to the equityholders. Under Subchapter C of the Internal Revenue Code, a corporation is treated as a taxpaying entity separate from its shareholders. Thus, in a sense, the profits are subject to "double taxation" since the corporation is taxed as an independent entity, and the shareholders, who are treated as separate and distinct from the corporation, are taxed on dividends paid by the corporation and capital gains on the sale of their stock. Subchapter S, permits qualified corporations to be treated as pass-through entities that pay no income taxes themselves, but their shareholders are taxed on their share of the corporation's income. S corporations tend to be more suitable for smaller corporations because IRS regulations limit the type of corporation, the number of shareholders, and equity capital structure. As a result, most large corporations and all publicly-traded corporations are C corporations.

---

[6]   Nevada is an exception to the Delaware and MBCA approach. The Nevada corporate statute provides:

> Except as otherwise provided in NRS 35.230, 90.660, 91.250, 452.200, 452.270, 668.045 and 694A.030, or unless the articles of incorporation or an amendment thereto, in each case filed on or after October 1, 2003, provide for greater individual liability, a director or officer is not individually liable to the corporation or its stockholders or creditors for any damages as a result of any act or failure to act in his or her capacity as a director or officer unless it is proven that: (a) The director's or officer's act or failure to act constituted a breach of his or her fiduciary duties as a director or officer; and (b) The breach of those duties involved intentional misconduct, fraud or a knowing violation of law.

Nevada Rev. Stat. § 78.138(7). The statute also provides: "The articles of incorporation may also contain any provision, not contrary to the laws of this State . . . Creating, defining, limiting or regulating the powers of the corporation or the rights, powers or duties of the directors, the officers or the stockholders, or any class of the stockholders, or the holders of bonds or other obligations of the corporation . . . ." *Id.* § 78.037. *See* Michal Barzuza, *Market Segmentation: The Rise of Nevada as a Liability-Free Jurisdiction*, 98 Va. L. Rev. 935, 949–58 (2012) (discussing the differences between Nevada and Delaware with respect to duties and liabilities of directors and officers).

Non-corporate business entities, can avoid double taxation by electing treatment as partnerships, the income of which is not taxed at the entity level but "passes through" and is taxed to the partners. Under IRS regulations popularly known as "check-the-box," partnerships and multi—member LLCs, can elect to be taxed as either partnerships or corporations.[7] A single-member LLC is treated as a "disregarded" (pass-through) entity, and thus cannot elect treatment as a corporation.

For some businesses, tax considerations are the determinative factor in choosing an organizational form. As important as they may be, however, tax considerations are not the only ones relevant to the choice of form of entity. The planner must consider all factors in determining entity choice.

7. CHOICE OF STATE OF ORGANIZATION

The decision as to the state under whose laws the entity is to be organized, depends in large part on the nature and scope of the entity's proposed business. There is requirement that a company be organized in the state in which it plans to operate. There are many Delaware corporations that do no business at all in Delaware, for example. However, state laws require that "foreign" corporations, limited partnerships, and LLCs that are "doing business" in the state "qualify" to do business by registering with the state, filing annual reports, and paying certain fees. Thus, if a company will conduct its business primarily in a single state, organizing in that state will reduce filing, reporting and tax burdens.

Lawyers generally recommend organizing under the laws of a jurisdiction other than where the business plans to operate only when there is good reason to do so. Because most states have adopted the ULPA (2001) or the RULPA, there is usually little reason to choose one state over another when organizing a limited partnership. Occasionally particular provisions of the corporation law or LLC statute of the local jurisdiction may be especially burdensome and justify organizing elsewhere (often in Delaware). This would be unusual for most small businesses.

Some of the other factors to be considered in deciding where to organize are state income and franchise tax rates; flexibility and ease of operation under corporate or LLC laws; regulation of the sale of stock and the payment of dividends; the existence of specific provisions for close corporations; and, although rare, the possible liability of equityholders for wages.

If a business is large, sophisticated, or complex, Delaware is often the preferred jurisdiction for organizing an entity. The Delaware laws of non-

---

[7]   If an LLC or a partnership is publicly traded, it will be ineligible for check-the-box election as a non-corporate business. Its tax treatment will be as a public corporation. 26 U.S.C. § 7704. *See* Laura D'Angelo & Phuc H. Lu, *Model Organizational Checklist for a Limited Liability Company*, 69 Bus. Law. 1251, 1270 n.30 (2014) (describing the tax treatment of partnerships and LLCs).

corporate entities tend to favor maximum freedom of contract.[8] The practical effect is that the organizers of a business are virtually free of most mandatory rules and can customize their entities to meet their needs. Delaware offers corporations an extensive, sophisticated body of corporation law and an expert judiciary that is attuned to the needs of businesses and their constituents in terms of handling cases efficiently and expeditiously. *See* Randy J. Holland, *Delaware's Business Courts: Litigation Leadership*, 34 J. Corp. L. 771 (2009). Because Delaware law is so widely known and understood, early-stage investors such as venture capital firms often insist that their portfolio companies incorporate in Delaware. Likewise, investment bankers tend to encourage companies that hope eventually to go public to incorporate there. Recognizing this, experienced counsel often recommend incorporating in Delaware for new businesses that hope to attract venture capital or eventually go public.

This does not mean that Delaware corporate law is necessarily "superior" in some normative sense. There have been many critics of Delaware law. *See, e.g.,* William J. Carney & George B. Shepherd, *The Mystery of Delaware Law's Continuing Success*, 2009 U. Ill. L. Rev. 1 (2009) (arguing that "since the 1980s Delaware law has become increasingly complex and uncertain, due largely to judicial decisions that appear to tailor doctrines to produce fairness in individual cases, at the expense of certainty in planning and executing transactions"). There is an old debate in corporation law over whether there has been a "race to the bottom" or a "race to the top" in the competition among states for chartering. Regardless of one's views on the question, it is indisputable that Delaware has won the race, and has become the jurisdiction of choice for the majority of public, and many private corporations.

8. FORMATION

The formation of a corporation requires formal action with the state. The filing requirements and procedures for forming a corporation and other limited liability entities are simple and ministerial. Most state governments maintain websites to provide information to businesses. These websites contain business entity statutes, descriptions of business entity types, instructions about the incorporation process and fee system, and forms for downloading and filing. Some states are moving towards on-line "paperless" registration systems.

Although the procedures vary slightly from state to state, MBCA §§ 2.01–2.07 illustrate the procedure generally required. The organization is formally accomplished by an "incorporator" who, after incorporation,

---

[8]   *See* Delaware Limited Liability Company Act § 18–1101(b) ("It is the policy of this chapter to give the maximum effect to the principle of freedom of contract and to the enforceability of limited liability company agreements."); Delaware Limited Partnership Act § 17–1101(b) ("It is the policy of this chapter to give maximum effect to the principle of freedom of contract and to the enforceability of partnership agreements.").

usually plays no other role in the corporation.[9] The incorporator signs and files the articles of incorporation (a public document) with the Secretary of State or another designated official, and, in some cases, with a county official in the county where the principal place of business of the corporation in that state will be located. The filing of the articles of incorporation is accompanied by the payment of a fee, part of which is usually calculated on the basis of the number of authorized shares or the aggregate legal capital of the company.

The articles of incorporation (called the certificate of incorporation in Delaware and some other states) *must* contain certain required information. *See, e.g.,* DGCL § 102(a); MBCA § 2.02(a). The mandatory disclosure requirement is largely ministerial, requiring the disclosure of: "(1) a corporate name for the corporation that satisfies the requirements of section 4.01;[10] (2) the number of shares the corporation is authorized to issue; (3) the street address of the corporation's initial registered office and the name of its initial registered agent at that office; and (4) the name and address of each incorporator." MBCA § 2.02(a). *See* DGCL § 102(a) (providing similar requirement).

Additionally, the articles *may* also contain other provisions that are not inconsistent with law. *See, e.g.,* DGCL § 102(b); MBCA § 2.02(b). Such provisions may include more complex provisions including "managing the business and regulating the affairs of the corporation" and "defining, limiting, and regulating the powers of the corporation, its board of directors, and shareholders." *See, e.g.,* MBCA §§ 2.02(b)(2)(ii), (iii). They also include a provision limiting the liability of directors for money damages in certain circumstances. *See, e.g.,* DGCL § 102(b)(7); MBCA § 2.02(b)(4).

The formal existence of a corporation commences with the completion of filing of the articles of incorporation, although the filing is subject to review and acceptance by the Secretary of State, who reviews the articles to assure that they conform to the minimum requirements of the statute. Thereafter, an organizational meeting must be held, either by the incorporator(s), who select the first members of the board of directors, or, where the initial board is named in the articles of incorporation, by the board members so named. In the first meeting, the board accomplishes a number of standard tasks, including the election of additional directors, if any; the adoption of bylaws; the appointment of officers; the adoption of a

---

[9] Under the MBCA and many state statutes there may be more than one incorporator, although only one is usually necessary.

[10] In practice, the selection of a corporate name can be challenging, as the name must be distinguishable from the names of other corporations incorporated or qualified as foreign corporations in the state. Moreover, careful counsel will do a trademark search to be sure that, even if the name chosen is available in the state, it does not create the possibility of infringing on a trademark owned by another business. Finally, if the corporation plans to do business in other states and may be required to register as a foreign corporation, it may want to assure that the name chosen is available in those states.

corporate seal; the designation of a bank as depository for corporate funds; and often the sale of stock to the initial shareholders. (*See* MBCA §§ 2.05, 2.06.)

Like a corporation, the organization of other limited liability entities (*e.g.*, LLC, limited partnership, and limited liability partnership) requires filing with the state. *See, e.g.,* RULLCA § 201; ULPA (2001) § 201; RUPA § 1001(c). The disclosure requirement is similarly threadbare: "The certificate must state: (1) the name of the limited partnership, which must comply with Section 108; (2) the street and mailing address of the initial designated office and the name and street and mailing address of the initial agent for service of process; (3) the name and the street and mailing address of each general partner; (4) whether the limited partnership is a limited liability limited partnership; and (5) any additional information required by [Article] 11." ULPA (2001) § 201(a). Typically, the partners or members also execute a written partnership or operating agreement.

In contrast to limited liability entities, a general partnership does not require filing with the state. Most partnerships are formed consensually when two or more persons enter into a partnership agreement that will govern the relationship of the partners, including such matters as managerial rights, distribution rights, interests in profits and losses, and rights upon dissolution of the enterprise. However, because the RUPA defines a partnership as "an association of two or more persons to carry on as co-owners a business for profit," a partnership also may be created by operation of law. Such accidentally-formed partnerships often give rise to undesirable and unforeseen consequences for the partners, such as liability for debts the partnership is deemed to have incurred.

As may be apparent from the foregoing description, the actual task of filing with the state with the minimal required information is a fairly ministerial function. It is not necessary to use a lawyer to incorporate a business. In many cases, the routine work associated with the incorporation process is done by a service company rather than a lawyer. What, then, is the business lawyer's role in formation? The business lawyer provides more value-added advisory service. Although corporate law requires only minimal disclosure requirement in the certificate of incorporation, public company charters are often lengthy and complex. Even for private companies, business lawyers are called on to draft the provisions of the articles and bylaws related to the capital structure, board of directors and committees, duties and responsibilities of corporate officers, indemnification of officers and directors, and processes of corporate governance. The consideration that go into these matters are not ministerial functions.

C. PLANNING AND STRUCTURING THE ENTITY

In addition to selecting form of entity and the jurisdiction in which it will be organized, the organizers must consider a variety of additional planning issues: What will the ownership structure be? How will control be allocated? How will the entity be managed?

1. CONTRACTING

As we have seen, the laws of business organizations provide certain default terms that give shape to each business entity. However, the laws provide, to varying degrees depending on the entity, considerable flexibility to alter default, non-mandatory rules.

Consequently, all well-planned business enterprises require some degree of contracting.

With respect to all closely-held businesses, there are several questions that the organizers should consider. For a corporation some may be addressed in the charter and bylaws. But there are others that require the creation of contractual relations among the shareholders, or between shareholders and the corporation. For partnerships and LLCs, these questions are generally addressed in the operating agreement.

At a minimum, the questions that the planner of a closely-held enterprise must consider include the following:

- **Ownership structure:** How will the economic risks and benefits of the enterprise be allocated among the owners?

- **Management structure:** How will management authority and rights of control be allocated?

- **Dissociation and investment exit:** What will happen when one of the owners dies or departs from the business?

- **Minority protection:** What protections will a minority owner have if there is a falling-out with the other owners?

- **Fiduciary duties:** What fiduciary duties will the owners have to each other, either as owners or as managers?

2. OWNERSHIP STRUCTURE

One of the most important considerations in designing a new business entity is how its ownership will be divided. In a general partnership, the default rule is: "Each partner is entitled to an equal share of the partnership profits and is chargeable with a share of the partnership losses in proportion to the partner's share of the profits." RUPA § 401(b). This rule may suffice in a simple case, but suppose different partners make different contributions to the partnership. This may create an expectation of division of profit commensurate with relative contribution. In a limited partnership, the default rule is: "A distribution by a limited partnership must be shared among the partners on the basis of the value . . . of the contributions the limited partnership has received from each partner." ULPA (2001) § 503.

In both general partnerships and limited partnerships, the partners may modify the default ownership structure in the partnership agreement. For example, partners in a general partnership may want to allocate ownership interest based on value, similar to a limited partnership. Partners in a limited partnership may want to create different classes of limited partners where a senior class of limited partners would have priority preferences as to profit or distribution compared to the junior class.

The rules for LLCs are similar. The default rule under the RULLC is that members are entitled to equal shares of any distribution. RULLC § 404(a). The operating agreement may, however, modify this rule in any way. The Delaware statute provides that distributions and allocations of profits or losses will be as specified in the operating agreement. If the operating agreement is silent, they are allocated in proportion to the members' contributions. Delaware Limited Liability Company Act §§ 18–503 and 18–504.

In a corporation, there must be at least one class of stock that is entitled to receive dividends, if any, and the net assets of the corporation upon dissolution. *E.g.,* MBCA § 6.01(b). However, corporate law enables the corporation to create an array of equity ownership structures through the issuance of different kinds and classes of stock. For example, MBCA § 6.01(c) provides:

The articles of incorporation may authorize one or more classes or series of shares that:

(1) have special, conditional, or limited voting rights, or no right to vote, except to the extent otherwise provided by this Act;

(2) are redeemable or convertible as specified in the articles of incorporation:

(i) at the option of the corporation, the shareholder, or another person or upon the occurrence of a specified event;

(ii) for cash, indebtedness, securities, or other property; and

(iii) at prices and in amounts specified, or determined in accordance with a formula;

(3) entitle the holders to distributions calculated in any manner, including dividends that may be cumulative, noncumulative, or partially cumulative; or

> (4) have preference over any other class or series of shares with respect to distributions, including distributions upon the dissolution of the corporation.

See also DGCL § 151(a). This permits a structure in which the economic rights are allocated separately to various classes of shareholders. For example, a corporation may have preferred stock and common stock. It may have different classes of common stock for which the economic benefits are the same, but one class has superior voting rights. It may have preferred stock convertible into common stock. In short, although the ownership interests of the owners of stock corporations must take the form of stock, the planner has considerable latitude to allocate those interests in different ways using various forms or classes of stock.

3. MANAGEMENT

The choice of entity provides only a default management structure. While this structure may meet the needs of the situation, it is more common that the situation will call on the planner to modify it to conform to the client's wishes.

In a general partnership, the default rule is: "Each partner has equal rights in the management and conduct of the partnership business." RUPA § 401(f). This rule may work for a small group of partners who work in an informal, collegial environment. However, as the partnership gets larger, such a rule may become unworkable. A partnership with 100 partners may require more centralized authority structure. What would such a structure look like? It could be, for example, that most day-to-day management decisions are vested in a managing partner or an executive committee of partners, and certain kinds of business decisions or transactions require the approval of a specified vote of all partners.

This is a structure that is similar to the default rule of a limited partnership where general partners have equal management rights, but limited partners have limited management rights. ULPA (2001) § 302, § 406(a). However, because limited partnerships are principally used as investment vehicles conceived by the general partners, there is often only one general partner. If there is more than one general partner, however, thought must be given to how decisions will be made. The general partners must determine whether the default rule of equal management rights work or not. If not, they must devise the proper management structure as well as any potential checks on management authority by the limited partners through the process of voting. But voting for what? Limited partners can vote on certain fundamental transactions such as mergers, acquisitions or disposals of substantial assets, approval of changes or amendments to the partnership agreement, ratification of conflict of interest transactions involving the general partner, etc. Such voting and approval process can place checks and controls on the general partner's authority to management the limited partnership. Of course, these kinds of devices are not limited to limited partnership, and are instead generally applicable to most business organizations.

In a corporation, management authority is centralized in the board of directors, which can have various committees empowered to act with respect to particular types of decision. Corporations may also establish specified officers and grant particular authority to them. Finally, the shareholders of a close corporation will normally be concerned about the composition of the board and how its members are elected. We have already considered in Chapter 6 some of the devices available to the planner to address these concerns, including shareholder agreements and the use of multiple classes of stock.

4. DISSOCIATION AND EXIT

What will happen when one of the owners dies, becomes disabled, or otherwise departs from the business? Because business entities are capable of perpetual existence, they maintain stability of the enterprise even as owners and managers come and go. In public corporations, investments and divestments by shareholders do not create planning issues because shares are freely transferable in the trading markets, and a transfer of shares normally will have little effect on the corporation.

In closely-held entities, however, the departure of an owner can have significant ramifications for the remaining owners. Among other things, if an owner transfers her interest to someone else (to the extent that the law permits such a transfer) the remaining owners may find a new owner thrust upon a closely-knit group, that may not wish to have a new member. Competent lawyers will therefore help their clients anticipate departures and provide for them in advance.

There are a number of questions to consider: What are the economic rights upon a departure? Does it matter what kind of a departure it is (*e.g.*, voluntary withdrawal, expulsion, death or disability, etc.)? What happens to the governance rights? Do those rights cancel upon transfer? If not, are those rights transferable to a transferee? If so, what are the implications on the owners and the entity? Do other owners have certain rights against the departing person? Must the firm repurchase the interest? Is there a right of first refusal by other owners or managers?

An owner who leaves a firm for whatever reason will not want her capital to be locked in the firm indefinitely. On the other hand, the current owners will not likely want to see capital exiting the firm. The problem is alleviated if the departing owner is permitted to sell her interest to another. However, for the remaining owners, a transfer of the ownership interest to someone new might not be desirable for obvious reasons.

Because partnership law presumes as a starting point a communitarian enterprise of co-equal partners, an interest in a partnership is conceived in two distinct parts: the economic rights, which are personal property and transferable by default, and the governance rights, which are not transferable. The same is true for LLCs. While this default structure may satisfy, it may be desirable to modify it in the partnership agreement or LLC operating agreement through some sort of buy-sell arrangement of the type discussed for close corporations in Chapter 6.

Shares of stock, by contrast, constitute a bundle of economic and governance rights; and corporate law presumes shares are freely transferable. As discussed in Chapter 6, however, it is possible to impose restrictions on transfers by contract, and such restrictions are widely used in close corporations. *See* MBCA § 6.27 and comment.

5.   PROTECTION OF THE MINORITY

People who join together in a business generally do so with mutual trust and shared commitment to the common good. They may be reluctant to contemplate that, in the future, one or more of the parties may seek to behave opportunistically—that is, to promote their interests at the expense of other owners. Unfortunately, over time, the owners of businesses sometimes do fall out with each other, in which case the owner or owners of a controlling interest may be tempted to treat minority owners unfairly.

In a close corporation, a minority shareholder unhappy with the direction of the business may want to sell her shares. But the majority shareholder is likely to be the only person interested in buying, probably at a price less than the minority shareholder would consider fair. The problem can be exacerbated if the shareholders are withdrawing much of the economic results of the business in the form of compensation as employees, and the majority attempt to terminate the employment of a minority owner.

As we saw in Chapter 7, some states allow a minority shareholder to seek a judicial order of involuntary dissolution or other forms of equitable relief on the grounds that the majority's actions are oppressive or have frustrated the minority's reasonable expectations. But the ability to obtain such relief is far less certain than the ability to withdraw unilaterally from an at-will partnership and obtain cash payment for the withdrawing partner's interest. Accordingly, minority stockholders may want some protection from the majority in the form of special voting rights.

As Professor O'Kelley has observed:

The downsides of corporate statutory governance norms, especially when compared to partnership statutory governance rules, are the relative lack of assurance that individual adaptive needs will be satisfied and the relatively greater risk of majority opportunism posed because minority shareholder[s] may not withdraw their money capital from the firm. If a partner finds it value-maximizing to withdraw her capital from the firm and invest it elsewhere, the at-will dissolution mechanism insures that she will be able to do so. In a corporation, a minority shareholder has no similar adaptive rights. On the other hand, the corporation law preference for majority adaptability combines with the lack of a unilateral minority withdrawal right to insulate the majority from the threat of minority opportunism. A minority shareholder simply has no ability to withdraw unilaterally, and thus, no ability to extort an objectively unjustifiable change in terms from the majority.

Charles R. O'Kelley, Jr., *Filling Gaps in the Close Corporation Contract: A Transaction Cost Analysis*, 87 Nw. U. L. Rev. 216, 240–41 (1992).

In a general partnership, the default rule allowing at-will dissolution is critical. The majority can bring about needed changes in the organization that otherwise would require unanimous consent by threatening to dissolve the partnership. Consider, for example, a situation in which one partner refuses to perform her share of the work and also refuses to retire. The majority can simply dissolve the old partnership, purchase the firm's assets at a judicial sale, and continue the business in a new partnership to which the non-performing partner does not belong. Of course, the majority might exclude a minority partner for less worthy reasons, such as to deny her a share in anticipated profits resulting from the excluded partner's efforts. Partnership law provides minority partners some protection against such unjustified squeeze outs if the minority partner can sustain the burden of proving that the majority has not acted in good faith.

Minority partners also can use at-will dissolution to deal opportunistically with the majority. Consider, for example, a situation in which a minority partner develops special business skills that would be hard to replace. The minority partner might be able to bargain for undeserved concessions from the majority by threatening to withdraw. Even if the majority believes it eventually could prove that the minority partner's withdrawal was wrongful, the cost of litigation and the available remedies might not fully compensate the majority.

LLCs present the same problems, although default rules differ. The RULLC, for example provides that a minority member may seek judicial dissolution on the grounds that the controlling members "have acted, are acting, or will act in a manner that is" illegal, fraudulent, or oppressive. RULLC § 701(a)(5). The default rule in Delaware is less helpful to an oppressed minority member, judicial dissolution being available only if "it is not reasonably practical to carry on the business in conformity with a limited liability company agreement." § 18–802.

To deal with problems of this nature, planners for any closely-held enterprise should consider drafting provisions that anticipate and address the possibility that a controlling faction may act oppressively toward the minority. The benefits of protections for the minority are not without costs. For example, a minority veto provides an owner with a say, but used pervasively it would mean that the minority would have significant control rights over the interests of the majority. An employment contract for a minority shareholder in a close corporation may result in a situation where the cost of an underperforming owner-employee becomes high. A buy-sell agreement may result in the availability of an easy exit by a minority owner, which may not be in the best interest of the firm. It should be evident that such a planning and drafting exercise is challenging, requiring considerable experience and lawyerly skill.

6. FIDUCIARY DUTIES

What fiduciary duties will the owners have to each other, either as owners or as managers? As we have already discussed, the laws of business organizations provide default fiduciary duties that vary among types of organization and from state to state. The planner must be cognizant of what these default duties are, and ready to modify them by contract if they do not meet the needs of the situation. In some cases, the owners of the business will expect to treat each other more or less as partners, and that as such they will have enforceable fiduciary duties to each other. In others, the owners may have other business interests and wish to be free to put those interests ahead of the new enterprise should a conflict arise. In that case, they may want to opt out of some aspects of the fiduciary duties that would exist by default. As we have seen, corporation law is less flexible in this regard than partnership and LLC statutes, which generally allow considerable flexibility in defining or limiting fiduciary duties.

Planning requires an assessment the default fiduciary duties applicable to the chosen business entity, the degree of contracting permitted by the law, and the reasons for contracting to expand, contract or potentially eliminate fiduciary duties. Fiduciary duties will impact both the production of the firm and the individual allocation of risk and return. Relaxing the duty of loyalty may result in opportunistic behavior by owners and managers, thus resulting in inequitable wealth transfers. Yet, certain categories of conduct, if fully disclosed, may be a necessity. Relaxing the duty of care may result in suboptimal effort and care by owners and managers in managing the firm. On the other hand, too stringent standards may result in unwanted litigation and its costs and risk averse behavior by managers, which may reduce the firm's production. Thus, the lawyer and the owners must carefully consider the implications of owing or being owed fiduciary duties.

Problem: Precision Tools—Part 11

We return to the Precision Tools problem. In the previous chapters, we saw that business enterprise can be conducted through various entities: general partnership, limited partnership, limited liability company, and corporation. Each has its unique features, and the collective set of features along with varying permissibility of contracting around default rules provides the internal set of rules applicable to the business enterprise and its participants. Consider, then, the menu of entities in light of the following two scenarios.

Michael Lane, Jessica Bacon, and Bernie Gould believe that they can raise $3.3 million of capital from various sources, including themselves, to finance the acquisition of Precision Tools. For now, we not consider the form and amounts of the individual investments by Michael, Jessica, and Bernie. It is sufficient to assume that they will be able to raise the money for the acquisition. The plan is to purchase all of Precision Tools' assets and assume all the liabilities listed on the company's balance sheet.[11] In year 2xx2, Precision Tools had assets of $8.04 million, liabilities of $5.775 million, and equity of $2.265 million. It had revenues of $11.25 million, operating profit of $1.38 million, and net profit of $0.585 million. After consulting with Michael, Jessica and Bernie, you learn more about the business plan. They have advised you that they anticipate two paths for Precision Tools.

One potential scenario is that Precision Tools would be a business that provides Michael, Jessica and Bernie a good economic return. There is no further plan other than to continue the business, grow the business as internal financing and market conditions permit, and run it as soundly as they can. Precision Tools would become the principal economic livelihood of the three investors, though Bernie may plan to take more of a passive role in the management. In year 2xx2, Precision Tools made net profit of $585,000. The three investors think that they can easily manage the business to generate recurring profits of $750,000, which they would split among themselves based on their investment stake.

Another potential scenario is a more ambitious one. Michael, Jessica and Bernie would use Precision Tools as a vehicle to "roll up" (acquire) other electronic component manufacturers. This would require additional financing beyond what Michael, Jessica and Bernie have already put into the business. The anticipated funding would come from venture private equity firms as well as debt financing from a large bank. Through the "roll up" the three investors seek to grow Precision Tools to about $100 million in assets and $10 million in net profit within a three-year period of aggressive expansion. At this anticipated size, they plan either to sell the

---

[11]   See Chapter 9, which presents the company's financial statements.

company to a large company (most likely a publicly traded industrial company) or to go public itself in an initial public offering (IPO).

Michael, Jessica and Bernie ask for advice on the choice of entity and thereafter the structure of the chosen entity.

What is your advice?

PART IV

THE CORPORATION

■ ■ ■

Part IV focuses on the large, publicly-held corporation. Chapters 12 through 15 are devoted to the increasingly important law relating to the governance of public corporations. Chapter 12 introduces different models of the large corporation developed by economists and corporate lawyers, the choice among which informs and shapes contemporary debates about governance. Chapters 13 and 14 are devoted to the distinct roles in governance of the board of directors and the shareholders. Chapter 15 discusses both federal and state laws on disclosures to shareholders. Chapter 16 explores the procedural implications of shareholder litigation, a familiarity with which is essential to understanding the cases in Chapters 17 through 19, which consider the law of the fiduciary duties of the board and controlling shareholders. Chapters 20 through 22 cover the principal elements of the law relating to corporate combinations, contests for corporate control, and insider trading.

CHAPTER 12

CORPORATE GOVERNANCE IN THE PUBLIC CORPORATION

■ ■ ■

A. INTRODUCTION

The term "corporate governance" can have many meanings. The OECD's *Principles of Corporate Governance (2004)* describes it as follows:

> Corporate governance involves a set of relationships between a company's management, its board, its shareholders and other stakeholders. Corporate governance also provides the structure through which the objectives of the company are set, and the means of attaining those objectives and monitoring performance are determined. Good corporate governance should provide proper incentives for the board and management to pursue objectives that are in the interests of the company and its shareholders and should facilitate effective monitoring. The presence of an effective corporate governance system, within an individual company and across an economy as a whole, helps to provide a degree of confidence that is necessary for the proper functioning of a market economy. As a result, the cost of capital is lower and firms are encouraged to use resources more efficiently, thereby underpinning growth.

> Corporate governance is only part of the larger economic context in which firms operate that includes, for example, macroeconomic policies and the degree of competition in product and factor markets. The corporate governance framework also depends on the legal, regulatory, and institutional environment. In addition, factors such as business ethics and corporate awareness of the environmental and societal interests of the communities in which a company operates can also have an impact on its reputation and its long-term success.

> Corporate governance is affected by the relationships among participants in the governance system. Controlling shareholders, which may be individuals, family holdings, bloc alliances, or other corporations acting through a holding company or cross shareholdings, can significantly influence corporate behaviour. As owners of equity, institutional investors are increasingly demanding a voice in corporate governance in some markets.

Individual shareholders usually do not seek to exercise governance rights but may be highly concerned about obtaining fair treatment from controlling shareholders and management. Creditors play an important role in a number of governance systems and can serve as external monitors over corporate performance. Employees and other stakeholders play an important role in contributing to the long-term success and performance of the corporation, while governments establish the overall institutional and legal framework for corporate governance. The role of each of these participants and their interactions vary widely among OECD countries and among non-OECD countries as well. These relationships are subject, in part, to law and regulation and, in part, to voluntary adaptation and, most importantly, to market forces.

As the foregoing passage indicates, "corporate governance" involves the structure and procedures followed by the two primary governing organs of a corporation, the board of directors and the shareholders. Until the last ten or twenty years, the rules of governance in public companies were fairly simple, established primarily by the corporate statute and, to a lesser extent, by provisions in the charter and bylaws. In recent years, however, a variety of widely-publicized corporate scandals has fostered growing dissatisfaction with aspects of the roles of large public companies in society, and the economic performance of some of them. This has focused increased attention on the rules and practices of governance and a variety of efforts to bring about changes in the roles of boards and shareholders in governance and, in particular, the nature of the relationship between them.

The debates over governance have been informed by various theoretical models of the corporation; the more important of which are described below. Chapter 13 looks more closely at current governance rules and practices regarding the structure and functioning of boards of directors; and Chapter 14 examines the role of shareholders in the governance of public companies.

B. MODELS OF CORPORATE GOVERNANCE

There is no single, generally accepted model of corporate governance. Over the years, a number of different models have been proposed. Each describes some aspect of the problems faced in corporate governance and proposes a way to understand the problem from a particular conceptual perspective.

1. THE SEPARATION OF OWNERSHIP
FROM CONTROL

The modern debate about the nature of the public corporation and the role of public shareholders dates from the 1933 publication of *The Modern Corporation and Private Property* by two Columbia professors, Adolf Berle (law) and Gardiner Means (economics). The book, which studied the characteristics of the 200 largest corporations listed on the New York Stock Exchange, identified a separation between ownership and control. According to Berle and Means, the large body of shareholders in public corporations had no control over the enterprise. Instead, control resided with the board of directors and the corporation's top executives—that is, with corporate management.

Berle and Means found that public shareholders had little real say in the composition of the board:

> In the election of the board the stockholder ordinarily has three alternatives. He can refrain from voting, he can attend the annual meeting and personally vote his stock, or he can sign a proxy transferring his voting power to certain individuals selected by the management of the corporation, the proxy committee. As his personal vote will count for little or nothing at the meeting unless he has a very large block of stock, the stockholder is practically reduced to the alternative of not voting at all or else of *handing over his vote to individuals over whom he has no control and in whose selection he did not participate.* In neither case will he be able to exercise any measure of control. Rather, control will tend to be in the hands of those who select the proxy committee by whom, in turn, the election of directors for the ensuing period may be made. Since the proxy committee is appointed by the existing management, the latter can virtually dictate their own successors. Where ownership is sufficiently sub-divided, the management can thus become a self-perpetuating body even though its share in the ownership is negligible. This form of control can properly be called "management control." (Emphasis in original.)

For Berle and Means, the prescription to the separation of ownership from control was added legal protection for shareholders to guard them against unfettered management self-interest. One solution was providing greater information to shareholders in the voting process; heightened fiduciary duties was another. The abuses exposed by the stock market crash of 1929 cast doubt on market forces as adequate protection against management overreaching.

Much of corporate law is devoted to addressing the perceived problems arising out of the "separation of ownership and control" that Berle and Means identified. Professors Klein and Coffee suggest that this legal construct is the natural result of the difficulties associated with having more than one person involved in a business.

There is no more sense in bemoaning the costs of disloyalty than there is in bemoaning the costs of friction in an engine. We lubricate engines to reduce friction, but we are willing to accept some residual level of friction. We continue to use engines, despite the cost of lubrication, and despite the residual friction, because we conclude we are better off by doing so than we would be otherwise. People with capital hire managers, despite the monitoring costs, because they feel they are better off than they would be with any alternative investment or venture. This observation is, of course, a tautology. It is a useful tautology in that it reminds us of the silliness of worrying about unavoidable departures from unattainable ideals. While the point may seem obvious in the present context, it is often ignored in the context of large, complex economic organizations such as publicly held corporations.

In other words, we must be careful about comparing the actual situation, with division of ownership and management, to the *mythical ideal of the owner-managed firm.* Once the principal decides, for whatever reason, that she does not want to manage the business, the standard of an owner-managed firm is unattainable. [The agent] simply cannot be expected to act as he would if he were the owner. He is not an owner; and he is a human being. [The principal] is not a manager any longer; she is an investor. Both think that they are better off with the other than without. If that were not so, they would not have made the deal they made. It seems more useful to compare their actual position to what they would have if they could not combine their resources (services and capital) than to what they would have in the unattainable combined-owner-manager situation. In the actual position, with separation of management from ownership of capital, both can be expected to try to bargain for as much as possible in the way of contributions by the other and returns to themselves. It is fatuous to expect that [the agent] will behave selflessly, as if all the returns to his efforts were his. [The principal] might hope for something close to that result, but she would be silly to expect to achieve it.

Suppose, however, that when [the principal hires the agent], she says, either explicitly or implicitly, she expects him, as manager, to behave just as she would behave, or as he would behave if he were the owner. And suppose that [the agent] accepts the job on those terms. To a considerable extent the legal system seems to infer, and even to impose, such bargains. This is what is contemplated by the law when it refers to a duty of loyalty or a *fiduciary obligation*. That duty or obligation is like a golden rule, a broad, vague constraint applied to employment relationships (a one-way rule in favor of the employer). It is the kind of duty associated not only with employees but with trustees, brokers, and a whole host of other kinds of people (fiduciaries) who undertake to accomplish some objective for another person. The need to rely on a vague concept such as the duty of loyalty stems from the difficulty of specifying precisely what it is that the employer expects of the employee (on the need, that is, for discretion in the employee). The rule of law that embodies the duty of loyalty is a useful one. Without it, mutually advantageous economic relationships might not be feasible. As we have seen, however, violations of the duty of loyalty may be extremely difficult to detect. To that extent, and given the infirmities of human nature, the duty of loyalty may to a significant extent embody an unattainable ideal. It is wholly unrealistic to expect that all employees will as a matter of conscience consistently act as faithful retainers, selflessly pursuing the interests of their employers even at their own expense, or that we can be fully effective in efforts to force them to do so. We can publicly deplore the departures from the ideal. It may be useful to do so—to establish ethical standards and use deprivation of respect as a tool for enforcing the loyalty aspect of the business agreement. But we must be careful not to refuse to recognize the reality and cope with it.

William A. Klein & John C. Coffee, Jr., Business Organization and Finance 37–39 (11th ed. 2010).

Since the publication of the Berle and Means book, their analysis has served as the background against which others have proposed alternative models of the corporation in efforts to explain how governance mechanisms do, or should, guide corporate behavior toward socially desirable ends. The following is a brief description of some of those models.

2. THE MARKET FOR CORPORATE CONTROL MODEL

In 1967, Henry Manne (a law professor at George Washington University) agreed that Berle and Means had correctly diagnosed the separation of ownership and control in the public corporation, but had written the wrong prescription. In an influential article, Manne asserted that centralized management is essential for the public corporation to raise large amounts of capital:

> If the principal economic function of the corporate form was to amass the funds of investors *qua* investors, we should not anticipate their demanding or wanting a direct role in the

management of the company. Management, and the selection of particular managers, is not, in theory at least, a function of capital investors. Management is a discrete economic service of function, and the selection of individuals to perform that function, whether undertaken at the outset or during the later life of a company, is a part of the entrepreneurial job. Centralizing management serves simply to specialize these various economic functions and to allow the system to operate more efficiently.

While recognizing the problems of centralized management identified by Berle and Means, Manne contended that the most efficient solution lay in the market for corporate control:

> The market for corporate control serves an extraordinarily important purpose in the functioning of the corporate system. Unless a publicly traded company is efficiently managed, the price of its shares on the open market will decline, thus lowering the price at which an outsider can take over control of the corporation. The constant pressure provided by the threat of a takeover probably plays a larger role in the successful functioning of our corporate system than has been generally recognized. It conditions managers to a specific point of view perfectly consistent with the shareholders' interest, to wit, keeping the price of the company's shares as high as possible. Even this, of course, is no guarantee that an outsider will not feel that he can do better; but if the management group performs relatively efficiently, the dangers of losing control are not great.

Our Two Corporation Systems: Law and Economics, 53 Va. L. Rev. 259, 261, 265–66 (1967).

3.　THE CONTRACTARIAN MODEL

In the late 1970s, a number of economists and law professors advanced a model of the corporation as a "nexus of contracts" among the corporate participants. Under this theory investment is voluntary, and the relationships among shareholders, and between shareholders and managers, are essentially contractual. [Freedom of contract dictates that the parties be permitted to structure their relations as they choose, and the role of the state is limited] to identifying and enforcing their voluntary consensual arrangements. Because corporations must compete for investors' capital, they will design governance structures to reduce the risks of management overreaching so as to attract investment.

Taken to its logical extreme, this reliance on market forces suggests a minimal role for corporate law as a means of protecting investors. As Henry Butler has written:

The contractual theory of the corporation is in stark contrast to the legal concept of the corporation as an entity created by the state. The entity theory of the corporation supports state intervention—in the form of either direct regulation or the facilitation of shareholder litigation—in the corporation on the ground that the state created the corporation by granting it a charter. The contractual theory views the corporation as founded in private contract, where the role of the state is limited to enforcing contracts. [F]reedom of contract requires that parties to the "nexus of contracts" must be allowed to structure their relations as they desire.

[T]he contractual theory of the corporation offers a new perspective on the corporation and the role of corporation law. [The corporation is in no sense a ward of the state; it is, rather, the product of contracts among the owners and others.] Once this point is fully recognized by the state legislators and legal commentators, the corporate form may finally be free of unnecessary and intrusive legal chains.

Henry N. Butler, *The Contractual Theory of the Corporation*, 11 Geo. Mason U. L. Rev. 99, 100, 123 (1989).

The contractarians recognized that market forces do not always protect against opportunistic managers. For example, in "final period" transactions (such as a merger) where there is no market after the transaction, managers may rationally seek to benefit themselves at the expense of shareholders. For the contractarians, the answer to such opportunism lay in corporate fiduciary duties that they viewed as filling the gaps in the corporation's contractual structure. *See, e.g.,* Daniel Fischel, *The Corporate Governance Movement*, 35 Vand. L. Rev. 1259 (1982).

The contractarian theory—the first systematic effort to respond to Berle and Means—has had a significant influence on the intellectual development of corporate law. Drawing on economic rather than legal literature, it suggested a new way to view the corporate structure. Predictably, the theory met with considerable opposition from traditional legal scholars. Those advocating fully developed fiduciary duties to protect shareholders believed that the contractarians, by relying on a market-based bargaining model, diluted the fiduciary protections afforded shareholders.

Other legal scholars argued that the contractarian theory did not fit the legal structure of the large public corporation. Robert Clark (professor and former Dean of the Harvard Law School) wrote:

Though lawyers use the concept of agency in a variety of senses, the core legal concept implies a relationship in which the principal retains the power to control and direct the activities of the agent.

A review of elementary corporate law shows that this power of the principal to direct the activities of the agent does not apply to the stockholders as against the directors or officers of their corporation. By statute in every state, the board of directors of a corporation has the power and duty to manage or supervise its business. The stockholders do not.

Ignoring the legal restrictions on stockholders' decision-making power makes it easier to talk as if stockholders and managers "bargain" over and "contract" about the terms of their relationship, or "implicitly" or "virtually" do so—this is the next, more serious pitfall of the agency costs literature.

It may be objected that some corporate law rules seem to fit the model of "standard presumptions" adopted because they fit the normal case, and that it is intuitively plausible that the relevant participants would actually agree to them, if the issue were put to them for explicit consideration and bargaining. This group of rules is likely to include the more elementary structural features of the corporate form of organization, such as limited liability of stockholders and free transferability of shares, which are often embodied in statutes.

Another objection might be that while most rules of corporate law are imposed on the parties subject to it, they are usually free to "bargain around" them. *Failure* to bargain around a rule then amounts to accepting it, and one might even argue that the nonbargainers "contract" to obey the rule.

But bargaining around is costly. If the cost of bargaining is expected to exceed the benefits, the standard legal rule is simply tolerated—but this does not mean that it is the best available rule to govern the behavior in question. An alternative rule might make some people better off and no one worse off. Yet the substitution need not occur. For example, bargaining around a waivable fiduciary duty might require the preparation and distribution of a special proxy statement and the collection of a stockholder vote. The associated expense may deter many such bargains with investors. A different version of the legal doctrine might eliminate the transaction costs and deterrent effects of the need to seek shareholder consent. Thus, at any given time, it is an open question whether the standard legal rule is better than some imagined or proposed one.

The basic pitfall with implicit-contracts reasoning is that it is frequently indeterminate and therefore manipulable. This is true whether the purpose of the reasoning is to advance positive or normative theory. It is especially true of complex, multi-faceted relationships, such as those among directors, officers, stockholders, and the large bureaucratic organizations with which they are associated.

Robert Charles Clark, *Agency Costs Versus Fiduciary Duties*, in Pratt & Zeckhauser, Principals and Agents: The Structure of Business 55–64, 66–69 (1985).

Although some writers continue to advocate a strict contractarian view that public shareholders have the control rights that they have voluntarily accepted, many came to recognize that the linchpin of the contractarian theory, the market for corporate control, has not operated as predicted. Frank Easterbrook & Daniel Fischel, The Economic Structure of Corporate Law (1991). First, the stock market upon which the market in corporate control depends has not been as efficient as contractarians supposed. Second, takeovers are expensive, and not every badly managed company is subject to their discipline. Third, management has installed anti-takeover devices, sometimes with shareholder consent, even though contractarian theory predicts that the managers should have faced market discipline for installing such devices and shareholders should have rejected them as contrary to their best interest. Finally, state anti-takeover statutes passed at the behest of corporate managers, generally without shareholder participation, have undermined the effectiveness of the market for corporate control.

4. THE POLITICAL PRODUCT MODEL

If the contractarian model does not explain the Berle and Means separation of ownership and control in the modern U.S. public corporation, what does? Some scholars have suggested the role of the public shareholder is the product of a combination of political and economic forces.

> The prevailing paradigm is that the modern corporation survived because it was the fittest means of dealing with large-scale organization. But if politics cut off lines of development, then whether it is the inevitable form for large-scale firms becomes doubtful. Politics and the organization of financial intermediaries cannot be left out of the equation.

> Another paradigm, a political paradigm, better explains the modern American corporation than the prevailing paradigm does alone. The size and technology story fails to fully explain ownership patterns. There are organizational alternatives to fragmented ownership; the most prominent concentrated institutional ownership, a result prevalent in other countries (such as bank ownership in Germany and the *keiretsu* corporate-bank alliances in Japan). Enterprises could have obtained economies of scale and investors could have obtained diversification through large financial intermediaries that brought small investors and large firms together. These

institutions could have shared power in the enterprise with the new managers. But American law and politics deliberately diminished the power of financial institutions to hold the large equity blocks that would foster serious oversight of managers. The origin of the modern corporation lies in technology, economics, and politics.

Think about it. Fragmented securities markets are not the only way to move savings from households to the large firm. One could move savings from people to firms directly through securities markets, or indirectly through large financial intermediaries, which could then take big blocks of stock, sit in boardrooms, and balance power with the CEO. The increasing institutionalization of American securities markets and the concentrated ownership abroad mean this was economically viable. The institutional alternatives would raise a distinctive set of problems: bad management in the intermediary, instability of the intermediary, and political discomfort with concentrated private accumulations of power. All these are possible, but do not refute the proposition that there is more than one way to organize large scale enterprise, and that the short list of alternatives has at least one clear contender with the securities markets, namely the powerful financial intermediary.

Mark J. Roe, Strong Managers and Weak Owners: The Political Roots of the Separation of Ownership From Control 20–21 (1994).

Professor Roe asserts that corporate structures with strong managers and weak owners developed in the United States partly due to path dependence—that is, a path that "winds and goes here instead of there, when a straight road would be a much easier drive." Like a road that meanders along a path taken decades before, corporate law does not necessarily reflect the approach that would be chosen if society were making the decision today. But, having invested in the original path and in the resources alongside the path, it is easier to keep the winding road than to build another.

The rules and practices that weakened financial intermediaries arose because the American public historically abhorred private concentrations of economic power—concentrations that more powerful financial institutions would create, concentrations that a more powerful central government would have made politically palatable, concentrations that would probably be regulated, not destroyed, were they first arising today.

As large-scale industry arose at the end of the nineteenth century, it faced two financing problems created by the absence of nationwide financial institutions: big industry needed to gather lots of capital nationally, and certain organizational forms that worked well with strong financial institutions were unavailable. We developed very good substitutes. We developed, for example, high-quality securities markets, which allowed firms to raise capital in a national market, to remedy the absence of truly national financial institutions. We developed antitrust rules that promoted competition and, because competition pushes even firms with substandard internal governance toward efficiency, the costs of internal governance problems were reduced. America's continent-sized economy allowed enough competition to prevent any corporate governance problems from being too costly.

In time, we adopted new legal and economic institutions that are still not as well developed in other advanced nations. Corporate boards now have well defined legal duties that partly constrain managers, and we have an active bar that pursues lawsuits, some of which are legitimate and functional. We have developed a professionalism that motivates some managers. We have had hostile takeovers, which constrained managers.

Whatever tasks strong financial institutions might have done, other institutions developed to do. Although this take sees efficiency driving business evolution, we did not have an economic battle between one form of corporate ownership and another—through decentralized securities markets versus ownership through powerful financial institutions—one winning and the other losing. We barred the second type, allowed only the first type, and the consequential evolution made that which was available work satisfactorily.

Mark J. Roe, *Chaos and Evolution in Law and Economics*, 109 Harv. L. Rev. 641, 645–46 (1996).

5. SHAREHOLDER PRIMACY AND THE TEAM PRODUCTION MODEL

None of the foregoing models of the public corporation resolve whether the corporation should be run primarily for the benefit of shareholders or should be shaped to serve broader social goals. Thus the famous Berle-Dodd debate which we first saw in Chapter 4 continues. Most commentators assert that the corporation should be run for shareholders—a "shareholder primacy" norm. They offer several principal justifications in support of that theory. First, the shareholders are viewed as the residual claimants in a corporation, entitled to whatever remains after fixed payments have been made pursuant to explicit contracts to nonshareholder groups such as employees, managers and creditors. Second, and closely related, is the idea that the shareholders are the "owners" of the corporation and are most sensitive to corporate performance.

But as we have seen, shareholders do not "own" the corporation in the same way a proprietor owns her own business. The shareholders cannot determine what products the corporation will sell, who will run the day-to-day operations, whether cash will be paid to the owners, when the business will take on new debt, or even whether the business should be sold. Further recall that a shareholder can diversify her financial capital so as to reduce the risk of loss in any specific investment but that an employee cannot diversify her human capital to guard against the risk of business failure. The large numbers of business failures and employee layoffs in recent years have brought this message home quite clearly. *See* Lynn A. Stout, *Bad and Not-So-Bad Arguments for Shareholder Primacy*, 75 S. Cal. L. Rev. 1189 (2002). Nevertheless, the shareholder primacy norm retains considerable support. *See, e.g.*, Henry Hansmann & Reinier Kraakman, *The End of History for Corporate Law*, 89 Geo. L.J. 439 (2001).

That norm, however, has its limitations. First, it is unclear what it means. Must directors make every business decision solely on the basis of maximizing the financial wealth of current shareholders? Corporate law does not require this, at least in the form of an enforceable fiduciary duty. There is no modern case where a shareholder successfully brought a derivative suit against a board on the specific ground that the board failed to pursue a business strategy or action that would have maximized corporate profit. Indeed, there are well-known cases that strongly suggests the opposite proposition—that shareholders cannot substitute their viewpoint of profit-maximizing strategy through the medium of a derivative suit for breach of duty though they may plausibly have better thoughts on the matters. *See, e.g.,* Kamin v. American Express Co., 387 N.Y.S.2d 993 (App.Div. 1976) (upholding a board's decision to forego a decision that would minimize tax liability); Shlensky v. Wrigley, 237 N.E.2d 776 (Ill.App. 1968) (upholding a board decision to forego installing lights on a stadium though it could generate greater business). Corporate fiduciary duties are generally understood as running to the "corporation" itself rather than primarily to shareholders. Matters of business strategy and corporate actions—whether right or wrong, smart or not so bright— are within the province of the board's authority to manage the business and affairs of the corporation. The business judgment rule gives directors broad latitude to make decisions that do not necessarily maximize shareholder value.

Furthermore, no corporate statute expressly mandates profit maximization. Instead, contemporary corporate statutes that authorize charitable contributions and, in some states, permit directors to consider nonshareholder constituencies seem inconsistent with shareholder wealth maximization. In fact, corporate management often say they operate by considering the impact of their business decisions on all the corporation's constituencies, not just shareholders.

Seeking to bridge theory and reality, Professors Margaret Blair (an economist) and Lynn Stout (a law professor) offer an alternative model that they describe as "team production." Drawing on work by financial economists, they argue that a business corporation "requires inputs from a large number of individuals, including shareholders, creditors, managers, and rank-and-file employees"—all of whom constitute a "team." Corporate law calls on team members to cede control of the enterprise to the board of directors. In so doing, "the team members have created a new and separate entity that takes on a life of its own and could, potentially, act against their interests, leading them to lose what they have invested in the enterprise."

Why would team members give up control to the board in this way? For Blair and Stout, the answer is that team members believe they will capture a greater share of the gains of team production than if they attempted to write contracts with the other corporate participants. In this model, the board becomes the focal point for resolving the claims of all the team members—a "mediating hierarchy."

> Our argument suggests that it is misleading to view a public corporation as merely a bundle of assets under common ownership. Rather, a public corporation is a team of people who enter into a complex agreement to work together for their mutual gain. Participants—including shareholders, employees, and perhaps other stakeholders such as creditors or the local community—enter into a "pactum subjectionis" under which they yield control over outputs and key inputs (time, intellectual skills, or financial capital) to the hierarchy. They enter into this mutual agreement in an effort to reduce wasteful shirking and rent-seeking by relegating to the internal hierarchy the right to determine the division of duties and resources in the joint enterprise. They thus agree not to specific terms or outcomes (as in a traditional "contract"), but to participation in a process of internal goal setting and dispute resolution.

> The mediating hierarchy model of the public corporation necessarily implies that authority for making some allocative decisions—those that take place "within" the firm—ultimately rests with the board of directors, whose decisions cannot be overturned by appealing to some outside authority, like a court. This claim should not be read too broadly. When members of the hierarchy behave in ways that threaten the hierarchy itself (as when corporate directors violate their duty of loyalty to the firm through self-dealing), courts will intervene.

> We realize that this approach may seem odd—even counterintuitive—to corporate theorists accustomed to thinking of corporations in terms of a grand-design principal-agent model where shareholders are the principals and directors are their

agents. Nevertheless, our claim that directors should be viewed as disinterested trustees charged with faithfully representing the interests not just of shareholders, but of all team members, is consistent with the way that many directors have historically described their own roles. Most importantly, our model of corporations is consistent with the law itself.

Margaret M. Blair & Lynn A. Stout, *A Team Production Theory of Corporate Law*, 85 Va. L. Rev. 247, 277–87 (1999).

6. THE DIRECTOR-CENTRIC MODEL

Notice that all of these various theories of the public corporation assume that legal (if not actual) control of the corporation resides with the board of directors. Some, such as Berle and Means, see this as a problem and favor increased regulation to move control back into the hands of shareholders. Others, such as the contractarians, see board centrality as the result of implicit bargaining and would only seek to ensure that markets, particularly the market in corporate control, remain functional. Yet others see the powerful role of the board as the outcome of politics (the political realists) or the current state of the law (the team production theorists)—without coming to a view on the efficiency of the status quo.

Some recent corporate scholars, including Professor Stephen Bainbridge, have resolved these questions by asserting that the separation of ownership and control is not only real, but highly efficient. By placing control in the board of directors, these scholars argue that the modern corporation, particularly in the United States, has succeeded in organizing resources (labor, capital, goods) to produce enormous social wealth. Further empowering shareholders, beyond minor modifications to existing rules, would be a mistake—for shareholders.

> Any model of corporate governance must answer two basic sets of questions: (1) Who decides? In other words, which corporate constituency possesses ultimate decisionmaking power? (2) When the ultimate decisionmaker, whoever it may be, is presented with a zero sum game in which it must prefer the interests of one corporate constituency over those of all others, whose interests prevail?

> On the means question, prior scholarship typically favored either shareholder primacy or managerialism. In contrast, the power and right to exercise decisionmaking fiat is vested neither in the shareholders nor the managers, but in the board of directors. According to this director primacy model, the board of directors is not a mere agent of the shareholders, but rather is a sort of Platonic guardian serving as the nexus of the various contracts making up the corporation. As a positive theory of corporate governance, the director primacy model strongly emphasizes the

role of fiat—*i.e.*, the centralized decisionmaking authority possessed by the board of directors.

The substantial virtues of fiat can be realized only by preserving the board's decisionmaking authority from being trumped by either shareholders or courts. At some point, greater accountability necessarily makes the decisionmaking process less efficient, while highly efficient decisionmaking structures necessarily reduce accountability. In general, that tension is resolved in favor of authority. Because only shareholders are entitled to elect directors, boards of public corporations are insulated from pressure by nonshareholder corporate constituencies, such as employees or creditors. At the same time, the diffuse nature of U.S. stock ownership and regulatory impediments to investor activism insulate directors from shareholder pressure. Accordingly, the board has virtually unconstrained freedom to exercise business judgment. Ultimately, fiat is both the defining characteristic of corporate governance and its overarching value.

On the ends questions, prior scholarship has tended to favor either shareholder primacy or various forms of stakeholderism. Again, the director primacy model rejects both approaches. Director primacy can be reconciled with a contractual obligation on the board's part to maximize the value of the shareholders' residual claim.

Stephen M. Bainbridge, *Director Primacy: The Means and Ends of Corporate Governance*, 97 Nw. U. L. Rev. 547, 605–06 (2003).

7. THE AGENCY CAPITALISM MODEL

Models of the legal and economic mechanisms that shape corporate behavior continue to evolve. In 2013 Professors Gordon and Gilson proposed an entirely new model. Ronald J. Gilson & Jeffrey N. Gordon, *The Agency Costs of Agency Capitalism: Activist Investors and the Revaluation of Governance Rights,* 113 Colum. L. Rev. 863 (2013). Their argument starts with the observation that the ownership of public companies today looks very different from what Berle and Means described *circa* 1933. In that era individual investors owned a majority of the shares of most public companies; today large institutions—primarily pension funds and mutual funds—own nearly three-quarters of the common stock of the 1,000 largest U.S. public corporations. These institutions hold this stock for the benefit of the many individuals to whom they provide retirement benefits or who have chosen to invest in the stock market through the diversified vehicle of a mutual fund. These institutions are thus, in a sense, agents for their beneficiaries in the holding of stock. This results in two agency relationships: corporate managers acting as agents for shareholders; and institutional shareholders acting as agents for their beneficiaries. The authors dub the resulting governance structure, "agency capitalism."

Gilson and Gordon argue that the business models of most institutional investors provide them little incentive to engage in active monitoring of their portfolio companies. They compete in the market for institutional fund management services by trying to provide superior returns, evaluated in terms of relative performance. Such institutions, "can be expected to be skilled at managing portfolios, not at developing more profitable alternatives to a portfolio company's business strategy." Moreover their portfolios usually consist of relatively small percentages of the stock of many different companies, and improvements in the strategy of any one of them would have a relatively small effect on the returns of the portfolio. Consequently, the benefits they would derive from efforts to improve the performance of under-performing companies by active monitoring or exercising rights as shareholders would usually be lower than the costs of engaging in such activity. In other words, the value to these institutional investors of their governance rights in portfolio companies is small. The rational economic choice for such investors is to sell the stock of an under-performer rather than attempt to improve it.

In recent years a new breed of investor has arisen that seeks to capitalize on underutilized governance rights. These "activist investors" seek to identify underperforming companies that could be made more profitable through the exercise of governance rights. The activists then purchase significant, but not controlling, stakes in these companies and seek to persuade more passive institutions to join them in bringing about changes in the companies' strategy or structure. They do this by exerting public pressure on management, and if this is not successful, by engaging in proxy contests. According to a study cited by Gilson and Gordon, during the period 2000 to 2007 these campaigns were successful approximately 30% of the time.

C. CORPORATE GOVERNANCE IN A FEDERAL SYSTEM

With the exception of a few corporations that have been chartered by Congress, corporations in the United States are all creatures of state law. States grant them their charters, and state statutory and case law establish the basic organic rules pursuant to which corporations operate. Federal law is not, however, entirely without effect on the manner in which corporations are governed. The federal government regulates corporations in many ways, under the antitrust laws, banking regulation, civil rights laws, environmental law, labor law and product safety laws. Moreover, in response to dissatisfaction over the efficacy of the state law of corporate governance, federal law has begun to play an increasingly important and direct role in the governance of publicly-traded corporations, principally through the laws of federal securities regulation. In a federal system, this necessarily implicates questions with respect to both the allocation of power over corporations among the states, and its allocation between individual states and the federal government. The following materials consider some of the more important of these questions.

1.   THE INTERNAL AFFAIRS DOCTRINE

Corporations are organized under the law of one particular state. There is no requirement that a corporation incorporate in the state of its principal place of business—or even in a state in which it has operations— and a business can choose to incorporate under the laws of whatever state best suits its needs. With relatively little difficulty, it can reincorporate in another state if subsequent needs are better served by the laws of the other state. The choice is made by the management of the corporation rather than by its shareholders, thereby raising the possibility that managers will choose a state whose statutory and case law favors them rather than shareholders.

As noted in Chapter 2, an important characteristic of U.S. corporate law is its choice of law rule: the law of the state of incorporation, with rare exceptions, governs the "internal affairs" of the corporation. Restatement (Second) of Conflicts of Laws §§ 296–310 (1971). This rule, known as the "internal affairs doctrine," means that the relationships between shareholders and managers (directors and officers) are governed by the corporate statutes and case law of the state where the corporation is incorporated. If a suit raising corporate law issues is brought in a state other than the state of incorporation, the courts must apply the substantive law of the state of incorporation, not the law of the forum state. This, for example, the internal affairs doctrine provides that a Texas court adjudicating a dispute regarding the internal affairs of Delaware corporation must apply Delaware rather than Texas law to the dispute.

Application of the internal affairs doctrine means that the law of the state of incorporation governs the right of shareholders to vote, to receive distributions of corporate property, to receive information from the management about the affairs of the corporation, to limit the powers of the corporation to specifically chosen fields of activity, and to bring suit on behalf of the corporation when the managers refuse to do so. Perhaps most importantly, the internal affairs doctrine applies to the set of rules defining the fiduciary duties that the managers of a corporation owe to the corporation and its shareholders. The law of the state of incorporation also determines the procedures by which the board of directors will act, the right and extent to which officers and directors may be indemnified by the corporation, and the corporation's right to issue stock and to merge with other companies.

Any other choice of law rule would be extremely difficult to administer when the corporation is a multi-state venture. How could it be decided, for example, which stockholders were entitled to vote at an annual meeting if it were necessary to follow each potentially conflicting law of every state in which the corporation did business? Obviously, with respect to such questions a choice must be made, and the internal affairs doctrine enables a court to make this choice by deciding these questions according to the law of the state of incorporation.

The "external affairs" of a corporation are generally governed by the law of the place where the activities occur rather than by the place of incorporation. For example, a state's labor laws govern conditions of employment and minimum wages of the operations of all businesses within the state, wherever the businesses might be incorporated. State tax laws generally apply to activities of any corporation within the state especially those that are imposed on corporate real estate and income. Franchise taxes, which are collected by the state of incorporation from companies incorporated there, do not depend on the situs of a corporation's activities or property.

Some activities are governed by both internal and external rules. For example, state corporation law controls the right to merge and the procedure to be followed, but mergers are also independently subject to antitrust laws and securities laws.

2. THE INTERNAL AFFAIRS DOCTRINE AS A CONSTITUTIONAL PRINCIPLE

a. Introduction

Under early doctrine, a state could exclude out-of-state corporations altogether from engaging in intrastate business within its borders, and thus could subject foreign corporations to conditions for doing business within the state. More recently, the Supreme Court has concluded that it is "now established that whatever the extent of a state's authority to exclude foreign corporations from doing business within its boundaries, that authority does not justify imposition of more onerous taxes or other burdens on foreign corporations than those imposed on domestic corporations, unless the discrimination between foreign and domestic corporations bears a rational relation to a legitimate state purpose." *Western & Southern Life Insurance Co. v. State Board of Equalization of California*, 451 U.S. 648 (1987).

In practice, states do not seek to exclude foreign corporations, but seek to assert some control, mainly for revenue raising purposes. Thus, if a company is to engage in "local" business in a foreign state, it must register within the state so as to qualify to do business there as a foreign corporation. But if the corporation's intrastate activities are an inseparable part of an interstate transaction, it may not be required to qualify as a foreign corporation because of the constitutional prohibition against interference with interstate commerce.

Originally, the main purpose of the registration requirement was to assure that foreign corporations would be subject to the jurisdiction of the courts of the state and amenable to service of process in the state, objectives that have been largely achieved by the expansion of long-arm jurisdiction. Today, sanctions for a failure to qualify to do business are relatively mild; they generally entail little more than a temporary bar of access to local courts. This may be embarrassing when the corporation is sued and is unable to file an answer or a counterclaim but under most statutes, registration, even after the suit is filed, removes this bar.

Although this book is not a constitutional law text, it is important to note that some courts have said the internal affairs doctrine presents questions of U.S. constitutional law. The primary constitutional argument addressed is that a state statute violates the federal "dormant commerce clause," which limits the extent to which state laws may reach outside the state's territory. Under this doctrine, a state statute would be unconstitutional if it either (1) treated domestic and foreign corporations differently, or (2) ran the risk of generating multiple and conflicting standards that would burden interstate commerce. (The dormant commerce clause is not an explicit constitutional provision, but instead is a negative implication of the Commerce Clause, which gives Congress—not the states—the power to regulate interstate commerce.) Another argument that some courts make is that a state statute covering the internal affairs of corporations incorporated in other states might violate the federal "due process" clause. According to this doctrine, a state may not apply its laws to corporations incorporated in other states if it lacks sufficient contacts with the corporation and its conduct. Other cases treat disputes regarding internal affairs as involving conflicts of laws questions, and do not reach the constitutional issues.

b.   Antitakeover Statutes: *CTS* and Its Progeny

During the takeover wave of the 1970s and 1980s, a number of states adopted laws designed to protect corporations conducting local business from uninvited takeover bids that were opposed by the target company's management.[1] These first generation laws gave state regulators the power to decide if tender offers could be made to residents in their states. During the 1980s, the Supreme Court passed on claims that two state antitakeover laws were unconstitutional because they violated the Supremacy and Commerce Clauses. The Supremacy Clause claims were based on the

---

[1] An uninvited takeover bid frequently involves an offer (called a "*tender offer*"), made directly to a corporation's shareholders, to purchase all or a large portion of that corporation's stock.

Williams Act, a measure Congress adopted in 1968 to regulate tender offers. The Act was intended to ensure that when a public company becomes the target of a tender offer, its shareholders will receive adequate information about the bid and have sufficient time to evaluate that information. The Act also was meant to treat bidders and targets equally in the conduct of tender offers.

Edgar v. MITE Corp., 457 U.S. 624 (1982), involved an Illinois law regulating tender offers for any corporation 10 percent or more of whose shares were owned by Illinois residents, if the corporation also was organized under Illinois law, had its principal office in Illinois, or had 10 percent of its assets in Illinois. MITE made a takeover bid for Chicago Rivet that satisfied all three conditions.

Rather than comply with the law, MITE sued to have it declared unconstitutional. Six Justices voted to hold the Illinois law unconstitutional on one or more grounds (three Justices opined only that the case was moot). Three concluded that the law was preempted because it conflicted with the Williams Act's "policy of neutrality" between the bidder and the target; four concluded the Illinois law violated the Commerce Clause because it directly regulated interstate commerce; and five concluded the law violated the Commerce Clause because the burdens it imposed on interstate commerce were excessive in comparison to the local benefits the law produced. The Court rejected Illinois's claim that the internal affairs doctrine protected the law from constitutional attack, noting that the law was not limited to Illinois corporations but also covered foreign corporations that had the requisite proportion of Illinois shareholders and either their principal office or 10 percent of their assets in Illinois.

In response to *MITE*, several states enacted "second generation" antitakeover laws of several different types. Indiana's statute, the Indiana Control Share Acquisitions law (ICSA), was the first to be challenged. The ICSA differed from the Illinois law involved in *MITE* in that it applied only to Indiana corporations. In an attempt to insulate the ICSA from challenge under the Commerce Clause, Indiana further limited ICSA to corporations that had: (1) at least 100 shareholders; (2) at least 10% of their stock owned by Indiana residents; and (3) their principal place of business or substantial assets in Indiana. The ICSA provided that any person who acquired a control block of stock would not be entitled to vote that stock unless a majority of that corporation's disinterested shareholders voted to approve the acquisition.

The ICSA effectively extended to 50 days the time a target company's managers had to defeat a hostile bid, since no potential acquiror would purchase stock in a target company unless it was sure it would be able to vote that stock. Thus the statute represented a substantial extension of the 20 business day period that the Williams Act allowed. But the ICSA also made it easier for a target company's shareholders to protect themselves against certain tactics that might coerce them into accepting a bid that they preferred to reject.

Dynamics, the owner of 9.6 percent of CTS, an Indiana corporation covered by ICSA, announced a tender offer for sufficient shares to increase its ownership interest to 27.5 percent, thus potentially triggering ICSA. Dynamics simultaneously sued to enjoin enforcement of the ICSA, claiming it was preempted by the Williams Act and violated the Commerce Clause. The Seventh Circuit, relying on MITE, agreed that ICSA was unconstitutional on both grounds.

CTS CORP. v. DYNAMICS CORP. OF AMERICA
481 U.S. 69 (1987).

JUSTICE POWELL delivered the opinion of the Court.

[The Court first reversed the Seventh Circuit's holding that the ICSA was preempted by the Williams Act.]

As an alternative basis for its decision, the Court of Appeals held that the Act violates the Commerce Clause of the Federal Constitution. We now address this holding. On its face, the Commerce Clause is nothing more than a grant to Congress of the power "[t]o regulate Commerce * * * among the several States * * *," Art. I, § 8, cl. 3. But it has been settled for more than a century that the Clause prohibits States from taking certain actions respecting interstate commerce even absent congressional action. The Court's interpretation of "these great silences of the Constitution" has not always been easy to follow. Rather, as the volume and complexity of commerce and regulation have grown in this country, the Court has articulated a variety of tests in an attempt to describe the difference between those regulations that the Commerce Clause permits and those regulations that it prohibits.

The principal objects of dormant Commerce Clause scrutiny are statutes that discriminate against interstate commerce. The Indiana Act is not such a statute. It has the same effects on tender offers whether or not the offeror is a domiciliary or resident of Indiana. Thus, it "visits its effects equally upon both interstate and local business."

Dynamics nevertheless contends that the statute is discriminatory because it will apply most often to out-of-state entities. This argument rests on the contention that, as a practical matter, most hostile tender offers are launched by offerors outside Indiana. But this argument avails Dynamics little. "The fact that the burden of a state regulation falls on some interstate companies does not, by itself, establish a claim of discrimination against interstate commerce." Because nothing in the Indiana Act imposes a greater burden on out-of-state offerors than it does on similarly situated

Indiana offerors, we reject the contention that the Act discriminates against interstate commerce.

This Court's recent Commerce Clause cases also have invalidated statutes that may adversely affect interstate commerce by subjecting activities to inconsistent regulations. The Indiana Act poses no such problem. So long as each State regulates voting rights only in the corporations it has created, each corporation will be subject to the law of only one State. No principle of corporation law and practice is more firmly established than a State's authority to regulate domestic corporations, including the authority to define the voting rights of shareholders. See Restatement (Second) of Conflict of Laws § 304 (1971) (concluding that the law of the incorporating State generally should "determine the right of a shareholder to participate in the administration of the affairs of the corporation"). Accordingly, we conclude that the Indiana Act does not create an impermissible risk of inconsistent regulation by different States.

The Court of Appeals did not find the Act unconstitutional for either of these threshold reasons. Rather, its decision rested on its view of the Act's potential to hinder tender offers. We think the Court of Appeals failed to appreciate the significance for Commerce Clause analysis of the fact that state regulation of corporate governance is regulation of entities whose very existence and attributes are a product of state law. Every State in this country has enacted laws regulating corporate governance. By prohibiting certain transactions, and regulating others, such laws necessarily affect certain aspects of interstate commerce. This necessarily is true with respect to corporations with shareholders in States other than the State of incorporation. Large corporations that are listed on national exchanges, or even regional exchanges, will have shareholders in many States and shares that are traded frequently. The markets that facilitate this national and international participation in ownership of corporations are essential for providing capital not only for new enterprises but also for established companies that need to expand their businesses. This beneficial free market system depends at its core upon the fact that a corporation—except in the rarest situations—is organized under, and governed by, the law of a single jurisdiction, traditionally the corporate law of the State of its incorporation.

These regulatory laws may affect directly a variety of corporate transactions. Mergers are a typical example. In view of the substantial effect that a merger may have on the shareholders' interests in a corporation, many States require supermajority votes to approve mergers. By requiring a greater vote for mergers than is required for other transactions, these laws make it more difficult for corporations to merge. State laws also may provide for "dissenters' rights" under which minority shareholders who disagree with corporate decisions to take particular actions are entitled to sell their shares to the corporation at fair market value. By requiring the corporation to purchase the shares of dissenting shareholders, these laws may inhibit a corporation from engaging in the specified transactions.[12]

It thus is an accepted part of the business landscape in this country for States to create corporations, to prescribe their powers, and to define the rights that are acquired by purchasing their shares. A State has an interest in promoting stable relationships among parties involved in the corporations it charters, as well as in ensuring that investors in such corporations have an effective voice in corporate affairs.

Dynamics argues in any event that the State has " 'no legitimate interest in protecting the nonresident shareholders.' " Dynamics relies heavily on the statement by the *MITE* Court that "[i]nsofar as the * * * law burdens out-of-state transactions, there is nothing to be weighed in the balance to sustain the law." But that comment was made in reference to an Illinois law that applied as well to out-of-state corporations as to in-state corporations. We agree that Indiana has no interest in protecting nonresident shareholders of nonresident corporations. But this Act applies only to corporations incorporated in Indiana. We reject the contention that Indiana has no interest in providing for the shareholders of its corporations the voting autonomy granted by the Act. Indiana has a substantial interest in preventing the corporate form from becoming a shield for unfair business dealing.

On its face, the Indiana Control Share Acquisitions Chapter evenhandedly determines the voting rights of shares of Indiana corporations. The Act does not conflict with the provisions or purposes of the Williams Act. To the limited extent that the Act affects interstate commerce, this is justified by the State's interests in defining the attributes of shares in its corporations and in protecting shareholders. Congress has never questioned the need for state regulation of these matters. Nor do we think such regulation offends the Constitution. Accordingly, we reverse the judgment of the Court of Appeals.

THE AFTERMATH OF CTS

More than twenty states enacted second generation statutes in the years between the *MITE* and *CTS* decisions. However, legislators and lobbyists were often reluctant to promote legislation for fear of constitutional infirmities.

---

[12] Numerous other common regulations may affect both nonresident and resident shareholders of a corporation. Specified votes may be required for the sale of all of the corporation's assets. The election of directors may be staggered over a period of years to prevent abrupt changes in management. Various classes of stock may be created with differences in voting rights as to dividends and on liquidation. Provisions may be made for cumulative voting. Corporations may adopt restrictions on payment of dividends to ensure that specified ratios of assets to liabilities are maintained for the benefit of the holders of corporate bonds or notes. Where the shares of a corporation are held in States other than that of incorporation, actions taken pursuant to these and similar provisions of state law will affect all shareholders alike wherever they reside or are domiciled.

After *CTS*, legislative views changed immediately. Fourteen states adopted new statutes within approximately six months. More important, several of these new "third generation" statutes strengthen the less restrictive second generation statutes by using Indiana as a model, and many tested *CTS*'s limits by mandating constraints on bidders that went further than the Indiana statute. These third generation or business-combination statutes seek to prevent an acquirer from entering into a range of transactions with the acquired corporation for the period of time specified in the statute. For example, after a bidder has acquired a controlling interest in the target corporation, the statute may prohibit the bidder from merging with the target or liquidating its assets until the statutory time period has elapsed or the target board of directors has approved the transaction.

Perhaps the most important reaction to *CTS* was that Delaware, the leading incorporation state, enacted a third generation statute. Why would Delaware adopt such a statute, which at least arguably hurt shareholders by permitting managers to defend against takeovers that would enable them to sell their shares for a premium? According to Professor Roberta Romano, Delaware was motivated, at least in part, by the threat that some Delaware corporations would reincorporate in states with antitakeover statutes if Delaware did not adopt its own law. Delaware feared, rightly or wrongly, that inaction would hurt its preeminence in the incorporation business. *See* Roberta Romano, *The Future of Hostile Takeovers: Legislation and Public Opinion,* 57 U. Cin. L. Rev. 457 (1988). In actuality, the Delaware statute is among the least restrictive of the third generation statutes.

3.   THE CHOICE OF THE STATE OF INCORPORATION

a.   The History of States' Competition for Corporate Charters

State corporation law varies from state to state, and the organizers of a corporation are free to choose the state in which to incorporate and therefore the law governing many aspects of its behavior. This freedom has had significant implications for the operation and development of U.S. corporate law. It means that states can compete for incorporations since the corporate participants choose where the corporation is incorporated or reincorporated. Whether such competition is harmful or beneficial to investors is a question that has been heavily debated. Does the competition lead to a law that systematically favors management, a "race for the bottom?" Or does the competition produce a corporate law that reflects the optimal bargain between shareholders and managers, a "race for the top?" Is there still real competition? Finally, how does actual and potential federal corporate legislation affect the nature of the competition? This section considers those questions and concludes with some thoughts about the nature of the U.S. corporate law system.

State corporation laws are essentially enabling statues that establish a relatively flexible organizational framework that allows considerable room for "self-ordering" and involves minimal regulatory intervention.

Things were not always so. The following excerpt from Mr. Justice Brandeis' famous dissenting opinion in *Liggett Co. v. Lee* recounts some of the historical development.

Louis K. Liggett Co. v. Lee
288 U.S. 517 (1933).

Mr. Justice Brandeis (dissenting in part).

[The case, itself, was a challenge to the constitutionality of a tax imposed by Florida on chain stores. The Court struck down the tax. Brandeis' dissenting view was that "Whether the corporate privilege shall be granted or withheld is always a matter of state policy * * *. If a state believes that adequate protection * * * can be secured, without revoking the corporate privilege, by imposing * * * upon corporations the handicap of higher, discriminatory license fees as compensation for the privilege, I know of nothing in the Fourteenth Amendment to prevent it from making the experiment."]

Second. The prevalence of the corporation in America has led men of this generation to act, at times, as if the privilege of doing business in corporate form were inherent in the citizen; and has led them to accept the evils attendant upon the free and unrestricted use of the corporate mechanism as if these evils were the inescapable price of civilized life, and, hence, to be borne with resignation. Throughout the greater part of our history a different view prevailed. Although the value of this instrumentality in commerce and industry was fully recognized, incorporation for business was commonly denied long after it had been freely granted for religious, educational, and charitable purposes. It was denied because of fear. Fear of encroachment upon the liberties and opportunities of the individual. Fear of the subjection of labor to capital. Fear of monopoly. Fear that the absorption of capital by corporations, and their perpetual life, might bring evils similar to those which attended mortmain. There was a sense of some insidious menace inherent in large aggregations of capital, particularly when held by corporations. So at first the corporate privilege was granted sparingly; and only when the grant seemed necessary in order to procure for the community some specific benefit otherwise unattainable. The later enactment of general incorporation laws does not signify that the apprehension of corporate domination had been overcome. The desire for business expansion created an irresistible demand for more charters; and it was believed that under general laws embodying safeguards of universal application the scandals and favoritism incident to special incorporation could be avoided. The general laws, which long embodied severe restrictions upon size and upon the scope of corporate activity, were, in part, an expression of the desire for equality of opportunity.

The removal by the leading industrial states of the limitations upon the size and powers of business corporations appears to have been due, not to their conviction that maintenance of the restrictions was undesirable in itself, but to the conviction that it was futile to insist upon them; because local restriction would be circumvented by foreign incorporation. Indeed, local restriction seemed worse than futile. Lesser states, eager for the revenue derived from the traffic in charters, had removed safeguards from their own incorporation laws. Companies were early formed to provide charters for corporations in states where the cost was lowest and the laws least restrictive. The states joined in advertising their wares. The race was one not of diligence but of laxity. Incorporation under such laws was possible; and the great industrial States yielded in order not to lose wholly the prospect of the revenue and the control incident to domestic incorporation.

———————

New Jersey was the first state to depart from the early philosophy of strict limitations on corporations beginning with its 1888 incorporation statute which was followed by a revision in 1896. With its 1899 statute, Delaware entered the competition, and eventually succeeded in becoming the leading state for the incorporation of large businesses. Charles Beard, the noted historian, described how this came about in testimony before a Senate Committee considering federal corporate legislation in 1937:

> Under the leadership of Woodrow Wilson, after he was challenged by Theodore Roosevelt to reform his own state, the legislature of New Jersey passed a series of laws doing away with corporate abuses and applying high standards to corporations. What was the result? The revenues of the State from taxes on corporations fell. Malefactors moved over into other states. In time the New Jersey Legislature repealed its strict and prudent legislation, and went back, not quite, but almost to old ways.

Federal Licensing of Corporations: Hearings on S. 10 Before a Subcommittee of the Senate Committee on the Judiciary, 75th Cong., 1st Sess. 74 (1937).

Since its ascendancy, Delaware corporate law has always been the subject of great controversy. Shortly after the 1967 adoption of major changes to the Delaware General Corporation Law, a writer observed:

> The sovereign state of Delaware is in the business of selling its corporation law. This is profitable business, for a corporation law is a good commodity to sell. The market is large, and relatively few producers compete on a national scale. The consumers of this commodity are corporations. Delaware, like any other good businessman, tries to give the consumer what he wants. In fact, those who will buy the product are not only consulted about their

preferences, but are also allowed to design the product and run the factory.

Comment, *Law for Sale: A Study of the Delaware Corporation Law of 1967*, 117 U. Pa. L. Rev. 861, 861–862 (1969).

Thereafter, in his seminal article, *Federalism and Corporate Law: Reflections Upon Delaware*, 83 Yale L.J. 663, 705 (1974), Professor William L. Cary argued that in its attempt to maintain its primacy as the home of large corporations, Delaware led a "race for the bottom" of corporate law. He contended that Delaware systematically had eliminated or reduced shareholder protections. As an example, he pointed to statutory provisions reducing the shareholder vote required to approve a merger from two-thirds to a majority. He also cited numerous decisions that he interpreted as giving an overly liberal application to the business judgment rule and making it easier for corporate managers to resist hostile tender offers.

Professor Cary's argument is based on the existence of the federal system. Because managers can choose where to incorporate, no state can use its corporate law to impose policies or governance structures that managers would determine contrary to the corporate interest. If the legislature were to do so, managers would simply "exit" and reincorporate in a more hospitable jurisdiction. Accordingly, he proposed that Congress adopt a federal minimum standards law for larger public companies that would impose federal fiduciary standards and other restrictions on corporate officers and directors.

It is possible to criticize Professor Cary's thesis on a number of grounds. The cases he cites are very carefully selected, tending to support his arguments and ignoring some that do not. And, although it is implicit in his argument that the principal purpose of a corporate statute is to protect shareholders, it is not clear what "protect" means. As Bayless Manning has argued, "There is nothing in the sky that informs us that 66 2/3 percent is a good number while 51 percent is a bad number for purposes of shareholder voting on mergers. No commentator or scholar ever attempts to establish, nor could it be established, that a higher numerical vote requirement would save incorporated enterprises from unwise mergers (whatever that might mean), even if one were to assume that the prevention of unwise economic transactions is a proper legislative function." Bayless Manning, *Thinking Straight About Corporate Law Reform*, 41 L. & Contemp. Prob. 3 (1977).

The most significant intellectual disagreement with Professor Cary has come from those who argue that market forces rather than legal doctrine will align the interests of shareholders and managers and that competition among states ultimately benefits investors. The principal response to Professor Cary is that of Professor (now Judge) Ralph K. Winter, Jr.

RALPH K. WINTER, JR., STATE LAW, SHAREHOLDER PROTECTION, AND THE THEORY OF THE CORPORATION

6 J. Legal Stud. 251, 256–257, 259, 275, 276 (1977).

[Professor Cary's] claim, it is absolutely critical to note, is not that an overriding social goal is sacrificed by state law, but simply that Delaware is preventing private parties from optimizing their private arrangements. With all due respect both to Professor Cary and to the almost universal academic support for his position, it is implausible on its face. The plausible argument runs in the opposite direction: (1) If Delaware permits corporate management to profit at the expense of shareholders and other states do not, then earnings of Delaware corporations must be less than earnings of comparable corporations chartered in other states and shares in the Delaware corporations must trade at lower prices. (2) Corporations with lower earnings will be at a disadvantage in raising debt or equity capital. (3) Corporations at a disadvantage in the capital market will be at a disadvantage in the product market and their share price will decline, thereby creating a threat of a takeover which may replace management. To avoid this result, corporations must seek out legal systems more attractive to capital. (4) States seeking corporate charters will thus try to provide legal systems which optimize the shareholder-corporation relationship.

The conclusion that Delaware shares sell for less is implicit in Professor Cary's analysis, for if a "higher" legal standard for management conduct will increase investor confidence, investor confidence in Delaware stock must have been less than in stocks of other states for more than a generation. This lack of confidence would have long been reflected in the price of Delaware shares. Moreover, a reduction in the earnings of a corporation will affect its ability to raise debt capital, as well as equity, since the risk of a lender is thereby increased and a higher interest rate will be charged. Delaware corporations, therefore, not only face a lower share price but also must pay higher interest rates.

Intervention in private transactions which impose no social cost can be justified only as a means of reducing the costs to the private parties. Thus, a prime function of state corporation codes is to supply standard terms which reduce the transaction costs, and thereby increase the benefits, of investing by eliminating costly bargaining which might otherwise accompany many routine corporate dealings. But substituting a mandatory legal rule for bargaining also may impose a cost in the form of the elimination of alternatives which the parties might prefer.

Much of the legal literature calling for further federal regulation either assumes that no costs will fall upon shareholders or merely undertakes a cursory "eyeballing" of the potential costs. To be sure, self-dealing and fraud exist in corporate affairs and their elimination is desirable. But at some point the exercise of control by general rules of law may impose costs on investors which damage them in both quantity and quality quite as much as self-dealing or fraud. A paradox thus results: maximizing the yield to investors generally may, indeed almost surely will, result in a number of cases of fraud or self-dealing; and eliminating all fraud or self-dealing may decrease the yield to shareholders generally.

A state which rigs its corporation code so as to reduce the yield to shareholders will spawn corporations which are less attractive as investment opportunities than comparable corporations chartered in other states or countries, as well as bonds, savings accounts, land, etc. Investors must be attracted before they can be cheated, and except for those seeking a "one shot," "take the money and run," opportunity to raid a corporation, management has no reason to seek out such a code. The chartering decision, therefore, so far as the capital market is concerned, will favor those states which offer the optimal yield to both shareholders and management.

So far as the capital market is concerned, it is not in the interest of management to seek out a corporate legal system which fails to protect investors, and the competition between states for charters is generally a competition as to which legal system provides an optimal return to both interests. Only when that competition between legal systems exists can we perceive which legal rules are most appropriate for the capital market. Once a single legal system governs that market, we can no longer compare investor reaction. Ironically, in view of the conventional wisdom, the greater danger is not that states will compete for charters but that they will not.

How do you decide which of these arguments is "correct?" Whatever your answer, it is clear that Cary's arguments and criticisms have had considerable force and continue to influence Delaware lawyers and judges to this day. Indeed, as one leading Delaware scholar has recently noted, "Professor Cary has also been personally responsible for much of the evolution of Delaware case law." Lawrence A. Hamermesh, *How We Make Law in Delaware, and What to Expect from Us in the Future*, 2 J. Bus. & Tech. L. 409, 411 (2007).

Judge Easterbrook and Professor Fischel support the "thesis that competition creates a powerful tendency for states to enact laws that operate to the benefit of investors." Frank H. Easterbrook & Daniel R. Fischel, The Economic Structure of Corporate Law 222 (1991). However, they characterize the market for state corporate law as less than efficient. They conclude that state competition for investors does not eliminate opportunistic behavior by managers. Similarly, competition for incorporation does not eliminate opportunistic behavior by states—even

Delaware has enacted an antitakeover statute. Ultimately, though, Easterbrook and Fischel oppose a federal corporate law "because Federal laws face less competition."

b. The Preeminence of Delaware

Stepping back from the welter of studies, the "race," whether for the bottom, as Cary described it, or the top, as Winter did, may be over. History has given Delaware an insurmountable lead.

Commentators generally agree on the reasons why Delaware has become preeminent. Roberta Romano, *The State Competition Debate in Corporate Law*, 8 Cardozo L. Rev. 709 (1987), notes that when publicly traded firms choose to reincorporate—move from one state where they are already incorporated to another—they choose Delaware 82% of the time. Firms tend to choose Delaware because of what Romano calls the "first mover advantage." Firms feel relatively confident that Delaware will respond promptly to the concerns of corporate managers in the future, because it has done so in the past.

Three factors bolster this belief. First, Delaware relies heavily on corporate franchise taxes and therefore would have much to lose by failing to amend its statute in order to provide firms with advantages offered elsewhere. Second, the Delaware state constitution requires a two-thirds vote of both houses of the legislature to change its corporate code. The supermajority requirement makes it particularly difficult for the legislature to deprive corporations of benefits they currently enjoy. Finally, Delaware has tremendous assets in terms of "legal capital" which includes a massive body of corporate case law, judicial expertise, and an administrative body that is geared to process corporate filings expeditiously.

In another article, Romano attaches particular importance to Delaware's judicial system. Courts in other jurisdictions increasingly look to and rely upon Delaware case law. Romano concludes:

> The value of a Delaware domicile to firms is more than an up-to-date code; Delaware also offers a comprehensive body of case law, which is not easily replicated by another state, and a handful of experienced judges. These factors afford firms greater predictability of the legal outcomes of their decisions, facilitating planning and reducing the costs of doing business. Indeed, the large number of corporations domiciled in Delaware contributes to the development of its case law, for the sheer numbers make it more likely that a particular issue will have been litigated.

Roberta Romano, *Law as a Product: Some Pieces of the Incorporation Puzzle,* 1 J. L. Econ. & Org. 225, 280 (1985).

Recent scholarship has provided a more nuanced analysis of the competition debate and reinforced the idea that Delaware is the pre-eminent corporate law state. Professors Marcel Kahan and Ehud Kamar have demonstrated that other states generally do not try to build up franchise tax revenues in the way that Delaware does. Moreover, they have not taken steps to create a business court similar to Delaware's Court of Chancery, nor do they amend their corporate statutes regularly as does Delaware. Marcel Kahan & Ehud Kamar, *The Myth of State Competition in Corporate Law*, 55 Stan. L.Rev. 679 (2002).

Similarly, drawing on a study of actual incorporations by public companies, Professors Lucian Bebchuk and Assaf Hamdani have argued that Delaware has no significant competitors for attracting and servicing out-of-state incorporations. Based on that study, they contend that rather than "fifty-one 'sellers' of corporate law rules compet[ing] in a 'national' market over any given firm," "the existing situation might be better understood as one in which there are fifty-one local markets, with the firms located in each of them making a choice between incorporating in their home state or out of it." See, Lucian A. Bebchuk & Assaf Hamdani, *Vigorous Race or Leisurely Walk: Reconsidering the Competition over Corporate Charters*, 112 Yale L.J. 553 (2002). And the vast majority of those firms that incorporate out of their home state do so in Delaware. Lucien A. Bebchuk & Alma Cohen, *Firms' Decisions Where to Incorporate*, 46 J.L. & Econ. (2003).

c. Delaware and Federal Law

If the state charter competition debate is largely over, does any competition remain for Delaware? Professor Mark Roe has argued that the long-standing "top or bottom" argument is now misconceived because Delaware's primary competition comes not from other states but from the federal government. Mark J. Roe, *Delaware's Competition*, 117 Harv. L. Rev. 588 (2003). According to Roe, it is the fear of federal incursion that keeps Delaware from going too far in one direction or the other.

In assessing this argument, it is important to keep in mind the nature of Delaware law. The Delaware corporate statute is essentially an enabling law that encourages private ordering by the participants in a business. And, as we will see throughout the book, Delaware courts are the quintessential common law courts, deciding only the cases before them and eschewing broad formulations of law. Federal law, by contrast, has broad coverage and is created largely by Congress and the SEC.

The responses of Delaware and the federal government to the Enron and WorldCom scandals in 2002 highlight some of these differences. Congress enacted the Sarbanes-Oxley Act and the stock exchanges, under prodding from the SEC, reformed their corporate governance standards for listed companies; but the Delaware legislature did not adopt any new legislation to deal with the scandals. As Professors Marcel Kahan and Ed Rock have noted, "given Delaware's traditional mode of addressing controversy, it had to wait until a legal dispute was brought in its courts. Since no case was brought, Delaware had no opportunity to address the scandals directly." Marcel Kahan & Edward Rock, *Symbiotic Federalism and the Structure of Corporate Law*, 58 Vand. L. Rev. 1573, 1617 (2005).

A number of commentators subsequently have developed the idea that the Delaware lawmaking system does not lend itself to immediate responses to large-scale crises in the way that federal law does. As Professor Lawrence Hamermesh has stated:

> The areas that the federal government handles much better than we do at the state level include market-oriented disclosure regulation, audit and accounting regulation, and insider trading enforcement. There is no way that the State of Delaware could ever systematically monitor an insider trading regime. Delaware, on the other hand, has a system primarily based on private enforcement, meaning that it is much better able to deal with insider conflict transactions, and merger and acquisition transactions.

The consequence, according to Hamermesh, is that we should not:

> expect detailed regulatory prescriptions from future Delaware lawmaking. Do not expect to see anything involving criminal or regulatory enforcement. Do not look for active attempts by the state legislature to head off further federal activity. Federal activity is going to come or it is not going to come, according to political factors that we in Delaware are not going to have much to say about. Nevertheless, you should expect us in Delaware to make every effort to maintain the stability and continuity of the existing balance of authority among managers and shareholders.

Lawrence A. Hamermesh, *How We Make Law in Delaware, and What to Expect from Us in the Future*, 2 J. Bus. & Tech. L. 409, 413–14 (2008). *See* Lawrence A. Hamermesh, *The Policy Foundations of Delaware Corporate Law*, 106 Colum. L. Rev. 1749 (2006).

Delaware judges are very much aware of the potential reach of federal law into Delaware corporate law and the tension that this reach can create but are not troubled by it. As Chancellor Chandler and Vice-Chancellor (now Chancellor) Strine have written:

> This division of responsibilities [between state and federal authorities] has never been marked by bright borders. To the contrary, many federal disclosure requirements have had the natural and (presumably) intended consequence of influencing boardroom practices. Similarly, the state law of fiduciary duties has been an important tool in evolving better disclosure practices,

particularly in the context of mergers and acquisitions requiring a stockholder vote or tendering decision. The tug-and-pull among the various policy actors has occurred in a civil manner.

William B. Chandler III & Leo E. Strine, Jr., *The New Federalism of the American Corporate Governance System: Preliminary Reflections of Two Residents of One Small State*, 152 U. Pa. L. Rev. 953, 974 (2003).

Strine has further written:

[T]he capacious constitutional authority of Congress over interstate commerce is something that Delaware and other state corporate lawmakers have constantly had to take into account. When state law appeared to substantial elements of the investment community to be insufficient to protect investor interests, calls for congressional action arose, calls that influenced state lawmakers to reexamine the balance of interests between managers and stockholders.

Leo E. Strine, Jr., *Breaking the Corporate Governance Logjam in Washington: Some Constructive Thoughts on a Responsible Path Forward*, 63 Bus. Law. 1079, 1081 (2008).

As we will see in much greater detail in Chapter 15, recent developments have emphasized the relationship between Delaware and federal law and the increasingly active role that the Delaware legislature has played in that relationship. In 2008, Delaware amended its Constitution to permit the SEC, among other government bodies, to certify questions of Delaware law to the Delaware courts. The SEC promptly used that provision to ask the Delaware Supreme Court to opine on the validity of a shareholder bylaw concerning shareholder access to the ballot in the nomination of directors. That litigation was followed by new Delaware legislation on the subject and an SEC rule to provide such access. Notwithstanding a judicial decision that invalidated the SEC rule without considering the federalism issues, it is fair to conclude that such issues remain an active work in progress.

4.   THE FUTURE SHAPE OF STATE CORPORATE LAW

If you are persuaded by Professor Cary's critique of Delaware law, is federalizing some or all of state corporate law the only answer, or can the latter be changed to give greater protection to shareholders? One way of beginning the answer to those questions is to inquire into the purpose of a corporate statute. Judge Winter believes that one of the most important purposes of the statute is "to supply standard terms which reduce the transaction costs, and thereby increase the benefits, of investing by eliminating costly bargaining which might otherwise accompany many routine corporate dealings." But that, by itself does not provide a complete answer. As we will see in subsequent chapters, very little actual bargaining does or can take place in public corporations. Another possible purpose is to consider the interests of shareholders, managers and other constituencies and have the statute strike a balance among these interests. In that context, consider a provision such as DGCL § 228 which permits a majority of a corporation's shareholders to act without a meeting by written consent. Professor Cary criticized this provision because it permits the managers of a public corporation to avoid holding an annual meeting at which they may face opposition. While this provision thus might seem to favor management over shareholders, shareholders may benefit because the consent procedure makes it easier for them to act when no meeting is imminent, no provisions exist to allow them to call a meeting, and management would oppose their actions.

In thinking about what a balanced statute might look like and the likelihood that it could be enacted, consider the following analysis by the late Professor Ernest Folk who was active in many state corporate law revisions including the Delaware General Corporation Law of 1967.

ERNEST L. FOLK, III, SOME REFLECTIONS OF A CORPORATION LAW DRAFTSMAN
42 Conn. Bar J. 409, 411–419 (1968).

Understanding the realities of corporate law revisions requires us to identify and assess a major fiction. Committees undertaking to rewrite corporation statutes usually believe, with varying degrees of devoutness, that they are pursuing an ideal of fairly and equitably balancing the varied and sometimes conflicting interests of the constituents of any corporation. In a large corporation, these constituents include management (which subdivides into the varying interests of the directors, both outside and inside), the officers, and others, the shareholders (which may subdivide into possibly conflicting groups), the creditors, employees, and the general public. In all events, corporation law revisers often suppose that they are balancing many such interests in the sense of hammering out compromises.

This is a fiction. Corporation law revision committees are not organized to work that way; they are not expected to do so; they do not do so; and the final product reflects no such approach. Clearly, the Delaware statute does not represent a balancing of interests. The excellent and able committee consisted chiefly of pro-management corporation attorneys, with a divided minority representing the specialized interests of the Secretary of State's office and of the derivative suit plaintiff. The majority was strengthened by two representatives of the service companies. Presumably, an acknowledged goal of balancing interests would dictate that no particular segment of the corporate community should command a majority, either singly or in coalition; but would require representatives of other potentially affected interests. Indeed, I find that the Delaware committee embraced a greater variety of interests than counterpart groups in other states. Thus, the inevitable structure of the groups charged with the revision belies the notion that interests are being balanced, for usually the only interest represented is management.

Naturally, the product reflects this fact. Yet it may be, and usually is, an excellent piece of work. In my view, this is true of the Delaware revision which has greatly influenced corporation law revisions since enactment in July 1967.

The short of the matter is that we do not in fact balance interests. We do not seek to protect shareholders or creditors or others; rather we limit their rights and remedies. We constantly enlarge the rights and freedom of management. Representing primarily management interests, we operate from a position of impregnable strength and prestige, and we produce a statute we think is best suited to running a corporation as management sees fit. This is not an unworthy purpose or result, but it is not an interest-balancing procedure.

The best that we can say of the fiction, even though it has little congruence with reality, is that it is benign. To the extent that corporate law revisers believe they are charged with protecting a variety of possibly inconsistent interests, it may generate a greater sense of responsibility and restraint than might be the case if they explicitly assumed that they can and will act only for one limited group. Whether this is so or not lies in the realm of imponderables, since no foundation is likely to finance a probe of the psychological processes of corporate law revisers in order to verify or discredit this hypothesis. Nor are there any evident adverse effects from the divergence between reality and the fiction.

Given the fact that state corporation statutes are now almost exclusively enabling-type enactments granting management maximum "flexibility", the next question is whether, indeed, any state today can effectively implement interests other than those of management, let alone those opposed by management. My considered conclusion is that this is not possible, even though many will be grieved at the thought that state power to regulate internal affairs of corporations is so drastically circumscribed.

A hypothetical example exhibits the reasons why the enabling-type statute is practically inevitable in the United States today. Suppose that a state, prompted by the loftiest motives, genuinely believes that abuses in corporations operating in that state can be prevented by legislation. By "prevent," in this context, we mean that detailed prescriptions of the structure, and regulation of the operations, of the corporation will likely prevent or correct abuses, especially acts hostile to shareholders. We can further assume, contrary to today's realities, that this is a politically realistic goal. Yet within the federal system the state cannot accomplish its objective. The regulatory approach of our hypothetical state will be almost immediately frustrated by the availability of other state statutes affording management the freedom it desires. The question then becomes whether local corporations can be compelled to stay home rather than migrate to a "liberal" jurisdiction. This would either require every corporation operating primarily in the particular state to incorporate there, or, if incorporated elsewhere, to impose local policies on it as a condition of doing business. As to the latter course, there is no serious doubt of the constitutionality of a state regulating the "pseudo-foreign" corporation, assuming sufficiency of substantial contacts between the state and the corporation, although the scope of power is by no means clear. Judicial decisions have imposed such regulation in various situations. More pertinent is the fact that an occasional state statute tries to regulate the "runaway" corporation, but with little success. For example, the North Carolina draftsmen submitted strict statutory provisions, but the legislature promptly struck them out although simultaneously enacting strict regulatory controls over domestic corporations. New York adopted more relaxed provisions than those rejected by North Carolina, but these have been watered down by the New York legislature. Most states do not give it a thought. In fact, those which follow the Model Act usually adopt a little-noted provision which would expressly bar the courts of the enacting state from regulating the internal affairs of any foreign corporation, thus denying the state any power to deal with abuses arising in a corporation which is, in every realistic sense, a domestic enterprise, measured by the fact of local shareholders, strictly local business, local creditors, etc.

Why should states so willingly abdicate regulatory powers which could be used to protect important local interests? One reason, of course, is that management wants this; and management is the only effective lobby in this area. Other interests are almost unrepresented except by an occasional lone legislator who may exact one or two minor concessions to some pet interest or theory of his. Another factor is that legislators, who often are cautious lawyers, like the idea of an option to take a corporate client to a "liberal" jurisdiction if the need ever should arise. By foreswearing their state's regulatory power over foreign corporations, they preserve this option.

Finally, there persists a deep-seated but irrational conviction that a strict corporation statute will inhibit the growth of the state's economy. This is a non sequitur. It ignores the distinction between (1) an enterprise incorporating in a particular state, and (2) a corporation, whether foreign or domestic, building plants there and employing the local citizenry. A strict statute may well deter some incorporations in that state, but it will rarely, if ever, control the decision to do business in the state. However, this asserted, but illogical, nexus between a liberal statute and economic growth has to my knowledge been used to coax corporations to build plants in a particular state. Particularly those states with undeveloped industrial economies will try to sell a package with a varying mix of highly permissive corporation statutes, heavily financed industrial development boards, and generous servings of industrial development bonds. In spite of this popular though illogical conception, there is no evidence that out-of-state corporations have been frightened away from states with a paternalistic statute but with an otherwise bracing business climate.

For whatever reasons—and however ill grounded they may be—most states abhor a restrictive corporation statute. They know in advance that if they adopt such a law, their domestic businesses will incorporate elsewhere and return as foreign corporations. Moreover, a state gains a very bad "image" in the eyes of the business community if its local businesses must obtain their charters elsewhere, and besides it may mean some revenue loss. The result of all these factors is the rapid spread of the enabling-type statute into almost every state.

509 - 527
53 9 - 54ᴸ
551 - 554

CHAPTER 13

THE ROLE OF DIRECTORS
IN GOVERNANCE

■ ■ ■

A. THE ROLE OF A CORPORATE DIRECTOR

1. INTRODUCTION

A defining feature of corporation law is its requirement that there be a board of directors. *See* MBCA § 8.01(a) ("each corporation must have a board of directors"). A board has the ultimate authority to manage the business and affairs of the corporation. *See* DGCL § 141(a); MBCA § 8.01(b). The statutes of non-corporate entities do not have such a formal requirement with respect to the management structure, though the law of limited partnerships require a two-tier partnership structure.

What does or should a board do? Myles Mace conducted the first major empirical study of corporate boards during the 1960s and concluded that they largely failed to fulfill their primary functions. He found that directors rarely challenged a CEO or initiated debate on an issue. Directors also generally did not effectively monitor management's performance because CEOs typically did not provide their boards with enough information to do so. Boardroom culture emphasized collegiality and the avoidance of controversy. Mace concluded that most outside directors were reluctant to replace an incumbent CEO, no matter how poor the corporation's performance, and directors usually relied on the CEO to nominate his successor. Finally, Mace found that most boards did not actually establish basic corporate objectives, strategies and policies. All too often, directors served as little more than "attractive ornaments on the corporate Christmas tree." Myles Mace, Directors: Myth And Reality (1971). Ten years later, Mace conducted a follow-up study and reaffirmed his conclusions. Myles L. Mace, *Directors: Myth and Reality—Ten Years Later*, 32 Rutgers L. Rev. 293 (1979).

As we have seen, state corporate statutes simply give directors the duty to manage the company's business. A board consisting of the company's senior officers could comply with the statutory mandate but would add little value to the corporation's governance structure because there would be no external check on their decisions.

Recently, there has been an increasing consensus, reflected in the listing standards of the stock exchanges, that a majority of the directors of every public corporation should be outside directors—individuals with no strong ties to management. Boards with a majority of outsiders could monitor managers' performance and thus reduce agency costs. There is, however, considerable disagreement as to what monitoring entails. Some writers suggest that boards should limit themselves to establishing financial goals for the corporation and evaluating senior executives' success in meeting those goals. Under this approach, a board's main functions are to discharge and replace top managers whose performance is unsatisfactory.

Other commentators argue for a more expansive approach. They believe boards of directors must review and approve major corporate actions and become more involved in establishing corporate priorities and long-term objectives. Still other commentators contend that a board should assume major responsibility for fixing the annual budget and allocating funds among a corporation's operating divisions, as well as reviewing regularly the extent to which the corporation was meeting the goals the board had set. Such a board might be proactive, initiating some proposals on its own, rather than simply reacting to management's proposals.

One influential formulation of directors' responsibilities is outlined in The Corporate Director's Guidebook, a publication of the American Bar Association's Business Law Section.

THE CORPORATE LAWS COMMITTEE, ABA SECTION OF BUSINESS LAW, CORPORATE DIRECTOR'S GUIDEBOOK—SIXTH EDITION
66 Bus. Law. 975, 985–89 (2011).

State corporate statutes emphasize the board's responsibility to make major decisions on behalf of the corporation and to oversee the management of the corporation. Although these statutes do not specifically define board responsibilities, the following tasks are generally undertaken by the board and its committees:

- monitoring the corporation's performance in light of its operating, financial, and other significant corporate plans, strategies, and objectives, and approving major changes in plans and strategies;

- selecting the CEO, setting goals for the CEO and other senior executives, reviewing their performance, evaluating and establishing their compensation, and making changes when appropriate;

- developing, approving, and implementing succession plans for the CEO and top senior executives;

- understanding the corporation's risk profile and reviewing and overseeing the corporation's management of risks;

- understanding the corporation's financial statements and other financial disclosures and monitoring the adequacy of its financial and other internal controls, as well as its disclosure controls and procedures;

- evaluating and approving major transactions such as mergers, acquisitions, significant expenditures, and the disposition of major assets; and

- establishing and monitoring effective systems for receiving and reporting information about the corporation's compliance with its legal and ethical obligations.

To be effective, a director must understand the corporation's business, operations, and competitive environment. This knowledge is fundamental to the director's ability to form an objective judgment about corporate and senior management performance and strategic direction, and to challenge, support, and reward management as warranted. Accordingly, a director's understanding of the corporation and its industry should include:

- the corporation's business plan;

- the key drivers underlying the corporation's profitability and cash flow—how the corporation makes money both as a whole and also in its significant business segments;

- the corporation's operational and financial plans, strategies, and objectives and how they further the goal of enhancing shareholder value;

- the corporation's economic, financial, regulatory, and competitive risks, as well as risks to the corporation's physical assets, intellectual property, personnel, and reputation;

- the corporation's financial condition and the results of its operations and those of its significant business segments for recent periods; and

- the corporation's performance compared with that of its competitors.

In addition, a director should be satisfied that effective systems exist for timely reporting to, and consideration by, the board or relevant board committees of the following:

- corporate objectives and strategic plans;

- current business and financial performance of the corporation and its significant business segments, as compared to board-approved objectives and plans;

- material risk and liability contingencies, including industry risk, current and threatened litigation, and regulatory matters; and

- systems of company controls designed to manage risk and to provide reasonable assurance of compliance with law and corporate policies.

Problem: Fibernet Corporation—Part 1

FiberNet Corporation, is a Columbia corporation that develops and markets optical networking equipment used in communications networks. It was organized five years ago, and has been financed primarily by venture capital investors. The company is about to make a public offering of its common stock, which it proposes to list on the NASDAQ Stock Market.

FiberNet's current board of seven directors includes the following:

- Sam Brown, 45 years old, is the Chairman, CEO and a co-founder of FiberNet. He has a PhD in electrical engineering from the Columbia Institute of Technology (CIT). He is an experienced entrepreneur, having started two other high-tech companies. One of them failed, and the other was sold to a large technology company at a substantial profit. He has never worked for a public company.

- James Grove, 36 years old, is the other co-founder of the company and is the Senior Vice President for Technology. He has a PhD in physics from CIT, where he met Brown. Prior to starting FiberNet, he worked for Ball Laboratories, a non-profit research organization. FiberNet is the first for-profit company he has worked for.

- Norma Axtell, 48 years old, is the Senior Vice President of finance and Chief Financial Officer. She is a CPA and was a partner at a major accounting firm before joining FiberNet. Although she has been the outside auditor of several public companies, this is the first time that she has been a corporate director.

- Richard Rogers, 50 years old, is a partner in Optical Ventures, a venture capital firm which was an early investor in FiberNet and holds 25% of its equity. He has served on numerous boards of directors of public and private companies.

- Sarah Hart, 35 years old, is a partner in Columbia Ventures, another venture capital firm that is the second largest investor in FiberNet, holding 20% of its equity. She only recently became a partner in Columbia Ventures, and this is the first time she has served on a board of directors.

- Susan Manning, 44 years old, is a partner in a national law firm that has served as FiberNet's outside counsel since it was organized. Last year the firm's billings to FiberNet were $500,000, which represents a very small percentage of the firm's revenues. Manning is a neighbor of Brown's and served as the principal lawyer for both of his other companies. She has been on the board since the company's inception.

- Stanley Friedman, 60 years old, is the dean of CIT's business school, a position he has held for ten years. He has known Brown since Brown was a student in two of his classes at CIT. Friedman joined the board only recently.

In preparation for its IPO, FiberNet has asked Lauren Peters, age 50, to join the board of directors. Lauren is a close friend of Brown, whom she met 15 years ago because their daughters were in the same class in elementary school. For the last several years, their two families have vacationed together. She holds a degree in electrical engineering from CIT and is an expert in optical communications. She spent most of her career managing technology development at a large producer of communications equipment. Five years ago, she left to become the Vice President for Technology at a startup venture. When it was acquired six months ago, she made enough money that she was able to retire.

You are a partner in a large law firm, and you have known Lauren socially for years. She has come to you to seek advice. She says, "I'm flattered to be asked to go on the FiberNet board, but I have several concerns that need to be resolved before I decide. It would help to begin with, if you would prepare a memorandum that addresses my principal questions. After I've looked at that, we can turn to more detailed questions about my duties and the risks of liability that I might face.

1. Starting at the beginning, what are my duties as a director and how am I supposed to fulfill them?

2. How much do I need to know about everything that the company is doing?

3. What does the law reasonably expect outside directors to do? Most of them have other full-time jobs so how can they devote substantial time to their board responsibilities?

4. I've read a lot about the need for more "independent" directors to "prevent another Enron," whatever that may mean. Are "outside" directors the same as "independent" directors?

5. And why is so much weight given to independent directors? Do they really make a big difference in corporate performance? Doesn't top management know the most about the company and, if so, shouldn't there be more management directors on the board?

6. Would I be considered "independent" so that I could be a member of the Audit, Nominating or Compensation Committees if I were asked?

I know why I was asked to be a director: Brown is an old friend. But what about the others? Who are typically chosen to be outside directors and how are they selected? Should Fashion be worried about diversity on the board and, if so, how can greater diversity be achieved?"

B. FORMALITIES OF BOARD ACTION

1. BOARD ACTION AT A MEETING

The board of directors traditionally takes formal action by vote at a meeting. Each director has one vote and may not vote by proxy. Unless the articles or by-laws provide otherwise, the vote of a majority of the directors present at a board meeting at which there is a quorum is necessary to pass a resolution.

Why must the board come together at a meeting to act? The board is a collegial body. By consulting together, board members may draw on each other's knowledge and experience. More ideas and points of view are likely to be considered in the formulation of decisions, which may produce better results than if the directors act without collegial consultation.

An illustration of the wisdom of the "meeting rule" can be found in Baldwin v. Canfield, 1 N.W. 261 (Minn. 1879), where all the directors had separately signed a real estate deed, but the board had never approved the transfer at a meeting. The court stated:

As we have already seen, the court below finds that, by its articles of incorporation, the government of the [corporation], and the management of its affairs, was vested in the board of directors. The legal effect of this was to invest the directors with such government and management *as a board,* and not otherwise. This is in accordance with the general rule that the governing body of a corporation, as such, are agents of the corporation only as a board, and not individually. Hence it follows that they have no authority to act, save when assembled at a board meeting. The separate action, individually, of the persons comprising such governing body, is not the action of the constituted body of men clothed with the corporate powers.

Had the board met, they might have discovered that the corporation's sole shareholder planned to give the deed to a third-party purchaser, even though the shareholder had before pledged his stock in the corporation for a bank loan. At a meeting, the directors might have been more disposed to question the transaction and ascertain whether the company's real estate was indirectly encumbered by the stock pledge.

Courts have refused to uphold informal action by directors without a meeting when the board's alleged authority to bind the corporation was challenged by the corporation, the directors of the corporation, the corporation's trustee in bankruptcy or pledgees of the corporation's stock. Although courts frequently fail to articulate their reasons for requiring formal board action, many courts rely on the policy of protecting shareholders and their investment from arbitrary or irresponsible decisions by directors.

Courts nonetheless recognize that informal board action, particularly in close corporations, is common. This reality has led courts to seek to protect innocent third parties from the strict application of the traditional meeting rule. Courts have relied on different justifications to bind corporations on agreements never approved at formal board meetings.

Unanimous director approval. When all the directors separately approve a transaction, a meeting will usually not serve any purpose. In such circumstances, even if a meeting had been held, the directors would probably not have discussed the matter or come to a different result, but would simply have approved the action.

Emergency. Situations arise where the board must make very quick decisions to prevent great harm or to take advantage of a great opportunity. In such a situation, it may be impossible to assemble the board at a meeting. The corporation must proceed on the opinions of those directors who can be contacted in whatever manner contact may be made.

Unanimous shareholder approval. If all the shareholders meet, the conclusion they reach will likely bind the corporation. The meeting rule, which is meant to protect shareholders from unconsidered board action, would work a hardship against third parties when shareholders approved the transaction.

Majority shareholder-director approval. If the directors who participate in the informal action constitute a majority of the board and own a majority of the corporation's issued and outstanding shares, the corporation is bound.

To buttress these common law exceptions to the general rule, most states have enacted statutory provisions allowing informal director action under some conditions. MBCA § 8.21, for example, allows board action to be taken without a meeting on the unanimous written consent of the directors. The Official Comment notes: "Under section 8.21 the requirement of unanimous consent precludes the possibility of stifling or ignoring opposing argument. A director opposed to an action that is proposed to be taken by unanimous consent, or uncertain about the desirability of that action, may compel the holding of a directors' meeting to discuss the matter simply by withholding his consent."

In addition, board meetings need not be conducted in person. MBCA § 8.20(b) permits the board to conduct a meeting by "any means of communication by which all directors participating may simultaneously hear each other during the meeting"—such as a telephone conference call. The Official Comment to MBCA § 8.20 states: "The advantage of the traditional meeting is the opportunity for interchange that is permitted by a meeting in a single room at which members are physically present. If this opportunity for interchange is thought to be available by the board of directors, a meeting may be conducted by electronic means although no two directors are physically present at the same place".

These sections of the MBCA, however, have led some courts to take a harder line towards corporations that disregard statutory requirements governing board actions. These courts reason that the liberalized statutory approaches pre-empt common law exceptions to the meeting rule. In Village of Brown Deer v. Milwaukee, 114 N.W.2d 493 (Wisc. 1962), the corporate president and majority shareholder, who had customarily made decisions without involving the board, signed a petition on behalf of the corporation for municipal annexation of land. Noting that the Wisconsin statute permits a board to act by unanimous written consent without a meeting, the court held the petition was invalid. The court explained:

> Corporations owe their existence to the statutes. Those who would enjoy the benefits that attend the corporate form of operation are obliged to conduct their affairs in accordance with the laws which authorized them.

> The legislature having specified the means whereby corporations could function informally, it becomes incumbent upon the courts to enforce such legislative pronouncements. The legislature has said that the corporation could act informally, without a meeting, by obtaining the consent in writing of all of the Directors. In our opinion, this pronouncement has preempted the field and prohibits corporations from acting informally without complying with [the statute].

114 N.W.2d at 497.

Some courts, however, have upheld informal board action in close corporations even when such action fails to comply with statutory rules. In *White v. Thatcher Financial Group, Inc.*, 940 P.2d 1034 (Colo. App.1996), two directors approved payments to the corporation's outgoing president. Although the statute required that the board have a minimum of three directors, vacancies on the four-person board had gone unfilled for several years, and the board consisted of only two members. The court pointed out that these two directors constituted a quorum of the statutory minimum and upheld the validity of the payments. In reaching this conclusion, the court noted it was the "custom and practice of the corporation" to operate with fewer than the required number of directors. The court explained that the "custom and practice" doctrine protected innocent third parties in dealing with a close corporation. Although the president was not such a person, the court nonetheless upheld the directors' action.

Technology, of course, often outruns statutory amendments. If a board meeting were held through an Internet chat room or text messaging on a cell phone, as a lawyer, could you advise that either or both of those would satisfy § 8.20(b)? How certain would you be of your advice? Note that in 2013, the ABA Model Rules of Professional Conduct were amended to make clear that a lawyer's duty to stay abreast of changes in the law and practice includes understanding the benefits and risks of relevant technology. Model Rules of Professional Conduct, Rule 1.1, cmt. 6.

2.   NOTICE AND QUORUM

Notice and quorum requirements apply to board meetings. Notice facilitates personal attendance by directors. For special meetings, MBCA § 8.22(b) requires that two days' notice be given of the date, time and place of meeting, unless the articles of incorporation or by-laws impose different requirements. For regular meetings, directors are assumed to know the schedule, and MBCA § 8.22(a) does not require notice. Nonetheless, many companies provide directors with notice of the purpose of all meetings, to better prepare directors to discuss the matters on the agenda. Action taken at a board meeting held without the required notice is invalid. Notice must be in writing unless oral notice is reasonable in the circumstances. Notice may be given or sent by any method of delivery including electronic transmission. In 2009, the MBCA was amended to include a series of electronic technology changes designed to incorporate concepts from the Uniform Electronic Transmissions Act and the federal E-SIGN Act. *See* MBCA § 1.40, Comment 4.

Any director who does not receive proper notice may waive notice by signing a waiver before or after the meeting, MBCA § 8.23(a), or by attending or participating in the meeting and not protesting the absence of notice. MBCA § 8.23(b). A director who attends a meeting solely to protest the manner it was convened is not deemed to have waived notice. MBCA § 8.23(b).

The quorum requirement is intended to preclude action by a minority of the directors. The statutory norm for a quorum is a majority of the total number of directors, although the articles of incorporation or by-laws may increase the quorum requirement or reduce it to no less than one-third of the board. MBCA § 8.24. Action taken in the absence of a quorum is invalid.

3.   COMMITTEES OF THE BOARD

Boards with many members, such as the boards of publicly-held corporations, are unwieldy and often find it difficult, when acting as a whole, effectively to discharge all of their responsibilities. The trend in recent years toward increasing the proportion of outside directors has exacerbated this problem. Many companies have responded by delegating responsibility for many board functions to committees empowered to exercise, in defined areas, the authority of the board. Corporate statutes authorize this practice.

The executive committee is a common board committee because it can have the full authority of the board in all but a few essential transactions such as the declaration of a dividend or approval of a merger. MBCA § 8.25(e). Thus the executive committee often is the vehicle through which the board acts between meetings on less important matters of corporate housekeeping which, for technical reasons, require board approval.

The audit committee is another common board committee, particularly in publicly-held corporations. Its functions usually include selection of the company's auditors, specification of the scope of the audit, review of audit results, and oversight of internal accounting procedures. Both the New York Stock Exchange and the NASDAQ Stock Market require publicly-held companies to have audit committees.

Other relatively common committees include finance (usually responsible for giving advice on financial structure, the issuance of new securities, and the management of the corporation's investments), nomination (responsible for nominating new directors and officers), governance (often combined with the nomination committee) and compensation (responsible for fixing the compensation of executives). Boards often create specialized committees to deal with specific problems such as the use of special litigation committees in connection with derivative suits.

A board committee can be permanent or temporary. Its functions can be active—making decisions on behalf of the board. Or the committee can be passive—doing research and presenting information so the full board can make more informed decisions. Case law and statutes increasingly reflect the view that committees are desirable because directors who are committee members have a greater incentive to develop expertise in the area of the committee's responsibility. MBCA § 8.30(b) recognizes the expanding use of committees and permits a director to rely on the reports or actions of a committee on which she does not serve so long as the committee reasonably merits her confidence.

Problem: Widget Corporation

You are counsel to the Widget Corporation, incorporated in an MBCA jurisdiction. Widget's by-laws provide for an eight-member board of directors. Widget's president advises you that she has just negotiated a sale of one of the corporation's plants on advantageous terms that will provide much-needed working capital for the corporation. The sale agreement requires board authorization. A further condition of the closing is that it occur within 36 hours. One of Widget's directors is in a local hospital for minor surgery, one is in London on business, and two are mountain climbing in Nepal.

1.   Would a unanimous vote by the four available directors at a special meeting of the board be effective?

2.   Suppose the president visits the ailing board member in the hospital, explains the sale fully, and has her execute a proxy authorizing the president to cast the director's vote in favor of the sale at the board meeting. At a special meeting, the four available directors and the president casting the proxy then vote unanimously to approve the transaction. Is this a valid board action?

3.   What other alternatives are available for the board to authorize the sale? Does it make a difference if the mobile satellite phone for the two mountain-climbing directors in Nepal is not working, but base camp has an Internet connection? What if the connection is not fast enough to support a voice call but could support instant messaging or text "chat?"

4.   How could the articles of incorporation and by-laws be modified to deal with some future crisis where it is not possible to assemble a majority of directors at a board meeting?

C. GOVERNANCE IN THE MODERN BOARD

Problem: Fibernet Corporation—Part 2

You have now been approached by Stanley Friedman, whom Brown has asked to chair the board's new Governance and Nominations Committee. Brown tells you that he has been so occupied with his administrative role as Dean for the last few years that he has not kept up with developments in corporate governance. He asks you for answers to the following questions:

1.   How many independent directors must the board have under the NASDAQ listing standards? Do enough of the current directors qualify as independent to meet this requirement?

2.   What committees must the board have, and what are the requirements for their composition?

3.   In addition to what is legally required, are their other structural or procedural practices that the board should consider establishing? As to each, what is the reason for it, and do you recommend that it be adopted?

1.   SOURCES OF CORPORATE GOVERNANCE REQUIREMENTS

There are three major sources of "rules" relating to the role of directors in corporate governance: state law, federal law, stock exchange requirements. While state law provides the foundation, it contains few rules to guide the actual operations of boards. In recent years Federal law and stock exchange requirements related to board governance have expanded to fill the gaps left open by state law.

a.   State Law

We have already looked at many of the rules of state corporate law that affect the basic procedural aspects of governance such as the requirement that boards act at meetings, the manner of calling meetings, the need for a quorum, etc. Most state corporation statutes describe directors' responsibilities only in general terms and do not give significant guidance as to how those responsibilities should be carried out. MBCA § 8.01(b), for example, states only: "All corporate powers shall be exercised by or under the authority of the board of directors of the corporation, and the business and affairs of the corporation shall be managed by or under the direction, and subject to the oversight, of its board of directors. . . ." DGCL § 141(a) is similar, providing: "The business and affairs of every corporation organized under this chapter shall be managed by or under the direction of a board of directors. . . ."

b.   Federal Law

Although there is no federal corporation law, some provisions of the Securities Exchange Act of 1934 (1934 Act) directly affect corporate governance and intersect with state law for public corporations. To a considerable extent, federal law exercises its influence on corporate governance through mandatory disclosure. Under the Sections 12 and 13 of the 1934 Act, public companies are required to provide certain periodic disclosures, some significant periodic disclosures being the financial information provided in the Form 10–K and 10–Q (as discussed in Chapter 9). Additionally, under Section 14(a) of the 1934 Act, public companies are governed by the SEC's proxy rules when a board makes disclosures or solicits proxies to shareholders. Thus, although the election of directors is a question of state law, the disclosures that corporate managers must make in connection with that election are governed by federal proxy rules.

In 2002, Congress enacted the Sarbanes-Oxley Act (SOX) in response to the scandals discussed in the previous chapter. SOX directly regulates several areas that had previously been left exclusively to state law. Thus, notwithstanding that state law permits shareholders to choose whichever directors they want, SOX requires that a corporation's audit committee be comprised of "independent" directors even if the shareholders would prefer to have a board with no independent directors. Many (although not all) of the provisions of the Act have been implemented through amendments to the 1934 Act and the SEC rules implementing that Act.

The most controversial provisions of SOX direct the SEC to require the chief executive officer and chief financial officer of a reporting company to certify that the company's quarterly and annual reports do not contain any material misstatements or omissions and that the company's financial information fairly presents the company's financial situation in all material respects. The signing officers are also responsible for establishing, maintaining and regularly evaluating the effectiveness of the internal controls, which must be designed to ensure material information about the company is known to the officers. These controls must be evaluated within 90 days of any periodic report, and their effectiveness and any significant changes must be discussed in the company's reports. SOX § 302, § 906. The annual report also must provide an assessment of the adequacy of the company's internal controls for financial reporting. *Id.* § 404. There are criminal penalties for false certifications.

In addition to these public disclosures, the officers must disclose to the company's audit committee any significant deficiencies in the internal controls that could adversely affect the company's ability to record, process, summarize and report financial data, as well as "any fraud" by those responsible for the controls.

As we have previously seen, public companies must file an annual report on Form 10–K with the SEC. In that report, the corporation must disclose that it has adopted a code of ethics for the principal executive officer, principal financial officer, principal accounting officer or controller, or persons performing similar functions. If a company has not adopted such a code, it must explain why it has not. The code of ethics must prescribe standards "reasonably necessary to promote honest and ethical conduct," including the ethical handling of conflicts of interest between personal and professional relationships, full and fair disclosure, and compliance with applicable governmental rules and regulations. The code must be made publicly available in a company's annual report, on its website with a cross-reference to the annual report, or by an undertaking in the annual report to send a copy free to any person who requests it. Amendments to and waivers of this code must be disclosed on the company's Form 8–K or on the company's website.

Both the New York Stock Exchange and the NASDAQ Stock Market also require a company to adopt a code of business conduct and ethics for employees. NASDAQ requires this code to include a mechanism to ensure prompt and consistent enforcement of the code, protection for persons reporting questionable behavior, clear and objective standards for compliance, and a fair process by which to determine violations.

The SEC has expanded its disclosure requirements with respect to corporate directors. As part of its executive compensation disclosures (discussed in Chapter 25), the SEC requires companies to identify, for each director and nominee for election, the specific experience, qualifications, attributes or skills that led the board to nominate the person. The SEC has emphasized that this disclosure should be provided on an individual basis and that grouping directors by particular attributes will not be sufficient.

In addition, a company must disclose its board leadership structure, including whether and why it has chosen to combine or separate the chief executive officer and board chairman positions. The company must also state why it believes that its leadership structure is the "most appropriate structure for it at the time of filing." If the same person serves as board chairman and chief executive officer, the company must disclose whether the board has a lead independent director and the nature of that director's role.

Finally, a company must explain its process for identifying and evaluating nominees including whether and how the nominating committee or the board considers diversity in identifying potential directors. If the company has a formal policy concerning diversity, it must discuss how that policy is implemented and how its effectiveness is assessed.

The rule does not define "diversity" although the SEC has made clear that the term is to be interpreted broadly including criteria such as differences in viewpoint, professional experience and education in addition to the traditional criteria of race, gender and national origin. Although the rule would appear to encourage boards to consider diversity, companies still have significant discretion in determining what disclosures and what policies, if any, are appropriate.

c.   Stock Exchange Listing Standards

Over the last decade, corporate scandals have led to increasing focus on the performance of corporate boards. One effort to remedy the perceived inadequacies in the functioning of public company boards has been the development of new rules and "best practices" with respect to the composition, structure, and operations of boards. The most detailed sets of mandatory rules on corporate governance are found in the listing requirements of the New York Stock Exchange and the NASDAQ Stock Market. By listing their securities on one of these exchanges, public companies voluntarily submit to their regulation in many areas that are not the subject of state law. Since virtually every large public corporation is traded on either the NYSE or NASDAQ, their rules have a major influence on board structure and procedures. The exchanges' requirements for board composition and committee membership far exceed anything that is found in state corporate law.

2. BOARD COMPOSITION AND STRUCTURE

a. Board Composition

The NYSE and NASDAQ rules are nearly identical, and both are revised and updated from time to time. The NYSE governance rules are found in § 303A of the Listed Company Manual. They require that the boards of listed companies consist of at least a majority of independent directors (§ 303A.01) who must meet regularly in executive session without management (§ 303A.93). The rules define "independence" as follows:

303A.02 Independence Tests

(a)(i)   No director qualifies as "independent" unless the board of directors affirmatively determines that the director has no material relationship with the listed company (either directly or as a partner, shareholder or officer of an organization that has a relationship with the company).

(b) In addition, a director is not independent if:

   (i)   The director is, or has been within the last three years, an employee of the listed company, or an immediate family member is, or has been within the last three years, an executive officer,[1] of the listed company.

   (ii) The director has received, or has an immediate family member who has received, during any twelve-month period within the last three years, more than $120,000 in direct compensation from the listed company, other than director and committee fees and pension or other forms of deferred compensation for prior service (provided such compensation is not contingent in any way on continued service).

   (iii)(A) The director is a current partner or employee of a firm that is the listed company's internal or external auditor; (B) the director has an immediate family member who is a current partner of such a firm; (C) the director has an immediate family member who is a current employee of such a firm and personally works on the listed company's audit; or (D) the director or an immediate family member was within the last three years a partner or employee of such a firm and personally worked on the listed company's audit within that time.

(iv) The director or an immediate family member is, or has been with the last three years, employed as an executive officer of another company where any of the listed company's present executive officers at the same time serves or served on that company's compensation committee.

(v) The director is a current employee, or an immediate family member is a current executive officer, of a company that has made payments to, or received payments from, the listed company for property or services in an amount which, in any of the last three fiscal years, exceeds the greater of $1 million, or 2% of such other company's consolidated gross revenues.

One of the principal effects of the listing standards is that boards of listed companies must now consist of a majority of independent directors. Together with various provisions of the Sarbanes-Oxley Act and SEC regulations, boards of listed companies must also assign responsibility for three key functions to committees comprised of independent directors. State corporate laws do not define "independence," so the listing standards include a definition. Note that "outside directors"—those who are not also employees of a corporation—are not necessarily "independent." As the chart above indicates, other significant relationships with the corporation may also render a director not "independent."

b. Board Committees

The listing standards of the NYSE and NASDAQ require that boards have at least three committees: audit, compensation, and nominating. The boards of larger public companies often also include additional committees, charged with oversight of such matters as strategy, finance, risk management, public policy, and environmental matters.

i. Audit Committee

The audit committee must have at least three members who are independent directors. Each must be "financially literate, as such qualification is interpreted by the board in its business judgment." Generally, this means a member must be able to read and understand fundamental financial statements. If an audit committee member is not financially literate, he or she "must become financially literate within a reasonable period of time after his or her appointment to the audit committee." One member of the audit committee must have accounting or related financial-management expertise, such that she understands GAAP and, through education or experience, is knowledgeable about preparing financial statements, reviewing financial controls and dealing with audit committees. A director may not serve on the audit committee of more than three public companies without permission from each company. Except in limited circumstances, audit committee members are barred from receiving any compensation (other than directors' fees) for any consulting, advisory or other services they may provide to the corporation.

The audit committee rather than the entire board is responsible for the appointment, compensation, and oversight of the corporation's public accounting firm. If there are disagreements between management and the auditor regarding financial reporting, the audit committee must resolve them. The public accountants report directly to the committee. A corporation must provide its audit committee with the funding that the committee decides is required to compensate the public accountants and to pay other advisers the committee retains.

Any public accounting firm hired to perform auditing or non-audit services such as tax services must disclose those services to the audit committee. In addition, the accounting firm must timely report to the audit committee about: critical accounting policies and practices used by the company; alternative treatments of financial information the auditors have discussed with management; the ramifications of those alternatives; and the alternative the accountants prefer. The accounting firm also must provide the audit committee with copies of material written communications with management, including their management letters—which typically point out weaknesses in the audited firm's financial controls—and schedules showing all adjustments proposed by the accountants that management did not accept.

Beyond monitoring the company's accounting policies and practices, the audit committee is required to establish procedures for receiving and evaluating anonymous submissions by employees concerning "questionable accounting or auditing matters." The audit committee also can retain outside counsel at the corporation's expense.

The consequence of these duties is that the audit committee becomes the monitor of a corporation's financial transactions and financial reports. It is responsible for preventing financial improprieties and is a direct link between the corporation's public accountants and the board of directors. Through its independent access to financial information and its contact with the public accountants, the audit committee also can better inform the board of the company's financial activities and improve the board's monitoring of management. Finally, the audit committee can shield the public accountants from undue management influence by providing a forum in which they can confer directly with board members about accounting practices, the quality of internal controls, and other potentially troublesome issues.

ii. Compensation Committee

The compensation committee must consist solely of independent directors. The committee oversees the form and amount of senior executives' compensation. Ideally, the committee will try to ensure that compensation arrangements provide managers with appropriate incentives but are not overly generous. The committee's goal should be "to retain management in a reasonable and cost-effective manner, considering relevant factors such as motivating and retaining executives." The Conference Board Commission on Public Trust and Private Enterprise, *Findings and Recommendations: Part 1: Executive Compensation* 5 (Sept. 17, 2002). The compensation committee may retain consultants to design or review the executive compensation plans. If past executive compensation levels have been excessive, the committee should not treat those levels as a baseline for setting future compensation. Controversies surrounding increasing levels of executive compensation in recent years indicate just how difficult all these tasks are.

iii. Nominating Committee

A corporation must certify that it has adopted a formal written charter or board resolution addressing the nomination process. This includes the creation of a nominating committee, the mandate of which also often includes corporate governance, which must also be comprised solely of independent directors.

The committee is responsible for nominating candidates for the board of directors and deciding whether current directors should be nominated for reelection. The committee can also review how well the board and its committees carry out their responsibilities and consider whether the board should change how it operates. For example, the committee might determine that the independent directors should meet periodically outside the presence of management or it might name a "lead director" to coordinate the work of the outside directors and ensure that they receive adequate and timely information.

3. "BEST PRACTICES"

In addition to mandatory rules, public companies have come under increasing pressure to adopt a variety of what may be considered to be "best practices." This pressure comes largely from institutional investors. The form in which the pressure is embodied varies but they can best be seen in by "codes" or "principles" published by organizations such as Institutional Shareholder Services, the Council of Institutional Investors and the Business Roundtable. Though no formal set of rules mandates that companies adhere to these policies and practices, many public companies have begun doing so. These best practices have varying degrees of support. A current list would include, among others:

- The separation of the offices of Chairman of the Board and CEO (with some pressure for the Chairman to be an independent director)

- The appointment of a "lead director" from among the independent directors

- Regular meetings of the independent directors in executive session

- Annual reviews of the performance of the board and individual board members

- Policies with respect to term limits or mandatory retirement ages

- Requirements that directors hold a specified amount of the company's stock

- Requirements that directors participate in continuing education programs

Some of these practices have their roots in SEC disclosure requirements. Thus, a company must disclose how often its board of directors met and the names of any directors who failed to attend at least 75 percent of the meetings. It must also disclose whether it has nominating and compensation committees. If it does not have either of these committees, it must explain the basis for the board's view that it is appropriate not to have the committee. (Since the rules of the New York Stock Exchange and the NASDAQ Stock Market now require that boards have these committees, this disclosure requirement has no practical effect on listed companies. It still exerts considerable pressure on unlisted public companies, however, as they are likely to find it easier to establish the committees than to explain why they have not done so.)

D. WHAT KIND OF BOARD?

1. INDEPENDENCE

DONALD C. CLARKE, THREE CONCEPTS OF THE INDEPENDENT DIRECTOR
32 Del. J. Corp. L. 73 (2007).

Despite the surprisingly shaky support in empirical research for the value of independent directors, their desirability seems to be taken for granted in policy-making circles. Yet important elements of the concept of and rationale for independent directors remain curiously obscure and unexamined. As a result, the empirical findings we do have may be misapplied, and judicial gap-filling may be harder than imagined when legislative intent cannot be divined or is contradictory.

This article attempts to unpack the concept broadly understood by the term "independent director" and to distinguish among its various concrete manifestations. In particular, I discuss the critical differences between independent, outside, and disinterested directors, arguing that these manifestations serve different purposes and should not be confused with each other. . . . I also argue that the whole purpose of having independent directors is surprisingly undertheorized, leading to inconsistent rules, in particular regarding the effect of director shareholding, both across countries and within the United States.

Independent directors have long been viewed as a solution to many corporate governance problems. Well before the Enron and WorldCom scandals, the New York Stock Exchange (NYSE) already required the presence of independent directors on audit committees, and in the United States, insider-dominated boards have been rare for years. Disinterested directors have, following the takeover boom in the 1980s, become increasingly important in related state-level litigation, and the modest role for independent directors contemplated in the listing rules of the NYSE has given way, in the wake of Enron and other corporate scandals, to a requirement that independent directors constitute a board majority in domestic companies as well as federal mandates for listed companies under the Sarbanes-Oxley Act (SOA).

A series of corporate scandals in Britain led to the Cadbury Report and subsequent similar reports and studies, all of which recommended a greater role for outside and independent directors. In the last decade Japan has undertaken several corporate law reforms designed to enhance the role of directors and auditors not affiliated with management. Even China has joined this trend: in August 2001, the China Securities Regulatory Commission (CSRC) issued a rule requiring that at least one third of the directors of listed companies be independent directors by the middle of 2003.

Board independence does not, of course, guarantee corporate success. As one commentator has noted:

> [B]oard independence has done little to prevent past mismanagement and fraud. For example, thirty years ago the SEC cast much of the blame for the collapse of the Penn Central Company on the passive nonmanagement directors. No corporate boards could be much more independent than those of Amtrak, which have managed that company into chronic failure and government dependence. Enron had a fully functional audit committee operating under the SEC's expanded rules on audit committee disclosure.

While anecdotal examples of failure do not prove the absence of success, more to the point are the results of several studies of the effect of independent directors on corporate performance in the United States. The overall weight of the findings is that there is no solid evidence suggesting that independent directors improve corporate performance. Some studies have even found a negative correlation between board independence and corporate performance. A recent comprehensive study by Bhagat and Black reviews other studies along with their own research and finds, among other things, that there is no evidence that greater board independence leads to better firm performance. Poor performance is correlated with subsequent greater independence, but there is no evidence that this strategy works to improve performance. While independent directors with significant stock positions may add value, others do not. Indeed, Bhagat and Black find that having insiders on the board can add value.

A study by April Klein finds that the audit, nomination, and compensation committees, traditionally dominated by outsiders, have little, if any, effect on firm performance regardless of how those committees are staffed. Indeed, in direct contrast to conventional wisdom, Klein found a positive correlation between firm performance and the presence of insiders on a board's finance and investment committees. Evans and Evans for their part found that the presence of independent directors on the board or on compensation committees had no effect on CEO pay levels.

Despite the surprisingly shaky support in empirical research for the value of independent directors, their desirability seems to be taken for granted in policy-making circles. Yet important elements of the concept of and rationale for independent directors remain curiously obscure and unexamined. As a result, the empirical findings we do have may be misapplied, and judicial gap-filling may be harder than imagined when legislative intent cannot be divined or is contradictory.

This article attempts to unpack the concept broadly understood by the term "independent director" and to distinguish among its various concrete manifestations. I argue that these manifestations serve different purposes and should not be confused with each other. I also argue that the whole purpose of having independent directors is surprisingly undertheorized, leading to inconsistent rules, in particular regarding the effect of director shareholding, both across countries and within the United States.

To canvass various conceptions of the independent director, we must first seek a more general term because not all jurisdictions place a great deal of importance on directors who might plausibly be called "independent." Different jurisdictions and corporate governance norms speak variously of directors who are "non-interested," "independent," "outside," "non-executive," "non-employee," and "disinterested." Each of these terms is defined differently and implies a different role for the director it describes, yet they are frequently discussed together as if they were all describing the same thing. Moreover, conclusions about directors of one type are often applied to directors of another.

SANJAI BHAGAT & BERNARD BLACK, THE NON-CORRELATION BETWEEN BOARD INDEPENDENCE AND LONG-TERM FIRM PERFORMANCE
27 J. Corp. L. 231 (2002).

Over the last thirty years, American corporate boards have undergone a gradual but dramatic change. In the 1960s, most had a majority of inside directors. Today, almost all have a majority (usually a large majority) of outside directors, most have a majority (often a large majority) of independent directors, and an increasing number have only one or two inside directors. This pattern reflects the conventional wisdom that the board's principal task is to monitor management, and only independent directors can be effective monitors. In contrast, an insider-dominated board is seen as a device for management entrenchment. For example, guidelines adopted by the Council of Institutional Investors call for at least 2/3 of a company's directors to be independent; guidelines adopted by the California Public Employees Retirement System and by the National Association of Corporate Directors call for boards to have a "substantial majority" of independent directors. American corporate governance experts and institutional investors are now exporting this conventional wisdom around the world. It has only an occasional dissenting voice. Even the Business Roundtable (an organization of large-firm CEOs), which once opposed proposals for more independent boards, now recommends that boards have a "substantial majority" of independent directors. Yet there are numerous anecdotes where a highly independent board hasn't prevented large-scale wealth destruction. Enron (with eleven independent directors on its fourteen-member board) is only the most recent example. When we turn from anecdote to quantitative evidence, the conventional wisdom favoring highly independent boards lacks a solid empirical foundation, in this or other studies.

We study in this Article three related questions. First, does greater board independence produce better corporate performance, as conventional wisdom predicts? Second, and conversely, does board composition respond to firm performance? Third, does board size predict firm performance? Prior quantitative research on the first two questions has been inconclusive; for the third, two studies report that firms with large boards perform worse than firms with smaller boards. We report here evidence from the first large-scale, long-time-horizon study of the relationship among board independence, board size, and the long-term performance of large American firms.

Our principal findings: We find evidence that low-profitability firms respond to their business troubles by following conventional wisdom and increasing the proportion of independent directors on their boards. There is no evidence, however, that this strategy works. Firms with more independent boards (proxied by the fraction of independent directors minus the fraction of inside directors) do not achieve improved profitability, and there are hints in our data that they perform worse than other firms. This evidence suggests that the conventional wisdom on the importance of board independence lacks empirical support. Board size also shows no consistent correlation with firm performance, though we find hints of the negative correlation found in other studies.

If our results are correct, the current focus on board independence as a core measure of board quality could detract from other, perhaps more effective strategies for addressing poor firm performance. At the least, corporate governance advisors and institutional investors should support efforts by firms to experiment with different board structures and be more tentative in their advice that other countries should adopt American-style monitoring boards.

We do not doubt that independent directors are important. No one else can effectively restrain insider self-dealing or fire the CEO when necessary. Indeed, one of us has stressed, in other recent work, the role of independent directors in controlling self-dealing. The policy question raised by our results is whether inside and affiliated directors also play valuable roles that may be lost in a single-minded drive for greater board independence.

The proportion of independent directors on public company boards has increased dramatically over the last several decades. In 1950 only about 20% of public company board members were independent; but by 2005 the proportion had grown to approximately 75%. Jeffrey N. Gordon, *The Rise of Independent Directors in the United States, 1950–2005: Of Shareholder Value and Stock Market Prices*, 59 STAN. L. REV. 1465, 1474–75 (2007).

One possible explanation of the mixed results described in the excerpts above is that having a reasonable number of inside directors on a board may add value. Other possible explanations focus on the characteristics of "independent" directors. They may not have sufficient financial incentives to care about the performance of the firms on whose boards they sit. They may have financial ties to those firms that, under the definitions in force until recently, did not call into question their "independence." They may have personal relationships with the CEO or feel indebted to him because he was responsible for inviting them to join the board. They may have served too long or grown too old. Directors who are CEOs of other companies may be too busy or may not be inclined to raise questions about matters, such as executive compensation, where their interests are aligned with those of managers. Another possibility is that " 'visibility' directors— well-known persons with limited board experience, often holding multiple directorships and adding gender or racial diversity to a board—are not effective on average."

Professor Gordon argues that, even though independent boards may not improve the relative performance of individual companies, they may contribute to an increase in overall social welfare by focusing corporate efforts on maximizing shareholder value. He suggests this is the result of three different effects of independent boards:

> First, they enhance the fidelity of managers to shareholder objectives, as opposed to managerial interests or stakeholder interests. Second, they enhance the reliability of the firm's public disclosure, which makes stock market prices a more reliable signal for capital allocation and for the monitoring of managers at *other* firms as well as their own. Third, and more controversially, they provide a mechanism that binds the responsiveness of firms to stock market signals but in a bounded way. The turn to independent directors serves a view that stock market signals are the most reliable measure of firm performance and the best guide to allocation of capital in the economy, but that a "visible hand," namely the independent board, is needed to balance the tendency of markets to overshoot.

Jeffrey N. Gordon, *The Rise of Independent Directors in the United States, 1950–2005: Of Shareholder Value and Stock Market Prices*, 59 Stan. L. Rev. 1465 (2007).

Ultimately, while changes in board committee structure and procedures may have some beneficial effects, it is unclear how significant these are. The empirical studies of the relationship between governance practices and corporate performance discussed above as well as others in the last ten or fifteen years, suggest a mixed result at best. See, *e.g.*, David

F. Larcker, et al, How Important is Corporate Governance? (2005) (available at http://papers.ssrn.com/sol3/papers.cfm?abstract_id=595821).

Some studies suggest that certain indicia of better corporate governance practices are positively correlated with improved operating performance although not with stockholder returns. *E.g.*, Sanjai Bhagat & Brian Bolton, *Corporate Governance and Firm Performance*, 14 J. Corp. Fin. 257 (2008). But not all of the various "indices" of governance quality developed either by scholars or by the institutional shareholder advisory services show a correlation between governance and performance. Sanjai Bhagat et. al., *The Promise and Peril of Corporate Governance Indices*, 108 Colum. L. Rev. 1803 (2008). Moreover positive correlation does not establish causation: it is possible that better-managed companies simply choose to follow better governance practices and would have achieved superior operating results even without them.

2. DIVERSITY

In the late 1980s, almost two-thirds of outside directors were CEOs of other companies, and nearly all were white males more than 55 years old. Changes in the larger society, amplified in some cases by pressure from "socially responsible investors," have begun to alter that landscape, although slowly. Some of the change may be the result of the SEC disclosure requirements discussed above. Today, almost all large public companies state that they are committed to diversity among their directors. Nevertheless, a recent study showed that in 2011 women constituted only 16% of independent directors on the boards of the S&P 500, a slight increase from 15% in 2006, and 12% in 2001. The percentage of racial and ethnic minorities appears to have remained nearly constant during the same period at about 15%. This under-representation relative to population and work force may be greater than these data indicate because minority and women directors often hold multiple directorships.

DEBORAH L. RHODE & AMANDA K. PACKEL, DIVERSITY ON CORPORATE BOARDS: HOW MUCH DIFFERENCE DOES DIFFERENCE MAKE?
39 Del. J. Corp. L. 377 (2014).

Close to three-quarters of members of corporate boards of the largest American companies are white men. According to the most recent data, women hold only 16.9% of the seats on Fortune 500 boards. Women occupy 14.8% of Fortune 501–1000 board seats and only 11.9% of board seats in Russell 3000 companies. The situation in other nations is not markedly better, with the exception of those countries that have mandated quotas.

In the U.S., people of color also occupy a very small percentage of board seats. Among the Standard and Poor's (S&P) 200, 13% of the companies have no minorities on their boards, and more than two thirds of the Fortune

500 have no women of color. Only 3.2% of directors are women of color. Within the S&P 100 companies, only 37% have minority women on their boards.

Although the overall percentage of women and minorities on corporate boards remains small, the actual number has been growing. By some measures, diversity has increased substantially over the last three decades. In 1973, only 7% of Fortune 1000 boards had any minority directors; thirty-five years later, 76% had at least one minority director. Over the same period, the number of Fortune 100 boards with at least one woman increased from 11% to 97% in 2006. In 2004, the majority of Fortune 100 companies had 0–30% board diversity; by 2012, the majority had 31% or more board diversity. For certain minority groups, the progress has been particularly striking. In the last decade, Asian-American board representation has tripled and Latino board representation has doubled. Among S&P 100 companies, 71% "have achieved [a] critical mass of three or more diverse directors[—]a 4% increase since 2010[;]" only 2% lack any diversity on their boards.

By other measures, however, progress—especially in the past decade—has stalled. For S&P 1500 companies, the share of board seats held by women has only grown from 11% in 2006 to 14% in 2012. Women are also underrepresented as chairs of compensation, audit, and nominating committees, which are among the most influential board positions. At current rates of change, it would take almost seventy years before women's representation on corporate boards reached parity with that of men.

Increases in minority representation pose still greater challenges. Total minority seats on Fortune 100 boards have barely increased since 2003, and the representation of women of color has grown less than 1% since 2003. African-American representation declined from 2010 to 2012. Outside of the largest, most high-profile corporations, progress has been harder to achieve, in part receive as much scrutiny from those promoting gender diversity in the boardroom. . . ."

Moreover, some of the most encouraging numbers on board diversity may conceal less promising trends. The Sarbanes-Oxley Act led many corporations to reduce overall board size, meaning that the same number of women and minority directors may comprise a greater percentage of a now smaller board. In addition, much of the increase in women and minority directors over the last decade may reflect the same individuals sitting on more boards rather than the appointment of new individuals as directors. Many commentators worry that these "trophy directors," who may serve on as many as seven boards, are spread too thin to provide adequate oversight. Another concern is that the appointment of one or two token female or minority members will decrease pressure for continued diversity efforts.

* * *

The growing consensus within the corporate community is that diversity is an important goal. The case for diversity rests on two primary claims. The first is that diversity provides equal opportunity to groups historically excluded from positions of power. The public has a "strong [ ] interest in ensuring that opportunities are available to all, . . . that women [and minorities] entering the labour market are able to fulfil their potential, and that we make full use of the wealth of talented women . . . " and minorities available for board service. The second claim is that diversity will improve organizational processes and performance. This "business case for diversity" tends to dominate debates in part because it appeals to a culture steeped in shareholder value as the metric for corporate decision making.

A. Diversity and Firm Performance

Despite increasing references to acceptance of the business case for diversity, empirical evidence on the issue is mixed. While some studies have found positive correlations between board diversity and various measures of firm performance, others have found the opposite or no significant relationship. One of the most significant constraints is the shortage of studies on racial and ethnic diversity. Most of the modern research focuses on gender, from which commentators often generalize without qualification.

B. Diversity and Board Process, Corporate Reputation and Good Governance

A common argument by scholars, as well as board members of both sexes, is that diversity enhances board decision-making and monitoring functions. This assertion draws on social science research on small-group decision making, as well as studies of board process and members' experiences. The basic premise is that diversity may lessen the tendency for boards to engage in groupthink—a phenomenon in which members' efforts to achieve consensus override their ability to "realistically appraise alternative courses of action."

The literature on board decision making reflects three different theories about the process through which diversity enhances performance. The first theory is that women and men have different strengths, and that greater inclusion can ensure representation of valuable capabilities. For instance, some empirical evidence suggests that women generally are more financially risk averse than men. For that reason, many commentators have speculated that women's increased participation in corporate financial decision making could have helped to curb tendencies that caused the most recent financial crisis. A widely discussed panel at a World Economic Forum in Davos put the question: "Would the world be in this financial mess if it had been Lehman Sisters?" Many Davos participants believed that the answer was no, and cited evidence suggesting that women were "more prudent" and less "ego driven" than men in financial management contexts. One study found presence of at least one woman on a company's board was associated with a reduction of almost 40% in the likelihood of a financial restatement. Other research pointed in similar directions, including studies from researchers at Harvard and Cambridge Universities, which found a correlation between high levels of testosterone and an appetite for risk.

Some commentators also cite evidence indicating women have higher levels of trustworthiness or collaborative styles that can improve board dynamics. As one female director put it, "[w]omen are more cooperative and less competitive in tone and approach. When there's an issue, men are ready to slash and burn, while women are ready to approach. . . . Women often provide a type of leadership that helps boards do their jobs better." Women's experience with uncomfortable situations may give them particular capabilities in championing difficult issues. Similarly, racial and ethnic minorities' experience of needing to relate to both dominant and subordinate groups provides a form of bicultural fluency that may enhance decision-making.

A second theory of how diversity enhances performance is that women and minorities have different life experiences than white men, and bringing different concerns and questions to the table allows the board to consider "a wider range of options and solutions to corporate issues." Diversity is productive by generating cognitive conflict: "conflicting opinions, knowledge, and perspectives that result in a more thorough consideration of a wide range of interpretations, alternatives, and consequences." For example, Phillips et al.'s study of group decision making found that when new members were "socially similar" to existing team members, subjective satisfaction was high but actual problem solving results were not. Although team members rated productivity much lower when newcomers were socially dissimilar, the more heterogeneous group was much better at accomplishing the problem-solving task. A diverse board can also enhance the quality of a board's decision-making and monitoring functions because diverse groups are less likely to take extreme positions and more likely to engage in higher-quality analysis.

Some scholars have also suggested that diverse boards can help prevent corporate corruption because they are "bold enough to ask management the tough questions." According to one study, female directors expanded the content of board discussions and were more likely than their male counterparts to raise issues concerning multiple stakeholders. Research has found that heterogeneous groups are associated with broader information networks as well as increased creativity and innovation. One study concluded that board racial diversity increased innovation by expanding access to information and networks, and prompting more thorough evaluation. Overall, studies on the relationship between board diversity and its capacity for strategic change have reached conflicting results.

A third theory on how diversity enhances performance is that the very existence of diversity alters board dynamics in ultimately positive ways. Mannix and Neale, for example, argue that the presence of visibly diverse members enhances a group's ability to handle conflict by signaling that differences of opinion are likely. A group that lacks diversity is less likely to handle conflict well because it is not expected. Other scholars have drawn on this signaling theory to argue "that a diverse board conveys a credible signal to relevant observers of corporate behavior. . . ." Board diversity can convey a commitment to equal opportunity, responsiveness to diverse stakeholders, and a general message of progressive leadership, which can enhance the corporation's public image.

Given the competing findings and methodological limitations of these studies, the financial benefits of board diversity should not be overstated. But neither should boards understate other justifications for diversity, including values such as fairness, justice, and equal opportunity, as well as the symbolic message it sends to corporate stakeholders. A diverse board signals that women's perspectives are important to the organization, and that the organization is committed to gender equity not only in principle but also in practice. Further, corporations with a commitment to diversity have access to a wider pool of talent and a broader mix of leadership skills than corporations that lack such a commitment. For example, the adverse publicity that Twitter received when it went public with a board of all white men is a case study in the reputational costs of a leadership structure that fails to reflect the diversity of the user community it serves.

CHAPTER 14

SHAREHOLDERS' ROLE IN GOVERNANCE

■ ■ ■

Although shareholders are often called the "owners" of the corporation, their governance rights are delimited by corporate law's basic tenet of centralized management. As we have seen, the board of directors rather than the body of shareholders has the authority to manage and direct the business and affairs of the corporation.

Shareholder voting is governed by both state and federal law, the latter applying only to public corporations. Under state law, shareholders have limited voting rights. They elect the board of directors and replace directors in some circumstances. They vote on certain (but not all) fundamental transactions such as mergers, the sale of all or substantially all of the corporation's assets, amendments to the articles of incorporation and voluntary dissolution of the corporation. They also have the right to amend the corporation's by-laws. In addition, shareholders can vote on matters on which directors seek their approval such as the appointment of auditors, the adoption of management compensation plans, or the ratification of decisions that a board has made during the last year. Shareholders do *not* have the power to direct the board of directors to take actions concerning business decisions although they may be able to adopt non-binding recommendations (including a non-binding vote on executive compensation packages of top executives). Federal law governs shareholder voting in public companies through the proxy solicitation process by which such voting occurs.

In this chapter, we begin by looking at the scope of shareholder voting rights and the procedures for calling a shareholders' meeting. We then examine the shareholders' power to elect and remove directors. These matters are governed by state law. Finally, we review the federal regulation of the proxy solicitation process used to facilitate the voting and shareholder participation process in public companies.

A. MECHANICS OF SHAREHOLDERS' MEETINGS

1. CALLING THE MEETING

A corporation's bylaws usually fix the date of the annual meeting. Most corporate statutes provide that the board of directors, owners of 10 percent of the shares, or any person so authorized by the articles of incorporation or bylaws may call a special meeting of shareholders.

DGCL § 211(d) does not include stock ownership as a qualification for calling such a meeting and only the board of directors or persons authorized by the articles of incorporation or bylaws may do so. Delaware courts never have addressed the question of whether a corporation's shareholders have the inherent power to call a special meeting. One could argue that shareholders should have such power, at least if the purpose of the meeting is to take an action such as the removal of a director for cause that itself is within the shareholders' inherent power. On the other hand, the statutory power to act by written consent pursuant to DGCL § 228 may provide an effective mechanism for shareholders to exercise their power, without having the inherent power to call a special meeting.

2. NOTICE

A corporation must give written notice of all meetings to shareholders entitled to vote at the meeting. Only matters "within the purpose or purposes described in the meeting notice" may be considered at a special meeting. However, shareholders can waive notice, either in writing or by attending the meeting and not objecting to the absence of notice.

To satisfy the notice requirement, a board must set a "record date" prior to the meeting and provide that only shareholders "of record" as of that date will be entitled to vote at the meeting. For a special meeting, only the board (not the shareholders who called the meeting) has the exclusive power to set the record date and send out notices, unless the articles provide otherwise.

DGCL § 213 (a) permits (but does not require) the board of directors to fix one record date for stockholders entitled to notice of a meeting (no more than 60 nor less than 10 days before the date of the meeting) and a separate record date for determining the stockholders entitled to vote at the meeting. The provision is intended to provide the board with greater flexibility in aligning stockholders' voting and economic interests while minimizing the issues that arise when a stockholder holds a voting interest for stock it no longer owns at the time of the meeting. Under this section, a board could set a record date for voting that is much closer to the date of the meeting than the record date for notice of the meeting. If the board does not fix a separate record date, the default record date will be the same as the record date set for determining the stockholders entitled to notice of the meeting.

3. QUORUM

A quorum must be represented at a shareholders' meeting, either in person or by proxy, for an action taken at the meeting to be effective. A quorum usually consists of a majority of the shares entitled to vote, unless the articles or bylaws provide otherwise. The MBCA sets no minimum or maximum quorum but requires an amendment establishing (or reducing) a supermajority quorum requirement to meet that same requirement. DGCL § 216 allows a majority of shares to amend a corporation's articles of incorporation or bylaws to increase the quorum requirement or to reduce it to as little as one-third of the shares entitled to vote, unless the articles or bylaws require some greater vote.

4. ACTION BY WRITTEN CONSENT

Both the MBCA and DGCL allow shareholders to act by written consent rather than at a meeting, but the two statutes vary considerably.

MBCA § 7.04(a) requires the consent in writing of *all* shareholders entitled to vote on an action. Consequently, all voting shareholders also must receive advance notice of the action to be taken. Unless the bylaws provide otherwise, the record date for determining which shareholders must consent to an action is the date the first shareholder consents in writing to that action.

DGCL § 228 allows a *majority* of the shareholders entitled to vote on an action to act by means of written consent. Prompt notice that action has been taken by consent must be given to nonconsenting shareholders, but no advance notice is required. Every consent must be dated when signed, and the period during which consents can be signed is effectively limited to 60 days from the date the first consent delivered to the corporation was signed. That date also serves as the record date for a consent solicitation initiated by shareholders; if the board is soliciting consents, it may set a record date. DGCL § 228 is a default provision and many Delaware corporations have provisions in their articles of incorporation that eliminate or restrict shareholders' power to act by written consent.

5. VOTING

Unless the articles of incorporation provide otherwise, each share is entitled to one vote. Unlike directors, shareholders may vote by proxy. A proxy is simply a limited form of agency power by which a shareholder authorizes another, who will be present at the meeting, to exercise the shareholder's voting rights. A proxy may give the proxy holder discretion to vote as she pleases or may direct her to vote in a particular way. In public corporations, management typically solicits proxies from shareholders that authorize one or more members of management to vote the shareholder's stock at the meeting. The proxy can be revoked by notice to the company or by submitting a later-dated proxy with different instructions.

The authorization for proxy voting is found in state corporate statutes. These statutes generally limit the validity of the proxy to a period of 11 months from the date of its execution (one annual meeting), unless the appointment form specifies a longer period. MBCA § 7.22; but see DGCL § 212 (no time limitation). For a shareholder vote to be effective there must be a quorum present at the meeting or represented by proxy. Assuming the existence of a quorum, the general principle governing shareholder voting on questions other than the election of directors is majority rule. But what majority? Under the MBCA, shareholders generally act when "the votes cast favoring the action exceed the votes cast opposing the action." MBCA § 7.25(c). Thus, shares that are represented at the meeting but are not voted are not counted in determining the outcome. If a corporation has 100 shares outstanding of which 60 are represented at the meeting, there is a quorum. If 25 shares are voted in favor of an action, 20 are voted against, and 15 abstain, the motion will pass, even though it was not approved by a majority of a quorum.

DGCL § 216 is slightly different, providing that "in all matters other than the election of directors, the affirmative vote of the majority of shares present in person or represented by proxy at the meeting and entitled to vote on the subject matter shall be the act of the stockholders." In our example, the resolution would not pass, since to do so would require 31 affirmative votes, a majority of the shares represented at the meeting. As a general rule, few shareholders who attend a meeting or grant a proxy abstain from voting, and so the difference between the MBCA and the DGCL is more theoretical than practical.

On particularly important questions, some statutes require the affirmative vote of the majority of the shares outstanding and entitled to vote. For example, DGCL § 251(c) requires such a vote for the approval of a merger.

Majority voting (by whatever majority) is a default rule, and statutes generally allow a corporation to include in its articles of incorporation a supermajority voting requirement for all or particular shareholder actions. MBCA § 7.27 provides that a supermajority voting requirement must be adopted and can only be amended by the same supermajority vote. DGCL § 242 provides that a majority of the shares entitled to vote may approve a supermajority requirement but that only the specified supermajority can modify such a requirement. Corporate statutes, however, do not allow provisions that waive the requirement of shareholder approval of certain fundamental transactions.

B. ELECTION AND REMOVAL OF DIRECTORS

1. ELECTION OF DIRECTORS

All directors are elected at the annual meeting unless the articles of incorporation provide for staggered terms, in which case shareholders elect directors for terms of two or three years. The shareholders' power to elect directors is exclusive except when a board seat is vacant. In that event, the vacancy can be filled either by shareholders or by the remaining directors, unless the articles provide otherwise.

[If an annual meeting has not been held in the previous 15 months, any holder of voting stock can require the corporation to convene an annual meeting, at which new directors can be elected.]

Under most state statutes, the default rule is plurality voting in which the candidates who receive the most votes win, regardless of whether those votes constitute a majority of the votes cast. In the normal uncontested election of a public company board, the management nominates a slate consisting of one candidate for each of the board seats to be filled. Shareholders get to vote as many times as there are open seats. For each seat they can either vote in favor of the management nominee (there being no other candidates) or withhold their vote. In theory, therefore, if all of the shareholders but one withheld their votes, a candidate would still be elected by the vote of the one shareholder who voted in favor of the candidate, even if that shareholder owned only one share of stock. Thus, since the managers will presumably vote their shares in favor their nominees, uncontested elections are essentially formalities in which the outcome is a foregone conclusion.

In recent years, as part of an effort to enhance director accountability, there has been a movement to implement mechanisms that provide for majority voting in the election of directors. This movement is reflected in legislative enactments, shareholder proposals and actions that an increasing number of public corporations have taken. The danger with such a system, of course, is that the election would fail because no candidate will receive a majority.

Absent special legislation, these changes must deal with the problem that corporate statutes typically provide that directors continue in office until a successor is elected or they resign. *E.g.*, DGCL 141(b). So if a corporation adopts a bylaw or charter amendment to implement majority voting, some provision must be made to prevent a director who fails to receive a majority vote for re-election from simply remaining in office. MBCA § 10.22 provides that directors will be elected by a plurality of the votes cast, but that a nominee who does not receive a majority will serve a maximum of 90 days unless the board of directors appoints her to a longer term. DGCL § 141(b) provides that a director's resignation can be declared effective upon the occurrence of certain events including the failure to receive a specified vote for reelection and, under DGCL § 216, if shareholders have adopted a bylaw amendment that specifies the vote necessary for the election of directors (*e.g.*, a majority), the board of directors cannot amend or repeal that bylaw. In states that have not adopted legislative provisions to implement majority voting, some corporations have adopted a policy or bylaw provision that requires directors who fail to receive a majority affirmative vote to resign. All of these provisions, however, create the possibility that, in case of a failed election, there will be a vacancy on the board.

2. REMOVAL AND REPLACEMENT OF DIRECTORS

Most corporate statutes make provision for the removal of directors, and most authorize shareholders to remove directors with or without cause, unless a corporation's articles of incorporation provide that directors can be removed only for cause. *E.g.,* MBCA § 8.08. Shareholders' power to remove directors for cause is mandatory and it cannot be restricted.

The rare case in which shareholders undertake to remove a director for cause presents two difficult issues: what constitutes "cause" justifying removal? And what process must be followed by the shareholders in determining that cause exists?

These difficulties are illustrated in *Campbell v. Loew's, Inc.* 134 A. 2d 852 (Del.Ch. 1957). Decided before Delaware amended its statute to provide for removal *without cause,* it involved a battle for control of Loew's Inc. One of the contending factions was headed by its President, Vogel, and the other by a major shareholder, Tomlinson. The two sides had reached an uneasy compromise in which each was to have six directors and a neutral director would complete the thirteen member board. The dispute remained unresolved, however, and two of the Vogel directors, one Tomlinson director and the neutral director resigned. Then Vogel, as president, sent out a notice calling a special shareholders' meeting for the purposes of (1) filling the director vacancies; (2) amending the by-laws to increase the number of board members to nineteen, increasing the quorum to ten, and electing the six additional directors; and (3) removing Tomlinson and one of his allies from the board and filling the vacancies thus created.

The plaintiff, a member of the Tomlinson faction, brought an action seeking to enjoin the special shareholder's meeting. The court rejected the plaintiff's argument that the Delaware statute only authorized the directors to fill vacancies on the board, and that therefore the shareholders lacked the power to do so; holding that the shareholders had the "inherent" right to elect directors to fill vacancies. The court then held that the shareholders also have the "inherent power" to remove directors for cause:

> This power must be implied when we consider that otherwise a
> director who is guilty of the worst sort of violation of his duty could
> nevertheless remain on the board. It is hardly to be believed that
> a director who is disclosing the corporation's trade secrets to a
> competitor would be immune from removal by the stockholders.
> Other examples, such as embezzlement of corporate funds, etc.,
> come readily to mind.

The court considered whether the charges against the directors described in a letter accompanying the proxy solicitation constituted cause for removal. The court summarized the contents of the letter:

First of all, it charges that the two directors failed to cooperate with Vogel in his announced program for rebuilding the company; that their purpose has been to put themselves in control; that they made baseless accusations against him and other management personnel and attempted to divert him from his normal duties as president by bombarding him with correspondence containing unfounded charges and other similar acts; that they moved into the company's building, accompanied by lawyers and accountants, and immediately proceeded upon a planned scheme of harassment. They called for many records, some going back twenty years, and were rude to the personnel. Tomlinson sent daily letters to the directors making serious charges directly and by means of innuendos and misinterpretations.

Are the foregoing charges, if proved, legally sufficient to justify the ouster of the two directors by the stockholders? I am satisfied that a charge that the directors desired to take over control of the corporation is not a reason for their ouster. Standing alone, it is a perfectly legitimate objective which is a part of the very fabric of corporate existence. Nor is a charge of lack of cooperation a legally sufficient basis for removal for cause.

The next charge is that these directors, in effect, engaged in a calculated plan of harassment to the detriment of the corporation. Certainly a director may examine books, ask questions, etc., in the discharge of his duty, but a point can be reached when his actions exceed the call of duty and become deliberately obstructive. In such a situation, if his actions constitute a real burden on the corporation then the stockholders are entitled to relief. The charges in this area made by the Vogel letter are legally sufficient to justify the stockholders in voting to remove such directors.

I therefore conclude that the charge of "a planned scheme of harassment" as detailed in the letter constitutes a justifiable legal basis for removing a director.

Although it held that the charges against Tomlinson and his fellow director, if true, constituted cause for removal, the court ruled that, in exercising the inherent power to remove them for cause, the shareholders could act "only after [the] director has been given adequate notice of charges of grave impropriety and afforded an opportunity to be heard." Quoting an earlier case, it ruled, "that when the shareholders attempt to remove a director for cause, 'there must be the service of specific charges, adequate notice and full opportunity of meeting the accusation.' " Although in this case, the court found that the two directors had been given adequate notice of the charges against them, they were entitled to have an opportunity to make their case to the shareholders before the special meeting was held. Accordingly, it issued an order enjoining the proxies that had been already given to the Vogel faction from being voted in favor of removing Tomlinson and his ally.

C. INSPECTION OF BOOKS AND RECORDS

1. INTRODUCTION

To exercise fully their right to vote, and especially their right to initiate litigation, shareholders may need access to a corporation's books and records, including the identity of fellow shareholders. At common law, shareholders were deemed to have a right to inspect corporate books and records deriving from their equitable ownership of the corporation's assets. The right extended beyond the formal minutes of official actions to include the documents, contracts, and papers of the corporation. However, to avoid disruption of the corporation's business, shareholders were restricted to exercising the right to inspection at reasonable times and places and, more importantly, only when inspection was for a "proper purpose."

Every state corporate statute now provides for a right of inspection, but statutory provisions vary considerably. Some have been construed simply to codify the common law right. Others impose limits on which shareholders are eligible to assert the right and which records are subject to inspection. Many states limit inspection rights to shareholders who own a certain percentage of a corporation's shares or who have held their shares for some minimum period. N.Y.B.C.L. § 624(b), which is typical, allows inspection by shareholders who own 5 percent of any class of stock or who have held their stock for at least six months. MBCA § 16.02 grants inspection rights to beneficial owners as well as shareholders of record, but divides corporate records into two categories. Shareholders can readily inspect the articles of incorporation, by-laws, minutes of shareholder meetings and like documents. But to inspect minutes of board meetings, accounting records, or the shareholder list, a shareholder must have a "proper purpose" and describe "with reasonable particularity" that purpose and the records to be inspected, which records must be "directly connected" with that purpose. MBCA § 16.02(d).

The traditional remedy of a shareholder seeking inspection is a writ of mandamus. To prevent obstruction of a shareholder's right to inspect, many statutes make a corporation that refuses to grant inspection liable for the shareholder's costs, including reasonable attorney's fees, unless the corporation can establish that it acted reasonably. *E.g.,* MBCA § 16.04(c).

Shareholder inspection rights under DGCL § 220 are also limited to inspection for a proper purpose, and also extend to beneficial owners. Section 220 has become increasingly important in recent years as Delaware courts have encouraged its use as a technique for a plaintiff to obtain facts about a corporation before bringing a derivative suit. Several judicial opinions have encouraged § 220 searches, and have permitted shareholders to examine records from before the date the shareholder bought her shares, or third-party records held by the defendant. Indeed, Delaware courts often assume that plaintiffs make § 220 requests before filing a complaint in order to assure that they can plead the requisite facts with specificity, and judges are more likely to dismiss cases if the plaintiff did not undertake such a request. At the same time, the courts also have imposed some restrictions on the searches and placed the burden on the shareholder to show that each category of inspection is relevant to a proper purpose of the inspection. A plaintiff cannot purely speculate on claims.

2.   PROPER PURPOSE

Probably the most difficult hurdle faced by a shareholder seeking inspection of corporate books and records is the establishment of a "proper purpose" for inspection. Statutes usually contain no definition of the term or define it only in vague terms such as "a purpose reasonably related to such person's interest as a stockholder." DGCL § 220(b).

In general, proper purposes include ascertaining information related to shares or dividends, mismanagement and litigation. Shareholders also can obtain a mailing list of other shareholders to solicit proxies. Improper purposes include obtaining information that might help the person seeking the information to compete with the subject company, such as customer lists or other trade secrets. In determining whether the shareholder has alleged or proved a proper purpose for inspection, courts usually have focused on whether the asserted purpose is germane to the shareholder's economic interest in the corporation.

A few courts have had occasion to consider whether inspection is available to a shareholder primarily concerned with a corporation's social or political policies. In *State ex rel. Pillsbury v. Honeywell, Inc.,* 191 N.W.2d 406, 411–413 (Minn. 1971), Pillsbury, a member of a prominent and wealthy Minneapolis family, wanted to stop Honeywell's production of anti-personnel fragmentation bombs used in Vietnam. He purchased 100 shares for the "sole purpose" of gaining a voice in Honeywell's affairs and then requested a shareholders list in order to solicit proxies for the election of new directors. When Honeywell refused his request, he filed for a writ of mandamus. The court denied relief, holding that the same result would pertain whether it applied Minnesota law or the law of Delaware, Honeywell's state of incorporation. The court stated:

> Because the power to inspect may be the power to destroy, it is important that only those with a bona fide interest in the corporation enjoy that power.

> Petitioner had utterly no interest in the affairs of Honeywell before he learned of Honeywell's production of fragmentation bombs. Immediately after obtaining this knowledge, he purchased stock in Honeywell for the sole purpose of asserting ownership

privileges in an effort to force Honeywell to cease such production. But for his opposition to Honeywell's policy, petitioner probably would not have bought Honeywell stock, would not be interested in Honeywell's profits and would not desire to communicate with Honeywell's shareholders. His avowed purpose in buying Honeywell stock was to place himself in a position to try to impress his opinions favoring a reordering of priorities upon Honeywell management and its other shareholders. Such a motivation can hardly be deemed a proper purpose germane to his economic interest as a shareholder.[5]

From the deposition, the trial court concluded that petitioner had already formed strong opinions on the immorality and the social and economic wastefulness of war long before he bought stock in Honeywell. His sole motivation was to change Honeywell's course of business because that course was incompatible with his political views. If unsuccessful, petitioner indicated that he would sell the Honeywell stock.

We do not mean to imply that a shareholder with a bona fide investment interest could not bring this suit if motivated by concern with the long-or short-term economic effects on Honeywell resulting from the production of war munitions. Similarly, this suit might be appropriate when a shareholder has a bona fide concern about the adverse effects of abstention from profitable war contracts on his investment in Honeywell.

In the instant case, however, the trial court, in effect, has found from all the facts that petitioner was not interested in even the long-term well-being of Honeywell or the enhancement of the value of his shares. His sole purpose was to persuade the company to adopt his social and political concerns, irrespective of any economic benefit to himself or Honeywell. This purpose on the part of one buying into the corporation does not entitle the petitioner to inspect Honeywell's books and records.

Petitioner argues that he wishes to inspect the stockholder ledger in order that he may correspond with other shareholders with the

---

[5]   We do not question petitioner's good faith incident to his political and social philosophy; nor did the trial court. In a well-prepared memorandum, the lower court stated: "By enumerating the foregoing this Court does not mean to belittle or to be derisive of Petitioner's motivation and intentions because this Court cannot but draw the conclusion that the Petitioner is sincere in his political and social philosophy, but this Court does not feel that this is a proper forum for the advancement of these political-social views by way of direct contact with the stockholders of Honeywell Company or any other company. If the courts were to grant these rights on the basis of the foregoing, anyone who has a political-social philosophy which differs with that of a company in which he becomes a shareholder can secure a writ and any company can be faced with a rash and multitude of these types of actions which are not bona fide efforts to engage in a proxy fight for the purpose of taking over the company or electing directors, which the courts have recognized as being perfectly legitimate and acceptable."

hope of electing to the board one or more directors who represent his particular viewpoint. While a plan to elect one or more directors is specific and the election of directors normally would be a proper purpose, here the purpose was not germane to petitioner's or Honeywell's economic interest. Instead, the plan was designed to further petitioner's political and social beliefs. Since the requisite propriety of purpose germane to his or Honeywell's economic interest is not present, the allegation that petitioner seeks to elect a new board of directors is insufficient to compel inspection.

Shortly thereafter, the Delaware courts criticized the decision and declined to follow it. *Credit Bureau of St. Paul, Inc. v. Credit Bureau Reports, Inc.*, 290 A.2d 689 (Del.Ch. 1972), *aff'd* 290 A.2d 691 (Del. 1972). Instead, as noted above, the Delaware courts have tended to grant broad inspection rights, so long as the plaintiff does not appear to be on a "fishing expedition." In the typical Delaware case, the court will consider the specific demands and will analyze, demand-by-demand, which ones are proper and which are not. For a comprehensive review of Delaware § 220 decisions, see Stephen A. Radin, *The New Stage of Corporate Governance Litigation: Section 220 Demands—Reprise*, 28 Cardozo L. Rev. 1287 (2006).

D. THE DYNAMICS OF SHAREHOLDER VOTING IN PUBLIC COMPANIES

Shareholders of public companies formally *elect* the directors, to be sure, but rarely do they play a meaningful role in *selecting* them. The current rules governing proxy voting make it impractical for most shareholders to nominate or solicit support for board candidates. Incumbent directors, who control access to the corporation's proxy materials and can use corporate funds for proxy solicitations, effectively determine who is nominated and thus who is elected. The corporation's CEO is far more likely to influence these decisions than any shareholder or shareholder group.

Not all observers believe this is a problem. In recent years, however, some shareholders, particularly institutional investors, have sought a more active role in corporate governance through bylaw amendments and increased access to the management proxy statement. Shareholder activism is not a new phenomenon, but it has been given increased impetus of late by regulatory initiatives from the SEC and statutory changes in both the DGCL and the MBCA. The current wave of activism, then, although it draws on past efforts, has a new and as yet uncharted dimension.

Problem: Universal Netware, Inc.—Part 1

Universal Netware, Inc. (UNI), a Delaware corporation, produces and installs computer networks and information management systems for large businesses and government agencies. UNI has 100 million shares of common stock outstanding, which are traded on the NASDAQ Stock Market. Officers and directors of UNI own approximately 15 million shares, and institutional investors own another 60 million.

UNI was organized 12 years ago, and its sales and earnings have increased rapidly. So has the price of its common stock. One year ago, UNI stock was selling at $45.00 per share. Over the next six months it rose to $60.00 per share.

Six months ago, Oxbridge Health Systems Inc. ("Oxbridge"), a health maintenance organization that was one of UNI's larger customers, announced that it had suffered a loss of $275 million allegedly due to billing errors caused by a UNI information management system. Oxbridge terminated all its contracts with UNI and filed suit against UNI to recover its losses.

In response, UNI issued a press release confirming that it had been sued by Oxbridge and stating that UNI was committed to rectifying any errors it might have made in designing Oxbridge's information management system. The following day, the price of UNI stock dropped to $35.00 per share. It has subsequently declined to $14 per share, where it is now trading.

Like many high-tech companies, UNI has used stock options liberally to motivate, reward and retain its managerial and professional employees. Officers and employees currently hold options to purchase roughly 20 million shares of UNI stock. Of those, options to purchase about 16 million shares are "under water"—they can be exercised only at prices in excess of the current price of UNI stock. UNI's three top executives hold 5 million of the "under water" options; about 350 employees hold the remaining 11 million.

Paul Linch, UNI's chief executive officer, has come to you, as UNI's principal outside counsel, to discuss a proposal to "reprice" (*i.e.*, lower the exercise price of) all the "under water" options[1] so that employees could exercise them at the current price of UNI stock. He notes that notwithstanding some general improvement in stock market prices, many companies were in a similar position with respect to options held by their executives and senior managers and were now repricing those options. He is concerned that if UNI does not act to increase the value of its options, it may lose key managerial and professional employees who could be better

---

[1]   Stock options are frequently used as a form of incentive compensation for executives. Options are typically granted at "out-of-the-money" prices. Suppose the company's current stock price at the time of the option grant was $10 per share; the exercise price of the option may be $15 per share. The option grant incentivizes executive to increase the stock price so that it exceeds the $15 exercise price. The theory is that the executives will work hard to increase the value of the firm. Suppose at the maturity of the option, the stock price is $20 per share. The executive profits from the exercise of the option by $5 per share. However, if the stock price is below the exercise price of $15 per share, the option is said to be "under water."

compensated elsewhere. If that were to happen, UNI would have difficulty both in pursuing new business and servicing its existing customers. Linch wants your advice about the potential risks of proceeding with the plan.

He recognizes that, in light of the current controversy surrounding executive compensation, repricing would be likely to meet significant opposition. Management holds far less stock in UNI than do institutional investors; and there has been organized institutional investor opposition to similar proposals."

How do you respond to Linch's questions? From where might opposition come? And what are the risks that UNI's shareholders will not approve the plan, even if there is no organized opposition?

1. THE COLLECTIVE ACTION PROBLEM

Shareholders in public corporations rarely use their voting rights to oppose management's slate of directors, to vote against management proposals, or to undertake their own proxy solicitations. Why not? The following is a classic answer.

ROBERT CHARLES CLARK, CORPORATE LAW
389–94 (1986).

Whenever shareholders of a publicly held company vote upon matters affecting the corporation, they engage in collective action that suffers from many systemic difficulties. Such difficulties include "rational apathy" of shareholders, the temptation of individual shareholders to take a "free ride," and unfairness to certain shareholders even where collective action is successful.

Often the aggregate cost to shareholders of informing themselves of potential corporate actions, independently assessing the wisdom of such actions, and casting their votes will greatly exceed the expected or actual benefits garnered from informed voting. Recognition of this phenomenon accounts for the usual rules that entrust corporate management with all ordinary business decisions. But the same problem still exists with respect to the major subjects of shareholder voting: the election of directors and the approval or rejection of major organic changes such as mergers.

Consider a simplified case. Outta Control Corp., with 1 million voting common shares outstanding, has 10,000 shareholders, each of whom owns 1 block of 100 shares. The directors propose to merge Outta Control into Purchaser Corp., which would result in the acquisition by the former Outta Control shareholders, in exchange for their old shares, of voting common shares in Purchaser with a total market value of $50 million. In fact, Purchaser would have been willing to exchange $60 million worth of its shares if it had not agreed, under prodding by Outta Control's managers and in return for their cooperation in recommending the merger, to give extraordinary salary increases to those officers of Outta Control who would continue their employment after the merger.

Assume that all of this information is contained in a 240-page proxy statement that is sent to Outta Control's shareholders and that any rational shareholder who reads it would decide to vote against the merger. Assume further that if the merger proposal were disapproved, a new one would be adopted that would yield these shareholders the additional $10 million gain which Purchaser Corp. was prepared to pay. Thus, the actual benefit to be derived from collective shareholder action against the merger plan would be $1000 per shareholder.

Shareholders do not expect, however, to discover a reason for concluding that disapproval will avert a corporate harm or open the door to a larger corporate gain every time they read a proxy statement. To make our problem complete, assume that the shareholders in it make a rational assessment of the probabilities of such an occurrence. Because of their assessment, they assign an expected benefit of $50 per shareholder to collective action of the sort described, that is, action based on each shareholder's reading the proxy statement, making up his mind, and voting.

Now suppose the average cost of informed shareholder action is simply the opportunity cost (the cost of doing one thing to the exclusion of others) of reading the proxy statement before sending in the proxy card and that this amount is $120 per shareholder (three hours of reading at $40 per hour—a rather low estimate). Thus the total cost of collective action would be $1.2 million. This cost would still be less than the actual benefit to be gained in this case, from collective action by informed voters. But the cost of such collective action greatly exceeds the expected benefit—$120 versus $50 per shareholder—so sensible shareholders will not read the proxy statement. They will be rationally apathetic.

One legal approach toward improving the efficiency of collective action is to make it cheaper for each shareholder to act in an informed way. Suppose that in our example the opportunity cost of reading the proxy statement concerning the proposed merger were only $10 per shareholder, because the SEC had devised a system of proxy rules that produced extremely concise, quickly understandable proxy statements that emphasize crucial data. Suppose that the SEC also monitors the statement and requires that the crucial information appear in bold face type. The expected benefit of collective action by informed voting is still $50 per shareholder, but the cost of such action is now only $10 per shareholder. The net expected benefit is therefore $40 per shareholder.

Yet the desired collective action still may not occur. Any one shareholder may realize that only 50 percent of the shareholders are needed to block the merger. If the shareholder believes that enough other shareholders will respond to the incentive of the $40 net expected benefit and will act accordingly to produce the desirable collective result, he might decide to save himself the cost of reading the streamlined proxy statement. He can still participate in any benefits of collective action that arise through the work of the other shareholders. He will be a free rider on their efforts. The net expected benefit of his action as a free rider would be $50 rather than $40.

Of course, it may also occur to him that if all the other shareholders thought similarly, no collective action would be taken, and everyone would lose the chance of reaping the benefits. He might realize that giving in to the temptation to achieve an individual gain superior to everyone else's would jeopardize the attainment of collective benefits. Conceivably this realization might prompt him to read the proxy statement. But it is doubtful whether this would happen in practice and, as a matter of theory (game theory, that is), a rational, self-interested shareholder would not do so.

Why not? Because, whether he assumes the other shareholders will read or will not read, he will expect to be better off if he doesn't. Assume the others will read: His own expected benefit is $50 if he doesn't read, and $40 if he does. Assume the others will not read (so the original merger plan goes through): His own expected benefit is $0 if he doesn't read, but minus $10 if he does. The situation is like the prisoner's dilemma of game theory and may call for solutions similar in strategy to those that would solve that dilemma.[2]

Let us again alter the hypothetical so that the free rider problem, like the rational apathy problem, effectively disappears. Suppose that one shareholder, Ajax, owns 200,000 shares, while every other shareholder owns only one block of 100 shares. The other facts remain the same. The expected benefit to Ajax is now $100,000, which is, let us assume, more than the expected cost of reading the proxy statement and convincing the holders of 300,100 other shares also to vote against the merger. (He would do this by waging a proxy contest.) Unless it deeply galls Ajax to think that he will be treated unfairly, he will take action to achieve the collective benefit even if he cannot be reimbursed for the costs and risks of such action.

Acting strictly for his own benefit, he will nevertheless have created a collective good for all the other shareholders in the company. The smaller shareholders will get the benefit of his concern without bearing a pro rata share of cost. This phenomenon is an example of what one economist calls

---

[2] You and a colleague are arrested for bank robbery. The police have insufficient evidence for a conviction and put you in separate cells. Each of you is offered the same deal: if you testify against your colleague and your colleague remains silent, you will go free and your silent accomplice will receive a full 10-year sentence. If you both stay silent, you will both be sentenced to only six months on a reduced charge. If each of you betrays the other, you will each receive a 2-year sentence. You must decide whether to testify or remain silent without knowing what the other will do. How do you act? [Eds.]

the systematic exploitation of the large by the small. (We can assume that Ajax will not try to be a free rider because his particular expected benefit is so high that he would not risk depending on action by other shareholders.)

The obvious problem here is one of fairness to the guardian shareholder. The prospect of being taken advantage of by the smaller shareholders may deter investors from becoming dominant shareholders in the first place. The problem once again resembles the prisoner's dilemma, but in this situation the players are all investors as they contemplate buying into any publicly held corporation. But in the real world there are many factors that tempt investors to obtain large percentage interests in companies, not the least of which is the chance of acquiring the various special benefits of controlling the corporation on an ongoing basis. Any force toward misallocation created by the phenomenon of exploitation of the large by the small is likely to be more than offset by these factors. Thus, the only remaining problem will be unfair treatment of the large, but not controlling, shareholder who undertakes a proxy contest or similar action for the corporation's benefit.

2. THE ROLE OF INSTITUTIONAL INVESTORS

The types of large institutions that manage portfolios of securities and the role they have played has evolved over time. For most of the twentieth century what may be called the "traditional institutional investors" were passive investors that generally followed the "Wall Street rule": vote with the management or sell the stock. They seldom intervened in the affairs of their portfolio companies and, as the "rule" suggests, they voted their shares as management recommended, and if they became dissatisfied with management, they sold their shares.

The end of the last century saw the emergence of activist hedge funds. Although their strategies vary, these funds consist generally of pools of capital that take significant minority positions in companies, pressing them for changes designed to increase their stock prices, and then selling their positions to capture a quick profit. These funds have not only had an effect on the corporations that become their targets, but have caused changes in the behavior of many traditional institutional investors as well as other public companies that have reacted to concerns that they may become targets.

a. Traditional Institutions

Today institutions that manage other people's money own the overwhelming majority of the stock of U.S. public companies. These institutional investors include mutual funds, pension funds—both private and public, insurance companies, bank trust and estate departments, and foundation and endowment funds. The rise of institutional investors has been relatively recent. In 1950 institutions held only 9% of U.S. stocks, in 1983 they crossed the 50% threshold, and today they hold more than 70% of the value of all U.S. voting shares and over three-quarters of the shares of the Fortune 1,000 largest public companies.

Public and private pension funds account for the largest share of institutional ownership. They own approximately 60% of the Fortune 1000. Mutual funds, which pool the investments of many investors under common management, account for the next largest (and still growing) share of institutional ownership. Growth in mutual funds was stagnant in the early years; their holdings remained around 3% of public company shares from 1950 to 1980. But they rose from 9% in 1990 to 20.9% today. This trend was accelerated by the shift of many U.S. employers from defined-benefit plans (where employees are assured defined payments on retirement) to defined-contribution plans (where employees are only assured defined contributions paid to their retirement accounts). Today mutual funds are the principal destination for employee retirement savings.

Institutional ownership is even more concentrated in the largest U.S. companies. For many of the companies in the S & P 500, institutions hold more than 75% of the outstanding shares. This concentration of institutional ownership is particularly pronounced for the middle-tier of U.S. companies. Equity ownership is also concentrated in the largest institutional shareholders. The top 50 institutional holders account for 63.7% of stock in the top 1,000 U.S. corporations, and the top 100 holders represent 66.9%.

In the early 1990s, as corporate governance shifted from shareholders exercising their "exit" rights in takeovers to using their "voice" in voting contests, attention turned to the role of institutional investors. Hopes ran high that institutional investors could overcome the rational apathy and collective action problems faced by individual investors—to improve corporate governance and corporate social responsibility. In theory, the gradual disappearance of individual investors and the growth of institutions would narrow the separation of ownership from control highlighted by Berle and Means.

Academic commentators have pointed out that the "rational apathy" described by Dean Clark becomes less rational as shareholdings grow; the more a shareholder holds, the more it has to gain from a favorable voting outcome and the more likely its vote will be decisive. That is, a shareholder who owns 100,000 shares will realize a gain that is 1,000 times larger and will be 1,000 times more likely to cast a decisive vote compared to a shareholder who owns 100 shares.

Institutional shareholders, because they hold diversified portfolios, also should find that monitoring is easier because of economies of scale. Many governance issues (such as classified boards and executive pay) arise in similar forms at different companies. An institutional shareholder that votes on the same proposal at a number of companies reduces its per-company governance costs.

But would institutional shareholders, themselves agents for their beneficiaries, behave like principals? As academic commentators also have noted, institutional shareholders face their own conflicting interests that discourage them from taking an activist role in corporate governance. That is, the institutional agents may not have incentives to act as the principal. These conflicts are different for each institution:

Mutual funds. Mutual funds (which obtain much of their business from employer-based savings plans, such as 401(k) plans) view portfolio companies as customers. Thus, fund managers face pressure, often subtle, from corporate management to vote according to management's interests or risk that management will withdraw its savings plan and move it elsewhere. This threat is even greater for mutual funds that are part of financial conglomerates, which also offer investment banking and corporate lending services.

State pension plans. State pension plans (which invest their assets for state employee retirements) face an entirely different set of pressures. Unlike their private counterparts, which worry about offending corporate management, public pension managers often have political aspirations and seek to be a thorn in the side of corporate management—to advance particular economic, social or political causes that may be at odds with maximizing fund performance.

Corporate pension plans. Corporate pension plans (which invest corporate moneys to provide retirement benefits to employees) are managed by an in-house plan administrator, almost always an executive of the plan sponsor. The administrator faces the conflict between managing the pension fund for the benefit of plan participants, as required by the Employee Retirement Income Security Act (ERISA), and managing the fund for the benefit of corporate management.

Insurance companies. Insurance companies (which invest their assets to cover their insurance liabilities and also manage insurance-based retirement plans) face similar pressures as mutual funds. The pressure may be very crude or more subtle.

Besides these conflicts, institutional investors that index their investments (tracking the performance of a particular stock index, such as the S & P 500) have little incentive to undertake the expense of shareholder activism, even if it might improve portfolio performance. Since such institutions compete on cost, they have an incentive *not* to engage in corporate governance activities that would increase costs more than those of competitors. For many institutional investors, indexing is a significant part of their investment strategy representing, for example in the case of pension funds, 60% of their overall portfolios.

It may, in fact, be economically irrational for even the managers of most non-indexed funds to engage in efforts to improve the performance of portfolio companies. In that connection, how persuasive is the "agency capitalism" analysis of Professors Gilson and Gordon discussed in Chapter 12, Section B.7?

Another explanation for institutional passivity is that institutions have a strong preference (sometimes mandated by law) for liquidity rather than control. Open-end mutual funds, for example, must stand ready to redeem their investors' shares. And many mutual funds and insurance companies see their business model as buying and selling stock in their portfolios, with annual turnover rates often exceeding 100%. They don't have time to treat portfolio companies as if they were really owners. Only when an institution is constrained from selling the stock because the size of its ownership will depress the market price does an institution have the incentive to exercise voice in corporate affairs.

The institutional culture also is at odds with shareholder activism. Institutional managers often feel an "obedience to the mores of the financial community," which disdains shareholder activism. Institutional managers sometimes express their worry about developing a reputation as an activist, as though it were a communicable disease.

Marbled into these conflicts are various legal impediments to an institutional governance role. Liability under the 1934 Act for short-swing profits by 10% shareholders and the disclosure rules applicable to 5% "toehold" positions impose additional costs on institutions seeking to take a meaningful ownership position. The possibility of short-swing profit liability also discourages institutional investors from installing representatives on company boards. Regulation FD (the rule against selective corporate disclosures) raises questions about the legality of behind-the-scenes communications with corporate insiders on governance issues. And any legal liability that may arise from over-activism is borne by the institutional investor alone—another free-riding cost.

Despite these problems, there has been a steady increase in institutional activism over the past two decades. Some institutions, primarily state pension plans and labor union pension funds, have become regular and effective users of the shareholder proposal rule. Their submissions on corporate governance reforms such as declassified boards, restrictions on poison pills, and redesigned executive compensation have received significant support from other shareholders. And management implementation of some majority-proposals, particularly those dealing with board declassification, has become more frequent.

Other institutions, particularly the retirement fund for college professors (TIAA) and the largest state pension plan (CalPERS), have targeted under-performing companies and engaged in behind-the-scenes negotiations with corporate management to seek desired reforms. Studies indicate that some of these negotiations have produced positive effects on stock prices.

Institutional shareholders have mounted "withhold" campaigns against directors who are viewed as unsympathetic to shareholder interests. (Remember that board voting procedures do not allow shareholders to vote "no" on the election of a director.) Where institutions once uniformly rubber-stamped management slates, some now regularly withhold votes from at least one director at a majority of portfolio companies. Institutional Shareholder Services (ISS), the dominant proxy advisory firm, has been a leader in recommending "withhold" votes against directors whose business dealings cause them not to meet its independence standards or who sit on compensation committees that approved high pay packages. Many institutions strictly adhere to ISS guidelines, a voting strategy that assures the institution is in the mainstream. As important as those guidelines may be, because of the recent "say-on-pay" voting requirements, ISS reports that there has been a significant decline in shareholder opposition to director elections.

Some institutions, particularly mutual funds and investment funds with social/political investment policies, invest only in companies that meet certain criteria. For example, Domini Social Investments, which manages more than $1.2 billion in assets for individual and institutional investors, invests only in firms that meet specified criteria for corporate citizenship, diversity in employment, employee relations, environment, overseas operations, and safe and useful products.

b. Activist Investors

The term "activist investors" is generally reserved for investment funds that acquire stock positions in public companies and then seek to induce them to make changes designed to raise their stock price. The changes they seek take a variety of forms, including changing management, modifying business strategy, taking actions related to the balance sheet (such as returning cash to shareholders through dividends or share repurchases), divestiture of specified business operations or splitting the company into parts, selling the company, or opposing an acquisition.

Activist investors use a variety of tactics to bring about change. The most common is seeking representation on the company's board via a proxy contest or shareholder nomination bylaws discussed below. Short of that, they may simply engage in discussions with management in efforts to persuade them to make changes, often making those discussions quite public, with the goal of bringing additional pressure to bear. While the size of the positions taken by individual activists is typically small, averaging around 7%, they often increase their strength by inducing other activists to join them in what are known as "wolf packs." Activist investors may also attempt to persuade traditional institutional investors to join their cause, arguing that the changes they seek are in the interest of all shareholders.

One result of the increasing influence of activist investors has been to increase communications between public companies and their larger shareholders. According to a 2016 report by Sullivan & Cromwell, "These more open lines of communication mean that institutional investors are less dependent on activists to serve as watchdogs for corporate efficiency, performance and governance. The ongoing engagement has relieved tensions and in certain cases addressed potential shareholder concerns before they became a catalyst for a successful activist campaign. In addition, the spread of activism among larger respected companies has largely removed the stigma of an activist campaign, reducing the effectiveness of an activist's threat to take its demands public."

On the other hand, some commentators, including some major institutional investors, have expressed concerns that activist campaigns too often focus on short-term profits at the expense of the interests of the longer-term welfare of the corporation, its long-term shareholders, and other stakeholders. This tends to put too much management focus on profits and stock prices for the next quarter or the next year. This may amplify the short-term economic incentives of senior executives who often benefit personally from higher bonuses and more valuable stock compensation when stock prices increase. In response to these pressures, they may, for example, cut expenditures on research and development, to the benefit of near-term stock prices, but usually to the detriment of profits in the long run.

This is not to say that all activist campaigns have negative long-term effects. The managers of large corporations, like all humans, can become too comfortable with doing things as they have always been done. An outsider with a different perspective can sometimes identify changes in strategy that have beneficial effects in both the short run and the long run. One thing seems certain: the movement set in place by activist investors will continue to evolve, with effects on corporate governance practices, and probably the legal rules that affect them.

E. FEDERAL PROXY REGULATION

As we have seen, state corporate statutes require that a corporation hold an annual meeting of shareholders to elect the board of directors. Besides voting on director nominees, shareholders can also propose to amend the corporate bylaws and submit resolutions for shareholder approval. In addition, the shareholders must approve certain fundamental transactions recommended by the board, such as amendments to the articles of incorporation, mergers, and sales of assets and vote on other matters that management submits to them.

1. INTRODUCTION

The federal law that regulates the process for obtaining proxies from shareholders in public corporations marks one of the great intersections of federal and state law. State law authorizes proxy voting and federal law prescribes how it may proceed. Section 14(a) of the 1934 Act makes it unlawful:

> in contravention of such rules and regulations as the Commission may prescribe as necessary or appropriate in the public interest or for the protection of investors, to solicit . . . any proxy or consent or authorization in respect of any security registered pursuant to section 12.

Thus, for companies whose securities are listed or traded on national stock exchanges such as the New York Stock Exchange and NASDAQ Stock Market or are otherwise required to register their stock with the SEC, a proxy solicitation must comply with the SEC proxy rules. Such companies also must file periodic and annual reports with the SEC.

Federal proxy regulation emphasizes disclosure. The legislative history of the 1934 Act indicates that Congress wanted to provide "fair corporate suffrage." The SEC's operating theory is that fairness is achieved by providing sufficient information to investors to allow them to make an informed choice. The SEC rules also try to neutralize management's control of the proxy solicitation process. Beyond mandating disclosure in a proxy statement distributed to shareholders, the SEC rules prescribe the form of proxy and require management to include shareholder proposals in the proxy materials the company sends to shareholders.

On closer examination, "fair suffrage" often is closely related to the substantive fairness of the corporate transaction on which the shareholders are voting. Thus, the extent of federal involvement in corporate law through federal regulation of proxies is more substantial than appears at first.

For example, a merger requires shareholder approval under state law. State law does not require the solicitation of proxies to obtain that approval but if there is a solicitation, it is largely regulated by federal law. If the terms of the merger are unfair, shareholders may seek their remedies under state law. If the terms of the merger are not correctly or fairly described in the proxy solicitation (a failing that often accompanies unfairness in the deal), that failure creates a federal claim giving rise to federal remedies. A federal court would have to decide whether certain aspects of the deal were so significant to an investor's decision that disclosure was required. The answer to that question may entail a federal inquiry into whether the terms of the merger were substantively fair—a question one would have thought to be solely one of state law. For reasons which will become clearer in Chapter 15, shareholders often prefer to argue over disclosure rather than substantive fairness, but the underlying issues often are the same. Framing the issue as one of full disclosure federalizes the controversy.

Why does management solicit proxies, if state law does not require it? First is a practical answer: without a majority of shares represented at the meeting (unlikely to happen without a solicitation), there would be no quorum as required by state law to conduct a shareholders' meeting. Second is a regulatory answer: stock exchanges require that listed companies solicit proxies for all shareholders' meetings.

2. THE PROXY PROCESS

Voting by public shareholders typically happens at an annual shareholders' meeting in which shareholders submit written proxies for the election of directors and the approval of various matters submitted by management. Proxy materials must be filed with the SEC and distributed to shareholders, who often hold their shares through intermediaries.

a. The Annual Meeting

The annual shareholders' meeting is a rite of spring, since most public corporations hold their annual meetings shortly after distributing their annual financial statements for the previous year. As described below, shareholders receive or have Internet access to proxy materials for the meetings of the companies in which they hold shares. The materials include notice of the annual meeting and proxy statement (usually one document), a proxy card (the ballot on which shareholders give their voting instructions) and the company's annual report (required by federal proxy regulation).

The proxy process begins when the board of directors selects the date of the annual meeting, usually as specified in the bylaws. Because the shareholder body changes daily, the board must also fix a "record date" to determine which shareholders are entitled to receive notice and to vote at the meeting. Only shareholders of record (as maintained by the corporation's transfer agent) on the date fixed by the board will vote.

b. Shareholder Voting

The board of directors, through the nominating committee, selects the director nominees on whose behalf proxies will be solicited. Most public companies have bylaws that require advance notice of any director nominees by the company. Rarely are there other nominees. Thus, the directors nominated by the board and identified in the proxy statement mailed to shareholders as the management candidates will be the only candidates.

At the annual meeting, the management slate of candidates will be placed in nomination, but the votes have already effectively been cast and the election decided when the shareholders submit their proxies. In a board election, shareholders typically can only give proxy instructions to vote "for," "withhold," or "abstain" for each candidate.

In addition to submitting director nominees, the board may also decide to submit other matters for action at the shareholders' meeting—such as approval of executive compensation plans involving the issuance of stock, amendments to the articles of incorporation, or ratification of the company's independent auditor. The directors usually recommend how to vote, and the form of proxy generally provides that shares will be voted in accordance with the board's recommendations unless instructions are given to the contrary.

The proxy materials may also include shareholder proposals that have been submitted pursuant to the procedure laid out in the SEC shareholder proposal rule, which is discussed below. If the proposal is presented by the submitting shareholder at the meeting, proxy votes will be cast for or against the proposal according to shareholder instructions.

c.   Filing Proxy Material

After the board has identified the matters on which shareholders will vote, the proxy materials (proxy statement and the form of proxy) must be filed with the SEC. Often the proxy materials are a markup of last year's materials, unless there are new nominees or agenda changes. Although the board of directors will review the proxy materials, most of the work is performed by corporate executives and company counsel. Under current SEC rules, the definitive proxy statement must always be filed with the SEC although a preliminary proxy statement usually need not be filed.

d.   Identifying Shareholders: Street Names

Who are the shareholders and how does the corporation send them the proxy materials? Although the corporation maintains a list of record shareholders, this list does not identify beneficial owners. Most shareholders of public companies are not actually the record owners of their shares. Instead, they have their shares registered in "street name." The actual record owner is the broker or a "nominee" which hold a global certificate representing the shares of many investors. When a customer sells shares held in street name, the broker simply adjusts its books to reflect the transfer of ownership to the new holder. When shares are transferred from one brokerage firm to another, the transfer is reflected only on the records of a central clearing depository.

Because of this widely-used system, the list of record owners does not tell the corporation who are the beneficial owners of its shares. If an issuer requests, however, brokers must furnish the names and addresses of "non-objecting beneficial owners" ("NOBOs") with whom the issuer may communicate directly. Issuers often are reluctant to generate NOBO lists because corporate inspection statutes require that the lists be turned over to requesting shareholders, including insurgents. Without such lists, the issuer can communicate only with record holders.

SEC Rules 14a–13, 14b–1 and 14b–2 establish a mechanism by which corporations must attempt to communicate with the beneficial owners of their shares and allow them to vote at shareholder meetings. In addition, the rules of the exchanges and the NASD require that brokers either request voting instructions from their customers who are the beneficial owners or forward to them proxy materials provided by the corporation. These rules also permit brokers to vote the proxy on behalf of their customers in certain routine, uncontested matters if the beneficial owner does not give timely instructions to the broker. *See, e.g.,* New York Stock Exchange Rule 451 and 452.

Amendments to Rule 452 adopted in 2009 and 2010 restrict the ability of brokers to vote in their discretion in the election of directors and on compensation matters. Under the amended rule, director elections are not considered "routine" even if the elections are uncontested nor are executive compensation votes. In both cases, shares held in street name will not be voted unless the holders specifically instruct their brokers on how to vote.

Because brokers traditionally voted undirected shares according to management recommendations, broker votes have been significant in establishing a quorum at shareholders' meetings and for electing directors. The New York Stock Exchange rule change could affect director elections, particularly for companies that have adopted a majority-vote standard for elections.

One problem that has arisen from stock held in street name is that of "overvoting"—the voting by investors (often institutional investors) of shares that they no longer hold. The problem stems from the extensive borrowing and lending of shares in today's stock markets. When investors "sell short" to take advantage of anticipated drops in stock prices, their brokers "lend" them shares that the broker may not actually own. The client then sells these "virtual shares" to other investors, whose brokers are permitted to lend the virtual shares to yet more short sellers. The resulting daisy chain can continue, in theory, forever.

Each investor in this chain believes that she has the right to vote every share she holds in "street name." But there is only one actual voting share at the central depositary (which makes possible the street name registration system), and only the last purchaser has the right to vote that share. The problem is that investors don't know if the broker has lent out their shares. When it comes time to vote, investors (and their brokers) vote the shares shown in their account even if the shares had been lent—hence, the overvoting.

e.   Control of the Proxy Machinery

From the foregoing description, it should be obvious that the solicitation of proxies, which is necessary if shareholders are to act as a body, requires an elaborate machinery. Detailed records of shareholders must be maintained, material must be prepared, reviewed, filed and mailed, and counsel must play a significant role. All of this is expensive. The expenses are borne by the company since they relate to a necessary function that management must discharge. If a shareholder seeks to oppose management's proposals, or if she wishes to offer a candidate in opposition to those nominated by the board of directors, she must duplicate the entire process and bear the expense on her own, subject to obtaining reimbursement of expenses in limited circumstances.

f.   Counting the Proxies

After the proxy holders present their proxies at the meeting and establish they are the agent for the shares represented, they cast their ballot. In an uncontested election, no one challenges the count which is reported in the company's next SEC quarterly filing. But if the election or proposed transaction is contested, the proxy count becomes crucial. SEC rules require public companies to report the results of a shareholder vote on SEC Form 8–K within four business days after the end of the meeting at which the vote was taken. If the vote relates to a contested election of directors and the results were not definitively determined at the end of the meeting, a corporation is required to disclose preliminary results within four business days and an amended report within four business days after the final results are certified.

In a contested vote, questions will often arise as to whether particular proxies are valid or have been revoked. To settle such questions, the board designates inspectors of election. In contested elections, these people are generally not members of management, but are professionals hired to do the job. What law applies? Usually, the practical answer is found in the practices of corporate lawyers who deal with proper signatures, fiduciary voting, dating of proxies and the like. In a contested election, the lawyers for each side customarily agree on a set of ground rules in advance of the meeting. These unofficial documents have guided courts when the issues are litigated.

In some instances, courts have intervened to review the actions of election inspectors. Courts have not hesitated to set aside some or all of the disputed proxies when they disagreed with how the inspectors resolved disputes. The courts must balance the need for quick resolution of an election and the protection of the shareholder franchise. DGCL § 231, for example, requires that public corporations (as defined in the statute) appoint one or more inspectors in advance of any shareholders' meeting and make a written report. The inspectors, who can be independent third parties or employees of the corporation, must ascertain the number of shares outstanding and the voting power of each, the shares represented at the meeting and the validity of proxies and ballots cast, count all votes and ballots and certify their result.

g. E-Proxy Rules

Under the SEC's e-proxy rules, every corporation must post its proxy soliciting materials on a website other than that of the SEC. These rules were adopted to enable shareholders to utilize Internet technology in their voting and to permit corporations to lower their proxy soliciting expenses significantly. The rules give public companies the option to furnish proxy materials to their shareholders by providing them notice that the materials are available from its website.

3. THE MEANING OF "PROXY SOLICITATION"

Problem: Universal Netware, Inc.—Part 2

Review the facts of Part 1 in Section D, above. Tanya White, UNI's general counsel, reviewed the repricing proposal and concluded that the language of UNI's stock option plan, which has been approved by stockholders, does not permit repricing without shareholder approval. Consequently, White recommended that the board ask the shareholders to approve an amendment to the plan that would authorize the board to reprice outstanding options.

After some discussion, all members of UNI's board agreed that UNI should take action along the lines recommended by Linch and White. After the board meeting, Linch asked you whether UNI should issue a press release announcing the board's action. Specifically, he asked you whether the release would violate the proxy rules, especially Rules 14a–1 and 14a–3, if it:

   a) Contained a brief description of the repricing plan; stated that the board had adopted a resolution recommending that the shareholders adopt an amendment to the stock option plan authorizing the repricing; and said that the amendment would be put to a shareholder vote at UNI's next annual meeting.

   b) In addition to the above, explained that management and the board believe that the plan is in the best interests of UNI's shareholders because it rewards UNI's employees for their loyal service; strengthens UNI's ability to hire new employees in a tight market; and thus enhances management's ability to promote the long-term interests of UNI and its shareholders.

How do you respond to his questions?

———————

What is a proxy solicitation? Rule 14a–1 defines "proxy" broadly to include proxies, consents and authorizations. The rule defines "solicitation" to include:

(i)   any request for a proxy whether or not accompanied by or included in a form of proxy;

(ii) any request to execute or not to execute, or to revoke, a proxy; or

(iii) the furnishing of a form of proxy or other communication to security holders under circumstances *reasonably calculated* to result in the procurement, withholding or revocation of a proxy.

The most important interpretive question is the meaning of "reasonably calculated." Does it mean an action "intended" to have shareholders eventually give their proxy, or does it mean an action "likely" to result in shareholder action?

Studebaker Corp. v. Gittlin, 360 F.2d 692 (2d Cir.1966) illustrates the broad interpretation that the SEC and some courts have given to "solicitation." Gittlin, a Studebaker shareholder, sought inspection of the company's shareholder list in preparation for an effort to gain control of the board of directors. Because he had not been a shareholder for six months, New York law required that he own or have the support of holders of 5% of Studebaker's stock in order to obtain the list. After Gittlin obtained written authorizations from 42 other shareholders, a state court ordered Studebaker to allow inspection.

The company then asked a federal court to enjoin the state court order, charging that Gittlin had violated the federal proxy rules in obtaining the authorizations. The SEC, appearing *amicus curiae*, argued that soliciting authorizations was subject to the proxy rules even if the request was not part of a planned proxy solicitation. The Second Circuit agreed:

We need not go that far to uphold the order of the district court. A shareholder communication becomes subject to the Proxy Rules if it was part of "a continuous plan" intended to end in solicitation and to prepare the way for success. This was the avowed purpose of Gittlin's demand for inspection of the stockholders list and, necessarily, for his soliciting authorizations sufficient to aggregate the 5% of the stock required by New York's Business Corporation Law. Presumably the stockholders who gave authorizations were told something and, as Judge L. Hand said, "one need only spread the misinformation adequately before beginning to solicit, and the Commission would be powerless to protect shareholders."

A controversy relating to a proposed merger of the Rock Island Railroad with the Union Pacific Railroad in 1963 led to two decisions that show the factors courts consider when deciding whether to subject a communication to the requirements of the proxy rules. On May 19, 1963, the Rock Island and Union Pacific announced an agreement to merge. On June 24, 1963, the Chicago and Northwestern Railway unveiled a competing offer for the Rock Island. For Northwestern's offer to succeed, the Rock Island's shareholders would have to vote down the merger with Union Pacific, which the boards of the two companies formally approved on June 27, 1963. Northwestern also needed regulatory approval of its offer and applied for that approval on July 3, 1963.

On July 26, 1963, Union Pacific published a newspaper advertisement explaining that it opposed Northwestern's offer because it would adversely affect railroad service. The advertisements appeared in cities served by the Rock Island and in Washington and New York, which the Rock Island did not serve.

A Rock Island shareholder filed suit, claiming that the advertisement was a communication reasonably calculated to procure a proxy and thus constituted an unlawful solicitation. The court disagreed, noting that the ad informed the public about an issue pending before a government agency and thus served a public interest independent of the decision the Rock Island's shareholders would have to make. The court also considered it significant that the Rock Island shareholders' meeting had not been called at the time the ad was published. In fact, the meeting scheduled for November 15, 1963 was not called until October 1. *Brown v. Chicago, R.I. & P.R.R. Co.*, 328 F.2d 122, 124–5 (7th Cir. 1964).

In contrast, once the contestants began to solicit proxies formally, a different court held that another communication not specifically directed at the Rock Island's shareholders nonetheless constituted a solicitation. A brokerage firm prepared a report concluding that the Rock Island's shareholders would benefit more from Northwestern's offer than from Union Pacific's and distributed the report to its customers. Northwestern, which had assisted the brokerage firm in preparing the report, distributed additional copies of the report to Rock Island shareholders. The court held that the report was reasonably calculated to influence a Rock Island shareholder's decision on whether to grant a proxy and therefore was a solicitation. *Union Pacific R.R. Co. v. Chicago & N.W. Ry. Co.*, 226 F.Supp. 400 (N.D.Ill. 1964).

Smallwood v. Pearl Brewing Company, 489 F.2d 579 (5th Cir.1974), illustrates that the breadth of the term "solicitation" is not unlimited. Approximately two months prior to mailing its proxy statement soliciting shareholder approval of a merger, a company advised its shareholders by letter of the proposed merger. The company also indicated that the board believed that the merger would be beneficial to shareholders. The court held that the letter was not a communication reasonably calculated to result in the procurement of a proxy. No proxies were actually mentioned and the correspondence "if not totally innocuous was not overwhelmingly prejudicial either." The court also noted that requiring compliance with the proxy rules would impede prompt disclosure to investors of a major, pending corporate transaction.

This last point has great significance. A constant tension exists between the timing requirements of the proxy rules and the SEC's policy urging prompt disclosure of significant corporate information. Both the courts and the SEC recognize that labeling a communication a "solicitation" stifles some communication; it often will be impractical promptly to prepare and circulate material that meets all requirements of the proxy rules. Consequently, the courts and the SEC have strived to maintain a reasonable balance between serving the needs of the marketplace and protecting the integrity of the proxy solicitation process.

LONG ISLAND LIGHTING COMPANY V. BARBASH
779 F.2d 793 (2d Cir.1985).

[The Long Island Lighting Company (LILCO) was the focus of a local political campaign, in which candidate Matthews urged public ownership of the utility. Matthews acquired sufficient shares to demand a special shareholders' meeting to consider his proposal.

Meanwhile, a group favorable to Matthews' proposal, Citizens to Replace LILCO, published a newspaper advertisement accusing LILCO of mismanagement and attempting to pass through to ratepayers needless costs relating to construction of the Seabrook nuclear power plant and urging support for a campaign to have the public power authority acquire LILCO.

LILCO complained that the ad was unlawful because it constituted a proxy solicitation for which no proxy statement had been filed and because it was false and misleading. LILCO sought to enjoin the group's ads until their allegedly false statements were corrected and an appropriate SEC filing had been made. The district court declined to hold that the ad represented a solicitation because it appeared in a general publication and could only indirectly affect the proxy contest at LILCO.]

CARDAMONE, CIRCUIT JUDGE:

In our view the district court erred in holding that the proxy rules cannot cover communications appearing in publications of general circulation and that are indirectly addressed to shareholders. The SEC proxy rules apply not only to direct requests to furnish, revoke or withhold proxies, but also to communications which may indirectly accomplish such a result or constitute a step in a chain of communications designed ultimately to accomplish such a result.

The question in every case is whether the challenged communication, seen in the totality of circumstances, is "reasonably calculated" to influence the shareholders' votes. Determination of the purpose of the communication depends upon the nature of the communication and the circumstances under which it was distributed.

Deciding whether a communication is a proxy solicitation does not depend upon whether it is "targeted directly" at shareholders. See Rule 14a–6(g) (requiring that solicitations in the form of "speeches, press releases, and television scripts" be filed with the SEC). As the SEC correctly notes in its amicus brief, it would "permit easy evasion of the proxy rules" to exempt all general and indirect communications to shareholders.

Because discovery here was so abbreviated and the district court's determination was predicated on a mistaken notion of what constitutes a proxy solicitation, the case must be remanded to the district court.

WINTER, CIRCUIT JUDGE, dissenting:

In order to avoid a serious first amendment issue, I would construe the federal regulations governing the solicitation of proxies as inapplicable to the newspaper advertisement in question.

The content of the Citizens' Committee's advertisement is of critical importance. First, it is on its face addressed solely to the public. Second, it makes no mention either of proxies or of the shareholders' meeting demanded by Matthews. Third, the issues the ad addresses are quintessentially matters of public political debate, namely, whether a public power authority would provide cheaper electricity than LILCO. Claims of LILCO mismanagement are discussed solely in the context of their effect on its customers. Finally, the ad was published in the middle of an election campaign in which LILCO's future was an issue.

On these facts, therefore, LILCO's claim raises a constitutional issue of the first magnitude. It asks nothing less than that a federal court act as a censor, empowered to determine the truth or falsity of the ad's claims about the merits of public power and to enjoin further advocacy containing false claims. We need not resolve this constitutional issue, however.

Where advertisements are critical of corporate conduct but are facially directed solely to the public, in no way mention the exercise of proxies, and debate only matters of conceded public concern, I would construe federal proxy regulation as inapplicable, whatever the motive of those who purchase them. This position, which is strongly suggested by relevant case law, *see infra,* maximizes public debate, avoids embroiling the federal judiciary in determining the rightness or wrongness of conflicting positions on public policy, and does not significantly impede achievement of Congress' goal that shareholders exercise proxy rights on the basis of accurate information.

It is of course true that LILCO shareholders may be concerned about public allegations of mismanagement on LILCO's part. However, shareholders are most unlikely to be misled into thinking that advertisements of this kind, particularly when purchased in the name of a committee so obviously disinterested in the return on investment to LILCO's shareholders, are either necessarily accurate or authoritative sources of information about LILCO's management. Such advertisements, which in no way suggest internal reforms shareholders might bring about through the exercise of their proxies, are sheer political advocacy and would be so recognized by any reasonable shareholder.

To be sure, the fact that a corporation has become a target of political advocacy might well justify unease among shareholders. No one seriously asserts, however, that the right to criticize corporate behavior as a matter of public concern diminishes as shareholders' meetings become imminent.

———————

When *LILCO* was decided, the SEC proxy rules required every person soliciting a proxy to deliver to every solicited shareholder a proxy statement with detailed information about the solicitor and the matters for which proxy authority was sought. Thus, to place a newspaper ad about an upcoming shareholders' meeting that the SEC deemed to be a proxy solicitation, the solicitor would first have to file a proxy statement with the SEC, receive staff clearance, and then mail copies of the statement to all shareholders. Although the soliciting shareholder could use Rule 14a–7 to have the company mail her proxy materials, she would have to bear the cost of the mailing. Only if the shareholder limited her solicitation to 10 or fewer shareholders did the SEC rules exempt her communications.

As shareholder voice became more important in the early 1990s, many people raised concerns that the SEC proxy rules discouraged shareholder participation in corporate voting. In 1992, the SEC responded with a set of "shareholder communications" rules that sought to make it easier for shareholder participation in corporate voting, while protecting the voting process from fraud.

As the SEC explained:

The best protection for shareholders and the marketplace is to identify those classes of solicitations that warrant application of the proxy statement disclosure requirement, and to foster the free and unrestrained expression of views by all other parties by the removal of any regulatory cost, burden or uncertainty that could have the effect of deterring the free expression of views by disinterested shareholders who do not seek authority for themselves.

Exchange Act Rel. No. 31,326 (Oct. 22, 1992).

The SEC exempted from the proxy rules' filing and delivery requirements any solicitation by a person, whether or not a shareholder, who does not seek proxy voting authority and does not furnish shareholders with a form of proxy. Rule 14a–2. Thus, a person (unless in an excluded group) can solicit support for a shareholder proposal, so long as she is not asking for voting authority.

Moreover, soliciting shareholders need not file notice with the SEC, if the solicitation is oral or is by a shareholder who owns less than $5 million of the company's shares. But a solicitor who solicits in writing and owns more than $5 million in company shares must file a notice, within three days *following* the first dissemination of the solicitation. The notice is simple: a statement of the solicitor's name and address and an attachment of the soliciting materials. The only significant regulatory constraint continues to be Rule 14a–9's prohibition against materially false and misleading statements in a proxy solicitation.

This exemption is not available to (i) the company whose shares are the subject of the solicitation, (ii) a person acting on behalf of or financed by the company, (iii) a person soliciting in opposition to a merger or other extraordinary transaction where that person has proposed or plans to propose an alternative transaction to which it will be a party, (iv) certain large shareholders interested in seeking control of the company, or (v) a person who would receive a benefit from a successful solicitation that she would not share *pro rata* with other shareholders.

The SEC also excluded from the 14a–1 definition of "solicitation" an announcement by a shareholder of how she intends to vote and her explanation of her decision. Such an announcement can, without limitation, be published, broadcast, or disseminated to the media. None of the proxy rules apply since it is not deemed a solicitation.

Finally, the SEC substantially eliminated staff review of soliciting materials—other than management's initial proxy statement. Most such materials now can be filed with the SEC in definitive form when disseminated. The SEC explained that "the most cost-effective means to address hyperbole and other claims and opinions viewed as objectionable is not government screening of the contentions or resort to the courts. Rather, the parties should be free to reply to the statements in a timely and cost-effective manner, challenging the basis for the claims and countering with their own views on the subject matter through the dissemination of additional soliciting material.

F. SHAREHOLDER PROPOSALS

Problem: Universal Netware, Inc.—Part 3

UNI maintains three manufacturing plants. One, near Lima, Ohio, employs 1,000 people and accounts for a significant portion of that community's payroll. The output of that plant accounts for less than 2% of UNI's revenues and profits. Press reports suggest that, as a cost-saving measure, UNI is likely to close at least that plant, and perhaps all three, in the near future and contract to purchase the components they produce from suppliers in South Korea and the Philippines.

Prior to last year's annual shareholder meeting, Columbia Municipal Employees Pension Fund (CMEPF), a public pension fund, purchased 100 shares of UNI stock that now is trading at $32 per share. CMEPF wants to submit a shareholder proposal for inclusion in UNI's proxy statement for this year's annual meeting. It has prepared the following resolution and supporting statement:

> RESOLVED, that the bylaws be amended to add the following provision: The corporation shall not substantially discontinue the use of any significant business or plant facility unless (1) the company gives one year's notice in writing to the affected employees and community representatives of the extent of the proposed closing or reduction, (2) a hearing is conducted at which an opportunity is provided to employees and citizens of the affected communities to express their views on any aspect of the proposed closing or reduction and (3) the Board of Directors is furnished with a written report of a detailed study on the economic, environmental and social consequences of the proposed action upon the affected community. Such report shall become a record of the Corporation and copies shall be made available to shareholders upon payment of reasonable costs.

> Supporting Statement: The power to discontinue a plant or other facility carries with it the power to visit major economic, environmental and social consequences upon a particular community—consequences that may be calamitous. The proposed request simply asks the Board of Directors to be aware of these consequences before the Corporation acts on such matters, which are neither routine nor trivial, and enables the owners of the Corporation to acquire some knowledge concerning the social impact of their company's activities. The Company's disregard for the welfare of its workers necessitates revised procedures in making these far-reaching decisions.

> The policy, once implemented, would impose burdens upon the Corporation that are similar to but far less extensive than those calling upon federal agencies to furnish environmental impact

statements before undertaking certain projects, and for much the same reasons. The policy is limited to actions affecting "significant" facilities so as to avoid harassment of the company. Implementation and interpretation will devolve upon the Board, which must decide the issue in good faith.

CMEPF has asked your advice as to whether UNI management is legally required to include the proposal in its proxy statement. CMEPF also has asked you if there are any changes it should make in its proposal or supporting statement to improve the prospects that UNI will be required to include the proposal in its proxy statement.

How do you respond to these questions?

————————

Although, as we will see, shareholder proposals are regulated by SEC Rule 14a–8, that rule is grounded in state law. Because a shareholder's right to vote is a matter of state law, the extent of that right is also a matter of state law. We have already seen that because provisions such as DGCL § 141(a) give full managerial power to the board of directors, shareholders cannot adopt (and are not entitled to vote on) a resolution directing the board to act or refrain from acting on a business decision.

Under state law, if shareholders are restricted from voting on a mandatory resolution, are they entitled to vote on a resolution which is cast in the form of a non-binding recommendation? If so, what limits are there on that power? Consider the following resolutions, all cast as recommendations:

a)   That the walls of all the company's offices be painted blue.

b)   That the company stop manufacturing a particular product, for example, a food company stop manufacturing creamed corn.

c)   That the company take all necessary steps to increase its hiring of minorities.

What is it about each of the subject matter of each recommendation that would make it appropriate or inappropriate for a shareholder vote?

If you conclude that, even if cast as a recommendation, one or more of these resolutions are not proper subjects for a shareholder vote, could a shareholder circumvent that limitation by putting the recommendation into a bylaw amendment on the theory that shareholders have the statutory power to amend the bylaws? Do the same limitations on voting apply equally to a bylaw amendment or does the statute give broader power to shareholders when a bylaw amendment is involved? We will study bylaw amendments in greater detail in Section D but you also should consider the tension between DGCL §§ 109 and 141 (a), for example, in reading the following material.

1. STATE LAW

AUER V. DRESSEL
118 N.E.2d 590 (N.Y. 1954).

[The plaintiffs, who owned a majority of the Class A stock of R. Hoe & Co., Inc., brought an action for an order to compel the president of the corporation to call a special shareholders' meeting pursuant to a bylaw provision requiring such a meeting when requested by holders of a majority of the stock. The articles of incorporation provided for an eleven-member board, nine of whom were to be elected by the Class A stockholders and two of whom were to be elected by the Common stockholders. The purposes of the special meeting were:

A. To vote on a resolution endorsing the administration of Joseph L. Auer, the former President and demanding his reinstatement;

B. to amend the articles of incorporation and bylaws to provide that vacancies on the board of directors arising from the removal of a director by the shareholders be filled only by the shareholders;

C. to consider and vote on charges to remove four Class A directors for cause and to elect their successors;

D. to amend the bylaws to reduce the quorum requirement for board action.

The president refused to call the meeting on the ground, among others, that the foregoing purposes were not proper subjects for a Class A shareholder meeting.]

DESMOND, JUDGE.

The obvious purpose of the meeting here sought to be called (aside from the indorsement and reinstatement of former president Auer) is to hear charges against four of the class A directors, to remove them if the charges be proven, to amend the by-laws so that the successor directors be elected by the class A stockholders, and further to amend the by-laws so that an effective quorum of directors will be made up of no fewer than half of the directors in office and no fewer than one third of the whole authorized number of directors. No reason appears why the class A stockholders should not be allowed to vote on any or all of those proposals.

The stockholders, by expressing their approval of Mr. Auer's conduct as president and their demand that he be put back in that office, will not be able, directly, to effect that change in officers, but there is nothing invalid in their so expressing themselves and thus putting on notice the directors who will stand for election at the annual meeting. As to purpose (B), that is, amending the charter and by-laws to authorize the stockholders to fill vacancies as to class A directors who have been removed on charges or who have resigned, it seems to be settled law that the stockholders who are empowered to elect directors have the inherent power to remove them for cause, *In re Koch*, 257 N.Y. 318, 321, 322, 178 N.E. 545, 546. Of course, as the *Koch* case points out, there must be the service of specific charges, adequate notice and full opportunity of meeting the accusations, but there is no present showing of any lack of any of those in this instance. Since these particular stockholders have the right to elect nine directors and to remove them on proven charges, it is not inappropriate that they should use their further power to amend the by-laws to elect the successors of such directors as shall be removed after hearing, or who shall resign pending hearing. Quite pertinent at this point is *Rogers v. Hill*, 289 U.S. 582, 589, 53 S.Ct. 731, 734, 77 L.Ed. 1385, which made light of an argument that stockholders, by giving power to the directors to make by-laws, had lost their own power to make them; quoting a New Jersey case, *In re A.A. Griffing Iron Co.*, 63 N.J.L. 168, 41 A. 931, the United States Supreme Court said: " 'It would be preposterous to leave the real owners of the corporate property at the mercy of their agents, and the law has not done so.' " Such a change in the by-laws, dealing with the class A directors only, has no effect on the voting rights of the common stockholders, which rights have to do with the selection of the remaining two directors only. True, the certificate of incorporation authorizes the board of directors to remove any director on charges, but we do not consider that provision as an abdication by the stockholders of their own traditional, inherent power to remove their own directors. Rather, it provides an additional method. Were that not so, the stockholders might find themselves without effective remedy in a case where a majority of the directors were accused of wrongdoing and, obviously, would be unwilling to remove themselves from office.

We fail to see, in the proposal to allow class A stockholders to fill vacancies as to class A directors, any impairment or any violation of paragraph (h) of article Third of the certificate of incorporation, which says that class A stock has exclusive voting rights with respect to all matters "other than the election of directors". That negative language should not be taken to mean that class A stockholders, who have an absolute right to elect nine of these eleven directors, cannot amend their by-laws to guarantee a similar right, in the class A stockholders and to the exclusion of common stockholders, to fill vacancies in the class A group of directors.

Any director illegally removed can have his remedy in the courts, see *People ex rel. Manice v. Powell*, 201 N.Y. 194, 94 N.E. 634.

The order should be affirmed, with costs, and the Special Term directed forthwith to make an order in the same form as the Appellate Division order with appropriate changes of dates.

[VAN VOORHIS, J., dissented on the grounds that none of the cited purposes were appropriate subjects for action by shareholders at the requested meeting. Proposal A, the indorsement of Auer's tenure as president, was only "an idle gesture." The second proposal was improper because the articles of incorporation authorized the directors to fill vacancies on the board, and the change sought would have denied the common stockholders their rights to a voice in the replacement of directors through their two representatives on the board. Such a change, it was argued could be made only through special voting procedures. Proposal C, the removal of directors, was improper because a shareholders meeting was "altogether unsuited to the performance of duties which partake of the nature of the judicial function." Since most shareholders would vote by proxy, their decision would have to be made before the meeting at which the charges against the directors would be made and discussed. The fourth proposal was treated as irrelevant without action on the other three.]

2. FEDERAL LAW: THE SHAREHOLDER PROPOSAL RULE

In theory, shareholders of public corporations have the right to attend the annual shareholder meeting and introduce resolutions to be acted on at the meeting. In practice, however, this right, standing alone, is meaningless. Only a relatively small number of shareholders attend annual meetings, and most of them vote by giving the management their proxy. The standard form of management proxy gives the holder discretion to vote on resolutions raised for the first time at the meeting, and management would seldom vote in favor of a shareholder proposal. As a result, were it not for the proxy rules, shareholders who want their proposals to receive serious consideration would, as a practical matter, have to solicit their own proxies.

The "shareholder proposal rule," Rule 14a–8, solves this problem by providing shareholders access to the management proxy machinery. Any shareholder who meets the ownership requirements of the rule and submits a proposal in a timely fashion, in proper form and whose subject matter is proper can have the proposal included in the company's proxy materials for a vote at the shareholder annual meeting.

Shareholders have used the rule for a variety of purposes. Many of the early proposals dealt with issues of shareholder democracy. In the 1970s, the focus of shareholder activism shifted to questions of corporate social responsibility. In the 1980s, the focus changed again with an increased emphasis on issues of corporate governance. More recently, shareholder proposals have reflected a blend of social and corporate governance issues.

a. Eligibility and Submission Procedures

To be eligible under the rule, the proponent must continuously have held at least 1 percent or $2,000 worth of the company voting shares for at least one year. The proponent must then continue to hold the shares and present the proposal at the meeting.

A proponent may submit no more than one proposal per company for a particular shareholders' meeting. The proposal, including any accompanying supporting statement, may not exceed 500 words. The proposal must be submitted to the company not less than 120 calendar days before the date of the company's last-year proxy statement. The deadline can be found in the prior year's proxy statement.

If the company includes the proposal in its proxy materials, it may (and usually does) recommend that shareholders vote against the proposal and give reasons for its opposition. The proponent has no chance for rebuttal, but can contact the SEC staff if she believes the company's opposition contains materially false or misleading statements in violation of Rule 14a–9.

b. The Interpretative Process

The flesh on the bones of Rule 14a–8 is provided primarily through interpretations by the staff of the Division of Corporation Finance of the SEC. The staff furnishes these interpretations in response to company requests that the staff advise that it will not recommend that the Commission take any enforcement action if the company omits a shareholder proposal from its proxy statement. Because the inquiries deal with possible Commission enforcement action, the staff responses are known as "no-action" letters.

The process by which a no-action letter is issued most closely resembles a ritual dance in which each party's steps can be clearly predicted. The shareholder sends a letter to the company which may be anything from a simple request that a proposal be included to an elaborate presentation with a legal opinion in support of inclusion, depending upon the sophistication and experience of the proponent. If the company decides to include the proposal, the SEC staff is not involved in the process. If, however, the company wishes to exclude the proposal, it must send a letter to the SEC advising of its intent to omit the proposal, accompanied by an opinion of counsel stating the grounds on which the proposal can be excluded. This opinion often includes a detailed analysis of past staff no-action letters on the same or related issues; it strongly resembles a traditional brief in litigation in which counsel analyzes and distinguishes existing case law. In some cases, the proponent will submit a reply which may or may not include a contrary legal opinion. When all the papers have been submitted, the staff responds. If the staff concludes that the proposal can be omitted, it advises the company that "[T]here appears to be some basis for your view that the proposal may be excluded pursuant to Rule 14a–8(i) [appropriate subparagraph number]," but does not state what that basis is. If the staff concludes that the proposal cannot be omitted, it states that "the Division is unable to concur in your view that the proposal may be excluded." In such a case, the staff briefly explains the basis for its position.

Shareholders have an implied right of action to seek injunctive relief against the company's omission of a proposal. In addition, the SEC can enforce its rules and seek an injunction to compel inclusion of a proper proposal. Rarely does either happen, however, since shareholders rarely are willing to undertake the expense to sue, and companies uniformly acquiesce to the SEC staff's views. Thus, the 14a–8 no-action process constitutes an alternative dispute mechanism that puts the SEC staff in the peculiar role as arbiter of the role of public shareholders in corporate governance.

Are no-action letters binding law? The SEC has taken the position that they do not constitute "rulings" or "decisions" on the merits. Courts have agreed and held that the no-action letters do not create any legal relationship or constitute a final order under the Administrative Procedure Act. As a consequence, a shareholder aggrieved by an SEC no-action letter cannot sue the SEC.

c.   Substantive Grounds for Exclusion

Rule 14a–8(i) specifies various grounds on which companies may exclude shareholder proposals. Most controversy relates to the following three subsections of Rule 14a–8(i):

> (1) Improper under state law: If the proposal is not a proper subject for action by shareholders under the laws of the jurisdiction of the company's organization;

> (5) Relevance: If the proposal relates to operations which account for less than 5 percent of the company's total assets at the end of its most recent fiscal year, and for less than 5 percent of its net earnings and gross sales for its most recent fiscal year, and is not otherwise significantly related to the company's business;

> (7) Management functions: If the proposal deals with a matter relating to the company's ordinary business operations;

Sections (i)(1) and (i)(7) both require applying the law of the issuer's state of incorporation; Section (i)(1) does so by express reference to state law. Section (i)(7) does so because, as we have seen, corporate statutes all provide that the business and affairs of a corporation are to be managed by, or under the direction of, the board of directors, thus limiting the role of shareholders to matters for which the statute requires a shareholder vote, issues on which management solicits shareholders' vote, or matters that shareholders properly can raise at a shareholders' meeting.

The problem is that there is very little state law on what constitutes a "proper subject for action by shareholder" or on the division between those matters that are "ordinary business operations" that exclusively within the discretion of the board and management and those on which the shareholders have a right to act.

The principal case on "proper subject" is *Auer v. Dressel* which we considered in section 1, above. One rationale for the decision in *Auer* was that the subject matter of the meeting was the governance of the corporation, the matter in which shareholders may have the most direct interest. Under Rule 14a–8, the SEC staff has extended this rationale to require inclusion of proposals dealing with corporate governance such as the composition, structure, and compensation of the board. And, as we will see below, the rationale has been extended beyond governance to cover matters of social policy.

Under section (i)(1), as the SEC staff has interpreted it, the form of the resolution is significant. The Note to the section states,

> Depending on the subject matter, some proposals are not considered proper under state law if they would be binding on the company if approved by shareholders. In our experience, most proposals that are cast as recommendations or requests that the board of directors take specified action are proper under state law. Accordingly, we will assume that a proposal drafted as a recommendation or suggestion is proper unless the company demonstrates otherwise.

Thus, for a resolution cast as a request or recommendation (often called a "precatory" resolution) the question of excludability turns on the nature of the subject matter of the proposal. State law contemplates that "ordinary business" decisions will be made by the company's management. Thus a mandatory resolution that deals with "ordinary business" can be excluded both under subsection (i)(7) and the broader rubric of (i)(1). If, on the other hand, a precatory resolution does not deal with "ordinary business," a shareholder has the right to present it at the meeting and the company cannot omit it under either subsection. The antithesis of "ordinary business" appears to be "public policy;" if a proposal that otherwise might be considered to involve "ordinary business" *also* implicates questions of public policy, it cannot be excluded under (i)(7).

A similar methodology is used in determining whether a proposal can be omitted under section (i)(5). The principal purpose of (i)(5) is to exclude proposals whose economic significance to the corporation would be *de minimis*; the measuring rod is 5% of sales, assets or earnings. Some proposals, however, may be significant even though they do not meet the statistical test, either because they relate to governance structure (*e.g.*, cumulative voting) or because they raise public policy issues that relate directly to the corporation's business. Such proposals cannot be excluded under (i)(5). In this sense, the "significantly related" standard set forth in (i)(5) is analytically very similar to the "ordinary business" standard of (i)(7).

LOVENHEIM V. IROQUOIS BRANDS, LTD.
618 F.Supp. 554 (D.D.C.1985).

GASCH, DISTRICT JUDGE:

Plaintiff Peter C. Lovenheim, owner of two hundred shares of common stock in Iroquois Brands, Ltd. (hereinafter "Iroquois/Delaware"), seeks to bar Iroquois/Delaware from excluding from the proxy materials being sent to all shareholders in preparation for an upcoming shareholder meeting information concerning a proposed resolution he intends to offer at the meeting. Mr. Lovenheim's proposed resolution relates to the procedure used to force-feed geese for production of paté de foie gras in France,[2] a type of paté imported by Iroquois/Delaware. Specifically, his resolution calls upon the Directors of Iroquois/Delaware to:

> form a committee to study the methods by which its French supplier produces paté de foie gras, and report to the shareholders its findings and opinions, based on expert consultation, on whether this production method causes undue distress, pain or suffering to the animals involved and, if so, whether further distribution of this product should be discontinued until a more humane production method is developed.

Iroquois/Delaware has refused to allow information concerning Mr. Lovenheim's proposal to be included in proxy materials being sent in connection with the next annual shareholders meeting. In doing so, Iroquois/Delaware relies on an exception to the general requirement of Rule 14a–8, Rule 14a–8(c)(5) [before the 1998 amendments, the (i)(5) exclusion was numbered (c)(5)].

---

[2]   Paté de foie gras is made from the liver of geese. According to Mr. Lovenheim's affidavit, force-feeding is frequently used in order to expand the liver and thereby produce a larger quantity of paté. Mr. Lovenheim's affidavit also contains a description of the force-feeding process:

> Force-feeding usually begins when the geese are four months old. On some farms where feeding is mechanized, the bird's body and wings are placed in a metal brace and its neck is stretched. Through a funnel inserted 10–12 inches down the throat of the goose, a machine pumps up to 400 grams of corn-based mash into its stomach. An elastic band around the goose's throat prevents regurgitation. When feeding is manual, a handler uses a funnel and stick to force the mash down.

Plaintiff contends that such force-feeding is a form of cruelty to animals. Plaintiff has offered no evidence that force-feeding is used by Iroquois/Delaware's supplier in producing the paté imported by Iroquois/Delaware. However his proposal calls upon the committee he seeks to create to investigate this question.

Iroquois/Delaware's reliance on the Rule 14a–8(c)(5) exception for proposals not "significantly related" to the company's business is based on the following information contained in the affidavit of its president: Iroquois/Delaware has annual revenues of $141 million with $6 million in annual profits and $78 million in assets. In contrast, its paté de foie gras sales were just $79,000 last year, representing a net loss on paté sales of $3,121. Iroquois/Delaware has only $34,000 in assets related to paté. Thus none of the company's net earnings and less than .05 percent of its assets are implicated by plaintiff's proposal. These levels are obviously far below the five percent threshold set forth in the first portion of the exception claimed by Iroquois/Delaware.

Plaintiff does not contest that his proposed resolution relates to a matter of little economic significance to Iroquois/Delaware. Nevertheless he contends that the Rule 14a–8(c)(5) exception is not applicable as it cannot be said that his proposal "is not otherwise significantly related to the issuer's business" as is required by the final portion of that exception. In other words, plaintiff's argument that Rule 14a–8 does not permit omission of his proposal rests on the assertion that the rule and statute on which it is based do not permit omission merely because a proposal is not economically significant where a proposal has "ethical or social significance."[8]

Iroquois/Delaware challenges plaintiff's view that ethical and social proposals cannot be excluded even if they do meet the economic or five percent test. Instead, Iroquois/Delaware views the exception solely in economic terms as permitting omission for any proposals relating to a de minimis share of assets and profits. Iroquois/Delaware asserts that since corporations are economic entities, only an economic test is appropriate.

The Court would note that the applicability of the Rule 14a–8(c)(5) exception to Mr. Lovenheim's proposal represents a close question given the lack of clarity in the exception itself. In effect, plaintiff relies on the word "otherwise," suggesting that it indicates the drafters of the rule intended that other noneconomic tests of significance be used. Iroquois/Delaware relies on the fact that the rule examines other significance in relation to the issuer's business. Because of the apparent ambiguity of the rule, the Court considers the history of the shareholder

---

[8]   The assertion that the proposal is significant in an ethical and social sense relies on plaintiff's argument that "the very availability of a market for products that may be obtained through the inhumane force-feeding of geese cannot help but contribute to the continuation of such treatment." Plaintiff's brief characterizes the humane treatment of animals as among the foundations of western culture and cites in support of this view the Seven Laws of Noah, an animal protection statute enacted by the Massachusetts Bay Colony in 1641, numerous federal statutes enacted since 1877, and animal protection laws existing in all fifty states and the District of Columbia. An additional indication of the significance of plaintiff's proposal is the support of such leading organizations in the field of animal care as the American Society for the Prevention of Cruelty to Animals and The Humane Society of the United States for measures aimed at discontinuing use of force-feeding.

proposal rule in determining the proper interpretation of the most recent version of that rule.

Prior to 1983, paragraph 14a–8(c)(5) excluded proposals "not significantly related to the issuer's business" but did not contain an objective economic significance test such as the five percent of sales, assets, and earnings specified in the first part of the current version. Although a series of SEC decisions through 1976 allowing issuers to exclude proposals challenging compliance with the Arab economic boycott of Israel allowed exclusion if the issuer did less than one percent of their business with Arab countries or Israel, the Commission stated later in 1976 that it did "not believe that subparagraph (c)(5) should be hinged solely on the economic relativity of a proposal." Securities Exchange Act Release No. 12,999 (1976). Thus the Commission required inclusion "in many situations in which the related business comprised less than one percent" of the company's revenues, profits or assets "where the proposal has raised *policy questions* important" enough to be considered "significantly related to the issuer's business."

As indicated above, the 1983 revision adopted the five percent test of economic significance in an effort to create a more objective standard. Nevertheless, in adopting this standard, the Commission stated that proposals will be includible notwithstanding their "failure to reach the specified economic thresholds if a significant relationship to the issuer's business is demonstrated on the face of the resolution or supporting statement." Securities Exchange Act Release No. 19,135 (1982). Thus it seems clear based on the history of the rule that "the meaning of 'significantly related' is not *limited* to economic significance."

The Court cannot ignore the history of the rule, which reveals no decision by the Commission to limit the determination to the economic criteria relied on by Iroquois/Delaware. The Court therefore holds that in light of the ethical and social significance of plaintiff's proposal and the fact that it implicates significant levels of sales, plaintiff has shown a likelihood of prevailing on the merits with regard to the issue of whether his proposal is "otherwise significantly related" to Iroquois/Delaware's business.

[The court then granted plaintiff's motion for a preliminary injunction.]

3. ORDINARY BUSINESS VS. PUBLIC POLICY

a. The Medical Committee Case

When does corporate action go beyond ordinary business and become a matter of public policy? Consider the case of *Medical Committee for Human Rights v. SEC*, 432 F.2d 659 (D.C.Cir.1970), *vacated as moot* 404 U.S. 403, 92 S.Ct. 577, 30 L.Ed.2d 560 (1972). The Medical Committee, a public interest group, opposed the Vietnam War and, particularly, the manufacture by Dow Chemical Company (Dow) of napalm for use in the war. Although napalm constituted a small and not very profitable part of Dow's business, napalm was important to the government's war effort and Dow management strongly defended its manufacture on patriotic grounds.

The Medical Committee submitted a shareholder proposal requesting that the Dow board adopt an amendment to Dow's certificate of incorporation that would bar the sale of napalm to any buyer unless the buyer gave reasonable assurance that the napalm would not be used on or against human beings. Dow refused to include the proposal on the grounds that it promoted a general political cause (which was then, but is no longer, a ground for exclusion under Rule 14a–8) and that it related to Dow's ordinary business.

In a strongly worded opinion, the D.C. Circuit held that Dow could not omit the proposal:

> The clear import of the language, legislative history, and record of administration of section 14(a) is that its overriding purpose is to assure to corporate shareholders the ability to exercise their right—some would say their duty—to control the important decisions which affect them in their capacity as stockholders and owners of the corporation.

> Here the proposal relates solely to a matter that is completely within the accepted sphere of corporate activity and control. No reason has been advanced in the present proceedings which leads to the conclusion that management may properly place obstacles in the path of shareholders who wish to present to their co-owners, in accord with applicable state law, the question of whether they wish to have their assets used in a manner which they believe to be more socially responsible but possibly less profitable than that which is dictated by present company policy. Thus, even accepting Dow's characterization of the purpose and intent of the Medical Committee's proposal, there is a strong argument that permitting the company to exclude it would contravene the purpose of section 14(a).

> However, the record in this case contains indications that we are confronted with quite a different situation. The management of Dow Chemical Company is repeatedly quoted in sources which include the company's own publications as proclaiming that the decision to continue manufacturing and marketing napalm was made not *because* of business considerations, but *in spite of* them; that management in essence decided to pursue a course of activity which generated little profit for the shareholders and actively impaired the company's public relations and recruitment activities because management considered this action morally and politically desirable.

The proper political and social role of modern corporations is, of course, a matter of philosophical argument extending far beyond the scope of our present concern; the substantive wisdom or propriety of particular corporate political decisions is also completely irrelevant to the resolution of the present controversy. What *is* of immediate concern, however, is the question of whether the corporate proxy rules can be employed as a shield to isolate such managerial decisions from shareholder control.

We think that there is a clear and compelling distinction between management's legitimate need for freedom to apply its expertise in matters of day-to-day business judgment, and management's patently illegitimate claim of power to treat modern corporations with their vast resources as personal satrapies implementing personal political or moral predilections. It could scarcely be argued that management is more qualified or more entitled to make these kinds of decisions than the shareholders who are the true beneficial owners of the corporation; and it seems equally implausible that an application of the proxy rules which permitted such a result could be harmonized with the philosophy of corporate democracy which Congress embodied in section 14(a) of the Securities Exchange Act of 1934.

432 F.2d at 680–681.

b. The 1976 SEC Interpretive Release

The *Medical Committee* decision seems to say that shareholder proposals are proper when they raise issues of corporate social responsibility or question the "political and moral predilections" of management. Does this mean that any issue taken from the headlines (such as climate change, electronic privacy, business outsourcing, and so on) becomes "significantly related" to a company's business and not "ordinary business"—thus a "proper subject" for shareholder consideration at company expense?

In 1976 the SEC attempted to draw the line in an interpretive release that continues to influence both the SEC and the courts:

The term "ordinary business operations" has been deemed on occasion to include certain matters which have significant policy, economic or other implications inherent in them. For instance, a proposal that a utility company not construct a proposed nuclear power plant has in the past been considered excludable. In retrospect, however, it seems apparent that the economic and safety considerations attendant to nuclear power plants are of such magnitude that a determination whether to construct one is not an "ordinary" business matter. Accordingly, proposals of that nature as well as others having major implications be considered beyond the realm of an issuer's ordinary business operations, and future interpretive letters of the Commission's staff will reflect that view.

Where proposals involve business matters that are mundane in nature and do not involve any substantial policy or other considerations, the subparagraph may be relied upon to omit them.

Adoption of Amendments Relating to Proposals by Security Holders, Exchange Act Release No. 12,999 (Dec. 3, 1976).

c. The Cracker Barrel Story

As you can imagine, drawing the line between "ordinary business" and "public policy" has generated an ongoing debate. A series of shareholder proposals on discrimination based on sexual orientation submitted to the restaurant chain Cracker Barrel raise the question whether such discrimination relates primarily to the terms and conditions of employment ("ordinary business") or whether they have significant implications to the corporation ("public policy").

**INVESTOR RESEARCH RESPONSIBILITY CENTER,
HISTORIC CRACKER BARREL VOTE
PROMPTS NEW POLICY**

Corporate Social Issue Reporter 1 (Oct. 2002).

A long-running campaign by the New York City Comptroller's Office ended in a decisive victory last month when a majority of shareholders supported a resolution asking CBRL Group, the parent of the Cracker Barrel Old Country Store restaurant chain, to implement nondiscriminatory policies relating to sexual orientation. CBRL's board of directors responded to the 58 percent support level at the annual meeting by immediately, and unanimously, announcing that it would accept the proposal as company employment policy despite earlier objections.

This vote marks the first time that a social policy shareholder resolution has received majority vote when management opposed the resolution. The resulting policy change also ends a decade-long effort by the New York City Employees Retirement System to have the company add explicit protections for gay employees.

Cracker Barrel first gained the ire of the gay and lesbian community in 1991. Cracker Barrel's then vice president of human resources issued a memo that said "It is inconsistent with our concept and values, and is perceived to be inconsistent with those of our customer base, to continue to employ individuals in our operating units whose sexual preferences fail to demonstrate normal heterosexual values which have been the foundation of families in our society." As the policy was implemented in the approximately 100 restaurant/gift shops that the company then operated primarily in the south and midwest, at least 11 of the company's 11,000 employees lost their jobs. One employee received a separation notice that said, "This employee is being terminated due to violation of company policy. The employee is gay."

NYCERS filed its first shareholder resolution at the company in 1992, but the SEC issued a "no-action" letter to the company that was to become known as the Cracker Barrel ruling. In the letter the SEC staff said it would not challenge the company's decision to omit the resolution. The staff articulated its view that all employment-related shareholder proposals raise ordinary business issues and could be omitted from proxy statements. In January 1993, the SEC commissioners voted 3–1 to uphold the staff policy.

New York City and two other proponents of the 1992 resolution then sued the commission, whose policy was upheld by the U.S. Court of Appeals for the Second Circuit in 1995. The U.S. Court of Appeals ruled that the SEC had broad latitude in advising companies on the omission of shareholder resolutions from proxy statements. Despite this vindication from the court, the SEC eventually unanimously reversed this controversial policy in May 1998.

NYCERS continued each year to submit its proposal to Cracker Barrel, until finally the proposal was approved by the company's shareholders. Patrick Doherty of the New York City Comptroller's Office said the vote demonstrates the "virtue of persistence." As an institutional investor with a long-term view, NYCERS "stuck with it," reintroducing the resolution year after year, noted Doherty. He applauded the board's decision to adopt the majority vote, calling it a "tremendous victory for corporate democracy."

The jump in support for the resolution from 17.8 percent of the shares voted in 2001 to more than 58 percent of the 31.3 million votes cast in 2002 may be the result of a convergence of factors. There is some speculation that the new SEC proposal to require mutual funds to disclose information on how they cast their proxy votes has triggered a review of proxy voting guidelines that is altering some votes. In addition, a major proxy voting advisor [Risk Metrics] also recently changed its voting recommendation on this type of resolution. Despite the board's public opposition, some observers also question whether some board members or executives with large holdings cast their shares in favor of the resolution to effect a policy change while avoiding a showdown with management and other board members.

d. A Current View

TRINITY WALL STREET V. WAL-MART STORES, INC.
792 F.3d 323 (3rd Cir. 2015).

AMBRO, CIRCUIT JUDGE.

I. INTRODUCTION

"[T]he secret of successful retailing is to give your customers what they want." Sam Walton, Sam Walton: Made in America 173 (1993). This case involves one shareholder's attempt to affect how Wal-Mart goes about doing that.

Appellant Wal-Mart Stores, Inc., the world's largest retailer, and one of its shareholders, Appellee Trinity Wall Street—an Episcopal parish headquartered in New York City that owns Wal-Mart stock—are locked in a heated dispute. It stems from Wal-Mart's rejection of Trinity's request to include its shareholder proposal in Wal-Mart's proxy materials for shareholder consideration.

Stripped to its essence, Trinity's proposal—although styled as promoting improved governance—goes to the heart of Wal-Mart's business: what it sells on its shelves. For the reasons that follow, we hold that it is excludable under Rule 14a–8(i)(7) and reverse the ruling of the District Court.

II. FACTS & PROCEDURAL HISTORY

A. *Trinity Objects to Wal-Mart's Sale of Assault Rifles.*

Alarmed by the spate of mass murders in America, in particular the shooting at Sandy Hook Elementary School in December 2012, Trinity resolved to use its investment portfolio to address the ease of access to rifles equipped with high-capacity magazines (the weapon of choice of the Sandy Hook shooter and other mass murderers). Its principal focus was Wal-Mart.

B. *Trinity's Shareholder Proposal.*

The proposal, which is the subject of this appeal, provides:

Resolved:

Stockholders request that the Board amend the Compensation, Nominating and Governance Committee charter . . . as follows:

"27. Providing oversight concerning [and the public reporting of] the formulation and implementation of . . . policies and standards that determine whether or not the Company should sell a product that:

1)   especially endangers public safety and well-being;

2)   has the substantial potential to impair the reputation of the Company; and/or

3)   would reasonably be considered by many offensive to the family and community values integral to the Company's promotion of its brand."

The narrative part of the proposal makes clear it is intended to cover Wal-Mart's sale of certain firearms. It provides that the

> oversight and reporting is intended to cover policies and standards that would be applicable to determining whether or not the company should sell guns equipped with magazines holding more than ten rounds of ammunition ("high capacity magazines") and to balancing the benefits of selling such guns against the risks that these sales pose to the public and to the Company's reputation and brand value.

C.   Wal-Mart Seeks a No-Action Letter from the SEC.

On January 30, 2014, Wal-Mart notified Trinity and the Corp. Fin. staff of its belief that it could exclude the proposal from its 2014 proxy materials under Rule 14a–8(i)(7).

On March 20, 2014, the Commission's Corp. Fin. staff issued a "no-action" letter siding with Wal-Mart. It noted that "there appears to be some basis for [Wal-Mart's] view that [it] may exclude the proposal under rule 14a–8(i)(7), as relating to [its] ordinary business operations[,]" because "[p]roposals concerning the sale of particular products and services are generally excludable under [the rule]." Consequently, the staff would "not recommend enforcement action to the Commission if Walmart [sic] omits the proposal from its proxy materials in reliance on rule 14a–8(i)(7)." *Id.*

IV. ANALYSIS

A.   Trinity's Proposal Relates to Wal-Mart's Ordinary Business Operations.

We employ a two-part analysis to determine whether Trinity's proposal "deals with a matter relating to the company's ordinary business operations[.]" 17 C.F.R. § 240.14a–8(i)(7). Under the first step, we discern the "subject matter" of the proposal. Under the second, we ask whether that subject matter relates to Wal-Mart's ordinary business operations. If the answer to the second question is yes, Wal-Mart must still convince us that Trinity's proposal does not raise a significant policy issue that transcends the nuts and bolts of the retailer's business.

1.   What is the subject matter of Trinity's proposal?

[E]ven though Trinity's proposal asks for the development of a specific merchandising policy—and not a review, report or examination—we still ask whether the subject matter of the action it calls for is a matter of ordinary business.

Trinity argues that the subject matter of its proposal is the improvement of "corporate governance over strategic matters of community responsibility, reputation for good corporate citizenship, and brand reputation, none of which can be considered ordinary business," and the focus is on the "shortcomings in Wal-Mart's corporate governance and oversight over policy matters." We cannot agree.

Contrary to what Trinity would have us believe, the immediate consequence of the adoption of a proposal—here the improvement of corporate governance through the formulation and implementation of a merchandising policy—is not its subject matter. If it were, then, analogizing to the review context, the subject matter of a review would be the review itself rather than the information sought by it. The subject matter of the proposal is instead its ultimate consequence—here a potential change in the way Wal-Mart decides which products to sell. Indeed, as even the District Court acknowledged, if the company were to adopt Trinity's proposal, then, whatever the nature of the forthcoming policy, it "could (and almost certainly would) shape what products are sold by Wal-Mart[.]"

> 2. *Does Wal-Mart's approach to whether it sells particular products relate to its ordinary business operations?*

Reaching the second step of the analysis, we ask whether the subject matter of Trinity's proposal relates to day-to-day matters of Wal-Mart's business. Wal-Mart says the answer is yes because, even though the proposal doesn't demand any specific changes to the make-up of its product offerings . . . it "seeks to have a [B]oard committee address policies that could (and almost certainly would) shape what products are sold by Wal-Mart." That is, Trinity's proposal is just a sidestep from "a shareholder referendum on how [Wal-Mart] selects its inventory." And thus its subject matter strikes at the core of Wal-Mart's business.

B. Trinity's Proposal Does Not Focus on a Significant Policy Issue that Transcends Wal-Mart's Day-to-Day Business Operations.

As discussed above, there is a significant social policy exception to the default rule of excludability for proposals that relate to a company's ordinary business operations.

We think the inquiry is again best split into two steps. The first is whether the proposal focuses on a significant policy (be it social or, as noted below, corporate). If it doesn't, the proposal fails to fit within the social-policy exception to Rule 14a–8(i)(7)'s exclusion. If it does, we reach the second step and ask whether the significant policy issue transcends the company's ordinary business operations.

1. *Does Trinity's proposal raise a significant social policy issue?*

[I]t is hard to counter that Trinity's proposal doesn't touch the bases of what are significant concerns in our society and corporations in that society. Thus we deem that its proposal raises a matter of sufficiently significant policy.

2. *Even if Trinity's proposal raises a significant policy issue, does that issue transcend Wal-Mart's ordinary business operations?*

For major retailers of myriad products, a policy issue is rarely transcendent if it treads on the meat of management's responsibility: crafting a product mix that satisfies consumer demand. On the other hand, if a significant policy issue disengages from the core of a retailer's business (deciding whether to sell certain goods that customers want), it is more likely to transcend its daily business dealings.

To illustrate the distinction, a proposal that asks a supermarket chain to evaluate its sale of sugary sodas because of the effect on childhood obesity should be excludable because, although the proposal raises a significant social policy issue, the request is too entwined with the fundamentals of the daily activities of a supermarket running its business: deciding which food products will occupy its shelves. . . . By contrast, a proposal raising the impropriety of a supermarket's discriminatory hiring or compensation practices generally is not excludable because, even though human resources management is a core business function, it is disengaged from the essence of a supermarket's business. The same goes for proposals asking for information on the environmental effect of constructing stores near environmentally sensitive sites.

With those principles in mind, we turn to Trinity's proposal. Trinity says it focuses on "both corporate policy and social policy"—specifically, the "transcendent policy issue of under what policies and standards and with what Board oversight Wal-Mart handles [ ] merchandising decisions" for products that are "especially dangerous to [the company's] reputation, brand value, or the community.". . . "In an age of mass shootings, increased violence, and concerns about product safety," Trinity argues, "the [p]roposal goes to the heart of Wal-Mart's impact on and approach to social welfare as well as the risks such impact and approach may have to Wal-Mart's reputation and brand image and its community."

But is how a retailer weighs safety in deciding which products to sell too enmeshed with its day-to-day business? We think it is in this instance. As we noted before, the essence of a retailer's business is deciding what products to put on its shelves—decisions made daily that involve a careful balancing of financial, marketing, reputational, competitive and other factors. The emphasis management places on safety to the consumer or the community is fundamental to its role in managing the company in the best interests of its shareholders and cannot, "as a practical matter, be subject to direct shareholder oversight." 1998 Adopting Release, 1998 SEC LEXIS 1001, 1998 WL 254809 at *4.

Trinity's claim that its proposal raises a "significant" and "transcendent" corporate policy is likewise insufficient to fit that proposal within the social-policy exception to exclusion. The relevant question to us is whether Wal-Mart's consideration of the risk that certain products pose to its "economic success" and "reputation for good corporate citizenship" is enmeshed with the way it runs its business and the retailer-consumer interaction. We think the answer is yes. Decisions relating to what products Wal-Mart sells in its rural locations versus its urban sites will vary considerably, and these are quintessentially calls made by management. . . [W]hether to put emphasis on brand integrity and brand protection, or none at all, is naturally a decision shareholders as well as directors entrust management to make in the exercise of their experience and business judgment.

. . . We thus hold that, even if Trinity's proposal raises sufficiently significant social and corporate policy issues, those policies do not transcend the ordinary business operations of Wal-Mart. For a policy issue here to transcend Wal-Mart's business operations, it must target something more than the choosing of one among tens of thousands of products it sells. Trinity's proposal fails that test and is properly excludable under Rule 14a–8(i)(7).

EPILOGUE

Walmart's victory in the 3rd Circuit was not the end of the story. As so often happens, the shareholder proponents lost the battle but won the war. One month after the case was decided Walmart announced that it would cease selling assault rifles in the U.S. Hiroku Tabuchi, Walmart to End Sales of Assault-Style Rifles in U.S. Stores, New York Times, Aug. 26, 2015.

e.   Proposals Relating to Risk

The SEC has traditionally taken the position that shareholder proposals that focus on a company's engaging in an internal assessment of the risks and liabilities that it faces from its operations may be excluded under Rule 14a–8(i)(7) as constituting "ordinary business." On October 27, 2009, the SEC's Division of Corporation Finance issued Staff Legal Bulletin 14E in which it reversed its prior position. The following excerpt sets out the new analytical framework.

STAFF LEGAL BULLETIN NO. 14E (CF)

B. What analytical framework will we apply in determining whether a company may exclude a proposal related to risk under Rule 14a–8(i)(7)?

Over the past decade, we have received numerous no-action requests from companies seeking to exclude proposals relating to environmental, financial or health risks under Rule 14a–8(i)(7). As we explained in SLB No. 14C, in analyzing such requests, we have sought to determine whether the proposal and supporting statement as a whole relate to the company engaging in an evaluation of risk, which is a matter we have viewed as relating to a company's ordinary business operations. To the extent that a proposal and supporting statement have focused on a company engaging in an internal assessment of the risks and liabilities that the company faces as a result of its operations, we have permitted companies to exclude these proposals under Rule 14a–8(i)(7) as relating to an evaluation of risk. To the extent that a proposal and supporting statement have focused on a company minimizing or eliminating operations that may adversely affect the environment or the public's health, we have not permitted companies to exclude these proposals under Rule 14a–8(i)(7).

We have recently witnessed a marked increase in the number of no-action requests in which companies seek to exclude proposals as relating to an evaluation of risk. In these requests, companies have frequently argued that proposals that do not explicitly request an evaluation of risk are nonetheless excludable under Rule 14a–8(i)(7) because they would require the company to engage in risk assessment.

Based on our experience in reviewing these requests, we are concerned that our application of the analytical framework discussed in SLB No. 14C may have resulted in the unwarranted exclusion of proposals that relate to the evaluation of risk but that focus on significant policy issues. Indeed, as most corporate decisions involve some evaluation of risk, the evaluation of risk should not be viewed as an end in itself, but rather, as a means to an end. In addition, we have become increasingly cognizant that the adequacy of risk management and oversight can have major consequences for a company and its shareholders. Accordingly, we have reexamined the analysis that we have used for risk proposals, and upon reexamination, we believe that there is a more appropriate framework to apply for analyzing these proposals.

On a going-forward basis, rather than focusing on whether a proposal and supporting statement relate to the company engaging in an evaluation of risk, we will instead focus on the subject matter to which the risk pertains or that gives rise to the risk. The fact that a proposal would require an evaluation of risk will not be dispositive of whether the proposal may be excluded under Rule 14a–8(i)(7). Instead, similar to the way in which we analyze proposals asking for the preparation of a report, the formation of a committee or the inclusion of disclosure in a Commission-prescribed document—where we look to the underlying subject matter of the report, committee or disclosure to determine whether the proposal relates to ordinary business—we will consider whether the underlying subject matter of the risk evaluation involves a matter of ordinary business to the company. In those cases in which a proposal's underlying subject matter transcends the day-to-day business matters of the company and raises policy issues so significant that it would be appropriate for a shareholder vote, the proposal generally will not be excludable under Rule 14a–8(i)(7) as long as a sufficient nexus exists between the nature of the proposal and the company. Conversely, in those cases in which a proposal's underlying subject matter involves an ordinary business matter to the company, the proposal generally will be excludable under Rule 14a–8(i)(7). In determining whether the subject matter raises significant policy issues and has a sufficient nexus to the company, as described above, we will apply the same standards that we apply to other types of proposals under Rule 14a–8(i)(7).

In addition, we note that there is widespread recognition that the board's role in the oversight of a company's management of risk is a significant policy matter regarding the governance of the corporation. In light of this recognition, a proposal that focuses on the board's role in the oversight of a company's management of risk may transcend the day-to-day business matters of a company and raise policy issues so significant that it would be appropriate for a shareholder vote.

4. EVALUATING THE SHAREHOLDER PROPOSAL RULE

The use of the shareholder proposal rule to gain attention on questions of corporate responsibility has a long tradition. The first major social/political proposal was submitted by The Project on Corporate Responsibility, targeted GM in 1970. Campaign GM sought shareholder approval of several resolutions designed to examine GM's social record, including minority representation on its board of directors. Although each proposal received less than 3% support, GM's board responded within months to create a Public Policy Committee and elect its first black board member. A year later, GM elected its first woman member. *See* Donald E. Schwartz, *The Public-Interest Proxy Contest: Reflections on Campaign GM*, 69 Mich. L.Rev. 419 (1971).

Over the past couple of decades the shareholder proposal rule has evolved to become a major tool for shareholder activism. The effects of resolutions submitted by individual activists and a few public pension funds, but supported by an awakened community of institutional investors, indicate that, within limits, it is possible for large shareholders to overcome the collective action problem and have a significant impact on corporate governance.

The mix of shareholder proposals has varied from year to year, although they generally fall into three broad categories: (1) corporate governance; (2) executive compensation; and (3) social and environmental issues. In recent years, proposals related to governance have become the most numerous and most likely to succeed. They include calls for election of independent board chairs, making it easier for shareholders to call special shareholder meetings or to act by written consent, declassifying the board, adoption of majority voting, and the elimination of supermajority voting requirements for actions such as removing directors or amending corporate charters. The 2012 and 2013 proxy seasons saw an increase in the number of resolutions calling for shareholders to be able to place board nominees on the management proxy materials. (These proposals often mirror an SEC rule adopted in 2010 and invalidated by the DC Circuit in 2011, as discussed below.) Among the S&P 500 companies, there were 164 governance-related proposals in the 2012 proxy season, of which 68 passed. Although most were precatory proposals, the major proxy advisory firms have indicated that in the future they may recommend votes against the re-election of directors who fail to implement shareholder governance proposals that have received majority support.

Social and environmental issues raised by shareholder proposals also vary from one proxy season to the next, tending to mirror the concerns of the day. In recent years, for example, many have related in one way or another to renewable energy and greenhouse gas emissions. The *Citizens United* decision discussed in Chapter 4 seems to have prompted a number of proposals related to disclosure of corporate lobbying and political donations. Another frequent topic in recent years is gender diversity on boards of directors.

Shareholder concerns with excessive executive compensation have led to a significant rise in the number of proposals related to that subject in recent years. The "say-on-pay" rules discussed in Section H, below, may have taken some of the steam out of these efforts, however, as they provide shareholders a regular opportunity to vote on compensation policies, which have generally received overwhelming approval.

Despite the seeming success of Rule 14a–8 over the past several years to transmit the shareholder "voice" to other shareholders and to management, the question remains how successful the proposals have been and how to measure success. Voting data on proposals, now regularly collected by proxy advisory firms, such as Institutional Shareholder Services, reveal a disparity in shareholder support for different types of proposals. Those dealing with social, environmental and political issues have fared much less well than traditional governance proposals although recent environmental proposals have received greater support. The difference in results may reflect the views of institutional shareholders as to how much proposals add to the corporate bottom line. Historically, fewer than 10% of social and environmental (including political) proposals received as much as 15% of the shares voted and very few received a majority vote. That result, however, may be changing. In the 2011 and 2012 proxy seasons, social and environmental proposals on the proxies of the S&P 500 firms received an *average* favorable vote of 19%, although none passed.

Even though social/political proposals rarely gain majority support, their proponents often find success simply by raising the issue with management. In fact, it is now a common occurrence for management to agree to changes in order to avoid annoying a vocal minority of shareholders and to garner a public relations victory. Many proposals are withdrawn or not even submitted after shareholder proponents negotiate changes that achieve their goals. In the last few years, shareholder proponents withdrew approximately one third of environmental and social issue proposals after discussions with management.

Despite greater shareholder activism and voting success, empirical studies are mixed on whether the activism increases shareholder wealth. As Professor Roberta Romano notes:

> The consistent findings of statistical insignificance for shareholders are most plausibly a function of the value of the corporate governance mechanisms that are the objects of the proposals. The governance mechanisms of greatest interest to shareholder activists—board reforms, takeover defenses, executive compensation, and confidential voting—have been the subject of extensive research. In brief, the types of board and compensation reforms advocated by proposal sponsors have not been found to be value-enhancing corporate governance devices; the results of the empirical research on antitakeover devices are ambiguous, with only some findings of a negative impact from some of the tactics that shareholder proposals seek to rescind; and the implementation of confidential voting has no impact on voting outcomes or on firm performance.

Roberta Romano, *Less Is More: Making Institutional Investor Activism A Valuable Mechanism of Corporate Governance,* 18 Yale J. Reg. 174, 191 (2001).

More recent studies sound a more optimistic note. A 2004 study investigated 24 types of governance provisions tracked by Interfaith Center on Corporate Responsibility (IRRC), a group that includes most of the activist union and pension funds. The study found a *negative* correlation with firm value and stockholder returns for four "constitutional provisions" limiting shareholder majority power (staggered boards, limits to shareholder bylaw amendments, supermajority requirements for mergers,

r charter amendments), and two anti-
lls, golden parachutes). But it found no
RRC-tracked provisions were negatively
tock returns during the period. Lucian A.
len Ferrell, *What Matters in Corporate*
es, 783 (2009). The implication of the study
can have a positive effect on shareholder
et governance issues that correlate with
e and management implements reforms as a

NOMINATION OF DIRECTORS LAW AMENDMENTS

Under corporate law, management controls the nomination process for board candidates in public corporations. Unless an insurgent shareholder proposes its own directors through a proxy contest waged at its own expense (a rare event), the only candidates for shareholders to vote on are those nominated by the incumbent board and its nominating committee. The shareholder proposal rule specifically excludes proposals that "relate to an election for membership on the company's board of directors." Rule 14a–8(i)(8). For some time, however, activist shareholders have been attempting to establish a mechanism that would allow them to nominate and elect candidates for the board without the expense of a proxy solicitation.

1. JUDICIAL APPROACH

In 2003 the SEC proposed a rule that would have given shareholders greater access to the nomination of directors to the boards of public corporations. This proposal provoked substantial opposition. Management groups claimed that the SEC was interfering with a matter of corporate governance beyond its authority and argued that shareholder-nominated board members would disrupt the collegial working relationship on corporate boards. As time passed, it became clear that the SEC would not adopt the rule.

Recognizing that they could not achieve their ends through SEC rule-making, a group of activist union and state pension funds submitted proposals of their own to adopt bylaw amendments that would replicate the mechanisms of the SEC rule at a company level. Although at first the SEC staff issued no-action letters accepting such proposals under Rule 14a–8, in December 2004 it reversed its position and permitted the exclusion of such proposals.

Disappointed by the reversal, one of the institutional proponents brought a lawsuit in federal district court against the American International Group to require the Delaware-incorporated insurance company to include a shareholder access proposal in its proxy statement. The district court concluded that neither Rule 14a–8 nor state law required inclusion of the proposal, suggesting that the litigants (and the law professors who had filed an amicus brief in the case) should turn to the regulatory and legislative processes. The proponents then appealed.

AMERICAN FEDERATION OF STATE, COUNTRY & MUNICIPAL EMPLOYEES, EMPLOYEES PENSION PLAN V. AMERICAN INT'L GROUP, INC.

462 F.3d 121 (2d Cir. 2006).

WESLEY, CIRCUIT JUDGE:

We hold that a shareholder proposal that seeks to amend the corporate bylaws to establish a procedure by which shareholder-nominated candidates may be included on the corporate ballot does not relate to an election within the meaning of the Rule 14a–8 and therefore cannot be excluded from corporate proxy materials under that regulation.

BACKGROUND

The American Federation of State, County & Municipal Employees ("AFSCME") is one of the country's largest public service employee unions. Through its pension plan, AFSCME holds 26,965 shares of voting common stock of American International Group ("AIG"), a multi-national corporation operating in the insurance and financial services sectors. On December 1, 2004, AFSCME submitted to AIG for inclusion in the Company's 2005 proxy statement a shareholder proposal that, if adopted by a majority of AIG shareholders at the Company's 2005 annual meeting,[2] would amend the AIG bylaws to require the Company, under certain circumstances, to publish the names of shareholder-nominated candidates for director positions together with any candidates nominated by AIG's board of directors.[3] AIG sought the input of the Division regarding whether

---

[2]   Delaware corporate law, which governs AIG's internal affairs, provides that shareholders have the power to amend bylaws by majority vote. *See* Del. Code Ann. tit. 8, § 109(a).

[3]   The AFSCME Proposal states in relevant part:

RESOLVED, pursuant to Section 6.9 of the By-laws (the "Bylaws") of American International Group Inc. ("AIG") and *section 109(a)* of the Delaware General Corporation Law, stockholders hereby amend the Bylaws to add section 6.10:

"The Corporation shall include in its proxy materials for a meeting of stockholders the name, together with the Disclosure and Statement (both defined below), of any person nominated for election to the Board of Directors by a stockholder or group thereof that satisfies the requirements of this section 6.10 (the "Nominator"), and allow stockholders to vote with respect to such nominee on the Corporation's proxy card. Each Nominator may nominate one candidate for election at a meeting.

To be eligible to make a nomination, a Nominator must:

(a) have beneficially owned 3% or more of the Corporation's outstanding common stock (the "Required Shares") for at least one year;

(b) provide written notice received by the Corporation's Secretary within the time period specified in section 1.11 of the Bylaws containing (i) with respect to the nominee, (A) the information required by Items 7(a), (b) and (c) of SEC Schedule 14A (such information is

AIG could exclude the Proposal from its proxy statement under the election exclusion on the basis that it "relates to an election." The Division issued a no-action letter in which it indicated that it would not recommend an enforcement action against AIG should the Company exclude the Proposal from its proxy statement. Armed with the no-action letter, AIG then proceeded to exclude the Proposal from the Company's proxy statement. In response, AFSCME brought suit in the United States District Court for the Southern District of New York seeking a court order compelling AIG to include the Proposal in its next proxy statement. The district court denied AFSCME's motion for a preliminary injunction, concluding that AFSCME's Proposal "on its face 'relates to an election.' Indeed, it relates to nothing else."

We must determine whether, under Rule 14a–8(i)(8),[3] a shareholder proposal "relates to an election" if it seeks to amend the corporate bylaws to establish a procedure by which certain shareholders are entitled to include in the corporate proxy materials their nominees for the board of directors. The relevant language here—"relates to an election"—is not particularly helpful. AFSCME reads the election exclusion as creating an obvious distinction between proposals addressing a particular seat in a particular election (which AFSCME concedes are excludable) and those, like AFSCME's proposal, that simply set the background rules governing elections generally (which AFSCME claims are not excludable). AFSCME's distinction rests on Rule 14a–8(i)(8)'s use of the article "an," which AFSCME claims "necessarily implies that the phrase 'relates to an election' is intended to relate to proposals that address *particular elections*, instead of simply 'elections' generally." It is at least plausible that the words "an election" were intended to narrow the scope of the election exclusion, confining its application to proposals relating to "a particular election *and not* elections generally." It is, however, also plausible that the phrase was intended to create a comparatively broader exclusion, one covering "a particular election *or* elections generally" since any proposal that relates to elections in general will necessarily relate to an election in particular. The

---

referred to herein as the "Disclosure") and (B) such nominee's consent to being named in the proxy statement and to serving as a director if elected; and (ii) with respect to the Nominator, proof of ownership of the Required Shares; and

(c) execute an undertaking that it agrees (i) to assume all liability of any violation of law or regulation arising out of the Nominator's communications with stockholders, including the Disclosure (ii) to the extent it uses soliciting material other than the Corporation's proxy materials, comply with all laws and regulations relating thereto.

The Nominator shall have the option to furnish a statement, not to exceed 500 words, in support of the nominee's candidacy (the "Statement"), at the time the Disclosure is submitted to the Corporation's Secretary. The Board of Directors shall adopt a procedure for timely resolving disputes over whether notice of a nomination was timely given and whether the Disclosure and Statement comply with this section 6.10 and SEC Rules."

[3] At the time this case arose, Rule 14a–8(i)(8) read as follows: "(8) Relates to election: If the proposal relates to an election for membership on the company's board of directors or analogous governing body" [Eds.]

language of Rule 14a–8(i)(8) provides no reason to adopt one interpretation over the other.

When the language of a regulation is ambiguous, we typically look for guidance in any interpretation made by the agency that promulgated the regulation in question. In its amicus brief, the SEC interprets Rule 14a–8(i)(8) as permitting the exclusion of shareholder proposals that "would result in contested elections." The SEC explains that "for purposes of Rule 14a–8, a proposal would result in a contested election if it is a means either to campaign for or against a director nominee or to require a company to include shareholder-nominated candidates in the company's proxy materials." Under this interpretation, a proxy access bylaw proposal like AFSCME's would be excludable under Rule 14a–8(i)(8) because it "is a means to require AIG to include shareholder-nominated candidates in the company's proxy materials." However, that interpretation is plainly at odds with the interpretation the SEC made in 1976.

In that year, the SEC amended Rule 14a–8(i)(8) in an effort to clarify the purpose of the existing election exclusion. The SEC explained that "with respect to corporate elections, Rule 14a–8 is not the proper means for conducting campaigns or effecting reforms in elections of that nature [*i.e.*, "corporate, political or other elections to office"], *since other proxy rules, including Rule 14a–11, are applicable thereto.*" The district court opinion quoted the 1976 Statement but omitted the italicized language and concluded that shareholder proposals were not intended to be used to accomplish any type of election reform. Clearly, however, that cannot be what the 1976 Statement means. Indeed, when the SEC finally adopted the revision of Rule 14a–8(i)(8) four months after publication of the 1976 Statement, it explained that it was rejecting a previous proposed rule (which would have authorized the exclusion of proposals that "relate to a corporate, political or other election to office") in favor of the current version (which authorizes the exclusion of proposals that simply "relate to an election") so as to avoid creating "the erroneous belief that the Commission intended to expand the scope of the existing exclusion to cover proposals dealing with matters previously held not excludable by the Commission, such as cumulative voting rights, general qualifications for directors, and political contributions by the issuer." And yet, all three of these shareholder proposal topics—cumulative voting rights, general qualifications for directors, and political contributions—fit comfortably within the category "election reform."

The 1976 Statement clearly reflects the view that the election exclusion is limited to shareholder proposals used to oppose solicitations dealing with an identified board seat in an upcoming election and rejects the somewhat broader interpretation that the election exclusion applies to shareholder proposals that would institute procedures making such election contests more likely.

That the 1976 statement adopted this narrower view of the election exclusion finds further support in the fact that it was also the view that the Division adopted for roughly sixteen years following publication of the SEC's 1976 Statement. It was not until 1990 that the Division first signaled a change of course by deeming excludable proposals that *might* result in contested elections, even if the proposal only purports to alter general procedures for nominating and electing directors.[7]

Because the interpretation of Rule 14a–8(i)(8) that the SEC advances in its amicus brief—that the election exclusion applies to proxy access bylaw proposals—conflicts with the 1976 Statement, it does not merit the usual deference we would reserve for an agency's interpretation of its own regulations. The SEC has not provided, nor to our knowledge has it or the Division ever provided, reasons for its changed position regarding the excludability of proxy access bylaw proposals. Although the SEC has substantial discretion to adopt new interpretations of its own regulations in light of, for example, changes in the capital markets or even simply because of a shift in the Commission's regulatory approach, it nevertheless has a "duty to explain its departure from prior norms."

In its amicus submission, the SEC fails to so much as acknowledge a changed position, let alone offer a reasoned analysis of the change. The amicus brief is curiously silent on any Division action prior to 1990 and characterizes the intermittent post-1990 no-action letters which continued to apply the pre-1990 position as mere "mistakes." We have a difficult time accepting the SEC's characterization of a policy that the Division consistently applied for sixteen years as nothing more than a "mistake."

Accordingly, we deem it appropriate to defer to the 1976 Statement, which represents the SEC's interpretation of the election exclusion the last time the Rule was substantively revised.[8] We therefore interpret the

---

[7] Even then, the Division's position was far from clear-cut. Between 1990 and 1998, the Division continued to issue intermittently no-action letters adopting its prior distinction between procedures governing elections generally and those dealing with specific election contests. Since roughly 1998, the Division has consistently adopted the position expressed in the AIG No-Action Letter, which is the same position the SEC advances in its amicus brief.

[8] AIG suggests that the interpretation of the election exclusion that we adopt here—that it does not apply to proxy access proposals—"improperly conflicts" with a proposed SEC rule that would require corporations in particular circumstances to include certain shareholder-nominated director candidates in the corporate proxy statement. Proposed Rule 14a–11 would entitle a holder of at least 5 of the corporation's voting stock to place a nominee on the corporate ballot but only if the proxy access rule had been "activated" by one of two triggering events, including the adoption, by majority vote, of a shareholder proposal submitted by a holder of more than 1 of the corporation's voting stock. Essentially, Proposed Rule 14a–11 establishes a process by which the shareholder proposal mechanism (subject to the heightened eligibility requirement that the proposal be submitted by a holder of more than 1 of the corporation's voting stock) may be employed to adopt a proxy access rule that is uniform across companies. We recognize that our holding facilitates a process, by means of shareholder proposals subject to the standard eligibility requirements, for adopting non-uniform proxy access rules that are less restrictive than that created by Proposed Rule 14a–11. Thus, there might very well be no reason for a rule based on Proposed Rule 14a–11 to co-exist with the procedure that our holding makes available to shareholders. Accordingly, if the Commission ultimately decides to adopt Proposed Rule 14a–11,

election exclusion as applying to shareholder proposals that relate to a particular election and not to proposals that, like AFSCME's, would establish the procedural rules governing elections generally.

In deeming proxy access bylaw proposals non-excludable under Rule 14a–8(i)(8), we take no side in the policy debate regarding shareholder access to the corporate ballot. There might be perfectly good reasons for permitting companies to exclude proposals like AFSCME's, just as there may well be valid policy reasons for rendering them non-excludable. However, Congress has determined that such issues are appropriately the province of the SEC, not the judiciary.

The fate of Rule 14a–8(i)(8) has followed a winding path. In January 2008, the SEC amended the rule to overrule the Second Circuit decision in *AIG* and confirm its own interpretation that a corporation may exclude a shareholder proposal to amend the bylaws to provide for the inclusion of shareholder board nominations on the management proxy. As amended, the Rule allowed the exclusion of a proposal if it "relates to a nomination or an election for membership on the company's board of directors or analogous governing body *or a procedure for such nomination or election.*" As discussed below, however, in 2010 the SEC reversed this position by again amending the rule in a way that prohibits the exclusion of such a proposal.

CA, INC. V. AFSCME EMPLOYEES PENSION PLAN
953 A.2d 227 (Del. 2008).

JACOBS, JUSTICE.

[Article IV Section 11(8) of the Delaware Constitution was amended in 2007 to authorize this Court to hear and determine questions of law certified to it by (in addition to the tribunals already specified therein) the United States Securities and Exchange Commission. This certification request is the first submitted by the SEC to this Court. This proceeding arises from a certification by the SEC to this Court, of two questions of law. On June 27, 2008, the SEC asked this Court to address two questions of Delaware law regarding a proposed stockholder bylaw submitted by the AFSCME Employees Pension Plan ("AFSCME") for inclusion in the proxy materials of CA, Inc. ("CA" or the "Company") for CA's 2008 annual stockholders' meeting. This is the decision of the Court on the certified questions.]

---

then such an action, although certainly not necessary, would likely be sufficient to modify the interpretation of Rule 14a–8(i)(8) that we have adopted here.

I. FACTS

CA is a Delaware corporation whose board of directors consists of twelve persons, all of whom sit for reelection each year. CA's annual meeting of stockholders is scheduled to be held on September 9, 2008. CA intends to file its definitive proxy materials with the SEC on or about July 24, 2008 in connection with that meeting.

AFSCME, a CA stockholder, is associated with the American Federation of State, County and Municipal Employees. On March 13, 2008, AFSCME submitted a proposed stockholder bylaw (the "Bylaw" or "proposed Bylaw") for inclusion in the Company's proxy materials for its 2008 annual meeting of stockholders. The Bylaw, if adopted by CA stockholders, would amend the Company's bylaws to provide as follows:

RESOLVED, that pursuant to section 109 of the Delaware General Corporation Law and Article IX of the bylaws of CA, Inc., stockholders of CA hereby amend the bylaws to add the following Section 14 to Article II:

> The board of directors shall cause the corporation to reimburse a stockholder or group of stockholders (together, the "Nominator") for reasonable expenses ("Expenses") incurred in connection with nominating one or more candidates in a contested election of directors to the corporation's board of directors, including, without limitation, printing, mailing, legal, solicitation, travel, advertising and public relations expenses, so long as (a) the election of fewer than 50% of the directors to be elected is contested in the election, (b) one or more candidates nominated by the Nominator are elected to the corporation's board of directors, (c) stockholders are not permitted to cumulate their votes for directors, and (d) the election occurred, and the Expenses were incurred, after this bylaw's adoption. The amount paid to a Nominator under this bylaw in respect of a contested election shall not exceed the amount expended by the corporation in connection with such election.

CA's current bylaws and Certificate of Incorporation have no provision that specifically addresses the reimbursement of proxy expenses. Of more general relevance, however, is Article SEVENTH, Section (1) of CA's Certificate of Incorporation, which tracks the language of 8 *Del. C.* § 141(a) and provides that:

> The management of the business and the conduct of the affairs of the corporation shall be vested in [CA's] Board of Directors.

It is undisputed that the decision whether to reimburse election expenses is presently vested in the discretion of CA's board of directors, subject to their fiduciary duties and applicable Delaware law.

On April 18, 2008, CA notified the SEC's Division of Corporation Finance (the "Division") of its intention to exclude the proposed Bylaw from its 2008 proxy materials. The Company requested from the Division a "no-action letter" stating that the Division would not recommend any enforcement action to the SEC if CA excluded the AFSCME proposal. CA's request for a no-action letter was accompanied by an opinion from its Delaware counsel, Richards Layton & Finger, P.A. ("RL & F"). The RL & F opinion concluded that the proposed Bylaw is not a proper subject for stockholder action, and that if implemented, the Bylaw would violate the Delaware General Corporation Law ("DGCL").

On May 21, 2008, AFSCME responded to CA's no-action request with a letter taking the opposite legal position. The AFSCME letter was accompanied by an opinion from AFSCME's Delaware counsel, Grant & Eisenhofer, P.A. ("G & E"). The G & E opinion concluded that the proposed Bylaw is a proper subject for shareholder action and that if adopted, would be permitted under Delaware law.

The Division was thus confronted with two conflicting legal opinions on Delaware law. Whether or not the Division would determine that CA may exclude the proposed Bylaw from its 2008 proxy materials would depend upon which of these conflicting views is legally correct. To obtain guidance, the SEC, at the Division's request, certified two questions of Delaware law to this Court.

II. *THE CERTIFIED QUESTIONS*

The two questions certified to us by the SEC are as follows:

1.   Is the AFSCME Proposal a proper subject for action by shareholders as a matter of Delaware law?

2.   Would the AFSCME Proposal, if adopted, cause CA to violate any Delaware law to which it is subject?

III. *THE FIRST QUESTION*

A. *Preliminary Comments*

The first question presented is whether the Bylaw is a proper subject for shareholder action, more precisely, whether the Bylaw may be proposed and enacted by shareholders without the concurrence of the Company's board of directors. Before proceeding further, we make some preliminary comments in an effort to delineate a framework within which to begin our analysis.

First, the DGCL empowers both the board of directors and the shareholders of a Delaware corporation to adopt, amend or repeal the corporation's bylaws. 8 *Del. C.* § 109(a) relevantly provides that:

> After a corporation has received any payment for any of its stock, the power to adopt, amend or repeal bylaws shall be in the

stockholders entitled to vote . . . ; provided, however, any corporation may, in its certificate of incorporation, confer the power to adopt, amend or repeal bylaws upon the directors. . . . The fact that such power has been so conferred upon the directors . . . shall not divest the stockholders . . . of the power, nor limit their power to adopt, amend or repeal bylaws.

Pursuant to Section 109(a), CA's Certificate of Incorporation confers the power to adopt, amend or repeal the bylaws upon the Company's board of directors. Because the statute commands that that conferral "shall not divest the stockholders . . . of . . . nor limit" their power, both the board and the shareholders of CA, independently and concurrently, possess the power to adopt, amend and repeal the bylaws.

Second, the vesting of that concurrent power in both the board and the shareholders raises the issue of whether the stockholders' power is coextensive with that of the board, and vice versa. As a purely theoretical matter that is possible, and were that the case, then the first certified question would be easily answered. That is, under such a regime any proposal to adopt, amend or repeal a bylaw would be a proper subject for either shareholder or board action, without distinction. But the DGCL has not allocated to the board and the shareholders the identical, coextensive power to adopt, amend and repeal the bylaws. Therefore, how that power is allocated between those two decision-making bodies requires an analysis that is more complex.

Moving from the theoretical to this case, by its terms Section 109(a) vests in the shareholders a power to adopt, amend or repeal bylaws that is legally sacrosanct, *i.e.,* the power cannot be non-consensually eliminated or limited by anyone other than the legislature itself. If viewed in isolation, Section 109(a) could be read to make the power of the board and the shareholders to adopt, amend or repeal bylaws identical and coextensive, but Section 109(a) does not exist in a vacuum. It must be read together with 8 *Del. C.* § 141(a), which pertinently provides that:

> The business and affairs of every corporation organized under this chapter shall be managed by or under the direction of a board of directors, except as may be otherwise provided in this chapter or in its certificate of incorporation.

No such broad management power is statutorily allocated to the shareholders. Indeed, it is well-established that stockholders of a corporation subject to the DGCL may not directly manage the business and affairs of the corporation, at least without specific authorization in either the statute or the certificate of incorporation. Therefore, the shareholders' statutory power to adopt, amend or repeal bylaws is not coextensive with the board's concurrent power and is limited by the board's management prerogatives under Section 141(a).

Third, it follows that, to decide whether the Bylaw proposed by AFSCME is a proper subject for shareholder action under Delaware law, we must first determine: (1) the scope or reach of the shareholders' power to adopt, alter or repeal the bylaws of a Delaware corporation, and then (2) whether the Bylaw at issue here falls within that permissible scope. Where, as here, the proposed bylaw is one that limits director authority, that is an elusively difficult task.

Two other provisions of the DGCL, 8 *Del. C.* §§ 109(b) and 102(b)(1), bear importantly on the first question and form the basis of contentions advanced by each side. Section 109(b), which deals generally with bylaws and what they must or may contain, provides that:

> The bylaws may contain any provision, not inconsistent with law or with the certificate of incorporation, relating to the business of the corporation, the conduct of its affairs, and its rights or powers or the rights or powers of its stockholders, directors, officers or employees.

And Section 102(b)(1), which is part of a broader provision that addresses what the certificate of incorporation must or may contain, relevantly states that:

> (b) In addition to the matters required to be set forth in the certificate of incorporation by subsection (a) of this section, the certificate of incorporation may also contain any or all of the following matters:
>
> > (1) Any provision for the management of the business and for the conduct of the affairs of the corporation, and any provision creating, defining, limiting and regulating the powers of the corporation, the directors and the stockholders, or any class of the stockholders. . . . ; if such provisions are not contrary to the laws of this State. Any provision which is required or permitted by any section of this chapter to be stated in the bylaws may instead be stated in the certificate of incorporation.

AFSCME relies heavily upon the language of Section 109(b), which permits the bylaws of a corporation to contain "any provision . . . relating to the . . . rights or powers of its stockholders [and] directors. . . ." The Bylaw, AFSCME argues, "relates to" the right of the stockholders meaningfully to participate in the process of electing directors, a right that necessarily "includes the right to nominate an opposing slate."

CA argues, in response, that Section 109(b) is not dispositive, because it cannot be read in isolation from, and without regard to, Section 102(b)(1). CA's argument runs as follows: the Bylaw would limit the substantive decision-making authority of CA's board to decide whether or not to expend corporate funds for a particular purpose, here, reimbursing director election expenses. Section 102(b)(1) contemplates that any provision that limits the broad statutory power of the directors must be contained in the certificate of incorporation. Therefore, the proposed Bylaw can only be in CA's Certificate of Incorporation, as distinguished from its bylaws. Accordingly, the proposed bylaw falls outside the universe of permissible bylaws authorized by Section 109(b).

Implicit in CA's argument is the premise that *any* bylaw that in *any* respect might be viewed as limiting or restricting the power of the board of directors automatically falls outside the scope of permissible bylaws. That simply cannot be. That reasoning, taken to its logical extreme, would result in eliminating altogether the shareholders' statutory right to adopt, amend or repeal bylaws. Bylaws, by their very nature, set down rules and procedures that bind a corporation's board and its shareholders. In that sense, most, if not all, bylaws could be said to limit the otherwise unlimited discretionary power of the board. Yet Section 109(a) carves out an area of shareholder power to adopt, amend or repeal bylaws that is expressly inviolate. Therefore, to argue that the Bylaw at issue here limits the board's power to manage the business and affairs of the Company only begins, but cannot end, the analysis needed to decide whether the Bylaw is a proper subject for shareholder action. The question left unanswered is what is the scope of shareholder action that Section 109(b) permits yet does not improperly intrude upon the directors' power to manage corporation's business and affairs under Section 141(a).

It is at this juncture that the statutory language becomes only marginally helpful in determining what the Delaware legislature intended to be the lawful scope of the shareholders' power to adopt, amend and repeal bylaws. To resolve that issue, the Court must resort to different tools, namely, decisions of this Court and of the Court of Chancery that bear on this question. Those tools do not enable us to articulate with doctrinal exactitude a bright line that divides those bylaws that shareholders may unilaterally adopt under Section 109(b) from those which they may not under Section 141(a). They do, however, enable us to decide the issue presented in this specific case.[14]

It is well-established Delaware law that a proper function of bylaws is not to mandate how the board should decide specific substantive business decisions, but rather, to define the process and procedures by which those decisions are made.

Examples of the procedural, process-oriented nature of bylaws are found in both the DGCL and the case law. For example, 8 *Del. C.* § 141(b) authorizes bylaws that fix the number of directors on the board, the

---

[14] We do not attempt to delineate the location of that bright line in this Opinion. What we do hold is case specific; that is, wherever may be the location of the bright line that separates the shareholders' bylaw-making power under Section 109 from the directors' exclusive managerial authority under Section 141(a), the proposed Bylaw at issue here does not invade the territory demarcated by Section 141(a).

number of directors required for a quorum (with certain limitations), and the vote requirements for board action. 8 *Del. C.* § 141(f) authorizes bylaws that preclude board action without a meeting. And, almost three decades ago this Court upheld a shareholder-enacted bylaw requiring unanimous board attendance and board approval for any board action, and unanimous ratification of any committee action. Such purely procedural bylaws do not improperly encroach upon the board's managerial authority under Section 141(a).

The process-creating function of bylaws provides a starting point to address the Bylaw at issue. It enables us to frame the issue in terms of whether the Bylaw is one that establishes or regulates a process for substantive director decision-making, or one that mandates the decision itself. Not surprisingly, the parties sharply divide on that question. We conclude that the Bylaw, even though infelicitously couched as a substantive-sounding mandate to expend corporate funds, has both the intent and the effect of regulating the process for electing directors of CA. Therefore, we determine that the Bylaw is a proper subject for shareholder action, and set forth our reasoning below.

Although CA concedes that "restrictive procedural bylaws (such as those requiring the presence of all directors and unanimous board consent to take action) are acceptable," it points out that even facially procedural bylaws can unduly intrude upon board authority. The Bylaw being proposed here is unduly intrusive, CA claims, because, by mandating reimbursement of a stockholder's proxy expenses, it limits the board's broad discretionary authority to decide whether to grant reimbursement at all. CA further claims that because (in defined circumstances) the Bylaw mandates the expenditure of corporate funds, its subject matter is necessarily substantive, not process-oriented, and, therefore falls outside the scope of what Section 109(b) permits.[19]

Because the Bylaw is couched as a command to reimburse ("The board of directors shall cause the corporation to reimburse a stockholder"), it lends itself to CA's criticism. But the Bylaw's wording, although relevant, is not dispositive of whether or not it is process-related. The Bylaw could easily have been worded differently, to emphasize its process, as distinguished from its mandatory payment, component.[20] By saying this

---

[19] CA actually conflates two separate arguments that, although facially similar, are analytically distinct. The first argument is that the Bylaw impermissibly intrudes upon board authority because it mandates the expenditure of corporate funds. The second is that the Bylaw impermissibly leaves no role for board discretion and would require reimbursement of the costs of a subset of CA's stockholders, even in circumstances where the board's fiduciary duties would counsel otherwise. Analytically, the first argument is relevant to the issue of whether the Bylaw is a proper subject for unilateral stockholder action, whereas the second argument more properly goes to the separate question of whether the Bylaw, if enacted, would violate Delaware law.

[20] For example, the Bylaw could have been phrased more benignly, to provide that "[a] stockholder or group of stockholders (together, the 'Nominator') shall be entitled to reimbursement from the corporation for reasonable expenses ('Expenses') incurred in connection with nominating one or more candidates in a contested election of directors to the corporation's board of directors

we do not mean to suggest that this Bylaw's reimbursement component can be ignored. What we do suggest is that a bylaw that requires the expenditure of corporate funds does not, for that reason alone, become automatically deprived of its process-related character. A hypothetical example illustrates the point. Suppose that the directors of a corporation live in different states and at a considerable distance from the corporation's headquarters. Suppose also that the shareholders enact a bylaw that requires all meetings of directors to take place in person at the corporation's headquarters. Such a bylaw would be clearly process-related, yet it cannot be supposed that the shareholders would lack the power to adopt the bylaw because it would require the corporation to expend its funds to reimburse the directors' travel expenses. Whether or not a bylaw is process-related must necessarily be determined in light of its context and purpose.

The context of the Bylaw at issue here is the process for electing directors-a subject in which shareholders of Delaware corporations have a legitimate and protected interest. The purpose of the Bylaw is to promote the integrity of that electoral process by facilitating the nomination of director candidates by stockholders or groups of stockholders. Generally, and under the current framework for electing directors in contested elections, only board-sponsored nominees for election are reimbursed for their election expenses. Dissident candidates are not, unless they succeed in replacing the entire board. The Bylaw would encourage the nomination of non-management board candidates by promising reimbursement of the nominating stockholders' proxy expenses if one or more of its candidates are elected. In that the shareholders also have a legitimate interest, because the Bylaw would facilitate the exercise of their right to participate in selecting the contestants. The Court of Chancery has so recognized:

> [T]he unadorned right to cast a ballot in a contest for [corporate] office . . . is meaningless without the right to participate in selecting the contestants. As the nominating process circumscribes the range of choice to be made, it is a fundamental and outcome-determinative step in the election of officeholders. To allow for voting while maintaining a closed selection process thus renders the former an empty exercise.

The shareholders of a Delaware corporation have the right "to participate in selecting the contestants" for election to the board. The shareholders are entitled to facilitate the exercise of that right by proposing a bylaw that would encourage candidates other than board-sponsored nominees to stand for election. The Bylaw would accomplish that by

---

in the following circumstances. . . ." Although the substance of the Bylaw would be no different, the emphasis would be upon the shareholders' entitlement to reimbursement, rather than upon the directors' obligation to reimburse. As discussed in Part IV, *infra,* of this Opinion, in order for the bylaw not to be "not inconsistent with law" as Section 109(b) mandates, it would also need to contain a provision that reserves the directors' full power to discharge their fiduciary duties.

committing the corporation to reimburse the election expenses of shareholders whose candidates are successfully elected. That the implementation of that proposal would require the expenditure of corporate funds will not, in and of itself, make such a bylaw an improper subject matter for shareholder action. Accordingly, we answer the first question certified to us in the affirmative.

That, however, concludes only part of the analysis. The DGCL also requires that the Bylaw be "not inconsistent with law." Accordingly, we turn to the second certified question, which is whether the proposed Bylaw, if adopted, would cause CA to violate any Delaware law to which it is subject.

In answering the first question, we have already determined that the Bylaw does not facially violate any provision of the DGCL or of CA's Certificate of Incorporation. The question thus becomes whether the Bylaw would violate any common law rule or precept. Were this issue being presented in the course of litigation involving the application of the Bylaw to a specific set of facts, we would start with the presumption that the Bylaw is valid and, if possible, construe it in a manner consistent with the law. The factual context in which the Bylaw was challenged would inform our analysis, and we would "exercise caution [before] invalidating corporate acts based upon hypothetical injuries. . . ." The certified questions, however, request a determination of the validity of the Bylaw in the abstract. Therefore, in response to the second question, we must necessarily consider any possible circumstance under which a board of directors might be required to act. Under at least one such hypothetical, the board of directors would breach their fiduciary duties if they complied with the Bylaw. Accordingly, we conclude that the Bylaw, as drafted, would violate the prohibition, which our decisions have derived from Section 141(a), against contractual arrangements that commit the board of directors to a course of action that would preclude them from fully discharging their fiduciary duties to the corporation and its shareholders.

[AFSCME's argument that the Bylaw does not preclude the board from discharging their fiduciary duty because it relieves the board of its duties with respect to reimbursement] is more semantical than substantive. No matter how artfully it may be phrased, the argument concedes the very proposition that renders the Bylaw, as written, invalid: the Bylaw mandates reimbursement of election expenses in circumstances that a proper application of fiduciary principles could preclude. That such circumstances could arise is not far fetched. Under Delaware law, a board may expend corporate funds to reimburse proxy expenses "[w]here the controversy is concerned with a question of policy as distinguished from personnel o[r] management." But in a situation where the proxy contest is motivated by personal or petty concerns, or to promote interests that do not further, or are adverse to, those of the corporation, the board's fiduciary duty could compel that reimbursement be denied altogether.

It is in this respect that the proposed Bylaw, as written, would violate Delaware law if enacted by CA's shareholders. As presently drafted, the Bylaw would afford CA's directors full discretion to determine what *amount* of reimbursement is appropriate, because the directors would be obligated to grant only the "reasonable" expenses of a successful short slate. Unfortunately, that does not go far enough, because the Bylaw contains no language or provision that would reserve to CA's directors their full power to exercise their fiduciary duty to decide whether or not it would be appropriate, in a specific case, to award reimbursement at all.

* * *

In arriving at this conclusion, we express no view on whether the Bylaw as currently drafted, would create a better governance scheme from a policy standpoint. We decide only what is, and is not, legally permitted under the DGCL. That statute, as currently drafted, is the expression of policy as decreed by the Delaware legislature. Those who believe that CA's shareholders should be permitted to make the proposed Bylaw as drafted part of CA's governance scheme, have two alternatives. They may seek to amend the Certificate of Incorporation to include the substance of the Bylaw; *or* they may seek recourse from the Delaware General Assembly.

Accordingly, we answer the second question certified to us in the affirmative.

It is possible to interpret Justice Jacobs' opinion in many ways. Because the court invalidated the proposed bylaw, the decision may be seen as a victory for CA and those who argue for director primacy and who are troubled by increasing shareholder activism. On the other hand, because the court found that the subject matter of the bylaw was a proper subject for shareholder action under Delaware law, the decision can be read as an important step in the emergence of shareholder power. The court itself, not surprisingly, permits both interpretations by making clear (footnote 14) that it is only deciding the case before it and is not establishing broad principles governing all shareholder proposed bylaws.

The opinion is significant in resolving the potential tension between DGCL §§ 109(b) and 141(a) insofar as the proper subject for shareholder action is concerned. That is the threshold question in any shareholder bylaw that impinges on management discretion, regardless of the subject matter of the bylaw. There is very little case on law on this subject but it is implicit in the analysis in *Auer v. Dressel*.

The decision still leaves open the question of how much of an intrusion into corporate governance can be tolerated in a shareholder bylaw. The issue that has generated the most controversy is a bylaw that injects shareholders into the adoption or repeal of a poison pill. In *International Brotherhood of Teamsters General Fund v. Fleming Cos.*, 975 P.2d 907 (Okla.1999), the Oklahoma Supreme Court upheld a shareholder bylaw dealing with poison pills. There has been much debate about whether Delaware courts would follow *Fleming*, a question that this decision does not resolve. On the other hand, if a bylaw can be drafted to emphasize process while leaving the target corporation's board of directors some discretion to exercise its fiduciary duties (the methodology that the court adopts), it is not clear that such a bylaw would be invalid. The court's emphasis on deciding just the case before it would suggest that the bylaw would not be per se invalid.

In determining the validity of the bylaw, the court uses the personnel/policy dichotomy that has been a part of Delaware jurisprudence for fifty years, going back to early cases involving proxy contests. That dichotomy was the linchpin in *Cheff v. Mathes* (Chapter 21), a case which, when decided, was widely criticized partly because of that reasoning. In the *CA* opinion, the court simply accepts the validity of the dichotomy without reexamining whether it ever made sense or whether it makes sense in a more contemporary context. Clearly any contest for control has elements of both and it is hard to know how a court can examine the motivations of the participants in a contest, particularly when determining the validity of a bylaw amendment.

2. THE DELAWARE RESPONSE

Although the bylaw in *CA* only concerned the reimbursement of expenses in a proxy contest in which fewer than all the board seats were contested, its real significance lies in the broader question of shareholder access to the ballot which is why the case was so closely watched. Corporate reimbursement clearly facilitates shareholder nominations; denial of corporate funds equally clearly impedes them.

In August 2009, the Delaware legislature inserted itself directly into these issues. DGCL § 112 authorizes a corporation to adopt a bylaw granting shareholders the right to include their nominees (if less than all the directors are to be elected) in a corporation's proxy soliciting materials subject to certain conditions contained in the section. DGCL § 113 codifies the decision in *CA* and permits a corporation to adopt a by-law providing for corporate reimbursement of shareholder expenses incurred in connection with an election of directors, again subject to certain conditions contained in the section. Bylaws adopted under these sections could be initiated either by the corporation's shareholders, or proactively before such initiation, by the corporation's board of directors. The text of §§ 112 and 113 is as follows:

§ 112.   Access to proxy solicitation materials.

The bylaws may provide that if the corporation solicits proxies with respect to an election of directors, it may be required, to the extent and subject to such procedures or conditions as may be provided in the bylaws, to include in its proxy solicitation materials (including any form of proxy it distributes), in addition to individuals nominated by the board of directors, one or more individuals nominated by a stockholder. Such procedures or conditions may include any of the following:

(1) A provision requiring a minimum record or beneficial ownership, or duration of ownership, of shares of the corporation capital stock, by the nominating stockholder, and defining beneficial ownership to take into account options or other rights in respect of or related to such stock;

(2) A provision requiring the nominating stockholder to submit specified information concerning the stockholder and the stockholder nominees, including information concerning ownership by such persons of shares of the corporation capital stock, or options or other rights in respect of or related to such stock;

(3) A provision conditioning eligibility to require inclusion in the corporation proxy solicitation materials upon the number or proportion of directors nominated by stockholders or whether the stockholder previously sought to require such inclusion;

(4) A provision precluding nominations by any person if such person, any nominee of such person, or any affiliate or associate of such person or nominee, has acquired or publicly proposed to acquire shares constituting a specified percentage of the voting power of the corporation outstanding voting stock within a specified period before the election of directors;

(5) A provision requiring that the nominating stockholder undertake to indemnify the corporation in respect of any loss arising as a result of any false or misleading information or statement submitted by the nominating stockholder in connection with a nomination; and

(6) Any other lawful condition.

§ 113.   Proxy Expense Reimbursement.

(a) The bylaws may provide for the reimbursement by the corporation of expenses incurred by a stockholder in soliciting proxies in connection with an election of directors, subject to such procedures or conditions as the bylaws may prescribe, including:

> (1) Conditioning eligibility for reimbursement upon the number or proportion of persons nominated by the stockholder seeking reimbursement or whether such stockholder previously sought reimbursement for similar expenses;

> (2) Limitations on the amount of reimbursement based upon the proportion of votes cast in favor of one or more of the persons nominated by the stockholder seeking reimbursement, or upon the amount spent by the corporation in soliciting proxies in connection with the election;

> (3) Limitations concerning elections of directors by cumulative voting pursuant to 214 of this title; or

> (4) Any other lawful condition.

(b) No bylaw so adopted shall apply to elections for which any record date precedes its adoption.

The effect of these provisions is to permit access to the ballot and the reimbursement of proxy soliciting expenses but it permits an individual corporation and its shareholders to tailor bylaws in manner appropriate for its own governance structure. It is important to note that § 112 simply authorizes a bylaw that permits shareholder access to the ballot. By itself, it does not necessarily guarantee that a shareholder will be able to have such a bylaw included in a corporation's proxy statement, leaving that issue to the SEC proxy rules, particularly Rule 14a–8(i)(8).

Section 113 also leaves certain questions open. Although intended to codify CA, it does not do so fully. In footnote 20, the court stated that "in order for the bylaw not to be 'inconsistent with law' as Section 109(b) mandates, it would also need to contain a provision that reserves the directors' full power to discharge their fiduciary duties." § 113 does not have such an express requirement and it is thus unclear whether, notwithstanding the express statutory authority for a proxy expenses reimbursement bylaw, the courts will read a fiduciary out requirement into a bylaw that does not expressly contain that limitation.

3. THE SEC SHAREHOLDER ACCESS PROPOSAL

In August 2010, the SEC, by a 3–2 vote, adopted an extensive series of rules, most importantly Rule 14a–11, to permit shareholders to nominate candidates for director and have those nominees included in the corporation's proxy statement. As mentioned above, the SEC also amended Rule 14a–8(i)(8) in a way that would allow proposals to amend the bylaws or charter to permit shareholder access. Soon thereafter, the Business Round Table and the Chamber of Commerce brought an action in the U.S. Court of Appeals seeking to set aside the SEC rules. On July 22, 2011 the D.C. Circuit vacated most of these rule changes, holding them invalid as arbitrary and capricious because the SEC failed to adequately assess their costs and benefits. *Business Roundtable v. SEC*, 647 F.3d 1144 (D.C. Cir. 2011). The court did not, however, invalidate the amendment to Rule 14a–8(i)(8). In May 2012, in testimony before the House Financial Services subcommittee, SEC Chairman Mary Schapiro indicated that because of resource limitations, the SEC was not likely to revisit a mandatory rule for proxy access in the immediate future.

The effect of *Business Roundtable* was effectively to relegate the question of shareholder access to the management proxy for director elections to private ordering under state law. The principal avenue left for shareholders seeking to establish access to the proxy is thus a resolution to amend the bylaws or charter. Under the version of Rule 14a–8(i)(8) left standing by *Business Roundtable,* corporations may not exclude such a resolution from the proxy statement under that rule. Such a proposal would still, however, have to be a proper subject under state law and would be subject to the other exclusion provisions of Rule 14a–8. There were quite a few such proposals in the 2012 proxy season, and they received an average of 36% favorable votes.

This ongoing saga raises two important policy questions. The first is whether such rules, in any form, are necessary and desirable. Supporters of mandatory proxy access rules see the rules as a good way to permit shareholders to have additional influence over nominations to the board of directors. The rules would also be an effective mechanism to improve board performance through the injection of new ideas and the threat of removal for poor performance. For the rules' supporters, the proposal would improve corporate governance. As SEC Chairman Schapiro stated:

> Corporate governance is about maintaining an appropriate balance of accountability between three key players: the corporation's owners, the directors whom the owners elect, and the managers whom the directors select. Accountability requires not only good transparency, but also an effective means to take action for poor performance or bad decisions.

I believe that the most effective means of ensuring corporations are accountable is to ensure that the shareholders' vote is both meaningful and freely exercised. That is why the SEC proposed rules which would remove obstacles to shareholders' ability to nominate candidates for the boards of directors of the companies that they own.

Opponents of the rules fear that they would turn corporate elections into costly and disruptive contests that would discourage qualified nominees from being willing to serve as directors. They also argue that proxy access can undermine valuable board cohesiveness by empowering special interest shareholders, through electing their own candidates, to pursue their own narrow agendas that are not in the best interest of the corporation as a whole.

4. SHAREHOLDER ACCESS BYLAWS

It may be that much of the controversy surrounding shareholder access to the management proxy will be overtaken by events. Delaware §§ 112 and 113, discussed above, facilitates the adoption of bylaws that would make it easier for shareholders to nominate directors; and the MBCA was amended in 2009 to allow proxy access for director nominations and reasonable reimbursement for shareholder expenses incurred in proxy contests for director elections.

With this express authorization in state statutes, institutions and activist investors have used Rule 14a–8 or have lobbied portfolio companies to amend their bylaws to permit larger shareholders to include their nominees to the board on the management proxy. Proxy access bylaws have generally received strong support from institutional investors, and as of 2016 approximately 400 public companies had adopted them, including 75% of the S&P 100. These bylaw changes obviously have made it significantly easier for activist investors to seek board seats.

The details of proxy access bylaws vary somewhat, but certain common terms seem to be emerging as more or less standard. These include that shareholders wishing to access the management proxy have held at least 3% of the outstanding stock for at least three years; that there be no more than 20 members in a group of shareholders seeking to nominate directors, and that shareholders be permitted to nominate no more than 20% of the members of the board.

5. ADVANCE NOTICE BYLAWS

Several recent Delaware cases have highlighted the possibility of activist shareholders using a state law procedure, the advance notice bylaw, as a way to nominate director candidates outside the parameters of Rule 14a–8.

The principal purpose of an advance notice bylaw is to facilitate ordinary business at a shareholders meeting. Such a bylaw requires a stockholder to submit "advance notice" of her intention to introduce business at a meeting such as the nomination of a candidate for director or the introduction of a shareholder proposal. The bylaw serves three important functions. First, it informs the company of the business that a stockholder will bring to the meeting with sufficient time to enable the company to prepare. Second, it provides an opportunity for shareholders to be fully informed of the matter in advance of the meeting. Finally, it enables the company's board to make informed recommendations or present alternatives to the shareholders regarding the matter. Although the language in the bylaw may vary, essentially the bylaw requires not only notice of the business to be introduced but also the information necessary to determined that the shareholder nominee is qualified to be elected and that the person proposing the matter is actually a shareholder.

In *Jana Master Fund Ltd v. CNET Networks, Inc.*, 2008 WL 660556 (Del.Ch.), aff'd, 947 A.2d 1120 (Del. 2008), Jana, an investment fund, tried to gain control of the classified board of CNet by increasing the size of the board and nominating candidates for director. Jana advised CNet that it would solicit proxies for its proposals in a self-financed mailing to stockholders rather than use CNet's proxy materials. CNet argued that because Jana would have owned CNet stock for only eight months by the date of the meeting, it had not complied with CNet's advance notice bylaw which required that a stockholder must have held $1,000 worth of stock for a full year in order to be eligible to "seek to transact other corporate business at the annual meeting."

Chancellor Chandler rejected CNet's argument. Because CNet's advance notice bylaw stated that the notice provided by the shareholder had to "comply with the federal securities laws governing shareholder proposals a corporation must include in its own proxy materials," the court held that it unambiguously applied only to proposals that shareholders wished to have included in the company proxy statement.

In ruling that the advance notice bylaw was simply inapplicable, the court found it unnecessary to decide whether the one year requirement was invalid because it constituted an unreasonable restriction of shareholder rights, the criterion for determining the validity of such bylaws under Delaware law.

Levitt Corp. v. Office Depot, Inc., 2008 WL 1724244 (Del.Ch.) also involved a shareholder's effort to nominate candidates for director at Office Depot's annual meeting. Shortly after the company filed its definitive proxy materials with the SEC, the shareholder filed its own proxy materials but did not give advance notice to the company of its intention to propose director candidates. Concurrently, the shareholder brought suit in the Court of Chancery to confirm that no additional notice was required.

The Office Depot bylaws required that "for business to be properly brought before an annual meeting by a stockholder, the stockholder must have given timely notice thereof in writing to the Secretary." Office Depot argued that this bylaw required advance notice for the shareholder nomination to be brought properly before the meeting. The shareholder argued that the bylaws did not require advance notice. Alternatively, if notice were required, Office Depot itself had already made nominations an item of business in its own notice of business, thus negating the need for advance notice by the shareholder.

As in *CNET*, the court did not reach the question of whether the provisions of the company's bylaw were unduly restrictive. Rather, the court focused on the part of the bylaw which provided that "At an annual meeting of the stockholders, only such business shall be conducted as shall have been properly brought before the meeting." The court agreed with the company that "business" included director nominations but concluded, perhaps unexpectedly, that although the bylaw required notice of nominations, the company itself had brought the business of nominating and electing directors—its own nominees and the competing slate—before the annual meeting through its notice to shareholders that accompanied the proxy statement

H. THE ROLE OF SHAREHOLDERS IN EXECUTIVE COMPENSATION: SAY-ON-PAY

The Dodd-Frank Act created a "say-on-pay" requirement, the name commonly given to the process by which shareholders are asked to give a non-binding advisory vote on executive compensation. Under Rule 14a–21, adopted by the SEC in response to the Dodd-Frank requirement, companies also must include a resolution in their proxy statements at least once every three years asking shareholders, in a non-binding vote, to approve the compensation of those executive officers listed under Item 402 of Regulation S–K. Separately, at least once every six years, a resolution is required to determine whether the shareholder vote should take place every one, two or three years.

The say-on-pay provisions also relate to compensation paid to senior executives in merger transactions. If any golden parachute compensation has not been approved in the say-on-pay vote, companies must solicit shareholder approval of such compensation in a separate nonbinding vote at the meeting where shareholders are asked to approve a merger or similar extraordinary transaction that would trigger payments under the golden parachute provisions (say-on-severance").

The theory behind say-on-pay is that giving shareholders a periodic referendum on executive compensation will decrease the likelihood that overly generous compensation packages will be paid to senior executives. The vote may also motivate companies to align manager compensation more closely with performance in the belief that shareholders respond most negatively to large compensation packages when stock performance is poor. Additionally, although the vote is non-binding, it might nonetheless powerfully influence the behavior of compensation committees who may wish to avoid the public opprobrium associated with a negative vote.

But as sensible as that theory may seem, the mechanism represents a dramatic deviation from the ordinary allocation of decision-making authority between management and shareholders. As the discussion of shareholder proposals above indicates, a corporation may exclude from its proxy materials any shareholder proposal dealing with the company's ordinary business operations. Absent the explicit statutory mandate in Dodd-Frank, a proposal dealing with excessive executive compensation might not have been required to be included under the SEC's traditional analysis unless the SEC staff considered it be a question of "public policy."

Rule 14a–21 does not explicitly mandate that companies disclose the manner in which their compensation practices relate to risk management and risk-taking; for example whether those practices may create incentives for executives to take greater risks in hopes of increasing their bonuses or the value of their stock options. However, the "Compensation Discussion and Analysis" report, that is also required by the proxy rules requires that "To the extent that risks arising from the registrant's compensation policies and practices for its employees are reasonably likely to have a material adverse effect on the registrant," the registrant must "discuss the registrant's policies and practices of compensating its employees, including non-executive officers, as they relate to risk management practices and risk-taking incentives."

Since the rule was adopted, shareholders have consistently approved the overwhelming majority of executive compensation plans. The numbers for 2016 are representative. Of nearly 2,000 companies that held votes, 93% of the plans passed with over 70% shareholder support, and only 1.6% failed to receive a majority vote.

The leading proxy advisory firms have played a role in say-on-pay votes. In 2016, ISS recommended a negative vote on approximately 12% of the proposals it reviewed. The principal reason for a negative recommendation appears to be a lack of a connection between the company's executive compensation package and its performance. Some companies that received negative recommendations from ISS were clearly troubled by the recommendation and responded by filing additional proxy soliciting materials that explained the reasons for their disagreement with the negative recommendations and defended their own methodologies. Perhaps more importantly, many companies appear to have tailored their executive pay plans to assure that they will receive a favorable recommendation under ISS's announced policies.

As to say-on-pay frequency, in the overwhelming majority of companies, shareholders have favored annual votes, a preference that may have been influenced by the ISS recommendation. A higher percentage of larger companies received recommendations for annual votes, than smaller companies, which more frequently received recommendations for a triennial vote.

CHAPTER 15

DISCLOSURE DUTIES TO SHAREHOLDERS

■ ■ ■

Disclosure lies at the heart of corporate accountability in public corporations, particularly when shareholder voting is involved. This chapter considers the disclosure duties owed to shareholders as decision-makers and the remedies available when deceit infects the voting process. Much of the duty of public corporations to make disclosures to their shareholders is a found in §§ 12, 13, and 14 of the Securities Exchange Act of 1934. Sections 12 and 13 and the rules under them require that unlisted public companies and listed companies, respectively, file and disseminate to stockholders annual and quarterly reports containing financial statements and descriptions of the company's business, as well as occasional reports upon the occurrence of certain specified events. A discussion of this kind of reporting is largely beyond the scope of this book; consequently the following materials focus primarily on disclosure in proxy statements.

Section 14 and its rules mandate disclosures in connection with the solicitation of proxies. Their purpose is to ensure that stockholders have all the material information necessary to make an informed voting decision. SEC Rule 14a–9 prohibits a solicitation made through a proxy statement that contains a material misstatement or omission. We begin by considering the implied private action for proxy fraud developed by federal courts under Rule 14a–9. We look at the elements of such an action: materiality, reliance, causation, and scienter. We then explore whether federal disclosure duties can be used to impose standards of substantive fairness in corporate transactions, even when shareholders do not vote. Finally, we describe disclosure duties under state law and their relationship to federal law.

Problem: National Metal Products

National Metal Products, Inc. ("National") is a Delaware corporation whose common stock is traded on the New York Stock Exchange. The company manufactures specialized metal products. Its sales for the most recent year were $500 million.

In February, the board of directors approved a merger with International Petroleum Corporation ("IPC") whereby National would issue additional shares of its common stock equal to 25% of the outstanding shares. The transaction required shareholder approval by both companies under state law. The proxy material sought approval of the merger and the election of directors. The candidates for election were the incumbent directors of National, as well as Sanford, the CEO of IPC. At the meeting in July, the shareholders voted overwhelmingly to approve the merger and management's slate of directors.

National's proxy statement contained all the information required by SEC rules concerning the merger and the candidates for election to the board. Among the statements made about the merger was the following: "The board of directors recommends approval of the merger. The board's recommendation is based upon its review of management's report and recommendations and the financial statements of IPC. It is the board's judgment, premised on this information, that the merger is in the best interests of the company and its shareholders."

Several months later, the following facts became known. No mention of them was made in the proxy statement:

A.   The merger was negotiated between Meacham, the CEO of National, and Sanford, the CEO of IPC. It was taken up by National's board at a regular meeting where Meacham and other members of management made a brief presentation and answered questions. Financial statements of IPC had been given to each member of the board two days before the meeting. After about 30 minutes of discussion, the board voted unanimously in favor of the merger. This was the same procedure that National had followed with three other acquisitions during the past two years.

B.   Several years before the merger, management of IPC learned that its field managers had engaged in a price-fixing scheme with several other independent oil producers. Senior management ordered the practice halted. Sanford informed Meacham of these past practices during the negotiations, and explained that it was common in the industry, but Meacham made no mention of this to the National board, nor was he asked any questions relating to possible price fixing.

The acquisition has proven costly to National. Several months after the merger, it was revealed that the price-fixing practices had continued even after the merger with National. As a result, substantial contracts between National (through IPC) and some refineries were cancelled, and large private suits and criminal prosecutions under the antitrust laws are likely. National has dismissed key managers who were engaged in the price-fixing activities.

C.   National entered into a settlement of a claim by two state environmental protection agencies that the company violated state emission controls. The violations were caused by furnaces in two older smelting plants of National, where management had decided to attempt compliance by patching up old emission control systems rather than replacing them with new and expensive electronic equipment. The company was fined $500,000. At the time the proxy statement was issued, the National board was aware of management's decision on the furnaces and the risks but decided, on advice of counsel, that no disclosure was necessary in the proxy statement.

Rogers, the owner of 1,000 shares of National common stock has consulted you about a lawsuit alleging that the proxy statement for the shareholders' meeting was materially false and misleading in violation of Rule 14a–9 of the SEC proxy rules. How would you answer the following questions?

1. Are there any material misstatements or omissions in the proxy statement in violation of Rule 14a–9?

2. Assuming that there are material misstatements or omissions, what causal connection can Rogers show between the violations he can establish and the injury of which he complains?

3. Suppose that Rogers believes that even if there were no material misstatements or omissions in the proxy statement, the merger was unfair because National paid too much to acquire IPC. Does Rogers have a valid claim under either the proxy rules or Rule 10b–5, either before or after the shareholder vote, based on a showing that the terms of the merger were unfair and that the unfairness was not directly disclosed?

4. Does Rogers have a claim under state law in connection with the proxy solicitation? If so, against whom? What must Rogers prove to prevail on his claim?

A. IMPLIED FEDERAL PRIVATE ACTION FOR PROXY FRAUD

A landmark decision at the intersection of state corporate law and federal securities regulation is *J.I. Case Co. v. Borak*, 377 U.S. 426 (1964), where the Supreme Court held that a private right of action existed under § 14(a) of the 1934 Act is. Plaintiff Carl Borak was a stockholder in J.I. Case Co., which had proposed to merge with American Tractor Corp. Borak believed the merger involved improper self-dealing by the Case managers and that the Case shareholders were being treated unfairly. He brought suit in federal district court to enjoin the merger, alleging a violation of the federal securities laws. The district court denied the injunction on the grounds that it had no power to grant a remedy, the merger was consummated, and Case ceased to exist. Borak appealed. In finding an implied private right of action for violations of § 14(a), the Court reasoned that § 14(a) grants jurisdiction to federal district courts over suits at equity. Because the stated purpose of § 14(a) is to protect investors, the Court found it reasonable to assume that those investors hurt by violations of § 14(a) had a right of action under it. The court further justified its holding by noting that because the SEC cannot review the accuracy of every proxy statement, providing investors with a private right of action would assist the enforcement of the section.

In the years immediately after *Borak,* the Supreme Court continued to support implied private rights of action under the federal securities laws. In the mid-1970s, however, the Court began to curtail the availability of such rights under federal law. In *Cort v. Ash,* 422 U.S. 66 (1975), a unanimous Court refused to imply a private right of action under the Federal Election Campaign Act. *Cort* moved away from the *Borak* analysis and reflected the Court's concerns about increasing judicial involvement in matters better left to state law. In 1979, the Court refused to imply a federal cause of action for a violation of § 17 of the 1934 Act, which requires securities firms to maintain records for the protection of their customers. *Touche Ross & Co. v. Redington,* 442 U.S. 560 (1979). The Court rejected the plaintiff's reliance on § 27, however, leaving the result of *Borak* intact.

Although class actions under Rule 10b–5 have largely replaced proxy fraud derivative suits, *Borak* remains an important federalism case. It created an implied private right of action for proxy fraud that provided both prospective and retrospective relief under federal law. Equally important, it made the determination of the parameters of such an action a matter of federal law rather than, as might have been expected with respect to shareholder voting, a question of state law. Indeed, the Court expressed skepticism about the possible effectiveness of state law as a means of protecting shareholders in the voting process, noting that "if the law of the State happened to attach no responsibility to the use of misleading proxy statements, the whole purpose of the section might be frustrated."

B. MATERIALITY

1. MATERIALITY ORTHODOXY

TSC INDUSTRIES, INC. V. NORTHWAY, INC.
426 U.S. 438 (1976).

[National Industries acquired 34% of TSC Industries stock by purchase from the founding family, and then placed five of its nominees on TSC's board of directors. The two companies agreed to a sale of TSC's assets to National in exchange for stock and warrants of National. A joint proxy statement was issued by the two companies. A shareholder of TSC sued for violation of § 14(a) of the 1934 Act and Rule 14a–9. The shareholder claimed, among other things, that the proxy statement failed to state that purchase of the 34% block of stock, which was disclosed, gave it control of

TSC. The District Court found no material omissions from the proxy statement, but the Court of Appeals reversed.]

MR. JUSTICE MARSHALL delivered the opinion of the Court:

The question of materiality, it is universally agreed, is an objective one, involving the significance of an omitted or misrepresented fact to a reasonable investor. Variations in the formulation of a general test of materiality occur in the articulation of just how significant a fact must be or, put another way, how certain it must be that the fact would affect a reasonable investor's judgment.

The Court of Appeals in this case concluded that material facts include "all facts which a reasonable shareholder *might* consider important." 512 F.2d at 330 (emphasis added). This formulation of the test of materiality has been explicitly rejected by at least two courts as setting too low a threshold for the imposition of liability under Rule 14a–9. In these cases, panels of the Second and Fifth Circuits opted for the conventional tort test of materiality—whether a reasonable man *would* attach importance to the fact misrepresented or omitted in determining his course of action.

In arriving at its broad definition of a material fact as one that a reasonable shareholder *might* consider important, the Court of Appeals in this case relied heavily upon language of this Court in *Mills v. Electric Auto-Lite Co.* That reliance was misplaced. The *Mills* Court did characterize a determination of materiality as at least "embod[ying] a conclusion that the defect was of such a character that it might have been considered important by a reasonable shareholder who was in the process of deciding how to vote." But if any language in *Mills* is to be read as suggesting a general notion of materiality, it can only be the opinion's subsequent reference to materiality as a "requirement that the defect have a significant *propensity* to affect the voting process." For it was that requirement that the Court said "adequately serves the purpose of ensuring that a cause of action cannot be established by proof of a defect so trivial, or so unrelated to the transaction for which approval is sought, that correction of the defect or imposition of liability would not further the interests protected by § 14(a)." Even this language must be read, however, with appreciation that the Court specifically declined to consider the materiality of the omissions in *Mills*. The references to materiality were simply preliminary to our consideration of the sole question in the case— whether proof of the materiality of an omission from a proxy statement must be supplemented by a showing that the defect actually caused the outcome of the vote. It is clear, then, that *Mills* did not intend to foreclose further inquiry into the meaning of materiality under Rule 14a–9.

In formulating a standard of materiality under Rule 14a–9, we are guided, of course, by the recognition in *Borak* and *Mills* of the Rule's broad remedial purpose. That purpose is not merely to ensure by judicial means that the transaction, when judged by its real terms, is fair and otherwise adequate, but to ensure disclosures by corporate management in order to enable the shareholders to make an informed choice. As an abstract proposition, the most desirable role for a court in a suit of this sort, coming after the consummation of the proposed transaction, would perhaps be to determine whether in fact the proposal would have been favored by the shareholders and consummated in the absence of any misstatement or omission. But as we recognized in *Mills,* such matters are not subject to determination with certainty. Doubts as to the critical nature of information misstated or omitted will be commonplace. And particularly in view of the prophylactic purpose of the Rule and the fact that the content of the proxy statement is within management's control, it is appropriate that these doubts be resolved in favor of those the statute is designed to protect.

We are aware, however, that the disclosure policy embodied in the proxy regulations is not without limit. Some information is of such dubious significance that insistence on its disclosure may accomplish more harm than good. The potential liability for Rule 14a–9 violation can be great indeed, and if the standard of materiality is unnecessarily low, not only may the corporation and its management be subjected to liability for insignificant omissions or misstatements, but also management's fear of exposing itself to substantial liability may cause it simply to bury the shareholders in an avalanche of trivial information—a result that is hardly conducive to informed decisionmaking. Precisely these dangers are presented, we think, by the definition of a material fact adopted by the Court of Appeals in this case—a fact which a reasonable shareholder *might* consider important. We agree with Judge Friendly, speaking for the Court of Appeals, that the "might" formulation is "too suggestive of mere possibility, however unlikely."

The general standard of materiality that we think best comports with the policies of Rule 14a–9 is as follows: An omitted fact is material if there is a substantial likelihood that a reasonable shareholder would consider it important in deciding how to vote. This standard is fully consistent with *Mills* general description of materiality as a requirement that "the defect have a significant *propensity* to affect the voting process." It does not require proof of a substantial likelihood that disclosure of the omitted fact would have caused the reasonable investor to change his vote. What the standard does contemplate is a showing of a substantial likelihood that, under all the circumstances, the omitted fact would have assumed actual significance in the deliberations of the reasonable shareholder. Put another way, there must be a substantial likelihood that the disclosure of the omitted fact would have been viewed by the reasonable investor as having significantly altered the "total mix" of information made available.

In considering whether summary judgment on the issue is appropriate, we must bear in mind that the underlying objective facts, which will often be free from dispute, are merely the starting point for the ultimate determination of materiality. The determination requires delicate assessments of the inferences a "reasonable shareholder" would draw from a given set of facts and the significance of those inferences to him, and these assessments are peculiarly ones for the trier of fact. Only if the established omissions are "so obviously important to an investor, that reasonable minds cannot differ on the question of materiality" is the ultimate issue of materiality appropriately resolved "as a matter of law" by summary judgment.

The omissions found by the Court of Appeals to have been materially misleading as a matter of law involved two general issues—the degree of National's control over TSC at the time of the proxy solicitation, and the favorability of the terms of the proposed transaction to TSC shareholders.

The Court of Appeals concluded that two omitted facts relating to National's potential influence, or control, over the management of TSC were material as a matter of law. First, the proxy statement failed to state that at the time the statement was issued, the chairman of the TSC board of directors was Stanley Yarmuth, National's president and chief executive officer, and the chairman of the TSC executive committee was Charles Simonelli, National's executive vice president. Second the statement did not disclose that in filing reports required by the SEC, both TSC and National had indicated that National "may be deemed to be a 'parent' of TSC as that term is defined in the Rules and Regulations under the Securities Act of 1933." The Court of Appeals noted that TSC shareholders were relying on the TSC board of directors to negotiate on their behalf for the best possible rate of exchange with National. It then concluded that the omitted facts were material because they were "persuasive indicators that the TSC board was in fact under the control of National, and that National thus 'sat on both sides of the table' in setting the terms of the exchange."

We do not agree that the omission of these facts, when viewed against the disclosures contained in the proxy statement, warrants the entry of summary judgment against TSC and National on this record. Our conclusion is the same whether the omissions are considered separately or together.

The proxy statement prominently displayed the facts that National owned 34% of the outstanding shares in TSC, and that no other person owned more than 10%. It also prominently revealed that 5 out of 10 TSC directors were National nominees, and it recited the positions of those National nominees with National—indicating, among other things, that Stanley Yarmuth was president and a director of National, and that Charles Simonelli was executive vice president and a director of National. These disclosures clearly revealed the nature of National's relationship with TSC and alerted the reasonable shareholder to the fact that National exercised a degree of influence over TSC. In view of these disclosures, we certainly cannot say that the additional facts that Yarmuth was chairman of the TSC board of directors and Simonelli chairman of its executive committee were, on this record, so obviously important that reasonable minds could not differ on their materiality.

[The Court also found that the other omissions concerning National's control of TSC were not material as a matter of law. It reversed the entry of summary judgment for the plaintiff and remanded for the fact-finder to determine the materiality of omissions concerning the favorability of the terms to TSC shareholders.]

BASIC, INC. V. LEVINSON
485 U.S. 224 (1988).

JUSTICE BLACKMUN delivered the opinion of the Court:

This case requires us to apply the materiality requirement of § 10(b) of the Securities Exchange Act of 1934, and the Securities and Exchange Commission's Rule 10b–5,[1] promulgated thereunder, in the context of preliminary corporate merger discussions.

Prior to December 20, 1978, Basic Incorporated was a publicly traded company primarily engaged in the business of manufacturing chemical refractories for the steel industry. As early as 1965 or 1966, Combustion Engineering, Inc., a company producing mostly alumina-based refractories, expressed some interest in acquiring Basic, but was deterred from pursuing this inclination seriously because of antitrust concerns it then entertained. In 1976, however, regulatory action opened the way to a renewal of Combustion's interest. The "Strategic Plan," dated October 25, 1976, for Combustion's Industrial Products Group included the objective: "Acquire Basic Inc. $30 million."

Beginning in September 1976, Combustion representatives had meetings and telephone conversations with Basic officers and directors, including petitioners here, concerning the possibility of a merger. During 1977 and 1978, Basic made three public statements denying that it was engaged in merger negotiations. On December 18, 1978, Basic asked the New York Stock Exchange to suspend trading in its shares and issued a release stating that it had been "approached" by another company concerning a merger. On December 19, Basic's board endorsed Combustion's offer of $46 per share for its common stock, and on the

---

[1]   Authors' note: SEC Rule 10b–5 is an antifraud provision. It provides: "It shall be unlawful for any person . . . (a) to employ any device, scheme, or artifice to defraud, (b) to make any untrue statement of a material fact or to omit to state a material fact necessary in order to make the statements made, in light of the circumstances under which they were made, not misleading, or (c) to engage in any act, practice, or course of business which operates or would operate as a fraud or deceit upon any person, in connection with the purchase or sale of any security."

following day publicly announced its approval of Combustion's tender offer for all outstanding shares.

[Respondents are former Basic shareholders who sold their stock after Basic's first public statement of October 21, 1977, and before the suspension of trading in December 1978. Respondents brought a class action against Basic and its directors, asserting that the defendants issued three false or misleading public statements and thereby were in violation of § 10(b) of the 1934 Act and of Rule 10b–5. Respondents alleged that they were injured by selling Basic shares at artificially depressed prices in a market affected by petitioners' misleading statements and in reliance thereon.]

We granted certiorari, to resolve the split, among the Courts of Appeals as to the standard of materiality applicable to preliminary merger discussions.

The 1934 Act was designed to protect investors against manipulation of stock prices. Underlying the adoption of extensive disclosure requirements was a legislative philosophy: "There cannot be honest markets without honest publicity. Manipulation and dishonest practices of the market place thrive upon mystery and secrecy." This Court "repeatedly has described the 'fundamental purpose' of the Act as implementing a 'philosophy of full disclosure.'"

The Court previously has addressed various positive and common-law requirements for a violation of § 10(b) or of Rule 10b–5. The Court also explicitly has defined a standard of materiality under the securities laws, see *TSC Industries, Inc. v. Northway, Inc.*, 426 U.S. 438 (1976), concluding in the proxy-solicitation context that ["[a]n omitted fact is material if there is a substantial likelihood that a reasonable shareholder would consider it important in deciding how to vote."] Acknowledging that certain information concerning corporate developments could well be of "dubious significance," the Court was careful not to set too low a standard of materiality; it was concerned that a minimal standard might bring an overabundance of information within its reach, and lead management "simply to bury the shareholders in an avalanche of trivial information—a result that is hardly conducive to informed decisionmaking." It further explained that to fulfill the materiality requirement "there must be a substantial likelihood that the disclosure of the omitted fact would have been viewed by the reasonable investor as having significantly altered the 'total mix' of information made available." We now expressly adopt the *TSC Industries* standard of materiality for the § 10(b) and Rule 10b–5 context.

The application of this materiality standard to preliminary merger discussions is not self-evident. Where the impact of the corporate development on the target's fortune is certain and clear, the *TSC Industries* materiality definition admits straightforward application. Where, on the other hand, the event is contingent or speculative in nature, it is difficult to ascertain whether the "reasonable investor" would have considered the omitted information significant at the time. Merger negotiations, because of the ever-present possibility that the contemplated transaction will not be effectuated, fall into the latter category.

Even before this Court's decision in *TSC Industries,* the Second Circuit had explained the role of the materiality requirement of Rule 10b–5, with respect to contingent or speculative information or events, in a manner that gave that term meaning that is independent of the other provisions of the Rule. Under such circumstances, materiality "will depend at any given time upon a balancing of both the indicated probability that the event will occur and the anticipated magnitude of the event in light of the totality of the company activity." Interestingly, neither the Third Circuit decision adopting the agreement-in-principle test nor petitioners here take issue with this general standard. Rather, they suggest that with respect to preliminary merger discussions, there are good reasons to draw a line at agreement on price and structure.

In a subsequent decision, Judge Friendly, writing for a Second Circuit panel, applied the *Texas Gulf Sulphur* probability/magnitude approach in the specific context of preliminary merger negotiations. After acknowledging that materiality is something to be determined on the basis of the particular facts of each case, he stated:

> "Since a merger in which it is bought out is the most important event that can occur in a small corporation's life, to wit, its death, we think that inside information, as regards a merger of this sort, can become material at an earlier stage than would be the case as regards lesser transactions—and this even though the mortality rate of mergers in such formative stages is doubtless high."

SEC v. Geon Industries, Inc., 531 F.2d 39, 47–48 (C.A.2 1976). We agree with that analysis.

Whether merger discussions in any particular case are material therefore depends on the facts. Generally, in order to assess the probability that the event will occur, a factfinder will need to look to indicia of interest in the transaction at the highest corporate levels. Without attempting to catalog all such possible factors, we note by way of example that board resolutions, instructions to investment bankers, and actual negotiations between principals or their intermediaries may serve as indicia of interest. To assess the magnitude of the transaction to the issuer of the securities allegedly manipulated, a factfinder will need to consider such facts as the size of the two corporate entities and of the potential premiums over market value. No particular event or factor short of closing the transaction need be either necessary or sufficient by itself to render merger discussions material.[17]

As we clarify today, materiality depends on the significance the reasonable investor would place on the withheld or misrepresented information.[18] The fact-specific inquiry we endorse here is consistent with the approach a number of courts have taken in assessing the materiality of merger negotiations. Because the standard of materiality we have adopted differs from that used by both courts below, we remand the case for reconsideration of the question whether a grant of summary judgment is appropriate on this record.

2. QUANTITATIVE AND QUALITATIVE MATERIALITY

As the Court makes clear in *TSC*, not every false or misleading statement is material. Must the statement have played a significant role in bringing about the matter submitted to a vote? Does only information bearing on financial matters have a bearing on a shareholder's voting decision? Or do other non-financial factors bear on a shareholder's decision? Are the proxy rules meant to protect more than the shareholder's financial interest?

Misstatements or omissions related to financial information are generally quantitative, but corporate disclosures generally contain a good deal of qualitative information that is not expressed in numbers. Courts and the SEC are generally more comfortable in assessing quantitative materiality; but they are often called on to apply standards of qualitative

---

[17] To be actionable, of course, a statement must also be misleading. Silence, absent a duty to disclose, is not misleading under Rule 10b–5. "No comment" statements are generally the functional equivalent of silence. *See In re Carnation Co., supra.* See also New York Stock Exchange Listed Company Manual § 202.01 (premature public announcement may properly be delayed for valid business purpose and where adequate security can be maintained); American Stock Exchange Company Guide §§ 401–405 (similar provisions).

It has been suggested that given current market practices, a "no comment" statement is tantamount to an admission that merger discussions are underway. That may well hold true to the extent that issuers adopt a policy of truthfully denying merger rumors when no discussions are underway, and of issuing "no comment" statements when they are in the midst of negotiations. There are, of course, other statement policies firms could adopt; we need not now advise issuers as to what kind of practice to follow, within the range permitted by law. Perhaps more importantly, we think that creating an exception to a regulatory scheme founded on a prodisclosure legislative philosophy, because complying with the regulation might be "bad for business," is a role for Congress, not this Court.

[18] We find no authority in the statute, the legislative history, or our previous decisions, for varying the standard of materiality depending on who brings the action or whether insiders are alleged to have profited.

We recognize that trading (and profit making) by insiders can serve as *an* indication of materiality. We are not prepared to agree, however, that "[i]n cases of the disclosure of inside information to a favored few, determination of materiality has a different aspect than when the issue is, for example, an inaccuracy in a publicly disseminated press release." Devising two different standards of materiality, one for situations where insiders have traded in abrogation of their duty to disclose or abstain (or for that matter when any disclosure duty has been breached), and another covering affirmative misrepresentations by those under no duty to disclose (but under the ever-present duty not to mislead), would effectively collapse the materiality requirement into the analysis of defendant's disclosure duties.

materiality. These standards often raise questions about "the subjective intentions and motivations of those involved in making disclosure decisions without reference to the economic significance of the information in question." John J. Jenkins, *The SEC's Renewed Embrace of Qualitative Materiality in Enforcement Proceedings*, 13 Corp. Gov. Advisor No. 5, 22, 24 (September/October 2005).

The Note to Rule 14a–9 sheds some light on these questions. In pertinent part, it provides that in some circumstances, a statement may be misleading if it relates to "material which directly or indirectly impugns character, integrity or personal reputation, or directly or indirectly makes charges concerning improper, illegal or immoral conduct or associations, without factual foundation."

These questions have jurisdictional significance. If a company must disclose information that is material in relation to some goal other than financial protection, great sweep is given to the federal securities laws and to the SEC's power to influence corporate conduct. Section 14(a) gives the Commission power to prescribe rules and regulations it deems "necessary or appropriate in the public interest or for the protection of investors." Presumably the words "in the public interest" have some meaning that, according to one writer (one of the co-authors of this Casebook) "would seem at least to permit the Commission to take into account the broader public interest when acting in areas near the margins of investor protection." Russell B. Stevenson, Jr., *The SEC and Foreign Bribery*, 32 Bus. Law. 53 (1976).

In some cases, the real focus of the shareholder's attack is management's conduct—a state fiduciary claim in federal disclosure garb. For example, if management proposes a patently unfair merger, but scrupulously discloses its financial terms, has there been a violation of the proxy rules? Must the unfairness be specifically identified and the merger characterized as unfair?

In *Golub v. PPD Corp.*, 576 F.2d 759 (8th Cir.1978), plaintiffs alleged that a corporation's sale of assets to a related person was unfair, and that the proxy statement did not disclose management's improper motives. The court upheld dismissal of the complaint, stating:

> [The] plaintiffs are not complaining about any absence of facts in the proxy statement. Their complaint is that those who prepared the statement did not "disclose" what the plaintiffs say was the true motivation of management in selling the assets of the company, and did not characterize the bonus aspects of the transaction as plaintiffs would have it characterized. Under the [1934] Act and regulations plaintiffs were not entitled to have such a "disclosure" or such a characterization.

It is quite possible that plaintiffs may have a claim against the defendants or some of them under applicable state law. If so, plaintiffs are free to pursue that claim in an appropriate forum.

Id. at 764–65.

In *In the Matter of Huntington Bancshares, Inc.*, S.E.C. Release No. 2251, 2005 WL 1797110 (June 2, 2005), the SEC signaled a potential return to enforcement actions based on the qualitative materiality of misstatements or omissions. In *Huntington Bancshares*, the SEC found that while the company's accounting misstatements may have been quantitatively immaterial, "the accounting practices at issue enabled Huntington Bancshares to 'meet or exceed analysts' expectations' and led to the receipt by the executives of incentive bonuses that were tied to earnings performance. The SEC cited Staff Accounting Bulletin No. 99 for the proposition that the 'materiality is defined in qualitative as well as quantitative terms' and that, under that standard, financial misstatements 'of even a small magnitude may be material depending on the surrounding facts and circumstances.' "

In thinking about the relationship between conduct and disclosure, consider whether the failure to disclose violations of the law is a material omission. One answer might be that law violations are material if the anticipated penalty imposed on the corporation would be financially significant under a traditional investment analysis. But suppose the violation would result in relatively insignificant penalties or, even better from the company's standpoint, would result in a substantial net benefit for the company. A company might have violated an environmental law that enabled it to dispose of waste products at a great saving. Or its bribes of a public official might have resulted in substantial financial benefits. Are investors interested in requiring disclosure of such information especially where the disclosure might undermine the company's profit-maximizing activities? The theory for requiring such disclosure is that the information relates to the integrity of corporate management which is material to investors when making a voting decision.

On February 2, 2010, the SEC issued an interpretative release to provide guidance on the application of its disclosure requirements as they apply to climate change matters. In the release, the SEC stated that the release did not affect existing disclosure obligations and that its purpose was to provide clarity with respect to climate change disclosures and to remind companies of the need to provide early notice to investors of potential material effects that might result from climate change developments. The SEC noted that disclosure might be necessary in a company's description of its risk factors, the nature of its business, legal proceedings and Management's Discussion and Analysis.

The SEC release came after a number of public petitions from environmental and other groups for rulemaking seeking increased disclosure on climate change matters. The release also followed numerous legislative, regulatory and other initiatives that the SEC noted in the release. The SEC acknowledged the significance of these developments and indicated that companies should consider them in determining whether disclosure would be required.

The SEC emphasized that disclosure would be required only if the climate changes are material to the company. Citing *TSC Industries, Inc. v. Northway, Inc.* and *Basic, Inc. v. Levinson*, the SEC stated that its release did not change the traditional standard of materiality. The SEC, however, did endorse the principle set out in *TSC* that doubts about materiality should be resolved in favor of disclosure. Thus, a company faced with the need to make a materiality determination involving climate change developments would need to consider both the present effect of those developments on the company's business and [the potential future effects of known trends and uncertainties that are reasonably likely to occur.]

3.   STATEMENTS OF OPINION OR BELIEF

a.   Federal Law

Another question that arises in claims under the antifraud provisions of the securities laws is whether statements of opinion can be considered materially false or misleading. Such claims can arise when a corporation's board or management make statements to shareholders about their opinion as to the fairness of a proposed transaction. The Supreme Court addressed the question in *Virginia Bankshares, Inc. v. Sandberg*, 501 U.S. 1083 (1991). The case was another one involving a merger designed to "freeze out" a minority shareholder interest. The proxy statement that recommended that the shareholders vote to approve the transaction stated: ["The Plan of Merger has been approved by the Board of Directors because it provides an opportunity for the Bank's public shareholders to achieve a high value for their shares."] The bank argued that this was merely an expression of opinion, and that such "statements of opinion or belief incorporating indefinite and unverifiable expressions" could not ever be material. The Supreme Court rejected that argument, holding that a statement of opinion did, after all amount to a statement of a fact, and that if the maker of the statement did not actually hold the opinion, the statement was false. Although it made a point that not all misstatements of an opinion are material, it was clear that one that met the *TSC Industries* test could be material to investors.

b.   State Law

Although arising under Delaware law rather than § 14(a), the following case raises an issue similar to the one in *Virginia Bankshares*, although rather than a statement of opinion or belief, the statement related to whether the board had, in fact, performed its fiduciary duty in evaluating a merger proposal before recommending it to the shareholders.

GANTLER V. STEPHENS
965 A.2d 695 (Del.2009).

JACOBS, JUSTICE.

First Niles, a Delaware corporation headquartered in Niles, Ohio, is a holding company whose sole business is to own and operate the Home Federal Savings and Loan Association of Niles ("Home Federal" or the "Bank"). The Bank is a federally chartered stock savings association that operates a single branch in Niles, Ohio.

In late 2003, First Niles was operating in a depressed local economy, with little to no growth in the Bank's assets and anticipated low growth for the future. At that time Stephens, who was Chairman, President, CEO and founder of First Niles and the Bank, was beyond retirement age and there was no heir apparent among the Company's officers. The acquisition market for banks like Home Federal was brisk, however, and First Niles was thought to be an excellent acquisition for another financial institution. Accordingly, the First Niles Board sought advice on strategic opportunities available to the Company, and in August 2004, decided that First Niles should put itself up for sale.

At the March 2005 board meeting rejected the only firm offer, that of First Place, by a 4–1 vote, allegedly without any discussion or deliberation. The dissenting director, who subsequently resigned, is the plaintiff in this litigation.

On April 18, 2005, Stephens circulated a recapitalization proposal that would reclassify the shares of holders of 300 or fewer shares of First Niles common stock into a new issue of Series A Preferred Stock with limited voting rights. On June 5, 2006, based on the advice of management and First Niles' general counsel, the board determined that the recapitalization plan was fair both to the First Niles shareholders who would receive the new preferred stock and those shareholders who would continue to hold First Niles common stock and on June 19, 2006, the board voted unanimously to amend the Company's articles of incorporation to reflect the features of the plan.

On November 16, 2006, the Board disseminated a definitive proxy statement ("Reclassification Proxy" or "Proxy") to the First Niles shareholders.

In the Reclassification Proxy, the Board represented that the proposed Reclassification would allow First Niles to "save significant legal, accounting and administrative expenses" relating to public disclosure and reporting requirements under the Exchange Act.

The Reclassification Proxy also disclosed alternative transactions that the Board had considered, including a cash-out merger, a reverse stock-split, an issue tender offer, expense reduction and a business combination. The Proxy stated that each of the directors and officers of First Niles had "a conflict of interest with respect to [the Reclassification] because he or she is in a position to structure it in such a way that benefits his or her interests differently from the interests of unaffiliated shareholders." The Proxy further disclosed that the Company had received one firm merger offer, and that "[a]fter careful deliberations, the board determined in its business judgment the proposal was not in the best interests of the Company or our shareholders and rejected the proposal."

We conclude that the Proxy disclosures concerning the Board's deliberations about the First Place bid were materially misleading.

It is well-settled law that "directors of Delaware corporations [have] a fiduciary duty to disclose fully and fairly all material information within the board's control when it seeks shareholder action." That duty "attaches to proxy statements and any other disclosures in contemplation of stockholder action." The essential inquiry here is whether the alleged omission or misrepresentation is material. The burden of establishing materiality rests with the plaintiff, who must demonstrate "a substantial likelihood that the disclosure of the omitted fact would have been viewed by the reasonable investor as having significantly altered the 'total mix' of information made available."

In the Reclassification Proxy, the Board disclosed that "[a]fter careful deliberations, the board determined in its business judgment that the [First Place merger] proposal was not in the best interest of the Company or our shareholders and rejected the [merger] proposal." Although boards are "not required to disclose all available information[,] . . ." "once [they] travel[ ] down the road of partial disclosure of . . . [prior bids] us[ing] . . . vague language . . . , they ha[ve] an obligation to provide the stockholders with an accurate, full, and fair characterization of those historic events."

By stating that they "careful[ly] deliberat[ed]," the Board was representing to the shareholders that it had considered the Sales Process on its objective merits and had determined that the Reclassification would better serve the Company than a merger. The Court of Chancery found, however, that the Board's Reclassification Proxy disclosure of "careful deliberations" about terminating the Sales Process was immaterial, because it would not alter the total mix of information to "omit[ ] that phrase in its entirety." We disagree and conclude that that disclosure was materially misleading.

The Reclassification Proxy specifically represented that the First Niles officers and directors "ha[d] a conflict of interest with respect to the [Reclassification] because he or she is in a position to structure it in a way that benefits his or her interests differently from the interests of unaffiliated shareholders." Given the defendant fiduciaries' admitted conflict of interest, a reasonable shareholder would likely find significant—indeed, reassuring—a representation by a conflicted Board that the Reclassification was superior to a potential merger which, after "careful deliberations," the Board had "carefully considered" and rejected. In such circumstances, it cannot be concluded as a matter of law, that disclosing that there was little or no deliberation would not alter the total mix of information provided to the shareholders.

The Vice Chancellor's finding that the challenged phrase could have been omitted in its entirety has the same infirmity. Had the "careful deliberations" representation never been made, the shareholders might well have evaluated the Reclassification more skeptically, and perhaps even less favorably on its merits, for two reasons. First, the shareholders would have had no information about the Reclassification's desirability vis-à-vis other alternatives. Second, they were told that the Board and Management had a conflict of interest in the one transaction that their fiduciaries had determined to endorse.

We are mindful of the case law holding that a corporate board is not obligated to disclose in a proxy statement the details of merger negotiations that have "gone south," since such information "would be [n]either viably practical [n]or material to shareholders in the meaningful way intended by . . . case law." Even so, a board cannot properly claim in a proxy statement that it had carefully deliberated and decided that its preferred transaction better served the corporation than the alternative, if in fact the Board rejected the alternative transaction without serious consideration. The complaint's allegation that at its March 9, 2005 meeting the Board voted to reject a merger with First Place without any discussion, supports a reasonable inference that the Board did not "carefully deliberate" on the merits of that transaction.

C. CAUSATION

In order for a misstatement or omission to be actionable under the proxy rules, it must not only be material, but it must cause some harm to the complaining shareholders. That raises a question as to what they must allege and prove to obtain a remedy. Must they show that the outcome of the vote would have been different were it not for the false statement or omission? That would obviously present difficult, if not insuperable, problems of proof. Moreover, what if the transaction does not require shareholder approval, but, as was the case in *Virginia Bankshares,* management solicits is anyway?

Handwritten note in top-left margin:
Merg owned 50+% of AL
AL owned 33% of Mer

LINK" IN THE TRANSACTION

ELECTRIC AUTO-LITE CO.
396 U.S. 375 (1970).

ed the opinion of the Court:

consider a basic aspect of the implied private § 14(a) of the Securities Exchange Act of 1934, I. Case Co. v. Borak. As in *Borak* the asserted erger was accomplished through the use of a terially false or misleading. [The question with ..l relationship must be shown between such a statement and the merger to establish a cause of action based on the violation of the Act.]

Petitioners were shareholders of the Electric Auto-Lite Company until 1963, when it was merged into Mergenthaler Linotype Company. They brought suit on the day before the shareholders' meeting at which the vote was to take place on the merger against Auto-Lite, Mergenthaler, and a third company, American Manufacturing Company, Inc. The complaint sought an injunction against the voting by Auto-Lite's management of all proxies obtained by means of an allegedly misleading proxy solicitation; however, it did not seek a temporary restraining order, and the voting went ahead as scheduled the following day. Several months later petitioners filed an amended complaint, seeking to have the merger set aside and to obtain such other relief as might be proper.

Petitioners alleged that the proxy statement sent out by the Auto-Lite management to solicit shareholders' votes in favor of the merger was misleading, in violation of § 14(a) of the Act and SEC Rule 14a–9 thereunder. Petitioners recited that before the merger Mergenthaler owned over 50% of the outstanding shares of Auto-Lite common stock, and had been in control of Auto-Lite for two years. American Manufacturing in turn owned about one-third of the outstanding shares of Mergenthaler, and for two years had been in voting control of Mergenthaler and, through it, of Auto-Lite. Petitioners charged that in light of these circumstances the proxy statement was misleading in that it told Auto-Lite shareholders that their board of directors recommended approval of the merger without also informing them that all 11 of Auto-Lite's directors were nominees of Mergenthaler and were under the "control and domination of Mergenthaler." Petitioners asserted the right to complain of this alleged violation both derivatively on behalf of Auto-Lite and as representatives of the class of all its minority shareholders.

On petitioners' motion for summary judgment with respect to Count II, the District Court for the Northern District of Illinois ruled as a matter of law that the claimed defect in the proxy statement was, in light of the circumstances in which the statement was made, a material omission. The District Court concluded, from its reading of the *Borak* opinion, that it had [to hold a hearing on the issue whether there was "a causal connection between the finding that there has been a violation of the disclosure requirements of § 14(a) and the alleged injury to the plaintiffs" before it could consider what remedies would be appropriate.]

After holding such a hearing, the court found that under the terms of the merger agreement, an affirmative vote of two-thirds of the Auto-Lite shares was required for approval of the merger, and that the respondent companies owned and controlled about 54% of the outstanding shares. Therefore, to obtain authorization of the merger, respondents had to secure the approval of a substantial number of the minority shareholders. At the stockholders' meeting, approximately, 950,000 shares, out of 1,160,000 shares outstanding were voted in favor of the merger. This included 317,000 votes obtained by proxy from the minority shareholders, votes that were "necessary and indispensable to the approval of the merger." The District Court concluded that a causal relationship had thus been shown, and it granted an interlocutory judgment in favor of petitioners on the issue of liability, referring the case to a master for consideration of appropriate relief.

The District Court made the certification required by 28 U.S.C. § 1292(b), and respondents took an interlocutory appeal to the Court of Appeals for the Seventh Circuit. That court affirmed the District Court's conclusion that the proxy statement was materially deficient, but reversed on the question of causation. The court acknowledged that, if an injunction had been sought a sufficient time before the stockholders' meeting, "corrective measures would have been appropriate." However, since this suit was brought too late for preventive action, the courts had to determine "whether the misleading statement and omission caused the submission of sufficient proxies," as a prerequisite to a determination of liability under the Act. [If the respondents could show, "by a preponderance of probabilities, that the merger would have received a sufficient vote even if the proxy statement had not been misleading in the respect found," petitioners would be entitled to no relief of any kind.]

The Court of Appeals acknowledged that this test corresponds to the common law fraud test of whether the injured party relied on the misrepresentation. However, rightly concluding that "[r]eliance by thousands of individuals, as here, can scarcely be inquired into", the court ruled that the issue was to be determined by proof of the fairness of the terms of the merger. If respondents could show that the merger had merit and was fair to the minority shareholders, the trial court would be justified in concluding that a sufficient number of shareholders would have approved the merger had there been no deficiency in the proxy statement. In that case respondents would be entitled to a judgment in their favor.

Claiming that the Court of Appeals has construed this Court's decision in *Borak* in a manner that frustrates the statute's policy of enforcement through private litigation, the petitioners then sought review in this Court. We granted certiorari, believing that resolution of this basic issue should be made at this stage of the litigation and not postponed until after a trial under the Court of Appeals' decision.

As we stressed in *Borak,* § 14(a) stemmed from a congressional belief that "[f]air corporate suffrage is an important right that should attach to every equity security bought on a public exchange." The decision below, by permitting all liability to be foreclosed on the basis of a finding that the merger was fair, would allow the stockholders to be bypassed, at least where the only legal challenge to the merger is a suit for retrospective relief after the meeting has been held. A judicial appraisal of the merger's merits could be substituted for the actual and informed vote of the stockholders.

The result would be to insulate from private redress an entire category of proxy violations—those relating to matters other than the terms of the merger. Even outrageous misrepresentations in a proxy solicitation, if they did not relate to the terms of the transaction, would give rise to no cause of action under § 14(a). Particularly if carried over to enforcement actions by the Securities and Exchange Commission itself, such a result would subvert the congressional purpose of ensuring full and fair disclosure to shareholders.

Further, recognition of the fairness of the merger as a complete defense would confront small shareholders with an additional obstacle to making a successful challenge to a proposal recommended through a defective proxy statement. The risk that they would be unable to rebut the corporation's evidence of the fairness of the proposal, and thus to establish their cause of action, would be bound to discourage such shareholders from the private enforcement of the proxy rules that "provides a necessary supplement to Commission action."[5]

Such a frustration of the congressional policy is not required by anything in the wording of the statute or in our opinion in the *Borak* case. Section 14(a) declares it "unlawful" to solicit proxies in contravention of Commission rules, and SEC Rule 14a–9 prohibits solicitations "containing

---

[5]   The Court of Appeals' ruling that "causation" may be negated by proof of the fairness of the merger also rests on a dubious behavioral assumption. There is no justification for presuming that the shareholders of every corporation are willing to accept any and every fair merger offer put before them; yet such a presumption is implicit in the opinion of the Court of Appeals. That court gave no indication of what evidence petitioners might adduce, once respondents had established that the merger proposal was equitable, in order to show that the shareholders would nevertheless have rejected it if the solicitation had not been misleading. Proof of actual reliance by thousands of individuals would, as the court acknowledged, not be feasible. In practice, therefore, the objective fairness of the proposal would seemingly be determinative of liability. But in view of the many other factors that might lead shareholders to prefer their current position to that of owners of a larger, combined enterprise, it is pure conjecture to assume that the fairness of the proposal will always be determinative of their vote.

any statement which is false or misleading with respect to any material fact, or which omits to state any material fact necessary in order to make the statements therein not false or misleading." Use of a solicitation that is materially misleading is itself a violation of law, as the Court of Appeals recognized in stating that injunctive relief would be available to remedy such a defect if sought prior to the stockholders' meeting. Referring to the argument made by petitioners there "that the merger can be dissolved only if it was fraudulent or non-beneficial, issues upon which the proxy material would not bear," the Court stated: "But the causal relationship of the proxy material and the merger are questions of fact to be resolved at trial, not here. We therefore do not discuss this point further." In the present case there has been a hearing specifically directed to the causation problem. The question before the Court is whether the facts found on the basis of that hearing are sufficient in law to establish petitioners' cause of action, and we conclude that they are.

Where the misstatement or omission in a proxy statement has been shown to be "material," as it was found to be here, that determination itself indubitably embodies a conclusion that the defect was of such a character that it might have been considered important by a reasonable shareholder who was in the process of deciding how to vote. This requirement that the defect have a significant *propensity* to affect the voting process is found in the express terms of Rule 14a–9, and it adequately serves the purpose of ensuring that a cause of action cannot be established by proof of a defect so trivial, or so unrelated to the transaction for which approval is sought, that correction of the defect or imposition of liability would not further the interests protected by § 14(a).

There is no need to supplement this requirement, as did the Court of Appeals, with a requirement of proof of whether the defect actually had a decisive effect on the voting. [Where there has been a finding of materiality, a shareholder has made a sufficient showing of causal relationship between the violation and the injury for which he seeks redress, if, as here, he proves that the proxy solicitation itself, rather than the particular defect in the solicitation materials, was an essential link in the accomplishment of the transaction.] This objective test will avoid the impracticalities of determining how many votes were affected, and, by resolving doubts in favor of those the statute is designed to protect, will effectuate the congressional policy of ensuring that the shareholders are able to make an informed choice when they are consulted on corporate transactions.[7]

---

[7] We need not decide in this case whether causation could be shown where the management controls a sufficient number of shares to approve the transaction without any votes from the minority. Even in that situation, if the management finds it necessary for legal or practical reasons to solicit proxies from minority shareholders, at least one court has held that the proxy solicitation might be sufficiently related to the merger to satisfy the causation requirement, *see Laurenzano v. Einbender*, 264 F.Supp. 356 (D.C.E.D.N.Y.1966).

Our conclusion that petitioners have established their case by showing that proxies necessary to approval of the merger were obtained by means of a materially misleading solicitation implies nothing about the form of relief to which they may be entitled. We held in *Borak* that upon finding a violation the courts were "to be alert to provide such remedies as are necessary to make effective the congressional purpose," noting specifically that such remedies are not to be limited to prospective relief. In devising retrospective relief for violation of the proxy rules, the federal courts should consider the same factors that would govern the relief granted for any similar illegality or fraud. One important factor may be the fairness of the terms of the merger. Possible forms of relief will include setting aside the merger or granting other equitable relief, but, as the Court of Appeals below noted, nothing in the statutory policy "requires the court to unscramble a corporate transaction merely because a violation occurred." In selecting a remedy the lower courts should exercise " 'the sound discretion which guides the determinations of courts of equity,' " keeping in mind the role of equity as "the instrument for nice adjustment and reconciliation between the public interest and private needs as well as between competing private claims."

Monetary relief will, of course, also be a possibility. Where the defect in the proxy solicitation relates to the specific terms of the merger, the district court might appropriately order an accounting to ensure that the shareholders receive the value that was represented as coming to them. On the other hand, where, as here, the misleading aspect of the solicitation did not relate to terms of the merger, monetary relief might be afforded to the shareholders only if the merger resulted in a reduction of the earnings or earnings potential of their holdings. In short, damages should be recoverable only to the extent that they can be shown. If commingling of the assets and operations of the merged companies makes it impossible to establish direct injury from the merger, relief might be predicated on a determination of the fairness of the terms of the merger at the time it was approved. These questions, of course, are for decision in the first instance by the District Court on remand, and our singling out of some of the possibilities is not intended to exclude others.

Although the question of relief must await further proceedings in the District Court, our conclusion that petitioners have established their cause of action indicates that the Court of Appeals should have affirmed the partial summary judgment on the issue of liability. The result would have been not only that respondents, rather than petitioners, would have borne the costs of the appeal, but also, we think, that petitioners would have been entitled to an interim award of litigation expenses and reasonable attorneys' fees. We agree with the position taken by petitioners, and by the United States as *amicus,* that petitioners, who have established a violation of the securities laws by their corporation and its officials, should be reimbursed by the corporation or its survivor for the costs of establishing the violation.

While the general American rule is that attorneys' fees are not ordinarily recoverable as costs, both the courts and Congress have developed exceptions to this rule for situations in which overriding considerations indicate the need for such a recovery. A primary judge-created exception has been to award expenses where a plaintiff has successfully maintained a suit, usually on behalf of a class, that benefits a group of others in the same manner as himself. To allow the others to obtain from the plaintiff's efforts without contributing equally to the litigation expenses would be to enrich the others unjustly at the plaintiff's expense. This suit presents such a situation. The dissemination of misleading proxy solicitations was a "deceit practiced on the stockholders as a group," and the expenses of petitioners' lawsuit have been incurred for the benefit of the corporation and the other shareholders.

The fact that this suit has not yet produced, and may never produce, a monetary recovery from which the fees could be paid does not preclude an award based on this rationale.

In many suits under § 14(a), particularly where the violation does not relate to the terms of the transaction for which proxies are solicited, it may be impossible to assign monetary value to the benefit. Nevertheless, the stress placed by Congress on the importance of fair and informed corporate suffrage leads to the conclusion that, in vindicating the statutory policy, petitioners have rendered a substantial service to the corporation and its shareholders. Whether petitioners are successful in showing a need for significant relief may be a factor in determining whether a further award should later be made. But regardless of the relief granted, private stockholders' actions of this sort "involve corporate therapeutics," and furnish a benefit to all shareholders by providing an important means of enforcement of the proxy statute. To award attorneys' fees in such a suit to a plaintiff who has succeeded in establishing a cause of action is not to saddle the unsuccessful party with the expenses but to impose them on the class that has benefited from them and that would have had to pay them had it brought the suit.

For the foregoing reasons we conclude that the judgment of the Court of Appeals should be vacated and the case remanded to that court for further proceedings consistent with this opinion.

2. CAUSATION WHEN SOLICITATION NOT REQUIRED

In some settings, corporations solicit shareholder approval of transactions although such approval is "not required by law or corporate bylaw." Are proxy solicitations in connection with transactions not requiring shareholder approval "essential," for purposes of demonstrating that a violation of Rule 14a–9 caused some cognizable injury to shareholders who were solicited?

VIRGINIA BANKSHARES, INC. V. SANDBERG
501 U.S. 1083 (1991).

[This case addressed two important issues regarding federal proxy regulation. The first, discussed above, was whether a false statement of opinion or belief could ever be considered materially misleading to investors. The second was whether such a statement could support an action under § 14(e). The transaction in question was a "freeze-out" merger in which First Virginia Bank, was merged into its parent holding company, Virginia Bankshares, Inc. Because the holding company owned all but 15% of the stock of the bank, under Virginia law there was no requirement that the bank secure the approval of the minority shareholders. The parent owned sufficient shares to approve the transaction without their vote. Nevertheless, for reasons not explained in the opinion, the bank decided to solicit proxies approving the transaction anyway, perhaps for the sake of appearance, or perhaps in hopes that a vote by the minority shareholders approving the transaction would help insulate it from challenge. The following excerpt from the case addresses the issue.]

The second issue before us, left open in *Mills v. Electric Auto-Lite Co.,* n. 7, is whether causation of damages compensable through the implied private right of action under § 14(a) can be demonstrated by a member of a class of minority shareholders whose votes are not required by law or corporate bylaw to authorize the transaction giving rise to the claim.

Although a majority stockholder in *Mills* controlled just over half the corporation's shares, a two-thirds vote was needed to approve the merger proposal. [The] Court found the solicitation essential, as contrasted with one addressed to a class of minority shareholders without votes required by law or by-law to authorize the action proposed, and left it for another day to decide whether such a minority shareholder could demonstrate causation.

In this case, respondents address *Mills'* open question by proffering two theories that the proxy solicitation addressed to them was an "essential link" under the *Mills* causation test. They argue, first, that a link existed and was essential simply because VBI and FABI would have been unwilling to proceed with the merger without the approval manifested by the minority shareholders' proxies, which would not have been obtained without the solicitation's express misstatements and misleading omissions. On this reasoning, the causal connection would depend on a desire to avoid bad shareholder or public relations, and the essential character of the causal link would stem not from the enforceable terms of the parties' corporate relationship, but from one party's apprehension of the ill will of the other.

In the alternative, respondents argue that the proxy statement was an essential link between the directors' proposal and the merger because it was the means to satisfy a state statutory requirement of minority shareholder approval, as a condition for saving the merger from voidability resulting from a conflict of interest on the part of one of the Bank's directors, Jack Beddow, who voted in favor of the merger while also serving as a director of FABI. On this theory, causation would depend on the use of the proxy statement for the purpose of obtaining votes sufficient to bar a minority shareholder from commencing proceedings to declare the merger void.

Although respondents have proffered each of these theories as establishing a chain of causal connection in which the proxy statement is claimed to have been an "essential link," neither theory presents the proxy solicitation as essential in the sense of *Mills'* causal sequence, in which the solicitation links a directors' proposal with the votes legally required to authorize the action proposed. As a consequence, each theory would, if adopted, extend the scope of *Borak* actions beyond the ambit of *Mills,* and expand the class of plaintiffs entitled to bring *Borak* actions to include shareholders whose initial authorization of the transaction prompting the proxy solicitation is unnecessary.

The rule that has emerged in the years since *Borak* and *Mills* came down is that recognition of any private right of action for violating a federal statute must ultimately rest on congressional intent to provide a private remedy. From this the corollary follows that the breadth of the right once recognized should not, as a general matter, grow beyond the scope congressionally intended.

[Justice Souter reviewed the text and legislative history of the 1934 Act and concluded that they provide no guidance with respect to the intended scope of a private right of action.]

The congressional silence that is thus a serious obstacle to the expansion of cognizable *Borak* causation is not, however, a necessarily insurmountable barrier. In *Blue Chip Stamps*, we looked to policy reasons for deciding where the outer limits of the right should lie. We may do no less here, in the face of respondents' pleas for a private remedy to place them on the same footing as shareholders with votes necessary for initial corporate action.

The same threats of speculative claims and procedural intractability that were present in *Blue Chip Stamps* are inherent in respondents' theory of causation linked through the directors' desire for a cosmetic vote. Causation would turn on inferences about what the corporate directors would have thought and done without the minority shareholder approval unneeded to authorize action. The issues would be hazy, their litigation protracted, and their resolution unreliable. Given a choice, we would reject any theory of causation that promised such prospects, and we reject this one.

The theory of causal necessity derived from the requirements of Virginia law dealing with postmerger ratification seeks to identify the essential character of the proxy solicitation from its function in obtaining the minority approval that would preclude a minority suit attacking the merger. Since the link is said to be a step in the process of barring a class of shareholders from resort to a state remedy otherwise available, this theory of causation rests upon the proposition of policy that § 14(a) should provide a federal remedy whenever a false or misleading proxy statement results in the loss under state law of a shareholder plaintiff's state remedy for the enforcement of a state right.

This case does not, however, require us to decide whether § 14(a) provides a cause of action for lost state remedies, since there is no indication in the law or facts before us that the proxy solicitation resulted in any such loss. The contrary appears to be the case. Assuming the soundness of respondents' characterization of the proxy statement as materially misleading, the very terms of the Virginia statute indicate that a favorable minority vote induced by the solicitation would not suffice to render the merger invulnerable to later attack on the ground of the conflict. The statute bars a shareholder from seeking to avoid a transaction tainted by a director's conflict if, inter alia, the minority shareholders ratified the transaction following disclosure of the material facts of the transaction and the conflict. Assuming that the material facts about the merger and Beddow's interests were not accurately disclosed, the minority votes were inadequate to ratify the merger under state law, and there was no loss of state remedy to connect the proxy solicitation with harm to minority shareholders irredressable under state law. Nor is there a claim here that the statement misled respondents into entertaining a false belief that they had no chance to upset the merger, until the time for bringing suit had run out.[14]

The judgment of the Court of Appeals is reversed.

3. CONSTRUCTIVE FRAUD: UNFAIRNESS AS DECEIT

Thus far, we have examined corporate transactions in which disclosures are made to shareholders who are asked to vote. When proxies

---

[14] Respondents do not claim that any other application of a theory of lost state remedies would avail them here. It is clear, for example, that no state appraisal remedy was lost through a § 14(a) violation in this case. Respondent Weinstein and others did seek appraisal under Virginia law in the Virginia courts; their claims were rejected on the explicit grounds that although "[s]tatutory appraisal is now considered the exclusive remedy for stockholders opposing a merger," "dissenting stockholders in bank mergers do not even have this solitary remedy available to them," because "Va. Code § 6.1–43 specifically excludes bank mergers from application of § 13.1–730 [the Virginia appraisal statute]." Weinstein does not claim that the Virginia court was wrong and does not rely on this claim in any way. Thus, the § 14(a) violation could have had no effect on the availability of an appraisal remedy, for there never was one.

are solicited in a deceptive manner and the proxy solicitation constitutes an "essential link" in effecting the transaction, shareholders can claim they have been deceived and sue under § 14(a) and Rule 14a–9. More difficult questions arise when the transaction does not require a shareholder vote or disclosure to shareholders, as when a parent corporation merges with a 90-percent-owned subsidiary in a "short form merger." Is financial unfairness in such transactions tantamount to deceit?

As we will see in Chapter 18, proof of financial unfairness may not be sufficient to establish a breach of fiduciary duty under state law. State law principles can sometimes insulate arguably unfair transactions from judicial scrutiny, especially if those transactions have been approved by independent directors. To avoid litigating their claims under state law and to obtain the procedural advantages available under federal law, aggrieved shareholders often have used federal securities law to challenge transactions they considered unfair. In the absence of a proxy solicitation, the most attractive alternative is a suit under Rule 10b–5.

Rule 10b–5 is concerned with decisions to purchase or sell stock, rather than with decisions about how to vote. As interpreted by the Supreme Court, Rule 10b–5 prohibits both false and misleading statements and fraudulent acts and practices in connection with the purchase or sale of any security. In early cases when plaintiffs attempted to use Rule 10b–5 to challenge unfair or "constructively fraudulent" transactions, the courts rebuffed their efforts.

However, in a series of decisions in the 1960s and 1970s, the Second Circuit suggested that shareholders could challenge a corporation's securities transactions that suffered from financial unfairness under Rule 10b–5, even if the corporation's shareholders neither voted nor sold shares. *See Schoenbaum v. Firstbrook*, 405 F.2d 215 (2d Cir.1968) (corporation's self-dealing securities transaction with controlling shareholder for "inadequate consideration" acted as a deceit on the corporation's shareholders, even though it had been approved by the corporation's independent directors).

This expansive view ended with the Supreme Court's decision in *Santa Fe Industries, Inc. v. Green*, 430 U.S. 462 (1977). The case involved a claim by minority shareholders of Kirby Lumber Company, of which Santa Fe had acquired 95% of the outstanding stock. To eliminate the remaining minority interest in Kirby, Santa Fe executed a short-form merger in which the minority shareholders received cash. Some of them sued Santa Fe, claiming that the price they received in the transaction was unfair and based on a "fraudulent" appraisal, and that this constituted a violation of Rule 10b–5. The Supreme Court rejected this claim, holding that the matter was essentially a question of a breach of state law fiduciary duty, not a material misrepresentation. As a matter of policy, the Court held, this was a matter "traditionally relegated to state law," and Delaware "has supplied minority shareholders with a cause of action in the Delaware Court of Chancery to recover the fair value of shares allegedly undervalued in a short-form merger." Accordingly, it was "entirely appropriate in this instance to relegate respondent and others in his situation to whatever remedy is created by state law."

In *Santa Fe,* the plaintiffs conceded that advance disclosure to shareholders would have served no function, not only because they had no vote but because their only remedy was appraisal. Hence, there could be no "material" omission in the failure to disclose. This reasoning left open the possibility that the availability of a federal cause of action under Rule 10b–5 could turn on whether shareholders, if fully informed, could maintain a state cause of action, presumably for breach of fiduciary duty. In such a case, the court would be placed back into the business of evaluating the fairness of a transaction which is what *Santa Fe* was intended to prevent.

Nevertheless, subsequent cases in the Courts of Appeal suggest that *Santa Fe* is not always an insuperable barrier to federal actions based on omissions to state facts relevant to the fairness of a transaction under state law. In *Goldberg v. Meridor,* 567 F.2d 209 (2d Cir.1977), a stockholder of Universal Gas & Oil Company, Inc. (UGO), Goldberg, brought suit against UGO's controlling parent, Maritimecor, S.A. and a number of other parties, challenging Maritimecor's sale of essentially all of its assets to UGO in exchange for up to 4,200,000 shares of UGO stock and the assumption by UGO of Maritimecor's debts. Goldberg alleged that this transaction, for which shareholder approval was neither required nor solicited, violated Rule 10b–5.

The essence of the amended complaint was that the exchange was unfair to UGO because Maritimecor had huge current liabilities and few liquid assets. Thus, UGO was likely to be rendered insolvent by the challenged transaction. The defendants moved to dismiss, on the ground that the amended complaint failed to allege any deception or non-disclosure necessary to state a claim under Rule 10b–5. In response, plaintiff submitted two press releases that described the Martimecor-UGO agreement, but failed to disclose that current liabilities of Maritimecor exceeded the shareholder's net equity and that Maritimecor had overstated its assets.

Judge Friendly, writing for the Second Circuit, concluded the press releases were materially misleading:

> Here the complaint alleged "deceit upon UGO's minority shareholders" and alleged misrepresentation as to the UGO-Maritimecor transaction at least in the sense of failure to state material facts "necessary in order to make the statements made, in the light of the circumstances under which they were made, not misleading," Rule 10b–5(b). The nub of the matter is that the conduct attacked in [*Santa Fe*] did not violate the "fundamental

purpose" of the Act as implementing a "philosophy of full disclosure", the conduct here attacked does.

Defendants contend that even if all this is true, the failure to make a public disclosure or even the making of a misleading disclosure would have no effect, since no action by stockholders to approve the UGO-Maritimecor transaction was required.

Here there is surely a significant likelihood that if a reasonable director of UGO had known the facts alleged by plaintiff rather than the barebones of the press releases, he would not have voted for the transaction with Maritimecor.

Beyond this Goldberg and other minority shareholders would not have been without remedy if the alleged facts had been disclosed. The doubts entertained by our brother as to the existence of injunctive remedies in New York, are unfounded. [There have been a number of New York cases involving] suits by stockholders acting in their own behalf to enjoin the sale of all corporate assets or a merger transaction as to which New York afforded dissenters the remedy of an appraisal. Where an appraisal remedy is not available, the courts of New York have displayed no hesitancy in granting injunctive relief.

The availability of injunctive relief if the defendants had not lulled the minority stockholders of UGO into security by a deceptive disclosure, as they allegedly did, is in sharp contrast to [*Santa Fe,*] where the disclosure following the merger transaction was full and fair, and, as to the premerger period, respondents accepted "the conclusion of both courts below that under Delaware law they could not have enjoined the merger because an appraisal proceeding is their sole remedy in the Delaware courts for any alleged unfairness in the terms of the merger."

Id. at 218–220.

Does *Goldberg* survive *Virginia Bankshares*? Arguably, *Virginia Bankshares* requires a stronger causal link between the alleged deception and the loss of state remedies than that the deception lulled shareholders into complacency. In *Virginia Bankshares* the Supreme Court rejected the minority shareholders' theory of causation on the grounds it "would turn on inferences about what the corporate directors might have done without the minority shareholder approval unneeded to authorize action." A major criticism of *Goldberg* has been its implicit presumption that but for the omission of material information, the plaintiffs would have rushed to state court to seek, and could have obtained, an injunction to prevent the merger. Is the Court's refusal in *Virginia Bankshares* to speculate about "what might have been" equally pertinent to a *Goldberg* claim? What if the plaintiffs can demonstrate that they would have acted differently?

Virginia Bankshares implicitly raises the question of what constitutes the "loss" of a state law remedy. Does being lulled by a deceptive disclosure into not seeking an injunction until it is too late constitute such a loss? Note that *Virginia Bankshares* closes with the caveat that there was no "claim here that the statement misled respondents into entertaining a false belief that they had no chance to upset the merger, until the time for bringing suit had run out." Does this mean that shareholders can complain if the corporate deception *discourages* them from pursuing a viable state law remedy or does it mean that the deception must actually cause shareholders to *forego* such a remedy?

D. CULPABILITY IN PROXY FRAUD ACTIONS

Virginia Bankshares left open the question of whether the standard of culpability to which directors are held in a § 14(a) action is negligence or scienter (the traditional fraud standard). The language of § 14(a), which simply prohibits the solicitation of proxies in violation of SEC rules, provides no guidance nor does the legislative history. Rule 10b–5 (promulgated pursuant to § 10(b), which prohibits "any manipulative or deceptive device or contrivance") requires a showing that the maker of the false or misleading statement acted intentionally, or at least with reckless disregard of the truth or falsity of the statement.

Lower federal courts are divided. A number of courts have held that negligence, not scienter, is the standard for those who solicit proxies, such as corporate directors. As the Third Circuit observed, even an outside director "would have known that the proxy statement in its final form was false if he had read it, which it was his duty to do as a member of the board of directors which was issuing the document to solicit the shareholders' proxies." *Gould v. American-Hawaiian Steamship Co.*, 535 F.2d 761, 776–77 (3d Cir.1976).

But when the defendant did not solicit proxies, some courts have been more demanding. In *Adams v. Standard Knitting Mills*, 623 F.2d 422 (6th Cir.1980), the Sixth Circuit held that scienter is the appropriate standard for the corporation's outside accountants. The court stated:

> Although we are not called on in this case to decide the standard of liability of the corporate issuer of proxy material, we are influenced by the fact that the accountant here, unlike the corporate issuer, does not directly benefit from the proxy vote and is not in privity with the stockholder. Unlike the corporate issuer, the preparation of financial statements to be appended to proxies and other reports is the daily fare of accountants, and the accountant's potential liability for relatively minor mistakes would be enormous under a negligence standard. [I]n the instant case there was no proof of investor reliance on the notes to the financial statements which erroneously described the restriction

on payment of dividends. We can see no reason for a different standard of liability for accountants under the proxy provisions than under 10(b).

Id. at 429.

The Third Circuit, however, has extended the negligence standard to outside advisers of the corporation, such as accountants and investment bankers. In *Herskowitz v. Nutri/System, Inc.,* 857 F.2d 179, 190 (3d Cir. 1988), the court rejected the scienter standard and stated, "since an investment banker rendering a fairness opinion in connection with a leveraged buyout knows full well that it will be used to solicit shareholder approval, and is well paid for the service it performs, we see no convincing reason for not holding it to the same standard of liability as the management it is assisting."

Nonetheless, when the false or misleading statements involve opinions, several District Courts have read the insistence in *Virginia Bankshares* on a showing of both objective and subjective falsity for an opinion to be actionable as imposing a "knowing falsity" requirement—effectively, requiring a showing of scienter. Under this heightened culpability standard, false or misleading fairness opinions given by investment bankers in a merger are not actionable under § 14(a) on a showing of negligence alone.

Further impediments are placed on federal proxy fraud actions by the Private Securities Litigation Reform Act of 1995, which requires that all damages suits brought under the 1934 Act where the defendant's state of mind is at issue must allege "with particularity facts giving rise to a strong inference that the defendant acted with the required state of mind." § 21D(b)(2). This requirement applies not only to cases where the culpability standard is scienter, but also negligence.

E. DUTY OF DISCLOSURE UNDER STATE LAW

1. SOURCE OF THE DUTY

State regulation of proxy solicitations is a logical outgrowth of state statutes governing notice to shareholders of shareholder meetings. Fewer cases have arisen under state law than federal law, however.

State corporate laws vary, but Delaware law is instructive in understanding how disclosure obligations apply to many corporations and their officers, directors, and controlling shareholders. The duty to disclose is not an independent duty but derives from the fiduciary duties of care and loyalty. *Gantler v. Stephens,* excerpted above, is regularly cited for its statement of the basic rule: "It is well-settled law that directors of Delaware corporations [have] a fiduciary duty to disclose fully and fairly all material information within the board's control when it seeks shareholder action.

That duty attaches to proxy statements and any other disclosures in contemplation of stockholder action." 965 A.2d 695, 710 (Del. 2009) (internal quotation marks omitted). Its scope and requirements depend on the context in which the duty arises.

In general, Delaware courts apply the duty of disclosure to directors or controlling shareholders when they place the shareholders in a position where they have to decide whether to sell their stock or seek appraisal. The duty comes into play most often when management solicits shareholder approval through proxy materials that contain a material misstatement or omission. It also applies to short-form mergers; even though no shareholder vote is required, inadequate or misleading disclosure may cause shareholders to forgo their appraisal remedy.

What if the fiduciary making the allegedly misleading disclosure does not seek shareholder action? The duty of disclosure probably does not extend to such cases. *Stroud v. Grace*, 606 A.2d 75 (Del. 1992). In *Stroud*, the board of a closely held corporation approved controversial bylaw amendments that established new qualifications for board membership. The board then sought shareholder ratification at the annual meeting, sending a notice of the meeting to the shareholders. As required by the statute, the notice included a copy of the amended bylaws but did not explain the purpose of the bylaw amendments or the meeting. In upholding the board's actions, the court reaffirmed the principle that "directors of Delaware corporations are under a fiduciary duty to disclose fully and fairly all material information within the board's control when it seeks shareholder action." But the court limited the principle, holding that the common law duty of disclosure did not override the bare-bones disclosure requirements for the notice of meeting specified by the statute—namely, the time and place of the meeting and a copy or summary of any amendment to the corporation's certificate of incorporation.

Although *Stroud* would seem to allow a board to bypass the duty of disclosure by foregoing a proxy solicitation and providing only bare-bones statutory notice, the chances of obtaining sufficient proxies in a public corporation would be slim. Moreover, such a tactic might be viewed as an inequitable manipulation of shareholder voting, in violation of the fiduciary duties laid out in *Schnell v. Chris-Craft Industries* discussed in Chapter 2.

For a good summary of the Delaware duty to disclose, see *In re Wayport, Inc. Litigation*, 76 A.3d 296 (Del.Ch. 2013).

2. LIABILITY FOR FALSE STATEMENTS

MALONE V. BRINCAT
722 A.2d 5 (Del.1998).

HOLLAND, JUSTICE:

Doran Malone, Joseph P. Danielle, and Adrienne M. Danielle, the plaintiffs-appellants, filed this individual and class action in the Court of Chancery. The complaint alleged that the directors of Mercury Finance Company ("Mercury"), a Delaware corporation, breached their fiduciary duty of disclosure. The complaint also alleged that the defendant-appellee, KPMG Peat Marwick LLP ("KPMG") aided and abetted the Mercury directors' breaches of fiduciary duty. The Court of Chancery dismissed the complaint with prejudice pursuant to Chancery Rule 12(b)(6) for failure to state a claim upon which relief may be granted.

The complaint alleged that the director defendants intentionally overstated the financial condition of Mercury on repeated occasions throughout a four-year period in disclosures to Mercury's shareholders. Plaintiffs contend that the complaint states a claim upon which relief can be granted for a breach of the fiduciary duty of disclosure. Plaintiffs also contend that, because the director defendants breached their fiduciary duty of disclosure to the Mercury shareholders, the Court of Chancery erroneously dismissed the aiding and abetting claim against KPMG.

This Court has concluded that the Court of Chancery properly granted the defendants' motions to dismiss the complaint. That dismissal, however, should have been without prejudice. Plaintiffs are entitled to file an amended complaint. Therefore, the judgment of the Court of Chancery is affirmed in part, reversed in part, and remanded for further proceedings consistent with this opinion.

Mercury is a publicly-traded company engaged primarily in purchasing installment sales contracts from automobile dealers and providing short-term installment loans directly to consumers. This action was filed on behalf of the named plaintiffs and all persons (excluding defendants) who owned common stock of Mercury from 1993 through the present and their successors in interest, heirs and assigns (the "putative class"). The complaint alleged that the directors "knowingly and intentionally breached their fiduciary duty of disclosure because the SEC filings made by the directors and every communication from the company to the shareholders since 1994 was materially false" and that "as a direct result of the false disclosures . . . the Company has lost all or virtually all of its value (about $2 billion)." The complaint also alleged that KPMG knowingly participated in the directors' breaches of their fiduciary duty of disclosure.

According to plaintiffs, since 1994, the director defendants caused Mercury to disseminate information containing overstatements of Mercury's earnings, financial performance and shareholders' equity. Mercury's earnings for 1996 were actually only $56.7 million, or $.33 a share, rather than the $120.7 million, or $.70 a share, as reported by the director defendants. Mercury's earnings in 1995 were actually $76.9 million, or $.44 a share, rather than $98.9 million, or $.57 a share, as reported by the director defendants. Mercury's earnings for 1994 were $83 million, or $.47 a share, rather than $86.5 million, or $.49 a share, as reported by the director defendants. Mercury's earnings for 1993 were $64.2 million, rather than $64.9 million, as reported by the director defendants. Shareholders' equity on December 31, 1996 was disclosed by the director defendants as $353 million, but was only $263 million or less. The complaint alleged that all of the foregoing inaccurate information was included or referenced in virtually every filing Mercury made with the SEC and every communication Mercury's directors made to the shareholders during this period of time.

Having alleged these violations of fiduciary duty, which (if true) are egregious, plaintiffs alleged that as "a direct result of [these] false disclosures the company has lost all or virtually all its value (about $2 billion)," and seeks class action status to pursue damages against the directors and KPMG for the individual plaintiffs and common stockholders. The individual director defendants filed a motion to dismiss, contending that they owed no fiduciary duty of disclosure under the circumstances alleged in the complaint. KPMG also filed a motion to dismiss the aiding and abetting claim asserted against it.

After briefing and oral argument, the Court of Chancery granted both of the motions to dismiss with prejudice. The Court of Chancery held that directors have no fiduciary duty of disclosure under Delaware law in the absence of a request for shareholder action. In so holding, the Court stated:

> The federal securities laws ensure the timely release of accurate information into the marketplace. The federal power to regulate should not be duplicated or impliedly usurped by Delaware. When a shareholder is damaged merely as a result of the release of inaccurate information into the marketplace, unconnected with any Delaware corporate governance issue, that shareholder must seek a remedy under federal law.

We disagree, and although we hold that the Complaint as drafted should have been dismissed, our rationale is different.

This Court has held that a board of directors is under a fiduciary duty to disclose material information when seeking shareholder action. The majority of opinions from the Court of Chancery have held that there may be a cause of action for disclosure violations only where directors seek shareholder action. The present appeal requires this Court to decide whether a director's fiduciary duty arising out of misdisclosure is implicated in the absence of a request for shareholder action. We hold that directors who knowingly disseminate false information that results in corporate injury or damage to an individual stockholder violate their fiduciary duty, and may be held accountable in a manner appropriate to the circumstances.

Although the fiduciary duty of a Delaware director is unremitting, the exact course of conduct that must be charted to properly discharge that responsibility will change in the specific context of the action the director is taking with regard to either the corporation or its shareholders. This Court has endeavored to provide the directors with clear signal beacons and brightly lined-channel markers as they navigate with due care, good faith, and loyalty on behalf of a Delaware corporation and its shareholders. This Court has also endeavored to mark the safe harbors clearly.

The shareholder constituents of a Delaware corporation are entitled to rely upon their elected directors to discharge their fiduciary duties at all times. Whenever directors communicate publicly or directly with shareholders about the corporation's affairs, with or without a request for shareholder action, directors have a fiduciary duty to shareholders to exercise due care, good faith and loyalty. It follows *a fortiori* that when directors communicate publicly or directly with shareholders about corporate matters the *sine qua non* of directors' fiduciary duty to shareholders is honesty.

According to the appellants, the focus of the fiduciary duty of disclosure is to protect shareholders as the "beneficiaries" of all material information disseminated by the directors. The duty of disclosure is, and always has been, a specific application of the general fiduciary duty owed by directors. The duty of disclosure obligates directors to provide the stockholders with accurate and complete information material to a transaction or other corporate event that is being presented to them for action.

The issue in this case is not whether Mercury's directors breached their duty of disclosure. It is whether they breached their more general fiduciary duty of loyalty and good faith by knowingly disseminating to the stockholders false information about the financial condition of the company. The directors' fiduciary duties include the duty to deal with their stockholders honestly.

Shareholders are entitled to rely upon the truthfulness of all information disseminated to them by the directors they elect to manage the corporate enterprise. Delaware directors disseminate information in at least three contexts: public statements made to the market, including shareholders; statements informing shareholders about the affairs of the corporation without a request for shareholder action; and, statements to shareholders in conjunction with a request for shareholder action.

Inaccurate information in these contexts may be the result of violation of the fiduciary duties of care, loyalty or good faith. We will examine the remedies that are available to shareholders for misrepresentations in each of these three contexts by the directors of a Delaware corporation.

In the absence of a request for stockholder action, the Delaware General Corporation Law does not require directors to provide shareholders with information concerning the finances or affairs of the corporation. Even when shareholder action is sought, the provisions in the General Corporation Law requiring notice to the shareholders of the proposed action do not require the directors to convey substantive information beyond a statutory minimum.

The duty of directors to observe proper disclosure requirements derives from the combination of the fiduciary duties of care, loyalty and good faith. The plaintiffs contend that, because directors' fiduciary responsibilities are not "intermittent duties," there is no reason why the duty of disclosure should not be implicated in every public communication by a corporate board of directors. The directors of a Delaware corporation are required to disclose fully and fairly all material information within the board's control when it seeks shareholder action. When the directors disseminate information to stockholders when no stockholder action is sought, the fiduciary duties of care, loyalty and good faith apply. Dissemination of false information could violate one or more of those duties.

When corporate directors impart information they must comport with the obligations imposed by both the Delaware law and the federal statutes and regulations of the United States Securities and Exchange Commission ("SEC"). Historically, federal law has regulated disclosures by corporate directors into the general interstate market. This Court has noted that "in observing its congressional mandate the SEC has adopted a 'basic philosophy of disclosure.' " Accordingly, this Court has held that there is "no legitimate basis to create a new cause of action which would replicate, by state decisional law, the provisions of the 1934 Act." In deference to the panoply of federal protections that are available to investors in connection with the purchase or sale of securities of Delaware corporations, this Court has decided not to recognize a state common law cause of action against the directors of Delaware corporations for "fraud on the market." Here, it is to be noted, the claim appears to be made by those who did not sell and, therefore, would not implicate federal securities laws which relate to the purchase or sale of securities.

The historic roles played by state and federal law in regulating corporate disclosures have been not only compatible but complementary. That symbiotic relationship has been perpetuated by the recently enacted federal Securities Litigation Uniform Standards Act of 1998. Although that statute by its terms does not apply to this case, the new statute will require securities class actions involving the purchase or sale of nationally traded securities, based upon false or misleading statements, to be brought exclusively in federal court under federal law. The 1998 Act, however, contains two important exceptions: the first provides that an "exclusively derivative action brought by one or more shareholders on behalf of a corporation" is not preempted; the second preserves the availability of state court class actions, where state law already provides that corporate directors have fiduciary disclosure obligations to shareholders. These exceptions have become known as the "Delaware carve-outs."

Delaware law also protects shareholders who receive false communications from directors even in the absence of a request for shareholder action. When the directors are not seeking shareholder action, but are deliberately misinforming shareholders about the business of the corporation, either directly or by a public statement, there is a violation of fiduciary duty. That violation may result in a derivative claim on behalf of the corporation or a cause of action for damages. There may also be a basis for equitable relief to remedy the violation.

Here the complaint alleges (if true) an egregious violation of fiduciary duty by the directors in knowingly disseminating materially false information. Then it alleges that the corporation lost about $2 billion in value as a result. Then it merely claims that the action is brought on behalf of the named plaintiffs and the putative class. It is a *non sequitur* rather than a syllogism.

The allegation in paragraph 3 that the false disclosures resulted in the corporation losing virtually all its equity seems obliquely to claim an injury to the corporation. The plaintiffs, however, never expressly assert a derivative claim on behalf of the corporation or allege compliance with Court of Chancery Rule 23.1, which requires pre-suit demand or cognizable and particularized allegations that demand is excused. If the plaintiffs intend to assert a derivative claim, they should be permitted to replead to assert such a claim and any damage or equitable remedy sought on behalf of the corporation.[46] Likewise, the plaintiffs should have the opportunity to replead to assert any individual cause of action and articulate a remedy that is appropriate on behalf of the named plaintiffs individually, or a properly recognizable class consistent with Court of Chancery Rule 23, and our decision in *Gaffin*.[47]

The judgment of the Court of Chancery to dismiss the complaint is affirmed. The judgment to dismiss the complaint with prejudice is

---

[46] We express no opinion whether equitable remedies such as injunctive relief, judicial removal of directors or disqualification from directorship could be asserted here. No such equitable relief has been sought in the current complaint.

[47] *Gaffin v. Teledyne, Inc.*, 611 A.2d at 474 ("A class action may not be maintained in a purely common law or equitable fraud case since individual questions of law or fact, particularly as to the element of justifiable reliance, will inevitably predominate over common questions of law or fact.").

reversed. This matter is remanded for further proceedings in accordance with this opinion.

3.   SECTION 102(b)(7) AND THE IMPLICATIONS OF MALONE V. BRINCAT

Malone is far more complex than it appears. One point is clear: directors have a duty to speak truthfully whenever they choose to speak, whether or not shareholder action is required. Beyond that, much is murky. The court does not make clear which duties the directors may have breached, what remedies may be available, or the extent to which a class action can be successfully maintained.

As noted earlier and as you will read in subsequent chapters, § 102(b)(7) permits Delaware corporations to adopt a provision in their certificates of incorporation that exculpate directors from any personal liability for money damages exclusively for breaches of their duty of care, but not for their duties of loyalty, good faith, or other conduct. The charters of most public corporations have such an exculpation provision. If the failure to disclose constitutes only a breach of the duty of care and the corporation has a § 102(b)(7) exculpatory provision in its certificate of incorporation, there can be no damages for the breach, although equitable relief may still be available. If there is no exculpation, the full range of remedies remains open as it would if the breach is considered to be of the duty of loyalty. The duty of good faith is discussed in Chapter 18.

In *Malone*, the court remanded the case to permit the plaintiffs to amend their complaint to assert either a derivative or a class action claim. The court's analysis, however, strongly suggested that plaintiffs may not be able to maintain a class action using a fraud-on-the-market theory under Delaware law.

At present, it is difficult to present established circumstances under which Delaware courts will find directors liable in claims involving violations of the duty to disclose. The courts' decisions vary and largely depend on the nature of the claim. In particular, courts often focus on the alleged motivation underlying the allegation. Violations may be triggered by a number of circumstances beyond proxy disclosure, including general communications with shareholders and among directors and officers.

4.   MATERIALITY UNDER STATE LAW

Fiduciaries must disclose "all material information." The Delaware Supreme Court has expressly adopted the Supreme Court's formulation of materiality set forth in *TSC Industries*: "There must be a substantial likelihood that the disclosure of the omitted fact would have been viewed by the reasonable investor as having significantly altered the 'total mix' of information made available." *Rosenblatt v. Getty Oil Co.*, 493 A.2d 929, 944 (Del. 1985). Although the Delaware and federal definitions of materiality are articulated identically, it is not clear that the different courts would apply them the same way.

One case in which the Delaware Supreme Court appears to have interpreted materiality in proxy fraud cases more broadly than federal courts was *Arnold v. Society for Sav. Bancorp, Inc.*, 650 A.2d 1270, 1277 (Del. 1994). *Arnold* involved the materiality of disclosures in a merger proxy statement. The principal misstatement concerned Bancorp's efforts to sell its most profitable subsidiary, Fidelity Acceptance Corporation (FAC) prior to the merger. These efforts resulted in a contingent bid, but the sale was never consummated. The ultimate merger proxy statement described the failed proposal but did not disclose the amount of the bid or the qualified estimates as to the value of the Bancorp shares that had been generated in connection with the proposal. In granting summary judgment for the defendants, the Court of Chancery held that the contingent FAC bid was immaterial as a matter of law under the circumstances. The Delaware Supreme Court reversed and held that the Bancorp directors had violated their duty of disclosure to the Bancorp shareholders. It remanded the question of whether, in light of DGCL § 102(b)(7), there was a remedy available against the corporate defendants.

The Delaware Supreme Court emphasized that it was "not deciding that the FAC bid was material as a matter of law." Rather, it held only that "once defendants traveled down the road of partial disclosure of the history leading up to the Merger and used the vague language described, they had an obligation to provide the stockholders with an accurate, full and fair characterization of those historic events."

This latter statement could be viewed as inconsistent with *Basic, Inc. v. Levinson*, which rejected the argument that "once a statement is made denying the existence of any [merger] discussions, even discussions that might not have been material in absence of the denial are material because they make the statement made untrue." This inconsistency illustrates the difficulty of distinguishing between materiality as a matter of fact and as a matter of law. Because *Arnold* arose on a motion for summary judgment, the court had to accept the facts in the light most favorable to the defendants. Thus the Delaware Supreme Court may be viewed as having held that, for purposes of summary judgment, the half-truths about the FAC offer could be viewed as creating a genuine issue of material fact so that summary judgment would be inappropriate. At the same time, the court was not prepared to say that the same half-truths would be material as a matter of law.

Does the Delaware disclosure duty compel revelation of unlawful or wrongful conduct? Recall that the federal cases under Rule 14a–9 do not require directors to characterize their conduct as unlawful or constituting a breach of fiduciary duty. Delaware law is consistent with those cases. *See, e.g., Brody v. Zaucha*, 697 A.2d 749, 754 (Del. 1997), in which the court noted that "[i]t is settled Delaware law that a director need not make self-accusatory statements nor engage in 'self-flagellation' by confessing to wrongdoing that has not been formally adjudicated by a court of law."

Although directors need not confess wrongdoing, good faith in an omission or false statement appears to be irrelevant to the disclosure's materiality. In *Shell Petroleum, Inc. v. Smith*, 606 A.2d 112 (Del. 1992), the controlling shareholder released erroneous information to minority shareholders concerning the value of the corporation. Although the error was inadvertent, the court nonetheless held the controlling shareholder liable for the omission because it controlled the preparation of the materials and thus had constructive knowledge of the error. "It is only logical that a majority shareholder who directs a subsidiary to prepare certain disclosure materials and then distributes those materials to minority shareholders should be held accountable for any errors contained therein."

5. "VOLUNTARY" DISCLOSURES AND STATE REMEDIES

What disclosure does a fiduciary owe to shareholders when a vote is sought but not required or needed to accomplish a contemplated transaction? Recall *Virginia Bankshares,* in which proxies were solicited even though management had sufficient votes to approve the transaction without the vote of the minority shareholders. Although *Virginia Bankshares* found causation lacking under § 14(a) of the 1934 Act in such a situation, Delaware has not yet directly addressed the question as a matter of state law. The Delaware Supreme Court has indicated, however, that a duty of full and fair disclosure arises whenever directors are either required to seek a shareholder vote or elect to do so. *Stroud v. Milliken Enterprises, Inc.*, 552 A.2d 476, 480 (Del. 1989).

In light of Delaware's seeming willingness to impose the duty of disclosure when a board "voluntarily" seeks approval of a transaction by a majority of the minority shareholders, how much insulation does *Virginia Bankshares* give the board, even if no action can be brought under federal law? Have developments under state law overtaken the Court's concern in *Borak* that if a victim of a deceptive proxy statement were "obliged to go into state courts for remedial relief [and] the law of the State happened to attach no responsibility to the use of misleading proxy statements, the whole purpose of [federal proxy regulation] might be frustrated?" Alternatively, does the reasoning the Court used in *Virginia Bankshares* suggest that, if state law provides a plaintiff with a remedy for an alleged violation of the duty of disclosure, she cannot assert a federal claim based on the theory that defendant's misrepresentation caused her to lose a remedy she otherwise would have had under state law?

Delaware courts have not imposed greater disclosure duties when a shareholder vote is unnecessary, such as when disclosure is relevant to the decision of minority shareholders to accept merger terms or to seek appraisal. Rejecting the arguments by minority shareholders that they should have been given all of the financial data necessary to make an independent determination of fair value, the Delaware Supreme Court refused to imply "a new disclosure standard where appraisal is an option." *Skeen v. Jo-Ann Stores, Inc.*, 750 A.2d 1170, 1174 (Del. 2000). Nonetheless, the court has stated that when a majority shareholder controls the outcome of the vote on a merger, there is a "more compelling case for the application of the recognized disclosure standards." *McMullin v. Beran*, 765 A.2d 910, 926 (Del. 2000). In *Beran* the court upheld a complaint that minority shareholders were unfairly forced to choose between an outside acquirer's tender offer and an appraisal when the controlling shareholder failed to disclose (1) indications of interest from other potential acquirers; (2) the handling of these potential offers; (3) the restrictions and constraints imposed by the controlling shareholder on the potential sale of company; (4) the information provided to the acquirer's investment banker and the valuation methodologies it used.

6. THE FEDERALISM ISSUE

In light of the extensive proxy disclosure requirements that we have previously studied, what is the relationship between federal and state law? Consider Professor Robert Thompson's analysis:

> Delaware cases show a yoking of disclosure obligations and fiduciary duty requirements as part of an integrated approach to protect the role of shareholders in corporate governance. Neither obligation is as straightforward as conventional wisdom might suggest. For disclosure, Delaware has neatly piggybacked on the massive disclosure developed by the SEC and required by the federal securities law. By decreeing, as a matter of fiduciary duty, that directors seeking a shareholder vote must disclose all material information, all disclosure deficiencies become potential violations of Delaware law. Though these deficiencies could be brought under federal law as well as state law, Delaware has an advantage because it alone (for the moment) provides law that insures not only that disclosure is accurate, but also that the space for shareholder voting is protected against encroachment by director or management action. The result is that the SEC provides the details of mandatory disclosure, but the Delaware courts are the front line in the application of those requirements to specific corporate transactions.
>
> This combination within Delaware law of disclosure to protect shareholder decision making and substantive protection of the

shareholder space to make decisions provides an interesting contrast to adjacent areas in which the federal government has itself sought to play both roles and Delaware has not tried to repel such a federal incursion. Early on in the history of securities regulation, the SEC recognized that the disclosure mandated by the 1934 Act would be less complete if shareholders lacked the ability to set the agenda at their own meeting and to have those items included on management's proxy solicitation, which is the means by which voting often occurs. Rule 14a–8 therefore provided a federal means for an individual shareholder to place an issue on the management's proxy solicitation. Although the rule provides that such access must be a matter on which state law permits shareholders to act, a long-standing note to that rule plunges deep into substantive shareholder rights by presuming that any precatory resolution, framed as a suggestion, is within the shareholder space, despite the absence of any significant state law on this point.

Robert B. Thompson, *Delaware's Disclosure: Moving the Line of Federal-State Corporate Regulation,* 2009 U. Ill. L. Rev. 167, 187–88 (2009).

Another aspect of the federalism issue arises from the Securities Law Uniform Standards Act (SLUSA) referred to in *Malone v. Brincat.* The Private Securities Litigation Reform Act of 1995 imposed various substantive and procedural limitations on class actions under Rule 10b–5 in an effort to stem perceived abuses. To avoid the limitations of that statute, plaintiffs' lawyers began to take their class actions to state court. Congress reacted by passing SLUSA, which effectively required that most class actions alleging what would constitute a violation of Rule 10b–5 must be brought in federal court, and if brought in state court can be removed to federal court. SLUSA excepts from its coverage derivative suits under state law and suits in which the allegedly false or misleading statement was made by the issuer and related to repurchases of its securities or recommendations regarding a tender or exchange offer. It would thus permit claims in state court based on an allegedly misleading solicitation of proxies to approve a merger or acquisition.

CHAPTER 16

SHAREHOLDER LITIGATION

■ ■ ■

Most lawsuits initiated by corporate shareholders are brought in a representative capacity as derivative suits or class actions. They typically concern alleged breaches of fiduciary duty by directors, officers or controlling shareholders. Although a variety of other forces including government regulation, oversight by outside directors, capital and product market forces and shareholder voting, impose some degree of accountability on managers and controlling shareholders, shareholder lawsuits constitute an important corporate accountability mechanism because they alone target specific instances of managerial misconduct and can be initiated without collective action by shareholders.

This chapter focuses on the derivative suit, which is the form in which most shareholder actions are cast. A derivative action is a suit against third parties (usually officers and directors) brought by a shareholder on behalf of the corporation in which she holds stock. Class actions also have a role in shareholder litigation, but they are more often the appropriate form in claims that shareholders have been misled than in claims of breach of fiduciary duty.

Almost all the cases in which the courts have developed the law of fiduciary duties take the form of derivative suits. Therefore, it is important to understand the mechanics of litigating a derivative action when studying those cases. Few derivative suits ever go to trial. All but a handful are decided on procedural motions or settled after the court decides a motion to dismiss or for summary judgment. As a consequence, the substantive legal principles of a board's duties developed in these cases are inextricably intertwined with the procedural aspects of derivative litigation.

A. INTRODUCTION

We have already seen how collective action problems limit the effectiveness of shareholder voting as an accountability mechanism. One might reasonably assume that similar collective action problems would limit shareholder litigation. A shareholder who chooses to devote resources to monitoring managers' performance must bear the costs of her efforts, as well as the risk that no wrongdoing will be found. Moreover, even if the shareholder succeeds in identifying a breach of fiduciary duty and remedying it through a derivative or class action, the only benefit she will realize is a pro rata portion of whatever increase in the value of the corporation results from a derivative suit or whatever is recovered in a class action. The following passage provides the essential rationale for a derivative action.

> A fundamental condition of the corporate form when stockholders are widely dispersed, as typically occurs in public corporations, is that individual shareholders have little incentive to bear the costs associated with activities that monitor board of director (or management) performance. Of course, a fundamental advantage that the corporate form offers to owners of capital is the utility that an investor gains through centralized management. Centralized management allows passive (low cost) ownership and promotes investor diversification. Limited liability and the entity status of a corporation similarly allow investors to be relatively passive. While the conditions that allow investors to be rationally passive are a primary source of utility, they can also lead to inefficiency to the extent centralized management may have incentives that are not perfectly aligned with those of the residual owners of the firm, which is inevitably the case. This imperfect alignment of incentives will inevitably lead to excess costs associated with centralized management. For that reason *some* expenditures for shareholder monitoring would be efficient. Such monitoring is, of course, more or less costly to the shareholder who engages in it. In a public company with widely distributed shares any particular shareholder has very little incentive to incur those costs himself in pursuit of a collective good, since unless there is some method to force a sharing of costs, he will bear all of the costs and only a (small) pro rata share of any gains that the monitoring yields. Thus, it is likely that in a public corporation there will be less shareholder monitoring expenditures than would be optimum from the point of the shareholders as a collectivity. One way the corporation law deals with this conundrum is through the derivative lawsuit and the recognized practice of awarding to successful shareholder champions and their attorney's risk-adjusted reimbursement payments (*i.e.,* contingency based attorneys fees). The derivative suit offers to risk-accepting shareholders and lawyers a method and incentives to pursue monitoring activities that are wealth increasing for the collectivity (the corporation or the body of its shareholders). Of course that remedy itself suffers from deep agency problems and can lead to a variety of problems that for the most part can be passed over today.

Bird v. Lida, Inc., 681 A.2d 399, 402–03 (Del.Ch. 1996).

In a derivative action, the shareholder asserts rights belonging to the corporation on behalf of the corporation after the board of directors has failed to do so. The corporation is named as a nominal defendant. Any amounts recovered belong to the corporation, not the shareholder-plaintiff. Counsel for plaintiffs play a major role in initiating derivative suit litigation, and they receive their fees from the corporation on the theory that they are entitled to compensation for conferring a benefit on the corporation.

To understand fully the policy issues that derivative suits raise, one must appreciate the economic incentives of the principal players in these suits and the conflicts that these incentives create. Because any recovery in a derivative suit goes to the corporation, the nominal shareholder-plaintiff receives no direct pecuniary benefit from successful litigation; her benefit comes from an increase in the corporation's stock price attributable to the recovery. Thus, the plaintiff wants to maximize the size of that recovery, an interest shared by the corporation itself. The defendants, usually senior officers or directors, seek to minimize their costs, which consist of any monies paid in judgment or settlement, plus attorneys' fees. As in any contingent fee litigation, plaintiff's counsel will receive a fee if the suit results in a favorable judgment or a settlement, whether involving monetary damages or some other benefit to the corporation. She earns nothing if the plaintiff loses. The size of the fee generally will be based either on the time spent on the litigation or on a percentage of the total recovery.

Unlike most litigation in which the plaintiff's gain comes at the defendant's expense, a derivative suit is not a zero-sum game; in fact both plaintiff *and* defendant can recover many of their litigation costs from the corporation. The defendant in a derivative suit, particularly if she is a director, is not like a defendant in other actions. Under most state corporate laws, a corporation may indemnify a director for her expenses in a derivative suit if she has not been adjudged to have breached her duty to the corporation and otherwise meets the standards for indemnification. These expenses include attorneys' fees—which can be substantial—and, in some jurisdictions, even the amounts paid in settlement. Thus, a risk-averse defendant has a strong incentive to agree to a relatively small settlement and be indemnified for substantially all her expenses rather than risk an adverse decision after trial. To the extent that the monetary settlement is reduced or eliminated through the inclusion of non-pecuniary relief, the defendant's economic risk is lessened still further. Because indemnification usually is paid by insurance, which the corporation purchases at its own expense, a settlement may result in the shareholders paying part of the cost of the defense.

Similarly, the plaintiff in a derivative suit is not like most plaintiffs, and her relationship with her lawyer is not like most lawyer-client relationships in contingent fee litigation. In most litigation, counsel must operate within the bounds set by her client. When the client tells counsel to litigate, counsel litigates; when the client prefers to settle, the lawyer settles. By contrast, the shareholder in a derivative suit has only a nominal economic interest and usually gives no directions. Additionally, in most contingent litigation the client knows she has been injured and seeks out a lawyer; in the derivative suit, it is not uncommon for the lawyer to seek out the client and advise her of the wrong that has occurred. Indeed, one commentator has called plaintiff's counsel "the engine that drives the derivative action." John C. Coffee, Jr., *American Law Institute's Corporate Governance Project: Remedies: Litigation and Corporate Governance: An Essay on Steering Between Scylla and Charybdis*, 52 Geo. Wash. L. Rev. 789, 800 (1984). Finally, in a derivative suit, the lawyer has far more at stake than the plaintiff shareholder. Thus, plaintiff's counsel has an incentive to agree to settlements that shareholders collectively might view as inadequate, in order to assure that she receives a fee for her work.

Some of the problems described above are present in any form of contingent fee litigation. They are more troublesome here because of the representative nature of the derivative suit. Nuisance suits are not peculiar to the corporate setting. Nevertheless, in order to discourage abuses by people purporting to act on the corporation's behalf, the law has singled out derivative suits for the imposition of special procedural restrictions and judicial oversight. Among other things, this chapter examines the reasons for these restrictions, how they operate, and how to evaluate their efficacy and desirability.

Problem: Prime Parts, Inc.—Part 1

Prime Parts, Inc. ("Prime") is in the business of manufacturing and selling parts used by major auto manufacturers in the production of new cars. It is incorporated in Delaware, and it has outstanding 100 million shares of common stock, which are traded on the NASDAQ Stock Market.

Prime's Chairman and CEO is Peter Bennett. He is the founder of the company, and has been its CEO and President for fifteen years. He owns approximately 5 million shares of common stock.

The other directors of Prime are:

- Cliff Fender, the Chief Financial Officer of Prime. He owns 100,000 shares of Prime common stock.

- Barbara Banks, a senior partner at Silverman Sachs, which has acted as Prime's investment banker since 1995. She owns 5,000 shares of Prime common stock.

- Richard Rains, the CEO of Autosoft, Inc., and a close friend of Bennett, whom he first met in business school. He owns 50,000 shares of Prime common stock.

- Paula Ritchie, Bennett's daughter, who is a senior managing director at McDonald Consulting, a leading business consultant. She owns 250,000 shares of Prime common stock.

- Sally Smart, the CEO of Smart Investors Group, Inc ("SIG"), a private equity fund that is one of Prime's largest stockholders.

- Seymour Smith, a professor at Harvard Business School, where he taught both Bennett and Rains. He owns 1,000 shares of Prime common stock.

Although Prime has over the years been quite profitable, it has never paid a dividend, and as a result has accumulated nearly $500 million in cash. Because of conditions in the auto industry Prime's current business has been flat for several years, and it has been under pressure from investors either to return some of the cash to stockholders or to expand into a new line of business by using some of the cash to purchase another company.

Five years ago, Bennett made a personal investment in Autosoft, Inc., which was then an early stage company that was developing the increasingly complex software that is used to operate modern automobiles. He also took a position on Autosoft's board of directors, on which he continues to serve. His investment currently represents approximately 8% of Autosoft's outstanding equity.

Two years ago, at dinner after a meeting of Prime's board of directors, Rains suggested to Bennett that Prime consider buying Autosoft. After some discussion they decided that the idea was worth exploring. Without informing the rest of the board, Bennett spoke to Banks, and engaged Silverman Sachs to analyze the possibility of a deal and to represent Prime in the transaction if it proceeded. A few weeks later, Banks sent Bennett an analysis that concluded with a favorable recommendation for an acquisition at a price of $400 million. Bennett called Rains to propose that Prime acquire Autosoft for $400 million in cash. After consultation with his own board, Rains told Bennett that Autosoft was inclined to accept the proposal.

At Prime's next board meeting, Bennett, Rains and Banks presented the acquisition proposal, including a copy of the Silverman Sachs analysis. After a brief discussion, the board voted unanimously to proceed with an exploration of the acquisition, subject to reaching final agreement on price and terms. Because of the obvious conflict of interest of Bennett and Rains, the board appointed a special committee, consisting of Banks, Smart and Smith, and empowered them to negotiate and agree on final terms.

After several weeks of conducting due diligence and negotiations, the committee voted to approve the purchase of Autosoft for $410 million in cash, and submitted an acquisition agreement to the full board for final approval. In the course of the negotiations, Autosoft insisted on accelerating the vesting of all of the unvested stock options of the Autosoft management, including options for 100,000 shares held by Rains. Because the effect of this provision resulted in the purchase price being divided among a higher number of shares, resulting in a lower per-share price, Autosoft's board insisted on increasing the purchase price by $10 million. The Prime board met by conference call, discussed the proposed transaction for approximately fifteen minutes, and voted unanimously to approve it. There was no discussion of the acceleration of the options or that it was the reason for increasing the price above the originally-proposed $400 million. The deal closed a week later. Prime issued a press release announcing the acquisition and filed with the SEC the required disclosure statement describing it. Neither the release nor the SEC filing discussed the details of the negotiations or the reason for increasing the price; nor did they disclose the numerous conflicts of interest involved.

A year later, it appears that the acquisition has been a failure. Prime's lack of experience in the software business turned out to be a severe handicap. It attempted to force the Autosoft subsidiary to follow Prime's management practices, several of the key employees of Autosoft left in disgust, leaving the development operation in disarray. Prime also laid off many of Autosoft's sales personnel with the view of having Prime's sales force sell the Autosoft product, which was another disaster.

A

You are a partner in a law firm that represents plaintiffs in shareholder litigation. Harry Patterson is a retired attorney who has been the named plaintiff in many shareholder suits in which your firm has been involved. He owns a few shares of stock in many public companies, including 10 shares of the stock of Prime. You are considering filing a lawsuit in state court on Harry's behalf asserting one or more of the followings claims: (1) against the directors of Prime for breaching their duty of care in approving the Autosoft acquisition and failing to pay sufficient attention to managing the integration of the two businesses; (2) against Bennett, Rains, and Banks for breaching their duty of loyalty; and (3) against the directors for violating their duty to disclose all material facts.

1. Can the claims outlined above be asserted in a direct action, which could be filed as a class action, or can one or more of them be asserted only as derivative claims?

2. What additional facts, if any, does your firm need in order to determine whether Harry has standing to file either a direct or a derivative suit?

3. Assuming Harry has standing; would he qualify as an adequate plaintiff in a derivative or class action?

4.   To the extent that the action is brought as a derivative suit, would Harry be required to make a demand on the board of Prime? If the demand requirement applies, is it likely that Harry could establish demand futility as to each of the claims that he might seek to assert?

B

The plaintiff has filed a derivative suit in the Delaware Court of Chancery alleging that the directors breached their duties of care and loyalty. He did not make a demand on the board, on the theory that a demand would have been futile. If you were Prime's in-house counsel how would you answer the following questions?

1.   Can you retain one firm to represent both the corporation and the directors?

2.   Should you retain Prime's regular outside counsel, to handle the lawsuit?

3.   Instead of filing a motion to dismiss for failure to make a demand, you are considering having the board appoint a special litigation committee to review the claims and decide whether it would be in the best interest of Prime to pursue them. Would this approach be preferable? Who, if anyone, on the current board would be considered independent for purposes of serving on such a committee? If you are concerned about whether a sufficiently independent committee could be formed from the existing board, is there any other way to create such a committee?

4.   If, on the special committee's recommendation, the corporation moved to dismiss the complaint, what standard of review would the court use in deciding the motion? How would you assess your chances of success on the motion?

Problem: Prime Parts, Inc.—Part 2

After preliminary motions, but before the court has ruled on any motions by defendants, the parties have submitted a proposed settlement of all actions in which they agree to the following terms:

(a)   Bennett and Rains will together pay Prime $10 million.

(b)   Prime's board will create a disclosure committee to assure that future disclosures to shareholders are complete and accurate.

(c)   Prime will pay the plaintiff's attorneys' fees in the amount of $850,000.

1.   What procedures must be followed for the settlement to be approved?

2. Should the court approve the settlement? Should it award $850,000 in attorneys' fees? What additional information, if any, should the court obtain before deciding these questions?

---

1. DIRECT AND DERIVATIVE ACTIONS

In shareholder litigation, a crucial distinction, present at the outset, is whether the nature of the injury to shareholders is direct or derivative. If a state court determines that the injury is direct, the likely suit will be a class action, often in federal court under the federal securities laws.

In theory, a shareholder can bring a derivative action against any party who has harmed the corporation, whether an insider or outsider. In practice, virtually all derivative actions are brought against directors or controlling shareholders who have allegedly breached duties to the corporation. Suing an outside party—for example, claiming breach of a contract with the corporation—is seen as a business decision reserved for the board of directors.

The shareholder-plaintiff who brings a derivative action represents the corporation to vindicate the interests of all shareholders. Federal Rule of Civil Procedure 23.1 requires that the plaintiff "fairly and adequately represent the interests of the shareholders similarly situated in enforcing the rights of the corporation." Courts have stressed the obligations that fall on a stockholder when she initiates a derivative suit. The Supreme Court has characterized the stockholder as assuming "a position, not technically as a trustee perhaps, but one of a fiduciary character. He sues, not for himself alone, but as representative of a class comprising all who are similarly situated." *Cohen v. Beneficial Industrial Loan Corp.*, 337 U.S. 541, 549 (1949).

Shareholders can also sue directly on their own behalf to vindicate individual rights, rather than corporate rights. In public corporations, direct actions are often brought as class actions, in which a shareholder-representative brings the action on behalf of similarly situated shareholders. Direct actions, although they have their own procedural rules, are attractive because they avoid the procedural hurdles that apply to derivative actions, principally, the requirement of pre-suit demand on the board and the board's power to seek dismissal of the derivative suit before trial.

Although some courts have sought to distinguish derivative actions from direct actions by looking at whether the shareholder plaintiff suffered a special injury (direct) or whether all shareholders are affected equally (derivative), that approach has created considerable uncertainty. In response, the American Law Institute, Principles of Corporate Governance and, more recently, the Delaware Supreme Court has tried to simplify the task of distinguishing the two actions.

ALI PRINCIPLES § 7.01

Direct and Derivative Actions Distinguished

(a) A derivative action may be brought in the name or right of a corporation by a holder to redress an injury sustained by, or enforce a duty owed to, a corporation. An action in which the holder can prevail only by showing an injury or breach of duty to the corporation should be treated as a derivative action.

(b) A direct action may be brought in the name or right of a holder to redress an injury sustained by, or enforce a duty owed to, the holder. An action in which the holder can prevail without showing an injury or breach of duty to the corporation should be treated as a direct action that may be maintained by the holder in an individual capacity.

(c) If a transaction gives rise to both direct and derivative claims, a holder may commence and maintain direct and derivative actions simultaneously, and any special restrictions or defenses pertaining to the maintenance, settlement, or dismissal of either action should not apply to the other.

COMMENT

d. Relevant criteria. In borderline cases, the following policy considerations deserve to be given close attention by the court:

First, a derivative action distributes the recovery more broadly and evenly than a direct action. Because the recovery in a derivative action goes to the corporation, creditors and others having a stake in the corporation benefit financially from a derivative action and not from a direct one. Similarly, although all shareholders share equally, if indirectly, in the corporate recovery that follows a successful derivative action, the injured shareholders other than the plaintiff will share in the recovery from a direct action only if the action is a class action brought on behalf of all these shareholders.

Second, once finally concluded, a derivative action will have a preclusive effect that spares the corporation and the defendants from being exposed to a multiplicity of actions.

Third, a successful plaintiff is entitled to an award of attorneys' fees in a derivative action directly from the corporation, but in a direct action the plaintiff must generally look to the fund, if any, created by the action.

Finally, characterizing the action as derivative may entitle the board to take over the action or to seek dismissal of the action. Accordingly, in some circumstances the characterization of the action will determine the available defenses.

TOOLEY V. DONALDSON, LUFKIN, & JENRETTE, INC.
845 A.2d 1031 (Del. 2004).

VEASEY, CHIEF JUSTICE.

Plaintiff-stockholders brought a purported class action in the Court of Chancery, alleging that the members of the board of directors of their corporation breached their fiduciary duties by agreeing to a 22-day delay in closing a proposed merger. Plaintiffs contend that the delay harmed them due to the lost time-value of the cash paid for their shares. The Court of Chancery granted the defendants' motion to dismiss on the sole ground that the claims were, "at most," claims of the corporation being asserted derivatively. They were, thus, held not to be direct claims of the stockholders, individually. Thereupon, the Court held that the plaintiffs lost their standing to bring this action when they tendered their shares in connection with the merger.

Although the trial court's legal analysis of whether the complaint alleges a direct or derivative claim reflects some concepts in our prior jurisprudence, we believe those concepts are not helpful and should be regarded as erroneous. We set forth in this Opinion the law to be applied henceforth in determining whether a stockholder's claim is derivative or direct. That issue must turn *solely* on the following questions: (1) who suffered the alleged harm (the corporation or the suing stockholders, individually); and (2) who would receive the benefit of any recovery or other remedy (the corporation or the stockholders, individually)?

[Plaintiffs] are former minority stockholders of Donaldson, Lufkin & Jenrette, Inc. (DLJ). DLJ was acquired by Credit Suisse Group (Credit Suisse) in the Fall of 2000. Before that acquisition, AXA Financial, Inc. (AXA), which owned 71% of DLJ stock, controlled DLJ. Pursuant to a stockholder agreement between AXA and Credit Suisse, AXA agreed to exchange with Credit Suisse its DLJ stockholdings for a mix of stock and cash.

The tender offer price was set at $90 per share in cash. The tender offer was to expire 20 days after its commencement. The merger agreement, however, authorized two types of extensions. First, Credit Suisse could unilaterally extend the tender offer if certain conditions were not met. Alternatively, DLJ and Credit Suisse could agree to postpone acceptance by Credit Suisse of DLJ stock tendered by the minority stockholders.

Credit Suisse availed itself of both types of extensions to postpone the closing of the tender offer. Plaintiffs challenge the second extension that resulted in a 22-day delay. They contend that this delay was not properly authorized and harmed minority stockholders while improperly benefiting AXA. They claim damages representing the time-value of money lost through the delay.

The order of the Court of Chancery dismissing the complaint is based on the plaintiffs' lack of standing to bring the claims asserted therein. Thus, when plaintiffs tendered their shares they lost standing under the contemporaneous holding rule. The ruling before us on appeal is that the plaintiffs' claim is derivative, purportedly brought on behalf of DLJ. The Court of Chancery, relying upon our confusing jurisprudence on the direct/derivative dichotomy, based its dismissal on the following ground: "Because this delay affected all DLJ shareholders equally, plaintiffs' injury was not a special injury, and this action is, thus, a derivative action, at most".

In our view, the concept of "special injury" that appears in some Supreme Court and Court of Chancery cases is not helpful to a proper analytical distinction between direct and derivative actions. We now disapprove the use of the concept of "special injury" as a tool in that analysis.

The analysis must be based solely on the following questions: Who suffered the alleged harm—the corporation or the suing stockholder individually—and who would receive the benefit of the recovery or other remedy? This simple analysis is well imbedded in our jurisprudence, but some cases have complicated it by injection of the amorphous and confusing concept of "special injury."

The Chancellor, in the very recent *Agostino* [*v. Hicks,* 845 A.2d 1110 (Del.Ch. 2004)] case, correctly points this out and strongly suggests that we should disavow the concept of "special injury." In a scholarly analysis of this area of the law, he also suggests that the inquiry should be whether the stockholder has demonstrated that he or she has suffered an injury that is not dependent on an injury to the corporation. In the context of a claim for breach of fiduciary duty, the Chancellor articulated the inquiry as follows: "Looking at the body of the complaint and considering the nature of the wrong alleged and the relief requested, has the plaintiff demonstrated that he or she can prevail without showing an injury to the corporation?"[9] We believe that this approach is helpful in analyzing the first prong of the analysis: what person or entity has suffered the alleged harm? The second prong of the analysis should logically follow.

Determining whether an action is derivative or direct is sometimes difficult and has many legal consequences, some of which may have an expensive impact on the parties to the action. For example, if an action is

---

[9] The Chancellor further explains that the focus should be on the person or entity to whom the relevant duty is owed. As noted in *Agostino*, this test is similar to that articulated by the American Law Institute (ALI), a test that we cited with approval in *Grimes v. Donald,* 673 A.2d 1207 (Del. 1996).

derivative, the plaintiffs are then required to comply with the requirements of Court of Chancery Rule 23.1, that the stockholder: (a) retain ownership of the shares throughout the litigation; (b) make presuit demand on the board; and (c) obtain court approval of any settlement. Further, the recovery, if any, flows only to the corporation. The decision whether a suit is direct or derivative may be outcome-determinative. Therefore, it is necessary that a standard to distinguish such actions be clear, simple and consistently articulated and applied by our courts.

[A] court should look to the nature of the wrong and to whom the relief should go. The stockholder's claimed direct injury must be independent of any alleged injury to the corporation. The stockholder must demonstrate that the duty breached was owed to the stockholder and that he or she can prevail without showing an injury to the corporation.

In this case it cannot be concluded that the complaint alleges a derivative claim. There is no derivative claim asserting injury to the corporate entity. There is no relief that would go the corporation. Accordingly, there is no basis to hold that the complaint states a derivative claim.

But, it does not necessarily follow that the complaint states a direct, individual claim. While the complaint purports to set forth a direct claim, in reality, it states no claim at all. The trial court analyzed the complaint and correctly concluded that it does not claim that the plaintiffs have any rights that have been injured. Their rights have not yet ripened. The contractual claim is nonexistent until it is ripe, and that claim will not be ripe until the terms of the merger are fulfilled, including the extensions of the closing at issue here. Therefore, there is no direct claim stated in the complaint before us.

Due to the reliance on the concept of "special injury" by the Court of Chancery, the ground set forth for the dismissal is erroneous, there being no derivative claim. That error is harmless, however, because, in our view, there is no direct claim either.

––––––––

Like many rules of law, the application of the *Tooley* test is clear in many instances but is sometimes elusive. Quintessential derivative claims are actions alleging mismanagement and breach of fiduciary duty including claims for self-dealing by directors and officers (fiduciary duties are discussed in Chapters 17–19). Additionally, claims challenging executive compensation, asset sales or purchases, and payment of special dividends are also derivative in nature.

On the other hand, direct claims arise when the "structural relationship" between the corporation and shareholders is harmed by the actions of directors or officers.

The Delaware General Corporation Law ("DGCL") establishes a structural relationship between the corporation and its officers, directors, and shareholders. Although the DGCL empowers corporate directors and officers to act for the corporation, the DGCL also imposes certain restraints on the use of this authority. If a corporate officer acts in a manner that the DGCL prohibits, then the officer has violated this structural relationship by disregarding the specific restraints placed on him or her by the shareholders. It is consequently the rights of the shareholders, not those of the corporation, that are injured by the encroachment. Thus, any shareholder who was harmed by the violation of the structural relationship established between the corporation and the shareholder is harmed directly and has an individual cause of action.

Grayson v. Imagination Station, Inc., 2010 WL 3221951, at *5 (Del.Ch. 2010). Examples of direct claims include a failure to enforce the terms of a stockholders' voting agreement, discrimination against particular shareholders, withholding of dividends, deprivation of preferred stockholders' contract-based rights, interference with shareholders' right to vote, challenges to price and process in a merger, and abdication of a board's statutory duties.

The policy reasons for requiring shareholders to sue derivatively when their claim is based on an alleged injury to the corporation may not be present when the suit involves a close corporation in which the shareholders are also the managers. In addition, litigation-related agency costs are much less likely to arise in a suit involving a close corporation because the plaintiff generally will have substantial financial interests in the action and will monitor closely the actions of her attorney. Nevertheless, there may be other reasons for requiring that such an action be maintained as a derivative suit; for example, having damages awarded to the corporation, rather than to an individual shareholder, may be necessary to protect creditors' interests.

In recognition of these differences, ALI Principles § 7.01(d) provides:

In the case of a closely held corporation, the court in its discretion may treat an action raising derivative claims as a direct action, exempt it from those restrictions and defenses applicable only to derivative actions, and order an individual recovery, if it finds that to do so will not (i) unfairly expose the corporation or the defendants to a multiplicity of actions, (ii) materially prejudice the interests of creditors of the corporation, or (iii) interfere with a fair distribution of the recovery among all interested persons.

2. ROLE OF COUNSEL

As we have seen, in a derivative action, the corporation is the nominal plaintiff but also is a defendant. It is being sued to compel it to bring an action against its co-defendants, who are directors and/or officers who are alleged to have caused it injury. Because any recovery from individual defendants would go to the corporation, the corporate and individual defendants have potentially conflicting interests. At the same time, the corporation and individual defendants have congruent interests if the corporation resists the plaintiffs' suit, because it does not wish to pursue a cause of action against the individuals. Does the potential conflict prevent regular corporate counsel from representing both the corporate and individual defendants in a derivative suit? Or does the potential alignment of interests permit dual representation until a conflict actually arises? Unfortunately, as one court has put it, "as a general matter, the case law is not uniform on the issue of joint representation of the corporation and individual defendants." *Bell Atlantic Corp. v. Bolger*, 2 F.3d 1304 (3d Cir. 1993).

One line of cases and commentary maintains that corporate counsel may never represent both the corporate and individual defendants in a derivative action. *See, e.g., In re Oracle Securities Litigation*, 829 F.Supp. 1176 (N.D. Cal. 1993); *Messing v. FDI, Inc.*, 439 F.Supp. 776 (D.N.J. 1977); *Cannon v. U.S. Acoustics*, 398 F.Supp. 209, 216–217 (N.D. Ill. 1975), *aff'd in relevant part per curiam*, 532 F.2d 1118 (7th Cir. 1976). The concern about such representation is that the interests of the corporation may not receive adequate consideration. Regular counsel is accustomed to working with and treating directors and officers as the voice of the company, and often develops personal relationships with them. As one court suggested, when directors and officers are defendants in the derivative action, it seems likely that counsel "would be reluctant to recommend that the corporation take any position adverse to these men, individual defendants for whom he works on a day-to-day basis and who control his future with the corporation." *Oracle, supra*, 829 F.Supp. at 1189. This scenario is especially an issue with respect to in-house counsel, although regular outside counsel also might be subject to the same subtle influences.

Another concern about dual representation is that counsel will have obtained confidential information from the individual clients in the course of representing the company. She has an obligation to keep this information confidential from parties who might use it to these clients' disadvantage, such as the corporation. While this theoretically is a legitimate concern, as a practical matter it arguably will be of less concern in a derivative suit. It is likely that in this type of case information has been and will be shared between the corporation and the individual defendants. *See Cannon, supra*, 398 F.Supp. at 216–217.

A second approach to dual representation in the derivative context is to prohibit it when plaintiffs allege fraud, intentional misconduct, or self-dealing. *See Bell Atlantic v. Bolger*, 2 F.3d 1304, 1317 (3d Cir. 1993) (prohibiting dual representation when such allegations are made, "except in patently frivolous cases"). The court suggested that this position reflects the fact that allegations of breaches of the duty of loyalty traditionally have been regarded as more serious than allegations of breaches of the duty of care. It went on to say that separate representation should be required "in cases where the line is blurred between duties of care and loyalty." Another court has held that separate representation is required when derivative plaintiffs allege fraud and self-dealing, even when an independent committee of the corporation has determined that the company should not pursue legal action against the individual defendants. *Musheno v. Gensemer*, 897 F.Supp. 833 (M.D. Pa. 1995).

The Model Rules of Professional Conduct appear to follow this second approach, which focuses on the nature of the plaintiffs' allegations. Comment 13 to Model Rule 1.13 states that a derivative action "may be brought nominally by the organization, but usually is, in fact, a legal controversy over management of the organization." And Comment 14 provides: "Most derivative actions are a normal incident of an organization's affairs, to be defended by the organization's lawyer like any other suit." If, however, "the claim involves serious charges of wrongdoing by those in control of the organization, a conflict may arise between the lawyer's duty to the organization and the lawyer's relationship with the board. In those circumstances, Rule 1.7 governs who should represent the directors and the organization."

When separate representation is required, the practice is that corporate counsel will represent the individual defendants because of her familiarity and past experience with them. *See Musheno*, 897 F.Supp. at 837; *Cannon*, 398 F.Supp. at 220; *Oracle*, 829 F.Supp. at 1189.

Finally, the American Law Institute's Restatement (Third) of the Law Governing Lawyers (2000) Section 131, Comment *g*, provides that a lawyer may represent both the corporate and individual defendants in a derivative action if the company's disinterested directors conclude that there is no basis for the claim. Because of the potential for conflict, such dual representation requires the consent of all clients; in the case of the corporate client, this means "responsible agents not named and not likely to be named in the case." The Comment further states that "if the advice of the lawyer acting for the organization was an important factor in the action of the officers and directors that gave rise to the suit, it is appropriate for the lawyer to represent, if anyone, the officers and directors and for the organization to obtain new counsel."

B. WHO QUALIFIES AS A PLAINTIFF?

1. ADEQUACY

Federal Rules of Civil Procedure 23 and 23.1, governing class actions and derivative suits, respectively, both require that a named plaintiff be capable of adequately and fairly representing the interests of the shareholders on whose behalf suit has been brought. Most states have similar requirements. However, the vast majority of decisions by federal and state courts have held that so long as a plaintiff is represented by a qualified attorney and does not have interests antagonistic to the class or the corporation, she satisfies the adequacy requirement.

For example, *Surowitz v. Hilton Hotels Corp.*, 383 U.S. 363 (1966), involved a derivative claim filed by a Polish immigrant who had a very limited grasp of English and who, when deposed by defendants, had demonstrated almost no understanding of the charges in the complaint. She had filed suit only after her attorney and her son-in-law, Irving Brilliant—who was a lawyer and investment advisor—had uncovered evidence of stock-price manipulation and egregious self-dealing. The Court noted that "derivative suits have played a rather important role in protecting shareholders of corporations from the designing schemes and wiles of insiders who are willing to betray their company's interests in order to enrich themselves." It held that it was error to dismiss an apparently meritorious claim simply because the plaintiff had advanced it on the advice of others.

Courts analyzing the adequacy requirement often look to the role the plaintiffs' lawyer plays in the litigation. The following case is representative.

IN RE FUQUA INDUSTRIES, INC. SHAREHOLDER LITIGATION
752 A.2d 126 (Del.Ch.1999).

CHANDLER, CHANCELLOR.

The question I must answer is whether I should disqualify a derivative plaintiff who is unfamiliar with the basic facts of his or her lawsuit and who exercises little, if any, control over the conduct of such suit?

[The first derivative plaintiff] Mrs. Abrams has held Fuqua shares for over thirty years. The quantity of her holdings has ranged from as much as 12,008 Fuqua shares to the current level of 8000 shares. The decision to purchase Fuqua shares, as most all of Abrams' investment decisions [including the decision to file this suit], was made jointly with her husband, Burton Abrams, a retired trial attorney.

During the long pendency of this litigation Mrs. Abrams fell ill. As she concedes, her memory and faculties have suffered as a result. In a 1998 deposition, it was evident that Mrs. Abrams lacked a meaningful grasp of the facts and allegations of the case prosecuted in her name. While at times she appeared able to provide a general understanding of her claim, she was unable to articulate the understanding with any particularity and she was obviously confused about basic facts regarding her lawsuit.

Alan Freberg, the second derivative plaintiff in this action, purchased twenty-five Fuqua shares in 1989. In 1991, presumably upon concluding that Fuqua directors and Triton had engaged in self-dealing transactions, Freberg retained counsel and filed his first complaint.

Freberg's deposition testimony evidences that his knowledge of the case is at best elliptical. Defendants argue that before his "cram" session immediately before the deposition, Freberg knew absolutely nothing about this matter and had not even been privy to the third amended complaint. Defendants also point out (with much scorn) Freberg's general ignorance of the six or seven other lawsuits in which he was, or still is, the named representative plaintiff. The subtext of defendants' motion is that Freberg has no knowledge of this case because he has no real economic interest at stake. In defendants' view, Freberg is a puppet for his fee-hungry lawyers.

[Court of Chancery decisions hold that a representative plaintiff will not be barred] from the courthouse for lack of proficiency in matters of law and finance and poor health so long as he or she has competent support from advisors and attorneys and is free from disabling conflicts. This conclusion is both just and sensible.

Defendants' attack on Abrams' and Freberg's adequacy raises serious concerns. The allegation that attorneys bring actions through puppet plaintiffs while the real parties in interest are the attorneys themselves in search of fees is an oft-heard complaint from defendants in derivative suits. Sometimes, no doubt, the allegation rings true.

By the same token, however, the mere fact that lawyers pursue their own economic interest in bringing derivative litigation cannot be held as grounds to disqualify a derivative plaintiff. To do so is to impeach a cornerstone of sound corporate governance. Our legal system has privatized in part the enforcement mechanism for policing fiduciaries by allowing private attorneys to bring suits on behalf of nominal shareholder plaintiffs. In so doing, corporations are safeguarded from fiduciary breaches and shareholders thereby benefit. Through the use of cost and fee shifting mechanisms, private attorneys are economically incentivized to perform this service on behalf of shareholders.

To be sure, a real possibility exists that the economic motives of attorneys may influence the remedy sought or the conduct of the litigation. This influence, however, is inherent in private enforcement mechanisms and does not necessarily vitiate the substantial beneficial impact upon the conduct of fiduciaries.

Nonetheless, in some instances, the attorney in pursuit of his own economic interests may usurp the role of the plaintiff and exploit the judicial system entirely for his own private gain. Such extreme facts call for the court to exercise its discretion and to curb the agency costs inherent in private regulatory and enforcement mechanisms. These agency costs should not be borne by society, defendant corporations, directors or the courts.

I cannot say that either Abrams or Freberg is an inadequate plaintiff in this case. Contrary to defendants' assertions, Freberg does in fact understand the basic nature of the derivative claims brought in his name, even if barely so.

Our legal system has long recognized that lawyers take a dominant role in prosecuting litigation on behalf of clients. A conscientious lawyer should indeed take a leadership role and thrust herself to the fore of a lawsuit. This maxim is particularly relevant in cases involving fairly abstruse issues of corporate governance and fiduciary duties.

I deny defendants' motions to disqualify Virginia Abrams and Alan Freberg as representative plaintiffs in this action.

2. STANDING

a. Contemporaneous Ownership

Because a derivative suit seeks to enforce a right in the name of the corporation, standing generally has been limited to those with an equity interest in the corporation. Moreover, in many jurisdictions, the plaintiff must have been a shareholder at the time of the wrong complained of and at the time suit is brought and must remain a shareholder throughout the litigation. Absent this requirement, a person could purchase stock in a company at a price that reflected the harm already done, bring a derivative suit and, if the suit succeeded, realize a windfall equal to her pro rata share of whatever amount the company recovered.

Where a derivative suit is filed on behalf of a typical public corporation the rationale supporting the contemporaneous ownership requirement is less compelling. Some shareholders almost always will have sold their stock at prices that reflect the harm the wrongdoers caused and will not share in any subsequent recovery, while some shareholders will have purchased their stock after the wrong occurred and will realize a windfall if the suit succeeds. This suggests that the main purpose of the contemporaneous ownership requirement, at least in public companies, may not be to prevent a windfall but to make it more difficult for a plaintiffs' attorney to "buy into a lawsuit." Some jurisdictions have relaxed the contemporaneous ownership requirement. California, for example, permits a suit if there is a strong prima facie case in favor of the claim asserted on behalf of the corporation, and the plaintiff acquired the shares before there was disclosure to the public or to the plaintiff of the wrongdoing.

b. Continuing Interest

Either directly or by implication from the applicable statute, many jurisdictions require that the plaintiff maintain an interest in her shares until a derivative suit is resolved. The issue often arises when shareholders assert a claim on behalf of a corporation that has been merged out of existence, or on behalf of the surviving corporation in a merger. The general rule is that a shareholder of a corporation that does not survive a merger lacks standing to sue derivatively for misconduct that occurred before the merger because the claim now is an asset of the surviving corporation. Courts generally do not apply this rule, however, where the merger itself is the subject of a claim, or where the merger involved a reorganization that did not eliminate the plaintiff's economic interest in the enterprise.

c. Security Ownership

In most jurisdictions, a derivative suit may be brought by either a shareholder of record or a beneficial owner of stock. MBCA § 7.40(e) includes in its definition of "shareholder" a person whose shares are held in a voting trust as well as the more traditional "street name" owner of shares.

Suppose the plaintiff is not and never was a shareholder of the corporation injured by the transaction of which she complains, but instead owns stock in a direct or indirect parent of that corporation. The action would then be a double derivative suit, or possibly a triple derivative suit. *Brown v. Tenney*, 532 N.E.2d 230 (Ill.1988), involved a derivative claim by a shareholder of P Corporation based on an alleged injury to S Corporation, a wholly owned subsidiary of P. The court allowed the shareholder to maintain the suit because both P and S were controlled by the alleged wrongdoers. The ALI would allow such suits "[w]here the shareholder's corporation holds at least a *de facto* controlling interest in the injured subsidiary." ALI Principles, § 7.02 Comment f.

C. THE DEMAND REQUIREMENT

Directors, not shareholders, manage the corporation. Derivative suits, which assert rights that belong to the corporation, depart from this norm insofar as they allow shareholders to act on behalf of the corporation in bringing, maintaining and settling such suits. In recognition of this departure, courts and legislatures have sought to maintain some balance between the board's managerial responsibilities and the desirability, in certain circumstances, of allowing shareholders to litigate on behalf of the corporation.

Two different approaches have evolved—a traditional approach, followed by Delaware and several other states, and a newer approach that is incorporated in the MBCA. The traditional approach places great emphasis on whether the shareholder-plaintiff is required to make a demand on the corporation's board of directors to take appropriate corrective action to remedy the alleged misconduct or whether demand should be excused as futile. The MBCA, by contrast, has a universal demand requirement in virtually all cases. It seeks to draw a balance between the interests of directors and shareholder-plaintiffs by specifying the conditions under which a court should defer to a decision by directors to reject a shareholder's demand.

The demand issue arises in two contexts. The first, discussed above, is that a shareholder must exhaust her intra-corporate remedies before bringing a derivative suit unless exhaustion would be futile because of the likelihood that the directors would refuse to act. The second is that, in some circumstances, the board of directors can act to cause the corporation to dismiss a derivative suit after it has been brought on the ground that the action is not in the best interest of the corporation. These two issues are closely related but ultimately are analytically distinct. Both recognize that given the incentives to initiate derivative suits, there is a risk that frivolous and opportunistic suits will be brought. Each is an attempt to screen out the frivolous suits from the meritorious. The problem is designing screening devices with the right mesh.

1. THE TRADITIONAL (DELAWARE) APPROACH

The requirement that a shareholder filing a derivative suit make a demand on the directors before filing suit is designed to ensure that all intra-corporate remedies are exhausted before a shareholder seeks to involve the courts. The demand requirement most often appears as a pleading rule. F.R.C.P. 23.1, for example, provides that the complaint in a derivative suit shall "allege with particularity the efforts, if any, made by the plaintiff to obtain the action plaintiff desires from the directors and the reasons for the plaintiff's failure to obtain the action or for not making the effort." Delaware Chancery Court Rule 23.1 contains an almost identical provision. Although the demand requirement is framed as a pleading rule, courts treat it as a matter of substantive law governing the allocation of power within the corporation.

Prior to the decision that follows, the demand requirement usually did not represent a significant impediment to shareholders seeking to prosecute derivative suits. Courts, in general, allowed shareholders to satisfy the requirement with boilerplate allegations to the effect that demand would be futile because the corporation's directors either had benefitted improperly from the transaction at issue or were dominated or controlled by whomever had benefitted. Alternatively, courts would allow shareholder-plaintiffs to name all directors as defendants and then assert that they could not be expected to sue because they were potentially liable for having approved the transaction at issue or for failing to seek to hold liable whoever was responsible for approving it. *Barr v. Wackman*, 329 N.E.2d 180 (N.Y. 1975), for example, recognized that a complaint naming a majority of the directors as defendants and making conclusory allegations of wrongdoing or control by wrongdoers "would only beg the question of actual futility and ignore the particularity requirement of the statute," the court then held that allegations that the corporation's unaffiliated directors had acquiesced in the allegedly wrongful transactions (from which they realized no personal benefits) stated a cause of action for breach of those directors' duty of due care and thus served to establish that demand would be futile.

ARONSON V. LEWIS
473 A.2d 805 (Del.1984).

MOORE, JUSTICE:

When is a stockholder's demand upon a board of directors, to redress an alleged wrong to the corporation, excused as futile prior to the filing of a derivative suit? We granted this interlocutory appeal to the defendants, Meyers Parking System, Inc. (Meyers), a Delaware corporation, and its directors, to review the Court of Chancery's denial of their motion to dismiss this action, pursuant to Chancery Rule 23.1, for the plaintiff's failure to make such a demand or otherwise demonstrate its futility. The Vice Chancellor ruled that plaintiff's allegations raised a "reasonable inference" that the directors' action was unprotected by the business judgment rule. Thus, the board could not have impartially considered and acted upon the demand.

We cannot agree with this formulation of the concept of demand futility. In our view demand can only be excused where facts are alleged with particularity which create a reasonable doubt that the directors' action was entitled to the protections of the business judgment rule. Because the plaintiff failed to make a demand, and to allege facts with particularity indicating that such demand would be futile, we reverse the Court of Chancery and remand with instructions that plaintiff be granted leave to amend the complaint.

The issues of demand futility rest upon the allegations of the complaint. The plaintiff, Harry Lewis, is a stockholder of Meyers. The defendants are Meyers and its ten directors, some of whom are also company officers.

In 1979, Prudential Building Maintenance Corp. (Prudential) spun off its shares of Meyers to Prudential's stockholders. Prior thereto Meyers was a wholly owned subsidiary of Prudential. Meyers provides parking lot facilities and related services throughout the country. Its stock is actively traded over-the-counter.

This suit challenges certain transactions between Meyers and one of its directors, Leo Fink, who owns 47% of its outstanding stock. Plaintiff claims that these transactions were approved only because Fink personally selected each director and officer of Meyers.

Prior to January 1, 1981, Fink had an employment agreement with Prudential which provided that upon retirement he was to become a consultant to that company for ten years. This provision became operable when Fink retired in April 1980. Thereafter, Meyers agreed with Prudential to share Fink's consulting services and reimburse Prudential for 25% of the fees paid Fink. Under this arrangement Meyers paid Prudential $48,332 in 1980 and $45,832 in 1981.

On January 1, 1981, the defendants approved an employment agreement between Meyers and Fink for a five year term with provision for automatic renewal each year thereafter, indefinitely. Meyers agreed to pay Fink $150,000 per year, plus a bonus of 5% of its pre-tax profits over $2,400,000. Fink could terminate the contract at any time, but Meyers could do so only upon six months' notice. At termination, Fink was to become a consultant to Meyers and be paid $150,000 per year for the first three years, $125,000 for the next three years, and $100,000 thereafter for life. Death benefits were also included. Fink agreed to devote his best efforts and substantially his entire business time to advancing Meyers' interests. The agreement also provided that Fink's compensation was not to be affected by any inability to perform services on Meyers' behalf. Fink was 75 years old when his employment agreement with Meyers was approved by the directors. There is no claim that he was, or is, in poor health.

Additionally, the Meyers board approved and made interest-free loans to Fink totaling $225,000. These loans were unpaid and outstanding as of August 1982 when the complaint was filed. At oral argument defendants' counsel represented that these loans had been repaid in full.

The complaint charges that these transactions had "no valid business purpose", and were a "waste of corporate assets" because the amounts to be paid are "grossly excessive", that Fink performs "no or little services", and because of his "advanced age" cannot be "expected to perform any such services". The plaintiff also charges that the existence of the Prudential consulting agreement with Fink prevents him from providing his "best efforts" on Meyers' behalf. Finally, it is alleged that the loans to Fink were in reality "additional compensation" without any "consideration" or "benefit" to Meyers.

The complaint alleged that no demand had been made on the Meyers board because:

13. Such attempt would be futile for the following reasons:

(a) All of the directors in office are named as defendants herein and they have participated in, expressly approved and/or acquiesced in, and are personally liable for, the wrongs complained of herein.

(b) Defendant Fink, having selected each director, controls and dominates every member of the Board and every officer of Meyers.

(c) Institution of this action by present directors would require the defendant-directors to sue themselves, thereby placing the conduct of this action in hostile hands and preventing its effective prosecution.

The relief sought included the cancellation of the Meyers-Fink employment contract and an accounting by the directors, including Fink, for all damage sustained by Meyers and for all profits derived by the directors and Fink.

A cardinal precept of the General Corporation Law of the State of Delaware is that directors, rather than shareholders, manage the business and affairs of the corporation. 8 Del.C. § 141(a). Section 141(a) states in pertinent part:

> "The *business and affairs* of a corporation organized under this chapter *shall be managed by or under the direction* of a board of directors except as may be otherwise provided in this chapter or in its certificate of incorporation."

8 Del.C. § 141(a) (Emphasis added). The existence and exercise of this power carries with it certain fundamental fiduciary obligations to the corporation and its shareholders. Moreover, a stockholder is not powerless to challenge director action which results in harm to the corporation. The machinery of corporate democracy and the derivative suit are potent tools to redress the conduct of a torpid or unfaithful management. The derivative action developed in equity to enable shareholders to sue in the corporation's name where those in control of the company refused to assert a claim belonging to it. The nature of the action is two-fold. First, it is the equivalent of a suit by the shareholders to compel the corporation to sue. Second, it is a suit by the corporation, asserted by the shareholders on its behalf, against those liable to it.

By its very nature the derivative action impinges on the managerial freedom of directors. Hence, the demand requirement of Chancery Rule 23.1 exists at the threshold, first to insure that a stockholder exhausts his intracorporate remedies, and then to provide a safeguard against strike suits. Thus, by promoting this form of alternate dispute resolution, rather than immediate recourse to litigation, the demand requirement is a recognition of the fundamental precept that directors manage the business and affairs of corporations.

In our view the entire question of demand futility is inextricably bound to issues of business judgment and the standards of that doctrine's applicability. The business judgment rule is an acknowledgment of the managerial prerogatives of Delaware directors under Section 141(a). It is a presumption that in making a business decision the directors of a corporation acted on an informed basis, in good faith and in the honest belief that the action taken was in the best interests of the company. Absent an abuse of discretion, that judgment will be respected by the courts. The burden is on the party challenging the decision to establish facts rebutting the presumption.

The function of the business judgment rule is of paramount significance in the context of a derivative action. It comes into play in several ways—in addressing a demand, in the determination of demand futility, in efforts by independent disinterested directors to dismiss the action as inimical to the corporation's best interests, and generally, as a defense to the merits of the suit. However, in each of these circumstances there are certain common principles governing the application and operation of the rule.

First, its protections can only be claimed by disinterested directors whose conduct otherwise meets the tests of business judgment. From the standpoint of interest, this means that directors can neither appear on both sides of a transaction nor expect to derive any personal financial benefit from it in the sense of self-dealing, as opposed to a benefit which devolves upon the corporation or all stockholders generally. Thus, if such director interest is present, and the transaction is not approved by a majority consisting of the disinterested directors, then the business judgment rule has no application whatever in determining demand futility.

Second, to invoke the rule's protection directors have a duty to inform themselves, prior to making a business decision, of all material information reasonably available to them. Having become so informed, they must then act with requisite care in the discharge of their duties. While the Delaware cases use a variety of terms to describe the applicable standard of care, our analysis satisfies us that under the business judgment rule director liability is predicated upon concepts of gross negligence.

However, it should be noted that the business judgment rule operates only in the context of director action. Technically speaking, it has no role where directors have either abdicated their functions, or absent a conscious decision, failed to act. But it also follows that under applicable principles, a conscious decision to refrain from acting may nonetheless be a valid exercise of business judgment and enjoy the protections of the rule.

Delaware courts have addressed the issue of demand futility on several earlier occasions. The rule emerging from these decisions is that where officers and directors are under an influence which sterilizes their discretion, they cannot be considered proper persons to conduct litigation on behalf of the corporation. Thus, demand would be futile.

However, those cases cannot be taken to mean that any board approval of a challenged transaction automatically connotes "hostile interest" and "guilty participation" by directors, or some other form of sterilizing influence upon them. Were that so, the demand requirements of our law would be meaningless, leaving the clear mandate of Chancery Rule 23.1 devoid of its purpose and substance.

The trial court correctly recognized that demand futility is inextricably bound to issues of business judgment, but stated the test to be based on allegations of fact, which, if true, "show that there is a reasonable inference" the business judgment rule is not applicable for purposes of a pre-suit demand.

The problem with this formulation is the concept of reasonable inferences to be drawn against a board of directors based on allegations in a complaint. As is clear from this case, and the conclusory allegations upon which the Vice Chancellor relied, demand futility becomes virtually automatic under such a test. Bearing in mind the presumptions with which director action is cloaked, we believe that the matter must be approached in a more balanced way.

Our view is that in determining demand futility the Court of Chancery in the proper exercise of its discretion must decide whether, under the particularized facts alleged, a reasonable doubt is created that: (1) the directors are disinterested and independent and (2) the challenged transaction was otherwise the product of a valid exercise of business judgment. Hence, the Court of Chancery must make two inquiries, one into the independence and disinterestedness of the directors and the other into the substantive nature of the challenged transaction and the board's approval thereof. As to the latter inquiry the court does not assume that the transaction is a wrong to the corporation requiring corrective steps by the board. Rather, the alleged wrong is substantively reviewed against the factual background alleged in the complaint. As to the former inquiry, directorial independence and disinterestedness, the court reviews the factual allegations to decide whether they raise a reasonable doubt, as a threshold matter, that the protections of the business judgment rule are available to the board. Certainly, if this is an "interested" director transaction, such that the business judgment rule is inapplicable to the board majority approving the transaction, then the inquiry ceases. In that event futility of demand has been established by any objective or subjective standard.[8]

However, the mere threat of personal liability for approving a questioned transaction, standing alone, is insufficient to challenge either the independence or disinterestedness of directors, although in rare cases a transaction may be so egregious on its face that board approval cannot meet the test of business judgment, and a substantial likelihood of director liability therefore exists. In sum the entire review is factual in nature. The Court of Chancery in the exercise of its sound discretion must be satisfied that a plaintiff has alleged facts with particularity which, taken as true, support a reasonable doubt that the challenged transaction was the product of a valid exercise of business judgment. Only in that context is demand excused.

Having outlined the legal framework within which these issues are to be determined, we consider plaintiff's claims of futility here: Fink's domination and control of the directors, board approval of the Fink-Meyers employment agreement, and board hostility to the plaintiff's derivative action due to the directors' status as defendants.

Plaintiff's claim that Fink dominates and controls the Meyers board is based on: (1) Fink's 47% ownership of Meyers' outstanding stock, and (2) that he "personally selected" each Meyers director. Plaintiff also alleges that mere approval of the employment agreement illustrates Fink's domination and control of the board. In addition, plaintiff argued on appeal that 47% stock ownership, though less than a majority, constituted control given the large number of shares outstanding, 1,245,745.

Such contentions do not support any claim under Delaware law that these directors lack independence. In *Kaplan v. Centex Corp.*, Del.Ch., 284 A.2d 119 (1971), the Court of Chancery stated that "[s]tock ownership alone, at least when it amounts to less than a majority, is not sufficient proof of domination or control". *Id.* at 123. Moreover, in the demand context even proof of majority ownership of a company does not strip the directors of the presumptions of independence, and that their acts have been taken in good faith and in the best interests of the corporation. There must be coupled with the allegation of control such facts as would demonstrate that through personal or other relationships the directors are beholden to the controlling person. To date the principal decisions dealing with the issue of control or domination arose only after a full trial on the merits. Thus, they

---

[8]   We recognize that drawing the line at a majority of the board may be an arguably arbitrary dividing point. Critics will charge that we are ignoring the structural bias common to corporate boards throughout America, as well as the other unseen socialization processes cutting against independent discussion and decisionmaking in the boardroom. The difficulty with structural bias in a demand futile case is simply one of establishing it in the complaint for purposes of Rule 23.1. We are satisfied that discretionary review by the Court of Chancery of complaints alleging specific facts pointing to bias on a particular board will be sufficient for determining demand futility.

are distinguishable in the demand context unless similar particularized facts are alleged to meet the test of Chancery Rule 23.1.

The requirement of director independence inheres in the conception and rationale of the business judgment rule. The presumption of propriety that flows from an exercise of business judgment is based in part on this unyielding precept. Independence means that a director's decision is based on the corporate merits of the subject before the board rather than extraneous considerations or influences. While directors may confer, debate, and resolve their differences through compromise, or by reasonable reliance upon the expertise of their colleagues and other qualified persons, the end result, nonetheless, must be that each director has brought his or her own informed business judgment to bear with specificity upon the corporate merits of the issues without regard for or succumbing to influences which convert an otherwise valid business decision into a faithless act.

Thus, it is not enough to charge that a director was nominated by or elected at the behest of those controlling the outcome of a corporate election. That is the usual way a person becomes a corporate director. It is the care, attention and sense of individual responsibility to the performance of one's duties, not the method of election, that generally touches on independence.

We conclude that in the demand-futile context a plaintiff charging domination and control of one or more directors must allege particularized facts manifesting "a direction of corporate conduct in such a way as to comport with the wishes or interests of the corporation (or persons) doing the controlling". *Kaplan,* 284 A.2d at 123. The shorthand shibboleth of "dominated and controlled directors" is insufficient. In recognizing that *Kaplan* was decided after trial and full discovery, we stress that the plaintiff need only allege specific facts; he need not plead evidence. Otherwise, he would be forced to make allegations which may not comport with his duties under Chancery Rule 11.

Here, plaintiff has not alleged any facts sufficient to support a claim of control. The personal-selection-of-directors allegation stands alone, unsupported. At best it is a conclusion devoid of factual support. The causal link between Fink's control and approval of the employment agreement is alluded to, but nowhere specified. The director's approval, alone, does not establish control, even in the face of Fink's 47% stock ownership. The claim that Fink is unlikely to perform any services under the agreement, because of his age, and his conflicting consultant work with Prudential, adds nothing to the control claim. Therefore, we cannot conclude that the complaint factually particularizes any circumstances of control and domination to overcome the presumption of board independence, and thus render the demand futile.

Turning to the board's approval of the Meyers-Fink employment agreement, plaintiff's argument is simple: all of the Meyers directors are named defendants, because they approved the wasteful agreement; if plaintiff prevails on the merits all the directors will be jointly and severally liable; therefore, the directors' interest in avoiding personal liability automatically and absolutely disqualifies them from passing on a shareholder's demand.

Such allegations are conclusory at best. In Delaware mere directorial approval of a transaction, absent particularized facts supporting a breach of fiduciary duty claim, or otherwise establishing the lack of independence or disinterestedness of a majority of the directors, is insufficient to excuse demand. Here, plaintiff's suit is premised on the notion that the Meyers-Fink employment agreement was a waste of corporate assets. So, the argument goes, by approving such waste the directors now face potential personal liability, thereby rendering futile any demand on them to bring suit. Unfortunately, plaintiff's claim fails in its initial premise. The complaint does not allege particularized facts indicating that the agreement is a waste of corporate assets. Indeed, the complaint as now drafted may not even state a cause of action, given the directors' broad corporate power to fix the compensation of officers.

In essence, the plaintiff alleged a lack of consideration flowing from Fink to Meyers, since the employment agreement provided that compensation was not contingent on Fink's ability to perform any services. The bare assertion that Fink performed "little or no services" was plaintiff's conclusion based solely on Fink's age and the *existence* of the Fink-Prudential employment agreement. As for Meyers' loans to Fink, beyond the bare allegation that they were made, the complaint does not allege facts indicating the wastefulness of such arrangements. Again, the mere existence of such loans, given the broad corporate powers conferred by Delaware law, does not even state a claim.

Plaintiff's final argument is the incantation that demand is excused because the directors otherwise would have to sue themselves, thereby placing the conduct of the litigation in hostile hands and preventing its effective prosecution. This bootstrap argument has been made to and dismissed by other courts. Its acceptance would effectively abrogate Rule 23.1 and weaken the managerial power of directors. Unless facts are alleged with particularity to overcome the presumptions of independence and a proper exercise of business judgment, in which case the directors could not be expected to sue themselves, a bare claim of this sort raises no legally cognizable issue under Delaware corporate law.

In sum, we conclude that the plaintiff has failed to allege facts with particularity indicating that the Meyers directors were tainted by interest, lacked independence, or took action contrary to Meyers' best interests in order to create a reasonable doubt as to the applicability of the business judgment rule. Only in the presence of such a reasonable doubt may a demand be deemed futile, hence, we reverse the Court of Chancery's denial of the motion to dismiss, and remand with instructions that plaintiff be granted leave to amend his complaint to bring it into compliance with Rule 23.1 based on the principles we have announced today.

Reversed and remanded.

———————

Justice Moore's opinion appears to be ambiguous on one respect. He writes that demand can be excused if the trial court finds that, "under the particularized facts alleged, a reasonable doubt is created that: (1) the directors are disinterested and independent *and* (2) the challenged transaction was otherwise the product of a valid exercise of business judgment." (Emphasis added.) This statement can be read to mean that the complaint must allege facts creating a reasonable doubt *both* that the current board cannot be relied on to make an independent decision with respect to the prosecution of the lawsuit *and* that the decision being challenged was the result of a valid business judgment. That reading is illogical, however, and subsequent cases have held that demand is excused if *either* of those statements is true. *E.g., Brehm v. Eisner*, 746 A.2d 244, 256 (Del. 2000).

Three other aspects of *Aronson* are particularly notable. First, the court explains that the demand requirement serves not only to ensure that intra-corporate remedies be exhausted, but also as a necessary adjunct to the mandate of DGCL § 141(a) that the board of directors shall manage or oversee the management of the corporation. Second, the court notes that if plaintiffs are allowed to proceed on the basis of "conclusory allegations, demand futility becomes virtually automatic." Some commentators argue that the considerations that justify judicial deference to directors' business judgments do not apply with equal force to decisions not to prosecute claims the corporation would be entitled to assert. Directors do not face any significant threat of personal liability if courts override decisions in the latter category, because the claim at issue then will be pursued by the shareholder-plaintiff. Moreover, courts are far more qualified to weigh directors' decisions as to whether potential derivative claims are worth pursuing than they are to assess commercial or financial judgments. Finally, *Aronson* is the first definitive holding by the Delaware Supreme Court "that under the business judgment rule director liability is predicated upon concepts of gross negligence." 473 A.2d at 812. *Aronson*'s holding that a plaintiff must demonstrate demand futility by setting forth "particularized facts," rather than "conclusory allegations" can put plaintiffs in a difficult situation: without discovery, a plaintiff will not be able to learn the facts necessary to establish demand futility, yet without those facts, a plaintiff will not be entitled to engage in discovery. Subsequent decisions demonstrate that *Aronson* did not create an insurmountable barrier; and, when the plaintiff in *Aronson* filed an amended, more particularized complaint, the Court of Chancery held it satisfied the new, more stringent, pleading requirement.

As is discussed at greater length below, later Delaware Supreme Court decisions have made clear that shareholders are to use their inspection rights under DGCL § 220 as an information-gathering tool to investigate the possibility of corporate wrongdoing. *See Rales v. Blasband*, 634 A.2d 927, 935 n. 10 (Del. 1993). As *Rales* implies, one "proper purpose" for inspection is to investigate suspected wrongdoing so as to establish a basis for a derivative suit. However, inspection cannot be used to engage in a "fishing expedition." The shareholder seeking inspection bears the burden of establishing, by a preponderance of the evidence, that she has a credible basis for believing that wrongdoing has occurred. *See Security First Corp. v. U.S. Die Casting & Development Co.*, 687 A.2d 563, 568 (Del. 1997). In addition, shareholders' inspection rights only extend to documents that are "essential" to their investigation and, as to documents within this category, a shareholder must "make specific and discrete identification, with rifled precision, of the documents sought." *Brehm v. Eisner*, 746 A.2d 244, 266–67 (Del. 2000).

Failure to establish demand futility usually signals the death knell of a derivative suit. Where demand has been made and refused, courts generally apply the business judgment rule to the board's refusal, creating a strong presumption in favor of the board's decision not to pursue the litigation. Moreover, a shareholder, once having made demand, cannot thereafter argue that demand should be excused as futile. Thus, if demand is made and rejected, almost the only circumstances in which a shareholder is allowed to proceed is if she can demonstrate, without the benefits of discovery, that the board rejected her demand without informing itself of the issues involves or that the board relied on attorneys who also represented or had represented the alleged wrongdoer. *See Stepak v. Addison*, 20 F.3d 398 (11th Cir. 1994) (holding refusal of demand wrongful where board's consideration dominated by attorneys who represented alleged wrongdoer in criminal proceedings relating to same subject as demand). A board's failure to object to a demand, however, is viewed as an approval for the shareholder to pursue the suit on the litigation on the corporation's behalf. Thus, a defendant-corporation can only argue demand is not excused if the board affirmatively objects to the continuation of the derivative suit.

RALES V. BLASBAND

Aronson establishes the test for demand futility in cases in which the board that is considering the demand is the board that has made the decision that is being challenged. Not every case, however, fits this model. In some cases, the board on which demand is made did not make the business decision which is the subject of the suit and thus an *Aronson* analysis would be inappropriate.

In *Rales v. Blasband,* 634 A.2d 927 (Del.1993), the Delaware Supreme Court confronted such a case and, recognizing the difficulty of applying *Aronson*, established a new test for these situations. The court stated:

> Under the unique circumstances of this case, an analysis of the Board's ability to consider a demand requires a departure here from the standards set forth in *Aronson*. The Board did not approve the transaction which is being challenged by Blasband in this action. In fact, the Danaher directors have made no decision relating to the subject of this derivative suit. Where there is no conscious decision by directors to act or refrain from acting, the business judgment rule has no application. The absence of board action, therefore, makes it impossible to perform the essential inquiry contemplated by *Aronson*—whether the directors have acted in conformity with the business judgment rule in approving the challenged transaction.

> Consistent with the context and rationale of the *Aronson* decision, a court should not apply the *Aronson* test for demand futility where the board that would be considering the demand did not make a business decision which is being challenged in the derivative suit. This situation would arise in three principal scenarios: (1) where a business decision was made by the board of a company, but a majority of the directors making the decision have been replaced; (2) where the subject of the derivative suit is not a business decision of the board; and (3) where, as here, the decision being challenged was made by the board of a different corporation.

> Instead, it is appropriate in these situations to examine whether the board that would be addressing the demand can impartially consider its merits without being influenced by improper considerations. Thus, a court must determine whether or not the particularized factual allegations of a derivative stockholder complaint create a reasonable doubt that, as of the time the complaint is filed, the board of directors could have properly exercised its independent and disinterested business judgment in responding to a demand. If the derivative plaintiff satisfies this burden, then demand will be futile.

634 A.2d at 933.

2. THE MBCA APPROACH

The MBCA sets forth detailed rules governing the conduct and disposition of derivative litigation. MBCA §§ 7.40–7.47. It takes the position that demand should be made in every case before a derivative suit is filed. The Official Comment to MBCA § 7.42 explains that this approach (1) gives the board an opportunity to review the conduct in question and take corrective action and (2) eliminates the time and expense involved in litigating whether demand is excused.

However, the MBCA often requires courts to make judgments similar to those they make where demand is required. A plaintiff must wait 90 days after making demand to file her complaint, unless the demand is rejected before that. Where demand is rejected, a plaintiff, without the benefit of discovery, must plead "with particularity facts establishing either (1) that a majority of the board [that rejected the demand] did not consist of independent directors" or (2) that the decision rejecting the demand was not made "in good faith after conducting a reasonable inquiry." MBCA § 7.44. Allegations sufficient to establish that a majority of the board was not independent shift to the corporation the burden of proving that the decision to reject the demand was made in good faith after reasonable inquiry. Thus, as the Official Comment acknowledges, § 7.44 carries forward the distinction between demand excused and demand required cases by assigning to plaintiff the threshold burden of alleging facts that establish a majority of the board is not independent and allocating the burden of proof on the basis of whether plaintiff has met this burden. Although the MBCA frames the relevant question in terms of directors' independence, rather than demand futility, the issues a court must address are much the same.

The decisions which have examined the qualifications of directors making the determination have required that they be both "disinterested" in the sense of not having a personal interest in the transaction being challenged as opposed to a benefit which devolves upon the corporation or all shareholders generally, and "independent" in the sense of not being influenced in favor of the defendants by reason of personal or other relationships. Only the word "independent" has been used in section 7.44(b) because it is believed that this word necessarily also includes the requirement that a person have no interest in the transaction. The concept of an independent director is not intended to be limited to non-officer or "outside" directors but may in appropriate circumstances include directors who are also officers.

Many of the special litigation committees involved in the reported cases consisted of directors who were elected after the alleged wrongful acts by the directors who were named as defendants in the action. Subsection (c)(1) makes it clear that the participation of non-independent directors or shareholders in the nomination or election of a new director shall not prevent the new director from being considered independent. This sentence therefore rejects the concept that the mere appointment of new directors by the non-independent directors makes the new directors not independent in making the necessary determination because of an inherent structural bias. Clauses (2) and (3) also confirm the decisions by a number of courts that the mere fact that a director has been named as a defendant or approved the action being challenged does not cause the director to be considered not independent.

MBCA § 7.44, Official Comment.

EINHORN V. CULEA

612 N.W.2d 78 (Wis. 2000).

SHIRLEY S. ABRAHAMSON, CHIEF JUSTICE.

Under Wis. Stat. § 180.0744, [which is based on MBCA § 7.44,] the [corporation may create a special litigation committee consisting of two or more independent directors appointed by a majority vote of independent directors present at a meeting of the board of directors.] The independent special litigation committee determines whether the derivative action is in the best interests of the corporation. If the independent special litigation committee acts in good faith, conducts a reasonable inquiry upon which it bases its conclusions and concludes that the maintenance of the derivative action is not in the best interests of the corporation, the circuit court shall dismiss the derivative action. The statute thus requires the circuit court to defer to the business judgment of a properly composed and properly operating special litigation committee.

[The most common challenge to the decision of a special litigation committee, and the one made in the present case, is that the members are not independent.] Given the finality of the ultimate decision of the committee to dismiss the action, judicial oversight is necessary to ensure that the special litigation committee is independent so that it acts in the corporation's best interest. [At issue is whether the special litigation committee created in the present case under Wis. Stat. § 180.0744 was composed of independent directors as required by statute.]

Although the plain language of Wis. Stat. § 180.0744 requires the directors who are members of the special litigation committee to be independent, the statute does not define the word "independent." Rather, § 180.0744(3) merely instructs that whether a director on the committee is independent should _not_ be determined solely on the basis of any of the following three factors set forth in the statute: [(1) whether the director is nominated to the special litigation committee or elected by persons who are defendants in the derivative action, (2) whether the director is a defendant in the action, or (3) whether the act being challenged in the derivative action was approved by the director if the act resulted in no personal benefit to the director.]

The legislature understood the significance of the factors it listed. It allows the circuit court to give weight to these factors; the statute simply states that the presence of one or more of these factors is not solely determinative of the issue of whether a director is independent.

PP

The legislature recognized, for example, that a shareholder could prevent the entire board of directors from serving on the special litigation committee merely by naming all the directors as defendants in the derivative action.

Judicial review to determine whether the members of the committee are independent and whether the committee's procedure complies with the statute is of utmost importance, because the court is bound by the substantive decision of a properly constituted and acting committee. The power of a corporate defendant to obtain a dismissal of an action by the ruling of a committee of independent directors selected by the board of directors is unique in the law. The threshold established by the legislature in Wis. Stat. § 180.0744 to determine whether members of a committee are independent is decidedly not "extremely low," as the circuit court stated. We conclude the legislature intended a circuit court to examine carefully whether members of a special litigation committee are independent.

We now discuss the appropriate test to be applied to determine whether directors who are members of a special litigation committee are independent under Wis. Stat. § 180.0744. This question is one of first impression in Wisconsin. Nothing in the statute expressly states the factors to be examined to determine whether directors who are members of a committee are independent.

The Model Business Corporation Act (upon which Wis. Stat. § 180.0744 is based) builds on the law relating to special litigation committees developed by a number of states. We are therefore informed by the case law of other states, and we derive from this case law the following test to determine whether a member of a special litigation committee is independent.

Standard

Whether members are independent is tested on an objective basis as of the time they are appointed to the special litigation committee. Considering the totality of the circumstances, a court shall determine whether a reasonable person in the position of a member of a special litigation committee can base his or her decision on the merits of the issue rather than on extraneous considerations or influences. [In other words, the test is whether a member of a committee has a relationship with an individual defendant or the corporation that would reasonably be expected to affect the member's judgment with respect to the litigation in issue.] The factors a court should examine to determine whether a committee member is independent include, but are not limited to, the following:

> (1) *A committee member's status as a defendant and potential liability.* Optimally members of a special litigation committee should not be defendants in the derivative action and should not be exposed to personal liability as a result of the action.

(2) *A committee member's participation in or approval of the alleged wrongdoing or financial benefits from the challenged transaction.* Optimally members of a special litigation committee should not have been members of the board of directors when the transaction in question occurred or was approved. Nor should they have participated in the transaction or events underlying the derivative action. Innocent or *pro forma* involvement does not necessarily render a member not independent, but substantial participation or approval or personal financial benefit should.

(3) *A committee member's past or present business or economic dealings with an individual defendant.* Evidence of a committee member's employment and financial relations with an individual defendant should be considered in determining whether the member is independent.

(4) *A committee member's past or present personal, family, or social relations with individual defendants.* Evidence of a committee member's non-financial relations with an individual defendant should be considered in determining whether the member is independent. A determination of whether a member is independent is affected by the extent to which a member is directly or indirectly dominated by, controlled by or beholden to an individual defendant.

(5) *A committee member's past or present business or economic relations with the corporation.* For example, if a member of the special litigation committee was outside counsel or a consultant to the corporation, this factor should be considered in determining whether the member is independent.

(6) *The number of members on a special litigation committee.* The more members on a special litigation committee, the less weight a circuit court may assign to a particular disabling interest affecting a single member of the committee.

(7) *The roles of corporate counsel and independent counsel.* Courts should be more likely to find a special litigation committee independent if the committee retains counsel who has not represented individual defendants or the corporation in the past.

Some courts and commentators have suggested that a "structural bias" exists in special litigation committees that taints their decisions. They argue that members of a committee, appointed by the directors of the corporation, are instinctively sympathetic and empathetic towards their colleagues on the board of directors and can be expected to vote for dismissal of any but the most egregious charges. They assert that the committees are inherently biased and untrustworthy. Wisconsin Stat.

§ 180.0744 and the Model Business Corporation Act are designed to combat this possibility.

A court should not presuppose that a special litigation committee is inherently biased. Although members of a special litigation committee may have experiences similar to those of the defendant directors and serve with them on the board of directors, the legislature has declared that independent members of a special litigation committee are capable of rendering an independent decision. The test we set forth today is designed, as is the statute, to overcome the effects of any "structural bias."

A circuit court is to look at the totality of the circumstances. A finding that a member of the special litigation committee is independent does not require the complete absence of any facts that might point to non-objectivity. A director may be independent even if he or she has had some personal or business relation with an individual director accused of wrongdoing. Although the totality of the circumstances test does not necessitate the complete absence of any facts that might point to a member not being independent, a circuit court is required to apply the test for determining whether a member is independent with care and rigor. If the members are not independent, the court will, in effect, be allowing the defendant directors to render a judgment on their own alleged misconduct. The value of a special litigation committee depends on the extent to which the members of the committee are independent.

It is vital for a circuit court to review whether each member of a special litigation committee is independent. The special litigation committee is, after all, the "only instance in American Jurisprudence where a defendant can free itself from a suit by merely appointing a committee to review the allegations of the complaint. . . ." [*Lewis v. Fuqua*, 502 A.2d 962, 967 (Del.Ch.1985).] We agree with the Delaware Court of Chancery that the trial court must be "certain that the SLC [special litigation committee] is truly independent." [*Id.*] While ill suited to assessing business judgments, courts are well suited by experience to evaluate whether members of a special litigation committee are independent.

The test we set forth attains the balance the legislature intended by empowering corporations to dismiss meritless derivative litigation through special litigation committees, while checking this power with appropriate judicial oversight over the composition and conduct of the special litigation committee.

D. INSPECTION OF BOOKS AND RECORDS

Shareholders have a right to inspect the books and records of a corporation for a "proper purpose." One purpose for inspecting books and records that *is* clearly "proper" is investigating possible corporate mismanagement in order to be in a position to bring a lawsuit challenging it. "Delaware courts have strongly encouraged stockholder-plaintiffs to utilize Section 220 before filing a derivative action, in order to satisfy the heightened demand futility pleading requirements of Court of Chancery Rule 23.1. To show demand futility, a stockholder-plaintiff in a derivative suit must allege with particularity why the stockholder was justified in having made no effort to obtain board action. By first prosecuting a Section 220 action to inspect books and records, the stockholder-plaintiff may be able to uncover particularized facts that would establish demand excusal in a subsequent derivative suit." *King v. VeriFone Holdings, Inc.*, 12 A.3d 1140, 1145–46 (Del. 2011). This principle is not without its limits, however, as the following cases illustrate.

SAITO V. MCKESSON HBOC, INC.
806 A.2d 113 (Del. 2002).

BERGER, JUSTICE.

In this appeal, we consider the limitations on a stockholder's statutory right to inspect corporate books and records. The statute, 8 Del.C. § 220, enables stockholders to investigate matters "reasonably related to [their] interest as [stockholders]" including, among other things, possible corporate wrongdoing. It does not open the door to the wide ranging discovery that would be available in support of litigation. For this statutory tool to be meaningful, however, it cannot be read narrowly to deprive a stockholder of necessary documents solely because the documents were prepared by third parties or because the documents predate the stockholder's first investment in the corporation. A stockholder who demands inspection for a proper purpose should be given access to all of the documents in the corporation's possession, custody or control, that are necessary to satisfy that proper purpose. Thus, where a § 220 claim is based on alleged corporate wrongdoing, and assuming the allegation is meritorious, the stockholder should be given enough information to effectively address the problem, either through derivative litigation or through direct contact with the corporation's directors and/or stockholders.

On October 17, 1998, McKesson Corporation entered into a stock-for-stock merger agreement with HBO & Company ("HBOC"). On October 20, 1998, appellant, Noel Saito, purchased McKesson stock. The merger was consummated in January 1999 and the combined company was renamed McKesson HBOC, Incorporated. HBOC continued its separate corporate existence as a wholly-owned subsidiary of McKesson HBOC.

Starting in April and continuing through July 1999, McKesson HBOC announced a series of financial restatements triggered by its year-end audit process. During that four month period, McKesson HBOC reduced its revenues by $327.4 million for the three prior fiscal years. The restatements all were attributed to HBOC accounting irregularities. The first announcement precipitated several lawsuits, including a derivative action pending in the Court of Chancery, captioned *Ash v. McCall,* Civil Action No. 17132. Saito was one of four plaintiffs in the *Ash* complaint, which alleged that: (i) McKesson's directors breached their duty of care by failing to discover the HBOC accounting irregularities before the merger; (ii) McKesson's directors committed corporate waste by entering into the merger with HBOC; (iii) HBOC's directors breached their fiduciary duties by failing to monitor the company's compliance with financial reporting requirements prior to the merger; and (iv) McKesson HBOC's directors failed in the same respect during the three months following the merger. Although the Court of Chancery granted defendants' motion to dismiss the complaint, the dismissal was without prejudice as to the pre-merger and post-merger oversight claims.

In its decision on the motion to dismiss, the Court of Chancery specifically suggested that Saito and the other plaintiffs "use the 'tools at hand,' most prominently § 220 books and records actions, to obtain information necessary to sue derivatively." Saito was the only *Ash* plaintiff to follow that advice. The stated purpose of Saito's demand was:

> (1) to further investigate breaches of fiduciary duties by the boards of directors of HBO & Co., Inc., McKesson, Inc., and/or McKesson HBOC, Inc. related to their oversight of their respective company's accounting procedures and financial reporting; (2) to investigate potential claims against advisors engaged by McKesson, Inc. and HBO & Co., Inc. to the acquisition of HBO & Co., Inc. by McKesson, Inc.; and (3) to gather information relating to the above in order to supplement the complaint in *Ash v. McCall, et al.,* . . . in accordance with the September 15, 2000 Opinion of the Court of Chancery.

Saito demanded access to eleven categories of documents, including those relating to Arthur Andersen's pre-merger review and verification of HBOC's financial condition; communications between or among HBOC, McKesson, and their investment bankers and accountants concerning HBOC's accounting practices; and discussions among members of the Boards of Directors of HBOC, McKesson, and/or McKesson HBOC concerning reports published in April 1997 and thereafter about HBOC's accounting practices or financial condition.

After trial, the Court of Chancery found that Saito stated a proper purpose for the inspection of books and records-to ferret out possible wrongdoing in connection with the merger of HBOC and McKesson. But the court held that Saito's proper purpose only extended to potential wrongdoing after the date on which Saito acquired his McKesson stock. The court also held that Saito did not have a proper purpose to inspect documents relating to potential claims against third party advisors who counseled the boards in connection with the merger. Finally, the court held that Saito was not entitled to HBOC documents because Saito was not a stockholder of pre-merger HBOC, and, with respect to post-merger HBOC, he did not establish a basis on which to disregard the separate existence of the wholly-owned subsidiary.]

Stockholders of Delaware corporations enjoy a qualified common law and statutory right to inspect the corporation's books and records. Inspection rights were recognized at common law because, "[a]s a matter of self-protection, the stockholder was entitled to know how his agents were conducting the affairs of the corporation of which he or she was a part owner." The common law right is codified in 8 Del.C. § 220, which provides in relevant part:

> (b) Any stockholder . . . shall, upon written demand under oath stating the purpose thereof, have the right . . . to inspect for any proper purpose the corporation's stock ledger, a list of its stockholders, and its other books and records, and to make copies or extracts therefrom. A proper purpose shall mean a purpose reasonably related to such person's interest as a stockholder.

Once a stockholder establishes a proper purpose under § 220, the right to relief will not be defeated by the fact that the stockholder may have secondary purposes that are improper. The scope of a stockholder's inspection, however, is limited to those books and records that are necessary and essential to accomplish the stated, proper purpose.

By statute, stockholders who bring derivative suits must allege that they were stockholders of the corporation "at the time of the transaction of which such stockholder complains. . . ." The Court of Chancery decided that this limitation on Saito's ability to maintain a derivative suit controlled the scope of his inspection rights. As a result, the court held that Saito was "effectively limited to examining conduct of McKesson and McKesson HBOC's boards *following* the negotiation and public announcement of the merger agreement."

Although we recognize that there may be some interplay between the two statutes, we do not read § 327 as defining the temporal scope of a stockholder's inspection rights under § 220. The books and records statute requires that a stockholder's purpose be one that is "reasonably related" to his or her interest as a stockholder. The standing statute, § 327, bars a stockholder from bringing a derivative action unless the stockholder owned the corporation's stock at the time of the alleged wrong.[If a stockholder wanted to investigate alleged wrongdoing that substantially predated his or her stock ownership, there could be a question as to whether the stockholder's purpose was reasonably related to his or her interest as a stockholder, especially if the stockholder's only purpose was to institute derivative litigation.] But stockholders may use information about corporate mismanagement in other ways, as well. They may seek an audience with the board to discuss proposed reforms or, failing in that, they may prepare a stockholder resolution for the next annual meeting, or mount a proxy fight to elect new directors. None of those activities would be prohibited by § 327.

Even where a stockholder's only purpose is to gather information for a derivative suit, the date of his or her stock purchase should not be used as an automatic "cut-off" date in a § 220 action. First, the potential derivative claim may involve a continuing wrong that both predates and postdates the stockholder's purchase date. In such a case, books and records from the inception of the alleged wrongdoing could be necessary and essential to the stockholder's purpose. Second, the alleged post-purchase date wrongs may have their foundation in events that transpired earlier. In this case, for example, Saito wants to investigate McKesson's apparent failure to learn of HBOC's accounting irregularities until months after the merger was consummated. Due diligence documents generated before the merger agreement was signed may be essential to that investigation. In sum, the date on which a stockholder first acquired the corporation's stock does not control the scope of records available under § 220. If activities that occurred before the purchase date are "reasonably related" to the stockholder's interest as a stockholder, then the stockholder should be given access to records necessary to an understanding of those activities.[10]

The Court of Chancery denied Saito access to documents in McKesson-HBOC's possession that the corporation obtained from financial and accounting advisors, on the ground that Saito could not use § 220 to develop potential claims against third parties. On appeal, Saito argues that he is seeking third party documents for the same reason he is seeking McKesson HBOC documents—to investigate possible wrongdoing by McKesson and McKesson HBOC. Since the trial court found that to be a proper purpose, Saito argues that he should not be precluded from seeing documents that are necessary to his purpose, and in McKesson HBOC's possession, simply because the documents were prepared by third party advisors.

We agree that, generally, the source of the documents in a corporation's possession should not control a stockholder's right to inspection under § 220. It is not entirely clear, however, that the trial court restricted Saito's access on that basis. The Court of Chancery decided that Saito's interest in pursuing claims against McKesson HBOC's advisors was not a proper purpose. It recognized that a secondary improper purpose usually is irrelevant if the stockholder establishes his need for the same documents to support a proper purpose. But the court apparently concluded that the categories of third party documents that Saito demanded did not

---

[10] [A] Section 220 proceeding does not open the door to wide ranging discovery. See *Brehm v. Eisner*, 746 A.2d 244, 266–67 (Del.2000) (Plaintiffs "bear the burden of showing a proper purpose and [must] make specific and discrete identification, with rifled precision . . . [to] establish that each category of books and records is essential to the accomplishment of their articulated purpose . . ."); *Security First Corp. v. U.S. Die Casting and Dev. Co.*, 687 A.2d 563, 568, 570 (Del.1997) ("mere curiosity or desire for a fishing expedition" is insufficient.).

support the proper purpose of investigating possible wrongdoing by McKesson and McKesson HBOC.

We cannot determine from the present record whether the Court of Chancery intended to exclude all third party documents, but such a blanket exclusion would be improper. The source of the documents and the manner in which they were obtained by the corporation have little or no bearing on a stockholder's inspection rights. The issue is whether the documents are necessary and essential to satisfy the stockholder's proper purpose. In this case, Saito wants to investigate possible wrongdoing relating to McKesson and McKesson HBOC's failure to discover HBOC's accounting irregularities. Since McKesson and McKesson HBOC relied on financial and accounting advisors to evaluate HBOC's financial condition and reporting, those advisors' reports and correspondence would be critical to Saito's investigation.

Finally, the Court of Chancery held that Saito was not entitled to any HBOC documents because he was not a stockholder of HBOC before or after the merger. Although Saito is a stockholder of HBOC's parent, McKesson HBOC, stockholders of a parent corporation are not entitled to inspect a subsidiary's books and records, "[a]bsent a showing of a fraud or that a subsidiary is in fact the mere alter ego of the parent. . . ." The Court of Chancery found no basis to disregard HBOC's separate existence and, therefore, denied access to its records.

We reaffirm this settled principle, which applies to those HBOC books and records that were never provided to McKesson or McKesson HBOC. But it does not apply to relevant documents that HBOC gave to McKesson before the merger, or to McKesson HBOC after the merger. We assume that HBOC provided financial and accounting information to its proposed merger partner and, later, to its parent company. As with the third party advisors' documents, Saito would need access to relevant HBOC documents in order to understand what his company's directors knew and why they failed to recognize HBOC's accounting irregularities.

SEINFELD V. VERIZON COMMUNICATIONS, INC.

909 A.2d 117 (Del. 2006).

HOLLAND, JUSTICE.

The plaintiff-appellant, Frank D. Seinfeld ("Seinfeld"), brought suit under section 220 of the Delaware General Corporation Law to compel the defendant-appellee, Verizon Communications, Inc. ("Verizon"), to produce, for his inspection, its books and records related to the compensation of Verizon's three highest corporate officers from 2000 to 2002. Seinfeld claimed that their executive compensation, individually and collectively, was excessive and wasteful. On cross-motions for summary judgment, the Court of Chancery applied well-established Delaware law and held that

Seinfeld had not met his evidentiary burden to demonstrate a proper purpose to justify the inspection of Verizon's records.

The settled law of Delaware required Seinfeld to present some evidence that established a credible basis from which the Court of Chancery could infer there were legitimate issues of possible waste, mismanagement or wrongdoing that warranted further investigation. Seinfeld argues that burden of proof "erects an insurmountable barrier for the minority shareholder of a public company." We have concluded that Seinfeld's argument is without merit.

We reaffirm the well-established law of Delaware that stockholders seeking inspection under section 220 must present "some evidence" to suggest a "credible basis" from which a court can infer that mismanagement, waste or wrongdoing may have occurred. The "credible basis" standard achieves an appropriate balance between providing stockholders who can offer some evidence of possible wrongdoing with access to corporate records and safeguarding the right of the corporation to deny requests for inspections that are based only upon suspicion or curiosity. Accordingly, the judgment of the Court of Chancery must be affirmed.

Seinfeld asserts that he is the beneficial owner of approximately 3,884 shares of Verizon, held in street name through a brokerage firm. His stated purpose for seeking Verizon's books and records was to investigate mismanagement and corporate waste regarding the executive compensations of Ivan G. Seidenberg, Lawrence T. Babbio, Jr. and Charles R. Lee. Seinfeld alleges that the three executives were all performing in the same job and were paid amounts, including stock options, above the compensation provided for in their employment contracts. Seinfeld's section 220 claim for inspection is further premised on various computations he performed which indicate that the three executives' compensation totaled $205 million over three years and was, therefore, excessive, given their responsibilities to the corporation.

During his deposition, Seinfeld acknowledged he had no factual support for his claim that mismanagement had taken place. He admitted that the three executives did not perform any duplicative work. Seinfeld conceded he had no factual basis to allege the executives "did not earn" the amounts paid to them under their respective employment agreements. Seinfeld also admitted "there is a possibility" that the $205 million executive compensation amount he calculated was wrong.

The issue before us is quite narrow: should a stockholder seeking inspection under section 220 be entitled to relief without being required to show some evidence to suggest a credible basis for wrongdoing? We conclude that the answer must be no.

Section 220 provides stockholders of Delaware corporations with a "powerful right." By properly asserting that right under section 220, stockholders are able to obtain information that can be used in a variety of contexts. Stockholders may use information about corporate mismanagement, waste or wrongdoing in several ways. For example, they may: institute derivative litigation; "seek an audience with the board [of directors] to discuss proposed reform or, failing in that, they may prepare a stockholder resolution for the next annual meeting, or mount a proxy fight to elect new directors."

More than a decade ago, we noted that "[s]urprisingly, little use has been made of section 220 as an information-gathering tool in the derivative [suit] context." Today, however, stockholders who have concerns about corporate governance are increasingly making a broad array of section 220 demands. The rise in books and records litigation is directly attributable to this Court's encouragement of stockholders, who can show a proper purpose, to use the "tools at hand" to obtain the necessary information before filing a derivative action. Section 220 is now recognized as "an important part of the corporate governance landscape."

The Court of Chancery determined that Seinfeld's deposition testimony established only that he was concerned about the large amount of compensation paid to the three executives. That court concluded that Seinfeld offered "no evidence from which [it] could evaluate whether there is a reasonable ground for suspicion that the executive's compensation rises to the level of waste." It also concluded that Seinfeld did not "submit any evidence showing that the executives were not entitled to [the stock] options." The Court of Chancery properly noted that a disagreement with the business judgment of Verizon's board of directors or its compensation committee is not evidence of wrongdoing and did not satisfy Seinfeld's burden under section 220. The Court of Chancery held:

> [V]iewing the evidence in the light most favorable to Seinfeld, the court must conclude that he has not carried his burden of showing that there is a credible basis from which the court can infer that the Verizon board of directors committed waste or mismanagement in compensating these three executives during the relevant period of time. Instead, the record clearly establishes that Seinfeld's Section 220 demand was made merely on the basis of suspicion or curiosity.

In this appeal, Seinfeld asserts that the "Court of Chancery's ruling erects an insurmountable barrier for the minority shareholder of a public company." Seinfeld argues that:

> This Court and the Court of Chancery have instructed shareholders to utilize § 220 as one of the tools at hand. Yet, the Court of Chancery at bar, in requiring *evidence* makes a § 220 application a mirage. If the shareholder had evidence, a derivative

suit would be brought. Unless there is a whistle blower, or a video cassette, the public shareholder, having no access to corporate records, will only have suspicions.

Seinfeld submits that "by requiring evidence, the shareholder is prevented from using the tools at hand." Seinfeld's brief concludes with a request for this Court to reduce the burden of proof that stockholders must meet in a section 220 action:

> Plaintiff submits that in a case involving public companies, minority shareholders who have access only to public documents and without a whistle blower or corporate documents should be permitted to have limited inspection based upon suspicions, reasonable beliefs, and logic arising from public disclosures.

[Seinfeld's arguments have caused us to] review the current balance between the rights of stockholders and corporations that is established by *Thomas & Betts Corp. v. Leviton Mfg. Co.* and *Security First Corp. v. U.S. Die Casting & Dev. Co.* and their progeny.

In a section 220 action, a stockholder has the burden of proof to demonstrate a proper purpose by a preponderance of the evidence. It is well established that a stockholder's desire to investigate wrongdoing or mismanagement is a "proper purpose." Such investigations are proper, because where the allegations of mismanagement prove meritorious, investigation furthers the interest of all stockholders and should increase stockholder return.

The evolution of Delaware's jurisprudence in section 220 actions reflects judicial efforts to maintain a proper balance between the rights of shareholders to obtain information based upon credible allegations of corporation mismanagement and the rights of directors to manage the business of the corporation without undue interference from stockholders. In *Thomas & Betts,* this Court held that, to meet its "burden of proof, a stockholder must present some *credible basis* from which the court can infer that waste or mismanagement may have occurred." Six months later, in *Security First,* this Court held "[t]here must be *some evidence* of possible mismanagement as would warrant further investigation of the matter."

Investigations of meritorious allegations of possible mismanagement, waste or wrongdoing, benefit the corporation, but investigations that are "indiscriminate fishing expeditions" do not. "At some point, the costs of generating more information fall short of the benefits of having more information. At that point, compelling production of information would be wealth-reducing, and so shareholders would not want it produced." Accordingly, this Court has held that an inspection to investigate possible wrongdoing where there is no "credible basis," is a license for "fishing expeditions" and thus adverse to the interests of the corporation.

[A stockholder is "not required to prove by a preponderance of the evidence that waste and [mis]management are actually occurring." Stockholders need only show, by a preponderance of the evidence, a credible basis from which the Court of Chancery can infer there is possible mismanagement that would warrant further investigation-a showing that "may ultimately fall well short of demonstrating that anything wrong occurred." That "threshold may be satisfied by a credible showing, through documents, logic, testimony or otherwise, that there are legitimate issues of wrongdoing."]

Although the threshold for a stockholder in a section 220 proceeding is not insubstantial, the "credible basis" standard sets the lowest possible burden of proof. The only way to reduce the burden of proof further would be to eliminate any requirement that a stockholder show *some evidence* of possible wrongdoing. That would be tantamount to permitting inspection based on the "mere suspicion" standard that Seinfeld advances in this appeal. However, such a standard has been repeatedly rejected as a basis to justify the enterprise cost of an inspection.

We remain convinced that the rights of stockholders and the interests of the corporation in a section 220 proceeding are properly balanced by requiring a stockholder to show "some evidence of *possible* mismanagement as would warrant further investigation." The "credible basis" standard maximizes stockholder value by limiting the range of permitted stockholder inspections to those that might have merit. Accordingly, our holdings in *Security First* and *Thomas & Betts* are ratified and reaffirmed.

E. BYLAW PROVISIONS DEALING WITH DERIVATIVE LITIGATION

In *ATP Tour, Inc. v. Deutscher Tennis Bund*, 91 A.3d 554 (Del. 2014), the Delaware Supreme Court upheld a bylaw provision in a non-stock corporation that reversed the so-called "American Rule" of litigation, which provides that, absent a contrary contractual provision, each party in a lawsuit must bear the cost of its own attorneys' fees and expenses. The bylaw in that case shifted liability for attorneys' fees to the losing party. In the wake of this decision, many Delaware corporations began adopting similar bylaws, largely a means of discouraging derivative suits. This trend did not last long, however. In response to heavy pressure from lawyers that handle corporate litigation in Delaware, the Delaware legislature amended DGCL § 109 and DGCL § 102 to prohibit bylaw provisions or charter provisions, respectively, that shifted the costs of litigation in suits alleging that an officer, director or shareholder had breached a duty or in which the DGCL confers jurisdiction on the Delaware Court of Chancery.

Meanwhile, Delaware corporations had also begun adopting provisions in the certificate or bylaws requiring that derivative suits be brought in the Delaware courts. The Delaware legislature viewed these provisions with more favor, and in the same bill that amended § 109, it added § 115, which expressly permits such provisions.

F. TERMINATION WHEN DEMAND IS EXCUSED

In response to a derivative suit, corporations often form a special litigation committee (SLC) to consider whether it is in the best interest of the corporation to take over the suit, allow it to continue, or move to dismiss it. Early cases held that the business judgment rule precluded judicial review of the substance of a recommendation by an SLC that a derivative suit be dismissed. *Auerbach v. Bennett*, 393 N.E.2d 994 (N.Y. 1979), the leading such decision, involved a derivative suit filed by shareholders of General Telephone and Electronics Corporation ("GTE") to recover from the responsible GTE officials more than $11 million in bribes and kickbacks that GTE, in a SEC filing, acknowledged it had paid. An SLC, comprised of three directors who had joined the GTE board after the incidents in question, was appointed to consider the shareholder's claim. The SLC conducted an investigation and concluded that none of the defendants had breached his duty of care or profited personally from the challenged payments and that it was not in GTE's best interest for the suit to proceed. (Had the suit proceeded to trial, GTE no doubt would have been forced to disclose publicly the identities of those to whom it had paid bribes and kickbacks—information that it had not disclosed in its SEC filing.) It then filed, and the trial court granted, a motion for summary judgment dismissing the shareholders' claim.

On appeal, the court held that the business judgment rule would not foreclose inquiry into either the disinterest and independence of the members of the SLC or the adequacy and appropriateness of the committee's investigative procedures and methodologies. However, plaintiffs had not called either of these matters into question. As for the plaintiffs' request that the court review the merits of the committee's "ultimate substantive decision" that it was not in GTE's interests to pursue the claims advanced, the New York Court of Appeals took the position that such an inquiry would be inappropriate.

> [The committee's substantive decision] falls squarely within the embrace of the business judgment doctrine, involving as it did the weighing and balancing of legal, ethical, commercial, promotional, public relations, fiscal and other factors familiar to the resolution of many if not most corporate problems. To this extent the conclusion reached by the special litigation committee is outside the scope of our review. Thus, the courts cannot inquire as to which factors were considered by that committee or the relative weight accorded them in reaching that substantive decision. Inquiry into such matters would go to the very core of the business judgment made by the committee. To permit judicial probing of

such issues would be to emasculate the business judgment doctrine as applied to actions and determinations of the special litigation committee.

Id. at 1002. Other courts have adopted this approach.

In contrast, *Zapata Corp. v. Maldonado*, 430 A.2d 779 (Del. 1981), rejected *Auerbach*'s deferential approach in part out of concern that "there but for the grace of God go I" empathy may make directors appointed to SLCs reluctant to support prosecution of claims asserted against their fellow board members. In Zapata, plaintiff alleged that certain actions constituted a breach of fiduciary duty and that demand was excused because a majority of the directors had benefited from the challenged decision. The corporation did not contest plaintiff's claim of demand futility. Instead, it created an "Independent Investigation Committee of Zapata Corporation," composed of two new directors. This Committee retained counsel, filed a report recommending that the suit be dismissed, and caused Zapata to move to have the suit dismissed. The Delaware Chancery Court denied Zapata's motion. The Delaware Supreme Court agreed, and proposed a two-part test for assessing an SLC's decision to dismiss a derivative suit:

> After an objective and thorough investigation of a derivative suit, an independent committee may cause its corporation to file a pretrial motion to dismiss in the Court of Chancery. The basis of the motion is the best interests of the corporation, as determined by the committee. The Court should apply a two-step test to the motion.
>
> First, the Court should inquire into the independence and good faith of the committee and the bases supporting its conclusions. Limited discovery may be ordered to facilitate such inquiries. The corporation should have the burden of proving independence, good faith and a reasonable investigation, rather than presuming independence, good faith and reasonableness. If the Court determines either that the committee is not independent or has not shown reasonable bases for its conclusions, or, if the Court is not satisfied for other reasons relating to the process, including but not limited to the good faith of the committee, the Court shall deny the corporation's motion. If, however, the Court is satisfied that the committee was independent and showed reasonable bases for good faith findings and recommendations, the Court may proceed, in its discretion, to the next step.
>
> The second step provides, we believe, the essential key in striking the balance between legitimate corporate claims as expressed in a derivative stockholder suit and a corporation's best interests as expressed by an independent investigating committee. The Court should determine, applying its own independent business

judgment, whether the motion should be granted.[18] This means, of course, that instances could arise where a committee can establish its independence and sound bases for its good faith decisions and still have the corporation's motion denied. The second step is intended to thwart instances where corporate actions meet the criteria of step one, but the result does not appear to satisfy its spirit, or where corporate actions would simply prematurely terminate a stockholder grievance deserving of further consideration in the corporation's interest. The Court of Chancery of course must carefully consider and weigh how compelling the corporate interest in dismissal is when faced with a non-frivolous lawsuit. The Court of Chancery should, when appropriate, give special consideration to matters of law and public policy in addition to the corporation's best interests.

430 A.2d at 788–89.

Other courts have expressed concern similar to those expressed in *Zapata*. In *Joy v. North*, 692 F.2d 880 (2d Cir.1982), the Second Circuit concluded that a Connecticut court would follow *Zapata*, noting: "It is not cynical to expect that [special litigation] committees will tend to view derivative actions against the other directors with skepticism. Indeed if the involved directors expected any results other than a recommendation of termination, at least as to them, they would probably never establish the committee." *Id.* at 888.

At least one Delaware court has expressed its concern about whether *Zapata* adds another layer of complexity and delay to derivative litigation. In *Kaplan v. Wyatt*, 484 A.2d 501 (Del.Ch.1984), *aff'd* 499 A.2d 1184 (Del.1985), Chancellor Brown stated:

> [I]t must be kept in mind that the entire [Special Litigation Committee] procedure is designed to provide a means, if warranted, to throw a derivative plaintiff out of Court before he has an opportunity to engage in any discovery whatever in support of the merits of his cause of action purportedly brought on the corporation's behalf. In fact, the *Zapata* procedure takes the case away from the plaintiff, turns his allegations over to special agents appointed on behalf of the corporation for the purpose of making an informal, internal investigation of his charges, and places the plaintiff on the defensive once a motion to dismiss is filed by the Special Litigation Committee, leaving him to snipe away at the bona fides of the Committee and its extra-judicial investigation in a last-ditch effort to salvage a right to present the case on the corporation's behalf as he sees it. The procedure also

---

[18] This step shares some of the same spirit and philosophy of the statement by the Vice Chancellor: "Under our system of law, courts and not litigants should decide the merits of litigation." 413 A.2d at 1263.

asks the Court to consider dismissing the case prior to the time that the facts pertaining to the plaintiff's allegations are developed in an adversarial context unlike the procedure that has existed heretofore. As to whether this new departure in derivative litigation is good or bad I offer no judgment. Certainly, it has its justification in legal theory as is ably expressed in *Zapata*. However, it is fraught with practical complications at the trial court level. It certainly does not speed up the course of derivative litigation and, based upon what I have seen so far, it is doubtful that it reduces the expense or inconvenience of derivative litigation to the corporation.

Experience since *Zapata*, including the activities in this case, indicates that procedurally the Special Litigation Committee approach has added at least three new hearings to a derivative suit brought by a shareholder in the absence of demand on the board of directors. [First, while the court has no choice but to grant a Committee's request for a stay of all discovery by the plaintiff, a hearing almost always is required on the length of the stay. Second, where the Committee recommends that the suit be dismissed, plaintiff inevitably will seek to take the "limited discovery" *Zapata* allows and the Committee will seek to limit the scope of that discovery. The court will need to read the Committee's report—customarily at least 150 pages in length—and hear argument in order to decide how much discovery to permit. Finally, the court must hold a hearing on the motion sponsored by the Special Litigation Committee to dismiss the suit, at which plaintiff, with his back to the wall, can be expected to pull out all stops and to throw every possible argument imaginable into the controversy, no matter how minor or picayune.]

In short, the new *Zapata* procedure, while perhaps laudatory in legal concept, has the pragmatic effect of setting up a form of litigation within litigation. [It] adds, in effect, a new party to derivative litigation—the Special Litigation Committee—and a new battery of lawyers—counsel for the Committee—with the attendant expense to the corporation. It sidetracks derivative litigation as we have heretofore known it for approximately two years at a minimum while the Committee goes through its functions and while the plaintiff passively awaits his chances to resist them. And in the process the *Zapata* procedure has imposed substantial additional burdens at the trial court level in each such derivative suit in which it has been employed.

484 A.2d at 509–12.

One of the central concerns about SLCs is the degree to which they might be influenced by other directors, including defendants in the relevant derivative action. As we have discussed, some courts and commentators have articulated concerns about potential "structural bias" among directors. For example, in *Miller v. Register and Tribune Syndicate, Inc.*, 336 N.W.2d 709, 716 (Iowa 1983), the Iowa Supreme Court stated that concerns about "structural bias" made it "unrealistic to assume that the members of independent committees are free from personal, financial or moral influences which flow from the directors who appoint them." The court rejected both *Zapata* and *Auerbach*, holding that under Iowa law a corporate board could not delegate to an SLC the power to act for the corporation in connection with a derivative suit; the board was limited to asking the court to appoint a "special panel" charged with investigating the shareholder's claim and taking binding action on the corporation's behalf.

Similar concerns seemed to underlie the North Carolina Supreme Court's conclusion in *Alford v. Shaw*, 358 S.E.2d 323, 327 (N.C. 1987), that a recommendation to dismiss a derivative suit should be closely scrutinized, whether demand was required or excused. "To rely blindly on the report of a corporation-appointed committee which assembled such materials on behalf of the corporation is to abdicate the judicial duty to consider the interests of shareholders imposed by the statute. This abdication is particularly inappropriate in a case such as this one, where shareholders allege serious breaches of fiduciary duties owed to them by the directors controlling the corporation."

Professors Cox and Munsinger argue that structural bias is particularly pertinent to SLCs.

> The directors called upon to evaluate a derivative suit against their colleagues are not, and generally have not been, isolated from the suit's defendants. As members of the board of directors they continue to interact with the defendants, who usually remain directors or officers of the corporation. Even members of a special litigation committee who were appointed *after* the derivative suit was initiated are legally bound under the organic requirements for committee membership to serve as directors on the full board. The new special litigation committee members and the defendant directors therefore serve as colleagues on the same corporate board in addressing an array of nonderivative suit issues. Consequently, the judges and those to be judged associate on a regular basis in discharging their many tasks as corporate directors during the preliminary derivative suit skirmishes. In doing so, they share a mutual duty to serve the corporate interest, and they often adopt a common view of that corporate interest. Analogous studies suggest that the effect of these shared experiences is not only to bond the directors and the defendants

together but also to form a basis upon which the directors can be expected to give greater weight to the defendant's values, attitudes, and perceptions than to those of outgroup members like the plaintiff. Indeed, the greater the interaction between the defendants and directors, in terms of frequency and degree of task complexity, the stronger the favoritism the directors can be expected to express toward the defendants. While this favoritism does not necessarily cause the outgroup member (the plaintiff) to be held at a lower level of esteem, in an absolute sense, than when there was no interaction between ingroup members, on a relative scale a greater regard results for ingroup members than for outgroup members.

More is involved in the dynamics of intergroup discrimination in the demand or special litigation committee context than the seemingly simple categorization of the nondefendant directors as 'directors,' a category which also includes the defendants. As seen earlier, individuals place great value on their selection to and membership on a corporation's board: They are attracted to their colleagues and value greatly the associations they reap from the directorship. The relative attractiveness and rewards of board membership to the nondefendant director are important considerations in the director's ability to be an impartial arbitrator of a colleague's behavior.

James D. Cox & Harry Munsinger, *Bias in the Boardroom: Psychological Foundations and Legal Implications of Corporate Cohesion*, 48 L. & Contemp. Probs., 83, 103–4 (1985).

G. ON THE INDEPENDENCE OF DIRECTORS

As the material above indicates, whether the members of a board or special litigation committee are "independent" can be determinative of the outcome of a derivative suit. As we will see in Chapter 18, director independence also can be critical to the effectiveness of a board decision on a transaction in which an officer or director has a conflict of interest.

The excerpt from *Orman v. Cullman* immediately below describes the difference between "independence" and "interest." A director is "interested" in a transaction if he or she has a direct financial interest in it that differs from the interests of other shareholders. Such a director is obviously also not "independent" in making a decision on the transaction. A director may be thought incapable of making an independent decision for a variety of reasons besides having a direct financial interest in it. As the succeeding cases illustrate, the concept of "independence" has evolved over time in recognition of human nature.

ORMAN V. CULLMAN

794 A.2d 5 (Del.Ch. 2002).

CHANDLER, J.

Although interest and independence are two separate and distinct issues, these two attributes are sometimes confused by parties.

A disabling "interest," as defined by Delaware common law, exists in two instances. The first is when (1) a director personally receives a benefit (or suffers a detriment), (2) as a result of, or from, the challenged transaction, (3) which is not generally shared with (or suffered by) the other shareholders of his corporation, and (4) that benefit (or detriment) is of such subjective material significance to that particular director that it is reasonable to question whether that director objectively considered the advisability of the challenged transaction to the corporation and its shareholders. The second instance is when a director stands on both sides of the challenged transaction. This latter situation frequently involves the first three elements listed above. As for the fourth element, whenever a director stands on both sides of the challenged transaction he is deemed interested and allegations of materiality have not been required.

"Independence" does not involve a question of whether the challenged director derives a benefit *from the transaction* that is not generally shared with the other shareholders. Rather, it involves an inquiry into whether the director's decision resulted from that director being *controlled* by another. A director can be controlled by another if in fact he is *dominated* by that other party, whether through close personal or familial relationship or through force of will. A director can also be controlled by another if the challenged director is *beholden* to the allegedly controlling entity. A director may be considered beholden to (and thus controlled by) another when the allegedly controlling entity has the unilateral power (whether direct or indirect through control over other decision makers), to decide whether the challenged director continues to receive a benefit, financial or otherwise, upon which the challenged director is so dependent or is of such subjective material importance to him that the threatened loss of that benefit might create a reason to question whether the controlled director is able to consider the corporate merits of the challenged transaction objectively.

Confusion over whether specific facts raise a question of interest or independence arises from the reality that similar factual circumstances may implicate *both* interest and independence, one but not the other, or neither. By way of example, consider the following: Director *A* is both a director and officer of company *X*. Company *X* is to be merged into company *Z*. Director *A*'s vote in favor of recommending shareholder approval of the merger is challenged by a plaintiff shareholder.

Scenario One. Assume that one of the terms of the merger agreement is that director *A* was to be an officer in surviving company *Z, and* that maintaining his position as a corporate officer in the surviving company was material to director *A*. That fact might, when considered in light of *all* of the facts alleged, lead the Court to conclude that director *A* had a disabling interest.

Scenario Two. Assume that director C is both a director and the majority shareholder of company X. Director C had the power plausibly to threaten director A's position as officer of corporation X should director A vote against the merger. Assume further that director A's position as a corporate officer is material to director A. Those circumstances, when considered in light of all of the facts alleged, might lead the Court to question director A's independence from director C, because it could reasonably be assumed that director A was controlled by director C, since director A was beholden to director C for his position as officer of the corporation. Confusion over whether to label this disability as a disqualifying "interest" or as a "lack of independence" may stem from the fact that, colloquially, director A was "interested" in keeping his job as a corporate officer. Scenario Two, however, raises only a question as to director A's independence since there is nothing that suggests that director A would receive something from the transaction that might implicate a disabling interest.

If a plaintiff's allegations combined all facts described in both Scenario One and Scenario Two, it might be reasonable to question both director A's interest and independence. Conversely, if all the facts in both scenarios were alleged except for the materiality of Director A's position as a corporate officer (perhaps because director A is a billionaire and his officer's position pays $20,000 per year and is not even of prestige value to him) then neither director A's interest nor his independence would be reasonably questioned. The key issue is not simply whether a particular director receives a benefit from a challenged transaction not shared with the other shareholders, or solely whether another person or entity has the ability to take some benefit away from a particular director, but whether the possibility of gaining some benefit or the fear of losing a benefit is likely to be of such importance to that director that it is reasonable for the Court to question whether valid business judgment or selfish considerations animated that director's vote on the challenged transaction.

IN RE INFOUSA, INC. SHAREHOLDERS LITIGATION

953 A.2d 963 (Del.Ch. 2007).

CHANDLER, J.

Before me is a complaint that tests the boundaries of the business judgment rule, the protection offered to defendant directors by Court of Chancery Rule 23.1, and the procedural rules by which a plaintiff brings a derivative complaint. After an activist shareholder petitioned this Court for access to books and records under 8 *Del. C.* § 220, two plaintiffs brought separate lawsuits on behalf of infoUSA against its directors. Both complaints alleged that the board either collaborated in or stood by idly in the face of a garish collection of self-interested transactions, principally engineered by the CEO, and largest shareholder, Vinod Gupta. Such extravagances included the lease of aircraft and office space for personal use, the provision of a yacht, and a collection of luxury and collectible cars that would leave James Bond green with envy.

Plaintiffs Dolphin Limited Partnership I, LP, Dolphin Financial Partners, LLC and Robert Bartow (hereafter, "Dolphin") sought to recover derivatively the benefits expropriated from the company by the CEO and the defendant directors through claims for breach of fiduciary duty and waste. Plaintiff Cardinal Value Equity Partners LP (hereafter, "Cardinal Value"), on the other hand, pursued a more novel form of redress. In response to an offer from Vinod Gupta to take the company private, infoUSA formed a Special Committee that considered, and eventually rejected, his proposal. After the rejection, the board of directors dissolved the committee before it could canvas the market for other offers. Cardinal Value asked this Court to order the reinstatement of the Special Committee so that it could "complete" its mission. While Dolphin's litany of related party transactions formed the basis of its complaint, Cardinal Value relied upon many of the same facts to suggest the impotency of the infoUSA board of directors in the face of the demand required of derivative plaintiffs under Court of Chancery Rule 23.1.

A Delaware corporation with its principle place of business in Omaha, Nebraska, infoUSA provides sales and marketing, database marketing, and data processing solutions. Founded in 1972, the company maintains a proprietary database of over 210 million consumers and fourteen million businesses, and it sells this information on to over three million customers. The company also provides direct marketing, e-mail marketing, and telemarketing services to clients.

Defendant Vinod Gupta has been a director and CEO of infoUSA since its founding in 1972, with the exception of a brief period between September 1997 and August 1998. According to a Schedule 13G filed on July 28, 2006, Vinod Gupta owns over 41% of the company's outstanding shares. This includes 4.4% of the company's shares held in irrevocable trust for his three sons and his charitable foundation.

Defendant George F. Haddix has served as a director since 1995. He chairs the Nominating and Governance Committee and is currently a member of the Compensation Committee. He runs PKWare, a software company, and is co-founder and former CEO and director of CSG Systems, and a member of the board of directors of Creighton University.

Defendant Vasant H. Raval, a director since 2002, chairs the Audit Committee and is a member of the Finance Committee. Since 2004, he has also held a seat on the Finance Committee, and was one of the three members of the Compensation Committee in 2004. A professor and chair of the Department of Accounting at Creighton University in Omaha, Nebraska, he also sits on Creighton University's board of directors.

Defendant Bill L. Fairfield was appointed to the board of directors on November 10, 2005, replacing defendant Harold Andersen. He serves on the Nominating and Governance Committee and Audit Committee, and chairs the Compensation Committee. He is also chairman of Dreamfield Capital Ventures LLC, a venture firm in Omaha, Nebraska, and is the former chairman of a wholly-owned subsidiary of infoUSA. On July 21, 2006, he was appointed the company's "lead independent director." He serves, along with Vinod Gupta, as a trustee of the University of Nebraska foundation.

Defendant Anshoo S. Gupta, a director since 2005, is not related to Vinod Gupta. He serves on the Audit Committee.

Defendant Elliot S. Kaplan, a senior partner in the law firm of Robins, Kaplan, Miller & Ciresi LLP, has served on infoUSA's board since 1988. Robins, Kaplan, Miller & Ciresi provided $1.1 million worth of legal services to infoUSA in 2006.

Defendant Martin F. Kahn, who began his service on the board in 2004, was a member of the Nominating and Governance Committee, and Chair of the Finance Committee after 2004. He resigned on February 2, 2007. He is the former Chairman and CEO of One Source Information Services, which was acquired by infoUSA in 2004.

Defendant Bernard W. Reznicek joined the infoUSA board in March 2006, replacing former director Charles Stryker. He serves on the Governance and Nominating Committee and the Audit Committee. The former president and CEO of Omaha Public Power in Omaha, Nebraska, and a former director of CSG Systems, he is presently the president and CEO of Premier Enterprises. He also served as dean of the Creighton University College of Business Administration.

Defendant Dennis P. Walker, a director of infoUSA since 2003, is a member of the Nominating and Governance Committee and the Compensation Committee. He is the president and CEO of Jet Linx Aviation, which sells fractional interests in private jets, and was a founder, board member and executive vice president of MemberWorks, Inc., a telemarketing company based in Stanford, Connecticut.

Defendant Harold W. Andersen, a former director of infoUSA, served from September 1993 until November 2005. An alumnus of the University of Nebraska, he is the former President, CEO, Chairman and publisher of the Omaha World Herald company. He served on the Audit Committee between 1997 and July 2005, chairing it between 2001 and 2003. He also served on the Nominating and Governance Committee and the Audit Committee. He has also served as a director of two mutual funds in the Everest Mutual Fund Family. Vinod Gupta is a director and owns 100% of Everest Asset Management and Everest Investment Management.

Defendant Charles W. Stryker, a former director of infoUSA, served from May 2005 until January 2006.

At the heart of the complaint lies the accusation that Vinod Gupta and, to a much lesser extent, the other individual defendants have long used infoUSA to enrich themselves at the expense of shareholders. Indeed, the bulk of the complaint presents a vast, gaudy panoply of gilded excess, expressed either through frequent and allegedly unquestioned related-party transactions or through payments made directly for the benefit of Vinod Gupta and his family.

The list of related-party transactions relating to transportation alone makes for lengthy reading. Between 2001 and 2005, infoUSA paid approximately $8.2 million to Annapurna Corporation, an entity 100% owned by V. Gupta. These expenditures covered the use of private jets, the use of the *American Princess* yacht, and the use of a personal residence in California, as well as unidentified travel expenses. Vinod Gupta himself incurred much of the travel expenses, and Dolphin alleges that none of the documents provided in response to its § 220 request identified a business purpose for a substantial number of these payments. The log books of the *American Princess* yacht reveal little regarding the justification for these "business" expenses. Nor did defendants produce minutes or consents reflecting board approval of these substantial transactions as part of their response to Dolphin's § 220 request. Plaintiffs allege that many of these travel expenditures were either personal in nature or provided as gifts by Vinod Gupta to personal or political friends.

In its annual reports for 2004 and 2005, the company disclosed approximately $1.5 million in payments to Annapurna, supposedly made for "usage of aircraft and related services." Defendant Raval, however, prepared a report to the board in February 2005 that revealed that about 40% of these payments had no relationship whatever to aircraft, and were instead payments for the *American Princess* yacht, use of personal residences, and other undefined travel services. According to the amended consolidated complaint, the company's 2004 and 2005 10–Ks, filed with the SEC no earlier than March 16, 2005, were signed by defendants Raval, Kaplan, Kahn, Haddix, and Walker, although each of these defendants had access to the internal report before issuing their SEC filings.

At least as alleged, these arrangements resulted in a very sweet deal for Vinod Gupta: using infoUSA's money, he was able to purchase services from his own leasing company, pocket the profit on those services and then provide them to his personal friends and political associates. Defendants insist, however, that the company has eliminated the conflict of interest through the expedient of purchasing Annapurna's interest in the private jets in two transactions totaling approximately $5.3 million. Dolphin's § 220 action, however, did not uncover board minutes, consents, or any evidence of board approval of these transactions. Similarly, the company now directly leases the *American Princess* yacht, rather than paying a Vinod Gupta-controlled entity for its use. Yet another Gupta firm, Aspen Leasing Services, received almost $100,000 from infoUSA over two years to provide the Gupta family with an H2 Hummer, a Honda Odyssey, a Mini-Cooper, a Lexus 330, a Mercedes SL500, and (presumably for the times when travel by land or air simply were not enough) a Glacier Bay catamaran. In 2005, the company directly purchased four of these luxury automobiles, again "eliminating" the conflict of interest. This strategy was also employed to internalize the costs of a skybox at the University of Nebraska football stadium previously leased from Annapurna.

Even after a thorough request for books and records, plaintiffs allege that they have received documentation reflecting board approval of only *two* of these related-party transactions: the acquisition of the skybox and the assumption of a mortgage on a building owned by Everest (another Gupta entity). On the other hand, the plaintiffs discovered the aforementioned report written by defendant Raval, which covered only a narrow sliver of the related party transactions alleged in the amended consolidated complaint. Raval restricted himself to payments made by the company in 2004, and did not address approximately $14 million of payments extending as far back as 1998. Even this report, however, conceded that the company had made $631,899 worth of payments for personal perquisites of Vinod Gupta, and commented that the company's practice of paying fixed monthly amounts to Annapurna for use of personal residences was "difficult to support under any circumstances."

Apart from the related-party transactions, the amended consolidated complaint alleges that Vinod Gupta plunders corporate assets for himself and his family, particularly through the receipt of shares and stock options. Since 1998, infoUSA has awarded Vinod Gupta options on 3.2 million shares, often allowing him to grant himself the lion's share of options allocated under the company's option plan. As a result, Vinod Gupta now controls over 41% of the company, and would control more if he exercised his other stock options.

This control has not always been exercised in a forthright manner. In 2005, the company asked for shareholder approval of an amendment to the 1997 Stock Option Plan in order to increase the number of shares available from five million to eight million. The amendment passed narrowly, by a vote of 28.2 million votes in favor to twenty million against, with the yea-votes bolstered significantly by Vinod Gupta's twenty-three million shares. Plaintiffs allege, however, that the proxy vote soliciting shareholder approval of the plan represented that Vinod Gupta owned only 20,135,006 shares and neglected to mention a further 2.4 million shares held by his sons' trusts and his charitable foundation.

The amended consolidated complaint loses its level of detail and particularity, however, when it begins to address related-party transactions with directors other than Vinod Gupta. Although most of the directors are the subject of a few allegations of interested conduct, the allegations frequently lack detail and substance.

1. *Director fees*

Each of the directors received compensation for their board membership. Of particular import, plaintiff alleges that defendant Raval, who holds a professorship at Creighton University, received approximately $450,000 in compensation from Creighton University between 2002 and 2006. During the same period, he received $399,000 in director and committee fees from infoUSA, excluding the value of stock options.

2. *Legal fees*

Plaintiffs allege that infoUSA paid an average of $500,000 per year to Robbins, Kaplan, Miller & Ciresi L.L.P. for legal services between 2002 and 2005, an amount that rose to $1.1 million in 2006. The firm continues as counsel for the company. According to the complaint, the average income per partner at Robbins, Kaplan, Miller & Ciresi in 2004 was $672,000. Kaplan is a named partner in this firm.

3. *Use of free office space*

Plaintiffs allege that defendants Anderson, Walker and Haddix benefited from the use of free office space for their own businesses in buildings owned indirectly by V. Gupta and later owned by infoUSA itself. The complaint does not specify the size or value of this office space to defendants, but does provide the intriguing details that in 2001 infoUSA paid for an interior designer to assist with the decorating of these offices.

4. *Co-directorships*

Plaintiffs allege that Anderson served both as a co-director of Everest Investments and a director of two mutual funds in the Everest Mutual Fund Family, a privately-held mutual fund group. V. Gupta is President and owns 100% of the voting stock in Everest Funds Management, LLC, a Delaware corporation, and 100% of Everest Asset Management. According to the complaint, infoUSA paid $415,000 to Everest Asset Management for acquisition related expenses and $1 million to a fund in Everest Funds Management, LLC. The complaint states that despite these business relationships, defendants represented to stockholders that Anderson was an independent overseer of V. Gupta's compensation. Further, Anderson chaired the Audit Committee meeting at which the company approved infoUSA's earlier acquisition of an office building from Everest Investment Management.

The amended consolidated complaint alludes to several other business relationships between infoUSA, Vinod Gupta, and his director co-defendants. Fairfield is the former chairman of businessCreditUSA.com, a wholly-owned subsidiary of the company. Haddix, co-founder and former CEO of CSG Systems, participated as a member of an investor group that executed a leveraged buyout of CSG. As part of this effort, infoUSA invested $500,000 in a CSG acquisition fund organized by Trident Capital. Reznicek currently serves as the non-executive chairman of CSG Systems. One Source Information Services, acquired by infoUSA in 2004, succumbed to acquisition by infoUSA in 2004. Stryker formerly served as chairman and CEO of Naviant, Inc, a firm with which infoUSA signed a $12 million licensing agreement in 2001.

5.   *Contributions to Creighton University*

Raval works as a professor at Creighton University and Reznicek is a former dean of the Creighton University College of Business Administration. V. Gupta allegedly provided a $50,000 grant to Raval through the V. Gupta School of Business Administration, and he continues to be a substantial economic contributor to the school. Further, Haddix sits on the board of Creighton University and on the advisory counsel to the school of business administration.

6.   *Travel*

The amended consolidated complaint alleges that several directors have followed Vinod Gupta's example in using corporate transportation for personal use. Kaplan is alleged to have flown on the corporate aircraft to resort locations. Haddix accompanied Vinod Gupta on at least one personal trip with Vinod Gupta and his wife, using the company jet. Plaintiff also alleges that Anderson accompanied V. Gupta on holiday trips to the Bahamas, Las Vegas and the Masters Tournament.

7.   *Form 10–K for 2005*

Finally, plaintiffs allege that defendants Raval, Kaplan, Haddix, Kahn, and Walker (as well as Vinod Gupta) all face a fundamental conflict of interest in this litigation due to their approval of the company's 2004 and 2005 Form 10–K. The company filed the 2004 10–K six weeks after the Raval Report provided considerable detail as to the company's related-party transactions. Nevertheless, the disclosure statements described these transactions simply as "usage of the aircraft and related services."

On October 17, 2006, I dismissed Cardinal Value's first amended derivative complaint for failure to show that demand upon infoUSA's board of directors was excused. The earlier complaint, like this one, regaled the Court at length with stories of fancy cars and favored perks for Vinod

Gupta and his family. Much of Cardinal Value's argument boiled down to an argument by excess, the proposition that no board of directors exercising their business judgment in good faith could ever have approved-or stood by idly while Vinod Gupta allocated to himself-the extensive array of perquisites that he has enjoyed over the years.

Mere recitations of elephantine compensation packages and executive perquisites, however amusingly described, will rarely be enough to excuse a derivative plaintiff from the obligation to make demand upon a defendant board of directors. Sensational allegations may be grist for the mill of business journalists, but a Court cannot declare a grant of executive compensation to be excessive without immediately inviting the subsequent question: "How much is too much?" The answer to that question depends greatly upon context. The acumen of the business executive, the competitive environment in the industry, and the recruitment and retention challenges faced by the hiring corporation all bear heavily on an appropriate level of compensation. "How much is too much?" is a question far better suited to the boardroom than the courtroom.

The amended consolidated complaint incorporates all of plaintiffs' myriad allegations. Based on this final pleading, I conclude that plaintiffs raise issues sufficient for this Court to conclude that any demand upon the board of infoUSA would have been futile. Similarly, I conclude that the amended consolidated complaint states claims for which relief may be granted.

There are two ways that a plaintiff can show that a director is unable to act objectively with respect to a pre-suit demand. Most obviously, a plaintiff can show that a given director is personally interested in the outcome of the litigation, in that the director will personally benefit or suffer as a result of the lawsuit. A plaintiff may also challenge a director's independence by putting forward allegations that raise a reasonable inference that a given director is dominated through a "close personal or familial relationship or through force of will," or is so beholden to an interested director that his or her "discretion would be sterilized." To demonstrate that a given director is beholden to a dominant director, plaintiffs must show that the beholden director receives a benefit "upon which the director is so dependent or is of such subjective material importance that its threatened loss might create a reason to question whether the director is able to consider the corporate merits of the challenged transaction objectively." In short, plaintiff is required to show that a majority of the board of directors is either interested or lacking in independence.

To excuse demand in this case it is not enough to show that the defendants approved a discriminatory poison pill, granted V. Gupta generous share options or allowed the Gupta family to carry out self-interested transactions. Instead, the plaintiff must provide the Court with reason to suspect that each director did so not because they felt it to be in the best interests of the company, but out of self-interest or a loyalty to, or fear of reprisal from, Vinod Gupta. It is to this analysis that I now turn.

The nine board members relevant to an analysis under either *Aronson* or *Rales* are Vinod Gupta, Haddix, Raval, Walker, Fairfield, Anshoo Gupta, Kahn, Kaplan, and Reznicek. Plaintiffs must show that a majority-or in a case where there are an even number of directors, exactly half-of the board was incapable of considering demand. Plaintiffs never solidly grapple with the issue, preferring to assert that the board must be conflicted solely because no non-conflicted board could confer such munificence on Vinod Gupta. Nevertheless, I conclude that the amended consolidated complaint contains allegations scattered throughout that allow me to determine that a majority of these directors were either interested or lacking in independence at the time Dolphin filed its first amended derivative complaint.

a.   V. Gupta

Neither party denies that V. Gupta was an interested party with respect to the amended consolidated complaint. Almost every paragraph of the complaint cites some transaction in which Vinod Gupta's interests are at stake and, if liability is imposed, he would almost certainly bear the brunt of any judgment. Plaintiffs' specific allegations of significant related party transactions suffice to suggest that he is interested with regard to the lawsuit.

b.   The misleading Form 10–K and the self-interest of Kaplan, Walker, Haddix, Kahn and Raval

Although the mere threat of personal liability is insufficient to render a director interested in a transaction, plaintiffs are entitled to a reasonable inference of interestedness where a complaint indicates a "substantial likelihood" of liability will be found. The standard is difficult to meet, and the vast majority of plaintiffs' allegations fail to rise to this considerable level. Nevertheless, the willingness of certain directors to issue Form 10–Ks that, allegedly, materially misrepresented the nature of benefits provided to Vinod Gupta strike me as egregious enough that the directors involved are likely to face personal liability.

When a Delaware corporation communicates with its shareholders, even in the absence of a request for shareholder action, shareholders are entitled to honest communication from directors, given with complete candor and in good faith. Communications that depart from this expectation, particularly where it can be shown that the directors involved issued their communication with the knowledge that it was deceptive or incomplete, violate the fiduciary duties that protect shareholders. Such violations are sufficient to subject directors to liability in a derivative claim.

The Raval Report was distributed to Walker, Haddix, Kahn and Kaplan on February 8, 2005, shortly before the company released its 2004 10–K on March 16, 2005. The 10–Ks affirmatively stated that payments made to Annapurna involved "usage of aircraft and related services." Yet the Raval Report indicates that almost $600,000 worth of the payments constituted compensation for the use of personal residences, the *American Princess* yacht, travel services or payments to contractors. No conceivable definition of candor will shoehorn such payments into services "related" to the use of aircraft.

The Court may reasonably infer, based upon these allegations, that the directors who signed the 2004 and 2005 10–Ks did so knowing that the information contained therein fell far below the standards of candor expected from them. Those allegedly false disclosures were made shortly before the board was to ask shareholders, in a closely-contested vote, to approve the expansion of the company's 2005 Stock Incentive Plan. I note that in 2006, after these and other related-party transactions had been disclosed, Vinod Gupta, Haddix and Raval were narrowly re-elected in a proxy contest that can only be described as an open revolt of unaffiliated shareholders. Despite himself controlling, directly or indirectly, approximately 40% of the voting power of the company, Vinod Gupta received only 50.7% of the shares voted, with the opposing slate receiving over 48. This rising tide of shareholder dissatisfaction suggests that defendants had every motivation before the 2005 elections to conceal the true nature of the massive hidden perquisites being provided to Vinod Gupta, and that their failure of candor misled stockholders and damaged the company.

Thus, not only Vinod Gupta, but also Haddix, Walker, Kahn, Kaplan and Raval face a significant likelihood of personal liability arising from the present lawsuit, and may be considered to be interested for purposes of demand. This alone discharges plaintiffs' duty to show that demand would be futile under Rule 23.1. Nevertheless, I also find plaintiffs' additional allegations against Kaplan, Raval, Haddix, and Walker to be sufficient to raise a reasonable inference that they are dominated by Vinod Gupta, and that their discretion has been sterilized.

c.   Kaplan

Plaintiffs contend that infoUSA's payments to Kaplan's law firm are material enough to raise a reasonable doubt as to his lack of interest and independence. I agree. The annual payments listed in the amended complaint come close to or exceed a reasonable estimate of the annual yearly income per partner of Robins, Kaplan, Miller & Ciresi L.L.P. The threat of withdrawal of such business is certainly enough, in the case of a legal professional, to raise a reasonable doubt as to a director's independence.

Defendants respond that this Court's conclusion in *In re The Limited,* in which this Court held that a $400,000 payment to a director's in-store music supply business was on its own insufficient to raise an inference that the director's judgment was tainted, applies by analogy to Kaplan. The payments, after all, constitute a miniscule proportion of the total revenues of Kaplan's firm. Yet there is a unique relationship between a law firm and its partners. Legal partnerships normally base the pay and prestige of their members upon the amount of revenue that partners (and, more importantly, their clients) bring to their firms. Indeed, with law becoming an ever-more competitive business, there is a notable trend for partners who fail to meet expectations to risk a loss of equity in their firms. The threat of withdrawal of one partner's worth of revenue from a law firm is arguably sufficient to exert considerable influence over a named partner such that, in my opinion, his independence may be called into question.

d. Raval

Plaintiffs attack Raval's independence as a director because (a) his remuneration as a board member exceeds the average salary reported for a professor at Creighton University, (b) he received a $50,000 grant from the V. Gupta School of Business Administration, and (c) both V. Gupta and Haddix have social and professional ties to his employer. Defendants point to a legitimate policy concern with plaintiff's reasoning, relying upon my decision in *In re Walt Disney Co. Derivative Litigation:*

> [T]he Delaware Supreme Court has held that "such allegations [of payment of director's fees], *without more,* do not establish any financial interest." . . . [To hold otherwise] would be to discourage the membership on corporate boards of people of less-than extraordinary means. Such "regular folks" would face allegations of being dominated by other board members, merely because of the relatively substantial compensation provided by the board membership compared to their outside salaries. I am especially unwilling to facilitate such a result.

My concern about this issue has not diminished. Nevertheless, plaintiffs do not rely upon Professor Raval's income alone. Raval's receipt of a financial grant deriving from his relationship with V. Gupta, as well as the presence of defendants on other boards that could affect his professional advancement, are sufficient to raise a reasonable inference necessary to call his independence into question.

e. Haddix and Walker

When the Court dismissed Cardinal Value's original amended complaint, it put significant emphasis on the failure of plaintiffs to allege facts sufficient to excuse demand against Haddix and Walker. Cardinal Value's allegations against Haddix and Walker, as originally pleaded, were simply too vague for the Court to make any reasonable inference as to their lack of independence. The consolidated plaintiffs, however, have now put forward facts that are sufficient to meet the requirements of Rule 23.1. Both Haddix and Walker receive rent free office space from which they allegedly operate their own independent businesses, and plaintiffs have put together a collection of allegations, albeit in a disjointed fashion, from which this Court can infer that this benefit is sufficiently material to question their independence.

Defendants object that the bare words "office space" cannot establish materiality, and there is some merit to this argument. Provision of a single slate-gray *Dilbert*-style cubicle to directors whose income, by plaintiff's own contention, almost certainly exceeds $100,000 a year amounts to an almost incidental benefit. On the other hand, several hundred square feet set up to allow JetLinks Aviation (Mr. Walker's company) or PKWare (Mr. Haddix's company) to operate a call center would certainly raise questions as to their impartiality and independence. Cardinal Value's original complaint provided almost no guidance on this issue and, thus, I determined that the accusation must be considered "vague or conclusory."

Plaintiffs maintain that, despite the recommendation of the report, no payments have been made to recompense the company for rent. Nor do any leases between the company and Haddix or Walker appear to have materialized over the course of Dolphin's extensive § 220 request.

From this, the Court could make two reasonable inferences. First, the Court could infer that Haddix and Walker occupy two relatively Spartan cubicles in the Everest Building, and that this benefit is, at best, a *de minimus* perquisite provided more for the convenience of the company than the directors. Alternatively, the Court could infer that Raval, himself a professor of business who can be presumed to know something about conflicts of interest, based his concerns upon a reasonable assessment of the personal interests of directors, and that the office space provided to Haddix and Walker may materially affect their judgment. If Raval believed the office space could raise a question as to independence, there is no reason this Court should not do so.

The amended consolidated complaint provides very little detail regarding the allegations against Haddix and Walker. It may appear, after discovery, that the offices occupied by these two directors possessed not even a window facing a grimy alleyway. Plaintiffs have not had the benefit of discovery, however, and it would be too much to expect for plaintiffs now to provide the Court with a detailed floor-plan of the Everest offices; an estimate of the cost of office space in Omaha, Nebraska; the square footage occupied by each defendant; an estimate of the personal net worth of Haddix and Walker; and any of the various other factors that would need to be presented to establish by a preponderance of the evidence that the two directors lack independence. For the moment, Raval's concerns, prepared for the board of directors before Cardinal Value brought its initial complaint, suffice to suggest that Haddix and Walker receive benefits sufficient to sterilize their discretion.

f.   The remaining directors

Plaintiffs make only half-hearted attempts, at best, to impugn the remaining directors. Reznicek is alleged to be the non-executive chairman of a company in which infoUSA has made an unquantified investment, as well as being the former dean of Creighton University. A similar allegation is leveled at Fairfield, a former chairman of an infoUSA subsidiary. Kahn also worked for a company acquired by infoUSA, and later recommended, as chair of the Special Committee, that its members receive compensation for their efforts. As for Anshoo Gupta, the sole grounds to question his independence seems to be that he graduated from the same *alma mater* as Vinod Gupta, with no allegation that the pair was ever classmates or associates.

Plaintiffs supplement these meager efforts with nothing that would allow the Court to reasonably infer that these benefits are sufficient to render the directors beholden to Vinod Gupta. The allegations against Reznicek, in sharp contrast to those concerning Raval, fail to outline the materiality of his relationship with Vinod Gupta. Nor does the amended consolidated complaint suggest that the current or prior business relationships of Fairfield or Kahn rise to the level where the "threatened loss [of these benefits] might create a reason to question whether the director is able to consider the corporate merits of the challenged transaction objectively."

Plaintiffs have shown that six directors-Vinod Gupta, Haddix, Walker, Raval, Kahn, and Kaplan-face a sufficient likelihood of liability that their own self-interest would prevent them from considering objectively a demand upon the board. Further, the allegations against Kaplan, Raval, Haddix, and Walker raise a reasonable inference that each is dominated by Vinod Gupta and, thus, incapable of impartially considering demand. As such, demand is excused, and defendants' motion must be denied so long as plaintiffs have stated a claim for which relief may be granted.

THE DISNEY LITIGATION

In *In re The Walt Disney Company Derivative Litigation,* 731 A.2d 342 (Del.Ch. 1998) to which Chancellor Chandler refers in the *infoUSA* opinion, he rejected plaintiffs' challenges to the independence of Father J. O'Donovan, a director of Disney and, at the time, president of Georgetown University, and Reveta Bowers, the principal of the elementary school that Eisner's children formerly attended.

Plaintiffs also allege that Father Leo J. O'Donovan, involved only in the decision to honor the Employment Agreement, is incapable of rendering independent business judgment. O'Donovan is the president of Georgetown University, the alma mater of one of Eisner's sons and the recipient of over $1 million of donations from Eisner since 1989. Accordingly, Plaintiffs allege that O'Donovan would not act contrary to Eisner's wishes.

The closest parallel to O'Donovan's situation faced by this Court occurred in *Lewis v. Fuqua*. Any reliance by Plaintiffs on that case, however, would be misplaced. In *Lewis*, the allegedly disinterested director, Sanford, was the President of Duke University. Duke was the recipient of a $10 million pledge from the dominant board member, Fuqua. Nevertheless, several differences exist that serve to distinguish that matter from the present one. First and foremost, Sanford had "numerous political and financial dealings" with Fuqua, while Plaintiffs here have not alleged any such relationship between Eisner and O'Donovan. Secondly, Fuqua and Sanford served as directors together both on the Board whose actions were being challenged and on the Duke University Board of Trustees. Such an interlocking directorship, a situation that would likely lead to a reasonable doubt of O'Donovan's independence, does not exist here, as Eisner has no formal relationship with Georgetown University. These two differences are sufficient to demonstrate that *Lewis* does not apply here.

The question, then, is whether Eisner exerted such an influence on O'Donovan that O'Donovan could not exercise independent judgment as a director. Plaintiffs do not allege any personal benefit received by O'Donovan—in fact, they admit that O'Donovan is forbidden, as a Jesuit priest, from collecting any director's fee. Plaintiffs cite the case of *Kahn v. Tremont Corp.* "Eisner's philanthropic largess to Georgetown is no less disqualifying than the financial arrangements enjoyed by the special committee members in *Kahn*." In that case, however, two of the three special committee members received a direct, personal financial benefit from their affiliation with the interested party, and the third sought membership on the boards of other entities controlled by the interested party. The distinction between *Kahn* and this matter then is clear, and I do not believe that Plaintiffs have presented a reasonable doubt as to the independence of O'Donovan.

Director Reveta F. Bowers is the principal of the elementary school that Eisner's children once attended. Plaintiffs suggest that because Bowers' salary as a teacher is low compared to her director's fees and stock options, "only the most rigidly formalistic or myopic analysis" would view Bowers as not beholden to Eisner.

Plaintiffs fail to recognize that the Delaware Supreme Court has held that "such allegations of payment of director's fees, without more, do not establish any financial interest." To follow Plaintiffs' urging to discard "formalistic notions of interest and independence in favor of a realistic approach" expressly would be to overrule the Delaware Supreme Court.

Furthermore, to do so would be to discourage the membership on corporate boards of people of less-than extraordinary means. Such "regular folks" would face allegations of being dominated by other board members, merely because of the relatively substantial compensation provided by the board membership compared to their outside salaries. I am especially unwilling to facilitate such a result. Without more, Plaintiffs have failed to allege facts that lead to a reasonable doubt as to the independence of Bowers.

THE ORACLE STORY

In many respects, *Disney* represents a traditional judicial inquiry into the connections, influence and biases among directors on a corporate board. Absent a clear showing of personal domination or financial ties, courts have generally assumed that directors can put aside personal and social connections, and be impartial and objective in the face of an interested colleague.

More recent cases, particularly since the Sarbanes-Oxley Act, have looked at board dynamics in a different light. Just as the federal legislation reflects doubts about director independence and seeks to shore up corporate boards of public companies by specifying the composition of the audit committee, mandating new stock exchange rules that define director independence, and prohibiting loans to company insiders, courts (particularly in Delaware) have shown more skepticism of director independence.

The following story describes an important Delaware Chancery Court case, and its aftermath, involving the question of director independence. The case arose as a derivative suit in which the board of Oracle Corporation appointed an SLC of two newly-elected directors to investigate and act on allegations of insider trading by the company's CEO and other prominent directors. *In re Oracle Corp. Derivative Litigation,* 824 A.2d 917 (Del. Ch. 2003). Vice Chancellor Strine ultimately determined that the two SLC members were not sufficiently independent of the defendants to decide to terminate the derivative suit. Strine reached this conclusion even though both SLC members were academics of great stature with impeccable credentials, who had undertaken a thorough review of the allegations and, assisted by outside counsel, had interviewed 70 witnesses, reviewed volumes of internal company communications, and prepared a 1110-page report that detailed their investigation and the reasons to terminate the litigation.

> The question of independence "turns on whether a director is, *for any substantial reason,* incapable of making a decision with only the best interests of the corporation in mind." That is, the independence test ultimately "focuses on impartiality and objectivity." In this case, the SLC has failed to demonstrate that no material factual question exists regarding its independence.

During discovery, it emerged that the two SLC members—both of whom are professors at Stanford University—are being asked to investigate fellow Oracle directors who have important ties to Stanford, too. One of the directors, another Stanford professor, had taught one of the SLC members as a Ph.D. student and now serves with him at a Stanford research institute; another director is a Stanford alumnus who has contributed millions of dollars to Stanford, including to Stanford units with which one of the SLC members is closely affiliated; and another director (Oracle's CEO) has donated large sums to Stanford through a personal foundation and through Oracle, and was considering making additional multi-million dollar donations when the SLC members joined the Oracle board. Taken together, these and other facts cause me to harbor a reasonable doubt about the impartiality of the SLC.

It is no easy task to decide whether to accuse a fellow director of insider trading. For Oracle to compound that difficulty by requiring SLC members to consider accusing a fellow professor and two large benefactors of their university of conduct that is rightly considered a violation of criminal law was unnecessary and inconsistent with the concept of independence recognized by our law. The possibility that these extraneous considerations biased the inquiry of the SLC is too substantial for this court to ignore. I therefore deny the SLC's motion to terminate.

824 A.2d at 920–21.

The insiders accused of insider trading (the Trading Defendants) included the company's leading directors: Lawrence Ellison (Oracle's chair, CEO and largest shareholder, a major figure in Silicon Valley, and one of the wealthiest men in America), Donald Lucas (chair of Oracle's executive committee and its finance and audit committee), and Michael Boskin (chair of Oracle's compensation committee, and a member of its finance and audit committee).

In response to the derivative suit alleging that the Trading Defendants had misappropriated and traded on inside information, the Oracle board formed the SLC to investigate the allegations and determine whether Oracle should press the claims raised by the plaintiffs, settle the case, or terminate it. The SLC was granted full authority to decide these matters without further approval by the Oracle board.

The two Oracle board members named to the SLC had joined the board about half a year after the alleged improper trading occurred. Both were tenured professors at Stanford University. Strine focused much of his attention on Professor Joseph Grundfest, a chaired professor of law and business at Stanford. Among his many impressive activities, Grundfest directed Stanford's well-known Directors' College, a two-day program for corporate directors on boardroom best practices and corporate ethics. (Strine noted that he had been a speaker at the College.) Immediately before coming to Stanford, Grundfest had served for five years as an SEC Commissioner.

Strine explained the applicable procedural standard for reviewing the SLC's recommendation that the derivative claims be terminated:

> In order to prevail on its motion to terminate the derivative action, the SLC must persuade me its members were independent, acted in good faith, and had a reasonable basis for their recommendation. If there is a material factual question about these issues causing doubt about any of these grounds, I read *Zapata* and its progeny as requiring a denial of the SLC's motion to terminate.

Id. at 928–29.

In its Report, the SLC had noted several factors that indicated that Grundfest was independent: he did not receive compensation from Oracle other than as a director; he was not on the Oracle board at the time of the alleged wrongdoing; he was willing to return his compensation as an SLC member if necessary to preserve his independent status; and he had no "material ties" with Oracle or the Trading Defendants. But absent from the SLC Report was any disclosure of the significant ties between the Trading Defendants and Stanford University—except that Boskin was a Stanford professor, and that Grundfest knew that Lucas had made donations to Stanford, including to the Law School after Grundfest gave a speech to a group of venture capitalists at Lucas's request.

During discovery it emerged that—although Grundfest was a highly-respected, tenured professor whose "ability to make a nice living" was not at risk—there existed a multitude of ties that raised questions about Grundfest's ability to be impartial. Boskin, besides being a chaired professor of economics at Stanford, had taught Grundfest as a Ph.D. candidate, and they both had become senior fellows and steering committee members at the Stanford Institute for Economic Policy Research (SIEPR). Lucas had been a "very loyal alumnus" of Stanford, personally contributing $4.1 million to the university, with a SIEPR conference center named after him. Finally, Ellison had made major contributions to Stanford through a personal foundation and large donations indirectly through Oracle. Ellison was also considering making donations of his $100 million house and $170 million for a scholarship program (modeled on the Rhodes Scholarship program of Oxford) around the time that Grundfest was added to the Oracle board.

The SLC argued that these facts did not impair Grundfest's independence. The SLC asserted that as a practical matter the Trading Defendants could not punish Grundfest, who both had tenure and had no official fundraising responsibilities as part of his job. The SLC also emphasized that prior cases on director independence had focused on economically consequential relationships between the interested party and the director, treating "personal wealth as the key to the independence inquiry." The court summarized the argument: "University professors simply are not inhibited types, unwilling to make tough decisions even as to fellow professors and large contributors."

Strine then turned to the meaning of independence, signaling a new approach under Delaware law:

According to the SLC, its members are independent unless they are essentially subservient to the Trading Defendants—*i.e.*, they are under the "domination and control" of the interested parties. If the SLC is correct and this is the central inquiry in the independence determination, they would win. Nothing in the record suggests to me that either member is dominated and controlled by any of the Trading Defendants, by Oracle, or even by Stanford.

But, in my view, an emphasis on "domination and control" would serve only to fetishize much-parroted language, at the cost of denuding the independence inquiry of its intellectual integrity. Take an easy example. Imagine if two brothers were on a corporate board, each successful in different businesses and not dependent in any way on the other's beneficence in order to be wealthy. The brothers are brothers, they stay in touch and consider each other family, but each is opinionated and strong-willed. A derivative action is filed targeting a transaction involving one of the brothers. The other brother is put on a special litigation committee to investigate the case. If the test is domination and control, then one brother could investigate the other. Does any sensible person think that is our law? I do not think it is.

And it should not be our law. Delaware law should not be based on a reductionist view of human nature that simplifies human motivations on the lines of the least sophisticated notions of the law and economics movement. *Homo sapiens* is not merely *homo economicus*. We may be thankful that an array of other motivations exist that influence human behavior; not all are any better than greed or avarice, think of envy, to name just one. But also think of motives like love, friendship, and collegiality, think of those among us who direct their behavior as best they can on a guiding creed or set of moral values.

Nor should our law ignore the social nature of humans. To be direct, corporate directors are generally the sort of people deeply enmeshed in social institutions. Such institutions have norms, expectations that, explicitly and implicitly, influence and channel the behavior of those who participate in their operation. Some things are "just not done," or only at a cost, which might not be so severe as a loss of position, but may involve a loss of standing in the institution. In being appropriately sensitive to this factor, our law also cannot assume—absent some proof of the point—that corporate directors are, as a general matter, persons of unusual social bravery, who operate heedless to the inhibitions that social norms generate for ordinary folk.

Without backtracking from these general propositions, it would be less than candid if I did not admit that Delaware courts have applied these general standards in a manner that has been less than wholly consistent. Different decisions take a different view about the bias-producing potential of family relationships, not all of which can be explained by mere degrees of consanguinity. Likewise, there is admittedly case law that gives little weight to ties of friendship in the independence inquiry. In this opinion, I undertake what I understand to be my duty and what is possible: the application of the independence inquiry that our Supreme Court has articulated in a manner that is faithful to its essential spirit.

Id. at 937–39.

Strine pointed out the "the extraordinary importance and difficulty" of the responsibility of a special litigation committee. In the SLC context, the difficulty of making a decision against a fellow director is compounded because the weight of making the moral judgment necessarily falls on less than the full board. A small number of directors feels the moral gravity—and social pressures—of this duty alone. For Professor Grundfest to declare that "Oracle should press insider trading claims against the Trading Defendants would have been, to put it mildly, news."

Using this "contextual approach," Strine concluded that the SLC (and Grundfest) had not met the burden to show the absence of a material factual question about the SLC's independence. Strine found the ties among the SLC members, the Trading Defendants, and Stanford "so substantial that they cause reasonable doubt about the SLC's ability to impartially consider whether the Trading Defendants should face suit."

Strine's discussion of Grundfest's relationship to Boskin, his former professor, is revealing:

As an SLC member, Grundfest was being asked to consider whether the company should level extremely serious accusations of wrongdoing against fellow board members. As to Boskin, Grundfest faced another layer of complexity: the determination of whether to have Oracle press insider trading claims against a fellow professor at his university. Even though Boskin was in a different academic department from Grundfest, it is reasonable to assume that the fact that Boskin was also on faculty would—to persons possessing typical sensibilities and institutional loyalty—be a matter of more than trivial concern. Universities are obviously places of at-times intense debate, but they also see themselves as communities.

In addition, Boskin was a professor who had taught Grundfest and with whom he had maintained contact over the years. Their areas of academic interest intersected, putting Grundfest in contact if not directly with Boskin, then regularly with Boskin's colleagues. Moreover, although I am told by the SLC that the title of senior fellow at SIEPR is an honorary one, the fact remains that Grundfest willingly accepted it and was one of a select number of faculty who attained that status. And, they both just happened to also be steering committee members. Having these ties, Grundfest would have more difficulty objectively determining whether Boskin engaged in improper insider trading than would a person without them.

In so concluding, I necessarily draw on a general sense of human nature. In this respect, it is critical to note that I do not infer that Grundfest would be less likely to recommend suit against Boskin than someone without these ties. Human nature being what it is, it is entirely possible that Grundfest would in fact be tougher on Boskin than he would on someone with whom he did not have such connections. The inference I draw is subtly, but importantly, different. What I infer is that a person in Grundfest's position would find it difficult to assess Boskin's conduct without pondering his own association with Boskin and their mutual affiliations. Although these connections might produce bias in either a tougher or laxer direction, the key inference is that these connections would be on the mind of a person in Grundfest's position, putting him in the position of either causing serious legal action to be brought against a person with whom he shares several connections (an awkward thing) or not doing so (and risking being seen as having engaged in favoritism toward his old professor and SIEPR colleague).

Id. at 942–43.

Strine came to similar conclusions about the difficulties Grundfest would face in separating Lucas and Ellison from their roles as benefactors of Stanford and its Law School. "A reasonable professor giving any thought to the matter would obviously consider the effect his decision might have on the University's relationship with Lucas [and Ellison], it being sensible to infer that a professor of reasonable collegiality and loyalty cares about the well-being of the institution he serves."

In closing, Strine addressed his own "undeniable awkwardness of opinions like this one." He explained that his doubts about the SLC's independence did not imply a finding about the subjective good faith of the SLC members, "both of whom are distinguished academics at one of this nation's most prestigious institutions of higher learning." He noted that nothing in the record suggested that the SLC members "had acted out of any conscious desire to favor the Trading Defendants or to do anything other than discharge their duties with fidelity. But that is not the purpose of the independence inquiry."

That inquiry recognizes that persons of integrity and reputation can be compromised in their ability to act without bias when they must make a decision adverse to others with whom they share material affiliations. To conclude that the Oracle SLC was not independent is not a conclusion that the two accomplished professors who comprise it are not persons of good faith and moral probity, it is solely to conclude that they were not situated to act with the required degree of impartiality. *Zapata* requires independence to ensure that stockholders do not have to rely upon special litigation committee members who must put aside personal considerations that are ordinarily influential in daily behavior in making the already difficult decision to accuse fellow directors of serious wrongdoing.

Id. at 947.

The Delaware Supreme Court has not decided how far *Oracle*'s behavioral analysis should reach. On one hand, *Oracle* might be seen applying only to directorial independence on a special litigation committee. On the other, it might be seen as establishing generally a new judicial measure of board independence, including in such contexts as whether a pre-suit demand on the board would be futile.

Soon after *Oracle* in a case involving demand futility, the Delaware Supreme Court limited *Oracle* to the specific SLC context, but suggested that specific allegations of friendship might be relevant to independence when considering demand futility. *Beam ex rel. Martha Stewart Living Omnimedia, Inc.* v. *Stewart*, 845 A.2d 1040 (Del. 2004). In the case the plaintiff had alleged that Martha Stewart breached her duties of loyalty and care by selling stock of another company (ImClone) and then making misleading statements to the media. Relying on *Oracle*, the plaintiff contended that demand was futile because social and business connections created a reasonable doubt as to the independence of a majority of the board of directors. The Court of Chancery held that demand was required because the plaintiff had not alleged specific facts to demonstrate a lack of independence, and the Delaware Supreme Court affirmed.

Addressing the question of personal friendship, the Delaware Supreme Court returned to earlier jurisprudence (recall that in *Oracle*, Vice Chancellor Strine noted that his decision was inconsistent with some Delaware opinions), stating:

> A variety of motivations, including friendship, may influence the demand futility inquiry. But, to render a director unable to consider demand, a relationship must be of a bias-producing nature. Allegations of mere personal friendship or a mere outside business relationship, standing alone, are insufficient to raise a reasonable doubt about a director's independence. In this connection, we adopt as our own the Chancellor's analysis in this case:

>> Some professional or personal friendships, which may border on or even exceed familial loyalty and closeness, may raise a reasonable doubt whether a director can appropriately consider demand. This is particularly true when the allegations raise serious questions of either civil or criminal liability of such a close friend. Not all friendships, or even most of them, rise to this level and the Court cannot make a *reasonable* inference that a particular friendship does so without specific factual allegations to support such a conclusion.

> The facts alleged by Beam regarding the relationships between Stewart and these other members of MSO's board of directors largely boil down to a "structural bias" argument, which presupposes that the professional and social relationships that naturally develop among members of a board impede independent decisionmaking.

Critics will charge that by requiring the independence of only a majority of the board we are ignoring the structural bias common to corporate boards throughout America, as well as the other unseen socialization processes cutting against independent discussion and decisionmaking in the boardroom. The difficulty with structural bias in a demand futile case is simply one of establishing it in the complaint for purposes of Rule 23.1. We are satisfied that discretionary review by the Court of Chancery of complaints alleging specific facts pointing to bias on a particular board will be sufficient for determining demand futility.

In the present case, the plaintiff attempted to plead affinity beyond mere friendship between Stewart and the other directors, but her attempt is not sufficient to demonstrate demand futility. Even if the alleged friendships may have preceded the directors' membership on MSO's board and did not necessarily arise out of that membership, these relationships are of the same nature as those giving rise to the structural bias argument.

Allegations that Stewart and the other directors moved in the same social circles, attended the same weddings, developed business relationships before joining the board, and described each other as "friends," even when coupled with Stewart's 94% voting power, are insufficient, without more, to rebut the presumption of independence. They do not provide a sufficient basis from which reasonably to infer that Martinez, Moore and Seligman may have been beholden to Stewart. Whether they arise before board membership or later as a result of collegial relationships among the board of directors, such affinities—standing alone—will not render presuit demand futile.

That is not to say that personal friendship is always irrelevant to the independence calculus. But, for presuit demand purposes, friendship must be accompanied by substantially more in the nature of serious allegations that would lead to a reasonable doubt as to a director's independence. To create a reasonable doubt about an outside director's independence, a plaintiff must plead facts that would support the inference that because of the nature of a relationship or additional circumstances other than the interested director's stock ownership or voting power, the non-interested director would be more willing to risk his or her reputation than risk the relationship with the interested director.

845 A.2d at 1050–52.

———

In a section titled "A Word About the Oracle Case," the Delaware Supreme Court addressed specifically the meaning of *Oracle*:

Oracle involved the issue of the independence of the Special Litigation Committee (SLC) appointed by the Oracle board to determine whether or not the corporation should cause the dismissal of a corporate claim by stockholder-plaintiffs against directors.

> We need not decide whether the substantive standard of independence in an SLC case differs from that in a presuit demand case. As a practical matter, the procedural distinction relating to the diametrically-opposed burdens and the availability of discovery into independence may be outcome-determinative on the issue of independence. Moreover, because the members of an SLC are vested with enormous power to seek dismissal of a derivative suit brought against their director-colleagues in a setting where presuit demand is already excused, the Court of Chancery must exercise careful oversight of the bona fides of the SLC and its process. Aside from the procedural distinctions, the Stanford connections in *Oracle* are factually distinct from the relationships present here.

Id. at 1055.

How might a plaintiff discover specific information about board connections and director independence? The Delaware Supreme Court reiterated the usefulness in demand-futility cases of inspection rights under Section 220:

> Beam's failure to plead sufficient facts to support her claim of demand futility may be due in part to her failure to exhaust all reasonably available means of gathering facts. As the Chancellor noted, had Beam first brought a Section 220 action seeking inspection of MSO's books and records, she might have uncovered facts that would have created a reasonable doubt. For example, irregularities or "cronyism" in MSO's process of nominating board members might possibly strengthen her claim concerning Stewart's control over MSO's directors. A books and records inspection might have revealed whether the board used a nominating committee to select directors and maintained a separation between the director-selection process and management. A books and records inspection might also have revealed whether Stewart unduly controlled the nominating process or whether the process incorporated procedural safeguards to ensure directors' independence. Beam might also have reviewed the minutes of the board's meetings to determine how the directors handled Stewart's proposals or conduct in various contexts. Whether or not the result of this exploration might create a reasonable doubt would be sheer speculation at this stage. But the point is that it was within the plaintiff's power to explore these matters and she elected not to make the effort.

Id. at 1056.

In short, the Delaware Supreme Court seemed amenable to a broader concept of director independence, though without diminishing the presumption that outside directors are independent even if they occasionally play golf with the CEO or attend his child's wedding. To show bias, there must be real evidence.

IN RE EBAY, INC. SHAREHOLDERS LITIGATION
2004 WL 253521 (Del. Ch. 2004).

CHANDLER, CHANCELLOR:

Shareholders of eBay, Inc. filed these consolidated derivative actions against certain eBay directors and officers for usurping corporate opportunities. Plaintiffs allege that eBay's investment banking advisor, Goldman Sachs Group, engaged in "spinning," a practice that involves allocating shares of lucrative initial public offerings of stock to favored clients. In effect, the plaintiff shareholders allege that Goldman Sachs bribed certain eBay insiders, using the currency of highly profitable investment opportunities—opportunities that should have been offered to, or provided for the benefit of, eBay rather than the favored insiders. Plaintiffs accuse Goldman Sachs of aiding and abetting the corporate insiders breach of their fiduciary duty of loyalty to eBay.

The facts, as alleged in the complaint, are straightforward. In 1995, defendants Pierre M. Omidyar and Jeffrey Skoll founded nominal defendant eBay, a Delaware corporation, as a sole proprietorship. eBay is a pioneer in online trading platforms, providing a virtual auction community for buyers and sellers to list items for sale and to bid on items of interest. In 1998, eBay retained Goldman Sachs and other investment banks to underwrite an initial public offering of common stock.

Goldman Sachs was the lead underwriter. The stock was priced at $18 per share. Goldman Sachs purchased about 1.2 million shares. Shares of eBay stock became immensely valuable during 1998 and 1999, rising to $175 per share in early April 1999. Around that time, eBay made a secondary offering, issuing 6.5 million shares of common stock at $170 per share for a total of $1.1 billion. Goldman Sachs again served as lead underwriter. Goldman Sachs was asked in 2001 to serve as eBay's financial advisor in connection with an acquisition by eBay of PayPal, Inc. For these services, eBay has paid Goldman Sachs over $8 million.

During this same time period, Goldman Sachs "rewarded" the individual defendants by allocating to them thousands of IPO shares, managed by Goldman Sachs, at the initial offering price. Because the IPO market during this particular period of time was extremely active, prices of initial stock offerings often doubled or tripled in a single day. Investors who were well connected, either to Goldman Sachs or to similarly situated investment banks serving as IPO underwriters, were able to flip these investments into instant profit by selling the equities in a few days or even in a few hours after they were initially purchased.

The essential allegation of the complaint is that Goldman Sachs provided these IPO share allocations to the individual defendants to show appreciation for eBay's business and to enhance Goldman Sachs' chances of obtaining future eBay business. In addition to co-founding eBay, defendant Omidyar has been eBay's CEO, CFO and President. He is eBay's largest stockholder, owning more than 23% of the company's equity. Goldman Sachs allocated Omidyar shares in at least forty IPOs at the initial offering price. Omidyar resold these securities in the public market for millions of dollars in profit.

Defendant Whitman owns 3.3% of eBay stock and has been President, CEO and a director since early 1998. Whitman also has been a director of Goldman Sachs since 2001. Goldman Sachs allocated Whitman shares in over a 100 IPOs at the initial offering price. Whitman sold these equities in the open market and reaped millions of dollars in profit.

Defendant Skoll, in addition to co-founding eBay, has served in various positions at the company, including Vice-President of Strategic Planning and Analysis and President. He served as an eBay director from December 1996 to March 1998. Skoll is eBay's second largest stockholder, owning about 13% of the company. Goldman Sachs has allocated Skoll shares in at least 75 IPOs at the initial offering price, which Skoll promptly resold on the open market, allowing him to realize millions of dollars in profit. Finally, defendant Robert C. Kagle has served as an eBay director since June 1997. Goldman Sachs allocated Kagle shares in at least 25 IPOs at the initial offering price. Kagle promptly resold these equities, and recorded millions of dollars in profit.

Plaintiffs bring these actions on behalf of nominal defendant eBay, seeking an accounting from the individual director defendants of their profits from the IPO transactions as well as compensatory damages from Goldman Sachs for its participation (aiding and abetting) in the eBay insiders' breach of fiduciary duty. Court of Chancery Rule 23.1 requires that a shareholder make a demand that the corporation's board pursue potential litigation before initiating such litigation on the corporation's behalf. When a plaintiff fails to make a demand on the board of directors, the plaintiff must plead with factual particularity why the demand is excused.

eBay's board of directors consists of seven members. Three are the individual defendants-Whitman, Omidyar and Kagle; defendant Skoll is not presently a director. All four of these individual defendants received IPO allocations from Goldman Sachs. As a result, the three current directors of eBay who received IPO allocations (Omidyar, Whitman and Kagle) are clearly interested in the transactions at the core of this controversy.

Although the other four directors of eBay (Cook, Lepore, Schultz and Bourguignon) did not participate in the "spinning," plaintiffs allege that they are not independent of the interested directors and, thus, demand is excused as futile. Since three of the seven present eBay directors are interested in the transactions that give rise to this litigation, plaintiffs need only demonstrate a reason to doubt the independence of one of the remaining four directors. Plaintiffs allege that directors Cook, Lepore, Schultz and Bourguignon all have "close business and personal ties with the individual defendants" and are incapable of exercising independent judgment to determine whether eBay should bring a breach of fiduciary duty action against the individual defendants. Plaintiffs allege, for example, that Schultz is a member of Maveron LLC, an investment advisory company in which Whitman has made significant personal investments. More significantly, plaintiffs allege that Cook, Lepore, Schultz and Bourguignon have received huge financial benefits as a result of their positions as eBay directors and, furthermore, that they owe their positions on the board to Omidyar, Whitman, Kagle and Skoll.

eBay pays no cash compensation to its directors, but it does award substantial stock options. For example, in 1998, when Cook joined eBay's board, it awarded him 900,000 options at an exercise price of $1.555. One fourth of these options (225,000) vested immediately, and an additional 2% vests each subsequent month so long as Cook remains a director. In 1998, after Cook had joined the board, eBay adopted a director's stock option plan pursuant to which each non-employee director was to be awarded 30,000 options each year (except for 1999, when no additional options were awarded). As of early 2002, Cook beneficially owned 903,750 currently exercisable options, and an additional 200,000 shares of eBay stock. The complaint notes that the exercise price on 900,000 of the options originally awarded to Cook is $1.555 per share. At the time the complaint was filed in this case, eBay stock was valued at $62.13 per share. At an exercise price of $1.555, Cook's original option grant is thus worth millions of dollars. In addition, the stock options awarded in 2000, 2001 and 2002, which are not yet fully vested, and will never vest unless Cook retains his position as a director, are worth potentially millions of dollars.

The complaint further alleges that director Schultz, Lepore and Bourguignon are similarly situated. That is, the stock options granted to these directors, which are both vested and unvested, are so valuable that they create a financial incentive for these directors to retain their positions as directors and make them beholden to the defendant directors. As a result, plaintiffs contend that it is more than reasonable to assume that an individual who has already received, and who expects to receive still more, options of such significant value could not objectively decide whether to commence legal proceedings against fellow directors who are directly responsible for the outside directors' continuing positions on the board.

I need not address each of the four outside directors, as I agree with plaintiffs that the particularized allegations of the complaint are sufficient to raise a reasonable doubt as to Cook's independence from the eBay insider directors who accepted Goldman Sachs' IPO allocations. Defendants resist this conclusion by pointing out that Whitman, Kagle, Omidyar and Skoll, collectively with management, control 40% of eBay's common stock, which they argue is insufficient to allege control or domination. Defendants also contend that the options represent past compensation and would not effectively disable a director from acting fairly and impartially with respect to a demand. These arguments are unpersuasive in these circumstances.

First, defendants must concede that certain stockholders, executive officers and directors control eBay. For example, eBay's form 10–K for the fiscal year ending December 31, 2000 notes that eBay's executive officers and directors Whitman, Omidyar, Kagle and Skoll (and their affiliates) own about one-half of eBay's outstanding common stock. As a result, these eBay officers and directors effectively have the ability to control eBay and to direct its affairs and business, including the election of directors and the approval of significant corporate transactions. Although the percentage of ownership may have decreased slightly from the time eBay filed the 2000 10–K, the decrease is insufficient to detract from the company's acknowledgement that these four individual defendants control the company and the election of directors.

Second, although many of the options awarded to Cook and the other purported outside directors have in fact vested, a significant number of options have not yet vested and will never vest unless the outside directors remain directors of eBay. Given that the value of the options for Cook (and allegedly for the other outside directors) potentially run into the millions of dollars, one cannot conclude realistically that Cook would be able to objectively and impartially consider a demand to bring litigation against those to whom he is beholden for his current position and future position on eBay's board. With the specific allegations of the complaint in mind, I conclude that plaintiffs have adequately demonstrated that demand on eBay's board should be excused as futile.

――――――――

CAN DIRECTORS BE TRULY INDEPENDENT?

Professor Charles Elson has questioned whether most directors can truly be independent.

> There are three problems with a management-appointed board that leads to ineffective oversight. First, personal and psychic ties to the individuals who are responsible for one's appointment to a board make it difficult to engage in necessary confrontation. It is always tough to challenge a fiend, particularly when the challenging party may one day, as an officer of another enterprise, end up in the same position. Second, conflicts with a manager who is also a member of one's own board may lead to future retribution on one's own turf, thus

reducing the incentive to act. Third, and most important, when one owes one's own board position to the largesse of management, any action taken that is inimical to management may result in a failure to be renominated to the board, which—given the large fees paid to directors and the great reputational advantage of board membership—malfunction as an effective club to stifle dissension. This is why the development of substantial director compensation, a consequence of management control, has acted to stifle board oversight of management, and has, in fact, enhanced management domination.

Charles M. Elson, *Director Compensation*, 50 S.M.U.L. Rev. 127, 161–62 (1996).

H. SETTLEMENT AND ATTORNEYS' FEES

The settlement of lawsuits has always played a major role in the American judicial system; and that is particularly true in derivative suit litigation. Few suits go to trial or are tried to a final judgment; most that are not dismissed at the pleading stage or on summary judgment settle.

The representative nature of a derivative suit helps explain why settlements occur frequently in shareholder litigation. Suits often are initiated by plaintiffs' attorneys who represent "figurehead" clients. Many plaintiffs' attorneys are committed to protecting the interests of the shareholders they represent, but almost all such attorneys work on a contingent fee basis. Thus, their personal financial interests lie in maximizing the fees they will earn for any given amount of work and minimizing the risk that they will receive no fee for their efforts. This produces a bias in favor of smaller, speedier settlements over trials that, if unsuccessful, will leave attorneys without compensation after years of work. In addition, plaintiffs' attorneys may find it financially attractive to initiate "strike suits" that have little prospect of success on the merits but that impose litigation costs on the defendant corporation, giving them nuisance, and thus settlement value.

A shareholder's financial interest, in contrast, lies in realizing the largest recovery, adjusted for litigation risk, that a suit has the potential to generate. At times, shareholders also may benefit from changes in the governance practices of the defendant corporation or from enhanced or corrective disclosure of material information. Shareholders, however, realize no benefits from strike suits or from settlements that produce only symbolic governance changes or meaningless disclosures.

The key safeguard against opportunism in shareholder litigation is the requirement in F.R.C.P. 23 and 23.1, and the comparable requirement in most states' statutes or rules, that a court both approve any settlement, compromise, discontinuance or dismissal of a derivative suit or shareholder class action and that the court also determine what fee should be awarded to plaintiffs' attorney(s).

A court must decide whether to approve a settlement that typically has been negotiated by plaintiffs' attorneys without input from many of the shareholders whose interests they represent. As the court observed in *Needham v. Cruver*, 1995 WL 510039 (Del.Ch. 1995), "the law promotes the value of fair settlements by affording a process in which some degree of assurance can be afforded to absent class members or shareholders that the settlement is fair to them at least in the judgment of a disinterested and experienced judge." The proponents of a settlement bear the burden of convincing the court that it is fair. In most cases, that determination will depend largely on the adequacy of the amount being recovered when compared to the potential recovery were plaintiff to succeed at trial. In making this evaluation, the court will discount the potential recovery at trial by the risk factors inherent in any litigation and the time value of money over the period during which recovery will be delayed. Most courts look to a list of factors similar to those enumerated by the Delaware Supreme Court in *Polk v. Good*, 507 A.2d 531, 536 (Del. 1986):

> (1) the probable validity of the claims, (2) the apparent difficulties in enforcing the claims through the courts, (3) the collectibility of any judgment recovered, (4) the delay, expense and trouble of litigation, (5) the amount of compromise as compared with the amount and collectibility of a judgment, and (6) the views of the parties involved, pro and con.

Evaluation of a settlement becomes more difficult when it involves nonpecuniary benefits to the corporation or the plaintiff class. For example, settlements of derivative suits may involve agreements to add outside directors to the board, to create more independent audit, compensation or nominating committees, or to require managers to surrender stock options. Class action settlements may require additional disclosure before a planned transaction is consummated. Although settlements calling for improved governance mechanisms may reduce the prospect of future wrongdoing, they raise a separate problem: in the words of the ALI, "such therapeutic relief can sometimes represent a counterfeit currency by which the parties can increase the apparent value of the settlement and thereby justify higher attorney's fees for plaintiff's counsel, who is often the real party in interest." To deal with this problem, the ALI recommends that the court review the value of non-pecuniary relief both when evaluating the settlement and when computing plaintiff's counsel fees. ALI Principles § 7.14, Comment c.

The integrity of the shareholder litigation process depends to a considerable degree on the rigor with which courts review proposed settlements and requests for attorneys' fees. However, a number of factors impair the effectiveness of courts' review. Perhaps the most important is that settlement hearings rarely are adversarial. As Judge Henry Friendly pointed out many years ago: "Once a settlement is agreed, the attorneys for the plaintiff stockholders link arms with their former adversaries to defend the joint handiwork. . . ." *Alleghany Corp. v. Kirby*, 333 F.2d 327, 347 (2d Cir.1964) (Friendly, J., dissenting), *aff'd per curiam*, 340 F.2d 311 (2d Cir.1965) (en banc). Absent a well prepared objector, courts thus must take the initiative in reviewing proposed settlements, yet courts often have an incentive to approve a proposed settlement, if for no other reason than to clear potentially complex cases from their (often overcrowded) dockets that otherwise are likely to require a great deal of judicial attention.

Affected shareholders are made aware of proposed settlements through the notices required by Federal Rules of Civil Procedure 23 and 23.1 and comparable provisions of state law. Largely as a consequence of collective action problems, though, affected shareholders rarely object. They usually do not have detailed information about the merits of the action or the manner in which the settlement has been negotiated. To obtain this information, a shareholder has to challenge both the plaintiffs' attorneys, who nominally represent the shareholder's interests but who always have a strong interest in having the settlement approved, and the attorneys representing the defendants and the corporation. In addition, a shareholder often will have only a relatively brief period in which to object before the hearing on the settlement is scheduled to be held. Despite these problems, courts usually treat the absence of a large number of objections as a factor supporting approval of a proposed settlement.

Even courts that are skeptical about the benefits of a proposed settlement often are reluctant to reject it. *In re Chicago and North Western Transportation Company Shareholders Litigation*, 1995 WL 389627 (Del.Ch.1995), involved an attempt to enjoin a merger on the grounds that its terms were not fair, the directors had failed to seek the highest value reasonably available to the shareholders, and there had not been full disclosure of all material facts in the merger proxy statement. On the eve of the injunction hearing, the parties settled the litigation by having the defendants make additional disclosures to the shareholders in a supplemental proxy statement. Plaintiffs' counsel then sought attorneys' fees and expenses of $525,000. A shareholder objected on the grounds that the settlement provided no benefit whatsoever to the shareholders; it only benefitted plaintiffs' counsel.

Vice Chancellor Chandler reluctantly approved the settlement. He acknowledged that causing a corporation's directors to provide shareholders with facts material to their vote on a merger benefits shareholders. He found, however, that only three facts in the defendant corporation's supplemental proxy statement were material and that any other benefits of the settlement were "meager." Those findings led him to conclude that the attorneys' fee request was disproportionate to the benefit obtained for the class; he awarded plaintiffs' attorneys only $300,000.

In contrast, in *Fruchter v. Florida Progress Corporation*, 2002 WL 1558220 (Fla.Cir.Ct.2002), the court refused to approve a proposed settlement of a class action that challenged the fairness of a merger, negotiated at arm's length, in which Florida Progress agreed to be acquired by Carolina Power & Light. The settlement, reached after the merger had closed, did not call for any additional consideration to be paid to the plaintiff class or for any additional disclosures. The only "benefit" it provided for the class was an assurance, provided by plaintiff's counsel after reviewing both public and non-public information, that the merger "was negotiated properly, at arms-length, and resulted in Class Members receiving fair and reasonable consideration for their [Florida Progress] stock" and that "the final proxy provided class members with a complete and accurate disclosure of all facts material to their decision to vote in favor of the Share Exchange." Defendants, in exchange, would receive a comprehensive release from all claims that had been made or could be made in connection with the merger. Defendants also agreed not to oppose an application by plaintiff's counsel for fees and expenses of up to $375,000 and to pay any court-awarded fee up to that amount.

The court summarized its reasons for rejecting the proposed settlement as follows:

> In summary, the Stipulation of Settlement contains no compensation for the class members. Indeed, all of the evidence suggests that class members are in precisely the same financial and legal position today, as they would have been had this litigation never been filed. In spite of the fact that it is devoid of benefits for class members, Class counsel has urged this court to approve the settlement, grant the Defendants their res judicata and presumably grant him several hundred thousand dollars in attorneys' fees. This action appears to be the class litigation equivalent of the 'Squeegee boys' who used to frequent major urban intersections and who would run up to a stopped car, splash soapy water on its perfectly clean windshield and expect payment for the uninvited service of wiping it off.

Id. at 10.

CHAPTER 17

THE DUTY OF CARE

■ ■ ■

Problem: FiberNet Corporation—Part 3

It has been a year since FiberNet went public. One of the original directors has decided to retire, and FiberNet has succeeded in recruiting Roger Roket to take his place. Roger is a well-known expert in optical technology who recently retired as Chief Operating Officer of Ball Laboratories, a privately-held company that has done a great deal of research and development in the field. Roger has had some experience in business, but he has never served on a board of directors, and he is concerned about what potential liabilities he might be exposed to and what he should do to avoid them. FiberNet's CEO has asked you to brief Roger on his responsibilities as a director and how he should go about fulfilling them. In a preliminary conversation Roger has told you that he is particularly interested in how well he should get to know FiberNet's business, and how much he should be concerned about areas in which he does not have much experience. In particular he asked the following questions:

- How much do I need to learn about everything that the company is doing?

- I know the optical networking industry and I have a basic understanding of finance, but in what depth must I understand the company's financial statements? To what extent can I rely on the accountants who have prepared them and on other directors who may have more experience?

- I also know that, like most public corporations, FiberNet is subject to a wide range of regulations, both federal and state, with which I have had little experience. What can and/or must I do, if anything, to be sure the company complies with these laws?

- Finally, a matter of great concern. I've run a business for a long time and I know that decisions can turn out badly. If they do, can I be personally liable for errors of judgment? In that connection, I understand that FiberNet's certificate of incorporation has a clause exculpating directors from liability. How much will that help if something goes wrong?

A. INTRODUCTION TO FIDUCIARY DUTIES

As we saw in Chapter 2, much of the law of corporations revolves around the application of principles of fiduciary duty. Perhaps because many of the earliest corporate cases involved charitable corporations, courts began to analogize the duties of a director in managing corporate property to the duties of a trustee in managing trust property. But as corporations began to play a more important role in an increasingly complex commercial world, the strictures based on trust law gradually eroded.

Today, the basic notion survives that director and officers owe enforceable duties to the corporation and, through the corporation, to the shareholders. Historically, courts have articulated these fiduciary duties as comprising a *duty of care* and a *duty of loyalty*. Controlling shareholders also owe a duty of loyalty to minority shareholders but do not owe a duty of care.

The duty of care is a duty that directors owe to act in the corporation's best interests and to exercise reasonable care in making decisions and in overseeing the corporation's affairs. The duty of loyalty is a duty that requires directors act in the good faith belief that their actions are in the best interests of the corporation and its stockholders rather than in their personal interest. Although the duties of care and loyalty are discrete concepts, the line between the two is often blurry.

B. INTRODUCTION TO THE STANDARDS OF CARE

Although the specific parameters of the duty of care have been primarily developed in the courts, § 8.30 of the MBCA is an effort to codify those standards:

(a) Each member of the board of directors, when discharging the duties of a director, shall act: (1) in good faith, and (2) in a manner the director reasonably believes to be in the best interests of the corporation.

(b) The members of the board of directors or a committee of the board, when becoming informed in connection with their decision-making function or devoting attention to their oversight function, shall discharge their duties with the care that a person in a like position would reasonably believe appropriate under similar circumstances.

Note the lack of specific guidance in the statutory language. The section provides a framework for understanding a director's duty of care but does not indicate what a director must do to satisfy the statutory standards. "Good faith" and "best interests" apply to each director and describe the director's duties generally—whether in a decision-making or oversight capacity. The standards concerning "becoming informed" and "devoting attention to oversight" apply when directors act together and focus on specific aspects of the directors' decision-making and oversight functions.

Perhaps one reason for the lack of specificity is that it is possible to divide the nature of directors' duties into two questions. First, how do shareholders hope directors will act in overseeing the corporation and becoming informed when making decisions? This question may be answered without taking into account the costs to the corporation of enforcing those aspirations. The harder question is the second: Under what circumstances do shareholders want directors to pay monetary damages if the corporation suffers losses from their breach of duty? The two questions, of course, are related. The closer the answers are to each other, the greater is the potential risk to directors of personal liability, which presumably increases the difficulty of persuading qualified individuals to serve. The issue is especially difficult with respect to the duty of care because, by definition, the directors have not benefitted personally from the alleged breach.

Put differently, the standards of care typically articulated in statutes and by commentators are mainly aspirational. They describe an ideal of director conduct. Falling short of these aspirational standards does not necessarily lead to personal liability. Positive enforcement of the duty of care through the imposition of liability is more complicated. For corporate lawyers, it is important to differentiate the aspirational and enforceable aspects of the duty of care. Lawyers who counsel corporations are usually asked to counsel directors as to the aspirational standards of proper behavior rather than what is necessary to avoid liability. In some situations, however, the question is whether particular conduct or decisions may result in liability.

Professor Eisenberg draws a useful distinction between standards of conduct and standards of liability:

> A standard of conduct states how an actor should conduct a given activity or play a given role. A standard of review states the test a court should apply when it reviews an actor's conduct to determine whether to impose liability or grant injunctive relief.

> In many or most areas of law, these two kinds of standards tend to be conflated. For example, the standard of conduct that governs automobile drivers is that they should drive carefully, and the standard of review in a liability claim against a driver is whether he drove carefully.

> The conflation of standards of conduct and standards of review is so common that it is easy to overlook the fact that whether the two kinds of standards are or should be identical in

any given area is a matter of prudential judgment. Perhaps standards of conduct and standards of review in corporate law would always be identical in a world in which information was perfect, the risk of liability for assuming a given corporate role was always commensurate with the incentives for assuming the role, and institutional considerations never required deference to a corporate organ. In the real world, however, these conditions seldom hold, and the standards of review in corporate law pervasively diverge from the standards of conduct.

Melvin Aron Eisenberg, *The Divergence of Standards of Conduct and Standards of Review in Corporate Law*, 62 Fordham L. Rev. 437, 437–438 (1993).

Corporate directors often are well compensated, and many prominent figures like to serve on corporate boards. But the modern director must work hard to satisfy her duties, and she inevitably puts her reputation at risk. Several decades ago, corporate directorships were not particularly demanding, and directors sometimes served on a large number of boards simultaneously, devoting little effort to each. Today, however, being a corporate director is much more demanding, requiring significantly greater attention and engagement.

It is significant that outside directors are almost never required to pay damages for breaching their duty of care. Several legal mechanisms are available to protect them. The business judgment rule precludes liability unless directors have been grossly negligent. Corporations also can include in their charters exculpation clauses that limit director liability for money damages for breaches of the duty of care unless (in Delaware at least) the directors have not acted in "good faith" (a complex subject that we will consider later in this chapter and Chapter 18). Corporations also can agree to indemnify directors in certain circumstances both for the expenses associated with litigation and for damages. And they can buy insurance for directors and officers.

Given the limited possibility of director liability, why is there an enforceable duty of care? One reason is that its bark can be as bad as its bite. The duty of care is a potential shaming mechanism for publicly evaluating the conduct of directors. Directors generally are successful and respected people, who worry about their reputations. They do not want to be found to have breached a duty, even if it doesn't cost them any money.

This chapter begins with a consideration of the business judgment rule, a key aspect of judicial enforcement of the duty of care. We then examine the oversight duties of directors. Next we look at the duty of directors to become informed in making decisions. Finally, we review the ways in which corporate law protects directors from personal liability through exculpation clauses, indemnification, and insurance.

C. BUSINESS JUDGMENT RULE

1. SCOPE OF THE BUSINESS JUDGMENT RULE

The duty of care and the business judgment rule are closely linked. A starting point to understanding this relationship is that, whereas the duty of care imposes potential liability for a breach of the duty, the business judgment rule requires that, in determining whether there has been a breach, courts defer to the informed, good faith judgment of a board in making the decision being challenged.

The business judgment rule has been part of the common law for at least one hundred fifty years. Traditionally, it has operated as a shield to protect directors from liability for their decisions. If the business judgment rule applies, courts will not interfere with or second-guess directors' decisions.

A leading formulation of the rule is that of the Delaware Supreme Court in *Aronson v. Lewis*, 473 A.2d 805, 812 (Del.1984):

> The business judgment rule is an acknowledgment of the managerial prerogatives of Delaware directors under Section 141(a) ["The business and affairs of every corporation organized under this chapter shall be managed by or under the direction of a board of directors"]. It is a presumption that in making a business decision the directors of a corporation acted on an informed basis, in good faith and in the honest belief that the action taken was in the best interests of the company. Absent an abuse of discretion, that judgment will be respected by the courts. The burden is on the party challenging the decision to establish facts rebutting the presumption.

The business judgment rule applies under two conditions: "First, did the Board reach its decision in the good faith pursuit of a legitimate corporate interest? Second, did the Board do so advisedly?" *Gantler v. Stephens*, 965 A.2d 695, 706 (Del. 2009). The business judgment rule does not apply when there has been no exercise of judgment resulting in a decision. Intentional omissions, being decisions to not take action, are protected. But neglectful inaction is not protected. *See, e.g., Francis v. United Jersey Bank,* 432 A.2d 814 (N.J. 1981). Another caveat is that the decision or action must meet a minimum standard of rationality. *See Sinclair Oil Corp. v. Levien*, 280 A.2d 717, 720 (Del. 1971); *Gagliardi v. Trifoods Int'l, Inc.*, 683 A.2d 1049, 1051–52 (Del.Ch. 1996). Irrationality is "the outer limit of the business judgment rule" and "the functional equivalent of the waste test." *Brehm v. Eisner*, 746 A.2d 244, 264 (Del. 2000). Waste occurs "only in the rare, 'unconscionable case' " where a board irrationally squanders corporate assets. *In re Walt Disney Co. Derivative Litig.*, 906 A.2d 27, 74 (Del. 2006).

The business judgment rule is essentially a creature of the courts, and its statutory treatment is ambiguous at best. The DGCL, for example, contains no statement of the required standards of care for directors or of the business judgment rule. Although the MBCA specifies standards of conduct for directors, the Official Comment to Section 8.31 (dealing with director liability) notes that "the fact that a director's performance fails to reach [the level of the standards of section 8.30] does not automatically establish personal liability for damages that the corporation may have suffered as a consequence." And although MBCA § 8.31 establishes general standards for director liability, it is not intended to codify the business judgment rule. Indeed, the Official Comment expresses a preference that courts continue the common law development of the business judgment rule, rather than attempt to "freeze the concept in a statute." Nevertheless, as the Official Comment explains, MBCA § 8.31(a)(2) retains the principal elements of the business judgment rule, as they relate to director liability under the case law.

The following well-known case illustrates the application of the business judgment rule. In reading the case, consider these questions: (1) If the plaintiff was right that night baseball would be profitable, should he be able to sue on the basis that his judgment is substantively better than the board's? (2) If the board made a poor business decision, shouldn't it be held liable for making a bad decision?

SHLENSKY V. WRIGLEY

237 N.E.2d 776 (Ill.App. 1968).

SULLIVAN, JUSTICE.

This is an appeal from a dismissal of plaintiff's amended complaint on motion of the defendants. The action was a stockholders' derivative suit against the directors for negligence and mismanagement. The corporation was also made a defendant. Plaintiff sought damages and an order that defendants cause the installation of lights in Wrigley Field and the scheduling of night baseball games.

Plaintiff is a minority stockholder of defendant corporation, Chicago National League Ball Club (Inc.), a Delaware corporation with its principal place of business in Chicago, Illinois. Defendant corporation owns and operates the major league professional baseball team known as the Chicago Cubs. The corporation also engages in the operation of Wrigley Field, the Cubs' home park, the concessionaire sales during Cubs' home games, television and radio broadcasts of Cubs' home games, the leasing of the field for football games and other events and receives its share, as visiting team, of admission moneys from games played in other National League stadia. The individual defendants are directors of the Cubs and have served for varying periods of years. Defendant Philip K. Wrigley is also president of the corporation and owner of approximately 80% of the stock therein.

Plaintiff alleges that since night baseball was first played in 1935 nineteen of the twenty major league teams have scheduled night games. In 1966, out of a total of 1620 games in the major leagues, 932 were played at night. Plaintiff alleges that every member of the major leagues, other than the Cubs, scheduled substantially all of its home games in 1966 at night, exclusive of opening days, Saturdays, Sundays, holidays and days prohibited by league rules. Allegedly this has been done for the specific purpose of maximizing attendance and thereby maximizing revenue and income.

The Cubs, in the years 1961–65, sustained operating losses from its direct baseball operations. Plaintiff attributes those losses to inadequate attendance at Cubs' home games. He concludes that if the directors continue to refuse to install lights at Wrigley Field and schedule night baseball games, the Cubs will continue to sustain comparable losses and its financial condition will continue to deteriorate.

Plaintiff alleges that, except for the year 1963, attendance at Cubs' home games has been substantially below that at their road games, many of which were played at night.

Plaintiff compares attendance at Cubs' games with that of the Chicago White Sox, an American League club, whose weekday games were generally played at night. The weekend attendance figures for the two teams was similar; however, the White Sox week-night games drew many more patrons than did the Cubs' weekday games.

Plaintiff alleges that the funds for the installation of lights can be readily obtained through financing and the cost of installation would be far more than offset and recaptured by increased revenues and incomes resulting from the increased attendance.

Plaintiff further alleges that defendant Wrigley has refused to install lights, not because of interest in the welfare of the corporation but because of his personal opinions "that baseball is a 'daytime sport' and that the installation of lights and night baseball games will have a deteriorating effect upon the surrounding neighborhood." It is alleged that he has admitted that he is not interested in whether the Cubs would benefit financially from such action because of his concern for the neighborhood, and that he would be willing for the team to play night games if a new stadium were built in Chicago.

Plaintiff alleges that the other defendant directors, with full knowledge of the foregoing matters, have acquiesced in the policy laid down by Wrigley and have permitted him to dominate the board of directors in matters involving the installation of lights and scheduling of night games, even though they knew he was not motivated by a good faith concern as to the best interests of defendant corporation, but solely by his personal views set forth above. It is charged that the directors are acting for a reason or reasons contrary and wholly unrelated to the business interests of the corporation; that such arbitrary and capricious acts constitute mismanagement and waste of corporate assets, and that the directors have been negligent in failing to exercise reasonable care and prudence in the management of the corporate affairs.

The question on appeal is whether plaintiff's amended complaint states a cause of action. It is plaintiff's position that fraud, illegality and conflict of interest are not the only bases for a stockholder's derivative action against the directors. Contrariwise, defendants argue that the courts will not step in and interfere with honest business judgment of the directors unless there is a showing of fraud, illegality or conflict of interest.

The cases in this area are numerous and each differs from the others on a factual basis. However, the courts have pronounced certain ground rules which appear in all cases and which are then applied to the given factual situation. The court in *Wheeler v. Pullman Iron & Steel Co.*, 32 N.E. 420, 423 (Ill. 1892), said:

> It is, however, fundamental in the law of corporations, that the majority of its stockholders shall control the policy of the corporation, and regulate and govern the lawful exercise of its franchise and business. * * * Every one purchasing or subscribing for stock in a corporation impliedly agrees that he will be bound by the acts and proceedings done or sanctioned by a majority of the shareholders, or by the agents of the corporation duly chosen by such majority, within the scope of the powers conferred by the charter, and courts of equity will not undertake to control the policy or business methods of a corporation, although it may be seen that a wiser policy might be adopted and the business more successful if other methods were pursued. The majority of shares of its stock, or the agents by the holders thereof lawfully chosen, must be permitted to control the business of the corporation in their discretion, when not in violation of its charter or some public law, or corruptly and fraudulently subversive of the rights and interests of the corporation or of a shareholder.

Plaintiff argues that the allegations of his amended complaint are sufficient to set forth a cause of action under the principles set out in *Dodge v. Ford Motor Co.*, 170 N.W. 668 (Mich. 1919).

From the authority relied upon in that case it is clear that the court felt that there must be fraud or a breach of that good faith which directors are bound to exercise toward the stockholders in order to justify the courts entering into the internal affairs of corporations. This is made clear when the court refused to interfere with the director[s'] decision to expand the business.

Plaintiff in the instant case argues that the directors are acting for reasons unrelated to the financial interest and welfare of the Cubs. However, we are not satisfied that the motives assigned to Philip K. Wrigley, and through him to the other directors, are contrary to the best interests of the corporation and the stockholders. For example, it appears to us that the effect on the surrounding neighborhood might well be considered by a director who was considering the patrons who would or would not attend the games if the park were in a poor neighborhood. Furthermore, the long run interest of the corporation in its property value at Wrigley Field might demand all efforts to keep the neighborhood from deteriorating. By these thoughts we do not mean to say that we have decided that the decision of the directors was a correct one. That is beyond our jurisdiction and ability. We are merely saying that the decision is one properly before directors and the motives alleged in the amended complaint showed no fraud, illegality or conflict of interest in their making of that decision.

Finally, we do not agree with plaintiff's contention that failure to follow the example of the other major league clubs in scheduling night games constituted negligence. [Plaintiff made no allegation that these teams' night schedules were profitable or that the purpose for which night baseball had been undertaken was fulfilled.] Furthermore, it cannot be said that directors, even those of corporations that are losing money, must follow the lead of the other corporations in the field. Directors are elected for their business capabilities and judgment and the courts cannot require them to forego their judgment because of the decisions of directors of other companies. Courts may not decide these questions in the absence of a clear showing of dereliction of duty on the part of the specific directors and mere failure to "follow the crowd" is not such a dereliction.

For the foregoing reasons the order of dismissal entered by the trial court is affirmed.

2. THE BUSINESS JUDGMENT RULE AND DIRECTORIAL NEGLIGENCE

Many statutes state that directors should exercise "the care an ordinarily prudent person in a like position would exercise under similar circumstances." Pre-1998 MBCA § 8.30(a)(2). The phrasing, sounding as it does in tort, suggests a negligence standard in evaluating a director's conduct. [However, under the business judgment rule courts do not review the decisions of courts to determine whether they were "reasonable" or "prudent."] Consider the following characterization of the duty of care by the Delaware Supreme Court.

As for the plaintiffs' contention that the directors failed to exercise "substantive due care," we should note that such a concept is foreign to the business judgment rule. Courts do not measure, weigh or quantify directors' judgments. We do not even decide if they are reasonable in this context. *Due care in the decisionmaking context is <u>process due care only</u>.*

Brehm v. Eisner, 746 A.2d 244, 264 (Del. 2000) (emphasis added). Other courts have made clear they would not impose liability for board actions even if they were "stupid, egregious or irrational" (*In re Caremark Int'l Inc. Derivative Litig.*, 698 A.2d 959, 967 (Del. Ch. 1996); or "foolishly risky! stupidly risky! egregiously risky" (*Gagliardi v. TriFoods Int'l, Inc.*, 683 A.2d 1049, 1052 (Del. Ch. 1996).

Contrast this corporate law rule with tort doctrine that has long rejected the stupid-person defense for the reasonable person standard. See, *e.g.*, *Vaughn v. Menlove*, 132 Eng. Rep. 490, 492 (1837) (rejecting the defense in a negligence action that the defendant "ought not to be responsible for the misfortune of not possessing the highest order of intelligence"). For this reason the amended MBCA drops the "ordinarily prudent person" language and calls on directors to "discharge their duties with the care that a person in a like position would reasonably believe appropriate under similar circumstances." MBCA § 8.30(b).

Why aren't directors subject to a negligence standard? Judge Ralph Winter has articulated a classic defense of the business judgment rule:

> While it is often stated that corporate directors and officers will be liable for negligence in carrying out their corporate duties, all seem agreed that such a statement is misleading. Whereas an automobile driver who makes a mistake in judgment as to speed or distance injuring a pedestrian will likely be called upon to respond in damages, a corporate officer who makes a mistake in judgment as to economic conditions, consumer tastes or production line efficiency will rarely, if ever, be found liable for damages suffered by the corporation. Whatever the terminology, the fact is that liability is rarely imposed upon corporate directors or officers simply for bad judgment and this reluctance to impose liability for unsuccessful business decisions has been doctrinally labeled the business judgment rule. Although the rule has suffered under academic criticism, see, *e.g.*, Cary, *Standards of Conduct Under Common Law, Present Day Statutes and the Model Act*, 27 Bus. Law. 61 (1972), it is not without rational basis.

> First, shareholders to a very real degree voluntarily undertake the risk of bad business judgment. Investors need not buy stock, for investment markets offer an array of opportunities less vulnerable to mistakes in judgment by corporate officers. Nor need investors buy stock in particular corporations. In the exercise of what is genuinely a free choice, the quality of a firm's management is often decisive and information is available from professional advisors. Since shareholders can and do select among

investments partly on the basis of management, the business judgment rule merely recognizes a certain voluntariness in undertaking the risk of bad business decisions.

Second, courts recognize that after-the-fact litigation is a most imperfect device to evaluate corporate business decisions. The circumstances surrounding a corporate decision are not easily reconstructed in a courtroom years later, since business imperatives often call for quick decisions, inevitably based on less than perfect information. The entrepreneur's function is to encounter risks and to confront uncertainty, and a reasoned decision at the time made may seem a wild hunch viewed years later against a background of perfect knowledge.

Third, because potential profit often corresponds to the potential risk, it is very much in the interest of shareholders that the law not create incentives for overly cautious corporate decisions. Some opportunities offer great profits at the risk of very substantial losses, while the alternatives offer less risk of loss but also less potential profit. Shareholders can reduce the volatility of risk by diversifying their holdings. In the case of the diversified shareholder, the seemingly more risky alternatives may well be the best choice since great losses in some stocks will over time be offset by even greater gains in others. Given mutual funds and similar forms of diversified investment, courts need not bend over backwards to give special protection to shareholders who refuse to reduce the volatility of risk by not diversifying. A rule which penalizes the choice of seemingly riskier alternatives thus may not be in the interest of shareholders generally.

Whatever its merit, however, the business judgment rule extends only as far as the reasons which justify its existence. Thus, it does not apply in cases, *e.g.*, in which the corporate decision lacks a business purpose, is tainted by a conflict of interest, is so egregious as to amount to a no-win decision, *Litwin v. Allen*, 25 N.Y.S.2d 667 (N.Y.Co.Sup.Ct.1940), or results from an obvious and prolonged failure to exercise oversight or supervision.

Joy v. North, 692 F.2d 880, 885–886 (2d Cir.1982).

As Professor Eisenberg has explained, a standard of "rationality" is quite different from one of "reasonableness":

[T]he prevalent formulation of the standard of review under the business-judgment rule, if [a judgment has been made, the director employed a reasonable decision-making process, the decision was made in subjective good faith, the director had no financial interest in the subject matter of the decision], is that the decision must be rational. This rationality standard of review is much easier to satisfy than a prudence or reasonability standard. To see how exceptional a rationality standard is, we need only think about the judgments we make in everyday life. It is common to characterize a person's conduct as imprudent or unreasonable, but it is very uncommon to characterize a person's conduct as irrational. Unlike a subjective-good-faith standard, a rationality standard preserves a minimum and necessary degree of director and officer accountability. Further, a rationality standard allows courts to enjoin directors and officers from taking actions that would waste the corporation's assets.

An obvious example of a decision that fails to satisfy the rationality standard is a decision that cannot be coherently explained. For example, in *Selheimer v. Manganese Corp. of America,* [224 A.2d 634 (Pa.1966),] 23 managers poured a corporation's funds into the development of a single plant even though they knew the plant could not be operated profitably because of various factors, including lack of a railroad siding and proper storage areas. The court imposed liability, because the managers' conduct "defie[d] explanation; in fact, the defendants have failed to give any satisfactory explanation or advance any justification for [the] expenditures." *Id.* at 646.

Melvin Aron Eisenberg, *The Divergence of Standards of Conduct and Standards of Review in Corporate Law*, 62 Fordham L. Rev. 437, 442–443 (1993).

3.   THE BUSINESS JUDGMENT RULE AND WASTE

The business judgment rule also can be overcome if board action lacked a "rational" business purpose. A challenge on these grounds typically takes the form of a claim that a transaction wholly lacks consideration, and the cases that address such claims often speak of "waste" or "spoliation" of corporate assets.

a.   The Meaning of "Corporate Waste"

How much business justification is sufficient? Under the waste standard, even board decisions that seem unquestionably unwise or imprudent are shielded from review and the directors from liability. As the Delaware Supreme Court has stated, there is waste only if "what the corporation has received is so inadequate in value that no person of ordinary, sound business judgment would deem it worth that which the corporation has paid." *Grobow v. Perot*, 539 A.2d 180, 189 (Del.1988).

Only if a corporate transaction results in no benefit to the corporation—such as issuing stock without consideration or using corporate funds to discharge personal obligations—have courts found corporate waste. As one court observed, "rarest of all—and indeed, like

Nessie, possibly non-existent—would be the case of disinterested business people making non-fraudulent deals (non-negligently) that meet the legal standard of waste." *Steiner v. Meyerson*, 1995 WL 441999 at 5 (Del.Ch.1995).

Under the waste standard good-faith board decisions are protected from judicial second-guessing. As we have seen in *Shlensky v. Wrigley* and in *Kamin v. American Express Co.*, courts are typically willing to uphold business decisions on the flimsiest of justifications. In only a handful of cases have courts found good-faith board action so imprudent as to fall outside the business judgment rule, such as when evidence of conflicts of interest or other malfeasance is submerged. For example, in a famous case involving high-risk bank transactions during the height of the Great Depression, the court imposed liability on bank directors for approving the transactions in the precarious financial markets after the 1929 stock market crash. *Litwin v. Allen*, 25 N.Y.S.2d 667 (Sup.Ct.1940). The court faulted the directors for approving a transaction "so improvident, so risky, so unusual and unnecessary to be contrary to fundamental conceptions of prudent banking practice." Although some commentators have explained the case as imposing higher duties on bank directors, who were often viewed as appropriate deep pockets before of federal bank deposit insurance, the case has overtones of self-dealing. The company that had been benefitted by the financing transactions was the holding company for a business group in which the bank's parent, J. P. Morgan & Company, was deeply committed. Although the court concluded the plaintiffs had failed to show a conflict of interest, the court's heightened scrutiny of the transaction suggested it had doubts about the good faith of the bank directors.

b. Options Backdating

One of the rare instances in which courts have found that board decisions constituted "waste" involved the so-called "options backdating" scandal. Stock options are a common component of executive compensation. They consist of rights to purchase a specified number of shares at a specified price. These options are normally not exercisable immediately but "vest" and become exercisable with the passage of time, typically in installments over four or five years. Because they involve the issuance of stock, options must be approved by the board of directors or, more often, its compensation committee. Exchange rules and the securities laws effectively require that employee stock options be issued pursuant to plans that have been approved by shareholders; and most plans require that the exercise price of the options be at or above the price of the stock on the date the option is granted.

In 2006 the Wall Street Journal published a front page article suggesting that some companies had violated this provision of their plans by "backdating" the grants of options to a date when the stock price was lower than on the price on the day the options were granted. Since such options were already "in the money," they conferred an unauthorized benefit on the recipients. Not only did this violate the option plans, but accounting rules require that companies that issue in-the-money options to employees recognize a compensation expense; and few, if any of these companies had done so. This led to a major scandal in which the SEC and the Justice Department conducted wide-ranging investigations, over two hundred public companies came forward to admit having engaged in options backdating, several corporate executives lost their jobs, and at least on CEO went to jail.

Typo

The publicity given these cases also prompted numerous shareholder derivative suits alleging that the directors had breached their fiduciary duty by approving backdated options. Since most of the options were issued to executives, and the grants were made by compensation committees consisting of independent directors, these suits raised the question whether the approval of in-the-money options constituted a breach of the directors' duty of care. As the material above demonstrates, normally the business judgment rule would protect a decision by directors to give some form of additional compensation to executives.

To get around that problem, the derivative suits generally alleged that the directors had been guilty of "waste." As we have seen, the waste doctrine constitutes a significant hurdle for a plaintiff claiming a breach of the duty of care. One way to overcome that hurdle is to show that the board's decision was irrational. As one opinion put it, "Irrationality is the outer limit of the business judgment rule" and "the functional equivalent of the waste test." *Brehm v. Eisner,* 746 A.2d 244, 264 (Del. 2000). Demonstrating this level of irrationality, absent evidence of "conflict of interest or improper motivation" has been described as "theoretical." *Gagliardi v. TriFoods Int'l,* Inc., 683 A.2d 1049, 1051–52 (Del.Ch. 1996).

The option backdating cases proved that there are still situations in which the "theoretical" possibility of waste can actually be real. In one such case Chancellor Chandler denied a motion to dismiss for failure to make a demand, saying, "A director who approves the backdating of options faces at the very *least* a substantial likelihood of liability, if only because it is difficult to conceive of a context in which a director may simultaneously lie to his shareholders (regarding his violations of a shareholder-approved plan, no less) and yet satisfy his duty of loyalty. Backdating options qualifies as one of those "rare cases [in which] a transaction may be so egregious on its face that board approval cannot meet the test of business judgment, and a substantial likelihood of director liability therefore exists." *Ryan v. Gifford,* 918 A.2d 341, 355–56 (Del. Ch. 2007), quoting *Aronson v. Lewis,* 473 A 2d 805, at 815 (set forth in Chapter 16).

4. THE BUSINESS JUDGMENT RULE AND EXECUTIVE COMPENSATION

Under state corporate law, compensation of employees and officers is generally a matter of business judgment. And even when the duty of loyalty is implicated—as when directors fix the compensation of the company's CEO who sits on the board—courts do not necessarily use a fairness standard of review. As you read the following materials, consider whether the permissive business judgment standard is sensible when directors and executives are designing compensation packages for other corporate managers. Given the potential for self-dealing inherent in executive compensation (a condition the courts refer to in other contexts as the "omnipresent specter of self-dealing," what standard do you believe is appropriate? Is review under a "waste" standard enough, and if so, how should "waste" be defined in this contrast? How, if at all, should the federal regime affect the state law determination of waste?

a. The Traditional "Waste" Standard

Litigation involving bonuses paid to officers of the American Tobacco Co. crystallized the traditional judicial approach to executive compensation. In 1912, American Tobacco's shareholders adopted a by-law providing for payment of annual bonus payments to the corporation's officers in amounts equal to a percentage of net profits in excess of a stated threshold. The soaring fortunes of American Tobacco led to a dramatic increase in those bonuses. A shareholder brought a derivative suit (under federal common law) to recover allegedly excessive compensation paid to the company's president and five vice presidents.

In *Rogers v. Hill*, 289 U.S. 582 (1933), the Supreme Court, reversing a Second Circuit decision dismissing plaintiff's complaint, stated:

It follows from what has been shown that when adopted the by-law was valid. But plaintiff alleges that the measure of compensation fixed by it is not now equitable or fair. And he prays that the court fix and determine the fair and reasonable compensation of the individual defendants, respectively, for each of the years in question. The only payments that plaintiff by this suit seeks to have restored to the company are the payments made to the individual defendants under the by-law.

We come to consider whether these amounts are subject to examination and revision in the District Court. As the amounts payable depend upon the gains of the business, the specified percentages are not per se unreasonable. The by-law was adopted in 1912 by an almost unanimous vote of the shares represented at the annual meeting and presumably the stockholders supporting the measure acted in good faith and according to their best judgment. Plaintiff does not complain of any payments made prior to 1921. Regard is to be had to the enormous increase of the company's profits in recent years. The 2½ per cent yielded President Hill $447,870.30 in 1929 and $842,507.72 in 1930. The 1½ per cent yielded to each of the vice-presidents, Neiley and Riggio, $115,141.86 in 1929 and $409,495.25 in 1930 and for these years payments under the by-law were in addition to the cash credits and fixed salaries shown in the statement.

While the amounts produced by the application of the prescribed percentages give rise to no inference of actual or constructive fraud, the payments under the by-law have by reason of increase of profits become so large as to warrant investigation in equity in the interest of the company. Much weight is to be given to the action of the stockholders, and the by-law is supported by the presumption of regularity and continuity. But the rule prescribed by it cannot, against the protest of a shareholder, be used to justify payments of sums as salaries so large as in substance and effect to amount to spoliation or waste of corporate property. The dissenting opinion of Judge Swan indicates the applicable rule: "If a bonus payment has no relation to the value of services for which it is given, it is in reality a gift in part and the majority stockholders have no power to give away corporate property against the protest of the minority." 60 F.2d 109, 113. The facts alleged by plaintiff are sufficient to require that the District Court, upon a consideration of all the relevant facts brought forward by the parties, determine whether and to what extent payments to the individual defendants under the by-law constitute misuse and waste of the money of the corporation.

Other shareholders subsequently sued (under state law) to recover American Tobacco bonus payments made in later years. A New York state court rejected their attack, stating:

Yes, the Court possesses the *power* to prune these payments, but openness forces the confession that the pruning would be synthetic and artificial rather than analytic or scientific. Whether or not it would be fair and just, is highly dubious. Yet, merely because the problem is perplexing is no reason for eschewing it. It is not timidity, however, which perturbs me. It is finding a rational or just gauge for revising these figures were I inclined to do so. No blueprints are furnished. The elements to be weighed are incalculable; the imponderables, manifold. To act out of whimsy or caprice or arbitrariness would be more than inexact— it would be the precise antithesis of justice; it would be a farce.

If comparisons are to be made, with whose compensation are they to be made—executives? Those connected with the motion picture industry? Radio artists? Justices of the Supreme Court of the United States? The President of the United States? Manifestly, the material at hand is not of adequate plasticity for fashioning into a pattern or standard. Many instances of positive underpayment will come to mind, just as instances of apparent rank overpayment abound. Haplessly, intrinsic worth is not always the criterion. A classic might perhaps produce trifling compensation for its author, whereas a popular novel might yield a titanic fortune. Merit is not always commensurately rewarded, whilst mediocrity sometimes unjustly brings incredibly lavish returns. Nothing is so divergent and contentious and inexplicable as values.

Courts are ill-equipped to solve or even to grapple with these entangled economic problems. Indeed, their solution is not within the juridical province. Courts are concerned that corporations be honestly and fairly operated by its directors, with the observance of the formal requirements of the law; but what is reasonable compensation for its officers is primarily for the stockholders. This does not mean that fiduciaries are to commit waste, or misuse or abuse trust property, with impunity. A just cause will find the Courts at guard and implemented to grant redress. But the stockholder must project a less amorphous plaint than is here presented.

On this branch of the case, I find for the defendants. Yet it does not follow that I affirmatively approve these huge payments. It means that I cannot by any reliable standard find them to be waste or spoliation; it means that I find no valid ground for disapproving what the great majority of stockholders have approved. In the circumstances, if a ceiling for these bonuses is to be erected, the stockholders who built and are responsible for the present structure must be the architects.

Heller v. Boylan, 29 N.Y.S.2d 653, 679–80 (Sup.Ct.1941), *aff'd mem.* 263 App.Div. 815, 32 N.Y.S.2d 131 (1st Dept.1941).

Following the American Tobacco litigation, most publicly-held corporations sought to minimize the risk of legal challenges to executive compensation plans by seeking approval from disinterested directors, disinterested shareholders, or both. By securing such approval, corporations shifted the burden to shareholders to prove that the compensation plan involved waste.

The judicial attitude is perhaps best exemplified by former Chancellor Allen's holding that a grant of immediately exercisable stock options is not corporate waste if "there is some rational basis for directors to conclude that the amount and form of compensation is appropriate." *Steiner v. Meyerson,* 1995 WL 441999 (Del.Ch.1995). Chancellor Allen observed:

Absent an allegation of fraud or conflict of interest courts will not review the substance of corporate contracts; the waste theory represents a theoretical exception to the statement very rarely encountered in the world of real transactions. There surely are cases of fraud; of unfair self-dealing and, much more rarely negligence. But rarest of all—and indeed, like Nessie, possibly non-existent—would be the case of disinterested business people making non-fraudulent deals (non-negligently) that meet the legal standard of waste!

b. The Disney Litigation

Perhaps the most celebrated recent case involving executive compensation arose from a $130 million severance package of cash and stock options paid by the Walt Disney Company to Michael Ovitz, a Hollywood talent agent who had been hired as the number-two executive at Disney even though he lacked any managerial experience in a public corporation. Terminated less than 13 months after being hired, Ovitz ended up receiving *daily* compensation of about $333,000 (or almost $14,000 per hour including sleeping time) even though his tenure at Disney was seen as a failure.

IN RE WALT DISNEY DERIVATIVE LITIGATION
906 A.2d 27 (Del. 2006).

[In 1995 Disney's board and its Chairman and CEO, Michael Eisner decided that the time had come to identify a successor to Eisner. Eisner's prime candidate for his replacement was Michael Ovitz, the leading partner of Creative Artists Agency ("CAA"), and one of the most powerful figures in Hollywood. Eisner and Ovitz had enjoyed a social and professional relationship that spanned nearly 25 years.

Eisner approached Ovitz about joining Disney, and there ensued extensive negotiations about the nature of his role and his compensation. During the negotiations Ovitz came to believe that he and Eisner would run Disney, and would work together in a relation akin to that of junior and senior partner. Unfortunately, Ovitz's belief was mistaken, as Eisner had a radically different view of what their respective roles at Disney should be.

Russell, another member of Disney's board, took the lead in negotiating the financial terms of the Ovitz employment agreement ("OEA"). Ovitz owned 55% of CAA, from which he received approximately $20 to $25 million a year and the right to receive a large share of future revenues. He made it clear that he would not give up his interest in CAA without "downside protection." Russell and Ovitz eventually reached agreement on terms of the OEA. It provided for a five-year contract with total compensation, including stock options, equal to approximately $23.6

million per year. It sought to protect both parties in the event that Ovitz's employment ended prematurely. If Disney fired Ovitz for any reason other than gross negligence or malfeasance (a Non-Fault Termination or "NFT"), Ovitz would be entitled to a payment consisting of his remaining salary, $7.5 million a year for unaccrued bonuses, and various provisions designed to compensate him for loss of the value of unvested options.

After reviewing and discussing the OLA, the compensation committee of Disney's board voted unanimously to approve and recommend it to the board, which, after further deliberation, voted unanimously to elect Ovitz as President, and he began work on October 1, 1995.

Within a year of his assuming office, it had become clear that Ovitz was "a poor fit with his fellow executives." By then the Disney directors were discussing that the disconnect between Ovitz and the Company was likely irreparable and that Ovitz would have to be terminated.

Eisner asked Litvak, Disney's General Counsel if Disney had cause to fire Ovitz and thereby avoid the costly NFT payment. After reviewing the issue and consulting with others, Litvack concluded there was no basis to terminate Ovitz for cause, and that it would be inappropriate, unethical and a bad idea to attempt to coerce Ovitz into negotiating for a smaller NFT package by threatening a for-cause termination.

Eisner, Litvack and Ovitz then worked out the terms of Ovitz' departure, and he resigned from Disney on December 31, 1996.]

In January 1997, several Disney shareholders brought derivative actions in the Court of Chancery, on behalf of Disney, against Ovitz and the directors of Disney who served at the time of the events complained of. The plaintiffs claimed that the $130 million severance payout was the product of fiduciary duty and contractual breaches by Ovitz, and breaches of fiduciary duty by the Disney defendants, and a waste of assets.

THE CLAIMS AGAINST THE DISNEY DEFENDANTS

1. The Due Care Determinations

Because no duty of loyalty claim was asserted against the Disney defendants, the only way to rebut the business judgment rule presumptions would be to show that the Disney defendants had either breached their duty of care or had not acted in good faith. At trial, the plaintiff-appellants attempted to establish both grounds, but the Chancellor determined that the plaintiffs had failed to prove either.

[T]he overall thrust of [appellants'] claim is that the compensation committee approved the OEA with NFT provisions that could potentially result in an enormous payout, without informing themselves of what the full magnitude of that payout could be. Rejecting that claim, the Court of Chancery found that the compensation committee members were adequately informed. The issue thus becomes whether that finding is supported by the evidence of record. We conclude that it is.

In our view, a helpful approach is to compare what actually happened here to what would have occurred had the committee followed a "best practices" (or "best case") scenario, from a process standpoint. In a "best case" scenario, all committee members would have received, before or at the committee's first meeting on September 26, 1995, a spreadsheet or similar document prepared by (or with the assistance of) a compensation expert. Making different, alternative assumptions, the spreadsheet would disclose the amounts that Ovitz could receive under the OEA in each circumstance that might foreseeably arise. That spreadsheet, which ultimately would become an exhibit to the minutes of the compensation committee meeting, would form the basis of the committee's deliberations and decision.

Had that scenario been followed, there would be no dispute (and no basis for litigation) over what information was furnished to the committee members or when it was furnished. Regrettably, the committee's informational and decisionmaking process used here was not so tidy.

[T]he compensation committee knew that in the event of an NFT, Ovitz's severance payment alone could be in the range of $40 million cash, plus the value of the accelerated options. Because the actual payout to Ovitz was approximately $130 million, of which roughly $38.5 million was cash, the value of the options at the time of the NFT payout would have been about $91.5 million. Thus, the issue may be framed as whether the compensation committee members knew, at the time they approved the OEA, that the value of the option component of the severance package could reach the $92 million order of magnitude if they terminated Ovitz without cause after one year. The evidentiary record shows that the committee members were so informed.

The OEA was specifically structured to compensate Ovitz for walking away from $150 million to $200 million of anticipated commissions from CAA over the five-year OEA contract term. This meant that if Ovitz was terminated without cause, the earlier in the contract term the termination occurred the larger the severance amount would be to replace the lost commissions. Indeed, because Ovitz was terminated after only one year, the total amount of his severance payment (about $130 million) closely approximated the lower end of the range of Ovitz's forfeited commissions ($150 million), less the compensation Ovitz received during his first and only year as Disney's President. Accordingly, the Court of Chancery had a sufficient evidentiary basis in the record from which to find that, at the time they approved the OEA, the compensation committee members were adequately informed of the potential magnitude of an early NFT severance payout.

For these reasons, we uphold the Chancellor's determination that the compensation committee members did not breach their fiduciary duty of care in approving the OEA.

2. The Good Faith Determinations

The Court of Chancery held that the business judgment rule presumptions protected the decisions of the compensation committee and the remaining Disney directors, not only because they had acted with due care but also because they had not acted in bad faith.

In its Opinion the Court of Chancery defined bad faith as follows:

> Upon long and careful consideration, I am of the opinion that the concept of intentional dereliction of duty, a conscious disregard for one's responsibilities, is an appropriate (although not the only) standard for determining whether fiduciaries have acted in good faith. Deliberate indifference and inaction in the face of a duty to act is, in my mind, conduct that is clearly disloyal to the corporation. It is the epitome of faithless conduct.

The precise question is whether the Chancellor's articulated standard for bad faith corporate fiduciary conduct—intentional dereliction of duty, a conscious disregard for one's responsibilities—is legally correct. In approaching that question, we note that the Chancellor characterized that definition as "an appropriate (although not the only) standard for determining whether fiduciaries have acted in good faith." That observation is accurate and helpful, because as a matter of simple logic, at least three different categories of fiduciary behavior are candidates for the "bad faith" pejorative label.

The first category involves so-called "subjective bad faith," that is, fiduciary conduct motivated by an actual intent to do harm. We need not dwell further on this category, because no such conduct is claimed to have occurred, or did occur, in this case.

The second category of conduct, which is at the opposite end of the spectrum, involves lack of due care—that is, fiduciary action taken solely by reason of gross negligence and without any malevolent intent. Although the Chancellor found, and we agree, that the appellants failed to establish gross negligence, to afford guidance we address the issue of whether gross negligence (including a failure to inform one's self of available material facts), without more, can also constitute bad faith. The answer is clearly no.

That leaves the third category of fiduciary conduct, which falls in between the first two categories. This third category is what the Chancellor's definition of bad faith—intentional dereliction of duty, a conscious disregard for one's responsibilities—is intended to capture. The question is whether such misconduct is properly treated as a non-exculpable, nonindemnifiable violation of the fiduciary duty to act in good faith. In our view it must be, for at least two reasons.

First, the universe of fiduciary misconduct is not limited to either disloyalty in the classic sense (*i.e.*, preferring the adverse self-interest of the fiduciary or of a related person to the interest of the corporation) or gross negligence. To protect the interests of the corporation and its shareholders, fiduciary conduct of this kind, which does not involve disloyalty (as traditionally defined) but is qualitatively more culpable than gross negligence, should be proscribed.

For these reasons, we uphold the Court of Chancery's definition as a legally appropriate, although not exclusive, definition of fiduciary bad faith.

THE WASTE CLAIM

The appellants' final claim is that even if the approval of the OEA was protected by the business judgment rule presumptions, the payment of the severance amount to Ovitz constituted waste. To recover on a claim of corporate waste, the plaintiffs must shoulder the burden of proving that the exchange was "so one sided that no business person of ordinary, sound judgment could conclude that the corporation has received adequate consideration." A claim of waste will arise only in the rare, "unconscionable case where directors irrationally squander or give away corporate assets." This onerous standard for waste is a corollary of the proposition that where business judgment presumptions are applicable, the board's decision will be upheld unless it cannot be "attributed to any rational business purpose."

Appellants claim that the NFT provisions of the OEA were wasteful because they incentivized Ovitz to perform poorly in order to obtain payment of the NFT provisions. That claim does not come close to satisfying the high hurdle required to establish waste. The approval of the NFT provisions in the OEA had a rational business purpose: to induce Ovitz to leave CAA, at what would otherwise be a considerable cost to him, in order to join Disney. The Chancellor found that the evidence does not support any notion that the OEA irrationally incentivized Ovitz to get himself fired. Ovitz had no control over whether or not he would be fired, either with or without cause. To suggest that at the time he entered into the OEA Ovitz would engineer an early departure at the cost of his extraordinary reputation in the entertainment industry and his historical friendship with Eisner, is not only fanciful but also without proof in the record. Indeed, the Chancellor found that it was "patently unreasonable to assume that Ovitz intended to perform just poorly enough to be fired quickly, but not so poorly that he could be terminated for cause."

We agree. Because the appellants have failed to show that the approval of the NFT terms of the OEA was not a rational business decision, their waste claim must fail.

[Handwritten note:]
Directors (mother) | Sons
Pritchard & Baird
- reinsurance
broker
← Creditor

× Company insolvent,
so creditors can
go after Company
& Sons.

OF OVERSIGHT

...ty of care is oversight of the corporation's ... ...ial Comment to MBCA § 8.30(b) states:

...01 duties associated with the board's ...lard of care entails primarily a duty ... with the board's decision-making ...volves informed action at a point in ...is concerned with a continuum and ...ccordingly involves participatory ...time.

1. SUPERVISION OF ONGOING BUSINESS

FRANCIS V. UNITED JERSEY BANK
432 A.2d 814 (N.J. 1981).

POLLOCK, J.

[Pritchard & Baird, Inc., was a reinsurance broker, a firm that arranged contracts between insurance companies by means of which companies that wrote large policies sold participations in those policies to other companies in order to share the risks.]According to the custom in the industry, the selling company pays the applicable portion of the premium to the broker, which deducts its commission and forwards the balance to the reinsuring company. The broker thus handles large amounts of money as a fiduciary for its clients.

As of 1964, all the stock of Pritchard & Baird was owned by Charles Pritchard, Sr., one of the firm's founders, and his wife and two sons, Charles, Jr. and William. They were also the four directors. Charles, Sr., dominated the corporation until 1971, when he became ill and the two sons took over management of the business. Charles, Sr. died in 1973, leaving Mrs. Pritchard and the sons the only remaining directors.

Contrary to the industry practice, Pritchard & Baird did not segregate its operating funds from those of its clients; instead, it deposited all funds in the same account. From this account Charles, Sr. had drawn "loans," that correlated with corporate profits and were repaid at the end of each year. After his death, Charles, Jr. and William began to draw ever larger sums (still characterizing them as "loans") that greatly exceeded profits. They were able to do so by taking advantage of the "float" available to them during the period between the time they received a premium and the time they had to forward it (less commission) to the reinsurer.

By 1975 the corporation was bankrupt. This action was brought by the trustees in bankruptcy against Mrs. Pritchard and the bank as administrator of her husband's estate. Mrs. Pritchard died during the

pendency of the proceedings, and her executrix was substituted as
defendant. As to Mrs. Pritchard, [the principal claim was that she had been
negligent in the conduct of her duties as a director of the corporation.]

The "loans" were reflected on financial statements that were prepared
annually as of January 31, the end of the corporate fiscal year. Although
an outside certified public accountant prepared the 1970 financial
statement, the corporation prepared only internal financial statements
from 1971–1975. In all instances, the statements were simple documents,
consisting of three or four 8 × 11 inch sheets.

The statements of financial condition from 1970 forward
demonstrated:

	Working Capital Deficit	Shareholders' Loans	Net Brokerage Income
1970	$ 389,022	$ 509,941	$ 807,229
1971	not available	not available	not available
1972	$ 1,684,289	$ 1,825,911	$ 1,546,263
1973	$ 3,506,460	$ 3,700,542	$ 1,736,349
1974	$ 6,939,007	$ 7,080,629	$ 876,182
1975	$10,176,419	$10,298,039	$ 551,598

Mrs. Pritchard was not active in the business of Pritchard & Baird and
knew virtually nothing of its corporate affairs. She briefly visited the
corporate offices in Morristown on only one occasion, and she never read or
obtained the annual financial statements. She was unfamiliar with the
rudiments of reinsurance and made no effort to assure that the policies and
practices of the corporation, particularly pertaining to the withdrawal of
funds, complied with industry custom or relevant law. Although her
husband had warned her that Charles, Jr. would "take the shirt off my
back," Mrs. Pritchard did not pay any attention to her duties as a director
or to the affairs of the corporation.

After her husband died in December 1973, Mrs. Pritchard became
incapacitated and was bedridden for a six-month period. She became
listless at this time and started to drink rather heavily. Her physical
condition deteriorated, and in 1978 she died. The trial court rejected
testimony seeking to exonerate her because she "was old, was grief-stricken
at the loss of her husband, sometimes consumed too much alcohol and was
psychologically overborne by her sons." That court found that she was
competent to act and that the reason Mrs. Pritchard never knew what her
sons "were doing was because she never made the slightest effort to
discharge any of her responsibilities as a director of Pritchard & Baird."

Individual liability of a corporate director for acts of the corporation is a prickly problem. Generally directors are accorded broad immunity and are not insurers of corporate activities. The problem is particularly nettlesome when a third party asserts that a director, because of nonfeasance, is liable for losses caused by acts of insiders, who in this case were officers, directors and shareholders.[Determination of the liability of Mrs. Pritchard requires findings that she had a duty to the clients of Pritchard & Baird, that she breached that duty and that her breach was a proximate cause of their losses.]

As a general rule, a director should acquire at least a rudimentary understanding of the business of the corporation. Accordingly, a director should become familiar with the fundamentals of the business in which the corporation is engaged. Because directors are bound to exercise ordinary care, they cannot set up as a defense lack of the knowledge needed to exercise the requisite degree of care. If one feels that he has not had sufficient business experience to qualify him to perform the duties of a director, he should either acquire the knowledge by inquiry, or refuse to act.

Directors are under a continuing obligation to keep informed about the activities of the corporation. Otherwise, they may not be able to participate in the overall management of corporate affairs. Directors may not shut their eyes to corporate misconduct and then claim that because they did not see the misconduct, they did not have a duty to look[The sentinel asleep at his post contributes nothing to the enterprise he is charged to protect.]

Directorial management does not require a detailed inspection of day-to-day activities, but rather a general monitoring of corporate affairs and policies. Accordingly, a director is well advised to attend board meetings regularly. Regular attendance does not mean that directors must attend every meeting, but that directors should attend meetings as a matter of practice. A director of a publicly held corporation might be expected to attend regular monthly meetings, but a director of a small, family corporation might be asked to attend only an annual meeting. The point is that one of the responsibilities of a director is to attend meetings of the board of which he or she is a member.

While directors are not required to audit corporate books, they should maintain familiarity with the financial status of the corporation by a regular review of financial statements. In some circumstances, directors may be charged with assuring that bookkeeping methods conform to industry custom and usage. The extent of review, as well as the nature and frequency of financial statements, depends not only on the customs of the industry, but also on the nature of the corporation and the business in which it is engaged. Financial statements of some small corporations may be prepared internally and only on an annual basis; in a large publicly held corporation, the statements may be produced monthly or at some other regular interval. Adequate financial review normally would be more informal in a private corporation than in a publicly held corporation.

The review of financial statements, however, may give rise to a duty to inquire further into matters revealed by those statements. Upon discovery of an illegal course of action, a director has a duty to object and, if the corporation does not correct the conduct, to resign.

In certain circumstances, the fulfillment of the duty of a director may call for more than mere objection and resignation. Sometimes a director may be required to seek the advice of counsel concerning the propriety of his or her own conduct, the conduct of other officers and directors or the conduct of the corporation. Sometimes the duty of a director may require more than consulting with outside counsel. A director may have a duty to take reasonable means to prevent illegal conduct by co-directors; in any appropriate case, this may include threat of suit.

A director is not an ornament, but an essential component of corporate governance. Consequently, a director cannot protect himself behind a paper shield bearing the motto, "dummy director." The New Jersey Business Corporation Act, in imposing a standard of ordinary care on all directors, confirms that dummy, figurehead and accommodation directors are anachronisms with no place in New Jersey law.

The factors that impel expanded responsibility in the large, publicly held corporation may not be present in a small, close corporation. Nonetheless, a close corporation may, because of the nature of its business, be affected with a public interest. For example, the stock of a bank may be closely held, but because of the nature of banking the directors would be subject to greater liability than those of another close corporation. Even in a small corporation, a director is held to the standard of that degree of care that an ordinarily prudent director would use under the circumstances.

A director's duty of care does not exist in the abstract, but must be considered in relation to specific obligees. In general, the relationship of a corporate director to the corporation and its stockholders is that of a fiduciary. Shareholders have a right to expect that directors will exercise reasonable supervision and control over the policies and practices of a corporation. The institutional integrity of a corporation depends upon the proper discharge by directors of those duties.

While directors may owe a fiduciary duty to creditors also, that obligation generally has not been recognized in the absence of insolvency. With certain corporations, however, directors are deemed to owe a duty to creditors and other third parties even when the corporation is solvent. Although depositors of a bank are considered in some respects to be creditors, courts have recognized that directors may owe them a fiduciary duty. Directors of nonbanking corporations may owe a similar duty when the corporation holds funds of others in trust.

As a reinsurance broker, Pritchard & Baird received annually as a fiduciary millions of dollars of clients' money which it was under a duty to segregate. To this extent, it resembled a bank rather than a small family business. Accordingly, Mrs. Pritchard's relationship to the clientele of Pritchard & Baird was akin to that of a director of a bank to its depositors.

As a director of a substantial reinsurance brokerage corporation, she should have known that it received annually millions of dollars of loss and premium funds which it held in trust for ceding and reinsurance companies. Mrs. Pritchard should have obtained and read the annual statements of financial condition of Pritchard & Baird. Although she had a right to rely upon financial statements prepared in accordance with [New Jersey law], such reliance would not excuse her conduct.

From those statements, she should have realized that, as of January 31, 1970, her sons were withdrawing substantial trust funds under the guise of "Shareholders' Loans." The financial statements for each fiscal year commencing with that of January 31, 1970, disclosed that the working capital deficits and the "loans" were escalating in tandem. Detecting a misappropriation of funds would not have required special expertise or extraordinary diligence; a cursory reading of the financial statements would have revealed the pillage.

The judgment of the Appellate Division is affirmed.

———————

In one sense, *Francis* is a relatively easy case because Mrs. Pritchard did virtually nothing as a director. But how much inquiry does the law require of her? The Official Comment to MBCA § 8.31(a) states:

> [T]he oversight function under section 8.01(b) involves ongoing monitoring of the corporation's business and affairs over a period of time. This involves the duty of ongoing attention, when actual knowledge of particular facts and circumstances arouse suspicions which indicate a need to make inquiry. While the facts will be outcome-determinative, deficient conduct involving a sustained failure to exercise oversight where found actionable has typically been characterized by the courts in terms of abdication and continued neglect of a director's duty of attention, not a brief distraction or temporary interruption. However, imbedded in the oversight function is the need to inquire when suspicions are aroused. This duty is not a component of ongoing oversight, and does not entail proactive vigilance, but arises when, and only when particular facts and circumstances of material concern (*e.g.*, evidence of embezzlement at a high level or the discovery of significant inventory shortages) suddenly surface.

The MBCA refers to "the care a person in a like position" would reasonably believe appropriate. Does that formulation mean there is a single, unitary standard of care, or is the director's background and experience relevant in determining the appropriate standard of care? For example, would a director with an accounting background have greater responsibilities to uncover accounting fraud? Would a labor union representative elected to the board under a collective bargaining agreement be more responsible for overseeing employee relations? Are lawyers serving on a board supposed to be particularly sensitive to legal compliance? What are the responsibilities of an investment banker whose only contribution at board meetings is in connection with proposed financings?

The trial court's opinion in *Francis v. United Jersey Bank*, 392 A.2d 1233 (N.J. Super.Ct. 1978) contains the following passage:

> It has been urged in this case that Mrs. Pritchard should not be held responsible for what happened while she was a director of Pritchard & Baird because she was a simple housewife who served as a director as an accommodation to her husband and sons. Let me start by saying that I reject the sexism which is unintended but which is implicit in such an argument. There is no reason why the average housewife could not adequately discharge the functions of a director of a corporation such as Pritchard & Baird, despite a lack of business career experience, if she gave some reasonable attention to what she was supposed to be doing. The problem is not that Mrs. Pritchard was a simple housewife. The problem is that she was a person who took a job which necessarily entailed certain responsibilities and she then failed to make any effort whatever to discharge those responsibilities. The ultimate insult to the fundamental dignity and equality of women would be to treat a grown woman as though she were a child not responsible for her acts and omissions.

> It has been argued that allowance should be made for the fact that during the last years in question Mrs. Pritchard was old, was grief-stricken at the loss of her husband, sometimes consumed too much alcohol and was psychologically overborne by her sons. I was not impressed by the testimony supporting that argument. There is no proof whatever that Mrs. Pritchard ever ceased to be fully competent. There is no proof that she ever made any effort as a director to question or stop the unlawful activities of Charles, Jr. and William. The actions of the sons were so blatantly wrongful that it is hard to see how they could have resisted any moderately firm objection to what they were doing. The fact is that Mrs. Pritchard never knew what they were doing because she never

made the slightest effort to discharge any of her responsibilities as a director of Pritchard & Baird.

Id. at 1241.

At the very least, there appears to be some minimum standard to which all directors will be held. The Official Comment to MBCA § 8.30(a) states:

> The combined phrase "in a like position under similar circumstances" is intended to recognize that (a) the nature and extent of responsibilities will vary, depending upon such factors as the size, complexity, urgency, and location of activities carried on by the particular corporation, (b) decisions must be made on the basis of the information known to the directors without the benefit of hindsight, and (c) the special background, qualifications, and management responsibilities of a particular director may be relevant in evaluating his compliance with the standard of care. Even though the quoted phrase takes into account the special background, qualifications and management responsibilities of a particular director, it does not excuse a director lacking business experience or particular expertise from exercising the common sense, practical wisdom, and informed judgment of an "ordinarily prudent person."

2. MONITORING LEGAL COMPLIANCE AND CONTROLS

Whether directors are legally required to establish monitoring systems to ensure management and other employees are complying with their legal responsibilities is a question that has received a great deal of attention. There has never been any doubt that directors *should* institute legal compliance programs (an aspirational standard). Historically, the question has been whether they faced *liability* for failure to do so. Questions also arose whether a monitoring duty arose only after a "triggering event" that put directors on notice that the corporation was not in compliance or whether such programs were part of a legal duty of care.

Although for a long time these questions were left largely to state law, in recent years federal law has played an increasing role in their resolution. As we saw in Chapter 13, after the corporate and accounting scandals in the early 2000s, in the Sarbanes-Oxley Act (SOX) Congress federalized a number of areas of corporate governance, including internal controls over financial accounting and disclosure systems in public companies. Among its numerous reforms, SOX mandates closer oversight of company financial reporting by corporate boards, senior management, and even company lawyers. One of the most onerous provisions of SOX is § 404, which requires that managers of public corporations establish and maintain an adequate internal control structure and procedures for financial reporting, and include an assessment of these controls in the corporation's annual report.

One much-cited statement of a director's state law duty to create legal compliance programs comes from *Graham v. Allis-Chalmers Manufacturing Co.*, 188 A.2d 125 (Del. 1963). The case involved a derivative action against the directors of Allis-Chalmers, a multi-division manufacturing firm with over 31,000 employees. Suit was brought after the company and four non-director employees were indicted for price-fixing violations of the federal antitrust laws.

The derivative action alleged that the director defendants either had actual knowledge of the illegal price-fixing or were aware of facts that should have put them on notice. However, discovery produced no evidence that any director actually knew of the price-fixing or of facts suggesting that lower-level employees were violating the antitrust laws. So the plaintiffs shifted their theory to claim the directors were liable for failing to institute a monitoring system that would have allowed directors to learn of and prevent the antitrust violations.

In rejecting plaintiffs' claim, the Delaware Supreme Court pointed out that the company's operating policy was to delegate price-setting authority "to the lowest possible management level capable of fulfilling the delegated responsibility." The board, although it annually reviewed departmental profit goals, did not participate in decisions setting specific product prices. The Court stated, "By reason of the extent and complexity of the company's operations, it is not practicable for the Board to consider in detail specific problems of the various divisions."

The plaintiffs pointed to two 1937 FTC decrees against Allis-Chalmers that had enjoined the company from fixing prices on certain electrical equipment. The plaintiffs argued that the decrees should have alerted the directors to past antitrust violations and put them on notice of the necessity to take steps to prevent future violations. The Court was not impressed:

> The difficulty the argument has is that only three of the present directors knew of the decrees, and all three of them satisfied themselves that Allis-Chalmers had not engaged in the practice enjoined and had consented to the decrees merely to avoid expense and the necessity of defending the company's position. Under the circumstances, we think knowledge by three of the directors that in 1937 the company had consented to the entry of decrees enjoining it from doing something they had satisfied themselves it had never done, did not put the Board on notice of the possibility of future illegal price fixing.

> Plaintiffs have wholly failed to establish either actual notice or imputed notice to the Board of Directors of facts which should have put them on guard, and have caused them to take steps to

prevent the future possibility of illegal price fixing and bid rigging. Plaintiffs say that as a minimum in this respect the Board should have taken the steps it took in 1960 when knowledge of the facts first actually came to their attention as a result of the Grand Jury investigation. Whatever duty, however, there was upon the Board to take such steps, the fact of the 1937 decrees has no bearing upon the question, for under the circumstances they were [put on] notice of nothing.

Plaintiffs are thus forced to rely solely upon the legal proposition advanced by them that directors of a corporation, as a matter of law, are liable for losses suffered by their corporations by reason of their gross inattention to the common law duty of actively supervising and managing the corporate affairs.

The precise charge made against these director defendants is that, even though they had no knowledge of any suspicion of wrongdoing on the part of the company's employees, they still should have put into effect a system of watchfulness which would have brought such misconduct to their attention in ample time to have brought it to an end. On the contrary, it appears that directors are entitled to rely on the honesty and integrity of their subordinates until something occurs to put them on suspicion that something is wrong. If such occurs and goes unheeded, then liability of the directors might well follow, but absent cause for suspicion there is no duty upon the directors to install and operate a corporate system of espionage to ferret out wrongdoing which they have no reason to suspect exists.

In the last analysis, the question of whether a corporate director has become liable for losses to the corporation through neglect of duty is determined by the circumstances. If he has recklessly reposed confidence in an obviously untrustworthy employee, has refused or neglected cavalierly to perform his duty as a director, or has ignored either willfully or through inattention obvious danger signs of employee wrongdoing, the law will cast the burden of liability upon him. This is not the case at bar, however, for as soon as it became evident that there were grounds for suspicion, the Board acted promptly to end it and prevent its recurrence.

Id. at 129–130.

Graham grew out of the heavy electrical equipment price fixing conspiracy, one of the first instances in which executives of major corporations received jail terms for antitrust violations. Despite evidence in the criminal cases and similar evidence in *Graham* that subordinate employees had concealed their illegal behavior from their supervisors, there was skepticism in the press and Congress that senior executives were, in fact, unaware of what was going on.

Instead, under Allis-Chalmers' decentralized structure, there were indications that the heads of the various organizational units faced significant pressure to show steadily increasing profits for their segments. Profits were expected regardless of the conditions in the particular markets in which the organizational units operated. Under these circumstances, was the court too quick to say that when a board creates such a mode of management it need not establish "a corporate system of espionage"?

The next case, *Caremark*, suggests that *Graham* would be decided differently now. At the same time, notice the procedural context of the case, which involved a hearing on the fairness of a settlement to which there were no objectors. Because there was no appeal, the Delaware Supreme Court did not review Chancellor Allen's evaluation of plaintiff's allegations at that time. Nevertheless, as George Orwell might have said, some statements of law are more equal than others, and *Caremark* is considered, at least in Delaware, to be an accurate statement of the law concerning the duty of oversight.

If *Caremark* accurately describes the standard for the duty of inquiry in Delaware, does it provide more or less protection to directors than *Graham*? *Graham* imposes a duty of inquiry only when there are "obvious signs" of employee wrongdoing. The red flag test, however, still requires directors to heed red flags when they are raised. But to what extent are they responsible for noticing the flags in the first place? *Graham* uses a "reasonable person" or negligence standard, focusing on the director's ability to notice the red flags.

Caremark, by contrast, seems to require some sort of monitoring system even absent a red flag. The directors' decisions with respect to the extent of those systems, however, will receive the protection of the business judgment rule and will lead to liability only in the absence of good faith. Therefore, as long as the directors establish some sort of monitoring system, they generally will not be held liable even if those systems fail.

In describing the standards of conduct for directors in their oversight function, the Official Comment accompanying MBCA § 8.30(b) seems to borrow from both *Graham* and *Caremark*. Although directors are urged to implement information systems, the MBCA minimizes the need to inquire into every possible future problem:

> The phrase "devoting attention," in the context of the oversight function, refers to concern with the corporation's information and reporting systems and not to proactive inquiry searching out system inadequacies or noncompliance. While directors typically give attention to future plans and trends as well as current activities, they should not be expected to anticipate the problems which the corporation may face except in those circumstances where something has occurred to make it obvious to the board that the corporation should be addressing a particular problem. The

standard of care associated with the oversight function involves gaining assurances from management and advisers that systems believed appropriate have been established coupled with ongoing monitoring of the systems in place, such as those concerned with legal compliance or internal controls—followed up with a proactive response when alerted to the need for inquiry.

Official Comment to MBCA § 8.30(b).

Caremark is one of the most important cases in contemporary Delaware jurisprudence. Although it arose as a duty of care case and deals only with the duty to institute a legal compliance system, its present significance comes from the standard of liability that it establishes. As we will see in the next chapter, that standard directly implicates the good faith exclusion in Delaware's director exculpation statute, and the case is now seen as involving the duty of loyalty rather than the duty of care.

IN RE CAREMARK INTERNATIONAL INC. DERIVATIVE LITIGATION
698 A.2d 959 (Del.Ch. 1996).

ALLEN, CHANCELLOR.

Pending is a motion pursuant to Chancery Rule 23.1 to approve as fair and reasonable a proposed settlement of a consolidated derivative action on behalf of Caremark International, Inc. ("Caremark"). The suit involves claims that the members of Caremark's board of directors (the "Board") breached their fiduciary duty of care to Caremark in connection with alleged violations by Caremark employees of federal and state laws and regulations applicable to health care providers. As a result of the alleged violations, Caremark was subject to an extensive four year investigation by the United States Department of Health and Human Services and the Department of Justice. In 1994 Caremark was charged in an indictment with multiple felonies. It thereafter entered into a number of agreements with the Department of Justice and others. Those agreements included a plea agreement in which Caremark pleaded guilty to a single felony of mail fraud and agreed to pay civil and criminal fines. Subsequently, Caremark agreed to make reimbursements to various private and public parties. In all, the payments that Caremark has been required to make total approximately $250 million.

This suit was filed in 1994, purporting to seek on behalf of the company recovery of these losses from the individual defendants who constitute the board of directors of Caremark. The parties now propose that it be settled and, after notice to Caremark shareholders, a hearing on the fairness of the proposal was held on August 16, 1996.

Legally, evaluation of the central claim made entails consideration of the legal standard governing a board of directors' obligation to supervise or monitor corporate performance. For the reasons set forth below I conclude, in light of the discovery record, that there is a very low probability that it would be determined that the directors of Caremark breached any duty to appropriately monitor and supervise the enterprise. Indeed the record tends to show an active consideration by Caremark management and its Board of the Caremark structures and programs that ultimately led to the company's indictment and to the large financial losses incurred in the settlement of those claims. It does not tend to show knowing or intentional violation of law. Neither the fact that the Board, although advised by lawyers and accountants, did not accurately predict the severe consequences to the company that would ultimately follow from the deployment by the company of the strategies and practices that ultimately led to this liability, nor the scale of the liability, gives rise to an inference of breach of any duty imposed by corporation law upon the directors of Caremark.

The complaint charges the director defendants with breach of their duty of attention or care in connection with the on-going operation of the corporation's business. The claim is that the directors allowed a situation to develop and continue which exposed the corporation to enormous legal liability and that in so doing they violated a duty to be active monitors of corporate performance. The complaint thus does not charge either director self-dealing or the more difficult loyalty-type problems arising from cases of suspect director motivation, such as entrenchment or sale of control contexts. The theory here advanced is possibly the most difficult theory in corporation law upon which a plaintiff might hope to win a judgment. The good policy reasons why it is so difficult to charge directors with responsibility for corporate losses for an alleged breach of care, where there is no conflict of interest or no facts suggesting suspect motivation involved, were recently described in *Gagliardi v. TriFoods Int'l Inc.*, 1996 WL 422330 at 7 (Del.Ch. July 19, 1996).

1. Potential liability for directorial decisions: Director liability for a breach of the duty to exercise appropriate attention may, in theory, arise in two distinct contexts. First, such liability may be said to follow from a board decision that results in a loss because that decision was ill advised or "negligent". Second, liability to the corporation for a loss may be said to arise from an unconsidered failure of the board to act in circumstances in which due attention would, arguably, have prevented the loss. The first class of cases will typically be subject to review under the director-protective business judgment rule, assuming the decision made was the product of a process that was either deliberately considered in good faith or was otherwise rational. What should be understood, but may not widely be understood by courts or commentators who are not often required to face such questions, is that compliance with a director's duty of care can never appropriately be judicially determined by reference to the content of the board decision that leads to a corporate loss, apart from consideration of

the good faith or rationality of the process employed. That is, whether a judge or jury considering the matter after the fact, believes a decision substantively wrong, or degrees of wrong extending through "stupid" to "egregious" or "irrational", provides no ground for director liability, so long as the court determines that the process employed was either rational or employed in a good faith effort to advance corporate interests. To employ a different rule—one that permitted an "objective" evaluation of the decision—would expose directors to substantive second guessing by ill-equipped judges or juries, which would, in the long-run, be injurious to investor interests. Thus, the business judgment rule is process oriented and informed by a deep respect for all good faith board decisions.]

Indeed, one wonders on what moral basis might shareholders attack a good faith business decision of a director as "unreasonable" or "irrational". Where a director in fact exercises a good faith effort to be informed and to exercise appropriate judgment, he or she should be deemed to satisfy fully the duty of attention. If the shareholders thought themselves entitled to some other quality of judgment than such a director produces in the good faith exercise of the powers of office, then the shareholders should have elected other directors. Judge Learned Hand made the point rather better than can I. In speaking of the passive director defendant Mr. Andrews in *Barnes v. Andrews*, Judge Hand said:

> True, he was not very suited by experience for the job he had undertaken, but I cannot hold him on that account. After all it is the same corporation that chose him that now seeks to charge him. . . . Directors are not specialists like lawyers or doctors. . . . They are the general advisors of the business and if they faithfully give such ability as they have to their charge, it would not be lawful to hold them liable. Must a director guarantee that his judgment is good? Can a shareholder call him to account for deficiencies that their votes assured him did not disqualify him for his office? While he may not have been the Cromwell for that Civil War, Andrews did not engage to play any such role.

In this formulation Learned Hand correctly identifies, in my opinion, the core element of any corporate law duty of care inquiry: whether there a good faith effort to be informed and exercise judgment.

2.   Liability for failure to monitor: The second class of cases in which director liability for inattention is theoretically possible entail circumstances in which a loss eventuates not from a decision but, from unconsidered inaction. Most of the decisions that a corporation, acting through its human agents, makes are, of course, not the subject of director attention. Legally, the board itself will be required only to authorize the most significant corporate acts or transactions: mergers, changes in capital structure, fundamental changes in business, appointment and compensation of the CEO, etc. As the facts of this case graphically

demonstrate, ordinary business decisions that are made by officers and employees deeper in the interior of the organization can, however, vitally affect the welfare of the corporation and its ability to achieve its various strategic and financial goals. If this case did not prove the point itself, recent business history would. Recall for example the displacement of senior management and much of the board of Salomon, Inc.; the replacement of senior management of Kidder, Peabody following the discovery of large trading losses resulting from phantom trades by a highly compensated trader; or the extensive financial loss and reputational injury suffered by Prudential Insurance as a result its junior officers misrepresentations in connection with the distribution of limited partnership interests. Financial and organizational disasters such as these raise the question, what is the board's responsibility with respect to the organization and monitoring of the enterprise to assure that the corporation functions within the law to achieve its purposes?

Modernly this question has been given special importance by an increasing tendency, especially under federal law, to employ the criminal law to assure corporate compliance with external legal requirements, including environmental, financial, employee and product safety as well as assorted other health and safety regulations. In 1991, pursuant to the Sentencing Reform Act of 1984, the United States Sentencing Commission adopted Organizational Sentencing Guidelines which impact importantly on the prospective effect these criminal sanctions might have on business corporations. The Guidelines set forth a uniform sentencing structure for organizations to be sentenced for violation of federal criminal statutes and provide for penalties that equal or often massively exceed those previously imposed on corporations. The Guidelines offer powerful incentives for corporations today to have in place compliance programs to detect violations of law, promptly to report violations to appropriate public officials when discovered, and to take prompt, voluntary remedial efforts.

In 1963, the Delaware Supreme Court in *Graham v. Allis-Chalmers Mfg. Co.* addressed the question of potential liability of board members for losses experienced by the corporation as a result of the corporation having violated the anti-trust laws of the United States. There was no claim in that case that the directors knew about the behavior of subordinate employees of the corporation that had resulted in the liability. Rather, as in this case, the claim asserted was that the directors ought to have known of it and if they had known they would have been under a duty to bring the corporation into compliance with the law and thus save the corporation from the loss. The Delaware Supreme Court concluded that, under the facts as they appeared, there was no basis to find that the directors had breached a duty to be informed of the ongoing operations of the firm. In notably colorful terms, the court stated that "absent cause for suspicion there is no duty upon the directors to install and operate a corporate system of espionage to ferret out wrongdoing which they have no reason to suspect exists." The Court found that there were no grounds for suspicion in that case and, thus, concluded that the directors were blamelessly unaware of the conduct leading to the corporate liability.

How does one generalize this holding today? Can it be said today that, absent some ground giving rise to suspicion of violation of law, that corporate directors have no duty to assure that a corporate information gathering and reporting systems exists which represents a good faith attempt to provide senior management and the Board with information respecting material acts, events or conditions within the corporation, including compliance with applicable statutes and regulations? I certainly do not believe so. I doubt that such a broad generalization of the Graham holding would have been accepted by the Supreme Court in 1963. The case can be more narrowly interpreted as standing for the proposition that, absent grounds to suspect deception, neither corporate boards nor senior officers can be charged with wrongdoing simply for assuming the integrity of employees and the honesty of their dealings on the company's behalf.

A broader interpretation of *Graham v. Allis-Chalmers*—that it means that a corporate board has no responsibility to assure that appropriate information and reporting systems are established by management— would not, in any event, be accepted by the Delaware Supreme Court in 1996, in my opinion. In stating the basis for this view, I start with the recognition that in recent years the Delaware Supreme Court has made it clear—especially in its jurisprudence concerning takeovers, from *Smith v. Van Gorkom* through *QVC v. Paramount Communications*—the seriousness with which the corporation law views the role of the corporate board. Secondly, I note the elementary fact that relevant and timely information is an essential predicate for satisfaction of the board's supervisory and monitoring role under Section 141 of the Delaware General Corporation Law. Thirdly, I note the potential impact of the federal organizational sentencing guidelines on any business organization. Any rational person attempting in good faith to meet an organizational governance responsibility would be bound to take into account this development and the enhanced penalties and the opportunities for reduced sanctions that it offers.

In light of these developments, it would, in my opinion, be a mistake to conclude that our Supreme Court's statement in *Graham* concerning "espionage" means that corporate boards may satisfy their obligation to be reasonably informed concerning the corporation, without assuring themselves that information and reporting systems exist in the organization that are reasonably designed to provide to senior management and to the board itself timely, accurate information sufficient to allow management and the board, each within its scope, to reach informed judgments concerning both the corporation's compliance with law and its business performance.

Obviously the level of detail that is appropriate for such an information system is a question of business judgment. And obviously too, no rationally designed information and reporting system will remove the possibility that the corporation will violate laws or regulations, or that senior officers or directors may nevertheless sometimes be misled or otherwise fail reasonably to detect acts material to the corporation's compliance with the law. But it is important that the board exercise a good faith judgment that the corporation's information and reporting system is in concept and design adequate to assure the board that appropriate information will come to its attention in a timely manner as a matter of ordinary operations, so that it may satisfy its responsibility.

Thus, I am of the view that a director's obligation includes a duty to attempt in good faith to assure that a corporate information and reporting system, which the board concludes is adequate, exists, and that failure to do so under some circumstances may, in theory at least, render a director liable for losses caused by non-compliance with applicable legal standards. I now turn to an analysis of the claims asserted with this concept of the directors duty of care, as a duty satisfied in part by assurance of adequate information flows to the board, in mind.

In order to show that the Caremark directors breached their duty of care by failing adequately to control Caremark's employees, plaintiffs would have to show either (1) that the directors knew or (2) should have known that violations of law were occurring and, in either event, (3) that the directors took no steps in a good faith effort to prevent or remedy that situation, and (4) that such failure proximately resulted in the losses complained of, although under *Cede & Co. v. Technicolor, Inc.*, 636 A.2d 956 (Del.1994) this last element may be thought to constitute an affirmative defense.

1.   Knowing violation for statute: Concerning the possibility that the Caremark directors knew of violations of law, none of the documents submitted for review, nor any of the deposition transcripts appear to provide evidence of it. Certainly the Board understood that the company had entered into a variety of contracts with physicians, researchers, and health care providers and it was understood that some of these contracts were with persons who had prescribed treatments that Caremark participated in providing. The board was informed that the company's reimbursement for patient care was frequently from government funded sources and that such services were subject to the ARPL. But the Board appears to have been informed by experts that the company's practices while contestable, were lawful. There is no evidence that reliance on such reports was not reasonable. Thus, this case presents no occasion to apply a principle to the effect that knowingly causing the corporation to violate a criminal statute constitutes a breach of a director's fiduciary duty. It is not clear that the Board knew the detail found, for example, in the indictments

arising from the Company's payments. But, of course, the duty to act in good faith to be informed cannot be thought to require directors to possess detailed information about all aspects of the operation of the enterprise. Such a requirement would simple be inconsistent with the scale and scope of efficient organization size in this technological age.

2. Failure to monitor: Since it does appears that the Board was to some extent unaware of the activities that led to liability, I turn to a consideration of the other potential avenue to director liability that the pleadings take: director inattention or "negligence". Generally where a claim of directorial liability for corporate loss is predicated upon ignorance of liability creating activities within the corporation, as in *Graham* or in this case, in my opinion only a sustained or systematic failure of the board to exercise oversight—such as an utter failure to attempt to assure a reasonable information and reporting system exits—will establish the lack of good faith that is a necessary condition to liability. (Such a test of liability—lack of good faith as evidenced by sustained or systematic failure of a director to exercise reasonable oversight—is quite high.) But, a demanding test of liability in the oversight context is probably beneficial to corporate shareholders as a class, as it is in the board decision context, since it makes board service by qualified persons more likely, while continuing to act as a stimulus to good faith performance of duty by such directors.

Here the record supplies essentially no evidence that the director defendants were guilty of a sustained failure to exercise their oversight function. To the contrary, insofar as I am able to tell on this record, the corporation's information systems appear to have represented a good faith attempt to be informed of relevant facts. If the directors did not know the specifics of the activities that lead to the indictments, they cannot be faulted.

The liability that eventuated in this instance was huge. But the fact that it resulted from a violation of criminal law alone does not create a breach of fiduciary duty by directors. The record at this stage does not support the conclusion that the defendants either lacked good faith in the exercise of their monitoring responsibilities or conscientiously permitted a known violation of law by the corporation to occur. The claims asserted against them must be viewed at this stage as extremely weak.

The proposed settlement provides very modest benefits. Under the settlement agreement, plaintiffs have been given express assurances that Caremark will have a more centralized, active supervisory system in the future. Specifically, the settlement mandates duties to be performed by the newly named Compliance and Ethics Committee on an ongoing basis and increases the responsibility for monitoring compliance with the law at the lower levels of management. In adopting the resolutions required under the settlement, Caremark has further clarified its policies concerning the prohibition of providing remuneration for referrals. These appear to be positive consequences of the settlement of the claims brought by the plaintiffs, even if they are not highly significant. Nonetheless, given the weakness of the plaintiffs' claims the proposed settlement appears to be an adequate, reasonable, and beneficial outcome for all of the parties. Thus, the proposed settlement will be approved.

NOTE

Caremark would seem to make clear that under Delaware law, directors have an affirmative duty to establish an effective legal compliance program that covers, at the very least, the most important laws to which the corporation is subject. In establishing the program and determining its scope, the opinion suggests that the directors will be protected by the business judgment rule. Because compliance costs can be substantial, are directors justified in considering cost-effectiveness as one of the factors in the program? To what extent must they monitor the effectiveness of the program? As one recent article has noted, discussing the Foreign Corrupt Practices Act, "although there is no expectation that any compliance program can be perfectly implemented, corporations must consider their business structure, existing controls, costs and corporate culture in fashioning a program that will actually be followed." Dan K. Webb and Robb C. Adkins, *Anti-Bribery Compliance Programs in the Real World*, National Law Journal (February 4, 2013).

Courts outside Delaware may be more inclined to permit oversight claims to go forward than are Delaware courts. In *McCall v. Scott*, 239 F.3d 808 (6th Cir.), *amended on denial of rehearing*, 250 F.3d 997 (6th Cir. 2001), the plaintiffs, citing *Caremark*, contended that the directors of Columbia/HCA should be held liable in damages for failing to monitor and prevent the company's senior management from engaging in fraudulent activities such as improper cost reporting, improper billing practices, improper referral incentives, and improper acquisition practices. The complaint alleged that the directors either recklessly or intentionally disregarded "red flags" that warned of the systematic fraudulent practices of management such as audit information, ongoing acquisition practices, allegations brought against the company in a legal proceeding, an extensive federal investigation, and a New York Times investigation. The Sixth Circuit found that plaintiffs had alleged, with the requisite specificity to survive a motion to dismiss for failure to make a demand, that the directors had consciously disregarded known risks, which proven, could not have been undertaken in good faith. The court considered the prior experience of the board members as directors or managers of health care organizations that were acquired by the company in reaching its decision.

In *In re Abbott Laboratories Derivative Shareholders Litigation*, 325 F.3d 795 (7th Cir. 2001), the Seventh Circuit reached the same result. Shareholders alleged that Abbott's directors breached their fiduciary duty by failing to provide appropriate oversight to prevent findings of violations of FDA rules with respect to Abbott's diagnostics division. The plaintiffs did not contend that the reporting system in place was inadequate, but rather that the members of the Abbott board were aware of prior FDA violations and warnings and took no corrective steps. The complaint further alleged that, given six years of noncompliance, inspections, warning letters and notice of violations in the press, the directors' failure to act was not in good faith. The Seventh Circuit held that the facts alleged were sufficient to show demand futility and supported the reasonable inference that there was an intentional, sustained and systematic failure of the board to exercise oversight, which if true, would be a breach of the duty of good faith and therefore not protected under Abbott's charter.

Lastly, although *Caremark* was litigated as a duty of care case and the chancery court decided the case on the duty of care, the Delaware Supreme Court subsequently in *Stone v. Ritter* (discussed in Chapter 18) endorsed the *Caremark* legal standard but recharacterized the standard as falling with the duty of loyalty. This facet of *Caremark* is referenced in the case below.

The cases considered above all involve directors' duty of oversight over *legal* risks. In the following case the plaintiffs sought to extend the *Caremark* principle to oversight over *business* risks.

IN RE CITIGROUP INC. SHAREHOLDER DERIVATIVE LITIGATION
964 A.2d 106 (Del.Ch. 2009).

CHANDLER, CHANCELLOR.

This is a shareholder derivative action brought on behalf of Citigroup Inc. ("Citigroup" or the "Company"), seeking to recover for the Company its losses arising from exposure to the subprime lending market. Plaintiffs, shareholders of Citigroup, brought this action against current and former directors and officers of Citigroup, alleging, in essence, that the defendants breached their fiduciary duties by failing to properly monitor and manage the risks the Company faced from problems in the subprime lending market and for failing to properly disclose Citigroup's exposure to subprime assets. Plaintiffs allege that there were extensive "red flags" that should have given defendants notice of the problems that were brewing in the real estate and credit markets and that defendants ignored these warnings in the pursuit of short term profits and at the expense of the Company's long term viability.

Defendants in this action are current and former directors and officers of Citigroup. The complaint names thirteen members of the Citigroup board of directors on November 9, 2007, when the first of plaintiffs' now-consolidated derivative actions was filed. Plaintiffs allege that a majority of the director defendants were members of the Audit and Risk

Management Committee ("ARM Committee") in 2007 and were considered audit committee financial experts as defined by the Securities and Exchange Commission.

Plaintiffs allege that since as early as 2006, defendants have caused and allowed Citigroup to engage in subprime lending that ultimately left the Company exposed to massive losses by late 2007. Beginning in late 2005, house prices, which many believe were artificially inflated by speculation and easily available credit, began to plateau, and then deflate. Adjustable rate mortgages issued earlier in the decade began to reset, leaving many homeowners with significantly increased monthly payments. Defaults and foreclosures increased, and assets backed by income from residential mortgages began to decrease in value. By February 2007, subprime mortgage lenders began filing for bankruptcy and subprime mortgages packaged into securities began experiencing increasing levels of delinquency. In mid-2007, rating agencies downgraded bonds backed by subprime mortgages.

Much of Citigroup's exposure to the subprime lending market arose from its involvement with collateralized debt obligations ("CDOs")-repackaged pools of lower rated securities that Citigroup created by acquiring asset-backed securities, including residential mortgage backed securities ("RMBSs"), and then selling rights to the cash flows from the securities in classes, or tranches, with different levels of risk and return. Included with at least some of the CDOs created by Citigroup was a "liquidity put"—an option that allowed the purchasers of the CDOs to sell them back to Citigroup at original value.

According to plaintiffs, Citigroup's alleged $55 billion subprime exposure was in two areas of the Company's Securities & Banking Unit. The first portion totaled $11.7 billion and included securities tied to subprime loans that were being held until they could be added to debt pools for investors. The second portion included $43 billion of super-senior securities, which are portions of CDOs backed in part by RMBS collateral.

Plaintiffs also allege that Citigroup was exposed to the subprime mortgage market through its use of SIVs. Banks can create SIVs by borrowing cash (by selling commercial paper) and using the proceeds to purchase loans; in other words, the SIVs sell short term debt and buy longer-term, higher yielding assets. According to plaintiffs, Citigroup's SIVs invested in riskier assets, such as home equity loans, rather than the low-risk assets traditionally used by SIVs.

The problems in the subprime market left Citigroup's SIVs unable to pay their investors. The SIVs held subprime mortgages that had decreased in value, and the normally liquid commercial paper market became illiquid. Because the SIVs could no longer meet their cash needs by attracting new investors, they had to sell assets at allegedly "fire sale" prices. In November 2007, Citigroup disclosed that it provided $7.6 billion of emergency financing to the seven SIVs the Company operated after they were unable to repay maturing debt. Ultimately, Citigroup was forced to bail out seven of its affiliated SIVs by bringing $49 billion in assets onto its balance sheet, notwithstanding that Citigroup previously represented that it would manage the SIVs on an arms-length basis.

Plaintiffs allege that defendants are liable to the Company for breach of fiduciary duty for (1) failing to adequately oversee and manage Citigroup's exposure to the problems in the subprime mortgage market, even in the face of alleged "red flags" and (2) failing to ensure that the Company's financial reporting and other disclosures were thorough and accurate.[6] As will be more fully explained below, the "red flags" alleged in the eighty-six page Complaint are generally statements from public documents that reflect worsening conditions in the financial markets, including the subprime and credit markets, and the effects those worsening conditions had on market participants, including Citigroup's peers.

Where, as here, a plaintiff does not make a pre-suit demand on the board of directors, the complaint must plead with particularity facts showing that a demand on the board would have been futile. The purpose of the demand requirement is not to insulate defendants from liability; rather, the demand requirement and the strict requirements of factual particularity under Rule 23.1 "exist[ ] to preserve the primacy of board decisionmaking regarding legal claims belonging to the corporation."

Plaintiffs have not alleged that a majority of the board was not independent for purposes of evaluating demand. Plaintiffs allege that demand is futile because the director defendants are not able to exercise disinterested business judgment in responding to a demand because their failure of oversight subjects them to a substantial likelihood of personal liability. According to plaintiffs, the director defendants face a substantial threat of personal liability because their conscious disregard of their duties and lack of proper supervision and oversight caused the Company to be overexposed to risk in the subprime mortgage market.

Plaintiffs' argument is based on a theory of director liability famously articulated by former-Chancellor Allen in *In re Caremark*.

With regard to director liability standards, the Court distinguished between (1) "*a board decision* that results in a loss because that decision

---

[6] Plaintiffs also assert a claim for "reckless and gross mismanagement." Delaware law does not recognize an independent cause of action against corporate directors and officers for reckless and gross mismanagement; such claims are treated as claims for breach of fiduciary duty. Delaware fiduciary duties are based in common law and have been carefully crafted to define the responsibilities of directors and managers, as fiduciaries, to the corporation. In defining these duties, the courts balance specific policy considerations such as the need to keep directors and officers accountable to shareholders and the degree to which the threat of personal liability may discourage beneficial risk taking. These common law standards thus govern the duties that directors and officers owe the corporation as well as claims such as those for "reckless and gross mismanagement," even if those claims are asserted separate and apart from claims of breach of fiduciary duty.

was ill advised or 'negligent' " and (2) "an *unconsidered failure of the board to act* in circumstances in which due attention would, arguably, have prevented the loss." In the former class of cases, director action is analyzed under the business judgment rule, which prevents judicial second guessing of the decision if the directors employed a rational process and considered all material information reasonably available-a standard measured by concepts of gross negligence. As former-Chancellor Allen explained:

> What should be understood, but may not widely be understood by courts or commentators who are not often required to face such questions, is that compliance with a director's duty of care can never appropriately be judicially determined by reference to *the content of the board decision* that leads to a corporate loss, apart from consideration of the good faith *or* rationality of the process employed. That is, whether a judge or jury considering the matter after the fact, believes a decision substantively wrong, or degrees of wrong extending through "stupid" to "egregious" or "irrational", provides no ground for director liability, so long as the court determines that the process employed was either rational or employed in *a good faith* effort to advance corporate interests. To employ a different rule-one that permitted an "objective" evaluation of the decision-would expose directors to substantive second guessing by ill-equipped judges or juries, which would, in the long-run, be injurious to investor interests. Thus, the business judgment rule is process oriented and informed by a deep respect for all *good faith* board decisions.

In the latter class of cases, where directors are alleged to be liable for a failure to monitor liability creating activities, the *Caremark* Court, in a reassessment of the holding in *Graham*, stated that while directors could be liable for a failure to monitor, "only a sustained or systematic failure of the board to exercise oversight-such as an utter failure to attempt to assure a reasonable information and reporting system exists-will establish the lack of good faith that is a necessary condition to liability."

In *Stone v. Ritter,* the Delaware Supreme Court approved the *Caremark* standard for director oversight liability and made clear that liability was based on the concept of good faith, which the *Stone* Court held was embedded in the fiduciary duty of loyalty and did not constitute a freestanding fiduciary duty that could independently give rise to liability. As the *Stone* Court explained:

> *Caremark* articulates the necessary conditions predicate for director oversight liability: (a) the directors utterly failed to implement any reporting or information system or controls; *or* (b) having implemented such a system or controls, consciously failed to monitor or oversee its operations thus disabling themselves from being informed of risks or problems requiring their attention.

In either case, imposition of liability requires a showing that the directors knew that they were not discharging their fiduciary obligations. Where directors fail to act in the face of a known duty to act, thereby demonstrating a conscious disregard for their responsibilities, they breach their duty of loyalty by failing to discharge that fiduciary obligation in good faith.]

Thus, to establish oversight liability a plaintiff must show that the directors _knew_ they were not discharging their fiduciary obligations or that the directors demonstrated a _conscious_ disregard for their responsibilities such as by failing to act in the face of a known duty to act. The test is rooted in concepts of bad faith; indeed, a showing of bad faith is a _necessary condition_ to director oversight liability.

Plaintiffs' theory of how the director defendants will face personal liability is a bit of a twist on the traditional _Caremark_ claim. In a typical [_Caremark_ case, plaintiffs argue that the defendants are liable for damages that arise from a failure to properly monitor or oversee employee misconduct or violations of law.] For example, in _Caremark_ the board allegedly failed to monitor employee actions in violation of the federal Anti-Referral Payments Law; in _Stone,_ the directors were charged with a failure of oversight that resulted in liability for the company because of employee violations of the federal Bank Secrecy Act.

* Different

In contrast, plaintiffs' _Caremark_ claims are based on defendants' alleged failure to properly monitor Citigroup's _business risk,_ specifically its exposure to the subprime mortgage market. In their answering brief, plaintiffs allege that the [director defendants are personally liable under _Caremark_ for failing to "make a good faith attempt to follow the procedures put in place or fail[ing] to assure that adequate and proper corporate information and reporting systems existed that would enable them to be fully informed regarding Citigroup's risk to the subprime mortgage market."] Plaintiffs point to so-called "red flags" that should have put defendants on notice of the problems in the subprime mortgage market and further allege that the board should have been especially conscious of these red flags because a majority of the directors (1) served on the Citigroup board during its previous Enron related conduct and (2) were members of the ARM Committee and considered financial experts.

Although these claims are framed by plaintiffs as _Caremark_ claims, plaintiffs' theory essentially amounts to a claim that the director defendants should be personally liable to the Company because they failed to fully recognize the risk posed by subprime securities. When one looks past the lofty allegations of duties of oversight and red flags used to dress up these claims, [what is left appears to be plaintiff shareholders attempting to hold the director defendants personally liable for making (or allowing to be made) business decisions that, in hindsight, turned out poorly for the Company.]

Citigroup has adopted a provision in its certificate of incorporation pursuant to 8 *Del. C.* § 102(b)(7) that exculpates directors from personal liability for violations of fiduciary duty, except for, among other things, breaches of the duty of loyalty or actions or omissions not in good faith or that involve intentional misconduct or a knowing violation of law. Because the director defendants are "exculpated from liability for certain conduct, 'then a serious threat of liability may only be found to exist if the plaintiff pleads a *non-exculpated* claim against the directors based on particularized facts.' " Here, plaintiffs have not alleged that the directors were interested in the transaction and instead root their theory of director personal liability in bad faith.

The Delaware Supreme Court has stated that bad faith conduct may be found where a director "intentionally acts with a purpose other than that of advancing the best interests of the corporation, . . . acts with the intent to violate applicable positive law, or . . . intentionally fails to act in the face of a known duty to act, demonstrating a conscious disregard for his duties." More recently, the Delaware Supreme Court held that when a plaintiff seeks to show that demand is excused because directors face a substantial likelihood of liability where "directors are exculpated from liability except for claims based on 'fraudulent,' 'illegal' or 'bad faith' conduct, a plaintiff must also plead particularized facts that demonstrate that the directors acted with scienter, *i.e.,* that they had 'actual or constructive knowledge' that their conduct was legally improper." A plaintiff can thus plead bad faith by alleging with particularity that a director *knowingly* violated a fiduciary duty or failed to act in violation of a *known* duty to act, demonstrating a *conscious* disregard for her duties.

The Delaware Supreme Court made clear in *Stone* that directors of Delaware corporations have certain responsibilities to implement and monitor a system of oversight; however, this obligation does not eviscerate the core protections of the business judgment rule—protections designed to allow corporate managers and directors to pursue risky transactions without the specter of being held personally liable if those decisions turn out poorly. Accordingly, the burden required for a plaintiff to rebut the presumption of the business judgment rule by showing gross negligence is a difficult one, and the burden to show bad faith is even higher. Additionally, as former-Chancellor Allen noted in *Caremark,* director liability based on the duty of oversight "is possibly the most difficult theory in corporation law upon which a plaintiff might hope to win a judgment." The presumption of the business judgment rule, the protection of an exculpatory § 102(b)(7) provision, and the difficulty of proving a *Caremark* claim together function to place an extremely high burden on a plaintiff to state a claim for personal director liability for a failure to see the extent of a company's business risk.

It is almost impossible for a court, in hindsight, to determine whether the directors of a company properly evaluated risk and thus made the "right" business decision. In any investment there is a chance that returns will turn out lower than expected, and generally a smaller chance that they will be far lower than expected. When investments turn out poorly, it is possible that the decision-maker evaluated the deal correctly but got "unlucky" in that a huge loss—the probability of which was very small— actually happened. It is also possible that the decision-maker improperly evaluated the risk posed by an investment and that the company suffered large losses as a result.

Business decision-makers must operate in the real world, with imperfect information, limited resources, and an uncertain future. To impose liability on directors for making a "wrong" business decision would cripple their ability to earn returns for investors by taking business risks. Indeed, this kind of judicial second guessing is what the business judgment rule was designed to prevent, and even if a complaint is framed under a *Caremark* theory, this Court will not abandon such bedrock principles of Delaware fiduciary duty law. With these considerations and the difficult standard required to show director oversight liability in mind, I turn to an evaluation of the allegations in the Complaint.

The allegations in the Complaint amount essentially to a claim that Citigroup suffered large losses and that there were certain warning signs that could or should have put defendants on notice of the business risks related to Citigroup's investments in subprime assets. Plaintiffs then conclude that because defendants failed to prevent the Company's losses associated with certain business risks, they must have consciously ignored these warning signs or knowingly failed to monitor the Company's risk in accordance with their fiduciary duties. Such conclusory allegations, however, are not sufficient to state a claim for failure of oversight that would give rise to a substantial likelihood of personal liability, which would require particularized factual allegations demonstrating bad faith by the director defendants.

Plaintiffs do not contest that Citigroup had procedures and controls in place that were designed to monitor risk. Plaintiffs admit that Citigroup established the ARM Committee and in 2004 amended the ARM Committee charter to include the fact that one of the purposes of the ARM Committee was to assist the board in fulfilling its oversight responsibility relating to policy standards and guidelines for risk assessment and risk management. The ARM Committee was also charged with, among other things, (1) discussing with management and independent auditors the annual audited financial statements, (2) reviewing with management an evaluation of Citigroup's internal control structure, and (3) discussing with management Citigroup's major credit, market, liquidity, and operational risk exposures and the steps taken by management to monitor and control such exposures, including Citigroup's risk assessment and risk management policies. According to plaintiffs' own allegations, the ARM Committee met eleven times in 2006 and twelve times in 2007.

Plaintiffs nevertheless argue that the director defendants breached their duty of oversight either because the oversight mechanisms were not adequate or because the director defendants did not make a good faith effort to comply with the established oversight procedures. To support this claim, the Complaint alleges numerous facts that plaintiffs argue should have put the director defendants on notice of the impending problems in the subprime mortgage market and Citigroup's exposure thereto.

Plaintiffs argue that demand is excused because a majority of the director defendants face a substantial likelihood of personal liability because they were charged with management of Citigroup's risk as members of the ARM Committee and as audit committee financial experts and failed to properly oversee and monitor such risk.[63] As explained above, however, to establish director oversight liability plaintiffs would ultimately have to prove bad faith conduct by the director defendants. Plaintiffs fail to plead any particularized factual allegations that raise a reasonable doubt that the director defendants acted in good faith.

The Complaint and plaintiffs' answering brief repeatedly make the conclusory allegation that the defendants have breached their duty of oversight, but nowhere do plaintiffs adequately explain what the director defendants actually did or failed to do that would constitute such a violation. Even while admitting that Citigroup had a risk monitoring system in place, plaintiffs seem to conclude that, because the director defendants (and the ARM Committee members in particular) were charged with monitoring Citigroup's risk, then they must be found liable because Citigroup experienced losses as a result of exposure to the subprime mortgage market. The only factual support plaintiffs provide for this conclusion are "red flags" that actually amount to nothing more than signs of continuing deterioration in the subprime mortgage market. These types of conclusory allegations are exactly the kinds of allegations that do not state a claim for relief under *Caremark*.

---

[63] Directors with special expertise are not held to a higher standard of care in the oversight context simply because of their status as an expert. Directors of a committee charged with oversight of a company's risk have additional responsibilities to monitor such risk; however, such responsibility does not change the standard of director liability under *Caremark* and its progeny, which requires a showing of bad faith. Evaluating director action under the bad faith standard is a contextual and fact specific inquiry and what a director knows and understands is, of course, relevant to such an inquiry. *See In re Emerging Commc'ns, Inc. S'holders Litig.*, C.A. No. 16415, 2004 WL 1305745, at *39–40 (Del.Ch. May 3, 2004). Even accepting, however, that a majority of the directors were members of the ARM Committee and considered audit committee financial experts, plaintiffs have not alleged facts showing that they demonstrated a conscious disregard for duty, or any other conduct or omission that would constitute bad faith. Even directors who are experts are shielded from judicial second guessing of their business decisions by the business judgment rule.

Director oversight duties are designed to ensure reasonable reporting and information systems exist that would allow directors to know about and prevent wrongdoing that could cause losses for the Company. [There are significant differences between failing to oversee employee fraudulent or criminal conduct and failing to recognize the extent of a Company's business risk.] Directors should, indeed must under Delaware law, ensure that reasonable information and reporting systems exist that would put them on notice of fraudulent or criminal conduct within the company. Such oversight programs allow directors to intervene and prevent frauds or other wrongdoing that could expose the company to risk of loss as a result of such conduct. While it may be tempting to say that directors have the same duties to monitor and oversee business risk, imposing *Caremark*-type duties on directors to monitor business risk is [fundamentally different.] Citigroup was in the business of taking on and managing investment and other business risks. To impose oversight liability on directors for failure to monitor "excessive" risk would involve courts in conducting hindsight evaluations of decisions at the heart of the business judgment of directors. Oversight duties under Delaware law are not designed to subject directors, even expert directors, to *personal liability* for failure to predict the future and to properly evaluate business risk.[78]

Instead of alleging facts that could demonstrate bad faith on the part of the directors, by presenting the Court with the so called "red flags," plaintiffs are inviting the Court to engage in the exact kind of judicial second guessing that is proscribed by the business judgment rule. In any business decision that turns out poorly there will likely be signs that one could point to and argue are evidence that the decision was wrong. Indeed, it is tempting in a case with such staggering losses for one to think that they could have made the "right" decision if they had been in the directors' position. This temptation, however, is one of the reasons for the presumption against an objective review of business decisions by judges, a presumption that is no less applicable when the losses to the Company are large.

Citigroup has suffered staggering losses, in part, as a result of the recent problems in the United States economy, particularly those in the subprime mortgage market. It is understandable that investors, and

---

[78] If defendants had been able to predict the extent of the problems in the subprime mortgage market, then they would not only have been able to avoid losses, but presumably would have been able to make significant gains for Citigroup by taking positions that would have produced a return when the value of subprime securities dropped. Query: if the Court were to adopt plaintiffs' theory of the case—that the defendants are personally liable for their failure to see the problems in the subprime mortgage market and Citigroup's exposure to them—then could not a plaintiff succeed on a theory that a director was personally liable for failure to predict the extent of the subprime mortgage crisis and profit from it, even if the company was not exposed to losses from the subprime mortgage market? If directors are going to be held liable for losses for failing to accurately predict market events, then why not hold them liable for failing to profit by predicting market events that, in hindsight, the director should have seen because of certain red (or green?) flags? If one expects director prescience in one direction, why not the other?

others, want to find someone to hold responsible for these losses, and it is often difficult to distinguish between a desire to blame *someone* and a desire to force those responsible to account for their wrongdoing. Our law, fortunately, provides guidance for precisely these situations in the form of doctrines governing the duties owed by officers and directors of Delaware corporations. This law has been refined over hundreds of years, which no doubt included many crises, and we must not let our desire to blame someone for our losses make us lose sight of the purpose of our law. Ultimately, the discretion granted directors and managers allows them to maximize shareholder value in the long term by taking risks without the debilitating fear that they will be held personally liable if the company experiences losses. This doctrine also means, however, that when the company suffers losses, shareholders may not be able to hold the directors personally liable.

———————

[Chancellor Chandler draws a distinction between liability for failure to monitor legal risks and failure to monitor business risks.]He says, "While it may be tempting to say that directors have the same duties to monitor and oversee business risk, imposing *Caremark*-type duties on directors to monitor business risk is fundamentally different." Do you agree? Or does the case really turn on the fact that Citigroup did have in place a detailed risk-management program, albeit one that failed to catch the particular risk that led to the losses at issue?

Interestingly, the issues that Chancellor Chandler addresses in *Citigroup* arose more than twenty-five years ago in a little noticed case, *Hoye v. Meek*, 795 F.2d 893 (10th Cir.1986). In that case, unlike *Citigroup*, the court looked to statutory standards of conduct and disregarded the teachings of the business judgment rule. In *Hoye*, the Guaranty Trust Company, of which Meek was a director and president, suffered large losses from some of its investments. In a suit by the trustee in bankruptcy, the trial court held that Meek had breached his duty of care by failing to curb the extent of the investment and to monitor the company's investment decisions and results, and by delegating excessive authority to his son. On appeal, the Tenth Circuit rejected Meek's argument that he was entitled to the protection of the business judgment rule and stated:

> We are not persuaded by appellant's argument that, because Maxwell had operated the company at a profit for seven years, the directors' and president's duty to monitor activities was dissipated. [D]irectors and officers are charged with knowledge of those things which it is their duty to know and ignorance is not a basis for escaping liability. Where suspicions are aroused, or should be aroused, it is the directors' duty to make necessary inquiries. We hold that appellant failed to make the necessary inquiries. He had a duty to keep abreast of Guaranty's

investments, particularly investments that posed a double risk of decrease in market price and an increase in transactional costs.

Appellant of course would not be required to have the ability to predict increasing interest rates during the two-year period here involved. A decision made in good faith, based on sound business judgment, would not alone subject appellant to liability. But in order to come within the ambit of the business judgment rule, a director must be diligent and careful in performing the duties he has undertaken. In the instant case, appellant's breach of duty resulted from both his delegation of authority to Maxwell without adequate supervision and his failure to avert Guaranty's continued exposure to increasing indebtedness. At each monthly board meeting during this two-year period, the directors could have decided to halt this increasing exposure to risk.

Assuming appellant's good faith, that alone was not sufficient to shield him from liability. It is undisputed that, as Guaranty was on the verge of filing for bankruptcy, appellant attempted to find other sources of capital for the company. This eleventh hour effort, however, was not sufficient to fulfill his duty of care as a director and president. The Oklahoma statute requires good faith *and* the diligence, care and skill of a prudent man.

795 F.2d at 896.

How do *Caremark* duties apply to directors of Delaware corporations that are operating in a global economy? *In re Puda Coal, Inc. Stockholders Litigation* (Del.Ch. 2013) (Bench Ruling) involved a Delaware corporation whose assets, located in China, were stolen by a Chinese director (two of the other directors were American). The theft went undetected for two years. Plaintiffs brought a *Caremark* claim against the other directors, two of whom had, by the time of the litigation, resigned.

Chancellor Strine denied a motion to dismiss for failure to make demand and a similar motion for failure to state a claim on which relief could be granted. Addressing the latter, with respect to corporations with overseas operations and assets, he stated:

[I]f you're going to have a company domiciled for purposes of its relations with its investors in Delaware and the assets and operations of that company are situated in China that, in order for you to meet your obligation of good faith, you better have your physical body in China an awful lot. You better have in place a system of controls to make sure that you know that you actually own the assets. You better have the language skills to navigate the environment in which the company is operating. You better have retained accountants and lawyers who are fit to the task of maintaining a system of controls over a public company.

Independent directors who step into these situations involving essentially the fiduciary oversight of assets in other parts of the world have a duty not to be dummy directors. I'm not mixing up care in the sense of negligence with loyalty here, in the sense of your duty of loyalty. I'm talking about the loyalty issue of understanding that if the assets are in Russia, if they're in Nigeria, if they're in the Middle East, if they're in China, that you're not going to be able to sit in your home in the U.S. and do a conference call four times a year and discharge your duty of loyalty. That won't cut it. That there will be special challenges that deal with linguistic, cultural and others in terms of the effort that you have to put in to discharge your duty of loyalty. There's no such thing as being a dummy director in Delaware, a shill, someone who just puts themselves up and represents to the investing public that they're a monitor. Because the only reason to have independent directors—remember, you don't pick them for their industry expertise. You pick them because of their independence and their ability to monitor the people who are managing the company.

If it's a situation where, frankly, all the flow of information is in the language that I don't understand, in a culture where there's, frankly, not legal strictures or structures or ethical mores yet that may be advanced to the level where I'm comfortable? It would be very difficult if I didn't know the language, the tools. You better be careful there. You have a duty to think. You can't just go on this [board] and act like this was an S&L regulated by the federal government in Iowa and you live in Iowa.

One commentator has noted that:

Chancellor Strine articulates a very broad vision of independent directors' oversight responsibilities for Delaware companies' foreign operations or assets. The expectation that independent directors physically visit and inspect the foreign operations and also speak the local language in the foreign locations may come as something of a shock to many outside directors. These days many companies have operations in multiple companies; larger companies have operations around the world. Chancellor Strine's expectation that outside directors must be both regularly physically present and culturally literate in the each of the locations of the company's overseas operations may represent a vision of board responsibility that likely would exceed the expectations of many company directors.

Kevin LaCroix, Delaware Chancery Court: A Sweeping Vision of Outside Directors' Foreign Operations Oversight Responsibilities?, The D & O Diary (February 27, 2013).

E. DUTY TO BECOME INFORMED

Problem: FiberNet Corporation—Part 4

You have just received a call from Lauren Peters, whom you have advised from time to time on a number of business and legal issues. She tells you that she has served on the board of FiberNet for three years, during which it has done quite well. She has just had a call from Sam Brown, the CEO, informing her of an emergency meeting of the board, to be held tomorrow. The purpose of the meeting is to consider a potential acquisition of LaserTek, Inc., which develops and sells a line of optical Ethernet switches. LaserTek has been struggling, and will require a significant capital infusion to keep its business alive.

Sam told Lauren that the board will receive at the meeting a detailed analysis of the proposed transaction, including LaserTek's financial statements for the last three years, an analysis prepared by Norma Axtell, the CFO, pro-forma projections of the combined results of the two companies, a valuation analysis prepared by FiberNet's investment bankers and Sam's own recommendation. The price of the proposed acquisition is approximately 25% of FiberNet's current market capitalization, so it represents a significant transaction. Apparently, it is essential that the board approve the transaction at the special meeting, or otherwise the letter of intent that Brown has negotiated will expire, and LaserTek will probably have to file for bankruptcy.

1. Lauren tells you that Sam worked with the CEO of LaserTek at another company, where they became close friends. She is concerned that FiberNet's management has never done an acquisition and does not know how difficult integrating two businesses will be, especially when one of them has been in financial difficulty. She suspects, however, that, as long as the deal looks reasonable, the rest of the board will go along with Sam, given his success so far in managing FiberNet. Lauren asks for your advice about what she should do at the board meeting. She says that she has heard of some recent cases in which boards of directors have been sued for breach of their fiduciary duties in making major decisions like this one.

2. Now assume you are Secretary and General Counsel at FiberNet. You have been deeply involved in negotiating the proposed acquisition of LaserTek, and you are working with Sam on preparing for the special board meeting. What should you do to minimize the risk that the board would be held liable for failing in its fiduciary duties if FiberNet purchases LaserTek and the acquisition turns out badly.

1. THE TRANS UNION CASE

SMITH V. VAN GORKOM
488 A.2d 858 (Del.1985).

[Trans Union Corporation was a publicly traded, diversified holding company. Its chairman and chief executive officer was Jerome W. Van Gorkom, who was then nearing retirement age. Its Board of Directors consisted of five company officers and five outside directors. Four of the latter were chief executive officers of large public corporations; the fifth was the former Dean of the University of Chicago Business School.

At the time of the events in the case, Trans Union faced a major business problem relating to investment tax credits (ITCs). Its competitors generated sufficient taxable income to allow them to make use of all ITCs they generated and took these tax benefits into account in setting the terms of lease notes. Trans Union did not have sufficient income to take advantage of all of its ITCs, but nevertheless had to match its competitors' prices. In July 1980, Trans Union management submitted its annual revision of the company's five year forecast to the board. That report discussed alternative solutions to the ITC problem and concluded that the company had sufficient time to develop its course of action. The report did not mention the possible sale of the company.

On August 27, Van Gorkom met with senior management to consider the ITC problem. Among the ideas mentioned were the sale of Trans Union to a company with a large amount of taxable income, or a leveraged buyout. This latter alternative was discussed again at a meeting on September 5. At that meeting, the chief financial officer, Donald Romans, presented preliminary calculations based on a price between $50 and $60 per share but did not state that these calculations established a fair price for the company. While Van Gorkom rejected the leveraged buy out idea, he stated that he would be willing to sell his own shares at $55 per share.

Without consulting the board of directors or any officers, Van Gorkom decided to meet with Jay A. Pritzker, a corporate takeover specialist whom he knew socially. Prior to that meeting, Van Gorkom instructed Trans Union's controller, Carl Peterson, to prepare a confidential calculation of the feasibility of a leveraged buy out at $55 per share. On September 13, Van Gorkom proposed a sale of Trans Union to Pritzker at $55 per share. Two days later, Pritzker advised Van Gorkom that he was interested in a purchase at that price. By September 18, after two more meetings that included two Trans Union officers and an outside consultant, Van Gorkom knew that Pritzker was ready to propose a cash-out merger at $55 per share if Pritzker could also have the option to buy one million shares of Trans Union treasury stock at $38 per share (a price which was 75 cents above the current market price). Pritzker also insisted that the Trans

Union board act on his proposal within three days, *i.e.,* by Sunday, September 21 and instructed his attorney to draft the merger documents.

On September 19, without consulting Trans Union's legal department, Van Gorkom engaged outside counsel as merger specialists. He called for meetings of senior management and the board of directors for the next day, but only those officers who had met with Pritzker knew the subject of the meetings.

Senior management's reaction to Pritzker's proposal was completely negative. Romans objected both to the price and to the sale of treasury shares as a "lock-up". Immediately after this meeting, Van Gorkom met with the board. He made an oral presentation outlining the Pritzker offer but did not furnish copies of the proposed merger agreement. Neither did he tell the board that he had approached Pritzker. He stated that Pritzker would purchase all outstanding Trans Union shares for $55 each and Trans Union would be merged into a wholly owned entity Pritzker formed for this purpose; for 90 days Trans Union would be free to receive but not to solicit competing offers; only published, rather than proprietary information could be furnished to other bidders; the Trans Union board had to act by Sunday evening, September 21; the offer was subject to Pritzker obtaining financing by October 10, 1980; and that if Pritzker met or waived the financing contingency, Trans Union was obliged to sell him one million newly issued shares at $38 per share. According to Van Gorkom, the issue for the board was whether $55 was a fair price rather than the best price. He said that putting Trans Union "up for auction" through a 90 day "market test" would allow the free market an opportunity to judge whether $55 was fair. Outside counsel advised the board that they might be sued if they did not accept the offer, and that a fairness opinion from an investment banker was not legally required.

At the board meeting, Romans stated that his prior studies in connection with a possible leveraged buy out did not indicate a fair price for the stock. However, it was his opinion that $55 was "at the beginning of the range" of a fair price.

The board meeting lasted two hours, at the end of which the board approved the merger, with two conditions:

(1) Trans Union reserved the right to accept any better offer during the 90 day market test period.

(2) Trans Union could share its proprietary information with other potential bidders.

At that time, however, the board did not reserve the right actively to solicit other bids.

Van Gorkom signed the as yet unamended merger agreement, still unread either by himself or the other board members, that evening "in the midst of a formal party which he hosted for the opening of the Chicago Lyric Opera."

On September 22, Trans Union issued a press release announcing a "definitive" merger agreement with Marmon Group, Inc., an affiliate of a Pritzker holding company. Within ten days, rebellious key officers threatened to resign. Van Gorkom met with Pritzker who agreed to modify the agreement provided that the "dissident" officers agreed to stay with Trans Union for at least six months following the merger.

The board reconvened on October 8 and, without seeing their text, approved the proposed amendments regarding the 90 day market test and solicitation of other bids. The board also authorized the company to employ its investment banker to solicit other offers.

Although the amendments had not yet been prepared, Trans Union issued a press release on the following day stating that it could actively seek other offers and had retained an investment banker for that purpose. The release also said that Pritzker had obtained the necessary financing commitments and had acquired one million shares of Trans Union at $38 per share and that if Trans Union had not received a more favorable offer by February 1, 1981, its shareholders would meet to vote on the Pritzker bid. Van Gorkom executed the amendments to the merger agreement on October 10, without consulting the board and apparently without fully understanding that the amendments significantly constrained Trans Union's ability to negotiate a better deal.

Trans Union received only two serious offers during the market test period. One, from General Electric Credit Corporation, fell through when Trans Union would not rescind its agreement with Pritzker to give GE Credit extra time. The other offer, a leveraged buyout by management (except Van Gorkom) arranged through Kohlberg, Kravis, Roberts & Co. ("KKR") was made in early December at $60 per share. It was contingent upon completing equity and bank financing, which KKR said was 80% complete, with terms and conditions substantially the same as the Pritzker deal. Van Gorkom, however, did not view the KKR deal as "firm" because of the financing contingency (even though the Pritzker offer had been similarly conditioned) and he refused to issue a press release about it. KKR planned to present its offer to the Trans Union board, but withdrew shortly before the scheduled meeting, noting that a senior Trans Union officer had withdrawn from the purchasing KKR group after Van Gorkom spoke to him. Van Gorkom denied influencing the officer's decision, and he made no mention of it to the board at the meeting later that day.

The shareholders commenced their lawsuit on December 19, 1980. Management's proxy statement was mailed on January 21 for a meeting scheduled for February 10, 1981. The Trans Union board met on January 26 and gave final approval to both the Pritzker merger and a supplement to its proxy statement which was mailed the next day. On February 10, 1981, the shareholders approved the Pritzker merger by a large majority.]

HORSEY, JUSTICE (for the majority):

We turn to the issue of the application of the business judgment rule to the September 20 meeting of the Board.

The Court of Chancery concluded from the evidence that the Board of Directors' approval of the Pritzker merger proposal fell within the protection of the business judgment rule. The Court found that the Board had given sufficient time and attention to the transaction, since the directors had considered the Pritzker proposal on three different occasions, on September 20, and on October 8, 1980 and finally on January 26, 1981. On that basis, the Court reasoned that the Board had acquired, over the four-month period, sufficient information to reach an informed business judgment on the cash-out merger proposal. The Court ruled:

> that given the market value of Trans Union's stock, the business acumen of the members of the board of Trans Union, the substantial premium over market offered by the Pritzkers and the ultimate effect on the merger price provided by the prospect of other bids for the stock in question, that the board of directors of Trans Union did not act recklessly or improvidently in determining on a course of action which they believed to be in the best interest of the stockholders of Trans Union.

The Court of Chancery made but one finding; *i.e.,* that the Board's conduct over the entire period from September 20 through January 26, 1981 was not reckless or improvident, but informed. This ultimate conclusion was premised upon three subordinate findings, one explicit and two implied. The Court's explicit finding was that Trans Union's Board was "free to turn down the Pritzker proposal" not only on September 20 but also on October 8, 1980 and on January 26, 1981. The Court's implied, subordinate findings were: (1) that no legally binding agreement was reached by the parties until January 26; and (2) that if a higher offer were to be forthcoming, the market test would have produced it, and Trans Union would have been contractually free to accept such higher offer. However, the Court offered no factual basis or legal support for any of these findings; and the record compels contrary conclusions.

Under Delaware law, the business judgment rule is the offspring of the fundamental principle, codified in 8 Del.C. § 141(a), that the business and affairs of a Delaware corporation are managed by or under its board of directors. In carrying out their managerial roles, directors are charged with an unyielding fiduciary duty to the corporation and its shareholders. The business judgment rule exists to protect and promote the full and free exercise of the managerial power granted to Delaware directors. The rule itself "is a presumption that in making a business decision, the directors of a corporation acted on an informed basis, in good faith and in the honest belief that the action taken was in the best interests of the company." [*Aronson v. Lewis*, 473 A.2d 805, 812 (Del.1984)] Thus, the party attacking a board decision as uninformed must rebut the presumption that its business judgment was an informed one. *Id.*

The determination of whether a business judgment is an informed one turns on whether the directors have informed themselves "prior to making a business decision, of all material information reasonably available to them." *Id.*

Under the business judgment rule there is no protection for directors who have made "an unintelligent or unadvised judgment." *Mitchell v. Highland-Western Glass*, 167 A. 831, 833 (Del.Ch.1933). A director's duty to inform himself in preparation for a decision derives from the fiduciary capacity in which he serves the corporation and its stockholders. Since a director is vested with the responsibility for the management of the affairs of the corporation, he must execute that duty with the recognition that he acts on behalf of others. Such obligation does not tolerate faithlessness or self-dealing. But fulfillment of the fiduciary function requires more than the mere absence of bad faith or fraud. Representation of the financial interests of others imposes on a director an affirmative duty to protect those interests and to proceed with a critical eye in assessing information of the type and under the circumstances present here.

Thus, a director's duty to exercise an informed business judgment is in the nature of a duty of care, as distinguished from a duty of loyalty. Here, there were no allegations of fraud, bad faith, or self-dealing, or proof thereof. Hence, it is presumed that the directors reached their business judgment in good faith, and considerations of motive are irrelevant to the issue before us.

The standard of care applicable to a director's duty of care has also been recently restated by this Court. In *Aronson, supra*, we stated:

> While the Delaware cases use a variety of terms to describe the applicable standard of care, our analysis satisfies us that under the business judgment rule director liability is predicated upon concepts of gross negligence. (footnote omitted)

473 A.2d at 812.

We again confirm that view. We think the concept of gross negligence is also the proper standard for determining whether a business judgment reached by a board of directors was an informed one.

In the specific context of a proposed merger of domestic corporations, a director has a duty under 8 Del.C. § 251(b), along with his fellow directors, to act in an informed and deliberate manner in determining whether to approve an agreement of merger before submitting the proposal to the stockholders. Certainly in the merger context, a director may not abdicate that duty by leaving to the shareholders alone the decision to approve or disapprove the agreement. Only an agreement of merger satisfying the requirements of 8 Del.C. § 251(b) may be submitted to the shareholders under § 251(c).

It is against those standards that the conduct of the directors of Trans Union must be tested, as a matter of law and as a matter of fact, regarding their exercise of an informed business judgment in voting to approve the Pritzker merger proposal.

The issue of whether the directors reached an informed decision to "sell" the Company on September 20, 1980 must be determined only upon the basis of the information then reasonably available to the directors and relevant to their decision to accept the Pritzker merger proposal. This is not to say that the directors were precluded from altering their original plan of action, had they done so in an informed manner. What we do say is that the question of whether the directors reached an informed business judgment in agreeing to sell the Company, pursuant to the terms of the September 20 Agreement presents, in reality, two questions: (A) whether the directors reached an informed business judgment on September 20, 1980; and (B) if they did not, whether the directors' actions taken subsequent to September 20 were adequate to cure any infirmity in their action taken on September 20. We first consider the directors' September 20 action in terms of their reaching an informed business judgment.

On the record before us, we must conclude that the Board of Directors did not reach an informed business judgment on September 20, 1980 in voting to "sell" the Company for $55 per share pursuant to the Pritzker cash-out merger proposal. Our reasons, in summary, are as follows:

The directors (1) did not adequately inform themselves as to Van Gorkom's role in forcing the "sale" of the Company and in establishing the per share purchase price; (2) were uninformed as to the intrinsic value of the Company; and (3) given these circumstances, at a minimum, were grossly negligent in approving the "sale" of the Company upon two hours' consideration, without prior notice, and without the exigency of a crisis or emergency.

As has been noted, the Board based its September 20 decision to approve the cash-out merger primarily on Van Gorkom's representations. None of the directors, other than Van Gorkom and Chelberg, had any prior knowledge that the purpose of the meeting was to propose a cash-out merger of Trans Union. No members of Senior Management were present, other than Chelberg, Romans and Peterson; and the latter two had only learned of the proposed sale an hour earlier. Both general counsel Moore and former general counsel Browder attended the meeting, but were equally uninformed as to the purpose of the meeting and the documents to be acted upon.

Without any documents before them concerning the proposed transaction, the members of the Board were required to rely entirely upon Van Gorkom's 20-minute oral presentation of the proposal. No written summary of the terms of the merger was presented; the directors were given no documentation to support the adequacy of $55 price per share for sale of the Company; and the Board had before it nothing more than Van Gorkom's statement of his understanding of the substance of an agreement which he admittedly had never read, nor which any member of the Board had ever seen.

Under 8 Del.C. § 141(e) "directors are fully protected in relying in good faith on reports made by officers." The term "report" has been liberally construed to include reports of informal personal investigations by corporate officers. However, there is no evidence that any "report," as defined under § 141(e), concerning the Pritzker proposal, was presented to the Board on September 20. Van Gorkom's oral presentation of his understanding of the terms of the proposed Merger Agreement, which he had not seen, and Romans' brief oral statement of his preliminary study regarding the feasibility of a leveraged buy-out of Trans Union do not qualify as § 141(e) "reports" for these reasons: The former lacked substance because Van Gorkom was basically uninformed as to the essential provisions of the very document about which he was talking. Romans' statement was irrelevant to the issues before the Board since it did not purport to be a valuation study. At a minimum for a report to enjoy the status conferred by § 141(e), it must be pertinent to the subject matter upon which a board is called to act, and otherwise be entitled to good faith, not blind, reliance. Considering all of the surrounding circumstances—hastily calling the meeting without prior notice of its subject matter, the proposed sale of the Company without any prior consideration of the issue or necessity therefor, the urgent time constraints imposed by Pritzker, and the total absence of any documentation whatsoever—the directors were duty bound to make reasonable inquiry of Van Gorkom and Romans, and if they had done so, the inadequacy of that upon which they now claim to have relied would have been apparent.

The defendants rely on the following factors to sustain the Trial Court's finding that the Board's decision was an informed one: (1) the magnitude of the premium or spread between the $55 Pritzker offering price and Trans Union's current market price of $38 per share; (2) the amendment of the Agreement as submitted on September 20 to permit the Board to accept any better offer during the "market test" period; (3) the collective experience and expertise of the Board's "inside" and "outside" directors; and (4) their reliance on Brennan's legal advice that the directors might be sued if they rejected the Pritzker proposal. We discuss each of these grounds *seriatim:*

(1)

A substantial premium may provide one reason to recommend a merger, but in the absence of other sound valuation information, the fact of a premium alone does not provide an adequate basis upon which to assess the fairness of an offering price. Here, the judgment reached as to the adequacy of the premium was based on a comparison between the historically depressed Trans Union market price and the amount of the Pritzker offer. Using market price as a basis for concluding that the premium adequately reflected the true value of the Company was a clearly faulty, indeed fallacious, premise, as the defendants' own evidence demonstrates.

The record is clear that before September 20, Van Gorkom and other members of Trans Union's Board knew that the market had consistently undervalued the worth of Trans Union's stock, despite steady increases in the Company's operating income in the seven years preceding the merger. The Board related this occurrence in large part to Trans Union's inability to use its ITCs as previously noted. Van Gorkom testified that he did not believe the market price accurately reflected Trans Union's true worth; and several of the directors testified that, as a general rule, most chief executives think that the market undervalues their companies' stock. Yet, on September 20, Trans Union's Board apparently believed that the market stock price accurately reflected the value of the Company for the purpose of determining the adequacy of the premium for its sale.

The parties do not dispute that a publicly-traded stock price is solely a measure of the value of a minority position and, thus, market price represents only the value of a single share. Nevertheless, on September 20, the Board assessed the adequacy of the premium over market, offered by Pritzker, solely by comparing it with Trans Union's current and historical stock price.

Indeed, as of September 20, the Board had no other information on which to base a determination of the intrinsic value of Trans Union as a going concern. As of September 20, the Board had made no evaluation of the Company designed to value the entire enterprise, nor had the Board ever previously considered selling the Company or consenting to a buy-out merger. Thus, the adequacy of a premium is indeterminate unless it is assessed in terms of other competent and sound valuation information that reflects the value of the particular business.

Despite the foregoing facts and circumstances, there was no call by the Board, either on September 20 or thereafter, for any valuation study or documentation of the $55 price per share as a measure of the fair value of the Company in a cash-out context. It is undisputed that the major asset of Trans Union was its cash flow. Yet, at no time did the Board call for a valuation study taking into account that highly significant element of the Company's assets.

We do not imply that an outside valuation study is essential to support an informed business judgment; nor do we state that fairness opinions by independent investment bankers are required as a matter of law. Often insiders familiar with the business of a going concern are in a better position than are outsiders to gather relevant information; and under appropriate circumstances, such directors may be fully protected in relying in good faith upon the valuation reports of their management.

Here, the record establishes that the Board did not request its Chief Financial Officer, Romans, to make any valuation study or review of the proposal to determine the adequacy of $55 per share for sale of the Company. The Board rested on Romans' elicited response that the $55 figure was within a "fair price range" within the context of a leveraged buy-out. No director sought any further information from Romans. No director asked him why he put $55 at the bottom of his range. No director asked Romans for any details as to his study, the reason why it had been undertaken or its depth. No director asked to see the study; and no director asked Romans whether Trans Union's finance department could do a fairness study within the remaining 36-hour period available under the Pritzker offer.

Had the Board, or any member, made an inquiry of Romans, he presumably would have responded as he testified: that his calculations were rough and preliminary; and, that the study was not designed to determine the fair value of the Company, but rather to assess the feasibility of a leveraged buy-out financed by the Company's projected cash flow, making certain assumptions as to the purchaser's borrowing needs. Romans would have presumably also informed the Board of his view, and the widespread view of Senior Management, that the timing of the offer was wrong and the offer inadequate.

The record also establishes that the Board accepted without scrutiny Van Gorkom's representation as to the fairness of the $55 price per share for sale of the Company—a subject that the Board had never previously considered. The Board thereby failed to discover that Van Gorkom had suggested the $55 price to Pritzker and, most crucially, that Van Gorkom had arrived at the $55 figure based on calculations designed solely to determine the feasibility of a leveraged buy-out.[19] No questions were raised either as to the tax implications of a cash-out merger or how the price for the one million share option granted Pritzker was calculated.

---

[19] As of September 20 the directors did not know: that Van Gorkom had arrived at the $55 figure alone, and subjectively, as the figure to be used by Controller Peterson in creating a feasible structure for a leveraged buy-out by a prospective purchaser; that Van Gorkom had not sought advice, information or assistance from either inside or outside Trans Union directors as to the value of the Company as an entity or the fair price per share for 100% of its stock; that Van Gorkom had not consulted with the Company's investment bankers or other financial analysts; that Van Gorkom had not consulted with or confided in any officer or director of the Company except Chelberg; and that Van Gorkom had deliberately chosen to ignore the advice and opinion of the members of his Senior Management group regarding the adequacy of the $55 price.

We do not say that the Board of Directors was not entitled to give some credence to Van Gorkom's representation that $55 was an adequate or fair price. Under § 141(e), the directors were entitled to rely upon their chairman's opinion of value and adequacy, provided that such opinion was reached on a sound basis. Here, the issue is whether the directors informed themselves as to all information that was reasonably available to them. Had they done so, they would have learned of the source and derivation of the $55 price and could not reasonably have relied thereupon in good faith.

None of the directors, Management or outside, were investment bankers or financial analysts. Yet the Board did not consider recessing the meeting until a later hour that day (or requesting an extension of Pritzker's Sunday evening deadline) to give it time to elicit more information as to the sufficiency of the offer, either from inside Management (in particular Romans) or from Trans Union's own investment banker, Salomon Brothers, whose Chicago specialist in merger and acquisitions was known to the Board and familiar with Trans Union's affairs.

Thus, the record compels the conclusion that on September 20 the Board lacked valuation information adequate to reach an informed business judgment as to the fairness of $55 per share for sale of the Company.

(2)

This brings us to the post-September 20 "market test" upon which the defendants ultimately rely to confirm the reasonableness of their September 20 decision to accept the Pritzker proposal. In this connection, the directors present a two-part argument: (a) that by making a "market test" of Pritzker's $55 per share offer a condition of their September 20 decision to accept his offer, they cannot be found to have acted impulsively or in an uninformed manner on September 20; and (b) that the adequacy of the $17 premium for sale of the Company was conclusively established over the following 90 to 120 days by the most reliable evidence available— the marketplace. Thus, the defendants impliedly contend that the "market test" eliminated the need for the Board to perform any other form of fairness test either on September 20, or thereafter.

Again, the facts of record do not support the defendants' argument. There is no evidence: (a) that the Merger Agreement was effectively amended to give the Board freedom to put Trans Union up for auction sale to the highest bidder; or (b) that a public auction was in fact permitted to occur.

(3)

The directors' unfounded reliance on both the premium and the market test as the basis for accepting the Pritzker proposal undermines the defendants' remaining contention that the Board's collective experience and sophistication was a sufficient basis for finding that it reached its

September 20 decision with informed, reasonable deliberation.[21] *Compare Gimbel v. Signal Companies, Inc.*, 316 A.2d 599 (Del.Ch.1974), *aff'd per curiam*, 316 A.2d 619 (Del.1974). There, the Court of Chancery [preliminarily] enjoined a board's sale of stock of its wholly-owned subsidiary for an alleged grossly inadequate price. It did so based on a finding that the business judgment rule had been pierced for failure of management to give its board "the opportunity to make a reasonable and reasoned decision." 316 A.2d at 615. The Court there reached this result notwithstanding the board's sophistication and experience; the company's need of immediate cash; and the board's need to act promptly due to the impact of an energy crisis on the value of the underlying assets being sold— all of its subsidiary's oil and gas interests. The Court found those factors denoting competence to be outweighed by evidence of gross negligence; that management in effect sprang the deal on the board by negotiating the asset sale without informing the board; that the buyer intended to "force a quick decision" by the board; that the board meeting was called on only one-and-a-half days' notice; that its outside directors were not notified of the meeting's purpose; that during a meeting spanning "a couple of hours" a sale of assets worth $480 million was approved; and that the Board failed to obtain a *current* appraisal of its oil and gas interests. The analogy of *Signal* to the case at bar is significant.

(4)

Part of the defense is based on a claim that the directors relied on legal advice rendered at the September 20 meeting by James Brennan, Esquire, who was present at Van Gorkom's request. Unfortunately, Brennan did not appear and testify at trial even though his firm participated in the defense of this action.

Several defendants testified that Brennan advised them that Delaware law did not require a fairness opinion or an outside valuation of the Company before the Board could act on the Pritzker proposal. If given, the advice was correct. However, that did not end the matter. Unless the directors had before them adequate information regarding the intrinsic value of the Company, upon which a proper exercise of business judgment

---

[21] Trans Union's five "inside" directors had backgrounds in law and accounting, 116 years of collective employment by the Company and 68 years of combined experience on its Board. Trans Union's five "outside" directors included four chief executives of major corporations and an economist who was a former dean of a major school of business and chancellor of a university. The "outside" directors had 78 years of combined experience as chief executive officers of major corporations and 50 years of cumulative experience as directors of Trans Union. Thus, defendants argue that the Board was eminently qualified to reach an informed judgment on the proposed "sale" of Trans Union notwithstanding their lack of any advance notice of the proposal, the shortness of their deliberation, and their determination not to consult with their investment banker or to obtain a fairness opinion.

could be made, mere advice of this type is meaningless; and, given this record of the defendants' failures, it constitutes no defense here.[22]]

A second claim is that counsel advised the Board it would be subject to lawsuits if it rejected the $55 per share offer. It is, of course, a fact of corporate life that today when faced with difficult or sensitive issues, directors often are subject to suit, irrespective of the decisions they make. However, counsel's mere acknowledgement of this circumstance cannot be rationally translated into a justification for a board permitting itself to be stampeded into a patently unadvised act. While suit might result from the rejection of a merger or tender offer, Delaware law makes clear that a board acting within the ambit of the business judgment rule faces no ultimate liability. Thus, we cannot conclude that the mere threat of litigation, acknowledged by counsel, constitutes either legal advice or any valid basis upon which to pursue an uninformed course.

[The court examined the board's post-September 20 conduct and determined that the board had been grossly negligent and that its conduct did not cure the deficiencies in its September 20 actions.]

[As to] questions which were not originally addressed by the parties in their briefing of this case [t]he parties' response, including reargument, has led the majority of the Court to conclude: (1) that since all of the defendant directors, outside as well as inside, take a unified position, we are required to treat all of the directors as one as to whether they are entitled to the protection of the business judgment rule; and (2) that considerations of good faith, including the presumption that the directors acted in good faith, are irrelevant in determining the threshold issue of whether the directors as a Board exercised an informed business judgment. For the same reason, we must reject defense counsel's *ad hominem* argument for affirmance: that reversal may result in a multi-million dollar class award against the defendants for having made an allegedly uninformed business judgment in a transaction not involving any personal gain, self-dealing or claim of bad faith.

[P]laintiffs have not claimed, nor did the Trial Court decide, that $55 was a grossly inadequate price per share for sale of the Company. That being so, the presumption that a board's judgment as to adequacy of price represents an honest exercise of business judgment (absent proof that the sale price was grossly inadequate) is irrelevant to the threshold question of whether an informed judgment was reached.

The defendants ultimately rely on the stockholder vote of February 10 for exoneration. The defendants contend that the stockholders' "overwhelming" vote approving the Pritzker Merger Agreement had the

---

[22] Nonetheless, we are satisfied that in an appropriate factual context a proper exercise of business judgment may include, as one of its aspects, reasonable reliance upon the advice of counsel. This is wholly outside the statutory protections of 8 Del.C. § 141(e) involving reliance upon reports of officers, certain experts and books and records of the company.

legal effect of curing any failure of the Board to reach an informed business judgment in its approval of the merger.

The parties tacitly agree that a discovered failure of the Board to reach an informed business judgment in approving the merger constitutes a voidable, rather than a void, act. Hence, the merger can be sustained, notwithstanding the infirmity of the Board's action, if its approval by majority vote of the shareholders is found to have been based on an informed electorate. *Cf. Michelson v. Duncan*, 407 A.2d 211 (Del.1979), *aff'g in part and rev'g in part*, 386 A.2d 1144 (Del.Ch.1978). The disagreement between the parties arises over: (1) the Board's burden of disclosing to the shareholders all relevant and material information; and (2) the sufficiency of the evidence as to whether the Board satisfied that burden.

The burden must fall on defendants who claim ratification based on shareholder vote to establish that the shareholder approval resulted from a fully informed electorate. On the record before us, it is clear that the Board failed to meet that burden.

To summarize: we hold that the directors of Trans Union breached their fiduciary duty to their stockholders (1) by their failure to inform themselves of all information reasonably available to them and relevant to their decision to recommend the Pritzker merger; and (2) by their failure to disclose all material information such as a reasonable stockholder would consider important in deciding whether to approve the Pritzker offer.

We hold, therefore, that the Trial Court committed reversible error in applying the business judgment rule in favor of the director defendants in this case.

On remand, the Court of Chancery shall conduct an evidentiary hearing to determine the fair value of the shares represented by the plaintiffs' class, based on the intrinsic value of Trans Union on September 20, 1980. Thereafter, an award of damages may be entered to the extent that the fair value of Trans Union exceeds $55 per share.

Reversed and Remanded for proceedings consistent herewith.

MCNEILLY, JUSTICE, dissenting:

The majority opinion reads like an advocate's closing address to a hostile jury. And I say that not lightly. Throughout the opinion great emphasis is directed only to the negative, with nothing more than lip service granted the positive aspects of this case. In my opinion Chancellor Marvel (retired) should have been affirmed. The Chancellor's opinion was the product of well reasoned conclusions, based upon a sound deductive process, clearly supported by the evidence and entitled to deference in this appeal. Because of my diametrical opposition to all evidentiary conclusions of the majority, I respectfully dissent.

It would serve no useful purpose, particularly at this late date, for me to dissent at great length. I restrain myself from doing so, but feel compelled to at least point out what I consider to be the most glaring deficiencies in the majority opinion. The majority has spoken and has effectively said that Trans Union's Directors have been the victims of a "fast shuffle" by Van Gorkom and Pritzker. That is the beginning of the majority's comedy of errors. The first and most important error made is the majority's assessment of the directors' knowledge of the affairs of Trans Union and their combined ability to act in this situation under the protection of the business judgment rule.

Trans Union's Board of Directors consisted of ten men, five of whom were "inside" directors and five of whom were "outside" directors. The "inside" directors were Van Gorkom, Chelberg, Bonser, William B. Browder, Senior Vice-President—Law, and Thomas P. O'Boyle, Senior Vice-President—Administration. At the time the merger was proposed the inside five directors had collectively been employed by the Company for 116 years and had 68 years of combined experience as directors. The "outside" directors were A.W. Wallis, William B. Johnson, Joseph B. Lanterman, Graham J. Morgan and Robert W. Reneker. With the exception of Wallis, these were all chief executive officers of Chicago based corporations that were at least as large as Trans Union. The five "outside" directors had 78 years of combined experience as chief executive officers, and 53 years cumulative service as Trans Union directors.

The inside directors wear their badge of expertise in the corporate affairs of Trans Union on their sleeves. But what about the outsiders? Dr. Wallis is or was an economist and math statistician, a professor of economics at Yale University, dean of the graduate school of business at the University of Chicago, and Chancellor of the University of Rochester. Dr. Wallis had been on the Board of Trans Union since 1962. He also was on the Board of Bausch & Lomb, Kodak, Metropolitan Life Insurance Company, Standard Oil and others.

William B. Johnson is a University of Pennsylvania law graduate, President of Railway Express until 1966, Chairman and Chief Executive of I.C. Industries Holding Company, and member of Trans Union's Board since 1968.

Joseph Lanterman, a Certified Public Accountant, is or was President and Chief Executive of American Steel, on the Board of International Harvester, Peoples Energy, Illinois Bell Telephone, Harris Bank and Trust Company, Kemper Insurance Company and a director of Trans Union for four years.

Graham Morgan is a chemist, was Chairman and Chief Executive Officer of U.S. Gypsum, and in the 17 and 18 years prior to the Trans Union transaction had been involved in 31 or 32 corporate takeovers.

Robert Reneker attended University of Chicago and Harvard Business Schools. He was President and Chief Executive of Swift and Company, director of Trans Union since 1971, and member of the Boards of seven other corporations including U.S. Gypsum and the Chicago Tribune.

Directors of this caliber are not ordinarily taken in by a "fast shuffle". I submit they were not taken into this multi-million dollar corporate transaction without being fully informed and aware of the state of the art as it pertained to the entire corporate panorama of Trans Union. True, even directors such as these, with their business acumen, interest and expertise, can go astray. I do not believe that to be the case here. These men knew Trans Union like the back of their hands and were more than well qualified to make on the spot informed business judgments concerning the affairs of Trans Union including a 100% sale of the corporation. Lest we forget, the corporate world of then and now operates on what is so aptly referred to as "the fast track". These men were at the time an integral part of that world, all professional business men, not intellectual figureheads.

The majority of this Court holds that the Board's decision, reached on September 20, 1980, to approve the merger was not the product of an *informed* business judgment, that the Board's subsequent efforts to amend the Merger Agreement and take other curative action were *legally and factually* ineffectual, and that the Board did *not deal with complete candor* with the stockholders by failing to disclose all material facts, which they knew or should have known, before securing the stockholders' approval of the merger. I disagree.

At the time of the September 20, 1980 meeting the Board was acutely aware of Trans Union and its prospects. The problems created by accumulated investment tax credits and accelerated depreciation were discussed repeatedly at Board meetings, and all of the directors understood the problem thoroughly. Moreover, at the July, 1980 Board meeting the directors had reviewed Trans Union's newly prepared five-year forecast, and at the August, 1980 meeting Van Gorkom presented the results of a comprehensive study of Trans Union made by The Boston Consulting Group. This study was prepared over an 18 month period and consisted of a detailed analysis of all Trans Union subsidiaries, including competitiveness, profitability, cash throw-off, cash consumption, technical competence and future prospects for contribution to Trans Union's combined net income.

At the September 20 meeting Van Gorkom reviewed all aspects of the proposed transaction and repeated the explanation of the Pritzker offer he had earlier given to senior management. Having heard Van Gorkom's explanation of the Pritzker's offer, and Brennan's explanation of the merger documents the directors discussed the matter. Out of this discussion arose an insistence on the part of the directors that two modifications to the offer be made. First, they required that any potential competing bidder be given access to the same information concerning Trans Union that had been provided to the Pritzkers. Second, the merger documents were to be modified to reflect the fact that the directors could accept a better offer and would not be required to recommend the Pritzker offer if a better offer was made.

I have no quarrel with the majority's analysis of the business judgment rule. It is the application of that rule to these facts which is wrong. An overview of the entire record, rather than the limited view of bits and pieces which the majority has exploded like popcorn, convinces me that the directors made an informed business judgment which was buttressed by their test of the market.

ON MOTIONS FOR REARGUMENT

Following this Court's decision, Thomas P. O'Boyle, one of the director defendants, sought, and was granted, leave for change of counsel. Thereafter, the individual director defendants, other than O'Boyle, filed a motion for reargument and director O'Boyle, through newly-appearing counsel, then filed a separate motion for reargument. Plaintiffs have responded to the several motions and this matter has now been duly considered.

Although O'Boyle continues to adopt his fellow directors' arguments, O'Boyle now asserts in the alternative that he has standing to take a position different from that of his fellow directors and that legal grounds exist for finding him not liable for the acts or omissions of his fellow directors.

We reject defendant O'Boyle's new argument as to standing because not timely asserted. Our reasons are several. *One,* in connection with the supplemental briefing of this case in March, 1984, a special opportunity was afforded the individual defendants, including O'Boyle, to present any factual or legal reasons why each or any of them should be individually treated. Thereafter, at argument before the Court on June 11, 1984, the following colloquy took place between this Court and counsel for the individual defendants at the outset of counsel's argument:

> Counsel: I'll make the argument on behalf of the nine individual defendants against whom the plaintiffs seek more than $100,000,000 in damages. That is the ultimate issue in this case, whether or not nine honest, experienced businessmen should be subject to damages in a case where—
>
> Justice Moore: Is there a distinction between Chelberg and Van Gorkom vis-à-vis the other defendants?
>
> Counsel: No, sir.
>
> Justice Moore: None whatsoever?
>
> Counsel: I think not.

Two, in this Court's Opinion dated January 29, 1985, the Court relied on the individual defendants as having presented a unified defense. We stated:

> The parties' response, including reargument, has led the majority of the Court to conclude: (1) that since all of the defendant directors, outside as well as inside, take a unified position, we are required to treat all of the directors as one as to whether they are entitled to the protection of the business judgment rule.

VAN GORKOM *AND ITS AFTERMATH*

1.   The defendant directors of Trans Union settled *Van Gorkom* by paying $23.5 million to the plaintiff class. The payments were made to approximately 12,000 former shareholders of Trans Union who held stock between September 19, 1980 and February 10, 1981. Of that amount, the directors' liability insurance carrier paid about $10 million. The $13.5 million balance was paid by the Pritzker group on behalf of the Trans Union directors, even though the Pritzker group was not a defendant. The Pritzker group did, however, have the directors pay 10 percent of their uninsured liability to charity, which in the case of some directors was paid by Van Gorkom. *Roundtable Discussion: Corporate Governance*, 77 Chi.-Kent L. Rev. 235, 238, 242 (2001) (comments of Robert Pritzker, CEO of the Marmon Group).

2.   *Van Gorkom* created a firestorm in much of the corporate community. Few had believed that the Delaware Supreme Court would hold experienced directors liable in a case in which the shareholders received a 50% premium over the existing market price for their stock, notwithstanding Justice Moore's colloquy with counsel in the final reargument. The embers of the firestorm still can be seen, as illustrated by a 2000 roundtable discussion of lawyers and corporate directors who reminisced about the decision:

> *Ira Millstein:* This case sent shock waves through the boardrooms of the United States because I guarantee you 99% of boards didn't think that anything wrong had happened. Most everybody wrote about the decision as "the Delaware courts are going nuts." Most academics thought it was crazy. Most directors were horrified.

> *Boris Yavitz:* What Ira is describing as a typical board is pretty much what I saw in the very early years of my service, which goes back to about 1975. Most boards were not much more than rubber stamps. The CEO said "Jump" and directors were allowed just one question: How high? It wasn't a matter of not arguing with the boss—you typically didn't even question him.

> *Steven Friedman:* Everybody seems to imply that the process was wrong but the end result was right. You see in the published accounts that KKR was willing to pay $60, and also that GE Capital was willing to pay more. Both of them were turned off by the fact that

there was a signed merger agreement and a clear message of "Don't mess with my deal." So I think that we should criticize this board not just for the process but for their decision.

Boris Yavitz: What happened is that all directors got the message: It is *procedure, procedure, procedure* that counts. Everything else doesn't mean very much. We were clearly panicked about what could happen if we didn't do what the lawyers said. We went through a tightly scripted process, which we hoped would end up with us not being sued but, even more hopefully, end up with the right decision. It was of great concern to me that we directors seemed to abandon much of our judgment to the security guards.

Ira Millstein: On behalf of the legal community, I will say that this was happening for a good reason, which was that you *hadn't* been doing your job. What happened with *Smith v. Van Gorkom* is it gave the lawyers an opportunity to act like lawyers for change. Most lawyers knew generally what was required—that the board had to make a good faith judgment. But if you went into a boardroom before *Smith v. Van Gorkom* and tried to talk about legal obligations, they'd say, "We have more important things to do than listen to you tell us about what we ought to be doing." When *Smith* came down, you were able to walk into a boardroom for the first time in my experience and really be heard. That was a good thing to have happen. Up until then it was more missionary work—talking about good and evil and how you really "ought" to do your jobs.

Roundtable: The Legacy of "Smith v. Van Gorkom," 24 Directors and Boards 28, 32–37 (Spring 2000).

3.   The fear of liability that arose after *Van Gorkom* has subsided. Almost immediately after the decision, Delaware adopted DGCL § 102(b)(7), which allows the exculpation of directors from personal liability for money damages for the breach of the duty of care. The landscape also looks very different from the way it appeared to the decision's initial critics. The "greater randomness and unpredictability on the part of future courts passing on future board decisions" that had been predicted does not seem to have occurred. More important, subsequent courts and scholars have reinterpreted the case. As Justice Moore has noted, "[i]t is said that the case pushed aside the business judgment rule and a court substituted its own business judgment. That is incorrect. *Van Gorkom* was much more a case about the process in the takeover environment than anything else." Andrew G.T. Moore II, *The 1980s—Did We Save the Stockholders While the Corporation Burned?* 70 Wash. U. L.Q. 277, 281 (1992). And recall that in *Caremark*, Chancellor Allen cited *Van Gorkom* as the first case involving the "jurisprudence concerning takeovers" in which the Delaware Supreme Court indicated its "seriousness" about the role of the corporate board.

4.   *Van Gorkom* focused attention on the board decision-making process. It also established "gross negligence" as the standard for liability. The Official

Comment to MBCA § 8.30(b) describes the standard of conduct for how directors should become informed:

> The phrase "becoming informed," in the context of the decision-making function, refers to the process of gaining sufficient familiarity with the background facts and circumstances in order to make an informed judgment. Unless the circumstances would permit a reasonable director to conclude that he or she is already sufficiently informed, the standard of care requires every director to take steps to become informed about the background facts and circumstances before taking action on the matter at hand. The process typically involves review of written materials provided before or at the meeting and attention to/participation in the deliberations leading up to a vote. It can involve consideration of information and data generated by persons other than legal counsel, public accountants, etc., retained by the corporation, as contemplated by subsection (e)(2); for example, review of industry studies or research articles prepared by unrelated parties could be very useful. It can also involve direct communications, outside of the boardroom, with members of management or other directors. There is no one way for "becoming informed," and both the method and measure—"how to" and "how much"—are matters of reasonable judgment for the director to exercise.

Note that the last sentence of the Official Comment suggests that "how to" and "how much" are themselves questions of business judgment that are subject to the same business judgment rule protection as other decisions. Chancellor Allen reached the same conclusion in *Caremark* when he stated that "the level of detail for such an information system is a question of business judgment."

5.   One significant issue in Van Gorkom was whether the board was required to seek a "fairness opinion" from an investment bank. (A fairness opinion is a letter or memorandum from an investment bank to the board of directors opining that the consideration to be received by shareholders in a transaction will be "fair from a financial point of view." Since, "Due care in the decisionmaking context is process due care only," *Brehm v. Eisner*, 746 A.2d 244, 264 (Del. 2000), a fairness opinion can support a demonstration that the board has employed a reasonable process in reaching its decision.) Although the court did not hold that such an opinion is legally required, many lawyers have assumed that a fairness opinion is a necessity in every corporate acquisition.

In fact, the Trans Union board may actually have been presented with a valuation study of the company before the September meeting. According to Robert Pritzker (brother of Jay Pritzker and later CEO of the Marmon Group), the Boston Consulting Group had prepared an 18-month study of Trans Union, which apparently concluded the company had a value of $55/share. *Roundtable Discussion: Corporate Governance*, 77 Chi.-Kent L. Rev. 235, 238, 242 ("As I understand it, the Boston Consulting Groups tried to make an evaluation [c]onsiderably before [the September 20 meeting]. It was told to me that it was

$55 a share."). The Delaware Supreme Court was aware of the Boston Consulting Group study. Justice McNeilly's dissent refers to it as "a comprehensive study" supporting his conclusion that the board was "acutely aware of Trans Union and its prospects." The majority opinion in a footnote, however, states "no one even referred to [the Boston Consulting Group study] at the September 20 meeting; and it is conceded that these materials do not represent valuation studies."

6.   Justice Moore has written of *Van Gorkom* that there was

> one aspect of the case that the Court found especially troublesome. Trans Union's directors were stalwart in their unified defense of what occurred. This position was taken even though it was obvious that certain directors were more culpable than others, and in the face of the Court's invitation that they take separate positions with a clear hint of exoneration for all but the most culpable insiders. Indeed, one of the directors was ill and did not even attend the meeting at which the merger was approved. In a way, they were "daring" us to find them all liable in a strategic maneuver to save certain insiders. In light of our decision finding all the directors liable, the strategic maneuver to cast down the gauntlet before the Delaware Supreme Court hardly appears to have been among the wisest decisions in the annals of corporate America.

Andrew G.T. Moore II, *The 1980s—Did We Save the Stockholders While the Corporation Burned?* 70 Wash. U. L.Q. 277, 281–282 (1992).

Suppose, however, that the Trans Union defendants had accepted the court's invitation to invoke individual defenses. What legal theory would the court have used to exonerate individual directors in light of the court's finding that the directors collectively had been grossly negligent in not being fully informed about the fair value of the Trans Union shares? Are there varying degrees of gross negligence for different directors?

7.   A significant change in MBCA § 8.30 is the emphasis on the board as a collective decision-making body. Although under MBCA § 8.30 (a) *each member* must perform her duties in good faith and in a manner she believes to be in the best interests of the corporation, the standard of conduct under MBCA § 8.30(b) involving board decision-making and oversight refers to *the members of the board* collectively. The Official Comment to MBCA § 8.30 notes that the board generally performs its duties through collegial action and, in several places, emphasizes that in evaluating board actions, it will be the conduct of the entire board rather than a particular director that will be most important:

> [D]irectors often act collegially in performing their functions and discharging their duties. If the observance of the directors' conduct is called into question, courts will typically evaluate the conduct of the entire board (or committee). Deficient performance of section 8.30 duties on the part of a particular director may be overcome, absent unusual circumstances, by acceptable conduct (meeting, for example, subsection (b)'s standard of care) on the part of other directors

sufficient in number to perform the function or discharge the duty in question. While not thereby remedied, the deficient performance becomes irrelevant in any evaluation of the action taken.

Similarly, when discussing the extent to which directors can rely on officers and outside experts, the Official Comment notes:

Recognition in the statute of the right of one director to rely on the expertise and experience of another director, in the context of board or committee deliberations, is unnecessary, for the group's reliance on shared experience and wisdom is an implicit underpinning of director conduct. In relying on another member of the board, a director would quite properly take advantage of the colleague's knowledge and experience in becoming informed about the matter at hand before taking action; however, the director would be expected to exercise independent judgment when it comes time to vote.

Nevertheless, when it comes to director liability, the MBCA standards of liability for directors focuses on the individual director, who can become liable if "not informed to an extent the director reasonably believed appropriate in the circumstances." MBCA § 8.31(a)(2)(ii)(B).

2. RELIANCE

In *Van Gorkom*, the court rejected the directors' argument that they were protected from liability because they relied on the information that Van Gorkom presented to them. Such reliance is not unusual. Indeed, directors—especially outside directors, who are necessarily less involved in the everyday affairs of a corporation—routinely rely on the chief executive officer and other top management for information and recommendations in connection with their decision-making. Such reliance is clearly efficient, and it is sound policy that directors generally should be entitled to rely on that information when the care with which they have acted is challenged.

There may be limits, however, on the extent to which reliance may be justified. Reports to the board may contain on their face sufficient warning of their own inadequacy to put a reasonable director on notice that better information should be demanded. And reports prepared by or under the supervision of corporate employees who have a personal interest in the outcome of the decision on which they bear may require closer than usual scrutiny.

Directors also frequently rely on opinions provided by attorneys, accountants, engineers, financial specialists, and other expert professional advisors. Here again the general rule is that such reliance is justified and protects directors who relied in good faith on such advice against liability if the advice turns out to be poor.

Reliance imposes certain standards of conduct on directors. MBCA § 8.30(d) provides:

In discharging board or committee duties a director, who does not have knowledge that makes reliance unwarranted, is entitled to rely on information, opinions, reports or statements, including financial statements and other financial data, prepared or presented by any of the persons specified in subsection (e).

The Official Comment to Section 8.30(d) suggests doing homework is part of the directorial standard of conduct, permitting reliance on information presented to a director "only if the director has read the information, opinion, report or statement in question, or was present at a meeting at which it was orally presented, or took other steps to become generally familiar with it." What does this statement mean? Can a director ever rely on a lengthy and technical report that she would not understand even if she read it? Or could such a report be the basis for reliance if it contained an executive summary understandable to the director? What "other steps" must the director take?

Absent from the MBCA, however, is any specific mention whether reliance (and reading reports presented to directors) is a defense to liability under § 8.31. The Official Comment explains that a director must reasonably believe her decisions are in the corporation's best interests after becoming sufficiently informed. In evaluating a particular decision, reasonable reliance may be important to a director in forming a subjective belief that the decision is in the corporation's best interests and an objective belief that the decision is within the realm of reason.

3. LACK OF OBJECTIVITY

Recall Justice McNeilly's dissent in *Van Gorkom* in which he asserted the majority had accepted that the Trans Union directors had been victims of a "fast shuffle" by Van Gorkom and Pritzker. Although the majority opinion focused on the directors' failure to become informed about the value of the company, the court presumed that "the directors reached their business judgment in good faith, and considerations of motive are irrelevant to the issue before us." What if this presumption were wrong, and the directors had passively sought to be accommodating to Van Gorkom? Could the directors have been liable for lacking independence and being dominated by Van Gorkom?

As we saw in Chapter 16, the question of director independence arises frequently in cases involving dismissal by the board (or a special litigation committee) of derivative litigation, authorization of conflict-of-interest transactions, and approval of takeover defenses. Typically, however, the issue in these cases has been the validity of the directors' action rather than their individual liability for succumbing to management pressure.

The MBCA expressly recognizes that a lack of objectivity or independence may create a conflict of interest that exposes a director to individual liability. MBCA § 8.31(a)(2)(iii). Under that provision, a director can become liable for the losses suffered in a corporate transaction if the transaction resulted from a director's lack of objectivity due to the director's familial, financial or business relationship with a person having a "material interest" in the transaction, or if the interested person dominates or controls the director.

Section 8.31, which codifies the "lack of objectivity" concept, distinguishes between a lack of objectivity due to a familial relationship and a lack of independence because the director is dominated. The Official Comment explains:

> If the matter at issue involves lack of independence, the proof of domination or control and its influence on the director's judgment will typically entail different (and perhaps more convincing) evidence than what may be involved in a lack of objectivity case. The variables are manifold, and the facts must be sorted out and weighed on a case-by-case basis. If that other person is the director's spouse or employer, the concern that the director's judgment might be improperly influenced would be substantially greater than if that person is the spouse of the director's step-grandchild or the director's partner in a vacation time-share.

If the plaintiff can establish that the relationship or domination could reasonably be expected to affect the director's judgment, the director is then given the opportunity to prove that she reasonably believed that her action was in the best interests of the corporation. The reasonableness of that belief is tested not only by the director's own honest and good faith belief, but also on considerations of the fairness of the transaction to the corporation.

4. CAUSATION

Claims that directors failed to exercise reasonable care generally fall into two categories. In nonfeasance cases, such as *Francis* and *Caremark*, the plaintiffs charge that if directors had carried out their oversight duties with more diligence, they would have prevented events that caused the corporation a loss. Cases involving allegedly deficient decisions can be said to involve misfeasance. For example, in transactional cases, such as *Van Gorkom,* the plaintiffs charge that if directors had been sufficiently informed they would not have approved a specific transaction which caused losses to the corporation or its shareholders. In each case, an essential element of the plaintiffs' case would seem to be that the defendant directors' breach of duty, and not other factors, was the proximate cause of the loss in question.

The "proximate cause" element can be traced to Judge Learned Hand's decision in *Barnes v. Andrews*, 298 F. 614, 616–617 (S.D.N.Y.1924). There Judge Hand found that Andrews, an accommodation director of a corporation that had become bankrupt, had been inexcusably inattentive in carrying out his directorial responsibilities. Nonetheless, Judge Hand declined to hold Andrews liable because plaintiff had not proven that Andrews' negligence had caused the corporation to fail:

> This cause of action rests upon a tort, as much though it be a tort of omission as though it had rested upon a positive act. The plaintiff must accept the burden of showing that the performance of the defendant's duties would have avoided loss, and what loss it would have avoided.
>
> When the corporate funds have been illegally lent, it is a fair inference that a protest would have stopped the loan, and that the director's neglect caused the loss, but when a business fails from general mismanagement, business incapacity, or bad judgment, how is it possible to say that a single director could have made the company successful, or how much in dollars he could have saved? Before this cause can go to a master, the plaintiff must show that, had Andrews done his full duty, he could have made the company prosper, or at least could have broken its fall. He must show what sum he could have saved the company. Neither of these has he made any effort to do.
>
> The defendant is not subject to the burden of proving that the loss would have happened, whether he had done his duty or not. If he were, it would come to this: That, if a director were once shown slack in his duties, he would stand charged prima facie with the difference between the corporate treasury as it was, and as it would be, judged by a hypothetical standard of success. How could such a standard be determined? How could any one guess how far a director's skill and judgment would have prevailed upon his fellows, and what would have been the ultimate fate of the business, if they had? How is it possible to set any measure of liability, or to tell what he would have contributed to the event? Men's fortunes may not be subjected to such uncertain and speculative conjectures. It is hard to see how there can be any remedy, except one can put one's finger on a definite loss and say with reasonable assurance that protest would have deterred, or counsel persuaded, the managers who caused it. No men of sense would take the office, if the law imposed upon them a guaranty of the general success of their companies as a penalty for any negligence.

As is evidenced by *Barnes,* requiring causal proof reduces considerably the likelihood that inattentive directors will be held liable in cases of general business failure. Even with the benefit of 20/20 hindsight, how can it be shown that an inattentive director might have made a difference in the business collapse? In a case of management misbehavior, as *Francis* demonstrates, this burden is not insurmountable. There the court defined

Mrs. Pritchard's duties so that her non-performance could be seen as the proximate cause of the corporation's losses:

> In this case, the scope of Mrs. Pritchard's duties was determined by the precarious financial condition of Pritchard & Baird, its fiduciary relationship to its clients and the implied trust in which it held their funds. Thus viewed, the scope of her duties encompassed all reasonable action to stop the continuing conversion. Her duties extended beyond mere objection and resignation to reasonable attempts to prevent the misappropriation of the trust funds.

> Within Pritchard & Baird, several factors contributed to the loss of the funds: commingling of corporate and client monies, conversion of funds by Charles, Jr. and William and dereliction of her duties by Mrs. Pritchard. The wrongdoing of her sons, although the immediate cause of the loss, should not excuse Mrs. Pritchard from her negligence which also was a substantial factor contributing to the loss. Her sons knew that she, the only other director, was not reviewing their conduct; they spawned their fraud in the backwater of her neglect. Her neglect of duty contributed to the climate of corruption; her failure to act contributed to the continuation of that corruption. Consequently, her conduct was a substantial factor contributing to the loss.

> Analysis of proximate cause is especially difficult in a corporate context where the allegation is that nonfeasance of a director is a proximate cause of damage to a third party. Nonetheless, where it is reasonable to conclude that the failure to act would produce a particular result and that result has followed, causation may be inferred. We conclude that even if Mrs. Pritchard's mere objection had not stopped the depredations of her sons, her consultation with an attorney and the threat of suit would have deterred them. That conclusion flows as a matter of common sense and logic from the record. Whether in other situations a director has a duty to do more than protest and resign is best left to case-by-case determinations. In this case, we are satisfied that there was a duty to do more than object and resign. Consequently, we find that Mrs. Pritchard's negligence was a proximate cause of the misappropriations.

> To conclude, by virtue of her office, Mrs. Pritchard had the power to prevent the losses sustained by the clients of Pritchard & Baird. With power comes responsibility. She had a duty to deter the depredation of the other insiders, her sons. She breached that duty and caused plaintiffs to sustain damages.

432 A.2d at 827–829.

In a transactional setting, it is easier to prove that a breach of the duty of care caused a given loss than in a case in which the directors failed to act. If the directors wrongfully approved a transaction, the plaintiff usually can plausibly contend that had the directors been more diligent, the transaction would not have occurred and the resulting loss would have been avoided. In *Van Gorkom,* for example, plaintiffs established that Trans Union's directors had been grossly negligent in agreeing to sell the company for $55 per share. That, however, did not necessarily mean the directors were liable. Indeed, the Delaware Supreme Court remanded the case with instructions that the Court of Chancery "conduct an evidentiary hearing to determine the fair value of [Trans Union's] stock as of the date of the board's decision. Thereafter, an award of damages *may be entered* to the extent that the fair value of Trans Union exceeds $55 per share." (emphasis added). The implication of the court's instructions, consistent with *Barnes'* causation requirement, appeared to be that if the Court of Chancery determined Trans Union had not been worth more than $55 per share, no damages would be awarded.

5. REBUTTING THE PRESUMPTION OF THE BUSINESS JUDGMENT RULE

Recall that the business judgment rule is often stated as a rebuttable presumption. The difficulty of rebutting the presumption has acted as a virtually impregnable shield for directors when the wisdom of their business decisions are challenged. But suppose that the plaintiff is able to rebut the presumption, either because the director was not independent and thus not acting in good faith or was not fully informed. Is rebuttal enough to establish the defendant's liability? If not, what happens in the next stage of the litigation?

Answering these questions involves the concept of fairness that will be developed more fully in the next chapter. In *Cede & Co. v. Technicolor, Inc.*, 634 A.2d 345 (Del. 1993) (*Cede II*), the Delaware Supreme Court held that "a breach of either the duty of loyalty or the duty of care rebuts the presumption that the directors have acted in the best interests of the shareholders, and requires the directors to prove that the transaction was entirely fair." Chancellor Allen interpreted this language to mean that "under the Delaware version of the 'business judgment rule,' if a shareholder establishes director negligence, thus overcoming the presumption, he or she has established a prima facie case of liability." *Cinerama, Inc. v. Technicolor, Inc. (Cede III)*, 663 A.2d 1134, 1137 (Del.Ch. 1994).

On appeal, the Delaware Supreme Court stated:

The business judgment rule "operates as both a procedural guide for litigants and a substantive rule of law." As a procedural guide the business judgment presumption is a rule of evidence that places the initial burden of proof on the plaintiff. In *Cede II*, this Court described the rule's evidentiary, or procedural, operation as follows:

> If a shareholder plaintiff fails to meet this evidentiary burden, the business judgment rule attaches to protect corporate officers and directors and the decisions they make, and our courts will not second-guess these business judgments. If the rule is rebutted, the burden shifts to the defendant directors, the proponents of the challenged transaction, to prove to the trier of fact the "entire fairness" of the transaction to the shareholder plaintiff.

Burden shifting does not create per se liability on the part of the directors. Rather, it "is a procedure by which Delaware courts of equity determine under what standard of review director liability is to be judged." In remanding this case for review under the entire fairness standard, this Court expressly acknowledged that its holding in *Cede II* did not establish liability.

Where, as in this case, the presumption of the business judgment rule has been rebutted, the board of directors' action is examined under the entire fairness standard. This Court has described the dual aspects of entire fairness, as follows:

> The concept of fairness has two basic aspects: fair dealing and fair price. The former embraces questions of when the transaction was timed, how it was initiated, structured, negotiated, disclosed to the directors, and how the approvals of the directors and the stockholders were obtained. The latter aspect of fairness relates to the economic and financial considerations of the proposed merger, including all relevant factors: assets, market value, earnings, future prospects, and any other elements that affect the intrinsic or inherent value of a company's stock. . . . However, the test for fairness is not a bifurcated one as between fair dealing and price. All aspects of the issue must be examined as a whole since the question is one of entire fairness.

Weinberger v. UOP, Inc., 457 A.2d at 711. Thus, the entire fairness standard requires the board of directors to establish "to the court's satisfaction that the transaction was the product of both fair dealing and fair price." *Cede II, 634 A.2d at 361*.

Because the decision that the procedural presumption of the business judgment rule has been rebutted does not establish substantive liability under the entire fairness standard, such a ruling does not necessarily present an insurmountable obstacle for a board of directors to overcome. Thus, an initial judicial determination that a given breach of a board's fiduciary duties has rebutted the presumption of the business judgment rule does not preclude a subsequent judicial determination that the board action was entirely fair, and is, therefore, not outcome-determinative per se. To avoid substantive liability, notwithstanding the quantum of adverse evidence that has defeated the business judgment rule's protective procedural presumption, the board will have to demonstrate entire fairness by presenting evidence of the cumulative manner by which it otherwise discharged all of its fiduciary duties.

Cinerama, Inc. v. Technicolor, Inc. (Cede IV), 663 A.2d. 1156, 1162–63 (Del. 1995).

The traditional concept of "fair price" is the range of values that two independent parties might agree to in an arms-length transaction. Where a director is financially interested in the transaction, that can be a useful measuring rod for determining the validity of the transaction although many questions arise in that determination.

But if, as was true in *Van Gorkom,* there is an arms-length transaction and the presumption of the business judgment rule is rebutted because the directors were not fully informed, is fairness an appropriate standard for determining liability? If so, how would it be determined? Does the failure to be informed constitute a *per se* breach of the fair dealing requirement so that a plaintiff would only have to prove an unfair price? Or can the directors successfully argue that their failure is evaluated differently when rebutting the presumption of the business judgment rule than when determining whether they have satisfied their duty of fair dealing? Consider the Delaware Supreme Court's discussion of *Van Gorkom* in *Cede IV*. Does it answer these questions satisfactorily?

F. AVOIDANCE OF LIABILITY

In the 1980s, many states enacted legislation to reduce the risk of directors' personal liability for monetary damages. The statutory exculpations took three different forms: the authorization of charter provisions eliminating or reducing the personal liability of directors for monetary damages, primarily in due care cases; a change in the standard of liability to require a higher degree of fault than ordinary negligence; and a limit on the monetary amount for which a director could be held personally liable.

Statutory exculpation and indemnification are closely related. As the ABA Committee on Corporate Laws has noted:

Liability limitation insulates the director from personal liability for acts or omissions that have not yet occurred but that might otherwise give rise to personal liability. Indemnification protects the director from personal liability for acts or omissions that occurred in the past. Both liability limitation and indemnification shift from the director to the corporation the ultimate economic cost for the director's acts and omissions. Both liability limitation and indemnification, therefore, are addressed to the issue of allocation, between the directors and the corporation, of the economic cost of certain actual or alleged wrongful conduct by a director.

American Bar Association Committee on Corporate Laws, *Changes in the Model Business Corporation Act—Amendments Pertaining to Indemnification and Advance for Expenses*, 49 Bus. Law. 741, 742 (1994).

Some critics recognize the need to reduce the risks and costs of frivolous litigation but argue that the risk shifting created by indemnification and insurance reduces management's incentive to act responsibly and thus impedes an effective system of management accountability. The congressional response to the corporate scandals of the 2000s in SOX, which imposes individual liability on corporate executives who certify financial statements and increases criminal sanctions for securities fraud, suggests a reinvigoration of the philosophy against risk shifting. Others have argued that greater liability is unnecessary, because shareholders are efficient risk bearers and can diversify their investments. In contrast, corporate managers are undiversified risk bearers who are not able to work for more than one firm at a time. Hence, unless they are paid to do otherwise, they will tend to evaluate business decisions with a risk-averse bias that may be detrimental to the best interests of the stockholders.

Problem: FiberNet Corporation—Part 5

FiberNet did acquire LaserTek, and, after just over a year, it has become clear that the acquisition was a failure. The software for LaserTek's principal product turns out to have been poorly designed. Bugs in the software have led to major outages at several of FiberNet's customers causing FiberNet to absorb millions of dollars in liquidated damages. The code has required a major rewrite, which has cost several million dollars of unplanned R&D expense that, together with the liquidated damages, has substantially reduced FiberNet's profitability. In the first six months after the acquisition, FiberNet's stock price fell almost 40%, although it has since begun to recover, as its original business has remained strong.

(A)

A shareholder derivative suit has been filed against the directors, alleging that they were grossly negligent in approving the acquisition. Sam Brown has asked for your advice on the following questions:

1. Can the corporation advance the directors money for their attorneys' fees in the lawsuit?

2. What procedure must be followed?

3. Must any conditions be imposed on the payments?

(B)

The lawsuit is eventually settled, with the defendants paying $15 million, all but $1 million of which is covered by the company's directors' and officers' liability policy. The directors also incurred an aggregate of $1.5 million in attorneys' fees and expenses. They have asked the corporation to indemnify them for the $1 million in uninsured settlement payments and the $1.5 million in fees and expenses. Sam has asked you the following questions:

1. May FiberNet indemnify the directors for the $1 million in damages not covered by the D&O policy?

2. May FiberNet reimburse the directors for the $1.5 million in attorneys' fees and expenses?

3. What procedure must be followed for any payments to the directors?

4. Are there any limitations on the payments that may be made?

5. If the corporation refuses to indemnify, do the defendants have any other means to recover their expenses?

1. STATUTORY EXCULPATION OF DIRECTORS

Although *Van Gorkom* dramatically increased the potential liability of directors for a breach of the duty of care, that magnification was short-lived. In response to the decision, the Delaware legislature enacted DGCL § 102(b)(7), which enables the exculpation of director liability for a breach of the duty of care. *See* MBCA § 2.02(b)(4) (similar exculpation provision).

> **DGCL § 102(b)(7)**
>
> (b) In addition to the matters required to be set forth in the certificate of incorporation by subsection (a) of this section, the certificate of incorporation may also contain any or all of the following matters: . . .
>
> > (7) A provision eliminating or limiting the personal liability of a director to the corporation or its stockholders for monetary damages for breach of fiduciary duty as a director, provided that such provision shall not eliminate or limit the liability of a director: (i) For any breach of the director's duty of loyalty to the corporation or its stockholders; (ii) for acts or omissions not in good faith or which involve intentional misconduct or a knowing violation of law; (iii) under § 174 of this title; or (iv) for any transaction from which the director derived an improper personal benefit. No such provision shall eliminate or limit the liability of a director for any act or omission occurring prior to the date when such provision becomes effective. All references in this paragraph to a director shall also be deemed to refer to such other person or persons, if any, who, pursuant to a provision of the certificate of incorporation in accordance with § 141(a) of this title, exercise or perform any of the powers or duties otherwise conferred or imposed upon the board of directors by this title.

After the enactment of Section 102(b)(7), most public companies have incorporated an exculpation provision in their charter. *See, e.g.,* Restated Certificate of Facebook, Inc., Art. 7, ¶ 1 (May 22, 2012) ("To the fullest extent permitted by law, no director of the corporation shall be personally liable to the corporation or its stockholders for monetary damages for breach of fiduciary duty as a director."). Section 102(b)(7) exemplifies a statute that permits a charter provision to reduce directors' personal liability for violations of the duty of due care. The section is not self-executing; it requires either that a corporation include an exculpation provision in its original certificate of incorporation or that the stockholders approve an amendment to the certificate. The statute limits exculpation by excluding from its coverage a breach of the director's duty of loyalty to the corporation or its shareholders, acts or omissions not in good faith, intentional misconduct, knowing violations of law, and transactions in which the director has obtained an improper personal benefit, such as from insider trading.

The MBCA contains a similar provision in § 2.02(b)(4). It excludes exculpation from liability for improperly received financial benefits, intentional infliction of harm on the corporation or the shareholders, intentional violations of criminal law or making unlawful distributions. Unlike Delaware, the MBCA does not provide for exculpation from liability for breach of the duty of loyalty or for "acts or omissions not in good faith." In rejecting this approach, the ABA Committee on Corporate Laws noted that the phrase "duty of loyalty" appeared nowhere else in the Delaware statute and that the "acts or omissions" standard was potentially too vague. Committee on Corporate Laws, *Changes in the Revised Model Business Corporation Act—Amendment Pertaining to the Liability of Directors*, 45 Bus. Law. 695, 697 (1990). Both statutes apply only to liability for monetary damages and have no effect on the availability of equitable relief for a breach of fiduciary duty.

Nearly all state corporate statutes now provide for some means of limiting director liability. Some two-thirds of states have followed the Delaware approach of authorizing exculpation provisions in the charter. In some states, the exceptions from exculpation differ from those allowed by DGCL § 102(b)(7) and MBCA § 2.02(b)(4), for example excluding actions that create liability to a third party and improper appropriations of business opportunities of the corporation. Many states have followed MBCA § 2.02(b)(4) in omitting a "duty of loyalty" exception.

A few states have amended their statutes to alter the standard of conduct giving rise to personal liability. For example, under Indiana law, a director who has breached or failed to perform her duties in accordance with the statutory standard of care will not be liable for the breach or failure unless her conduct constituted "willful misconduct or recklessness." Ind.Code Ann. § 23–1–35(1)(e)(2). This limitation applies to actions for equitable relief as well as damages, and includes suits by both third parties and stockholders. Unlike the charter option provisions, these statutes are self-executing. They do not require shareholder approval to become effective nor do they permit the corporation to opt out of the liability limitation provisions, even if the stockholders wish to do so.

Exculpatory clauses in corporate charters may not have eliminated liability for breaches of the duty of care altogether. In *RBC Capital Markets, LLC v. Jervis*, 129 A.3d 816 (Del. 2015) the court found that the board of directors of a corporation had breached its duty of care in approving the sale of the corporation. Although the directors were exculpated from liability pursuant to a § 102(b)(7) provision in the certificate, the court held that the investment banking firm that had advised the board was liable for aiding and abetting the breach. *See also In re Rural Metro Corp.*, 88 A.3d 54, 110 (Del.Ch. 2014). Moreover, as the discussion after *Caremark*, above, indicates, cases that once might have been brought against directors under the duty of care may survive exculpation clauses by being cast as a breach of the duty of loyalty, which cannot be exculpated.

2. INDEMNIFICATION

The right of a corporate officer or director to be indemnified and the power of the corporation to indemnify her voluntarily against damages, fines, or penalties growing out of the performance of corporate duties are governed by both corporate statutes and the articles of incorporation, by-laws or private contracts of the corporation.

The common law concerning the right of a corporate officer or director to indemnification was long confused. Little precedent guided corporations as to the limitations on their power to indemnify directors and officers. Dissatisfaction with the judicial handling of indemnification eventually led New York to enact the first indemnification statute in 1941. Today every jurisdiction has adopted legislation dealing with the matter, and most have enacted comprehensive indemnification statutes.

Indemnification provisions are of two types, permissive and mandatory; comprehensive statutes include both. A permissive, or enabling, provision gives a corporation the power to indemnify its corporate managers under certain circumstances. Mandatory statutes accord a director or officer who meets the statutory standards a right to indemnification.

AMERICAN BAR ASSOCIATION COMMITTEE ON CORPORATE LAWS, CHANGES IN THE MODEL BUSINESS CORPORATION ACT—AMENDMENTS PERTAINING TO INDEMNIFICATION AND ADVANCE FOR EXPENSES
49 Bus. Law. 741, 749–50 (1994).

The provisions for indemnification and advance for expenses of the Model Act are among the most complex and important in the entire Act. Subchapter E of chapter 8 is an integrated treatment of this subject and strikes a balance among important social policies. Its substance is based almost entirely on an amendment to the 1969 Model Act adopted in 1980 and substantially revised in 1994.

Indemnification (including advance for expenses) provides financial protection by the corporation for its directors against exposure to expenses and liabilities that may be incurred by them in connection with legal proceedings based on an alleged breach of duty in their service to or on behalf of the corporation. Today, when both the volume and the cost of litigation have increased dramatically, it would be difficult to persuade responsible persons to serve as directors if they were compelled to bear personally the cost of vindicating the propriety of their conduct in every instance in which it might be challenged. While reasonable people may differ as to what constitutes a meritorious case, almost all would agree that corporate directors should have appropriate protection against personal risk and that the rule of *New York Dock Co. v. McCollom*, 16 N.Y.S.2d 844

(N.Y.Sup.Ct.1939), which denied reimbursement to directors who successfully defended their case on the merits, should as a matter of policy be overruled by statute.

The concept of indemnification recognizes that there will be situations in which the director does not satisfy all of the elements of the standard of conduct set forth in section 8.30(a) or the requirements of some other applicable law but where the corporation should nevertheless be permitted (or required) to absorb the economic costs of any ensuing litigation. A carefully constructed indemnification statute should identify these situations.

If permitted too broadly, however, indemnification may violate equally basic tenets of public policy. It is inappropriate to permit management to use corporate funds to avoid the consequences of certain conduct. For example, a director who intentionally inflicts harm on the corporation should not expect to receive assistance from the corporation for legal or other expenses and should be required to satisfy from his personal assets not only any adverse judgment but also expenses incurred in connection with the proceeding. Any other rule would tend to encourage socially undesirable conduct.

A further policy issue is raised in connection with indemnification against liabilities or sanctions imposed under state or federal civil or criminal statutes. A shift of the economic cost of these liabilities from the individual director to the corporation by way of indemnification may in some instances frustrate the public policy of those statutes.

The fundamental issue that must be addressed by an indemnification statute is the establishment of policies consistent with these broad principles: to ensure that indemnification is permitted only where it will further sound corporate policies and to prohibit indemnification where it might protect or encourage wrongful or improper conduct. As phrased by one commentator, the goal of indemnification is to "seek the middle ground between encouraging fiduciaries to violate their trust, and discouraging them from serving at all." Joseph F. Johnston, *Corporate Indemnification and Liability Insurance for Directors and Officers*, 33 Bus. Law. 1993, 1994 (1978). The increasing number of suits against directors, the increasing cost of defense, and the increasing emphasis on diversifying the membership of boards of directors all militate in favor of workable arrangements to protect directors against liability to the extent consistent with established principles.

E. NORMAN VEASEY, JESSE A. FINKELSTEIN & C. STEPHEN BIGLER, DELAWARE SUPPORTS DIRECTORS WITH A THREE-LEGGED STOOL OF LIMITED LIABILITY, INDEMNIFICATION AND INSURANCE

42 Bus. Law. 401, 404–412 (1987).

Section 145 of the Delaware General Corporation Law is the statutory authority for indemnification. It combines specific statutory rights and limitations on indemnification. It applies to any person involved (as a plaintiff or defendant) in actual or threatened litigation or an investigation by reason of the status of such person as an officer, director, employee, or agent of the corporation or of another corporation, trust, partnership, joint venture, or other enterprise he served at the request of the indemnifying corporation.

The general statutory framework of the entitlement to ultimate indemnification is found in subsections (a) and (b) of section 145. Section 145(a) permits indemnification of officers, directors, employees, and agents for attorneys' fees and other expenses as well as judgments or amounts paid in settlement in civil cases. This subsection applies only to third-party actions, not to actions brought by or in the right of the corporation. The person seeking indemnification must have acted in good faith and in a manner he reasonably believed to be in or not opposed to the best interests of the corporation in respect of the claim made against him. In criminal cases the indemnitee may be indemnified for fines and costs provided that, in addition to the foregoing standard of conduct, he did not have reasonable cause to believe his conduct was unlawful.

Section 145(b) pertains to actions brought by or in the right of the corporation. Most frequently, of course, it applies to derivative suits. This subsection permits indemnification only for attorneys' fees and other expenses. It does not permit indemnification of judgments or amounts paid in settlement. The principal difference between section 145(a) and section 145(b), aside from the fact that the latter permits indemnification only for expenses and attorneys' fees, is that section 145(b) does not permit any indemnification "in respect of any claim, issue or matter as to which such person shall have been adjudged to be liable to the corporation," although it does permit some limited court relief "to the extent that the Court of Chancery or the court in which such action or suit was brought shall determine upon application that, despite the adjudication of liability but in view of all the circumstances of the case, such person is fairly and reasonably entitled to indemnity for such expenses [as the] court shall deem proper." There are no definitive criteria in the statute or the case law articulating the showing that must be made to satisfy the court that indemnification is proper.

[Under section 145(b)] it seems that indemnification may not be made (absent court relief provided in the statute) if the director has been adjudged liable to the corporation on any recognized basis of personal liability such as self-dealing, statutory violations, or gross negligence. This provision must be harmonized with the contemporaneously adopted section 102(b)(7) authorizing the limitation on or elimination of liability of directors in certain cases.

It is important to keep in mind the distinctions between indemnification in respect of third-party actions and that applicable to derivative actions. Section 145(b) permits indemnification only of expenses in derivative suits and does not authorize indemnification of judgments or amounts paid in settlement in derivative suits. On the other hand, such broader indemnification power is expressly authorized for third-party actions by section 145(a). It can be argued that since section 145(b) does not expressly prohibit indemnification of judgments or amounts paid in settlement in derivative suits, such indemnification may be provided under the "nonexclusive" provision of section 145(f). It would seem that since subsections (a) and (b) should be read in *pari materia,* the express inclusion of the broader indemnification power in (a) and its exclusion in (b) demonstrates a legislative intent to prohibit indemnification of judgments or amounts paid in settlement in derivative suits. The policy behind this distinction is based on the fact that in a derivative action the ultimate plaintiff is the corporation on whose behalf the suit is brought. Consequently, any resulting money judgment against, or settlement funds provided by, the defendant is paid to the corporation in order to make it whole. The corporation would not receive that benefit if it were to reimburse a defendant for the amount of the judgment or settlement funds that the defendant is required to pay the corporation.

As mentioned above, section 145(a) authorizes indemnification for various classes of indemnitees in third-party actions, while section 145(b) does so for actions brought by or in the right of the corporation. Although the scope of the permitted indemnification differs, these statutes are permissive. Implementation of the authority granted requires action by the corporation. Indemnification may, therefore, be denied unless it is made mandatory by statute or otherwise.

Mandatory indemnification by statute is provided in section 145(c).

The phrase found in section 145(c), "on the merits or otherwise," permits the indemnitee to be indemnified as a matter of right in the event he wins a judgment on the merits in his favor or if he successfully asserts a "technical" defense, such as a defense based upon a statute of limitations. The same statutory language contemplates the dismissal of the suit in conjunction with a negotiated settlement where the dismissal is with prejudice and without any payment or assumption of liability. A dismissal without prejudice, however, is insufficient to invoke mandatory indemnification under the statute.[1]

One of the biggest problems facing a potential indemnitee is that she will be required to incur immediate expenses such as legal fees long before a final determination is made as to the propriety of her conduct. Can the corporation make advance payments to her to meet these ongoing costs? If so, must someone make a determination as to the probable outcome of the litigation and whether she is likely to satisfy the standard of conduct after the dust settles? Must an advance for litigation expenses be secured? If so, then a dichotomy is created between rich directors who can afford to pay litigation expenses, regardless of whether the corporation advances these expenses, and less affluent directors, who might be unable to afford either litigation or the security for any bond that might be required to secure the advances.

Some statutes eliminate the statutory requirement for such a bond and permit advances upon the giving of an undertaking to repay and the satisfaction of other conditions. MBCA § 8.58(a) does not distinguish between indemnification and the right to receive an advance for expenses. As the Official Comment notes, "a provision requiring indemnification to the fullest extent permitted by law shall be deemed, absent an express statement to the contrary, to include an obligation to advance expenses under section 8.53." Such provisions are prevalent in corporations incorporated in MBCA jurisdictions.

Litigation creates a number of different expenses, including court costs, attorneys' fees, fines, judgments and amounts paid in settlement. Clear public policy reasons require differentiating among them, and the statutes do so. For example, if a corporation could indemnify a director for amounts paid in settlement of a derivative suit, it would be taking from the director with one hand while giving the same amount with the other, a situation that would not be true in a third-party action.

DGCL § 145(b) expressly excludes amounts paid in settlement from expenses that can be indemnified in a derivative suit. By contrast, MBCA § 8.54(a)(3) gives the court the power to order indemnification of the amounts paid in settlement in a derivative suit if, as the Official Comment states, "there are facts peculiar to [the director's] situation that make it fair

---

[1] In 2009, Delaware amended Section 145(f) to provide that rights to indemnification may not be eliminated after the occurrence of the act or omission giving rise to a claim in respect of which indemnification is sought unless the relevant indemnification provision expressly permits such elimination. In 2011, Delaware amended Section 145(f) again to clarify that indemnification or advanced rights in a certificate of incorporation or bylaw cannot be eliminated or impaired by an amendment to either of those documents after the occurrence of the event to which the indemnification or advancement relates unless the original document expressly authorized such elimination or limitation [Ed.]

and reasonable to both the corporation and to the director to override an intra-corporate declination or any otherwise applicable statutory prohibition against indemnification." The presumption in the MBCA is that such situations will be extremely rare.

Among the hardest questions are those connected with the required standard of conduct for indemnification. If after trial, a court determines that an indemnitee is innocent of the charges leveled against her, that determination is sufficient to warrant indemnification. But suppose the indemnitee wins on a technical defense such as the statute of limitations? What about a nolo contendere plea? And suppose the case is settled rather than going to trial so that the court never passes on the merits of the plaintiff's claim concerning the indemnitee's conduct?

Closely related to the standard of conduct is the question of who determines whether it has been met. The statutes suggest four possibilities: the board of directors, the stockholders, independent legal counsel, or a court. Consider the pros and cons of each. In connection with a determination by the board, be aware of a potential trap. Suppose that the board is hostile to the indemnitee and refuses to indemnify her, notwithstanding the statute. Should she have an alternate route to secure the indemnification which the statute contemplates?

The 1994 amendments to the MBCA permit the determinations made under the statute to be made by the board through a majority of its disinterested directors. § 8.50 defines a "disinterested director" as one who, at the time of the vote, "is not (i) a party to the proceeding, or (ii) an individual having a familial, financial, professional, or employment relationship with the director whose indemnification or advance for expenses is the subject of the decision being made, which relationship would, in the circumstances, reasonably be expected to exert an influence on the director's judgment when voting on the decision being made." Keep this definition in mind when you read the next chapter, which focuses, among other things, on the significance of decisions made by disinterested directors.

As lawyers, you should be concerned whether there can be such an animal as an "independent" legal counsel when the issue is whether management is entitled to indemnification. The by-laws of some corporations contain a definition of independent legal counsel similar to the following: "A law firm, or a member of a law firm that is experienced in matters of corporation law and neither presently is, nor in the past five years has been, retained to represent: (1) the company or indemnitee in any matter material to either such party, or (2) any other party to the proceeding giving rise to a claim for indemnification hereunder." The by-law also includes any person who would be considered to have a conflict of interest under the applicable standards of professional conduct. *See* Ohio Gen.Corp.L. § 1701.13(E)(4)(b).

Critics argue that the problems of indemnification are exacerbated because no state or federal law requires the corporation to disclose indemnification payments to the stockholders. They contend that a corporation which must disclose such payments will be more careful in making them; presumably, the payments themselves might be the subject of a further derivative suit by a stockholder alleging a waste of corporate assets. Because such payments are not considered to be compensation, they do not come within the SEC's proxy rules. MBCA, § 16.21(a) requires disclosure in the corporation's annual report to stockholders but most state statutes, including Delaware, do not have a similar requirement.

Whether because of uncertainty as to the scope of indemnification allowed or required under the applicable statutory and case law or because of a desire to amplify or clarify the various rights and obligations of the corporation and its executives, many corporations include in their articles of incorporation or by-laws some provision relating to indemnification. In addition, in recent years, directors' increasing fear of liability and the higher cost or actual unavailability of liability insurance has led many corporations to enter into indemnification agreements with their management that are separate from the indemnification provided for in corporate articles of incorporation and by-laws.

In many cases, the corporate by-law will do nothing more than track the statute while the indemnification agreement will contain provisions that go beyond the express indemnification sections of the statute. MBCA § 8.59 limits these provisions to those consistent with the statute but, as previously noted, the statutory provisions are extremely broad. DGCL § 145(f) provides specifically that statutory rights and procedures concerning indemnification are not exclusive. Thus, a corporation may indemnify a director through its own policies under circumstances not prescribed in the statute. It is doubtful, however, that a corporation could agree to indemnify a director for *any* action undertaken. As one article noted:

> Some commentators have criticized section 145(f) as too liberal and have expressed concern that public policy could be subverted if, for instance, a director is indemnified according to a by-law in spite of a finding in a derivative suit that he had breached his fiduciary duty to the corporation. Although there is no case law on point, it is probable that a Delaware court would not allow indemnification under a by-law or pursuant to a contract when the proposed indemnification is prohibited by law or public policy. To the extent the statute can be read to embody the public policy limitations of indemnification, a by-law or agreement purporting to expand these limits would likely be void as violative of public policy.

E. Norman Veasey et.al., *Delaware Supports Directors With a Three-Legged Stool of Limited Liability, Indemnification and Insurance*, 42 Bus. Law. 399, 414 (1987).

3. DIRECTORS' AND OFFICERS' INSURANCE

Directors' and officers' liability insurance ("D&O insurance") has experienced an ebb and flow over the last several decades. It was only in the mid-1960s, when an increasing number of lawsuits began to generate fears of liability, that insurance companies began to offer D&O coverage. During the corporate litigation explosion of the 1980s, which coincided with a rise in merger and acquisition activity, some insurance companies cut back on their D&O coverage and significantly increased premiums. In the 1990s, coverage returned and premiums stabilized. Following the spate of corporate scandals in the early 2000s, D&O premiums and deductibles significantly increased, fewer items were covered, and the number of insurance companies offering coverage dwindled. In the past few years, premiums again have begun to stabilize.

D&O policies consist of two separate but integral parts. The first part reimburses the corporation for its lawful expenses in connection with indemnifying its directors and officers, thus encouraging indemnification by the corporation. The second part of the D&O policy covers claims against corporate directors or officers in their corporate capacity, thus reducing their exposure when the corporation is unable or unwilling to indemnify. This coverage often extends to claims (including judgments, settlements and attorneys' fees) arising in court litigation, as well as administrative, regulatory and investigative proceedings.

A third type of coverage, entity coverage, is increasingly offered in D & O policies. Through entity coverage, a corporation is insured against claims, such as securities violations, made against the corporation itself for its own negligent acts, errors or omissions. In addition, D & O policies are negotiated documents and may contain other types of coverage, such as coverage for special litigation committee investigations and workplace torts.

D&O insurance protects beyond corporate indemnification. First, amounts paid in judgment or settlement in a derivative suit can be recovered under the standard D&O policy. Second, D&O insurance may cover conduct that does not satisfy the statutory standard for indemnification. For example, in *Van Gorkom*, because the directors were found grossly negligent in not informing themselves sufficiently prior to approving the merger, statutory indemnification might have been unlikely. Nonetheless, since the directors had not been "dishonest or fraudulent," the corporation's insurance carrier paid $10,000,000—the full policy limit—as part of the $23,000,000 settlement of the case. Finally, D&O coverage is available even if the corporation becomes insolvent or refuses to pay indemnification, assuming the policy requirements are satisfied.

D&O coverage, however, is subject to significant limitations. Many policies have a deductible amount for each director and officer and for the corporation. Sometimes there are co-pays, which means the insured bears a certain percentage (such as 5%) of the loss above the deductible amount. In addition, D&O exclusions are many and significant, and they vary from policy to policy:

- Dishonest, fraudulent or criminal acts are not covered. Sometimes these exclusions are triggered merely if there are *allegations* of such conduct, while others require an actual *adjudication*.

- Claims alleging conduct by directors or officers detrimental to the corporation for their own person gain or profit are excluded. A usual, specific example of this exclusion is any claim for "short-swing profits" made under § 16(d) of the 1934 Act.

- Claims involving ERISA, libel and slander, bodily harm or property damages, and pollution are all excluded.

- Claims against a director or officer brought directly by the corporation, although not necessarily derivative suits, are excluded since most insurers seek to stay clear of internal disputes.

The exclusion of "dishonest, fraudulent or criminal conduct" has potentially important ramifications for executives in corporations that have experienced "accounting irregularities" and have had to restate their financial statements. Some policy exclusions only apply if there is a *judgment* finding such conduct, creating incentives for executives to settle the charges without admitting liability. When a corporation restates its financials, coverage may also turn on whether the financial misstatements were dishonest or intentional, or merely the result of an honest error in accounting or business judgment. Under some policies, mere *allegations* of dishonest or intentional conduct are enough to exclude coverage. The broadened criminal liability under SOX has led to a new market for insurance companies, which are now offering non-rescindable coverage to corporate officers and directors. In addition, many insurance companies offer independent director liability policies for non-employee directors.

D&O policies, like other insurance policies, can be rescinded if there were "material misrepresentations" in the policy application. As you would expect, D&O policy applications include extensive descriptions of the corporation and its finances, including the latest annual report, and financial statements. In addition, the insured must disclose knowledge of "any act, error or omission which might give rise to a claim under the policy."

An additional issue the financial scandals brought to light was the effect of rescission on outside directors. Outside directors for both Enron and WorldCom agreed to contribute personal assets toward a settlement with shareholders in part because their D & O insurers claimed that a false statement by a single officer rescinded coverage for all directors and officers. In response, outside directors have become increasingly concerned about liability for acts of which they had no knowledge. Thus, many outside directors now demand that their D & O Policies include severability provisions. Under severability provisions, coverage is preserved for innocent officers and directors even if others misrepresent material information to the insurer.

Most state statutes expressly authorize corporations to purchase D&O insurance. MBCA § 8.57; DGCL § 145(g). New York's statute goes further and states "it is the public policy of this state to spread the risk of corporate management, notwithstanding any other general or special law of this state or of any other jurisdiction including the federal government." N.Y. B.C.L. § 726(e).

To some, it is troubling that corporate law permits a corporation to insure its executives for conduct sufficiently egregious to be outside the scope of indemnification. Moreover, these critics point out, D&O insurance is expensive and is paid for almost entirely by the corporation. "The question is whether wrongful acts should be indemnified at all. Why should an executive of a drug company be indemnified for the costs of a criminal fine if he is convicted of allowing a harmful drug to injure several thousand people when the same act as a private individual would send him to jail? An untenable double standard has been created. The more powerful an executive becomes, the less likely he is to pay for an abuse of power." Ralph Nader et al., Taming the Giant Corporation 108 (1976).

Defenders of D&O insurance respond with a simple argument: the scope of D & O insurance coverage is a question of insurance law rather than corporate law. The statute only authorizes the purchase of insurance and leaves the determination of the limits on that insurance to insurance companies and state insurance commissioners. In addition, if corporations did not purchase D&O insurance for their executives, one would expect that the executives would demand additional compensation to purchase it for themselves.

Who should bear the risks of executive malfeasance? Supporters of the present system argue that insurance companies (and their regulators) should decide this through exclusions and pricing decisions. And if D&O insurance is harmful from a corporate perspective, shareholders can choose to invest in corporations that do not insure, although this argument assumes shareholders have information about the D&O coverage and payments—an assumption often not true. Thus, if the market is to set limits on corporate behavior, whether the market is informed and sensitive to the insurance issue becomes relevant.

CHAPTER 18

DUTY OF LOYALTY

∎ ∎ ∎

A. INTRODUCTION

Directors have fiduciary duties in various contexts: when they make decisions for the corporation, when they oversee corporate activities and when they engage in transactions that affect the corporation. While the duty of care focuses on board decision-making where director interests are aligned with those of the corporation, the duty of loyalty arises when a director has personal interests that are contrary to those of the corporation. In the most basic terms, the duty of loyalty requires a director to place the corporation's best interests above his own.

The chapter begins with an overview of the issues presented in director self-dealing transactions and the historical evolution of the duty of loyalty, including the traditional statutory approach to director self-dealing transactions and the newer approach under the MBCA. We next consider the elements that courts examine in determining the fairness of a transaction—namely, fair price and approval by disinterested decision-makers. The next section deals with the important concept of good faith and its integral role in the duty of loyalty. We conclude with a discussion of the ability of corporate directors and executives to take business opportunities that may belong to the corporation.

In subsequent chapters, we will consider conflicting loyalties in other contexts: transactions by controlling shareholders, insider trading, and protection and sale of control. One theme that runs throughout these chapters is what it means for a director to be "independent" in a wide range of contexts and to what extent true "independence" is possible. The nature of judicial review may differ with each context, but the question remains the same: how should a court evaluate business transactions that affect the corporation when a corporate fiduciary has a personal interest that may conflict with corporate interests?

As you read the materials in these chapters, it is important to keep in mind that, as a number of judges and scholars have recently written, the duty of loyalty is implicated by all director actions and is at the core of the entire jurisprudence of fiduciary duties. *See*, Randy J. Holland, *Delaware Directors' Fiduciary Duties: The Focus on Loyalty,* 11 U. Pa. J. Bus. L. 675 (2009); Leo E. Strine, Jr., Lawrence A. Hamermesh, R. Franklin Balotti &

Jeffrey M. Gorris, *Loyalty's Core Demand: The Defining Role of Good Faith in Corporation Law,* 98 Geo. L.J. 629 (2010).

Problem: Starcrest Corporation—Part 1

Starcrest is a public company, founded by the Adams family in 1935. In 1955, Starcrest sold 60% of its stock to public investors, and it is now listed on the New York Stock Exchange. Members of the Adams family continue to own 40% of the stock. Elizabeth Adams, the president and chief executive officer, owns 25% and other family members who are not active in the business own the remaining 15%. The company constructs, owns and operates hotels and restaurants throughout the United States. It has built many of these hotels and restaurants after acquiring the raw land on which they sit.

The board of directors consists of Elizabeth Adams; Paul Baker, the chief financial officer; Robert Crown, the vice-president for sales; Linda Diamond, a partner in the law firm that is one of Starcrest's outside counsel; and Michael Brown, Sarah Green, Ruth Grey and Robert White, each of whom is a prominent business executive having no business connections with Starcrest.

Baker and Crown have been officers for more than ten years. Adams, Brown and Green were in the same business school class and they remain close personal friends, often socializing together. Last year, Starcrest used 25 different law firms for its legal work; the billings to Starcrest from Diamond's law firm were $900,000.

Many years ago, Adams inherited a large tract of raw land from a distant uncle. Until recently, she had paid little attention to it, but she recently decided to sell it. Although Adams knows very little about real estate in the area, conversations with her uncle's lawyer (who specialized in probate work) have convinced her that the land is worth $10 million. She initially sought to sell the land privately to sophisticated buyers in the area, but none offered more than $5 million. Somewhat daunted, she listed the land with a real estate broker for a thirty-day period at price of $7.5 million, but received no offers.

Meanwhile, Starcrest began to consider building a new hotel nearby. In early March, at Adams' request, Patricia Jones, the head of the Corporation's real estate department, looked into whether Adams' property would be a suitable site for the hotel. After looking at other sites, Jones concluded that it was superior to any of the other possibilities. She prepared a valuation study based on prices of other land that had recently sold in the area, concluding that the Adams property was worth the $7.5 million Elizabeth was asking. On March 15, Adams formally offered to sell the land to Starcrest for $7.5 million. She accompanied her offer with a copy of the Jones appraisal. She did not disclose that she had unsuccessfully tried to sell the land before offering it to the Corporation because she did not believe that this information was material to the board of directors in making its decision.

In response to the offer, the board of directors established a committee consisting of Brown, Grey and Diamond to evaluate the offer. Because none of the committee members were experts in real estate, they hired an outside consultant who opined that the land might conceivably be worth $7.5 million but that he wouldn't pay that price. The committee also obtained a formal appraisal from an outside appraiser, who valued the land at $5 million.

In June, relying primarily on the Jones valuation study and the independent appraisal, the committee recommended that the Corporation offer to purchase the land for $6.5 million, a price that Elizabeth had indicated she was willing to accept. The committee's report set out in detail the procedures it had followed and the basis for the recommendation. Grey dissented from the recommendation on the grounds that there was no reason to pay more than $5 million. The board accepted the committee's recommendation by a vote of 5 to 1. Grey again dissented, and White did not attend the meeting. Elizabeth did not participate in the deliberations of either the committee or the board and did not vote on the transaction.

On Diamond's advice, the Corporation submitted the transaction to the shareholders for ratification at the annual meeting in October. The proxy statement disclosed all the information available to the board of directors and the process by which the board reached its decision. At the meeting, the shareholders ratified the transaction, with Elizabeth and other Adams family members voting. 54% of the outstanding stock (including Elizabeth's 25% and the 15% held by her relatives) voted in favor; 22% opposed.

It is now one week after the meeting and two days before the parties are scheduled to close the transaction. Grant, a shareholder of the corporation, learned of the transaction through reading the proxy statement. He believes that the transaction constitutes a windfall to Adams and has consulted you to see what liabilities Adams and the board of directors may have in connection with the transaction and what remedies may be available.

In advising Grant, answer the following questions, assuming that the applicable law is either DGCL § 144 or MBCA Subchapter F:

1. Under the applicable statute, what standard of review will a court use to determine whether to enjoin the transaction or to impose personal liability on Adams or the board of directors?

    a. Does approval by disinterested directors or by shareholders affect the court's standard of review?

    b. Who will have the burden of proof in the litigation?

c.   Could the burden be met in this case?

2.   Can the shares of the Adams family be counted in determining whether the transaction has been effectively ratified? What effect does shareholder ratification have on any claim for liability?

B. DIRECTOR SELF-DEALING AND CONFLICT OF INTEREST

1. NATURE OF DIRECTOR SELF-DEALING

Consider the paradigm case in which a director, the CEO of the corporation, has a conflict of interest: a transaction in which she proposes to sell property that she owns to the corporation on whose board she sits. Her conflict is obvious. As the property owner, she wants to receive the highest possible price. As director, she has a duty to see that the corporation pays the lowest possible price. The law characterizes such a transaction as "self-dealing." That conflicting interests exist does not necessarily mean, however, that the transaction will be unfair to the corporation.

> It is important to keep firmly in mind that it is a contingent risk we are dealing with—that an interest conflict is not in itself a crime or a tort or necessarily injurious to others. Contrary to much popular usage, having a "conflict of interest" is not something one is "guilty of"; it is simply a state of affairs. Indeed, in many situations, the corporation and the shareholders may secure major benefits from a transaction despite the presence of a director's conflicting interest. Further, while history is replete with selfish acts, it is also oddly counterpointed by numberless acts taken contrary to self interest.

MBCA Subchapter F, Introductory Comment.

Self-dealing transactions can be both fair and beneficial to a corporation. An "interested" director will frequently be uniquely situated to help the corporation. She may have knowledge about how the corporation will benefit from the transaction and the ability to effectuate the transaction at minimal cost.

Some self-dealing transactions *are* unfair to the corporation. When such a transaction occurs the interested director appropriates the difference between the fair market value of the transaction and the payment actually made. The effect of an unfair self-dealing transaction is no different from the direct diversion of corporate assets. Self-dealing is apt to be more common than flagrant diversion, however, because the interested director may more easily rationalize an inflated purchase price than outright stealing. It is frequently possible to identify and exaggerate some reasons why a corporation should pay dearly for some particular piece of land or property. That having been done, the director may continue to think of himself as a just and honorable man.

Robert Charles Clark, Corporate Law 143 (1986).

But director conflicts of interest are not limited to the director who directly benefits from the transaction. In our paradigm land transaction, other directors who do not have a financial interest in the transaction may have corporate or other positions that depend on the good will or authority of the interested CEO. For example, another director may be a member of a law firm that depends on the CEO for some of the legal work that the firm does for the corporation. Some directors may also be employees of the corporation whose positions may be dependent on the CEO. And even if a director had no financial interest, there may be personal dimensions if she is a family member or lifelong friend of the CEO.

The principal difficulty in this area of the law is establishing appropriate criteria for measuring the validity of the transaction. The business judgment rule, which is premised on the director's independent judgment, does not provide an appropriate standard in a conflict transaction because, by definition, the director's judgment cannot be independent. A substitute test, however, has proved difficult to articulate. A director who engages in a transaction with the corporation may well be acting in good faith, but how is that to be tested? The law requires that the transaction be "fair" to the corporation, but fairness itself can be difficult to determine. Should a court focus on the terms of the transaction or the process by which it was authorized?

2. CONTEMPORARY STATUTORY APPROACHES

Statutes now govern director self-dealing transactions in most states. Statutes, such as DGCL § 144 and former MBCA § 8.31 codify the common law development that conflict transactions are not automatically invalid. They do not, however, specify when a transaction is valid. Over time, courts have had to resolve whether approval by directors or shareholders should be determinative or whether the court should engage in its own review of director self-dealing.

Subchapter F of the MBCA seeks to overcome these interpretive problems. Subchapter F, adopted in 1989 and revised in 2005, uses a safe harbor approach. Although the basic provisions of Subchapter F do not differ from existing law in many respects, by providing bright line definitions of who is an "interested" director, what constitutes a "conflicting interest transaction," and who are "qualified directors," Subchapter F attempts to provide greater prospective certainty and reduce judicial intervention.

a. Traditional Analysis

The following case involved a transaction approved by interested directors, who also owned a majority of the voting stock. The defendants argued that the transaction had been approved in their capacity as shareholders and therefore the court could not inquire into its fairness. The decision prompted a change in the California statute to disqualify shares being voted by interested directors in a shareholder vote.

REMILLARD BRICK CO. v. REMILLARD-DANDINI CO.
241 P.2d 66 (Cal.App. 1952).

[The case involved three corporations: Remillard-Dandini Company and its wholly-owned subsidiary, San Jose Brick & Tile, Ltd, (the "manufacturing companies") and Remillard-Dandini Sales Corporation (the "sales corporation"). Stanley and Sturgis controlled a majority of the shares of Remillard-Dandini Company, and were executive officers of both of the manufacturing companies. Stanley and Sturgis established an arrangement pursuant to which the manufacturing companies sold bricks to the sales corporation, which they, controlled and operated.

Plaintiff, a minority shareholder of Remillard-Dandini Company, alleged that the directors of the manufacturing companies caused them to be stripped of the their sales function, thus permitting Stanley and Sturgis to realize profits that should have gone to the manufacturing companies. Stanley and Sturgis maintained that the minority shareholder and the minority directors of the manufacturing companies were informed of their interests in the contracts.]

PETERS, PRESIDING JUSTICE:

It is argued that, since the fact of common directorship was fully known to the boards of the contracting corporations, and because the majority stockholders consented to the transaction, the minority stockholder and directors of the manufacturing companies have no legal cause to complain. In other words, it is argued that if the majority directors and stockholders inform the minority that they are going to mulct the corporation, section 820 of the Corporations Code[1] constitutes an

---

[1] Section 820 of the Corporations Code, enacted in 1947 and based on former section 311 of the Civil Code, provided:

> Directors and officers shall exercise their powers in good faith, and with a view to the interests of the corporation. No contract or other transaction between a corporation and one or more of its directors, or between a corporation and any corporation, firm, or association in which one or more of its directors are directors or are financially interested, is either void or voidable because such director or directors are present at the meeting of the board of directors or a committee thereof which authorizes or approves the contract

impervious armor against any attack on the transaction short of actual fraud. If this interpretation of the section were sound, it would be a shocking reflection on the law of California. It would completely disregard the first sentence of section 820 setting forth the elementary rule that "Directors and officers shall exercise their powers in good faith, and with a view to the interests of the corporation", and would mean that if conniving directors simply disclose their dereliction to the powerless minority, any transaction by which the majority desire to mulct the minority is immune from attack. That is not and cannot be the law.

Section 820 of the Corporations Code is based on former section 311 of the Civil Code, first added to our law in 1931. Before the adoption of that section it was the law that the mere existence of a common directorate, at least where the vote of the common director was essential to consummate the transaction, invalidated the contract. That rule was changed in 1931 when section 311 was added to the Civil Code, and limited to a greater extent by the adoption of section 820 of the Corporations Code. If the conditions provided for in the section appear, the transaction cannot be set aside simply because there is a common directorate. Here, undoubtedly, there was a literal compliance with subdivision b of the section. The fact of the common directorship was disclosed to the stockholders, and the majority stockholders, did approve the contracts.

But neither section 820 of the Corporations Code nor any other provision of the law automatically validates such transactions simply because there has been a disclosure and approval by the majority of the stockholders. That section does not operate to limit the fiduciary duties owed by a director to all the stockholders, nor does it operate to condone acts which, without the existence of a common directorate, would not be countenanced. That section does not permit an officer or director, by an abuse of his power, to obtain an unfair advantage or profit for himself at the expense of the corporation. The director cannot, by reason of his position, drive a harsh and unfair bargain with the corporation he is supposed to represent. If he does so, he may be compelled to account for

---

or transaction, or because his or their votes are counted for such purpose, if the circumstances specified in any of the following subdivisions exist:

   (a) The fact of the common directorship or financial interest is disclosed or known to the board of directors or committee and noted in the minutes, and the board or committee authorizes, approves, or ratifies the contract or transaction in good faith by a vote sufficient for the purpose without counting the vote or votes of such director or directors.

   (b) The fact of the common directorship or financial interest is disclosed or known to the shareholders, and they approve or ratify the contract or transaction in good faith by a majority vote or written consent of shareholders entitled to vote.

   (c) The contract or transaction is just and reasonable as to the corporation at the time it is authorized or approved.

Common or interested directors may be counted in determining the presence of a quorum at a meeting of the board of directors or a committee thereof which authorizes, approves, or ratifies a contract or transaction.

unfair profits made in disregard of his duty. Even though the requirements of section 820 are technically met, transactions that are unfair and unreasonable to the corporation may be avoided. California Corporation Laws by Ballantine and Sterling (1949 ed.), p. 102, § 84. [It would be a shocking concept of corporate morality to hold that because the majority directors or stockholders disclose their purpose and interest, they may strip a corporation of its assets to their own financial advantage, and that the minority is without legal redress.]

Here the unchallenged findings demonstrate that Stanley and Sturgis used their majority power for their own personal advantage and to the detriment of the minority stockholder. They used it to strip the manufacturing companies of their sales functions—functions which it was their duty to carry out as officers and directors of those companies. There was not one thing done by them acting as the sales corporation that they could not and should not have done as officers and directors and in control of the stock of the manufacturing companies. It is no answer to say that the manufacturing companies made a profit on the deal, or that Stanley and Sturgis did a good job. The point is that those large profits that should have gone to the manufacturing companies were diverted to the sales corporation. The good job done by Stanley and Sturgis should and could have been done for the manufacturing companies. If Stanley and Sturgis, with control of the board of directors and the majority stock of the manufacturing companies, could thus lawfully, to their own advantage, strip the manufacturing companies of their sales functions, they could just as well strip them of their other functions. If the sales functions could be stripped from the companies in this fashion to the personal advantage of Stanley and Sturgis, there would be nothing to prevent them from next organizing a manufacturing company, and transferring to it the manufacturing functions of these companies, thus leaving the manufacturing companies but hollow shells. This should not, is not, and cannot be the law.

It is hornbook law that directors, while not strictly trustees, are fiduciaries, and bear a fiduciary relationship to the corporation, and to all the stockholders. They owe a duty to all stockholders, including the minority stockholders, and must administer their duties for the common benefit. The concept that a corporation is an entity cannot operate so as to lessen the duties owed to all of the stockholders. Directors owe a duty of highest good faith to the corporation and its stockholders. It is a cardinal principle of corporate law that a director cannot, at the expense of the corporation, make an unfair profit from his position. He is precluded from receiving any personal advantage without fullest disclosure to and consent of *all* those affected. The law zealously regards contracts between corporations with interlocking directorates, will carefully scrutinize all such transactions, and in case of unfair dealing to the detriment of minority stockholders, will grant appropriate relief. Where the transaction greatly benefits one corporation at the expense of another, and especially if it personally benefits the majority directors, it will and should be set aside. In other words, while the transaction is not voidable simply because an interested director participated, it will not be upheld if it is unfair to the minority stockholders. These principles are the law in practically all jurisdictions.

---

b.   DGCL § 144

DGCL § 144 is a typical director self-dealing statute. It provides that an interested director transaction will not automatically be void or voidable solely because of the interest if *either* there has been informed, disinterested board approval *or* informed shareholder approval *or* the transaction is fair to the corporation.

DGCL § 144

(a)   No contract or transaction between a corporation and 1 or more of its directors or officers, or between a corporation and any other corporation, partnership, association, or other organization in which 1 or more of its directors or officers, are directors or officers, or have a financial interest, shall be void or voidable solely for this reason, or solely because the director or officer is present at or participates in the meeting of the board or committee which authorizes the contract or transaction, or solely because any such director's or officer's votes are counted for such purpose, if:

(1)   The material facts as to the director's or officer's relationship or interest and as to the contract or transaction are disclosed or are known to the board of directors or the committee, and the board or committee in good faith authorizes the contract or transaction by the affirmative votes of a majority of the disinterested directors, even though the disinterested directors be less than a quorum; or

(2)   The material facts as to the director's or officer's relationship or interest and as to the contract or transaction are disclosed or are known to the stockholders entitled to vote thereon, and the contract or transaction is specifically approved in good faith by vote of the stockholders; or

> (3) The contract or transaction is fair as to the corporation as of the time it is authorized, approved or ratified, by the board of directors, a committee or the stockholders.
>
> (b) Common or interested directors may be counted in determining the presence of a quorum at a meeting of the board of directors or of a committee which authorizes the contract or transaction.

Under this section, what role does a court have in reviewing the fairness of the transaction to the corporation? Because the statute is written in the disjunctive, one possible answer is that there should be judicial review for fairness only if there has been no prior approval by an informed, disinterested decision-maker. If this interpretation were correct, it would reduce judicial scrutiny (and, hence, potentially be less protective for minority shareholders), particularly when compared to the early days of the common law. This approach, however, could be viewed as efficient because it would give prospective certainty to a transaction in which the decisional process has been reliable, presumably on the theory that good process will lead to substantively fair decisions in most instances.

Alternatively, the statute might be read as removing the absolute bar against interested director transactions but specifying no clear standard in its stead. Support for this reading comes from the language in the statute that a transaction that satisfies one or more of the tests will not be void or voidable *solely* because of the director's interest. Under this construction, the statute might relate primarily to the burden of proof in litigation challenging a conflict of interest transaction rather than establishing the validity of the transaction itself. Thus, the burden of establishing validity initially would be on the interested director but would shift to the shareholder challenging the transaction if there had been full disclosure and approval by a disinterested decision-maker. This interpretation leaves to the court the question of the transaction's fairness; approval by a disinterested decision-maker only shifts the burden of who must establish fairness or unfairness.

Delaware court decisions illustrate the difficulties in interpreting § 144. Some decisions state that the court retains a role in determining fairness, even if the self-dealing transaction is approved by informed, disinterested decision-makers. Others suggest that the review by appropriate corporate decision-makers affords business judgment rule protection to the transaction, limiting judicial review to determining waste.

In *Fliegler v. Lawrence,* 361 A.2d 218 (Del. 1976), a shareholder brought a derivative suit on behalf of Agau Mines against its officers and directors (including the named defendant Lawrence), and another corporation, United States Antimony Corp. (USAC), which was owned primarily by Lawrence and the other defendants. Lawrence had acquired, in his individual capacity, certain mining properties which he transferred to USAC. Agau later acquired USAC in exchange for 800,000 shares of Agau stock. Fliegler, a minority shareholder of Agau, challenged Agau's acquisition of USAC, claiming it was unfair. The defendants contended that they had been relieved of the burden of proving fairness because Agau's shareholders had ratified the transaction pursuant to § 144(a)(2).

The court held that the purported ratification did not affect the burden of proof because the majority of shares voted in favor of the acquisition were cast by the defendants in their capacity as Agau stockholders. Only one-third of the disinterested shareholders cast votes. Thus, the *Fliegler* court determined that despite the absence of any provision in § 144(a)(2) requiring *disinterested* shareholder approval of an interested director transaction, it would impose such a requirement before shifting the burden of proof from the interested director to the challenging shareholder.

The court then addressed the proper interpretation of the disjunctive language of § 144. The court rejected the argument that compliance with § 144(a)(2) automatically validated the transaction and concluded that the statute "merely removes an 'interested director' cloud when its terms are met and provides against invalidation of an agreement 'solely' because such a director or officer is involved. Nothing in the statute sanctions unfairness to Agau or removes the transaction from judicial scrutiny."

In *Marciano v. Nakash,* 535 A.2d 400 (Del. 1987), the court found to be fair a director self-dealing transaction that, because of a deadlock at both the shareholder and director level, had not been approved by either disinterested shareholders or directors. The court characterized *Fliegler* as having "refused to view § 144 as either completely preemptive of the common law duty of director fidelity of as constituting a grant of broad immunity" and cited with approval *Fliegler*'s "merely removes an 'interested director' cloud" language. In footnote 3, however, the court observed:

> Although in this case none of the curative steps afforded under section 144(a) were available because of the director-shareholder deadlock, a non-disclosing director seeking to remove the cloud of interestedness would appear to have the same burden under section 144(a)(3), as under prior case law, of proving the intrinsic fairness of a questioned transaction which had been approved or ratified by the directors or shareholders. On the other hand, approval by fully-informed disinterested directors under section 144(a)(1), or disinterested stockholders under section 144(a)(2), permits invocation of the business judgment rule and limits judicial review to issues of gift or waste with the burden of proof upon the party attacking the transaction.

Without explicitly addressing the tension between *Fliegler* and *Marciano* and without explanation, the following decision by the Delaware Supreme Court embraces the view that compliance with § 144(a)(1) establishes a business judgment rule standard of review for director self-dealing transactions.

BENIHANA OF TOKYO, INC. V. BENIHANA, INC.

906 A.2d 114 (Del. 2006).

BERGER, JUSTICE:

In this appeal, we consider whether Benihana, Inc. was authorized to issue $20 million in preferred stock and whether Benihana's board of directors acted properly in approving the transaction. We conclude that the Court of Chancery's factual findings are supported by the record and that it correctly applied settled law in holding that the stock issuance was lawful and that the directors did not breach their fiduciary duties. Accordingly, we affirm.

Rocky Aoki founded Benihana of Tokyo, Inc. (BOT), and its subsidiary, Benihana, which own and operate Benihana restaurants in the United States and other countries. Aoki owned 100% of BOT until 1998, when he pled guilty to insider trading charges. In order to avoid licensing problems created by his status as a convicted felon, Aoki transferred his stock to the Benihana Protective Trust. The trustees of the Trust were Aoki's three children and the family's attorney.

Benihana, a Delaware corporation, has two classes of common stock. There are approximately 6 million shares of Class A common stock outstanding. Each share has 1/10 vote and the holders of Class A common are entitled to elect 25% of the directors. There are approximately 3 million shares of Common stock outstanding. Each share of Common has one vote and the holders of Common stock are entitled to elect the remaining 75% of Benihana's directors. Before the transaction at issue, BOT owned 50.9% of the Common stock and 2% of the Class A stock. The nine member board of directors is classified and the directors serve three-year terms.

In 2003, conflicts arose between Aoki and his children. In August, the children were upset to learn that Aoki had changed his will to give his new wife Keiko control over BOT.

The Aoki family's turmoil came at a time when Benihana also was facing challenges. Many of its restaurants were old and outmoded. Benihana hired WD Partners to evaluate its facilities and to plan and design appropriate renovations. The resulting Construction and Renovation Plan anticipated that the project would take at least five years and cost $56 million or more. Wachovia offered to provide Benihana a $60 million line of credit for the Construction and Renovation Plan, but the restrictions Wachovia imposed made it unlikely that Benihana would be able to borrow the full amount. Because the Wachovia line of credit did not assure that Benihana would have the capital it needed, the company retained Morgan Joseph & Co. to develop other financing options.

On January 9, 2004, after evaluating Benihana's financial situation and needs, Fred Joseph, of Morgan Joseph, met with Joel Schwartz (Benihana's CEO), Darwin Dornbush (Benihana's general counsel) and John E. Abdo (a member of the board's executive committee). Joseph expressed concern that Benihana would not have sufficient available capital to complete the Construction and Renovation Plan and pursue appropriate acquisitions. Benihana was conservatively leveraged, and Joseph discussed various financing alternatives, including bank debt, high yield debt, convertible debt or preferred stock, equity and sale/leaseback options.

The full board met with Joseph on January 29, 2004. He reviewed all the financing alternatives that he had discussed with the executive committee, and recommended that Benihana issue convertible preferred stock. Joseph explained that the preferred stock would provide the funds needed for the Construction and Renovation Plan and also put the company in a better negotiating position if it sought additional financing from its bank.

Joseph gave the directors a board book, marked "Confidential," containing an analysis of the proposed stock issuance (the Transaction). The book included, among others, the following anticipated terms: (i) issuance of $20,000,000 of preferred stock, convertible into Common stock; (ii) dividend of 6% +/- 0.5%; (iii) conversion premium of 20% +/- 2.5%; (iv) buyer's approval required for material corporate transactions; and (v) one to two board seats to the buyer. At trial, Joseph testified that the terms had been chosen by looking at comparable stock issuances and analyzing the Morgan Joseph proposal under a theoretical model.

The board met again on February 17, 2004, to review the terms of the Transaction. The directors discussed Benihana's preferences and Joseph predicted what a buyer likely would expect or require. For example, Schwartz asked Joseph to try to negotiate a minimum on the dollar value for transactions that would be deemed "material corporation transactions" and subject to the buyer's approval. Schwartz wanted to give the buyer only one board seat, but Joseph said that Benihana might have to give up two. Joseph told the board that he was not sure that a buyer would agree to an issuance in two tranches, and that it would be difficult to make the second tranche non-mandatory. As the Court of Chancery found, the board understood that the preferred terms were akin to a "wish list."

Shortly after the February meeting, Abdo contacted Joseph and told him that BFC Financial Corporation was interested in buying the new convertible stock. In April 2005, Joseph sent BFC a private placement memorandum. Abdo negotiated with Joseph for several weeks.[5] They agreed to the Transaction on the following basic terms: (i) $20 million issuance in two tranches of $10 million each, with the second tranche to be issued one to three years after the first; (ii) BFC obtained one seat on the board, and one additional seat if Benihana failed to pay dividends for two consecutive quarters; (iii) BFC obtained preemptive rights on any new voting securities; (iv) 5% dividend; (v) 15% conversion premium; (vi) BFC had the right to force Benihana to redeem the preferred stock in full after ten years; and (vii) the stock would have immediate "as if converted" voting rights. Joseph testified that he was satisfied with the negotiations, as he had obtained what he wanted with respect to the most important points.

On April 22, 2004, Abdo sent a memorandum to Dornbush, Schwartz and Joseph, listing the agreed terms of the Transaction. He did not send the memorandum to any other members of the Benihana board. Schwartz did tell four directors that BFC was the potential buyer. At its next meeting, held on May 6, 2004, the entire board was officially informed of BFC's involvement in the Transaction. Abdo made a presentation on behalf of BFC and then left the meeting. Joseph distributed an updated board book, which explained that Abdo had approached Morgan Joseph on behalf of BFC, and included the negotiated terms. The trial court found that the board was not informed that Abdo had negotiated the deal on behalf of BFC. But the board did know that Abdo was a principal of BFC. After discussion, the board reviewed and approved the Transaction, subject to the receipt of a fairness opinion.

On May 18, 2004, after he learned that Morgan Joseph was providing a fairness opinion, Schwartz publicly announced the stock issuance. Two days later, Aoki's counsel sent a letter asking the board to abandon the Transaction and pursue other, more favorable, financing alternatives. The letter expressed concern about the directors' conflicts, the dilutive effect of the stock issuance, and its "questionable legality." Schwartz gave copies of the letter to the directors at the May 20 board meeting, and Dornbush advised that he did not believe that Aoki's concerns had merit. Joseph and another Morgan Joseph representative then joined the meeting by telephone and opined that the Transaction was fair from a financial point of view. The board then approved the Transaction.

During the following two weeks, Benihana received three alternative financing proposals. Schwartz asked three outside directors to act as an independent committee and review the first offer. The committee decided that the offer was inferior and not worth pursuing. Morgan Joseph agreed with that assessment. Schwartz referred the next two proposals to Morgan Joseph, with the same result.

---

[5]　BFC, a publicly traded Florida corporation, is a holding company for several investments. Abdo is a director and vice chairman. He owns 30% of BFC's stock.

On June 8, 2004, Benihana and BFC executed the Stock Purchase Agreement. On June 11, 2004, the board met and approved resolutions ratifying the execution of the Stock Purchase Agreement and authorizing the stock issuance. Schwartz then reported on the three alternative proposals that had been rejected by the ad hoc committee and Morgan Joseph. On July 2, 2004, BOT filed this action against all of Benihana's directors, except Kevin Aoki, alleging breaches of fiduciary duties; and against BFC, alleging that it aided and abetted the fiduciary violations.

The Court of Chancery held that Benihana was authorized to issue the preferred stock with preemptive rights, and that the board's approval of the Transaction was a valid exercise of business judgment. This appeal followed.

[The court first decided that Benihana's certificate of incorporation authorized the board to issue preferred stock with preemptive rights.]

Section 144 of the Delaware General Corporation Law provides a safe harbor for interested transactions, like this one, if "the material facts as to the director's relationship or interest and as to the contract or transaction are disclosed or are known to the board of directors . . . and the board . . . in good faith authorizes the contract or transaction by the affirmative votes of a majority of the disinterested directors."

After approval by disinterested directors, courts review the interested transaction under the business judgment rule,[12] which "is a presumption that in making a business decision, the directors of a corporation acted on an informed basis, in good faith and in the honest belief that the action taken was in the best interest of the company."

[The Court concludes that the disinterested directors possessed all the material information regarding Abdo's interest in the transaction, including that he had negotiated it on behalf of BFC.]

BOT next argues that the Court of Chancery should have reviewed the Transaction under an entire fairness standard because Abdo breached his duty of loyalty when he used Benihana's confidential information to negotiate on behalf of BFC. This argument starts with a flawed premise. The record does not support BOT's contention that Abdo used any confidential information against Benihana. Even without Joseph's comments at the February 17 board meeting, Abdo knew the terms a buyer could expect to obtain in a deal like this. Moreover, as the trial court found, "the negotiations involved give and take on a number of points" and Benihana "ended up where it wanted to be" for the most important terms. Abdo did not set the terms of the deal; he did not deceive the board; and he did not dominate or control the other directors' approval of the Transaction.

---

[12] *See Cede & Co. v. Technicolor, Inc.,* 634 A.2d 345, 366 n.34 (Del. 1993); *Marciano v. Nakash,* 535 A.2d 400, 405 n.3 (Del. 1987).

In short, the record does not support the claim that Abdo breached his duty of loyalty.

 Finally, BOT argues that the board's primary purpose in approving the Transaction was to dilute BOT's voting control. BOT points out that Schwartz was concerned about BOT's control in 2003 and even discussed with Dornbush the possibility of issuing a huge number of Class A shares. Then, despite the availability of other financing options, the board decided on a stock issuance, and agreed to give BFC "as if converted" voting rights. According to BOT, the trial court overlooked this powerful evidence of the board's improper purpose.

Here, however, the trial court found that "the primary purpose of the . . . Transaction was to provide what the directors subjectively believed to be the best financing vehicle available for securing the necessary funds to pursue the agreed upon Construction and Renovation Plan for the Benihana restaurants." That factual determination has ample record support, especially in light of the trial court's credibility determinations. Accordingly, we defer to the Court of Chancery's conclusion that the board's approval of the Transaction was a valid exercise of its business judgment, for a proper corporate purpose.

---

c.   MBCA Subchapter F

In 1989, the Committee on Corporate Laws of the American Bar Association adopted Subchapter F to replace the then existing MBCA § 8.31 whose language was similar to that of DGCL § 144. (Former MBCA § 8.31 should not be confused with the present MBCA § 8.31, which deals with director liability when there is no conflict of interest transaction.) In 2005, Subchapter F was revised to clarify its coverage and specify the procedures necessary to validate a director self-dealing transaction.

Subchapter F adopts a disjunctive safe-harbor approach in which a director self-dealing transaction is immunized from attack if authorized by either "qualified directors," disinterested shareholders, or the court under a fairness standard. The statute also provides specific "bright line" definitions of who is an "interested" director and what constitutes a "director's conflicting interest transaction" (DCIT) to which Subchapter F is applicable. To date, approximately thirteen states have adopted some version of Subchapter F.

Subchapter F defines a DCIT as a transaction by the corporation in which the director (i) is a party, (ii) has a "material financial interest," or (3) knows that a "related person" is party or had a material financial interest. A "material financial interest" is defined as one that would reasonably be expected to impair the director's judgment when authorizing the transaction. A "related person" is defined to include someone on a precisely enumerated family tree (from spouse to half sibling), someone who lives in the director's house, an entity controlled by the director or someone on the family tree, an entity in which the director serves as director, partner or trustee, or an entity controlled by the director's employer.

In short, Subchapter F opts for precision over generality. The Official Comment explains:

> Section 8.61(a) makes clear that a transaction between a corporation and another person cannot be the subject of judicial review on the ground that the director has an interest respecting the transaction, unless the transaction falls within the bright-line definition of "director's conflicting interest transaction" in section 8.60. So, for example, a transaction will not constitute a director's conflicting interest transaction and, therefore, will not be subject to judicial review on the ground that a director had an interest in the transaction, where the transaction is made with a [cousin] of a director who is not one of the relatives specified in section 8.60(5), or on the ground of an alleged interest other than a material financial interest, such as a nonfinancial interest.

Official Comment to Section 8.61(a).

> Sections 8.60 and 8.61 attempt to frame a tight definition of who is "interested" in a transaction, and what constitutes a "conflict of interest transaction."

> Section 8.61(a) is a key component in the design of subchapter F. It draws a bright-line circle, declaring that the definitions of section 8.60 wholly occupy and preempt the field of directors' conflicting interest transactions. Of course, outside this circle there is a penumbra of director interests, desires, goals, loyalties, and prejudices that may, in a particular context, run at odds with the best interests of the corporation, but section 8.61(a) forbids a court to ground remedial action on any of them.

For DCITs approved by qualified directors, Subchapter F specifies the procedures that must be followed to insulate the transaction from judicial review. The DCIT, after required disclosure by the conflicted director, must be authorized by a majority of the qualified directors (at least two) who voted on the transaction. The qualified directors must have deliberated and voted by themselves, without the presence or participation of the conflicted director. Normal quorum requirements are relaxed, and a quorum exists if a majority of the board's qualified directors (at least two) are present.

Who is a "qualified director"? MBCA § 1.43 (described by its drafters as a "critical component of the governance provisions of the MBCA") defines the term in various situations involving director conflicts of interests— such as dismissal of derivative suits, indemnification or advancement of expenses, and rejection of corporate opportunities. For purposes of approval of a DCIT, a "qualified director" is one who does not have a conflicting interest in the transaction and has no "material relationship" with a conflicted director (that is, there is no "actual or potential benefit or detriment that would reasonably be expected to impair the director's judgment" when considering the DCIT). A director does not become unqualified simply because he was nominated or elected to the board by a conflicted director, or serves with the conflicted director on the board of another corporation.

The either-or framework of Subchapter F is tempered by the new MBCA § 8.31 (standards of liability for directors). Under that section, if a person challenging a corporate transaction can show that a board's approval of the transaction was influenced by any director's relationship with the other party to that transaction, the burden shifts to the director with such a relationship to show that she reasonably believed the challenged transaction was in the corporation's best interests. In effect, § 8.31 creates an intermediate standard of review for a transaction involving a related director who does not have a full-blown "conflicting interest" as defined in § 8.60(1).

As you can see, the MBCA creates a framework that seeks to provide clear yes-or-no answers. For example, a conflicted director who fails to disclose to the board his interest in the transaction (where the other directors do not know) or fails to reveal material information (such as that the land he is selling is sinking into an abandoned coal mine) cannot claim the MBCA safe harbor for board approval. On the other hand, if the DCIT is approved by directors who have neither a conflicting interest in the transaction nor financial ties to the conflicted director, the transaction falls within the safe harbor even if the directors are all close personal friends.

Perhaps because relatively few states have adopted Subchapter F, there has been virtually no litigation interpreting the statute. What is clear thus far is that courts have recognized the significance of the safe harbors of Subchapter F. *See Fisher v. State Mutual Ins. Co.,* 290 F.3d 1256 (11th Cir. 2002) (finding compliance with Georgia's statute based on Subchapter F, where conflicted directors involved in a DCIT had fully disclosed their interest and did not participate in negotiating or voting on the transaction).

3. THE MEANING OF "FAIRNESS"

Unless approved by an independent board or board committee, or disinterested shareholders, a transaction in which an officer or director is interested is subject to challenge on the grounds that it is unfair to the corporation. A great deal of judicial ink has been spilled in efforts to define what "fairness" means.

While the concept of "fairness" is incapable of precise definition, courts have stressed such factors as whether the corporation received in the transaction full value in all the commodities purchased; the corporation's need for the property; its ability to finance the purchase; whether the transaction was at the market price, or below, or constituted a better bargain than the corporation could have otherwise obtained in dealings with others; whether there was a detriment to the corporation as a result of the transaction; whether there was a possibility of corporate gain siphoned off by the directors directly or through corporations they controlled; and whether there was full disclosure—although neither disclosure nor shareholder assent can convert a dishonest transaction into a fair one.

Shlensky v. South Parkway Building Corp., 166 N.E.2d 793, 801–02 (Ill. 1960).

The Delaware courts have established the greatest body of law on fairness in cases involving the duty of loyalty. More recent Delaware decisions have applied a test of "entire fairness." (The courts sometimes use the terms, "intrinsic fairness" or "inherent fairness," but most commentators believe they mean the same thing.) The Delaware Supreme Court described what this means in the following passage:

The concept of fairness has two basic aspects: fair dealing and fair price. The former embraces questions of when the transaction was timed, how it was initiated, structured, negotiated, disclosed to the directors, and how the approvals of the directors and the stockholders were obtained. The latter aspect of fairness relates to the economic and financial considerations of the proposed merger, including all relevant factors: assets, market value, earnings, future prospects, and any other elements that affect the intrinsic or inherent value of a company's stock. However, the test for fairness is not a bifurcated one as between fair dealing and price. All aspects of the issue must be examined as a whole since the question is one of entire fairness. However, in a non-fraudulent transaction we recognize that price may be the preponderant consideration outweighing other features of the merger.

Weinberger v. UOP, Inc., 457 A.2d 701, 711 (Del. 1983). *See also Kahn v. Lynch Communication Systems, Inc.*, 638 A.2d 1110 (Del. 1994).

Under this standard, a transaction must be both substantively and procedurally fair to the corporation. As one case put it, "[T]he entire fairness standard requires the board of directors to establish "to the *court's* satisfaction that the transaction was the product of both fair dealing *and* fair price." *Cinerama, Inc. v. Technicolor, Inc.*, 663 A.2d 1156, 1163 (Del. 1995).

The MBCA takes a similar approach, defining "fair to the corporation" as follows:

> [T]he transaction as a whole was beneficial to the corporation, taking into appropriate account whether it was (i) fair in terms of the director's dealings with the corporation, and (ii) comparable to what might have been obtainable in an arm's length transaction, given the consideration paid or received by the corporation.

MBCA § 8.60(6).

a. Substantive Fairness

Despite the safe harbors created by Subchapter F and perhaps DGCL § 144, courts are often called on to review the "fairness" of director self-dealing transactions. Director self-dealing transactions that fail to satisfy the procedural conditions become subject to judicial review for fairness.

Substantive fairness focuses on a comparison of the fair market value of the transaction to the price the corporation actually paid as well as the corporation's need for and ability to consummate the transaction. The test has been articulated as "whether the proposition submitted would have commended itself to an independent corporation." *Johnston v. Greene,* 121 A.2d 919, 925 (Del. Ch. 1956). To the extent that this formulation contemplates independent arms-length negotiation as providing the basis for fair market value, a range of prices can satisfy the test of substantive fairness. Consider the Official Comment to MBCA § 8.60:

> *Terms of the transaction.* If the issue in a transaction is the "fairness" of a price, "fair" is not to be taken to imply that there is one single "fair" price, all others being "unfair." It is settled law that a "fair" price is any price within a range that an unrelated party might have been willing to pay or willing to accept, as the case may be, for the relevant property, asset, service or commitment, following a normal arm's-length business negotiation. The same approach applies not only to gauging the fairness of price, but also to the fairness evaluation of any other key term of the deal.

> *Benefit to the corporation.* In considering the "fairness" of the transaction, the court will be required to consider not only the market fairness of the terms of the deal—whether it is comparable to what might have been obtainable in an arm's length transaction—but also whether the transaction was one that was reasonably likely to yield favorable results. Thus, if a manufacturing company that lacks sufficient working capital allocates some of its scarce funds to purchase a sailing yacht owned by one of its directors, it will not be easy to persuade the court that the transaction was "fair" in the sense that it was

reasonably made to further the business interests of the corporation. The facts that the price paid for the yacht was a "fair" market price, and that the full measure of disclosures made by the director is beyond challenge, may still not be enough to defend and uphold the transaction.

Although MBCA § 8.61(b)(3) makes clear that a director self-dealing transaction that is "fair" should be upheld, even if it was not approved by qualified directors or disinterested shareholders, the process by which the transaction was approved remains relevant:

> *Process of decision.* In some circumstances, the behavior of the director having the conflicting interest may affect the finding and content of "fairness." Fair dealing requires that the director make required disclosure at the relevant time even if the director plays no role in arranging or negotiating the terms of the transaction. One illustration of unfair dealing is the director's failure to disclose fully the director's interest or hidden defects known to the director regarding the transaction. Another illustration would be the exertion by the director of improper pressure upon the other directors or other parties that might be involved with the transaction. Whether a transaction can be successfully challenged by reason of deficient or improper conduct, notwithstanding the fairness of the economic terms, will turn on the court's evaluation of the conduct and its impact on the transaction.

Official Comment to MBCA § 8.60.

Another part of the Official Comment also suggests that the protection of the business judgment rule may not be as absolute under Subchapter F as it is in other contexts:

> Consider, for example, a situation in which it is established that the board of a manufacturing corporation approved a cash loan to a director where the duration, security and interest terms of the loan were at prevailing commercial rates, but (i) the loan was not made in the course of the corporation's business activities and (ii) the loan required a commitment of limited working capital that would otherwise have been used in furtherance of the corporation's business activities. Such a loan transaction would not be afforded safe-harbor protection by section 8.62(b)(1) since the board did not comply with the requirement in section 8.30(a) that the board's action be, in its reasonable judgment, in the best interests of the corporation—that is, that the action will, as the board judges the circumstances at hand, yield favorable results (or reduce detrimental results) as judged from the perspective of furthering the corporation's business activities.

If a determination is made that the terms of a director's conflicting interest transaction, judged according to the circumstances at the time of commitment, were manifestly unfavorable to the corporation, that determination would be relevant to an allegation that the directors' action was not taken in good faith and therefore did not comply with section 8.30(a).

Official Comment to Section 8.61.

Does this comment thrust the courts back into determining fairness, notwithstanding Subchapter F's attempt to limit judicial intervention? Or should Subchapter F be read to shield a conflict of interest transaction whose terms are fair by market standards and from which the corporation benefits, even if the interested director failed to disclose material facts about the transaction? This result would overrule those decisions which have held that disclosure is an indispensable element of fairness. In view of the philosophy underlying Subchapter F, would that be a desirable result?

b. Procedural Fairness

Because they seem more comfortable reviewing the process of decision-making than the substance of a transaction, in determining entire fairness, courts have increasingly given greater weight to procedural considerations. They have focused primarily on (1) the disclosure given the corporate decision-makers, (2) the interest of directors in the transaction, and (3) the effect of shareholder ratification.

i. *Disclosure*

Procedural fairness—whether through approval by disinterested directors or disinterested shareholders—requires full disclosure of the existence of the interested director's conflict and other "material" information concerning the substance of the transaction. The importance of disclosure in director self-dealing transactions antedates modern statutes. Consider the case of a supply contract between a utility company and a manufacturing company owned and managed by one of the utility's directors. *Globe Woolen Co. v. Utica Gas & Electric Co.*, 121 N.E. 378 (N.Y. 1918). The court found that the interested director had dominated the utility board and had negotiated the contract, which proved disastrous for the utility. Although his refusal to vote gave the transaction a presumption of propriety, the court held that the transaction unfair and voidable by the utility company. Judge Cardozo wrote:

> As a result of the contract, Utica Gas has supplied the plaintiff with electric current for nothing, and owes, if the contract stands, about $11,000 for the privilege. These elements of unfairness, Mr. Maynard must have known, if indeed his knowledge be material. He may not have known how great the loss would be. He may have

trusted to the superior technical skill of Mr. Greenidge [an employee of Utica Gas] to compute with approximate accuracy the comparative cost of steam and electricity. But he cannot have failed to know that he held a one-sided contract, which left the defendant at his mercy. He was not blind to the likelihood that in a term of ten years there would be changes in the business. The swiftness with which some of the changes followed permits the inference that they were premeditated. But whether these and other changes were premeditated or not, at least they were recognized as possible. With that recognition, no word of warning was uttered to Greenidge or to any of the defendant's officers. There slumbered within these contracts a potency of profit which the plaintiff neither ignored in their making nor forgot in their enforcement.

It is no answer to say that this potency, if obvious to Maynard, ought also to have been obvious to other members of the committee. They did not know, as he did, the likelihood or the significance of changes in the business. There was need, too, of reflection and analysis before the dangers stood revealed. For the man who framed the contracts there was opportunity to consider and to judge. His fellow members, hearing them for the first time, and trustful of his loyalty, would have no thought of latent peril. That they had none is sufficiently attested by the fact that the contracts were approved. There was inequality, therefore, both in knowledge and in the opportunity for knowledge. It is not important in such circumstances whether the trustee foresaw the precise evils that developed. The inference that he did, might not be unsupported by the evidence. But the indefinite possibilities of hardship, the opportunity in changing circumstances to wrest unlooked-for profits and impose unlooked-for losses, these must have been foreseen. Foreseen or not, they were there, and their presence permeates the contracts with oppression and inequity.

We hold, therefore, that the refusal to vote does not nullify as of course an influence and predominance exerted without a vote. We hold that the constant duty rests on a trustee to seek no harsh advantage to the detriment of his trust, but rather to protest and renounce if through the blindness of those who treat with him he gains what is unfair. And because there is evidence that in the making of these contracts, that duty was ignored, the power of equity was fittingly exercised to bring them to an end.

121 N.E. at 380–81.

Some cases suggest that the failure to make full disclosure constitutes per se unfairness. One such case involved a director, who also was corporate president and a substantial shareholder, who arranged for the sale of corporate properties to another corporation in which he was to have an interest. *State ex rel. Hayes Oyster Co. v. Keypoint Oyster Co.*, 391 P.2d 979, 984 (Wash. 1964). The transaction was submitted to the shareholders for their approval, but without disclosure of the director's interest. In invalidating the transaction, the court stated:

> This court has abolished the mechanical rule whereby any transaction involving corporate property in which a director has an interest is voidable at the option of the corporation. Such a contract cannot be voided if the director or officer can show that the transaction was fair to the corporation. However, non-disclosure by an interested director or officer is, in itself, unfair. This wholesome rule can be applied automatically without any of the unsatisfactory results which flowed from a rigid bar against any self-dealing.

> The shareholders and directors had the right to know of Hayes' interest in the properties in order to intelligently determine the advisability of retaining Hayes as president and manager under the circumstances, and to determine whether or not it was wise to enter into the contract at all, in view of Hayes' conduct. In all fairness, they were entitled to know that their president and director might be placed in a position where he must choose between the interests of the two corporations in conducting their business with one another.

Although this language suggests that only the existence of the director's interest in the transaction need be disclosed, the court (like other courts) also said that the director was obligated to disclose fully all relevant or material information concerning the transaction itself to the directors and shareholders.

ii. *Approval by Directors*

As we have seen DGCL § 144 provides that a transaction is not void or voidable by reason of a conflict of interest if it is approved by "disinterested" directors. The former § 8.31 of the MBCA, some version of which is still in effect in many states, is similar in that it requires approval by directors "who have no direct or indirect interest in the transaction."

In challenges to self-dealing transactions, one of the most often litigated questions is whether the decision-makers are "interested." While it is clear that a decision-maker is interested if she has a direct or indirect financial interest in the transaction, it is less clear whether a *non-financial relationship* with an interested director will call into question the approval by a person who otherwise would be considered disinterested. Official Comment 5 to former MBCA § 8.31 suggests that a person with such a non-financial interest would be considered "interested" if he had "a relationship with the other parties to the transaction such that the relationship might reasonably be expected to affect his judgment in the particular matter in a manner adverse to the corporation."

Delaware law on this point is less clear. While the statute requires approval of the "disinterested" directors, as we saw above in the discussion of *Fliegler v. Lawrence*, such an approval merely renders the transaction not void or voidable, and does not necessarily eliminate the possibility that it can be challenged as unfair. Moreover, there is a suggestion in some cases that the approval of the disinterested directors must be in "good faith." Consequently, even if the approving directors were "disinterested," their approval is ineffective if they were not acting indepently and in good faith. *E.g., In re Walt Disney Co. Derivative Litig.*, 907 A.2d 693, 756 n. 46, 778 (Del.Ch. 2005) aff'd, 906 A.2d 27 (Del. 2006).

iii. Approval by Shareholders

A director self-dealing transaction can also be seen as fair if approved or subsequently ratified by shareholders, if the material facts as to the transaction and the director's interest were disclosed to the shareholders. At common law, informed shareholder ratification created a presumption that the transaction was fair. Thus, many courts indicated that shareholder ratification had the effect of shifting the burden of proof to the party challenging the transaction to show that the terms were so unequal as to amount to waste. Where, however, the interested directors owned a majority of the shares, shareholder ratification generally did not shift the burden of proof to the challenging party.

The shareholder approval provisions of the interested director statutes seem to codify the common law. Thus, an interested director transaction is not void or voidable if the director's interest is disclosed to the shareholders and the shareholders approve the transaction. Technical compliance with the statutory procedures, however, will not immunize a transaction from scrutiny for fairness where the interested directors are also majority shareholders who voted in favor of the transaction.

To avoid the uncertainty of whether shareholder approval is valid if the interested directors vote their shares, it is now common to obtain "majority of the minority" shareholder approval as a condition of the transaction. In fact, some statutes do not permit the voting of shares owned by interested directors when shareholders are asked to approve a director self-dealing transaction. *See* Calif.Corp.Code § 310(a)(1).

Approval by shareholders, compared to that by directors, has the disadvantage that shareholders are not in a position to negotiate the terms of the transaction. Their approval or ratification is on a "take it or leave it" basis. Consider the comments of Harold Marsh:

> The rule permitting shareholder approval of an interested director transaction after full disclosure has been justified on the basis

that where there is shareholder ratification the case is precisely analogous to that of a trustee dealing with his cestui que trust after full disclosure, and is not at all a case of a trustee dealing with himself. However, the validity of this analogy may be seriously questioned. When a trustee deals with his cestui que trust who is an individual that is sui juris, after full disclosure, then the cestui que trust is able to negotiate for himself and there is no more danger of fraud or over-reaching than in any other business transaction. However, when the shareholders of a publicly-held company are asked to ratify a transaction with interested directors they cannot as a practical matter *negotiate* for the corporation. They are, they must be, limited to rejecting or accepting the deal formulated by the interested directors. Even if it be assumed that the deal is fair, that is not what the shareholders are entitled to. They are entitled to have someone negotiate the best deal obtainable for their corporation, fair or unfair.

Harold Marsh, *Are Directors Trustees? Conflict of Interest and Corporate Morality*, 22 Bus. Law. 35, 48–49 (1966).

Should approval by a majority of disinterested shareholders be given conclusive weight? Or is there still a role for the court to ensure fairness? The following cases discuss these questions. The following excerpt considers the effect of shareholder approval of option granted by a board to its own members has on the a challenge based on the obvious conflict of interest involved.

LEWIS V. VOGELSTEIN
699 A.2d 327 (Del.Ch. 1997).

ALLEN, CHANCELLOR:

This shareholders' suit challenges a stock option compensation plan for the directors of Mattel, Inc., which was approved or ratified by the shareholders of the company at its 1996 Annual Meeting of Shareholders ["1996 Plan" or "Plan"]

The facts as they appear in the pleading are as follows. The Plan was adopted in 1996 and ratified by the company's shareholders at the 1996 annual meeting. It contemplates two forms of stock option grants to the company's directors: a one-time grant of options on a block of stock and subsequent, smaller annual grants of further options.

With respect to the one-time grant, the Plan provides that each outside director will qualify for a grant of options on 15,000 shares of Mattel common stock at the market price on the day such options are granted (the "one-time options"). The one-time options are alleged to be exercisable immediately upon being granted although they will achieve economic value, if ever, only with the passage of time. It is alleged that if not exercised, they remain valid for ten years.

With respect to the second type of option grant, the Plan qualifies each director for a grant of options upon his or her re-election to the board each year (the "Annual Options"). The maximum number of options grantable to a director pursuant to the annual options provision depends on the number of years the director has served on the Mattel board. Those outside directors with five or fewer years of service will qualify to receive options on no more than 5,000 shares, while those with more than five years service will qualify for options to purchase up to 10,000 shares. Once granted, these options vest over a four year period, at a rate of 25% per year. When exercisable, they entitle the holder to buy stock at the market price on the day of the grant. According to the complaint, options granted pursuant to the annual options provision also expire ten years from their grant date, whether or not the holder has remained on the board.

When the shareholders were asked to ratify the adoption of the Plan, as is typically true, no estimated present value of options that were authorized to be granted under the Plan was stated in the proxy solicitation materials.

As the presence of valid shareholder ratification of executive or director compensation plans importantly affects the form of judicial review of such grants, it is logical to begin an analysis of the legal sufficiency of the complaint by analyzing the sufficiency of the attack on the disclosures made in connection with the ratification vote.

[The court rejected plaintiff's claim that defendants had a duty to disclose the estimated present value of the stock option grants to which directors might become entitled under the 1996 Plan.]

I turn to the motion to dismiss the complaint's allegation to the effect that the Plan, or grants under it, constitute a breach of the directors' fiduciary duty of loyalty. As the Plan contemplates grants to the directors that approved the Plan and who recommended it to the shareholders, we start by observing that it constitutes self-dealing that would ordinarily require that the directors prove that the grants involved were, in the circumstances, entirely fair to the corporation. However, it is the case that the shareholders have ratified the directors' action. That ratification is attacked only on the ground just treated. Thus, for these purposes I assume that the ratification was effective. The question then becomes what is the effect of informed shareholder ratification on a transaction of this type (*i.e.*, officer or director pay).

What is the effect under Delaware corporation law of shareholder ratification of an interested transaction? The answer to this apparently simple question appears less clear than one would hope or indeed expect. Four possible effects of shareholder ratification appear logically available:

First, one might conclude that an effective shareholder ratification acts as a complete defense to any charge of breach of duty. **Second**, one might conclude that the effect of such ratification is to shift the substantive test on judicial review of the act from one of fairness that would otherwise be obtained (because the transaction is an interested one) to one of waste. **Third**, one might conclude that the ratification shifts the burden of proof of unfairness to plaintiff, but leaves that shareholder-protective test in place. **Fourth**, one might conclude (perhaps because of great respect for the collective action disabilities that attend shareholder action in public corporations) that shareholder ratification offers no assurance of assent of a character that deserves judicial recognition. Thus, under this approach, ratification on full information would be afforded no effect. Excepting the fourth of these effects, there are cases in this jurisdiction that reflect each of these approaches to the effect of shareholder voting to approve a transaction.

In order to state my own understanding I first note that by shareholder ratification I do not refer to every instance in which shareholders vote affirmatively with respect to a question placed before them. I exclude from the question those instances in which shareholder votes are a necessary step in authorizing a transaction. Thus the law of ratification as here discussed has no direct bearing on shareholder action to amend a certificate of incorporation or bylaws. Nor does that law bear on shareholder votes necessary to authorize a merger, a sale of substantially all the corporation's assets, or to dissolve the enterprise. For analytical purposes one can set such cases aside.

1. *Ratification generally:* I start with principles broader than those of corporation law. Ratification is a concept deriving from the law of agency which contemplates the ex post conferring upon or confirming of the legal authority of an agent in circumstances in which the agent had no authority or arguably had no authority. To be effective, of course, the agent must fully disclose all relevant circumstances with respect to the transaction to the principal prior to the ratification. Beyond that, since the relationship between a principal and agent is fiduciary in character, the agent in seeking ratification must act not only with candor, but with loyalty. Thus an attempt to coerce the principal's consent improperly will invalidate the effectiveness of the ratification.

Assuming that a ratification by an agent [*sic*] is validly obtained, what is its effect? One way of conceptualizing that effect is that it provides, after the fact, the grant of authority that may have been wanting at the time of the agent's act. Another might be to view the ratification as consent or as an estoppel by the principal to deny a lack of authority. In either event the effect of informed ratification is to validate or affirm the act of the agent as the act of the principal.

Application of these general ratification principles to shareholder ratification is complicated by three other factors. **First**, most generally, in the case of shareholder ratification there is of course no single individual acting as principal, but rather a class or group of divergent individuals— the class of shareholders. This aggregate quality of the principal means that decisions to affirm or ratify an act will be subject to collective action disabilities; that some portion of the body doing the ratifying may in fact have conflicting interests in the transaction; and some dissenting members of the class may be able to assert more or less convincingly that the "will" of the principal is wrong, or even corrupt and ought not to be binding on the class. In the case of individual ratification these issues won't arise, assuming that the principal does not suffer from multiple personality disorder. Thus the collective nature of shareholder ratification makes it more likely that following a claimed shareholder ratification, nevertheless, there is a litigated claim on behalf of the principal that the agent lacked authority or breached its duty. The **second**, mildly complicating factor present in shareholder ratification is the fact that in corporation law the "ratification" that shareholders provide will often not be directed to lack of legal authority of an agent but will relate to the consistency of some authorized director action with the equitable duty of loyalty. Thus shareholder ratification sometimes acts not to confer legal authority—but as in this case—to affirm that action taken is consistent with shareholder interests. **Third**, when what is "ratified" is a director conflict transaction, the statutory law—in Delaware Section 144 of the Delaware General Corporation Law—may bear on the effect.

2. *Shareholder ratification:* These differences between shareholder ratification of director action and classic ratification by a single principal, do lead to a difference in the effect of a valid ratification in the shareholder context. The principal novelty added to ratification law generally by the shareholder context, is the idea—no doubt analogously present in other contexts in which common interests are held—that, in addition to a claim that ratification was defective because of incomplete information or coercion, shareholder ratification is subject to a claim by a member of the class that the ratification is ineffectual (1) because a majority of those affirming the transaction had a conflicting interest with respect to it or (2) because the transaction that is ratified constituted a corporate waste. As to the second of these, it has long been held that shareholders may not ratify a waste except by a unanimous vote. The idea behind this rule is apparently that a transaction that satisfies the high standard of waste constitutes a gift of corporate property and no one should be forced against their will to make a gift of their property. In all events, informed, uncoerced, disinterested shareholder ratification of a transaction in which corporate directors have a material conflict of interest has the effect of protecting the transaction from judicial review except on the basis of waste.

The judicial standard for determination of corporate waste is well developed. Roughly, a waste entails an exchange of corporate assets for consideration so disproportionately small as to lie beyond the range at which any reasonable person might be willing to trade. Most often the claim is associated with a transfer of corporate assets that serves no corporate purpose; or for which no consideration at all is received. Such a transfer is in effect a gift. If, however, there is *any substantial* consideration received by the corporation, and if there is a *good faith judgment* that in the circumstances the transaction is worthwhile, there should be no finding of waste, even if the fact finder would conclude *ex post* that the transaction was unreasonably risky. Any other rule would deter corporate boards from the optimal rational acceptance of risk. Courts are ill-fitted to attempt to weigh the "adequacy" of consideration under the waste standard or, ex post, to judge appropriate degrees of business risk.

[The court concluded that plaintiff's complaint should not be dismissed because the one time option grants to the directors were sufficiently unusual as to require further inquiry into whether they constituted waste.]

HARBOR FINANCE PARTNERS V. HUIZENGA
751 A.2d 879 (Del.Ch. 1999).

STRINE, VICE CHANCELLOR:

This matter involves a challenge to the acquisition of AutoNation, Incorporated by Republic Industries, Inc. A shareholder plaintiff contends that this acquisition (the "Merger") was a self-interested transaction effected for the benefit of Republic directors who owned a substantial block of AutoNation shares, that the terms of the transaction were unfair to Republic and its public stockholders, and that stockholder approval of the transaction was procured through a materially misleading proxy statement (the "Proxy Statement").

The Rule 12(b)(6) motion: The complaint fails to state a claim that the disclosures in connection with the Merger were misleading or incomplete. The affirmative stockholder vote on the Merger was informed and uncoerced, and disinterested shares constituted the overwhelming proportion of the Republic electorate. As a result, the business judgment rule standard of review is invoked and the Merger may only be attacked as wasteful. As a matter of logic and sound policy, one might think that a fair vote of disinterested stockholders in support of the transaction would dispose of the case altogether because a waste claim must be supported by facts demonstrating that "no person of ordinary sound business judgment" could consider the merger fair to Republic and because many disinterested and presumably rational Republic stockholders voted for the Merger. But under an unbroken line of authority dating from early in this century, a non-unanimous, although overwhelming, free and fair vote of disinterested stockholders does not extinguish a claim for waste. The waste vestige does not aid the plaintiff here, however, because the complaint at best alleges that the Merger was unfair and does not plead facts demonstrating that no reasonable person of ordinary business judgment could believe the transaction advisable for Republic. Thus I grant the defendants' motion to dismiss under Chancery Court Rule 12(b)(6).

Although I recognize that our law has long afforded plaintiffs the vestigial right to prove that a transaction that a majority of fully informed, uncoerced independent stockholders approved by a non-unanimous vote was wasteful, I question the continued utility of this "equitable safety valve."

The origin of this rule is rooted in the distinction between voidable and void acts, a distinction that appears to have grown out of the now largely abolished ultra vires doctrine. Voidable acts are traditionally held to be ratifiable because the corporation can lawfully accomplish them if it does so in the appropriate manner. Thus if directors who could not lawfully effect a transaction without stockholder approval did so anyway, and the requisite approval of the stockholders was later attained, the transaction is deemed fully ratified because the subsequent approval of the stockholders cured the defect.

In contrast, void acts are said to be non-ratifiable because the corporation cannot, in any case, lawfully accomplish them. Such void acts are often described in conclusory terms such as "ultra vires" or "fraudulent" or as "gifts or waste of corporate assets." Because at first blush it seems it would be a shocking, if not theoretically impossible, thing for stockholders to be able to sanction the directors in committing illegal acts or acts beyond the authority of the corporation, it is unsurprising that it has been held that stockholders cannot validate such action by the directors, even on an informed basis.

One of the many practical problems with this seemingly sensible doctrine is that its actual application has no apparent modern day utility insofar as the doctrine covers claims of waste or gift, except as an opportunity for Delaware courts to second-guess stockholders. There are several reasons I believe this to be so.

First, the types of "void" acts susceptible to being styled as waste claims have little of the flavor of patent illegality about them, nor are they categorically ultra vires. Put another way, the oft-stated proposition that "waste cannot be ratified" is a tautology that, upon close examination, has little substantive meaning. I mean, what rational person would ratify "waste"? Stating the question that way, the answer is, of course, no one. But in the real world stockholders are not asked to ratify obviously wasteful transactions. Rather than lacking any plausible business rationale or being clearly prohibited by statutory or common law, the transactions attacked as waste in Delaware courts are ones that are quite ordinary in the modern business world. Thus a review of the Delaware cases reveals that our courts have reexamined the merits of stockholder votes approving such transactions as: stock option plans; the fee agreement between a mutual fund and its investment advisor; corporate mergers; the purchase of a business in the same industry as the acquiring corporation; and the repurchase of a corporate insider's shares in the company. These are all garden variety transactions that may be validly accomplished by a Delaware corporation if supported by sufficient consideration, and what is sufficient consideration is a question that fully informed stockholders seem as well positioned as courts to answer. That is, these transactions are neither per se ultra vires or illegal; they only become "void" upon a determination that the corporation received no fair consideration for entering upon them.

Second, the waste vestige is not necessary to protect stockholders and it has no other apparent purpose. While I would hesitate to permit stockholders to ratify a blatantly illegal act—such as a board's decision to indemnify itself against personal liability for intentionally violating applicable environmental laws or bribing government officials to benefit the corporation—the vestigial exception for waste has little to do with corporate integrity in the sense of the corporation's responsibility to society as a whole. Rather, if there is any benefit in the waste vestige, it must consist in protecting stockholders. And where disinterested stockholders are given the information necessary to decide whether a transaction is beneficial to the corporation or wasteful to it, I see little reason to leave the door open for a judicial reconsideration of the matter.

The fact that a plaintiff can challenge the adequacy of the disclosure is in itself a substantial safeguard against stockholder approval of waste. If the corporate board failed to provide the voters with material information undermining the integrity or financial fairness of the transaction subject to the vote, no ratification effect will be accorded to the vote and the plaintiffs may press all of their claims. As a result, it is difficult to imagine how elimination of the waste vestige will permit the accomplishment of unconscionable corporate transactions, unless one presumes that stockholders are, as a class, irrational and that they will rubber stamp outrageous transactions contrary to their own economic interests.

In this regard, it is noteworthy that Delaware law does not make it easy for a board of directors to obtain "ratification effect" from a stockholder vote. The burden to prove that the vote was fair, uncoerced, and fully informed falls squarely on the board. Given the fact that Delaware law imposes no heightened pleading standards on plaintiffs alleging material nondisclosures or voting coercion and given the pro-plaintiff bias inherent in Rule 12(b)(6), it is difficult for a board to prove ratification at the pleading stage. If the board cannot prevail on a motion to dismiss, the defendant directors will be required to submit to discovery and possibly to a trial.

Nor is the waste vestige necessary to protect minority stockholders from oppression by majority or controlling stockholders. Chancellor Allen recently noted that the justification for the waste vestige is "apparently that a transaction that satisfies the high standard of waste constitutes a gift of corporate property and no one should be forced against their will to make a gift of their property." This justification is inadequate to support continued application of the exception. As an initial matter, I note that property of the corporation is not typically thought of as personal property of the stockholders, and that it is common for corporations to undertake important value-affecting transactions over the objection of some of the voters or without a vote at all.

In any event, my larger point is that this solicitude for dissenters' property rights is already adequately accounted for elsewhere in our corporation law. Delaware fiduciary law ensures that a majority or controlling stockholder cannot use a stockholder vote to insulate a transaction benefiting that stockholder from judicial examination. Only votes controlled by stockholders who are not "interested" in the transaction at issue are eligible for ratification effect in the sense of invoking the business judgment rule rather than the entire fairness form of review. That is, only the votes of those stockholders with no economic incentive to approve a wasteful transaction count.

Indeed, it appears that a corporation with a controlling or majority stockholder may, under current Delaware law, never escape the exacting entire fairness standard through a stockholder vote, even one expressly conditioned on approval by a "majority of the minority." Because of sensitivity about the structural coercion that might be thought to exist in such circumstances, our law limits an otherwise fully informed, uncoerced vote in such circumstances to having the effect of making the plaintiffs prove that the transaction was unfair. Doubtless defendants appreciate this shift, but it still subjects them to a proceeding in which the substantive fairness of their actions comes under close scrutiny by the court—the type of scrutiny that is inappropriate when the business judgment rule's presumption attaches to a decision.

Third, I find it logically difficult to conceptualize how a plaintiff can ultimately prove a waste or gift claim in the face of a decision by fully informed, uncoerced, independent stockholders to ratify the transaction. The test for waste is whether any person of ordinary sound business judgment could view the transaction as fair.

If fully informed, uncoerced, independent stockholders have approved the transaction, they have, it seems to me, made the decision that the transaction is "a fair exchange." As such, it is difficult to see the utility of allowing litigation to proceed in which the plaintiffs are permitted discovery and a possible trial, at great expense to the corporate defendants, in order to prove to the court that the transaction was so devoid of merit that each and every one of the voters comprising the majority must be disregarded as too hopelessly misguided to be considered a "person of ordinary sound business judgment." In this day and age in which investors also have access to an abundance of information about corporate transactions from sources other than boards of directors, it seems presumptuous and paternalistic to assume that the court knows better in a particular instance than a fully informed corporate electorate with real money riding on the corporation's performance.

Finally, it is unclear why it is in the best interests of disinterested stockholders to subject their corporation to the substantial costs of litigation in a situation where they have approved the transaction under attack. Enabling a dissident who failed to get her way at the ballot box in a fair election to divert the corporation's resources to defending her claim on the battlefield of litigation seems, if anything, contrary to the economic well-being of the disinterested stockholders as a class. Why should the law give the dissenters the right to command the corporate treasury over the contrary will of a majority of the disinterested stockholders? The costs to corporations of litigating waste claims are not trifling.

Although there appears to be a trend in the other direction, binding case law still emphasizes the ease with which a plaintiff may state a waste claim and the difficulty of resolving such a claim without a trial. As in this case, proxy statements and other public filings often contain facts that, if true, would render waste claims wholly without merit. Plaintiffs' lawyers (for good reason) rarely put such facts in their complaints and it is doubtful that the court can look to them to resolve a motion to dismiss a waste claim even where the plaintiff has not pled that the facts in the public filings are not true. Given this reality and the teaching of prior cases, claims with no genuine likelihood of success can make it to discovery and perhaps to trial. To the extent that there is corporate waste in such cases, it appears to be some place other than in the corporate transactions under scrutiny.

For all these reasons, a reexamination of the waste vestige would seem to be in order. Although there may be valid reasons for its continuation, those reasons should be articulated and weighed against the costs the vestige imposes on stockholders and the judicial system. Otherwise, inertia alone may perpetuate an outdated rule fashioned in a very different time.

GANTLER V. STEPHENS

965 A.2d 695 (Del. 2009).

[The relevant facts are set forth in Chapter 15, Section B.3.]

JACOBS, JUSTICE.

Finally, we address the issues generated by the dismissal of Count III. That Count alleges that the defendants breached their duty of loyalty by recommending the Reclassification Proposal to the shareholders for purely self-interested reasons (to enlarge their ability to engage in stock buy-backs and to trigger their ESOP put and appraisal rights). The Vice Chancellor concluded that the complaint sufficiently alleged that a majority of the directors that approved the Reclassification Proposal lacked independence. Despite having so concluded, the court dismissed the claim on the ground that a disinterested majority of the shareholders had "ratified" the Reclassification by voting to approve it.

We conclude that the Court of Chancery legally erred in upholding Count III on shareholder ratification grounds, for two reasons. First, because a shareholder vote was required to amend the certificate of incorporation, that approving vote could not also operate to "ratify" the challenged conduct of the interested directors. Second, the adjudicated cognizable claim that the Reclassification Proxy contained a material misrepresentation, eliminates an essential predicate for applying the doctrine, namely, that the shareholder vote was fully informed.

Under current Delaware case law, the scope and effect of the common law doctrine of shareholder ratification is unclear, making it difficult to apply that doctrine in a coherent manner. As the Court of Chancery has noted in *In re Wheelabrator Technologies, Inc., Shareholder Litigation:*

> [The doctrine of ratification] might be thought to lack coherence because the decisions addressing the effect of shareholder "ratification" have fragmented that subject into three distinct compartments, . . . In its "classic" . . . form, shareholder ratification describes the situation where shareholders approve board action that, legally speaking, could be accomplished without any shareholder approval. . . . "[C]lassic" ratification involves the voluntary addition of an independent layer of shareholder approval in circumstances where shareholder approval is not legally required. But "shareholder ratification" has also been used to describe the effect of an informed shareholder vote that was statutorily required for the transaction to have legal existence. . . . That [the Delaware courts] have used the same term is such highly diverse sets of factual circumstances, without regard to their possible functional differences, suggests that "shareholder ratification" has now acquired an expanded meaning intended to describe any approval of challenged board action by a fully

informed vote of shareholders, irrespective of whether that shareholder vote is legally required for the transaction to attain legal existence.

To restore coherence and clarity to this area of our law, we hold that the scope of the shareholder ratification doctrine must be limited to its so-called "classic" form; that is, to circumstances where a fully informed shareholder vote approves director action that does *not* legally require shareholder approval in order to become legally effective. Moreover, the only director action or conduct that can be ratified is that which the shareholders are specifically asked to approve. With one exception, the "cleansing" effect of such a ratifying shareholder vote is to subject the challenged director action to business judgment review, as opposed to "extinguishing" the claim altogether (*i.e.*, obviating all judicial review of the challenged action).[54]

The Court of Chancery held that although Count III of the complaint pled facts establishing that the Reclassification Proposal was an interested transaction not entitled to business judgment protection, the shareholders' fully informed vote "ratifying" that Proposal reinstated the business judgment presumption. That ruling was legally erroneous, for several reasons. First, the ratification doctrine does not apply to transactions where shareholder approval is statutorily required. Here, the Reclassification could not become legally effective without a statutorily mandated shareholder vote approving the amendment to First Niles' certificate of incorporation. Second, because we have determined that the complaint states a cognizable claim that the Reclassification Proxy was materially misleading, that precludes ruling at this procedural juncture, as a matter of law, that the Reclassification was fully informed. Therefore, the approving shareholder vote did not operate as a "ratification" of the challenged conduct in any legally meaningful sense.

C. THE EVOLUTION OF "GOOD FAITH"

1. GOOD FAITH AS A PART OF THE DUTY OF LOYALTY

The concept of "good faith" arises in several aspects of directors' fiduciary duties. The business judgment rule presumes that directors act in good faith. When directors rely on experts, courts ask whether the

---

[54] To the extent that *Smith v. Van Gorkom* holds otherwise, it is overruled. 488 A.2d 858, 889–90 (Del.1985). The only species of claim that shareholder ratification can validly extinguish is a claim that the directors lacked the authority to take action that was later ratified. Nothing herein should be read as altering the well-established principle that void acts such as fraud, gift, waste and ultra vires acts cannot be ratified by a less than unanimous shareholder vote.

To avoid confusion about the doctrinal clarifications set forth in Part III A of this Opinion, we note that they apply only to the common law doctrine of shareholder ratification. They are not intended to affect or alter our jurisprudence governing the effect of an approving vote of disinterested shareholders under 8 *Del. C.* § 144.

reliance was made in good faith. When judges analyze the independence of directors, they often inquire into whether decisions were made in good faith. Indemnification requires that the indemnified director have acted in good faith and, as we have seen, DGCL § 102(b)(7) specifically excludes exculpation for actions "not in good faith." In other words, even if a company adopts a provision limiting director liability to the full extent permitted by that section, directors still can be liable if they do not act in "good faith."

The evolving concept of good faith raises serious questions about the extent to which directors can be held liable for monetary damages for their conduct, whether in exercising their oversight function or engaging in decision-making. On the one hand, if good faith is broadly interpreted, director exculpation clauses authorized by Section 102(b)(7) will have relatively little value. On the other hand, if it is too narrowly interpreted, it runs the risk of being almost meaningless.

The question whether directors acted in "good faith" can arise in two different types of claims, which might be characterized as claims of "misfeasance" and "nonfeasance." In the first type, the claim is that the directors failed to act in good faith in making a business decision. The *Disney* case, discussed below, is an example, in which the decision was the approval of an executive compensation agreement. Other types of decisions that might be challenged include approval of a merger or a decision not to pursue litigation.

The second type of claim involves allegations that directors failed to monitor or oversee corporate activity. Such allegations generally are known as "*Caremark* claims." In the *Citigroup* case in the previous chapter, the court considered and rejected a claim that the directors had acted in bad faith, thereby breaching their duty of loyalty.

We considered the Walt Disney litigation above in the context of the discussion of the duty of care. In another part of his opinion in the Delaware Supreme Court's decision, Justice Jacobs discusses the meaning of "good faith."

IN RE WALT DISNEY CO. DERIVATIVE LITIGATION
906 A.2d 27 (Del. 2006).

JACOBS, JUSTICE:

The first category involves so-called "subjective bad faith," that is, fiduciary conduct motivated by an actual intent to do harm. That such conduct constitutes classic, quintessential bad faith is a proposition so well accepted in the liturgy of fiduciary law that it borders on axiomatic.

The second category of conduct, which is at the opposite end of the spectrum, involves lack of due care—that is, fiduciary action taken solely by reason of gross negligence and without any malevolent intent. Although the Chancellor found, and we agree, that the appellants failed to establish gross negligence, to afford guidance we address the issue of whether gross negligence (including a failure to inform one's self of available material facts), without more, can also constitute bad faith. The answer is clearly no.

The Delaware General Assembly has addressed the distinction between bad faith and a failure to exercise due care (*i.e.*, gross negligence) in two separate contexts. The first is Section 102(b)(7) of the DGCL, which authorizes Delaware corporations, by a provision in the certificate of incorporation, to exculpate their directors from monetary damage liability for a breach of the duty of care. The statute carves out several exceptions, however, including most relevantly, "for acts or omissions not in good faith. . . ." To adopt a definition of bad faith that would cause a violation of the duty of care automatically to become an act or omission "not in good faith," would eviscerate the protections accorded to directors by the General Assembly's adoption of Section 102(b)(7).

A second legislative recognition of the distinction between fiduciary conduct that is grossly negligent and conduct that is not in good faith, is Delaware's indemnification statute, found at 8 Del. C. § 145. To oversimplify, under Delaware statutory law a director or officer of a corporation can be indemnified for liability (and litigation expenses) incurred by reason of a violation of the duty of care, but not for a violation of the duty to act in good faith.

Section 145, like Section 102(b)(7), evidences the intent of the Delaware General Assembly to afford significant protections to directors of Delaware corporations. To adopt a definition that conflates the duty of care with the duty to act in good faith by making a violation of the former an automatic violation of the latter, would nullify those legislative protections and defeat the General Assembly's intent. There is no basis in policy, precedent or common sense that would justify dismantling the distinction between gross negligence and bad faith.

That leaves the third category of fiduciary conduct, which falls in between the first two categories of (1) conduct motivated by subjective bad intent and (2) conduct resulting from gross negligence. This third category is what the Chancellor's definition of bad faith—intentional dereliction of duty, a conscious disregard for one's responsibilities—is intended to capture. The question is whether such misconduct is properly treated as a non-exculpable, non-indemnifiable violation of the fiduciary duty to act in good faith. In our view it must be, for at least two reasons.

First, to protect the interests of the corporation and its shareholders, fiduciary conduct of this kind, which does not involve disloyalty (as traditionally defined) but is qualitatively more culpable than gross negligence, should be proscribed. The Chancellor identified different examples of bad faith as follows:

> A failure to act in good faith may be shown, for instance, where the fiduciary intentionally acts with a purpose other than that of advancing the best interests of the corporation, where the fiduciary acts with the intent to violate applicable positive law, or where the fiduciary intentionally fails to act in the face of a known duty to act, demonstrating a conscious disregard for his duties.

> Second, the legislature has also recognized this intermediate category of fiduciary misconduct, which ranks between conduct involving subjective bad faith and gross negligence. Section 102(b)(7)(ii) of the DGCL expressly denies money damage exculpation for "acts or omissions not in good faith or which involve intentional misconduct or a knowing violation of law." By its very terms that provision distinguishes between "intentional misconduct" and a "knowing violation of law" (both examples of subjective bad faith) on the one hand, and "acts . . . not in good faith," on the other. Because the statute exculpates directors only for conduct amounting to gross negligence, the statutory denial of exculpation for "acts . . . not in good faith" must encompass the intermediate category of misconduct captured by the Chancellor's definition of bad faith.

> For these reasons, we uphold the Court of Chancery's definition as a legally appropriate, although not the exclusive, definition of fiduciary bad faith. We need go no further. To engage in an effort to craft (in the Court's words) "a definitive and categorical definition of the universe of acts that would constitute bad faith" would be unwise and is unnecessary to dispose of the issues presented on this appear.

906 A.2d at 67.

In *Stone v. Ritter,* the Delaware Supreme Court reached what many observers consider the surprising conclusion that the duty of good faith is a branch of the duty of loyalty.

STONE V. RITTER
911 A.2d 362 (Del. 2006).

HOLLAND, JUSTICE:

This is an appeal from a final judgment of the Court of Chancery dismissing a derivative complaint against fifteen present and former directors of AmSouth Bancorporation ("AmSouth"), a Delaware corporation. The plaintiffs-appellants, William and Sandra Stone, are AmSouth shareholders and filed their derivative complaint without making a pre-suit demand on AmSouth's board of directors (the "Board"). The Court of Chancery held that the plaintiffs had failed to adequately plead that such a demand would have been futile.

The Court of Chancery characterized the allegations in the derivative complaint as a "classic *Caremark* claim," a claim that derives its name from *In re Caremark Int'l Deriv. Litig.* In *Caremark*, the Court of Chancery recognized that: "[g]enerally where a claim of directorial liability for corporate loss is predicated upon ignorance of liability creating activities within the corporation . . . only a sustained or systematic failure of the board to exercise oversight—such as an utter failure to attempt to assure a reasonable information and reporting system exists—will establish the lack of good faith that is a necessary condition to liability."

In this appeal, the plaintiffs acknowledge that the directors neither "knew [n]or should have known that violations of law were occurring," *i.e.*, that there were no "red flags" before the directors. Nevertheless, the plaintiffs argue that the Court of Chancery erred by dismissing the derivative complaint which alleged that "the defendants had utterly failed to implement any sort of statutorily required monitoring, reporting or information controls that would have enabled them to learn of problems requiring their attention." The defendants argue that the plaintiffs' assertions are contradicted by the derivative complaint itself and by the documents incorporated therein by reference.

During the relevant period, AmSouth's wholly-owned subsidiary, AmSouth Bank, operated about 600 commercial banking branches in six states throughout the southeastern United States and employed more than 11,600 people. In 2004, AmSouth and AmSouth Bank paid $40 million in fines and $10 million in civil penalties to resolve government and regulatory investigations pertaining principally to the failure by bank employees to file "Suspicious Activity Reports" ("SARs"), as required by the federal Bank Secrecy Act ("BSA") and various anti-money-laundering ("AML") regulations. No fines or penalties were imposed on AmSouth's directors, and no other regulatory action was taken against them.

The government investigations arose originally from an unlawful "Ponzi" scheme operated by Louis D. Hamric, II and Victor G. Nance. In August 2000, Hamric, then a licensed attorney, and Nance, then a registered investment advisor with Mutual of New York, contacted an AmSouth branch bank in Tennessee to arrange for custodial trust accounts to be created for "investors" in a "business venture." That venture (Hamric and Nance represented) involved the construction of medical clinics overseas. In reality, Nance had convinced more than forty of his clients to invest in promissory notes bearing high rates of return, by misrepresenting the nature and the risk of that investment. Relying on similar misrepresentations by Hamric and Nance, the AmSouth branch employees in Tennessee agreed to provide custodial accounts for the investors and to distribute monthly interest payments to each account upon receipt of a check from Hamric and instructions from Nance.

The Hamric-Nance scheme was discovered in March 2002, when the investors did not receive their monthly interest payments. Thereafter, Hamric and Nance became the subject of several civil actions brought by the defrauded investors in Tennessee and Mississippi (and in which AmSouth also was named as a defendant), and also the subject of a federal grand jury investigation in the Southern District of Mississippi. Hamric and Nance were indicted on federal money-laundering charges, and both pled guilty.

[The government authorities found that AmSouth was in violation of the anti-money-laundering program requirements of the Bank Secrecy Act, that "AmSouth's compliance program lacked adequate board and management oversight," and that "reporting to management for the purposes of monitoring and oversight of compliance activities was materially deficient." The investigations culminated in fines and penalties totaling $50 million and a cease and desist order that, among other things, required AmSouth to engage an independent consultant, KPMG Forensic Services, to study its operations. The resulting "KPMG Report" contained a variety of recommendations regarding improved compliance procedures.]

It is a fundamental principle of the Delaware General Corporation Law that "[t]he business and affairs of every corporation organized under this chapter shall be managed by or under the direction of a board of directors. . . ." Thus, "by its very nature [a] derivative action impinges on the managerial freedom of directors." Therefore, the right of a stockholder to prosecute a derivative suit is limited to situations where either the stockholder has demanded the directors pursue a corporate claim and the directors have wrongfully refused to do so, or where demand is excused because the directors are incapable of making an impartial decision regarding whether to institute such litigation. Court of Chancery Rule 23.1, accordingly, requires that the complaint in a derivative action "allege with particularity the efforts, if any, made by the plaintiff to obtain the action the plaintiff desires from the directors [or] the reasons for the plaintiff's failure to obtain the action or for not making the effort."

To excuse demand "a court must determine whether or not the particularized factual allegations of a derivative stockholder complaint create a reasonable doubt that, as of the time the complaint is filed, the board of directors could have properly exercised its independent and disinterested business judgment in responding to a demand." The plaintiffs assert that the incumbent defendant directors "face a substantial likelihood of liability" that renders them "personally interested in the outcome of the decision on whether to pursue the claims asserted in the complaint," and are therefore not disinterested or independent.[12]

Critical to this demand excused argument is the fact that the directors' potential personal liability depends upon whether or not their conduct can be exculpated by the section 102(b)(7) provision contained in the AmSouth certificate of incorporation. Such a provision can exculpate directors from monetary liability for a breach of the duty of care, but not for conduct that is not in good faith or a breach of the duty of loyalty. The standard for assessing a director's potential personal liability for failing to act in good faith in discharging his or her oversight responsibilities has evolved beginning with our decision in Graham v. Allis-Chalmers Manufacturing Company, through the Court of Chancery's Caremark decision to our most recent decision in Disney. A brief discussion of that evolution will help illuminate the standard that we adopt in this case.

Graham was a derivative action brought against the directors of Allis-Chalmers for failure to prevent violations of federal anti-trust laws by Allis-Chalmers employees. There was no claim that the Allis-Chalmers directors knew of the employees' conduct that resulted in the corporation's liability. Rather, the plaintiffs claimed that the Allis-Chalmers directors should have known of the illegal conduct by the corporation's employees. In Graham, this Court held that "absent cause for suspicion there is no duty upon the directors to install and operate a corporate system of espionage to ferret out wrongdoing which they have no reason to suspect exists."

In *Caremark*, the Court of Chancery reassessed the applicability of our holding in Graham when called upon to approve a settlement of a derivative lawsuit brought against the directors of Caremark International, Inc. The plaintiffs claimed that the Caremark directors should have known that certain officers and employees of Caremark were involved in violations of the federal Anti-Referral Payments Law. That law prohibits health care providers from paying any form of remuneration to induce the referral of Medicare or Medicaid patients. The plaintiffs claimed that the Caremark directors breached their fiduciary duty for having "allowed a situation to develop and continue which exposed the corporation to enormous legal liability and that in so doing they violated a duty to be active monitors of corporate performance."

In evaluating whether to approve the proposed settlement agreement in *Caremark,* the Court of Chancery narrowly construed our holding in *Graham* "as standing for the proposition that, absent grounds to suspect deception, neither corporate boards nor senior officers can be charged with

---

[12] The fifteen defendants include eight current and seven former directors. The complaint concedes that seven of the eight current directors are outside directors who have never been employed by AmSouth. One board member, C. Dowd Ritter, the Chairman, is an officer or employee of AmSouth.

wrongdoing simply for assuming the integrity of employees and the honesty of their dealings on the company's behalf." The *Caremark* Court opined it would be a "mistake" to interpret this Court's decision in *Graham* to mean that corporate boards may satisfy their obligation to be reasonably informed concerning the corporation, without assuring themselves that information and reporting systems exist in the organization that are reasonably designed to provide to senior management and to the board itself timely, accurate information sufficient to allow management and the board, each within its scope, to reach informed judgments concerning both the corporation's compliance with law and its business performance.

To the contrary, the *Caremark* Court stated, "it is important that the board exercise a good faith judgment that the corporation's information and reporting system is in concept and design adequate to assure the board that appropriate information will come to its attention in a timely manner as a matter of ordinary operations, so that it may satisfy its responsibility." The *Caremark* Court recognized, however, that "the duty to act in good faith to be informed cannot be thought to require directors to possess detailed information about all aspects of the operation of the enterprise." The Court of Chancery then formulated the following standard for assessing the liability of directors where the directors are unaware of employee misconduct that results in the corporation being held liable:

> Generally where a claim of directorial liability for corporate loss is predicated upon ignorance of liability creating activities within the corporation, as in *Graham* or in this case, . . . only a sustained or systematic failure of the board to exercise oversight-such as an utter failure to attempt to assure a reasonable information and reporting system exists—will establish the lack of good faith that is a necessary condition to liability.

As evidenced by the language quoted above, the *Caremark* standard for so-called "oversight" liability draws heavily upon the concept of director failure to act in good faith. That is consistent with the definition(s) of bad faith recently approved by this Court in its recent *Disney* decision, where we held that a failure to act in good faith requires conduct that is qualitatively different from, and more culpable than, the conduct giving rise to a violation of the fiduciary duty of care (*i.e.*, gross negligence). In *Disney*, we identified the following examples of conduct that would establish a failure to act in good faith:

> A failure to act in good faith may be shown, for instance, where the fiduciary intentionally acts with a purpose other than that of advancing the best interests of the corporation, where the fiduciary acts with the intent to violate applicable positive law, or where the fiduciary intentionally fails to act in the face of a known duty to act, demonstrating a conscious disregard for his duties.

There may be other examples of bad faith yet to be proven or alleged, but these three are the most salient.

The third of these examples describes, and is fully consistent with, the lack of good faith conduct that the *Caremark* court held was a "necessary condition" for director oversight liability, *i.e.*, "a sustained or systematic failure of the board to exercise oversight—such as an utter failure to attempt to assure a reasonable information and reporting system exists. . . ." Indeed, our opinion in *Disney* cited *Caremark* with approval for that proposition. Accordingly, the Court of Chancery applied the correct standard in assessing whether demand was excused in this case where failure to exercise oversight was the basis or theory of the plaintiffs' claim for relief.

It is important, in this context, to clarify a doctrinal issue that is critical to understanding fiduciary liability under *Caremark* as we construe that case. The phraseology used in *Caremark* and that we employ here—describing the lack of good faith as a "necessary condition to liability"—is deliberate. The purpose of that formulation is to communicate that a failure to act in good faith is not conduct that results, ipso facto, in the direct imposition of fiduciary liability. The failure to act in good faith may result in liability because the requirement to act in good faith "is a subsidiary element[,]" *i.e.*, a condition, "of the fundamental duty of loyalty." It follows that because a showing of bad faith conduct, in the sense described in *Disney* and *Caremark*, is essential to establish director oversight liability, the fiduciary duty violated by that conduct is the duty of loyalty.

This view of a failure to act in good faith results in two additional doctrinal consequences. First, although good faith may be described colloquially as part of a "triad" of fiduciary duties that includes the duties of care and loyalty, the obligation to act in good faith does not establish an independent fiduciary duty that stands on the same footing as the duties of care and loyalty. Only the latter two duties, where violated, may directly result in liability, whereas a failure to act in good faith may do so, but indirectly. The second doctrinal consequence is that the fiduciary duty of loyalty is not limited to cases involving a financial or other cognizable fiduciary conflict of interest. It also encompasses cases where the fiduciary fails to act in good faith. As the Court of Chancery aptly put it in *Guttman*, "[a] director cannot act loyally towards the corporation unless she acts in the good faith belief that her actions are in the corporation's best interest."

We hold that *Caremark* articulates the necessary conditions predicate for director oversight liability: (a) the directors utterly failed to implement any reporting or information system or controls; or (b) having implemented such a system or controls, consciously failed to monitor or oversee its operations thus disabling themselves from being informed of risks or problems requiring their attention. In either case, imposition of liability requires a showing that the directors knew that they were not discharging their fiduciary obligations. Where directors fail to act in the face of a known duty to act, thereby demonstrating a conscious disregard for their responsibilities, they breach their duty of loyalty by failing to discharge that fiduciary obligation in good faith.

The plaintiffs contend that demand is excused under *Rule 23.1* because AmSouth's directors breached their oversight duty and, as a result, face a "substantial likelihood of liability" as a result of their "utter failure" to act in good faith to put into place policies and procedures to ensure compliance with BSA and AML obligations. The Court of Chancery found that the plaintiffs did not plead the existence of "red flags"—"facts showing that the board ever was aware that AmSouth's internal controls were inadequate, that these inadequacies would result in illegal activity, and that the board chose to do nothing about problems it allegedly knew existed." In dismissing the derivative complaint in this action, the Court of Chancery concluded:

> This case is not about a board's failure to carefully consider a material corporate decision that was presented to the board. This is a case where information was not reaching the board because of ineffective internal controls. . . . With the benefit of hindsight, it is beyond question that AmSouth's internal controls with respect to the Bank Secrecy Act and anti-money laundering regulations compliance were inadequate. Neither party disputes that the lack of internal controls resulted in a huge fine—$50 million, alleged to be the largest ever of its kind. The fact of those losses, however, is not alone enough for a court to conclude that a majority of the corporation's board of directors is disqualified from considering demand that AmSouth bring suit against those responsible.

The KPMG Report evaluated the various components of AmSouth's longstanding BSA/AML compliance program. The KPMG Report reflects that AmSouth's Board dedicated considerable resources to the BSA/AML compliance program and put into place numerous procedures and systems to attempt to ensure compliance. According to KPMG, the program's various components exhibited between a low and high degree of compliance with applicable laws and regulations.

The KPMG Report describes the numerous AmSouth employees, departments and committees established by the Board to oversee AmSouth's compliance with the BSA and to report violations to management and the Board:

> **BSA Officer.** Since 1998, AmSouth has had a "BSA Officer" "responsible for all BSA/AML-related matters including employee training, general communications, CTR reporting and SAR reporting," and "presenting AML policy and program changes to the Board of Directors, the managers at the various lines of

business, and participants in the annual training of security and audit personnel[;]"

BSA/AML Compliance Department. AmSouth has had for years a BSA/AML Compliance Department, headed by the BSA Officer and comprised of nineteen professionals, including a BSA/AML Compliance Manager and a Compliance Reporting Manager;

Corporate Security Department. AmSouth's Corporate Security Department has been at all relevant times responsible for the detection and reporting of suspicious activity as it relates to fraudulent activity, and William Burch, the head of Corporate Security, has been with AmSouth since 1998 and served in the U.S. Secret Service from 1969 to 1998; and

Suspicious Activity Oversight Committee. Since 2001, the "Suspicious Activity Oversight Committee" and its predecessor, the "AML Committee," have actively overseen AmSouth's BSA/AML compliance program. The Suspicious Activity Oversight Committee's mission has for years been to "oversee the policy, procedure, and process issues affecting the Corporate Security and BSA/AML Compliance Programs, to ensure that an effective program exists at AmSouth to deter, detect, and report money laundering, suspicious activity and other fraudulent activity."

The KPMG Report reflects that the directors not only discharged their oversight responsibility to establish an information and reporting system, but also proved that the system was designed to permit the directors to periodically monitor AmSouth's compliance with BSA and AML regulations. For example, as KPMG noted in 2004, AmSouth's designated BSA Officer "has made annual high-level presentations to the Board of Directors in each of the last five years." Further, the Board's Audit and Community Responsibility Committee (the "Audit Committee") oversaw AmSouth's BSA/AML compliance program on a quarterly basis. The KPMG Report states that "the BSA Officer presents BSA/AML training to the Board of Directors annually," and the "Corporate Security training is also presented to the Board of Directors."

The KPMG Report shows that AmSouth's Board at various times enacted written policies and procedures designed to ensure compliance with the BSA and AML regulations. For example, the Board adopted an amended bank-wide "BSA/AML Policy" on July 17, 2003—four months before AmSouth became aware that it was the target of a government investigation. That policy was produced to plaintiffs in response to their demand to inspect AmSouth's books and records pursuant to section 220 and is included in plaintiffs' appendix. Among other things, the July 17, 2003, BSA/AML Policy directs all AmSouth employees to immediately report suspicious transactions or activity to the BSA/AML Compliance Department or Corporate Security.

In this case, the adequacy of the plaintiffs' assertion that demand is excused depends on whether the complaint alleges facts sufficient to show that the defendant directors are potentially personally liable for the failure of non-director bank employees to file SARs. Delaware courts have recognized that "[m]ost of the decisions that a corporation, acting through its human agents, makes are, of course, not the subject of director attention." Consequently, a claim that directors are subject to personal liability for employee failures is "possibly the most difficult theory in corporation law upon which a plaintiff might hope to win a judgment."

For the plaintiffs' derivative complaint to withstand a motion to dismiss, "only a sustained or systematic failure of the board to exercise oversight—such as an utter failure to attempt to assure a reasonable information and reporting system exists—will establish the lack of good faith that is a necessary condition to liability." As the *Caremark* decision noted:

> Such a test of liability—lack of good faith as evidenced by sustained or systematic failure of a director to exercise reasonable oversight—is quite high. But, a demanding test of liability in the oversight context is probably beneficial to corporate shareholders as a class, as it is in the board decision context, since it makes board service by qualified persons more likely, while continuing to act as a stimulus to good faith performance of duty by such directors.

The KPMG Report—which the plaintiffs explicitly incorporated by reference into their derivative complaint—refutes the assertion that the directors "never took the necessary steps . . . to ensure that a reasonable BSA compliance and reporting system existed." KPMG's findings reflect that the Board received and approved relevant policies and procedures, delegated to certain employees and departments the responsibility for filing SARs and monitoring compliance, and exercised oversight by relying on periodic reports from them. Although there ultimately may have been failures by employees to report deficiencies to the Board, there is no basis for an oversight claim seeking to hold the directors personally liable for such failures by the employees.

With the benefit of hindsight, the plaintiffs' complaint seeks to equate a bad outcome with bad faith. The lacuna in the plaintiffs' argument is a failure to recognize that the directors' good faith exercise of oversight responsibility may not invariably prevent employees from violating criminal laws, or from causing the corporation to incur significant financial liability, or both, as occurred in *Graham*, *Caremark* and this very case. In the absence of red flags, good faith in the context of oversight must be measured by the directors' actions "to assure a reasonable information and reporting system exists" and not by second-guessing after the occurrence of employee conduct that results in an unintended adverse outcome.

Accordingly, we hold that the Court of Chancery properly applied *Caremark* and dismissed the plaintiffs' derivative complaint for failure to excuse demand by alleging particularized facts that created reason to doubt whether the directors had acted in good faith in exercising their oversight responsibilities.

The judgment of the Court of Chancery is affirmed.

You will have noted that the *Stone* opinion speaks favorably of *Caremark* and its extensive discussion of a board's duty to monitor. *Caremark* was decided only a few weeks before *Stone*, and, as mentioned in the preceding chapter, Chancellor Allen analyzed it under traditional notions of the duty of care. In a passage quoted by the *Stone* court, however, Chancellor Allen writes, "only a sustained or systematic failure of the board to exercise oversight . . . will establish *the lack of good faith* that is a necessary condition to liability." (Emphasis added.) What is significant, and came as a surprise to many commentators, is that *Stone* held that a failure of good faith was not only a breach of the duty of care, but that it was, in fact, a breach of the duty of loyalty. Professor Bainbridge opined that *Stone* "ripped the Caremark claim from its original home in the duty of care and reinvented it as a duty of loyalty." Stephen M. Bainbridge, *Caremark and Enterprise Risk Management*, 34 J. Corp. L. 967, 974–75 (2009). Importantly, breaches of the duty of loyalty are not exculpable under a § 102(b)(7) clause in the certificate of incorporation.

2.   THE DUTY OF GOOD FAITH APPLIED

ATR-KIM ENG FINANCIAL CORP. V. ARANETA
2006 WL 3783520 (Del.Ch. 2006).

STRINE, VICE CHANCELLOR.

Plaintiffs ATR-Kim Eng Financial Corp. ("ATR Financial") and ATR-Kim Eng Capital Partners, Inc. ("ATR Capital") (collectively, "ATR") own 10% of the shares of a holding company—PMHI Holdings Corp. (f/k/a LBC Global Corp.) (the "Delaware Holding Company"). ATR claims that defendant Carlos Araneta, who controlled the remaining 90% of the Delaware Holding Company's equity and served as chairman of its board, caused the corporation to transfer its key assets—its ownership of several businesses worth over $35 million (the "LBC Operating Companies")—to members of his family in violation of his fiduciary duties. The Delaware Holding Company was formed precisely to enable ATR to share with Araneta in the benefits of owning the LBC Operating Companies. But, after Araneta denuded the Delaware Holding Company of those assets, ATR was left with only a minority stock ownership position in a floundering joint venture that it had undertaken with Araneta, a position that is worth very little. Meanwhile, Araneta and his family were left with sole control of the LBC Operating Companies, which, from the record, appear to be thriving.

Furthermore, ATR claims that the other members of the board of directors of the Delaware Holding Company, defendants Hugo Bonilla and Liza Berenguer, are jointly and severally liable for this harm because they failed to take any steps to monitor Araneta and prevent his self-dealing. Bonilla was the head of Araneta's operations in the United States, and Berenguer served as the Chief Financial Officer of his worldwide enterprise. They essentially admit that they regarded themselves as mere employees of Araneta and failed to take any steps to fulfill their fiduciary duties to the Delaware Holding Company. As directors, they were charged with protecting the interests of their corporation and its stockholders. Yet, Bonilla and Berenguer allowed Araneta to do whatever he wanted, without any examination of whether his conduct benefited the Delaware Holding Company and all of its stockholders, rather than simply Araneta personally.

In this post-trial opinion, I find that Araneta breached his duty of loyalty by impoverishing the Delaware Holding Company for his own personal enrichment. Bonilla and Berenguer also breached their duty of loyalty. Having assumed the important fiduciary duties that come with a directorship in a Delaware corporation, Bonilla and Berenguer acted as— no other word captures it so accurately—stooges for Araneta, seeking to please him and only him, and having no regard for their obligations to act loyally towards the corporation and all of its stockholders. Such behavior is not indicative of a good faith error in judgment; it reflects a conscious decision to approach one's role in a faithless manner by acting as a tool of a particular stockholder rather than an independent and impartial fiduciary honestly seeking to make decisions for the best interests of the corporation. Although it is clearly the case that Araneta is the most culpable of the defendants, Bonilla and Berenguer are accountable for their complicity in his wrongful endeavors.

I now come to a slightly more difficult issue. Namely, to what extent should Araneta's fellow directors, Bonilla and Berenguer, share responsibility for harming the Delaware Holding Company and ATR? Making this more challenging is that ATR does not allege that either Berenguer or Bonilla participated in, approved of, or directly profited from Araneta's removal of the LBC Operating Companies. Rather, ATR claims that Bonilla and Berenguer consciously breached the important duties articulated in this court's *Caremark* decision and recently reaffirmed by our Supreme Court in *Stone v. Ritter*. Specifically, ATR alleges that Bonilla and Berenguer failed to monitor Araneta's conduct thereby allowing his self-dealing to continue.

Under Delaware law, it is fundamental that a director cannot act loyally towards the corporation unless she tries—*i.e.*, makes a genuine, good faith effort—to do her job as a director. One cannot accept the important role of director in a Delaware corporation and thereafter consciously avoid any attempt to carry out one's duties.

One of the most important duties of a corporate director is to monitor the potential that others within the organization will violate their duties. Thus, "a director's obligation includes a duty to attempt in good faith to assure that a corporate information and reporting system, which the board considers to be adequate, exists." Obviously, such a reporting system will not remove the possibility of illegal or improper acts, but it is the directors' charge to "exercise a good faith judgment that the corporation's information and reporting system is in concept and design adequate to assure the board that appropriate information will come to its attention in a timely manner as a matter of ordinary questions, so that it may satisfy its responsibility."

From the testimony of the directors of the Delaware Holding Company, it is apparent that no reporting system was in place and that no other information systems or controls were ever considered, let alone implemented, by the Delaware Holding Company's board of directors. They did not even have regular board meetings. As a result, the directors were often unaware of corporate activities—despite how easy that would have been given the Delaware Holding Company's modest size. Berenguer testified that although there had been meetings regarding the Delaware Holding Company before the LBC Operating Companies were transferred into the corporation in January 2001, she did not remember any meetings of the board of directors or of the shareholders after that time. Bonilla confirmed this fact, explaining that when the Delaware Holding Company's name was changed from LBC Global, Corp. to PMHI Holdings, Corp., he was never informed about the change, never voted to approve it, and did not even know what the initials PMHI in the new corporate name stood for at the time he signed the certificate of amendment as the corporation's authorized agent. Even when corporate activities involved them directly— as in the case of their supposed resignations from the board of directors— neither Berenguer nor Bonilla questioned the wisdom of Araneta's actions nor insisted that corporate procedures be followed.[120]

Moreover, both Berenguer and Bonilla testified that they entirely deferred to Araneta in matters relating to the Delaware Holding Company.

---

[120] Notwithstanding the issues regarding the date of their resignation as directors, the process by which Berenguer and Bonilla were removed by Araneta is telling. Bonilla testified that he received a phone call from Araneta informing them that he was no longer a director of the Delaware Holding Company. Berenguer explained that she did not give formal written notice of her resignation; instead, Araneta just "took it [she] wanted to resign" from the Delaware Holding Company based on her general "verbal intention" to "resign in all LBC" and eventually "replaced" her.

Berenguer is, as mentioned, Araneta's niece and served as the CFO for the LBC group of companies worldwide. She testified that she would not insert herself into a disagreement between ATR and Araneta about how the Delaware Holding Company should proceed on an issue because such a disagreement would be between those parties and would not affect her as a director of the Delaware Holding Company. Similarly, she stated that she would take Araneta's word as authoritative if he claimed that he had agreed with ATR to take certain actions. Bonilla, the head of Araneta's U.S. operations, was more explicit—explaining that to him Araneta and the Delaware Holding Company were basically one and the same and that he took the word of Araneta as being the word of the company. Moreover, when pressed regarding whether he would undertake an independent inquiry if told to act by Araneta, Bonilla responded, "Why should I ask him all these questions? He's telling me they have already agreed. . . . It's not like I'm going to go out there and check on him, doesn't make sense."

Based on these failures, neither Berenguer nor Bonilla can be said to have upheld their fiduciary obligations. Although it was Araneta who ran amok by emptying the Delaware Holding Company of its major assets, the other directors did nothing to make themselves aware of this blatant misconduct or to stop it. Put in plain terms, it is no safe harbor to claim that one was a paid stooge for a controlling stockholder. Berenguer and Bonilla voluntarily assumed the fiduciary roles of directors of the Delaware Holding Company. For them to say that they never bothered to check whether the Delaware Holding Company retained its primary assets and never took any steps to recover the LBC Operating Companies once they realized that those assets were gone is not a defense. To the contrary, it is a confession that they consciously abandoned any attempt to perform their duties independently and impartially, as they were required to do by law. Their behavior was not the product of a lapse in attention or judgment; it was the product of a willingness to serve the needs of their employer, Araneta, even when that meant intentionally abandoning the important obligations they had taken on to the Delaware Holding Company and its minority stockholder, ATR.

When required by their office to be loyal to the Delaware Holding Company, Bonilla and Berenguer chose total fealty to Araneta's conflicting interests instead. Consequently, I find them jointly liable for Araneta's fiduciary violations.

McPADDEN V. SIDHU
964 A.2d 1262 (Del.Ch. 2008).

CHANDLER, CHANCELLOR.

Though what must be shown for bad faith conduct has not yet been completely defined, it is quite clearly established that gross negligence, alone, cannot constitute bad faith. Thus, a board of directors may act "badly" without acting in bad faith. This sometimes fine distinction between a breach of care (through gross negligence) and a breach of loyalty (through bad faith) is one illustrated by the actions of the board in this case.

In June 2005, the board of directors of i2 Technologies, Inc. ("i2" or the "Company") approved the sale of i2's wholly owned subsidiary, Trade Services Corporation ("TSC"), to a management team led by then-TSC vice president, defendant Anthony Dubreville ("Dubreville") for $3 million. Two years later, after first rejecting an offer of $18.5 million as too low just six months after the sale, Dubreville sold TSC to another company for over $25 million. These transactions engendered this lawsuit and the motions to dismiss presently before me. Plaintiff alleges that the Company's directors caused the Company to sell TSC to Dubreville's team for a price that the directors knew to be a mere fraction of TSC's fair market value.

The gravamen of plaintiff's complaint is that i2's directors caused the Company to sell TSC, its wholly owned subsidiary, to members of TSC's management in bad faith for a price that defendants knew was a fraction of TSC's fair market value.

Though defendants insist that plaintiff has failed to plead particularized facts to excuse his failure to make a demand upon i2's board, I find that demand is excused as futile, as explained below. I then consider the effect of the section 102(b)(7) provision on plaintiff's claims for breach of fiduciary duty against the Director Defendants and Dubreville and for unjust enrichment against Dubreville.

In evaluating the decisions of boards, the courts of this State have consistently noted the limited nature of such judicial determinations of due care: "Due care in the decisionmaking context is *process* due care only." Where, as here, the board has retained an expert to assist the board in its decision making process, the Delaware Supreme Court has specified that a complaint will survive a motion to dismiss in a due care case if it alleges particularized facts that, if proven, would show that "the subject matter . . . that was material and reasonably available was so obvious that the board's failure to consider it was grossly negligent regardless of the expert's advice or lack of advice." Contrary to defendants' cursory treatment of this argument, I conclude that the complaint does plead particularized facts demonstrating that material and reasonably available information was not considered by the board and that such lack of consideration constituted gross negligence, irrespective of any reliance on the Sonenshine fairness opinion.

The challenged transaction at issue—the sale of TSC to Dubreville's group—is analytically a series of discrete board actions. Plaintiff has sufficiently alleged facts to create a reasonable doubt that they, together, cannot be the product of a valid exercise of the board's business judgment. The board's first step in the series of actions culminating in the sale of TSC to Dubreville was also its most egregious: tasking Dubreville with the sale process of TSC when the board knew that Dubreville was interested in purchasing TSC. Certainly Dubreville's interest as a potential purchaser was material to the board's decision in determining to whom to assign the task of soliciting bids and offers for TSC. It would be in Dubreville's own self-interest to obtain low offers for TSC; the more diligent he was about seeking the best offers for TSC, the higher Dubreville himself would have to bid. Had the board not known of Dubreville's interest in the sale, its decision to charge him with finding a buyer for TSC might be less perplexing. Yet, this material information was not merely reasonably available to the board, it was actually known. Dubreville had already discussed with i2 the possibility of leading a management buyout of TSC, an idea that Sidhu, Clemmer, Cash, Crandall, and McGrath discussed at the February 1, 2005 board meeting (and a topic that was later revisited during the March 9, 2005 meeting). Nevertheless, the board decided that Dubreville, whom the board knew was conflicted, would conduct the sale process. From this point forward, the board's actions only exacerbated a misstep that was presumably otherwise correctable or perhaps even unactionable.

Despite having tasked a potential purchaser of TSC with its sale, the board appears to have engaged in little to no oversight of that sale process, providing no check on Dubreville's half-hearted (or, worse, intentionally misdirected) efforts in soliciting bids for TSC. Dubreville's limited attempts to find a buyer for TSC did not include contacting the most obvious potential buyers: TSC's direct competitors, particularly a competitor that had previously offered as much as $25 million for TSC in 2003. Perhaps unsurprisingly, Dubreville's group emerged as the highest bidder for TSC from the sale process.

The board, during its consideration of the offers for TSC at the April 18, 2005 meeting, discussed the Sonenshine Document, which clearly described Dubreville's efforts in selectively contacting potential buyers. Thus, the Director Defendants knew that Dubreville did not contact any TSC competitors. Yet the Director Defendants did nothing to remedy the situation they created by tasking an interested purchaser with the sale of an asset of the Company. Instead, they authorized further discussions with TSH and, on April 22, 2005, signed a letter of intent for i2 to sell TSC to Dubreville and his group and, in doing so, missed another opportunity to rectify the situation they had created.

In addition, the two sets of projections described in the Sonenshine Document should have alerted the board to carefully consider whether Dubreville's offer was high enough. The Directors Defendants knew that Sonenshine's preliminary valuation of TSC was based on projections provided by management, which were prepared at the direction of Dubreville. The Director Defendants therefore also knew that the valuation was calculated using these "buyer" projections. The January projections valued TSC at $6 to $10.8 million. Even the February projections, which plaintiff alleges were adjusted to make TSC appear significantly less profitable than it was, valued TSC at $3 to $7 million. Despite this, the board agreed to proceed with an offer of $3 million, which would only ultimately result in a net gain of $2.2 million because of terms in the agreement favorable to Dubreville. The entire offer of $3 million, not even considering its ultimate net value, was at the lowest end of the valuation range of TSC using even the February projections.

The board's actions, to this point, are quite puzzling. In making its decisions, the board had no shortage of information that was both material—because it affected the process and ultimate result of the sale—and reasonably available (or, even, actually known as evidenced by the discussions at the board meetings): Dubreville's interest in leading a management buyout of TSC; Dubreville's limited efforts in soliciting offers for TSC, including his failure to contact TSC competitors, including one he knew had previously expressed concrete interest in purchasing TSC; the circumstances under which the January and February projections were produced; the use of those projections in Sonenshine's preliminary valuations of TSC; and that TSH was a group led by Dubreville. That the board would want to consider this information seems, to me, so obvious that it is equally obvious that the Directors Defendants' failure to do so was grossly negligent.

Finally, on June 28, 2008, the board and the special committee approved the sale of TSC to Dubreville. As detailed above, plaintiff argues strenuously that the Sonenshine fairness opinion was flawed and that the Director Defendants cannot reasonably have relied on it. Because, however, I conclude that the Director Defendants' actions, culminating with the approval of the sale of TSC, were grossly negligent, I need not further consider the board's reliance on the Sonenshine fairness opinion or the reliability of the opinion in finding that demand is excused as futile.

Though plaintiff has demonstrated that it would have been futile to make a demand upon the board, plaintiff fails to state a claim against the Director Defendants, who have the benefit of a section 102(b)(7) exculpatory provision in the i2 certificate, because plaintiff has not adequately alleged that the Director Defendants acted in bad faith. In contrast, however, plaintiff has stated a claim for both breach of fiduciary duty and unjust enrichment as to Dubreville. Dubreville, though he, as an officer, owes the same duties to the Company as the Director Defendants, does not benefit from the same protections as the Director Defendants because the section 102(b)(7) provision operates to exculpate only directors, not officers.

As authorized by Section 102(b)(7), i2's certificate of incorporation contains an exculpatory provision, limiting the personal liability of directors for certain conduct. Certain conduct, however, cannot be exculpated, including bad faith actions. Gross negligence, in contrast, is exculpated because such conduct breaches the duty of care. Traditionally, "[i]n the duty of care context gross negligence has been defined as 'reckless indifference to or a deliberate disregard of the whole body of stockholders or actions which are without the bounds of reason.'" Recently, however, the Supreme Court has modified Delaware's understanding of the definition of gross negligence in the context of fiduciary duty. In analyzing "three different categories of fiduciary behavior [that] are candidates for the 'bad faith' pejorative label," the Court made quite clear that gross negligence cannot be such an example of bad faith conduct: "[t]here is no basis in policy, precedent or common sense that would justify dismantling the distinction between gross negligence and bad faith." Instead, the Court concluded that conduct motivated by subjective bad intent and that resulting from gross negligence are at opposite ends of the spectrum. The Court then considered a third category of conduct: the intentional dereliction of duty or the conscious disregard for one's responsibilities. The Court determined that such misconduct must be treated as a non-exculpable, non-indemnifiable violation of the fiduciary duty to act in good faith, a duty that the Court later confirmed was squarely within the duty of loyalty. Thus, from the sphere of actions that was once classified as grossly negligent conduct that gives rise to a violation of the duty of care, the Court has carved out one specific type of conduct—the intentional dereliction of duty or the conscious disregard for one's responsibilities—and redefined it as bad faith conduct, which results in a breach of the duty of loyalty. Therefore, Delaware's current understanding of gross negligence is conduct that constitutes reckless indifference or actions that are without the bounds of reason.

The conduct of the Director Defendants here fits precisely within this revised understanding of gross negligence. In finding that demand is excused as futile, I have already concluded that plaintiff has pleaded with particularity so as to raise a reasonable doubt that the actions of the board were a product of the valid exercise of their business judgment. Thus, for the reasons explained above, the Director Defendants' actions, beginning with placing Dubreville in charge of the sale process of TSC and continuing through their failure to act in any way so as to ensure that the sale process employed was thorough and complete, are properly characterized as either recklessly indifferent or unreasonable. Plaintiff has not, however, sufficiently alleged that the Director Defendants acted in bad faith through a conscious disregard for their duties. Instead, plaintiff has ably pleaded that the Director Defendants quite clearly were not careful enough in the discharge of their duties—that is, they acted with gross negligence or else reckless indifference. Because such conduct breaches the Director Defendants' duty of care, this violation is exculpated by the Section

102(b)(7) provision in the Company's charter and therefore the Director Defendants' motion to dismiss for failure to state a claim must be granted.

3. WHITHER GOOD FAITH?

McPadden seems to raise as many questions as it answers. Chancellor Chandler wants to make clear that the conscious disregard of a known duty does not, by itself, destroy the exculpation protections of § 102(b)(7). As he notes, "a board of directors may act 'badly' without acting in bad faith." On the other hand, as the court in *Disney* made clear, its examples of bad faith were illustrative and not exhaustive. In *McPadden*, the transaction involved a sale to an insider who the directors knew had a conflict of interest in circumstances in which the directors also knew that the sale process was problematic. In such circumstances, arguably the directors' recklessness could still fall within the concept of bad faith.

Nevertheless, in another case decided contemporaneously with *McPadden*, Vice-Chancellor Strine examined the concept of bad faith in a transactional (rather than oversight) context and also adopted a broad view of the exception in Section 102(b)(7).

> To this point, the plaintiffs' use of this body of law also makes clear the policy danger raised by transporting a doctrine rooted in the monitoring context and importing it into a context where a discrete transaction was approved by the board. When a discrete transaction is under consideration, a board will always face the question of how much process should be devoted to that transaction given its overall importance in light of the myriad of other decisions the board must make. Seizing specific opportunities is an important business skill, and that involves some measure of risk. Boards may have to choose between acting rapidly to seize a valuable opportunity without the luxury of months, or even weeks, of deliberation—such as a large premium offer—or losing it altogether. Likewise, a managerial commitment to timely decision making is likely to have systemic benefits but occasionally result in certain decisions being made that, with more time, might have come out differently. Courts should therefore be extremely chary about labeling what they perceive as deficiencies in the deliberations of an independent board majority over a discrete transaction as not merely negligence or even gross negligence, but as involving bad faith. In the transactional context, a very extreme set of facts would seem to be required to sustain a disloyalty claim premised on the notion that disinterested directors were intentionally disregarding their duties. Where, as here, the board employed a special committee that met frequently, hired reputable advisors, and met frequently itself, a *Caremark*-based liability theory is untenable.

In re Lear Corporation Shareholders Litig., 967 A.2d 640, 654–655 (Del.Ch. 2008).

Another question about the reach of good faith comes from the Delaware Supreme Court's holding in *Stone v. Ritter* that a conscious and systematic disregard of directors' responsibilities constitutes a breach of the duty of loyalty. As we have already seen in the traditional standard of review in a duty of loyalty case is fairness which consists of fair dealing and fair price. If, however, there is such a disregard in a *Caremark/Stone* type of case, what would a fairness review consist of and what would the remedy be?

D. CORPORATE OPPORTUNITY DOCTRINE

The corporate opportunity doctrine is a "default mechanism for allocating property rights between a corporation and those who manage it." Eric Talley, *Turning Servile Opportunities to Gold: A Strategic Analysis of the Corporate Opportunities Doctrine*, 108 Yale L.J. 277, 280 (1998). Analyzed under the duty of loyalty, the doctrine forbids a director, officer or managerial employee from diverting to himself any business opportunity that "belongs" to the corporation. In a famous case laying out the doctrine, the Delaware Supreme Court stated a corporate fiduciary cannot take a business opportunity for himself if it is one that the corporation can financially undertake; is within the line of the corporation's business and is advantageous to the corporation; and is one in which the corporation has an interest or a reasonable expectancy. *Guth v. Loft*, 5 A.2d 503, 511 (Del. 1939).

As with many loyalty concepts, the proposition is simple to state but difficult to apply. Which "opportunities" should be turned over to the corporation and which can properly be exploited by the individual? When a business opportunity is presented to a corporate insider (usually a director or officer), can she accept it for herself or must she first offer it to the corporation? And are there some opportunities that belong to the corporation so that the insider cannot take them even if the corporation, for some reason, is unable to do so?

To answer these questions requires balancing competing interests. The corporation must be able to further its own legitimate business interests. Those in positions of trust and confidence cannot be permitted to abuse their positions to enhance their own economic interests at the expense of their employers. On the other hand, by cordoning off a class of business opportunities, the doctrine effectively prohibits managers from exploiting their own entrepreneurial interests through competing with the corporation, even in the absence of an explicit non-competition agreement. Moreover, society benefits when persons are permitted to develop and exploit new business possibilities.

The corporate opportunity doctrine differs from other types of fiduciary duties by focusing on *potential* harm to the corporation rather than actual harm. The unlawful usurpation of a corporate opportunity happens when the corporate manager takes the opportunity for herself, without presenting it to the corporation. The corporation might have rejected the opportunity, and even if the corporation had accepted it, the opportunity might not have been profitable. For this reason, the usual remedy for the unlawful taking of a corporate opportunity is for the corporation to receive whatever profits the manager derived from the opportunity.

Problem: Starcrest Corporation—Part 2

Review the facts about Starcrest at the beginning of this chapter. A little over a year ago, Starcrest began to discuss the possibility of buying or building a gambling casino. After a management presentation to the directors on the advantages and disadvantages of such a step, the board authorized the officers to begin an active search for specific prospects. Management's initial investigations in the United States turned up nothing that seemed appropriate.

Robert White, a director of Starcrest, has extensive personal investments in a variety of fields, including substantial real estate holdings. He is also the president and chairman of the board of Petro Investments, Inc., a real estate holding company. Shortly after the board meeting at which the directors of Starcrest were informed of management's initial investigations, White met an old business acquaintance while on a trip to the Bahamas. White's friend told him that a casino there had just come on the market at a very attractive price. The friend further advised White that if he acted quickly the seller would take $10 million in cash for the casino. White immediately called the real estate broker who was handling the casino, and within two days signed a contract on behalf of Petro to purchase it. Twelve months later, Petro resold the casino at a $6 million profit.

You are a lawyer who specializes in shareholder litigation. Beatrice Parker, a Starcrest shareholder, has told you these facts and asked whether they might provide the basis for a lawsuit against White. How should you advise her under the traditional corporate opportunity doctrine? The ALI's version of the corporate opportunity doctrine? What additional information would you need?

1. TRADITIONAL CORPORATE OPPORTUNITY DOCTRINE

FARBER V. SERVAN LAND COMPANY, INC.
662 F.2d 371 (5th Cir. 1981).

[In 1959, Charles Serianni and other investors formed Servan Land Company, (Servan) to build and operate a golf course and country club near Fort Lauderdale, Florida. Serianni and A.I. Savin owned a majority of the stock and were Servan's principal officers. There were eight other stockholders, including Jack Farber, the plaintiff in this action. Servan acquired 160 acres of land on which to build the course and, shortly thereafter acquired an additional twenty acres abutting the course.

At the 1968 annual stockholders' meeting, a Servan director and stockholder said that James Farquhar, the vendor of the twenty acre tract, was willing to sell another 160 acres of abutting land to the corporation that was suitable for use as an additional golf course. After some discussion, the stockholders took no action to authorize the purchase of the land. In March 1969, Serianni and Savin, in their individual capacities, bought the 160 acres that had been discussed at the stockholders' meeting.

There was no discussion of the purchase at the 1969 annual stockholders' meeting, held in April 1969. In 1970, Farber learned of the purchase from a third party, and at the annual stockholders' meeting, he inquired about it. Savin and Serianni acknowledged the purchase, but there is conflicting evidence as to whether the stockholders ratified the purchase.

In 1973, Serianni, Savin and the corporation entered into an agreement with a purchaser to sell as a package the corporation's assets and the 160 acres of adjoining land Serianni and Savin had bought; each contract of sale was conditioned upon execution of the other. Of the aggregate sales price, the defendants allocated $5,000,000 to the corporation and $3,353,700 to Savin and Serianni, though this division was not based on any appraisal of the respective properties.

At a special directors' and stockholders' meeting, all the stockholders except Farber approved the sale and voted to liquidate Servan. After the sale was completed Farber brought a derivative suit alleging that Savin and Serianni's purchase constituted the taking of a corporate opportunity. Farber also sought appointment of an appraiser to determine the proper allocation of the purchase price.

The district court found that Serianni had been the "driving force" of Servan from its inception. The court also found that, although there was a possibility of real estate development, such development was not one of the purposes for which Servan had been formed. After reviewing the events of the 1968 stockholders' meeting, the court said that Serianni and Savin should have called a special stockholders' meeting to give the stockholders the opportunity to have the corporation purchase the land before Serianni and Savin did so individually. The court noted, however, that the corporation benefitted from their purchase because the entire package was worth more when the assets and real estate were sold in 1973. Finally, the court found that Farber was entitled to an appraisal to determine whether the corporation should have received a larger portion of the total sale price of the properties than the $5 million allocated by Serianni and Savin.

The appraiser subsequently valued the corporation's properties at $4,065,915, and the Serianni-Savin property at $3,950,925. Thus Serianni and Savin had allotted to the corporation a greater percentage of the proceeds of the sale than would have been allocated using the appraiser's figures.

After the appraisal, the district court issued a memorandum opinion which set forth its earlier findings and incorporated the results of the appraisal. The court again noted that Servan had profited from the purchase by Serianni and Savin. It also found that the acreage did not constitute a corporate opportunity because the property bore no substantial relationship to Servan's primary purpose of operating a golf course. Thus the purchase was not "antagonistic to any significant corporate purpose."]

TJOFLAT, CIRCUIT JUDGE:

Farber appealed the district court's decision, and this court vacated and remanded it for clarification, stating: "if, as seems to be clearly expressed, there was no corporate opportunity, why should, as is three times stated, Serianni and Savin have offered the 160 adjacent acres to the corporation? The holdings are inconsistent." *Farber v. Servan Land Co., Inc.*, 541 F.2d 1086, 1088 (5th Cir.1976). We stated:

> If the corporate opportunity doctrine is otherwise applicable it is not made inapplicable by the realization of a substantial gain from a fortuitous sale of its assets at the same time as the sale of the property asserted to be a corporate opportunity to a lone buyer who would not have bought either property without the other. If a corporate opportunity existed the corporation and its stockholders would have been entitled to the profits from the sale of both parcels.

On remand, the district court failed to explain why it found that Serianni and Savin had a duty to offer the opportunity to purchase the 160 acres to the corporation, but it reaffirmed its finding that "Seriani (sic) and Savin had satisfactorily sustained the burden of establishing the propriety of the transaction."

Farber appeals once again.

In reviewing the district court's decision we must evaluate its resolution of four key issues: whether a corporate opportunity existed; whether the stockholders declined the opportunity by failing to act; whether the stockholders ratified Serianni and Savin's purchase; and whether the subsequent benefit the corporation received in selling its assets in conjunction with Serianni and Savin's 160 acres rectifies any wrong it might have suffered through the defendants' initial purchase of the land.

In Florida, a corporate director or officer "occupies a quasi-fiduciary relation to the corporation and the existing stockholders. He is bound to act with fidelity and the utmost good faith." Because he "occupies a fiduciary relationship to the corporation, (he) will not be allowed to act in hostility to it by acquiring for his own benefit any intangible assets of the corporation. He cannot make a private profit from his position or, while acting in that capacity, acquire an interest adverse to that of the corporation."

If one occupying a fiduciary relationship to a corporation acquires, "in opposition to the corporation, property in which the corporation has an interest or tangible expectancy or which is essential to its existence," he violates what has come to be known as the "doctrine of 'corporate opportunity'." Florida has long recognized the doctrine of corporate opportunity, and has described a corporate opportunity as a business opportunity in which the corporation has an interest for a "valid and significant corporate purpose." The opportunity need not be "of the utmost importance to the welfare of the corporation," to be protected from preemption by the corporation's directors and officers. As we elaborated in the first appeal of this case, however, the opportunity must "fit into the present activities of the corporation or fit into an established corporate policy which the acquisition of the opportunity would forward."

In its initial opinion the district court found that no corporate opportunity existed:

> The court finds the possibility of real estate development was contemplated by the stockholders. For example, Mr. Forman testified, via deposition, that scarcely a meeting of the stockholders occurred without discussing the acquiring of additional property from Mr. Farquhar. However, the possibility of real estate development would always be in the minds of a group of affluent businessmen. This does not mean that real estate development was actually part of the corporate purpose and the court specifically finds that real estate development was not a purpose for which the corporation was formed.
>
> The mere fact that the land was adjacent to the corporate land in itself does not support a conclusion that therefore the acreage was a corporate opportunity. The property had no substantial relation to the corporation's primary purpose of operating a golf course and

the individual purpose was not antagonistic to any significant corporate purpose and thus the facts do not fall within the general proposition that an officer of a corporation cannot acquire title to or an interest in property prejudicial to the corporation.

We find that the district court's findings of fact do not support its legal conclusion that the opportunity to buy Farquhar's 160 acres was not a corporate opportunity.

It should be noted that the district court not only found that the stockholders frequently discussed acquisition of Mr. Farquhar's land at their meetings; it also found that the stockholders had discussed this matter at the last meeting, just shortly before Serianni and Savin made their purchase, and that they had "indicated a sense of approval to the idea of acquiring abutting land from Mr. Farquhar." Further, the court heard testimony that the corporation needed the land on the perimeter of the golf course, and evidence that the corporation had bought additional land from Mr. Farquhar in the past and that it had bought and operated a lodge located on part of that land. These facts make it clear that the opportunity to acquire the Farquhar land was an advantageous one that fit into a present, significant corporate purpose, as well as an ongoing corporate policy, and that the corporation had an active interest in it. Accordingly, the opportunity to buy the land constituted a corporate opportunity.

In addition to finding that no corporate opportunity existed, the district court found that if one did exist, "it was rejected by the corporation." The court apparently reached this conclusion because after deciding at their annual meeting that the opportunity to purchase the land should be investigated, the stockholders did not vote, at that meeting, to commit the funds available from the refinancing to purchase the Farquhar property. We find that this failure does not indicate a decision to refrain from pursuing the opportunity to purchase. Indeed, since the stockholders apparently lacked specific information about Mr. Farquhar's terms of sale, it would have been illogical to make a commitment of funds at that time. It is true that there is no evidence to indicate that the stockholders undertook formal investigation of the potential purchase between the time of the meeting and the time of Serianni and Savin's purchase. It should be noted, however, that Serianni was the president of the corporation and the only active director. The other stockholders customarily relied upon him to exercise the executive powers of the corporation, since most of them resided in other states. Because the other stockholders relied upon Serianni to initiate the investigation on the corporation's behalf, he may not now translate his own inaction into a corporate rejection of the opportunity, thus allowing him to buy the land personally. The district court's finding that the corporation rejected the opportunity is clearly erroneous.

As another ground for its decision, the district court held that the stockholders ratified Serianni and Savin's purchase at their May 9, 1970 meeting. Farber attacks this finding on two grounds. First, he argues that it was clearly erroneous to rely on the corporate minutes, which indicated a vote to ratify, rather than on his court reporter's transcript of the meeting, which indicates no ratification attempt.

The district court received adequate evidence that the corporate minutes were valid and reliable. This left it with an issue of credibility, and this court, on appeal, cannot say that the district judge's decision to rely on the corporate minutes was clearly erroneous. This is especially so since official minutes of corporate meetings are generally considered the best evidence of corporate business transacted.

Farber also argues that even if the ratification vote did take place, it cannot be used to prohibit his derivative action. We agree. When ratification is possible and the proceedings are proper, stockholders may sanction the act of a corporate officer or director and thus abolish any cause of action that the corporation might have against that individual. Not all acts may be ratified, and the Florida courts have not indicated whether stockholders are capable of ratifying a director or officer's breach of fiduciary duty. We do not need to decide whether ratification was possible here, however, because even if it was, the manner of ratification in this case renders the ratification a nullity.

According to the corporate minutes, all of the directors present at the annual meeting, except the plaintiff, voted to ratify the land purchase. Both of the purchasing directors were present, and between the two of them, they held four-sevenths of the stock. While it is true that directors ordinarily may vote their stock on measures in which they have a personal interest, most authorities agree that "the violation of their duty by corporate directors cannot be ratified by the action of those who were guilty of participation in the wrongful acts, even though they constitute a majority of the directors or of the stockholders." Thus, Serianni and Savin may not bind Farber by ratifying their own inappropriate acts. Farber is entitled to bring a derivative action.

Finally, in finding in favor of the defendants, the district court relied heavily on the notion that by valuing the two properties favorably for the corporation when they were sold jointly, and by selling the properties together, thus raising the value of each, Serianni and Savin benefitted the corporation. This benefit, according to the court, precluded any recovery for breach of fiduciary duty in obtaining the Farquhar acres in the first place.

As we stated in the first appeal, however:

> If the corporate opportunity doctrine is otherwise applicable it is not made inapplicable by the realization of a substantial gain from a fortuitous sale of its assets at the same time as the sale of the property asserted to be a corporate opportunity to a lone buyer who would not have bought either property without the other. *If*

*a corporate opportunity existed the corporation and its
stockholders would have been entitled to the profits from the sale
of both parcels.* (Emphasis added).

Further, it has already been established that Serianni and Savin
apportioned the proceeds of the joint sale without the benefit of an
appraisal of the individual properties. While it may be to their credit that
they overvalued the corporate property in the apportionment, they have
not contended, nor has the district court found, that this overvaluation
constituted a deliberate settlement between the parties for damages
incurred in the defendants' acquisition of the Farquhar property. Despite
the undervaluation of their own property relative to the corporation's
assets, Serianni and Savin made a handsome profit on the sale. The two
directors must hold those profits in trust for the corporation.

We find that the opportunity to buy Mr. Farquhar's 160 acres
constituted a corporate opportunity and that the defendants, Serianni and
Savin, breached their fiduciary duties to the corporation by preempting
that opportunity. We also find that the attempted ratification of the
preemption does not preclude Farber from bringing a derivative suit on
behalf of the corporation.

The corporation is entitled to the profits of the directors' subsequent
sale of the 160 acres. We remand the case to the district court to determine
the proper amount of damages and the appropriate method for distributing
those damages.

2.   WHAT IS A CORPORATE OPPORTUNITY?

Courts have traditionally used one or more of three tests to determine
whether a corporate opportunity exists: (1) interest or expectancy; (2) line
of business; and (3) fairness.

a.   Interest or Expectancy

The interest or expectancy test is the earliest approach developed by
the courts. The concept underlying "interest or expectancy" appears to be
"something much less tenable than ownership—less than a legal right to
exclude independent third parties from acquiring the project; and less even
contingent contractual claims." Victor Brudney & Robert Charles Clark, *A
New Look at Corporate Opportunities*, 94 Harv. L. Rev. 997, 1013–14
(1981).

This test is difficult to apply. In *Litwin v. Allen*, 25 N.Y.S.2d 667, 686
(Sup.Ct. 1940), the court suggested how to discern whether the corporation
has an interest or expectancy:

This corporate right or expectancy, this mandate upon directors
to act for the corporation, may arise from various circumstances,
such as, for example, the fact that directors had undertaken to

negotiate in the field on behalf of the corporation, or that the corporation was in need of the particular business opportunity to the knowledge of the directors, or that the business opportunity was seized and developed at the expense, and with the facilities of the corporation. It is noteworthy that in cases which have imposed this type of liability upon fiduciaries, the thing determined by the court to be the subject of the trust was a thing of special and unique value to the beneficiary; for example, real estate, a proprietary formula valuable to the corporation's business, patents indispensable or valuable to its business, a competing enterprise or one required for the growth and expansion of the corporation's business or the like.

b. Line of Business

Under the line of business test, a corporation has a prior claim to a business opportunity presented to an officer or director that falls within the firm's particular line of business. The test is closely related to the "interest or expectancy" standard, but includes a realistic assessment of the corporation's ability to take on the business opportunity. In *Guth v. Loft*, 5 A.2d 503, 514 (Del.Ch. 1939), the court explained the concept as follows:

> The phrase is not within the field of precise definition, nor is it one that can be bounded by a set formula. It has a flexible meaning, which is to be applied reasonably and sensibly to the facts and circumstances of the particular case. Where a corporation is engaged in a certain business, and an opportunity is presented to it embracing an activity as to which it has fundamental knowledge, practical experience and ability to pursue, which, logically and naturally is adaptable to its business having regard for its financial position, and is one that is consonant with its reasonable needs and aspirations for expansion, it may be properly said that the opportunity is in the line of the corporation's business.

Thus, if a business proposition would require a corporation to modify its operating infrastructure beyond a certain threshold, the business opportunity would be found to be outside the corporation's line of business. Courts typically will apply the test to extend beyond a corporation's existing operations. The rationale for such an application is simple. Courts recognize that corporations are dynamic entities. Furthermore, shareholders reasonably expect that a corporation will go beyond the status quo and take advantage of highly profitable, but safe, opportunities.

The difficulties involved in applying the line of business test are increased when a director or officer holds positions in two or more corporations or is a corporate manager in one corporation and a substantial shareholder in another and dominates the latter through her ability to select its officers and directors. Potential conflicts are exacerbated in the venture capital business, in which venture capitalists often sit on the boards of several corporations in similar lines of business.

In *Johnston v. Greene*, 121 A.2d 919 (Del. 1956), Odlum, a financier, who was an officer and director of numerous corporations, was offered, in his individual capacity, the chance to acquire the stock of Nutt-Shel, a corporation 100% owned by Hutson, and several patents pertaining to its business. The business of Nutt-Shel had no close relation to the business of Airfleets, Inc., of which Odlum was president. Odlum turned over to Airfleets the opportunity to buy the stock of Nutt-Shel, but purchased the patents for his friends and associates and, to a limited extent, for himself. Airfleets, a corporation with a large amount of cash, possessed the financial capability to buy the patents. The board of Airfleets, dominated by Odlum, voted to buy only the stock. In a shareholders' derivative action against Odlum and the directors, the Delaware Supreme Court found that Odlum had not breached his duty in the sale of the patents. In discussing the problem of multiple conflicting loyalties, the court stated:

> At the time when the Nutt-Shel business was offered to Odlum, his position was this: He was the part-time president of Airfleets. He was also president of Atlas—an investment company. He was a director of other corporations and a trustee of foundations interested in making investments. If it was his fiduciary duty, upon being offered any investment opportunity, to submit it to a corporation of which he was a director, the question arises, Which corporation? Why Airfleets instead of Atlas? Why Airfleets instead of one of the foundations? So far as appears, there was no specific tie between the Nutt-Shel business and any of these corporations or foundations. Odlum testified that many of his companies had money to invest, and this appears entirely reasonable. How, then, can it be said that Odlum was under any obligation to offer the opportunity to one particular corporation? And if he was not under such an obligation, why could he not keep it for himself?

> Plaintiff suggests that if Odlum elects to assume fiduciary relationships to competing corporations he must assume the obligations that are entailed by such relationships. So he must, but what are the obligations? The mere fact of having funds to invest does not ordinarily put the corporations "in competition" with each other, as that phrase is used in the law of corporate opportunity. There is nothing inherently wrong in a man of large business and financial interests serving as a director of two or more investment companies, and both Airfleets and Atlas (to mention only two companies) must reasonably have expected that Odlum would be free either to offer to any of his companies any

business opportunity that came to him personally, or to retain it for himself—provided always that there was no tie between any of such companies and the new venture or any specific duty resting upon him with respect to it.

It is clear to us that the reason why the Nutt-Shel business was offered to Airfleets was because Odlum, having determined that he did not want it for himself, chose to place the investment in that one of his companies whose tax situation was best adapted to receive it. He chose to do so, although he could probably have sold the stock to an outside company at a profit to himself. If he had done so, who could have complained? If a stockholder of Airfleets could have done so, why not a stockholder of Atlas as well?

121 A.2d at 924–25.

c. Fairness

A few courts have adopted a fairness test, either by itself or in combination with other standards. In *Durfee v. Durfee & Canning, Inc.*, 80 N.E.2d 522, 529 (Mass. 1948), the court stated:

> The true basis of the governing doctrine of corporate opportunity rests fundamentally on the unfairness in the particular circumstances of a director, whose relation to the corporation is fiduciary, taking advantage of an opportunity when the interests of the corporation justly call for protection. This calls for the application of ethical standards of what is fair and equitable in particular sets of facts.

The fairness test is premised on removing the temptation for officers and directors to breach their fiduciary duty by making such breaches profitless. However, an amorphous fairness test produces uncertainty in application and unpredictability in result. Thus, the test does not provide a reliable guide to an officer or director concerning the scope of her duty to offer a specific opportunity to the corporation.

As a result of this uncertainty, some courts have attempted to combine the line of business doctrine with the fairness test. In *Miller v. Miller*, 222 N.W.2d 71, 81 (Minn. 1974), the court first determined that an opportunity was a corporate opportunity under the line of business test. Then under a second test, the court asked whether the corporate insider could sustain the burden of showing he had satisfied his duties of good faith, loyalty, and fair dealing. The court identified the following factors as relevant to whether the taking of an opportunity was fair to the corporation:

> [T]he nature of the officer's relationship to the management and control of the corporation; whether the opportunity was presented to him in his official or individual capacity; his prior disclosure of the opportunity to the board of directors or shareholders and their

response; whether or not he used or exploited corporate facilities, assets, or personnel in acquiring the opportunity; whether his acquisition harmed or benefited the corporation; and all other facts and circumstances bearing on an officer's good faith and whether he exercised the diligence, devotion, care and fairness toward the corporation which ordinarily prudent men would exercise under similar circumstances in like position.

The *Miller* approach appears to give an officer or director who may have usurped a corporate opportunity another line of defense under the fairness rubric. Brudney and Clark have criticized the *Miller* approach as "adding only a new layer of confusion to an already murky area of the law, without forwarding the analysis in any significant fashion." Because of the multitude of factors relevant to determining "fairness," particularly whether an individual's usurpation of the opportunity harmed the corporation, the *Miller* test is not useful as a planning vehicle or litigation predictor.

3. WHEN CAN A MANAGER TAKE A CORPORATE OPPORTUNITY?

Various factors enter into determining whether a corporation can insist that the manager not take a corporate opportunity. Some cases suggest that the corporation loses its claim to the opportunity if lacks the financial capacity to take it. Other cases state that the manager must present the opportunity to the corporation (and its independent decision-makers) for a decision as to whether the corporation wants to accept the opportunity. This is also the approach of the ALI Principles of Corporate Governance, which some courts have cited in requiring that the manager always present the corporate opportunity for corporate rejection.

BURG V. HORN
380 F.2d 897 (2d Cir.1967).

LUMBARD, CHIEF JUSTICE:

Darand was incorporated in September 1953 with a capital of $5500, subscribed equally by the three stockholders, Mrs. Burg and George and Max Horn, all of whom became directors, and immediately purchased a low-rent building in Brooklyn. The Horns, who were engaged in the produce business and had already acquired three similar buildings in Brooklyn through wholly-owned corporations, urged the Burgs, who were close friends then also residing in Brooklyn, to 'get their feet wet' in real estate, and the result was the formation of Darand. The Burgs testified that they expected the Horns to offer any low-rent properties they found in Brooklyn to Darand, but that there was not discussion or agreement to that effect. The Horns carried on the active management of Darand's properties.

Darand sold its first property and acquired another in 1956, and purchased two more buildings in 1959. From 1953 to 1963, nine similar properties were purchased by the Horns, individually or through wholly-owned corporations.

In 1962 the Burgs moved to California, and disagreements thereafter arose between them and the Horns concerning the accounting for rent receipts and expenditures of Darand. This action seeking an accounting for receipts and expenditures and the imposition of a constructive trust on the alleged corporate opportunities was brought in 1964. After a six-day trial, [the trial judge] held that the Horns had failed to account for $7,893.36 of rent receipts for 1961–1964. This holding has not been appealed. He found, however, that there was no agreement that all low-rent buildings found by the Horns should be offered to Darand, and that the Burgs were aware of the purposes of the loans from Darand and Louis Burg and of at least some of the Horns' post-1953 acquisitions. He therefore declined to hold that those acquisitions were corporate opportunities of Darand.

[There is no evidence that the properties in question were sought by or offered to Darand, or necessary to its success.] Plaintiff apparently contends that defendants were as a matter of law under a duty to acquire for Darand further properties like those it was operating. She is seemingly supported by several commentators, who have stated that any opportunity within a corporation's 'line of business' is a corporate opportunity. *E.g.,* Note, *Corporate Opportunity*, 74 Harv. L. Rev. 765, 768–69 (1961); Note, *A Survey of Corporate Opportunity*, 45 Geo. L. J. 99, 100–01 (1956). This statement seems to us too broad a generalization. We think that under New York law a court must determine in each case, by considering the relationship between the director and the corporation, whether a duty to offer the corporation all opportunities within its 'line of business' is fairly to be implied. Had the Horns been full-time employees of Darand with no prior real estate ventures of their own, New York law might well uphold a finding that they were subject to such an implied duty. But as they spent most of their time in unrelated produce and real estate enterprises and already owned corporations holding similar properties when Darand was formed, as plaintiff knew, we agree with [the trial judge] that a duty to offer Darand all such properties coming to their attention cannot be implied absent some further evidence of an agreement or understanding to that effect.

HAYS, CIRCUIT JUDGE (dissenting):

I dissent.

My brothers hold that the scope of a director's duty to his corporation must be measured by the facts of each case. However, although they are unable to find any New York case presenting the same facts as those before us, they conclude that New York law does not support the imposition of liability in the circumstances of this case. I do not agree.

In an often quoted passage, the New York Court of Appeals laid down the principles of fiduciary conduct:

Many forms of conduct permissible in a workaday world for those acting at arm's length, are forbidden to those bound by fiduciary ties. A trustee is held to something stricter than the morals of the market place. Not honesty alone, but the punctilio of an honor the most sensitive, is then the standard of behavior. As to this there has developed a tradition that is unbending an inveterate. Uncompromising rigidity has been the attitude of courts of equity when petitioned to undermine the rule of undivided loyalty by the "disintegrating erosion" of particular exceptions. Only thus has the level of conduct for fiduciaries been kept at a level higher than that trodden by the crowd. *Meinhard v. Salmon*, 249 N.Y. 458, 464, 164 N.E. 545, 546, 62 A.L.R.1 (1928).

Applying these standards to the instant case it seems clear that in the absence of a contrary agreement or understanding between the parties, the Horns, who were majority stockholders and managing officers of the Darand Corporation and whose primary function was to locate suitable properties for the company were under a fiduciary obligation to offer such properties to Darand before buying the properties for themselves. That the Horns used Darand's funds to effectuate certain of these purchases reinforces the conclusion that their conduct was improper and failed to comport with the standards established by law.

Since the Horns were under a fiduciary duty imposed by law not to take advantage for themselves of corporate opportunities, it is irrelevant that, as the district court found, there was no agreement under which "the Horns would contract their real estate activities or offer every property they located to Darand." *A fortiori* the Horns were not free to select the best properties for themselves.

―――――――――

a. Economic Capacity

The inquiry into whether the corporation has the economic capacity to take the opportunity is derived from the financial ability prong of the Guth analysis.

The general rule seems to be that if a corporation is financially incapable of exploiting a business proposition, that proposition cannot be said to "belong" to the corporation. Thus, at this stage of the decision-making process, a fiduciary who correctly determines that a proposition is beyond her corporation's financial means cannot be said to have appropriated a corporate opportunity if she later exploits it for herself. The capacity inquiry seems to have underpinnings in economic efficiency. Courts would apparently prefer to see a business proposition developed rather than allow it to languish because of economic constraints. At the capacity-inquiry waypoint, therefore, the integrity of the fiduciary relationship is trumped by a preference for vigorous economic competition.

DeLarme R. Landes, *Economic Efficiency and the Corporate Opportunity Doctrine: In Defense of a Contextual Disclosure Rule*, 74 Temp. L. Rev. 837, 850 (2001).

Courts differ on whether the financial difficulty is one of insolvency or merely lack of liquid assets. As one court stated:

> Nevertheless, these facts which raise some question whether the corporation actually lacked the funds or credit necessary for carrying out a contract tend to show the wisdom of a rigid rule forbidding directors of a solvent corporation to take over for their own profit a corporate contract on the plea of the corporation's financial inability to perform. If the directors are uncertain whether the corporation can make the necessary outlays, they need not embark it upon the venture; if they do, they may not substitute themselves for the corporation any place along the line and divert possible benefits into their own pockets.

Irving Trust Co. v. Deutsch, 73 F.2d 121, 124 (2d Cir.1934), *rev'g in part* 2 F.Supp. 971 (S.D.N.Y.1932).

Other courts are less rigid. Some allow corporate managers to retain an opportunity if the corporation did not then "have the liquid funds available" to take advantage of it. Corporate managers must use their best efforts to uncover the financing needed by their corporation to acquire an opportunity. A director or officer, however, need not advance funds to enable a corporation to take advantage of a business opportunity.

Professors Brudney and Clark point out that the corporate incapacity defense may be different for public corporations, compared to close corporations:

> There is no reason to allow the diverters to exploit opportunities that they claim the corporation is unable to exploit, if the claimed inability may be feasibly eliminated. To permit claims of disability to become the subject of judicial controversy when they can only be disproved by outsiders with great difficulty and at considerable expense is to tempt participants to actions whose impropriety is visible but rarely subject to effective challenge. Availability of the defense of corporate incapacity reduces the incentive to solve corporate financing and other problems.

The argument against the defense of incapacity or disability may be less forceful for close corporations than for public corporations because of the greater familiarity of the participants with the affairs of the firm, their better access to relevant information, and the relative manageability of the problems. But the arguments against the defense are not without power in the close corporation context as well, as several courts have noted. Moreover, the possibility of obtaining consent to non-pro rata participation in a venture that the corporation appears unable to exploit should remove the seeming harshness of a rule that does not allow the defense of corporate incapacity. Indeed, rejection by the other participants of a request to assist in curing the incapacity might occur in circumstances that imply consent to the requesting person's taking the opportunity.

94 Harv. L. Rev. at 1022.

b. Corporate Rejection

Courts broadly accept the notion that a manager can take a corporate opportunity if the corporation has rejected it. The important question is whether the opportunity was presented to and rejected after full disclosure by disinterested, independent corporate decision-makers. By accepting the opportunity, the corporation precludes the manager from developing it individually. Proper rejection, however, precludes the corporation from later claiming the corporate opportunity.

ALI PRINCIPLES OF CORPORATE GOVERNANCE

§ 5.05   TAKING OF CORPORATE OPPORTUNITIES BY DIRECTORS OR SENIOR EXECUTIVES

(a) General Rule. A director or senior executive may not take advantage of a corporate opportunity unless:

(1) The director or senior executive first offers the corporate opportunity to the corporation and makes disclosure concerning the conflict of interest and the corporate opportunity;

(2) The corporate opportunity is rejected by the corporation; and

(3) Either:

(A) The rejection of the opportunity is fair to the corporation;

(B) The opportunity is rejected in advance, following such disclosure, by disinterested directors or, in the case of a senior executive who is not a director, by a disinterested superior, in a manner that satisfies the standards of the business judgment rule; or

(C) The rejection is authorized in advance or ratified, following such disclosure, by disinterested shareholders and the rejection is not equivalent to a waste of corporate assets.

(b) Definition of a Corporate Opportunity. For purposes of this Section, a corporate opportunity means:

(1) Any opportunity to engage in a business activity of which a director or senior executive becomes aware, either:

(A) In connection with the performance of functions as a director or senior executive, or under circumstances that should reasonably lead the director or senior executive to believe that the person offering the opportunity expects it to be offered to the corporation; or

(B) Through the use of corporate information or property, if the resulting opportunity is one that the director or senior executive should reasonably be expected to believe would be of interest to the corporation; or

(2) Any opportunity to engage in a business activity of which a senior executive becomes aware and knows is closely related to a business in which the corporation is engaged or expects to engage.

(c) Burden of Proof. A party who challenges the taking of a corporate opportunity has the burden of proof, except that if such party establishes that the requirements of Subsection (a)(3)(B) or (C) are not met, the director or the senior executive has the burden of proving that the rejection and the taking of the opportunity were fair to the corporation.

(d) Ratification of Defective Disclosure. A good faith but defective disclosure of the facts concerning the corporate opportunity may be cured if at any time (but no later than a reasonable time after suit is filed challenging the taking of the corporate opportunity) the original rejection of the corporate opportunity is ratified, following the required disclosure, by the board, the shareholders, or the corporate decisionmaker who initially approved the rejection of the corporate opportunity, or such decisionmaker's successor.

———————

The central feature of ALI § 5.05 is the strict requirement of full disclosure prior to taking advantage of any corporate opportunity. The corporate manager may not take a corporate opportunity unless she has made full disclosure of her conflict of interest and the corporation has rejected the opportunity. The rejection must be made in advance by disinterested directors or shareholders, or must be fair to the corporation. If the rejection is made by disinterested directors, it must satisfy the business judgment rule. If the rejection is made by disinterested shareholders, it must not constitute a waste of corporate assets.

To date, two courts have explicitly adopted the ALI approach. The Maine Supreme Judicial Court noted:

> The disclosure-oriented approach provides a clear procedure whereby a corporate officer may insulate herself through prompt and complete disclosure from the possibility of a legal challenge. The requirement of disclosure recognizes the paramount importance of the corporate fiduciary's duty of loyalty. At the same time it protects the fiduciary's ability pursuant to the proper procedure to pursue her own business ventures free from the possibility of a lawsuit.

Northeast Harbor Golf Club, Inc. v. Harris, 661 A.2d 1146, 1152 (Me.1995). *See also, Klinicki v. Lundgren*, 695 P.2d 906 (Ore. 1985) (adopting an earlier version of § 5.05 which remained unchanged).

Courts in other states, including Delaware, have been unwilling to make disclosure an absolute pre-requisite to the validity of the taking of corporate opportunities. The Delaware Supreme Court has held that the financial inability of a corporation to take an opportunity was conclusive, even though the opportunity had not been formally presented to the corporation's board of directors. *Broz v. Cellular Information Systems, Inc.*, 673 A.2d 148 (Del. 1996). In the case, Broz, an outside director of Cellular Information Systems (CIS) learned of the availability of a cellular telephone license and acquired it for another corporation of which he was the sole shareholder. The court concluded that CIS itself lacked an interest in the license since it did not have the financial ability to make the acquisition.

The court found that the license opportunity had come to Broz individually and that he had ascertained from CIS's top management and some of its directors that CIS did not wish to acquire the license for itself. The court noted that although a director might be shielded from liability had the director formally offered the opportunity to the corporation, there was no legal requirement to do so. The court recognized that the manner in which Broz had discussed the issue with the other directors did not constitute formal board assent. Nevertheless, given Broz's attempts to determine whether CIS might be interested, the court concluded that his failure to present the opportunity formally did not result in the improper usurpation of a corporate opportunity. The court declined to impose "a new requirement onto the law of corporate opportunity, *viz.*, the requirement of formal presentation under circumstances where the corporation does not have an interest, expectancy or financial ability."

MBCA § 8.70, adopted in 2005, takes a similar approach, permitting a director to have the corporation "disclaim" an interest in a specific business opportunity. The disclaimer procedure, like that of the ALI Principles, requires action by previously-informed qualified directors or disinterested shareholders. But if a director fails to present such opportunity to the corporation before taking advantage of it himself, such failure "shall not create an inference that the opportunity should have been first presented to the corporation or alter the burden of proof otherwise applicable to establish that the director breached a duty to the corporation."

Should the procedures for disinterested rejection of a corporate opportunity be different for public and close corporations? Brudney and Clark have argued that the proxy process in the public corporation usually will not result in truly informed consent. They maintain that "consent to the officer's taking a corporate opportunity approaches the kind of waste for which unanimous stockholder approval is traditionally required." Thus, they conclude that all officers and inside directors of public corporations should be precluded from taking any active, outside business opportunities. They point out that a strict rule would protect the usually powerless shareholders in public corporations from diversions of corporate opportunities. The pursuit of active, outside business interests would distract full-time officers from corporate affairs. As to outside directors, however, they conclude that a corporate opportunity would exist only when such a director has used corporate resources in acquiring or developing an opportunity. The narrower duty rests on the basis of the more limited responsibilities and remuneration of outside directors.

Brudney and Clark, however, urge a more flexible approach for close corporations in light of the basically contractual nature of such ventures. They reason:

> Investors in private ventures are fairly small in number and tend to know one another. They make more conscious choices when selecting managers from among themselves. They are likely to be active participants rather than merely passive contributors of funds. And they can consent in a more meaningful way to diversions of corporate assets by fellow participants, either when they form or join enterprises, or on the occasion of the diversion. Accordingly, such investors have less need of categorical strictures on such diversions.

c.   A Statutory Approach: Omnibus Waiver

Both the MBCA and the DCGL permit corporations to include in their charters a provision waiving the protections of the corporate opportunity doctrine. MBCA § 2.02(b)(6) permits:

> a provision limiting or eliminating any duty of a directoror any other person to offer the corporation the right to have or participate in any, or one or more classes or categories of, business opportunities, prior to the pursuit or taking of the opportunity of the director or other person; provided that any application of such a provision to an officer or a related person of that officer (i) also requires a determination by the board of directors by action of

qualified directors . . . subsequent to the effective date of the provision applying the provision to a particular officer or any related person of that officer, and may be limited by the authorizing action of the board.

Why does this provision treat officers differently from directors?

DGCL § 122(17) permits a corporation to:

Renounce, in its certificate of incorporation or by action of its board of directors, any interest or expectancy of the corporation in, or in being offered an opportunity to participate in, specified business opportunities or specified classes or categories of business opportunities that are presented to the corporation or one or more of its officers, directors or stockholders.

The possibility of including such a provision in a corporation's charter is likely to be of particular interest to some types of potential investors, especially venture capitalists, who take positions in numerous companies in the same or related industries and who are interested in being represented on portfolio corporations' boards of directors.

The waiver permitted by these statutory provisions raises some interesting questions. (1) Does the absence of a renunciation permitted suggest that the corporation has an interest or expectancy in an opportunity? (2) What should be the standard of review if the board renounces a business opportunity? Should the court review the board's decision under the business judgment rule on the theory renunciation of business deals is simply ordinary business? Or should the court review the renunciation for fairness, since the taking of a corporate opportunity implicates the duty of loyalty? (3) Will it matter whether the renunciation is made in the corporation's certificate of incorporation or by board resolution?

4. REMEDIES FOR USURPING A CORPORATE OPPORTUNITY

In general, the remedy for a breach of fiduciary duty is the award of damages in the amount of the harm the corporation suffered from the breach. When dealing with the taking of a corporate opportunity, however, the problem of the appropriate remedy is more complex. Recall that the harm when a corporate manager takes a corporate opportunity occurs before it is known how the corporation might have developed it and whether it will be profitable. The harm to the corporation is not *actual*, but instead the deprivation of the right to take the opportunity for itself.

One possible remedy for usurpation of a corporate opportunity is to assess damages according to the *potential profits* lost by the corporation, based on a calculation of the estimated value of the opportunity at the time of the taking given its likely returns and their risk. Another possible remedy is to assess the *profits realized* by the usurping manager on the theory of unjust enrichment. Such profits would be easy to measure if the manager had already sold the opportunity—although as *Farber* illustrates, valuation problems may sometimes arise.

Courts have chosen the latter approach. The traditional remedy is the imposition of a constructive trust on the manager's new business. This approach eliminates messy (and sometimes speculative) valuation problems and assumes that the manager's actual profits approximate the corporation's potential lost profits. The offending manager, however, is entitled to expenditures she may have made in pursuing and developing the opportunity, including her reasonable compensation.

CHAPTER 19

DUTIES OF CONTROLLING SHAREHOLDERS

■ ■ ■

A. INTRODUCTION

In Chapters 17 and 18, our discussion of fiduciary duties focused exclusively on directors and officers. But no analysis of fiduciary duties, and particularly the duty of loyalty, would be complete without examining the position of controlling shareholders. It may seem curious that controlling shareholders have duties to minority shareholders. Directors and officers have voluntarily assumed the role of fiduciary that is inherent in a corporate office; controlling shareholders have never formally assented to a fiduciary role toward minority shareholders. Yet courts have imposed special duties when shareholders have control—duties analogous to those of directors and officers, but different in subtle and important ways.

A long line of cases supports the proposition that the ordinary shareholder may vote her stock as she pleases and has no fiduciary obligation to her fellow shareholders. Courts treat the actions of *controlling* shareholders differently, however. When they engage in transactions with the corporation they control, they have duties similar to those of directors and officers. The theory underlying this approach appears to be that the directors of the controlled corporations, who must approve or authorize such transactions, should be viewed as agents of the controlling shareholders.

Generally, "control" means the power to determine the policies of a corporation's business. Control can exist in several ways. First, there can be *de jure* control. Absent special voting rules for board of director elections or shareholder voting, the owner of more than 50 percent of a corporation's stock controls that corporation because she can elect a majority of the board of directors and decide any matters submitted to a shareholder vote.

Second, there can be *de facto* control. An owner of a significant block of stock, less than 50 percent, may be able to mobilize sufficient votes to elect a board majority. For example, in a public corporation with dispersed shareholders, holding more than 20 percent of the company's stock (without any other large block owners) can constitute control. The question is whether the shareholder dominates through actual control of the corporation's actions. The presumption is that non-majority shareholders are not dominant, and the plaintiff bears the burden to prove domination.

Courts have examined the block owner's relationship with board members, and whether the block owner can dictate the terms of the transaction.

Finally, control also can arise from incumbency. In public corporations where ownership is fragmented among many shareholders, incumbent directors and managers usually possess de facto control because of their power to nominate management's candidates for election as directors and to use corporate resources to support their election of those candidates.

Corporate statutes generally do not address transactions between corporations and their controlling shareholders. Although courts have looked to duties imposed on directors for guidance in treating controlling shareholders, there is no provision analogous to DGCL § 144. The traditional standard of review for controlling stockholder transactions has been fairness. Unlike interested director transactions, approval by a majority of disinterested directors or the minority stockholders does not give the controlling stockholder the benefit of the business judgment rule. Rather, such approval shifts the burden to the complaining shareholder to demonstrate that the transaction was unfair. The *MFW* case (Section B of this chapter) suggests that business judgment review may be possible if both disinterested directors *and* informed minority stockholders have approved the transaction.

You will notice that the fiduciary duties of controlling shareholders are not the same as those of directors and officers. Unlike corporate managers, controlling shareholders usually have paid for their control on the assumption that certain managerial privileges come with control. Minority shareholders know this (or should), and their reasonable expectations recognize the prerogatives afforded the controlling shareholder. In addition, while the duties of officers and directors run to the corporation, the duties of controlling shareholders are said to run directly to the minority.

This chapter explores fiduciary duties in corporate groups in two distinct settings, both presenting a conflict between the interests of the controlling shareholder (parent) and the interests of the controlled corporation (subsidiary) and its minority shareholders. First, we look at transactions within the corporate group, such as parent-subsidiary dealings and dealings between the subsidiary and other corporations controlled by the parent (affiliates). Second, we review the process and judicial review of cashing out the minority shareholders, usually accomplished through a merger in which the parent acquires all the stock of the subsidiary and the minority shareholders receive cash for their shares.

Problem: Starcrest Corporation—Part 3

Review the facts of Part 1 of the problem in Chapter 18.

Many years ago, members of the Adams family purchased all the stock of Universal Produce Company, a leading supplier of fresh fruits and vegetables to hotels and restaurants. Harold Adams, the chief executive officer of Universal and Elizabeth's brother, owns 25% of Universal stock (and also owns 3% of Starcrest stock). Elizabeth owns 20% of Universal. Initially, Starcrest hotels purchased fruit and vegetables from Universal at then current market prices but have not done so in recent years.

Because of recent weather conditions, Starcrest has had increasing difficulty in obtaining a regular supply of several kinds of gourmet vegetables at reasonable prices. Starcrest uses these vegetables to prepare "signature" dishes that it serves at most of its restaurants. These dishes account for a large portion of those restaurants' volume and substantially increase their profitability.

Elizabeth recently mentioned this vegetable supply problem to Harold. He responded by proposing that Universal enter into a long term supply contract with Starcrest pursuant to which Universal would supply Starcrest with the vegetables it needs. Because performing the contract would force Universal to give up some of its existing customers and devote more of its facilities to Starcrest's needs, and because of unpredictable future weather and market prices, Harold has suggested that the average price for the vegetables that Universal supplies be 110% of the average price Starcrest has paid for those vegetables for the past two years.

Elizabeth has asked you, as counsel to the Adams family, to advise her of the legal risks to her, the Adams family, Universal and Starcrest if Starcrest were to enter into such a contract. She also has asked you to advise her of what steps, if any, she or Starcrest could take to minimize those risks.

B. TRANSACTIONS WITHIN CORPORATE GROUPS

One reason to obtain control of a corporation is to be able to engage in transactions with the controlled corporation. Such transactions occur regularly and rarely give rise to litigation. But fairness is always on the minds of the parent.

SINCLAIR OIL CORP. V. LEVIEN
280 A.2d 717 (Del. 1971).

WOLCOTT, CHIEF JUSTICE:

This is an appeal by the defendant, Sinclair Oil Corporation (hereafter Sinclair), from an order of the Court of Chancery, in a derivative action requiring Sinclair to account for damages sustained by its subsidiary, Sinclair Venezuelan Oil Company (hereafter Sinven), organized by Sinclair for the purpose of operating in Venezuela, as a result of dividends paid by Sinven, the denial to Sinven of industrial development, and a breach of contract between Sinclair's wholly-owned subsidiary, Sinclair International Oil Company, and Sinven.

Sinclair, operating primarily as a holding company, is in the business of exploring for oil and of producing and marketing crude oil and oil products. At all times relevant to this litigation, it owned about 97% of Sinven's stock. The plaintiff owns about 3000 of 120,000 publicly held shares of Sinven. Sinven, incorporated in 1922, has been engaged in petroleum operations primarily in Venezuela and since 1959 has operated exclusively in Venezuela.

2.5%

Sinclair nominates all members of Sinven's board of directors. The Chancellor found as a fact that the directors were not independent of Sinclair. Almost without exception, they were officers, directors, or employees of corporations in the Sinclair complex. By reason of Sinclair's domination, it is clear that Sinclair owed Sinven a fiduciary duty. Sinclair concedes this.

The Chancellor held that because of Sinclair's fiduciary duty and its control over Sinven, its relationship with Sinven must meet the test of intrinsic fairness. The standard of intrinsic fairness involves both a high degree of fairness and a shift in the burden of proof. Under this standard the burden is on Sinclair to prove, subject to careful judicial scrutiny, that its transactions with Sinven were objectively fair.

Sinclair Arg.

Sinclair argues that the transactions between it and Sinven should be tested, not by the test of intrinsic fairness with the accompanying shift of the burden of proof, but by the business judgment rule under which a court will not interfere with the judgment of a board of directors unless there is a showing of gross and palpable overreaching. *Meyerson v. El Paso Natural Gas Co.,* 246 A.2d 789 (Del.Ch. 1967). A board of directors enjoys a presumption of sound business judgment, and its decisions will not be disturbed if they can be attributed to any rational business purpose. A court under such circumstances will not substitute its own notions of what is or is not sound business judgment.

We think, however, that Sinclair's argument in this respect is misconceived. When the situation involves a parent and a subsidiary with the parent controlling the transaction and fixing the terms, the test of intrinsic fairness, with its resulting shifting of the burden of proof, is applied. The basic situation for the application of the rule is the one in which the parent has received a benefit to the exclusion and at the expense of the subsidiary.

Parent - Sub ↓

Recently, this court dealt with the question of fairness in parent-subsidiary dealings in *Getty Oil Co. v. Skelly Oil Co.,* 267 A.2d 883 (Del.1970). In that case, both parent and subsidiary were in the business of refining and marketing crude oil and crude oil products. The Oil Import Board ruled that the subsidiary, because it was controlled by the parent, was no longer entitled to a separate allocation of imported crude oil. The subsidiary then contended that it had a right to share the quota of crude oil allotted to the parent. We ruled that the business judgment standard should be applied to determine this contention. Although the subsidiary suffered a loss through the administration of the oil import quotas, the parent gained nothing. The parent's quota was derived solely from its own past use. The past use of the subsidiary did not cause an increase in the parent's quota. Nor did the parent usurp a quota of the subsidiary. Since the parent received nothing from the subsidiary to the exclusion of the minority stockholders of the subsidiary, there was no self-dealing. Therefore, the business judgment standard was properly applied.

A parent does indeed owe a fiduciary duty to its subsidiary when there are parent-subsidiary dealings. However, this alone will not evoke the intrinsic fairness standard. This standard will be applied only when the fiduciary duty is accompanied by self-dealing—the situation when a parent is on both sides of a transaction with its subsidiary. Self-dealing occurs when the parent, by virtue of its domination of the subsidiary, causes the subsidiary to act in such a way that the parent receives something from the subsidiary to the exclusion of, and detriment to, the minority stockholders of the subsidiary.

We turn now to the facts. The plaintiff argues that, from 1960 through 1966, Sinclair caused Sinven to pay out such excessive dividends that the industrial development of Sinven was effectively prevented, and it became in reality a corporation in dissolution.

From 1960 through 1966, Sinven paid out $108,000,000 in dividends ($38,000,000 in excess of Sinven's earnings during the same period). The Chancellor held that Sinclair caused these dividends to be paid during a period when it had a need for large amounts of cash. Although the dividends paid exceeded earnings, the plaintiff concedes that the payments were made in compliance with 8 Del.C. § 170, authorizing payment of dividends out of surplus or net profits. However, the plaintiff attacks these dividends on the ground that they resulted from an improper motive— Sinclair's need for cash. The Chancellor, applying the intrinsic fairness standard, held that Sinclair did not sustain its burden of proving that these dividends were intrinsically fair to the minority stockholders of Sinven.

Since it is admitted that the dividends were paid in strict compliance with 8 Del.C. § 170, the alleged excessiveness of the payments alone would not state a cause of action. Nevertheless, compliance with the applicable statute may not, under all circumstances, justify all dividend payments. If a plaintiff can meet his burden of proving that a dividend cannot be grounded on any reasonable business objective, then the courts can and will interfere with the board's decision to pay the dividend.

Sinclair contends that it is improper to apply the intrinsic fairness standard to dividend payments even when the board which voted for the dividends is completely dominated.] In support of this contention, Sinclair relies heavily on *American District Telegraph Co. [ADT] v. Grinnell Corp.* (N.Y.Sup.Ct.1969) *aff'd*, 33 A.D.2d 769, 306 N.Y.S.2d 209 (1969). Plaintiffs were minority stockholders of ADT, a subsidiary of Grinnell. The plaintiffs alleged that Grinnell, realizing that it would soon have to sell its ADT stock because of a pending anti-trust action, caused ADT to pay excessive dividends. Because the dividend payments conformed with applicable statutory law, and the plaintiffs could not prove an abuse of discretion, the court ruled that the complaint did not state a cause of action. Other decisions seem to support Sinclair's contention.

We do not accept the argument that the intrinsic fairness test can never be applied to a dividend declaration by a dominated board, although a dividend declaration by a dominated board will not inevitably demand the application of the intrinsic fairness standard. If such a dividend is in essence self-dealing by the parent, then the intrinsic fairness standard is the proper standard. For example, suppose a parent dominates a subsidiary and its board of directors. The subsidiary has outstanding two classes of stock, X and Y. Class X is owned by the parent and Class Y is owned by minority stockholders of the subsidiary. If the subsidiary, at the direction of the parent, declares a dividend on its Class X stock only, this might well be self-dealing by the parent. It would be receiving something from the subsidiary to the exclusion of and detrimental to its minority stockholders.] This self-dealing, coupled with the parent's fiduciary duty, would make intrinsic fairness the proper standard by which to evaluate the dividend payments.

Consequently it must be determined whether the dividend payments by Sinven were, in essence, self-dealing by Sinclair. The dividends resulted in great sums of money being transferred from Sinven to Sinclair. However, a proportionate share of this money was received by the minority shareholders of Sinven. Sinclair received nothing from Sinven to the exclusion of its minority stockholders. As such, these dividends were not self-dealing. We hold therefore that the Chancellor erred in applying the intrinsic fairness test as to these dividend payments. The business judgment standard should have been applied.

We conclude that the facts demonstrate that the dividend payments complied with the business judgment standard and with 8 Del.C. § 170. The motives for causing the declaration of dividends are immaterial unless the plaintiff can show that the dividend payments resulted from improper motives and amounted to waste. The plaintiff contends only that the dividend payments drained Sinven of cash to such an extent that it was prevented from expanding.

The plaintiff proved no business opportunities which came to Sinven independently and which Sinclair either took to itself or denied to Sinven. As a matter of fact, with two minor exceptions which resulted in losses, all of Sinven's operations have been conducted in Venezuela, and Sinclair had a policy of exploiting its oil properties located in different countries by subsidiaries located in the particular countries.

From 1960 to 1966 Sinclair purchased or developed oil fields in Alaska, Canada, Paraguay, and other places around the world. The plaintiff contends that these were all opportunities which could have been taken by Sinven. The Chancellor concluded that Sinclair had not proved that its denial of expansion opportunities to Sinven was intrinsically fair. He based this conclusion on the following findings of fact. Sinclair made no real effort to expand Sinven. The excessive dividends paid by Sinven resulted in so great a cash drain as to effectively deny to Sinven any ability to expand. During this same period Sinclair actively pursued a company-wide policy of developing through its subsidiaries new sources of revenue, but Sinven was not permitted to participate and was confined in its activities to Venezuela.

However, the plaintiff could point to no opportunities which came to Sinven. Therefore, Sinclair usurped no business opportunity belonging to Sinven. Since Sinclair received nothing from Sinven to the exclusion of and detriment to Sinven's minority stockholders, there was no self-dealing. Therefore, business judgment is the proper standard by which to evaluate Sinclair's expansion policies.

Since there is no proof of self-dealing on the part of Sinclair, it follows that the expansion policy of Sinclair and the methods used to achieve the desired result must, as far as Sinclair's treatment of Sinven is concerned, be tested by the standards of the business judgment rule. Accordingly, Sinclair's decision, absent fraud or gross overreaching, to achieve expansion through the medium of its subsidiaries, other than Sinven, must be upheld.

Even if Sinclair was wrong in developing these opportunities as it did, the question arises, with which subsidiaries should these opportunities have been shared? No evidence indicates a unique need or ability of Sinven to develop these opportunities. The decision of which subsidiaries would be used to implement Sinclair's expansion policy was one of business judgment with which a court will not interfere absent a showing of gross and palpable overreaching. *Meyerson v. El Paso Natural Gas Co.*, 246 A.2d 789 (Del.Ch.1967). No such showing has been made here.

Next, Sinclair argues that the Chancellor committed error when he held it liable to Sinven for breach of contract.

In 1961 Sinclair created Sinclair International Oil Company (hereafter International), a wholly owned subsidiary used for the purpose of coordinating all of Sinclair's foreign operations. All crude purchases by Sinclair were made thereafter through International.

On September 28, 1961, Sinclair caused Sinven to contract with International whereby Sinven agreed to sell all of its crude oil and refined products to International at specified prices. The contract provided for minimum and maximum quantities and prices. The plaintiff contends that Sinclair caused this contract to be breached in two respects. Although the contract called for payment on receipt, International's payments lagged as much as 30 days after receipt. Also, the contract required International to purchase at least a fixed minimum amount of crude and refined products from Sinven. International did not comply with this requirement.

Clearly, Sinclair's act of contracting with its dominated subsidiary was self-dealing. Under the contract Sinclair received the products produced by Sinven, and of course the minority shareholders of Sinven were not able to share in the receipt of these products. If the contract was breached, then Sinclair received these products to the detriment of Sinven's minority shareholders. We agree with the Chancellor's finding that the contract was breached by Sinclair, both as to the time of payments and the amounts purchased.

Although a parent need not bind itself by a contract with its dominated subsidiary, Sinclair chose to operate in this manner. As Sinclair has received the benefits of this contract, so must it comply with the contractual duties.

Under the intrinsic fairness standard, Sinclair must prove that its causing Sinven not to enforce the contract was intrinsically fair to the minority shareholders of Sinven. Sinclair has failed to meet this burden. Late payments were clearly breaches for which Sinven should have sought and received adequate damages. As to the quantities purchased, Sinclair argues that it purchased all the products produced by Sinven. This, however, does not satisfy the standard of intrinsic fairness. Sinclair has failed to prove that Sinven could not possibly have produced or someway have obtained the contract minimums. As such, Sinclair must account on this claim.

Finally, Sinclair argues that the Chancellor committed error in refusing to allow it a credit or setoff of all benefits provided by it to Sinven with respect to all the alleged damages. The Chancellor held that setoff should be allowed on specific transactions, *e.g.*, benefits to Sinven under the contract with International, but denied an over all setoff against all damages claimed. We agree with the Chancellor, although the point may well be moot in view of our holding that Sinclair is not required to account for the alleged excessiveness of the dividend payments.

We will therefore reverse that part of the Chancellor's order that requires Sinclair to account to Sinven for damages sustained as a result of dividends paid between 1960 and 1966, and by reason of the denial to Sinven of expansion during that period. We will affirm the remaining portion of that order and remand the cause for further proceedings.

NOTES AND QUESTIONS

1.   Although it is not discussed in the opinion, Levien acquired his stock *after* Sinclair already owned 97% of Sinven. In light of the court's two holdings, why do you think he bought the stock? When he bought it, how did Levien expect Sinclair to conduct its business? Wasn't he on notice that Sinclair was likely to cause Sinven to pay large dividends at the end of each year? Should that affect the nature of the fiduciary duties that Sinclair owes to the minority shareholders of Sinven?

2.   Which of the two claims do you think Levien believed was more important and/or likely to succeed? Do your answers help answer the question of why he purchased Sinven stock?

3.   Do you agree with the court's holding on the dividend issue? It appears that Levien was unable to show that the payment of dividends caused Sinven to forego otherwise profitable investments. Would the result have changed if he had been able to demonstrate such a loss?

4.   The Supreme Court accepted, as had the Court of Chancery, that it was "fair" for Sinclair to enter into the contract with Sinven, even though it specified prices of 5–10% below market and minimum quantities. The problem arose when International failed to pay on time or to purchase the minimum quantities specified in the contract—apparently because Sinclair found it more attractive to buy on the spot market. If Sinven was producing at full capacity, as the trial court found, should Sinclair have been forced to buy on the spot market through Sinven?

5.   What burdens does the court's holding place on contract dealings among affiliated corporations in a corporate group? In that connection, consider that Sinven won a judgment for $5.6 million on the contract claim, providing an (indirect) benefit for the public shareholders of approximately $168,000. Plaintiff's attorneys were awarded fees in excess of $1 million for recovering the $5.6 million.

C. CASH-OUT TRANSACTIONS

1. INTRODUCTION

The most common (and frequently litigated) form of controlling shareholder transaction is the cash-out merger in which the controlling shareholder of a corporation seeks to terminate, or cash out, other shareholders' equity interest in that corporation, usually by forcing them to accept cash for their stock. The potential for conflicting interests between the controlling shareholder and the minority shareholder is fairly obvious: (1) the controlling shareholder would be inclined to minimize the consideration to the minority; (2) minority shareholders would exit the investment in the company though some may not want to exit, whereas the controlling shareholder would gain the entire ownership of the company.

At first blush, the very concept that a shareholder can be forced to sell her stock at all may seem strange. But in a corporation, the system of "majority rule" allows controlling shareholders to structure transactions that force minority shareholders to accept cash for their shares.

Eliminating minority shareholders can be accomplished in several different ways:

(1) **Cash-out merger.** In this most common of the available techniques, the parent corporation uses its control of the subsidiary's board and its voting majority to arrange a merger typically between the partially-owned subsidiary and another wholly-owned subsidiary of the parent. In the process, the minority shareholders receive cash in the merger or, if they are dissatisfied with the merger terms, in a judicial appraisal proceeding.

(2) **Tender offer followed by short-form merger.** A bidder corporation (sometimes already with a controlling interest) makes a tender offer conditioned on acquiring at least 90 percent of a corporation's stock. If successful, the bidder then merges with the corporation in a short-form merger, which requires only approval of the parent corporation's board of directors.

(3) **Sale to outside buyer.** The parent corporation, rather than acquiring 100 percent ownership of the subsidiary, arranges for the subsidiary to be merged with an outside buyer. In the merger, the parent corporation and minority shareholders receive the consideration, usually cash, specified in the merger plan.

(4) **Reverse stock split.** A controlling shareholder of a corporation can effect a reverse split of the corporation's shares in a transaction in which cash is issued in lieu of fractional shares. If the ratio of old shares to new is set high enough, all of the minority shareholders will be left with only fractional shares and will therefore be forced to accept cash for their stock.

Over the last thirty years, the cash-out merger has been widely used as the second step in the completion of corporate takeovers. When a corporate bidder acquires majority control of a target company, the cash-out merger provides the simplest means to consolidate control. Once the target becomes a wholly-owned subsidiary, the parent gains the significant advantage of using the cash flow and assets of the subsidiary to repay the debt it assumed to acquire the target. Freed of nettlesome minority shareholders, the parent can deal with the subsidiary as it chooses, and its dealings are not subject to challenge as self-dealing.

Cashing out minority shareholders in a controlled subsidiary is relatively straightforward. Typically, the parent corporation (P) organizes a new shell corporation (Newco) to which it transfers all its stock in the partially-owned subsidiary (S). Next, P has the boards of S and Newco enter into a merger agreement providing that, upon the merger of Newco into S, all the shareholders of S will receive cash for their S stock. P then votes all the stock of Newco in favor of the merger. P also votes its S stock for the merger and, if necessary, uses its control over the S proxy machinery to obtain the support of any additional shares needed to approve the merger. Under most corporate statutes, subject to certain exceptions, S shareholders who are dissatisfied with the merger terms can dissent and seek a judicial appraisal of the "fair value" of their stock, payable in cash.

Cash-out mergers are fraught with conflicts. If P owns a majority of S stock, it can use its control of S's board and its ability to vote for approval of the merger to dictate the terms on which S's minority shareholders will be cashed out. Unless S's non-controlling shareholders can induce a court to intervene on equitable grounds, they will be powerless to alter the terms of the merger or to retain their equity interest in S.

Even if P has only de facto control of S and needs the support of other S shareholders to accomplish the cash-out, S's non-controlling shareholders may have difficulty blocking an unfair cash-out merger. In a public corporation, the shareholders face collective action problems and lack a mechanism for bargaining with P. These problems are exacerbated by P's better understanding of S's business and assets—and thus its value. P also will be in a position to time a cash-out merger so as to take advantage of shifts in interest rates, fluctuations in S's stock price, or changes in the value of S's assets.

Despite the potential for abuse, a cash-out merger is not inevitably exploitative. P may have bona fide reasons for the transaction. P may anticipate operating efficiencies by combining P and S. P may wish to engage in concededly fair transactions with S without the threat of litigation. P may wish to eliminate the expense of having public shareholders, thus avoiding the reporting requirements of the Securities Exchange Act of 1934. Or, significantly, if P has acquired a controlling interest in S through a cash tender offer, a subsequent cash-out merger will give P access to the cash flows and assets of S that can be used to repay the acquisition debt P incurred in the tender offer. And, whatever the business reasons for the cash-out, P may, in fact, offer the minority shareholders a fair price for their stock.

The availability of appraisal only mitigates the potential for P's abuse. Dissenting shareholders (at least in Delaware) must bear the significant out-of-pocket costs of appraisal. Thus, even if they obtain an award higher than the merger price, the effort may not be economically worthwhile. Suppose P proposes a cash-out merger at $9 per share, and the owner of 1,000 shares of S stock believes her stock is worth $12. With a maximum potential gain of $3,000, that shareholder probably will be reluctant to incur the legal fees, expert witness fees, and other costs involved in an appraisal. Even if most of the non-controlling shareholders of S similarly valued their stock at $12, collective action problems will impede them from coordinating their joint efforts to pursue appraisal. Recognizing this, P may try to set the merger price just high enough to make appraisal cost-ineffective.

All that said, several factors almost guarantee that litigation will be brought challenging most cash-out mergers: the conflicts of interest and inherent potential for abuse; the large stakes involved; and the likelihood that any attorney who successfully challenges a cash-out merger will receive a substantial contingent fee. Faced with this situation, courts are sensitive to the need to provide corporate planners with some degree of certainty when planning cash-out mergers. Courts have sought to balance the potential for abuse by controlling shareholders with the potential for abuse when the litigation is driven by a desire for attorneys' fees.

2. *WEINBERGER* AND ITS ANTECEDENTS

Weinberger v. UOP lays out the analytical framework for cash-out mergers of Delaware corporations. To appreciate *Weinberger*, it is useful to understand its antecedents. In 1977, the Delaware Supreme Court had held that a merger "made for the sole purpose of freezing-out minority stockholders is an abuse of the corporate process." *Singer v. Magnavox Co.,* 380 A.2d 969 (Del.1977) (overruling earlier cases). In addition, the court reiterated the long-standing rule that the controlling shareholder bears the burden of demonstrating the "entire fairness" of the proposed merger. See *Sterling v. Mayflower Hotel Corp.,* 93 A.2d 107 (Del. 1952).

Singer (and two other contemporaneous decisions) established that a shareholder dissatisfied with the terms of a cash-out merger could avoid appraisal by challenging the merger's purpose. The *Singer* trilogy, which provided little guidance as to what constitutes a proper purpose or when a merger is "entirely fair," opened cash-out mergers to extended litigation. An aggrieved shareholder could simply allege that the merger had been effectuated "solely to cash-out minority shareholders at an inadequate price"—thus creating a factual issue as to whether the merger had a proper purpose and shifting the burden to the controlling shareholder to prove the merger was "entirely fair."

Decided at the beginning of the 1980s takeover movement, *Weinberger* answers a number of important questions, including the judicial standard of review (entire fairness), the relevance of approval by disinterested directors and minority shareholders (shifts burden of proof), and the method by which Delaware courts are to value minority shares (generally accepted financial methods).

After *Weinberger*, we take up some of the other issues that the case raises: whether the controlling shareholder must have a proper business purpose for eliminating the minority; when appraisal is the exclusive

Signal
_officer : Crawford

UOP
- CEO Crawford

Board:
Arledge
Chitiea
others

Board:
Arledge
Chitiea
others

...rs; what constitutes fair dealing in ...transaction; the relation of these ...liability of directors who approve a ...lly, we look at recent cases that decide ...k should be extended to tender offers ...ales of partially-owned subsidiaries to ...the question is whether heightened ...fairness standard should apply to ...minority shareholders.

R V. UOP, INC.

...01 (Del. 1983).

MOORE, JUSTICE:

This post-trial appeal was reheard en banc from a decision of the Court of Chancery. It was brought by the class action plaintiff below, a former shareholder of UOP, Inc., who challenged the elimination of UOP's minority shareholders by a cash-out merger between UOP and its majority owner, The Signal Companies, Inc. Originally, the defendants in this action were Signal, UOP, certain officers and directors of those companies, and UOP's investment banker, Lehman Brothers Kuhn Loeb, Inc. The present Chancellor held that the terms of the merger were fair to the plaintiff and the other minority shareholders of UOP. Accordingly, he entered judgment in favor of the defendants.

Numerous points were raised by the parties, but we address only the following questions presented by the trial court's opinion:

1) The plaintiff's duty to plead sufficient facts demonstrating the unfairness of the challenged merger;

2) The burden of proof upon the parties where the merger has been approved by the purportedly informed vote of a majority of the minority shareholders;

3) The fairness of the merger in terms of adequacy of the defendants' disclosures to the minority shareholders;

4) The fairness of the merger in terms of adequacy of the price paid for the minority shares and the remedy appropriate to that issue; and

5) The continued force and effect of *Singer v. Magnavox Co.*, Del.Supr., 380 A.2d 969, 980 (1977), and its progeny.

In ruling for the defendants, the Chancellor re-stated his earlier conclusion that the plaintiff in a suit challenging a cash-out merger must allege specific acts of fraud, misrepresentation or other items of misconduct to demonstrate the unfairness of the merger terms to the minority. We approve this rule and affirm it.

The Chancellor also held that even though the ultimate burden of proof is on the majority shareholder to show by a preponderance of the evidence that the transaction is fair, it is first the burden of the plaintiff attacking the merger to demonstrate some basis for invoking the fairness obligation. We agree with that principle. However, where corporate action has been approved by an informed vote of a majority of the minority shareholders, we conclude that the burden entirely shifts to the plaintiff to show that the transaction was unfair to the minority. But in all this, the burden clearly remains on those relying on the vote to show that they completely disclosed all material facts relevant to the transaction.

Here, the record does not support a conclusion that the minority stockholder vote was an informed one. Material information, necessary to acquaint those shareholders with the bargaining positions of Signal and UOP, was withheld under circumstances amounting to a breach of fiduciary duty. We therefore conclude that this merger does not meet the test of fairness, at least as we address that concept, and no burden thus shifted to the plaintiff by reason of the minority shareholder vote. Accordingly, we reverse and remand for further proceedings consistent herewith.

In considering the nature of the remedy available under our law to minority shareholders in a cash-out merger, we believe that it is, and hereafter should be, an appraisal under 8 Del.C. § 262 as hereinafter construed. To give full effect to section 262 within the framework of the General Corporation Law we adopt a more liberal, less rigid and stylized, approach to the valuation process than has heretofore been permitted by our courts. While the present state of these proceedings does not admit the plaintiff to the appraisal remedy per se, the practical effect of the remedy we do grant him will be co-extensive with the liberalized valuation and appraisal methods we herein approve for cases coming after this decision.

Our treatment of these matters has necessarily led us to a reconsideration of the business purpose rule announced in the trilogy of *Singer v. Magnavox Co.*, supra; *Tanzer v. International General Industries, Inc.*, Del.Supr., 379 A.2d 1121 (1977); and *Roland International Corp. v. Najjar*, Del.Supr., 407 A.2d 1032 (1979). For the reasons hereafter set forth we consider that the business purpose requirement of these cases is no longer the law of Delaware.

I.

Signal is a diversified, technically based company operating through various subsidiaries. Its stock is publicly traded on the New York, Philadelphia and Pacific Stock Exchanges. UOP, formerly known as Universal Oil Products Company, was a diversified industrial company engaged in various lines of business, including petroleum and petro-chemical services and related products, construction, fabricated metal products, transportation equipment products, chemicals and plastics, and other products and services including land development, lumber products and waste disposal. Its stock was publicly held and listed on the New York Stock Exchange.

In 1974 Signal sold one of its wholly-owned subsidiaries for $420,000,000 in cash. See *Gimbel v. Signal Companies, Inc.*, Del.Ch., 316 A.2d 599, aff'd, Del.Supr., 316 A.2d 619 (1974). While looking to invest this cash surplus, Signal became interested in UOP as a possible acquisition. Friendly negotiations ensued, and Signal proposed to acquire a controlling interest in UOP at a price of $19 per share. UOP's representatives sought $25 per share. In the arm's length bargaining that followed, an understanding was reached whereby Signal agreed to purchase from UOP 1,500,000 shares of UOP's authorized but unissued stock at $21 per share.

This purchase was contingent upon Signal making a successful cash tender offer for 4,300,000 publicly held shares of UOP, also at a price of $21 per share. This combined method of acquisition permitted Signal to acquire 5,800,000 shares of stock, representing 50.5% of UOP's outstanding shares. The UOP board of directors advised the company's shareholders that it had no objection to Signal's tender offer at that price. Immediately before the announcement of the tender offer, UOP's common stock had been trading on the New York Stock Exchange at a fraction under $14 per share.

The negotiations between Signal and UOP occurred during April 1975, and the resulting tender offer was greatly oversubscribed. However, Signal limited its total purchase of the tendered shares so that, when coupled with the stock bought from UOP, it had achieved its goal of becoming a 50.5% shareholder of UOP.

Although UOP's board consisted of thirteen directors, Signal nominated and elected only six. Of these, five were either directors or employees of Signal. The sixth, a partner in the banking firm of Lazard Freres & Co., had been one of Signal's representatives in the negotiations and bargaining with UOP concerning the tender offer and purchase price of the UOP shares.

However, the president and chief executive officer of UOP retired during 1975, and Signal caused him to be replaced by James V. Crawford, a long-time employee and senior executive vice president of one of Signal's wholly-owned subsidiaries. Crawford succeeded his predecessor on UOP's board of directors and also was made a director of Signal.

By the end of 1977 Signal basically was unsuccessful in finding other suitable investment candidates for its excess cash, and by February 1978 considered that it had no other realistic acquisitions available to it on a friendly basis. Once again its attention turned to UOP.

The trial court found that at the instigation of certain Signal management personnel, including William W. Walkup, its board chairman, and Forrest N. Shumway, its president, a feasibility study was made

[handwritten note in top margin: UOP – Signal was shareholder & wanted to acquire the rest of UOP]

isition of the balance of UOP's outstanding
formed by two Signal officers, Charles S.
ctor of planning), and Andrew J. Chitiea,
nancial officer). Messrs. Walkup, Shumway,
all directors of UOP in addition to their
ard.

luded that it would be a good investment for
ing 49.5% of UOP shares at any price up to
scussed between Walkup and Shumway who,
and Brewster L. Arms, internal counsel for
enior management. In particular, they talked
be paid if the acquisition was pursued,
purportedly keeping in mind that as UOP's majority shareholder, Signal
owed a fiduciary responsibility to both its own stockholders as well as to
UOP's minority. It was ultimately agreed that a meeting of Signal's
Executive Committee would be called to propose that Signal acquire the
remaining outstanding stock of UOP through a cash-out merger in the
range of $20 to $21 per share.

The Executive Committee meeting was set for February 28, 1978. As
a courtesy, UOP's president, Crawford, was invited to attend, although he
was not a member of Signal's executive committee. On his arrival, and prior
to the meeting, Crawford was asked to meet privately with Walkup and
Shumway. He was then told of Signal's plan to acquire full ownership of
UOP and was asked for his reaction to the proposed price range of $20 to
$21 per share. Crawford said he thought such a price would be "generous",
and that it was certainly one which should be submitted to UOP's minority
shareholders for their ultimate consideration.

Thus, Crawford voiced no objection to the $20 to $21 price range, nor
did he suggest that Signal should consider paying more than $21 per share
for the minority interests. Later, at the Executive Committee meeting the
same factors were discussed, with Crawford repeating the position he
earlier took with Walkup and Shumway. Also considered was the 1975
tender offer and the fact that it had been greatly oversubscribed at $21 per
share. For many reasons, Signal's management concluded that the
acquisition of UOP's minority shares provided the solution to a number of
its business problems.

Thus, it was the consensus that a price of $20 to $21 per share would
be fair to both Signal and the minority shareholders of UOP. Signal's
executive committee authorized its management "to negotiate" with UOP
"for a cash acquisition of the minority ownership in UOP, Inc., with the
intention of presenting a proposal to Signal's board of directors on March
6, 1978". Immediately after this February 28, 1978 meeting, Signal issued
a press release stating:

The Signal Companies, Inc. and UOP, Inc. are conducting negotiations for the acquisition for cash by Signal of the 49.5 per cent of UOP which it does not presently own, announced Forrest N. Shumway, president and chief executive officer of Signal, and James V. Crawford, UOP president.

Price and other terms of the proposed transaction have not yet been finalized and would be subject to approval of the boards of directors of Signal and UOP, scheduled to meet early next week, the stockholders of UOP and certain federal agencies.

The announcement also referred to the fact that the closing price of UOP's common stock on that day was $14.50 per share.

Two days later, on March 2, 1978, Signal issued a second press release stating that its management would recommend a price in the range of $20 to $21 per share for UOP's 49.5% minority interest. This announcement referred to Signal's earlier statement that "negotiations" were being conducted for the acquisition of the minority shares.

Between Tuesday, February 28, 1978 and Monday, March 6, 1978, a total of four business days, Crawford spoke by telephone with all of UOP's non-Signal, *i.e.*, outside, directors. Also during that period, Crawford retained Lehman Brothers to render a fairness opinion as to the price offered the minority for its stock. He gave two reasons for this choice. First, the time schedule between the announcement and the board meetings was short (by then only three business days) and since Lehman Brothers had been acting as UOP's investment banker for many years, Crawford felt that it would be in the best position to respond on such brief notice. Second, James W. Glanville, a long-time director of UOP and a partner in Lehman Brothers, had acted as a financial advisor to UOP for many years. Crawford believed that Glanville's familiarity with UOP, as a member of its board, would also be of assistance in enabling Lehman Brothers to render a fairness opinion within the existing time constraints.

Crawford telephoned Glanville, who gave his assurance that Lehman Brothers had no conflicts that would prevent it from accepting the task. Glanville's immediate personal reaction was that a price of $20 to $21 would certainly be fair, since it represented almost a 50% premium over UOP's market price. Glanville sought a $250,000 fee for Lehman Brothers' services, but Crawford thought this too much. After further discussions Glanville finally agreed that Lehman Brothers would render its fairness opinion for $150,000.

During this period Crawford also had several telephone contacts with Signal officials. In only one of them, however, was the price of the shares discussed. In a conversation with Walkup, Crawford advised that as a result of his communications with UOP's non-Signal directors, it was his feeling that the price would have to be the top of the proposed range, or $21 per share, if the approval of UOP's outside directors was to be obtained. But again, he did not seek any price higher than $21.

Glanville assembled a three-man Lehman Brothers team to do the work on the fairness opinion. These persons examined relevant documents and information concerning UOP, including its annual reports and its Securities and Exchange Commission filings from 1973 through 1976, as well as its audited financial statements for 1977, its interim reports to shareholders, and its recent and historical market prices and trading volumes. In addition, on Friday, March 3, 1978, two members of the Lehman Brothers team flew to UOP's headquarters in Des Plaines, Illinois, to perform a "due diligence" visit, during the course of which they interviewed Crawford as well as UOP's general counsel, its chief financial officer, and other key executives and personnel.

As a result, the Lehman Brothers team concluded that "the price of either $20 or $21 would be a fair price for the remaining shares of UOP". They telephoned this impression to Glanville, who was spending the weekend in Vermont.

On Monday morning, March 6, 1978, Glanville and the senior member of the Lehman Brothers team flew to Des Plaines to attend the scheduled UOP directors meeting. Glanville looked over the assembled information during the flight. The two had with them the draft of a "fairness opinion letter" in which the price had been left blank. Either during or immediately prior to the directors' meeting, the two-page "fairness opinion letter" was typed in final form and the price of $21 per share was inserted.

On March 6, 1978, both the Signal and UOP boards were convened to consider the proposed merger. Telephone communications were maintained between the two meetings. Walkup, Signal's board chairman, and also a UOP director, attended UOP's meeting with Crawford in order to present Signal's position and answer any questions that UOP's non-Signal directors might have. Arledge and Chitiea, along with Signal's other designees on UOP's board, participated by conference telephone. All of UOP's outside directors attended the meeting either in person or by conference telephone.

First, Signal's board unanimously adopted a resolution authorizing Signal to propose to UOP a cash merger of $21 per share as outlined in a certain merger agreement, and other supporting documents. This proposal required that the merger be approved by a majority of UOP's outstanding minority shares voting at the stockholders meeting at which the merger would be considered, and that the minority shares voting in favor of the merger, when coupled with Signal's 50.5% interest would have to comprise at least two-thirds of all UOP shares. Otherwise the proposed merger would be deemed disapproved.

UOP's board then considered the proposal. Copies of the agreement were delivered to the directors in attendance, and other copies had been forwarded earlier to the directors participating by telephone. They also had before them UOP financial data for 1974–1977, UOP's most recent financial statements, market price information, and budget projections for 1978. In addition they had Lehman Brothers' hurriedly prepared fairness opinion letter finding the price of $21 to be fair. Glanville, the Lehman Brothers partner, and UOP director, commented on the information that had gone into preparation of the letter.

Signal also suggests that the Arledge-Chitiea feasibility study, indicating that a price of up to $24 per share would be a "good investment" for Signal, was discussed at the UOP directors' meeting. The Chancellor made no such finding, and our independent review of the record, detailed infra, satisfies us by a preponderance of the evidence that there was no discussion of this document at UOP's board meeting. Furthermore, it is clear beyond peradventure that nothing in that report was ever disclosed to UOP's minority shareholders prior to their approval of the merger.

After consideration of Signal's proposal, Walkup and Crawford left the meeting to permit a free and uninhibited exchange between UOP's non-Signal directors. Upon their return a resolution to accept Signal's offer was then proposed and adopted. While Signal's men on UOP's board participated in various aspects of the meeting, they abstained from voting. However, the minutes show that each of them "if voting would have voted yes".

On March 7, 1978, UOP sent a letter to its shareholders advising them of the action taken by UOP's board with respect to Signal's offer. This document pointed out, among other things, that on February 28, 1978 "both companies had announced negotiations were being conducted".

Despite the swift board action of the two companies, the merger was not submitted to UOP's shareholders until their annual meeting on May 26, 1978. In the notice of that meeting and proxy statement sent to shareholders in May, UOP's management and board urged that the merger be approved. The proxy statement also advised:

> The price was determined after *discussions* between James V. Crawford, a director of Signal and Chief Executive Officer of UOP, and officers of Signal which took place during meetings on February 28, 1978, and in the course of several subsequent telephone conversations. (Emphasis added.)

In the original draft of the proxy statement the word "negotiations" had been used rather than "discussions". However, when the Securities and Exchange Commission sought details of the "negotiations" as part of its review of these materials, the term was deleted and the word "discussions" was substituted. The proxy statement indicated that the vote of UOP's board in approving the merger had been unanimous. It also advised the shareholders that Lehman Brothers had given its opinion that the merger price of $21 per share was fair to UOP's minority. However, it did not disclose the hurried method by which this conclusion was reached.

As of the record date of UOP's annual meeting, there were 11,488,302 shares of UOP common stock outstanding, 5,688,302 of which were owned by the minority. At the meeting only 56%, or 3,208,652, of the minority shares were voted. Of these, 2,953,812, or 51.9% of the total minority, voted for the merger, and 254,840 voted against it. When Signal's stock was added to the minority shares voting in favor, a total of 76.2% of UOP's outstanding shares approved the merger while only 2.2% opposed it.

By its terms the merger became effective on May 26, 1978, and each share of UOP's stock held by the minority was automatically converted into a right to receive $21 cash.

II.

A primary issue mandating reversal is the preparation by two UOP directors, Arledge and Chitiea, of their feasibility study for the exclusive use and benefit of Signal. This document was of obvious significance to both Signal and UOP. Using UOP data, it described the advantages to Signal of ousting the minority at a price range of $21–$24 per share. Mr. Arledge, one of the authors, outlined the benefits to Signal:

Purpose of the Merger

1) Provides an outstanding investment opportunity for Signal— (Better than any recent acquisition we have seen.)

2) Increases Signal's earnings.

3) Facilitates the flow of resources between Signal and its subsidiaries—(Big factor—works both ways.)

4) Provides cost savings potential for Signal and UOP.

5) Improves the percentage of Signal's "operating earnings" as opposed to "holding company earnings."

6) Simplifies the understanding of Signal.

7) Facilitates technological exchange among Signal's subsidiaries.

8) Eliminates potential conflicts of interest.

Having written those words, solely for the use of Signal it is clear from the record that neither Arledge nor Chitiea shared this report with their fellow directors of UOP. We are satisfied that no one else did either. This conduct hardly meets the fiduciary standards applicable to such a transaction.

The Arledge-Chitiea report speaks for itself in supporting the Chancellor's finding that a price of up to $24 was a "good investment" for

Signal. It shows that a return on the investment at $21 would be 15.7% versus 15.5% at $24 per share. This was a difference of only two-tenths of one percent, while it meant over $17,000,000 to the minority. Under such circumstances, paying UOP's minority shareholders $24 would have had relatively little long-term effect on Signal, and the Chancellor's findings concerning the benefit to Signal, even at a price of $24, were obviously correct.

Certainly, this was a matter of material significance to UOP and its shareholders. Since the study was prepared by two UOP directors, using UOP information for the exclusive benefit of Signal, and nothing whatever was done to disclose it to the outside UOP directors or the minority shareholders, a question of breach of fiduciary duty arises. This problem occurs because there were common Signal-UOP directors participating, at least to some extent, in the UOP board's decision-making processes without full disclosure of the conflicts they faced.[7]

In assessing this situation, the Court of Chancery was required to:

> examine what information defendants had and to measure it against what they gave to the minority stockholders, in a context in which "complete candor" is required. In other words, the limited function of the Court was to determine whether defendants had disclosed all information in their possession germane to the transaction in issue. And by "germane" we mean, for present purposes, information such as a reasonable shareholder would consider important in deciding whether to sell or retain stock.

This is merely stating in another way the long-existing principle of Delaware law that these Signal designated directors on UOP's board still owed UOP and its shareholders an uncompromising duty of loyalty.

Given the absence of any attempt to structure this transaction on an arm's length basis, Signal cannot escape the effects of the conflicts it faced, particularly when its designees on UOP's board did not totally abstain from participation in the matter. There is no "safe harbor" for such divided loyalties in Delaware. When directors of a Delaware corporation are on both sides of a transaction, they are required to demonstrate their utmost good faith and the most scrupulous inherent fairness of the bargain. The requirement of fairness is unflinching in its demand that where one stands on both sides of a transaction, he has the burden of establishing its entire fairness, sufficient to pass the test of careful scrutiny by the courts.

---

[7] Although perfection is not possible, or expected, the result here could have been entirely different if UOP had appointed an independent negotiating committee of its outside directors to deal with Signal at arm's length. Since fairness in this context can be equated to conduct by a theoretical, wholly independent, board of directors acting upon the matter before them, it is unfortunate that this course apparently was neither considered nor pursued. Particularly in a parent-subsidiary context, a showing that the action taken was as though each of the contending parties had in fact exerted its bargaining power against the other at arm's length is strong evidence that the transaction meets the test of fairness.

There is no dilution of this obligation where one holds dual or multiple directorships, as in a parent-subsidiary context. *Levien v. Sinclair Oil Corp.*, Del.Ch., 261 A.2d 911, 915 (1969). Thus, individuals who act in a dual capacity as directors of two corporations, one of whom is parent and the other subsidiary, owe the same duty of good management to both corporations, and in the absence of an independent negotiating structure (see note 7, supra), or the directors' total abstention from any participation in the matter, this duty is to be exercised in light of what is best for both companies. The record demonstrates that Signal has not met this obligation.

The concept of fairness has two basic aspects: fair dealing and fair price. The former embraces questions of when the transaction was timed, how it was initiated, structured, negotiated, disclosed to the directors, and how the approvals of the directors and the stockholders were obtained. The latter aspect of fairness relates to the economic and financial considerations of the proposed merger, including all relevant factors: assets, market value, earnings, future prospects, and any other elements that affect the intrinsic or inherent value of a company's stock. However, the test for fairness is not a bifurcated one as between fair dealing and price. All aspects of the issue must be examined as a whole since the question is one of entire fairness. However, in a non-fraudulent transaction we recognize that price may be the preponderant consideration outweighing other features of the merger. Here, we address the two basic aspects of fairness separately because we find reversible error as to both.

Part of fair dealing is the obvious duty of candor. Moreover, one possessing superior knowledge may not mislead any stockholder by use of corporate information to which the latter is not privy. Delaware has long imposed this duty even upon persons who are not corporate officers or directors, but who nonetheless are privy to matters of interest or significance to their company. With the well-established Delaware law on the subject, and the Court of Chancery's findings of fact here, it is inevitable that the obvious conflicts posed by Arledge and Chitiea's preparation of their "feasibility study", derived from UOP information, for the sole use and benefit of Signal, cannot pass muster.

Fair dealing issues — The Arledge-Chitiea report is but one aspect of the element of fair dealing. How did this merger evolve? It is clear that it was entirely initiated by Signal. The serious time constraints under which the principals acted were all set by Signal. It had not found a suitable outlet for its excess cash and considered UOP a desirable investment, particularly since it was now in a position to acquire the whole company for itself. For whatever reasons, and they were only Signal's, the entire transaction was presented to and approved by UOP's board within four business days. Standing alone, this is not necessarily indicative of any lack of fairness by a majority shareholder. It was what occurred, or more properly, what did not occur, during this brief period that makes the time constraints imposed by Signal relevant to the issue of fairness.

The structure of the transaction, again, was Signal's doing. So far as negotiations were concerned, it is clear that they were modest at best. Crawford, Signal's man at UOP, never really talked price with Signal, except to accede to its management's statements on the subject, and to convey to Signal the UOP outside directors' view that as between the $20–$21 range under consideration, it would have to be $21. The latter is not a surprising outcome, but hardly arm's length negotiations. Only the protection of benefits for UOP's key employees and the issue of Lehman Brothers' fee approached any concept of bargaining.

As we have noted, the matter of disclosure to the UOP directors was wholly flawed by the conflicts of interest raised by the Arledge-Chitiea report. All of those conflicts were resolved by Signal in its own favor without divulging any aspect of them to UOP.

This cannot but undermine a conclusion that this merger meets any reasonable test of fairness. The outside UOP directors lacked one material piece of information generated by two of their colleagues, but shared only with Signal. True, the UOP board had the Lehman Brothers' fairness opinion, but that firm has been blamed by the plaintiff for the hurried task it performed, when more properly the responsibility for this lies with Signal. There was no disclosure of the circumstances surrounding the rather cursory preparation of the Lehman Brothers' fairness opinion. Instead, the impression was given UOP's minority that a careful study had been made, when in fact speed was the hallmark, and Mr. Glanville, Lehman's partner in charge of the matter, and also a UOP director, having spent the weekend in Vermont, brought a draft of the "fairness opinion letter" to the UOP directors' meeting on March 6, 1978 with the price left blank. We can only conclude from the record that the rush imposed on Lehman Brothers by Signal's timetable contributed to the difficulties under which this investment banking firm attempted to perform its responsibilities. Yet, none of this was disclosed to UOP's minority.

Finally, the minority stockholders were denied the critical information that Signal considered a price of $24 to be a good investment. Since this would have meant over $17,000,000 more to the minority, we cannot conclude that the shareholder vote was an informed one. Under the circumstances, an approval by a majority of the minority was meaningless.

Given these particulars and the Delaware law on the subject, the record does not establish that this transaction satisfies any reasonable concept of fair dealing, and the Chancellor's findings in that regard must be reversed.

Turning to the matter of price, plaintiff also challenges its fairness. His evidence was that on the date the merger was approved the stock was worth at least $26 per share. In support, he offered the testimony of a chartered investment analyst who used two basic approaches to valuation: a comparative analysis of the premium paid over market in ten other tender offer-merger combinations, and a discounted cash flow analysis.

In this breach of fiduciary duty case, the Chancellor perceived that the approach to valuation was the same as that in an appraisal proceeding. Consistent with precedent, he rejected plaintiff's method of proof and accepted defendants' evidence of value as being in accord with practice under prior case law. This means that the so-called "Delaware block" or weighted average method was employed wherein the elements of value, *i.e.*, assets, market price, earnings, etc., were assigned a particular weight and the resulting amounts added to determine the value per share. This procedure has been in use for decades. However, to the extent it excludes other generally accepted techniques used in the financial community and the courts, it is now clearly outmoded. It is time we recognize this in appraisal and other stock valuation proceedings and bring our law current on the subject.

While the Chancellor rejected plaintiff's discounted cash flow method of valuing UOP's stock, as not corresponding with "either logic or the existing law", it is significant that this was essentially the focus, *i.e.*, earnings potential of UOP, of Messrs. Arledge and Chitiea in their evaluation of the merger. Accordingly, the standard "Delaware block" or weighted average method of valuation, formerly employed in appraisal and other stock valuation cases, shall no longer exclusively control such proceedings. We believe that a more liberal approach must include proof of value by any techniques or methods which are generally considered acceptable in the financial community and otherwise admissible in court, subject only to our interpretation of 8 Del.C. § 262(h), infra. This will obviate the very structured and mechanistic procedure that has heretofore governed such matters.

Fair price obviously requires consideration of all relevant factors involving the value of a company. This has long been the law of Delaware:

> The basic concept of value under the appraisal statute is that the stockholder is entitled to be paid for that which has been taken from him, viz., his proportionate interest in a going concern. By value of the stockholder's proportionate interest in the corporate enterprise is meant the true or intrinsic value of his stock which has been taken by the merger. In determining what figure represents this true or intrinsic value, the appraiser and the courts must take into consideration all factors and elements which reasonably might enter into the fixing of value. Thus, market value, asset value, dividends, earning prospects, the nature of the enterprise and any other facts which were known or which could be ascertained as of the date of merger and which throw any light

on *future prospects* of the merged corporation are not only pertinent to an inquiry as to the value of the dissenting stockholders' interest, but must be considered by the agency fixing the value. (Emphasis added.)

It is significant that section 262 now mandates the determination of "fair" value based upon "all relevant factors". Only the speculative elements of value that may arise from the "accomplishment or expectation" of the merger are excluded. We take this to be a very narrow exception to the appraisal process, designed to eliminate use of pro forma data and projections of a speculative variety relating to the completion of a merger. But elements of future value, including the nature of the enterprise, which are known or susceptible of proof as of the date of the merger and not the product of speculation, may be considered. When the trial court deems it appropriate, fair value also includes any damages, resulting from the taking, which the stockholders sustain as a class. If that was not the case, then the obligation to consider "all relevant factors" in the valuation process would be eroded.

Although the Chancellor received the plaintiff's evidence, his opinion indicates that the use of it was precluded because of past Delaware practice. While we do not suggest a monetary result one way or the other, we do think the plaintiff's evidence should be part of the factual mix and weighed as such. Until the $21 price is measured on remand by the valuation standards mandated by Delaware law, there can be no finding at the present stage of these proceedings that the price is fair. Given the lack of any candid disclosure of the material facts surrounding establishment of the $21 price, the majority of the minority vote, approving the merger, is meaningless.

The plaintiff has not sought an appraisal, but rescissory damages [that is, damages that measured what the value of the plaintiff's shares would have been had the merger not taken place]. In view of the approach to valuation that we announce today, we see no basis in our law for an exclusive monetary formula for relief. On remand the plaintiff will be permitted to test the fairness of the $21 price by the standards we herein establish, in conformity with the principle applicable to an appraisal—that fair value be determined by taking "into account all relevant factors" see 8 Del.C. § 262(h). In our view this includes the elements of rescissory damages if the Chancellor considers them susceptible of proof and a remedy appropriate to all the issues of fairness before him.

While a plaintiff's monetary remedy ordinarily should be confined to the more liberalized appraisal proceeding herein established, we do not intend any limitation on the historic powers of the Chancellor to grant such other relief as the facts of a particular case may dictate. The appraisal remedy we approve may not be adequate in certain cases, particularly where fraud, misrepresentation, self-dealing, deliberate waste of corporate assets, or gross and palpable overreaching are involved. Under such circumstances, the Chancellor's powers are complete to fashion any form of equitable and monetary relief as may be appropriate, including rescissory damages. Since it is apparent that this long completed transaction is too involved to undo, and in view of the Chancellor's discretion, the award, if any, should be in the form of monetary damages based upon entire fairness standards, *i.e.*, fair dealing and fair price.

Going forward, the provisions of 8 Del.C. § 262, as herein construed, respecting the scope of an appraisal and the means for perfecting the same, shall govern the financial remedy available to minority shareholders in a cash-out merger.

III.

Finally, we address the matter of business purpose. The defendants contend that the purpose of this merger was not a proper subject of inquiry by the trial court. The plaintiff says that no valid purpose existed—the entire transaction was a mere subterfuge designed to eliminate the minority. The Chancellor ruled otherwise, but in so doing he clearly circumscribed the thrust and effect of *Singer*. This has led to the thoroughly sound observation that the business purpose test "may be virtually interpreted out of existence, as it was in *Weinberger*."

The requirement of a business purpose is new to our law of mergers and was a departure from prior case law. In view of the fairness test which has long been applicable to parent-subsidiary mergers, the expanded appraisal remedy now available to shareholders, and the broad discretion of the Chancellor to fashion such relief as the facts of a given case may dictate, we do not believe that any additional meaningful protection is afforded minority shareholders by the business purpose requirement of the trilogy of Singer, Tanzer, Najjar, and their progeny. Accordingly, such requirement shall no longer be of any force or effect.

The judgment of the Court of Chancery, finding both the circumstances of the merger and the price paid the minority shareholders to be fair, is reversed. The matter is remanded for further proceedings consistent herewith. Upon remand the plaintiff's post-trial motion to enlarge the class should be granted.

Reversed and remanded.

NOTES AND QUESTIONS

1. On remand in *Weinberger*, the Court of Chancery seemed unimpressed with the Delaware Supreme Court's finding that Signal had dealt unfairly with the UOP minority shareholders. It interpreted the Supreme Court's holding as equating "to a finding that Signal was guilty of a misrepresentation," though not necessarily deliberate fraud. Chancellor Brown stated that he felt free to make a damage award without reference to

"the results of an appraisal of the value of a share of UOP stock either at the merger date or at some other date." Accordingly, he awarded $1 per share (about $5.7 million) together with interest from the date of the Supreme Court's opinion. He declined to award rescissory damages because of the speculative nature of the offered proof.

2.   *Weinberger* strongly suggested that the parent in a cash-out merger must disclose its internal reports and "reservation price" (the top price it would be willing to pay) to minority shareholders. One year later, the Delaware Supreme Court attempted to allay the fears that this suggestion had been raised, stating, "While it has been suggested that *Weinberger* stands for the proposition that a majority shareholder must under all circumstances disclose its top bid to the minority, that clearly is a misconception of what we said there. [The sole basis for our conclusions in *Weinberger* regarding the non-disclosure of the Arledge-Chitiea report was because Signal appointed directors on UOP's board, who thus stood on both sides of the transaction, violated their undiminished duty of loyalty to UOP.] It had nothing to do with Signal's duty, as the majority stockholder, to the other shareholders of UOP." *Rosenblatt v. Getty Oil Company*, 493 A.2d 929, 939 (Del. 1985). Under this analysis, how did Signal (as distinct from Arledge and Chitiea) breach its duty to the minority shareholders?

3.   In *Weinberger*, the court held that those relying on a shareholder vote to shift the burden of proof must show that they fully disclosed all material facts. If UOP had set up an independent negotiating committee as described in footnote 7, would Arledge and Chitiea have owed the same duty to disclose their report to the committee (and then to the shareholders) that they owed to the full UOP board? If so, how much protection would the footnote 7 committee have provided?

3.   BUSINESS PURPOSE TEST OUTSIDE OF DELAWARE

Although *Weinberger* rejects the business purpose test for Delaware corporations, courts in other states have continued to require that cash-out mergers have a proper purpose. In addition, the cash-out of minority shareholders in a public corporation triggers disclosure obligations under the federal securities laws, which require a description of the transaction's business purposes.

Some courts have adopted a broad understanding of proper purpose—in the context of close corporations. The New York Court of Appeals, in a case involving a cash-out of minority shareholders in a closely-held corporation that owned a valuable building, commented:

> Fair dealing and fair price alone will not render the merger acceptable. As mentioned, there exists a fiduciary duty to treat all shareholders equally. The fact remains, however, that in a freeze-out merger the minority shareholders are being treated in a different manner: the majority is permitted continued

participation in the equity of the surviving corporation while the minority has no choice but to surrender their shares for cash. On its face, the majority's conduct would appear to breach this fiduciary obligation.

In the context of a freeze-out merger, variant treatment of the minority shareholders—*i.e.*, causing their removal—will be justified when related to the advancement of a general corporate interest. The benefit need not be great, but it must be for the corporation. For example, if the sole purpose of the merger is reduction of the number of profit sharers—in contrast to increasing the corporation's capital or profits, or improving its management structure—there will exist no "independent corporate interest." What distinguishes a proper corporate purpose from an improper one is that, with the former, removal of the minority shareholders furthers the objective of conferring some general gain upon the corporation. Only then will the fiduciary duty of good and prudent management of the corporation serve to override the concurrent duty to treat all shareholders fairly.

Without passing on all of the business purposes cited by Supreme Court as underlying the merger, it is sufficient to note that at least one justified the exclusion of plaintiffs' interests: attracting additional capital to effect needed repairs of the building. There is proof that there was a good-faith belief that additional, [outside capital was required.] Moreover, this record supports the conclusion that this capital would not have been available through the merger had not plaintiffs' interest in the corporation been eliminated.

Alpert v. 28 Williams St. Corp., 473 N.E.2d 19, 27–29 (N.Y. 1984).

Other courts have used the proper purpose test to decide disputes in close corporations. The Massachusetts Supreme Judicial Court stated, "Unlike the *Weinberger* court, we believe that the 'business-purpose' test is an additional useful means under our statutes and case law for examining a transaction in which a controlling stockholder eliminates the minority interest in a corporation." The court then affirmed a trial court ruling that it was not proper for a controlling shareholder to effectuate a cash-out merger solely to gain access to the corporation's assets for the purpose of repaying personal debts that he had incurred to finance his purchase of control. *Coggins v. New England Patriots Football Club*, 492 N.E.2d 1112 (Mass. 1986).

Even in cases subject to the *Weinberger* standard, SEC rules require disclosure of the reasons for (or purposes of) cash-out mergers involving a public corporation. SEC Rule 13e–3, which adopts a disclosure-based approach to regulating "going private transactions," requires the filing with the SEC and distribution to shareholders of a Schedule 13E that discusses, among other things, the purpose and fairness of the cash-out. Specifically, the person seeking to accomplish the transaction must state the purpose of the transaction, describe briefly any alternative means considered to accomplish that purpose, explain why the alternatives were rejected, and give reasons for structuring the transaction as a cash-out. In addition, the person must state whether she believes the terms of the merger are reasonably fair to the shareholders who will be cashed out and discuss "in reasonable detail the material factors upon which the belief is based, and, to the extent practicable, the weight assigned to each factor" in a list of valuation factors. Schedule 13E, Item 8.

4. EXCLUSIVITY OF APPRAISAL AFTER *WEINBERGER*

Although *Weinberger* states that appraisal is to be considered the exclusive remedy, it recognizes that appraisal might "not be adequate where fraud, misrepresentation, self-dealing, deliberate waste of corporate assets, or gross and palpable overreaching are involved." In such a case, equitable relief or monetary damages would be appropriate.

Other states are divided on whether appraisal is the exclusive remedy in a cash-out merger. Some state courts have interpreted their corporate statutes to make appraisal exclusive in all circumstances. Others permit a dissatisfied shareholder to seek to enjoin a transaction fraught with "fraud or fundamental unfairness." And some courts permit shareholders entitled to seek appraisal to also bring a collateral attack against an unfair transaction.

What happens when a shareholder brings an appraisal action (seeking fair value at the time of the merger) and discovers evidence that she could have brought a fraud-based action for rescission based on value based on post-merger events? In a 1988 decision, the Delaware Supreme Court allowed a cashed-out shareholder who had exercised dissenters' rights to file a second action challenging the fairness of the merger on the basis of a later-discovered fraud:

> An appraisal proceeding is a limited legislative remedy intended to provide shareholders dissenting from a merger on grounds of inadequacy of the offering price with a judicial determination of the intrinsic worth (fair value) of their stock. Value was traditionally arrived at by determining "the true or intrinsic value" of the shareholders' proportionate interest in the company, valued on a going-concern rather than a liquidated basis.

> *Weinberger* broadens or liberalizes the process for determining the "fair value" of the company's outstanding shares by including all generally accepted techniques of valuation used in the financial community, thereby supplementing the previously employed rigid or stylized approach to valuation. *Weinberger* directs that this

"liberalized approach" to appraisal shall be used to determine the value of a cashed-out minority's share interest on the day of the merger, reflecting all relevant information regarding the company and its shares. This includes information concerning future events not arising solely "from the accomplishment or expectation of the merger," 8 Del.C. § 262(h), which, if made public, can affect the current value of the shares and "which are known or susceptible of proof as of the date of the merger."

In contrast to appraisal, entire fairness—fair price and fair dealing—is the focal point against which the merger transaction and consideration arrived at can be measured. The appraisal remedy may not be adequate in certain cases, particularly where fraud, misrepresentation, self-dealing, deliberate waste of corporate assets, or gross and palpable overreaching are involved. It is important to emphasize that "the test for fairness is not a bifurcated one as between fair dealing and price. *All aspects of the issue must be examined as a whole* since the question is one of fairness."

To summarize, in a section 262 appraisal action the only litigable issue is the determination of the value of the appraisal petitioners' shares on the date of the merger, the only party defendant is the surviving corporation and the only relief available is a judgment against the surviving corporation for the fair value of the dissenters' shares. In contrast, a fraud action asserting fair dealing and fair price claims affords an expansive remedy and is brought against the alleged wrongdoers to provide whatever relief the facts of a particular case may require. In evaluating claims involving violations of entire fairness, the trial court may include in its relief any damages sustained by the shareholders. An appraisal action may not provide a complete remedy for unfair dealing or fraud because a damage award in a fraud action may include "rescissory damages if the trier of fact considers them susceptible of proof and a remedy appropriate to all issues of fairness before him."

Cede & Co. v. Technicolor, Inc., 542 A.2d 1182, 1186–88 (Del. 1988).

5. ENTIRE FAIRNESS; RELATIONSHIP OF FAIR DEALING AND FAIR PRICE

Weinberger holds that "entire fairness encompasses consideration of both whether the merger was the product of fair dealing and whether it involved a fair price." Fair dealing requires inquiry into the process by which the transaction was negotiated and approved. Fair price involves a review of the substantive terms of the merger.

Courts, particularly in Delaware, are more comfortable with issues of process than with issues of value, especially when there is no ready market, as in a cash-out merger. Determining a fair price calls for financial skills and business judgment that courts lack. Decision-making processes, however, are easier to gauge, and courts assume that fair price follows fair dealing.

This explains the importance of the guidance *Weinberger* gives in footnote 7 on how fair dealing can be promoted in parent-subsidiary mergers: "Although perfection is not possible, or expected, the result could have been better if UOP had appointed an independent negotiating committee of its outside directors to deal with Signal at arm's length." In addition, *Weinberger* states that if a merger is "approved by an informed vote of a majority of the minority shareholders, the burden entirely shifts to the plaintiff to show that the transaction was unfair to the minority."

As might be expected, after *Weinberger* it became common for corporations involved in cash-out mergers to create independent negotiating committees of outside directors to negotiate with controlling shareholders and to condition such mergers on the approval of a majority of the minority shareholders. For an interesting argument that these decisions (and others involving fiduciary duties) are more concerned with establishing standards of conduct to guide directors and their counsel rather than liability rules, see Edward B. Rock, *Saints and Sinners: How Does Delaware Corporate Law Work*, 44 UCLA L. Rev. 1009 (1997).

As you read the following materials, consider whether fair dealing, particularly an independent negotiating committee, can be a substitute for judicial review of fair price. Consider also whether you think the courts have been sufficiently inquisitive and demanding of board processes.

WILLIAM T. ALLEN, INDEPENDENT DIRECTORS IN MBO TRANSACTIONS: ARE THEY FACT OR FANTASY?
45 Bus. Law. 2055–58, 2060–63 (1990).

I want to inquire into the role of outside directors—special committees of outside directors—when the corporation is to be sold, and whether such committees can or do function adequately to protect appropriate interests in such a setting. Addressing that subject requires, as well, that one explore, a bit, the role of the investment bankers and lawyers who guide the board in a change of control transaction.

To relieve any suspense, I will report now that I am going to conclude that, as one who has reviewed in one way or another a fair number of special committees in a sale context, I remain open to the possibility that such committees can be employed effectively to protect corporate and shareholder interests. But I must confess a painful awareness of the ways in which the device may be subverted and rendered less than useful. I conclude, as well, that it is the lawyers and the investment bankers who in many cases hold the key to the effectiveness of the special committee.

Now, the foundation for an inquiry into whether special committees are worthy of respect by courts is the question whether outside directors can be expected to exercise independent judgment on matters in which the corporation's CEO has a conflicting interest—the paradigm case of such conflict and the one that I presently have in mind being the management affiliated leveraged buyout.

On this foundational question, there is a disturbing dichotomy of views. A prominent view is the view that outside directors serve a largely ornamental role in the month-to-month direction of the enterprise.

Yet our statutory corporation law has long assumed that disinterested directors can exercise a business judgment unaffected by the fact that the CEO of the firm may be self-interested. Indeed, one of the principal threads in the development of corporation law over the past 20 years has been the emphasis on bringing more outside directors onto boards, and the creation of more board committees comprised of outside directors.

What is going on here? How do we explain the dissonance between what the established organs of corporation law—statutes, court decrees, statements by the organized bar—imply, and what those who purport to be realists say, about the likelihood that outside directors will act as an effective constraint upon self-interested management?

Consider the outside director who is asked to serve on a special committee to preside over a sale of the company. While he may receive some modest special remuneration for this service, he and his fellow committee members are likely to be the only persons intensely involved in the process who do not entertain the fervent hope of either making a killing or earning a princely fee. Couple that with the pressure that the seriousness and urgency of the assignment generate; the unpleasantness that may be required if the job is done right; and, the fact that no matter what the director does he will probably be sued for it, and you have, I think, a fairly unappetizing assignment.

Combine these factors with those mentioned earlier that create feelings of solidarity with management directors, particularly the corporation's CEO, and it becomes, I would think, quite easy to understand how some special committees appear as no more than, in T.S. Eliot's phrase, "an easy tool, deferential, glad to be of use."

Only one factor stands against these pressures towards accommodation of the CEO: that is a sense of duty. When special committees have appeared to push and resist their colleagues, it has been, I submit, because the men and women who comprised the committee have understood that as a result of accepting this special assignment, they have a new duty and stand in a new and different relationship to the firm's management or its controlling shareholder.

I fully appreciate that corrupt conduct does occur. But I believe—especially in the context of the larger public companies—that when outside directors serving on a special committee fail to meet our expectations, it is likely that they fail because they have not understood what was expected of them. Directors must know what is right before courts can expect them to do what is right.

Thus, I come to the role of the committee's advisors—the lawyers and investment bankers who guide the committee through the process of the sale of a public company. I regard the role of the advisors in establishing the integrity of this process as absolutely crucial. Indeed, the motives and performance of the lawyers and bankers who specialize in the field of mergers and acquisitions is to my mind the great, largely unexamined variable in the process. In all events, it is plain that quite often the special committee relies upon the advisors almost totally. It is understandable why. Frequently, the outside directors who find themselves in control of a corporate sale process have had little or no experience in the sale of a public company. They are in terra incognito. Naturally, they turn for guidance to their specialist advisors who will typically have had a great deal of relevant experience.

unexplored territory

Thus, in my opinion, if the special committee process is to have integrity, it falls in the first instance to the lawyers to unwrap the bindings that have joined the directors into a single board; to instill in the committee a clear understanding of the radically altered state in which it finds itself and to lead the committee to a full understanding of its new duty.

Please don't mistake me. This is not a call to pay even greater attention to appearances; it is advice to abandon the theatrical and to accept and to implement the substance of an arm's-length process. To do this, the lawyers and the bankers must be independent of management. They must accept in their hearts that in the MBO or the auction context, their client is the committee and not management. They must clearly and emphatically remind their client that, at this juncture, the CEO and his associates are to be treated at arm's-length. And the lawyers and bankers must act on that view. That means that from the outset, the advisors must be prepared to forego future business. It comes to that.

My intuition is that the jury is still out on the question whether the special committee device works well enough, often enough, for the law to continue to accord it weight. I am sure, however, of this: if the future leads us to view that that process does offer to shareholders protections that are consistent with justice, it will in large measure be because lawyers have been true to their professional responsibilities and have used their talent and power to see that outside directors understand and strive to satisfy their duty.

KAHN V. LYNCH COMMUNICATION SYS., INC. ("*LYNCH I*")

638 A.2d 1110 (Del. 1994).

[Lynch Communication Systems, Inc. (Lynch), a Delaware corporation, designed and manufactured electronic telecommunications equipment, primarily for sale to telephone operating companies. Alcatel U.S.A. Corp. (Alcatel), a holding company, is a subsidiary of Alcatel (S.A.), a French company involved in public telecommunications, business communications, electronics, and optronics, which itself was a subsidiary of Compagnie Generale d'Electricite (CGE), another French corporation.

In 1981, Alcatel acquired 30.6 percent of Lynch's common stock pursuant to a stock purchase agreement under which the parties agreed to reciprocal obligations. Lynch agreed to amend its certificate of incorporation to require an 80 percent affirmative vote of its shareholders for approval of any business combination. Alcatel also obtained proportional representation on the Lynch board of directors and the right to purchase 40% of any equity securities offered by Lynch to third parties. Alcatel agreed it would not hold more than 45 percent of Lynch's stock prior to October 1, 1986.

In the spring of 1986, Lynch's management recommended that Lynch acquire Telco Systems, Inc. (Telco), which possessed fiber optics technology that Lynch needed to remain competitive in the rapidly changing telecommunications field. Because of the supermajority voting provision, Lynch needed Alcatel's consent to acquire Telco. Alcatel advised Ellsworth F. Dertinger ("Dertinger"), CEO and chairman of the board of directors of Lynch, that it opposed Lynch's acquisition of Telco. Alcatel proposed that Lynch instead acquire Celwave Systems, Inc. ("Celwave"), an indirect subsidiary of CGE that manufactured and sold telephone wire, cable and related products.

At a Lynch board meeting held on August 1, 1986, Dertinger said that Celwave would not be of interest to Lynch if Alcatel did not own it. The Lynch board, five of whose eleven members were designees of Alcatel, nonetheless voted unanimously to establish an Independent Committee, consisting of Hubert L. Kertz ("Kertz"), Paul B. Wineman ("Wineman"), and Stuart M. Beringer ("Beringer"), to make recommendations concerning the appropriate terms and conditions of a combination with Celwave. Alcatel's investment banking firm, Dillon, Read & Co., Inc. ("Dillon Read") subsequently proposed to the Independent Committee that Lynch acquire Celwave in a stock-for-stock merger. After the Committee's investment bankers advised that Dillon Read's proposal overvalued Celwave, the Committee, on October 31, 1986, voted to reject Dillon Read's proposal and to oppose a merger of Celwave into Lynch.

Alcatel responded on November 4, 1986, by simultaneously withdrawing the Celwave proposal and offering to acquire the 56.7% of

Lynch's outstanding stock that it did not own for $14 cash per share. Three days later, the Lynch board authorized the Independent Committee to negotiate with Alcatel the terms of its cash merger offer. The Committee began that process by concluding that Alcatel's $14 per share offer was inadequate.

On November 12, 1986, Beringer, as chairman of the Independent Committee, made a counteroffer to Alcatel of $17 per share. Alcatel responded with an offer of $15 per share, which the Independent Committee's rejected as insufficient. Alcatel raised its offer to $15.25 per share. which the Committee also rejected. Alcatel then made a final offer of $15.50 per share.

At a meeting on November 24, 1986 Beringer told the other two members of the Independent Committee that Alcatel was "ready to proceed with an unfriendly tender at a lower price" if the Independent Committee did not recommend and the Lynch board of directors did not approve Alcatel's $15.50 per share offer. Beringer also advised that alternatives to a cash-out merger had been investigated but were impracticable. The Independent Committee met with its financial and legal advisors and then voted unanimously to recommend that the Lynch board of directors approve Alcatel's proposal for a $15.50 cash merger. Later that day, the Lynch board approved the Committee's recommendation, Alcatel's nominees abstaining.]

HOLLAND, JUSTICE:

This Court has held that "a shareholder owes a fiduciary duty only if it owns a majority interest in or exercises control over the business affairs of the corporation." Alcatel held a 43.3 percent minority share of stock in Lynch. Therefore, the threshold question to be answered by the Court of Chancery was whether, despite its minority ownership, Alcatel exercised control over Lynch's business affairs.

At the August 1 Lynch board meeting, Alcatel opposed the renewal of compensation contracts for Lynch's top five managers. Christian Fayard ("Fayard"), an Alcatel director, told the board members, "You must listen to us. We are 43 percent owner. You have to do what we tell you." The minutes recite that Fayard also declared, "you are pushing us very much to take control of the company. Our opinion is not taken into consideration."

At the same meeting, Alcatel vetoed Lynch's acquisition of the target company, which, according to the minutes, Beringer considered "an immediate fit" for Lynch. Dertinger agreed with Beringer, stating that the "target company is extremely important as they have the products that Lynch needs now." Nonetheless, Alcatel prevailed. The minutes reflect that Fayard advised the board: "Alcatel, with its 44% equity position, would not approve such an acquisition as it does not wish to be diluted from being the main shareholder in Lynch."

The record thus supports the Court of Chancery's underlying factual finding that "the non-Alcatel independent directors deferred to Alcatel because of its position as a significant stockholder and not because they decided in the exercise of their own business judgment that Alcatel's position was correct." The record also supports the subsequent factual finding that, notwithstanding its 43.3 percent minority shareholder interest, Alcatel did exercise actual control over Lynch by dominating its corporate affairs. The Court of Chancery's legal conclusion that Alcatel owed the fiduciary duties of a controlling shareholder to the other Lynch shareholders followed syllogistically as the logical result of its cogent analysis of the record.

A controlling or dominating shareholder standing on both sides of a transaction, as in a parent-subsidiary context, bears the burden of proving its entire fairness. *Weinberger v. UOP, Inc.*, Del.Supr., 457 A.2d 701, 710 (1983). The logical question raised by this Court's holding in *Weinberger* was what type of evidence would be reliable to demonstrate entire fairness. That question was not only anticipated but also initially addressed in the *Weinberger* suggestion regarding the use of an independent negotiating committee of outside directors. *Id.* at 709–10 n. 7.

In this case, the Vice Chancellor noted that the Court of Chancery has expressed "differing views" regarding the effect that an approval of a cash-out merger by a special committee of disinterested directors has upon the controlling or dominating shareholder's burden of demonstrating entire fairness. One view is that such approval shifts to the plaintiff the burden of proving that the transaction was unfair. The other view is that such an approval renders the business judgment rule the applicable standard of judicial review.

"It is often of critical importance whether a particular decision is one to which the business judgment rule applies or the entire fairness rule applies." This Court has recognized that it would be inconsistent with its holding in *Weinberger* abolishing the business purpose test to apply the business judgment rule in the context of an interested merger transaction which, by its very nature, did not require a business purpose.

The policy rationale for the exclusive application of the entire fairness standard to interested merger transactions has been stated as follows:

> Parent subsidiary mergers, unlike stock options, are proposed by a party that controls, and will continue to control, the corporation, whether or not the minority stockholders vote to approve or reject the transaction. The controlling stockholder relationship has the potential to influence, however subtly, the vote of ratifying minority stockholders in a manner that is not likely to occur in a transaction with a noncontrolling party.

> Even where no coercion is intended, shareholders voting on a parent subsidiary merger might perceive that their disapproval could risk retaliation of some kind by the controlling stockholder. For example, the controlling stockholder might decide to stop dividend payments or to effect a subsequent cash-out merger at a less favorable price, for which the remedy would be time consuming and costly litigation. At the very least, the potential for that perception, and its possible impact upon a shareholder vote, could never be fully eliminated.

Citron v. E.I. Du Pont de Nemours & Co., 584 A.2d at 502.

Once again, this Court holds that the exclusive standard of judicial review in examining the propriety of an interested cash-out merger transaction by a controlling or dominating shareholder is entire fairness. The initial burden of establishing entire fairness rests upon the party who stands on both sides of the transaction. However, an approval of the transaction by an independent committee of directors or an informed majority of minority shareholders shifts the burden of proof on the issue of fairness from the controlling or dominating shareholder to the challenging shareholder-plaintiff. Nevertheless, even when an interested cash-out merger transaction receives the informed approval of a majority of minority stockholders or an independent committee of disinterested directors, an entire fairness analysis is the only proper standard of judicial review.

The same policy rationale which requires judicial review of interested cash-out mergers exclusively for entire fairness also mandates careful judicial scrutiny of a special committee's real bargaining power before shifting the burden of proof on the issue of entire fairness.

> The mere existence of an independent special committee does not itself shift the burden. At least two factors are required. First, the majority shareholder must not dictate the terms of the merger. Second, the special committee must have real bargaining power that it can exercise with the majority shareholder on an arms length basis.

The performance of the Independent Committee merits careful judicial scrutiny to determine whether Alcatel's demonstrated pattern of domination was effectively neutralized so that "each of the contending parties had in fact exerted its bargaining power against the other at arm's length." The fact that the same independent directors had submitted to Alcatel's demands on August 1, 1986 was part of the basis for the Court of Chancery's finding of Alcatel's domination of Lynch. Therefore, the Independent Committee's ability to bargain at arm's length with Alcatel was suspect from the outset.

The Independent Committee's original assignment was to examine the merger with Celwave which had been proposed by Alcatel. The record reflects that the Independent Committee effectively discharged that assignment and, in fact, recommended that the Lynch board reject the merger on Alcatel's terms. Alcatel's response to the Independent Committee's adverse recommendation was not the pursuit of further negotiations regarding its Celwave proposal, but rather its response was an offer to buy Lynch. That offer was consistent with Alcatel's August 1, 1986 expressions of an intention to dominate Lynch, since an acquisition would effectively eliminate once and for all Lynch's remaining vestiges of independence.

The Independent Committee's second assignment was to consider Alcatel's proposal to purchase Lynch. The Independent Committee proceeded on that task with full knowledge of Alcatel's demonstrated pattern of domination. The Independent Committee was also obviously aware of Alcatel's refusal to negotiate with it on the Celwave matter.

The Court of Chancery gave credence to the testimony of Kertz, one of the members of the Independent Committee, to the effect that he did not believe that $15.50 was a fair price but that he voted in favor of the merger because he felt there was no alternative. The Court of Chancery also found that Kertz understood Alcatel's position to be that it was ready to proceed with an unfriendly tender offer at a lower price if Lynch did not accept the $15.50 offer, and that Kertz perceived this to be a threat by Alcatel. The Court of Chancery concluded that Kertz ultimately decided that, "although $15.50 was not fair, a tender offer and merger at that price would be better for Lynch's stockholders than an unfriendly tender offer at a significantly lower price." The Court of Chancery determined that "Kertz failed either to satisfy himself that the offered price was fair or oppose the merger."

The record reflects that Alcatel was "ready to proceed" with a hostile bid. This was a conclusion reached by Beringer, the Independent Committee's chairman and spokesman, based upon communications to him from Alcatel. Beringer testified that although there was no reference to a particular price for a hostile bid during his discussions with Alcatel, or even specific mention of a "lower" price, "the implication was clear to him that it probably would be at a lower price."

According to the Court of Chancery, the Independent Committee rejected three lower offers for Lynch from Alcatel and then accepted the $15.50 offer "after being advised that it was fair and after considering the absence of alternatives." The Vice Chancellor expressly acknowledged the impracticability of Lynch's Independent Committee's alternatives to a merger with Alcatel: Lynch was not in a position to shop for other acquirors, since Alcatel could block any alternative transaction. Alcatel also made it clear that it was not interested in having its shares repurchased by Lynch. The Independent Committee decided that a stockholder rights plan was not viable because of the increased debt it would entail.

Nevertheless, based upon the record before it, the Court of Chancery found that the Independent Committee had "appropriately simulated a third-party transaction, where negotiations are conducted at arms-length and there is no compulsion to reach an agreement." The Court of Chancery concluded that the Independent Committee's actions "as a whole" were "sufficiently well informed and aggressive to simulate an arms-length transaction," so that the burden of proof as to entire fairness shifted from Alcatel to the contending Lynch shareholder, Kahn. The Court of Chancery's reservations about that finding are apparent in its written decision.

The Court of Chancery properly noted that limitations on the alternatives to Alcatel's offer did not mean that the Independent Committee should have agreed to a price that was unfair:

> The power to say no is a significant power. It is the duty of directors serving on an independent committee to approve only a transaction that is in the best interests of the public shareholders, to say no to any transaction that is not fair to those shareholders and is not the best transaction available. It is not sufficient for such directors to achieve the best price that a fiduciary will pay if that price is not a fair price.

In this case the coercion was extant and directed at a specific price offer which was, in effect, presented in the form of a "take it or leave it" ultimatum by a controlling shareholder with the capability of following through on its threat of a hostile takeover.

The Court of Chancery's determination that the Independent Committee "appropriately simulated a third-party transaction, where negotiations are conducted at arm's-length and there is no compulsion to reach an agreement," is not supported by the record. The record reflects that the ability of the Committee effectively to negotiate at arm's length was compromised by Alcatel's threats to proceed with a hostile tender offer if the $15.50 price was not approved by the Committee and the Lynch board. The fact that the Independent Committee rejected three initial offers, which were well below the Independent Committee's estimated valuation for Lynch and were not combined with an explicit threat that Alcatel was "ready to proceed" with a hostile bid, cannot alter the conclusion that any semblance of arm's length bargaining ended when the Independent Committee surrendered to the ultimatum that accompanied Alcatel's final offer.

Accordingly, the judgment of the Court of Chancery is reversed. This matter is remanded for further proceedings consistent herewith, including a redetermination of the entire fairness of the cash-out merger to Kahn and the other Lynch minority shareholders with the burden of proof remaining on Alcatel, the dominant and interested shareholder.

KAHN V. LYNCH COMMUNICATION SYS., INC. (*"LYNCH II"*)

669 A.2d 79 (Del. 1995).

WALSH, JUSTICE:

[Following the remand, the Court of Chancery reexamined the cash-out merger, relying solely on the existing record, and once again held that the defendants had carried the burden of showing that the merger was entirely fair to Lynch's public shareholders. The Court of Chancery concluded that, despite Alcatel's coercion of the Independent Committee, defendants had met their burden of proving fair dealing because they had satisfied other relevant factors set forth in *Weinberger v. UOP, Inc.*, 457 A.2d 701 (Del. 1983)—specifically, the transaction's timing, initiation, structure and negotiation. On the issue of fair price, the Court of Chancery found the evaluation of the plaintiffs' expert flawed and concluded that the defendants had also met their burden of establishing the fairness of the price received by the stockholders. 1995 Decision at 5–6. Thus, the Court of Chancery held for the defendants because they had established the entire fairness of the transaction. Kahn again appealed.]

While we agree that our decision in *Lynch I* limited the range of findings available to the Court of Chancery upon remand, our previous review of the record focused upon the threshold question of burden of proof. Our reversal on burden of proof left open the question whether the transaction was entirely fair. Indeed, Kahn concedes that our ruling on burden shifting did not create per se liability, an obvious concession since we did not address the fair price element in *Lynch I*, except to note that the Independent Committee's ability to negotiate price had been compromised by Alcatel's threat to proceed with a hostile tender offer.

As we noted in *Lynch I*, "a controlling or dominating shareholder standing on both sides of a transaction, as in a parent-subsidiary context, bears the burden of proving its entire fairness." The standard for demonstrating entire fairness is the oft-repeated one announced in *Weinberger*: fair dealing and fair price. Fair dealing addresses the timing and structure of negotiations as well as the method of approval of the transaction, while fair price relates to all the factors which affect the value of the stock of the merged company. An important teaching of *Weinberger*, however, is that the test is not bifurcated or compartmentalized but one requiring an examination of all aspects of the transaction to gain a sense of whether the deal in its entirety is fair.

In addressing the fair dealing component of the transaction, the Court of Chancery determined that the initiation and timing of the transactions were responsive to Lynch's needs. This conclusion was based on the fact that Lynch's marketing strategy was handicapped by the lack of a fiber optic technology. Alcatel proposed the merger with Celwave to remedy this competitive weakness but Lynch management and the non-Alcatel directors did not believe this combination would be beneficial to Lynch. Dertinger, Lynch's CEO, suggested to Alcatel that, under the circumstances, a cash merger with Alcatel will be preferable to a Celwave merger. Thus, the Alcatel offer to acquire the minority interests in Lynch was viewed as an alternative to the disfavored Celwave transaction.

Kahn argues that the Telco acquisition, which Lynch management strongly supported, was vetoed by Alcatel to force Lynch to accept Celwave as a merger partner or agree to a cash-out merger with Alcatel. The benefits of the Telco transaction, however, are clearly debatable. Telco was not profitable and had a limited fiber optic capability. There is no assurance that Lynch's shareholders would have benefitted from the acquisition. More to the point, the timing of a merger transaction cannot be viewed solely from the perspective of the acquired entity. A majority shareholder is naturally motivated by economic self-interest in initiating a transaction. Otherwise, there is no reason to do it. Thus, mere initiation by the acquirer is not reprehensible so long as the controlling shareholder does not gain a financial advantage at the expense of the minority.

In support of its claim of coercion, Kahn contends that Alcatel timed its merger offer, with a thinly-veiled threat of using its controlling position to force the result, to take advantage of the opportunity to buy Lynch on the cheap. As will be discussed at greater length in our fair price analysis, Lynch was experiencing a difficult and rapidly changing competitive situation. Its current financial results reflected that fact. Although its stock was trading at low levels, this may simply have been a reflection of its competitive problems. Alcatel is not to be faulted for taking advantage of the objective reality of Lynch's financial situation. Thus the mere fact that the transaction was initiated at Alcatel's discretion, does not dictate a finding of unfairness in the absence of a determination that the minority shareholders of Lynch were harmed by the timing. The Court of Chancery rejected such a claim and we agree.

With respect to the negotiations and structure of the transaction, the Court of Chancery, while acknowledging that the Court in *Lynch I* found the negotiations coercive, commented that the negotiations "certainly were no less fair than if there had been no negotiations at all." The court noted that a committee of non-Alcatel directors negotiated an increase in price from $14 per share to $15.50. The committee also retained two investment banking firms who were well acquainted with Lynch's prospects based on their work on the Celwave proposal. Moreover, the committee had the benefit of outside legal counsel.

It is true that the committee and the Board agreed to a price which at least one member of the committee later opined was not a fair price. But there is no requirement of unanimity in such matters either at the Independent Committee level or by the Board. A finding of unfair dealing based on lack of unanimity could discourage the use of special committees in majority dominated cash-out mergers. Here Alcatel could have presented a merger offer directly to the Lynch Board, which it controlled, and received a quick approval. Had it done so, of course, it would have borne the burden of demonstrating entire fairness in the event the transaction was later questioned. Where, ultimately, it has been required to assume the same burden, it should fare no worse in a judicial review of the fairness of its negotiations with the Independent Committee.

Kahn asserts that the Court of Chancery did not properly consider our finding of coercion in *Lynch I*. Generally, as in this case, the burden rests on the party that engaged in coercive conduct to demonstrate the equity of their actions. But to be actionable, the coercive conduct directed at selling shareholders must be a "material" influence on the decision to sell.

Where other economic forces are at work and more likely produced the decision to sell, as the Court of Chancery determined here, the specter of coercion may not be deemed material with respect to the transaction as a whole, and will not prevent a finding of entire fairness. In this case, no shareholder was treated differently in the transaction from any other shareholder nor subjected to a two-tiered or squeeze-out treatment. Alcatel offered cash for all the minority shares and paid cash for all shares tendered. Clearly there was no coercion exerted which was material to this aspect of the transaction, and thus no finding of per se liability is required.

As previously noted, in *Lynch I* this Court did not address the fair price aspect of the merger transaction since our remand required a reexamination of fair dealing at the trial level.

In considering whether Alcatel had discharged its burden with respect to fairness of price, the Court of Chancery placed reliance upon the testimony of Michael McCarty, a senior officer at Dillon Read, who prepared Alcatel's proposal to the Independent Committee. He valued Lynch at $15.50 to $16.00 per share—a range determined by using the closing market price of $11 per share of October 17, 1988 and adding a merger premium of 41% to 46%. Dillon Read's valuation had been prepared in October, 1986 in connection with the Lynch/Celwave combination proposed at a time when Lynch was experiencing a downward trend in earnings and prospects. Subsequent to the October valuation, Lynch management revised its three year forecast downward to reflect disappointing third quarter results.

The Court of Chancery also considered the valuation reports issued by both Kidder Peabody and Thompson McKinmon who were retained by the Independent Committee at the time of the Celwave proposal in October. At that time both bankers valued Lynch at $16.50 to $17.50 per share. These valuations, however, were made in response to Alcatel's Celwave proposal and were not, strictly speaking, fairness opinions. When Lynch later revised downward its financial forecasts based on poor third quarter operating results both firms opined that the Alcatel merger price was fair as of the later merger date.

Kahn supported his claim of inadequate price principally through the expert testimony of Fred Shinagle, an independent financial analyst, who opined that the fair value of Lynch on November 24, 1986 was $18.25 per share. He reached that conclusion by averaging equally the values he derived from market price, book value, earning power and capitalization.

In addition to the testimony of his valuation expert, Kahn offered the view of Dertinger, Lynch's CEO at the time of the merger, who testified that he thought the fair value of Lynch at the time of the merger was $20 per share. Dertinger considered "two values of Lynch: Our marketing value—that is in the eyes of our customers—and the value of Lynch on Wall Street as exemplified primarily by the stock price. But I think that is definitely secondary to a company's potential." Board member Hubert Kertz also testified that in his opinion Lynch's value was well above the $14 merger price. Although conceding that "not being a financial man but being a manager" he thought that "even under almost the worst scenario, it ought to be somewhere in the high teens or $20 a share."

In its fair price analysis, the Court of Chancery accepted the fairness opinions tendered by Alcatel and found the merger price fair. The court rejected Kahn's attack on the merger price because it found the Shinagle valuation methodology to be flawed.[1]

In resolving issues of valuation the Court of Chancery undertakes a mixed determination of law and fact. When faced with differing methodologies or opinions the court is entitled to draw its own conclusions from the evidence. So long as the court's ultimate determination of value is based on the application of recognized valuation standards, its acceptance of one expert's opinion, to the exclusion of another, will not be disturbed.

Although the burden of proving fair price had shifted to Alcatel, once a sufficient showing of fair value of the company was presented, the party attacking the merger was required to come forward with sufficient credible evidence to persuade the finder of fact of the merit of a greater figure proposed. See *Cinerama, Inc. v. Technicolor, Inc.*, 663 A.2d at 1177; *Citron*, 584 A.2d at 508; *Rosenblatt*, 493 A.2d at 942. The Court of Chancery was not persuaded that Kahn had presented evidence of sufficient quality to prove the inadequacy of the merger price. We find that ruling to be logically determined and supported by the evidence and accordingly affirm.

---

[1] [Shinagle estimated that Lynch had a capitalization value of $27.92 per share, which he calculated using the highest capitalization ratio of any comparable company. Had Shinagle used the average ratio of comparable companies, as he did in his other calculations, Lynch's capitalization value would have been $13.18 per share and its fair value would have been $14.44 per share.—Ed.]

6. WHEN BUSINESS JUDGMENT IS THE STANDARD OF REVIEW

KAHN V. M & F WORLDWIDE CORP.

88 A.3d 635 (Del. 2014).

HOLLAND, JUSTICE:

This is an appeal from a final judgment entered by the Court of Chancery in a proceeding that arises from a 2011 acquisition by MacAndrews & Forbes Holdings, Inc. ("M & F" or "MacAndrews & Forbes")—a 43% stockholder in M & F Worldwide Corp. ("MFW")—of the remaining common stock of MFW (the "Merger"). From the outset, M & F's proposal to take MFW private was made contingent upon two stockholder-protective procedural conditions. First, M & F required the Merger to be negotiated and approved by a special committee of independent MFW directors (the "Special Committee"). Second, M & F required that the Merger be approved by a majority of stockholders unaffiliated with M & F. The Merger closed in December 2011, after it was approved by a vote of 65.4% of MFW's minority stockholders.

The Appellants initially sought to enjoin the transaction. They withdrew their request for injunctive relief after taking expedited discovery, including several depositions. The Appellants then sought post-closing relief against M & F, Ronald O. Perelman, and MFW's directors (including the members of the Special Committee) for breach of fiduciary duty. Again, the Appellants were provided with extensive discovery. The Defendants then moved for summary judgment, which the Court of Chancery granted.

FACTS

MFW is a holding company incorporated in Delaware. Before the Merger that is the subject of this dispute, MFW was 43.4% owned by MacAndrews & Forbes, which in turn is entirely owned by Ronald O. Perelman.

In May 2011, Perelman began to explore the possibility of taking MFW private. At that time, MFW's stock price traded in the $20 to $24 per share range. MacAndrews & Forbes engaged a bank, Moelis & Company, to advise it. After preparing valuations based on projections that had been supplied to lenders by MFW in April and May 2011, Moelis valued MFW at between $10 and $32 a share.

On June 10, 2011, MFW's shares closed on the New York Stock Exchange at $16.96. The next business day, June 13, 2011, Schwartz [an officer of McAndrews & Forbes and a member of MFW's board] sent a letter proposal ("Proposal") to the MFW board to buy the remaining MFW shares for $24 in cash. The Proposal stated, in relevant part:

The proposed transaction would be subject to the approval of the Board of Directors of the Company [*i.e.,* MFW] and the negotiation and execution of mutually acceptable definitive transaction documents. It is our expectation that the Board of Directors will appoint a special committee of independent directors to consider our proposal and make a recommendation to the Board of Directors. *We will not move forward with the transaction unless it is approved by such a special committee. In addition, the transaction will be subject to a non-waivable condition requiring the approval of a majority of the shares of the Company not owned by M & F or its affiliates. . . .*[3]

[The MFW board met the following day to consider the Proposal. The directors who were not independent recused themselves, and the independent directors, with the advice of special counsel, formed a Special Committee and adopted a resolution to evaluate the Proposal, negotiate the terms of a definitive agreement and make a recommendation to the board "as to whether the Proposal is fair and in the best interests of the stockholders of the Company."]

ANALYSIS

What Should Be The Review Standard?

Where a transaction involving self-dealing by a controlling stockholder is challenged, the applicable standard of judicial review is "entire fairness," with the defendants having the burden of persuasion.[5] In other words, the defendants bear the ultimate burden of proving that the transaction with the controlling stockholder was entirely fair to the minority stockholders. In *Kahn v. Lynch Communication Systems, Inc.,* however, this Court held that in "entire fairness" cases, the defendants may shift the burden of persuasion to the plaintiff if either (1) they show that the transaction was approved by a well-functioning committee of independent directors; **or** (2) they show that the transaction was approved by an informed vote of a majority of the minority stockholders.

This appeal presents a question of first impression: what should be the standard of review for a merger between a controlling stockholder and its subsidiary, where the merger is conditioned *ab initio* upon the approval of **both** an independent, adequately-empowered Special Committee that fulfills its duty of care, and the uncoerced, informed vote of a majority of the minority stockholders. The question has never been put directly to this Court.

Almost two decades ago, in *Kahn v. Lynch,* we held that the approval by *either* a Special Committee *or* the majority of the noncontrolling stockholders of a merger with a buying controlling stockholder would shift the burden of proof under the entire fairness standard from the defendant

---

[3]   Emphasis added.

to the plaintiff. *Lynch* did not involve a merger conditioned by the controlling stockholder on both procedural protections. The Appellants submit, nonetheless, that statements in *Lynch* and its progeny could be (and were) read to suggest that even if both procedural protections were used, the standard of review would remain entire fairness. However, in *Lynch* and the other cases that Appellants cited, the controller did not give up its voting power by agreeing to a non-waivable majority-of-the-minority condition. That is the vital distinction between those cases and this one. The question is what the legal consequence of that distinction

Business Judgment Review Standard Adopted

We hold that business judgment is the standard of review that should govern mergers between a controlling stockholder and its corporate subsidiary, where the merger is conditioned *ab initio* upon both the approval of an independent, adequately-empowered Special Committee that fulfills its duty of care; and the uncoerced, informed vote of a majority of the minority stockholders. We so conclude for several reasons.

First, entire fairness is the highest standard of review in corporate law. It is applied in the controller merger context as a substitute for the dual statutory protections of disinterested board and stockholder approval, because both protections are potentially undermined by the influence of the controller. However, as this case establishes, that undermining influence does not exist in every controlled merger setting, regardless of the circumstances. The simultaneous deployment of the procedural protections employed here create a countervailing, offsetting influence of equal—if not greater—force. That is, where the controller irrevocably and publicly disables itself from using its control to dictate the outcome of the negotiations and the shareholder vote, the controlled merger then acquires the shareholder-protective characteristics of third-party, arm's-length mergers, which are reviewed under the business judgment standard.

Second, the dual procedural protection merger structure optimally protects the minority stockholders in controller buyouts. As the Court of Chancery explained:

> [W]hen these two protections are established up-front, a potent tool to extract good value for the minority is established. From inception, the controlling stockholder knows that it cannot bypass the special committee's ability to say no. And, the controlling stockholder knows it cannot dangle a majority-of-the-minority vote before the special committee late in the process as a deal-closer rather than having to make a price move.

Third, and as the Court of Chancery reasoned, applying the business judgment standard to the dual protection merger structure:

> . . . is consistent with the central tradition of Delaware law, which defers to the informed decisions of impartial directors, especially

when those decisions have been approved by the disinterested stockholders on full information and without coercion. Not only that, the adoption of this rule will be of benefit to minority stockholders because it will provide a strong incentive for controlling stockholders to accord minority investors the transactional structure that respected scholars believe will provide them the best protection, a structure where stockholders get the benefits of independent, empowered negotiating agents to bargain for the best price and say no if the agents believe the deal is not advisable for any proper reason, plus the critical ability to determine for themselves whether to accept any deal that their negotiating agents recommend to them. A transactional structure with both these protections is fundamentally different from one with only one protection.

Fourth, the underlying purposes of the dual protection merger structure utilized here and the entire fairness standard of review both converge and are fulfilled at the same critical point: **price.** Following *Weinberger v. UOP, Inc.,* this Court has consistently held that, although entire fairness review comprises the dual components of fair dealing and fair price, in a non-fraudulent transaction "price may be the preponderant consideration outweighing other features of the merger." The dual protection merger structure requires two price-related pretrial determinations: first, that a fair price was achieved by an empowered, independent committee that acted with care; and, second, that a fully-informed, uncoerced majority of the minority stockholders voted in favor of the price that was recommended by the independent committee.

The New Standard Summarized

To summarize our holding, in controller buyouts, the business judgment standard of review will be applied *if and only if:* (i) the controller conditions the procession of the transaction on the approval of both a Special Committee and a majority of the minority stockholders; (ii) the Special Committee is independent; (iii) the Special Committee is empowered to freely select its own advisors and to say no definitively; (iv) the Special Committee meets its duty of care in negotiating a fair price; (v) the vote of the minority is informed; and (vi) there is no coercion of the minority.

If a plaintiff that can plead a reasonably conceivable set of facts showing that any or all of those enumerated conditions did not exist, that complaint would state a claim for relief that would entitle the plaintiff to proceed and conduct discovery. If, after discovery, triable issues of fact remain about whether either or both of the dual procedural protections were established, or if established were effective, the case will proceed to a trial in which the court will conduct an entire fairness review.

This approach is consistent with *Weinberger, Lynch* and their progeny. A controller that employs and/or establishes only one of these dual procedural protections would continue to receive burden-shifting within the entire fairness standard of review framework. Stated differently, unless *both* procedural protections for the minority stockholders are established *prior to trial,* the ultimate judicial scrutiny of controller buyouts will continue to be the entire fairness standard of review.

7. DIRECTOR LIABILITY IN CASH-OUT TRANSACTION

Weinberger focuses on the duties of the controlling shareholder. But directors on the subsidiary's board, particularly outside directors on the negotiating committee, have even clearer duties to the minority shareholders. They can be liable for breaching their duty of loyalty—when they act to advance their personal economic interests in the cash-out transaction. They can also be liable for breaching their duty of care—though personal liability is tempered by the exculpation clauses permitted by statute, particularly DGCL § 102(b)(7). Finally, directors can be liable for not acting in good faith if they consciously disregard their duties to minority shareholders, and that cannot be exculpated by a § 102(b)(7).

In re Emerging Communications, Inc. Shareholders Litigation 2004 WL 1305745 (Del.Ch. 2004) involved the question whether directors of a partially-owned subsidiary in a cash-out merger can be liable for the difference between what the minority shares are worth and what was offered in the merger. The case is remarkable in its conclusion that the liability of outside directors can vary according to their level of expertise. Specifically, a director on the negotiating committee who had financial expertise may have special responsibilities to recognize and respond to price unfairness, compared with less knowledgeable outside directors. The court stated:

> Muoio is culpable because he voted to approve the transaction even though he knew, or at the very least had strong reasons to believe, that the $10.25 per share merger price was unfair. Muoio was in a unique position to know that. He was a principal and general partner of an investment advising firm, with significant experience in finance and the telecommunications sector. From 1995 to 1996, Muoio had been a securities analyst for, and a vice president of, Lazard Freres & Co. in the telecommunications and media sector. From 1985 to 1995, he was a securities analyst for Gabelli & Co., Inc., in the communications sector, and from 1993 to 1995, he was a portfolio manager for Gabelli Global Communications Fund, Inc.

> Hence, Muoio possessed a specialized financial expertise, and an ability to understand ECM's intrinsic value, that was unique to the ECM board members (other than, perhaps, Prosser). Informed

by his specialized expertise and knowledge, Muoio conceded that the $10.25 price was 'at the low end of any kind of fair value you would put,' and expressed to Goodwin his view that the Special Committee might be able to get up to $20 per share from Prosser. In these circumstances, it was incumbent upon Muoio, as a fiduciary, to advocate that the board reject the $10.25 price that the Special Committee was recommending. As a fiduciary knowledgeable of ECM's intrinsic value, Muoio should also have gone on record as voting against the proposed transaction at the $10.25 per share merger price. Muoio did neither. Instead he joined the other directors in voting, without objection, to approve the transaction.

ECM's directors other than Prosser and Raynor could plausibly argue that they voted for the transaction in reliance on Houlihan's opinion that the merger term price was fair. In Muoio's case, however, that argument would be implausible. Muoio's expertise in this industry was equivalent, if not superior, to that of Houlihan, the Special Committee's financial advisor. That expertise gave Muoio far less reason to defer to Houlihan's valuation. Knowing (or at least having very strong reasons to suspect) that the price was unfair, why, then, would Muoio vote to approve this deal? The only explanation that makes sense is that Muoio, who was seeking future business opportunities from Prosser, decided that it would disserve his interests to oppose Prosser and become the minority's advocate.

Admittedly, divining the operations of a person's mind is an inherently elusive endeavor. Concededly, the possibility exists that Muoio's decision was driven not by his overriding loyalty to Prosser, but by a sincere belief that the $10.25 price was minimally fair, even if not the fairest or highest price attainable. But in this case that possibility is not sufficient to carry the day, because to establish a director's exculpation from liability under 8 Del. C. § 102(b)(7), the burden falls upon the director to show that "his failure to withstand an entire fairness analysis is *exclusively* attributable to a violation of the duty of care." Muoio has not carried that burden.

The credible evidence persuades the Court that Muoio's conduct is explainable in terms of only one of two possible mindsets. The first is that Muoio made a deliberate judgment that to further his personal business interests, it was of paramount importance for him to exhibit his primary loyalty to Prosser. The second was that Muoio, for whatever reason, "consciously and intentionally disregarded" his responsibility to safeguard the minority stockholders from the risk, of which he had unique knowledge, that the transaction was unfair. If motivated by either of those mindsets, Muoio's conduct would have amounted to a violation of his duty of loyalty and/or good faith. Because Muoio has not established to the satisfaction of the Court, after careful scrutiny of the record, that his motivation was of a benign character, he is not exculpated from liability to Greenlight and the shareholder class.

8. ALTERNATIVES TO CASH-OUT MERGER

A cash-out merger imposes on the controlling stockholder the burden to demonstrate the entire fairness of the transaction, including the fairness of the price paid to the minority. But there are other techniques, besides a cash-out merger, for a controlling shareholder to cash-out minority shareholders. What standard of review is appropriate for these other techniques?

a. Short-Form Merger

DGCL § 253 (like many similar state statutes) authorizes a "short-form merger" between a parent corporation and its subsidiary, if the parent owns at least 90 percent of the subsidiary's stock. To effectuate the merger, the parent simply files a certificate setting forth its stock ownership and the terms of the merger, as set by the board of directors of the parent corporation. No action is required of either the board of directors or the shareholders of the subsidiary. The parent corporation, however, must inform the subsidiary's minority shareholders of the terms of the merger and advise them of their appraisal rights if they are dissatisfied with the consideration offered by the parent.

A short-form merger, by definition, involves self-dealing by the parent corporation. After *Weinberger,* attorneys and commentators generally have assumed that in a cash-out merger, the parent corporation also bears the burden of proving that the terms of the merger are entirely fair. In 2001, however, the Delaware Supreme Court held that the entire fairness standard does not apply to short-form mergers. Instead the exclusive remedy for minority shareholders is appraisal:

> Under settled principles, a parent corporation and its directors undertaking a short-form merger are self-dealing fiduciaries who should be required to establish entire fairness, including fair dealing and fair price. The problem is that § 253 authorizes a summary procedure that is inconsistent with any reasonable notion of fair dealing. In a short-form merger, there is no agreement of merger negotiated by two companies; there is only a unilateral act—a decision by the parent company that its 90% owned subsidiary shall no longer exist as a separate entity. The minority stockholders receive no advance notice of the merger;

their directors do not consider or approve it; and there is no vote. Those who object are given the right to obtain fair value for their shares through appraisal.

The equitable claim plainly conflicts with the statute. If a corporate fiduciary follows the truncated process authorized by § 253, it will not be able to establish the fair dealing prong of entire fairness. If, instead, the corporate fiduciary sets up negotiating committees, hires independent financial and legal experts, etc., then it will have lost the very benefit provided by the statute—a simple, fast and inexpensive process for accomplishing a merger. We resolve this conflict by giving effect the intent of the General Assembly. In order to serve its purpose, § 253 must be construed to obviate the requirement to establish entire fairness.

Thus, we hold that, absent fraud or illegality, appraisal is the exclusive remedy available to a minority stockholder who objects to a short-form merger. In doing so, we also reaffirm *Weinberger's* statements about the scope of appraisal. The determination of fair value must be based on *all* relevant factors, including damages and elements of future value, where appropriate. So, for example, if the merger was timed to take advantage of a depressed market, or a low point in the company's cyclical earnings, or to precede an anticipated positive development, the appraised value may be adjusted to account for those factors. We recognize that these are the types of issues frequently raised in entire fairness claims, and we have held that claims for unfair dealing cannot be litigated in an appraisal. But those decisions should not be read to restrict the elements of value that properly may be considered in an appraisal.

Although fiduciaries are not required to establish entire fairness in a short-form merger, the duty of full disclosure remains, in the context of this request for stockholder action. Where the only choice for the minority stockholders is whether to accept the merger consideration or seek appraisal, they must be given all the factual information that is material to that decision.

Glassman v. Unocal Exploration Corp., 777 A.2d 242, 247–48 (Del. 2001).

In *Berger v. Pubco Corp.*, 976 A.2d 132 (Del. 2009), the Delaware Supreme Court held that the remedy for minority shareholders in a short-form merger in which the parent had breached its duty of disclosure is "quasi-appraisal." In this procedure, the minority shareholders automatically become members of a class (rather than having to opt in) and are not required to escrow a portion of the proceeds they received.

b.   Tender Offer Followed by Short-Form Merger

A controlling shareholder with less than 90 percent ownership can take advantage of the short-form merger technique by first making a tender offer directly to minority shareholders to reach 90 percent ownership, followed by a short-form merger. In such a case, the directors of the controlled corporation have no direct decisional role. Whether the offer succeeds depends on whether the minority shareholders choose to accept it.

The Delaware Supreme Court has held that "in the case of totally voluntary tender offers, courts do not impose any right of the shareholders to receive a particular price. Delaware law recognizes that, as to allegedly voluntary tender offers (in contrast to cash-out mergers), the determinative factor as to voluntariness is whether coercion is present, or whether full disclosure has been made." *Solomon v. Pathe Communications Corp.*, 672 A.2d 35, 39 (Del.1996).

Since the economic substance of a cash-out merger and a tender offer followed by a short-form merger is much the same, should the standards of review be different? The case below addresses the question, choosing a review standard that focuses on the structure of the tender offer and the disclosure to shareholders, but not the offer's entire fairness.

IN RE PURE RESOURCES, INC., SHAREHOLDERS LITIGATION
808 A.2d 421 (Del.Ch. 2002).

STRINE, VICE CHANCELLOR:

[Unocal Corporation is a large, independent natural gas and oil exploration with extensive operations in the Gulf of Mexico. Before May 2000, Unocal also had operations in the Permian Basin of western Texas and southeastern New Mexico, but it spun them off and combined them with Titan Exploration, Inc. The resulting entity was Pure Resources, Inc. Unocal owned 65.4% of Pure's issued and outstanding common stock. The remaining shares were held by Titan's former stockholders, the largest of which was Jack D. Hightower, Pure's Chairman and Chief Executive Officer, who owned 6.1% of Pure's outstanding stock before the exercise of options. As a group, Pure's management controls between a quarter and a third of the Pure stock not owned by Unocal, when options are considered.

Several important agreements were entered into when Pure was formed. The first was a Stockholders Voting Agreement which required Unocal and Hightower to elect five persons designated by Unocal, two persons designated by Hightower, and one jointly designated person. Unocal also entered into a Business Opportunities Agreement ("BOA") providing that at as long as it owned at least 35% of Pure, Pure's exploration and production activities would be limited to certain designated areas where it operated at the time of the agreement. The BOA expressly stated that Unocal could compete with Pure in its areas of operation and implied that Pure board members affiliated with Unocal could bring a corporate opportunity in Pure's area of operation to Unocal for exploitation, but could not pursue the opportunity personally.

Finally, members of Pure's management team entered into Put Agreements with Unocal pursuant to which Pure managers, including Hightower and Staley, had the right to put their Pure stock to Unocal upon the occurrence of certain triggering events. The Put Agreements required Unocal to pay the managers the "per share net asset value" or "NAV" of Pure, determined by a complex formula, upon the occurrence of a triggering event. One of the triggering events was a transaction in which Unocal obtained 85% of Pure's shares, which could include the Offer if it results in Unocal obtaining that level of ownership. Although it was not clear whether the Put holders could themselves tender into the Offer in order to create a triggering transaction and receive the higher of the Offer price or the NAV, it was clear that the Put Agreements could create materially different incentives for the holders than if they were simply holders of Pure common stock.

In addition to the Put Agreements, senior members of Pure's management team have severance agreements that will (if they choose) be triggered in the event the Offer succeeds. In his case, Hightower will be eligible for a severance payment of three times his annual salary and bonus, or nearly four million dollars, an amount that while quite large, is not substantial in comparison to the economic consequences of the treatment of his equity interest in Pure. Staley has a smaller, but similar package, and the economic consequences of the treatment of his equity also appear to be more consequential than any incentive to receive severance.

From the time of Pure's formation, its board realized that "the day would come when Pure either had to become wholly-owned by Unocal or independent of it." Pure sought and received limited waivers of the BOA to enable it to take advantage of exploration opportunities beyond those specified in the original agreement. In operating Pure aggressively, Hightower made clear that Unocal should decide whether to acquire the remainder of Pure or let it become independent.

In the summer of 2001, Unocal explored the feasibility of acquiring the rest of Pure and, with the permission of Pure's management, collected non-public information about Pure. The terrorist attack in September 2001 forestalled what had appeared to be Unocal's forthcoming merger proposal.

In August 2002, Unocal sent a letter to the Pure board of directors stating that it had decided to take Pure private. The letter also set forth the terms of the offer which Unocal intended to make. The offer, when ultimately made, bore a 27% premium over the closing price of Pure common stock. The offer contained a non-waivable "majority of the minority" provision, a waivable condition that Unocal receive enough tenders to give it 90% ownership, and a description of a planned second-step short-form merger. The Pure board met to consider the offer and established a Special Committee of two directors. The Unocal employee directors recused themselves from considering the offer, and Hightower and Staley were excluded from the committee because of the possibility that the Put Agreements could give them incentives that differed from the other Pure shareholders.

The initial authority of the Special Committee was unclear and seemed limited to retaining independent advisers, taking a position on the advisability of the offer to Pure, and negotiating with Unocal to obtain an increase in the offer price. As negotiations continued, the Committee's authority appeared to have been reduced. Because the Committee invoked the attorney-client privilege with respect to its operations, it was impossible to "know what really went on." The most reasonable inference that can be drawn from the record is that the special committee was unwilling to confront Unocal as aggressively as it would have confronted a third-party bidder.

Ultimately, Unocal refused to raise its bid and the Special Committee voted not to recommend the offer based on the advice of its financial advisers. It also recommended that the Pure minority shareholders not tender into the offer. Because Hightower and Staley announced that they would not tender their stock, it was nearly impossible for Unocal to obtain 90% of Pure stock in the offer.]

This is the court's decision on a motion for preliminary injunction. The lead plaintiff in the case holds a large block of stock in Pure Resources, Inc., 65% of the shares of which are owned by Unocal Corporation. The lead plaintiff and its fellow plaintiffs seek to enjoin a now-pending exchange offer (the "Offer") by which Unocal hopes to acquire the rest of the shares of Pure in exchange for shares of its own stock.

The plaintiffs believe that the Offer is inadequate and is subject to entire fairness review, consistent with the rationale of *Kahn v. Lynch Communication Systems, Inc.* and its progeny. Moreover, they claim that the defendants, who include Unocal and Pure's board of directors, have not made adequate and non-misleading disclosure of the material facts necessary for Pure stockholders to make an informed decision whether to tender into the Offer.

By contrast, the defendants argue that the Offer is a non-coercive one that is accompanied by complete disclosure of all material facts. As such, they argue that the Offer is not subject to the entire fairness standard, but to the standards set forth in cases like *Solomon v. Pathe Communications Corp.,* standards which they argue have been fully met.

In this opinion, I conclude that the Offer is subject, as a general matter, to the *Solomon* standards, rather than the *Lynch* entire fairness standard. I conclude, however, that many of the concerns that justify the *Lynch* standard are implicated by tender offers initiated by controlling stockholders, which have as their goal the acquisition of the rest of the subsidiary's shares. These concerns should be accommodated within the *Solomon* form of review, by requiring that tender offers by controlling shareholders be structured in a manner that reduces the distorting effect of the tendering process on free stockholder choice and by ensuring minority stockholders a candid and unfettered tendering recommendation from the independent directors of the target board. In this case, the Offer for the most part meets this standard, with one exception that Unocal may cure.

The primary argument of the plaintiffs is that the Offer should be governed by the entire fairness standard of review. In their view, the structural power of Unocal over Pure and its board, as well as Unocal's involvement in determining the scope of the Special Committee's authority, make the Offer other than a voluntary, non-coercive transaction. In the plaintiffs' mind, the Offer poses the same threat of (what I will call) "inherent coercion" that motivated the Supreme Court in *Kahn v. Lynch Communication Systems, Inc.* to impose the entire fairness standard of review on any interested merger involving a controlling stockholder, even when the merger was approved by an independent board majority, negotiated by an independent special committee, and subject to a majority of the minority vote condition.

In support of their argument, the plaintiffs contend that the tender offer method of acquisition poses, if anything, a greater threat of unfairness to minority stockholders and should be subject to the same equitable constraints. More case-specifically, they claim that Unocal has used inside information from Pure to foist an inadequate bid on Pure stockholders at a time advantageous to Unocal. Then, Unocal acted self-interestedly to keep the Pure Special Committee from obtaining all the authority necessary to respond to the Offer. As a result, the plaintiffs argue, Unocal has breached its fiduciary duties as majority stockholder, and the Pure board has breached its duties by either acting on behalf of Unocal (in the case of Chessum and Ling) or by acting supinely in response to Unocal's inadequate offer (the Special Committee and the rest of the board). Instead of wielding the power to stop Unocal in its tracks and make it really negotiate, the Pure board has taken only the insufficient course of telling the Pure minority to say no.

In response to these arguments, Unocal asserts that the plaintiffs misunderstand the relevant legal principles. Because Unocal has proceeded by way of an exchange offer and not a negotiated merger, the rule of *Lynch* is inapplicable. Instead, Unocal is free to make a tender offer at whatever price it chooses so long as it does not: i) "structurally coerce" the Pure minority by suggesting explicitly or implicitly that injurious events will occur to those stockholders who fail to tender; or ii) mislead the Pure minority into tendering by concealing or misstating the material facts. Because Unocal has conditioned its Offer on a majority of the minority provision and intends to consummate a short-form merger at the same price, it argues that the Offer poses no threat of structural coercion and that the Pure minority can make a voluntary decision.

This case therefore involves an aspect of Delaware law fraught with doctrinal tension: what equitable standard of fiduciary conduct applies when a controlling shareholder seeks to acquire the rest of the company's shares?

When a transaction to buy out the minority is proposed, is it more important to the development of strong capital markets to hold controlling stockholders and target boards to very strict (and litigation-intensive) standards of fiduciary conduct? Or is more stockholder wealth generated if less rigorous protections are adopted, which permit acquisitions to proceed so long as the majority has not misled or strong-armed the minority? Is such flexibility in fact beneficial to minority stockholders because it encourages liquidity-generating tender offers to them and provides incentives for acquirors to pay hefty premiums to buy control, knowing that control will be accompanied by legal rules that permit a later "going private" transaction to occur in a relatively non-litigious manner?

At present, the Delaware case law has two strands of authority that answer these questions differently. In one strand, which deals with situations in which controlling stockholders negotiate a merger agreement with the target board to buy out the minority, our decisional law emphasizes the protection of minority stockholders against unfairness. In the other strand, which deals with situations when a controlling stockholder seeks to acquire the rest of the company's shares through a tender offer followed by a short-form merger under 8 *Del.C.* § 253, Delaware case precedent facilitates the free flow of capital between willing buyers and willing sellers of shares, so long as the consent of the sellers is not procured by inadequate or misleading information or by wrongful compulsion.

These strands appear to treat economically similar transactions as categorically different simply because the method by which the controlling stockholder proceeds varies. This disparity in treatment persists even though the two basic methods (negotiated merger versus tender offer/short-form merger) pose similar threats to minority stockholders. Indeed, it can be argued that the distinction in approach subjects the transaction that is more protective of minority stockholders when implemented with appropriate protective devices—a merger negotiated by an independent committee with the power to say no and conditioned on a majority of the minority vote—to more stringent review than the more dangerous form of a going private deal—an unnegotiated tender offer made by a majority stockholder. The latter transaction is arguably less protective than a merger of the kind described, because the majority stockholder-offeror has access to inside information, and the offer requires disaggregated stockholders to decide whether to tender quickly, pressured by the risk of being squeezed out in a short-form merger at a different price later or being left as part of a much smaller public minority. This disparity creates a possible incoherence in our law.

Because no consent or involvement of the target board is statutorily mandated for tender offers, our courts have recognized that "in the case of totally voluntary tender offers courts do not impose any right of the shareholders to receive a particular price. Delaware law recognizes that, as to allegedly voluntary tender offers (in contrast to cash-out mergers), the determinative factors as to voluntariness are whether coercion is present, or whether there are materially false or misleading disclosures made to stockholders in connection with the offer."

The differences between this approach, which I will identify with the *Solomon* line of cases, and that of *Lynch* are stark. To begin with, the controlling stockholder is said to have no duty to pay a fair price, irrespective of its power over the subsidiary. Even more striking is the different manner in which the coercion concept is deployed. In the tender offer context addressed by *Solomon* and its progeny, coercion is defined in the more traditional sense as a wrongful threat that has the effect of forcing stockholders to tender at the wrong price to avoid an even worse fate later on, a type of coercion I will call structural coercion. The inherent coercion that *Lynch* found to exist when controlling stockholders seek to acquire the minority's stake is not even a cognizable concern for the common law of corporations if the tender offer method is employed.

Because tender offers are not treated exceptionally in the third-party context, it is important to ask why the tender offer method should be consequential in formulating the equitable standards of fiduciary conduct by which courts review acquisition proposals made by controlling stockholders. Is there reason to believe that the tender offer method of acquisition is more protective of the minority, with the result that less scrutiny is required than of negotiated mergers with controlling stockholders?

Unocal's answer to that question is yes and primarily rests on an inarguable proposition: in a negotiated merger involving a controlling stockholder, the controlling stockholder is on both sides of the transaction. That is, the negotiated merger is a self-dealing transaction, whereas in a tender offer, the controlling stockholder is only on the offering side and the minority remain free not to sell.

The problem is that nothing about the tender offer method of corporate acquisition makes the 800-pound gorilla's retributive capabilities less daunting to minority stockholders. Indeed, many commentators would argue that the tender offer form is more coercive than a merger vote. In a merger vote, stockholders can vote no and still receive the transactional consideration if the merger prevails. In a tender offer, however, a non-tendering shareholder individually faces an uncertain fate. That stockholder could be one of the few who holds out, leaving herself in an even more thinly traded stock with little hope of liquidity and subject to a § 253 merger at a lower price or at the same price but at a later (and, given the time value of money, a less valuable) time.

Furthermore, the common law of corporations has long had a structural answer to the formal self-dealing point Unocal makes: a non-waivable majority of the minority vote condition to a merger. By this technique, the ability of the controlling stockholder to both offer and accept is taken away, and the sell-side decision-making authority is given to the minority stockholders. That method of proceeding replicates the tender offer made by Unocal here, with the advantage of not distorting the stockholders' vote on price adequacy in the way that a tendering decision arguably does.

I admit being troubled by the imbalance in Delaware law exposed by the *Solomon/Lynch* lines of cases. Under *Solomon,* the policy emphasis is on the right of willing buyers and sellers of stock to deal with each other freely, with only such judicial intervention as is necessary to ensure fair disclosure and to prevent structural coercion. The advantage of this emphasis is that it provides a relatively non-litigious way to effect going private transactions and relies upon minority stockholders to protect themselves. The cost of this approach is that it arguably exposes minority stockholders to the more subtle form of coercion that *Lynch* addresses and leaves them without adequate redress for unfairly timed and priced offers. The approach also minimizes the potential for the minority to get the best price, by arguably giving them only enough protection to keep them from being structurally coerced into accepting grossly insufficient bids but not necessarily merely inadequate ones.

[T]he preferable policy choice is to continue to adhere to the more flexible and less constraining *Solomon* approach, while giving some greater recognition to the inherent coercion and structural bias concerns that motivate the *Lynch* line of cases. Adherence to the *Solomon* rubric as a general matter, moreover, is advisable in view of the increased activism of institutional investors and the greater information flows available to them. Investors have demonstrated themselves capable of resisting tender offers made by controlling stockholders on occasion, and even the lead plaintiff here expresses no fear of retribution. This does not mean that controlling stockholder tender offers do not pose risks to minority stockholders; it is only to acknowledge that the corporate law should not be designed on the assumption that diversified investors are infirm but instead should give great deference to transactions approved by them voluntarily and knowledgeably.

To be more specific about the application of *Solomon* in these circumstances, it is important to note that the *Solomon* line of cases does not eliminate the fiduciary duties of controlling stockholders or target boards in connection with tender offers made by controlling stockholders. Rather, the question is the contextual extent and nature of those duties, a question I will now tentatively, and incompletely, answer.

The potential for coercion and unfairness posed by controlling stockholders who seek to acquire the balance of the company's shares by acquisition requires some equitable reinforcement, in order to give proper effect to the concerns undergirding *Lynch*. In order to address the prisoner's dilemma problem, our law should consider an acquisition tender offer by a controlling stockholder non-coercive only when: 1) it is subject to a non-waivable majority of the minority tender condition; 2) the controlling stockholder promises to consummate a prompt § 253 merger at the same price if it obtains more than 90% of the shares; and 3) the controlling stockholder has made no retributive threats. Those protections—also stressed in this court's recent *Aquila* decision—minimize the distorting influence of the tendering process on voluntary choice. They also recognize the adverse conditions that confront stockholders who find themselves owning what have become very thinly traded shares. These conditions also provide a partial cure to the disaggregation problem, by providing a realistic non-tendering goal the minority can achieve to prevent the offer from proceeding altogether.

The informational and timing advantages possessed by controlling stockholders also require some countervailing protection if the minority is to truly be afforded the opportunity to make an informed, voluntary tender decision. In this regard, the majority stockholder owes a duty to permit the independent directors on the target board both free rein and adequate time to react to the tender offer, by (at the very least) hiring their own advisors, providing the minority with a recommendation as to the advisability of the offer, and disclosing adequate information for the minority to make an informed judgment. For their part, the independent directors have a duty to undertake these tasks in good faith and diligently, and to pursue the best interests of the minority.

When a tender offer is non-coercive in the sense I have identified and the independent directors of the target are permitted to make an informed recommendation and provide fair disclosure, the law should be chary about superimposing the full fiduciary requirement of entire fairness upon the statutory tender offer process. Here, the plaintiffs argue that the Pure board breached its fiduciary duties by not giving the Special Committee the power to block the Offer by, among other means, deploying a poison pill. Indeed, the plaintiffs argue that the full board's decision not to grant that authority is subject to the entire fairness standard of review because a majority of the full board was not independent of Unocal.

That argument has some analytical and normative appeal, embodying as it does the rough fairness of the goose and gander rule. I am reluctant, however, to burden the common law of corporations with a new rule that would tend to compel the use of a device that our statutory law only obliquely sanctions and that in other contexts is subject to misuse, especially when used to block a high value bid that is not structurally coercive. When a controlling stockholder makes a tender offer that is not coercive in the sense I have articulated, therefore, the better rule is that there is no duty on its part to permit the target board to block the bid through use of the pill. Nor is there any duty on the part of the independent directors to seek blocking power. But it is important to be mindful of one of the reasons that make a contrary rule problematic—the awkwardness of a legal rule requiring a board to take aggressive action against a structurally non-coercive offer by the controlling stockholder that elects it. This recognition of the sociology of controlled subsidiaries puts a point on the increased vulnerability that stockholders face from controlling stockholder tenders, because the minority stockholders are denied the full range of protection offered by boards in response to third party offers. This factor illustrates the utility of the protective conditions that I have identified as necessary to prevent abuse of the minority.

Turning specifically to Unocal's Offer, I conclude that the application of these principles yields the following result. The Offer, in its present form, is coercive because it includes within the definition of the "minority" those stockholders who are affiliated with Unocal as directors and officers. It also includes the management of Pure, whose incentives are skewed by their employment, their severance agreements, and their Put Agreements. This is, of course, a problem that can be cured if Unocal amends the Offer to condition it on approval of a majority of Pure's unaffiliated stockholders. Requiring the minority to be defined exclusive of stockholders whose independence from the controlling stockholder is compromised is the better legal rule (and result). Too often, it will be the case that officers and directors of controlled subsidiaries have voting incentives that are not perfectly aligned with their economic interest in their stock and who are more than acceptably susceptible to influence from controlling stockholders. Aside, however, from this glitch in the majority of the minority condition, I conclude that Unocal's Offer satisfies the other requirements of "non-coerciveness." Its promise to consummate a prompt § 253 merger is sufficiently specific, and Unocal has made no retributive threats.

D. SALE OF A CONTROLLING INTEREST

Problem: Gotham Tribune

Gotham Tribune, Inc. (GTI), publisher of the Gotham Tribune, is a publicly owned Columbia corporation whose stock is traded on the New York Stock Exchange. In recent months the price of the stock has been fairly stable at about $15 per share. Burt and Ernie, sons of the founder of the paper, each owns 15 percent of the stock and holds office as co-chief executive of GTI. GTI has 10 million shares of common stock outstanding.

GTI Timber, Inc. (Timber), a wholly-owned subsidiary of GTI, owns substantial timber property in Canada and is a large producer of newsprint. Timber supplies all of the Tribune's needs and sells to other users as well. The Tribune pays the same price as Timber's other customers. There is a growing shortage of newsprint and prices are on the rise. For this reason and others, the Tribune has contributed a relatively declining amount to GTI's profits and Timber has contributed increasingly more. GTI earned $15 million, or $1.50 per share last year, of which $5 million was contributed by Timber. Were it not for Timber, GTI stock probably would sell for six or seven times its remaining earnings of $1.00 per share. However, the Tribune is the pride of GTI's management and is generally acclaimed to be one of the region's finest papers.

World Publishers, Inc. publishes more than 50 newspapers. Most of them are highly profitable; all are very different from the Tribune. Some of the differences suggest why those papers are more profitable than the Tribune. The papers are directed at a mass market; they emphasize the sensational; and they rely heavily on wire services, rather than separate and expensive news gathering bureaus, for national and international news.

World recently offered to buy Timber from GTI for $50 million in cash and long-term debentures, subject to a commitment to continue supplying newsprint to the Tribune. GTI's board, composed of Burt, Ernie, GTI's attorney, the president of Timber and five business people who have no other connection with GTI, voted unanimously to reject World's offer as inadequate, since it was only ten times Timber's earnings for the prior year.

World then approached Burt and Ernie and offered to buy their stock for $21 per share, or a total of $63 million. Burt wanted to accept the offer; he is anxious to get out of the newspaper business and enter politics. Ernie, however, initially decided not to sell. That appeared to scuttle the deal, since World's offer was for both their shares.

Ernie subsequently became apprehensive that World might make another offer to Burt or might make a tender offer directly to GTI's public shareholders, which could leave him as a minority stockholder with little influence over GTI. Moreover, World agreed that if Ernie stepped down as co-CEO, it would continue him as a director and as publisher of the

Tribune, at a salary higher than his present salary. Under these circumstances, Ernie tentatively agreed with Burt to accept World's $63 million offer.

As part of their contract with World, Burt and Ernie also would have to arrange for GTI's other directors to resign and to elect a slate of candidates suggested by World in their stead. Burt and Ernie know little about any of World's candidates. They are aware that World's CEO has a reputation as a flamboyant entrepreneur. They also are familiar with the details of an exposé the Tribune published last year linking World's second-in-command to payoffs of labor racketeers tied to newspaper distribution companies.

Before proceeding to sign a contract with World, Ernie has sought the advice of counsel. The partner in charge of this matter has sent you a memorandum setting forth the facts stated above and further noting:

> This is the kind of situation for which shareholder suits are made, and I have advised our client of the high probability of litigation. I asked Ernie whether World could be induced to pay the same price for all GTI stock now held by public shareholders; he said World has made clear they are not willing to proceed in that fashion. That eliminates what probably would be the best way to minimize litigation problems.

> Assume that Ernie wants to go forward only if we conclude that he is likely to prevail in any lawsuits that may be brought by GTI shareholders. The threshold issue is whether this transaction involves a sale of control. Assuming it does, could shareholders sustain claims of looting, sale of corporate office, or usurpation of corporate opportunity or other breaches of fiduciary duty. Is there anything that Ernie should do prior to closing to protect himself against such claims? Does he have any responsibility for what happens to GTI or its shareholders after World assumes control? Could a shareholder successfully claim that by giving World control of Timber, Ernie has converted a corporate opportunity into a personal profit? Even if we assume that Ernie will take any protective actions that we believe are necessary, can he nonetheless be required to give up some or all of the premium he will receive for his stock? If so, is there some other way to restructure the deal so as to avoid such liability?

> Respond to the partner's questions.

1. INTRODUCTION

Control is valuable. The power to dictate how corporate assets are used eliminates many of the agency costs associated with the separation of ownership from control. Controlling shareholders can command a premium price when they sell their stock because it carries the power to exercise control of the corporation's assets. Buyers who believe they can manage the company more efficiently than current management may be willing to pay a premium over current market prices to obtain that control.

Control also can be exploited. The owner of control may find it easy to misappropriate corporate assets, to appoint herself to corporate office and be paid excessive compensation, or to enter into self-dealing transactions with the corporation on unfair terms. To be sure, the duties of care and loyalty apply to such conduct, but breaches of those duties often are difficult to detect, challenge, and remedy.

When control is sold at a premium price, it may be unclear whether the transaction will put corporate assets in the hands of a more efficient manager or allow an unscrupulous buyer to enrich herself at the expense of a corporation's remaining shareholders and even the corporation's creditors. Every sale of stock by a controlling person, if it is accompanied by the departure of the controlling person from the company, as is customary, necessarily carries with it a change in management and dominion over the company's assets. If more than 50% of the stock is sold, the investment properties and the control properties of that stock are inseparable. It is impossible to sell one without selling the other. It almost defies nature to say that, in such circumstances, one can sell stock but cannot sell control.

Perhaps the problem could be solved by not permitting controlling shareholders to be the sole shareholders who realize a control premium. Some commentators believe that exploitation of minority shareholders presents a great danger. William D. Andrews, *The Stockholder's Right to Equal Opportunity in the Sale of Shares*, 78 Harv. L. Rev. 505 (1965), argues that "a controlling shareholder should not be free to sell, at least to an outsider, except pursuant to a purchase offer made equally available to other shareholders."

Other commentators maintain that the law should impose few if any restrictions on transfers of control because most such transfers are beneficial; they move corporate resources into the hands of those who value them most highly and therefore are apt to utilize them most efficiently. Frank E. Easterbrook and Daniel R. Fischel assert "that those who produce a gain through a transfer of control should be allowed to keep it, subject to the constraint that other parties to the transaction be at least as well off as before the transaction." Consequently, "any attempt to require sharing simply reduces the likelihood that there will be gains to share." *Corporate Control Transactions,* 91 Yale L.J. 698, 698 (1982).

Professor Einer Elhauge has pointed out that the rules advanced by Andrews and Easterbrook and Fischel both may serve useful purposes, but both also have drawbacks. Any rule designed to facilitate transfers of control also is certain to facilitate some potentially exploitative transactions, while any rule designed to discourage all exploitative transfers of control surely will deter some potentially beneficial transactions. Consequently, Professor Elhauge suggests that the debate focus not on absolutes, but on the trade-offs involved. Einer Elhauge, *The Triggering Function of Sale of Control Doctrine*, 59 U. Chi. L. Rev. 1465 (1992).

Courts also largely have rejected the extreme positions. The basic rule is that control can be sold at a premium price, subject to exceptions only in special circumstances. The New York Court of Appeals has summarized this rule as follows:

> Recognizing that those who invest the capital necessary to acquire a dominant position in the ownership of a corporation have the right of controlling that corporation, it has long been settled law that, absent looting of corporate assets, conversion of a corporate opportunity, fraud or other acts of bad faith, a controlling stockholder is free to sell, and a purchaser is free to buy, that controlling interest at a premium price.

Zetlin v. Hanson Holdings, Inc., 397 N.E.2d 387, 388 (N.Y. 1979).

2. DUTY OF CARE

HARRIS V. CARTER
582 A.2d 222 (Del.Ch. 1990).

ALLEN, CHANCELLOR:

The litigation arises from the negotiation and sale by one group of defendants (the Carter group) of a control block of Atlas stock to Frederic Mascolo; the resignation of the Carter group as directors and the appointment of the Mascolo defendants as directors of Atlas, and, finally, the alleged looting of Atlas by Mascolo and persons associated with him. Insofar as the Carter defendants are concerned it is alleged that they were negligent and that their negligence breached a duty that, in the circumstances, they owed to the corporation. It is not claimed that they stand as an insurer of the corporation generally, but that the specific circumstances of their sale of control should have raised a warning that Mascolo was dishonest. The claims against Mascolo are more conventional: effectuation of self-dealing transactions on unfair terms. The Mascolo group is principally Messrs. Mascolo and Ager. They are two of the four alleged co-conspirators who orchestrated the wrongs alleged. The other two named co-conspirators—a convicted felon named Riefler and a lawyer named Beall—were not named as defendants since they are not amenable to service of process in the jurisdiction.

Plaintiff is a minority shareholder of Atlas. He brought this action after the change in control from the Carter group to the Mascolo group had occurred.

It is alleged that the Carter group, *qua* shareholders, owed a duty of care to Atlas to take the steps that a reasonable person would take in the circumstances to investigate the *bona fides* of the person to whom they sold control. It is said that the duty was breached here, and that if it had been met the corporation would have been spared the losses that are alleged to have resulted from the transactions effected by the board under the domination of Mascolo. There is no allegation that the Carter group conspired with Mascolo. Indeed the Carter group did not sell for cash but for shares of common stock of a corporation that plaintiff claims was a worthless shell and which was later employed in the transactions that are said to constitute a looting of Atlas. Thus, accepting the allegations of the complaint, they suggest that the Carter group was misled to its own injury as well as the injury of Atlas and its other shareholders.

With respect to the second group of defendants—the Mascolo defendants—the amended complaint alleges a series of complex corporate transactions effectuated once Mascolo took control of Atlas, and claims that those transactions wrongfully injured Atlas.

Atlas Energy Corporation is a Delaware corporation which, before Mascolo acquired control of it, engaged in oil and gas exploration and production. It conducted its business primarily through the acquisition of oil and gas properties which were resold to drilling programs. It then acted as sponsor and general partner of the drilling programs.

The Carter group, which collectively owned 52% of the stock of Atlas, and Mascolo entered into a Stock Exchange Agreement dated as of March 28, 1986. That agreement provided that the Carter group would exchange its Atlas stock for shares of stock held by Mascolo in a company called Insuranshares of America ("ISA") and contemplated a later merger between ISA and Atlas. ISA was described in the preamble to the Stock Exchange Agreement as "a company engaged in the insurance field by and through wholly-owned subsidiaries." The Stock Exchange Agreement contained representations and warranties by Mascolo to the effect that ISA owned all of the issued and outstanding capital stock of Pioneer National Life Insurance Company and Western National Life Insurance Company. It is alleged that those representations were false. ISA did not own stock in either company and had no insurance subsidiaries.

In the course of negotiations, the Mascolo group furnished the Carter group with a draft financial statement of ISA that reflected an investment in Life Insurance Company of America, a Washington corporation ("LICA"). No representation concerning LICA was made in the Stock Exchange Agreement, however. The existence of a purported investment by ISA in LICA was fictitious. It is alleged that the draft ISA financial statement was sufficiently suspicious to put any reasonably prudent business person on notice that further investigation should be made. Indeed Atlas' chief financial officer analyzed the financial statement and raised several questions concerning its accuracy, none of which were pursued by the Carter group.

The Stock Exchange Agreement further provided that Mascolo would place in escrow 50,000 shares of Louisiana Bankshares Inc. 8% cumulative preferred stock, $10 par value. It was agreed that if Atlas consummated an exchange merger for all of the outstanding common stock of ISA on agreed upon terms within 365 days of the date of the Stock Exchange Agreement, the bank stock would be returned to Mascolo. If no merger took place within the specified time, then that stock was to be distributed *pro rata* to the Carter group members.

It was agreed, finally, that as part of the stock exchange transaction, the members of the Carter group would resign their positions as Atlas directors in a procedure that assured that Mascolo and his designees would be appointed as replacements.

The gist of plaintiff's claim against the Carter defendants is the allegation that those defendants had reason to suspect the integrity of the Mascolo group, but failed to conduct even a cursory investigation into any of several suspicious aspects of the transaction: the unaudited financial statement, the mention of LICA in negotiations but not in the representations concerning ISA's subsidiaries, and the ownership of the subsidiaries themselves. Such an investigation, argues plaintiff, would have revealed the structure of ISA to be fragile indeed, with minimal capitalization and no productive assets.

The charges against the Mascolo defendants are that the Mascolo defendants caused the effectuation of self-dealing transactions designed to benefit members of the Mascolo group, at the expense of Atlas.

Mascolo purchased the Carter group's stock on March 28, 1986. Also on that day the newly elected Atlas board (*i.e.,* the Mascolo defendants) adopted resolutions that, among other things:

(a)   changed Atlas' name to Insuranshares of America, Inc.;

(b)   effectuated a reverse stock split converting each existing Atlas share into .037245092 new shares, thus reducing the 26,849,175 Atlas shares to approximately 1,000,000 shares;

(c)   reduced Atlas authorized capitalization to 10,000,000 shares, $.10 par value;

(d)   approved the acquisition of all of the outstanding common stock of ISA in consideration for 3,000,000 post-reverse stock split Atlas shares;

(e)   elected defendant Mascolo as chairman of the board, Johnson as president, Devaney as treasurer and Ager as vice president;

(f)   approved the negotiation of the sale of Atlas' oil properties "with a series of potential buyers";

(g)   approved the purchase of 200,000 shares of the common stock of Hughes Chemical Corporation at $3 per share with an option to acquire an additional 1,000,000 shares at $5 per share for a 12-month period and for $10 per share for a consecutive 12-month period;

(h) ratified the actions of the company's prior officers and directors and released them from any liability arising as a consequence of their relationship to the company.

It is alleged, essentially, that defendants Devaney, Demunck, and Johnson approved the ISA and Hughes chemical transactions without any credible information about the business or assets of either of those companies. Messrs. Mascolo and Ager, it is alleged, knew of the poor financial condition of ISA and Hughes Chemical and fraudulently approved the challenged transaction.

Plaintiff asserts that ISA is nothing more than a corporate shell. Pursuant to the Stock Exchange Agreement Mascolo acquired a controlling (52%) stock interest in Atlas in exchange for 518,335 ISA shares. Atlas then acquired all the outstanding ISA shares in exchange for 3,000,000 newly issued shares of Atlas common stock. As a result of that transaction, the Mascolo group as a whole came to own 75% of Atlas' shares. The minority shareholders of Atlas saw their proportionate ownership of Atlas reduced from 48% before the ISA transaction to 12% upon its consummation. For Atlas to exchange 3,000,000 of its shares for the stock of this "corporate shell" was, argues plaintiff, equivalent to issuing Atlas stock to the Mascolo group (the holders of the ISA stock) without consideration.

Hughes Chemical Corporation is a North Carolina corporation with its sole place of operations in Fletcher, North Carolina. Mr. Mascolo and two of his associates (who are referred to in the amended complaint as members of the Mascolo group but who are not named as defendants) were stockholders and directors of Hughes Chemical. Plaintiff asserts that in March, 1986, Mascolo caused Atlas to acquire shares of Hughes Chemical at a price unfair to Atlas and its stockholders.

Defendant Devaney, elected by Mascolo to the Atlas board, was president and a principal stockholder of MPA Associates, Inc., a Utah corporation ("MPA"). On April 20, 1986, Atlas entered into an agreement with MPA for the sale to MPA of Atlas' oil and gas properties. In exchange for those properties, MPA issued to Atlas a $5,000,000 secured promissory note, and 2,000,000 shares of MPA common stock, representing 31.8% of the MPA shares issued and outstanding after such issuance. It was agreed that until the MPA Note was fully paid, Atlas would receive 40% of the net cash flow from the oil and gas properties attributable to sales of oil and gas in excess of certain specified prices. Plaintiff alleges that, as a result of the MPA transaction, the MPA Note and stock became Atlas' principal assets.

After MPA's acquisition of the oil and gas properties, Devaney discovered that certain Atlas creditors had claims on the cash flow from those properties. MPA did not make the payments to Atlas required by the MPA Note. On June 2, 1987, Devaney and Mascolo reached an agreement which essentially rescinded the MPA Agreement. Mascolo transferred his Atlas stock to Devaney in exchange for shares of an unrelated corporation. The MPA Note was canceled and Atlas transferred its 2,000,000 MPA shares to MPA, all in exchange for a return of the oil and gas properties originally sold to MPA. Devaney and/or his nominees assumed control of Atlas.

Finally, I turn to the Carter defendants motion to dismiss for failure to state a claim upon which relief may be granted. This motion raises novel questions of Delaware law. Stated generally the most basic of these questions is whether a controlling shareholder or group may under any circumstances owe a duty of care to the corporation in connection with the sale of a control block of stock. If such a duty may be said to exist under certain circumstances the questions in this case then become whether the facts alleged in the amended complaint would permit the finding that such a duty arose in connection with the sale to the Mascolo group and was breached.

[The court first surveyed the case law, which generally imposes a duty on the owners of control "not to transfer it to outsiders if the circumstances surrounding the proposed transfer are such as to awaken suspicion and put a prudent man on his guard—unless a reasonably adequate investigation discloses such facts as would convince a reasonable person that no fraud is intended or likely to result." The court found that the leading cases rejected the notion that the transferor "must have actual notice that the transferee intends to loot the corporation." To require proof that the seller knew of the intended looting would, according to the cases, create a "head in the sand" approach to corporate control sales.]

While Delaware law has not addressed this specific question, one is not left without guidance from our decided cases. Several principles deducible from that law are pertinent. First, is the principle that a shareholder has a right to sell his or her stock and in the ordinary case owes no duty in that connection to other shareholders when acting in good faith.

Equally well established is the principle that when a shareholder presumes to exercise control over a corporation, to direct its actions, that shareholder assumes a fiduciary duty of the same kind as that owed by a director to the corporation. A sale of controlling interest in a corporation, at least where, as is alleged here, that sale is coupled with an agreement for the sellers to resign from the board of directors in such a way as to assure that the buyer's designees assume that corporate office, does, in my opinion, involve or implicate the corporate mechanisms so as to call this principle into operation.

More generally, it does not follow from the proposition that ordinarily a shareholder has a right to sell her stock to whom and on such terms as she deems expedient, that no duty may arise from the particular circumstances to take care in the exercise of that right. It is established American legal doctrine that, unless privileged, each person owes a duty to those who may foreseeably be harmed by her action to take such steps as a reasonably prudent person would take in similar circumstances to avoid such harm to others. While this principle arises from the law of torts and not the law of corporations or of fiduciary duties, that distinction is not, I think, significant unless the law of corporations or of fiduciary duties somehow privileges a selling shareholder by exempting her from the reach of this principle. The principle itself is one of great generality and, if not negated by privilege, would apply to a controlling shareholder who negligently places others foreseeably in the path of injury.

That a shareholder may sell her stock (or that a director may resign his office) is a right that, with respect to the principle involved, is no different, for example, than the right that a licensed driver has to operate a motor vehicle upon a highway. The right exists, but it is not without conditions and limitations, some established by positive regulation, some by common-law. Thus, to continue the parallel, the driver owes a duty of care to her passengers because it is foreseeable that they may be injured if, through inattention or otherwise, the driver involves the car she is operating in a collision. In the typical instance a seller of corporate stock can be expected to have no similar apprehension of risks to others from her own inattention. But, in some circumstances, the seller of a control block of stock may or should reasonably foresee danger to other shareholders; with her sale of stock will also go control over the corporation and with it the opportunity to misuse that power to the injury of such other shareholders. Thus, the reason that a duty of care is recognized in any situation is fully present in this situation. I can find no universal privilege arising from the corporate form that exempts a controlling shareholder who sells corporate control from the wholesome reach of this common-law duty.

Thus, I conclude that while a person who transfers corporate control to another is surely not a surety for his buyer, when the circumstances would alert a reasonably prudent person to a risk that his buyer is dishonest or in some material respect not truthful, a duty devolves upon the seller to make such inquiry as a reasonably prudent person would make, and generally to exercise care so that others who will be affected by his actions should not be injured by wrongful conduct.

The cases that have announced this principle have laid some stress on the fact that they involved not merely a sale of stock, but a sale of control over the corporation. Thus, the agreement that the sellers would resign from the board in a way that would facilitate the buyers immediately assuming office was given importance. That circumstance is pleaded here as well.

One cannot determine (and may not on this type of motion determine) whether Mr. Carter and those who acted with him were in fact negligent in a way that proximately caused injury to the corporation. Indeed one cannot determine now whether the circumstances that surrounded the negotiations with Mascolo were such as to have awakened suspicion in a person of ordinary prudence. The test of a Rule 12(b)(6) motion is, as noted above, permissive. It is sufficient to require denial of this motion to dismiss that I cannot now say as a matter of law that under no state of facts that might be proven could it be held that a duty arose, to the corporation and its other shareholders, to make further inquiry and was breached. In so concluding I assume without deciding that a duty of care of a controlling shareholder that may in special circumstances arise in connection with a sale of corporate control is breached only by grossly negligent conduct.

That Mr. Carter may well have been misled to his own detriment may be a factor affecting the question whether a duty to inquire arose, as Carter might be assumed to be a prudent man when dealing with his own property. But that assumption is essentially evidentiary and can be given no weight on this motion.

For the foregoing reasons the pending motions will be denied.

THE DUTY TO INVESTIGATE

1.   Chancellor Allen adopts a test that requires a corporate seller to investigate the buyer if put on notice that the buyer is deceptive or not truthful. What if the buyer has a reputation for damaging businesses through sheer incompetence? Does the duty of investigate extend to investigating the business practices of reckless corporate managers?

2.   In many cases, the purchase price may seem abnormally high for a particular type of business. In such a case, if the buyer is unknown to the seller, does the seller have a duty to investigate? How much above current market prices must the offered price be before the duty is triggered?

3. SALE OF OFFICE

Control of a corporation's business is vested in the board of directors. Therefore, acquiring a majority of the corporation's stock does not give a new owner immediate control of the corporation's business. For this reason, when a controlling block of stock is sold, the usual practice is to accompany the sale with the resignation of some or all of the existing directors and their replacement by new directors chosen by the purchaser. At the same time, because directors are generally elected by all the shareholders, it is illegal to transfer a corporate office for value. The following case, arising in the unusual circumstance of a seller wishing to renege on a contract of sale, illustrates the tension between these two concepts.

ESSEX UNIVERSAL CORP. V. YATES
305 F.2d 572 (2d Cir. 1962).

[Plaintiff contracted to purchase defendant's 28.3% interest in Republic Pictures for $8 per share, approximately $2 above the price at which the stock sold on the New York Stock Exchange. The contract required the seller to deliver resignations of a majority of Republic's directors and to cause the election of persons designated by the buyer. The seller refused to go ahead with this condition and claimed as a defense in a suit for breach of contract that to do so would be illegal.

The court unanimously reversed a judgment for the defendant-seller.]

LUMBARD, CHIEF JUDGE:

Despite the disagreement evidenced by the diversity of our opinions, my brethren and I agree that such a provision does not on its face render the contract illegal and unenforceable, and thus that it was improper to grant summary judgment. Judge Friendly would reject the defense of illegality without further inquiry concerning the provision itself (as distinguished from any contention that control could not be safely transferred to the particular purchaser). Judge Clark and I are agreed that on remand, which must be had in any event to consider other defenses raised by the pleadings, further factual issues may be raised by the parties upon which the legality of the clause in question will depend; we disagree, however, on the nature of those factual issues, as our separate opinions reveal. Accordingly, the grant of summary judgment is reversed and the case is remanded for trial of the question of the legality of the contested provision and such further proceedings as may be proper on the other issues raised by the pleadings.

It is established beyond question under New York law that it is illegal to sell a corporate office or management control by itself (that is, accompanied by no stock or insufficient stock to carry voting control). The rationale of the rule is undisputable: persons enjoying management control hold it on behalf of the corporation's stockholders, and therefore may not regard it as their own personal property to dispose of as they wish. Any other rule would violate the most fundamental principle of corporate democracy, that management must represent and be chosen by, or at least with the consent of, those who own the corporation.

Essex was, however, contracting with Yates for the purchase of a very substantial percentage of Republic stock. If, by virtue of the voting power carried by this stock, it could have elected a majority of the board of directors, then the contract was not a simple agreement for the sale of office to one having no ownership interest in the corporation, and the question of its legality would require further analysis. Such stock voting control would incontestably belong to the owner of a majority of the voting stock, and it is commonly known that equivalent power usually accrues to the owner of 28.3% of the stock. For the purpose of this analysis, I shall assume that Essex was contracting to acquire a majority of the Republic stock, deferring consideration of the situation where, as here, only 28.3% is to be acquired.

Republic's board of directors at the time of the aborted closing had fourteen members divided into three classes, each class being "as nearly as may be" of the same size. Directors were elected for terms of three years, one class being elected at each annual shareholder meeting on the first Tuesday in April. Thus, absent the immediate replacement of directors provided for in this contract, Essex as the hypothetical new majority shareholder of the corporation could not have obtained managing control in the form of a majority of the board in the normal course of events until April 1959, some eighteen months after the sale of the stock. The first question before us then is whether an agreement to accelerate the transfer of management control, in a manner legal in form under the corporation's charter and by-laws, violates the public policy of New York.

There is no question of the right of a controlling shareholder under New York law normally to derive a premium from the sale of a controlling block of stock. In other words, there was no impropriety per se in the fact that Yates was to receive more per share than the generally prevailing market price for Republic stock.

The next question is whether it is legal to give and receive payment for the immediate transfer of management control to one who has achieved majority share control but would not otherwise be able to convert that share control into operating control for some time. I think that it is.

A fair generalization may be that a holder of corporate control will not, as a fiduciary, be permitted to profit from facilitating actions on the part of the purchasers of control which are detrimental to the interests of the corporation or the remaining shareholders. There is, however, no suggestion that the transfer of control over Republic to Essex carried any such threat to the interests of the corporation or its other shareholders.

Given this principle that it is permissible for a seller thus to choose to facilitate immediate transfer of management control, I can see no objection to a contractual provision requiring him to do so as a condition of the sale. Indeed, a New York court has upheld an analogous contractual term requiring the board of directors to elect the nominees of the purchasers of a majority stock interest to officerships. *San Remo Copper Mining Co. v. Moneuse*, 149 App.Div. 26, 133 N.Y.S. 509 (1st Dept.1912). The court said that since the purchaser was about to acquire "absolute control" of the corporation, "it certainly did not destroy the validity of the contract that by one of its terms defendant was to be invested with this power of control at once, upon acquiring the stock, instead of waiting for the next annual meeting."

The easy and immediate transfer of corporate control to new interests is ordinarily beneficial to the economy and it seems inevitable that such transactions would be discouraged if the purchaser of a majority stock interest were required to wait some period before his purchase of control could become effective. Conversely it would greatly hamper the efforts of any existing majority group to dispose of its interest if it could not assure the purchaser of immediate control over corporation operations. I can see no reason why a purchaser of majority control should not ordinarily be permitted to make his control effective from the moment of the transfer of stock.

Thus if Essex had been contracting to purchase a majority of the stock of Republic, it would have been entirely proper for the contract to contain the provision for immediate replacement of directors. Although in the case at bar only 28.3 per cent of the stock was involved, it is commonly known that a person or group owning so large a percentage of the voting stock of a corporation which, like Republic, has at least the 1,500 shareholders normally requisite to listing on the New York Stock Exchange, is almost certain to have share control as a practical matter. If Essex was contracting to acquire what in reality would be equivalent to ownership of a majority of stock, *i.e.*, if it would as a practical certainty have been guaranteed of the stock voting power to choose a majority of the directors of Republic in due course, there is no reason why the contract should not similarly be legal. Whether Essex was thus to acquire the equivalent of majority stock control would, if the issue is properly raised by the defendants, be a factual issue to be determined by the district court on remand.

Because 28.3 per cent of the voting stock of a publicly owned corporation is usually tantamount to majority control, I would place the burden of proof on this issue on Yates as the party attacking the legality of the transaction. Thus, unless on remand Yates chooses to raise the question whether the block of stock in question carried the equivalent of majority control, it is my view that the trial court should regard the contract as legal and proceed to consider the other issues raised by the pleadings. If Yates chooses to raise the issue, it will, on my view, be necessary for him to prove the existence of circumstances which would have prevented Essex from electing a majority of the Republic board of directors in due course. It will not be enough for Yates to raise merely hypothetical possibilities of opposition by the other Republic shareholders to Essex' assumption of management control. Rather, it will be necessary for him to show that, assuming neutrality on the part of the retiring management, there was at the time some concretely foreseeable reason why Essex' wishes would not have prevailed in shareholder voting held in due course. In other words, I would require him to show that there was at the time of the contract some other organized block of stock of sufficient size to outvote the block Essex was buying, or else some circumstance making it likely that enough of the holders of the remaining Republic stock would band together to keep Essex from control.

Reversed and remanded for further proceedings not inconsistent with the judgment of this court.

FRIENDLY, CIRCUIT JUDGE concurring:

Chief Judge Lumbard's thoughtful opinion illustrates a difficulty, inherent in our dual judicial system, which has led at least one state to authorize its courts to answer questions about its law that a Federal court may ask. Here we are forced to decide a question of New York law, of enormous importance to all New York corporations and their stockholders, on which there is hardly enough New York authority for a really informed prediction what the New York Court of Appeals would decide on the facts here presented.

I have no doubt that many contracts, drawn by competent and responsible counsel, for the purchase of blocks of stock from interests thought to "control" a corporation although owning less than a majority, have contained provisions like paragraph 6 of the contract sub judice. However, developments over the past decades seem to me to show that such a clause violates basic principles of corporate democracy. To be sure, stockholders who have allowed a set of directors to be placed in office, whether by their vote or their failure to vote, must recognize that death, incapacity or other hazard may prevent a director from serving a full term, and that they will have no voice as to his immediate successor. But the stockholders are entitled to expect that, in that event, the remaining directors will fill the vacancy in the exercise of their fiduciary responsibility. A mass seriatim resignation directed by a selling stockholder, and the filling of vacancies by his henchmen at the dictation of a purchaser and without any consideration of the character of the latter's nominees, are beyond what the stockholders contemplated or should have been expected to contemplate. This seems to me a wrong to the corporation and the other stockholders which the law ought not countenance, whether the selling stockholder has received a premium or not. Right in this Court we have seen many cases where sudden shifts of corporate control have caused serious injury. To hold the seller for delinquencies of the new directors only if he knew the purchaser was an intending looter is not a sufficient sanction. The difficulties of proof are formidable even if receipt of too high a premium creates a presumption of such knowledge, and, all too often, the doors are locked only after the horses have been stolen. Stronger medicines are needed—refusal to enforce a contract with such a clause, even though this confers an unwarranted benefit on a defaulter, and continuing responsibility of the former directors for negligence of the new ones until an election has been held. Such prophylactics are not contraindicated, as Judge Lumbard suggests, by the conceded desirability of preventing the dead hand of a former "controlling" group from continuing to dominate the board after a sale, or of protecting a would-be purchaser from finding himself without a majority of the board after he has spent his money. A special meeting of stockholders to replace a board may always be called, and there could be no objection to making the closing of a purchase contingent on the results of such an election. I perceive some of the difficulties of mechanics such a procedure presents, but I have enough confidence in the ingenuity of the corporate bar to believe these would be surmounted.

Hence, I am inclined to think that if I were sitting on the New York Court of Appeals, I would hold a provision like Paragraph 6 violative of public policy save when it was entirely plain that a new election would be a mere formality—*i.e.*, when the seller owned more than 50% of the stock. I put it thus tentatively because, before making such a decision, I would want the help of briefs, including those of amici curiae, dealing with the serious problems of corporate policy and practice more fully than did those here, which were primarily devoted to argument as to what the New York law has been rather than what it ought to be. Moreover, in view of the perhaps unexpected character of such a holding, I doubt that I would give it retrospective effect.

As a judge of this Court, my task is the more modest one of predicting how the judges of the New York Court of Appeals would rule, and I must make this prediction on the basis of legal materials rather than of personal acquaintance or hunch. Also, for obvious reasons, the prospective technique is unavailable when a Federal court is deciding an issue of state law. Although *Barnes v. Brown,* 80 N.Y. 527 (1880), dealt with the sale of a majority interest, I am unable to find any real indication that the doctrine there announced has been thus limited. True, there are New York cases saying that the sale of corporate offices is forbidden; but the New York decisions do not tell us what this means and I can find nothing, save perhaps one unexplained sentence in the opinion of a trial court in *Ballantine v. Ferretti*, 28 N.Y.S.2d 668, 682 (1941), to indicate that New York would not apply *Barnes v. Brown* to a case where a stockholder with much less than a majority conditioned a sale on his causing the resignation of a majority of the directors and the election of the purchaser's nominees.

Chief Judge Lumbard's proposal goes part of the way toward meeting the policy problem I have suggested. Doubtless proceeding from what, as it seems to me, is the only justification in principle for permitting even a majority stockholder to condition a sale on delivery of control of the board— namely that in such a case a vote of the stockholders would be a useless formality, he sets the allowable bounds at the line where there is "a practical certainty" that the buyer would be able to elect his nominees and, in this case, puts the burden of disproving that on the person claiming illegality.

Attractive as the proposal is in some respects, I find difficulties with it. One is that I discern no sufficient intimation of the distinction in the New York cases, or even in the writers, who either would go further in voiding such a clause. When an issue does arise, the "practical certainty" test is difficult to apply. Judge Lumbard correctly recognizes that, from a policy standpoint, the pertinent question must be the buyer's prospects of election, not the seller's—yet this inevitably requires the court to canvass the likely reaction of stockholders to a group of whom they know nothing and seems rather hard to reconcile with a position that it is "right" to insert such a condition if a seller has a larger proportion of the stock and "wrong" if he has a smaller. At the very least the problems and uncertainties arising from the proposed line of demarcation are great enough, and its advantages small enough, that in my view a Federal court would do better simply to overrule the defense here, thereby accomplishing what is obviously the "just" result in this particular case, and leave the development of doctrine in this area to the State, which has primary concern for it.

I would reverse the grant of summary judgment and remand for consideration of defenses other than a claim that the inclusion of paragraph 6 ex mero motu renders the contract void.

SELLING CORPORATE OFFICE

1.   When a buyer buys a minority interest in a corporation, are shareholders disenfranchised if their elected directors resign and replace themselves with nominees chosen by the buyer? Is it enough if the shareholders receive notice of the change and have the opportunity to elect a different slate of directors at the next election?

2.   Does the analysis of the legality of the sale of shares by a shareholder-director who promises he will resign his board seat depend on the size of the holding? In *Carter v. Muscat*, 251 N.Y.S.2d 378 (1st Dept.1964), the directors of Republic Corporation chose a new majority of the board in connection with the sale of 9.7 percent of the stock, by Republic's former management, at a price slightly above market. The sale occurred approximately nine months before the next regularly scheduled shareholders' meeting; an interim report on the board's action was furnished to shareholders. At their next meeting, the shareholders reelected the new directors. A dissident shareholder then petitioned to set the directors' election aside.

The court rejected the petition, remarking: "When a situation involving less than 50% of the ownership of stock exists, the question of what percentage of stock is sufficient to constitute working control is likely to be a matter of fact, at least in most circumstances." The interim notice and subsequent election established that there was no deception of Republic's shareholders.

Brecher v. Gregg, 392 N.Y.S.2d 776 (Sup.Ct. 1975), involved the sale by Gregg, the president of Lin Broadcasting Corporation, of his 4 percent stock interest to the Saturday Evening Post. Gregg also promised to resign and cause the Post's president and two others to be elected directors of Lin and the Post's president to be elected Lin's president.

A Lin shareholder sued to recover from Gregg and the other directors the premium paid by the Post. The court held Gregg, but not the other directors, liable, reasoning as follows:

> The Court concludes as a matter of law that the agreement insofar as it provided for a premium in exchange for a promise of control, with only 4% of the outstanding shares actually being transferred, was contrary to public policy and illegal.

> In summary, an officer's transfer of fewer than a majority of his corporation's shares, at a price in excess of that prevailing in the market, accompanied by his promise to effect the transfer of offices and control in the corporation to the vendee, is a transaction which breaches the fiduciary duty owed the corporation and upon application to a court of equity; the officer will be made to forfeit that portion of his profit ascribable to the unlawful promise as he has been unjustly enriched; and an accounting made on behalf of the corporation, since it is, of the two, the party more entitled to the proceeds.

CHAPTER 20

THE MECHANICS OF CORPORATE COMBINATIONS

■ ■ ■

Problem: LaFrance Cosmetics—Part 1

LaFrance Cosmetics, Inc., a Columbia corporation, manufactures a line of cosmetics. Its articles of incorporation authorize two million shares of common stock, of which one million shares are issued and outstanding. They are owned as follows:

- Mimi, the founder of LaFrance and board chair—400,000 shares.

- Pierre, Mimi's son and company CEO—100,000 shares.

- Margaret, Mimi's daughter, who is not otherwise involved in the business—100,000 shares.

- Columbia Museum of Modern Art, held in trust by the Third National Bank, from a bequest by Mimi's late husband, Maurice—400,000 shares.

The board of LaFrance consists of Mimi, Pierre, Margaret, Victor Gauguin, a retired businessman, and Lauren Miller, the senior vice-president responsible for the bank's trust department.

Pierre, with Mimi's support, has been seeking to expand LaFrance's business into related lines. He recently approached Sweet Violet, Inc. another Columbia corporation, about a business combination. Sweet Violet, which manufactures perfume and related toiletries, has about 250 shareholders, none of whom owns more than 10% of the 100,000 shares of Sweet Violet common stock currently outstanding. After extensive negotiations, Pierre and Sweet Violet's management agreed in principle on a transaction in which LaFrance would acquire Sweet Violet for 400,000 shares of LaFrance common stock.

Pierre then sought the LaFrance board of directors' approval of the proposed acquisition. Margaret objected strongly. In recent years, LaFrance has reinvested most of its income in an effort to become a more effective competitor of the large, publicly-held companies that dominate the cosmetics business. Margaret, dissatisfied with the relatively modest dividends LaFrance has been paying, has urged Pierre and Mimi to abandon this effort and sell LaFrance to one of those companies. She argued that the acquisition of Sweet Violet was inconsistent with her preferred strategy. LaFrance's other two directors, however, supported the proposed acquisition, Victor Gauguin strongly and Lauren Miller more moderately. Lauren also remarked that, while she favored the move, some other members of the Bank's investment committee had questioned whether this was a good time for LaFrance to expand. The LaFrance board then voted 4–1 to approve the proposed acquisition of Sweet Violet for 400,000 shares of LaFrance stock.

As counsel to LaFrance, Pierre has asked you to advise him on how to structure the proposed acquisition of Sweet Violet. Pierre is concerned about the possibility that Margaret will vote against the transaction and seek to obtain the fair value of her shares by exercising appraisal rights. The latter possibility would be particularly troublesome, because LaFrance already is strapped for cash. Pierre's preference is to avoid a vote by LaFrance's shareholders and, in all events, to avoid giving Margaret appraisal rights. Pierre also has advised you that Sweet Violet's management is indifferent as to how the proposed transaction is structured, so long as Sweet Violet's shareholders end up with 400,000 shares of LaFrance stock.

The proposed acquisition could be structured as either (1) a statutory merger of Sweet Violet into LaFrance, (2) a "triangular" merger of Sweet Violet into a subsidiary of LaFrance, (3) a "reverse triangular" merger of La France into a subsidiary of Sweet Violet, (4) a statutory share exchange, or (5) an exchange of LaFrance stock for Sweet Violet's assets, followed by the dissolution of Sweet Violet.

1.   For each of these alternatives:

(a)   Is a vote by LaFrance's shareholders required?

(b)   Are LaFrance's shareholders entitled to appraisal rights?

(c)   Is Margaret likely to succeed in a suit to block the transaction if LaFrance's shareholders are not given voting or appraisal rights?

2.   How would your answers to these questions differ if LaFrance were a Delaware corporation?

3.   Would your answer to question 1 change if LaFrance and Sweet Violet restructured their transaction so that LaFrance first sold 400,000 already-authorized shares for cash and then used the proceeds to acquire all the stock of Sweet Violet? Would LaFrance shareholders have "de facto" voting or appraisal rights under the MBCA in this transaction?

A. INTRODUCTION

Corporate statutes recognize that some changes in a shareholder's investment are so significant that special procedures should be required to accomplish them. The "organic" or "fundamental" changes include amendments to the corporate charter, dissolution of the corporation, and many types of acquisition—that is, transactions that change a firm's form, scope or continuity of existence. Although state laws vary, these transactions usually require shareholder approval and, in some circumstances, the right for shareholders to exit at a fair price by seeking appraisal of their shares.

Although these are sometimes called "fundamental transactions," that is a misnomer. Statutes do not require shareholder approval for many transactions which could be viewed as being "fundamental" such as the acquisition of a new line of business or a major change in the corporation's products, notwithstanding their impact on the shareholders' investment. Thus often it is the form rather than the substance of a transaction that determines whether shareholders have voting and appraisal rights.

At common law, fundamental corporate changes required unanimous shareholder approval. One shareholder could block the corporation from making the desired change, even one as simple as extending the life of a corporation beyond its expiration date. The corporate charter was considered to be a contract, both among the corporation's shareholders and between the corporation and the state, in which every shareholder had vested rights. Majority shareholders were powerless to change the corporation unless they convinced the dissenting shareholder to approve or bought her shares.

State legislatures began to recognize that the unanimous consent requirement created the potential for tyranny by the minority. Situations arose in which an enterprising investor would purchase stock in a company after some fundamental change had been proposed, threaten to veto the change, and force the majority to repurchase her shares at a premium. Legislatures responded by amending corporation statutes to allow fundamental changes approved by a corporation's board of directors and a majority or supermajority of its shareholders.

Because these amendments diluted the veto power of minority shareholders, legislatures granted minority shareholders a right to opt out of certain fundamental changes. Today a shareholder who votes against such a change can demand that the corporation pay her in cash for the value of her shares as determined by a court in an appraisal proceeding. In some transactions, appraisal may not be available if there is a public market for the corporation's stock. These veto and exit rights are entirely statutory, and there is considerable variation among statutes as to who has these rights.

B. STRUCTURING CORPORATE COMBINATIONS

Perhaps the most common type of organic change involves combining two corporations in a merger or other form of acquisition, which practitioners often call "M & A transactions." These transactions can be structured in several different ways, and the structure selected can have implications for the formalities that must be observed, the tax consequences, and the rights of shareholders. Many of the cases that you will read in previous chapters involve challenges to corporate combinations. Here we focus on the statutory and planning aspects of such combinations rather than on the litigation that can arise from them.

This chapter describes the transactional dynamics and the voting and appraisal rights in four basic negotiated combination techniques: (1) a statutory merger or consolidation, (2) a triangular merger, (3) a purchase by one corporation of the assets of another; and (4) a statutory share exchange. We will also examine the mechanics of a tender offer (another form of corporate combination) although tender offers will be treated in greater detail in Chapter 21. In the following discussion, the acquiring corporation is designated as P (for Purchaser), the corporation to be acquired is designated as T (for Target) and a subsidiary that P may create to be a party to the transaction is designated as S (for Subsidiary). In the next section, we will study how courts treat the conflicts that can arise between form and substance.

Corporate planners can choose different techniques to combine two or more firms into one firm. Business and tax considerations often dominate the choice. For example, if the sale of a corporation's assets would trigger significant financial or tax obligations, the combination can be structured so the corporation holding the assets either survives the transaction or is extinguished by operation of law. Whatever transactional technique is used, the functional result largely will be the same: the former shareholders of P and T will be the shareholders of P and P will own, directly or through a wholly owned subsidiary, both its assets and those of T. What were two or more separate business enterprises now will operate under the control of one board of directors.

Shareholder voting and appraisal rights vary by statute. (All corporate combinations require the approval of the board of directors of the combining corporations). Under Delaware law, the choice of form determines the voting and appraisal rights of the shareholders of the combining corporations. MBCA § 6.21(f), takes a fundamentally different approach. It seeks to harmonize voting rights in corporate combinations, regardless of how the transaction is structured. Thus it focuses on whether a business combination, whatever its form, will dilute substantially the voting power of the acquiring corporation's shareholders. If the combination involves issuance of shares with voting power equal to more than 20 percent of the voting power that existed prior to the combination (a "dilutive share issuance"), the acquiring corporation's shareholders must vote to approve the combination. This requirement is the same as that of the New York Stock Exchange and NASDAQ Stock Market, which also base shareholder voting rights on the dilutive impact of a proposed share issuance rather than the form of a proposed business combination.

The MBCA also restricts the availability of appraisal rights, which are available only when a corporate transaction fundamentally affects share rights and there is uncertainty about the fairness of the price of the transaction. Appraisal rights are no longer available to a shareholder simply because she opposes the transaction.

1. STATUTORY MERGER

A statutory merger, the simplest form of combination, takes effect pursuant to a corporate statute's merger provisions. In a statutory merger, T is merged into P. T's assets and liabilities become P's assets and liabilities by operation of law (rather than by formal conveyance or assignment) and T ceases to exist. All shares of T are converted into shares of P unless the plan of merger provides for consideration in the form of cash or other property.[1]

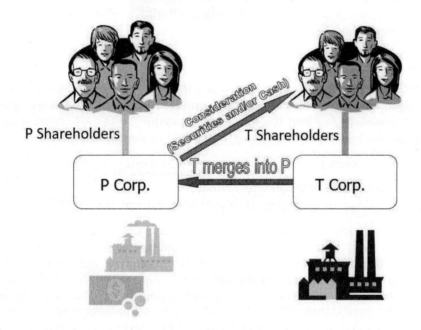

---

[1]   A "statutory consolidation" is a rarely-used variant of this structure in which P and T are "consolidated" into a new corporation, PT, with both P and T ceasing to exist. The voting, appraisal and tax consequences of this form are identical to those for a statutory merger, so we will refer to both here as "mergers."

AFTER

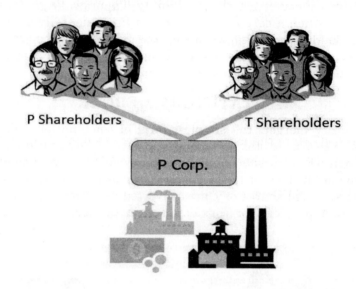

MBCA

P shareholders vote only if there is a dilutive share issuance. If a vote is required, the combination can be approved by a simple majority of the votes at a meeting at which a quorum is present. P shareholders do not have appraisal rights unless they are entitled to vote on the merger.

T shareholders always must vote on a statutory merger. They have appraisal rights unless (1) their stock was publicly traded before the merger and (2) they receive cash or publicly traded stock in the merger. This "market exception" is based on the premise that if the stock is publicly traded, shareholders who are not satisfied with the terms of the merger can simply sell their stock on the open market and do not need the protection of judicial valuation. The market exception assumes that the stock's current market price will more accurately reflect the stock's value than would a later valuation by a judge or judicially appointed appraiser. Because the availability of a public market may not be adequate protection in a merger involving a conflict of interest, the market exception does not apply to mergers involving a 20 percent shareholder (such as in a cash-out merger) or an insider group controlling 25 percent of the corporation's board of directors (a management buyout).

DGCL

Under Delaware law, a majority of the outstanding shares (an absolute majority) of both P and T must approve a statutory merger, subject to two exceptions. Neither P nor T shareholder approval is required for a short-form merger in which P owns at least 90 percent of T's stock prior to the merger. The approval of P shareholders also is not required for a merger that does not increase P's outstanding voting stock by more than 20 percent.

P shareholders have appraisal rights if (1) they were entitled to vote on the merger and (2) the "market out exception" does not apply. T shareholders have appraisal rights, regardless of whether they were entitled to vote on the merger, if the market out exception does not apply. The market out exception (which is extremely complex) generally provides that P and T shareholders do not have appraisal rights if their stock was publicly traded before the merger and they receive publicly traded shares after the merger. If the shareholders receive consideration other than cash or stock in a publicly traded corporation (either in P or a third party), however, appraisal rights are available. DGCL § 262(b).

2.   TRIANGULAR MERGER

Sometimes an acquiring corporation will want to use the statutory merger technique because of the relative ease with which assets can be transferred and liabilities assumed but will seek to avoid certain legal or business consequences of a statutory merger. For example, P may be concerned about subjecting its own assets to unknown or contingent liabilities associated with T's business. In such a situation, P can employ a "triangular merger," which leaves T's assets and liabilities in a separate subsidiary.

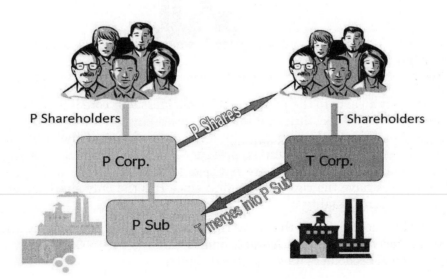

A triangular merger is a form of statutory merger in which P creates a wholly-owned subsidiary, S, and merges T into S. T's assets and liabilities become the assets and liabilities of S by operation of law as they would in a traditional statutory merger. T shareholders receive the merger consideration, usually cash or securities (often P stock). This leaves S as an operating corporation wholly owned by P. It is also possible to structure the transaction as a "reverse triangular merger" in which S merges into T, the T shareholders receive the merger consideration, and P becomes the sole shareholder of T.

AFTER

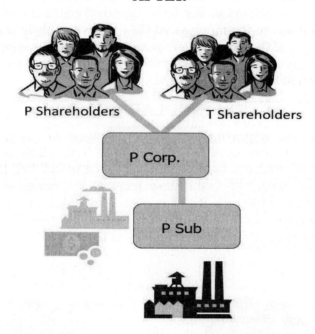

MBCA

P is not a party to the merger. P shareholders will vote but only if the shares issued by P constitute a dilutive share issuance. If a vote is required, the combination can be approved by a simple majority of the votes at a meeting at which a quorum is present. P shareholders do not have appraisal rights unless they are entitled to vote on the merger. The S shareholders have the right to vote, but since P is the only shareholder of S, the vote is a formality.

T shareholders have the same rights as in a statutory merger. They are entitled to vote on the merger, and, if there is no market exception, dissenting shareholders have appraisal rights.

DGCL

P shareholders do not vote on the merger because P is not a party to the merger. Only S and T are parties. Only the shareholder of S (which is

P) votes on the merger. The decision on how to vote S's stock thus is made by P's board of directors, which has already approved the merger. Because P shareholders are denied the right to vote on a triangular merger, they cannot exercise appraisal rights. In short, by structuring the combination as a triangular merger, P's board can deny P's shareholders the right to vote on the business combination or to exercise any appraisal rights. Note that, if P is listed on the New York Stock Exchange or the NASDAQ Stock Market, their rules require that P shareholders approve the transaction if it involves the issuance of P shares representing 20% or more of the shares outstanding.

T shareholders have the same rights as in a statutory merger. They are entitled to vote on the merger, and, if there is no market exception, dissenting shareholders have appraisal rights.

3.   STATUTORY SHARE EXCHANGE

The statutory share exchange is a form of business combination provided for by the MBCA. It does not exist under Delaware law.

A statutory share exchange achieves the same results as a triangular merger. Upon shareholder approval, T shareholders receive P shares (or cash or other property) in exchange for their stock. The status of P shareholders is unchanged. After the exchange, T is a wholly-owned subsidiary of P, creating a corporate structure identical to the structure resulting from a triangular merger.

P shareholders vote only if there is a dilutive share issuance and do not have appraisal rights because they retain their shares. T shareholders must approve the plan of exchange and dissenters may seek appraisal unless the market exception applies.

4.   SALE OF ASSETS

In a sale of assets transaction, P purchases all or substantially all of T's assets and assumes some or all of T's liabilities in exchange for P stock or other consideration. T's assets must be transferred by deed or other form of conveyance, a process that can generate a good deal of paperwork. T may retain sufficient liquid assets to pay off its liabilities. In many jurisdictions, statutory requirements or common law principles relating to "successor liability" may result in P being held responsible for certain of T's obligations, even if not formally transferred.

If, as is usually the case, T is dissolved following the sale of its assets and assumption or payment of its liabilities, it will distribute the consideration it received from P to its shareholders. The resulting corporate structure of P will be functionally identical to that produced by a statutory merger. P will own all of the assets of T and will be owned by its existing shareholders and the former shareholders of T.

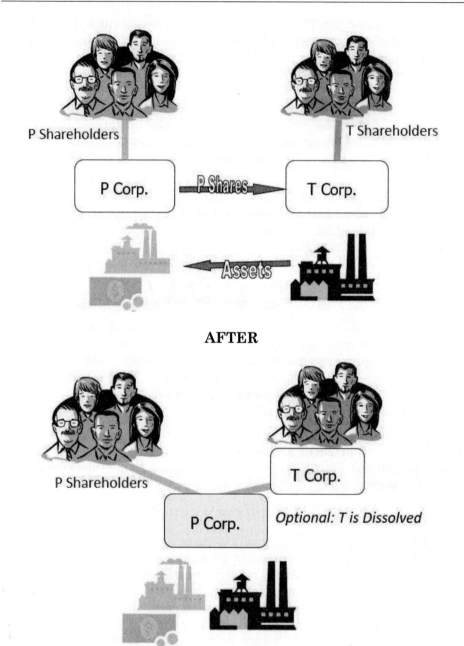

AFTER

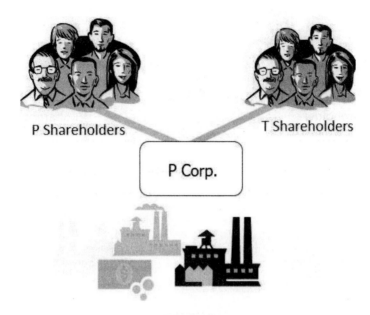

MBCA

P shareholders vote only if there is a dilutive share issuance. They do not have appraisal rights because they retain their shares.

T shareholders must approve the terms of the sale, and if there is no market exception, dissenting shareholders have appraisal rights.

DGCL

T shareholders must approve the transaction, but unlike in other forms of corporate combinations they do not have appraisal rights.

5. TENDER OFFERS

P can also seek to acquire control of T by offering to purchase T shares directly from T shareholders, either for P stock or for cash or other property. Through a tender offer, P can acquire control of T without the approval of T's board of directors. Unlike the other forms of acquisition, T shareholders "approve" the transaction by individually accepting P's offer rather than through a formal vote. Similarly, there are no appraisal rights; T shareholders who do not wish to accept P's offer can simply refuse to tender their shares.

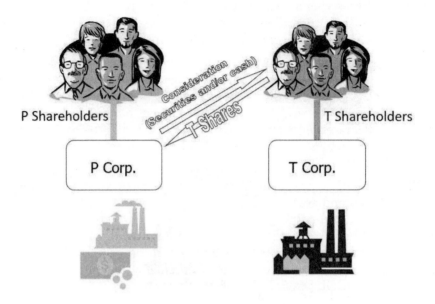

AFTER

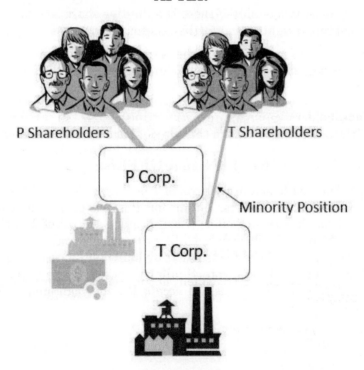

If the holders of a majority of T's shares tender their stock (and no state antitakeover law or provision of T's articles of incorporation prevents P from voting the shares it acquires), P will have the power to control T after it purchases this majority interest. P then often will seek to acquire the remaining T shares in some form of "second-step" transaction so P can operate T without the presence of a minority interest in T.

P can make a tender offer without any vote by its shareholders, unless P offers its shares as consideration and either lacks sufficient authorized shares to effectuate the exchange or the issuance would constitute a "dilutive share issuance." P's shareholders do not have appraisal rights in the tender offer, since their shares are not reduced in the transaction. Under the pre-1999 MBCA, P's shareholders have no voting or appraisal rights if there are sufficient shares already authorized.

Whether either company's shareholders have voting or appraisal rights in the second step will depend on the form of that transaction and the corporate statutes that govern shareholder rights. Most state statutes provide for "short-form" mergers between a parent corporation and a subsidiary of which the parent holds a high percentage (usually 90%) of the subsidiary's outstanding shares. No stockholder vote is required for such mergers. *E.g.*, DGCL § 253; MBCA § 11.05.

Of course an acquiror that succeeds in acquiring a majority, but less than 90%, of the target's shares can still effect a second-step merger by having a shareholder vote in which its stock ownership will allow it to approve the transaction without the vote of the remaining stockholders. In 2013 the DGCL was amended to adopt a new subsection 251(h) which eliminates the 90% requirement so long as certain conditions are met. These include that the merger take place promptly after the consummation of a tender offer for all of the target's outstanding shares and that following the tender offer, the acquiror owns at least the percentage of the target that otherwise would be required to adopt the merger agreement (usually 50%). The new subsection does not change the fiduciary duties of directors (including the duty of loyalty) in connection with such mergers or the level of judicial scrutiny that would apply to the decision to enter into the merger agreement.

C. TAX ASPECTS OF CORPORATE REORGANIZATIONS

The federal income tax treatment of corporate reorganizations, which include mergers and acquisitions as well as recapitalizations and liquidations, is one of the most complex areas in the entire field of tax. Since tax considerations often play a substantial role in planning corporate combinations, it is helpful to have a general understanding of how the Internal Revenue Code deals with them.

The basic philosophy of the reorganization sections of the Code is that, to the extent possible, the tax laws should not influence the form in which businesses choose to carry on their operations. The effort of the drafters, therefore, was to permit reorganization transactions to be effected without tax consequences, even though most of them involve some "sale or exchange" of assets that would ordinarily require the taxpayers—both the corporations involved and their shareholders—to recognize some gain or loss that would have tax consequences. Those reorganizations that qualify as tax-exempt are treated as "non-recognition" transactions in which, in general, no gains or losses are realized for tax purposes. It is also necessary, however, that these gains (or losses) not escape taxation altogether, otherwise it would be possible to avoid taxation by simply engaging periodically in some form of reorganization that qualified for nonrecognition treatment. As a corollary to non-recognition, therefore, the Code provides, in effect, for deferral of the taxation of these gains through its treatment of the basis of the assets transferred in the reorganization. As a general rule the Code provides that the basis of such an asset is "carried over" in the transaction. The surviving corporation in a merger or consolidation holds the assets it receives in the transaction at the same basis those assets had in the hands of the transferor corporation (or corporations). Thus, although any appreciation in the value of those assets goes untaxed at the time of the transaction, it will eventually be taxed upon any subsequent transfer of the assets by the surviving corporation in a taxable transaction.

To illustrate, assume that the balance sheet of the acquired corporation looks like this:

Assets		Liabilities	
Current assets	1,000	Current liabilities	500
Fixed assets	3,000	Long-term debt	2,000
		Equity	1,500
TOTAL ASSETS	4,000	TOTAL LIABILITY & EQUITY	4,000

Now suppose that the acquiring corporation is willing to pay $5000 to acquire the assets of the acquired corporation ($1000 in excess of their book value). This $5000 is made up of $2500 worth of stock issued by the acquiring corporation and the assumption of all of the $2500 of liabilities owed by the acquired corporation. If the acquisition were taxable, the $1000 paid for the assets in excess of their basis would be taxed as a gain on the sale of property. If the transaction qualifies as a tax-free reorganization, however, the $1000 gain is not recognized, and no tax need be paid on the transaction. Even though it has paid $5000 for them, the acquiring corporation holds the assets at the same $4000 basis as they had in the hands of the acquired corporation: $1000 for current assets and $3000 for fixed assets. Should the acquiring corporation subsequently sell the assets for $5000, it will be taxed on the $1000 "profit" from the sale, a profit that it has earned only in the eyes of the I.R.S.

By the same token, the shareholders of the corporations that are parties to a reorganization are in general deemed to hold any securities they receive as a result of the transaction at a basis equal in the securities they surrendered. Thus, although they, too, recognize no gain or loss in the transaction even though their original securities may have increased or decreased in value, the carryover of their basis to the new securities means that they will eventually be taxed (or be allowed to take whatever loss deductions they would be entitled to) on the change in value when they eventually dispose of the new securities.

To continue the illustration, assume that the acquired corporation has two equal shareholders, Able and Baker. Able originally paid $1000 for his stock; Baker paid $1500 for hers. This establishes their tax basis in their stock. In the acquisition transaction, each receives stock of the acquiring corporation worth $1250. Neither, however, recognizes any gain or loss on the exchange. And they hold the new stock at a basis equal to the stock they gave up. Thus if they each sell later for $1600, Able realizes a taxable gain of $600, and Baker a gain of $100.

Just as the Code provides for the carryover of the basis of assets transferred from one corporation to another, the transferee corporation also succeeds to certain other tax attributes of the transferor corporation in a merger, consolidation, or sale of assets. Since the acquired corporation remains in existence, continuing to hold its assets, in a stock-swap transaction, there is no need for special treatment of its tax attributes. The relevant provisions of the Code here are those providing for the filing of one consolidated return by a parent and its subsidiaries. The effect of these provisions on a stock swap is quite similar to the effect of the carryover provisions on the transactions to which they apply.

It should be emphasized that this brief description greatly oversimplifies an extremely complex topic, and that, notwithstanding the Internal Revenue Code's underlying philosophy of "tax neutrality" toward reorganizations, it is impossible to plan such transactions without careful attention to their tax aspects.

D. DE FACTO MERGER DOCTRINE

When a corporate combination is structured so the applicable statute does not provide for voting or appraisal rights, can a shareholder nonetheless assert these rights by asking a court to treat the combination as if it were a merger? Under the de facto merger doctrine, some courts have looked beyond the form of the combination, and recognized shareholder rights if the substance of the combination is that of a merger. A threshold problem with the doctrine is to determine precisely what a "merger" is. The MBCA and DGCL have extensive procedures for effecting a merger but neither statute defines the term itself.

Like the MBCA approach in § 6.21(f), discussed above, the American Law Institute Principles adopted a functional approach to determining shareholder voting and appraisal rights, in part to avoid the kinds of fact-specific inquiries in de facto merger cases. Under this approach, shareholders are entitled to vote on any transaction that qualifies as a "transaction in control." ALI Principles § 6.01(b). In addition, shareholders are entitled to appraisal rights in connection with any business combination, whatever its form, "unless those persons who were shareholders of the corporation immediately before the combination own 60 percent or more of the total voting power of the surviving corporation immediately thereafter." *Id.* § 7.21(a).

In the comment to the definition of "transaction in control" in ALI Principles § 1.38, the drafters explained:

A central theme of § 1.38 is that the mere form in which a transaction is cast should not determine the manner in which the transaction is characterized. A continuing problem in corporation law is to identify those transactions that are so different from the day-to-day operation of the corporation's business that a different decisionmaking process, appraisal rights for shareholders who disapprove, or both, are appropriate. The traditional approach to this problem has been to specify the covered transactions by reference to the form in which those planning the transactions have cast them.

This approach has resulted in an important problem. From the perspective of the managers who plan commercial transactions, the transaction often can be cast in a variety of forms without altering its economic substance. Thus, the assertion of something akin to what has become to be called the de facto merger doctrine was inevitable.

There are substantial difficulties associated with each of the four approaches to the de facto merger problem. The provision of different shareholder approval and appraisal procedures for substantially identical transactions is difficult to justify, whether accomplished by statute or through judicial deference to the equal dignity the legislature may have accorded different transactional forms. Judicial efforts to identify the essential characteristics of a merger may result in the imposition of the most restrictive procedures on all transactions because sales of assets and triangular mergers are substantially identical to two-party mergers. Finally, legislative efforts to incorporate the de facto merger doctrine into the corporate statute have reduced the problem, but not eliminated it. Although the net is cast more broadly, its reach is still determined by transaction form, leaving planners room to recast transactions to avoid shareholder approval and appraisal procedures.

The following case is one approach to the de facto merger doctrine in Delaware. Many courts in other jurisdictions also have been reluctant to adopt the doctrine, believing that it is the province of the legislature rather than the judiciary to make such a change. Thus, to a substantial extent, courts have respected the parties' choice of form, whatever the economic substance of the transaction.

HARITON V. ARCO ELECTRONICS, INC.
182 A.2d 22 (Del.Ch. 1962).

SHORT, VICE CHANCELLOR.

Plaintiff is a stockholder of defendant Arco Electronics, Inc., a Delaware corporation. The complaint challenges the validity of the purchase by Loral Electronics Corporation, a New York corporation, of all the assets of Arco. Two causes of action are asserted, namely (1) that the transaction is unfair to Arco stockholders, and (2) that the transaction constituted a de facto merger and is unlawful since the merger provisions of the Delaware law were not complied with.

Plaintiff now concedes that he is unable to sustain the charge of unfairness. The only issue before the court, therefore, is whether the transaction was by its nature a de facto merger with a consequent right of appraisal in plaintiff.

Prior to the transaction of which plaintiff complains Arco was principally engaged in the business of the wholesale distribution of components or parts for electronics and electrical equipment.

Loral was engaged, primarily, in the research, development and production of electronic equipment.

In the summer of 1961 Arco commenced negotiations with Loral with a view to the purchase by Loral of all of the assets of Arco in exchange for shares of Loral common stock. [A]n agreement for the purchase was entered into between Loral and Arco on October 27, 1961. This agreement provides, among other things, as follows:

> 1.   Arco will convey and transfer to Loral all of its assets and property of every kind, tangible and intangible; and will grant to Loral the use of its name and slogans.

> 2.   Loral will assume and pay all of Arco's debts and liabilities.

> 3.   Loral will issue to Arco 283,000 shares of its common stock.

4. Upon the closing of the transaction Arco will dissolve and distribute to its shareholders, pro rata, the shares of the common stock of Loral.

5. Arco will call a meeting of its stockholders to be held December 21, 1961 to authorize and approve the conveyance and delivery of all the assets of Arco to Loral.

6. After the closing date Arco will not engage in any business or activity except as may be required to complete the liquidation and dissolution of Arco.

Pursuant to its undertaking in the agreement for purchase and sale Arco caused a special meeting of its stockholders to be called for December 27, 1961. At the meeting 652,050 shares were voted in favor of the sale and none against. The proposals to change the name of the corporation and to dissolve it and distribute the Loral stock were also approved. The transaction was thereafter consummated.

Plaintiff contends that the transaction, though in form a sale of assets of Arco, is in substance and effect a merger, and that it is unlawful because the merger statute has not been complied with, thereby depriving plaintiff of his right of appraisal.

Defendant contends that since all the formalities of a sale of assets pursuant to 8 Del.C. § 271 have been complied with the transaction is in fact a sale of assets and not a merger. In this connection it is to be noted that plaintiffs nowhere allege or claim that defendant has not complied to the letter with the provisions of said section.

The question here presented is one which has not been heretofore passed upon by any court in this state. In *Heilbrunn v. Sun Chemical Corporation*, Del., 150 A.2d 755, the Supreme Court was called upon to determine whether or not a stockholder of the *purchasing* corporation could, in circumstances like those here presented, obtain relief on the theory of a de facto merger. The court held that relief was not available to such a stockholder. It expressly observed that the question here presented was not before the court for determination. It pointed out also that while Delaware does not grant appraisal rights to a stockholder dissenting from a sale, citing *Argenbright v. Phoenix Finance Co.*, 21 Del.Ch. 288, 187 A. 124, and *Finch v. Warrior Cement Corp.*, 16 Del.Ch. 44, 141 A. 54, those cases are distinguishable from the facts here presented, "because dissolution of the seller and distribution of the stock of the purchaser were not required as a part of the sale in either case." In speaking of the form of the transaction the Supreme Court observes:

> The argument that the result of this transaction is substantially the same as the result that would have followed a merger may be readily accepted. As plaintiffs correctly say, the Ansbacher enterprise [seller] is continued in altered form as a part of Sun

[purchaser]. This is ordinarily a typical characteristic of a merger. *Sterling v. Mayflower Hotel Corp.*, 33 Del.Ch. 293, 303, 93 A.2d 107, 38 A.L.R.2d 425 (Sup.1952). Moreover the plan of reorganization *requires* the dissolution of Ansbacher and the distribution to its stockholders of the Sun stock received by it for the assets. As a part of the plan, the Ansbacher stockholders are compelled to receive Sun stock. From the viewpoint of Ansbacher, the result is the same as if Ansbacher had formally merged into Sun.

This result is made possible, of course, by the overlapping scope of the merger statute and the statute authorizing the sale of all the corporate assets. This possibility of overlapping was noticed in our opinion in the *Mayflower* case.

There is nothing new about such a result. For many years drafters of plans of corporate reorganization have increasingly resorted to the use of the sale-of-assets method in preference to the method by merger. Historically at least, there were reasons for this quite apart from the avoidance of the appraisal right given to stockholders dissenting from a merger.

The doctrine of de facto merger in comparable circumstances has been recognized and applied by the Pennsylvania courts, both state and federal, *Lauman v. Lebanon Valley Railroad Co.*, 30 Pa. 42; *Marks v. Autocar Co.*, D.C., 153 F.Supp. 768; *Farris v. Glen Alden Corporation*, 393 Pa. 427, 143 A.2d 25. The *Farris* case demonstrates the length to which the Pennsylvania courts have gone in applying this principle. It was there applied in favor of a stockholder of the purchasing corporation, an application which our Supreme Court expressly rejected in *Heilbrunn*.

The right of appraisal accorded to a dissenting stockholder by the merger statutes is in compensation for the right which he had at common law to prevent a merger.

While plaintiff's contention that the doctrine of de facto merger should be applied in the present circumstances is not without appeal, the subject is one which, in my opinion, is within the legislative domain. The argument underlying the applicability of the doctrine of de facto merger, namely, that the stockholder is forced against his will to accept a new investment in an enterprise foreign to that of which he was a part has little pertinency. The right of the corporation to sell all of its assets for stock in another corporation was expressly accorded to Arco by § 271 of Title 8, Del.C. The stockholder was, in contemplation of law, aware of this right when he acquired his stock. He was also aware of the fact that the situation might develop whereby he would be ultimately forced to accept a new investment, as would have been the case here had the resolution authorizing dissolution followed consummation of the sale.

There is authority in decisions of courts of this state for the proposition that the various sections of the Delaware Corporation Law conferring authority for corporate action are independent of each other and that a given result may be accomplished by proceeding under one section which is not possible, or is even forbidden under another.

In a footnote to Judge Leahy's opinion [in *Langfelder v. Universal Laboratories*, 68 F.Supp. 209, 211 n. 5 (D.Del.1946), aff'd 163 F.2d 804 (3d Cir.1947)] the following comment appears:

> The text is but a particularization of the general theory of the Delaware Corporation Law that action taken pursuant to the authority of the various sections of that law constitute acts of independent legal significance and their validity is not dependent on other sections of the Act.

I conclude that the transaction complained of was not a de facto merger, either in the sense that there was a failure to comply with one or more of the requirements of § 271 of the Delaware Corporation Law, or that the result accomplished was in effect a merger entitling plaintiff to a right of appraisal.

Defendant's motion for summary judgment is granted.

E. SALE OF ALL OR SUBSTANTIALLY ALL OF THE CORPORATION'S ASSETS

Problem: LaFrance Cosmetics—Part 2

Five years have passed since LaFrance acquired Sweet Violet. LaFrance's board of directors is unchanged; its stock is now held as follows:

Mimi LaFrance	400,000 shares
Pierre LaFrance	100,000 shares
Margaret LaFrance	100,000 shares
Third National Bank, Trustee	400,000 shares
Former shareholders of Sweet Violet and others	400,000 shares
Total	1,400,000 shares

LaFrance has invested heavily in the perfume business; the Sweet Violet division now accounts for nearly two-thirds of the book value of LaFrance's assets. LaFrance's investment produced a sharp increase in perfume sales; they have accounted for about 70% of LaFrance's total sales last year. But this investment has not produced the profits Mimi and Pierre anticipated. The perfume business has become more competitive, profit margins have declined, and LaFrance has had difficulty integrating perfume into its cosmetics business. Despite increased sales, the Sweet

Violet division produced only 20% of LaFrance's net income last year. These disappointing results have depressed the price of LaFrance stock, for which a limited trading market has developed.

LaBelle, S.A., a large French perfume manufacturer, recently approached LaFrance with an offer to buy the Sweet Violet division for $50 million in cash, which is slightly more than the division's book value. Mimi and Pierre are anxious to accept the offer. Margaret continues to believe the entire company should be sold. She opposes the sale of Sweet Violet alone, fearing that Mimi and Pierre will use the proceeds to finance another ill-advised expansion effort. Lauren Miller now supports Margaret's position, but Victor Gauguin continues to side with Mimi and Pierre.

While a majority of LaFrance's directors thus will vote to accept LaBelle's offer, it is unclear whether a majority of LaFrance's shareholders would concur. Although Mimi and Pierre would vote for the sale, Margaret and the bank almost certainly would oppose it. The views of the remaining shareholders are unknown, but many of them no doubt have been disappointed with LaFrance's results in recent years. Consequently, they might well be inclined to support Margaret's view that the entire company, not merely Sweet Violet, should be sold.

Pierre has asked for your advice in connection with two conditions of LaBelle's offer. The first is that, at the closing, LaFrance deliver an unqualified opinion of counsel to the effect that LaFrance has complied with all applicable provisions of Columbia law in effectuating the sale of Sweet Violet. The other is that the closing occur within 120 days of today.

Pierre has asked what procedures LaFrance must follow to effectuate the sale of the Sweet Violet division. He wants to know, in particular, (i) if you are prepared to give a legal opinion that shareholder approval is not required and (ii) assuming you are, how likely is it that Margaret or some other shareholder nonetheless could assert a claim that would survive a motion to dismiss for failure to state a claim and/or a motion for summary judgment, thus preventing the sale from closing within 120 days. In developing your response, consider MBCA §§ 12.01 and 12.02, and the Official Comments.

GIMBEL V. SIGNAL COMPANIES, INC.
316 A.2d 599 (Del.Ch. 1974).

[On December 21, 1973, at a special meeting, the board of directors of Signal Companies, Inc. ("Signal") approved a proposal to sell its wholly owned subsidiary Signal Gas & Oil Co. ("Signal Oil") to Burmah Oil Inc. ("Burmah") for a price of $480 million. Based on Signal's books, Signal Oil represented 26% of Signal's total assets, 41% of its net worth, and produced 15% of Signal's revenues and earnings. The contract provided that the sale would take place on January 15, 1974 or upon obtaining the necessary governmental consents, whichever was later, but, in no event, after February 15, 1974, unless mutually agreed.

On December 24, 1973, plaintiff, a Signal shareholder, sued for a preliminary injunction to prevent consummation of the sale. The plaintiff, among other contentions, alleged that approval only by Signal's board was insufficient and that a favorable vote from a majority of the outstanding shares of Signal was necessary to authorize the sale].

QUILLEN, CHANCELLOR.

I turn first to the question of 8 Del.C. § 271(a) which requires majority stockholder approval for the sale of "all or substantially all" of the assets of a Delaware corporation. A sale of less than all or substantially all assets is not covered by negative implication from the statute. Folk, The Delaware General Corporation Law, Section 271, p. 400, ftnt. 3; 8 Del.C. § 141(a).

It is important to note in the first instance that the statute does not speak of a requirement of shareholder approval simply because an independent, important branch of a corporate business is being sold. The plaintiff cites several non-Delaware cases for the proposition that shareholder approval of such a sale is required. But that is not the language of our statute. Similarly, it is not our law that shareholder approval is required upon every "major" restructuring of the corporation. Again, it is not necessary to go beyond the statute. The statute requires shareholder approval upon the sale of "all or substantially all" of the corporation's assets. That is the sole test to be applied. While it is true that test does not lend itself to a strict mathematical standard to be applied in every case, the qualitative factor can be defined to some degree notwithstanding the limited Delaware authority. But the definition must begin with and ultimately necessarily relate to our statutory language.

In interpreting the statute the plaintiff relies on *Philadelphia National Bank v. B.S.F. Co.*, 41 Del.Ch. 509, 199 A.2d 557 (1964), *rev'd on other grounds*, 42 Del.Ch. 106, 204 A.2d 746 (Sup.1964). In that case, B.S.F. Company owned stock in two corporations. It sold its stock in one of the corporations, and retained the stock in the other corporation. The Court found that the stock sold was the principal asset B.S.F. Company had available for sale and that the value of the stock retained was declining. The Court rejected the defendant's contention that the stock sold represented only 47.4% of consolidated assets, and looked to the actual value of the stock sold. On this basis, the Court held that the stock constituted at least 75% of the total assets and the sale of the stock was a sale of substantially all assets.

The key language in the Court of Chancery opinion in *Philadelphia National Bank* is the suggestion that "the critical factor in determining the character of a sale of assets is generally considered not the amount of property sold but whether the sale is in fact an unusual transaction or one made in the regular course of business of the seller." (41 Del.Ch. at 515, 199 A.2d at 561). Professor Folk suggests from the opinion that "the statute would be inapplicable if the assets sale is 'one made in furtherance of express corporate objects in the ordinary and regular course of the business'" (referring to language in 41 Del.Ch. at 516, 199 A.2d at 561). Folk, *supra,* Section 271, p. 401.

But any "ordinary and regular course of the business" test in this context obviously is not intended to limit the directors to customary daily business activities. Indeed, a question concerning the statute would not arise unless the transaction was somewhat out of the ordinary. While it is true that a transaction in the ordinary course of business does not require shareholder approval, the converse is not true. Every transaction out of normal routine does not necessarily require shareholder approval. The unusual nature of the transaction must strike at the heart of the corporate existence and purpose. As it is written at 6A Fletcher, Cyclopedia Corporations (Perm.Ed.1968 Rev.) § 2949.2, p. 648:

> The purpose of the consent statutes is to protect the shareholders from fundamental change, or more specifically to protect the shareholder from the destruction of the means to accomplish the purposes or objects for which the corporation was incorporated and actually performs.

It is in this sense that the "unusual transaction" judgment is to be made and the statute's applicability determined. If the sale is of assets quantitatively vital to the operation of the corporation and is out of the ordinary and substantially affects the existence and purpose of the corporation, then it is beyond the power of the Board of Directors. With these guidelines, I turn to Signal and the transaction in this case.

Signal or its predecessor was incorporated in the oil business in 1922. But, beginning in 1952 Signal diversified its interests. In 1952, Signal acquired a substantial stock interest in American President Lines. From 1957 to 1962 Signal was the sole owner of Laura Scudders, a nationwide snack food business. In 1964, Signal acquired Garrett Corporation which is engaged in the aircraft, aerospace, and uranium enrichment business. In 1967, Signal acquired Mack Trucks, Inc., which is engaged in the manufacture and sale of trucks and related equipment. Also in 1968, the oil and gas business was transferred to a separate division and later in 1970 to the Signal Oil subsidiary. Since 1967, Signal has made acquisition of or formed substantial companies none of which are involved or related with the oil and gas industry. As indicated previously, the oil and gas production development of Signal's business is now carried on by Signal Oil, the sale of the stock of which is an issue in this lawsuit.

Based on the company's figures, Signal Oil represents only about 26% of the total assets of Signal. While Signal Oil represents 41% of the Signal's total net worth, it produces only about 15% of Signal's revenues and earnings.

While it is true, based on the experience of the Signal-Burmah transaction and the record in this lawsuit, that Signal Oil is more valuable than shown by the company's books, even if, as plaintiff suggests in his brief, the $761,000,000 value attached to Signal Oil's properties by the plaintiff's expert Paul V. Keyser, Jr., were substituted [for $376.2 million] as the asset figure, the oil and gas properties would still constitute less than half the value of Signal's total assets. Thus, from a straight quantitative approach, I agree with Signal's position that the sale to Burmah does not constitute a sale of "all or substantially all" of Signal's assets.

In addition, if the character of the transaction is examined, the plaintiff's position is also weak. While it is true that Signal's original purpose was oil and gas and while oil and gas is still listed first in the certificate of incorporation, the simple fact is that Signal is now a conglomerate engaged in the aircraft and aerospace business, the manufacture and sale of trucks and related equipment, and other businesses besides oil and gas. The very nature of its business, as it now in fact exists, contemplates the acquisition and disposal of independent branches of its corporate business. Indeed, given the operations since 1952, it can be said that such acquisitions and dispositions have become part of the ordinary course of business. The facts that the oil and gas business was historically first and that authorization for such operations are listed first in the certificate do not prohibit disposal of such interest. As Director Harold M. Williams testified, business history is not "compelling" and "many companies go down the drain because they try to be historic."

It is perhaps true, as plaintiff has argued, that the advent of multi-business corporations has in one sense emasculated § 271 since one business may be sold without shareholder approval when other substantial businesses are retained. But it is one thing for a corporation to evolve over a period of years into a multi-business corporation, the operations of which include the purchase and sale of whole businesses, and another for a single business corporation by a one transaction revolution to sell the entire means of operating its business in exchange for money or a separate business. In the former situation, the processes of corporate democracy customarily have had the opportunity to restrain or otherwise control over a period of years. Thus, there is a chance for some shareholder participation. The Signal development illustrates the difference. For example, when Signal, itself formerly called Signal Oil and Gas Company, changed its name in 1968, it was for the announced "need for a new name appropriate to the broadly diversified activities of Signal's multi-industry complex."

I conclude that measured quantitatively and qualitatively, the sale of the stock of Signal Oil by Signal to Burmah does not constitute a sale of "all or substantially all" of Signal's assets. Accordingly, insofar as the complaint rests on 8 Del.C. § 271(a), in my judgment, it has no reasonable probability of ultimate success.

Official Comment 1 to § 12.01 of the 1984 MBCA, addressed the interpretative problems that courts had faced in determining what constituted "all or substantially all." The Comment stated:

> The phrase "all or substantially all" chosen by the draftsmen of the Model Act is intended to mean what it literally says, "all or substantially all." The phrase "substantially all" is synonymous with "nearly all" and was added to make it clear that the statutory requirements could not be avoided by retention of some minimal or nominal residue of the original assets.

> Some court decisions have adopted a narrower construction of somewhat similar statutory language. These decisions should be viewed as resting on the diverse statutory language involved in those cases and should not be viewed as illustrating the meaning of "all or substantially all" intended by the draftsmen of the Model Act.

This language seemingly gave shareholders relatively little voting power in this type of transaction. Nevertheless, in 1999, MBCA § 12.02(a) was amended to take a different approach to defining when shareholders are entitled to vote on a sale of assets. It introduces new terminology by jettisoning the term "all or substantially all" in favor of requiring approval "if the disposition would leave the corporation without a significant continuing business activity."

Further, in keeping with the MBCA drafters' approach in other sections of the statute, Section 12.02(a) also adds a bright-line test for delineating which asset dispositions require shareholder approval. It provides that a corporation retains a "significant continuing business activity" (and shareholder approval therefore is not required) if the retained business constitute at least 25 percent of the corporation's consolidated assets and 25 percent of either its consolidated revenues or pre-tax earnings from pre-transaction operations.

In *Katz v. Bregman*, 431 A.2d 1274 (Del.Ch. 1981), the court held that a corporation's sale of assets that constituted more than 51 percent of its total assets and generated approximately 45 percent of its net sales in the previous year, and that would cause the corporation to depart radically from its historically successful line of business, constituted a sale of substantially all of the corporation's assets.

How would *Katz v. Bregman* be decided under MBCA § 12.02?

CHAPTER 21

PROTECTING AND SELLING CONTROL

■ ■ ■

Most changes in control of publicly held corporations are negotiated. The managers of the buyer and the seller bargain at arm's length over the terms, conditions, future management, and precise legal form of the transaction. The managers represent the interests of the shareholders. If the managers do not reach an agreement, the negotiations are terminated. Although corporate law may require shareholder approval, and federal securities law may require full disclosure to shareholders, the managers and directors structure the deal. In a truly arm's length transaction, the business judgment rule largely insulates directors from liability. As long as the board acts in good faith, exercises due care and does not engage in self-dealing, directors may negotiate a change of control with little risk of legal liability.

This chapter deals with contested changes in control in which one company (the *bidder*) seeks to acquire control of another company (the *target*) without the initial consent of the target company's board by appealing directly to the target's shareholders. The bidder can select the form of its challenge. It can start a proxy contest to persuade a majority of the target shareholders to elect a slate of directors that the bidder has chosen, or it can make a tender offer for all or a majority of the target's stock. In a tender offer, the bidder proposes to the target's shareholders that they tender their shares for purchase by the bidder, usually at a premium over the market price. The offer is often conditioned on the bidder's being able to acquire a majority interest, and it succeeds, the bidder can then replace the incumbent directors with its own nominees. Today, because of the poison pill and other takeover defenses, bidders often conduct a simultaneous proxy contest and tender offer.

A. SETTING THE SCENE

Contested changes of control take a form today different from twenty-five or thirty years ago when much of the relevant case law developed. That law was a response to the large increase in the number of tender offers and the variety of innovative defensive tactics that target boards implemented to forestall or defeat unwanted takeovers. No single technique created an absolute bar to hostile takeovers, but each helped to deter them by slowing the process, raising the economic cost to the bidder, or providing shareholders with an attractive alternative to the takeover bid.

Until recent years, almost all changes of control were driven by operating companies wanting to expand their businesses. While this kind of transaction is still common, today many changes of control are driven by institutional investors, primarily private equity and hedge funds.

Private equity funds are pools of capital raised from qualified investors, including pension funds, financial institutions and high-net worth individuals. They are higher risk investments but offer the potential for higher returns, often 20% to 30% per year. Private equity funds raise billions of dollars of capital, which they then leverage with large amounts of debt. The resulting pools of capital enable the funds to buy large publicly traded corporations. When a private equity firm makes an offer for a public corporation, in addition to offering the target shareholders a substantial premium to tender their shares, it often offers the target board and senior officers an opportunity to remain with the newly formed corporation and to receive lucrative compensation packages. The conflicts of interest are clear: the board will recommend that the shareholders tender their shares at a premium but the board will also realize personal gains if the transaction is consummated.

Hedge funds are also private investment pools available only to wealthy individuals or institutional investors. Like private equity funds, they charge high fees in exchange for attempting to achieve above-normal returns. Hedge funds take various roles in the market, including buying and selling shares in the market and activist investing. They look for undervalued corporations in which to buy shares at a low price. They often choose corporations because they believe that the managements are not doing a good job or the assets are not being fully utilized. Then, either through a proxy contest or negotiation, they seek to obtain board representation and to get the board to improve the company's performance. Activist hedge funds generally are not looking to buy and operate companies but rather to take stock positions companies and try to increase the value of those positions and sell them for a quick profit.

The activity of hedge funds highlights the tensions between activist investors and corporate managers when control may be at stake. Hedge funds have the ability to launch proxy contests to obtain control of, or at least representation on, the board of directors. This threat can be as troublesome to the incumbent management as a hostile tender offer.

This chapter focuses on the basic governance questions that arise in contests for control. Put simply, the fundamental question, with which we have been concerned throughout the book, is for whose benefit the corporation should be run. In the context of takeovers, the question is who should decide as to whether a corporation should continue its existence in its present form. More specifically, under what circumstances should the management of a target company be allowed to employ defensive tactics against a takeover offer that the target shareholders might want to accept?

The first part of the chapter deals with the policy questions raised by contests for control. What role do takeovers play in the economy? What role do they play in a system of corporate governance? What role should the legal system play in regulating takeovers? What standard of review should a court employ in adjudicating control disputes that involve both business decisions and conflicts of interest?

The next two sections deal with the structure and regulation of takeovers. The majority of the chapter then examines how the Delaware courts have dealt with control contests, tracing the historical evolution of takeover jurisprudence. The last section considers the limits on the "deal protection" measures that can be used in structuring negotiated acquisitions in efforts to prevent competing offers.

B. THE POLICY DEBATE

1. CORPORATE GOVERNANCE

Takeover jurisprudence implicates a fundamental issue of corporate governance: How should power be allocated between a corporation's shareholders and its board of directors? A negotiated acquisition must generally be approved by both the board of a corporation and its shareholders. In a hostile tender offer, by contrast, the offeror can essentially go over the heads of the board and offer to buy control of the corporation from the shareholders over the objection of the board. On the other hand, the board of a target company has available powerful defenses to deter a tender offer, often undertaking major corporate transactions they would not have undertaken otherwise and incurring heavy debt in the process. When courts first started considering the propriety of defensive tactics, they had difficulty determining which of two standards of review to apply—the business judgment rule for claims that management violated its duty of care, or the intrinsic fairness test for claims that management breached its duty of loyalty. Hostile takeover defense tactics seemed a cross between the two duties. While the desirability of an acquisition is an issue of business judgment for the target, its management has conflicted interests because the transaction directly threatens their jobs. Therefore, the defensive tactics they employ are interested director transactions that should perhaps be reviewed under the stricter standard of entire fairness. It became apparent that corporate law had left open the question of what standard to apply and who, ultimately, should decide whether a corporation should accept a hostile takeover bid. *See* Ronald J. Gilson, *Unocal Fifteen Years Later (And What We Can Do About It)*, 26 Del. J. Corp. L. 491, 495 (2001).

This controversy reflects the debate about the nature and purpose of the corporation that we studied in Chapters 4 and 5. Those who view the corporation as the "property" of its owners argue that boards should only be able to adopt limited defensive measures, such as providing shareholders with the information they need to make informed decisions and helping shareholders overcome collective action problems. Because shareholders are the owners of the corporation, they should be permitted to sell their shares to a willing buyer without interference by the managers.

In contrast, those who embrace the "entity" concept of the corporation argue that managers should have more discretion to resist unwanted tender offers. When the corporation is seen as a social institution with a public purpose, the issue is not simply whether shareholders should have the unfettered discretion to accept a bidder's premium offer. Rather, a target's board of directors should have the ability to defend the corporation from a takeover that the board genuinely believes undervalues the long-term productivity of the company and threatens other legitimate corporate interests, such as the company's employees, customers, or the local community.

Whether courts should give management broad freedom to resist an unwanted tender offer depends not only on whether one accepts Chancellor Allen's entity view of the corporation, but also on whether one believes that directors confronting a hostile takeover bid are more likely to be motivated by self-interest or by a concern for the corporation's long-term well being. Defensive tactics are entrenchment mechanisms. As such, those who believe managers' decisions are influenced or dominated by self-interested motives oppose giving management unfettered discretion to resist an unwanted takeover bid. Those who advocate increasing shareholders' power in corporate takeovers argue that, because shareholders have a common investment interest in maximizing firm value, they can effectively discipline management overreaching.

Delaware courts have not chosen sides in the debate. In part, the case law adheres to the property model in holding that a corporation's purpose is to maximize shareholder wealth. The decisions also reflect the entity model because they permit directors to consider the best interests of the corporation in the long term, which may include consideration of constituents other than the shareholders. Directors can block a takeover that seems to be in the best interests of the current shareholders if the directors determine that the corporation will generate greater economic return in the long run under the current management's strategy. In making their decision, directors can, to a limited extent, consider the interest of constituents other than the shareholders. For a thoughtful discussion of this issue by three respected Delaware judges, *see* William T. Allen, Jack B. Jacobs & Leo E. Strine, Jr., *The Great Takeover Debate: A Meditation on Bridging the Conceptual Divide*, 69 U. Chi. L. Rev. 1067 (2002).

2. MANAGEMENT DISCIPLINE

The threat of hostile takeovers may curb management incompetence and misconduct. An active market for corporate control arguably encourages management to run the business profitably because, if the company's stock price falls, the company would be vulnerable to a takeover bid. Under this view of corporate governance, target company shareholders should be allowed to accept a tender offer for a premium over the current market price of their shares because it motivates entrenched managers to run the company in a way that maximizes shareholder value. This perspective assumes an efficient market in which stock prices accurately reflect a company's true value. In such a market, the bidder will look for a target company whose stock price is below the bidder's own assessment of value of the target's assets. A low stock-market valuation thus indicates that the company is underperforming, either because of bad management or because of underutilized assets.

The problem with this argument is that financial markets are less than perfectly efficient, and therefore the price of a stock does not always reflect a company's true value. A successful hostile offer for a stock that is valued too low by the market, can mean good managers are replaced by individuals who are interested only in making a quick profit and are unconcerned about the long-term health of the corporation.

3. ECONOMIC THEORY

A fundamental question about takeovers is whether they create, or simply redistribute, wealth. Because shareholders of target companies often enjoy great gains and shareholders of bidder companies usually receive slight gains, some economists conclude that the higher stock prices are evidence that tender offers create wealth. *See* Michael Jensen & Richard Ruback, *The Market for Corporate Control: The Scientific Evidence,* 11 J. Fin. Econ. 5 (1983). Although the source is uncertain, Jensen and Ruback believe that the gains do not result from monopoly profits. They suggest that the clear public policy implication is that no impediments to hostile takeover bids should be allowed.

However, others find the results of empirical studies of corporate takeovers less clear. In some situations, shareholders of target and bidder companies may be hurt by takeovers. Although an unsuccessful tender offer followed by a successful second offer for a higher price results in better gains for target shareholders, when an initial offer is defeated and there is no second offer, the target corporation's share prices eventually return to its pre-bid levels and the target shareholders have lost the opportunity to tender their shares for a premium. In addition, the shareholders of the acquiring corporation may only break even, at best, in merger transactions.

Even if corporate takeovers do increase shareholder wealth, the public policy directive is unclear. Shareholders are not the only group whose interests are implicated in a takeover. A takeover affects every corporate constituency—shareholders, managers, employees, customers, creditors, suppliers, and the local communities where the company operates. These constituents' interests often conflict. While the shareholders of the target company might sell their shares for a premium, thousands of employees might lose their jobs. Although the stock gains are objectively measurable, they do not reflect the gains and losses of the other constituents. The added wealth to shareholders may not justify the significant losses to the constituents of the target corporation.

Ultimately, society can be worse off from a takeover bid that benefits shareholders. For example, bidders may be willing to terminate implicit long-term contracts with other stakeholders (employees, suppliers and the community) that existing management would honor. Sometimes these terminations result in benefits to the community as well as to stockholders, when the stakeholders can replace their old relationships without cost. In that event, assets have been moved to more productive users. The stock gains measure society's gains. But at times the stakeholder losses may exceed shareholder gains if the consequences of job and supplier losses produce a ripple effect of further community losses. *See* Andrei Shleifer & Lawrence Summers, *Hostile Takeovers as Breaches of Trust*, in A.J. Auerbach, (ed.), Corporate Takeovers: Causes and Consequences (1988).

C. CONTESTS FOR CONTROL: METHODS AND DEFENSES

1. TENDER OFFERS

Bidders select their targets for a variety of reasons. The target may be a company that the bidder believes will operate more profitably under new and better management. Alternatively, the bidder may believe that target's operations can efficiently be combined with those of the bidder. Finally, the target's assets may be worth more sold separately than the value of those assets as reflected in the stock market price.

Bidders often first attempt to negotiate a friendly acquisition with the target, commencing a hostile offer only if those overtures fail. There are two substantial risks to proceeding with a bid that the target's management opposes. First, there is uncertainty. Unlike a negotiated acquisition, where the would-be acquirer has an opportunity to investigate fully the proposed target's business, assets and liabilities, in a hostile takeover, the bidder has no opportunity to learn about the target from the inside and must proceed on the basis of publicly available information, which is inevitably less complete.

Second, there is a financial risk. Another bidder (a "white knight"), sometimes chosen by the target, may be prepared to make a higher offer. If a contest for control develops, the original bidder must choose whether to increase its bid (and risk overpaying) or to abandon the takeover. If the offer fails, the offeror loses the (usually substantial) costs it has incurred. Bidders often mitigate this risk by first acquiring a block of the target's stock, which they can sell at a profit to the successful rival bidder.

Bidders typically form shell corporations to act as the offeror. If the shell corporation acquires control of the target company, the bidder usually rids itself of the remaining minority by merging the shell corporation into the target and forcing the minority to take cash or a debt security.

Target company shareholders that believe the offer is inadequate are in a "prisoner's dilemma." They must choose between tendering their shares for the offered price, or refusing to tender and risking that a successful offer will leave them in a minority position. If the offer succeeds, they face the unattractive choice of accepting whatever consideration is offered in the second-step merger or dissenting from that transaction and dealing with the costs and uncertainty involved in seeking appraisal.

The amount of pressure that target company's shareholders feel depends on the terms of the tender offer. The shareholders will feel the most pressure to tender their shares when the terms of the second-step merger differ materially from the initial offer. They will feel less pressure when the bidder commits to consummate the second-step merger for the same consideration as the initial offer. Then (putting aside the possibility of appraisal) the only risk a non-tendering shareholder faces is that she will not receive payment for her stock until some later date.

Although targets have many available defensive tactics to deter or defeat an unwanted tender offer, two measures have proved most effective, particularly when used together: the poison pill and the staggered board. We have considered each of these briefly in earlier chapters. The following sections describe them in greater detail. As you read the material, keep in mind that there are numerous variations of each that are not discussed here.

a.   Poison Pills

A shareholder rights plan, referred to as a "poison pill," is an inexpensive way for a company to protect itself from a hostile takeover. A rights plan is designed to prevent a bidder from employing certain types of takeover tactics and to encourage it to negotiate with the target's board. The poison pill does not prevent hostile takeovers entirely but strengthens the target board's powers in responding to a takeover attempt.

In general, a rights plan gives the target shareholders (other than the potential bidder) the right to buy additional stock in the target corporation at a significant discount from the prevailing market price. In a rights plan, the board creates a mechanism to authorize a dividend to all of the company's holders of common stock of one "right" for each share of stock. Initially, each right entitles the holder to buy a fraction of a share of a new series of preferred stock—intended to be the economic equivalent of the common stock. The exercise price of the right is significantly higher than the current market price (supposedly equal to the expected long-term trading value over the term of the plan). The exercise price often reflects a 300% to 500% premium over the current market.

The rights become exercisable upon the occurrence of a triggering event specified in the plan. This event is usually either the acquisition by a potential bidder of a specified percentage (often 15 or 20%) of the target company's stock or the consummation of a tender offer that would result in the bidder's ownership of that percentage. When the rights become exercisable, the target distributes rights certificates to the holders of common stock so that the common stock and the rights can trade separately.

The rights expire after a certain term, generally 10 years, unless they are redeemed by the corporation before they expire. The board can redeem them at a nominal price (such as $0.0001 per right) until a triggering event occurs.

The structure of the rights is such that their exercise would result in substantial dilution of the acquiror's position if it proceeded with the offer, in effect causing it to pay several times what the position is worth. As a consequence, in practice bidders always condition their offers on the redemption of the rights. Thus, it is unlikely that there will ever be a triggering event. Instead, the target board can use its power to redeem the pill as a sword to force the bidder to raise its price. When the price is high enough, the target board will then redeem the rights and the offer will proceed. In such a case, of course, what started as a hostile offer ends as a negotiated "friendly" deal.[1]

In recent years, as a result of pressures from the shareholder community there has been a marked decline in the number of poison pill rights plans in place. This decline, however, does not mean that poison pills have lost their desirability or effectiveness. Many corporations have chosen to have a rights plan "on the shelf" so that the board of directors can adopt it on short notice if a threat materializes that requires such a response. These plans are not required to be disclosed publicly until they have been formally adopted and implemented. Institutional Shareholder Services, the leading proxy advisory firm, discourages the use of rights plans and will recommend a "withhold" vote against a board of directors if the corporation

---

[1] The foregoing description was adapted from a memorandum entitled "Stockholder Rights Plan" prepared by the law firms of Baker & McKenzie and Richards, Layton & Finger (March 2002).

does not provide a mechanism for the shareholders to ratify or remove the plan after 12 months.

b.   Staggered Boards

A staggered (or classified) board lengthens the time required for a successful bidder to take control of the target board. Under Delaware law, directors are elected annually for one-year terms. Delaware law also permits corporations to change that structure by dividing the board into two or three classes, with each class to serve for two or three years. The staggered board may be provided for in either the certificate of incorporation or bylaws. If the staggered board structure is in the certificate of incorporation, it can be removed only by a vote of both the board and the shareholders. By contrast, if the board structure is in the bylaws, the shareholders can remove it unilaterally by amending the bylaws. The consequence of a staggered board is that a successful bidder must, at least in theory, wait two years before obtaining control of the board.

Although it is not without controversy, there is a considerable body of empirical research that purports to show that the existence of a staggered board depresses shareholder value. *See, e.g.,* Lucian A. Bebchuk and Alma Cohen, The *Costs of Entrenched Boards*, 78 J. Fin. Econ. 409 (2005); *but see* Thomas W. Bates, et al., *Board Classification and Managerial Entrenchment: Evidence from the Market for Corporate Control*, 87 J. Fin. Econ. 656 (2008). Over the last few years, pressure from institutional investors and shareholder activists, led largely by the Harvard Shareholder Rights Project, has resulted in a substantial reduction in the number of classified boards of larger public companies. In 2002, over 60 percent of the S&P 500 companies had classified boards. By the beginning of 2012, that number had declined to 126. And in 2012 42 of those companies declassified their boards.

Notwithstanding this trend, the majority of companies that conduct initial public offerings still elect to have classified boards. One explanation for this seeming contradiction is that lawyers continue to advise clients preparing for their IPOs that the existence of a staggered board gives directors more power to negotiate with a hostile offeror to obtain better terms. Ira Ross Sorkin, *The Case Against Staggered Boards*, New York Times (March 20, 2012).

2.   PROXY CONTESTS

As an alternative to making a tender offer, the bidder may seek to acquire control of the target through a proxy contest. In a proxy contest, the stockholders choose between competing slates of directors—one favored by the target's incumbent board and the other favored by the bidder. Each slate sends the stockholders various soliciting materials, the most important of which is the proxy statement.

Target management has two major advantages in a proxy contest. First, existing shareholders tend to support the incumbent management. Second, management can draw on the corporate treasury to finance its proxy solicitations. The bidder must fund its own solicitations and will only recover its expenses if it prevails. Proxy contests are costly for the bidder because proxies are revocable, so several rounds of solicitation may be required to wean away support from the other side or safeguard the votes of one's supporters. Proxy contests often involve litigation, which is also costly for the bidder, whereas the target's management can finance it with corporate funds. A plausible claim almost always can be made that the other side's solicitations are false or misleading in one or more material respects in violation of SEC Rule 14a–9.

Because of the widespread use of poison pills and staggered boards, most contests for control now couple a tender offer with a proxy contest. The bidder will condition its tender offer upon the redemption of the rights, something that a hostile target board will refuse to do. Thus the only way that the bidder can achieve its goals is to remove the target board and replace the board with its own directors. DGCL § 228 permits the bidder to effect such removal without a shareholder meeting by soliciting consents from the holders of a majority of the outstanding shares of the target. The solicitation may also involve amending the target's bylaws to remove the staggered board structure so that the bidder can take immediate control of the target board upon the successful completion of the tender offer. A solicitation under DGCL § 228 is subject to the SEC proxy rules in the same way that it would have been had there been a formal shareholder meeting.

D. THE REGULATORY FRAMEWORK

1. FEDERAL REGULATION

Federal regulation of proxy contests and tender offers has three main objectives: (1) ensure that shareholders receive the information they need to make informed decisions; (2) protect shareholders from deceptive acts and practices; and (3) outlaw certain coercive tactics that otherwise could be employed by bidders or target companies during tender offers. The regulation also imposes costs on both bidders and target companies in some circumstances, which affects the dynamics of contests for corporate control.

a. Tender Offers

The regulation of tender offers is found in the Williams Act amendments to the Securities Exchange Act of 1934 and the SEC rules thereunder. Both the legislation and the rules reflect the Congressional decision to maintain neutrality in the regulation of tender offers.

The following are the principal provisions that apply to tender offers:

- Any person (that is, "natural person, company, government, or political subdivision, agency, or instrumentality of a government") that makes a tender offer for more than 5% of a public corporation's stock must file the offer with the SEC, and publish, as part of its offer, information about the bidder and its controlling shareholders, the bidder's purpose, and the terms on which the bidder plans to consummate any second-step transaction. § 14(d)(1).

- A tender offer must remain open for a minimum of 20 business days. Rule 14e–1.

- Shares that are tendered may be withdrawn any time before the offer expires. § 14(d)(5) and Rule 14d–7.

- A new offer, or an increase in the price of the original offer, extends the duration of the offer and the withdrawal periods by 10 business days. Rule 14e–1.

- If the offer is for less than all of the corporation's shares, the bidder must accept tendered shares on a pro-rata basis. § 14(d)(6) and Rule 14d–8.

- If the bidder raises its offering price during the offer, it must pay the higher price to all tendering shareholders, including those who tendered in response to its previous, lower offer. § 14(d)(7).

- It is unlawful for any person, including the bidder and the target company, "to make any untrue statement of a material fact or omit to state any material fact necessary in order to make the statements made . . . not misleading, or to engage in any fraudulent, deceptive, or manipulative acts or practices, in connection with any tender offer." Rule 14e–3.

b. Proxy Contests

All of the proxy rules adopted pursuant to § 14(a) of the 1934 Act—including the Rule 14a–9 prohibition of materially false or misleading statements in a proxy solicitation—apply to proxy contests. Because, as we saw in Chapter 14, Rule 14a–8 allows a company to exclude proposals relating to the election of directors, a bidder must seek the power to vote shareholders' stock.

Two additional proxy rules apply to contests for corporate control. Rule 14a–7 requires a target company to provide a challenger seeking to solicit proxies (the bidder) with estimates of the number of its shareholders and estimates of the cost of mailing proxy materials to those holders. The target company must either promptly mail the bidder's proxy materials to the shareholders (for which the bidder pays the reasonable costs of mailing) or furnish the bidder with a mailing list of all shareholders. The mailing list does not have to indicate how many shares each shareholder owns. Target companies usually choose to mail the proxy materials for the bidder, so bidders rarely take advantage of this rule. Instead, bidders obtain shareholders' names, addresses and share holdings using shareholders' state law rights to inspect the target's shareholder list.

Under Rule 14a–11 all participants in an "election contest," which is defined as a proxy solicitation in opposition to another candidate for director, must disclose their biographical information and their securities holdings in the target company. Rule 14a–11 treats as a "participant" the issuer, its directors, all nominees for election as directors, and committees or groups soliciting proxies or financing a solicitation.

Although proxy contests are fought openly, bidders try to get organized before the target's management knows much about them or their plans. The goal is to contact potential supporters and launch their effort before management can enact takeover defenses. The SEC's rules, however, make it difficult for a bidder to proceed secretly. Section 13(d) of the 1934 Act requires any person who acquires more than 5% of the stock of a public company to file a Schedule 13D within 10 days after reaching the 5% threshold; and "person" is defined to include any "group" acting together. Thus, although the proxy rules allow limited contact with other shareholders without any disclosure, under § 13(d), if contacts lead to the formation of a "group," they trigger a filing obligation.

2. STATE REGULATION

Many states have adopted legislation to strengthen the ability of target companies to resist hostile takeover bids. To avoid running afoul of the Commerce Clause, they are generally framed as regulations of the internal affairs of their domestic corporations. Most take one of the following forms:

- Control share laws, which bar any bidder who acquires more than a stated percentage of a target company's stock from voting that stock unless the bidder first obtains approval of the target's board of directors to make the bid. If the board opposes the takeover bid, the bidder must conduct a proxy contest and secure support from of a majority or supermajority of the target's shares.

- Business combination laws, which bar for three to five years any business combination (such as a second-step merger) involving a target company and a bidder that has acquired more than a given percentage of a target's stock without first securing the approval of the target's board of directors,. These laws do not preclude a bidder from acquiring a controlling interest in a target company through a hostile bid, but do make it extremely difficult for the bidder to use the target's assets as collateral to finance its bid. They also give the bidder the burden of demonstrating that all of its transactions with the target, for a number of years, are "entirely fair."

- Poison pill laws, which explicitly authorize the use of shareholder rights plans, or poison pills. These laws have been passed primarily in states where there was dispute over whether a target board had authority to adopt a shareholder rights plan.

- Constituency statutes, which permit the board of directors of a target company to take account of the interests of employees, customers, creditors, suppliers, the community and other constituencies, in addition to the interests of shareholders, when deciding how to respond to an unsolicited takeover bid.

Delaware has adopted a relatively mild form of business combination law. DGCL § 203 bars for three years a business combination between a covered corporation and an "interested stockholder," defined as a person holding more than 15% of the corporation's stock or an entity controlled by such a person, *unless*:

- the target corporation's board of directors gave prior approval to the business combination or the transaction in which the bidder became an interested stockholder;

- the interested stockholder (the bidder) acquires more than 85% of the corporation's stock (excluding certain stock held or controlled by management) in the transaction in which it became an interested stockholder; or

- following the transaction in which the bidder became an interested stockholder but did not acquire more than 85% of the corporation's stock, the target corporation's board (which presumably will have been elected by the interested stockholder) and holders of at least two-thirds of the target's stock held by persons other than the interested stockholder vote to approve the business combination.

Thus, if a hostile bid is attractive enough to garner the support of more than 85% of a Delaware corporation's non-management shareholders, DGCL § 203 imposes no burdens on the bidder.

All state anti-takeover laws are either mandatory or establish the default rule. In the latter case, they apply unless a corporation opts out of the rule through a provision in its charter.

E. JUDICIAL REVIEW OF TAKEOVER DEFENSES

The Delaware courts have struggled with what standard of review to apply when evaluating a board's response to a perceived threat to control of the corporation. Neither the business judgment rule nor the entire fairness test quite work. The following cases trace the development of the Delaware law regarding tender offers and the evolution of the standards of review the courts use to evaluate board responses to threats to control.

1. THE BUSINESS JUDGMENT RULE

A transaction approved by a majority of independent, disinterested directors normally receives the protection of the business judgment rule. However, a board's response to a perceived threat to control—though partly a decision based on what the board believes to be in the best interests of the shareholders—is also motivated by self-interest. The directors want to keep their positions.

In *Cheff v. Mathes*, a shareholder who acquired more than 15% of Holland Furnace stock, after being denied a seat on the board, offered to sell his stock to the corporation for a substantial premium or, alternatively, threatened to make a tender offer for the remainder of the corporation's stock at the same price. The Holland Furnace board decided to repurchase the stock. The issue before the court was whether that decision would be protected by the business judgment rule.

CHEFF V. MATHES
199 A.2d 548 (Del.Ch. 1964).

CAREY, JUSTICE:

This is an appeal from the decision of the Vice-Chancellor in a derivative suit holding certain directors of Holland Furnace Company liable for loss allegedly resulting from improper use of corporate funds to purchase shares of the company. Because a meaningful decision upon review turns upon a complete understanding of the factual background, a somewhat detailed summary of the evidence is required.

Holland Furnace Company, a corporation of the State of Delaware, manufactures warm air furnaces, air conditioning equipment, and other home heating equipment. At the time of the relevant transactions, the board of directors was composed of the seven individual defendants:

Mr. Cheff had been Holland's Chief Executive Officer since 1933, received an annual salary of $77,400, and personally owned 6,000 shares of the company. He was also a director.

Mrs. Cheff, the wife of Mr. Cheff, was a daughter of the founder of Holland and had served as a director since 1922. She personally owned 5,804 shares of Holland and owned 47.9 percent of Hazelbank United

Interest. Hazelbank is an investment vehicle for Mrs. Cheff and members of the Cheff-Landwehr family group, which owned 164,950 shares of the 883,585 outstanding Holland shares. As a director, Mrs. Cheff received $200 for each monthly board meeting, whether or not she attended the meeting.

Edgar P. Landwehr was the nephew of Mrs. Cheff and personally owned 24,010 shares of Holland and 8.6 percent of the outstanding shares of Hazelbank. He received no compensation from Holland other than the monthly director's fee.

Robert H. Trenkamp is an attorney who first represented Holland in 1946. In May 1953, he became a director of Holland and acted as general counsel for the company. During the period in question, he received no retainer from the company, but did receive substantial sums for legal services rendered the company. Apart from the above-described payments, he received no compensation from Holland other than the monthly director's fee. He owned 200 shares of Holland stock. Although he owned no shares of Hazelbank, at the time relevant to this controversy, he was serving as a director and counsel of Hazelbank.

John D. Ames was a partner in the Chicago investment firm of Bacon, Whipple & Co. and joined the Holland board at the request of Mr. Cheff. During the periods in question, his stock ownership varied between ownership of no shares to ownership of 300 shares. He was considered by the other members of the Holland board to be the financial advisor to the board. He received no compensation from Holland other than the normal director's fee.

Ralph G. Boalt was the Vice President of J.R. Watkins Company, a manufacturer and distributor of cosmetics. In 1953, at the request of Mr. Cheff, he became a member of the board of directors. Apart from the normal director's fee, he received no compensation from Holland for his services.

George Spatta was the President of Clark Equipment Company, a large manufacturer of earth moving equipment. In 1951, at the request of Mr. Cheff, he joined the board of directors of Holland. Apart from the normal director's fee, he received no compensation from the company.

The board of directors of Hazelbank included the five principal shareholders: Mrs Cheff; Leona Kolb, who was Mrs. Cheff's daughter; Landwehr; Mrs. Bowles, who was Landwehr's sister; Mrs. Putnam, also Landwehr's sister; Trenkamp; and William DeLong, an accountant.

Prior to the events in question, Holland employed approximately 8,500 persons and maintained 400 branch sales offices, located in 43 states. The volume of sales had declined from more than $41,000,000 in 1948 to less than $32,000,000 in 1956. Defendants contend that the decline in earnings is attributable to the artificial post-war demand generated in the 1946 to 1948 period. In order to stabilize the condition of the company, the sales department apparently was reorganized and certain unprofitable branch offices were closed. By 1957, this reorganization had been completed and the management was convinced that the changes were manifesting beneficial results. The practice of the company was to directly employ the retail salesman, and the management considered that practice—unique in the furnace business—to be a vital factor in the company's success.

During the first five months of 1957, the monthly trading volume of Holland's stock on the New York Stock Exchange ranged between 10,300 shares to 24,200 shares. In the last week of June 1957, however, the trading increased to 37,800 shares, with a corresponding increase in the market price. In June of 1957, Mr. Cheff met with Arnold H. Maremont, president of Maremont Automotive Products and chairman of the boards of Motor Products Corporation and Allied Paper Corporation. Cheff testified, on deposition, that Maremont generally inquired about the feasibility of a merger between Motor Products and Holland. Cheff testified that, in view of the difference in sales practices between the two companies, he informed Maremont that a merger did not seem feasible. In reply, Maremont stated that, in the light of Cheff's decision, he had no further interest in Holland nor did he wish to buy any of the stock of Holland.

None of the members of the board apparently connected the interest of Maremont with the increased activity of Holland stock. However, Trenkamp and Staal, treasurer of Holland, unsuccessfully made an informal investigation in order to ascertain the identity of the purchaser or purchasers. The mystery was resolved, however, when Maremont called Ames in July of 1957 to inform him that Maremont then owned 55,000 shares of Holland stock. At that juncture, no requests for change in corporate policy were made, and Maremont made no demand to be made a member of the board of Holland.

Ames reported the above information to the board at its July 30, 1957, meeting. Because of the position now occupied by Maremont, the board elected to investigate the financial and business history of Maremont and the corporations controlled by him. Apart from the documentary evidence produced by this investigation, which will be considered below, Staal testified, on deposition, that "leading bank officials" had indicated that Maremont "had been a participant, or had attempted to be, in the liquidation of a number of companies."

On August 23, 1957, at the request of Maremont, a meeting was held between Maremont and Cheff. At this meeting, Cheff was informed that Motor Products then owned approximately 100,000 shares of Holland stock. Maremont then made a demand that he be named to the board of directors, but Cheff refused to consider it. Since considerable controversy has been generated by Maremont's alleged threat to liquidate the company or substantially alter the sales force of Holland, we believe it desirable to set forth the testimony of Cheff on this point: "Now we have 8,500 men, direct employees, so the problem is entirely different. He indicated immediately that he had no interest in that type of distribution, that he didn't think it was modern, that he felt furnaces could be sold as he sold mufflers, through half a dozen salesmen in a wholesale way."

Testimony was introduced by the defendants tending to show that substantial unrest was present among the employees of Holland as a result of the threat of Maremont to seek control of Holland. Moreover, at approximately this time, the company was furnished with a Dun and Bradstreet report, which indicated the practice of Maremont to achieve quick profits by sales or liquidations of companies acquired by him. The defendants were also supplied with an income statement of Motor Products, showing a loss of $336,121 in 1957.

On August 30, 1957, the board was informed by Cheff of Maremont's demand to be placed upon the board and of Maremont's belief that the retail sales organization of Holland was obsolete. The board was also informed of the results of the investigation by Cheff and Staal. Predicated upon this information, the board authorized the purchase of company stock on the market with corporate funds, ostensibly for use in a stock option plan.

Subsequent to this meeting, substantial numbers of shares were purchased and, in addition, Mrs. Cheff made personal purchases of Holland stock. As a result of purchases by Maremont, Holland and Mrs. Cheff, the market price rose. On September 4, Maremont proposed to sell his current holdings of Holland to the corporation for $14 a share. However, because of delay in responding to this offer, Maremont withdrew the offer. At this time, Mrs. Cheff was obviously quite concerned over the prospect of a Maremont acquisition, and had stated her willingness to expend her personal resources to prevent it.

On September 30, 1957, Motor Products, by letter to Mrs. Bowles, made a buy-sell offer to Hazelbank. At the Hazelbank meeting of October 3, 1957, Bowles presented the letter to the board. The board took no action, but referred the proposal to its finance committee. Although Bowles and Putnam were opposed to any acquisition of Holland stock by Hazelbank, Landwehr conceded that a majority of the board were in favor of the purchase. Despite this fact, the finance committee elected to refer the offer to the Holland board on the grounds that it was the primary concern of Holland.

Thereafter, Trenkamp arranged for a meeting with Maremont on October 14 to 15, 1957, in Chicago. Prior to this meeting, Trenkamp was aware of the intentions of Hazelbank and Mrs. Cheff to purchase all or portions of the stock then owned by Motor Products if Holland did not so act. As a result of the meeting, there was a tentative agreement on the part of Motor Products to sell its 155,000 shares at $14.40 per share. On October 23, 1957, at a special meeting of the Holland board, the purchase was considered. All directors, except Spatta, were present. The dangers allegedly posed by Maremont were again reviewed by the board. Trenkamp and Mrs. Cheff agree that the latter informed the board that either she or Hazelbank would purchase part or all of the block of Holland stock owned by Motor Products if the Holland board did not so act. The board was also informed that in order for the corporation to finance the purchase, substantial sums would have to be borrowed from commercial lending institutions. A resolution authorizing the purchase of 155,000 shares from Motor Products was adopted by the board. The price paid was in excess of the market price prevailing at the time, and the book value of the stock was approximately $20 as compared to approximately $14 for the net quick asset value. The transaction was subsequently consummated. The stock option plan mentioned in the minutes has never been implemented. In 1959, Holland stock reached a high of $15.25 a share.

On February 6, 1958, plaintiffs, owners of 60 shares of Holland stock, filed a derivative suit in the court below naming all of the individual directors of Holland, Holland itself and Motor Products as defendants. The complaint alleged that all of the purchases of stock by Holland in 1957 were for the purpose of insuring the perpetuation of control by the incumbent directors. The complaint requested that the transaction between Motor Products and Holland be rescinded and that the individual defendants account to Holland for the alleged damages. Since Motor Products was never served with process, the initial remedy became inapplicable. Ames was never served nor did he enter an appearance.

After trial, the Vice Chancellor found the following facts: (a) Holland directly sells to retail consumers by means of numerous branch offices. There were no intermediate dealers. (b) Immediately prior to the complained-of transactions, the sales and earnings of Holland had declined and its marketing practices were under investigation by the Federal Trade Commission. (c) Mr. Cheff and Trenkamp had received substantial sums as Chief Executive and attorney of the company, respectively. (d) Maremont, on August 23, 1957, demanded a place on the board. (e) At the October 14 meeting between Trenkamp, Staal and Maremont, Trenkamp and Staal were authorized to speak for Hazelbank and Mrs. Cheff as well as Holland. (f) Only Mr. Cheff, Mrs. Cheff, Landwehr, and Trenkamp clearly understood, prior to the October meeting, that either Hazelbank or Mrs. Cheff would have utilized their funds to purchase the Holland stock if Holland had not acted. (g) There was no real threat posed by Maremont and no substantial evidence of intention by Maremont to liquidate Holland. (h) Any employee unrest could have been caused by factors other than Maremont's intrusion and "only one important employee was shown to have left, and his motive for leaving is not clear."

The Court rejected the stock option plan as a meaningful rationale for the purchase from Maremont or the prior open market purchases. The

Court then found that the actual purpose behind the purchase was the desire to perpetuate control, but because of its finding that only the four above-named directors knew of the "alternative," the remaining directors were exonerated. No appeal was taken by plaintiffs from that decision.

Under the provisions of 8 Del. C. § 160, a corporation is granted statutory power to purchase and sell shares of its own stock. The charge here is not one of violation of statute, but the allegation is that the true motives behind such purchases were improperly centered upon perpetuation of control. In an analogous field, courts have sustained the use of proxy funds to inform stockholders of management's views upon the policy questions inherent in an election to a board of directors, but have not sanctioned the use of corporate funds to advance the selfish desires of directors to perpetuate themselves in office. Similarly, if the actions of the board were motivated by a sincere belief that the buying out of the dissident stockholder was necessary to maintain what the board believed to be proper business practices, the board will not be held liable for such decision, even though hindsight indicates the decision was not the wisest course. *See Kors v. Carey*, 39 Del. Ch. 47. On the other hand, if the board has acted solely or primarily because of the desire to perpetuate themselves in office, the use of corporate funds for such purposes is improper. *See Bennett v. Propp*, 41 Del Ch. 14, and *Yasik v. Wachtel*, 25 Del.Ch. 247.

Our first problem is the allocation of the burden of proof to show the presence or lack of good faith on the part of the board in authorizing the purchase of shares. Initially, the decision of the board of directors in authorizing a purchase was presumed to be in good faith and could be overturned only by a conclusive showing by plaintiffs of fraud or other misconduct. In *Kors,* the court merely indicated that the directors are presumed to act in good faith and the burden of proof to show the contrary falls upon the plaintiff. However, in *Bennett*, we stated:

> We must bear in mind the inherent danger in the purchase of shares with corporate funds to remove a threat to corporate policy when a threat to control is involved. The directors are of necessity confronted with a conflict of interest, and an objective decision is difficult. Hence, in our opinion, the burden should be on the directors to justify such a purchase as one primarily in the corporate interest.

To say that the burden of proof is upon the defendants is not to indicate, however, that the directors have the same "self-dealing interest" as is present, for example, when a director sells property to the corporation. The only clear pecuniary interest shown on the record was held by Mr. Cheff, as an executive of the corporation, and Trenkamp, as its attorney. The mere fact that some of the other directors were substantial shareholders does not create a personal pecuniary interest in the decisions made by the board of directors, since all shareholders would presumably share the benefit flowing to the substantial shareholder. Accordingly, these directors other than Trenkamp and Cheff, while called upon to justify their actions, will not be held to the same standard of proof required of those directors having personal and pecuniary interest in the transaction.

Plaintiffs urge that the sale price was unfair in view of the fact that the price was in excess of that prevailing on the open market. However, as conceded by all parties, a substantial block of stock will normally sell at a higher price than that prevailing on the open market, the increment being attributable to a "control premium." Plaintiffs argue that it is inappropriate to require the defendant corporation to pay a control premium, since control is meaningless to an acquisition by a corporation of its own shares. However, it is elementary that a holder of a substantial number of shares would expect to receive the control premium as part of his selling price, and if the corporation desired to obtain the stock, it is unreasonable to expect that the corporation could avoid paying what any other purchaser would be required to pay for the stock. In any event, the financial expert produced by defendant at trial indicated that the price paid was fair and there was no rebuttal.

The question then presented is whether or not defendants satisfied the burden of proof of showing reasonable grounds to believe a danger to corporate policy and effectiveness existed by the presence of the Maremont stock ownership. It is important to remember that the directors satisfy their burden by showing good faith and reasonable investigation; the directors will not be penalized for an honest mistake of judgment, if the judgment appeared reasonable at the time the decision was made.

We are of the opinion that the evidence presented in the court below leads inevitably to the conclusion that the board of directors, based upon direct investigation, receipt of professional advice, and personal observations of the contradictory action of Maremont and his explanation of corporate purpose, believed, with justification, that there was a reasonable threat to the continued existence of Holland, or at least existence in its present form, by the plan of Maremont to continue building up his stock holdings. We find no evidence in the record sufficient to justify a contrary conclusion. The opinion of the Vice Chancellor that employee unrest may have been engendered by other factors or that the board had no grounds to suspect Maremont is not supported in any manner by the evidence.

As noted above, the Vice Chancellor found that the purpose of the acquisition was the improper desire to maintain control, but, at the same time, he exonerated those individual directors whom he believed to be unaware of the possibility of using non-corporate funds to accomplish this purpose. Such a decision is inconsistent with his finding that the motive was improper, within the rule enunciated in *Bennett*. If the actions were in fact improper because of a desire to maintain control, then the presence or absence of a non-corporate alternative is irrelevant, as corporate funds may not be used to advance an improper purpose even if there is no non-corporate alternative available. Conversely, if the actions were proper because of a decision by the board made in good faith that the corporate interest was served thereby, they are not rendered improper by the fact that some individual directors were willing to advance personal funds if the corporation did not. It is conceivable that the Vice Chancellor considered this feature of the case to be of significance because of his apparent belief that any excess corporate funds should have been used to finance a subsidiary corporation. That action would not have solved the problem of Holland's over-capitalization. In any event, this question was a matter of business judgment, which furnishes no justification for holding the directors personally responsible in this case.

Accordingly, the judgment of the court below is reversed and remanded with instruction to enter judgment for the defendants.

NOTE

In *Cheff* the court drew a distinction between the protection of a corporate policy and the entrenchment of the current management. The "corporate policy" in issue in *Cheff* came to light in a proceeding before the Federal Trade Commission challenging Holland Furnace Company's sales practices. In upholding the FTC's order directing Holland to cease and desist from unfair trade practices, the 7th Circuit found that the record established that Holland had carried on a systematic sales program in which it:

1) Represented that its employees were employees or representatives of governmental agencies or of gas or utility companies;

2) Represented that its employees were heating engineers;

3) Misrepresented the condition of competitors' furnaces, or that the manufacturers of such furnaces were out of business or that parts therefor were unobtainable;

4) Dismantled furnaces without permission of the owners;

5) Misrepresented the condition of dismantled furnaces;

6) Required owners of furnaces dismantled by Holland to sign a release absolving Holland of liability as a condition precedent to reassembling the furnaces; and

7) Refused to reassemble, at the request of the owners, furnaces which it had dismantled.

Holland Furnace Co. v. F. T. C., 295 F.2d 302, 305 (7th Cir. 1961).

QUESTIONS

Before the Delaware Supreme Court's decision in *Cheff*, it would have seemed unlikely that a corporation could use its funds to selectively repurchase the stock of one non-controlling shareholder at a premium over the existing market price. As you will see, *Cheff* has provided the analytic framework for much subsequent Delaware jurisprudence concerning target directors' duties when faced with an actual or potential hostile takeover.

1.   Why should Holland Furnace have been permitted to use corporate funds to purchase Maremont's stock at a premium over the existing market price? The court says that "it is elementary that a holder of a substantial number of shares would expect to receive the control premium as part of his selling price." Given the existing stock ownership of Holland Furnace, did Maremont's ownership constitute "control" such that his expectation of a premium was reasonable?

2.   In justifying the use of corporate funds, the court says that "in an analogous field, courts have sustained the use of proxy funds to inform stockholders of management's views upon the policy questions inherent in an election to a board of directors, but have not sanctioned the use of corporate funds to advance the selfish desires of directors to perpetuate themselves in office." How good is the analogy? Is a proxy contest in which shareholders choose between two competing views of the corporation's future similar to a situation in which a potential hostile bidder is being paid a premium to go away?

3.   How thorough was the board's investigation of Maremont? If, as the court states, "directors satisfy their burden by showing good faith and reasonable investigation," what should be required to satisfy the "reasonable investigation" standard? In light of what you learned in Chapter 17 about the role of courts in reviewing business decisions, what should the court's standard of review be in this case?

2.   INTERMEDIATE STANDARD OF REVIEW: THE PROPORTIONALITY TEST

Most case law on corporation law issues develops at a snail's pace. Landmark decisions resolving major issues and changing the law's direction are separated by decades. Between 1985 and 1995, however, the law relating to corporate managers' responsibilities when they resist threats to control or agree to sell control was almost completely reshaped by the Delaware courts in a series of decisions that have been followed by many other jurisdictions.

Stimulated by the unprecedented surge in takeover activity that began in the late 1970s and continued into the early 1990s, and by the creativity of lawyers and investment bankers who were retained to advise bidders and target companies, the Delaware courts ended up revising their approach to transactions involving control on something approaching a "real time" basis. Within days or weeks after a court passed on the validity of a new takeover tactic employed by a bidder or target, another bidder or target tried out another new and innovative tactic that tested the limits of the court's previous decision. The Delaware courts, aware that they were operating in uncharted waters, "hewed largely to the traditional approach of writing narrowly and only for the case at hand, and have generally avoided sweeping pronouncements. This case-specific approach lends itself to low-cost innovations and mid-course corrections, because a carefully-cabined policy experiment can be abandoned or tempered with greater ease and grace than one that is broadly gauged and expansive." William T. Allen, Jack B. Jacobs & Leo E. Strine, Jr., *The Great Takeover Debate: A Meditation on Bridging the Conceptual Divide*, 69 U. Chi. L. Rev. 1067, 1069 (2002).

In *Unocal Corporation v. Mesa Petroleum Co.,* Mesa made a hostile takeover bid after which it would own 51% of Unocal stock. Unocal believed the offer was both coercive and inadequate. In response, Unocal offered to repurchase its own securities from its shareholders but excluded Mesa from the offer. In determining the validity of excluding Mesa, the court declined to use a business judgment rule standard of review. Rather, the court created an intermediate standard utilizing a proportionality test to determine whether the board had reasonable grounds for believing a threat to the corporation existed and whether the defensive measures taken were reasonable in relation to the perceived threat.

UNOCAL CORPORATION V. MESA PETROLEUM CO.

493 A.2d 946 (Del. 1985).

MOORE, JUSTICE:

We confront an issue of first impression in Delaware—the validity of a corporation's self-tender for its own shares which excludes from participation a stockholder making a hostile tender offer for the company's stock.

The Court of Chancery granted a preliminary injunction to the plaintiffs, Mesa Petroleum Co., Mesa Asset Co., Mesa Partners II, and Mesa Eastern, Inc. (collectively "Mesa")[1] enjoining an exchange offer of the defendant, Unocal Corporation for its own stock. The trial court concluded that a selective exchange offer, excluding Mesa, was legally impermissible. We cannot agree with such a blanket rule. The factual findings of the Vice Chancellor, fully supported by the record, establish that Unocal's board, consisting of a majority of independent directors, acted in good faith, and after reasonable investigation found that Mesa's tender offer was both inadequate and coercive. Under the circumstances the board had both the

---

[1]   T. Boone Pickens, Jr., is President and Chairman of the Board of Mesa Petroleum and President of Mesa Asset and controls the related Mesa entities.

Known corporate raider / Takeover operator

power and duty to oppose a bid it perceived to be harmful to the corporate enterprise. On this record we are satisfied that the device Unocal adopted is reasonable in relation to the threat posed, and that the board acted in the proper exercise of sound business judgment. We will not substitute our views for those of the board if the latter's decision can be "attributed to any rational business purpose." Accordingly, we reverse the decision of the Court of Chancery and order the preliminary injunction vacated.

The factual background of this matter bears a significant relationship to its ultimate outcome.

On April 8, 1985, Mesa, the owner of approximately 13% of Unocal's stock, commenced a two-tier "front loaded" cash tender offer for 64 million shares, or approximately 37%, of Unocal's outstanding stock at a price of $54 per share. The "back-end" was designed to eliminate the remaining publicly held shares by an exchange of securities purportedly worth $54 per share. However, pursuant to an order entered by the United States District Court for the Central District of California on April 26, 1985, Mesa issued a supplemental proxy statement to Unocal's stockholders disclosing that the securities offered in the second-step merger would be highly subordinated, and that Unocal's capitalization would differ significantly from its present structure. Unocal has rather aptly termed such securities "junk bonds."

Unocal's board consists of eight independent, outside directors and six insiders. It met on April 13, 1985, to consider the Mesa tender offer. Thirteen directors were present, and the meeting lasted nine and one-half hours. The directors were given no agenda or written materials prior to the session. However, detailed presentations were made by legal counsel regarding the board's obligations under both Delaware corporate law and the federal securities laws. The board then received a presentation from Peter Sachs on behalf of Goldman Sachs & Co. and Dillon, Read & Co. discussing the bases for their opinions that the Mesa proposal was wholly inadequate. Mr. Sachs opined that the minimum cash value that could be expected from a sale or orderly liquidation for 100% of Unocal's stock was in excess of $60 per share. In making his presentation, Mr. Sachs showed slides outlining the valuation techniques used by the financial advisors, and others, depicting recent business combinations in the oil and gas industry. The Court of Chancery found that the Sachs presentation was designed to apprise the directors of the scope of the analyses performed rather than the facts and numbers used in reaching the conclusion that Mesa's tender offer price was inadequate.

Mr. Sachs also presented various defensive strategies available to the board if it concluded that Mesa's two-step tender offer was inadequate and should be opposed. One of the devices outlined was a self-tender by Unocal for its own stock with a reasonable price range of $70 to $75 per share. The cost of such a proposal would cause the company to incur $6.1–6.5 billion of additional debt, and a presentation was made informing the board of Unocal's ability to handle it. The directors were told that the primary effect of this obligation would be to reduce exploratory drilling, but that the company would nonetheless remain a viable entity.

The eight outside directors, comprising a clear majority of the thirteen members present, then met separately with Unocal's financial advisors and attorneys. Thereafter, they unanimously agreed to advise the board that it should reject Mesa's tender offer as inadequate, and that Unocal should pursue a self-tender to provide the stockholders with a fairly priced alternative to the Mesa proposal. The board then reconvened and unanimously adopted a resolution rejecting as grossly inadequate Mesa's tender offer. Despite the nine and one-half hour length of the meeting, no formal decision was made on the proposed defensive self-tender.

On April 15, the board met again with one member still absent. This session lasted two hours. Unocal's Vice President of Finance and its Assistant General Counsel made a detailed presentation of the proposed terms of the exchange offer. A price range between $70 and $80 per share was considered, and ultimately the directors agreed upon $72. The board was also advised about the debt securities that would be issued, and the necessity of placing restrictive covenants upon certain corporate activities until the obligations were paid. The board's decisions were made in reliance on the advice of its investment bankers, including the terms and conditions upon which the securities were to be issued. Based upon this advice, and the board's own deliberations, the directors unanimously approved the exchange offer. Their resolution provided that if Mesa acquired 64 million shares of Unocal stock through its own offer (the Mesa Purchase Condition), Unocal would buy the remaining 49% outstanding for an exchange of debt securities having an aggregate par value of $72 per share. The board resolution also stated that the offer would be subject to other conditions that had been described to the board at the meeting, or which were deemed necessary by Unocal's officers, including the exclusion of Mesa from the proposal (the Mesa exclusion). Any such conditions were required to be in accordance with the "purport and intent" of the offer.

Unocal's exchange offer was commenced on April 17, 1985, and Mesa promptly challenged it by filing this suit in the Court of Chancery. On April 22, the Unocal board met again and was advised by Goldman Sachs and Dillon Read to waive the Mesa Purchase Condition as to 50 million shares. This recommendation was in response to a perceived concern of the shareholders that, if shares were tendered to Unocal, no shares would be purchased by either offeror. The directors were also advised that they should tender their own Unocal stock into the exchange offer as a mark of their confidence in it.

Another focus of the board was the Mesa exclusion. Legal counsel advised that under Delaware law Mesa could only be excluded for what the directors reasonably believed to be a valid corporate purpose. The directors' discussion centered on the objective of adequately compensating shareholders at the "back-end" of Mesa's proposal, which the latter would finance with "junk bonds". To include Mesa would defeat that goal, because under the proration aspect of the exchange offer (49%) every Mesa share accepted by Unocal would displace one held by another stockholder. Further, if Mesa were permitted to tender to Unocal, the latter would in effect be financing Mesa's own inadequate proposal.

On April 29, 1985, the Vice Chancellor temporarily restrained Unocal from proceeding with the exchange offer unless it included Mesa. The trial court recognized that directors could oppose, and attempt to defeat, a hostile takeover which they considered adverse to the best interests of the corporation. However, the Vice Chancellor decided that in a selective purchase of the company's stock, the corporation bears the burden of showing: (1) a valid corporate purpose, and (2) that the transaction was fair to all of the stockholders, including those excluded.

The issues we address involve these fundamental questions: Did the Unocal board have the power and duty to oppose a takeover threat it reasonably perceived to be harmful to the corporate enterprise, and if so, is its action here entitled to the protection of the business judgment rule?

Mesa contends that the discriminatory exchange offer violates the fiduciary duties Unocal owes it. Mesa argues that because of the Mesa exclusion the business judgment rule is inapplicable, because the directors by tendering their own shares will derive a financial benefit that is not available to all Unocal stockholders. Thus, it is Mesa's ultimate contention that Unocal cannot establish that the exchange offer is fair to all shareholders, and argues that the Court of Chancery was correct in concluding that Unocal was unable to meet this burden.

Unocal answers that it does not owe a duty of "fairness" to Mesa, given the facts here. Specifically, Unocal contends that its board of directors reasonably and in good faith concluded that Mesa's $54 two-tier tender offer was coercive and inadequate, and that Mesa sought selective treatment for itself. Furthermore, Unocal argues that the board's approval of the exchange offer was made in good faith, on an informed basis, and in the exercise of due care. Under these circumstances, Unocal contends that its directors properly employed this device to protect the company and its stockholders from Mesa's harmful tactics.

We begin with the basic issue of the power of a board of directors of a Delaware corporation to adopt a defensive measure of this type. Absent such authority, all other questions are moot. Neither issues of fairness nor business judgment are pertinent without the basic underpinning of a board's legal power to act.

The board has a large reservoir of authority upon which to draw. Its duties and responsibilities proceed from the inherent powers conferred by 8 Del.C. § 141(a), respecting management of the corporation's "business and affairs." Additionally, the powers here being exercised derive from 8 Del.C. § 160(a), conferring broad authority upon a corporation to deal in its own stock. From this it is now well established that in the acquisition of its shares a Delaware corporation may deal selectively with its stockholders, provided the directors have not acted out of a sole or primary purpose to entrench themselves in office.

Finally, the board's power to act derives from its fundamental duty and obligation to protect the corporate enterprise, which includes stockholders, from harm reasonably perceived, irrespective of its source. Thus, we are satisfied that in the broad context of corporate governance, including issues of fundamental corporate change, a board of directors is not a passive instrumentality.

Given the foregoing principles, we turn to the standards by which director action is to be measured. In *Pogostin v. Rice*, Del.Supr., 480 A.2d 619 (1984), we held that the business judgment rule, including the standards by which director conduct is judged, is applicable in the context of a takeover.

When a board addresses a pending takeover bid it has an obligation to determine whether the offer is in the best interests of the corporation and its shareholders. In that respect a board's duty is no different from any other responsibility it shoulders, and its decisions should be no less entitled to the respect they otherwise would be accorded in the realm of business judgment. There are, however, certain caveats to a proper exercise of this function. Because of the omnipresent specter that a board may be acting primarily in its own interests, rather than those of the corporation and its shareholders, there is an enhanced duty which calls for judicial examination at the threshold before the protections of the business judgment rule may be conferred.

This Court has long recognized that:

> We must bear in mind the inherent danger in the purchase of shares with corporate funds to remove a threat to corporate policy when a threat to control is involved. The directors are of necessity confronted with a conflict of interest, and an objective decision is difficult.

Bennett v. Propp, Del.Supr., 187 A.2d 405, 409 (1962). In the face of this inherent conflict, directors must show that they had reasonable grounds for believing that a danger to corporate policy and effectiveness existed because of another person's stock ownership. *Cheff v. Mathes*, 199 A.2d at 554–55. However, they satisfy that burden "by showing good faith and reasonable investigation." Furthermore, such proof is materially enhanced, as here, by the approval of a board comprised of a majority of outside, independent directors who have acted in accordance with the foregoing standards.

In the board's exercise of corporate power to forestall a takeover bid, our analysis begins with the basic principle that corporate directors have a fiduciary duty to act in the best interests of the corporation's stockholders. As we have noted, their duty of care extends to protecting the corporation and its owners from perceived harm whether a threat originates from third parties or other shareholders. But such powers are not absolute. A corporation does not have unbridled discretion to defeat any perceived threat by any Draconian means available.

The restriction placed upon a selective stock repurchase is that the directors may not have acted solely or primarily out of a desire to perpetuate themselves in office. Of course, to this is added the further caveat that inequitable action may not be taken under the guise of law. The standard of proof established in *Cheff v. Mathes* is designed to ensure that a defensive measure to thwart or impede a takeover is indeed motivated by a good faith concern for the welfare of the corporation and its stockholders, which in all circumstances must be free of any fraud or other misconduct. However, this does not end the inquiry.

A further aspect is the element of balance. If a defensive measure is to come within the ambit of the business judgment rule, it must be reasonable in relation to the threat posed. This entails an analysis by the directors of the nature of the takeover bid and its effect on the corporate enterprise. Examples of such concerns may include: inadequacy of the price offered, nature and timing of the offer, questions of illegality, the impact on "constituencies" other than shareholders (*i.e.*, creditors, customers, employees, and perhaps even the community generally), the risk of non-consummation, and the quality of securities being offered in the exchange. While not a controlling factor, it also seems to us that a board may reasonably consider the basic stockholder interests at stake, including those of short-term speculators, whose actions may have fueled the coercive aspect of the offer at the expense of the long-term investor. Here, the threat posed was viewed by the Unocal board as a grossly inadequate two-tier coercive tender offer coupled with the threat of greenmail.

Specifically, the Unocal directors had concluded that the value of Unocal was substantially above the $54 per share offered in cash at the front end. Furthermore, they determined that the subordinated securities to be exchanged in Mesa's announced squeeze-out of the remaining shareholders in the "back-end" merger were "junk bonds" worth far less than $54. It is now well recognized that such offers are a classic coercive measure designed to stampede shareholders into tendering at the first tier, even if the price is inadequate, out of fear of what they will receive at the back end of the transaction. Wholly beyond the coercive aspect of an inadequate two-tier tender offer, the threat was posed by a corporate raider with a national reputation as a "greenmailer."[13]

In adopting the selective exchange offer, the board stated that its objective was either to defeat the inadequate Mesa offer or, should the offer still succeed, provide the 49% of its stockholders, who would otherwise be forced to accept "junk bonds," with $72 worth of senior debt. We find that both purposes are valid.

However, such efforts would have been thwarted by Mesa's participation in the exchange offer. First, if Mesa could tender its shares, Unocal would effectively be subsidizing Mesa's continuing effort to buy Unocal stock at $54 per share. Second, Mesa could not, by definition, fit within the class of shareholders being protected from its own coercive and inadequate tender offer.

Thus, we are satisfied that the selective exchange offer is reasonably related to the threats posed. The board's decision to offer what it determined to be the fair value of the corporation to the 49% of its shareholders, who would otherwise be forced to accept highly subordinated "junk bonds," is reasonable and consistent with the directors' duty to ensure that the minority stockholders receive equal value for their shares.

Mesa contends that it is unlawful, and the trial court agreed, for a corporation to discriminate in this fashion against one shareholder. It argues correctly that no case has ever sanctioned a device that precludes a raider from sharing in a benefit available to all other stockholders. However, as we have noted earlier, the principle of selective stock repurchases by a Delaware corporation is neither unknown nor unauthorized. The only difference is that heretofore the approved transaction was the payment of "greenmail" to a raider or dissident posing a threat to the corporate enterprise. All other stockholders were denied such favored treatment, and given Mesa's past history of greenmail, its claims here are rather ironic.

Thus, while the exchange offer is a form of selective treatment, given the nature of the threat posed here the response is neither unlawful nor unreasonable. If the board of directors is disinterested, has acted in good faith and with due care, its decision in the absence of an abuse of discretion will be upheld as a proper exercise of business judgment.

To this Mesa responds that the board is not disinterested, because the directors are receiving a benefit from the tender of their own shares, which because of the Mesa exclusion, does not devolve upon all stockholders equally. However, Mesa concedes that if the exclusion is valid, then the

---

[13] The Chancery Court noted that "Mesa has made tremendous profits from its takeover activities although in the past few years it has not been successful in acquiring any of the target companies on an unfriendly basis." Moreover, the trial court specifically found that the actions of the Unocal board were taken in good faith to eliminate both the inadequacies of the tender offer and to forestall the payment of "greenmail."

directors and all other stockholders share the same benefit. The answer of course is that the exclusion is valid, and the directors' participation in the exchange offer does not rise to the level of a disqualifying interest.

In conclusion, there was directorial power to oppose the Mesa tender offer, and to undertake a selective stock exchange made in good faith and upon a reasonable investigation pursuant to a clear duty to protect the corporate enterprise. Further, the selective stock repurchase plan chosen by Unocal is reasonable in relation to the threat that the board rationally and reasonably believed was posed by Mesa's inadequate and coercive two-tier tender offer. Under those circumstances the board's action is entitled to be measured by the standards of the business judgment rule. Thus, unless it is shown by a preponderance of the evidence that the directors' decisions were primarily based on perpetuating themselves in office, or some other breach of fiduciary duty such as fraud, overreaching, lack of good faith, or being uninformed, a Court will not substitute its judgment for that of the board.

With the Court of Chancery's findings that the exchange offer was based on the board's good faith belief that the Mesa offer was inadequate, that the board's action was informed and taken with due care, that Mesa's prior activities justify a reasonable inference that its principle objective was greenmail, and implicitly, that the substance of the offer itself was reasonable and fair to the corporation and its stockholders if Mesa were included, we cannot say that the Unocal directors have acted in such a manner as to have passed an "unintelligent and unadvised judgment". The decision of the Court of Chancery is therefore REVERSED, and the preliminary injunction is VACATED.

NOTES AND QUESTIONS

In reading *Unocal*, it is important to understand the economics of the transaction and the way in which the Williams Act requirements affected Unocal's actions.

1.   Why was it necessary for Unocal to exclude Mesa from its exchange offer?

    a.   The court says that "under the proration aspect of the exchange offer, every Mesa share accepted by Unocal would displace one held by another stockholder." Under SEC Rule 14d–8, how does proration work?

    b.   The court also says that "if Mesa were permitted to tender to Unocal, the latter would in effect be financing Mesa's own inadequate proposal." What does the court mean?

2.   Why did Unocal waive the Mesa Purchase Condition?

3.   The court says that in evaluating a threat, a target board may consider "the impact on "constituencies" other than shareholders (*i.e.*, creditors, customers, employees, and perhaps even the community generally)." Does this language expand the board's ability to resist an unwanted offer? If not, what limits are there on this concept?

4.   Note the importance of *Cheff*, which the court cites throughout the opinion (although we have removed some of the citations in the edited version). At a critical point in the opinion, the court states that "as we have noted earlier, the principle of selective stock repurchases by a Delaware corporation is neither unknown nor unauthorized." How persuasive is the court's reliance on *Cheff*?

Unocal marks the beginning of Delaware's contemporary approach to regulating transactions involving a change of control. In *Unocal*, the Delaware Supreme Court abjured the fairness test that earlier decisions suggested would invalidate any board decision that discriminated between existing shareholders. After *Unocal*, target company's directors must satisfy a two-pronged test. Directors must show that: (1) they had reasonable grounds to believe that a danger to corporate policy and effectiveness existed; and (2) the defensive measure adopted was proportionate to the threat posed.

Moran v. Household International, Inc., 500 A.2d 1346 (Del. 1985), held that DGCL § 157, which authorizes a board to distribute rights to purchase a corporation's stock, gives the board of a Delaware corporation authority to adopt a shareholder rights plan—a "poison pill"—without the shareholders' approval. Relying on *Unocal*, the court also found that it was reasonable for Household's board to adopt a pill, given its conclusion that Household was likely to become the target of an uninvited takeover bid. However, the court emphasized that it would review under *Unocal's* proportionality test a decision by Household's board not to redeem the pill were such a bid be made. The court did not address what kinds of actions, other than a coercive tender offer, would justify a board's refusal to redeem a poison pill.

Despite this uncertainty, poison pills proliferated after *Moran*, largely because a poison pill often constitutes the most powerful takeover defense a board can adopt without the shareholders' approval. Poison pills therefore became many companies' first line of defense against hostile bids, and many takeover cases decided after *Moran*—although relatively few Delaware Supreme Court decisions—focus on when a target's directors are obliged to redeem a poison pill and, in particular, whether and when a target's directors can rely on a pill to "just say no" to a bidder who offers to purchase all of a company's stock for cash in an amount most shareholders are prepared to accept.

F. STATUTORY LIMITATIONS

In addition to the limits on takeover defenses arising out of directors' fiduciary duties, the courts have also found some defenses to violate Delaware statutory law. This has been particularly true with respect to certain provisions of poison pills.

For example, to neutralize pills the acquirors often wage proxy contests to remove the incumbent directors and replace them with nominees of the acquiror who can then be expected to vote to redeem the pill. To counter that tactic, during the late 1990s some companies adopted pills that incorporated a so-called "dead-hand provision," pursuant to which the pill could only be redeemed by vote of the directors in office at the time the pill was adopted. In *Carmody v. Toll Brothers, Inc.*, 723 A.2d 1180 (Del.Ch. 1998), the Delaware Chancery Court ruled that such a pill violated DGCL § 141. First, the court pointed out that, although § 141(d) permits creating distinctions among the voting rights of different classes of directors, it requires that the distinction be established in the certificate of incorporation, not in a shareholder rights plan created by the board. Second, "§ 141(d) mandates that the 'right to elect 1 or more directors who shall . . . have such [greater] voting powers' is reserved to the stockholders, not to the directors or a subset thereof. Third, the "dead hand" provision interferes with the directors' statutory power to manage the business and affairs of the corporation pursuant to DGCL § 141(a), which provides: "The business and affairs of every corporation organized under this chapter shall be managed by or under the direction of a board of directors, except as may be otherwise provided in this chapter or in its certificate of incorporation."

Citing *Blasius Industries, Inc. v. Atlas Corp.*, 564 A.2d 651 (Del.Ch. 1988) (discussed below) the Vice Chancellor held that the adoption of the dead-hand provision also violated the board's fiduciary duty of loyalty in that it "purposefully interferes with the shareholder voting franchise without any compelling justification" and "is a 'disproportionate' defensive measure, because it either precludes or materially abridges the shareholders' rights to receive tender offers and to wage a proxy contest to replace the board."

In *Quickturn Design Systems, Inc. v. Shapiro*, 721 A.2d 1281 (Del. 1998), the Delaware Supreme Court considered the "delayed redemption" provision of a poison pill that prohibited its redemption by a new board of directors until six months after it had taken office. Following the same reasoning as *Carmody,* it struck down this provision on the grounds that it improperly "restricts the board's power in an area of fundamental importance to the shareholders—negotiating a possible sale of the corporation."

Carmody and *Quickturn* do not hold that *all* restrictions on a board's discretion violate DGCL § 141, only that to be valid such restrictions must be included in the certificate of incorporation. They leave open the question of how much of an intrusion into corporate governance can be tolerated in a shareholder-initiated bylaw. The issue that has generated the most controversy is a bylaw that injects shareholders into the adoption or repeal of a poison pill. In *International Brotherhood of Teamsters General Fund v. Fleming Cos.*, 975 P.2d 907 (Okla. 1999), the Oklahoma Supreme Court upheld a shareholder bylaw dealing with poison pills.

There has been much debate about whether Delaware courts would follow *Fleming*. If a bylaw can be drafted to emphasize process while leaving the target corporation's board of directors some discretion to exercise its fiduciary duties, it is not clear that such a bylaw would be invalid. Or can these decisions be understood as merely stating that "the board's authority to manage the business and affairs of a corporation is inherently limited by the power of the stockholders to exercise decision-making authority for the voting and sale decisions assigned to them." Robert B. Thompson & D. Gordon Smith, *Toward a New Theory of the Shareholder Role: "Sacred Space" in Corporate Takeovers*, 80 Tex. L. Rev. 261, 311 (2001). Does the Delaware Supreme Court's 2008 opinion in *CA, Inc. v. AFSCME Employees Pension Plan*, which we reviewed in Chapter 14, shed any light on this question?

G. WHEN THE CORPORATION IS "FOR SALE"

1. *REVLON*—WHEN MUST THE BOARD SEEK TO MAXIMIZE PRESENT SHAREHOLDER VALUE?

In the events leading up to *Revlon, Inc. v. MacAndrews & Forbes Holdings, Inc.*, Ronald Perelman, a successful American businessman who was chairman of the board and CEO of Pantry Pride, met with Michel Bergerac, a Frenchman who was chairman of the board and CEO of Revlon, to discuss Pantry Pride's possible friendly acquisition of Revlon. The meeting went badly, with Bergerac dismissing Perelman's offer of $40 to $50 a share as considerably below Revlon's intrinsic value. Perhaps in part because of Bergerac's strong personal antipathy for Perelman, Revlon rebuffed all of Pantry Pride's subsequent attempts to discuss a possible acquisition.

Faced with the possibility of a hostile takeover bid by Pantry Pride, the Revlon board took several defensive measures, including adopting a poison pill and entering merger negotiations with a white knight, Forstmann Little & Co. The merger negotiations eventually led to a bidding war between Pantry Pride and Forstmann to acquire Revlon.

The *Revlon* court considered whether the directors have unlimited powers to defend the corporation from a threat to its policy and effectiveness or whether, at a certain point, their obligations to the corporation and the shareholders changed. As you read *Revlon*, consider at what point the board's duty changes from preserving the corporation to maximizing the corporation's value for the benefit of the shareholders, and whether the board would have recognized that such a change had occurred.

REVLON, INC. V. MACANDREWS & FORBES HOLDINGS, INC.
506 A.2d 173 (Del. 1986).

[In August 1985, after the meeting between CEOs Ronald Perelman of Pantry Pride and Michel Bergerac of Revlon, in which Bergerac rejected Perelman's offer to acquire Revlon at $40 to $50 per share, Perelman made another attempt. This time, Pantry Pride offered to acquire Revlon in a negotiated transaction at $42 to $43 per share or in a hostile tender offer at $45. Again, Bergerac rejected any possible Pantry Pride acquisition.

Revlon had a 14-member board of directors. Six directors held senior management positions and two others owned significant blocks of Revlon stock. Four of the remaining six directors had been associated with entities that had business relationships with Revlon. The Revlon board met with counsel and investment banker Lazard Freres to consider the impending hostile takeover bid. The board voted to repurchase up to 5 million shares of its common stock and to adopt a Note Purchase Rights plan. The plan permitted the rights holders to exchange their stock for a $65 one-year note unless someone acquired all the Revlon stock at $65 per share.

On August 23, Pantry Pride made an all-cash, all-shares tender offer at $47.50 per share, subject to obtaining financing and to the redemption of the rights. The Revlon board rejected the offer, then made its own offer to the Revlon shareholders to exchange notes for 10 million shares of common stock. The notes contained various covenants, the most important of which was a covenant against incurring future debt. Ultimately, Revlon accepted the full 10 million shares in the exchange offer.

On September 16, Pantry Pride announced a revised offer at $42 per share, conditioned on receiving 90% of the stock (or less, if Revlon removed the rights). Because of the exchange offer, the revised offer was the economic equivalent of Pantry Pride's earlier higher bid. Again the Revlon board rejected the offer. Pantry Pride increased its bid to $50 per share, then again to $53.

Meanwhile, the Revlon board agreed to a leveraged buyout in the form of a merger with Forstmann Little in which the Revlon shareholders would receive $56 per share, Forstmann would assume the debt incurred in the exchange offer, and Revlon would redeem the rights and waive the note covenants for Forstmann or any offer superior to Forstmann's. Immediately after the merger was announced, the market price of the notes fell substantially.

On October 7, Pantry Pride increased its bid to $56.25, subject to cancellation of the rights and the waiver of the note covenants. Two days later, it declared its intention to top any competing bid.

In response, Forstmann offered $57.25 per share and agreed to support the market price of the notes after the covenants were removed. The offer also required Revlon to grant Forstmann a lock-up option on two of its divisions at a price well below Lazard Freres' valuation if anyone else acquired 40% of the Revlon stock. Finally, Revlon was to pay a $25 million cancellation fee if the merger agreement was terminated or anyone else acquired more than 19.9% of Revlon's stock. The Revlon board accepted the offer because the price exceeded Pantry Pride's bid, the noteholders were protected against a decline in value of their notes, and Forstmann's financing was secure.

Pantry Pride promptly sued to invalidate the agreement and, on October 22, raised its bid to $58, conditioned upon the nullification of the rights, the waiver of the note covenants, and the granting of an injunction against the lock-up.]

MOORE, JUSTICE:

In this battle for corporate control of Revlon, Inc., the Court of Chancery enjoined certain transactions designed to thwart the efforts of Pantry Pride, Inc., to acquire Revlon.[1] The defendants are Revlon, its board of directors, and Forstmann Little & Co. and the latter's affiliated limited partnership (collectively, Forstmann). The injunction barred consummation of an option granted Forstmann to purchase certain Revlon assets (the lock-up option), a promise by Revlon to deal exclusively with Forstmann in the face of a takeover (the no-shop provision), and the payment of a $25 million cancellation fee to Forstmann if the transaction was aborted. The Court of Chancery found that the Revlon directors had breached their duty of care by entering into the foregoing transactions and effectively ending an active auction for the company. The trial court ruled that such arrangements are not illegal per se under Delaware law, but that their use under the circumstances here was impermissible. We agree.

If the business judgment rule applies, there is a "presumption that in making a business decision the directors of a corporation acted on an informed basis, in good faith and in the honest belief that the action taken was in the best interests of the company." However, when a board implements anti-takeover measures there arises "the omnipresent specter that a board may be acting primarily in its own interests, rather than those of the corporation and its shareholders." This potential for conflict places upon the directors the burden of proving that they had reasonable grounds for believing there was a danger to corporate policy and effectiveness, a

---

[1]   The nominal plaintiff, MacAndrews & Forbes Holdings, Inc., is the controlling stockholder of Pantry Pride. For all practical purposes their interests in this litigation are virtually identical, and we hereafter will refer to Pantry Pride as the plaintiff.

burden satisfied by a showing of good faith and reasonable investigation. In addition, the directors must analyze the nature of the takeover and its effect on the corporation in order to ensure balance—that the responsive action taken is reasonable in relation to the threat posed.

The first relevant defensive measure adopted by the Revlon board was the Rights Plan, which would be considered a "poison pill" in the current language of corporate takeovers—a plan by which shareholders receive the right to be bought out by the corporation at a substantial premium on the occurrence of a stated triggering event. By 8 *Del.C.* §§ 141 and 122(13), the board clearly had the power to adopt the measure. Thus, the focus becomes one of reasonableness and purpose.

The Revlon board approved the Rights Plan in the face of an impending hostile takeover bid by Pantry Pride at $45 per share, a price which Revlon reasonably concluded was grossly inadequate. Lazard Freres had so advised the directors, and had also informed them that Pantry Pride was a small, highly leveraged company bent on a "bust-up" takeover by using "junk bond" financing to buy Revlon cheaply, sell the acquired assets to pay the debts incurred, and retain the profit for itself.[12] In adopting the Plan, the board protected the shareholders from a hostile takeover at a price below the company's intrinsic value, while retaining sufficient flexibility to address any proposal deemed to be in the stockholders' best interests.

To that extent the board acted in good faith and upon reasonable investigation. Under the circumstances it cannot be said that the Rights Plan as employed was unreasonable, considering the threat posed. Indeed, the Plan was a factor in causing Pantry Pride to raise its bids from a low of $42 to an eventual high of $58. At the time of its adoption, the Rights Plan afforded a measure of protection consistent with the directors' fiduciary duty in facing a takeover threat perceived as detrimental to corporate interests. Far from being a "show-stopper," as the plaintiffs had contended in *Moran*, the measure spurred the bidding to new heights, a proper result of its implementation.

Although we consider adoption of the Plan to have been valid under the circumstances, its continued usefulness was rendered moot by the directors' actions on October 3 and October 12. At the October 3 meeting the board redeemed the Rights conditioned upon consummation of a merger with Forstmann, but further acknowledged that they would also be redeemed to facilitate any more favorable offer. On October 12, the board unanimously passed a resolution redeeming the Rights in connection with any cash proposal of $57.25 or more per share. Because all the pertinent offers eventually equaled or surpassed that amount, the Rights clearly

---

[12] A "bust-up" takeover generally refers to a situation in which one seeks to finance an acquisition by selling off pieces of the acquired company, presumably at a substantial profit.

were no longer any impediment in the contest for Revlon. This mooted any question of their propriety under *Moran* or *Unocal*.

The second defensive measure adopted by Revlon to thwart a Pantry Pride takeover was the company's own exchange offer for 10 million of its shares. The directors' general broad powers to manage the business and affairs of the corporation are augmented by the specific authority conferred under 8 *Del.C.* § 160(a), permitting the company to deal in its own stock. However, when exercising that power in an effort to forestall a hostile takeover, the board's actions are strictly held to the fiduciary standards outlined in *Unocal*. These standards require the directors to determine the best interests of the corporation and its stockholders, and impose an enhanced duty to abjure any action that is motivated by considerations other than a good faith concern for such interests.

The Revlon directors concluded that Pantry Pride's $47.50 offer was grossly inadequate. In that regard the board acted in good faith, and on an informed basis, with reasonable grounds to believe that there existed a harmful threat to the corporate enterprise. The adoption of a defensive measure, reasonable in relation to the threat posed, was proper and fully accorded with the powers, duties, and responsibilities conferred upon directors under our law.

However, when Pantry Pride increased its offer to $50 per share, and then to $53, it became apparent to all that the break-up of the company was inevitable. The Revlon board's authorization permitting management to negotiate a merger or buyout with a third party was a recognition that the company was for sale. The duty of the board had thus changed from the preservation of Revlon as a corporate entity to the maximization of the company's value at a sale for the stockholders' benefit. This significantly altered the board's responsibilities under the *Unocal* standards. It no longer faced threats to corporate policy and effectiveness, or to the stockholders' interests, from a grossly inadequate bid. The whole question of defensive measures became moot. The directors' role changed from defenders of the corporate bastion to auctioneers charged with getting the best price for the stockholders at a sale of the company.

This brings us to the lock-up with Forstmann and its emphasis on shoring up the sagging market value of the Notes in the face of threatened litigation by their holders. Such a focus was inconsistent with the changed concept of the directors' responsibilities at this stage of the developments. The impending waiver of the Notes covenants had caused the value of the Notes to fall, and the board was aware of the noteholders' ire as well as their subsequent threats of suit. The directors thus made support of the Notes an integral part of the company's dealings with Forstmann, even though their primary responsibility at this stage was to the equity owners.

The original threat posed by Pantry Pride—the break-up of the company—had become a reality which even the directors embraced.

Selective dealing to fend off a hostile-but-determined bidder was no longer a proper objective. Instead, obtaining the highest price for the benefit of the stockholders should have been the central theme guiding director action. Thus, the Revlon board could not make the requisite showing of good faith by preferring the noteholders and ignoring its duty of loyalty to the shareholders. The rights of the former already were fixed by contract. The noteholders required no further protection, and when the Revlon board entered into an auction-ending lock-up agreement with Forstmann on the basis of impermissible considerations at the expense of the shareholders, the directors breached their primary duty of loyalty.

The Revlon board argued that it acted in good faith in protecting the noteholders because Unocal permits consideration of other corporate constituencies. Although such considerations may be permissible, there are fundamental limitations upon that prerogative. A board may have regard for various constituencies in discharging its responsibilities, provided there are rationally related benefits accruing to the stockholders. However, such concern for non-stockholder interests is inappropriate when an auction among active bidders is in progress, and the object no longer is to protect or maintain the corporate enterprise but to sell it to the highest bidder.

Revlon also contended that it had contractual and good faith obligations to consider the noteholders. However, any such duties are limited to the principle that one may not interfere with contractual relationships by improper actions. Here, the rights of the noteholders were fixed by agreement, and there is nothing of substance to suggest that any of those terms were violated. The Notes covenants specifically contemplated a waiver to permit sale of the company at a fair price. The Notes were accepted by the holders on that basis, including the risk of an adverse market effect stemming from a waiver. Thus, nothing remained for Revlon to legitimately protect, and no rationally related benefit thereby accrued to the stockholders. Under such circumstances we must conclude that the merger agreement with Forstmann was unreasonable in relation to the threat posed.

A lock-up is not per se illegal under Delaware law. Its use has been approved in an earlier case. Such options can entice other bidders to enter a contest for control of the corporation, creating an auction for the company and maximizing shareholder profit. Current economic conditions in the takeover market are such that a "white knight" like Forstmann might only enter the bidding for the target company if it receives some form of compensation to cover the risks and costs involved. However, while those lock-ups which draw bidders into the battle benefit shareholders, similar measures which end an active auction and foreclose further bidding operate to the shareholders' detriment.

The Forstmann option had a . . . destructive effect on the auction process. Forstmann had already been drawn into the contest on a preferred basis, so the result of the lock-up was not to foster bidding, but to destroy it. The board's stated reasons for approving the transactions were: (1) better financing, (2) noteholder protection, and (3) higher price. As the Court of Chancery found, and we agree, any distinctions between the rival bidders' methods of financing the proposal were nominal at best, and such a consideration has little or no significance in a cash offer for any and all shares. The principal object, contrary to the board's duty of care, appears to have been protection of the noteholders over the shareholders' interests.

While Forstmann's $57.25 offer was objectively higher than Pantry Pride's $56.25 bid, the margin of superiority is less when the Forstmann price is adjusted for the time value of money. In reality, the Revlon board ended the auction in return for very little actual improvement in the final bid. The principal benefit went to the directors, who avoided personal liability to a class of creditors to whom the board owed no further duty under the circumstances. Thus, when a board ends an intense bidding contest on an insubstantial basis, and where a significant by-product of that action is to protect the directors against a perceived threat of personal liability for consequences stemming from the adoption of previous defensive measures, the action cannot withstand the enhanced scrutiny which *Unocal* requires of director conduct.

In addition to the lock-up option, the Court of Chancery enjoined the no-shop provision as part of the attempt to foreclose further bidding by Pantry Pride. The no-shop provision, like the lock-up option, while not per se illegal, is impermissible under the *Unocal* standards when a board's primary duty becomes that of an auctioneer responsible for selling the company to the highest bidder. The agreement to negotiate only with Forstmann ended rather than intensified the board's involvement in the bidding contest.

It is ironic that the parties even considered a no-shop agreement when Revlon had dealt preferentially, and almost exclusively, with Forstmann throughout the contest. After the directors authorized management to negotiate with other parties, Forstmann was given every negotiating advantage that Pantry Pride had been denied: cooperation from management, access to financial data, and the exclusive opportunity to present merger proposals directly to the board of directors. Favoritism for a white knight to the total exclusion of a hostile bidder might be justifiable when the latter's offer adversely affects shareholder interests, but when bidders make relatively similar offers, or dissolution of the company becomes inevitable, the directors cannot fulfill their enhanced Unocal duties by playing favorites with the contending factions. Market forces must be allowed to operate freely to bring the target's shareholders the best price available for their equity. Thus, as the trial court ruled, the shareholders' interests necessitated that the board remain free to negotiate in the fulfillment of that duty.

In conclusion, the Revlon board was confronted with a situation not uncommon in the current wave of corporate takeovers. A hostile and determined bidder sought the company at a price the board was convinced was inadequate. The initial defensive tactics worked to the benefit of the shareholders, and thus the board was able to sustain its *Unocal* burdens in justifying those measures. However, in granting an asset option lock-up to Forstmann, we must conclude that under all the circumstances the directors allowed considerations other than the maximization of shareholder profit to affect their judgment, and followed a course that ended the auction for Revlon, absent court intervention, to the ultimate detriment of its shareholders. No such defensive measure can be sustained when it represents a breach of the directors' fundamental duty of care. In that context the board's action is not entitled to the deference accorded it by the business judgment rule. The measures were properly enjoined. The decision of the Court of Chancery, therefore, is AFFIRMED.

NOTE

1.   *Revlon* established that the board of a target company does not have unfettered discretion to counter a hostile bid. The court made it clear that, consistent with *Unocal*, a target company's board can use a poison pill and other takeover defenses to oppose a bid that it reasonably concludes is clearly inadequate but *cannot* employ a takeover defense directed at protecting the interests of a non-shareholder constituency unless that defense also provides some significant financial benefit to the target company's shareholders. Most importantly, *Revlon* established that once a company clearly is "for sale," the board's duty shifts from preserving the corporate entity to getting the best price available for its stockholders. Long-term considerations disappear; the short-term selling price becomes paramount.

What does it mean to say that a company is "for sale"? In *Revlon,* the moment arrived when "it became apparent to all that the break-up of the company was inevitable," and at that moment an auction was required. However, *Revlon* left unanswered the question of when, apart from seeking out a "white knight" prepared to pay cash for all its stock, a company will be deemed to be for sale so that "*Revlon* duties" will apply.

2.   *Lyondell Chemical Company v. Ryan*, 970 A.2d 235 (Del. 2009) suggests that the Delaware courts will give the directors wide latitude in determining when their duty shifts to obtaining the best price for the shareholders under *Revlon*. The trial court had ruled that the filing of a Schedule 13D by Basell AF, the offeror, had put the company "in play," and thus triggered the board's *Revlon* duties. It said the failure of the board to take any action during the next two months "raised the specter of 'bad faith' that precluded granting the defendants' motion for summary judgment. The Delaware Supreme Court reversed, saying:

> The problem with the trial court's analysis is that *Revlon* duties do not arise simply because a company is "in play." The duty to seek the

best available price applies only when a company embarks on a transaction—on its own initiative or in response to an unsolicited offer—that will result in a change of control. Basell's Schedule 13D did put the Lyondell directors, and the market in general, on notice that Basell was interested in acquiring Lyondell. The directors responded by promptly holding a special meeting to consider whether Lyondell should take any action. The directors decided that they would neither put the company up for sale nor institute defensive measures to fend off a possible hostile offer. Instead, they decided to take a "wait and see" approach. That decision was an entirely appropriate exercise of the directors' business judgment. The time for action under *Revlon* did not begin until July 10, 2007, when the directors began negotiating the sale of Lyondell.

The case indicates that the business judgment rule gives directors broad latitude in deciding how to respond to an unsolicited offer absent the use of defensive measures or an affirmative decision to initiate a sale of control. The court stated that "the relevant question is whether the Director Defendants 'utterly failed to attempt to obtain the best sale price' " rather than whether the process was perfect.

In *Gantler v. Stephens*, 965 A.2d 695 (Del. 2009), a case decided contemporaneously with *Lyondell*, the Delaware Supreme Court stated:

A board's decision not to pursue a merger opportunity is normally reviewed within the traditional business judgment framework. In that context, the board is entitled to a strong presumption in its favor, because implicit in the board's authority to propose a merger, is also the power to decline to do so.

2.   PARAMOUNT V. TIME—WHEN CAN THE BOARD "JUST SAY NO"?

In *Paramount Communications, Inc. v. Time, Inc.*, 571 A.2d 1140 (Del. 1989), the Delaware Supreme Court attempted to clarify when the board's *Revlon* duties are triggered so that it must auction the corporation to the highest bidder. A corporation is not automatically "for sale" every time a board enters negotiations with a third party about a possible acquisition. Although the board has an obligation to secure the highest possible price for the corporation's shareholders, the board does not necessarily have to auction the corporation to the highest bidder. In other words, there are situations in which a board can "just say no."

PARAMOUNT COMMUNICATIONS, INC. V. TIME, INC.
571 A.2d 1140 (Del. 1989).

[Some directors of Time, Inc., a Delaware corporation, wanted the corporation to expand into the entertainment industry. Time's traditional business was book and magazine publishing, and it owned cable television franchises and provided pay television programming through its Home Box Office and Cinemax subsidiaries. The plan to expand, however, was met with resistance by several of Time's outside directors who viewed such a move as a threat to "Time Culture." They feared that a merger with an entertainment company would divert Time's focus from news journalism and threaten Time's editorial integrity.

In June 1988, management distributed a comprehensive long-range plan that examined strategies for the 1990s. Warner Communications was named as a potential acquisition candidate. Time's chairman and CEO J. Richard Munro and president and COO N.J. Nicholas then met with each outside director to discuss long-term strategies, specifically a combination with Warner, whose business they felt complemented Time better than other potential merger candidates. After these discussions, Time's board approved, in principle, a strategic plan for expansion and authorized continued merger discussions with Warner.

Talks between Time and Warner began in August 1988. Although Time had preferred an acquisition involving all cash or cash and securities, it agreed to a stock-for-stock exchange so that Warner's stockholders could retain an equity interest in the new corporation. Time also insisted on having control of the board in order to preserve "a management committed to Time's journalistic integrity." Negotiations failed when the parties could not agree on who would be the top executives of the new corporation. Time pursued other merger alternatives.

In January 1989, Time resumed talks with Warner. Time's board ultimately approved a stock-for-stock merger with Warner on March 3, 1989. The merger would give the Warner shareholders 62% of the combined company. The new company would have a 24-member board, with Time and Warner each initially represented by 12 directors. The board would have entertainment and editorial committees controlled respectively by Warner and Time directors. The rules of the New York Stock Exchange (NYSE) required Time's shareholders to approve the merger. But, because the transaction was cast as a triangular merger, Delaware law did not.

At the March 3 meeting, Time's board adopted several defensive tactics. It agreed to an automatic share exchange with Warner that gave Warner the right to receive 11.1% of Time's outstanding common stock. Time also sought and paid for "confidence letters" from its banks in which the banks agreed to not finance a hostile acquisition of Time. Time agreed to a no-shop clause preventing it from considering any other consolidation proposal regardless of the merits. After the announcement of the transaction, Time publicized the lack of debt in the transaction as being one of its chief benefits. Time scheduled the shareholder vote for June 23 and sent out its proxy materials for the merger on May 24.

On June 7, Paramount Communications announced a $175 per share, all-cash, all-shares "fully negotiable" offer for Time. Time's board found that Paramount's offer was subject to three conditions: (1) that Time terminate its merger agreement and share exchange agreement with Warner; (2) that Paramount obtain acceptable cable franchise transfers from Time; and (3) that DGCL § 203 (the anti-takeover statute) not apply to any subsequent Time-Paramount merger. Time believed that it would take at least several months to satisfy these conditions.

Although Time's financial advisers informed the board that Time's per share value was materially higher than Paramount's $175 offer, the board was concerned that shareholders would not appreciate the long-term benefits of the Warner merger if given the opportunity to accept the Paramount offer. Therefore, Time sought the NYSE's approval to complete the merger without stockholder approval. The NYSE refused.

A day after Paramount announced its offer, Time formally rejected it. Because it continued to believe that the offer presented a threat to Time's control of its own destiny and the "Time Culture," the board chose to recast the form of the Warner transaction. Under the new proposal, Time would make an immediate all-cash offer for 51% of Warner's outstanding stock at $70 per share. The remaining 49% would be purchased at some later date for a mixture of cash and securities worth $70 per share. Time would fund the acquisition of Warner by incurring $7 billion to $10 billion of debt, despite its original assertion that the debt-free nature of the combination was one of its principal benefits. Time also agreed to pay $9 billion to Warner for its goodwill. As a condition of accepting the revised transaction, Warner received a control premium and guarantee that the corporate governance provisions in the original merger agreement would remain. Time agreed not to employ its poison pill against Warner, and unless enjoined, to complete the transaction.

On June 23, 1989, Paramount raised its offer to $200 per share while continuing to maintain that all aspects of the offer were negotiable. On June 26, Time's board rejected the second offer on the grounds that it was still inadequate and that Time's acquisition of Warner "offered a greater long-term value for the stockholders and, unlike Paramount, was not a threat to Time's survival or 'culture.'"

Two groups of Time shareholders (collectively referred to as "Shareholder Plaintiffs") and Paramount sought to enjoin Time's tender offer. The Court of Chancery denied the plaintiffs' motions. The plaintiffs appealed.]

HORSEY, JUSTICE:

The Shareholder Plaintiffs first assert a *Revlon* claim. They contend that the March 4 Time-Warner agreement effectively put Time up for sale, triggering *Revlon* duties, requiring Time's board to enhance short-term shareholder value and to treat all other interested acquirers on an equal basis. The Shareholder Plaintiffs base this argument on two facts: (i) the ultimate Time-Warner exchange ratio of .465 favoring Warner, resulting in Warner shareholders' receipt of 62% of the combined company; and (ii) the subjective intent of Time's directors as evidenced in their statements that the market might perceive the Time-Warner merger as putting Time up "for sale" and their adoption of various defensive measures.

The Shareholder Plaintiffs further contend that Time's directors, in structuring the original merger transaction to be "takeover-proof," triggered *Revlon* duties by foreclosing their shareholders from any prospect of obtaining a control premium. In short, plaintiffs argue that Time's board's decision to merge with Warner imposed a fiduciary duty to maximize immediate share value and not erect unreasonable barriers to further bids. Therefore, they argue, the Chancellor erred in finding: that Paramount's bid for Time did not place Time "for sale;" that Time's transaction with Warner did not result in any transfer of control; and that the combined Time-Warner was not so large as to preclude the possibility of the stockholders of Time-Warner receiving a future control premium.

Paramount asserts only a *Unocal* claim in which the shareholder plaintiffs join. Paramount contends that the Chancellor, in applying the first part of the *Unocal* test, erred in finding that Time's board had reasonable grounds to believe that Paramount posed both a legally cognizable threat to Time shareholders and a danger to Time's corporate policy and effectiveness. Paramount also contests the court's finding that Time's board made a reasonable and objective investigation of Paramount's offer so as to be informed before rejecting it. Paramount further claims that the court erred in applying *Unocal*'s second part in finding Time's response to be "reasonable." Paramount points primarily to the preclusive effect of the revised agreement which denied Time shareholders the opportunity both to vote on the agreement and to respond to Paramount's tender offer. Paramount argues that the underlying motivation of Time's board in adopting these defensive measures was management's desire to perpetuate itself in office.

We first take up plaintiffs' principal *Revlon* argument, summarized above. In rejecting this argument, the Chancellor found the original Time-Warner merger agreement not to constitute a "change of control" and concluded that the transaction did not trigger *Revlon* duties. The Chancellor's conclusion is premised on a finding that "[b]efore the merger agreement was signed, control of the corporation existed in a fluid aggregation of unaffiliated shareholders representing a voting majority— in other words, in the market." The Chancellor's findings of fact are supported by the record and his conclusion is correct as a matter of law. However, we premise our rejection of plaintiffs' *Revlon* claim on different grounds, namely, the absence of any substantial evidence to conclude that

Time's board, in negotiating with Warner, made the dissolution or break-up of the corporate entity inevitable, as was the case in *Revlon*.

Under Delaware law there are, generally speaking and without excluding other possibilities, two circumstances which may implicate *Revlon* duties. The first, and clearer one, is when a corporation initiates an active bidding process seeking to sell itself or to effect a business reorganization involving a clear break-up of the company. Thus, in *Revlon*, when the board responded to Pantry Pride's offer by contemplating a "bust-up" sale of assets in a leveraged acquisition, we imposed upon the board a duty to maximize immediate shareholder value and an obligation to auction the company fairly. If, however, the board's reaction to a hostile tender offer is found to constitute only a defensive response and not an abandonment of the corporation's continued existence, *Revlon* duties are not triggered, though *Unocal* duties attach.[14]

The plaintiffs insist that even though the original Time-Warner agreement may not have worked "an objective change of control," the transaction made a "sale" of Time inevitable. Plaintiffs rely on the subjective intent of Time's board of directors and principally upon certain board members' expressions of concern that the Warner transaction *might* be viewed as effectively putting Time up for sale. Plaintiffs argue that the use of a lock-up agreement, a no-shop clause, and so-called "dry-up" agreements prevented shareholders from obtaining a control premium in the immediate future and thus violated *Revlon*.

We agree with the Chancellor that such evidence is entirely insufficient to invoke *Revlon* duties; and we decline to extend *Revlon*'s application to corporate transactions simply because they might be construed as putting a corporation either "in play" or "up for sale." The adoption of structural safety devices alone does not trigger *Revlon*. Rather, as the Chancellor stated, such devices are properly subject to a *Unocal* analysis.

Finally, we do not find in Time's recasting of its merger agreement with Warner from a share exchange to a share purchase a basis to conclude that Time had either abandoned its strategic plan or made a sale of Time inevitable. The Chancellor found that although the merged Time-Warner company would be large (with a value approaching approximately $30 billion), recent takeover cases have proven that acquisition of the combined company might nonetheless be possible. The legal consequence is that

---

[14] Within the auction process, any action taken by the board must be reasonably related to the threat posed or reasonable in relation to the advantage sought. Thus, a *Unocal* analysis may be appropriate when a corporation is in a *Revlon* situation and *Revlon* duties may be triggered by a defensive action taken in response to a hostile offer. Since *Revlon*, we have stated that differing treatment of various bidders is not actionable when such action reasonably relates to achieving the best price available for the stockholders.

Unocal alone applies to determine whether the business judgment rule attaches to the revised agreement.

We turn now to plaintiffs' *Unocal* claim. We begin by noting, as did the Chancellor, that our decision does not require us to pass on the wisdom of the board's decision to enter into the original Time-Warner agreement. That is not a court's task. Our task is simply to review the record to determine whether there is sufficient evidence to support the Chancellor's conclusion that the initial Time-Warner agreement was the product of a proper exercise of business judgment.

[There is] detailed the evidence of the Time board's deliberative approach to expand, [beginning in 1983]. Time's decision to combine with Warner was made only after what could be fairly characterized as an exhaustive appraisal of Time's future as a corporation. After concluding that the corporation must expand to survive, and beyond journalism into entertainment, the board combed the field of available entertainment companies. By 1987, Time had focused upon Warner; by late July 1988 Time's board was convinced that Warner would provide the best "fit" for Time to achieve its strategic objectives. The record attests to the zealousness of Time's executives, fully supported by their directors, in seeing to the preservation of Time's "culture," *i.e.*, its perceived editorial integrity in journalism. We find ample evidence in the record to support the Chancellor's conclusion that the Time board's decision to expand the business of the company through its March 3 merger with Warner was entitled to the protection of the business judgment rule.

The Chancellor reached a different conclusion in addressing the Time-Warner transaction as revised three months later. He found that the revised agreement was defense-motivated and designed to avoid the potentially disruptive effect that Paramount's offer would have had on consummation of the proposed merger were it put to a shareholder vote. Thus, the court declined to apply the traditional business judgment rule to the revised transaction and instead analyzed the Time board's June 16 decision under *Unocal*. The court ruled that *Unocal* applied to all director actions taken, following receipt of Paramount's hostile tender offer, that were reasonably determined to be defensive. Clearly that was a correct ruling and no party disputes that ruling.

Unocal involved a two-tier, highly coercive tender offer. In such a case, the threat is obvious: shareholders may be compelled to tender to avoid being treated adversely in the second stage of the transaction. In subsequent cases, the Court of Chancery has suggested that an all-cash, all-shares offer, falling within a range of values that a shareholder might reasonably prefer, cannot constitute a legally recognized "threat" to shareholder interests sufficient to withstand a *Unocal* analysis. *AC Acquisitions Corp. v. Anderson, Clayton & Co.,* Del.Ch., 519 A.2d 103 (1986); *Grand Metropolitan, PLC v. Pillsbury Co.,* Del.Ch., 558 A.2d 1049

(1988); *City Capital Associates v. Interco, Inc.,* Del.Ch., 551 A.2d 787 (1988). In those cases, the Court of Chancery determined that whatever threat existed related only to the shareholders and only to price and not to the corporation.

From those decisions, Paramount and the individual plaintiffs extrapolate a rule of law that an all-cash, all-shares offer with values reasonably in the range of acceptable price cannot pose any objective threat to a corporation or its shareholders. Thus, Paramount would have us hold that only if the value of Paramount's offer were determined to be clearly inferior to the value created by management's plan to merge with Warner could the offer be viewed—objectively—as a threat.

Implicit in the plaintiffs' argument is the view that a hostile tender offer can pose only two types of threats: the threat of coercion that results from a two-tier offer promising unequal treatment for non-tendering shareholders; and the threat of inadequate value from an all-shares, all-cash offer at a price below what a target board in good faith deems to be the present value of its shares. Since Paramount's offer was all-cash, the only conceivable "threat," plaintiffs argue, was inadequate value. We disapprove of such a narrow and rigid construction of *Unocal,* for the reasons which follow.

Plaintiffs' position represents a fundamental misconception of our standard of review under *Unocal* principally because it would involve the court in substituting its judgment as to what is a "better" deal for that of a corporation's board of directors. To the extent that the Court of Chancery has recently done so in certain of its opinions, we hereby reject such approach as not in keeping with a proper *Unocal* analysis.

The usefulness of *Unocal* as an analytical tool is precisely its flexibility in the face of a variety of fact scenarios. *Unocal* is not intended as an abstract standard; neither is it a structured and mechanistic procedure of appraisal. Thus, we have said that directors may consider, when evaluating the threat posed by a takeover bid, the "inadequacy of the price offered, nature and timing of the offer, questions of illegality, the impact on 'constituencies' other than shareholders, the risk of nonconsummation, and the quality of securities being offered in the exchange." The open-ended analysis mandated by *Unocal* is not intended to lead to a simple mathematical exercise: that is, of comparing the discounted value of Time-Warner's expected trading price at some future date with Paramount's offer and determining which is the higher. Indeed, in our view, precepts underlying the business judgment rule militate against a court's engaging in the process of attempting to appraise and evaluate the relative merits of a long-term versus a short-term investment goal for shareholders. To engage in such an exercise is a distortion of the *Unocal* process and, in particular, the application of the second part of *Unocal*'s test, discussed below.

In this case, the Time board reasonably determined that inadequate value was not the only legally cognizable threat that Paramount's all-cash, all-shares offer could present. Time's board concluded that Paramount's eleventh-hour offer posed other threats. One concern was that Time shareholders might elect to tender into Paramount's cash offer in ignorance or a mistaken belief of the strategic benefit which a business combination with Warner might produce. Moreover, Time viewed the conditions attached to Paramount's offer as introducing a degree of uncertainty that skewed a comparative analysis. Further, the timing of Paramount's offer to follow issuance of Time's proxy notice was viewed as arguably designed to upset, if not confuse, the Time stockholders' vote. Given this record evidence, we cannot conclude that the Time board's decision of June 6 that Paramount's offer posed a threat to corporate policy and effectiveness was lacking in good faith or dominated by motives of either entrenchment or self-interest.

Paramount also contends that the Time board had not duly investigated Paramount's offer. Therefore, Paramount argues, Time was unable to make an informed decision that the offer posed a threat to Time's corporate policy. Although the Chancellor did not address this issue directly, his findings of fact do detail Time's exploration of the available entertainment companies, including Paramount, before determining that Warner provided the best strategic "fit." In addition, the court found that Time's board rejected Paramount's offer because Paramount did not serve Time's objectives or meet Time's needs. Thus, the record does, in our judgment, demonstrate that Time's board was adequately informed of the potential benefits of a transaction with Paramount. We agree with the Chancellor that the Time board's lengthy pre-June investigation of potential merger candidates, including Paramount, mooted any obligation on Time's part to halt its merger process with Warner to reconsider Paramount. Time's board was under no obligation to negotiate with Paramount. Time's failure to negotiate cannot be fairly found to have been uninformed. The evidence supporting this finding is materially enhanced by the fact that twelve of Time's sixteen board members were outside, independent directors.

We turn to the second part of the *Unocal* analysis. The obvious requisite to determining the reasonableness of a defensive action is a clear identification of the nature of the threat. As the Chancellor correctly noted, this "requires an evaluation of the importance of the corporate objective threatened; alternative methods of protecting that objective; impacts of the 'defensive' action, and other relevant factors."

Paramount argues that, assuming its tender offer posed a threat, Time's response was unreasonable in precluding Time's shareholders from accepting the tender offer or receiving a control premium in the immediately foreseeable future. Once again, the contention stems, we believe, from a fundamental misunderstanding of where the power of corporate governance lies. Delaware law confers the management of the corporate enterprise to the stockholders' duly elected board representatives. The fiduciary duty to manage a corporate enterprise includes the selection of a time frame for achievement of corporate goals. That duty may not be delegated to the stockholders. Directors are not obliged to abandon a deliberately conceived corporate plan for a short-term shareholder profit unless there is clearly no basis to sustain the corporate strategy.

Here, on the record facts, the Chancellor found that Time's responsive action to Paramount's tender offer was not aimed at "cramming down" on its shareholders a management-sponsored alternative, but rather had as its goal the carrying forward of a pre-existing transaction in an altered form. Thus, the response was reasonably related to the threat.

Applying the test for grant or denial of preliminary injunctive relief, we find plaintiffs failed to establish a reasonable likelihood of ultimate success on the merits. Therefore, we affirm.

Time seemingly exposed a doctrinal tension between the Delaware Chancery Court and the Delaware Supreme Court concerning the nature of corporations and the question of for whose benefit the corporation is run. The Court of Chancery held that *Revlon* was inapplicable because, both before and after the merger, "control of the corporation existed [and would exist] in a fluid aggregation of unaffiliated shareholders representing a voting majority—in other words, in the market." The Supreme Court appeared to reject this line of reasoning. It stated:

> The Chancellor's findings of fact are supported by the record and his conclusion is correct as a matter of law. However, we premise our rejection of plaintiffs' *Revlon* claim on broader grounds, namely the absence of any substantial evidence to conclude that Time's board, in negotiating with Warner, made the dissolution or breakup of the corporate entity inevitable, as was the case in *Revlon*.

> Under Delaware law there are, generally speaking and without excluding other possibilities, two circumstances which may implicate *Revlon* duties. The first, and clearer one, is when a corporation initiates an active bidding process seeking to sell itself or to effect a business reorganization involving a clear break-up of the company. However, *Revlon* duties may also be triggered where, in response to a bidder's offer, a target abandons its long-term strategy and seeks an alternative transaction also involving the breakup of the company.

In its decisions from *Unocal* through *Time*, the Delaware Supreme Court established two regimes governing sales of control and responses to threats to control. When a board, in response to a hostile takeover bid, takes defensive actions but does not seek to sell control, *Unocal* governs. If a corporation is for sale, *Revlon* applies. However, *when* a corporation is "for sale," and what *Revlon* allows a board to do were not clearly resolved, although, as noted, *Time* appeared to limit sharply the situations in which directors have "*Revlon* duties." After *Unocal*, coercive takeover bids pretty much disappeared. *Moran* legitimated the adoption of poison pills, and *Time* left unresolved the question of whether, and in what circumstances, a board can rely on a poison pill (or other defense) to "just say no" to an all-cash offer for all of a corporation's stock.

3. PARAMOUNT V. QVC—*REVLON* DUTIES AND SALE OF CONTROL

The court's willingness to sustain the strategic merger in *Time-Warner*, made it appear that *Revlon* duties would apply only when a company puts itself up for sale or takes steps as to make the break-up of the company inevitable. In reliance on that analysis, Paramount tried again, and, as in *Time-Warner*, lost again. *Paramount Communications Inc. v. QVC Network Inc.*, 637 A.2d 34 (Del. 1994).

Paramount owned and operated various entertainment businesses, including motion picture and television studios, book publishers, professional sports teams, and amusement parks. The Paramount board consisted of 15 members, including 11 outside directors who were all present or former senior executives of public corporations or financial institutions. In the late 1980s, the Paramount board began to investigate the possibility of acquiring or merging with other companies in the entertainment, media or communications industries to stay competitive in a rapidly evolving industry. The unsuccessful bid for Time had been part of Paramount's goal of strategic expansion.

In 1990, Paramount first considered a possible combination with Viacom, which had a range of entertainment operations. Viacom was controlled by its Chairman and CEO Sumner M. Redstone, who indirectly owned approximately 85.2 percent of Viacom's voting Class A stock and approximately 69.2 percent of Viacom's nonvoting Class B stock through National Amusements, Inc. ("NAI"), an entity 91.7 percent owned by Redstone. In September 1993, after a few months of negotiations between the companies, the Paramount board unanimously approved an agreement to merge Paramount into Viacom. Under that agreement, Paramount Board agreed to amend its poison pill plan to exempt the proposed merger with Viacom. In addition, the agreement had several defensive provisions designed to make competing bids more difficult, including a no-shop provision, a termination fee, and a stock option agreement.

Under the no-shop provision, Paramount agreed not to solicit, encourage, discuss, negotiate, or endorse any competing transaction unless: (a) a third party made an unsolicited proposal not subject to any material financing contingencies and (b) the Paramount Board determined that it must negotiate with the third party to comply with its fiduciary duties.

The termination fee provision provided that Viacom would receive $100 million if: (a) Paramount terminated the merger agreement because of a competing transaction; (b) Paramount's stockholders did not approve the merger; or (c) the Paramount Board recommended a competing transaction.

The most significant defensive measure, the stock option agreement, gave Viacom an option to purchase approximately 19.9 percent of Paramount's outstanding common stock at $69.14 per share if the termination fee was triggered. The agreement also had two unusual provisions that were highly beneficial to Viacom: (a) Viacom was to pay for the shares with a senior subordinated note of questionable marketability rather than cash, avoiding the need to raise the $1.6 billion purchase price; and (b) Viacom could require Paramount to pay a cash sum equal to the difference between the purchase price and the market price of Paramount's stock. The stock option agreement had no limit to its maximum dollar value.

Paramount and Viacom publicly announced their proposed merger and indicated that it was a virtual certainty. Redstone described it as a 'marriage' that would 'never be torn asunder' and stated that only a 'nuclear attack' could break the deal. Further, aware that QVC was also interested in acquiring Paramount, Redstone called QVC Chairman and CEO Barry Diller to discourage him from making a competing bid.

QVC was not discouraged. Instead, it proposed a merger with Paramount in which QVC would acquire Paramount for approximately $80 per share (0.893 shares of QVC common stock and $30 in cash) and indicated its willingness to negotiate further with Paramount. The Paramount board ignored this proposal without investigating its value. Thereafter, QVC moved to enjoin the Paramount-Viacom merger and announced an $80 tender offer for 51% of Paramount's outstanding shares (the remaining shares to be converted into QVC common stock in a second-step merger). This bid was $10 more per share than the consideration the Paramount shareholders would receive in the proposed Viacom merger. Viacom realized that it needed to revise the terms of the merger agreement and thus, as the Delaware Supreme Court stated, "in effect, the opportunity for a 'new deal' with Viacom was at hand for the Paramount Board. With the QVC hostile bid offering greater value to the Paramount stockholders, the Paramount Board had considerable leverage with Viacom."

The amended merger agreement did not substantially change the terms of the transaction other than offering the Paramount shareholders more consideration and providing the Paramount board slightly more flexibility. The defensive measures were not removed. Paramount did not use its leverage to eliminate the no-shop provision, the termination fee or the stock option agreement.

A bidding war between Viacom and QVC ensued. Viacom's highest tender offer price was $85 a share. QVC's was $90. The Paramount board continued to reject QVC's bid, despite its higher price, because the board determined that QVC's offer was not in the best interests of the shareholders. Several directors believed the Viacom merger would be more advantageous to Paramount's future business prospects that a QVC merger would be.

The Court of Chancery preliminarily enjoined Paramount's defensive measures designed to facilitate the strategic alliance with Viacom and thwart QVC's unsolicited, more valuable tender offer. The Delaware Supreme Court affirmed, holding that Paramount's merger agreement with Viacom constituted a sale of control, triggering the board's *Revlon* duties to auction the corporation to the highest bidder. The court determined that the board violated its fiduciary duties in favoring the less-valuable Viacom merger over the QVC offer without adequately informing itself as to the terms of the QVC offer.

First, the Delaware Supreme Court explained, public shareholders owned a majority of Paramount's voting stock, so control of the corporation was maintained in "the fluid aggregation of unaffiliated shareholders" and not by a single entity. In the Paramount-Viacom transaction, the Paramount shareholders would receive a minority voting position in the new company. The new controlling shareholder would have the voting power to effect various corporate changes, including materially altering the nature of the corporation. Even though the Paramount board intended the merger with Viacom to further Paramount's long-term strategy, upon sale of control, the new controlling stockholder would have the power to alter that vision. Further, after the sale of the control, the former Paramount shareholders would no longer have leverage to demand a control premium for their shares. "As a result, the Paramount stockholders are entitled to receive, and should receive, a control premium and/or protective devices of significant value. There being no such protective provisions in the Viacom-Paramount transaction, the Paramount directors had an obligation to take the maximum advantage of the current opportunity to realize for the stockholders the best value reasonably available."

The court then held that when *Revlon* applied, the target board has a primary obligation to act reasonably to realize the best value available for the shareholders. This obligation required the board to be particularly diligent and adequately informed in its negotiations, including a consideration of the cash value, non-cash value, and future value of a strategic alliance in the context of the entire situation and the likelihood of each alternative.

Most important, the court rejected Paramount's argument that the proposed merger did not trigger *Revlon* duties because the transaction did not contemplate a break-up or dissolution of the corporation as *Time-Warner* had suggested. Rather, returning to Chancellor Allen's decision in *Time-Warner,* the court noted that there had been "no change of control in the original stock-for-stock merger between Time and Warner because Time would be owned by a fluid aggregation of stockholders both before and after the merger." By contrast, if the Paramount-Viacom merger took effect, because CEO Redstone had 89% voting control of Viacom, control of the surviving corporation would no longer exist in a fluid market and the minority shareholders (the former Paramount shareholders) could no longer demand a control premium for their stock.

The court emphasized that in *Time-Warner*, it had stated that there were "generally speaking and *without excluding other possibilities,* two circumstances which may implicate *Revlon* duties." (Emphasis added.) Here, the Paramount board did in fact contemplate a change in control because it unintentionally initiated a bidding war by agreeing to sell control of the corporation to Viacom when there was another potential acquirer, QVC, equally interested in bidding on the corporation. Thus the court held that:

> When a corporation undertakes a transaction which will cause: (a) a change in corporate control; or (b) a break-up of the corporate entity, the directors' obligation is to seek the best value reasonably available to the stockholders. This obligation arises because the effect of the Viacom-Paramount transaction, if consummated, is to shift control of Paramount from the public stockholders to a controlling stockholder, Viacom. Neither *Time-Warner* nor any other decision of this Court holds that a 'break-up' of the company is essential to give rise to this obligation where there is a sale of control.

The court held that the Paramount board had breached its fiduciary obligations by: (1) ignoring QVC's offer, failing to examine critically the competing transactions; (2) failing to obtain and act with due care on reasonably available information that was necessary to compare the two offers to determine which transaction, or an alternative course of action, would provide the best value reasonably available to the shareholders; and (3) failing to negotiate with both Viacom and QVC to achieve that value.

Even though provisions in the Paramount-Viacom merger agreement precluded the board from negotiating with QVC, the court held that the board's fiduciary duties overrode the terms of the contract. The court noted that the QVC offer gave Paramount an opportunity to renegotiate its contract with Viacom and modify the favorable defensive measures which impeded the board's ability to realize the best value available for the Paramount shareholders and was harshly critical of Paramount's failure to make any such effort in an effort to "cling to its vision of a strategic alliance with Viacom." While Paramount was not obligated to sell the corporation to QVC, it was obligated to evaluate QVC's bid carefully. Indeed, as the court found, at one point, QVC's offer exceeded Viacom's by $1 billion, yet the Paramount board never considered it.

After *Revlon* and *QVC*, Chancellor Allen described the duties of a target board in a sale of control as follows:

> [E]xisting uncertainty respecting the meaning of "*Revlon* duties" was substantially dissipated by the Delaware Supreme Court's opinion in [*QVC*]. The case teaches a great deal, but it may be said to support these generalizations at least: (1) where a transaction constituted a "change in corporate control", such that the shareholders would thereafter lose a further opportunity to participate in a change of control premium, (2) the board's duty of loyalty requires it to try in good faith to get the best price reasonably available (which specifically means that the board must at least discuss an interest expressed by any financially capable buyer), and (3) in such context courts will employ an (objective) "reasonableness" standard of review (both to the process and the result!) to evaluate whether the directors have complied with their fundamental duties of care and good faith (loyalty). Thus, [*QVC*] in effect mediates between the "normalizing" tendency of some prior cases and the more highly regulatory approach of others. It adopts an intermediate level of judicial review which recognizes the broad power of the board to make decisions in the process of negotiating and recommending a "sale of control" transaction, so long as the board is informed, motivated by good faith desire to achieve the best available transaction, and proceeds "reasonably."

> With respect to the important question of when these duties are enhanced—specifically, the duty to try in good faith to maximize current share value and the duty to reasonably explore all options (*i.e.*, to talk with all financially responsible parties)—the court's teaching ironically narrowed the range of corporate transactions to which the principle of *Revlon* applies. That is, it explicitly recognized that where a stock for stock merger is involved, the business judgment of the board, concerning the quality and prospects of the stock the shareholders would receive in the merger, would be reviewed deferentially, as in other settings. The holding of [*QVC*], however, was that where the stock to be received in the merger was the stock of a corporation under the control of

a single individual or a control group, then the transaction should be treated for "*Revlon* duty" purposes as a cash merger would be treated. How this "change in control" trigger works in instances of mixed cash and stock or other paper awaits future cases.

Equity-Linked Investors, L.P. v. Adams, 705 A.2d 1040, 1053–55 (Del.Ch.1997).

4.   WHO GETS TO DECIDE?

In *Blasius Industries, Inc. v. Atlas Corp.*, 564 A.2d 651 (Del.Ch. 1988) Blasius, an insurgent shareholder, urged the board to engage in a leveraged restructuring and declare a large dividend. When the corporation responded coolly to this proposal, Blasius announced that he planned to solicit shareholder consents to amend Atlas's bylaws to increase the board from seven to fifteen members and to elect eight new directors named by him. In response, the board held an emergency meeting at which it voted to amend the bylaws to increase the number of directors to nine and elected two new members to fill the vacancies thus created. (This would have left the old board on the long side of a nine-to-eight split if Blasius succeeded.)

Chancellor Allen found that the board's action was motivated by a sincere desire to protect the corporation against what they believed was an unwise recapitalization proposal. That did not resolve the dispute, however. The Chancellor analyzed the legal question thus:

> The real question the case presents, to my mind, is whether, in these circumstances, the board, even if it *is* acting with subjective good faith, may validly act for the principal purpose of preventing the shareholders from electing a majority of new directors. The question thus posed is not one of intentional wrong (or even negligence), but one of authority *as between the fiduciary and the beneficiary.*

> The shareholder franchise is the ideological underpinning upon which the legitimacy of directorial power rests. Generally, shareholders have only two protections against perceived inadequate business performance. They may sell their stock (which, if done in sufficient numbers, may so affect security prices as to create an incentive for altered managerial performance), or they may vote to replace incumbent board members.

> It has, for a long time, been conventional to dismiss the stockholder vote as a vestige or ritual of little practical importance. It may be that we are now witnessing the emergence of new institutional voices and arrangements that will make the stockholder vote a less predictable affair than it has been. Be that as it may, however, whether the vote is seen functionally as an unimportant formalism, or as an important tool of discipline, it is

clear that it is critical to the theory that legitimates the exercise of power by some (directors and officers) over vast aggregations of property that they do not own. Thus, when viewed from a broad, institutional perspective, it can be seen that matters involving the integrity of the shareholder voting process involve consideration not present in any other context in which directors exercise delegated power.

The distinctive nature of the shareholder franchise context also appears when the matter is viewed from a less generalized, doctrinal point of view. From this point of view, as well, it appears that the ordinary considerations to which the business judgment rule originally responded are simply not present in the shareholder voting context. That is, a decision by the board to act for the primary purpose of preventing the effectiveness of a shareholder vote inevitably involves the question who, as between the principal and the agent, has authority with respect to a matter of internal corporate governance. That, of course, is true in a very specific way in this case which deals with the question who should constitute the board of directors of the corporation, but it will be true in every instance in which an incumbent board seeks to thwart a shareholder majority. A board's decision to act to prevent the shareholders from creating a majority of new board positions and filling them does not involve the exercise of the corporation's power over its property, or with respect to its rights or obligations; rather, it involves allocation, between shareholders as a class and the board, of effective power with respect to governance of the corporation. Action designed principally to interfere with the effectiveness of a vote inevitably involves a conflict between the board and a shareholder majority. Judicial review of such action involves a determination of the legal and equitable obligations of an agent towards his principal. This is not, in my opinion, a question that a court may leave to the agent finally to decide so long as he does so honestly and competently; that is, it may not be left to the agent's business judgment.

Blasius is important both for its holding concerning the importance of shareholders' electoral rights and for its approach to how power is allocated between shareholders and directors. In contrast to *Unocal*, which allows a board considerable scope to decide whether a takeover bid is in the shareholders' best interests, *Blasius* held that, with respect to board elections, incumbent directors are not entitled to act as "Platonic masters" who "know better than do the shareholders what is in the corporation's best interest." Consequently, the board must provide a "compelling justification" for any "acts done for the primary purpose of impeding the exercise of the stockholder voting power."

In all of these cases, the courts are striving to develop rules that protect shareholders—but *which* shareholders? When a tender offer is announced, the stock price of the target naturally rises to just below—or occasionally even above—the tender offer price. Many shareholders sell at this point, wanting to cash in immediately or unwilling to hold on to see if the offer is successful. The buyers are typically "arbitrageurs"—or "arbs" in industry parlance—who hope to make a quick profit on the spread between the market price and the tender offer price or are speculating that a bidding war will occur that drives the price up even further. This leaves the corporation with two types of shareholders: those who have invested for the long term and who may believe in the current managements plans for the future, and the arbs, who are financial speculators hoping for a quick profit. The Delaware Chancery Court wrestled with the conundrum posed by this distinction in *Air Products and Chemicals, Inc. v. Airgas, Inc.*, 16 A.3d 48 (Del.Ch.2011), a case involving a tender offer for all of the stock of Airgas by Air Products and Chemicals.

In a lengthy opinion, Chancellor Chandler pointed out that directors were entitled to act to protect shareholders from a "coercive" offer, "so structured as to put undue pressure on shareholders to tender." He also recognized that Air Products' tender offer had caused a substantial percentage—perhaps a majority—of the Airgas shares to move into the hands of arbitrageurs. There was thus a risk that, "if management advises stockholders, in good faith, that it believes Air Products' hostile offer is inadequate because in its view the future earnings potential of the company is greater than the price offered, Airgas's stockholders might nevertheless reject the board's advice and tender."

Citing a law review article,[2] Chancellor Chandler recognized three different types of "coercion": "(1) structural coercion—'the risk that disparate treatment of non-tendering shareholders might distort shareholders' tender decisions' (*i.e.*, the situation involving a two-tiered offer where the back end gets less than the front end); (2) opportunity loss— the 'dilemma that a hostile offer might deprive target shareholders of the opportunity to select a superior alternative offered by target management;' and (3) substantive coercion—'the risk that shareholders will mistakenly accept an underpriced offer because they disbelieve management's representations of intrinsic value.' " He found that the offer in question did not fall into either of the first two categories, but was "substantively coercive" because there was "sufficient evidence that a majority of stockholders might be willing to tender their shares regardless of whether the price is adequate or not—thereby ceding control of Airgas to Air Products." Accordingly, the Chancellor found, Airgas had met the first part of the *Unocal* test by demonstrating a reasonable threat to corporate policy.

---

[2] Ronald Gilson & Reinier Kraakman, *Delaware's Intermediate Standard for Defensive Tactics: Is There Substance to Proportionality Review?*, 44 Bus. Law. 247, 258 (1989).

He went on to say that Airgas had also met the second part of the *Unocal* test: whether the Airgas board's use of the poison pill to block the offer were a proportionate response to the threat. He pointed out that Air Products could complete its tender offer and then use its majority position to replace the board with its own nominees. Airgas had a staggered board, but three of its nine members had been selected by Air Products as a result of earlier maneuvering. This meant that, in order to have a majority of the board, Air Products would either have to call a special meeting and remove the remaining directors or wait until the next annual meeting. Such a delay would not, in practice, be "preclusive" of the Air Products' ability to close its tender offer and ultimately take control.

Chancellor Chandler's opinion reflects a longstanding tension between the Chancery Court and the Supreme Court in Delaware; a tension that is reflected in the ongoing debate discussed in Chapter 12 between those who advocate a "shareholder primacy" model of corporate governance and those who advocate a "director primacy" model. It is clear that the Chancellor feels compelled by Supreme Court precedent to defer to the decision of the directors as long as, acting in good faith, they determine that there is "a legally cognizable threat" to the corporation and adopt reasonable defenses that are proportionate to the threat. It also appears that he is uncomfortable with that result. Which view do you think is the better one?

How one answers the question, "who gets to decide?" is likely to be influenced by whether one believes takeovers are, on the whole, good or bad. As we have seen, proponents of takeovers argue that an effective market for corporate control allows the replacement of ineffective managements and leads to greater economic efficiency. They therefore generally oppose legal rules that impede takeovers and favor leaving the decision to shareholders. Other observers are concerned that an unrestricted takeover regime can lead managements to focus on the short term, with results that can be economically inefficient. To counter that, they generally support giving directors greater power to resist hostile offers that they believe not to be in the best long-term interests of the corporation. An intermediate view is that while takeovers may generally be economically efficient in the aggregate, the effect of a takeover—or the threat of a takeover—on any individual company may be good or bad depending on its particular circumstances. Professors Enrique, Gilson and Pacces, writing about European takeover laws, suggest that the solution is to give corporations the ability to choose between more or less restrictive takeover rules. Luca Enrique, Ronald Gilson, Alessio Pacces, The Case for an Unbiased Takeover Law (with an Application to the European Union), European Corporate Governance Institute Working Paper Series in Law (May 2013).

H. THE INTERSECTION OF PROXY CONTESTS AND TENDER OFFERS

With the advent of the poison pill and other takeover defenses, a bidder corporation seeking to acquire a target corporation over the opposition of the target's board must now conduct both a proxy contest and a tender offer. If the bidder wins the proxy contest, it can replace the target's board of directors with a new slate of directors who will redeem the poison pill. Delaware's requirement that bidders submit the acquisition proposal to a vote has shifted defensive energy into proxy contests.

Blasius is one of a number of Delaware cases in which the court has had to determine how to treat defensive actions that may have the effect of disenfranchising shareholders. In *Unitrin, Inc. v. American General Corp.*, 651 A.2d 1361 (Del. 1995), which arose in the context of a joint tender offer and proxy contest, the Delaware Supreme Court upheld the use of defensive tactics that served to limit the ability of a bidder to wage a successful proxy contest.

Unitrin involved a hostile takeover offer by American General for all of the outstanding shares of Unitrin at a 30 percent premium above the market price of Unitrin's stock. The Unitrin board unanimously rejected American General's merger proposal as inadequate and implemented several defensive measures to thwart American General's bid, including approval of a stock repurchase plan to buy back up to 10 million shares of Unitrin's outstanding stock. The repurchase program increased the Unitrin board's stock ownership from 23% to 28%, making it more difficult for a bidder to wage a successful proxy contest. American General commenced litigation to enjoin Unitrin's repurchase plan.

The Delaware Chancery Court enjoined Unitrin's stock repurchase plan, finding that the repurchase program "went beyond what was necessary to protect the Unitrin stockholders from a 'low ball' negotiating strategy." The court also concluded that repurchase program was intended to keep the merger decision within the control of Unitrin's board because the program would materially affect an insurgent stockholder's ability to win a proxy contest.

The Delaware Supreme Court reversed the Chancery Court ruling and upheld the stock repurchase program. First, the court reasoned that the risk of substantive coercion justified Unitrin's defensive tactics: "The record appears to support Unitrin's argument that the Board's justification for adopting the Repurchase Program was its reasonably perceived risk of substantive coercion, *i.e.*, that Unitrin's shareholders might accept American General's inadequate Offer because of 'ignorance or mistaken belief' regarding the Board's assessment of the long-term value of Unitrin's stock."

Further, the Supreme Court determined that the board's response was proportionate to the threat posed by American General's bid. *Unitrin* refined the proportionality prong of *Unocal*, ruling that where a defensive action is neither "coercive" nor "preclusive" the court should exercise deference so long as the board's conduct falls within a "range of reasonable responses." After cautioning that it "has been and remains assiduous in its concern about defensive actions designed to thwart the essence of corporate democracy by disenfranchising shareholders," the court held that the repurchase program was not preclusive because so long as a bidder did not acquire more than 15 percent of Unitrin's stock, it would be able to wage a proxy contest to elect directors to redeem the poison pill.

The Supreme Court stressed that a board needs "latitude in discharging its fiduciary duties to the corporation and its shareholders when defending against perceived threats." 651 A. 2d at 1388. It described this latitude in colorful terms: "When a corporation is not for sale, the board of directors is the defender of the metaphorical medieval corporate bastion and the protector of the corporation's shareholders." *Id.*

> [I]f a board reasonably perceives that a threat is on the horizon, it has broad authority to respond with a panoply of individual or combined defensive precautions, *e.g.*, staffing the barbican, raising the drawbridge, and lowering the portcullis. Stated more directly, depending upon the circumstances, the board may respond to a reasonably perceived threat by adopting individually or sometimes in combination: advance notice by-laws, supermajority voting provisions, shareholder rights plans, repurchase programs, etc.

Id. at n. 38.

Unitrin made clear that a decision by a target company's board to fend off a hostile takeover bid—even an all-cash, all-shares bid that includes a substantial premium over target's current market price—should not be viewed as preclusive or coercive so long as the board's defensive action does not preclude a successful proxy fight. However, *Unitrin* left open the possibility that the Delaware courts could invalidate a target board's response to an unsolicited offer that completely foreclosed a proxy contest or was unreasonably disproportionate to the threat.

I. LIMITATIONS ON PROTECTING NEGOTIATED ACQUISITIONS

The great majority of corporate acquisitions are "friendly." Indeed, even situations that begin with a hostile offer often end in negotiated transactions between the target and either the original bidder or a "white knight." Today, the focus of Delaware cases has shifted from sale of control to the validity and nature of "deal-protection" measures.[3] Although such measures have the ability to forestall other offers, if they were forbidden completely, there would be few deals. No potential buyer would enter negotiations with a target corporation, knowing that the only way it could actually acquire the target corporation would be if it outbid any subsequent, competing bidders. Therefore, some amount of deal protection must be permitted so that deals can be consummated. The following excerpt describes some of the approaches that have been developed to accomplish that goal.

BRIAN J.M. QUINN, BULLETPROOF: MANDATORY RULES FOR DEAL PROTECTION
32 J. Corp. L. 865 (2007).

A. Voting Protections

Voting protections enable a seller to "bank" a high percentage of the shareholders' votes in favor of the agreed upon transaction prior to an actual shareholder vote. A seller can ensure the success of its preferred transaction by securing voting agreements from stockholders holding a majority of the shares or voting power. Where ownership of the seller is closely-held, the transaction costs associated with assembling a majority bloc in support of the transaction can be reasonably low since many of the major stockholders are often directly represented on the seller's board of directors and the universe of stockholders is limited in size. Where voting agreements are used, the merger agreement is usually signed contingent upon or contemporaneous with their delivery.

In public company transactions, where there is typically not a controlling bloc of shares that can be easily assembled in favor of the sale, sellers can offer lesser voting protections. The most attractive from the buyer's point of view is the commitment that the seller's board will continue to recommend the transaction regardless of whether a better offer arises before the time of the vote or, in the event of a better subsequent offer, that the seller's shareholders must be given an opportunity to vote on the initial transaction before being allowed to terminate the merger agreement. The "force-the-vote" provision, which requires boards to call such votes prior to terminating a merger agreement, can be an effective deterrent to a subsequent bid.

There are a number of other voting provisions that provide incremental defensive security for buyers. These measures include provisions that require sellers to call stockholder meetings or set time limits on how long a selling board may delay its obligation to call a meeting.

---

[3] For an excellent treatment of the history of mergers and acquisitions in the last thirty years, including the role of lawyers in structuring transactions, see Steven M. Davidoff, Gods at War: Shotgun Takeovers, Government by Deal, and the Private Equity Implosion (2009).

Other provisions include "best efforts" provisions relating to regulatory approvals that also provide incremental security for buyers. Though these provisions provide buyers with some additional deal security, voting agreements and the force-the-vote provisions are clearly the most valuable to buyers.

B. Exclusivity Measures

Exclusivity measures prevent selling boards from considering or negotiating with a potential rival acquirer. No-shop and no-talk provisions are the most common variants of exclusivity measures. No-shop, or no-solicitation, measures restrict selling boards from actively seeking an alternative buyer. No-shop provisions allow a seller to respond to an unsolicited bid but do not allow a seller to initiate discussions with a potential bidder or use a signed agreement to actively shop a target. No-talk provisions go further by prohibiting sellers from sharing proprietary and non-public information or engaging in any discussions with a potential subsequent bidder. In preventing sellers from sharing any non-public information or speaking with subsequent bidders, no-talk provisions can shut down a potential bid by starving a subsequent bidder of the information required to generate a competitive bid. Common versions of the no-shop and no-talk provisions, also known as no-solicitation provisions, prohibit sellers from initiating any contact with a potential subsequent bidder, but do allow sellers to terminate the initial transaction in order to respond to unsolicited superior offers from subsequent bidders.

Rights of first refusal, or matching rights, are another type of exclusivity measure. A right of first refusal provides that in the event that a subsequent bid is made, the buyer with a right of first refusal has the right to match the subsequent bid. The presence of rights of first refusal can be a strong deterrent against subsequent bids and is therefore a potentially potent protective measure in the non-Revlon context. A subsequent bidder faces a real risk of incurring the expense of evaluating a target and making a bid only to see the initial bidder exercise its right of first refusal and buy the company. While a subsequent bidder is always free to make a topping bid, it may have only limited access to information regarding the seller. The subsequent bidder knows that it can win only in the event its bid (based on limited information regarding the seller) is larger than the bid of the incumbent (based on extensive information regarding the seller). Success under these circumstances may involve paying too much and suffering the "winner's curse."

C. Compensatory Devices

The final general category of deal protection devices are compensatory devices. Stock lockups, termination fees, and topping fees are all intended both to compensate bidders in the event of an unsuccessful bid and to deter third party bids. A stock lockup is an option granted to the initial buyer to purchase shares of the seller's stock upon the occurrence of a triggering event, such as the seller's termination of the initial merger agreement in order to pursue an alternative transaction. A termination fee is a cash payment to the initial buyer in the event the merger agreement with the seller is terminated due to a triggering event. A topping fee is a cash payment made to the initial buyer by the seller in the event the seller terminates the initial buyer's transaction in order to accept a topping bid. The size of the fee is equal to a percentage of the difference between the price offered by the initial buyer and the topping bid. An asset lockup is an option issued to the initial bidder to purchase a division or other asset of the seller; such an asset may be the "crown jewel" of the seller or may involve assets that are of particular interest to the non-preferred bidder.

From the point of view of a subsequent bidder, compensatory devices act as a tax on its bid. Depending on the size of the compensatory device, the third party's valuation of the seller and the price at which the third party can acquire the seller, these mechanisms can render a seller unattractive to a third party.

By agreeing to some deal-protection measure, the seller's board is reducing whatever possibility there may have been that another buyer might come along with a better deal for the seller's shareholders. The Delaware courts have insisted that boards must be cognizant of their fiduciary obligations when negotiating to sell the company. The following is the leading case in Delaware on the issue.

OMNICARE, INC. V. NCS HEALTHCARE, INC.
818 A.2d 914 (Del. 2003).

[NCS, provided pharmacy services to long-term care institutions. Its common stock consisted of Class A shares and Class B shares. The Class B shares were entitled to ten votes per share and the Class A shares were entitled to one vote per share.

The NCS board consisted of four members: Outcalt, the Chairman; Shaw, the CEO; and Sells and Osborne, both outside directors. Outcalt owned 202,063 shares of NCS Class A common stock and 3,476,086 shares of Class B common stock. Shaw owned 28,905 shares of NCS Class A common stock and 1,141,134 shares of Class B common stock.

Genesis and Omnicare were both also in the healthcare services businesses and were competitors of NCS.

Beginning in late 1999, due to changes in the healthcare industry, NCS began experiencing severe financial difficulties, and by early 2001 it was in default on its debt, and its stock was trading at pennies a share. During 2000, NCS began serious efforts to find a way to address its problems.

In the summer of 2001, NCS invited Omnicare, Inc. to begin discussions with regarding a possible transaction. On July 20, Omnicare made a proposal, subject to a due diligence investigation, to acquire NCS in a bankruptcy sale at a price below the value of the outstanding debt, which would have left the NCS stockholders with nothing.

Dissatisfied with Omnicare's offer, in March, 2002, the NCS board established an independent committee, consisting of Sells and Osborne, and authorized it to negotiate a sale of the company. The committee, through its investment banker, approached Genesis to inquire about its interest in a transaction. Genesis said that it might be interested, but that it did not want to be a "stalking horse" and therefore insisted on some degree of certainty that if it negotiated a merger agreement, the transaction would be consummated.

After further discussions, Genesis proposed a merger that would pay the creditors in full and provide $24 million to the stockholders. At Genesis' insistence, NCS executed an exclusivity agreement providing that it would negotiate only with Genesis for a specified period. Negotiations on the final terms of a merger then commenced.

Meanwhile, Omnicare came to believe that NCS was moving forward with a transaction with another competitor that would potentially present a competitive threat to Omnicare. It sent NCS a letter outlining an offer to acquire NCS in a merger (rather than in bankruptcy) on terms that would give the NCS stockholders $3 per share in cash.

NCS was precluded by the exclusivity agreement with Genesis from replying to Omnicare's overture. NCS did tell Genesis of Omnicare's proposal in hopes of getting Genesis to improve its deal. Genesis did so, but only on condition that NCS formally approve the merger by the end of the next day. The NCS board then approved the Genesis transaction, including a provision pursuant to which Outcalt and Shaw, who together held a majority of the stockholder voting power, committed to vote their shares to approve it.

The merger agreement provided, among other things that:

- NCS would submit the merger agreement to NCS stockholders regardless of whether the NCS board continued to recommend the merger.

- NCS would not enter into discussions with third parties concerning an alternative acquisition of NCS, or provide non-public information to such parties, unless the NCS board believed in good faith that the proposal was or was likely to result in an acquisition on terms superior to those contemplated by the NCS/Genesis merger agreement.

- If the merger agreement were to be terminated, under certain circumstances NCS would be required to pay Genesis a $6 million termination fee and/or Genesis's documented expenses, up to $5 million.

When the transaction was announced, OmniCare filed a lawsuit attempting to enjoin the NCS/Genesis merger, and announced that it intended to launch a tender offer for NCS's shares. It dropped its due diligence condition and irrevocably committed itself to a transaction with NCS. As a result of this irrevocable offer, the NCS board withdrew its recommendation that the stockholders vote in favor of the NCS/Genesis merger agreement, and NCS's financial advisor withdrew its fairness opinion. These changes could have no effect on the ultimate outcome, however, since NCS had committed to submit the merger to a stockholder vote, and Outcalt and Shaw, who controlled a majority of the votes, had committed to vote in favor.]

HOLLAND, JUSTICE, for the majority:

Business Judgment or Enhanced Scrutiny

The "defining tension" in corporate governance today has been characterized as "the tension between deference to directors' decisions and the scope of judicial review." The appropriate standard of judicial review is dispositive of which party has the burden of proof as any litigation proceeds from stage to stage until there is a substantive determination on the merits. Accordingly, identification of the correct analytical framework is essential to a proper judicial review of challenges to the decision-making process of a corporation's board of directors.

"The business judgment rule, as a standard of judicial review, is a common-law recognition of the statutory authority to manage a corporation that is vested in the board of directors."[8] The business judgment rule is a "presumption that in making a business decision the directors of a corporation acted on an informed basis, in good faith and in the honest belief that the action taken was in the best interests of the company." "An application of the traditional business judgment rule places the burden on the 'party challenging the [board's] decision to establish facts rebutting the presumption.' "[9] The effect of a proper invocation of the business judgment rule, as a standard of judicial review, is powerful because it operates deferentially. Unless the procedural presumption of the business judgment rule is rebutted, a "court will not substitute its judgment for that of the board if the [board's] decision can be 'attributed to any rational business purpose.' "[11]

---

[8]   *MM Companies v. Liquid Audio, Inc.,* 813 A.2d 1118, 1127 (Del. 2003).

[9]   *Id.*

[11]   *Id.* at 1373 (quoting *Unocal Corp. v. Mesa Petroleum Co.,* 493 A.2d 946, 954 (Del. 1985) (citation omitted)).

The business judgment rule embodies the deference that is accorded to managerial decisions of a board of directors. "Under normal circumstances, neither the courts nor the stockholders should interfere with the managerial decision of the directors."[12] There are certain circumstances, however, "which mandate that a court take a more direct and active role in overseeing the decisions made and actions taken by directors. In these situations, a court subjects the directors' conduct to enhanced scrutiny to ensure that it is reasonable,"[13] "before the protections of the business judgment rule may be conferred."[14]

Deal Protection Devices Require Enhanced Scrutiny

The dispositive issues in this appeal involve the defensive devices that protected the Genesis merger agreement.

It is well established that conflicts of interest arise when a board of directors acts to prevent stockholders from effectively exercising their right to vote contrary to the will of the board. The "omnipresent specter" of such conflict may be present whenever a board adopts defensive devices to protect a merger agreement. The stockholders' ability to effectively reject a merger agreement is likely to bear an inversely proportionate relationship to the structural and economic devices that the board has approved to protect the transaction.

Accordingly, in *Paramount v. Time,* we held that the business judgment rule applied to the Time board's original decision to merge with Warner. We further held, however, that defensive devices adopted by the board to protect the original merger transaction must withstand enhanced judicial scrutiny under the *Unocal* standard of review, even when that merger transaction does not result in a change of control.

Enhanced Scrutiny Generally

In *Paramount v. QVC,* this Court identified the key features of an enhanced judicial scrutiny test. The first feature is a "judicial determination regarding the adequacy of the decisionmaking process employed by the directors, including the information on which the directors based their decision."[35] The second feature is "a judicial examination of the reasonableness of the directors' action in light of the circumstances then existing." We also held that "the directors have the burden of proving that they were adequately informed and acted reasonably."

In *QVC,* we explained that the application of an enhanced judicial scrutiny test involves a judicial "review of the reasonableness of the substantive merits of the board's actions." In applying that standard, we held that "a court should not ignore the complexity of the directors' task"

---

[12] *Paramount Communications Inc. v. QVC Network Inc.,* 637 A.2d 34, 42 (Del. 1993).

[13] *Id.*

[14] *Unocal Corp. v. Mesa Petroleum Co.,* 493 A.2d at 954.

[35] *Paramount Communications Inc. v. QVC Network Inc.,* 637 A.2d 34, 45 (Del. 1993).

in the context in which action was taken. Accordingly, we concluded that a court applying enhanced judicial scrutiny should not decide whether the directors made a perfect decision but instead should decide whether "the directors' decision was, on balance, within a range of reasonableness."

A board's decision to protect its decision to enter a merger agreement with defensive devices against uninvited competing transactions that may emerge is analogous to a board's decision to protect against dangers to corporate policy and effectiveness when it adopts defensive measures in a hostile takeover contest.

Therefore, in applying enhanced judicial scrutiny to defensive devices designed to protect a merger agreement, a court must first determine that those measures are not preclusive or coercive *before* its focus shifts to the "range of reasonableness" in making a proportionality determination. If the trial court determines that the defensive devices protecting a merger are not preclusive or coercive, the proportionality paradigm of *Unocal* is applicable. The board must demonstrate that it has reasonable grounds for believing that a danger to the corporation and its stockholders exists if the merger transaction is not consummated. That burden is satisfied "by showing good faith and reasonable investigation." Such proof is materially enhanced if it is approved by a board comprised of a majority of outside directors or by an independent committee.

Deal Protection Devices

Defensive devices, as that term is used in this opinion, is a synonym for what are frequently referred to as "deal protection devices." Both terms are used interchangeably to describe any measure or combination of measures that are intended to protect the consummation of a merger transaction. Defensive devices can be economic, structural, or both.

Deal protection devices need not all be in the merger agreement itself. In this case, for example, the Section 251(c) provision in the merger agreement was combined with the separate voting agreements to provide a structural defense for the Genesis merger agreement against any subsequent superior transaction. Genesis made the NCS board's defense of its transaction absolute by insisting on the omission of any effective fiduciary out clause in the NCS merger agreement.

These Deal Protection Devices Unenforceable

Pursuant to the judicial scrutiny required under *Unocal's* two-stage analysis, the NCS directors must first demonstrate "that they had reasonable grounds for believing that a danger to corporate policy and effectiveness existed. . . ." To satisfy that burden, the NCS directors are required to show they acted in good faith after conducting a reasonable investigation. The threat identified by the NCS board was the possibility of losing the Genesis offer and being left with no comparable alternative transaction.

The second stage of the *Unocal* test requires the NCS directors to demonstrate that their defensive response was "reasonable in relation to the threat posed." This inquiry involves a two-step analysis. The NCS directors must first establish that the merger deal protection devices adopted in response to the threat were not "coercive" or "preclusive," and then demonstrate that their response was within a "range of reasonable responses" to the threat perceived.

This aspect of the *Unocal* standard provides for a disjunctive analysis. If defensive measures are either preclusive or coercive they are draconian and impermissible. In this case, the deal protection devices of the NCS board were *both* preclusive and coercive.

The deal protection devices adopted by the NCS board were designed to coerce the consummation of the Genesis merger and preclude the consideration of any superior transaction. The NCS directors' defensive devices are not within a reasonable range of responses to the perceived threat of losing the Genesis offer because they are preclusive and coercive. Accordingly, we hold that those deal protection devices are unenforceable.

Effective Fiduciary Out Required

The defensive measures that protected the merger transaction are unenforceable not only because they are preclusive and coercive but, alternatively, they are unenforceable because they are invalid as they operate in this case. Given the specifically enforceable irrevocable voting agreements, the provision in the merger agreement requiring the board to submit the transaction for a stockholder vote and the omission of a fiduciary out clause in the merger agreement completely prevented the board from discharging its fiduciary responsibilities to the minority stockholders when Omnicare presented its superior transaction.

In *QVC*, this Court recognized that "[w]hen a majority of a corporation's voting shares are acquired by a single person or entity, or by *a cohesive group acting together* [as in this case], there is a significant diminution in the voting power of those who thereby become minority stockholders." Therefore, we acknowledged that "[i]n the absence of devices protecting the minority stockholders, stockholder votes are likely to become mere formalities," where a cohesive group acting together to exercise majority voting powers have already decided the outcome. Consequently, we concluded that since the minority stockholders lost the power to influence corporate direction through the ballot, "minority stockholders must rely for protection solely on the fiduciary duties owed to them by the directors."

The directors of a Delaware corporation have a continuing obligation to discharge their fiduciary responsibilities, as future circumstances develop, after a merger agreement is announced. Genesis anticipated the likelihood of a superior offer after its merger agreement was announced and demanded defensive measures from the NCS board that *completely* protected its transaction. Instead of agreeing to the absolute defense of the Genesis merger from a superior offer, however, the NCS board was required to negotiate a fiduciary out clause to protect the NCS stockholders if the Genesis transaction became an inferior offer. By acceding to Genesis' ultimatum for complete protection *in futuro,* the NCS board disabled itself from exercising its own fiduciary obligations at a time when the board's own judgment is most important, *i.e.* receipt of a subsequent superior offer.

In the context of this preclusive and coercive lock up case, the protection of Genesis' contractual expectations must yield to the supervening responsibility of the directors to discharge their fiduciary duties on a continuing basis. The merger agreement and voting agreements, as they were combined to operate in concert in this case, are inconsistent with the NCS directors' fiduciary duties. To that extent, we hold that they are invalid and unenforceable.

CHAPTER 22

REGULATION OF INSIDER TRADING

$\blacksquare \ \blacksquare \ \blacksquare$

We study the regulation of insider trading in a corporations course for two reasons. First, corporate managers who trade in their corporation's shares are subject to fiduciary duties to the corporation and other shareholders. Second, securities trading affects the market for a corporation's stock, a critical factor in corporate governance.

In this chapter we consider the duties of insiders who trade in their companies' securities, both under state corporate law and the federal regulatory regime of § 10(b) of the Securities Exchange Act of 1934 and Rule 10b–5. We also look at those who are not traditional insiders but whose trading or other activities may implicate fiduciary duties. Finally, we also consider the special disclosure and disgorgement rules that apply to corporate executives and large shareholders under § 16 of that Act.

A. WHAT IS WRONG WITH INSIDER TRADING?

Consider a paradigm case of insider trading: The president of a high-technology company whose stock is traded on the NASDAQ Stock Market learns that the first prototypes of a new product in which the company has invested substantial resources are not performing as anticipated. As a result, the company will not be able to bring the product to market on schedule and may have to abandon it entirely, very likely causing the price of the company's stock to decline. Before the company discloses this prototype failure, the president sells much of the stock she owns on the open market. Immediately after the bad news is disclosed, the company's stock price drops sharply and remains at the lower price. It is clear that this violates federal, and perhaps state law, and would expose the president to enforcement actions and potential civil and criminal liability.

One of the questions this chapter explores is why the law should prohibit trading by the president on the basis of this information. Over the years, courts and commentators have proposed a number of different answers to what may seem, at first, a relatively simple question. Consider the various arguments discussed below:

1. INSIDER TRADING HARMS INVESTORS

Who is hurt by insider trading? The answer would seem obvious. When an insider trades on the basis of an informational advantage, investors who trade contemporaneously sell or buy at a "false price," which does not reflect the undisclosed information known to the insider. Intuitively, it seems fundamentally unfair to permit such insiders to take advantage of other investors, particularly when the insider benefits from information generated for a corporate purpose, not individual gain.

But is this intuitive argument valid? Trading in the securities of publicly-held companies occurs primarily on stock exchanges or electronic markets rather than in face-to-face transactions. Such markets are anonymous; buyers and sellers are randomly matched with each other. As Professor James D. Cox has noted:

> [T]rading is at most a fortuity for the investor because the investor is no worse off when the insider trades than when the insider does not trade. The investor's decision to sell or purchase is unaffected by whether the insider is also secretly buying or selling shares in the open market. If the insider neither trades nor discloses his confidential material information, one can nevertheless expect the investor to pursue his trading plan. Sellers naturally are disadvantaged by the nondisclosure of good news, just as buyers are disadvantaged by the nondisclosure of bad news. These considerations, however, cast no light on why the insider's decision to trade should prompt disclosure.

James D. Cox, *Insider Trading and Contracting: A Critical Response to the "Chicago School,"* 1986 Duke L.J. 628, 635 (1986).

A more innovative theory is based on a phenomenon called "The Law of Conservation of Securities." William K. S. Wang, *Trading on Material, Non Public Information on Impersonal Markets: Who is Harmed, and Who Can Sue Whom Under SEC Rule 10b–5?*, 54 S. Cal. L. Rev. 1217 (1981). Wang argues that insider trading does harm specific individuals, although not necessarily the investors who trade with insiders. He contends that the insider's trades preempt (and thereby injure) those who would otherwise buy or sell the shares traded by the insider. An insider also induces trades that otherwise would not have occurred. Under Wang's analysis, if an insider's buying causes the price to rise, those investors induced to sell are harmed when they fail to profit from the subsequent good news. Similarly, if an insider's selling causes the price to fall, those investors induced to buy suffer a price decrease when bad news is ultimately disclosed.

Like other theories, Wang's argument is valid only if the insider's trading significantly affects stock prices. Although studies suggest that the market reacts when insiders are known to be trading (especially when they are buying), it is unclear whether these price effects are sufficient to induce trading by those who would not otherwise have traded. Instead, many investors trade regardless of the presence of trading by insiders, and some of them will garner the same benefits as the insiders. As Professor Cox has noted, even if insider trading induces others to trade, "the insider's trading causes the parallel trader to dispose of a dog or acquire a pearl."

2. INSIDER TRADING DISTORTS COMPANY DISCLOSURES

Insider trading, if permitted, might interfere with informational efficiency in stock markets as insiders manipulate or delay public disclosure to the markets so they can exploit their informational advantage. In fact, the motivating reason for the rules against short-swing trading by designated insiders under § 16 of the Securities Exchange Act of 1934 may have been to reduce the incentive of corporate insiders to manipulate stock prices for their own trading benefit.

Besides encouraging manipulation, the possibility of insider trading could encourage insiders to delay truthful corporate disclosures. This delay would be exacerbated if information flowed up the corporate ladder, permitting insiders at each rung to take advantage of it before passing it along. But rules permitting insider trading might also motivate insiders, once they had traded, to release the information expeditiously to assure their trading profits.

The extent of the delay, if there is any, may turn on whether the inside information is good news or bad news. Professor Kenneth E. Scott has argued that insiders who can profit from delayed disclosure have more incentive to cause the corporation to disclose information when the information is positive than when it is negative. Positive news about the firm benefits all stockholders, including the insiders, so that insiders will be anxious to profit from it, whereas they can delay the impact of negative news by simply not trading. Kenneth E. Scott, *Insider Trading: Rule 10b–5, Disclosure and Corporate Privacy*, 9 J. Legal Stud. 801, 810–811 (1980).

Judge (formerly Professor) Frank Easterbrook disagrees that insiders will manipulate or delay disclosure, arguing that firms need to be credible in communicating to investors and that this credibility is furthered only if the firm promptly releases bad news along with the good. Frank H. Easterbrook, *Insider Trading, Secret Agents, Evidentiary Privileges, and the Production of Information*, 1981 Sup. Ct. Rev. 309, 327 (1981). But this argument may be wishful thinking. It assumes that the incentives of insiders to create corporate credibility outweigh their individual incentives to trade profitably in their company's stock.

3. INSIDER TRADING SIGNALS INFORMATION TO STOCK MARKETS

A contrary view is that insider trading actually promotes market efficiency. In a famous and provocative defense of the practice, Professor Henry Manne argued that insider trading transmits critical information to the stock markets, permitting smoother price changes before inside information is ultimately disclosed. Henry Manne, Insider Trading and the Stock Market 78–104 (1966). Manne contended that insider trading (like any other trading) affects stock prices. Insiders who buy on undisclosed good news drive up the price, and insiders who sell on undisclosed bad news drive it down. Sometimes insider trading can signal information that might not be readily communicable to the market. For example, the undisclosed information might be competitively sensitive, and insider trading signals its existence without disclosing its content.

Professor Cox has argued that the signaling argument is seriously flawed. He points out that for the investor who trades with the insider, smoother prices are a poor second choice to having the information being disclosed prior to the trade. Moreover, he argues that price changes occur much more quickly and efficiently through public disclosure than through trading because there are too many other factors affecting a stock price to permit an investor to discern clearly that there is undisclosed inside information reflected in that price. Cox also contends that the signaling argument proves too much. "If accepted, this position justifies massive trading and tipping to ensure that sufficient trading occurs to propel the stock to the equilibrium price appropriate for the nondisclosed information. Such widespread trading, however, compromises the corporate interest that justified nondisclosure in the first place."

In addition, the premise that stock prices respond to trading volume is also questionable. Moreover, even when markets know that insiders are trading (as required by federal reporting requirements), price responses are skewed. Studies indicate that markets react quickly when insiders buy (presumably believing good news is afoot), but only slightly when insiders sell (perhaps uncertain why the insider is selling).

4. INSIDER TRADING HARMS MARKETS AND INCREASES FIRMS' COST OF CAPITAL

Many condemn insider trading for undermining investor confidence in stock markets. Under the theory, if insider trading were permitted, investors would discount a company's stock price, thereby raising the company's cost of capital. When investors cannot distinguish which firms have material non-public information and when insiders are trading on that information, they will assume every investment in the market presents the same risk of insider trading. In such a case, some investors will refrain completely from investing, and others will protect themselves by discounting all stocks by the risk of insider trading for all firms. In markets lacking effective prohibitions against insider trading, this investor self-insurance has been shown to increase firms' cost of capital by the amount that investors discount the price of their securities.

To reduce this discount, firms may incur bonding and monitoring costs to signal to investors their lower likelihood of insider trading. In fact, most U.S. public companies now limit when insiders can trade in their company's stock. Using "blackouts" and "trading windows," many companies permit insiders to trade only for a specified period after earnings announcements and other important corporate announcements are released. One study found that this self-regulation both suppresses trading by insiders and narrows the bid-ask spread for the company's stock. The study also indicates that not only do company-imposed policies affect insider trading, but that market intermediaries (such as brokers) price securities to reflect the reduced risk of insider trading once companies adopt such policies.

5. INSIDER TRADING CONSTITUTES THEFT OF A COMPANY ASSET

Insider trading involves the use of private information for the benefit of the trader. As such, insider trading regulation can be seen as protection of intellectual property. As Professor Stephen Bainbridge has explained, "[t]here is an emerging consensus that the federal insider trading prohibition is most easily justified as a means of protecting property rights in information". Stephen Bainbridge, *Insider Trading*, Encyclopedia of Law and Economics 791 (2000).

Just as trade secrets, patents and other informational property are protected to encourage the production of socially valuable information, Bainbridge has argued that insider information should be protected to encourage companies to create it. Stephen Bainbridge, *Incorporating State Law Fiduciary Duties into the Federal Insider Trading Prohibition*, 52 Wash. & Lee L. Rev. 1189, 1256–57 (1995). For example, a mining company that strikes a rich ore deposit will want to use this information to obtain rights from adjacent property owners, without disclosing to them information about the strike.

Insider trading regulation simply recognizes that, as between the company and the insider, valuable company information belongs to the company, not the insider. Although insiders might exploit proprietary information in various ways, the prohibition against insider trading is a way of protecting company information. Not only does treating inside information as company property encourage its production (good news), but protecting adverse information from insider exploitation (bad news) reduces the company's cost of capital and increases its reputation for integrity.

A property-based justification for insider trading regulation, however, has some weaknesses. If insider trading exploits company property, private enforcement would seem likely. Certainly, companies enforce their patents, trademarks and other valuable proprietary information. Instead, public enforcement of insider trading rules is the norm, with private enforcement often piggy-backing on public prosecutions. Nor is insider trading as exploitative or damaging as patent infringement or copyright theft. In fact, there are doubts that insider trading causes actual injury to the corporation. For example, it is unclear whether insider trading systematically does delay the public release of company information, cause companies to lose opportunities (such as by preventing the acquisition of mineral rights), or injure a corporate reputation.

Nonetheless, viewing insider trading as theft of proprietary information—where detection is costly and difficult—explains why public enforcement may be necessary. Since detection of insider trading requires systems of securities surveillance, private civil enforcement may be inadequate to create sufficient disincentives. Only through public systems of surveillance (stock markets and government regulators) and public enforcement (including criminal sanctions) is inside information adequately protected from insider exploitation.

B. MATERIALITY

The concept of materiality pervades federal securities law and also makes regular appearance in state corporate law cases. For obvious reasons, trading on non-public information is prohibited only if the information is "material." The classic test for materiality, articulated by the Supreme Court in *TSC Industries, Inc. v. Northway, Inc.*, 426 U.S. 438 (1976), is that "there must be a substantial likelihood that the disclosure of the omitted fact would have been viewed by the reasonable investor as having significantly altered the 'total mix' of the information made available." Where the misstatement or omission relates to contingent or speculative information or events, the test has been expanded so that materiality "will depend at any given time upon a balancing of both the indicated probability that the event will occur and the anticipated magnitude of the event in light of the totality of the company activity." *Basic Inc. v. Levinson*, 485 U.S. 224, 238 (1988) (quoting *SEC v. Texas Gulf Sulphur Co.*, 401 F.2d 833, 849 (1968)).

C. INSIDER TRADING: STATE CORPORATE LAW

The law governing the trading of securities is today largely federal law, more specifically, law developed under § 10(b) of the 1934 Act and Rule 10b–5. But state law remains relevant for several reasons. First, federal law on insider trading builds on common law concepts pertaining to fraud and fiduciary duty. As a consequence, you should understand state law to appreciate the doctrinal choices that federal courts have made. Second, shareholders continue to seek remedies under state law against insiders who induce them to sell their shares at an inadequate price. Delaware has noted that the regulatory competition between state corporate law and federal securities law is a tension in corporate governance. Thus, state law on insider trading is also relevant to the federalism issues that we have considered elsewhere in this book.

1. DUTY TO SHAREHOLDERS AND INVESTORS

GOODWIN V. AGASSIZ
186 N.E. 659 (Mass. 1933).

RUGG, CHIEF JUSTICE:

[A stockholder of the Cliff Mining Company, the stock of which was listed on the Boston Stock Exchange, sought relief for losses suffered in the sale through the exchange of 700 shares of the company's stock to the defendants, who were officers and directors of the corporation. The court accepted the trial judge's findings that Cliff had started exploration for copper on its land in 1925, acting on certain geological surveys. The exploration was not successful, however, and the company removed its equipment in May, 1926.

Meanwhile, in March, 1926, an experienced geologist wrote a report theorizing as to the existence of copper deposits in the region of the company's holdings. The defendants, believing there was merit to the theory, secured options to land adjacent to the copper belt. Also, anticipating an increase in the value of the stock if the theory proved correct, the defendants purchased shares of the company's stock through an agent.

When the plaintiff learned of the termination of the original exploratory operations from a newspaper article—for which defendants were in no way responsible—he immediately sold his stock.]

The contention of the plaintiff is that the purchase of his stock in the company by the defendants without disclosing to him as a stockholder their knowledge of the geologist's theory, their belief that the theory was true, had value, the keeping secret the existence of the theory, discontinuance by the defendants of exploratory operations begun in 1925 on property of the Cliff Mining Company and their plan ultimately to test the value of the theory, constitute actionable wrong for which he as stockholder can recover.

The directors of a commercial corporation stand in a relation of trust to the corporation and are bound to exercise the strictest good faith in respect to its property and business. The contention that directors also occupy the position of trustee toward individual stockholders in the corporation is plainly contrary to repeated decisions of this court and cannot be supported. In *Smith v. Hurd*, 12 Metc. 371, 384, 46 Am.Dec. 690, it was said by Chief Justice Shaw: "There is no legal privity, relation, or immediate connection, between the holders of shares in a bank, in their individual capacity, on the one side, and the directors of the bank on the other. The directors are not the bailees, the factors, agents or trustees of such individual stockholders." * * *

While the general principle is as stated, circumstances may exist requiring that transactions between a director and a stockholder as to stock in the corporation be set aside. The knowledge naturally in the possession of a director as to the condition of a corporation places upon him a peculiar obligation to observe every requirement of fair dealing when directly buying or selling its stock. Mere silence does not usually amount to a breach of duty, but parties may stand in such relation to each other that an equitable responsibility arises to communicate facts. Purchases and sales of stock dealt in on the stock exchange are commonly impersonal affairs. An honest director would be in a difficult situation if he could neither buy nor sell on the stock exchange shares of stock in his corporation without first seeking out the other actual ultimate party to the transaction and disclosing to him everything which a court or jury might later find that he then knew affecting the real or speculative value of such shares. Business of that nature is a matter to be governed by practical rules. Fiduciary obligations of directors ought not to be made so onerous that men of experience and ability will be deterred from accepting such office. Law in its sanctions is not coextensive with morality. It cannot undertake to put all parties to every contract on an equality as to knowledge, experience, skill and shrewdness. It cannot undertake to relieve against hard bargains made between competent parties without fraud. On the other hand, directors cannot rightly be allowed to indulge with impunity in practices which do violence to prevailing standards of upright businessmen. Therefore, where a director personally seeks a stockholder for the purpose of buying his shares without making disclosure of material facts within his peculiar knowledge and not within reach of the stockholder, the transaction will be closely scrutinized and relief may be granted in appropriate instances. *Strong v. Repide*, 213 U.S. 419 * * * .

The precise question to be decided in the case at bar is whether on the facts found the defendants as directors had a right to buy stock of the plaintiff, a stockholder. Every element of actual fraud or misdoing by the defendants is negated by the findings. Fraud cannot be presumed; it must be proved. *Brown v. Little, Brown & Co., Inc.*, 269 Mass. 102, 117, 168 N.E. 521. The facts found afford no ground for inferring fraud or conspiracy. The only knowledge possessed by the defendants not open to the plaintiff was the existence of a theory formulated in a thesis by a geologist as to the possible existence of copper deposits where certain geological conditions existed common to the property of the Cliff Mining Company and that of other mining companies in its neighborhood. This thesis did not express an opinion that copper deposits would be found at any particular spot or on property of any specified owner. Whether that theory was sound or fallacious, no one knew, and so far as appears has never been demonstrated. The defendants made no representations to anybody about the theory. No facts found placed upon them any obligation to disclose the theory. A few days after the thesis expounding the theory was brought to the attention of the defendants, the annual report by the directors of the Cliff Mining Company for the calendar year 1925, signed by Agassiz for the directors, was issued. It did not cover the time when the theory was formulated. The report described the status of the operations under the exploration which had been begun in 1925. At the annual meeting of the stockholders of the company held early in April, 1926, no reference was made to the theory. It was then at most a hope, possibly an expectation. It had not passed the nebulous stage. No disclosure was made of it. The Cliff Mining Company was not harmed by the nondisclosure. There would have been no advantage to it, so far as appears, from a disclosure.

The disclosure would have been detrimental to the interests of another mining corporation in which the defendants were directors. In the circumstances there was no duty on the part of the defendants to set forth to the stockholders at the annual meeting their faith, aspirations and plans for the future. Events as they developed might render advisable radical changes in such views. Disclosure of the theory, if it ultimately was proved to be erroneous or without foundation in fact, might involve the defendants in litigation with those who might act on the hypothesis that it was correct. The stock of the Cliff Mining Company was bought and sold on the stock exchange. The identity of buyers and sellers of the stock in question in fact was not known to the parties and perhaps could not readily have been ascertained. The defendants caused the shares to be bought through brokers on the stock exchange. They said nothing to anybody as to the reasons actuating them. The plaintiff was no novice. He was a member of the Boston stock exchange and had kept a record of sales of Cliff Mining Company stock. He acted upon his own judgment in selling his stock. He made no inquiries of the defendants or of other officers of the company. The result is that the plaintiff cannot prevail.

Decree dismissing bill affirmed with costs.

Goodwin sets out what is generally considered to be the "majority rule": directors and officers owe a fiduciary duty only to the corporation and have no duty to disclose material non-public information when purchasing or selling securities in an impersonal market. Nevertheless, *Goodwin* recognized that a different rule might apply to when insiders purchase stock in face-to-face transactions—the "special facts doctrine" enunciated in *Strong v. Repide*, 213 U.S. 419 (1909). Under this doctrine, although an insider normally owes no fiduciary duty to individual shareholders, a plaintiff may be afforded a remedy when, in particular circumstances, non-disclosure amounts to unconscionable behavior by the insider.

The defendant in *Strong* was a director, the majority stockholder, and general manager of the corporation. He was authorized by the board of directors to conduct negotiations leading to the sale to the United States government of otherwise worthless land that was one of the corporation's principal assets. At the time of the transaction in question, he alone knew that the government was prepared to pay a substantial price for that land. To keep secret his identity, the defendant used an agent to purchase shares owned by plaintiff, in a face-to-face transaction, at a price that did not reflect the price the government was prepared to pay for the land. The Supreme Court granted rescission of the sale of stock, saying, "That the defendant was a director of the corporation is but one of the facts upon which the liability is asserted, the existence of all the others in addition making such a combination as rendered it the plain duty of the defendant to speak."

A third "rule" that has steadily attracted more adherents among state courts, is that officers and directors have a fiduciary duty to disclose material nonpublic information in any face-to-face stock transaction with a shareholder, regardless of whether there are special circumstances. This duty "exists because the stockholders have placed the directors in a strategic position where they can secure firsthand knowledge of important developments. * * * [T]he detailed information a director has of corporate affairs is in a very real sense property of the corporation, and * * * no director should be permitted to use such information for his own benefit at the expense of his stockholders." *Taylor v. Wright*, 159 P.2d 980, 984–85 (Cal.App. 1945).

This "strict" or "Kansas" rule had its origin in *Hotchkiss v. Fischer*, 16 P.2d 531 (Kan. 1932). The plaintiff, an impoverished widow from Burr Oak, Kansas, came to Topeka shortly before a board meeting to inquire of the defendant, who was president and a director of the corporation, whether she could expect a dividend. If not, she believed she would have to sell her stock. The president replied that he could not say whether a dividend would be declared until the board met. He showed her the corporation's financial statements, explained them, but maintained a rather pessimistic stance. The widow sold her stock to him for $1.25 per share. Three days later, the corporation declared a dividend of $1 per share. The court held that in such a transaction, the officer or director "acts in a relation of scrupulous trust and confidence," and his behavior is therefore subject to the closest scrutiny.

Courts have applied the "special facts" doctrine and the "Kansas rule" only to transactions between insiders and existing shareholders. If an insider sold stock to someone who was not a shareholder, courts held that there was no breach of fiduciary duty because the purchaser did not become a shareholder until after the transaction was completed. They have also held that where an insider purchased stock in an impersonal market, the fact she had not made any representation directly to her counterparty relieved her from liability.

2.   DUTY TO THE CORPORATION

Because courts had held that directors and officers generally owe no duty to individual participants who trade in the open market, common law was largely unable to control insider trading abuses. In *Brophy v. Cities Service Co.,* 70 A.2d 5 (Del. Ch. 1949), however, the Delaware Court of Chancery broke new ground by recognizing for the first time that *the corporation* could state a cause of action against insiders for insider trading. In *Brophy,* an employee of Cities Service Co. learned through his position as the "confidential secretary" to a corporate officer that Cities Service Co. intended to repurchase shares of its own stock, which was likely to drive up the price of the shares. The employee then used this confidential information to buy shares for himself and later resold the shares for a substantial profit. The court found that although the employee was not in a position of trust or confidence, because he had obtained confidential information, he should be treated as "analogous to a fiduciary." As such, his duty was not to use the information "in competition with or to the injury of the corporation." The court further noted that it was immaterial whether the insider trading had caused the corporation to suffer any actual loss. Citing *Guth v. Loft, Inc.*, 5 A.2d 503 (Del. 1939) the court concluded that "[p]ublic policy will not permit an employee occupying a position of trust and confidence toward his employer to abuse that relation to his own profit, regardless of whether his employer suffers a loss."

DIAMOND V. OREAMUNO
248 N.E.2d 910 (N.Y. 1969).

FULD, CHIEF JUDGE:

The complaint was filed by a shareholder of Management Assistance, Inc. (MAI) asserting a derivative action against a number of its officers and directors to compel an accounting for profits allegedly acquired as a result of a breach of fiduciary duty. It charges that two of the defendants—Oreamuno, chairman of the board of directors, and Gonzalez, its president—had used inside information, acquired by them solely by virtue of their positions, in order to reap large personal profits from the sale of MAI shares and that these profits rightfully belong to the corporation.

MAI is in the business of financing computer installations through sale and lease back arrangements with various commercial and industrial users. Under its lease provisions, MAI was required to maintain and repair the computers but, at the time of this suit, it lacked the capacity to perform this function itself and was forced to engage the manufacturer of the computers, International Business Machines (IBM), to service the machines. As a result of a sharp increase by IBM of its charges for such service, MAI's expenses for August of 1966 rose considerably and its net earnings declined from $262,253 in July to $66,233 in August, a decrease of about 75%. This information, although earlier known to the defendants, was not made public until October of 1966. Prior to the release of the information, however, Oreamuno and Gonzalez sold off a total of 56,500 shares of their MAI stock at the then current market price of $28 a share.

After the information concerning the drop in earnings was made available to the public, the value of a share of MAI stock immediately fell from the $28 realized by the defendants to $11. Thus, the plaintiff alleges, by taking advantage of their privileged position and their access to confidential information, Oreamuno and Gonzalez were able to realize $800,000 more for their securities than they would have had this inside information not been available to them. A motion by the defendants to dismiss the complaint for failure to state a cause of action was granted by the court at Special Term.

It is well established, as a general proposition, that a person who acquires special knowledge or information by virtue of a confidential or fiduciary relationship with another is not free to exploit that knowledge or information for his own personal benefit but must account to his principal for any profits derived therefrom. This, in turn, is merely a corollary of the broader principle, inherent in the nature of the fiduciary relationship, that prohibits a trustee or agent from extracting secret profits from his position of trust.

In support of their claim that the complaint fails to state a cause of action, the defendants take the position that, although it is admittedly wrong for an officer or director to use his position to obtain trading profits for himself in the stock of his corporation, the action ascribed to them did not injure or damage MAI in any way. Accordingly, the defendants continue, the corporation should not be permitted to recover the proceeds. They acknowledge that, by virtue of the exclusive access which officers and directors have to inside information, they possess an unfair advantage over other shareholders and, particularly, the persons who had purchased the stock from them but, they contend, the corporation itself was unaffected and, for that reason, a derivative action is an inappropriate remedy.

The primary concern, in a case such as this, is not to determine whether the corporation has been damaged but to decide, as between the corporation and the defendants, who has a higher claim to the proceeds derived from the exploitation of the information. In our opinion, there can be no justification for permitting officers and directors, such as the defendants, to retain for themselves profits which, it is alleged, they derived solely from exploiting information gained by virtue of their inside position as corporate officials.

In addition, it is pertinent to observe that, despite the lack of any specific allegation of damage, it may well be inferred that the defendants' actions might have caused some harm to the enterprise. Although the corporation may have little concern with the day-to-day transactions in its shares, it has a great interest in maintaining a reputation of integrity, an image of probity, for its management and in insuring the continued public acceptance and marketability of its stock. When officers and directors abuse their position in order to gain personal profits, the effect may be to cast a cloud on the corporation's name, injure stockholder relations and undermine public regard for the corporation's securities.

Although no appellate court in this State has had occasion to pass upon the precise question before us, the concept underlying the present cause of action is hardly a new one. (See, *e.g.*, Securities Exchange Act of 1934 § 16[b]; *Brophy v. Cities Serv. Co.*, 31 Del.Ch. 241 [70 A.2d 5 (1949)]; Restatement, 2d, Agency, § 388, comment c.) Under Federal law (Securities Exchange Act of 1934, § 16[b]), for example, it is conclusively presumed that, when a director, officer or 10% shareholder buys and sells securities of his corporation within a six-month period, he is trading on inside information. The remedy which the Federal statute provides in that situation is precisely the same as that sought in the present case under State law, namely, an action brought by the corporation or on its behalf to recover all profits derived from the transactions.

Although the provisions of section 16(b) may not apply to all cases of trading on inside information, it demonstrates that a derivative action can be an effective method for dealing with such abuses which may be used to accomplish a similar purpose in cases not specifically covered by the statute. In *Brophy v. Cities Serv. Co.*, *supra*, for example, the Chancery Court of Delaware allowed a similar remedy in a situation not covered by the Federal legislation. And a similar view has been expressed in the Restatement, 2d Agency (§ 388, comment c):

> c.   *Use of confidential information.* An agent who acquires confidential information in the course of his employment or in violation of his duties has a duty * * * to account for any profits made by the use of such information, although this does not harm the principal. So, if [a corporate officer] has "inside" information that the corporation is about to purchase or sell securities, or to declare or to pass a dividend, profits made by him in stock transactions undertaken because of his knowledge are held in constructive trust for the principal.

In view of the practical difficulties inherent in an action under the Federal law, the desirability of creating an effective common-law remedy is manifest. "Dishonest directors should not find absolution from retributive justice", Ballantine observed in his work on Corporations, "by concealing their identity from their victims under the mask of the stock exchange." There is ample room in a situation such as is here presented for a "private Attorney General" to come forward and enforce proper behavior on the part of corporate officials through the medium of the derivative action brought in the name of the corporation. Only by sanctioning such a cause of action will there be any effective method to prevent the type of abuse of corporate office complained of in this case.

The order appealed from should be affirmed, with costs, and the question certified answered in the affirmative.

Diamond has been widely cited for the proposition that corporate officers and directors may be held liable for insider trading under state law without showing harm to the corporation. Nevertheless, *Diamond* has not been followed in any jurisdiction since being decided 45 years ago. Initially, the Florida Supreme Court refused to adopt the "innovative ruling" of the New York Court of Appeals in *Diamond,* holding that Florida courts would continue to require that the corporation prove that it had suffered actual damage from the insider trading to be entitled to relief. *Schein v. Chasen,* 313 So.2d 739 (Fla.1975). Three years later the Seventh Circuit also disallowed recovery in derivative claims absent a showing of actual harm to the corporation. *Freeman v. Decio,* 584 F.2d 186 (7th Cir. 1978). The *Freeman* court noted that in the years following *Diamond*, federal law had evolved so as to provide effective remedies against insider trading. That is, *Diamond* had been superseded.

3. INSIDER TRADING: DELAWARE AND CALIFORNIA

Does state law have any relevance to insider trading? Consider the litigation in Delaware and California, considered above in Chapter 16, involving Oracle Corporation's Chairman and CEO, Lawrence J. Ellison.

The *Oracle* cases arose from allegations that Ellison illegally sold $900 million in Oracle shares less than a month before the software giant announced publicly that it would miss its market estimates for the third quarter of 2001. During an analyst conference call held on December 14, 2000, Ellison announced that Oracle was "off to a great start" for the upcoming third quarter 2001. Between January 22 and January 31, 2001, Ellison then sold 29 million shares of Oracle stock (two percent of Ellison's total Oracle holdings). As Oracle's third quarter of 2001 drew to a close it became apparent that Oracle would not meet its December 2000 projections. On March 1, 2001, Oracle publicly disclosed that it would fall short of its market projections for the third quarter 2001. The announcement triggered a 50 percent drop in Oracle's stock price to around $14 per share. By selling his shares before the negative news became public, Oracle's shareholders alleged that Ellison potentially avoided $400 million in losses.

Oracle's shareholders filed derivative suits in Delaware (Oracle's state of incorporation) and California (Oracle's headquarters), and a federal class action lawsuit against Ellison in the U.S. District Court in San Francisco. The Delaware litigation ended in a dismissal. Vice-Chancellor Strine concluded the complaint failed to show that Ellison knew about Oracle's forthcoming negative announcement when he sold his shares. *In re Oracle Corp. Deriv. Litig.*, 808 A.2d 1206 (Del.Ch. 2002). The California litigation, however, resulted in a novel $124 million settlement pursuant to which Ellison, without admitting wrongdoing for the 2001 stock sales, agreed to donate $100 million to charitable organizations and pay $24 million in plaintiffs' legal fees to resolve the insider trading allegations.

The main issue in *Oracle* was whether *Brophy* continued to provide a remedy for insider trading under Delaware law. Vice-Chancellor Strine noted that the *Brophy* doctrine is "so venerable as to pre-date much of the pertinent federal law, in particular that arising under Securities Exchange Commission Rule 10b–5." Nevertheless, he acknowledged that its continuing vitality was an "unsettled question." Indeed, in light of the powerful federal role governing insider trading, several Delaware decisions, while upholding *Brophy*, questioned whether insider trading should be regulated primarily, if not exclusively, by federal securities law.

Vice-Chancellor Strine declined "to conclude that *Brophy* is an outdated precedent that ought to be abandoned" and found for the defendants "under a reasoned application of *Brophy*." Nevertheless, he seemed strongly inclined to overrule *Brophy*. He pointed out that while *Brophy* has been cited frequently by Delaware courts, the doctrine had never been applied to award damages to an issuer. He was also clearly influenced by countervailing jurisprudence in other jurisdictions and by the risk of duplicative liability. Most important, however, were the federalism questions that *Brophy* raises. For Vice-Chancellor Strine, the potentially dangerous regulatory conflict between Delaware law and the federal insider trading regime was such that he appeared willing to view insider trading as predominantly a question of federal regulation.

Unlike Delaware, California has adopted an express statutory prohibition against insider trading. Section 25402 of the California Corporate Securities Law of 1968 makes it unlawful for an issuer of securities, or an officer, director, controlling shareholder, or any person with a relationship affords access to material information of the company to:

> Purchase or sell any security of [an] issuer in this state at a time when he knows material nonpublic information about the issuer . . . which would significantly affect the market price of that security and which is not generally available to the public, and which he knows is not intended to be so available.

Cal. Corp. Code § 25402 (West 1977).

California's approach to regulating insider trading is singular in several respects. First, it provides extensive express remedies for insider trading violations. California Corporations Code § 25502 allows private investors who bought or sold securities from a person in violation of § 25402 to recover damages equal to the difference between the price at which the investor bought or sold the security and the market value of the stock had the information been publicly disclosed. Additionally, California is the only state that has a derivative remedy that allows the corporation to recover treble damages. California Corporations Code § 25502.5 makes violators of § 25402 liable to the issuer for up to three times the illegal trading profits. Only issuers who have more than $1 million in assets and more than 500 shareholders may bring an action under § 25502.5. Because § 25502.5 is a disgorgement statute, the issuer does not need to show actual harm to the corporation to recover damages. While § 25502.5 remains largely untested, the *Oracle* settlement suggests that this provision may have teeth. The plaintiffs' lawyers believe that the risk of treble damages liability under California law (upwards of $1.2 million) motivated Ellison to settle the insider trading claim rather than risk a trial.

California's insider trading law is also unusual is that its jurisdictional reach is not limited to companies incorporated in California. California's legislature in enacting the Corporate Securities Law of 1968, including § 25402, intended that the basis of jurisdiction and regulation should be the offer or sale of securities in California, not the principal place of business or corporate domicile. Consequently, insiders of Delaware corporations who engage in securities transactions in California may be liable under California's insider trading law.

One California court has interpreted § 25402 to reach insider trading claims brought against executives of a Delaware corporation. In *Friese v. Superior Court of San Diego County,* 36 Cal.Rptr.3d 558 (App. 2005), the plaintiffs alleged that several executives of Peregrine Systems, Inc., a publicly traded Delaware corporation that had its headquarters in San Diego, had engaged in insider trading in California. In finding that California's insider trading law was applicable, the court held that § 25402 should be construed as a "securities" law whose reach is not limited to corporations incorporated in California. The court reasoned that on its face, the statute is not limited to domestic corporations. Further, the court rejected the argument that Delaware's internal affairs doctrine shielded Delaware defendants from liability under California's insider trading law. The court imported an exception to the internal affairs doctrine set forth in § 309 of Restatement of Conflicts (Second), which provides that with respect to a particular issue, where there is no local statute (*i.e.,* securities laws) and where another state has a more significant relationship to the parties and the transaction than the state of incorporation, the local law of the other state will be applied. The court concluded that "the prohibition on insider trading was adopted as a means of protecting investor confidence in the securities market and more broadly as a means of punishing what is perceived by the public as immoral conduct." Thus, "given the public and regulatory interests [the Section] serves, it is not subject to the internal affairs doctrine."

For an excellent discussion of the federalism issues involved in the Delaware and California approaches to insider trading, see Donald C. Langevoort, *Federalism in Corporate/Securities Law: Reflections on Delaware, California and State Regulation of Insider Trading*, 40 U.S.F. L. Rev. 889 (2005–2006).

D. INSIDER TRADING: RULE 10b–5

1. OVERVIEW

Section 10(b) and Rule 10b–5 contain no express language prohibiting insider trading. Nevertheless, over the years the SEC and the courts have broadly interpreted Rule 10b–5 to contain a general prohibition against insider trading in open market transactions as well as in face-to-face dealings. Further, courts have implied a private right of action under the rule, even though as drafted, Rule 10b–5 provides no express private action for damages. Rule 10b5–1 incorporates this understanding:

> **(a) General.** The "manipulative and deceptive devices" prohibited by Section 10(b) of the [Securities Exchange Act] and [Rule 10b–5] include, among other things, the purchase or sale of a security of any issuer, on the basis of material nonpublic information about that security or issuer, in breach of a duty of trust or confidence that is owed directly, indirectly, or derivatively, to the issuer of that security or the shareholders of that issuer, or to any other person who is the source of the material nonpublic information.
>
> **(b) Definition of "on the basis of."** Subject to the affirmative defenses under Rule 10b5–1, discussed below, a purchase or sale of a security of an issuer is "on the basis of" material nonpublic information about that security or issuer if the person making the purchase or sale was aware of the material nonpublic information when the person made the purchase or sale.

Under Rule 10b–5, it is unlawful for a director, executive, or other employee of a corporation to engage in purchases or sales of the corporation's stock motivated by material non-public information. A person other than a traditional corporate insider may be treated as an insider for purposes of Rule 10b–5 where confidential corporate information is disclosed legitimately to such person in connection with her work for the corporation (*e.g.*, an underwriter, attorney, or accountant).

Rule 10b–5 may also prohibit trading by a person who is an outsider. Under the misappropriation theory such a person may be deemed to have violated Rule 10b–5 because she has misappropriated material, non-public information from its source in a breach of a fiduciary duty owing to the source rather than to the person with whom she trades.

Rule 10b–5 does not prohibit disclosure of material, non-public information if the person who receives such information (a "tippee") does not trade. The tippee is prohibited from trading only if the person who disclosed the information (the tipper") did so in breach of a fiduciary duty and the tippee knew of the breach. In determining whether there has been such a breach, the test is whether the tipper personally benefited from the disclosure.

In addition to Rule 10b–5, some insider trading is regulated by § 16(b) of the 1934 Act. Under that section, any director, executive officer or holder of 10% of a class of equity securities is liable to the corporation for any profits realized from a purchase and sale or sale and purchase within a six-month period. The SEC has adopted extensive rules implementing this section.

2.   DUTY TO "DISCLOSE OR ABSTAIN"

The first unambiguous statement about insider trading under federal law was *In the Matter of Cady, Roberts & Co.*, 40 S.E.C. 907 (1961), an administrative proceeding against a brokerage firm and two of its members, one of whom had traded on material non-public information given him by the other, who was a member of the board of the corporation in question. In the opinion in the proceeding, Chairman William Cary wrote, "We, and the courts have consistently held that insiders must disclose material facts which are known to them by virtue of their position but which are not known to persons with whom they deal and which, if known, would affect their investment judgment. . . . If, on the other hand, disclosure prior to effecting a purchase or sale would be improper or unrealistic under the circumstances, we believe the alternative is to forego the transaction." Thus was born the so-called "disclose or abstain rule," sometimes called the "*Cady, Roberts* duty."

CHIARELLA V. UNITED STATES
445 U.S. 222 (1980).

MR. JUSTICE POWELL delivered the opinion of the Court:

The question in this case is whether a person who learns from the confidential documents of one corporation that it is planning an attempt to secure control of a second corporation violates § 10(b) of the Securities Exchange Act of 1934 if he fails to disclose the impending takeover before trading in the target company's securities.

Petitioner is a printer by trade. In 1975 and 1976, he worked as a "markup man" in the New York composing room of Pandick Press, a financial printer. Among documents that petitioner handled were five announcements of corporate takeover bids. When these documents were delivered to the printer, the identities of the acquiring and target corporations were concealed by blank spaces or false names. The true names were sent to the printer on the night of the final printing.

The petitioner, however, was able to deduce the names of the target companies before the final printing from other information contained in the documents. Without disclosing his knowledge, petitioner purchased stock in the target companies and sold the shares immediately after the takeover attempts were made public. By this method, petitioner realized a gain of slightly more than $30,000 in the course of 14 months.

[A]dministrative and judicial interpretations have established that silence in connection with the purchase or sale of securities may operate as a fraud actionable under § 10(b) despite the absence of statutory language or legislative history specifically addressing the legality of nondisclosure. But such liability is premised upon a duty to disclose arising from a relationship of trust and confidence between parties to a transaction. Application of a duty to disclose prior to trading guarantees that corporate insiders, who have an obligation to place the shareholder's welfare before their own, will not benefit personally through fraudulent use of material nonpublic information.

[N]ot every instance of financial unfairness constitutes fraudulent activity under § 10(b). . . . [T]he element required to make silence fraudulent—a duty to disclose—is absent in this case. No duty could arise from petitioner's relationship with the sellers of the target company's securities, for petitioner had no prior dealings with them. He was not their agent, he was not a fiduciary, he was not a person in whom the sellers had placed their trust and confidence. He was, in fact, a complete stranger who dealt with the sellers only through impersonal market transactions.

We cannot affirm petitioner's conviction without recognizing a general duty between all participants in market transactions to forgo actions based on material, nonpublic information. Formulation of such a broad duty, which departs radically from the established doctrine that duty arises from a specific relationship between two parties, should not be undertaken absent some explicit evidence of congressional intent.

As we have seen, no such evidence emerges from the language or legislative history of § 10(b). Moreover, neither the Congress nor the Commission ever has adopted a parity-of-information rule. Instead the problems caused by misuse of market information have been addressed by detailed and sophisticated regulation that recognizes when use of market information may not harm operation of the securities markets. For example, the Williams Act limits but does not completely prohibit a tender offeror's purchases of target corporation stock before public announcement of the offer. Congress' careful action in this and other areas contrasts, and is in some tension, with the broad rule of liability we are asked to adopt in this case.

Indeed, the theory upon which the petitioner was convicted is at odds with the Commission's view of § 10(b) as applied to activity that has the same effect on sellers as the petitioner's purchases. "Warehousing" takes place when a corporation gives advance notice of its intention to launch a tender offer to institutional investors who then are able to purchase stock in the target company before the tender offer is made public and the price of shares rises. In this case, as in warehousing, a buyer of securities purchases stock in a target corporation on the basis of market information which is unknown to the seller. In both of these situations, the seller's behavior presumably would be altered if he had the nonpublic information. Significantly, however, the Commission has acted to bar warehousing under its authority to regulate tender offers after recognizing that action under § 10(b) would rest on a "somewhat different theory" than that previously used to regulate insider trading as fraudulent activity.

We see no basis for applying such a new and different theory of liability in this case. As we have emphasized before, the 1934 Act cannot be read " 'more broadly than its language and the statutory scheme reasonably permit.' " Section 10(b) is aptly described as a catch-all provision, but what it catches must be fraud. When an allegation of fraud is based upon nondisclosure, there can be no fraud absent a duty to speak. We hold that a duty to disclose under § 10(b) does not arise from the mere possession of nonpublic market information. The contrary result is without support in the legislative history of § 10(b) and would be inconsistent with the careful plan that Congress has enacted for regulation of the securities markets.

In its brief to this Court, the United States offers an alternative theory to support petitioner's conviction. It argues that petitioner breached a duty to the acquiring corporation when he acted upon information that he obtained by virtue of his position as an employee of a printer employed by the corporation. The breach of this duty is said to support a conviction under § 10(b) for fraud perpetrated upon both the acquiring corporation and the sellers.

We need not decide whether this theory has merit for it was not submitted to the jury.

The jury instructions demonstrate that petitioner was convicted merely because of his failure to disclose material, nonpublic information to sellers from whom he bought the stock of target corporations. The jury was not instructed on the nature or elements of a duty owed by petitioner to anyone other than the sellers. Because we cannot affirm a criminal conviction on the basis of a theory not presented to the jury, we will not speculate upon whether such a duty exists, whether it has been breached, or whether such a breach constitutes a violation of § 10(b).

The judgment of the Court of Appeals is reversed.

MR. CHIEF JUSTICE BURGER, dissenting.

I believe that the jury instructions in this case properly charged a violation of § 10(b) and Rule 10b–5, and I would affirm the conviction.

As a general rule, neither party to an arm's-length business transaction has an obligation to disclose information to the other unless the parties stand in some confidential or fiduciary relation. This rule permits a businessman to capitalize on his experience and skill in securing and evaluating relevant information; it provides incentive for hard work, careful analysis, and astute forecasting. But the policies that underlie the rule also should limit its scope. In particular, the rule should give way when an informational advantage is obtained, not by superior experience, foresight, or industry, but by some unlawful means. I would read § 10(b) and Rule 10b–5 to encompass and build on this principle: to mean that a person who has misappropriated nonpublic information has an absolute duty to disclose that information or to refrain from trading.

The Court's opinion, as I read it, leaves open the question whether § 10(b) and Rule 10b–5 prohibit trading on misappropriated nonpublic information. Instead, the Court apparently concludes that this theory of the case was not submitted to the jury. In the Court's view, the instructions given the jury were premised on the erroneous notion that the mere failure to disclose nonpublic information, however acquired, is a deceptive practice. And because of this premise, the jury was not instructed that the means by which Chiarella acquired his informational advantage—by violating a duty owed to the acquiring companies—was an element of the offense.

The Court's reading of the District Court's charge is unduly restrictive. Fairly read as a whole and in the context of the trial, the instructions required the jury to find that Chiarella obtained his trading advantage by misappropriating the property of his employer's customers.

[T]he evidence shows beyond all doubt that Chiarella, working literally in the shadows of the warning signs in the printshop, misappropriated—stole to put it bluntly—valuable nonpublic information entrusted to him in the utmost confidence. He then exploited his ill-gotten informational advantage by purchasing securities in the market. In my view, such conduct plainly violates § 10(b) and Rule 10b–5. Accordingly, I would affirm the judgment of the Court of Appeals.

3. TIPPER-TIPPEE LIABILITY

It is clear that under § 10(b) and Rule 10b–5 it is unlawful as a matter of "classical" insider trading law for a director, senior executive or other employee of a public corporation to use material nonpublic information to purchase or sell that corporation's stock. The same is true for "constructive insiders," such as lawyers, accountants, or consultants, who by nature of their relationship have a fiduciary duty to a corporation. Does the same prohibition apply to an outsider who has obtained material nonpublic information? And if the outsider obtains the information as a "tip" from an insider, has the "tipper" violated the law?

DIRKS V. SECURITIES AND EXCHANGE COMMISSION
463 U.S. 646 (1983).

JUSTICE POWELL delivered the opinion of the Court:

Petitioner Raymond Dirks received material nonpublic information from "insiders" of a corporation with which he had no connection. He disclosed this information to investors who relied on it in trading in the shares of the corporation. The question is whether Dirks violated the antifraud provisions of the federal securities laws by this disclosure.

In 1973, Dirks was an officer of a New York broker-dealer firm who specialized in providing investment analysis of insurance company securities to institutional investors. On March 6, Dirks received information from Ronald Secrist, a former officer of Equity Funding of America. Secrist alleged that the assets of Equity Funding, a diversified corporation primarily engaged in selling life insurance and mutual funds, were vastly overstated as the result of fraudulent corporate practices. Secrist also stated that various regulatory agencies had failed to act on similar charges made by Equity Funding employees. He urged Dirks to verify the fraud and disclose it publicly.

Dirks decided to investigate the allegations. He visited Equity Funding's headquarters in Los Angeles and interviewed several officers and employees of the corporation. The senior management denied any wrongdoing, but certain corporation employees corroborated the charges of fraud. Neither Dirks nor his firm owned or traded any Equity Funding stock, but throughout his investigation he openly discussed the information he had obtained with a number of clients and investors. Some of these persons sold their holdings of Equity Funding securities, including five investment advisers who liquidated holdings of more than $16 million.[2]

---

[2]   Dirks received from his firm a salary plus a commission for securities transactions above a certain amount that his clients directed through his firm. But "[i]t is not clear how many of those with whom Dirks spoke promised to direct some brokerage business through [Dirks' firm] to compensate Dirks, or how many actually did so." The Boston Company Institutional Investors,

During the two-week period in which Dirks pursued his investigation and spread word of Secrist's charges, the price of Equity Funding stock fell from $26 per share to less than $15 per share. This led the New York Stock Exchange to halt trading on March 27. Shortly thereafter California insurance authorities impounded Equity Funding's records and uncovered evidence of the fraud. Only then did the Securities and Exchange Commission (SEC) file a complaint against Equity Funding[3] and only then, on April 2, did the *Wall Street Journal* publish a front-page story based largely on information assembled by Dirks. Equity Funding immediately went into receivership.

The SEC began an investigation into Dirks' role in the exposure of the fraud. After a hearing by an administrative law judge, the SEC found that Dirks had aided and abetted violations of § 17(a) of the Securities Act of 1933, § 10(b) of the Securities Exchange Act of 1934, and SEC Rule 10b–5, by repeating the allegations of fraud to members of the investment community who later sold their Equity Funding stock. The SEC concluded: "Where 'tippees'—regardless of their motivation or occupation—come into possession of material 'information that they know is confidential and know or should know came from a corporate insider,' they must either publicly disclose that information or refrain from trading." Recognizing, however, that Dirks "played an important role in bringing [Equity Funding's] massive fraud to light," the SEC only censured him.

We were explicit in *Chiarella* in saying that there can be no duty to disclose where the person who has traded on inside information "was not [the corporation's] agent, * * * was not a fiduciary, [or] was not a person in whom the sellers [of the securities] had placed their trust and confidence." Not to require such a fiduciary relationship, we recognized, would "depar[t] radically from the established doctrine that duty arises from a specific relationship between two parties" and would amount to "recognizing a general duty between all participants in market transactions to forego actions based on material, nonpublic information."

The conclusion that recipients of inside information do not invariably acquire a duty to disclose or abstain does not mean that such tippees always are free to trade on the information. The need for a ban on some tippee trading is clear. Not only are insiders forbidden by their fiduciary relationship from personally using undisclosed corporate information to their advantage, but they may not give such information to an outsider for the same improper purpose of exploiting the information for their personal gain. Similarly, the transactions of those who knowingly participate with

---

Inc., promised Dirks about $25,000 in commissions, but it is unclear whether Boston actually generated any brokerage business for his firm.

[3] As early as 1971, the SEC had received allegations of fraudulent accounting practices at Equity Funding. Moreover, on March 9, 1973, an official of the California Insurance Department informed the SEC's regional office in Los Angeles of Secrist's charges of fraud. Dirks himself voluntarily presented his information at the SEC's regional office beginning on March 27.

the fiduciary in such a breach are "as forbidden" as transactions "on behalf of the trustee himself." Thus, the tippee's duty to disclose or abstain is derivative from that of the insider's duty. As we noted in *Chiarella,* "[t]he tippee's obligation has been viewed as arising from his role as a participant after the fact in the insider's breach of a fiduciary duty."

Thus, a tippee assumes a fiduciary duty to the shareholders of a corporation not to trade on material nonpublic information only when the insider has breached his fiduciary duty to the shareholders by disclosing the information to the tippee and the tippee knows or should know that there has been a breach.

Under the inside-trading and tipping rules set forth above, we find that there was no actionable violation by Dirks. It is undisputed that Dirks himself was a stranger to Equity Funding, with no pre-existing fiduciary duty to its shareholders. He took no action, directly or indirectly, that induced the shareholders or officers of Equity Funding to repose trust or confidence in him. There was no expectation by Dirks' sources that he would keep their information in confidence. Nor did Dirks misappropriate or illegally obtain the information about Equity Funding. Unless the insiders breached their *Cady, Roberts* duty to shareholders in disclosing the nonpublic information to Dirks, he breached no duty when he passed it on to investors as well as to the *Wall Street Journal.*

It is clear that neither Secrist nor the other Equity Funding employees violated their *Cady, Roberts* duty to the corporation's shareholders by providing information to Dirks. The tippers received no monetary or personal benefit for revealing Equity Funding's secrets, nor was their purpose to make a gift of valuable information to Dirks. As the facts of this case clearly indicate, the tippers were motivated by a desire to expose the fraud. In the absence of a breach of duty to shareholders by the insiders, there was no derivative breach by Dirks. Dirks therefore could not have been "a participant after the fact in [an] insider's breach of a fiduciary duty."

We conclude that Dirks, in the circumstances of this case, had no duty to abstain from use of the inside information that he obtained. The judgment of the Court of Appeals therefore is

Reversed.

JUSTICE BLACKMUN, with whom JUSTICE BRENNAN and JUSTICE MARSHALL join, dissenting.

The Court today takes still another step to limit the protections provided investors by § 10(b) of the Securities Exchange Act of 1934. The device employed in this case engrafts a special motivational requirement on the fiduciary duty doctrine. This innovation excuses a knowing and intentional violation of an insider's duty to shareholders if the insider does not act from a motive of personal gain. Even on the extraordinary facts of this case, such an innovation is not justified.

No one questions that Secrist himself could not trade on his inside information to the disadvantage of uninformed shareholders and purchasers of Equity Funding securities. Unlike the printer in *Chiarella,* Secrist stood in a fiduciary relationship with these shareholders. As the Court states, corporate insiders have an affirmative duty of disclosure when trading with shareholders of the corporation. This duty extends as well to purchasers of the corporation's securities.

In my view, Secrist violated his duty to Equity Funding shareholders by transmitting material nonpublic information to Dirks with the intention that Dirks would cause his clients to trade on that information. Dirks, therefore, was under a duty to make the information publicly available or to refrain from actions that he knew would lead to trading. Because Dirks caused his clients to trade, he violated § 10(b) and Rule 10b–5. Any other result is a disservice to this country's attempt to provide fair and efficient capital markets. I dissent.

4. MISAPPROPRIATION

Chiarella and *Dirks* left open the question of whether § 10(b) and Rule 10b–5 make it unlawful for a person who has no connection to a corporation to trade that corporation's securities on the basis of material, nonpublic information that she misappropriated from some third party. After *Chiarella,* circuit courts were split on the question of whether such "outsider trading" is unlawful and the theory on which such liability is based.

The misappropriation theory raises two difficult conceptual issues. One concerns the distinction between constructive and informational fraud. A fiduciary commits "constructive fraud" when she engages in conduct that is financially unfair to her beneficiary; she engages in "informational fraud"—or "deception"—when she misrepresents a material fact or fails to disclose such a fact in violation of a duty to disclose. In *Santa Fe Industries, Inc. v. Green*, 430 U.S. 462, 97 S.Ct. 1292, 51 L.Ed.2d 480 (1977), the Supreme Court held that because Rule 10b–5 speaks only to deception or manipulation, it does not provide a remedy for actions that are merely unfair, but only for those involving deception. Thus, even if trading on misappropriated information is unfair, the question is whether it constitutes "deception."

The other issue is whether the misappropriation is "in connection with" the purchase or sale of a security. If the person injured by the misappropriator's breach of fiduciary duty is not a participant in a securities transaction, even if the misappropriation somehow could be viewed as "deceptive," the deception arguably is not "in connection with" a purchase or sale of a security as Rule 10b–5 requires.

UNITED STATES V. O'HAGAN

521 U.S. 642 (1997).

JUSTICE GINSBURG delivered the opinion of the Court:

Respondent James Herman O'Hagan was a partner in the law firm of Dorsey & Whitney in Minneapolis, Minnesota. In July 1988, Grand Metropolitan PLC (Grand Met), a company based in London, England, retained Dorsey & Whitney as local counsel to represent Grand Met regarding a potential tender offer for the common stock of the Pillsbury Company, headquartered in Minneapolis. Both Grand Met and Dorsey & Whitney took precautions to protect the confidentiality of Grand Met's tender offer plans. O'Hagan did no work on the Grand Met representation. Dorsey & Whitney withdrew from representing Grand Met on September 9, 1988. Less than a month later, on October 4, 1988, Grand Met publicly announced its tender offer for Pillsbury stock.

On August 18, 1988, while Dorsey & Whitney was still representing Grand Met, O'Hagan began purchasing call options for Pillsbury stock. Each option gave him the right to purchase 100 shares of Pillsbury stock. By the end of September, he owned 2,500 unexpired Pillsbury options, apparently more than any other individual investor. O'Hagan also purchased, in September 1988, some 5,000 shares of Pillsbury common stock, at a price just under $39 per share. When Grand Met announced its tender offer in October, the price of Pillsbury stock rose to nearly $60 per share. O'Hagan then sold his Pillsbury call options and common stock, making a profit of more than $4.3 million.

The Securities and Exchange Commission initiated an investigation into O'Hagan's transactions, culminating in a 57-count indictment. The indictment alleged that O'Hagan defrauded his law firm and its client, Grand Met, by using for his own trading purposes material, nonpublic information regarding Grand Met's planned tender offer. According to the indictment, O'Hagan used the profits he gained through this trading to conceal his previous embezzlement and conversion of unrelated client trust funds. A jury convicted O'Hagan on all counts, and he was sentenced to a 41-month term of imprisonment.

[On appeal,] the Eighth Circuit rejected the misappropriation theory as a basis for § 10(b) liability. We hold, in accord with several other Courts of Appeals that criminal liability under § 10(b) may be predicated on the misappropriation theory.

The "misappropriation theory" holds that a person commits fraud "in connection with" a securities transaction, and thereby violates § 10(b) and Rule 10b–5, when he misappropriates confidential information for securities trading purposes, in breach of a duty owed to the source of the information. Under this theory, a fiduciary's undisclosed, self-serving use of a principal's information to purchase or sell securities, in breach of a duty of loyalty and confidentiality, defrauds the principal of the exclusive use of that information. In lieu of premising liability on a fiduciary relationship between company insider and purchaser or seller of the company's stock, the misappropriation theory premises liability on a fiduciary-turned-trader's deception of those who entrusted him with access to confidential information.

The classical theory [of insider trading] targets a corporate insider's breach of duty to shareholders with whom the insider transacts; the misappropriation theory outlaws trading on the basis of nonpublic information by a corporate "outsider" in breach of a duty owed not to a trading party, but to the source of the information. The misappropriation theory is . . . designed to "protec[t] the integrity of the securities markets against abuses by 'outsiders' to a corporation who have access to confidential information that will affect th[e] corporation's security price when revealed, but who owe no fiduciary or other duty to that corporation's shareholders." [Quoting *Dirks*.]

In this case, the indictment alleged that O'Hagan, in breach of a duty of trust and confidence he owed to his law firm, Dorsey & Whitney, and to its client, Grand Met, traded on the basis of nonpublic information regarding Grand Met's planned tender offer for Pillsbury common stock. This conduct, the Government charged, constituted a fraudulent device in connection with the purchase and sale of securities.[5]

We agree with the Government that misappropriation, as just defined, satisfies § 10(b)'s requirement that chargeable conduct involve a "deceptive device or contrivance" used "in connection with" the purchase or sale of securities. We observe, first, that misappropriators, as the Government describes them, deal in deception. A fiduciary who "[pretends] loyalty to the principal while secretly converting the principal's information for personal gain," "dupes" or defrauds the principal.

Deception through nondisclosure is central to the theory of liability for which the Government seeks recognition. As counsel for the Government stated in explanation of the theory at oral argument: "To satisfy the common law rule that a trustee may not use the property that [has] been entrusted [to] him, there would have to be consent. To satisfy the requirement of the Securities Act that there be no deception, there would only have to be disclosure."[6]

---

[5] The Government could not have prosecuted O'Hagan under the classical theory, for O'Hagan was not an "insider" of Pillsbury, the corporation in whose stock he traded. Although an "outsider" with respect to Pillsbury, O'Hagan had an intimate association with, and was found to have traded on confidential information from, Dorsey & Whitney, counsel to tender offeror Grand Met. Under the misappropriation theory, O'Hagan's securities trading does not escape Exchange Act sanction, as it would under the dissent's reasoning, simply because he was associated with, and gained nonpublic information from, the bidder, rather than the target.

[6] Under the misappropriation theory urged in this case, the disclosure obligation runs to the source of the information, here, Dorsey & Whitney and Grand Met. Chief Justice Burger, dissenting in *Chiarella*, advanced a broader reading of § 10(b) and Rule 10b–5; the disclosure

The misappropriation theory advanced by the Government is consistent with *Santa Fe Industries, Inc. v. Green*, a decision underscoring that § 10(b) is not an all-purpose breach of fiduciary duty ban; rather, it trains on conduct involving manipulation or deception. In contrast to the Government's allegations in this case, in *Santa Fe Industries,* all pertinent facts were disclosed by the persons charged with violating § 10(b) and Rule 10b–5, therefore, there was no deception through nondisclosure to which liability under those provisions could attach. Similarly, full disclosure forecloses liability under the misappropriation theory: because the deception essential to the misappropriation theory involves feigning fidelity to the source of information, if the fiduciary discloses to the source that he plans to trade on the nonpublic information, there is no "deceptive device" and thus no § 10(b) violation—although the fiduciary-turned-trader may remain liable under state law for breach of a duty of loyalty.[7]

We turn next to the § 10(b) requirement that the misappropriator's deceptive use of information be "in connection with the purchase or sale of [a] security." This element is satisfied because the fiduciary's fraud is consummated, not when the fiduciary gains the confidential information, but when, without disclosure to his principal, he uses the information to purchase or sell securities. The securities transaction and the breach of duty thus coincide. This is so even though the person or entity defrauded is not the other party to the trade, but is, instead, the source of the nonpublic information. A misappropriator who trades on the basis of material, nonpublic information, in short, gains his advantageous market position through deception; he deceives the source of the information and simultaneously harms members of the investing public.

The misappropriation theory targets information of a sort that misappropriators ordinarily capitalize upon to gain no-risk profits through the purchase or sale of securities. Should a misappropriator put such information to other use, the statute's prohibition would not be implicated. The theory does not catch all conceivable forms of fraud involving confidential information; rather, it catches fraudulent means of capitalizing on such information through securities transactions.

The dissent's charge that the misappropriation theory is incoherent because information, like funds, can be put to multiple uses, misses the point. The Exchange Act was enacted in part "to insure the maintenance of fair and honest markets," and there is no question that fraudulent uses of confidential information fall within § 10(b)'s prohibition if the fraud is "in

---

obligation, as he envisioned it, ran to those with whom the misappropriator trades. ("a person who has misappropriated nonpublic information has an absolute duty to disclose that information or to refrain from trading"). The Government does not propose that we adopt a misappropriation theory of that breadth.

[7] Where, however, a person trading on the basis of material, nonpublic information owes a duty of loyalty and confidentiality to two entities or persons—for example, a law firm and its client—but makes disclosure to only one, the trader may still be liable under the misappropriation theory.

connection with" a securities transaction. It is hardly remarkable that a rule suitably applied to the fraudulent uses of certain kinds of information would be stretched beyond reason were it applied to the fraudulent use of money.

The misappropriation theory comports with § 10(b)'s language, which requires deception "in connection with the purchase or sale of any security," not deception of an identifiable purchaser or seller. The theory is also well-tuned to an animating purpose of the Exchange Act: to insure honest securities markets and thereby promote investor confidence. Although informational disparity is inevitable in the securities markets, investors likely would hesitate to venture their capital in a market where trading based on misappropriated nonpublic information is unchecked by law. An investor's informational disadvantage vis-à-vis a misappropriator with material, nonpublic information stems from contrivance, not luck; it is a disadvantage that cannot be overcome with research or skill.

In sum, considering the inhibiting impact on market participation of trading on misappropriated information, and the congressional purposes underlying § 10(b), it makes scant sense to hold a lawyer like O'Hagan a § 10(b) violator if he works for a law firm representing the target of a tender offer, but not if he works for a law firm representing the bidder. The text of the statute requires no such result.[9] The misappropriation at issue here was properly made the subject of a § 10(b) charge because it meets the statutory requirement that there be "deceptive" conduct "in connection with" securities transactions.

The Eighth Circuit erred in holding that the misappropriation theory is inconsistent with § 10(b).

[The Court also reversed the Eight Circuit's rulings that the SEC had exceeded its authority by adopting Rule 14e–3(a), which proscribes trading on undisclosed information in the tender offer setting, even in the absence of a duty to disclose, and that O'Hagan could not be convicted for mail fraud.]

---

[9] As noted earlier, however, *see supra*, at 9–10, the textual requirement of deception precludes § 10(b) liability when a person trading on the basis of nonpublic information has disclosed his trading plans to, or obtained authorization from, the principal-even though such conduct may affect the securities markets in the same manner as the conduct reached by the misappropriation theory. Contrary to the dissent's suggestion, the fact that § 10(b) is only a partial antidote to the problems it was designed to alleviate does not call into question its prohibition of conduct that falls within its textual proscription. Moreover, once a disloyal agent discloses his imminent breach of duty, his principal may seek appropriate equitable relief under state law. Furthermore, in the context of a tender offer, the principal who authorizes an agent's trading on confidential information may, in the Commission's view, incur liability for an Exchange Act violation under Rule 14e–3(a).

JUSTICE THOMAS, with whom THE CHIEF JUSTICE joins, concurring in the judgment in part and dissenting in part.

Central to the majority's holding is the need to interpret § 10(b)'s requirement that a deceptive device be "use[d] or employ[ed], in connection with the purchase or sale of any security." Because the Commission's misappropriation theory fails to provide a coherent and consistent interpretation of this essential requirement for liability under § 10(b), I dissent.

I do not take issue with the majority's determination that the undisclosed misappropriation of confidential information by a fiduciary can constitute a "deceptive device" within the meaning of § 10(b). Nondisclosure where there is a pre-existing duty to disclose satisfies our definitions of fraud and deceit for purposes of the securities laws.

Unlike the majority, however, I cannot accept the Commission's interpretation of when a deceptive device is "use[d] . . . in connection with" a securities transaction. Although the Commission and the majority at points seem to suggest that *any* relation to a securities transaction satisfies the "in connection with" requirement of § 10(b), both ultimately reject such an overly expansive construction and require a more integral connection between the fraud and the securities transaction. The majority states, for example, that the misappropriation theory applies to undisclosed misappropriation of confidential information "for securities trading purposes," thus seeming to require a particular intent by the misappropriator in order to satisfy the "in connection with" language. The Commission goes further, and argues that the misappropriation theory satisfies the "in connection with" requirement because it "depends on an *inherent* connection between the deceptive conduct and the purchase or sale of a security." *See also* (the "misappropriated information had personal value to respondent *only* because of its utility in securities trading") (emphasis added).

As the majority concedes, because "the deception essential to the misappropriation theory involves feigning fidelity to the source of information, if the fiduciary discloses *to the source* that he plans to trade on the nonpublic information, there is no 'deceptive device' and thus no § 10(b) violation." Indeed, were the source expressly to authorize its agents to trade on the confidential information—as a perk or bonus, perhaps—there would likewise be no § 10(b) violation. Yet in either case—disclosed misuse or authorized use—the hypothesized "inhibiting impact on market participation," would be identical to that from behavior violating the misappropriation theory: "Outsiders" would still be trading based on nonpublic information that the average investor has no hope of obtaining through his own diligence.[6]

The majority's statement that a "misappropriator who trades on the basis of material, nonpublic information, in short, *gains his advantageous market position through deception; he deceives the source of the information and simultaneously harms members of the investing public*," (emphasis added), thus focuses on the wrong point. Even if it is true that trading on nonpublic information hurts the public, it is true whether or not there is any deception of the source of the information. Moreover, as we have repeatedly held, use of nonpublic information to trade is not itself a violation of § 10(b). Rather, it is the use of fraud "in connection with" a securities transaction that is forbidden. Where the relevant element of fraud has no impact on the integrity of the subsequent transactions as distinct from the nonfraudulent element of using nonpublic information, one can reasonably question whether the fraud was used in connection with a securities transaction. And one can likewise question whether removing that aspect of fraud, though perhaps laudable, has anything to do with the confidence or integrity of the market.

5. APPLYING THE PRINCIPLES

The Supreme Court's three insider-trading decisions—*Chiarella*, *Dirks* and *O'Hagan*—constitute the core of United States insider trading law. They provide broad guidelines for determining when a person violates § 10(b) and Rule 10b–5 by trading on the basis of material, nonpublic information. Applying these guidelines to particular fact situations is not always so easy, however.

a. Duties of "Trust or Confidence" in Non-Business Relationships

The misappropriation theory, upheld by the Supreme Court in *O'Hagan*, hinges on the finding that a person breached a duty of trust or confidence by misappropriating and trading on inside information. The theory's application is clearest in cases involving the misappropriation of confidential information in breach of an established business relationship, such as lawyer-client or employer-employee. Its application is less clear with respect to other business and personal relationships. For example, does a person have a duty to disclose or abstain from trading if she learns of material nonpublic information from a wealthy relative during a dinner conversation?

---

[6] That the dishonesty aspect of misappropriation might be eliminated via disclosure or authorization is wholly besides the point. The dishonesty in misappropriation is in the relationship between the fiduciary and the principal, not in any relationship between the misappropriator and the market. No market transaction is made more or less honest by disclosure to a third-party principal, rather than to the market as a whole. As far as the market is concerned, a trade based on confidential information is no more "honest" because some third party may know of it so long as those on the other side of the trade remain in the dark.

In 2000, the SEC adopted Rule 10b5–2 to clarify how the misappropriation theory applies to non-business relationships. Under the rule, a person receiving material nonpublic information under any of the following circumstances owes a duty of trust or confidence, and thus can be liable under the misappropriation theory if the recipient trades on the basis of such information, and:

- The recipient agreed to maintain the information in confidence. Rule 10b5–2(b)(1).

- The persons involved in the communication have a history, pattern or practice of sharing confidences (both business and non-business confidences) so the recipient had reason to know the communicator expected the recipient to maintain the information's confidentiality. Rule 10b5–2(b)(2).

- The communicator of the information was a spouse, parent, child or sibling of the recipient, unless the recipient could show (based on the facts and circumstances of that family relationship) that there was no reasonable expectation of confidentiality. Rule 10b5–2(b)(3).

The rule's first two categories, by their terms, clarify the duty of trust or confidence in both non-business and business settings. Thus, a contractual relationship (though not necessarily creating a fiduciary relationship) could give rise to a duty not to use confidential information, if that is what the parties had agreed or mutually understood. In addition, as the SEC stated in its preliminary note to the rule, the list is not exclusive, and a relationship of trust or confidence among family members or others also can be established in other ways.

Rule 10b5–2 also addressed the troublesome issue of when a family relationship gives rise to a fiduciary duty not to trade on information learned from another family member. Several lower court decisions had wrestled with that issue, with not always consistent results. *See, e.g., United States v. Chestman,* 947 F.2d 551 (2d Cir.1991) (en banc) (holding that son-in-law who learned of plans to sell family-controlled corporation did not owe a duty to family, since "[k]inship alone does not create the necessary relationship" and no duty arose when son-in-law asked to keep the plans confidential); *SEC v. Yun,* 327 F.3d 1263 (11th Cir. 2003) (ruling that a spouse had violated Rule 10b–5 by tipping confidential information about her husband's company to a co-worker after she had promised not to disclose this information).

b. Deception When There Is No Breach of Fiduciary Duty

As we have seen, both classical insider trading rules and those involving tipping and trading by outsiders, generally depend on the breach of a duty. Is it possible that some form of deception not involving the breach of a duty can give rise to insider trading liability? The Second Circuit was confronted by such a case in *S.E.C. v. Dorozhko*, 574 F.3d 42 (2d.Cir. 2009). The case involved a Ukrainian computer hacker who gained access to the computer server of Thomson Financial, Inc., and based on information thus obtained about an upcoming earnings release, bought put options that netted him a profit of approximately $286,000. On appeal from a District Court order imposing sanctions, the court held that the relevant question was whether the manner of accessing the server involved deception. Ruling that the record was insufficiently clear on that point, the court remanded the case to the District Court to determine "whether the computer hacking in this case involved a fraudulent misrepresentation that was 'deceptive' within the ordinary meaning of Section 10(b)."

Interestingly enough, this sort of activity seems to be becoming more common in this age of cyberespionage. *See, e.g.,* Christian Bertelson, *Chinese Hackers Charged With Trading on Stolen Law Firm Data*, Bloomberg News (December 27, 2016), https://www.bloomberg.com/news/articles/2016-12-27/china-residents-charged-with-insider-trading-on-hacked-m-a-data.

c. State of Mind and Rule 10b5–1

What state of mind triggers liability in a case of insider trading? In *O'Hagan*, the Supreme Court said only that the trading must be "on the basis" of material nonpublic information. It left unresolved exactly what that meant. Must the trade be motivated by the knowledge of material nonpublic information? Or is it enough that the trader knows she is in possession of such information and trades anyway? Lower courts split on whether insider trading liability requires a showing merely that the trader was in "knowing possession" of inside information or a more difficult proof that the trader "used" the information in trading.

This issue was of particular concern to corporate executives who are regularly aware of non-public information about their companies that may or may not be material. If they wish to buy because they believe their company is a good long-term investment, or sell to raise money to pay their daughter's law school tuition, they must worry about whether any of the many non-public facts they know about their company might, in hindsight, be considered material.

In response to these concerns, in 2000, the SEC adopted Rule 10b5–1 to clarify the meaning of "on the basis of." The rule provides that, for purposes of insider trading, a person trades "on the basis" of material nonpublic information if the trader is "aware" of the material nonpublic information when making the purchase or sale. Rule 10b5–1(b). In its release, the SEC explained that "aware" is a commonly-used English word, implying "conscious knowledge," with clearer meaning than "knowing possession."

Having thus taken an expansive view of the meaning of "trading on the basis of," the rule established several affirmative defenses designed to allow corporate insiders and others to implement securities trading plans without concern about liability. These "10b5–1 plans" are intended to eliminate the possibility that a trade was motivated by inside information. They must be established "in good faith" at a time when the insider does not have knowledge of material non-public information, and they must direct future trades in a manner that takes control of the trade out of the hands of the insider. The typical plan consists of instructions (preferably, but not mandatorily, written) to a broker to buy or to sell according to some defined rule. For example, an insider wishing to diversify her holdings or to raise money for some other purpose might direct the broker to sell a specified number of shares on the first trading day of each week. Or an insider might direct the broker to sell a specified number of shares if the reaches a specified level.

Rule 10b5–1 plans are now widely used by officers and directors in their sales of stock. It is not clear whether such plans have led to greater return for the insiders who use them or whether the rule has provided cover for what otherwise would have been considered illegal trading. Malloy & Lukasz Pomorski, *Decoding Insider Information*, 67 J. Fin. 1009 (2012).

The courts have generally recognized that individual trading plans executed pursuant to Rule 10b5–1 may provide a defense against insider trading charges. *E.g. SEC v. Healthsouth Corp.*, 261 F.Supp.2d 1298 (N.D. Ala. 2003), *Wietschner v. Monterey Pasta Co.*, 294 F.Supp.2d 1102 (N.D. Cal. 2003). On the other hand, regulators do scrutinize trades made under Rule 10b5–1 plans and have brought some enforcement actions. For example, the SEC accused Countrywide Financial's former chief executive, Angelo R. Mozilo, of selling $140 million of shares through multiple plans he adopted after he is said to have learned of serious problems in the company's subprime mortgage operations. And Qwest's former chief executive, Joseph P. Naccio, was convicted of insider trading after a finding that he sold stock under a Rule 10b5–1 plan that accelerated his trading after he learned that the company would not meet its internal revenue projections.

d. Benefit to Tipper

The Supreme Court held in *Dirks* that for a tipper to breach her fiduciary duty, she must receive some "personal benefit" in exchange for that tip. While the courts have consistently held that the benefit received from making a gift to a friend or relative in the form of a tip was sufficient, the courts have difficulty in applying the test in a consistent fashion. In *U.S v. Newman*, 773 F.3d 438 (2nd Cir. 2014) the Second Circuit took a view of the issue that surprised many securities lawyers as particularly narrow. In describing the nature of the benefit that must be received in exchange for a tip, the Court ruled that in order to secure a conviction the government provide "proof of a meaningfully close personal relationship that generates an exchange that is objective, consequential, and represents at least a potential gain of a pecuniary or similarly valuable nature. 773 F.2d at 452. It was not long before the Supreme Court was called on to address the question.

SALMAN V. UNITED STATES
137 S.Ct. 420 (2016).

ALITO, J.

[Salman was married to the sister of Mounir Kara (known as Michael) and Maher Kara, an investment banker in Citigroup's healthcare investment banking group. After Maher started at Citigroup, he began discussing aspects of his job with Michael. At first he relied on Michael's chemistry background to help him grasp scientific concepts relevant to his new job. After awhile, Michael began to trade on the information Maher shared with him. At first, Maher was unaware of his brother's trading activity, but eventually he began to suspect that it was taking place.

Without his younger brother's knowledge, Michael fed the information to others—including Salman, whom Michael considered a close friend as well as a brother-in-law. By the time the authorities caught on, Salman had made over $1.5 million in profits that he split with another relative who executed trades via a brokerage account on Salman's behalf.

Salman was indicted and convicted of securities fraud and conspiracy to commit securities fraud. Facing charges of their own, both Maher and Michael pleaded guilty and testified at Salman's trial. Salman appealed to the U.S. Court of Appeals for the 9th Circuit, arguing that under *U.S. v. Newman* it was necessary for the tipper to receive a pecuniary benefit for the tip to violate Rule 10b–5. The Ninth Circuit affirmed Salman's conviction, and the Supreme Court granted certiorari.]

We adhere to *Dirks*, which easily resolves the narrow issue presented here.

In *Dirks*, we explained that a tippee is exposed to liability for trading on inside information only if the tippee participates in a breach of the tipper's fiduciary duty. Whether the tipper breached that duty depends "in large part on the purpose of the disclosure" to the tippee. 463 U.S., at 662, 103 S.Ct. 3255. "[T]he test," we explained, "is whether the insider personally will benefit, directly or indirectly, from his disclosure." Ibid. Thus, the disclosure of confidential information without personal benefit is not enough. In determining whether a tipper derived a personal benefit, we instructed courts to "focus on objective criteria, *i.e.*, whether the insider receives a direct or indirect personal benefit from the disclosure, such as a pecuniary gain or a reputational benefit that will translate into future earnings." *Id.*, at 663, 103 S.Ct. 3255. This personal benefit can "often" be inferred "from objective facts and circumstances," we explained, such as "a relationship between the insider and the recipient that suggests a quid pro quo from the latter, or an intention to benefit the particular recipient." *Id.*, at 664, 103 S.Ct. 3255. In particular, we held that "[t]he elements of fiduciary duty and exploitation of nonpublic information also exist when an insider makes a gift of confidential information to a trading relative or friend." Ibid. In such cases, "[t]he tip and trade resemble trading by the insider followed by a gift of the profits to the recipient." Ibid. We then applied this gift-giving principle to resolve *Dirks* itself, finding it dispositive that the tippers "received no monetary or personal benefit" from their tips to Dirks, "nor was their purpose to make a gift of valuable information to Dirks." *Id.*, at 667, 103 S.Ct. 3255.

Our discussion of gift giving resolves this case. Maher, the tipper, provided inside information to a close relative, his brother Michael. Dirks makes clear that a tipper breaches a fiduciary duty by making a gift of confidential information to "a trading relative," and that rule is sufficient to resolve the case at hand. As Salman's counsel acknowledged at oral argument, Maher would have breached his duty had he personally traded on the information here himself then given the proceeds as a gift to his brother. It is obvious that Maher would personally benefit in that situation. But Maher effectively achieved the same result by disclosing the information to Michael, and allowing him to trade on it. Dirks appropriately prohibits that approach, as well. Cf. 463 U.S., at 659, 103 S.Ct. 3255 (holding that "insiders [are] forbidden" both "from personally using undisclosed corporate information to their advantage" and from "giv[ing] such information to an outsider for the same improper purpose of exploiting the information for their personal gain"). Dirks specifies that when a tipper gives inside information to "a trading relative or friend," the jury can infer that the tipper meant to provide the equivalent of a cash gift. In such situations, the tipper benefits personally because giving a gift of trading information is the same thing as trading by the tipper followed by a gift of the proceeds. Here, by disclosing confidential information as a gift to his brother with the expectation that he would trade on it, Maher breached his duty of trust and confidence to Citigroup and its clients—a duty Salman acquired, and breached himself, by trading on the information with full knowledge that it had been improperly disclosed.

To the extent the Second Circuit held that the tipper must also receive something of a "pecuniary or similarly valuable nature" in exchange for a gift to family or friends, *Newman*, 773 F.3d, at 452, we agree with the Ninth Circuit that this requirement is inconsistent with Dirks.

We reject Salman's argument that Dirks's gift-giving standard is unconstitutionally vague as applied to this case. Dirks created a simple and clear "guiding principle" for determining tippee liability, 463 U.S., at 664, 103 S.Ct. 3255 and Salman has not demonstrated that either § 10(b) itself or the Dirks gift-giving standard "leav[e] grave uncertainty about how to estimate the risk posed by a crime" or are plagued by "hopeless indeterminacy," *Johnson v. United States*, 576 U.S. ___, ___, ___, 135 S.Ct. 2551, 2557, 2558, 192 L.Ed.2d 569 (2015). At most, Salman shows that in some factual circumstances assessing liability for gift-giving will be difficult. That alone cannot render "shapeless" a federal criminal prohibition, for even clear rules "produce close cases." *Id.*, at ___, ___, 135 S.Ct., at 2560. We also reject Salman's appeal to the rule of lenity, as he has shown "no grievous ambiguity or uncertainty that would trigger the rule's application." *Barber v. Thomas*, 560 U.S. 474, 492 (internal quotation marks omitted). To the contrary, Salman's conduct is in the heartland of Dirks's rule concerning gifts. It remains the case that "[d]etermining whether an insider personally benefits from a particular disclosure, a question of fact, will not always be easy for courts." 463 U.S., at 664. But there is no need for us to address those difficult cases today, because this case involves "precisely the 'gift of confidential information to a trading relative' that Dirks envisioned." 792 F.3d, at 1092 (quoting 463 U.S., at 664, 103 S.Ct. 3255).

Accordingly, the Ninth Circuit's judgment is affirmed.

Problem: Standard Electronics Corporation

Standard Electronics Corporation (Standard) is a large Delaware corporation that manufactures products are used in high technology communications industries. It went public six years ago, and its common stock is listed on the New York Stock Exchange. In the last year, Standard's stock has traded between $19 and $28 per share. In order to provide incentives for its staff, it introduced an employee stock option plan almost immediately after going public and, to provide stock for that plan, Standard has been purchasing its own stock on the New York Stock Exchange on alternate Fridays pursuant to a prearranged schedule. The three trustees of the plan are the company's president, Herbert Jones, its treasurer, and one of its outside directors.

In March of this year, engineers in Standard's information storage division discovered a process that promises to significantly decrease the cost of digital data storage. Developing and producing a new generation of data storage products using the process will require major capital investments.

On April 2, Jones met with the company's general counsel, Abigail Benedict, to discuss the stock market implications of the new process. The two decided that the information was to be kept highly confidential within the company and was to be referred to only by the code name "Nirvana." The company's code of conduct requires senior officers to obtain advance clearance from her office for their securities transactions. After meeting with Jones Benedict sent a memo to all senior officers reminding them of this and indicating that she would not approved purchases of company stock by officers until further notice.

The next day, Steve Davis, a marketing vice-president, asked Benedict for permission to buy some stock. He was told that senior management was temporarily barred from trading but was not told why. Nevertheless, he bought 3,000 shares at about $26 per share on the same day. In addition, on April 7, without asking anyone, Amy Stevens, the research director of the Nirvana project, bought 5,000 shares at $24 per share.

On April 5, Jones met with the board of directors to discuss how best to finance the development of the new product. The meeting was attended by Ted Long, a partner of Goldwin & Co., an investment banking firm that had underwritten the company's public offering. Long proposed several alternative means of financing the project, including, among others, a merger with a company with substantial capital or the sale of a large block of stock. The Board reached no decision and retained Goldwin to advise how best to finance the development.

On May 5, one week before the company's annual meeting of stockholders, Long reported to the board that Goldwin was engaged in confidential discussions with several possible investors but that it was not prepared to present a formal recommendation. At the annual meeting, a stockholder asked Jones about new developments or products. Jones replied that "there is nothing I can report on now, although we are always hopeful that something exciting will emerge from the company's on-going research." His statement was accurately quoted on the Dow Jones News Service and in the Wall Street Journal.

On June 7, Long presented Goldwin's formal report to full board. The report stated that if the new products could be successfully commercialized, Goldwin projected Standard's value at between $40 and $45 per share. Long also told the board that Goldwin had approached Universal Products, Inc. (Universal) concerning a merger between the two companies at a price of $45–50 per share. The board authorized Jones to enter into formal negotiations with Universal and to furnish them any necessary confidential information.

From June 15–30, representatives of Standard and Universal met to review and discuss confidential and public financial data concerning Standard. At the end of the June 30 meeting, Universal's president said that he would seek authorization from his board to acquire Standard at a price of slightly more than $50 per share for each share of Standard stock. Later that day, both companies received calls from the New York Stock Exchange, asking them to comment on the rumors of a possible merger. The companies advised the Exchange that they were not in a position to comment because they had not reached a definitive agreement on a merger.

On July 7 both boards approved a merger in which Universal would issue stock having a value of $51 per share for 100% of the stock of Standard. The final agreement was signed and announced on July 10. By the following day, Standard stock was trading at $49 per share.

You are a senior associate in a law firm that has represented Standard for a number of years. The partner responsible for the Standard account has just sent a memorandum describing the above facts, and asking you to prepare a memo addressing the following:

I certainly hope we don't have another major insider trading scandal on our hands. I would like to know about any potential liabilities here, both personal as well as corporate.

1. For trading to be unlawful, it must be based on material non-public information. Which facts here might fit that description? The trading embargo? The technical discovery? The merger? What additional information do we need to know?

2. Are there any potential state law liabilities, and, if so, who could recover?

3. Would either Davis or Stevens be considered insiders for purposes of 10b–5 liability?

4. Long tells me that, after a squash game, he said to Bill Baker, one of his partners, "It looks like Standard had hit the jackpot in a deal with Universal." Long says it was a casual remark and was inadvertent, and I am inclined to believe him. But there seems some possibility that Baker may have used the information to benefit any some of Goldwin's institutional clients that he handles. If so, who might be liable?

    a) Look at footnote 14 in *Dirks*. Are Goldwin, Long and Baker insiders for purposes of this deal?

    b) Baker had nothing to do with the Universal-Standard deal, and only stumbled into information about it. Does the misappropriation theory apply to him? If so, who can recover from him?

    c) We don't know what Baker told his clients. Could he or Goldwin be liable for the clients' trades if Baker recommended the purchase of Standard stock but did not specifically disclose material non-public information?

5. It appears that Pamela Hobbes, one of the lawyers at the law firm representing Universal in the transaction, bought 1,000 shares of Standard stock for herself and

told various members of her family who bought an additional 5,000 shares.

a)   Could Hobbes be considered an insider in these circumstances even though she had no relationship with Standard?

b)   Does the misappropriation theory apply to Hobbes and, if so, who could bring suit against her? What damages or other relief might be granted?

c)   How does the tipper-tippee analysis apply to Hobbes and her family?

E.   REMEDIES FOR INSIDER TRADING VIOLATIONS

Section 20A of the 1934 Act creates a private right of action on behalf of contemporaneous traders against insiders, constructive insiders, tippers, and tippees (as well as their controlling persons) who trade while in possession of material nonpublic information. Liability in such cases is limited to the actual profits realized or losses avoided, reduced by the amount of any disgorgement obtained by the SEC under its broad authority to seek injunctive relief. Courts have generally required the same disgorgement of insiders' gains. The liability of controlling persons is governed by § 20(a) of the 1934 Act, which permits such persons to defend by showing that they acted in good faith and did not know of the violation of their controlled person. Because of the limited application and recovery afforded under § 20A, it has not been widely used in private litigation.

Pursuant to § 21A of the 1934 Act, which has been used significantly more than § 20A, the SEC is authorized to seek judicially imposed civil penalties against insiders, constructive insiders, tippers, and tippees. In addition to the disgorgement of profits, the penalty may be in an amount not exceeding the greater of $1,000,000 or three times the amount of the profit gained or loss avoided. These civil penalties are *in addition* to other remedies. The civil penalty can be imposed only at the instance of the SEC.

Section 21A(b) also permits the imposition of civil penalties on controlling persons, such as employers, of up to $1 million or three times the insider's profits (whichever is greater) if the controlling person knowingly or recklessly disregards the insider trading by persons under its control. Section 21A(e) of the 1934 Act also encourages private watchdogs by providing for the payment of bounties to people who provide information concerning insider trading.

The penalties for criminal securities violations include sentences of up to a maximum of ten years and maximum fines of $1 million for individuals and $2 million for nonnatural persons. 1934 Act § 32(a).

The Securities Enforcement and Penny Stock Act of 1990, which amended § 8 of the 1933 Act and § 21 of the 1934 Act, gives the SEC administrative "cease and desist" authority, and authorizes the SEC to impose civil penalties under § 21B of the 1934 Act.

F. DISGORGEMENT LIABILITY: SECTION 16

Insider trading was one of the principal problems Congress addressed in the 1934 Act. Responding to a public outcry against the practice and the perceived inadequacy of state common law, Congress created a novel regulatory scheme. Rather than prohibit trading on the basis of material nonpublic information, Congress attacked one narrow type of stock trading often associated with the misuse of inside information—namely short-swing trading—the purchase and resale by insiders of company stock within a relatively short period of time.

Since the capital gains period of the tax laws was then six months, there was good reason to suspect that in most cases someone with access to inside information who bought and sold within six months (and therefore forewent the favorable tax treatment available for profits made on trades separated by a longer period) was doing so to take advantage of some special knowledge. It was only a step from this perception to the simple and readily enforceable, if crude, principle of § 16(b), which provides that any profits realized by an insider on a purchase followed by a sale, or a sale followed by a purchase, within a six-month period, "shall inure to and be recoverable by the issuer." Although the section explicitly states that its purpose is "preventing the unfair use of information which may have been obtained by [the insider] by reason of his relationship to the issuer," there is no need to show any such "unfair use." All that is necessary is offsetting trades within six months by someone with the necessary relationship to the corporation.

Section 16 applies to the directors and officers, as well as any person who is the "beneficial owner" of more than 10 percent of a class of equity securities, of any corporation registered under § 12 of the 1934 Act. An "officer" for purposes of § 16 includes executive officers, chief financial or accounting officers, as well as any person, regardless of title, who performs significant "policy-making functions." A corporation or partnership may be considered to be a "director" under § 16 if a member or officer of the entity is "deputized" to represent the partnership or corporation as a director of the corporation in whose shares it trades. Whether the director is "deputized" is a question of fact that must be proved by the plaintiff. Section 16(b) applies to officers and directors so long as they held office at either the time of the purchase or the sale.

Beneficial ownership, solely for purposes of determining a person's status as a 10 percent shareholder, is defined with reference to § 13(d) of the 1934 Act. For all other purposes under § 16, beneficial ownership is determined by whether a § 16 insider has a pecuniary interest (as defined) in the security. In computing the 10 percent ownership, it is necessary to count the beneficial ownership of all equity securities, including those securities which could be acquired through the exercise of options or conversion rights. Unlike officers and directors, a beneficial owner may be liable under § 16(b) only if he owned more than 10 percent of the stock at the time of both purchase and sale. Officers and directors are treated differently from beneficial owners because the former are deemed to have more ready access to confidential business information that allows them to directly affect the market value of stock.

The problems that have generated the greatest amount of litigation under § 16(b) are those related to the definitions of "purchase" and "sale." When a transaction involves cash for stock, it is clearly subject to § 16. However certain "unorthodox" transactions, such as a merger, stock reclassification, or securities conversion, may also constitute a purchase or sale for § 16 purposes. When faced with the question of whether a particular transaction involves a purchase or sale, the courts have generally taken a pragmatic approach, depending on the presence or absence of the potential for speculative abuse in the transaction.

To ensure that potential plaintiffs can learn about short-swing trading, § 16(a) requires those covered by the statute to file reports with the SEC disclosing the ownership of their equity securities as well as any changes in that ownership. Initial reports must be filed electronically 10 days after a person becomes an insider, and updating reports must be filed electronically 2 days after any changes in the insider's holdings. These reports must be posted on the company's website within one day after filing.

Section 16(b) has a self-contained remedy with procedures of a hybrid derivative suit. A security holder, who need not be a contemporaneous owner, must make a demand on the directors unless demand would be futile. Thereafter, the corporation has sixty days to decide whether to institute suit. If it does not, the action may be maintained by the holder, who must hold the security at the institution of the suit and through trial. Any "profit" that is recovered, which courts compute from a series of several purchases and sales within six months so as to produce the maximum damages, goes to the corporation.

Why would a security holder bring a § 16(b) action if any recovery goes to the corporation, producing only the remotest benefit to him? As with conventional derivative suits, attorney's fees are available for a successful § 16(b) plaintiff. The plaintiff's counsel thus becomes the moving force in § 16(b) litigation. Indeed, courts have held that it is no defense to a § 16(b) action that the suit was motivated primarily by the desire to obtain such fees.

INDEX

References are to Pages